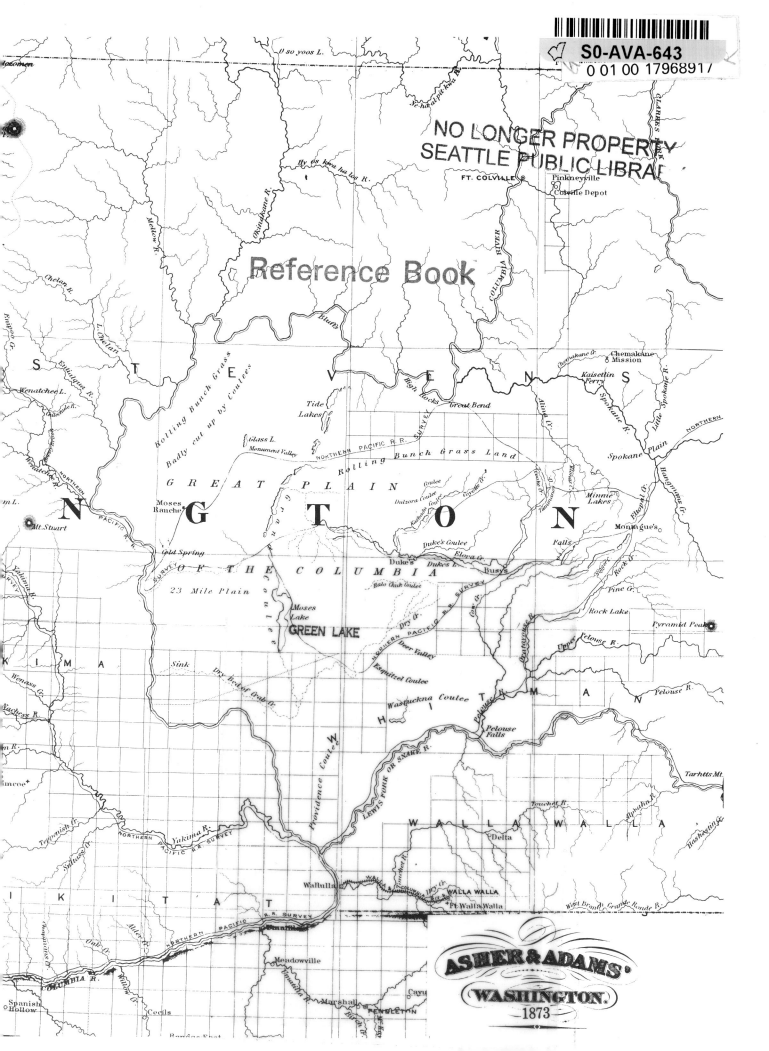

ASHER & ADAMS'
WASHINGTON.
1873

PLACE NAMES
OF WASHINGTON

By Robert Hitchman

Published by
Washington State Historical Society

1985

Copyright   1985
By The Washington State Historical Society.
All rights reserved. No part of this book may be
reproduced in any form without permission in writ-
ing from the publisher.
                 ISBN 0-917048-57-1
Manufactured in the United States of America

Library of Congress Cataloging-in-Publication Data

Hitchman, Robert.
   Place names of Washington State

     1. Washington (State) — Gazetteers.
I. Washington State Historical Society   II. Title.
F889.H57   1985   917.97'003'21   85-24683
ISBN 0-917048-57-1

PREFACE

Naming is a process that must have begun with creation, for how else could Genesis tell us that up there were the heavens and down here the earth? All through recorded time names have been used as identifiers for what the eye can see. Even primitive societies had names, spoken and remembered, but not written.

The selection and application of names all through time has been a most undisciplined procedure with few rules or guidelines. Names, whether applied to new-born humans, creations, inventions, discoveries or products usually are chosen somewhat at random, sometimes after careful thought and sometimes not. But one rule has prevailed for geographic names — respect for precedence. A name first applied must be respected because, whether one likes it or not, names go into records, onto maps and into common usage and are not easily or often changed.

During the exploration of the earth, each explorer had a pleasant obligation. To whatever he found he was privileged to attach a name of his own selection so that a record of what had been discovered could be made.

But the explorers could not name everything, and those who came after — settlers, pioneers, railroad builders and others — had to decide on and apply names all across the land.

Because a name once applied is so enduring, the selection of names would seem to be a solemn responsibility, and in truth it is, and yet the process of naming has been, at least until recent times, a most haphazard, casual and sometimes even whimsical undertaking.

The author of this place names book, Robert Hitchman, found all this particularly intriguing as he began while still quite young to pursue what became a lifelong passionate interest, the study of Pacific Northwest history. This study included the search for the origins of names not included in the book produced by an earlier historian who was similarly interested — Edmund Meany, the grey-bearded professor of history at the University of Washington who produced the classic ''Origin of Washington Geographic Names'', published first in the Washington Historical Quarterly and then in book form in 1923.

Bob Hitchman was a meticulous compiler. History was so worthy a subject, he felt, that it deserved scholarly treatment and he went about collecting place names with the same care that went into his extensive collecting of books, pamphlets and maps about the Northwest. He delighted in collecting and in finding others who shared that delight. The rambling Seattle home where he lived for many years had a third floor with high dormers. He called it the Crow's Nest. Just to make sure other collectors didn't miss new offerings in regional history, he produced a listing of them, together with his evaluations, which he printed and distributed without charge. It had a name, of course: *Sighted from the Crow's Nest.*

But the book collecting and the name researches could only be an avocation. Bob Hitchman was a busy insurance executive, rising to become president of the Unigard company, and an active participant in a variety of endeavors, none of which inspired his enthusiasm more than the ones relating to his great love, the history of the region. From 1952 until he died he was an active member of the State Historical Society. He was, in fact, president of the Society when struck by a fatal heart attack while attending a meeting of the board of councilors of the second oldest historical society in the country, the American Antiquarian Society in Worcester, Mass. Fewer than 300 persons can belong to that Society and Bob Hitchman felt honored to be elected its secretary of domestic correspondence. He was a member of the Washington Board on Geographic Names, created in recent times to be the final arbiter in the heretofore hit or miss procedure of applying names in the natural domain in Washington.

History is a serious business and the collecting and study of it was a serious matter for Bob Hitchman, but so strong was his sense of the humor to be seen in so many situations and circumstances that he was constantly expressing his amusement with what went on in the past. To him the work of history was fun. He took delight in recording the origins of such whimsical names as Poodle Dog Pass, Paddy Go East Pass, Jimmy Come Lately Creek, Dirty Face Mountain, Fisher's Hornpipe Creek and Laughing Jacob Lake.

Many names in Washington originated with the Indians, who could only pronounce them, not write them, and so what resulted was the phonetic spelling by the pioneers of what they thought the Indians were saying, and the resulting words were often strange indeed. Sorting them out was not easy. At least a dozen different spellings of the name Cowlitz, for example, can be found in the journals of the explorers and fur traders. Washington is the only state, Bob Hitchman found, where Chinook jargon, a curious mixture of English, French and several Indian languages left its imprint.

The years went on and the Hitchman compilation of name origins grew into the thousands. He assembled the names by counties on index cards, and on other sheets cited the sources of his information, often several sources, showing how names were spelled differently in early printed records and written documents. The legal description of each place was determined and added to the record.

In the late 1950s he began to see that what he was producing could be a successor to Meany's book — an updated and greatly expanded listing of the place names in Washington. It became his objective then to finish the work and submit it for publication. He even retained an assistant at one point, the late Donald Clark, well known as the originator and only president of a largely paper organization called Cannon Hunters Association of Seattle —

CHAOS for short. Clark did considerable editing, sorting and typing of the mostly handwritten Hitchman notes.

But Bob Hitchman was never quite ready to declare the task finished. New material kept turning up, more names remained to be researched, more work to be done. And yet every county had a voluminous file. Then came his untimely death in 1979. Helen Hitchman turned her husband's great file over to the Washington State Historical Society, to which her husband had been devoted all his adult life, together with a generous bequest he had made, and in 1982 the work of preparing it for publication began.

The first task was to get the names assembled, not by counties, but in alphabetical order, for ready reference purposes. Helen Hitchman did this. Next a standard style for the descriptions was decided upon and a means found for editing the whole on word processors and storing it with codes that would make it unnecessary to re-keyboard for typesetting. This was done—and it took more than a year—by Brenda Peterson and Linda Hillesheim of Seattle.

As the lengthy printouts were produced they were proofread by one of Bob Hitchman's close friends of many years and a Pacific Northwest historian, Father William Bishoff, S.J. A second reading was done by another friend, Prof. Keith Murray of Western Washington University.

The typesetting and make-up of the pages was presided over by Robert Phillips and the page proofs were read and corrected by Frank Green.

And so, in the course of a long time, this labor of love, as it must be called, came at last to completion with the publication of this volume by the Washington State Historical Society.

The question is asked: Was the work really finished when Bob Hitchman died? And the answer is: A work of this kind is never finished because the naming process goes on. When the Board of Geographic Names meets, changes and corrections are made to already applied names and new names are approved. About 100 name decisions are made each year. So, such a compilation as this cannot be completed; it can only be updated from time to time.

This compilation of name origins is the most comprehensive ever undertaken for Washington and the State Historical Society takes considerable pride and satisfaction in bringing it to publication after the many years Bob Hitchman diligently pursued his goal, which was to bring to his fellow citizens the fascination, the factual knowledge and fun he found in the pursuit of a lifetime.

John McClelland, Jr.
President
Washington State Historical Society
1985

Introduction

Several of Robert Hitchman's talks about place names were taped. What follows, as an introduction to the book of place names he produced, are excerpts from these talks.

By Robert Hitchman

My interest in place names has been the very root of my interest in Northwest history, and I have had a great deal of fun over the years in following it, prowling through it and finding stories that haven't been recorded. A tremendous amount of research work remains to be done in this area — some very important, vital and interesting. I find that studying place names, tracing origins, finding out who named various geographic features, when they were named, why they were named and what the names mean, and what other names may have been used in the past, is a most interesting endeavor. A lot of it borders on folklore, although a great deal is fact. Unfortunately the best stories relating to place names often aren't true, but some are and they are fun.

For example, one of my favorites is *Sedro Woolley*. It is such an unusual name that a real estate man there, when he was traveling, used to send postcards home to his friends and address them "the only Sedro Woolley in the world." And they were invariably delivered. The story began in 1848 when Mortimer Cook settled on the Skagit River and opened a little store or trading post. Gradually other pioneers settled around his place which was just a clearing in a cedar forest. When there seemed to be enough people for a town, Mortimer applied for a post office and the town was to be called, naturally, Cook. But there already was a Cook in Washington territory. The post office department suggested a name be chosen that was descriptive of something in the region. It being summer, with gnats, no-see-ums, mosquitoes and flies all around, Mortimer said: "All right, if that's what we are supposed to do, let's call the town 'Bug'." But that didn't go over very well with his fellow townsmen and someone suggested a Spanish name. They were considered quite romantic.

Since the townsite was located in a grove of cedars, it was suggested that the Spanish name for cedar would be appropriate. That would be "Cedra." But when the handwritten letter went to the Post Office Department someone at the receiving end read the word as "Sedro." And that became the name in 1886. Then, four years later, P. A. Woolley started his own little settlement nearby and called it "Woolley." Great rivalry developed. When one put up a flag pole for the Fourth of July, the other erected one a little taller. This went on for some time. Then the citizens got together and agreed that a merger would be in order and that they would decide by ballot whether the name should be "Sedro" or "Woolley." The elections held in 1898 came in with "Sedro" winning by one vote which distressed Mr. Woolley considerably. He called for a re-count. And while the ballots were being counted again, his nephew stole one "Sedro" ballot and destroyed it by eating it. So the re-count produced a tie which left them with an obvious solution — put a hyphen between the two words Sedro-Woolley.

Everyone seemed content. But 38 years later, in 1936, an old-timer raised a question: Since one ballot had been stolen and eaten, wasn't the decision in 1898 wrongfully made? He circulated a petition calling for another election to decide whether the then well-established name, *Sedro-Woolley*, should be changed. People signed the petition, but when the vote was taken it was 874 against the change and only 27 for it.

So there you have a bit of folklore, homey history and fun. It is typical of a great many place name stories.

Now let's go back 197 years when there were no names on the map and practically no maps. It was then that the first white men came into this region. They were Spaniards. They were not the first to apply names. The Indians were first. I'm particularly fond of them. They add spice and flavor to our whole area: *Snoqualmie, Snohomish, Stillaguamish, Walla Walla, Spokane, Seattle, Tacoma, Inchaleum, Nespellum, Chelan, Wahkiakum.* We have a real problem with Indian names. People ask: What do they mean? Often it is hard to determine. There were a number of completely independent Indian languages in the region. They were as different from each other as English and Turkish.

Indian names are a special problem because there were so many Indian languages and dialects. In addition there was Chinook jargon, a kind of inter-tribal language made up of Indian words and later mingled with French and English words. My count shows that at least 200 Chinook jargon names are still in use in Washington. Chinook jargon became a sort of international language. I'm not sure when it developed — maybe after the traders came — maybe before — but it could be used by one Indian speaking one language to communicate with another Indian speaking another language, or between the Indians and the whites, and sometimes between the whites and the whites.

When I was a lad, quite a few Chinook jargon words would slip into conversation. Many Chinook jargon words and terms have been placed on maps, largely through the work of the Forest Service and the mountaineers. There is *Tillicum Creek*. Tillicum (Tillica) means friend. *Tipsu Lake* is on the slopes of Mt. Rainier. Tipsu means grassy or hairy. And this is typical of Chinook jargon. Sometimes one word will mean several things and you can see a relationship between grass and hair, for instance, once it is brought to your attention. Skookum means big or powerful or strong, and Skookum Chuck is strong water — a rapids. Skookum Chuck also means whiskey. Here again we have one word meaning two things, and there is an association. Chuck means water. People used refer to the Sound as the Salt Chuck.

It is difficult to define Indian names because the Indians had a different attitude, a different concept of what is a geographic feature. We always think that a river, certainly, is a geographic feature and that everybody would have a name for the river. No so with the Indians. They might have a name for a bend in a river, but not for the river itself. Or they might have a name for a particular rock but not for a mountain range. They might have a name for a beach but not for the Sound or for a bay.

Then there is also the problem of translation. Many of the first white people working with Indians were not interested or did not care, and didn't do an adequate job of communicating with the Indians. James Swan was one of the few who did. He understood the Indians and worked well with them. There was tremendous difficulty in trying to record sounds in the Indian languages because so many sounds just don't fit our alphabet at all. As you know, the anthropologists used the Americanus alphabet which has strange symbols to record the strange sounds. So here we have all sorts of difficulty, and when people ask me what does an Indian name mean, I get quite nervous and shy away from it. I'm not specialized here. But we do have Chinook jargon names. *Mowich* is on the slopes of Rainier. Mowich means deer. *Tyee* is sprinkled all over the maps. Tyee means chief or leader or a hit man. There are lots of Olallies -- *Olallie Lake, Olallie Mountain.* Olallie refers to berries. Kalitin means arrow. *Kalitin Peak* near *Snoqualmie Pass* is a very sharp peak.

Cultus Bay is on Whidbey Island. Cultus means useless. *Cultus Bay* is hardly a bay at all when the tide goes out. Right next to *Cultus Bay* is *Useless Bay.* There used to be a settlement called Useless and I suppose that there was a school there. I would like to think there was a school called Useless School. There are *Chickamin Peak, Chickamin Creek,* and *Chickamin Pass.* Chickamin means metal or money. Here again we have two translations or two meanings to one word. There are several *Mimoluse Islands.* This means the island of death or the island of the dead, where Indians took their dead. *Melakwa Lake* near *Snoqualmie Pass* is another of the mountaineers' names. Melakwa means mosquito. La Push is a Chinook jargon name meaning mouth — mouth of the river.

So the oldest names are the Indian names. Next oldest are those brought here by the Spaniards. They came in 1774 from the tiny port of San Blason on the west coast of Mexico — New Spain in those days. The Spaniards came to see what the Russians were doing, for while the Spaniards claimed this part of the world as their own, they never came to investigate or really explore it. They came in tiny ships, some only 36 feet long, sailing up from the west coast of Mexico as far north as the *Queen Charlotte Islands,* probing, looking, fighting the winds and the currents. Fresh water and adequate provisions were a continuous problem. The journals of some Spanish explorers are fascinating to read. In 1774, Juan Perez, sailing as far as the *Queen Charlottes,* saw *Mt. Olympus* and named it *Sierra Nevada* (dele Santa Rosalia) the snow mountain of Saint Rosalia.

In 1790 Quimper arrived. He took possession of the land in the name of the King of Spain. His journal tells us that he landed near James Town, by *Dungeness,* to take possession of the land. And this is the record that is translated into English: ''The commander and the greater part of the seamen and soldiers having disembarked took ashore a cross which they adored, on their knees, and everybody in a loud voice proclaimed that in the name of his Majesty the King, Don Carlos, the 4th, the commander of the sloop took possession of this country. As sign of possession, laying hands on his sword which he carried in his belt, he cut with it trees — and branches — and grass and he moved stones and walked over the fields of the beach without contradiction from anyone, asking those present to be witness of it.''

Here he could slash down a bush, or some grass and since nobody said ''don't do it'', apparently nobody owned it.

''Then, immediately taking a large cross on their shoulders, the men of the vessel being arranged in martial order with their muskets and other arms, they carried this in procession, chanting a litany, with all responding. The procession being concluded, the commander planted the cross and erected a pile of stones at the foot of it as a memorial and sign of possession, and he named the bay *Puerto de Quimper.''* It is now *New Dungeness Bay.*

Here we visualize 10 or 12 men, rowing in from their anchored ships in small boats, and assembling on the gravelly beach of the bay to take possession, in the name of Spain, of this new land, which could be said to include all of what is now Washington. I find such reports fascinating.

Spaniards were here from 1774 to 1792, coming in the summer, setting up their headquarters at *Nootka Sound* on *Vancouver Island,* trying to establish a fortress or a settlement at *Cape Flattery.* It didn't last beyond the summer. They bestowed quite a few geographical names. *Port Angeles* was originally a Spanish name: *Puerta Veyartay;* ''Port of the Angels.'' The *San Juan Islands, Wayvess Island, Rosario Strait, Orcas Island, Fidalgo Island, Camino Island, Strait of Harrow, Badillo/Fidalgo* or *Badilla Bay, Susha Island, Mahia, Potos* — all these were names that trace back to these Spanish explorations.

Now it happens that some of these don't apply to the same spots that the Spaniards applied them to, because over the years they were not well recorded. The Spanish tried to keep their explorations secret, or undercover. But in 1846 a British naval officer, Captain Henry (Cowut/Cullut/Callut) came to explore this region and he had gotten access to some of the Spanish records and had the good sense to put some of these names on the map. They got moved around a little bit, but at least they're there.

In 1778, Captain James Cook was off the coast of what is now Washington. He was a tremendous man, an amazing man. The more we learn about him, the more highly we regard him. Cook made three voyages of discovery. He sailed from Britain in July 1776 and reached this part of the world in 1778, exploring, charting, mapping. As Cook sailed along the Northwest coast, he thought he saw an opening to the East, but sailed by it. The fog closed in and he was not sure it was an opening. He said he was flattered by the idea that here was an opening, and so named it *Cape Flattery.* What he actually saw was the *Strait of Juan de Fuca.*

The remarkable thing about the Cook exploration was that Cook's men traded trinkets to the Indians for furs — sea otter furs. It is remarkable because the men were not traders. They had no knowledge of commerce. Visualize them in ships that had no heat — no comforts at all — and they could get a very fine sea otter pelt from an Indian for some buttons or a piece of cloth. The furs, they thought, could be used as bedding, but they didn't have in mind making money until they got to China. The Chinese saw the sea otter pelts, most beautiful of all furs, and were willing to pay high prices for them. For a few days there was threat of a mutiny because the seamen wanted to go back to the Northwest and establish a fur trade. Here was a gold mine, they reasoned, better than gold, better than platinum, maybe as good as diamonds. But the ship returned to England, and when it did the word spread about the sea otter furs. So there followed a great fur rush to this part of the world. Ships hurried in from India, Britain and other parts of Europe, and from the New England states. The sea otter fur trade was launched in a hurry through the 1780s and the 1790s.

One of the merchant adventurers who came was John Veehrs/Meares. He was something of a scoundrel and a liar, but he saw the mountain that had been named *Sierra Nevada de Santa Rosalia* and called it *Mt. Olympus,* having in mind the Greek legend and the Greek mountain that was a home of the gods. Because John Veehrs chose this name and put it on the map in 1788, we now have the *Olympic Peninsula,* the *Olympic National Park,* and the city of *Olympia.* We also have the Olympic Hotel in Seattle, and Olympia beer — all tracing back to John Veehrs in 1788.

Robert Gray, a merchant adventurer from New England, an astute trader, drove his vessel, the *Columbia (re de Beva)* across the bar of a great river. He named it for his vessel on May 11th, 1792, the *Columbia River.* Because Gray made this discovery, the United States had an especially strong claim on this part of the world when the ownership of the Oregon country later was in dispute between Britain and the United States. Gray didn't realize it, but he certainly was making history. Gray's Harbor was named for him, although when he entered it he gave it another name.

The fur traders kept coming. Charles William Barclay came in 1787, age 29. He was sailing a British ship that had Austrian colors and pretended to be an Austrian vessel because of the monopoly that the East India Company then had on all trade in the Pacific. But Charles Barclay brought with him his bride, Frances Hornby Trevor Barclay, a girl of 17, the first white woman to see this region. Apparently a very fine person, alert and sensitive, she was the daughter of a Church of England clergyman. Mrs. Barclay kept a record of what she saw, and by strange coincidence her journal got back to Vancouver Island, over a hundred years later, where an amateur historian borrowed it and copied some excerpts. They give information about names in use as early as 1787.

In 1792, George Vancouver, British naval officer, came here with two vessels: *The Discovery* and the *Chatham. The Discovery* was only 99 feet 2 inches long. *The Chatham* was even smaller. The *Discovery* carried 100 men and officers; the *Chatham* fewer. Vancouver and his crew were the first Englishmen to come into the Puget Sound country. Others came into the strait, but none undertook to explore the Sound. Vancouver went on virtually a naming spree on this trip. Of course *Vancouver Island* commemorates him, as does *Vancouver,* Washington and *Vancouver,* B.C. He was 35 years of age and the voyage lasted 4-1/4 years. He determined that *Vancouver Island is* an island. His charts were so fine that they were in use until fairly recent times.

Vancouver named *Whidbey Island* for one of his officers, *Mt. Baker* for another, *Puget Sound* for Peter Puget. He said he would "honor" the largest mountain by naming it for Admiral Rainier. And, he didn't anticipate the intense feud that later would erupt between Seattle and Tacoma over the name of the mountain. The dispute was taken to the legislature, taken to Congress and the courts. Thousands of dollars, probably $100,000 or more, were spent fighting over whether the name of *Mt. Rainier* should be retained or whether the mountain should be called *Mt. Tacoma.*

Hood Canal was named "Hood's Channel" by Vancouver, using the old meaning of the word canal. A canal could be a long natural waterway. *Mt. St. Helen's* he named for the British ambassador to the court at Madrid. *Possession Point* is near where he took possession of the land in the name of the King of England. *Deception Pass* is where he was deceived. He didn't see it until Joseph Whidbey made the circuit of Whidbey Island in a long boat. *Protection Island* is the island that protects the bay where he took his ships for repair on the way into the sound — *Discovery Bay. Mt. Chatham* is named for his other vessel.

One of the surprising things we learn in the study of history is that so many people were young. There, on the muster roll of 127 men who were with the Vancouver only one was as old as 45. There were 14 between the ages of 30 and 38, 22 between the ages of 26 and 29, 56 between the ages of 20 and 25. 26 percent of his crew — 34 in all — were teenagers and 71 percent were 25 or less.

All through the study of Northwest history I meet young men, very young men. One of the most successful fur traders was a man named Sturgiss who became the skipper of a fur trading vessel at 17. He was a third mate. It happened that the captain died, then the first mate died, and finally the second mate died, leaving Sturgiss to take over command. He made an extremely successful trading voyage, continued in the trade, became a wealthy man and later a member of the Massachusetts legislature.

The first Americans who came overland to cross the continent were members of the Lewis and Clark expedition. Here were young men, too -- Meriwhether Lewis 31, William Clark 35. They did not do much about naming, but they did draw maps, using some new names along the way. They named, of course, *Ft. Klatsum (Clatsop)* where they wintered. They used the names of the Walla Walla Indians for the *Walla Walla River,* and the name of the *Kawitz/Kallitz* Indians for the Kawitz *(Cowlitz)* River. A good many things were named for the two explorers themselves in later years.

When the reports of Lewis and Clark were published, one businessman was astute enough to see that he might make money by establishing a fur trading post on the Pacific Coast. He was

John Jacob Astor, and because of Astor's vision and his astuteness, Ft. Astoria was established where Astoria is now. He sent out two parties. His Pacific Fur Company established posts at *Ft. Spokane* and *Ft. Okanagan*. Then the war of 1812 came along and some Canadians came down and said: ''Look, if you don't sell out to us you will be captured by the British and so why don't you sell.'' And since most of those who manned or staffed *Ft. Astoria* were Canadians or British, they agreed and sold out to the Northwest Company. On the Northwest Company staff was David Thompson, a great geographer. Then came the Hudson's Bay Company, and the Northwest Company was merged with it. This was the edge of the world, but the Hudson's Bay Company was here — a business enterprise — a commercial enterprise — here before government — here even before missionaries and settlers.

During all this time French was spoken more commonly than English since most of their servants, as they were called, came from French Canada. So we have a number of French names on our map, such as *(Nezpurse)/Nez Pours, Palous, Samon Le Sac, Ponderay, Nisqualley, S'Quer Nous* — the Dalles. One of my favorites, dating back to the time of the fur traders, is *Grand Coulee*.

The missionaries started coming in the 1830s. Marcus Whitman came in 1836, and we have *Whitman College* and *Whitman County*. Blanchett came in 1838. Quite a few high schools are named for him. And also in 1838 came the Walkers, *Walker Prairie* is named for them, north of Spokane.

Then in 1841 this region was visited by Lt. Charles Wilkes, commanding the United States Navy exploring expedition. Wilkes applied a lot of names from the war of 1812. *Mt. Constitution* he named for the frigate *Constitution*, and *Bainbridge Island* for a naval hero. *McNeil Island* happened to be for one of the Hudson's Bay people. Wilkes was a great man for naming in patterns, and if you can get the key to the pattern, you can solve a whole lot of name problems. He scattered lots of names around on passages and passes, naming them for civilian technicians who came with him: Artists, ethnographers, scientists, geologists, naturalists and so on. In this region are seven passes named for these civilian technicians: *Pickering Passage, Peal's Passage, Hale's Passage, Dana Pass, Rich's Pass, Geaton/Breton Passage* and *Agate Pass*.

When I was a kid I searched all around *Agate Pass* for agates, not knowing that it was named for Alfred T. Agate, one of Wilkes' artists. He named *Point Defiance* saying that a fortress there could defy the navies of the world. He named *Port Madison, Port Ludlow, Port Gamble. Commencement Bay* was where he commenced some of his surveys. He named several harbors after quartermasters aboard his vessels. Also points: *Point Minor, Point Neil, Point Higher* (phonetic), *Point Sanford, Point Southworth* and *Point Fouly/Folly* which is commonly known as *Three-tree Point*. Down in the South Seas, in the Fijis, Wilkes kidnapped a native chief who had been sort of a gangster and probably murdered some American whalers. His name was Bendovee. He named *Bendovee Island* for this poor kidnapped Fiji Islander. Bendovee, by the way, led the parade when Wilkes returned to the United States, because he was the ''chief'' and the most attractive specimen Wilkes brought back.

Washington Territory was established on February 8, 1853. The proposal was made that this be the Territory of Columbia, but Richard H. Stanton of Kentucky objected. He said if we have Columbia Territory and the District of Columbia, there will be great confusion, so let's name the territory Washington. He did not think there would be confusion between Washington Territory and Washington, D.C. Congress agreed with him, and it became *Washington Territory*.

Most names on the maps relate to early settlers, and rightly so. These people really built the country, not the explorers or discoverers or the Hudson's Bay people. A lot of the names are monuments to their work. *Bremerton* for the Bremer family, *Coupeville* for the Coup family, *La Connor* for Louisa A. Connor. They wanted to make it sound a little Spanish, so they added her two initials ''L.A.''. *Anacortes* resulted from another try to make it sound a little romantic. Ana Curtis Bowman was to be honored, but Anacurtis became *Anacortes*. *Bothell, Renton, Woodinville, Belltown, Ballard, Wilbur* — dozens of place names — all were family names. *Stevens Pass* was named for John F. Stevens, who located the pass for the railroad, not Gov. Isaac Stevens.

Many names related to the old home places where people came from. *Machias* for Machias, Maine; *Kenmore* for Kenmore, Ontario; *Elgin* for Elgin, Illinois; *Stillwater* for Stillwater, Maine; *Greenbank* for Greenbank, Delaware; *Lowell* for Lowell, Massachusetts; *Burlington* for Burlington, Iowa. Then there is one of my favorites — *Wilmaloop Creek* in the *Methow Valley*. It was named for *Wilmaloop Bay* in Australia. Some unknown, lonesome Australian prospector put the name of his hometown bay on the map.

There was naming for a purpose. General Winlock Miller (he wasn't a general but he liked the title and everybody was polite enough to give it to him), going from Kelso to Olympia, found some people hard at work on a settlement and he asked ''What are you going to call it?'' And they answered that they did not know yet. So he said: ''If you will let me name this town, I will give you a school bell.'' He chose the name *Winlock*, his first name and his mother's maiden name. But he forgot to send the bell. When he died the people of Winlock wrote to Mrs. Miller and asked about the school bell. And she did send the bell which was in use for a long time. *Starbuck* was named for General Starbuck of New York, an official of one of the companies behind the Oregon Railroad and Navigation Company, and he sent the town a church bell. *Buckley* was named for a Northern Pacific Railroad official with the hope that if the town was named for him he would give the town better railroad service. *Cheney* was named for Benjamin P. Cheney of Boston, a financier who was right behind the financing of the Northern Pacific Railroad. He was so flattered by this honor, that he sent the town $10,000. The money was used to establish Cheney Academy later to become Eastern Washington University.

The people in a southeast Washington town were not sure what name to choose for their town, so they looked over a list of rich people and selected George M. Pullman, the Pullman car millionaire. They wrote to ask for his permission to use his name, and he responded saying that he was tremendously flattered, the greatest compliment ever paid him, and wanted to do something for the town. He sent a check for $50. What do you do with $50? They bought fireworks for the 4th of July.

We have towns that are named for certain pioneer qualities, such as *Enterprise, Thrift, Opportunity* and *Equality*. There are some humorous names. There used to be a town on Vashon Island called *Aquarium* because Capt. Fish and his family lived there.

And of course, we have the town of *George*, in Eastern Washington, which gets lots of national publicity.

Place names can remind us of the many persons who helped shape the destiny of our state and its communities. It was a great anonymous group of Indians, fur traders, merchant adventurers, missionaries, explorers, settlers, farmers, prospectors, sheep herders who helped build what we have today. We have monuments to them in our place names.

Note: After each place name in the text of this volume is the abbreviated legal description, enabling one to find a place precisely on a map. The meaning of the abbreviated symbols are as follows:

S — Section
T — Township
R — Range
    (A small s after a letter indicates
    a multiple listing.)
N — North
S — South
E — East
W — West
uns. — unsurveyed
USBGN — United States Board of
            Geographic Names

A

A.E.C. Reservation (Grant, Benton, Franklin counties) *see* U.S. Atomic Energy Reservation

Abbey Island *(S.32;T.26N;R.13W)*
A rock island, including a large cave, 3 miles south of Hoh River mouth in Pacific Ocean, directly west of Ruby Beach, west central Jefferson County. It has been heavily eroded by wave action. In 1866, it was named by U.S. Coast Survey, because of a fancied resemblance to an ancient abbey.

Aberdeen *(T.17N;R.9W)*
City at the mouth of Chehalis and Wishkah rivers, east end of Grays Harbor, southwest Grays Harbor County. An important forest products industry city, it was founded in 1867 by Samuel Benn. The name was chosen by B. A. Seaborg, who established fish-packing plants here and at Ilwaco in Pacific County. He objected to the original name, *Wishkah*, and named the place for Aberdeen, Scotland.

Abernathy Creek (Cowlitz County) *see* Abernethy Creek

Abernethy Creek *(Ts.8,9N;R.4W)*
The stream of the creek heads 12 miles north of Columbia River, northwest Cowlitz County; flows to the river near Oak Point. It was named for George Abernethy, an Oregon pioneer, who built a mill near Oak Point before 1850. This stream has borne a number of other names in the past, including *Nequally, Negisticook, Ordway, Mill* and *Abernathy*. It is carried on some recent maps under the latter name.

Abiel Lake *(S.36;T.22N;R.10E)*
A 1-1/2-acre lake, south side of Abiel Peak at Cascade Mountain summit, Snoqualmie National Forest, east central King County. It was named for Abiel Peak.

Abiel Peak *(S.36;T.22N;R.10E)*
The peak rises from a ridge between Silver and Tinkham peaks, at Cascade Mountain summit, 6 miles south of Snoqualmie Pass, extreme east central King County. The name was given by The Mountaineers for Abiel W. Tinkham. (*see* Tinkham Peak)

Acme *(S.6;T.37N;R.5E)*
Village 4-1/2 miles east of Lake Whatcom, on South Fork, Nooksack River, southwest Whatcom County. The name was suggested by the *Acme Hymnal* which Samuel Parks used in church, and which, in 1887, became the name of the post office.

Active Cove *(T.38N;R.2W.) Cove protected by a small island, 7 miles northwest of East Sound, southwest end of Patos Island, north central San Juan County. It was named by U.S. Coast Survey for the U.S. Revenue Cutter Active*, purchased in 1853 from Pacific Mail Steamship Company, and used as a survey vessel in the San Juan Islands under command of Lieut. Cmdr. James Alden.

Ada Creek *(Mt. Rainier National Park)*
The stream of the creek rises in Sourdough Mountains, northeast quarter of the park; flows northwest into Huckleberry Creek. On April 8 and 9, 1914, the name was presented for approval to a Tacoma group by Park Ranger Thomas E. O'Farrell. O'Farrell stated that it had been in use for many years. (USBGN)

Adair (Grant County) *see* Odair

Adams County
This county in southeastern Washington was established by an act of the Territorial Legislature on November 28, 1883, from a portion of Whitman County. Wheat, cattle, and sheep are the major products of the county's 1,895 sq. miles. It is bounded on the north by Lincoln County, on the east and southeast by Whitman, on the south by Franklin, and on the west by Grant. It was named for John Adams, first vice president of the United States and the second president. The name was proposed by Samuel A. Wells, known as "Adams County's first politician."

Adams Creek
(Ts.9,10N;Rs.9,10E.uns)
The stream of the creek rises at the foot of Adams Glacier, northwest slope of Mt. Adams, extreme east central Skamania County; flows northwest to Cispus River at Adams Crossing, just south of the south end of Blue Lake Ridge. In spring and summer, when the glacier melts rapidly, the creek carries a heavy load of glacial flour, which discolors Cispus River. It was named for Adams Glacier, in which it originates.

Adams Glacier *(T.10N;Rs.10,11E)*
An active glacier on the northwest slope of Mt. Adams, southwest Yakima County. It is one of 8 glaciers on Mt. Adams, and was named, in 1901, for John Adams, second president of the United States, by C. E. Rusk. Rusk accompanied Prof. Harry Fielding Reid, a glaciologist from Johns Hopkins University. Reid evidently protested when Rusk named this feature *Reid Glacier*, and suggested that the name of John Adams be applied to this ice field, as well as to the mountain.

Adco *(S.12;T.22N;R.27E)*
Village 5-1/2 miles east of Soap Lake (town), north central Grant County. In 1910, the name was coined by Northern Pacific Railway Company officials, when a rail line was built between Adrian and Connell, Franklin County. It uses the first two letters in each name.

Addy *(S.13;T.33N;R.39E.)*
Community on Colville River, 14 miles south of Colville, central Stevens County. The site is on a land claim patented in 1854 by a pioneer settler named Fatzger, who built a grist mill near the mouth of Addy Creek in the late 1870s. In 1890, Addy became a settlement, when the Spokane Falls & Northern Railway was built. In 1894, it survived a very destructive flood. The town was named for Mrs. Adeline (Addy) Dudrey, an early resident and wife of the first postmaster, Elias S. Dudrey.

Adelaide *((S.1;T.21N;R.3E)*
Small settlement, 6 miles northwest of Auburn, east shore of East Passage, southwest King County. In 1886, it was named for a local girl, Miss Adelaide

Dixon, when a post office was established.

Adkins *(S.20;T.9N;R.33E)*

Community 15 miles northeast of Attalia, west central Walla Walla County. The original name of this place was *Fairfield*. In 1892, the Northern Pacific Railway changed the name of its station to honor W. M. Adkins, from whom a right-of-way had been acquired.

Admiralty Bay *(T.31N;R.1E)*

A west shore bay of Whidbey Island, on Admiralty Inlet, west central Island County. The name was borrowed from Admiralty Inlet. This area was the scene of many early land speculations, some of them quite fantastic. One involved a railroad terminus on the north shore of the bay, with trains to be ferried to the mainland and then to Sedro-Woolley on standard tracks.

Admiralty Head *(S.22;T.31N;R.1E)*

The head projects into Admiralty Inlet, at the site of Ft. Casey on the west coast of Whidbey Island, 6 miles northeast of Port Townsend, Island County. It was named after Admiralty Inlet. An earlier name was *Keelog's Point* or *Keelog Point*, for Dr. J. C. Keelog, who owned an early Donation Land Claim on this site. In 1841, Cmdr. Charles Wilkes called it *Red Bluff* from a reddish tinge on the seaward side.

Admiralty Inlet

The portion of northern Puget Sound which extends northward from Foulweather Bluff to the Strait of Juan de Fuca, between Whidbey Island on the east, and Kitsap and Jefferson counties on the west. In 1790, these waters were explored by Manuel Quimper, and were named *Ensenada de Caamano*. In 1791, Juan Francisco de Eliza cruised here, and applied the present name, in honor of the British Board of Admiralty, which supervised the Royal Navy. In 1841, Cmdr. Charles Wilkes charted these waters as *Admiralty Sound*, although Vancouver's name persisted, and is official today. (USBGN)

Adna *(S.9;T.13N;R.3E)*

Little settlement, 6 miles west of Chehalis, on Chehalis River, west central Lewis County. It has borne a succession of interesting names. When a post office was established, a pioneer named Browning suggested the name *Willoway* for his wife's favorite quota-

tion, "Where there's a will there's a way." Postal authorities objected because there was too much resemblance to *Willapa*. They accepted an alternative suggestion of *Pomona*, which was used for several years. When the Northern Pacific Railway built through here, the locating engineer, W. C. Marion, called the station *Edna*, for Mrs. Edna Browning. Postal authorities changed the name of the post office to *Adna*, however, as there already was a post office called *Edna* in the state.

Adolphus Island

One of 2 small islands, near Skipjack Island, 1 mile north of Waldron Island, San Juan County. In 1841, Cmdr. Charles Wilkes charted this and Gordon Island; but, in 1853, Davidson proved these places non-existent.

Adrian *(S.24;T.22N;R.28E)*

Community 5 miles east of Soap Lake (town), north central Grant County. It was named for Adrian, Michigan, by a Northern Pacific Railway Company superintendent who formerly resided in that town.

Aeneas *(S.6;T.35N;R.31E)*

Small settlement on West Fork, San Poil River, 20 miles southwest of Republic, east central Okanogan County. It was named for an Indian chief, Aeneas Somday, who was a government guide for Lieut. Mullan and others. He died about 1880, at an age estimated to be over 100 years. His first name is a distortion of the French *Ignace*.

Aeneas Creek (2) *(T.35N;Rs.29,30E)* *(T.37N;R.26E)*

These two creeks in Okanogan County bear the same name, and are namesakes of the Indian described under the heading of Aeneas. The creek in Township 35 is the principal western headwater of West Fork, San Poil River, east central Okanogan County. The stream farther west, in Township 37, is a small tributary of the Okanogan River from the west, located southwest of Tonasket.

Aeneas Lake *(S.25;T.37N;R.26E)*

A small lake, 3 miles southwest of Tonasket, central Okanogan County. It is near the south end of Horse Springs Coulee. *(see Aeneas)*

Aeneas Mountain *(S.31;T.38N;R.26E)*

One of 2 mountains with identical names at the south end of a ridge east of

Sinlahekin Creek, south of Loomis, north central Okanogan County. The other mountain is 14 miles northeast of Disautel, Colville National Forest, east central Okanogan County. The mountains have the same name origin. *(see Aeneas)*

Aeneas Valley *(T.36N;R.29E)*

Mountain valley several miles long, which extends from the head of West Fork, San Poil River, to Bonaparte Creek, east central Okanogan County. *(see Aeneas)*

Affi Falls *(Mt. Rainier National Park)*

These very scenic falls are in Lodi Creek, near the west end of Cold Basin, north central area of the park. A group of park officials and supporters approved this name at a meeting in Tacoma on April 8 and 9, 1914. It had been presented by Park Ranger Thomas E. O'Farrell, who considered it eligible because of very long use. (USBGN)

Agate Bay *(S.25;T.38N;R.3E)*

Small settlement located near the north end of Lake Whatcom, on a distinct bay in that lake, southwest Whatcom County. In 1883, it was named *Woodlawn* by Paul Woodard, when it was a grassy clearing surrounded by beautiful, old-growth timber. The present, locally-applied name appears to have no particular significance.

Agate Passage *(T.26N;R.2E)*

Passage between Port Madison Indian Reservation and the northwest tip of Bainbridge Island, north central Kitsap County. A bridge connects Bainbridge Island with the mainland here. In 1841, Cmdr. Charles Wilkes named this feature *Agates Passage*. *(see Agate Point)*

Agate Point *(T.26N;R.2E) A north end point of Bainbridge Island, on Port Madison Bay, northeast Kitsap County. In 1841, the point was named by Cmdr. Charles Wilkes for Alfred T. Agate, an artist and draughtsman on the Wilkes Expedition staff.*

Agnew *(S7;T.30N;R.4W)*

Town 8 miles east of Port Angeles and 1/2 mile inland from nearby Strait of Juan de Fuca, northeast Clallam County. On older maps it is shown as *Fuca* or *De Fuca* -- the latter being the name of the post office. It was named for Charles Agnew, a farmer and logger, who settled here in 1865.

Ahtanum *(S.6;T.12N;R.18E)*

Settlement 8-1/2 miles southwest of Yakima and 1 mile north of Ahtanum Creek, central Yakima County. It was started in 1869 when W. P. Crosno claimed land here. This Indian name, when applied to Ahtanum Creek, meant "creek by the long mountain." The long mountain was Ahtanum Ridge, which stretches west to east over 16 miles. Alternate spellings which have been used include *Atahnum, Atanum, Ahtahnam, Altahnum* and *Atinam*.

Ahtanum Creek
(Ts.11,12N;Rs.13-19E)

The north and south forks of this creek head in a wide area from Yakima Indian Reservation boundary to mountains south of Tieton Reservoir, Yakima County; flow east about 15 miles to join at Tampico; thence about 25 miles east to Yakima River near Wapato Dam. *(see Ahtanum)*

Ahtanum Ridge *(T.12N;Rs.16-18E)*

A 16-mile-long ridge, from west to east, on Yakima Indian Reservation, near its north boundary, south of Ahtanum Creek, central Yakima County. The western end is 2 miles south of Tampico; the eastern terminus is 4 miles south of Yakima. *(see Ahtanum)*

Ainsworth *(S.3;T.8N;R.30E)*

This long-abandoned railroad construction town was 2 miles east of present-day Pasco, near the mouth of Snake River, Franklin County. It was founded in October 1879, by Northern Pacific Railway engineers as a western base for operations. Its importance terminated when rail traffic between Pasco and Tacoma started to move through Stampede Tunnel in the Cascades, rather than via the Wallula route. Building of a bridge across Snake River and the elimination of a ferry were contributing factors. It was named for Capt. J. C. Ainsworth, a prominent official of the Oregon Steam Navigation Company.

Ainsworth Junction (Franklin County) *see* Ainsworth

Airport Lake *(S.19;T.14N;R.2W)*

A narrow, 1,200-ft. lake, with a varying area from 4 to 7 acres, 2-1/2 miles south of Centralia, adjacent to City-County Airport, northwest Lewis County. It was named for its proximity to the airport.

Airway Heights *(S.20;T.25N;R.41E)*

Town 9 miles west of Spokane and directly north of Fairchild Air Force Base, west central Spokane County. It was established in 1942 and incorporated in 1955. The name is for the nearby military air base.

Ajlune *(S.21;T.12N;R.3E)*

Small settlement, 11 miles southwest of Morton, central Lewis County. In 1914, it was named by G. Ghosn, storekeeper at Mossy Rock, for the town of *Ajlun* in Trans-Jordan, east of Jordan River, which was reputed to be the site of the oldest Christian church in the world.

Aladdin *(S.5;T.37N;R.41E)*

Settlement 16 miles northeast of Colville, Colville National Forest, east central Stevens County. It was established on Deep Creek when the nearby Morning Mine was developed. At one time it had 2 stores, a large school, and other town facilities. The closing of the Morning Mine and the inception of rural, free-delivery mail service changed the place from a town to a name along the highway. Better roads enabled the inhabitants to shop in Colville stores. The name remains on the highway and on the mail route.

Alameda *(S.4;T.30N;R.29E)*

Community on south bank of Columbia River, 10 miles north by west of Grand Coulee, northeast Douglas County. In 1907, it was named when a post office was established by an early settler, Vernile F. Hopkins, evidently for the city of that name in California.

Alamicut River (Wahkiakum County) *see* Deep River

Alan (Allen) Point (Island County) *see* Point Allen

Alaska Lake *(Ss.24,25;T.23N;R.11E)*

An eastern slope lake near Cascade Mountain summit, directly southwest of Alaska Mountain, 5 miles northeast of Snoqualmie Pass, Kittitas County. It was named for nearby Alaska Mountain. The Mountaineers applied the name *Gingerless Lake*, although it evidently does not appear on standard maps.

Albion *(S.15;T.15N;R.44E)*

Town on South Fork, Palouse River, 5 miles northwest of Pullman, southeast Whitman County. When settled in the 1880s, the place was called *Guy*. In March 1901, it was changed to *Albion*

through the persuasion of a British settler named Thomas, who thereby perpetuated the early British name for this region -- *New Albion.*

Albion Hill *(S.35;T.37N;R.34E)*

A Colville National Forest peak, elevation 5,707 ft., 12 miles east of Republic, in the mountain range which runs north and south through the middle of central Ferry County. By definition, it would be a mountain rather than a hill. It was named for *Albian* Eastman, an early ranger in the U.S. Forest Service. Even Forest Service maps include the spelling error.

Alden Bank *(T.38N;R.1W)*

Bank 2-1/2 miles northeast of Sucia Island, in the middle of Georgia Strait, extreme west central Whatcom County. In 1853, the bank was named by U.S. Coast Survey for Lieut. Cmdr. James Alden, an artist, who discovered the shoal in that year while in command of U.S. Revenue Cutter and survey ship *Active*. In 1841, Alden had been master of *U.S.S. Vincennes* under Cmdr. Charles Wilkes.

Alden Point *(S.17;T.38N;R.2W)*

A west end point of Patos Island, 7 miles northwest of East Sound, extreme north central San Juan County. The point was named by U.S. Coast Survey for Lieut. Cmdr. James Alden. *(see Alden Bank)*

Alder Creek *(Ts.27,28N;Rs.17,18E)*

The stream of the creek rises on the west slope of Entiat Mountains, Wenatchee National Forest, 2 miles south of Mad Lake, northwest Chelan County; flows 5 miles south to Chiwawa River. It was named by pioneers for abundant alder trees where the main trail crosses this creek.

Alder Creek *(Ts.4,5N;Rs.22,23E)*

The stream of the creek rises in extreme east central Klickitat County; flows south and east 10 miles to Columbia River at Alderdale. It was named for the abundant alder trees along portions of its course.

Alder Creek *(T.34N;Rs.8,9E)*

The stream of the creek rises in a mountainous area, 8-1/2 miles southwest of Rockport, central Skagit County; flows 4 miles northeast and east to North Fork, Stillaguamish River. It was so named because it flows through many patches of hardwood forest which consist mostly of native red alder.

Alder Creek *(Ts.29,30N;R.37E)*

The stream of the creek rises at Boundary Butte on Spokane Indian Reservation, southwest Stevens County; flows northeast and northwest to Columbia River at Fruitland -- a distance of about 12-1/2 miles. Originally, it was called *Powwow Creek* because local Indians held council meetings here. The present name has been placed on several streams in the region, where fringes of white alder often grow along the banks of water courses.

Alder Creek Slough (Skagit County) *see* Hamilton Slough

Alder Dam Lake (Pierce County) *see* Lake Alder

Alderdale *(S.9;T.4N;R.23E)*

Town on Columbia River, at mouth of Alder Creek, extreme southeast Klickitat County. The name was borrowed from Alder Creek when the town was platted by William Warner of Western Investment Company.

Aldrich (Walla Walla County) *see* Buroker

Aleck Rocks *(S.19;T.34N;R.1W)*

Several rocky islets at entrance to Aleck Bay, south end of Lopez Island, southeast San Juan County. The name was locally applied for a pioneer who settled on the bay before the San Juan boundary dispute. (USBGN)

Alfalfa *(S.33;T.10N;R.21E)*

Community 4 miles southeast of Toppenish, southeast Yakima County. In 1897, it was named by Northern Pacific Railway personnel when a spur was built here. At the time, very large volumes of alfalfa hay were shipped from this location. In 1905, a town developed which boasted a 20-room hotel, a school, and a post office. Its importance diminished in later years when rural free mail delivery caused abandonment of the post office.

Algona *(S.26;T.21N;R.4E)*

Town 2 miles southwest of Auburn, extreme southwest King County. In 1910, the town was named at a mass meeting of residents called by C. D. Hillman, a real estate promoter. The meeting adopted the name *Algoma*, which Hillman suggested, and which was for a town in Wisconsin. This Indian name means "valley of flowers." Citizens later used the name *Valley City*, but dropped it when the post office confused it with *Valley Grove* in Walla Walla County. The misspelling of the town's present name was done either by error or intent by postal officials when a post office was established.

Alice Falls *(Mt. Rainier National Park)*

Waterfall on Spunkwush (Spukwash, Spuckwush) Creek, a northern tributary of Carbon River, north central zone of the park. This name was well established by common usage prior to April 1914, according to Park Ranger Thomas E. O'Farrell. It is for an unidentified park visitor who made a strong impression on the early park staff. (USBGN)

Alice Lake *(Ss.26,27;T.24N;R.7E)*

A 1/2-mile-long, irregularly-shaped lake, 2 miles south of Fall City, central King County. Its original name, *Mud Lake*, was changed by sensitive citizens to that of a local belle.

Alice Lakes (King County) *see* Mt. Kent Lakes

Alki *(S.10;T.24N;R.3E)*

The first settlement on Elliott Bay, at the mouth of a small stream which flowed into the bay on the north side of Alki Point, King County. The stream is no longer visible, having been placed underground in subsequent realty developments. It can be traced in Schmitz Park in the upper part of its course. Alki was the ancestor of Seattle, and was founded in 1851 by the Denny Party. It was platted by C. C. Terry, after most of the original party had moved to the east shore of Elliott Bay. Its Chinook Indian name means "bye and bye," "after a while," or "soon." A nickname, based on the Indian meaning, was *New York Alki*. The origin of this nickname came from the original name *New York* which the Denny Party used for the place after they settled in the fall of 1851. When the settlement developed more slowly than they had expected, the Indian name for "soon" was added.

Alki Crest *(Mt. Rainier National Park)*

Mountain ridge, elevation 5,200 ft., northwest of Tolmie Peak, northwest area of the park; it forms a divide between Tolmie Creek and Carbon River. (USBGN) (*see* Alki)

Alki Point *(Ss.10,15;T.24N;R.3E)*

An abandoned townsite, originally a flat, sandy spit which extended 1/2 mile into Puget Sound from hills to the east, west central King County. On November 13, 1851, 24 persons landed here from the schooner *Exact* to form a settlement which later developed into the City of Seattle. The Denny Party, as they were called, found no safe boat landing here, and most of them moved to the east shore of Elliott Bay in February 1852. In 1858, Charles C. Terry platted the townsite on part of the point that was later abandoned. (*see* Alki)

Alkire (Ferry County) *see* West Fork

Allan Island *(Ss.4,5;T.34N;R.1E)*

An island on Rosario Strait at the entrance to Burrows Bay, 3-1/2 miles southwest of Anacortes, southwest Skagit County. In 1790, Dionisio Galiano named this island and adjacent Burrows Island as *Las Islas Morros*. The present name was chosen by Cmdr. Charles Wilkes for Capt. William Henry Allan, a naval hero of the War of 1812. Wilkes charted the name as *Allan's Island*, which since has been shortened to the present spelling.

Allard *(S.6;T.13N;R.26E)*

Community 6-1/2 miles west of White Bluff, on south bank of Columbia River, northwest Benton County. It was given the name of a pioneer settler, Samuel Allard, when the Chicago, Milwaukee & St. Paul Railway established a station at this point.

Allen *(S.14;T.35N;R.3E)*

Community 3 miles northwest of Burlington, on Samish River, west central Skagit County. It was named for a colorful pioneer sheriff, George Washington Lafayette Allen, who also founded the town of Atlanta on Samish Island.

Allen (Snohomish County) *see* Oso

Allen Bank *(T.24N;R.2E)*

A 10-fathom bank, at the north entrance to West (Colvos) Passage, southeast of Blake Island, southeast Kitsap County. In 1857, George Davidson of U.S. Coast Survey charted this feature, and is reported to have named it for a member of the survey party. It is not shown on most recent maps.

Allen Mountain
(Ss.35,36;T.14N;R.7E)

A 5,103-ft. peak, 9 miles northeast of Randle, northeast Lewis County. It was named in the 1920s for Grenville F. Allen, who then was forest supervisor of this area.

Alloweze (Grant County) *see* Burke

Allyn *(S.20;T.22N;R.1W)*

Town on the northwest shore of North Bay, 4 miles southeast of Hood Canal, east central Mason County. Formerly a logging town, it is now largely dependent on berry culture. When the town was platted in 1889, it was named for Judge Frank Allyn, a prominent Tacoma jurist, who was active in promoting the town.

Alma (Okanogan County) *see* Okanogan

Alma Creek *(T.27N;R.18E)*

The very short stream of the creek rises on Miners Ridge, Wenatchee National Forest, Central Chelan County; flows 2 miles northeast to Mad Creek. It was named by Forest Ranger John Brender for one of his two daughters. He named Wilma Creek for the other daughter.

Almira *(S.32;T.26N;R.31E)*

Town 35 miles west of Davenport, extreme west central Lincoln County. When founded in 1889, the place was named *Davisine*, for Charles C. Davis, owner of the site and first merchant in the area. He later sold part of his interest to 2 men, Odgers and Reed, who wanted to establish a townsite. When Mrs. Davis signed a deed, the 2 purchasers noticed that her given name was Almira, and christened the new town with that designation. Another report states that the name of Mrs. Davis was chosen for the town by the chief engineer of Northern Pacific Railway Company when Davis sold him a right-of-way across the property.

Almota *(S.13;T.14N;R.42E)*

Community on north bank of Snake River, 36 miles northwest of Clarkston, extreme south central Whitman County. In 1877, the town was founded by L. M. Ringer, who established a store. It was an important wheat-shipping point during the days of river navigation. The location is on a prehistoric Indian site which Nez Perce tribesmen called *Allamotin* or *Almotine*. The translation is "torchlight fishing" or "moonlight fishing." A distortion of this name, *La Monte*, was used in early days.

Aloha *(S.22;T.20N;R.12W)*

A sawmill and shingle mill community 2 miles east of Pacific Ocean at Pacific Beach, on Beaver Creek, west central Grays Harbor County. In 1905, it was founded by R. D. Emerson and W. H. Dole. The name, a Hawaiian greeting, was chosen by members of the Dole family, who had heavy interests in Hawaii.

Alocaman (Alokomin) River (Wahkiakum County) *see* Elokomin River

Alpha *(S.18;T.13N;R.2E)*

Small settlement 18 miles east of Chehalis, near South Fork, Newaukum River, central Lewis County. It has been called *Shoestring, Tilton* and *Alpha Prairie*. The name chosen by Postmaster James Vickery was the Greek word meaning "first."

Alpha *(S.7;T.21N;R.45E)*

A faded town with a few remains, 3 miles north of Latah, near Latah Creek, southeast Spokane County. In 1872, R. H. Wimpy and David T. Ham started the first town in this county, naming it Alpha because it was "first." Local names used for the community before 1872 were *Centerview* and *Hangman's Creek*.

Alpine *(S.26;T.26N;R.12E)*

Community 8 miles west of Cascade Mountain summit and 5-1/2 miles east of Skykomish, Snoqualmie National Forest, northeast King County. A former sawmill center, it was first named *Nippon* because of Japanese labor employed in one of the sawmills. The present name was substituted in January 1915, through the influence of C. L. Clemans, a sawmill owner. The name is descriptive, as the town is in rough, mountainous terrain. Both names are used on some local maps.

Alpine Creek *(T.30N;R.16E)*

This short, glacier-fed stream of the creek rises on Wenatchee National Forest, northwest Chelan County; flows about 2 miles from the southeast slope of Buck Mountain to Chiwawa River. In 1925, it was named by Jay Lonergan, mining engineer of Royal Development Company, for the alpine nature of the surrounding country.

Alpowa *(S.17;T.11N;R.44E)*

Town on Alpowa Creek, 12 miles west of Clarkston, east central Garfield County. It evidently took the name of an Indian village to the east, where Alpowa Creek enters Snake River. A translation from the Nez Perce word *alpaha* is said to mean "spring forming a creek" or "mouth of a spring-fed creek." Other spellings of the Indian word are *alpahwha* and *elpawawe*. Another version of the name's derivation comes from pioneer missionaries who were familiar with Nez Perce, and who recorded the word *halahpawit* as meaning "Sabbath" or "Sabbath rest." They stated that this was applied to the Indian village on Snake River by an Indian convert named Timothy, alias "Indian Tim." This name may have later been distorted to Alpowa, and applied to the town and to the creek on which it is located.

Alpowa *(S.20;T.11N;R.45E)*

Community on north bank of Snake River, 9 miles west of Clarkston, southeast Whitman County. There are numerous springs in the locality. (*see* Alpowa, Garfield County)

Alpowa Creek *(Ts.10,11N;Rs.42-44E)*

The stream of the creek rises in Umatilla National Forest, south Garfield County; flows northeast for 31 miles through Garfield and Asotin counties to Snake River, 7 miles west of Clarkston. The stream is intermittent in its upper course, and sinks before reaching Snake River. (*see* Alpowa, Garfield County)

Alpowa City (Asotin County) *see* Silcott

Alstown *(S.19;T.24N;R.23E)*

A station on a branch of Great Northern Railway on Moses Creek, 13 miles east of Columbia River, south central Douglas County. It was named for Albert ("Al") Luther Rogers, a civil engineer, merchant (Rogers & Howe Store), and civic leader of nearby Waterville. From 1909 to 1913, he served as a University of Washington regent.

Alta Creek *(T.25N;R.8W)*

The stream of the creek rises in 3 small lakes, 11 miles south of Mt. Olympus summit, central Olympic National Park, Jefferson County; flows 5-1/2 miles northwest to Queets River. This creek, like several other tributaries of Queets River, carries a Chinook jargon name; *alta* means "now" or "at the present time." It should not be confused with Pelton Creek, directly west. (USBGN)

Alta Lake *(Ss.10,15;T.29N;R.23E)*

A 1-1/2-mile-long lake, 2 miles

southwest of Pateros and 2 miles west of Columbia River, extreme southwest Okanogan County. Alta Lake State Park, 160 acres in extent, is on the lake. Why the name was applied to this lake is evidently not of public record. (*see* Alta)

Alta Lake State Park
(Ss.10,15;T.29N;R23E)

A 160-acre state park on Alta Lake, 2 miles southwest of Pateros and 2 miles west of Columbia River, extreme southwest Okanogan County. Camping, swimming, and fishing are the main attractions. (*see* Alta)

Alta Vista *(Mt. Rainier National Park)*

A ridge camp in Paradise Valley near the snow line, on the south central slope of Mt. Rainier. It was named by John P. Hartman of Tacoma, who camped here in 1889 with a party of Tacoma climbers. His Spanish phrase means "high view." (USBGN)

Altapus (Kittitas County) *see* Coleman Creek

Alto *(S.31;T.11N;R.38E)*

Community on McKay Creek, 8 miles northwest of Dayton, at an altitude of 1,900 ft., northwest Columbia County. The name was given by railroad location engineers because it is at the summit of a divide between Whetstone Hollow and Tucannon River drainage area.

Alyea *(S.2;T.30N;R.37E)*

Abandoned settlement on Hunter Creek, 6 miles east of Columbia River, southwest Stevens County. In 1889, it was established with a post office and store, but declined and is no longer carried on current maps. It was named by local residents for a pioneer family when the post office was established.

Amanda Park *(T.23N;R.10W)*

Settlement at the outlet of Quinault Lake into lower Quinault River, north central Grays Harbor County. It was founded in 1925 as a tourist camp with summer homes for rent or sale. The name is for the wife of J. J. Southard, co-founder of the place.

Amber *(S.36;T.22N;R.40E)*

Community 11 miles southwest of Cheney, on the north shore of Calvert Lake, extreme southwest Spokane County. Originally it was called *Calvert* for the lake on which it is located, and which was named for an early settler

here. It was changed to the name of a nearby post office, Amber, for conformity, and to secure better postal service.

Amber Creek *(T.29N;Rs.14,15E)*

The stream of the creek rises 2-1/2 miles east of Cascade Mountain summit, east slope of Indian Head Peak, Wenatchee National Forest, northwest Chelan County; flows 2-1/2 miles northeast to White River. It was named by U.S. Forest Supervisor A. H. Sylvester for the water's amber color, due to glacial silt.

Amboy *(S.16;T.5N;R.3E)*

Village 5 miles south of Lake Merwin on Cedar Creek, north central Clark County. The name is a composite arranged by the A. M. Ball family who settled here in 1879, and operated the post office when it was established in 1880. They combined the initials "A. M." with "boy" for their popular son. The family came from Amboy, Minnesota, which was named by them in the same manner.

Amboy Park *(S.16;T.5N;R.3E)*

A 5-acre park in the town of Amboy on Cedar Creek, north central Clark County. It is used mostly by local people. (*see* Amboy)

Amelia *(S.17;T.21N;R.3W)*

Once a town 4 miles south of Union on Hood Canal, central Mason County. There is no substantial settlement now, although it did have some town facilities and a post office. It was named for Amelia Emmonds, postmistress.

American Camp *(T.34N;R.2W)*

A state historical site near Cattle Point at the southeast end of San Juan Island, south central San Juan County. It was the site of a U.S. military camp during the San Juan boundary dispute of 1859-1872. Under the command of Capt. George Pickett, it was occupied by the 9th U.S. Infantry. Other names that have been applied to this site are *Ft. San Juan* and *Camp Pickett*. Neither has persisted.

American Prairie *(T.19N;R.2E)*

A prairie around Sequalitchew Lake, 1 mile west of Camp Murray, northwest Pierce County. The first name, chosen by early traders, was *Big Prairie*. When a missionary station for Indians was established here, the name was changed to *Mission Prairie* After members of the Wilkes Expedition chose this place for an Independence Day celebration in 1841,

the name was again changed -- this time to its present name.

American River
(Ts.16,17N;Rs.11-14E.partly uns)

A Snoqualmie National Park river which heads at Cascade Mountain summit in forks north and south of Chinook Pass, northwest Yakima County; flows east by north about 20 miles to Naches River near Sawmill Flat. The original name of the river was *Miners Creek*. As the area developed, local citizens chose a patriotic title which was not used for other rivers in the state.

Anacortes *(T.35N;Rs.1,2E)*

Town on the north end of Fidalgo Island, west central Skagit County. It experienced many early-day booms, and now has several very substantial industries. Amos Bowman, who platted the town in 1876, chose the name of his wife, *Anna Curtis* Bowman. The postal authorities altered the post office name to the present form. As it happened, however, the family name of Curtis had a Spanish origin of *Cortes*, which nullified the error of postal officials. Earlier names for the place were *Ship Harbor, Squaw Harbor* and *Magic City*.

Anacortes Lake (Skagit County) *see* Cranberry Lake

Anatone *(S.26;T.8N;R.46E)*

Small town at the foot of Blue Mountains, 25 miles south of Clarkston on Mill Creek, south central Asotin County. In June 1787, it was established by Charles Isecks and Daniel McIvor. Isecks operated a trading post which was a stop-off point on the Asotin route to Salmon River gold mines in Idaho. *Anatone* is a Nez Perce name for Tenmile Creek, 2-1/2 miles to the east, which was applied to this town by the founders. Two legends state that the name comes from that of a well-liked Nez Perce Indian woman in the area. Some say Anatone was her name; others that it was *Tony Ann*, reversed by Charles Isecke to produce Anatone. Judge Elgin V. Kuykendall, who gave particular attention to this name, reported that he could find no meaning for it.

Anatone Creek (Asotin County) *see* Tenmile Creek

Anderson Bay *(S.20;T.25N;R.5E)*

A small, narrow cove on the east shore of Lake Washington, east of Hunts Point and west of Yarrow, northwest

King County. It was named for one of the earliest land owners on this bay. An alternate name, in early days, was *Cosy Cove*.

Anderson Creek *(T.37N;R.9E)*

The stream of the creek heads in several small lakes, west of Mt. Watson, south central Whatcom County; flows 6 miles west to Baker River. This creek should not be confused with Anderson Creek, a tributary of North Fork, Nooksack River, although they appear to have the same name origin. (*see* Anderson Creek in T.39N;R.8E)

Anderson Creek *(T.39N;R.8E.uns)*

The stream of the creek heads in Galena Chain Lakes, Mt. Baker National Forest, central Whatcom County; flows 4-1/2 miles north to North Fork, Nooksack River. The creek should not be confused with Anderson Creek in the Baker Lake drainage area, although the lakes appear to have the same name origin. The name was applied locally in the 1890s for Hon. Michael Anderson, who represented this district in the State Legislature. Another local name was *Fern Roots Creek*, for a dense fern growth along the banks.

Anderson Glacier
(Ss.28,29,32,33;T.26N;R.5W)

One of 4 glaciers on Mt. Anderson slopes, at the head of Quinault River, between Mt. Anderson and Anderson Pass, east central Olympic National Park, Jefferson County. (*see* Anderson Pass)

Anderson Island *(Ts.19,20N;R.1E)*

A large island with many lakes bounded by Drayton Passage on the northwest, Balch Passage on the north, and Nisqually Reach on the south and east, northwest Pierce County. In 1841, it was named by Cmdr. Charles Wilkes to acknowledge many favors received from Alexander Caulfield Anderson, chief trader of Hudson's Bay Company at Fort Nisqually. In 1846, it was charted as *Fisgard Island* by Capt. R. N. Inskip, for H. M. Frigate *Fisgard*, on station in the Pacific northwest from 1844 until 1847. His name never came into common use. Another name which did not persist was *Wallace Island*, named for Leander C. Wallace, who was killed by Snoqualmie Indians at Ft. Nisqually during the early years of Indian unrest.

Anderson Lakes *(S.26;T.37N;R.9E)*

Four small, connected lakes on the northwest side of Mt. Watson, 11 miles northeast of Concrete, south central Whatcom County. The lakes are separated by 700 to 2,600 ft., and with elevations from 4,425 to 5,050 ft. The lake areas are: No. 1, 4 acres; No. 2, 4 acres; No. 3, 2 acres, and No. 4, 2 acres. The name is for Anderson Creek which drains the lakes.

Anderson Pass *(Ts.25,26N;R.5W)*

An Olympic National Park pass between the headwaters of West Creek and Quinault River, directly south of Anderson Glacier, east central Jefferson County. It was named by Lieut. Joseph P. O'Neil, U.S.A., who was in charge of an army mapping party in the Olympic Mountains in 1885 and 1890. In 1890, he named it for Maj. Gen. T. M. Anderson, commandant at Vancouver barracks from 1886 until 1898. O'Neil named Anderson Glacier at the same time for the same person.

Anderson Range
(Ts.25,26N;Rs.5,6W)

A series of high peaks with many glaciers, including elevations to 7,800 ft., located in the center of Olympic National Park; the area extends from Mt. Anderson northwest to East Peak, Jefferson County. This range name was conceived by Lieut. Joseph P. O'Neil, U.S.A., during his exploration of the Olympic Mountains in 1890. It did not receive recognition. (*see* Anderson Pass)

Andrews Creek *(T.28N;R.2W)*

The stream of the creek rises on Olympic National Forest, southeast Clallam County; flows northeast through Jefferson County, 4-1/2 miles to Lake Crocker. It was locally named for a homesteader who claimed land here in the 1870s.

Angeles Point *(S.27;T.31N;R.7W)*

A point on Strait of Juan de Fuca, 2 miles west of Port Angeles, north central Clallam County. The name was borrowed by local residents from nearby Port Angeles.

Angels Lake (Clallam County) *see* Lake Angeles

Angle Lake *(S.3;T.22N;R.4E)*

A 102-acre lake shaped like a "lazy L," 4 miles southwest of Renton, west central King County. It is popular for recreation and summer residence, and was named by local residents for its shape.

Angle Peak *(S.10;T.28N;R.19E)*

A boundary peak between Okanogan and Wenatchee national forests, 3 miles northwest of Entiat River in Chelan Mountains, central Chelan County. It was named by Forest Supervisor A. H. Sylvester because of a sharp bend in the ridge at this peak.

Angry Mountain *(S.17;T.12N;R.10E)*

A Gifford Pinchot National Forest peak, elevation 5,200 ft., 8 miles southeast of Packwood, southeast Lewis County. The name is of local origin, and refers to frequent storm clouds and turbulence surrounding the mountain top.

Ankeny *(S.27;T.16N;R.37E)*

Village 8 miles north of Palouse Falls, southeast Adams County. It was named by railroad officials for U.S. Sen. Levi Ankeny, a local landowner.

Annas Bay *(Ts.21,22N;Rs.3,4W)*

A south side bay of Hood Canal at the Great Bend, west of Union, central Mason County. Most of the shore land is within Skokomish Indian Reservation. In 1841, it was named *Anna's Bay* by Cmdr. Charles Wilkes. On some maps, the place is called *Annos Bay* and on others, *Anna Bay*. The present form is generally accepted as correct. Identity of Anna is not known.

Annette Lake *(S.25;T.22N;R.10E)*

A 19.7-acre lake at the head of Humpback Creek, directly west of Silver Peak at Cascade Mountain summit, east central King County. It was named by The Mountaineers for one of their lady members, Annette Wiestling, at the suggestion of George E. Wright.

Annette Lake (King County) *see* Lake Annette

Anthem Creek *(T.30N;R.17E.uns)*

The stream of the creek heads in Choral Lake, between Choral Creek and North Fork, Entiat River, Wenatchee National Forest, northwest Chelan County; flows 5 miles southwest to Entiat River. It was named by U.S. Forest Supervisor A. H. Sylvester, because it is "a singing stream."

Anvil Rock *(Mt. Rainier National Park)*

A rocky island, elevation 9,584 ft., on the upper reaches of Paradise Glacier, south slope of Mt. Rainier, below Cowlitz Cleaver, near the trail from Paradise Valley to the summit. It offers a view of 100 miles in all directions, except north. This descriptive name of the rock's shape was applied by a party which climbed the mountain before 1890. (USBGN)

Apple Lake (Snohomish County) *see* Grass Lake

Appledale *(S.33;T.22N;R.23E)*

Community in Moses Coulee, 10 miles east by south of Wenatchee, extreme southwest Douglas County. In 1909, it was named by Great Northern Railway officials when that railroad built through here; the name was transferred from the town which now is Mansfield. Its name is descriptive, as many orchards flourish here.

Appletree Cove *(T.27N;R.2E)*

Small cove on Puget Sound, directly south of Kingston, northeast Kitsap County. In 1841, it was named by Cmdr. Charles Wilkes for the many native apple trees in blossom. Land clearing has removed most of these wild apple trees *(Pyrus rivularis)*, although some remain today. In April and May, they are covered with small, white blossoms.

Appleyard *(S.21;T.22N;R.20E)*

A Great Northern Railway terminal for icing and assembling apple shipments, South Wenatchee, southeast Chelan County. This very descriptive name was chosen by the railway.

Arbuthnot Lake (Whatcom County) *see* Galena Chain Lakes

Arcadia *(S.28;T.20N;R.2W)*

Town on a point at the south entrance to Hammersley Inlet, southeast Mason County. In the early days of Shelton, it was a wide-open, booming trade center, much-frequented by loggers. Local residents named it for a country in ancient Greece, although there was little resemblance.

Arcadia Point *(S.28;T.20N;R.2W)*

A south side point on Hammersley Inlet entrance, on Pickering Passage, southeast Mason County. In 1841, it was named by Cmdr. Charles Wilkes as *Cook Point.* When this area was developed by settlers, that name was dropped in favor of the present name. (*see* Arcadia)

Arch Island *(S.16;T.23N;R.13W)*

A rock island in Pacific Ocean at the mouth of Whale Creek, northwest Grays Harbor County. The name was applied by local residents because of a water-worn arch in the island. (*see* Grenville Arch)

Arch Rock *(S.22;T.18N;R.11E)*

A scenic, sheer cliff, towering about 1,000 ft. above the headwaters of Greenwater River, on the Cascade Crest Trail between Government Meadows on the north and Big Crow Basin on the south, extreme northeast Pierce County. Formerly, it was a natural arch, but much of the rock has crumbled and fallen.

Archawat Village *(S.12;T.33N;R.16W)*

A former Indian village on Makah Indian Reservation on Pacific Ocean, 2 miles southeast of Cape Flattery, extreme northwest Clallam County. It had a Makah name which meant "good beach." The name has been spelled *Hacha-wa, Ah-ah-a-wat* and *Arch-a-wat.*

Archipelago de Arro (San Juan County) *see* San Juan Archipelago

Arden *(S.10;T.34N;R.39E)*

Small community on Little Pend Oreille River, 6 miles south of Colville, central Stevens County. In 1859, Marcus Oppenheimer built a grist mill here on the river, the second grist mill to operate in the Colville Valley. He later added a sawmill. In 1890, when the Spokane Falls & Northern Railway was built through Arden, the town became a lumber-shipping point of some importance. It was named by an early settler, Jack Mooney, but the name's origin has not been established.

Ardenvoir *(S.20;T.26N;R.20E)*

A sawmill community in Entiat Valley, on Entiat River, 10 miles northwest of Entiat, east central Chelan County. In 1919, it was established by C. A. Harris, and moved 3 miles in 1931 to its present location. It was named by Harris for his son, Arden Harris.

Argyle *(S.23;T.35N;R.3W)*

A scattered community on North Bay, northwest end of Griffin Bay, on the southeastern shore of San Juan Island, south central San Juan County. It is reported to have been named by a local settler for *Argyll*, Scotland.

Ariel Point (Jefferson Point) *see* Nodule Point

Ariels Point (Island County) *see* Double Bluff

Argus Bay (Skagit County) *see* Burrows Bay

Arkansas Creek *(T.9N;R.3W)*

A short stream tributary to Cowlitz River, near Castle Rock, southwest Cowlitz County. The name originated from the large number of settlers who came here from Arkansas in the 1850s.

Arletta *(S.22;T.21N;R.1E)*

Small settlement at the north end of Hales Passage, 5 miles southwest of Gig Harbor, northwest Pierce County. In 1892, the name was composed by Mrs. George Powell, a local resident. She combined the name of her daughter, Arla, with a portion of the name of Valetta, a beautiful city on the island of Malta.

Arlington *(T.31N;R.5E)*

Town 12 miles north of Everett, at the junctions of North and South forks, Stillaguamish River, northwest Snohomish County. In March 1889, when a townsite was platted here by Morris G. Haller, the name chosen was *Haller* for Col. Granville O. Haller, father of the founder. it is shown on some older maps as *Haller City.* An adjoining townsite, purchased by J. W. McLeod, a railroad contractor, was named *Arlington* for the National Cemetery in Washington, D.C. In June 1903, the 2 townsites were joined under the name of Arlington in a popular election.

Armitage Island *(S.10;T.35N;R.1W)*

An island directly south of the south point of Blakely Island, in Thatcher Pass, east central San Juan County. The name appears to have been applied locally for a pioneer family who settled here. (USBGN)

Armstrong Bay *(T.17N;R.12W)*

A bay inside a long, sand spit at the north entrance to Grays Harbor, in North Bay, southwest Grays Harbor County. It was named for a pioneer who established a sawmill on Chehalis River in 1850. His name also was used in early days for the spit at the south entrance of Grays Harbor, now called *Point Chehalis.*

Armstrongs Point (Grays Harbor County) *see* Point Chehalis

Arro Islands (San Juan County) *see* San Juan Islands

Arrow Point *(S.8;T.25N;R.2E)*

A west shore point on Bainbridge Island, northeast of Battle Point, central Kitsap County. In 1906, it was named by Albert H. Lord, when he platted the point into 33 waterfront tracts. His name was appropriate, as many arrow points and other Indian artifacts have been found here.

Arrowhead Mountain
(S.15;T.26N;R.15E)

A Wenatchee National Forest mountain, 5-1/2 miles east of Cascade Mountain summit, 1 mile south of Nason Creek, southwest Chelan County. It was named by Forest Supervisor A. H. Sylvester for a slide-rock area on the south slope, which is shaped like an arrowhead.

Art Creek *(T.38N;Rs.33-34E)*

The stream of the creek heads 2 miles east of Malo, Colville National Forest, northwest Ferry County; flows west to the San Poil River near that town. It was named for Arthur Radigan, one of the first U.S. Forest Service rangers on Colville National Forest.

Artic *(S.8;T.16N;R.8W)*

Community on North River, 6 miles south of Cosmopolis, south central Grays Harbor County. The name is for Arta Saunders, wife of the first postmaster. Her name was suggested when a post office was established, but postal authorities mistook the final "a" for "ic" and the error was not corrected. Many such errors happened in the days of handwritten letters compiled by persons who were not skilled in penmanship. Some maps show the name as *Arctic*, in an attempt to correct a presumed error.

Artesian *(S.5;T.12N;R.20E)*

Community 1-1/2 miles east of Moxee, east central Yakima County. In April 1900, a post office was established in the home of James H. Gano. The name was chosen by Gano because of many artesian wells in the vicinity. At one time, these were used extensively for irrigation. A few are reported to be still in use.

Artesian Coulee *(Ts.4,5N;R.24E)*

A narrow valley, 3 miles long, terminating at Columbia River, northwest of Crow Butte and across the river from Castle Rock, Oregon, extreme southwest Benton County. The coulee was named in pioneer days for flowing artesian wells that were struck in exploring for water.

Arthur Peak *(Mt. Rainier National Park)*

A Mt. Rainier National Park peak, elevation 5,471 ft., above Ranger Creek and northeast of Tolmie Peak, northwest corner of the park. It was named for Arthur Rust of Tacoma, a frequent park visitor and son of W. R. Rust, a prominent Tacoma citizen.

Arupp (Douglas County) *see* Lamoine

Arzina *(S.14;T.34N;R.37E)*

Village 12 miles south by west of Kettle Falls, 4 miles east of Columbia River, west central Stevens County. In 1898, it was founded by Charles H. Chamberlin on purchased land. A post office, school, and store were established; the school remains. It was named for Mrs. Arzina Chamberlin, first postmistress, wife of the founder, and pioneer music teacher.

Asahel Curtis Grove *(T.22N;R.11E)*

Snoqualmie National Forest park and picnic grove at the last crossing of Snoqualmie River and Sunset Hwy., west of Snoqualmie Pass, east central King County. The grove has a bronze plaque in memory of Asahel Curtis, a famous photographer, who produced classic studies of Indians and Indian life, particularly in this state.

Ash (Skamania County) *see* Carson

Ashford *(S.27;T.15N;R.6E)*

Village in upper Nisqually Valley, 6 miles west of Nisqually Park entrance to Mt. Rainier National Park, southeast Pierce County. It was named for Walter A. Ashford, who platted it in 1904, after purchasing the land from Northern Pacific Railway Company.

Ashnola River *(Ts.39,40N;Rs.20,21E)*

The stream of the river originates in North Cascade Primitive Area, northwest Okanogan County; flows north across the Canadian boundary to join Similkameen River, British Columbia. It carries the original Indian name, which has been variously spelled as *Ashtnulon, Ashanola, Na-is-nu-lah, Naisnuloh, Nais-nu-loh, Naisnulho* and *Ashtnoulou.* (USBGN)

Asotin *(S.16;T.10N;R.46E)*

Town on Snake River, at the mouth of Asotin Creek, 6 miles south of Clarkston, northeast Asotin County. In 1878, it was settled following the Nez Perce Indian War. In 1881, a ferry was built here by J. J. Kanawyer to cross the river. The name was officially approved October 27, 1883, by Washington's Territorial Legislature. The source is said to be the Nez Perce word *Hashotin*, meaning "Eel Creek," which Indians applied because of numerous eels in the stream. At one time, there were 2 rival towns platted next to each other: Asotin and Assotin City, both vying to become county seat. The former was successful, which included an act by the Territorial Legislature, in 1886, to change the spelling of Assotin City by eliminating one "s."

Asotin City (Asotin County) *see* Asotin

Asotin County

A small county, containing only 627 sq. miles, extreme southeast corner of Washington. It is bounded on the north by Whitman and Garfield counties; on the east by Snake River; on the south by Oregon, and on the west by Garfield County. It was created from Garfield County on October 27, 1883, by an act of the Territorial Legislature. (*see* Asotin)

Asotin Creek *(Ts.9,10N;Rs.43-46E)*

The stream of the creek rises in Umatilla National Forest, west central Asotin County; flows 35 miles east by north to Snake River at Asotin. (*see* Asotin)

Atlanta *(S.27;T.36N;R.2E)*

Abandoned town on Samish Island, adjoining the town of Samish, northwest Skagit County. In the early 1880s, Atlanta and Samish were platted side by side, and were deadly rivals for the cordwood trade of sternwheel steamships. The plat of Atlanta was vacated on May 4, 1886, and only rubble remains of its buildings. It was named by George Washington Lafayette Allen, when he platted the town in 1883. He was a very strong Confederate sympathizer, and planned the town as a refuge for persecuted southerners. Atlanta had been his home town in Georgia.

Attalia *(S.10;T.7N;R.31E)*

Community 15 miles southeast of Pasco and adjacent to Lake Wallula, southwest Walla Walla County. In 1906, the place was platted as a townsite and an irrigated area by V. K. Loose of Seattle. The name is reported to have been given to the plat by Mrs. Loose, for a small village in Italy, on her return from a trip to that country. The place now is the site of a large and modern paper manufacturing plant operated by Boise-Cascade Corporation.

Auburn *(T.21N;Rs.4,5E)*

City 21 miles south of Seattle in White River valley, southwest King County. Once a hop-growing center, it is now an industrial town surrounded by farms and dairy ranches. The original name was *Slaughter*, in honor of Lieut. W. A. Slaughter, who was killed by Indians near here on December 4, 1855. In 1893, local objection to this name caused the state legislature to substitute the present name. It was for "Sweet Auburn, loveliest village of the plain," from Oliver Goldsmith's poem, "The Deserted Village."

Augsburger Mountain
(S.17;T.3N;R.9E)

A south boundary peak of Gifford Pinchot National Forest, 9 miles west of White Salmon and 4 miles north of Columbia River, southeast corner of Skamania County. It was named by Forest Service officials for Pvt. Stanley R. Augsburger, a Forest Service employee, who lost his life in World War I while serving overseas with the 20th U.S. Engineers. A prior name was *Bald Mountain*.

Aurora Creek
(Ss.1-3;T.30N;R.17E.uns)

The stream of this short creek rises on the southeast slope of Chelan Mountains, Wenatchee National Forest, northwest Chelan County; flows 2-1/2 miles to Entiat River. In 1909, it was named by Forest Supervisor A. H. Sylvester when he witnessed a brilliant display of Northern Lights from this point.

Austin Pass *(S.30;T.39N;R.9E.uns)*

A Mt. Baker National Forest pass, between the north slopes of Mt. Baker and Mt. Shuksan, central Whatcom County. The pass was named for Banning N. Austin, state road surveyor, who explored the pass in the summer of 1885.

Austin Pass Lake *(S.19;T.39N;R.9E)*

An 8-acre lake elevation 4,450 ft., 800 ft. north of Austin Pass, near Mr. Baker Lodge, central Whatcom County. It was named for nearby Austin Pass.

Austins Landing (Whatcom County) *see* South Bay

Avalanche Camp *(Mt. Rainier National Park)*

A high camping ground on the north slope of Mt. Rainier, 1-1/2 miles north of the summit, east side of Willis Wall. In 1909, the camp was named by The Mountaineers for frequent snow slides on Willis Wall. The term is said to have been in use prior to this formal naming. (USBGN)

Avalanche Lake *(S.10;T.23N;R.12E)*

A 3-acre lake, 7 miles northeast of Snoqualmie Pass near Cascade Mountain summit, Snoqualmie National Forest, northeast King County. The name is descriptive, as it is in a glacial region which has heavy snowfall and many avalanches. An alternate name is *Lower Burnt Boot Lake*.

Avery *(S.10;T.2N;R.14E)*

Community 3 miles west of Wishram and 1-1/2 miles north of Columbia River, south central Klickitat County. It was named by officials of Spokane, Portland & Seattle Railway for A. G. Avery, their right-of-way attorney.

Avon *(S.11;T.34N;R.3E)*

Settlement on the west bank of Skagit River, 2-1/2 miles northwest of Mt. Vernon, west central Skagit County. In 1882, the name was chosen by W. H. Miller, founder of the settlement, for the Avon River in England, famous as the home of William Shakespeare.

Axford *(S.29;T.20N;R.10W)*

Community on Axford Prarie, 14 miles north by east of Aberdeen, southwest Grays Harbor County. It was named for the first settler, who claimed a homestead here in the fall of 1880.

Axford Creek *(T.20N;Rs.10,11W)*

The stream of the creek rises south of Humptulips, southwest Grays Harbor County; flows 9 miles southwest to Humptulips River. (*see* Axford)

Axford Prairie *(T.20N;Rs.10,11W)*

A prairie 14 miles north by west of Aberdeen, southwest Grays Harbor County. (*see* Axford)

Ayers Ridge *(T.9N;R.46E)*

A parallel ridge to Ayers Gulch, about 6 miles west of Snake River, east

central Asotin County. It was named for its first settler, Ben Ayers.

Ayock Point *(S.3;T.23N;R.3W)*

A western shore point of Hood Canal, 2-1/2 miles south of Hamma Hamma River mouth, north central Mason County. In 1841, it was named by Cmdr. Charles Wilkes as *Ayock's Point*. The name has been shortened to the present form over 120 years of use. Most probably, it was named for a member of the Wilkes Expedition. (USBGN)

Ayres Point *(S.19;T.22N;R.3W)*

A north side point on the Great Bend in Hood Canal, 1-1/2 miles north of Union and 2 miles east of Potlatch, central Mason County. In 1841, the name was given by Cmdr. Charles Wilkes to honor John Ayres, a crew member. Five years later, it was erroneously charted as *Ayos Point* by Capt. Henry Kellett. The present name is generally accepted.

Azure Lake *(S.21;T.38N;R.12E)*

A deep, 89-acre lake, elevation 4,200 ft., at the head of Stetattle Creek, 6-1/2 miles north of Newhalem, southeast Whatcom County. It is reported to have been named by Seattle City Light personnel for its deep blue color.

Azurite Lake *(S.14;T.24N;R.12E)*

A 43.9-acre lake, 3-1/2 miles west of Cascade Mountain summit, Snoqualmie National Forest, northeast King County. The lake is in a deep, mountain basin which is heavily mineralized. It was named for the blue copper carbonate ore found here by prospectors.

Azurite Peak *(S.5;T.36N;R.16E)*

An 8,443-ft. peak on Cascade Mountain summit, between north Skagit and northwest Okanogan counties. Its western slope is on Mt. Baker National Forest; its eastern slope on Chelan National Forest. The name is from that of the Azurite Mine, 3 miles northwest of the peak.

Azwell *(S.7;T.28N;R.23E)*

Orchard settlement on Columbia River, 10 miles northeast of Chelan, extreme east Chelan County. It was named by Great Northern Railway officials for A. Z. Wells of Wenatchee, who owned the land on which Azwell was built. Originally the name was *Wells*, but, in 1936, it was altered to the present name.

B

Baada Point *(S.12;T.33N;R.15W)*

Site of a former Indian fishing village (moved to Neah Bay in 1863), on Strait of Juan de Fuca, east entrance to Neah Bay, on Makah Indian Reservation, northwest Clallam County. In 1841, Cmdr. Charles Wilkes of the Wilkes Expedition named this feature *Mecena Point*, using the name of the Indian village. U.S. Coast Survey used the present name in 1852, although they spelled it Baadah Point. The present form has been approved by the USBGN.

Babcock *(S.20;T.10N;R.34E)*

Village 20 miles northwest of Walla Walla, west central Walla Walla County. Northern Pacific Railway officials named their station here for W. H. Babcock, a "wheat king," from whom they acquired a right-of-way.

Baby Island (Island County) *see* Hackney Island

Baby Island (Pacific County) *see* Round Island

Baby Lake *(T.37N;R.7E.uns)*

Small snow-fed mountain lake, south slope of Mt. Baker, south central Whatcom County. In 1909, it was named because of its small size by C. F. Easton of Bellingham, on a Mazama trip.

Bachelor Island *(T.4N;R.1W)*

An island between the main channel of Columbia River and Lake River, 11 miles north by west of Vancouver, west Clark County. On March 29, 1806, Lewis and Clark named the island *Cathlapole* for a local Indian tribe. In 1841, the Wilkes Expedition mapped this feature as *Pasauks Island*. The present name is of local origin, and there is some evidence that it was named for an unmarried man who took a donation claim here. Early maps show it as *Bachelor's Island*.

Bachelor Island Slough *(T.4N;R.1W)*

A channel between the main channel of Columbia River and Lake River, forming the southeast boundary of Bachelor Island, west Clark County. An early name was *Pigeon Creek*.

Bachelor Lake (Skagit County) *see* Mule Lake

Bachelor Point *(S.35;T.4N;R.1W)*

A south end point of Bachelor Island on the north side of Columbia River, west central Clark County. It is shown on some recent maps, in error, as *Bachelor Island Point*. (USBGN) (*see* Bachelor Island)

Backbone Lake *(S.30;T.14N;R.10E)*

A 3-1/2-acre lake, maximum depth 40 ft., 6 miles northeast of Packwood and 8 miles west of Cascade Mountain summit, northeast Lewis County. The name is from Backbone Ridge; an alternate name is *Jasper Lake*.

Backbone Ridge (Mt. Rainier National Park) *see* Cowlitz Divide

Bacon *(S.8;T.23N;R.28E)*

A railroad point, 7 miles south of Coulee City, north central Grant County. In 1902, it was named by railroad builders as a joke, possibly because of its proximity to Coffee Pot.

Bacon Creek *(Ts.36,37N;R.11E)*

The stream of the creek rises in several small lakes in North Cascade Primitive Area, south central Whatcom County; flows 15 miles south to Skagit River, 5 miles above Marblemount, Skagit County. It was named for County Commissioner Albert Bacon of Skagit County, who settled at the creek's mouth before 1884.

Bacon Creek (Whatcom County) *see* Noisy Creek

Badger; Badger Canyon; Badger Springs *(T.8N;R.28E)*

These features are from 8 to 10 miles west and southwest of Kennewick, southeast Benton County. In 1885, when Northern Pacific Railway built through here, the station received its present name from Badger Springs and Badger Canyon. The former is said to have been so named because spring water was found flowing from a badger hole. Badger Canyon took its name from the large number of these animals found in the area.

Badger Mountain *(S.28;T.9N;R.28E)*

A locally-named mountain, 3 miles southwest of Richland, east central Benton County. As in the case of several other features in this general area, the mountain was named for the abundance of the burrowing animal which scientists call *Meles taxus*.

Badger Mountain *(Ts.23,24N;Rs.12,22E)*

A spur of Cascade Mountains which extends about 14 miles northwest and southeast, maximum elevation 4,300 ft., southwest Douglas County. On June 7, 1841, it was named by Lieut. Robert E. Johnson of the Wilkes Expedition, who applied the name *Mount St. Pierre* to it. Its present name dates to pioneer days and relates to the common burrowing mammal that inhabits this range.

Bag Island (Wahkiakum County) *see* Brown's Island

Bagley Creek *(T.39N;R.9E.uns)*

The stream of the creek rises in Bagley Lakes, northeast of Table Mountain, central Whatcom County; flows 5 miles north and northeast to North Fork, Nooksack River. (*see* Bagley Lakes)

Bagley Lakes *(S.19;T.39N;R.9E.uns)*

Two lakes directly northeast of Table Mountain at the headwaters of Bagley Creek, Whatcom County. They were locally named for a popular engineer of the Bellingham Bay and British Columbia Railroad.

Bagley Lakes (Whatcom County) *see* Picture Lake; Highwood Lake

Bahia de Nunez Gaona (Clallam County) *see* Neah Bay (bay)

Bahobohosh Point *(S.29;T.33N;R.15W)*

A rocky point on Mukkaw Bay north of Sooes River mouth, Makah Indian Reservation, extreme northwest Clallam County. It retains the original Makah Indian name, which is pronounced *Baho-bo-hosh*.

Bailey Range *(T.28N;Rs.7,8W.uns)*

A group of precipitous Olympic National Park mountains with elevations to over 7,000 ft., 5 miles southwest of

Elwha Reservoir, Clallam County. On April 19, 1890, this mountain group was named by Seattle Press Expedition for William E. Bailey, proprietor of *The Seattle Press*, which sponsored the exploration.

Bainbridge Island *(Ts.24-26N;R.2E)*

A large island, over 11 miles long, 4 miles in average width, between Port Orchard Bay on the west and Puget Sound on the east, east central Kitsap County. Capt. George Vancouver sighted it, but failed to recognize its status as an island. Cmdr. Charles Wilkes discovered that it was an island when he traversed Agate Pass, and named it for Capt. William Bainbridge, naval hero of the War of 1812. Local Indians had no name for the entire island. It is now largely residential.

Baird *(S.28;T.25N;R.27E)*

Community 7-1/2 miles west of Coulee City, southeast Douglas County. When a post office was established, it was named for James Baird, who was the first postmaster, and on whose homestead the post office was located.

Baker *(S.31;T.20N;R.15E)*

A railway spur, 3 miles west of Cle Elum, west central Kittitas County. In 1906, when installed, it was named by Northern Pacific Railway officials for a local logger who loaded logs at this siding.

Baker (Skagit County) *see* Concrete

Baker Bay *(Ts.9,10N;R.11W)*

A large, circular bay with Sand Island across its mouth, near the mouth of Columbia River, separated from the ocean by Cape Disappointment, southwest Pacific County. In 1792, it was named by Lieut. W. R. Broughton of the Vancouver Expedition for Capt. James Baker of the brig *Jenny*, which was at anchor in the bay when Broughton arrived. In 1805, Lewis and Clark named it *Haley's Bay*. It also has borne the names *Deception Bay* and *Rogue's Harbor* in early years.

Baker Hot Springs
(S.19;T.38N;R.9E.uns)

A Mt. Baker National Forest hot springs near Morovitz Creek, between Mt. Baker and Mt. Shuksan, south central Whatcom County. The springs were named for Mt. Baker.

Baker Lake *(Ts.37,38N;R.9E)*

A Mt. Baker National Forest lake in

Baker River, 6-1/2 miles south of Mt. Shuksan, south central Whatcom County. Inundated by Baker Dam, it is now a 10-mile-long reservoir behind the hydroelectric dam which flooded the original Baker Lake and created a 5,000-acre basin. It was named for Mt. Baker.

Baker Pass *(S.6;T.37N;R.7E.uns)*

A south slope pass of Mt. Baker, near Mazama Park, between Baker River drainage and the headwaters of Nooksack River, south central Whatcom County. In 1904, it was named by Bert W. Huntoon, for Mt. Baker.

Baker Reservoir (Upper) *(T.37N;R.9E)*

A 3,616-acre reservoir, 9-3/4 miles long, 283 ft. maximum depth, on upper Baker River, 8 miles north of Concrete, south central Whatcom County. It was created by Puget Sound Power & Light Company for hydroelectric power development. It was named for Baker River; an alternate name is *Upper Baker River Reservoir*.

Baker River
(Ts.36-39N;Rs.8-11E.partly uns)

The stream of the river heads at Hannegan Pass near Whatcom Peak, east central Whatcom County; flows south and west via Baker Lake and Lake Shannon, through Skagit County to Skagit River at Concrete. In 1877, it was named by Otto Klement, a prospector, for Mt. Baker, which is visible from the river in many places. The Indian name was *Nuh-cul-lum* or *Nah-cul-lum*.

Balch *(S.1;T.15N;R.5W)*

Community near Chehalis River, 2 miles south of Oakville, extreme southeast Grays Harbor County. It was named for Capt. Lafayette Balch, a very early pioneer on Puget Sound who founded Steilacoom, served as a member of the first Territorial Legislature, and was an operator of trade boats and trade stores.

Balch Passage *(T.20N;R.1E)*

A Puget Sound passage between McNeil and Anderson islands, 4 miles west of Steilacoom, northwest Pierce County. In 1846, the passage was charted as *Ryder Channel* by Capt. R. N. Inskip, but his choice did not remain in use. The present name is for Capt. Lafayette Balch. (*see* Balch)

Balch's Cove (Pierce County) *see* Glen Cove

Bald Eagle Mountain
(S.34;T.29N;R.12E)

Mountain 12-1/2 miles southwest of Glacier Peak summit, east central Snohomish County. It was named by U.S. Forest Service personnel because of several nests of bald eagles on its slopes in high tree tops.

Bald Lake *(S.18;T.35N;R.10E)*

A 2-1/2-acre lake, elevation 3,750 ft., 8-1/2 miles east of Concrete, central Skagit County. It was named for Bald Mountain, directly to the west. An alternate name is *Baldy Lake*.

Bald Mountain *(Ss.11,12;T.30N;R.9E)*

A 4,773-ft. mountain 1-1/2 miles northwest of Silverton and directly south of Kelcema Lake, north central Snohomish County. This peak is in a mineralized area. Its very common name was applied by early prospectors, and it is one of many peaks in the state which have been so named by local people.

Bald Mountain (Skamania County) *see* Augspurger Mountain

Bald Mountain (Whatcom County) *see* Mt. Blum

Bald Mountain Lakes (Snohomish County) *see* Cutthroat Lakes

Bald Peak (Skagit County) *see* Eagle Cliff

Bald Peak (Spokane County) *see* Mt. Spokane

Bald Rock *(Mt.Rainier Naitonal Park)*

A 5,411-ft. rock mountain on the east slope of Cowlitz Divide, 2 miles west of Ohanapecosh River, southeast sector of the park. It is directly north of the Pierce-Lewis County boundary. Park personnel named the mountain for its barren summit.

Baldy Lake (Skagit County) *see* Sauk Lake; Bald Lake.

Baldy Mount (Spokane County) *see* Mt. Spokane.

Baldy Mountain
(Ss.4,9;T.27N;R.20E)

A 6,432-ft. peak in Chelan Mountains, 6 miles west of Lake Chelan, central Chelan County; it is located on the boundary between Okanogan and Wenatchee national forests. The name, applied by early stockmen, is used over and over throughout the west for mountains that do not have a heavy head of timber.

Balky Mule Canyon *(T.29N;R.36E)*

An isolated canyon area south of Enterprise, 5 to 6 miles north of old Ft. Spokane, southwest Stevens County. It is reported that a pioneer German settler here brewed beer for soldiers of old Ft. Spokane when that post was active. It is a typical pioneer name, indicating the trouble which was encountered by early packers who drove mules over difficult trails.

Ballard *(T.25N;R.3E)*

An annex of Seattle, northwest of the main business area, east of Shilshole Bay and north of the ship canal, King County. Formerly it was a separate town; annexed in 1907. Before the turn of the century, and for some years afterward, the Ballard shore of Salmon Bay was lined with sawmills and shingle mills that usually ran 2 shifts daily. It was named for Capt. William Rankin Ballard, who bought several hundred acres here in 1882. At one time the settlement was named *Salmon Bay City*. In 1887, an 800-acre tract called *Gilman Park Addition* was platted on adjoining ground by West Coast Improvement Company. In 1890, the name of Ballard was legally confirmed by the state legislature to avoid confusion in existing names, and was incorporated as a city under that name.

Ballast Island *(S.5;T.24N;R.4E)*

A small, artificial island which formerly was located on Seattle's waterfront in Elliott Bay, near the "Ocean Dock" at the foot of Washington St., King County. In the 1880s and 1890s, it was used as a campground for Indians enroute to hop fields in the area south of Seattle. The locally-applied name was chosen because the island was composed of rock and gravel ballast that was discharged here by ships in early days.

Ballow *(S.12;T.20N;R.1W)*

Settlement on the west shore of Cases Inlet, 11 miles east of Shelton, extreme southeast Mason County. The name is a modification of the Indian word *Bala*, and refers to a mythical monster which roamed the country, creating the Olympic Mountains.

Ball's Landing (Skagit County) *see* Sterling

Ballsom Bay (Whatcom County) *see* Bellingham Bay

Bancroft *(T.34N;R.1E)*

A failed townsite on Fidalgo Island, adjacent to Alder Academy, west central Skagit County. Neither Bancroft nor Alder Academy are carried on recent maps. The townsite was platted in 1883, by Rev. E. O. Tade, and it was named for Hubert H. Bancroft, author of the authoritative Pacific Coast histories.

Bandana Lake *(S.10;T.31N;R.8E)*

A very small, 3-acre lake, elevation 3,235 ft., 6 miles south of Hazel on Mt. Baker National Forest, north central Snohomish County. The original, local name was *Meadow Lake*. Because this name was in common use, members of a U.S. Forest Service trail crew devised the present name as a substitute.

Bandera *(S.16;T.22N;R.10E)*

Community 4-1/2 miles west of Cascade Mountain summit on Carter Creek, east central King County. It was named by officials of the Milwaukee Railroad, although company records do not disclose the name origin.

Bandera Mountain *(S.4;T.22N;R.10E)*

A 5,255-ft. peak, 6 miles west of Snoqualmie Pass, east central King County. It was named by The Mountaineers, evidently for the railroad station of Bandera, 1-1/2 miles to the south. (USBGN)

Bangor *(S.25;T.26N;R.1W)*

Community on the east shore of Hood Canal, 10 miles northwest of Bremerton, northwest Kitsap County. It is the location of Bangor Naval Station, a submarine base. The name was chosen when a post office was established. Residents are presumed to have picked the name out of a newspaper dispatch. An earlier name was *Three Spits*, which was quite descriptive.

Bangor Lake *(S.19;T.26N;R.1E)*

A 4.6-acre lake on Bangor Naval Station, 1-1/4 miles north of Bangor, northwest Kitsap County. It is open to Navy personnel only, and was named for Bangor.

Banks Lake *(Ts.25-28N;Rs.28-30E)*

A man-made reservoir, about 30 miles long, with an area of 43 sq. miles in Columbia River's prehistoric channel, from Dry Falls Dam (South Dam) near Coulee City, northeasterly to Grand Coulee, Grant County. It was named by reclamation engineers for Frank A. Banks, who supervised construction of Grand Coulee Dam and other reclama-

tion structures. He died in 1957. (USBGN).

FL. Bannock Mountain *(Ss.22,27;T.32N;R.14E)*

A 7,600-ft. peak at Cascade Mountain summit, 11 miles northeast of Glacier Peak summit, extreme northeast Snohomish County. It was named by early land surveyors. The record indicates that it was named for the meal-cake bread which they baked over campfires.

Barber Creek (Grays Harbor County) *see* Garrard Creek.

FL. Barberton *(S.5;T.2N;R.2E)*

A small settlement 4 miles northeast of Vancouver, southwest Clark County. It was named for Len Barber who ran a store here and who was postmaster in the early days of the place.

Bare Island *(T.37N;R.3W)*

An island 1/2 mile north of Waldron Island, east of Skipjack Island, north central San Juan County. In 1841, it was included with Wooded Island, now called Skipjack Island, by Cmdr. Charles Wilkes as *Skipjack Islands*. In 1853, the present name was charted by U.S. Coast Survey because it is barren of trees, in contrast with heavily-wooded Skipjack Island. A previous name, not shown on U.S. maps, was *Penguin Island*.

Baring *(S.2;T.26N;R.10E)*

Station 8 miles northwest of Skykomish in Skykomish River drainage area, northeast King County. Formerly it was a scene of prospecting and mining on a large scale. It was named for Mt. Baring, 2 miles east. Former local names were *Big Index* and *East Index*.

Baring Lake (King County) *see* Grotto Lake.

Baring Mountain (King County) *see* Mt. Baring.

Barlow Bay *(S.13;T.34N;R.2W)*

A small, partly-enclosed harbor at the south end of Mackaye Harbor, south shore of Lopez Island, southeast San Juan County. It was named for Capt. Arthur Barlow, who left a British sailing vessel to settle here during the San Juan boundary dispute, and who remained during his life.

Barlow Pass *(Ss.6,7;T.29N;R.11E)*

A Mt. Baker National Forest pass 4 miles northwest of Monte Cristo, east central Snohomish County. Since 1892, it was used by miners and was on the route of Everett & Monte Cristo Railroad. It was named for Capt. S. K. Barlow, a pioneer road locater and builder.

Barnaby Buttes *(S.18;T.35N;R.35E)*

A group of 3 peaks on Colville National Forest, 15 miles southeast of Republic, central Ferry County. The highest of the peaks has an elevation of 6,527 ft. They were named for a Colville Indian, Chief Barnaby, by early Forest Service officers. The chief's Indian name was *Skoyelpe*.

Barnaby Creek *(Ts.34,35N;Rs.35-37E)*

The stream of the creek heads on the east slope of White Mountain, east central Ferry County; flows east and southeast, 15 miles to Columbia River, 9 miles north of Inchelium. (*see* Barnaby Buttes)

Barnes (Benton County) *see* Chandler

Barnes Creek *(T.29N;Rs.8,9W)*

The stream of the creek rises south of Mt. Storm King, central Clallam County; flows west into Lake Crescent at Singers. It was named for the pioneer Barnes family, who homesteaded on the lake at the creek's mouth.

Barnes Forest Corridor *(T.10N;R.2W)*

A 1,000-acre patch of virgin timber along the old highway, 5 miles north of Castle Rock, Cowlitz County. It was designated as a Washington State Natural Area, and named for Sen. Frank Grant Barnes of Cowlitz County, who secured the state legislation for establishment of the corridor.

Barnes Island *(T.37N;R.1W)*

A northeast shore island, 1-1/2 miles off Orcas Island, directly west of Clark Island, northeast San Juan County. This island, with Clark Island, acquired the name *Islas de Arguayo* from Lieut. Juan Francisco de Eliza. The name was one of many used by the Viceroy of Mexico in 1791 when Eliza applied it. In 1841, the present name was charted by Cmdr. Charles Wilkes for a naval hero of the War of 1812.

Barnes Lake (Thurston County) *see* Ferguson Lake

Barneston *(S.13;T.22N;R.7W)*

A small logging community on Cedar River, 17 miles east of Kent, central King County. The name was selected when a post office was established

here on June 12, 1901. It was for John G. Barnes of Seattle, who owned much of the property.

Barren Island *(S.14;T.36N;R.4W)*

An island on Spieden Channel, 1/2 mile west of the northwest end of San Juan Island and directly north of Roche Harbor, west central San Juan County. The name was locally applied because the island is entirely devoid of vegetation.

Barrett Butte *(S.24;T.35N;R.32E)*

A low peak, elevation 3,362 ft., on Colville National Forest, 10 miles south of Republic, west central Ferry County. The name is for Thomas Barrett, who died in 1924, and who was the first administrative assistant on Colville National Forest.

Barrett Creek *(T.37N;R.32E)*

The stream of the creek rises on the north slope of Klondike Mountain, west central Ferry County; flows north and east 3-1/2 miles to Curlew Lake. It is in Colville National Forest. (*see* Barrett Butte)

Barrett Lake *(S.21;T.39N;R.2E)*

Early settlement near Nooksack River, 1 mile east of Ferndale, west central Whatcom County. In 1874, it was first named *Trudder* by homesteader Thomas E. Barrett, for his home town in Ireland. In 1876, the name was changed to that of the homesteader.

Barrier Peak *(Mt. Rainier National Park)*

A 6,614-ft. peak at the south end of Governors Ridge, 1 mile southeast of Owyhigh Lakes, at the head of West Branch Boundary Creek, east central zone of the park. The name is quite descriptive and was applied by park officers. (USBGN)

Barrier River (Okanogan County) *see* Methow River

Barrington (Snohomish County) *see* Darrington

Barron *(S.35;T.38N;R.17E.uns)*

An abandoned mining camp on Slate Creek, 3 miles from Harts Pass at Cascade Mountain summit, extreme southeast Whatcom County. Once it boasted 2,000 inhabitants. It was named by early miners for Alex Barron, who owned the famous Eureka and Black Jack mining claims here.

Barrons Bay (Kitsap County) *see* Yukon Harbor

Barry *(S.12;T.29N;R.30E)*

Village on west bank of Columbia River, 5 miles north of Grand Coulee Dam, extreme northwest Douglas County. In 1893, it was named for A. J. Barry, postmaster, when a post office was established. At that time Barry was located some distance west of the river. When the post office was moved to Stenson Ferry on the Columbia, the name was transferred with it.

Barstow *(Ss.20,21;T.38N;R.37E)*

A small settlement on Kettle River, 8 miles above the river's mouth, northeast Ferry County. It was named for an early settler who operated a store and way station here.

Barstow's Point (Island County) *see* Coveland

Bartow (Kitsap County) *see* Suquamish

Basalt Peak *(T.29N;R.17E)*

A Wenatchee National Forest peak between Chiwawa Creek and Chikamin Creek, at the head of Minnow Creek, northwest Chelan County. It was named by U.S. Forest Supervisor A. H. Sylvester for a basaltic rock formation on its northwest slope.

Basalt Point *(S.33;T.29N;R.1E)*

An Admiralty Inlet point south of the entrance to Mats Mats Bay and 2-1/2 miles north of Port Ludlow, east central Jefferson County. In 1855, the present name was applied by U.S. Coast Survey as there are extensive outcroppings of basaltic rock here. It is quarried in Mats Mats Bay at present. A previous name was *Point Kanawi*, charted by Cmdr. Charles Wilkes in 1841, as the original Indian name of the point.

Basaltic Falls *(Mt. Rainier National Park)*

Waterfall in a small tributary of Muddy Fork, Cowlitz River, elevation 5,666 ft., east central area of the park. The location is 1 mile east of Cowlitz Glacier terminus, at the south end of Cowlitz Park. The name was chosen by Prof. J. B. Flett and H. H. Garretson, while on a trip with The Mountaineers. It describes the basaltic rocks surrounding the waterfall.

Basin Creek *(Ts.25,26N;Rs.13,14E)*

The stream of the creek rises in Hope Lake, directly east of Cascade Mountain summit, southwest Chelan County; flows 2 miles southeast to Trapper Creek. It was named by U.S. Forest Supervisor A. H. Sylvester because its source at Hope Lake is in a small mountain basin.

Basin Lake *(S.5;T.24N;R.14E)*

A 7-acre glacial lake on Snoqualmie National Forest, Cascade Mountain summit, 1 mile northeast of Deception Pass, northeast King County. The lake is in a rather deep mountain basin, thus the descriptive name. An alternative name is *Trico Mountain Lake.*

Bassett Junction *(S.18;T.18N;R.30E)*

Settlement between Connell and Adco, 9 miles southeast of Moses Lake (town), southeast Grant County. In 1910, it started when a railroad branch line was built to this point, and was named by railroad officials for John D. Bassett, a Ritzville banker from whom the right-of-way was secured.

Bastile Glacier
(Ss.35,36;T.38N;R.7E.uns)

A rocky ridge with precipitous walls on the north slope of Mt. Baker, below Roosevelt and Coleman glaciers, south central Whatcom County. In 1911, the glacier was named by the Engberg-Wright climbing party, because its steep walls appeared somewhat similar to those of the *Bastille,* the famous prison in Paris. The error in spelling has persisted.

Bath Lake (Skagit County) *see* Itswoot Lake

Bathtub Lakes *(S.28;T.30N;R.8E)*

A group of 8 very small lakes, elevation about 4,800 ft., on Pilchuck Mountain, 3 miles southwest of Gold Basin, central Snohomish County. The name is appropriate, as the 8 lakes total only 10 acres, and some are little larger than a king-sized bathtub.

Battle Canyon *(T.25N;Rs.16,17E)*

A Wenatchee National Forest canyon which rises on Big Jim Mountain near the head of Painter Creek; extends 5 miles northeast to Chiwaukum Creek, southwest Chelan County. It was named by U.S. Forest Supervisor A. H. Sylvestor for a fight which took place here between a packer and a sheepherder.

Battle Point *(Ss.7,18;T.25N;R.2E)*

A west shore point of Bainbridge Island, 8 miles north of Bremerton, central Kitsap County. The name is for an ancient battle between Kitsap Indians and northern Indian raiders. Tradition states that the Kitsaps were victorious.

Battleground *(S.35;T.4N;R.2E)*

Town 11 miles northeast of Vancouver, central Clark County. It was named for an action between *Cast-la-poodle* Indians and a detachment of the 21st U.S. Infantry during the early period of Indian unrest. A number of Indians who had been held in the stockade at Ft. Vancouver escaped and stole cattle from settlers. The soldiers overtook the Indians at the present site of Crawford and killed Chief Umtuck while recovering the livestock.

Battleground Lake *(S.30;T.4N;R.3E)*

A 28-acre lake 2 miles northeast of Battleground and 12 miles northeast of Vancouver, Washington, central Clark County. The oyster-shaped lake is in an old volcanic crater. Its name is for the town of Battleground.

Battleship Island *(S.10;T.36N;R.4W)*

A Haro Strait island at the southwest entrance to Spieden Channel, 1/2 mile northwest of the west tip of Henry Island, west central San Juan County. In 1841, it was charted by Cmdr. Charles Wilkes as *Morse's Island* for William H. Morse, purser's steward on the expedition's brig *Porpoise.* The present name was applied by U.S. Coast Survey for the island's shape, which vaguely resembles a battleship. (USBGN)

Batum *(S.28;T.20N;R.32E)*

Village 20 miles northwest of Lind, northwest Adams County. Because of the many Russian wheat farmers who moved into this area, the place was named for a city in the Caucasus, a territory of old Russia on the east coast of the Black Sea. It now is Adzhar, U.S.S.R. The naming agents were officials of Chicago, Milwaukee & St. Paul Railway.

Bauerman Ridge *(T.40N;R.22E.uns)*

A mountain ridge, maximum elevation 8,072 ft., in an unsurveyed part of Chelan National Forest, northeast corner of Cascade Primitive Area, Okanogan County. It was named by an International Boundary Survey party for Hilary Bauerman, a British geologist employed by the First International Boundary Commission from 1857 until 1861. (USBGN)

Baugh (Lewis County) *see* Riffe

Baw Faw (Lewis County) *see* Boisfort; Boistfort

Bay Center *(S.8;T.13N;R.10W)*

Settlement on Goose Point, where Palix River enters Willapa Bay, northwest Pacific County. In 1849, native oysters were first discovered here. The settlement's first name was *Palix.* In 1875, it was changed to the present name by Mrs. Leonard Rhoades because the site is the middle of the landward side of Willapa Bay.

Bay City *(S.21;T.16N;R.11W)*

A small, scattered community on the southeast side of South Bay in Grays Harbor, extreme southeast Grays Harbor County. It was the former site of a large whaling plant installed by American Pacific Whaling Company in the early 1900s, and was named for its location on South Bay.

Bay Lake *(Ss.1,2;T.20N;R.1W)*

Bay 1 mile south of Lake Bay on Carrs Inlet, northwest Pierce County (see Lake Bay)

Bayne *(S.22;T.21N;R.7E)*

A small settlement, 7 miles northeast of Enumclaw, south central King County. In 1908, it was named by Northern Pacific Railway Company officials for George Bayne, who discovered and developed a coal mine here.

Bay Shore *(S.3;T.20N;R.3W)*

Settlement on the west shore of Oakland Bay, 3 miles northeast of Shelton, Mason County. It was named by local landowners after its location.

Bayview *(S17;T.29N;R.3E)*

A scattered settlement and school district on southern Whidbey Island, 2 miles north of Useless Bay, southeast Island County. The locally-chosen name is descriptive, as it overlooks Useless Bay.

Bayview *(S.30;T.35N;R.3E)*

A small settlement on the east shore of Padilla Bay, directly south of Bayview State Park, west central Skagit County. On April 17, 1884, it was given this descriptive name when a townsite was platted by William J. McKenna.

Bayview State Park
(S.30;T.35N;R.3E)

A 19-acre tideland park on the east shore of Padilla Bay, 7 miles northwest of Mount Vernon, west central Skagit

County. The park offers public camping and swimming. Its name describes a sweeping view of Padilla Bay.

Bazalgette Point *(S.23;T.36N;R.4W)*

An extreme northwest point of San Juan Island, directly south of Roche Harbor, west central San Juan County. In 1868, it was named by Capt. Pender, R.N., while he was in command of the H.M. surveying vessel *Beaver*, for Capt. George Bazalgette, R.M.L.I. He commanded British occupation forces at this place from 1860 to 1867, during the San Juan boundary dispute.

Beach *(S.9;T.37N;R.1E)*

A small town on the east shore of Lummi Island on Hale Passage, southwest Whatcom County. Formerly it was an important steamer landing. It was locally named for Wade S. Beach, who homesteaded here on November 20, 1884.

Beach Creek (Clallam County) *see* Titakoclos Creek

Beach Lake *(S.27;T.31N;R.7W)*

A 7-acre, fresh water lake near Strait of Juan de Fuca, at a point 1/2 mile east of Elwha River's mouth, north central Clallam County. The name is for the lake's proximity to a salt water beach.

Beacon Hill *(Ss.4,9;T.24N;R.4E)*

An elevated residential section of Seattle, southeast of the main business section, between Madrona Park and Jefferson Park, King County. Originally settled by the Hanford and Holgate families, it is one of Seattle's 12 official hills, with a maximum elevation of 336 ft. at Beacon Ave. and Holgate St. It was named by M. H. Young of Boston, part owner of Union Trunk Line, an electric street car system on this hill. He named it for Beacon Hill in Boston.

Beacon Rock *(S.27;T.2N;R.6E)*

A conical, columnar lava monolith, 900 ft. above the north bank of Columbia River, 36 miles east of Vancouver, southwest Skamania County. Beacon Rock State Park now administers this site. The name was given because early river navigators installed beacons on the rock to guide them at night or during heavy weather. An alternate name, not now in use, was *Castle Rock*.

Beacon Rock State Park
(S.27;T.2N;R.6E)

A 3,052-acre park built around the striking, scenic Beacon Rock, on north bank of Columbia River, 36 miles east of Portland, southwest Skamania County. Camping, fishing, and other privileges are available to the public. (*see* Beacon Rock)

Bead Island *(T.1N;R.3E)*

A locally-named island near the confluence of Washougal and Columbia rivers, on the eastern outskirts of Camas, southeast Clark County. The name was chosen because of many beads found here around Indian burials.

Bead Lake *(Ts.32,33N;R.45E)*

A large lake 8 miles north by west of Newport and 3 miles west of the Idaho line, southeast Pend Oreille County. It is very irregular, with 6 or more long arms. It was named by early settlers who saw a resemblance to beads in the many rock ledges that jutted into the lake.

Bean's Point (Kitsap County) *see* Restoration Point

Bear Creek *(Ts.36,37N;R.3E)*

The stream of the creek rises at the west end of Lake Samish, southwest Whatcom County; flows 4 miles east and southeast to Friday Creek, near Alger, northwest Skagit County. It should not be confused with Bear Creek near Lake Shannon, Skagit County. The creek was once the center of a legendary "black bear country." Two brothers named Smith are presumed to have killed about 400 bears in this area.

Bear Creek *(T.36N;R.8E)*

The stream of the creek rises in several branches at Dock Butte and Blue Lake, extreme north central Skagit County; flows southeast to Lake Shannon, a distance of about 5 miles. It should not be confused with Bear Creek near Lake Samish in Whatcom and Skagit counties. The lake was named by Joseph Morowitz, who killed a bear on the creek while building trail.

Bear Lake *(T.28N;R.19E)*

A Wenatchee National Forest lake at the head of Lake Creek in Chelan Mountains, central Chelan County. It was named by Forest Ranger James McKenzie because of numerous bears around the lake in berry season.

Bear Lake *(S.15;T.24N;R.11E)*

A 49-acre mountain lake on Snoqualmie National Forest, 11 miles northeast of Snoqualmie Lake, northeast King County. The name is appropriate for any feature in this area. Also appro-

priate would have been deer, cougar, marmot, coyote, or porcupine.

Bear Mountain *(S.14;T.35N;R.33E)*

A Colville National Forest mountain, elevation 4,649 ft., 9 miles southeast of Republic, west central Ferry County. It was named by an early settler, Harsy Davis, for the large number of bears that he killed around this mountain.

Bear River *(Ts.9,10N;R.10W)*

The stream of the river heads 2 miles north of Megler, southwest Pacific County; flows 12 miles northwest to the south end of Willapa Bay. Its course is winding, with many small tributaries. "Bear" is the translation of the Indian name for the river, which was *At-ee-so-will*.

Beards Hollow *(S.32;T.10N;R.11W)*

A circular beach in a hollow at the base of a cliff, on Pacific Ocean, 1 mile west of Ilwaco, southwest Pacific County. It was named for Capt. E. N. Beard whose ship, the bark *Vandalia*, foundered off the mouth of Columbia River in 1853. All hands were lost, and Beard's body was found on the beach near this hollow.

Beasley Spring (Grant County) *see* Ephrata

Beatrice *(S.14;T.16N;R.32E)*

Community 10 miles southwest of Lind, central Adams County. In 1905, it was named by H. J. Horn, general manager of Northern Pacific Railway Company, for Beatrice Ayer Patton, wife of Maj. Patton, U.S.A.

Beaux Arts Village *(S.3;T.24N;R.5E)*

A 50-acre artist colony on the east shore of Lake Washington, south of Bellevue and 3/4 mile north of East Channel Bridge, northwest King County. In 1908, it was founded by artists, writers, architects, and other artistic persons. It was established by Frank Calvert and Alfred T. Renfro and named by Renfro for the Western Academy of Beaux Arts which was within the colony boundaries.

Beaver *(S.36;T.30N;R.13W)*

A former logging camp on Beaver Creek, directly south of Lake Pleasant, west central Clallam County. It is now Lake Tyee Forest Camp. (Lake Tyee is an alternate name for Lake Pleasant.) It was named for Beaver Creek.

Beaver Creek *(Ts.26,27N;Rs.17,18E)*

The stream of the creek rises on Miners Ridge, 7 miles east of Wenatchee Lake, Wenatchee National Forest, southeast Chelan County; flows 6 miles southwest to Plain on Wenatchee River. The name was applied in early days for beaver dams and swamps in the lower course of the creek, which is quite level.

Beaver Creek *(T.16N;Rs.10,11W)*

The stream of the creek rises 2 miles east of Markham, southwest Grays Harbor County; flows west to Johns River near Markham. It was named by Charles Stevens, who built a dam in this creek in 1881 to secure power for a grist mill. He later converted it into a sawmill. An earlier name, because of these milling operations, was the much-used *Mill Creek.*

Beaver Dam Lake *(S.18;T.24N;R.1E)*

A narrow, 4.9-acre lake, 1 mile west of Lake Kitsap, central Kitsap County. Approximately 1,000 ft. long, it was formed by beaver dams in Dickerson Creek and was named for the beaver dams that originally impounded the lake.

Beaver Lake
(S.9;T.30N;R.12W)

A 36-acre lake, 3 miles northeast of Sappho, west central Clallam County. It drains into Beaver Creek through an 80-acre swamp and was named for the creek that drains it. Evidently the swamp was caused by a beaver dam in past years.

Beaver Lake *(Ss.1.2,11;T.24N;R.6E)*

An irregular lake about 1 mile long, 4-1/2 miles east of Lake Sammamish and 3-1/2 miles northeast of Issaquah, west central King County. It was named by early settlers for beaver that then lived in the lake. This lake should not be confused with Beaver Lake south of Black Diamond.

Beaver Lake *(S.35;T.20N;R.6E)*

A 13-acre lake 2-1/4 miles south of Black Diamond, south central King County. According to old-time residents, it was formed by a large beaver dam in a swampy stream. It should not be confused with Beaver Lake which is north of Issaquah.

Beaver Lake *(S.14;T.13N;R.10E)*

A 7-acre lake 7-1/4 miles east of Packwood and 5 miles west of Cascade Mountain summit, Gifford Pinchot National Forest, northeast Lewis County.

The name indicates that the lake was formed by beaver dams in upper Coal Creek, on which the lake is located.

Beaver Lake *(S.7;T.34N;R.5E)*

A 73.4-acre lake 1/4 mile southeast of Clear Lake, west central Skagit County. It is in a swampy area fed by Clear Lake. The name appears to have been chosen for its shape, rather than as a result of beaver dams. An aerial photograph of the lake shows a strong resemblance to the outline of a beaver -- tail and all.

Beaver Lake *(King County) see* Ravensdale Lake

Beaver Lakes *(Ss.1,11;T.24N;R.6E)*

A string of 3 connected lakes, 4 miles east of Lake Sammamish, west central King County. On some maps they are shown as a single lake; their respective areas are 11.6 acres, 61.9 acres, and 3.4 acres. As in the case of many lowland lakes around which hardwood trees are abundant, this group evidently was formed by dams built by one or more beaver colonies.

Beaverdam Lake *(S.9;T.20N;R.8E)*

A 1.8-acre lake 10 miles northeast of Enumclaw, on Tacoma City watershed, south central King County. It is reported to have been formed by beaver dams in Charley Creek.

Beckett Point *(S.25;T.30N;R.2W)*

An east shore point of Port Discovery Bay, 2 miles south of Cape George, northeast Jefferson County. In 1841, Cmdr. Charles Wilkes named this feature *Sandy Point.* Early settlers called it *Ft. Point* for a rather extensive, fortified and stockaded village of Clallam Indians there. In 1846, the present name was chosen by Capt. Henry Kellett. He stated that this was the local name for the Indian fort.

Bedal Camp *(T.30N;R.11E)*

A mining camp 14 miles southeast of Darrington on Mt. Baker National Forest, east central Snohomish County. It was very popular in early mining days as an overnight stop on the ''Tote Road'' between Sauk City and the Monte Cristo mines. (*see* Bedal Peak)

Bedal Lake *(S.14;T.30N;R.11E)*

A 3-acre lake, elevation 3,500 ft., Snoqualmie National Forest, on a tributary of North Fork, Sauk River, 1 mile north of Bedal Peak, west central Snohomish County. It was named for Bedal

Peak. An alternative name is *Nels Lake.* (*see* Bedal Peak)

Bedal Peak *(S.23;T.30N;R.11E)*

A 6,250-ft. peak, 11 miles southwest of Glacier Peak summit, 1-1/2 miles nrth of Bedal Mining Camp. It was named for James Bedal, founder of Bedal mines in this area.

Bedrock Springs (Benton County) *see* Horse Heaven

Bee *(S.26;T.20N;R.1E)*

Community on the southeast shore of McNeil Island, opposite Steilacoom on the mainland, northwest Pierce County. The name was chosen because an apiary was operating here when residents needed a name for a post office.

Beebe *(S.16;T.27N;R.23E)*

Community on east bank of Columbia River, 3 miles east of Chelan, northwest Douglas County. It was named in December 1912, when a post office was established, for James Beebe of Wakefield, Mass. Beebe was president of Wenatchee-Chelan Orchard Company, which established a large orchard tract here.

Beede Lake (King County) *see* Lake Geneva

Beehive Pinnacle *(Mt. Rainier National Park)*

A large rock protrusion in Cowlitz Glacier, on the southeast slope of Mt. Rainier, southeast sector of the park. In 1888, this feature was named by Maj. E. S. Ingraham, for its resemblance to an old-type beehive. (USBGN)

Beekman (Kittitas County) *see* Jonesville

Belcher Mountain
(Ss.8,17,18;T.37N;R.34E)

A Colville National Forest mountain, elevation 5,750 ft., 10 miles northeast of Republic, at the head of North Fork, San Poil River, north central Ferry County. It is about 1-1/2 miles long and located in a heavily mineralized area. The name is from nearby Belcher Mine.

Belfair *(S.29;T.23N;R.1W)*

Community directly east of the eastern extremity of Hood Canal, on Union River, northeast Mason County. In 1888, the town was platted as *Clifton.* In 1918, when the Navy Yard Highway was built, Clifton was bypassed; the town was re-established on the new highway, but postal officials forced a name change. Residents coined the present name. In 1934, when the highway route was altered, Belfair was again bypassed, and was moved to a location on the highway. The Indian name was *Duhlay-lip*, meaning "head of the bay."

Belfair State Park *(S.1;T.22N;R.2W)*

A north shore park of Hood Canal, 3 miles west of Belfair, northeast Mason County. This 53-acre park offers camping, fishing, and swimming. *(see* Belfair)

Belfast *(S.6;T.35N;R.4E)*

Small settlement near Samish River, 5 miles north of Burlington, northwest Skagit County. For some years it was the headquarters of an extensive logging operation. It was named for a local resident when a post office was established in 1890. Prior to that time it was known as *Moody's Camp*.

Belfast (Garfield County) *see* Mentor

Beljacka Mountain (Pierce County) *see* Mt. Beljicka

Beljica Meadows Lake
(S.17;T.15N;R.7E)

A shallow lake on the north side of Mt. Beljica, at the head of South Puyallup River, southeast Pierce County. It was named for Mt. Beljica; an alternate spelling which appears in some records is *Beljaca*.

Belle Rock *(S.25;T.35N;R.1W)*

A dangerous rock in Rosario Strait, 2-1/2 miles east of Decatur Island, southeast San Juan County. Many vessels were wrecked here before the rock was charted and a beacon established. This name was used when the rock was charted by George Davidson of U.S. Coast Survey in 1854. The name source appears to be unrecorded.

Bellevue *(Ts.24,25N;Rs.4,5E)*

A rapidly-developing Seattle suburb, with metropolitan facilities, on the east shore of Lake Washington, south of Kirkland, west central King County. Formerly it was a base for the 6-ship fleet of American-Pacific Whaling Company. This ornamental name, with no special significance, was chosen by Oliver F. Franz when he platted the townsite here in 1904.

Bellingham *(Ts.37,38N;Rs.2,3E)*

A city on the east shore of Bellingham Bay, extending east to Lake What-

com, southwest Whatcom County. It includes several small towns and settlements founded between 1854 and 1900, and combined into the present city in 1903. These towns included Sehome, Fairhaven, Whatcom, and New Whatcom. The name is from the bay on which the city is located.

Bellingham Bay *(Ts.37,38N;Rs.1,2E)*

A large, navigable bay off Rosario Strait, southwest Whatcom County. It constitutes the waterfront of Bellingham. Shoals at the north end are caused by silt from Nooksack River. In 1791, the bay was called *Bahia de Gaston* by Lieut. Juan Francisco de Eliza. The present name was used by Capt. George Vancouver on June 11, 1792; although the actual charting under that name was made by Joseph Whidbey, acting under Vancouver's orders. It was in honor of Sir William Bellingham, controller of the storekeeper's account of His Majesty's Navy. The name *Ballsom Bay* appears on an 1845 map of Puget Sound made by the North West Company.

Bellingham Channel
(Ts.35,36N;R.1E)

A 5-mile-long channel, average width 1 mile, between Cypress and Guemes islands, extreme northwest Skagit County. In 1853, it was named by U.S. Coast Survey because of its geographical position with regard to Bellingham Bay. In the early 1790s, Juan Francisco de Eliza named this feature *Canal de Guemes*. The Samish Indian name was *Tut-segh*.

Bells Bluff (Skamania County) *see* Cape Horn

Bells Creek *(T.39N;R.5E)*

The stream of the creek heads 4 miles north of Deming, west central Whatcom County; flows south and southeast 5 miles to North Fork, Nooksack River. It was named for mountaineer and former U.S. Forest Ranger Carl Bell, who discovered the creek.

Bells Mountain *(Ss.23,26;T.4N;R.3E)*

A low mountain 19 miles northeast of Vancouver, 6 miles east of Battleground, central Clark County. It was named for a man who homesteaded at the foot of this mountain in 1880.

Belltown *(S.31;T.25N;R.4E)*

An area of hotels and small businesses (most in very old structures) on the east shore of Elliott Bay, in the northern

business section of Seattle, King County. In the 1850s, it was named for William Nathaniel Bell, who was one of the Denny Party which landed on Alki Point in 1851. In 1852, Bell took a Donation Land Claim here between the claims of Arthur Denny and David Denny.

Bellville (Whitman County) *see* Colfax

Bellvue (San Juan County) *see* Friday Harbor

Bellvue Island (San Juan County) *see* San Juan Island

Bellvue Lake (King County) *see* Sturtevant Lake

Bellvue Point *(S.14;T.35N;R.4W)*

A southwest shore point of San Juan Island on Haro Strait, 7 miles west of Friday Harbor, San Juan County. This name was used by Hudson's Bay Company when a settlement was established here in 1859 for farming and trading. The post was named *Bellvue*. The same nomenclature had been used by the U.S. Coast Survey when the point was charted in 1855.

Belma *(S.28;T.9N;R.25E)*

Community 3-1/2 miles northeast of Mabton, southeast Yakima County. When established early in 1894, Belma had a post office and a trade store. In 1909, the post office was moved to Mabton. The name, which remains on the community, was chosen by T. W. Howell, a Mabton realtor. His mother's favorite song was "Sweet Bell Mahoney" When she sang this old favorite, she combined the "Bell" with the first syllable of "Mahoney."

Belmont *(S.5;T.18N;R.45E)*

A railroad point, 12 miles north of Palouse, northeast Whitman County. In 1885, it was named by Northern Pacific Railway Company officials for August Belmont, New York financier and director of the Northern Pacific.

Belmont (Stevens County) *see* Colville

Bemis *(S.33;T.17N;R.36E)*

A small, scattered farm community, 15 miles south of Ritzville, on Rattlesnake Flat, southeast Adams County. It was named for Alfred F. Bemis, who settled here in the spring of 1889.

Ben Muir Island (Island County) *see* Ben Ure Island

Ben Ure Island *(S.25;T.34N;R.1E)*

A small, 12-acre island in Deception

Pass, between Whidbey and Fidalgo islands, extreme north Island County. It has 2,500 ft. of shoreland. This island, like many features in the area, was named for a pioneer settler. It also has been recorded as *Ure's Island, Ben Ure's Island, Ben Muir Island*, and *Big Tenif Island*. (USBGN)

Bench Creek *(S.11;T.39N;R.45E)*

The stream of the creek heads on Kaniksu National Forest, northeast Pend Oreille County; flows northeasterly into Idaho. Originally it was called *Big Creek*. Because that name was too common, it was changed to a descriptive appellation for a 50-acre, level area at the mouth of the creek. (USBGN)

Bench Lake *(Mt. Rainier National Park)*

A 7.9-acre lake, elevation 4,600 ft., 1-1/2 miles southeast of Reflection Lakes, between Tatoosh Range and Stevens Canyon, south central area of the park. It is directly below a rocky protrusion called "The Bench," for which it was named. (USBGN)

Bench Lake *(S.16;T.33N;R.13E)*

A Mt. Baker National Forest lake at the head of Bench Creek, 4-1/2 miles west of Cascade Mountain summit, extreme southeast Skagit County. It was named by U.S. Forest Service personnel because it is on a bench-like plateau.

Bench Mark Mountain
(S.12;T.28N;R.12E)

A 5,815-ft. peak, 1-1/4 miles west of Cascade Mountain summit, 13-1/2 miles southwest of Glacier Peak summit, southeast Snohomish County. It is used for a forest fire lookout in season. In 1896, the name was applied by government surveyors when they established a bench mark on the mountain.

Bender (Benton County) *see* Gibbon

Bender Canyon (Chelan County) *see* Brender Canyon

Bender Creek *(T.30N;R.9E)*

The stream of the creek heads 2 miles south of South Fork, Stillaguamish River, east central Snohomish County; flows north to that river between Weigle and Silverton. It was locally named for J. F. Bender, an early miner and prospector in the Silverton district.

Benge *(S.1;T.16N;R.37E)*

Community 12 miles northeast of Palouse Falls, southeast Adams County. Benge was named by the Northern Pacific Railway Company for Frank H. Benge, a pioneer stockman and owner of land on which the station was erected.

Benson (Lincoln County) *see* Creston

Benton City *(S.18;T.9N;R.27E)*

Town on Yakima River, 9 miles west of Richland, central Benton County. A railroad station, established here in 1909, was named to honor Benton S. Grosscup, by E. L. Pitman, chief engineer on Northern Pacific Railway location, and by his right-of-way superintendent, C. E. Woods. Grosscup had been very active in the establishment of Benton County from Yakima and Klickitat counties in 1905.

Benton County

County in southeast Washington bounded on the north by Grant County; on the east by Walla Walla and Franklin counties; on the south by Columbia River; and, on the west by Yakima and Klickitat counties. It was created by the state legislature on March 8, 1905, from portions of Yakima and Klickitat counties, totaling 1,738 sq. miles. When the county was established, the name chosen was that of Thomas Hart Benton, senator from Missouri (1820-1851), a man of great vision and activity in all matters concerned with expansion of western portions of the United States.

Berg Creek *(T.27N;R.18E)*

A short stream with 3 branches that heads 8 miles northwest of Wenatchee Lake, Wenatchee National Forest, central Chelan County; flows 2-1/2 miles southwest to Mad River. It was named by Forest Ranger James McKenzie for Ed Berg, an honored resident of Entiat Valley.

Berkeley Park *(Mt. Rainier National Park)*

Small plateau, elevation 5,700-5,800 ft., at headwaters of Lodi Creek and foot of Burroughs Mountain, 1 mile west of Frozen Lake, north central area of the park. Flowers and small, stunted trees cover the area. Park Ranger Thomas E. O'Farrell recommended the adoption of this name since it had been in use since at least 1914. (USBGN)

Berlin *(S.33;T.12N;R.42E)*

Townsite on Pataha Creek, between Pataha and Pomeroy, north central Garfield County. Platted on January 9,

1883, by Charles and Sarah Ward, it never developed into an inhabited town. The platters chose the name for unknown reasons.

Berlin (King County) *see* Miller River

Berne *(S.8;T.26N;R.15E)*

Railroad station at east portal of Great Northern Railway tunnel through Cascade Mountains, Wenatchee National Forest, southwest Chelan County. It was named by railroad officials for the rugged mountain scenery, which they compared with Bern, Switzerland.

Bernier Creek *(Ts.13,14N;R.2E)*

The stream of this short creek rises 4 miles northeast of Alpha, north central Lewis County; flows 3 miles south to Newaukum River. It was named by and for Marcel Bernier, a French-Canadian trapper for Hudson's Bay Company, who camped and trapped on this creek in the 1840s.

Berrian *(S36;T.5N;R.29E)*

Settlement near Columbia River, 18 miles south of Kennewick, southeast Benton County. When a post office was established, it was named for the first settler, Gus Berrian. An earlier name was *Colbia*.

Berry Creek (King County) *see* Tibbetts Creek

Bertha May Lakes *(S.16;T.14N;R.7E)*

Two small, connected lakes, elevation 4,163 ft., on the northeast side of Sawtooth Ridge, Snoqualmie National Forest, northeast Lewis County. The upper lake covers 30 acres; lower lake, 1,000 ft. from the upper lake, covers approximately 6 acres. Peter Hershey, an early settler at Ashford, named the lakes for his 2 daughters.

Bertrand Creek *(T.40N;R.2E)*

The stream of the creek rises near the Canadian boundary, north of Delta, northwest Whatcom County; flows south 9 miles to Nooksack River. It was named for James Bertrand, who, in 1858, was the first white settler on the creek. Bertrand Prairie, on the Canadian side, is also named for him.

Bessemer *(S.9;T.35N;R.5E)*

Community 4 miles northeast of Sedro Woolley, west central Skagit County. Platted in 1890 when Cokedale mines opened nearby, the town was expected to be a big steel-producing center, but never developed. It was named for Sir Henry Bessemer, who invented the steel-producing process in 1858-59.

Beulah *(T.36N;R.37E)*

Small settlement on the west bank of Columbia River, east central Ferry County. It was the western terminus of a ferry which ran across the river to the old town of Kettle Falls. The site was inundated in the reservoir created by Grand Coulee Dam, and does not appear on recent maps. It was named by Ben Camp for his sister. A versatile pioneer, he not only built and owned the ferry, but homesteaded land on the east bank, and taught in the Kettle Falls school.

Beulah Land (Douglas County) *see* Palisades

Beverly *(S.34;T.16N;R.23E)*

Village 6 miles south by east of Vantage near the east bank of Columbia River, southwest Grant County. During the days of heavy navigation on the river, it was an active shipping point. It was named for Beverly, Massachusetts, by H.R. Williams, vice president of Chicago, Milwaukee & St. Paul Railway.

Bickleton *(S.22;T.6N;R.20E)*

Community 19 miles north of Columbia River, 3 miles south of Simcoe Mountains, northeast Klickitat County. It was named for Charlie Bickle, an early settler and horse trader.

Biddle Butte *(T.1N;R.3E)*

Butte on the north side of Columbia River, 8 miles east of Vancouver near Cape Horn, Clark County. It was named for Henry J. Biddle, a financier from Portland, Oregon, who bought land nearby in the 1890s.

Biddle Lake *(S.3;T.1N;R.2E)*

A 1-acre lake on the north bank of Columbia River, in the river's flood area, north of Government Island, 6-1/2 miles east of Vancouver, south central Clark County. (*see* Biddle Butte)

Big Bear Lake (Skagit County) *see* Itswoot Lake

Big Bear Mountain *(Ss.19,20;T.31N;R.9E)*

A Mt. Baker National Forest peak, elevation 5,612 ft., 6 miles north of Gold Basin, at the head of South Fork, Canyon Creek, north central Snohomish County. It is used as a forest fire lookout in season. The name developed through local usage. The mountain should not be confused with another by the same name, located 3 miles northwest. (USBGN)

Big Bear Mountain *(S.23;T.31N;R.8E)*

A 4,565-ft. peak 8-1/2 miles south of Fortson, north central Snohomish County. This mountain should not be confused with another of the same name, located 3 miles southeast. Each mountain's name developed through local usage, but the other peak's name has been approved by USBGN.

Big Bend Country

Large area south and east of Columbia River, where the river bends and changes course from west to south and southeast, Lincoln, Douglas, Grant, and Okanogan counties. As early as 1826, David Douglas referred to it as *The Big* or *Great Bend*.

Big Boulder Ridge (Ferry County) *see* Taylor Ridge

Big Camass Plain (Stevens County) *see* Camas Prairie

Big Chopaka Mountain *(Ss.14,23;T.40N;R.24E)*

A 7,870-ft. peak 3 miles south of the Canadian boundary and 8 miles northwest of Loomis, north central Okanogan County. It is one of 2 peaks in the area named "Chopaka." The lower peak is Little Chopaka Mountain. (*see* Chopaka)

Big Chutes (Klickitat County) *see* The Dalles

Big Creek *(Ts.19,20N;Rs.13,14E)*

The stream of the creek rises on the east slope of Cascade Mountain summit, southwest Kittitas County; flows northeast 14 miles through Wenatchee National Forest to Yakima River at Avendar. The name, while not exactly original, is descriptive. The stream has many tributaries, drains an extensive area of high mountain country, and carries a heavier volume of water in the summer season.

Big Creek *(T.33N;R.11E)*

The stream of the creek rises in Crater Lake, high in the mountains on Mt. Baker National Forest, southeast Skagit County; flows 9-1/2 miles west, joining Suiattle River, 3 miles northeast of Gyppo. The name is in contrast with Tenas Creek, directly to the south. In Chinook Indian jargon *tenas* means "small." While the creeks are almost the same length, Big Creek carries a much heavier volume of water in the spring run-off.

Big Four Mountain *(S.33;T.30N;R.10E)*

A 6,053-ft. peak 20 miles east of Granite Falls and 5 miles west of Monte Cristo mining area, east central Snohomish County. It is studded with glaciers and has extensive ice caves. The name is said to have been chosen because of a huge figure "4" which appears on the mountain's flank in certain weather phases. A local legend ascribes the name to 4 brothers who trapped and prospected in the area, and who built a cabin on the later site of Big Four Inn. They were said to have been huge men, and locally called the "Big Four."

Big Granite Lake (Skagit County) *see* Granite Lake

Big Hidden Lake (Skamania County) *see* Hidden Lake

Big Index, East Index (King County) *see* Baring

Big Island (Benton County) *see* Blalock Island

Big Jim Mountain *(S.15;T.25N;R.16E)*

A Wenatchee National Forest peak, elevation 7,775 ft., on a high spur of Icicle Ridge, 1 mile north of Lake Augusta, southwest Chelan County. This very prominent peak was named by U.S. Forest Supervisor A. H. Sylvester, whose associates believed he chose it in honor of James J. Hill of Great Northern Railway Company.

Big Joes Lake *(S.28;T.30N;R.14W)*

A 15-acre lake 10 miles northwest of Forks, west central Clallam County. According to local information, it was christened with the nickname of a very early resident. It also is known as *Joes Lake*.

Big Lake *(Ts.33,34N;Rs.4,5E)*

A 3-mile-long by 1/2-mile-wide lake, 3-1/2 miles east of Mt. Vernon, southwest Skagit County. It was the location of very active logging and sawmilling until the exhaustion of the timber supply. On very early maps it is shown as *DeLacey's Lake*. The present name describes its size in relation to other lakes in the immediate area.

Big Lake *(S.25;T.34N;R.4E)*

Town at the north end of Big Lake, 4 miles east of Mt. Vernon, southwest

Skagit County. Formerly a sawmill and logging center, it lost its importance with the depletion of old-growth timber. It was named for the lake on which it is located. Montborne, on the east shore of the lake, was called "Big Lake" until 1890 when it was changed by Seattle, Lake Shore & Eastern Railway.

Big Lake (Clallam County) *see* Lake Crescent

Big Lake (King County) *see* Lodge Lake

Big Lava Bed *(Ts.4,5N;Rs.8,9E)*
Volcanic lava bed directly east of Cascade Crest Trail, Gifford Pinchot National Forest, southeast Skamania County. Covering over 25 sq. miles, it is about 10 miles long from north to south and averages 3 to 4 miles in width. The bed, deserving its descriptive name, was created during the active volcanic period on Mt. Adams.

Big Mason Lake (King County) *see* Mason Lake

Big Meadow Creek
(Ts.27,28N;Rs.16,17E.partly uns)
The stream of the creek rises on Chiwawa Ridge between McCall Mountain and Dirtyface Peak, Wenatchee National Forest, northwest Chelan County; flows 7-1/2 miles southeast to Chiwawa River. Early settlers named it for a large, swampy meadow that borders the creek midway in its course.

Big Muddy Creek *(T.8N;Rs.11,12E)*
The stream of the creek rises in Klickitat Glacier, southeast slope of Mt. Adams, southwest corner Yakima County; plunges 10 miles eastward to Klickitat River, north of Glenwood. It is one of the state's most remarkable streams, carrying an enormous load of glacial debris and boulders when Klickitat Glacier melts. The heavy rocks, coupled with the stream's steep gradient, cause strong earth vibrations when the creek is in flood. The locally-applied name refers to the extremely muddy color of the stream during late spring and summer.

Big Prairie (Pierce County) *see* American Prairie

Big Quilcene River *(T.27N;Rs.2,3W)*
The stream of the river rises in Marmot Pass, Olympic Primitive Area; flows east into Quilcene Bay, east central Jefferson County. In early days, mining camps were in operation near the

headwaters. (*see* Quilcene)

Big Rattlesnake Lake (King County) *see* Rattlesnake Lake

Big Sheep Creek *(T.40N;Rs.38,39E)*
The stream of the creek rises at the Canadian boundary, Colville National Forest, north central Stevens County; flows east and southeast to Columbia River. The Indian name was *Yome-tsin*, the meaning of which has not been ascertained. The present name and that of a tributary, "Little Sheep Creek," were given by settlers, evidently from early use of this area for domestic sheep range.

Big Tenif Island (Island County) *see* Ben Ure Island

Big Twin Lake (Snohomish County) *see* Twin Lakes

Bill Point *(S.36;T.25N;R.2E)*
A southern shore point at the entrance to Eagle Harbor, southeast Bainbridge Island, east central Kitsap County. In 1841, it was named by Cmdr. Charles Wilkes in connection with Eagle Harbor and Wing Point.

Bill of Orcas (San Juan County) *see* Point Doughty

Billings (Spokane County) *see* Cheney

Billington (Adams County) *see* Hamlet

Billy Creek *(T.27N;Rs.18,19E)*
The stream of the creek rises on Tyee Mountain, 2-1/2 miles west of Entiat River, Wenatchee National Forest, central Chelan County; flows 3-1/2 miles southwest to Cougar Creek near junction with Mad River. It was named by U.S. Forest Supervisor A. H. Sylvester, for Billy Young, who had ranged his sheep in this area.

Billy Ridge *(T.27N;Rs.18,19E)*
A 4-mile-long ridge between Billy Creek and Young Creek from Tyee Mountain to Mad River, Wenatchee National Forest, central Chelan County. (*see* Billy Creek)

Bingen *(S.30;T.3N;R.11E)*
Town on a narrow flat between the north bank of Columbia River and a bluff, opposite Oregon's Hood River, southwest Klickitat County. In 1892, it was established by P. J. Suksdorf and other German settlers, who named it for "Bingen-On-The-Rhine." In 1931, the town went to court over the controversial naming of a Spokane, Portland & Seattle

Railway station in the town. White Salmon, adjoining Bingen on the northwest, also wanted its name on the station. At present, the station carries both names.

Biological Hill
(Ss.1,2,11,12;T.35N;R.3W)
Hill northwest of Friday Harbor Laboratories of the University of Washington, north of Friday Harbor, east central San Juan Island, San Juan County. It was named by university personnel for their laboratories, which formerly were called "Puget Sound Biological Station."

Birch *(S.18;T.20N;R.7E)*
Village 1-1/4 miles northeast of Enumclaw on Newaukum Creek, south central King County. In the 1880s, Northern Pacific Railway established a station here. Railroad officials named the place for native birch trees growing in the area, south of the normal range of that species.

Birch Bay *(Ts.39,40N;R.1W)*
Bay in Georgia Strait, 5 miles south of the Canadian boundary, extreme northwest Whatcom County. In 1791, members of the Francisco de Eliza expedition named it *Ensenada de Garzon* to honor Miguel Garzon, a Spanish Naval officer. On June 11, 1792, Capt. George Vancouver gave the bay its present name when his ships anchored here for 5 days. Abundant birches around the shore of the bay, which Vancouver called "black birches," inspired the name. In 1841, Cmdr. Charles Wilkes used Vancouver's name on his charts of the bay. Semiahmoo Indians called it *Tsan-wuch*. Lummi Indians called it *Say-wak*, meaning "people saved from a flood by building a raft."

Birch Mountain (Chelan County) *see* Burch Mountain

Birch Point *(T.40N;R.1W)*
A northern shore point of Birch Bay on Georgia Strait, northwest Whatcom County. In 1791, it was named *Punta de Senor Jose* by Lieut. Juan Francisco de Eliza. In 1858, Capt. Richards called it *South Bluff* on British Admiralty charts. The present name is from nearby Birch Bay.

Birchfield *(S.27;T.13N;R.19E)*
Community 2-1/2 miles southeast of Yakima, central Yakima County. Northern Pacific Railway officials

named it for W. A. *Burchfield*, a local landowner.

Bird Creek *(Ts.6-8N;Rs.11,12E)*

The stream of the creek rises at South Butte, southeast slope of Mt. Adams, southwest Yakima County; flows 26 miles southeast through Glenwood to Gilmer Creek near Conboy Lake, Klickitat County. According to local residents, early settlers chose the name for the large population of native grouse that inhabited heavy brush along the stream's lower reaches.

Bird Creek Meadows *(T.8N;R.11E)*

Park-like belt of mountain meadows near head of Bird Creek, southeast slope of Mt. Adams, between the 5,000-ft. contour and snowline, southwest Yakima County. Fires and over-grazing by sheep have severely damaged the area. (*see* Bird Creek)

Bird Rock (San Juan County) *see* Cormorant Rock

Bird Rocks *(T.35N;R.1W)*

Three small, low, rocky islands barren of soil, 2 miles southeast of Decatur Island in Rosario Strait, southeast San Juan County. In 1841, Cmdr. Charles Wilkes charted the name for the multitude of sea birds that nested on these rocks.

Birdsview *(S.15;T.35N;R.7E)*

Community on the north bank of Skagit River, between Hamilton and Concrete, central Skagit County. In 1878, Birdsley D. Minkler built a water-powered sawmill here, and also erected a hotel. The name was derived from Minkler's nickname "Bird."

Birmingham *(S.13;T.31N;R.3E)*

A resort and summer colony on Port Susan, 6 miles south of Stanwood, northwest Snohomish County. The plat was named for Birmingham, Alabama, by C. D. Hillman, a real estate speculator and promoter, who promised to build a city that would rival its namesake. A 1-mile tidal runout produces very warm water in summer, providing reason for the alternate name *Warm Beach*.

Birnie's Retreat, Birnie's Trading Post (Wahkiakum County) *see* Cathlamet

Bishop *(S.28;T.13N;R.44E)*

Settlement 1/2 mile north of Bishop Bar, north bank of Snake River at mouth of Yakawawa Canyon, southeast Whitman County. It was named by officials

of Camas Prairie Railway for Bishop Brothers, who settled on the nearby river bar in 1877.

Bissell *(S.33;T.32N;R.37E)*

Settlement near the east bank of Columbia River on Lake Creek near Charles Lake, 6 miles south of Gifford, southwest Stevens County. In 1895 it had a post office, and was named for Wilson S. Bissell, postmaster general. Presently, the place is little more than a settlement with a school.

Bismarck (Pierce County) *see* Hillsdale

Black Buttes *(Ss.26,27;T.38N;R.7E.uns)*

Buttes on the southwest slope of Mt. Baker, between Thunder and Deming glaciers, Mt. Baker National Forest, south central Whatcom County. The descriptive name was chosen by the Mazamas for these black, jagged precipices.

Black Creek *(T.32N;R.11E)*

The stream of the creek rises on Whitechuck Mountain, Mt. Baker National Forest, 9 miles east of Darrington, northeast Snohomish County; flows 4 miles north to Straight Creek. The name was given by Forest Service personnel to the West Fork, Straight Creek, because of the black appearance of dense timber on the creek's watershed, as viewed form the air.

Black Creek (Lewis County) *see* Skokomish River

Black Diamond *(S.14;T.21N;R.6E)*

Town 6 miles north of Enumclaw, 1-1/2 miles north of Green River, south central King County. Between 1880 and 1885, the entire population of Nortonville, Contra Costa County, California, moved here to live in this coal-mining town that was established and named for the Black Diamond Coal Company. By 1885, the Black Diamond mines had the largest production in King County. A high majority of the population was from Welsh ancestry.

Black Diamond Lake *(S.22;T.21N;R.6E)*

A 9-acre lake, 1 mile southwest of Black Diamond, south central King County. Originally it was called *Chub Lake*. The present name is for the town of Black Diamond.

Black Hills *(Ss.19,30,31;T.18N;R.2W)*

A range of hills, maximum elevation

760 ft., 3 miles southwest of Olympia and directly north of Black Lake, west central Thurston County. These low mountains were named for Black Lake.

Black Lake *(S.28;T.10N;R.11W)*

Lake directly north of Ilwaco, near the mouth of Columbia River, extreme southwest Pacific County. The name, of local origin, relates to the lake's very dark-colored water.

Black Lake *(Ts.17,18N;R.2W)*

A 2-1/2-mile-long lake at the source of Black River, directly south of Black Hills, 3 miles southwest of Olympia, west central Thurston County. In 1841, the Wilkes Expedition applied the Indian name *Sa-chal*. *Pacific Railroad Reports*, published in 1854, used *Sat-chall* on their maps. The present name was chosen locally for the very dark color of the lake's water.

Black Lake (Pacific County) *see* Johnson Lake

Black Mountain *(Ss.13,24;T.30N;R.12E)*

A 7,192-ft. mountain 5 miles southwest of Glacier Peak on its rugged slope, east central Snohomish County. In 1896, a survey party, consisting of Sam Strom, Thomas Gardine and Alex Dubor, named the mountain for the very dark color of its rock mass.

Black River *(T.23N;Rs.4,5E)*

Former river extending from the south end of Lake Washington to White River, southwest of Renton, west central King County. The short stream flowed either from Lake Washington to White River or vice versa, depending on the lake's water height. When the lake was lowered to connect it with Puget Sound via Lake Union and the Seattle ship canal, the river was eliminated. Early settlers named the river for the contrast of its dark water with that of the White River, which carried light-colored, glacial "flour."

Black River *(Ts.15,16,17N;Rs.2,3,4,5W)*

The stream of the river rises in Black Lake, 3 miles southwest of Olympia, central Thurston County; flows southwest to Chehalis River, south of Oakville, extreme southeast Grays Harbor County. It was named for Black Lake.

Black River Junction *(S.14;T.23N;R.4E)*

Railroad junction 2 miles west of Renton on the former channel of Black River, west central King County. Railroad officials named it for Black River, which met White River at this point before Black River was eliminated by the lowering of Lake Washington. (*see* Black River)

Black River Bridge (King County) *see* Renton

Black Rock *(S.2;T.35N;R.1W)*

A low, dark-colored rock 1/2 mile off the southeast coast of Blakely Island, east central San Juan County. In 1854, this descriptive name was charted by the U.S. Coast Survey. The rock is one of "The Pointers," with Pointer Island and Lawson Rock, which point the entrance to Thatcher Pass. This group name was applied in 1841 by Cmdr. Charles Wilkes.

Blackman's Lake (Snohomish County) *see* Stillaguamish Lake

Blackrock *(S.24;T.12N;R.22E)*

A settlement on Blackrock Creek, 16 miles east of Moxee, northeast Yakima County. In early 1906, a store and post office were established by Abraham Vanderlinde, postmaster from 1906 to 1911. Attempts were made to irrigate this barren area with the waters of Blackrock Creek, but it reverted to sagebrush. Farming has recently been revived. The place was named for a nearby large, black rock.

Blackwater Lake (Clallam County) *see* Lake Aldwell

Blackwood Creek *(S.30;T.29N;R.9W)*

The stream of the creek rises in Blackwood Lake, Olympic National Park, south central Clallam County; flows 3-1/2 miles north-northeast to Soleduck River near Sol Duc Hot Springs. Both the creek and lake are reported to bear the name of a pioneer settler in this area. On some maps the stream is labeled *Manden, Mauden* or *Munden* Creek. (USBGN)

Blackwood Lake *(S.17;T.28N;R.9W)*

A 16-acre lake, 3 miles west of Sol Duc Hot Springs, Olympic National Park, south central Clallam County. It is said to have been named for a pioneer prospector and trapper.

Blaine *(Ts.40,41N;R.1W,1E)*

Town directly south of the Canadian boundary, on Drayton Harbor, extreme

northwest Whatcom County. The International Peace Arch is located near here at the boundary, as well as U.S. and Canadian Customs and Immigration stations. In 1884, the town was named by Gen. McPherson for James G. Blaine, a presidential candidate. In 1858, during the Fraser River gold rush, it was called *Semiahmoo* for a local Indian tribe. Another early name was *Concord*

Blaine Glacier *(Pierce County)* *see* Emmons Glacier

Blake Island *(T.24N;R.2E)*

Island in Puget Sound, 4 miles west of Seattle's south suburbs, east central Kitsap County. In the 1850s, it was logged over, and has had several owners. It now is state-owned for park purposes. An early name was *High Island*, although the maximum elevation is only 160 ft. In early days, a local name was *Smugglers Island*. Early in the century, it was renamed *Trimble Island* while owned by William Pitt Trimble of Seattle. In spite of all these name changes, the name given in 1841 by Cmdr. Charles Wilkes endures. It was for George S. Blake, who headed the U.S. Coast Survey at the time of the Wilkes Expedition, and who assisted Wilkes in his preparations.

Blakely Harbor (Kitsap County) *see* Port Blakely

Blakely Hill *(Ss.27,34;T.36N;R.1W)*

Hill near the northeast shore of Blakely Island, east central San Juan County. The name source is the same as that of Blakely Island. (USBGN)

Blakely Island *(Ts.35,36N;R.1W)*

Island with an area about 8 sq. miles, between Decatur and Obstruction islands, east central San Juan County. It slopes steeply from the water to stony heights. In 1841, Cmdr. Charles Wilkes named it for Capt. Johnston Blakely, who was killed in the War of 1812 on the ship WASP. The Lummi Indian name for the island was *Com-com-rach*.

Blakely Lake (San Juan County) *see* Horseshoe Lake

Blakely Rock *(S.1;T.24N;R.3E)*

Rock at the entrance to Blakely Harbor, southeast shore of Bainbridge Island, east central Kitsap County. (*see* Port Blakely)

Blalock Island *(Ts.4,5N;Rs.25,26E)*

A whale-shaped island, 7 miles long

and 2 miles wide at mid-length tapering to points, between two channels of Columbia River, 20 miles south of Prosser, southwest Benton County. The island is largely inundated by the John Day Dam. In 1831, John Work of Hudson's Bay Company applied the name *Big Island*. Later, fur traders traveling the Columbia named it *Long Island*. The entire island was purchased in April 1899, by Dr. Nelson G. Blalock, a Civil War surgeon and pioneer railroad developer. He built a pumping plant for irrigation and planted extensive orchards. The island bears his name.

Blanchard *(S.22;T.36N;R.3E)*

Settlement on Whitehall Creek, 1/2 mile east of Samish Bay, northwest Skagit County. An early name was *Fravel* for a pioneer who built most of the Fraser River Trail in 1858, during the Fraser River gold rush. In 1913, it was renamed for a local timber owner when a shingle mill was established.

Blewett *(S.1;T.22N;R.17E)*

Town 15 miles west of Wenatchee and 5 miles north of Blewett Pass on Blewett Pass Hwy., Wenatchee National Forest, southwest Chelan County. In 1860, it was established in this mineralized area by miners returning from British Columbia. At one time, over 300 miners worked around this settlement. (*see* Blewett Pass)

Blewett Pass *(S.2;T.21N;R.17E)*

Important highway pass, elevation 4,071 ft., at Wenatchee Mountains summit, 25 miles north of Ellensburg, between southwest Chelan and north central Kittitas counties. It was named for Edward Blewett, an early miner who operated a mine here in the 1880s. In 1889, he and H. C. Henry, his partner from Seattle, installed a 10-stamp ore mill, and later built a 20-stamp mill and a sawmill near this pass. An earlier name was *Swauk Pass*.

Blind Bay *(S.27;T.36N;R.2W)*

North shore bay of Shaw Island, directly south of Orcas on Orcas Island, central San Juan County. It was locally named because the bay is visible only from the direct north.

Blind Island *(S.27;T.36N;R.2W)*

A very small island at the entrance to Blind Bay, north shore of Shaw Island, central San Juan County. It was locally named for the bay in which it is located. (*see* Blind Bay)

Blocher Falls (Pierce County) *see* Bloucher Falls

Blockhouse *(S.16;T.4N;R.15E)*

Once a fort 5 miles west of Goldendale, central Klickitat County. It was located on the wagon road between Ft. Dalles and Ft. Simcoe, Yakima County, and was named for a small blockhouse built here in 1855 during the Indian Wars. The log structure was moved to Goldendale, and later to Brooks Memorial Park near Satus Pass. Another name for the place is *Old Fort Klickitat.*

Bloucher Falls *(Mt. Rainier National Park)*

A 5,000-ft. falls in East Fork, Van Trump Creek, near the junction with West Fork, southwest zone of the park. This small but beautiful falls is 12-1/2 miles by highway and trail from Nisqually Entrance. It was named by a party of early mountain climbers for one of its members. Some maps name it, in error, *Blocher Falls.*

Blowers Bluff *(Ss.14,23;T.32N;R.1E)*

East shore bluff on Whidbey Island, facing Saratoga Passage, directly south of Oak Harbor, east central Island County. The first name was *Ford's Point*, for an early family of settlers. When the Fords moved, the name was changed to that of another family in the vicinity.

Blue Canyon *(S.22;T.37N;R.4E)*

A mining "ghost" town on the east shore of Lake Whatcom, 1 mile northwest of Park, southwest Whatcom County. It once produced the best steam coal on the Pacific Coast. The mine started in 1890 and was closed in 1920. The town was named by James F. Wardner, one of the town's promoters, for the blue tinge on ridges surrounding the mine when mist was in the air.

Blue Creek *(T.28N;R.18E)*

The stream of this very short creek rises near Two Little Lakes, Wenatchee National Forest, central Chelan County; flows 2 miles south to Mad Creek. It was named by sheepmen for a bluish cast which it acquires in late fall and winter.

Blue Creek *(T.21N;R.17E)*

The stream of this short creek flows east 4 miles from Teanaway Ridge to Swauk Creek, central Kittitas County. It was named by local settlers because of a blue-clay slide on a mountainside along the creek.

Blue Creek *(S.31;T.33N;R.40E)*

Community 16 miles south of Colville, central Stevens County. It was an early sawmill town and stage station, named for nearby Blue Creek, a tributary of Colville River. That stream was named for John Blue, an early settler, at whose station the stage drivers changed horses.

Blue Creek Station (Stevens County) *see* Blue Creek (town)

Blue Glacier
(Ss.27,34;T.27N;R.8W.uns)

A north slope glacier of East Peak, Mt. Olympus, at the headwaters of Glacier Creek, north central Jefferson County. It was named for its clear, blue color by Edward W. Allen of Seattle, who climbed the West Peak in 1913 with Charles Farrer and Earl Rice.

Blue Lake *(S.13;T.8N;R.4E)*

An 8-acre lake in Coldspring Creek, 1-1/2 miles northeast of Goat Marsh Lakes, east central Cowlitz County. It was named by local settlers who admired its dark blue color. *Coldspring Lake* and *Steamboat Lake* were earlier names.

Blue Lake *(Ss.20,21,29;T.24N;R.27E)*

A 3-mile-long lake, 1/2 mile in average width, 6 miles southwest of Coulee City, north Grant County. It is one of several prehistoric lakes in the Grand Coulee chain, used for bathing and camping. The name is reasonably descriptive.

Blue Lake *(S.32;T.11N;R.9E.uns)*

Lake 1/4 mile north of Skamania County boundary, southeast Lewis County. It drains through Blue Lake Creek into Cispus River. The name was locally chosen for the lake's intense blue color during summer months.

Blue Lake *(S.6;T.39N;R.27E)*

Small lake, 6-1/2 miles south of the Canadian boundary, 1 mile northwest of Wannacut Lake, north central Okanogan County. The name derives from its deep, cobalt-blue color. The lake is enhanced by an outcropping of smooth, white rock at the shoreline.

Blue Lake *(S.32;T.37N;R.8E.uns)*

Lake 9 miles south of Mt. Baker summit, Mt. Baker National Forest, south central Whatcom County. The name, describing the lake's color, was used by local sheepherders, and was adopted by U.S. Forest Service personnel.

Blue Lake (Grant County) *see* Sun Lakes State Park

Blue Lake (King County) *see* Lake Talapus

Blue Lake (Snohomish County) *see* Indigo Lake

Blue Mountains

Mountain range, elevations to 6,250 ft., mostly within Umatilla National Forest, Columbia, Garfield and Asotin counties in southeast Washington, and adjoining areas of Oregon. Rough and scenic, these mountains were an obstacle to early emigrants, travelers and stockmen, as evidenced by names that were applied in pioneer days. In 1811, David Thompson named the range for the blue or azure appearance of the higher peaks as seen from a distance. The Indian name is said to have been *Shawpatin.*

Blue Ridge *(T.10N;R.9E.uns)*

A 5-mile-long ridge, maximum elevation 5,049 ft., in a south bend of Cispus River, northwest of Mt. Adams, northeast Skamania County. The name was chosen by early settlers because the south side of the ridge acquires a bluish tinge under certain atmospheric conditions.

Blue Town *(S.14;T.36N;R.37E)*

A short-lived store and small community, between Kettle Falls (town) 1/2 mile north and Marcus, northwest Stevens County. In 1889, it was established during the Kettle Falls boom. It was named by and for Louis Blue, a Jewish merchant who established the store to compete with Kettle Falls for trade and settlers. Not on recent maps.

Blueberry Lake (King County) *see* Larsen Lake

Bluelight
(S.3;T.6N;&S.34;T.7N;R.21E)

Community 6 miles northeast of Bickleton, on Yakima-Klickitat county line. In 1889, it was named by Julius Martinet, postmaster. Local settlers speculated the reason for his choice, with no very logical answers.

Blue's Station (Stevens County) *see* Blue Creek (town)

Blueslide *(S.11;T.35N;R.43E)*

Small settlement on the west bank of Pend Oreille River, at its confluence with Little Ruby Creek, central Pend Oreille County. It is named for the color of a clay slide on the river bank, which has a bluish tinge when wet.

Bluestem *(S.34;T.24N;R.37E)*

Grain station 8 miles south of Harrington, east Lincoln County. In the early 1890s, it was platted by Ulysses Sheridan Long as *Moscow*. Later, the settlers changed its name to designate the principal wheat species raised in this area.

Blunt's Island (Island County) *see* Smith Island

Blustery Point (Pacific County) *see* Point Ellice

Bly *(S.9;T.6N;R.46E)*

Formerly a post office at the confluence of Cottonwood and Joseph creeks, 1-1/2 miles north of the Oregon boundary, extreme southeast Asotin County. It was named for Joseph Bly, the postmaster.

Blyn *(S.12;T.29N;R.3W)*

Once an important logging center at the southwest end of Sequim Bay, northeast Clallam County. Now it includes only a store and a few residences. It was named for Capt. Blyn, who lived here in early days, and about whom little is known.

Boat Channel *(S.18;T.35N;R.2W)*

A narrow channel, leading north to Friday Harbor, between San Juan Island and Twin Island, central San Juan County. This descriptive name was applied by British Admiralty surveyors.

Boat Harbor *(S.5;T.35N;R.2E)*

A small, square-shaped bay on the east shore of Guemes Island, north end of Padilla Bay, northwest Skagit County. An early, local name was *Square Bay*, because of its contour. The present name was substituted later by local navigators.

Boat Harbor (Jefferson County) *see* Mats Mats Bay

Bobbie Burns Creek (King County) *see* Burns Creek

Boca de Alava *(T.31N;R.16W)*

An entrance near Cape Alava, Clallam County. On August 6, 1790, Manuel Quimper named it for Jose Manuel de Alava, Spanish naval commandant at Acapulco. "Formed by a point," it probably was the mouth of Ozette River, as he described it.

Boca de Fidalgo (Skagit, San Juan, Whatcom counties) *see* Rosario Strait

Boca de Flon (Skagit, Island counties) *see* Deception Pass

Boca de Florida Blanca (Whatcom County) *see* Boundary Bay

Bocas de Horcasitas (San Juan County) *see* San Juan Channel

Bodie *(S.3;T.38N;R.31E)*

A mining "ghost" town, on Toroda Creek, Colville National Forest, 19 miles south of the Canadian boundary, northeast Okanogan County. It was named for nearby Bodie Mine.

Bogachiel Lake *(T.28N;R.9W.uns)*

Small mountain lake at the head of a north tributary of Bogachiel River, 1 mile northwest of Bogachiel Peak, Olympic National Park, south central Clallam County. (USBGN) *(see* Bogachiel River)

Bogachiel Park *(T.28N;R.9W)*

A mountain meadow with several small lakes, 2 miles south of Sol Duc Hot Springs, near head of Soleduck River, south central Clallam County. (USBGN)

Bogachiel Peak *(T.28N;R.9W.uns)*

A 5,474-ft. peak at head of Bogachiel River, 8 miles northwest of Mt. Olympus, Olympic National Park, north central Clallam County. (USBGN) *(see* Bogachiel River)

Bogachiel River
(Ts.27,28N;Rs.9-14W)

The stream of the river rises on Bogachiel Peak near High Divide, Olympic National Park, south central Clallam County; flows 40 miles west along Clallam-Jefferson county line to Soleduck River, 5 miles from Pacific Ocean. The Indian name *Bo-qua-tchiel* means "muddy after rain." (USBGN)

Bogachiel State Park *(T.27N;R.13W)*

A 123-acre park on Bogachiel River, 6 miles south of Forks, northwest Jefferson County. Camping and fishing are available to the public in this "rain forest" park. It was named for Bogachiel River. (USBGN)

Boggy Creek *(T.25N;R.16E)*

The stream of this short creek rises on the south side of Grindstone Mountain, Icicle Ridge, southeast Chelan County; flows 1-1/2 miles to Icicle Creek, Wenatchee National Forest. It

was named by U.S. Forest Supervisor A. H. Sylvester because of a muddy ford at a trail crossing.

Boise *(S.35;T.20N;R.6E)*

Railroad station on White River, 2 miles southwest of Enumclaw, extreme south central King County. In 1885, Northern Pacific Railway officials named it for Boise, Idaho.

Boise Creek (King County) *see* Boise

Boise Lake *(S.28;T.20N;R.7E)*

A 23-acre pond in Boise Creek, 3 miles east of Enumclaw, southwest King County. It was named for the settlement of Boise. Locally, it is called *White River Mill Pond* for White River Lumber Company which uses it for sorting and storing logs.

Boisfort Peak *(S.32;T.12N;R.4W)*

Highest peak in Willapa Hills, elevation 3,111 ft., between Chehalis River and Stillman Creek, 6-1/2 miles northwest of Wildwood, southwest Lewis County. It was named by French-Canadian employees of Hudson's Bay Company during fur-trading days. A literal translation from the French is "strong wood." Locally, the name is often pronounced "Baw Faw" or "Boo Foo."

Boistfort *(S.1;T.12N;R.4W)*

A farming area on South Fork, Chehalis River, 15 miles southwest of Chehalis, southwest Lewis County. It was considered as a possible site for the University of Washington. Many Donation Land Claims dating back to the 1850s are located here, most of which bear French-Canadian names. *Boisfort*, the original French name, may be translated as "strong wood" or "heavy forest." The surplus "t" was evidently added by map makers in early years. *(see* Boisfort Peak)

Bolster *(S.9;T.40N;R.30E)*

Settlement 20 miles east of Oroville, 8 miles east of Molson and 2 miles south of the Canadian boundary, Okanogan County. It was one of the rough-and-tumble mining camps which flourished in boom days of the country. George Tindall and Grant Stewart named the place for Mr. H. Bolster, a Spokane mining promoter.

Bolt Camp *(S.33;T.30N;R.9E)*

An abandoned camp on Mallardy Creek, 2 miles south of South Fork, Stillaguamish River, central Snohomish

County. The locally-selected name refers to extensive shingle-bolt cutting in the area between 1922 and 1927.

Bolton Peninsula *(T.27N;R.1W)*

A 4-mile-long peninsula, 1-1/2 miles in average width, between Dabob Bay and Quilcene Bay, 2 miles west of Quilcene, east central Jefferson County. In 1841, Cmdr. Charles Wilkes named it for Midshipman William F. Bolton of his command.

Bonaparte Creek *(T.38N;R.30E)*

The stream of the creek heads in Bonaparte Lake, Colville National Forest, northeast Okanogan County; flows to the south and west in a wide curve, to the Okanogan River at Tonasket. In 1841, Cmdr. Charles Wilkes mapped this water course as *River Bonaparte*, which had been previously used by Hudson's Bay Company officials. There is some evidence that the name was first applied by Peter Skene Ogden, who was chief factor of that company around the time Napoleon Bonaparte died. The Indian name for the stream was *Hy-as-kwa-ha-loos*.

Bonaparte Lake
(Ss.8,9,16,17;T.38N;R.30E)

A sausage-shaped lake at the head of Bonaparte Creek, Colville National Forest, 14 miles south of the Canadian boundary, northeast Okanogan County. The name origin is listed under Bonaparte Creek.

Bonaparte Mountain (Okanogan County) *see* Mt. Bonaparte

Bone Lake (Grays Harbor County) *see* Klone Lakes

Bone River *(Ss.34-36;T.14N;R.10W)*

The stream of the river rises 2 miles west of South Bend, northwest Pacific County; flows west to Willapa Bay, between Stony Point and Palix River. It is about 5 miles long and 200 feet wide at its mouth. The name is of local origin, and relates to numerous elk and deer bones found around an old Indian campsite at the river's mouth.

Bong *(T.25N;R.41E)*

A 4th-class post office, 7-1/2 miles west of Spokane, on the western boundary of Spokane Air Force Base, Spokane County. In 1948, it was originally named for Maj. Richard I. Bong, a World War II fighter pilot, who won the Congressional Medal of Honor, and who was killed in a post-war jet fighter plane

crash. It was later changed to *Fairchild*, and now is officially called *Fairchild Air Force Base*.

Bonita *(S.30;T.29N;R.24E)*

Settlement on the east bank of Columbia River, 9 miles west of Bridgeport, northwest Douglas County. In 1902, it was named by Lieut. Edward Nasler for a place or person in the Philippine Islands he had known in the Spanish-American War.

Bonneville Pool *(T.2N;R.7E.at dam)*

A 20,200-acre reservoir in lower Columbia River, with depths over 30 ft., upstream from Bonneville Dam which is at river mile 145.3 from the river's mouth, Skamania County. It extends a river distance of 45 miles to The Dalles Dam. It was named for Capt. B. L. D. Bonneville, a romantic frontier soldier who was commandant at Ft. Vancouver from 1852 to 1856, and who became brevet brigadier general in 1865. An alternate name is *Bonneville Dam Reservoir*.

Booker Mountain
(S.2;T.34N;R.15E.uns)

An Okanogan National Forest mountain, elevation 8,300 ft., between Stehekin River and Park Creek, near Cascade Mountain summit, Chelan County. It was named for Booker T. Washington by Mrs. Frank R. Hill of Tacoma. Mrs. Hill painted a display canvas of the peak for the Great Northern Railway, to be used at the 1904 Louisiana Purchase Exposition. At that time the peak had not been named, and her painting was called "No Name Mountain."

Boone Creek *(T.19N;R.12W)*

The stream of the creek rises 6 miles east of Pacific Ocean, west central Grays Harbor County; flows west by south to the ocean at Iron Springs. It was named for 2 Boone brothers who lived on the creek in pioneer days.

Bordeaux *(S.5;T.16N;R.3W)*

Settlement on Mima Creek and Mima Prairie, 12 miles southwest of Olympia, southwest Thurston County. Once a logging and sawmill town, it has suffered from timber depletion, and now is a scattered settlement. In 1900, it was named for Tom Bordeaux, manager of Mumby Lumber & Shingle Company.

Borealis Ridge *(T.30N;R.17E.uns)*

A 5-mile-long ridge between Entiat

River and Chelan Mountains summit, draining into Aurora Creek on the north and Snowbrushy Creek on the south, Wenatchee National Forest, north central Chelan County. In 1909, it was named by U.S. Forest Supervisor A. H. Sylvester when he witnessed a fine display of the Northern Lights from this ridge.

Boren Lake (King County) *see* Etta Cartney Lake

Borgeau Lake *(S.36;T.32N;R.36E)*

A 1/2-mile-long lake, 1-1/2 miles west of Columbia River, 5 miles south of Inchelium, on Colville Indian Reservation, east central Ferry County. It was named for Charley Borgeau, a part-Indian resident, to whom the lake, with adjacent land, was allotted. On some maps the name is spelled *Bourgeau*.

Borst Blockhouse (Lewis County) *see* Ft. Borst

Borst Lake *(S.6;T.14N;R.2W)*

A 5-acre, artificial lake in Centralia's Ft. Borst Park, northwest Lewis County. It is named for Ft. Borst. An alternate name is *Ft. Borst Park Lake*.

Borup *(S.3;T.20N;R.11E)*

Community 3 miles west of Cascade Mountain summit, between Stampede and Kennedy, southeast King County. A system of switchbacks started at this point to reach Stampede Tunnel through the Cascade Mountains summit. Northern Pacific Railway personnel evidently used railroad slang when they named this working station.

Bossburg *(S.36;T.38N;R.37E)*

Village on Columbia River, 9 miles east of Marcus, west central Stevens County. Established in 1888, it was named *Young America* after an adjoining silver mine. On May 1, 1893, it was platted as a townsite by the Consolidated Bonanza Mining & Smelting Company as *Millington*. It was later renamed for Chester S. Boss, first postmaster and storekeeper, and John Berg, a pioneer.

Boston (Clallam County) *see* Mora

Boston Harbor
(Ss.11,14;T.19N;R.2W)

Residential area at east entrance to Budd Inlet, north central Thurston County. In the early 1900s, it was boomed unsuccessfully as an industrial town by Boston Harbor Railroad, Steamship & Land Company. The name, chosen by this corporation, was considered to be excellent for an industrial city. Names used for short periods in the early boom days were *Harriman* and *Hillman*, for persons who were instrumental in boosting the proposed city.

Boston Peak (Chelan, Skagit counties) *see* Sahala Mountain

Boston Point (*S.11;T.25N;R.2W*)
A west shore point of Hood Canal, at south entrance to Pleasant Harbor, 1 mile south of Brinnon, southeast Jefferson County. In 1841, it was named by Cmdr. Charles Wilkes for Boston, Massachusetts. It does not appear on recent maps.

Bothell (*S.3;T.26N;R.5E*)
Town on Sammamish River, 5 miles east of Lake Washington's north end, 23 miles north of Seattle, northwest King County. It was named for David C. Bothell, who established a logging camp and shingle mill here in 1886. An earlier name was *Brackett's Landing*.

Bottomless Lake (*S.12;T.35N;R.4E*)
A 3.4-acre lake 2 miles north of Sedro-Woolley, west central Skagit County. Located in a very boggy area, it has a very soft, silty bottom which would cause difficulty in sounding with a lead line.

Bottomless Pond (*S.12;T.28N;R.3E*)
A 5-acre lake on Whidbey Island, 3-1/4 miles south of Columbia Beach, extreme south Island County. While the name can hardly be supported by facts, soundings show the lake to be very deep.

Boulder Creek (*T.29N;R.15E.uns*)
The stream of the creek rises on the southeast slope of Clark Mountain, northwest Chelan County; flows south and southwest 3-1/2 miles to White River, Wenatchee National Forest. The name, chosen by early settlers, has been applied to many Washington mountain streams. It may be taken for granted that the bed and borders of creeks in rocky terrain will be well supplied with large rocks.

Boulder Creek (*Ts.38,39N;Rs.34-36E*)
The stream of the creek rises in north central Ferry County; flows east in 2 main branches, almost 20 miles, to the Kettle River, 2-1/2 miles south of Orient. An Indian travel route along this creek became known as "Little Moun-

tain Trail" in early mining days. It later acquired the name "The Curlew Cutoff." The creek was named by early prospectors for its rock-strewn bed.

Boulder Creek
(*Ts.37,38N;Rs.8,9E.uns*)
The stream of the creek rises in Boulder Glacier, southeast slope of Mt. Baker, south central Whatcom County; flows southwest 5 miles to Baker River, 2 miles below Baker Lake. It was named by Joseph Morovitz, a local homesteader, because of the huge, rounded boulders at the ford in this creek where his trail crossed. It should not be confused with another Boulder Creek, which is a tributary to Nooksack River, north central Whatcom County.

Boulder Creek (*T.40N;R.6E*)
The stream of the creek heads on Bear Paw Mountain, 2 miles south of the Canadian boundary, north central Whatcom County; flows 5 miles southwest to North Fork, Nooksack River. The name, locally applied, refers to the stream's bed, strewn with large, water-worn boulders. This over-used name could logically be applied to nearly all mountain streams in the Cascade Mountains area and its slopes. It should not be confused with another Boulder Creek in the county that runs from the southeast slope of Mt. Baker to Baker River near Baker Lake.

Boulder Hill (Jefferson County) *see* Kloochman Peak

Boulder Island (*S.22;T.34N;R.1W*)
Island at the extreme southeast end of Lopez Island, at the entrance to Watmough Bay, southeast San Juan County. This descriptive name was charted in 1855 by the U.S. Coast Guard.

Boulder Lake (*S.24;T.33N;R.11E*)
A 55-acre lake in a deep, crater-like depression, 50 ft. deep at one point, elevation 5,000 ft., 13-1/2 miles northeast of Darrington, southeast Skagit County. The boulders for which the lake was named are large rock fragments which have fallen from adjacent rock cliffs.

Boulder Reef (*S.4;T.36N;R.1E*)
A dangerous reef 1/2 mile north of Sinclair Island in Rosario Strait, extreme northwest Skagit County. In 1854, the U.S. Coast Guard named it for the huge, granite boulders inside the reef proper. In 1859, British Admiralty surveyors

named it *Panama Reef*, but their name did not persist.

Boundary (*S.9;T.40N;R.41E*)
Once a town on Columbia River, 1 mile south of the Canadian boundary, 9 miles northeast of Northport, northeast Stevens County. Founded during the 1889-90 mining boom, it became prosperous during the building of Spokane Falls & Northern Railway in 1892-93, when it had a population of 1,200, with dance halls, saloons, a gambling house, and a "hostess house." When railroad building terminated, the town folded. Most of the population moved to Rossland, British Columbia. By 1904, there remained one family, one store and the post office. It was named for its proximity to the Canadian boundary. The town of New Boundary, on the same location, took its name from the old town.

Boundary (*S.35;T.40N;R.9E*)
Town on Silesia Creek, on the international boundary between the U.S. and Canada, 12 miles north of Mt. Shuksan, Whatcom County and British Columbia.

Boundary Bay (*T.41N;R.1W*)
A wide bay between Point Roberts, Whatcom County; and White Rock, British Columbia. It includes western Semiamhoo Bay and the mouth of Noemeki River, British Columbia. Spanish explorers named it *Boca de Bodega*, *Boca de Florida Blanca* and *Ensenada del Engano*. On the first chart, made in 1855 by U.S. Coast Survey, it was named *Mud Bay*. On the second chart of that year, it appeared with its present name, because the bay is on both sides of the international boundary.

Boundary Creek (*Mt. Rainier National Park*)
A north tributary of Kotsuk Creek, Mt. Rainier National Park; flows south and southeast from the east side of Governors Ridge in the east central sector of the park. The name stems from the creek's course along the former east boundary of the park. (USBGN)

Boundary Creek
(*Ss.31,32;T.18N;R.10E*)
The stream of the creek heads on the west slope of Dalles Ridge, Snoqualmie National Forest, northeast Pierce County; flows 2 miles west to White River. The name was applied by Forest Service personnel. It may have been the boundary of a livestock range; no other boundary indications are apparent.

Boundary Lake (Whatcom County) *see* Judson Lake

Boundary Lakes *(S.1;T.21N;R.5W)*

Two shallow, connected lakes, 12 miles northwest of Shelton, central Mason County. No. 1 covers 2-1/2 acres, and No. 2 has an area of 3-1/2 acres. The name was chosen by Forest Service employees because the lakes are on the south boundary of Olympic National Forest.

Boundary Mountain *(S.4;T.40N;R.44E)*

A Kaniksu National Forest peak on the north end of Boundary Ridge, 11 miles northeast of Metaline Falls, sloping to within 1/4 mile of the Canadian boundary, north central Pend Oreille County. The Forest Service operates a fire lookout here. The name is for the mountain's proximity to the Canadian boundary.

Boundary Peak *(Mt. Rainier National Park)*

A Mt. Rainier National Park peak, southwest of Stevens Peak, in the center of Tatoosh Range, extreme south central area of the park. The name was selected by park personnel because the mountain is very close to the southern park boundary.

Boundary Ridge *(T.40N;R.44E)*

A 3-mile-long ridge directly south of the Canadian boundary, 8 miles northeast of Metaline Falls, north central Pend Oreille County. It is oriented in a north-south direction, with Boundary Mountain at the north end. The name is for the ridge's proximity to the Canadian boundary.

Bourgeau Lake (Ferry County) *see* Borgeau Lake

Bow *(S.35;T.36N;R.3E)*

Village on North Samish River, 2 miles east of Samish Bay, northwest Skagit County. The settlement's first name was *Brownsville*, for William J. Brown who operated a sawmill here in pioneer days. When a post office was established in 1901, he suggested the present name, which was accepted. At that time, the Great Northern Railway was building through the town, and Brown wanted the station named after the great railway station in London.

Bowlder Reef (Skagit County) *see* Boulder Reef

Bowmans Bay (Skagit County) *see* Reservation Bay

Bowman's Creek (San Juan County) *see* Cascade Creek

Box Canyon *(Ss.19,20;T.38N;R.43E)*

A scenic canyon in Pend Oreille River, 54 miles north of Newport, between Ione and Metaline Falls, north central Pend Oreille County. The river boils through this narrow channel for 1,200 ft., with rock walls from 20 to 100 ft. high. The name is descriptive of the ''boxed in'' nature of the canyon.

Box Creek *(T.30N;R.16E.uns)*

The stream of the creek rises at the north end of Entiat Mountains, Wenatchee National Forest, northwest Chelan County; flows 1-1/2 miles southwest to Phelps Creek. It was named by former Forest Ranger Robert E. Nickles because the creek flows through a closed canyon with fairly steep walls.

Boxer Cove (Skagit County) *see* Flounder Bay

Brown Lake (town)
(Ss.1,2;T.34N;R.25E
Ss.6,7;T.34N;R.26E)

Small settlement 5 miles north of Okanogan and 6 miles southwest of Riverside, central Okanogan County. It was named for William (''Horse'') Brown, who settled here in 1889.

Browns Cove (Kitsap County) *see* Nellita

Brown's Island *(S.19;T.8N;R.5W)*

Island in Cathlamet Channel of Columbia River, between Puget Island and the river's north bank, southeast Wahkiakum County. In 1841, the Wilkes Expedition named it *Bag Island*. The present name developed from local usage for a pioneer settler on the island.

Brown's Junction (Pierce County) *see* Elbe

Brown's Lake *(S.31;T.32N;R.40E)*

A small lake 5 miles southwest of Chewelah, at the head of Woodberry Creek, south central Stevens County. In 1862, it was named for Henry Brown, a settler who often camped here with his family.

Brown's Point (Island County) *see* Sandy Point

Browns Point *(S.14;T.26N;R.1E)*

A west shore point of Hood Canal, on Toandos Peninsula, 2-1/2 miles north of Bangor, east Jefferson County. In 1841, it was named by Cmdr. Charles Wilkes; the record does not indicate which of the 14 Browns on the expedition was honored. The place appears on some recent maps incorrectly as *Brown Point*.

Browns Point *(Ss.16,21;T.21N;R.3E)*

A residential and summer-home area at the east entrance of Commencement Bay, northwest Pierce County. The first name applied to this point was *Point Harris* in 1841, the choice of Cmdr. Charles Wilkes. It was for Alvin Harris, one of Wilkes's sailmaker's mates. When the point was settled, local residents substituted the name of an early landowner.

Browns Slough *(T.33N;R.3E)*

A tidal slough on Skagit Delta, southwest Skagit County. As a discharge branch of North Fork, Skagit River, it flows 3 miles south from the North Fork to Skagit Bay. It was locally named for William Brown, who, in 1865, settled at the slough's mouth.

Brownsville (Skagit County) *see* Bow

Bruce *(S.28;T.16N;R.30E)*

Once a railway junction, 6 miles east of Othello, southwest Adams County. It was named by Northern Pacific Railway Company for Thomas W. Bruce, from whom the railroad acquired a right-of-way.

Bruce Creek *(Ts.37,38N;R.39E)*

The stream of the creek heads in Phalon Lake, north central Stevens County; flows southwest 5 miles, and sinks, or becomes intermittent, about 4 miles east of Evans. It was named for Robert Bruce, a Scottish homesteader here.

Bruceport *(S.27;T.14N;R.10W)*

South side settlement of Willapa Harbor, 5 miles west of South Bend, northwest Pacific County. In 1851, it was named for an oyster schooner, *Robert Bruce*, which was burned in Willapa Harbor by a crew member. The crew, called the ''Bruce Party,'' settled ashore at this place, which at first was named *Bruceville*. The settlement is on the site of an old Indian village called *Wharhoots*.

Brule Creek *(T.26N;R.15E)*

The stream of this short creek rises on the north slope of Icicle Ridge, north of Doelle Lakes, southwest Chelan County; flows 3 miles northeast to Whitepine Creek, Wenatchee National Forest. In naming this creek, U.S. Forest Supervisor A. H. Sylvester used the French adjective for "burned," as there were extensive areas along the creek which had been severely burned between 1870 and 1880. Planting by the Forest Service from 1912 to 1916 partly restored the forest.

Brush Creek *(T.28N;Rs.16,17E.partly uns)*

The stream of the creek rises on the southeast slope of McCall Mountain, 2 miles east of Twin Lakes, Wenatchee National Forest, northwest Chelan County; flows east 4-1/2 miles to Chiwawa River. It was named by U.S. Forest Supervisor A. H. Sylvester, who considered it a "very brushy stream."

Brush Prairie *(S.22;T.3N;R.2E)*

Town 8 miles northeast of Vancouver, central Clark County. It was named by Elmorine Bowman for a very brushy prairie and swamp on her father's homestead. Several attempts to change the name have been voted down.

Bruster (Okanogan County) *see* Brewster

Bryant *(S.22;T.32N;R.5E)*

A small community 3 miles north of Arlington, northwest Snohomish County. A sawmill town many years ago, it was named for John H. Bryant, who was a vice president and director of Seattle, Lake Shore & Eastern Railroad. This railroad is now the Seattle-Sumas branch of Northern Pacific Railway.

Bryant Lake *(S.27;T.32N;R.5E)*

A 20.2-acre lake, maximum depth 40 ft., 1/2 mile southeast of Bryant, northwest Snohomish County. It was locally named for the town of Bryant.

Bryant Peak *(S.1;T.28N;R.13E)*

A Wenatchee National Forest peak 4 miles east of Cascade Mountain summit, at the head of Papoose Creek, 1-1/2 miles north of Longfellow Mountain, northwest Chelan County. It is one of 5 peaks which circle the headwaters of Panther Creek, and which A. H. Sylvester named for early American authors; this peak is named for poet William Cullen Bryant.

Bryant Peak *(S.30;T.23N;R.11E)*

A 5,900-ft. peak directly west of Cascade Mountain summit, between Chair Peak and The Tooth, 2-1/2 miles northwest of Snoqualmie Pass, east central King County. On October 9, 1924, it was named by The Mountaineers for one of its members, Sidney Bryant of Seattle. Earlier names were *Hemlock Peak* and *Kidd's Peak.* (USBGN)

Bryn Mawr *(S.7;T.23N;R.5E)*

Townsite at the south end of Lake Washington, directly northwest of Renton, west central King County. On April 19, 1890, it was platted by William E. and Lillie R. Parker on the site of an old Indian village. The Parkers gave the place a name of Welsh origin, which means "windy hill." The Indian name was *Sext-i-tcib*, which translates "place where one wades."

Buck Bay *(S.16;T.36N;R.1W)*

An east shore bay of East Sound, on the southeast peninsula of Orcas Island, directly south of Olga, San Juan County. In 1858, this inlet was charted as *Stockade Bay* by Capt. Henry Richards, British Admiralty surveyor. The present name has become official by local use.

Buck Creek *(T.30N;Rs.15,16E.uns)*

The stream of this high mountain creek rises at Buck Creek Pass, Cascade Mountain summit, Wenatchee National Forest, northeast Chelan County; flows 5 miles southeast to Chiwawa River. The name, in use before 1908, is common for many features in areas like this Glacier Peak wilderness, where deer are very abundant. The person responsible for the name is not recorded.

Buck Creek Pass
(S.35;T.31N;R.15E.uns)

A 5,796-ft. pass, crossing Cascade Mountain summit at the head of Buck Creek, 8 miles east by north of Glacier Peak summit, on the boundaries of northwest Chelan and northeast Snohomish counties. Some of the world's best mountain scenery is visible from this high pass. (*see* Buck Creek)

Buck Island *(S.10;T.34N;R.2W)*

Island at the entrance to Davis Bay and southwest of Lopez Island, 1 mile west of Richardson, San Juan County. It is one of the Geese Islets, named individually and as a group in 1841 by Cmdr. Charles Wilkes. (*see* Geese Islets)

Buck Lake *(S.9;T.25N;R.5W.uns)*

A small lake less than 1 mile east-northeast of Lake LaCrosse, Olympic National Park, southeast Jefferson County; drains south to Duckabush River. This common name was applied by early hunters and trappers. There still are many deer in this mountain area. (USBGN)

Buck Mountain
(S.17;T.30N;R.16E.uns)

An 8,573-ft. peak 3 miles east of Cascade Mountain summit on Chiwawa Ridge, northwest Chelan County. It supports 2 small glaciers, several cascades, and many waterfalls. The mountain is named for Buck Creek, directly to the north.

Buck Mountain *(S.16;T.36N;R.1W)*

A 350-ft. hill on the southeast point of Orcas Island, 1/2 mile southeast of Buck Bay, east central San Juan County. Locally named for nearby Buck Bay, it should not be confused with a mountain by the same name, which is 2 miles east of East Sound (town).

Buck Mountain *(S.18;T.37N;R.1W)*

Mountain on north central Orcas Island, 2 miles east of East Sound (town), northeast San Juan County. The name was applied locally, presumably because of the abundance of deer on the island in early days. Many deer can still be found here. This feature should not be confused with a mountain which bears the same name, located on the southeast end of the island.

Buck Spring *(S.22;T.25N;R.19E)*

Settlement high on the east slope of Chumstick Mountain, Wenatchee National Forest, southeast Chelan County. It was named by early sheepmen, for whom this was a favorite campe. (*see* Buck Creek)

Buckeye (Spokane County) *see* Denison

Buckeye Basin (Snohomish County) *see* Buckeye Creek

Buckeye Creek *(Ts.31,32N;R.9E)*

The stream of the creek rises on the east slope of White Horse Mountain, Mt. Baker National Forest, north central Snohomish County; flows 3 miles northeast to Squire Creek. It was named by W. C. Hiles, the first postmaster at Darrington in 1894, for his home state, Ohio, which bears this nickname.

Buckingham (*S.33;T.28N;R.26E*)

A small settlement 5 miles northeast of Mansfield, north central Douglas County. It was named for James A. Buckingham, a local landowner.

Buckley (*S.3;T.19N;R.6E*)

Trade center for a farming area 2-1/2 miles south of Enumclaw on White River, extreme north central Pierce County. Originally, it was an important sawmill and logging center. Early names were *Perkin's Landing* and *Perkins' Prairie*. When the Northern Pacific Railway built through here, officials chose the name *White River Siding*. In 1888, when a townsite was platted by Alexander Wickersham, he named the town for John M. Buckley, division superintendent of Northern Pacific and a coal mine promoter.

Buckley (Garfield County) *see* Dodge

Buckskin Mountain
(*S.29;T.31N;R.17E.uns*)

A 7,300-ft. peak on Chelan Ridge, between Railroad Creek and the headwaters of Entiat River, 3 miles south of Holden, on the boundary between Okanogan and Wenatchee national forests, northwest Chelan County. It is reported to have been named by W. P. Robinson, a miner who had prospects in nearby Cooper Draw. He named it for his buckskin horse, which drowned while fording Railroad Creek.

Bucoda (*S.12;T.15N;R.2W*)

Town on Skookumchuck River, 18 miles south of Olympia, south central Thurston County. In 1873, it was named *Seatco* by Northern Pacific Railway officials. This Indian name means "ghost" or "devil." In 1890, the Territorial Legislature changed it to the present name. Bucoda is a combination of the first 2 letters in the last names of 3 men: John M. Buckley, division superintendent of Northern Pacific Railway; Samuel Colter, a coal mine promoter; and John D. David, a capitalist from Portland, Oregon.

Budd Inlet (*Ts.18,19N;R.2W*)

A wide, navigable body of water extending north from Olympia about 6 miles to Boston Harbor, north central Thurston County. It is a valuable bay in the commercial life of Olympia, and quite scenic. In 1841, it was named by the Wilkes Expedition for Thomas A. Budd, acting master of *Peacock*, one of the expedition's ships.

Budd's Harbor (Clallam County) *see* Sequim Bay

Buell Peak (*Mt. Rainier National Park*)

A 5,938-ft. peak between Kotsuck and Chinook creeks, 3 miles south of Cayuse Pass, east central zone of the park. Mountain goats are often seen on this peak. It was named for John L. Buell, a merchant. (USBGN)

Buena (*S.22;T.11N;R.20E*)

Railroad station 15 miles southeast of Yakima, east central Yakima County. It was named by Northern Pacific Railway officials when a station was established here in 1910. They used the Spanish word for "good" or "pleasant."

Buesch Lake (*S.23;T.14N;R.11E.uns*)

A 10-acre lake, 1/2 mile west of Cascade Mountain summit and 14 miles northeast of Packwood, northeast Lewis County. It was named for Otto Buesch, a local resident, who died in 1936 from injuries suffered on a trip to stock the lake with fish. An earlier name was the much-used *Lost Lake*.

Buffalo Rapids (*S.8;T.8N;R.47E*)

Rapids in the Snake River, 16-1/2 miles south of Clarkston, between east central Asotin County and Idaho. It was named in the very early days of river navigation for Buffalo Rock, across the river in Idaho.

Bug (Skagit County) *see* Sedro Woolley

Bullen Mountain (*Ss.6,7;T.31N;R.9E*)

A 5,940-ft. peak at the head of Boulder Creek, Mt. Baker National Forest, 6 miles southwest of Darrington, north central Snohomish County. It was named locally for Chauncey Bullen, a Forest Service timber scaler, who was killed at Darrington in 1919 by logs slipping from a railroad car. On some maps the peak is called *Mt. Bullen*.

Bullfinch's (Bulfinch's) Harbor (Grays Harbor County) *see* Grays Harbor

Bull's Head (*T.28N;R.1E*)

A south shore point of Port Ludlow Bay, east central Jefferson County. In 1841, Cmdr. Charles Wilkes named the point for its resemblance to a bull's head, complete with horns. It does not appear on recent maps.

Bulls Tooth Mountain
(*S.5;T.25N;R.15E*)

A Wenatchee National Forest peak 1/2 mile south of main Icicle Divide, above Doelle Lakes, southeast Chelan County. It was named by U.S. Forest Supervisor A. H. Sylvester, to whom it appeared "as a great fang on the jawbone of Icicle Ridge."

Bumping Lake
(*Ss.27,28;T.16N;R.12E.uns*)

Lake in Snoqualmie National Forest, elevation 3,265 ft., 8 miles east of Chinook Pass at the head of Bumping River, northwest Yakima County. It is a reservoir for irrigation in Yakima Valley. In 1856, it was mapped as *Lake Plehnam*, and, in 1897, as *Tannum Lake*. Other names used in the past include *Tanum* and *Taneum*. (*see* Bumping River)

Bumping River
(*Ts.16,17N;Rs.12,13E.partly uns*)

The stream of the river rises in Bumping Lake, 6 miles east of Cascade Mountain summit, northwest Yakima County; flows 10 miles northeast to American River. Stockmen stated that the name was given because the stream carries heavy boulders when in freshet, causing a rumbling vibration along its banks. (USBGN)

Bunch Lake (*S.3;T.23N;R.8W*)

A 16-acre lake in Olympic Primitive Area, at the head of Bunch Canyon, 7 miles east of Quinault, northeast Grays Harbor County. It is named for Bunch Canyon, through which it drains.

Bundy Hollow (*S.21;T.9N;R.38E*)

A 3-mile-long hollow, or draw, 4 to 5 miles southeast of Waitsburg, southwest Columbia County. It carries the name of Mr. and Mrs. Alex Bundy, who came from Illinois by ox team to settle here in 1865.

Bunker (*S.7;T.13N;R.3W*)

Settlement on Chehalis River, 3 miles west of Adna, northwest Lewis County. It was named by Northern Pacific Railway officials for John Elijah Bunker, who owned a land claim here in early days. The settlement grew up around a large sawmill and shingle mill at the mouth of Bunker Creek. A post office, established near the Bunker home, was named *Eagleton*. It closed when an RFD mail route from Chehalis was installed.

Bunker Creek *(Ts.13,14N;Rs.3,4,5W)*

The stream of the creek heads 4 miles north of Doty, northwest Lewis County; runs southeasterly to Chehalis River at Bunker. (*see* Bunker)

Bunker Hill *(S.22;T.4N;R.7E)*

A 2,350-ft. hill on Gifford Pinchot National Forest, 1-1/2 miles north of Stabler, south central Skamania County. A Forest Service fire lookout is maintained on its summit during fire season. It was named by settlers M. McGinty and B. Tillotson for historic Bunker Hill near Boston Harbor, even though this hill is much more heavily forested.

Burbank *(S.1;T.8N;R.30E)*

Farming green 7 miles southeast of Pasco, near the confluence of Snake and Columbia rivers, extreme west Walla Walla County. It formerly was the center of an irrigation district, which failed in the early 1930s. In 1907, it was named by Northern Pacific Railway officials for Burbank Power & Water Company, which had a power-house here. The company name had been applied by Will H. Parry of Seattle, in honor of the famous horticulturist Luther Burbank.

Burbank Creek, Burbank Valley
(Ss.22,23,25,26;T.15N;R.19E)

The valley follows the course of the creek, which rises near Yakima County line, southeast Kittitas County; flows northwest about 8 miles to Yakima River, below Roza. They were named for Henry Burbank, a successful cattleman, who came here in 1871.

Burch Mountain *(S.30;T.24N;R.20E)*

Peak 4 mile west of Lincoln Rock on Columbia River, southeast end of Entiat Mountains, southeast Chelan County. It was named by early settlers for the Burch family, who homesteaded at the mountain's base. A misspelling of the name is *Birch Mountain.*

Burge *(S.14;T.16N;R.16E)*

A former post office and store on Wenas Creek, 26 miles northwest of Yakima, north central Yakima County. Established on August 7, 1883, the post office location became rather vague as legislative actions switched it back and forth between Yakima and Kittitas counties. It was named for Andrew Burge, who founded the place in the mid 1880s.

Burgoyne Lake (Skamania County) *see* Snow Lake

Burke *(S.36;T.19N;R.23E)*

Community 9 miles south of Quincy, west central Grant County. The first name, *Alloweze,* is reported to have been borrowed by German settlers from that of a midwestern town. In 1907, it was changed by petition to honor James H. Burke, postmaster.

Burke Island *(S.10;T.5N;R.1W)*

Island in Columbia River, 2 miles north of Woodland, directly south of Martin Island, southwest Cowlitz County. In 1841, it was charted by the Wilkes Expedition as *Paia.* In April 1914, the U.S. Coast and Geodetic Survey applied the present name, which is that of an early resident.

Burksville (Columbia County) *see* Marengo

Burley *(S.11;T.22N;R.1E)*

Utopian village at the head of Burley Lagoon in Henderson Bay, 10 miles northwest of Tacoma, extreme south Kitsap County. Established in the 1890s by the "Co-operative Brotherhood," it was named *Circle City,* with buildings laid out on the periphery of a circle. When the colony plan failed in 1908, the present name was adopted by local residents, for a pioneer settler who was not a member of the colony.

Burley Creek (Kitsap County)*see* Burley Lagoon

Burley Lagoon *(T.22N;R.1E)*

Lagoon at the head of Henderson Bay, at the outlet of Burley Creek, northwest Pierce and southwest Kitsap counties. The lagoon, and the creek which drains into it, were named for a pioneer settler, who claimed land on both shores of the lagoon.

Burlington *(T.34N;R.4E)*

Town on Skagit River, 4 miles north of Mt. Vernon, west central Skagit County. It is reported to have been named by T. W. Soules, an early resident, for Burlington, Vermont.

Burnboot Creek *(T.23N;Rs.11,12E)*

The stream of the creek rises in Iceberg Lake, 1/2 mile west of Cascade Mountain summit, extreme east central King County; flows 4-1/2 miles west to Middle Fork, Snoqualmie River, at Goldmeyer Hot Springs. Records do not reveal the name source, but a minor tragedy in earlier days is indicated. A one-booted man in the high Cascades might consider it a major tragedy. An alternate

name is *Burnt Boot Creek.*

Burnett *(S.16;T.19N;R.6E)*

Village on South Prairie Creek, 6 miles southwest of Enumclaw, north central Pierce County. At the turn of the century, it was a very important coalmining center; but, in 1927, the mines closed. It was named for Charles H. Burnett, operator of the local South Prairie Coal Company.

Burns Creek *(T.28N;R.19E)*

The stream of the creek rises on Fourmile Ridge in Chelan Mountains; flows 3 miles southwest to Entiat River, Wenatchee National Forest, central Chelan County. It was named by Forest Service personnel for a family of squatters who settled at the creek's mouth.

Burns Creek *(T.19N;R.10E)*

The stream of this short creek rises on the south slope of Huckleberry Mountain, Snoqualmie National Forest, southeast King County; flows 2 miles south to Greenwater River, downstream from Last Crossing. In 1910, it was named by a Forest Service officer when he found a band of sheep in trespass near this creek on the national forest. The herder was a Scotsman whose assets consisted of a handful of flour and a book of poems by Robert Burns. The name originally given was *Bobbie Burns Creek,* but subsequent mapping reduced it to the present form.

Buroker *(S.5;T.7N;R.37E)*

Community on Dry Creek, 6 miles northeast of Walla Walla, southeast Walla Walla County. In 1889, it was named *Aldrich* when a railroad came through. In June 1908, it was changed to the present name in honor of J. Buroker, a pioneer of 1864.

Burroughs Mountain *(Mt. Rainier National Park)*

A 2-mile mountain ridge, maximum elevation 7,830 ft., extending northeast from the vicinity of Winthrop Glacier to within 1 mile of Sunrise Park (Yakima Park), north central sector of the park. It was named for James Burroughs, the famous naturalist, by a committee of The Mountaineers, headed by Asahel Curtis.

Burrows Bay *(Ts.34,35N;R.1E)*

A west shore bay of Fidalgo Island, 2 miles southwest of Anacortes, southwest Skagit County. It was originally charted in 1841 by Cmdr. Charles Wilkes as *Argus Bay,* for the American naval ship *Argus.* He later altered his charts to the present name, for Lieut. William Burroughs, a naval hero of the War of 1812.

Burrows Island
(Ss.32,33;T.35N;R.1E)

Island at the west entrance to Burrows Bay, west coast of Fidalgo Island, southwest Skagit County. In 1790, this island and adjacent Allan Island were named *Las Isles Morrows* by Dionisio Galiano. In 1841, it received its present name. (*see* Burrows Bay)

Burt *(S.28;T.14N;R.6W)*

Settlement on Elk Creek, 12 miles east of Raymond, northeast Pacific County. It was named for an early logger, who established a camp here.

Burton *(S.22;T.2N;R.2E)*

Small community 2-1/2 miles east of Vancouver, south central Clark County. It bore the delightful name of *Pucker Brush* until 1906, when it was changed to recognize George Burton, who furnished an acre of land for a school site.

Burton *(S.12;T.22N;R.3E)*

Community on Vashon Island, north end of Quartermaster Harbor, southwest King County. A scattered community, it was established in 1892 as the site of Vashon College. It was named when the town was founded by Mrs. M. F. Hatch, for her birthplace in England, Burton-In-Kendall.

Bush *(S.12;T.17N;R.2W)*

Hamlet 4 miles south of Olympia on Bush Prairie, east boundary of Olympia Airport, central Thurston County. (*see* Bush Prairie)

Bush Elier Lake (Pierce County) *see* Spanaway Lake

Bush Pacific Pioneer State Park
(S.8;T.13N;R.10W)

A 42-acre park at the mouth of Palia River, at Bay Center, west Pacific County.

Bush Point *(S.6;T.29N;R.2E)*

A wooded, west shore point projecting 1/2 mile beyond the general shoreline of Whidbey Island, north of Mutiny Bay and 3 miles east of Freeland, Island County. In 1841, it was named *Point*

Leavett by Cmdr. Charles Wilkes for a member of his crew. In 1855, it was changed by U.S. Coast Survey for the point's heavy growth of trees and bushes.

Bush Prairie *(T.17N;R.2W)*

Prairie between Tumwater and Olympia Airport, north central Thurston County. It was named for George W. Bush, a black freeman, or West Indian, who came overland with the Simmons party, and who, in 1845, was the first settler here.

Butcher Creek *(Ts.26,27N;R.16E)*

The stream of this short creek rises from the steep south slope of Nason Ridge, east of Round Mountain, Wenatchee National Forest, southwest Chelan County; flows 2-1/2 miles east to Nason Creek. It was named by A. H. Sylvester, former supervisor of Wenatchee National Forest. He applied original and descriptive names to hundreds of anonymous features on that forest, as well as mapping and recording name origins of even the most remote places. This creek appears to be one which he mapped, but gave no name source.

Bute Prairie (Thurston County) *see* Mound Prairie

Butler (Kitsap County) *see* Gorst

Butler (Skamania County) *see* Skamania

Butlers Cove *(S.33;T.19N;R.2W)*

A west shore cove of Budd Inlet, adjoining Olympia on the northwest, northwest Thurston County. It is named for John L. Butler, who filed a Donation Land Claim in the 1850s on adjacent land.

Butte Creek *(T.29N;R.18E.uns)*

The stream of the creek rises in Chelan Mountains, Wenatchee National Forest, south central Chelan County; flows between Sheep and Corral creeks, 2-1/2 miles east to South Pyramid Creek. A. H. Sylvester, a forester with a lively sense of humor, named this creek and the creeks which it flows between. It seems possible that he conceived the idea of putting a butte between the sheep and the corral.

Butte Hill *(T.5N;R.1W)*

Finnish settlement near Woodland, Cowlitz County. During World War I, many Finns came here, "building first the barn; second, the sauna; and third, the residence." It was named for Butte, Montana, from where many Finns had moved, and where many returned periodically to earn money and to keep up a homestead.

Butter Creek *(Ts.13-15N;R.9E)*

The stream of the creek rises near Pinnacle Peak, south central Mt. Rainier National Park; flows 12 miles south by east to Cowlitz River, 2 miles east of Packwood, northeast Lewis County. It was named in pioneer days by J. T. Chilcoat. He left no record of his name source, but during the melting season, the creek's color is a light yellow from clay and glacial "flour."

Butterfly Butte
(S.27;T.30N;R.15E.uns)

A low ridge, elevation 5,979 ft., between 2 upper branches of Napeequa River, 3 miles southeast of Cascade Mountain summit, Wenatchee National Forest, northwest Chelan County. It is heavily timbered, in a glacial environment. The name was first used about 1900 by a shepherd for Lauzier Brothers. Butterflies are very abundant here in season.

Buttonhole Island *(S.21;T.36N;R.1E)*

Most westerly of the Cone Islands, northeast coastal area off Cypress Island, northwest Skagit County. The name origin is from a small hole in the thin, jagged rock which constitutes the island.

Byron *(S.12;T.8N;R.23E)*

Townsite 6 miles east of Mabton, extreme southeast Yakima County. In 1908, it was named by Byron Improvement Company, when the townsite was platted. Local settlers state that the name was chosen because townsite surveyors found a post marked "Byron," set in 1890, by Northern Pacific Railway Company employees.

C

CCA Creek *(S.32;T.34N;R.44E)*

The stream of the creek rises east of CCA Peak, south central Pend Oreille County; flows 11 miles southwest to Pend Oreille River. It was named in pioneer days for *Si-Si-Ah*, an Indian chief. Later generations of settlers mispronounced the name, and it was placed on recent maps under the present meaningless spelling.

CCA Peak *(S.2;T.34N;R.44E)*

A Kaniksu National Forest peak between Loop and CCA creeks, 4 miles east of Jared, south central Pend Oreille County. It is used by the Forest Service as a fire lookout in season. (*see* CCA Creek)

Cabin Creek *(T.25N;Rs.16,17E)*

The stream of the creek rises in Lake Augusta on south slope of Big Jim Mountain, central Chelan County; flows east by south to Wenatchee River in Tumwater Canyon, 6-1/2 miles into Wenatchee National Forest.

Cabo de San Roque (Pacific County) *see* Cape Disappointment

Cactus *(S.16;T.13N;R.31E)*

Railroad siding 5 miles southwest of Connell, north central Franklin County. In 1905, Northern Pacific Railway Company named the station *Cliff* for G. B. Cliff, who had been superintendent of Seattle Division of that road. In June 1907, railroad officials changed it to the present name for cactus growth which was prevalent in this sagebrush country.

Cactus Islands *(T.36N;R.4W)*

Two low, rocky islands in New Channel, 1/2 mile north of Spieden Island, northwest San Juan County. In 1858, they were charted under the present name by Capt. Henry Richards, British Admiralty surveyor, who mapped the San Juan Archipelago. He named them for the abundant, low-growing cacti which cover most of the island area.

Cad Lake *(S.1;T.22N;R.10E)*

A 1/2-acre lake 1/2 mile north of Granite Mountain Peak and 2-1/2 miles west of Snoqualmie Pass, east central King County. It is one of 3 Granite Mountain Lakes, with Denny and Crystal lakes. Local legend states that the name is a combination of the initials of a pioneer miner.

Cadet Creek *(Ts.29,30N;R.12E)*

The stream of the creek rises on Cadet Peak, between Curry Gap and Pride Basin; flows 8 miles north by east to North Fork, Sauk River, Mt. Baker National Forest, east central Snohomish County. Its name derives from Cadet Peak, which was named in 1890 by an early land survey party in honor of the United States Cadets, then in existence.

Cadet Lake *(S.12;T.29N;R.11E)*

A very scenic, 2-acre lake, elevation 5,500 ft., Mt. Baker National Forest, 4 miles northeast of Monte Cristo, west central Snohomish County. It was named for Cadet Creek which drains it. An alternate name, of unknown origin, is *Harold Lake*. (*see* Cadet Creek)

Cadet Peak *(S.23;T.29N;R.11E)*

A large, irregular peak, elevation 6,280 ft., 2 miles east of Monte Cristo, east central Snohomish County. (*see* Cadet Creek)

Cady Creek *(T.28N;R.13E.uns)*

The stream of the creek rises in Cady Pass at Cascade Mountain summit, Wenatchee National Forest, northwest Chelan County; flows 5 miles southeast to Little Wenatchee River, with 5 branches to the north. It was named for Capt. Cady, who built a military trail over Cady Pass, and for whom the town of Snohomish was originally named. This stream should not be confused with West Cady Creek, on the west side of the pass.

Cady Pass *(S.5;T.28N;R.13E.uns)*

A Cascade Mountain summit pass in Glacier Peak Wilderness Area, between Chelan County on the east and Snohomish County on the west. Cady Creek heads on its eastern slope, and Pass Creek heads on the western slope. In 1870-71, Northern Pacific Railway Company surveyed a route over this pass, on the possibility of using Mukilteo as a western terminus. (*see* Cady Creek)

Cady Pass *(S.8;T.37N;R.17E.uns)*

A Mt. Baker National Forest pass through a ridge between South Fork, Slate Creek, and Mill Creek, extreme southeast Whatcom County. In the 1890s, this heavily mineralized area was the scene of mining excitement. The pass was named by early miners for James Cady, who, in 1902, built a narrow wagon road from Slate Creek to his mine on Mill Creek.

Cady Ridge *(T.28N;R.13E.uns)*

Ridge directly east of Cascade Mountain summit, between Cady Creek and the upper reaches of Little Wenatchee River, west central Chelan County. (*see* Cady Creek)

Cadyville (Snohomish County) *see* Snohomish

Calawah River
(Ts.28,29N;Rs.10-14W.partly uns)

The river's North Fork rises on Olympic National Forest, and South Fork on Olympic National Park, between headwaters of Bogachiel and Soleduck rivers, southwest Clallam County; flows 28 miles west to Bogachiel River, 4 miles east of Quillayute. This Quillayute Indian name means "Middle River," appropriate since the river flows between two large rivers throughout its course. The name is variously spelled *Calawa, Kalowa,* and *Ca-la-wa.*

California Creek *(Ts.39,40N;Rs.1,2E)*

The stream of the creek rises 1-1/2 miles northwest of Ferndale, northwest Whatcom County; flows 9 miles northwest to Drayton Harbor. It was locally named for a number of California miners who headquartered here in 1858 during the Fraser River gold rush.

Calispel Creek, River (Pend Oreille County) *see* Calispell Creek

Calispell Creek
(Ts.32,33N;Rs.43,44E)

The stream of the creek heads in a small, unnamed lake west of Grayback Mountain, southwest Pend Oreille County; winds northerly for 13 miles, through Calispell Lake to Pend Oreille River at Cusick. It was named for a sub-tribe of Pend Oreille Indians, the

Kalispel. Some maps show it as *Calispel River.* (USBGN)

Calispell Lake *(S.14;T.32N;R.43E)*

A pear-shaped lake, about 2 miles long, in Calispell Creek, 3 miles southwest of Usk, south central Pend Oreille County. (USBGN) (*see* Calispell Creek)

Callepuya River (Clark County) *see* Lake River

Calvert (Spokane County) *see* Amber

Camano Head *(T.30N;R.3E)*

A low headland on the south end of Camano Island, between Saratoga Passage and Port Susan, southeast Island County. Long ago, it was the scene of a great landslide which killed a number of Indians. The name derives from Camano Island, which was named *Caamano* or *Isla de Caamano* by Lieut. Francisco de Eliza in 1790 for Lieut. Cmdr. Jacinto Caamano of the Spanish Navy. In 1841, Cmdr. Charles Wilkes named the island *McDonough's Island* for Cmdt. Thomas MacDonough, commander of the flagship *Saratoga* in Lake Champlain during the War of 1812. British reports state that Eliza applied ''Caamano'' to part of Admiralty Inlet near Port Townsend, and that Capt. Henry Kellet, RN, transposed the name to this island in 1847, in an effort to retain original Spanish names. Whatever the train of events, the name, as altered, has become official.

Camano Island *(Ts.30-32N;Rs.2,3E)*

A long, narrow island directly east of Whidbey Island, Island County. It is bounded on the north by Skagit Bay, on the east by Port Susan, on the south by Possession Sound, and on the west by Saratoga Passage. At the northeast tip, it is separated from the mainland of Snohomish County by Davis Slough, which is dry at extreme low tides. Miles of shallow tideland adjoin the island in this vicinity. (*see* Camano Head)

Camano Island State Park
(T.31N;R.3E)

A 136-acre public park on the east shore of Camano Island, facing Port Susan, east central Island County. The park offers camping, swimming, fishing and clamming. (*see* Camano Head)

Camas *(T.1N;R.3E)*

Town on the north bank of Columbia River, 14 miles east of Vancouver, southeast Clark County. Its economy is based on Crown-Zellerbach's large pulp and paper mill plant located here. The

name derives from an edible root which was a favorite Indian food they called *quamash*; botanists named it *Camassia,* and the common name became *camas.* Several attempts have been made to combine this town with Washougal as ''Twin Cities,'' without success; an alternate plan was to combine the names as ''Camas-Washougal.'' Each town, however, retains its own name at present. Until 1894, the post office was designated as *La Camas,* when it was altered to the present spelling to avoid confusion with La Center and La Conner. Residents continued to use La Camas as the town's name, except on mail, until 1909, when the present name was adopted, by petition, as official.

Camas Prairie *(T.29N;R.39E)*

An extensive prairie 5 miles west of Springdale, on Camas Creek, central Stevens County. When early fur traders arrived, there was an abundance of *camas,* a starchy root which was an Indian staple. When John Work of Hudson's Bay company passed through the prairie on September 20, 1825, he called it *Big Camass Plain.* (*see* Camas)

Camas Prairie *(T.6N;R.12E)*

Meadow west of Conboy Lake, directly south of Glenwood, northwest Klickitat County. Not shown on recent maps, it was once an important stop on the annual ''food route'' of Yakima Indians. The Indian name, as mapped by Capt. George B. McClellan in 1853, was *Tahk,* meaning ''a meadow or grassy place.'' The present name, first appearing on the U.S. Land Office map of 1897, refers to the abundance of camas, an edible root. (*see* Camas)

Cameron Creek *(Ts.27,28N;Rs.3-5W)*

The stream of the creek rises in Cameron Glaciers, 20 miles southeast of Port Angeles, northeast Jefferson County. flows 8 miles northeast through Olympic National Park to Greywolf River, southeast Clallam County. Local residents state that it was named ''by a map sketcher from Portland, Oregon, for a rancher-hunter-packer named Cameron who homesteaded on the creek in 1899.''

Cameron Glaciers
(S.16;T.27N;R.5W.uns)

A group of 4 small glaciers, 2 which are joined, at the head of Cameron Creek, north of Dosewallips, northeast Jefferson County. (*see* Cameron Creek)

Camp Chelan *(T.27N;Rs.22,23E)*

A fort built prior to 1880 on Columbia River, east central Chelan County. In 1880, it was moved to a plateau on the north side of the river where the lake narrows into the creek. (*see* Chelan)

Camp Comfort *(Mt. Rainier National Park)*

A rocky outpost in a saddle near the summit of Gibraltar rock, directly southeast of Mt. Rainier's summit, central part of the park. It is a rather poor campsite, and originally was named *Camp No Camp.* In 1888, it received its present name from Maj. E. S. Ingraham to contrast with Camp Misery below Gibraltar, which is much worse.

Camp Creek *(T.27N;R.16E)*

The stream of the creek rises on Wenatchee National Forest, west central Chelan County; flows 1-1/2 miles south from Wenatchee Ridge to Little Wenatchee River, at a point 4 miles west of Wenatchee Lake. It was named by Forest Ranger Rush J. Huston for a camp which he established here during trail construction.

Camp Creek *(Ts.30,31N;R.12E)*

The stream of the creek rises in Camp Lake on the west slope of Glacier Peak, east central Snohomish County; flows 5 miles northwest to Whitechuck River. It was named for Camp Lake, which was named in 1917 by Nels Bruseth and Chauncey Bullen after they established a camp on the lake.

Camp Curtis *(Mt. Rainier National Park)*

Camp on Steamboat Prow, between Emmons and Winthrop glaciers, on the northeast slope of Mt. Rainier, central sector of the park. In 1909, it was used as a high camp by The Mountaineers on an outing lead by the famous photographer Asahel Curtis. It was named for Curtis at the suggestion of Edmond S. Meany. (USBGN)

Camp Delight (Mt. Rainier National Park) *see* Camp of the Stars

Camp Dodson *(T.38N;R.8E.uns)*

A timberline camp between Park and Boulder glaciers, on the east side of Mt. Baker, Mt. Baker National Forest, central Whatcom County. In 1908, it was named by The Mountaineers, when they found Harley Dodson's 1907 blazes on the last tree at snowline.

Camp Grisdale
(Ss.31,32;T.22N;R.7W)

A modern forest community on Olympic National Forest, between Wynooche and Satsop rivers, northeast Grays Harbor County. It was built by Simpson Timber Company, which has a 99-year contract for utilization of Forest Service timber. It is occupied by employees of the company, and has adequate town facilities. Officers of the company named the camp for George Grisdale, superintendent of all Simpson logging camps for many years.

Camp Hayden *(S.7;T.33N;R.15W)*

A 194-acre military reservation on Cape Flattery, on Makah Indian Reservation, north of Mukkaw Bay, extreme northwest Clallam County. Originally a harbor defense unit, it is now a radar base. When established in 1941, it was named *Fort Hayden* for Brig. Gen. John L. Hayden, who commanded Puget Sound Harbor defenses from 1919 until 1922. On April 1, 1944, the official name was changed to Camp Hayden by G.O. No. 27, War Department.

Camp Hazard *(Mt. Rainier National Park)*

A bivouac camp on the south slope of Mt. Rainier, on the Kautz route to the summit, south central sector of the park. It was named by The Mountaineers for Joseph T. Hazard, who located and used the camp during a 1923 exploration of the Kautz route.

Camp Lake (King County) *see* Rainbow Lake

Camp Marion *(S.25;T.27N;R.5W.uns)*

A north bank camp of upper Dosewallips River, 2 miles southwest of Deception Mountain, east central Jefferson County. It was named for Marion Vincent, who lived here with her husband Frank, a hunter and packer.

Camp Misery *(Mt. Rainier National Park)*

A 11,300-ft. camp at the base of Beehive Pinnacle near Cowlitz Glacier, southeast sector of the park. In 1888, it was named by Maj. E. S. Ingraham, when an expedition which he led to the summit camped here overnight. It proved to be an uncomfortable glacier camp, with icy winds and little protection. The name contrasts with that of Camp Comfort.

Camp Muir *(Mt. Rainier National Park)*

A 10,000-ft. camp on the southeast slope of Mt. Rainier, near the summit at the west margin of Cowlitz Glacier, in a saddle beneath Cowlitz Cleaver, central sector of the park. In 1888, it was named by Maj. E. S. Ingraham, during an expedition of The Mountaineers, for the famous explorer and naturalist John Muir.

Camp No Camp (Mt. Rainier National Park) *see* Camp Comfort

Camp of the Clouds *(Mt. Rainier National Park)*

A south slope camp of Mt. Rainier, directly above Paradise Valley, in the central area of the park. On August 12, 1886, it was named by Charles E. Kehoe, Charles A. Billings, and George N. Talcott, of Olympia. The party witnessed a superb mountain view when the clouds parted.

Camp of the Stars *(Mt. Rainier National Park)*

A southeast slope camp of Mt. Rainier, near the foot of Gibraltar, about 1-1/2 miles southeast of the summit. It is located on a narrow, rocky shelf which is limited in size, but offers a magnificent view of the landscape and sky. This descriptive name was chosen by early mountain climbers whose names were not recorded. An earlier name was *Camp Delight*.

Camp Robber Lake
(S.11;T.24N;R.11E)

A 4-1/2-acre lake on Snoqualmie National Forest, 3/4 of a mile east of Lake Dorothy inlet, east central King County. It was named for an abundance of Canada jays, which are nicknamed "Camp Robber." The nickname is accurately applied, as western campers know. An alternate name is *Charlie Lake No. 4*.

Camp Washington
(S.13;T.26N;R.41E)

An historic campsite at the east end of Four Mound Prairie, at the Forks of Coulee Creek, 5 miles northwest of Spokane, central Spokane County. It was established and occupied from October 17 to 30, 1853, by Isaac I. Stevens, first territorial governor of Washington, and was used as headquarters for several side trips. He was moving from Fort Snelling, Minnesota, to Olympia with a military party of 243 persons, to take over as governor. He named his first camp in this state for the first president of the United States.

Campbell Creek *(T.20N;Rs.2,3W)*

The stream of the creek heads in Phillips Lake, southeast Mason County; flows 4-1/2 miles southwest and west to Chapman Cove on the east shore of Oakland Bay. Its first name was *Swindall*, for Calvin W. Swindall, who was postmaster and storekeeper at Oakland. The present name is for a more recent local resident.

Campbell Lake
(Ss.29,30;T.30N;R.2W)

A small lake on Miller Peninsula, between Sequim Bay and Port Discovery Bay, northeast Clallam County. It was first given the local name *Catfish Lake*, which was shortened to *Cat Lake* by common usage. The present name is for a local landowner.

Campbell Lake *(T.34N;Rs.1,2E)*

The largest lake on Fidalgo Island, 4 miles south of Anacortes, west central Skagit County. It was named for a pioneer settler, who claimed land adjoining the lake.

Canaan Lake *(S.26;T.27N;R.15E)*

Lake at the head of Royal Creek, on a steep south slope of Nason Ridge, Wenatchee National Forest, southwest Chelan County. It was named by A. H. Sylvester, who considered it a "promised land" of mountainous beauty.

Canal de Arro (San Juan County) *see* Haro Strait

Canal de Fidalgo (San Juan County) *see* Rosario Strait

Canal de Guemes (Skagit County) *see* Bellingham Channel

Canal de Lopez de Haro (San Juan County) *see* Haro Strait

Canal de Pacheco (Whatcom County) *see* Hale Passage

Candy Creek
(Ss.2,3;T.30N;R.17E.uns)

The stream of the creek rises on the southwest slope of Chelan Mountains at Pinnacle Mountain, Wenatchee National Forest, north central Chelan County; flows 3 miles southwest to upper Entiat River. It was named by U.S. Forest Supervisor A. H. Sylvester because he found the water to have a sweet taste.

Canel River (Clallam County) *see* Pysht River; Twin River

Canim Point (Jefferson County) *see* Kanem Point

Cannery Lake *(S.21;T.35N;R.1E)*

An 18-acre lake at Shannon Point, directly west of Anacortes, and adjacent to the beach of Guemes Channel, west central Skagit County. The name was applied several years ago when a fish cannery operated at the site.

Cannonball Creek *(T.13N;R.5W)*

The stream of the creek rises 2 miles northwest of Pe Ell, west central Lewis County; flows 2 miles to Chehalis River. The name was coined locally because the bed of the creek was originally covered with spherical rocks, varying from marble to cannonball size. Old-timers state that the rocks were "perfectly round," and that each had a seashell at the center.

Cannonball Island
(S.23;T.31N;R.16W)

A high tide island, low tide promontory, in Pacific Ocean, a few hundred yards west of Cape Alava, extreme northwest Clallam County. It was named for the thousands of wave-rounded rocks which are found on the island and along its shore. The Indian name was *Wah-yah.*

Canoe Creek *(T.30N;R.19E)*

The stream of the creek rises on Vie Mountain, Okanogan National Forest, Chelan County; flows southwest 4 miles to Lake Chelan. In 1866, it was named by William Sanders and Henry Dumpke when they were forced to build a canoe, by axe and fire, after their pack horse was killed here.

Canoe Creek (Klickitat County) *see* White Salmon River

Canoe Island *(S.34;T.36N;R.2W)*

Island at the entrance to Indian Cove, on the southeast shore of Shaw Island, Upright Channel, central San Juan County. In 1858, the name was placed on British Admiralty charts by Capt. Henry Richards, evidently to harmonize with Indian Cove. In early days, the cove was the site of an extensive Indian village.

Canoe Island (Skagit County) *see* Pass Island

Canoe Pass *(T.34N;R.1E)*

A very narrow pass at the south tip of Fidalgo Island, between Pass Island and Fidalgo Island, southwest Skagit County. The name was applied by pioneers because no vessel much larger than a canoe could safely navigate this pass.

Canon (Kittitas County) *see* Bristol

Canton (King County) *see* Humphrey

Canvasback Lake
(Ss.14,23;T.4N;R.1W)

A whale-shaped lake, 1-1/2 miles long, on Bachelor Island, directly south of the mouth of Lewis River, west Clark County. It was named for the multitude of canvasback ducks which frequented the lake in early days.

Canyon *(S.9;T.13N;R.38E)*

Village in an 8-mile-long canyon of Alkali Flat Creek, 4 miles north of Snake River, southwest Whitman County. It was named for the canyon, which is 500 ft. deep in places.

Canyon (Kittitas County) *see* Wymer

Canyon Creek *(T.28N;R.15E)*

This short creek, which carries a heavy volume of water, rises on the northeast slope of Wenatchee Ridge, Wenatchee National Forest, northwest Chelan County; flows 4-1/2 miles to White River. The name was applied by Forest Ranger Robert E. Nuckles because the stream emerges from a deep canyon.

Canyon Creek *(Ts.30,31N;Rs.7-9E)*

The stream of the creek rises near Granite Pass on Mt. Baker National Forest, central Snohomish County; flows west and south to Stillaguamish River, 1 mile north of Granite Falls. It was first named *Pearson Creek* for a pioneer Stanwood merchant, who grub-staked prospectors who, in turn, named the creek in his honor. After his death, the name was changed to Canyon Creek.

Canyon Creek *(T.39N;Rs.5,6E)*

The stream of the creek rises 5 miles southeast of Kulshan, Mt. Baker National Forest, central Whatcom County; flows through Canyon Lake to North Fork, Nooksack River, near Kulshan. It was locally named for Canyon Lake. This creek should not be confused with another of the same name near Glacier, northeast Whatcom County.

Canyon Creek *(T.40N;Rs.6-8E.partly uns)*

The stream of the creek rises in Canyon Lake, 4 miles south of the Canadian boundary, northeast Whatcom County; flows west and south to North Fork, Nooksack River, 2 miles north-

west of Glacier. It was locally named for the deep canyon through which it runs most of its course. The Indian name was *Cowap* or *Cowsap.* This creek should not be confused with another of the same name, which enters the North Fork, Nooksack River, near Kulshan, central Whatcom County.

Canyon Lake *(S.30;T.39N;R.6E)*

A 45-acre lake, elevation 3,400 ft., in Canyon Creek, 6 miles south of Maple Falls, central Whatcom County. This lake should not be confused with another of the same name, 8 miles northeast of Glacier. (*see* Canyon Creek, central Whatcom County)

Canyon Lake *(S.20;T.40N;R.8E)*

A 2-acre lake, elevation 4,775 ft., at the headwaters of Canyon Creek, 8 miles northeast of Glacier, north central Whatcom County. This lake should not be confused with another of the same name, 6 miles south of Maple Falls. (*see* Canyon Creek, northeast Whatcom County)

Canyon Lake (Snohomish County) *see* Twenty-two Lake

Canyon Rim *(Mt. Rainier National Park)*

A 4,500-ft. canyon 2 miles beyond Ricksecker Point on Paradise Hwy., 14.3 miles east of Nisqually entrance, southwest sector of the park. It affords a fine view of Silver Forest. The descriptive name was chosen by park personnel shortly after the park was established.

Cap Sante *(S.18;T.35N;R.2E)*

A prominent headland in the city of Anacortes, northeast tip of Fidalgo Island, west central Skagit County. The name, carried on some maps as *Capsante,* is a corruption of a Spanish name applied in the early 1790s by a Spanish explorer, who was not identified.

Cape Alava *(S.23;T.31N;R.16W)*

The most westerly point in the state of Washington, and in the United States until Alaska became a state; on Pacific Ocean, 3 miles northwest of Lake Ozette, on the old Ozette Indian Reservation, west central Clallam County. On August 6, 1790, Manuel Quimper named the cape *Punta de Hijosa.* The name was changed on later Spanish charts to *Punta de Alava* for Jose Manuel de Alava, naval commandant at Acapulco in Mexico. In 1847, Capt. Henry Kellett charted it as *Point Alava.* The present name, however, has become generally accepted.

Cape Classet (Claaset) (Clallam County) *see* Cape Flattery

Cape Disappointment *(T.9N;R.11W)*
A high headland surmounted by a lighthouse at the north entrance to Columbia River, southwest Pacific County. On July 6, 1788, it was named by Capt. John Meares when he failed to locate the ''River of the West'' at a point charted by Bruno de Heceta on August 17, 1775. On that date, Heceta charted the cape as *Cabo de San Roque.* In 1792, it was named *Cape Hancock* by Robert Gray. The original Indian name was *Kah-eese.*

Cape Elizabeth *(S.34;T.22N;R.13W)*
Cape on Pacific Ocean, 2 miles north of Quinault River mouth, northwest Grays Harbor County. The present name is probably a modification of a name applied by early Russian sea-otter hunters, although the record is not clear. An alternate name, not used on modern maps, was *Point Quinault.*

Cape Flattery *(T.33N;R.16W)*
A high, rocky bluff, overlooking Tatoosh Island and Pacific Ocean, on Makah Indian Reservation, at the entrance to Strait of Juan de Fuca from the ocean, extreme northwest Clallam County. This name, charted by Capt. James Cook of the British Navy on March 22, 1778, is the oldest name now in use on maps of the state of Washington, other than that of the Pacific Ocean. Capt. Cook chose it because the cape flattered him with the hope of a passage or opening between the cape and the island beyond, which was Vancouver Island. Cook, failing to find the Strait of Juan de Fuca because of bad weather, discredited its existence. Other names applied to the cape by early explorers were *Cape Claaset, Cape Classet,* and *Punta de Martinez.* The Indian name was *Klasset.*

Cape Foulweather (Pacific County) *see* Cape Shoalwater

Cape George *(S.12;T.30N;R.2W)*
Cape at the east entrance to Port Discovery Bay, 3 miles west of Port Townsend, northeast Jefferson County. In 1841, Cmdr. Charles Wilkes named it *East Bluff* In 1846, Capt. Henry Kellett, R.N., in H.M. surveying vessel *Herald,* renamed it using the present name to honor Capt. George Vancouver.

Cape Hancock (Pacific County) *see* Cape Disappointment

Cape Heron (Skamania County) *see* Cape Horn

Cape Horn *(S.24;T.25N;R.15E)*
A steep peak on Icicle Ridge, just east of Ladies Pass, Wenatchee National Forest, west central Chelan County. In 1910, it was named by U.S. Forest Supervisor A. H. Sylvester because the peak is forbidding, and dangerous to climb.

Cape Horn *(S.16;T.1N;R.5E)*
A steep, jagged promontory with perpendicular cliffs, which is a landmark on the north bank of Columbia River, 25 miles east of Vancouver, extreme southwest Skamania County. In 1826, John Work, an official of Hudson's Bay Company, named this feature *Cape Heron* for the large number of those waterbirds in the vicinity. The present name is a distortion of Work's name, and has lost its significance. A local name, entirely unofficial, is *Bell's Bluff.*

Cape Horn *(S.27;T.8N;R.5W)*
A rounded cape on the north bank of Columbia River, 1 mile west of Waterford, southeast Wahkiakum County. The name was applied by early river navigators because of rough water frequently encountered off the cape.

Cape Johnson *(Ss.5,6;T.28N;R.15W)*
Cape on Pacific Ocean, 4 miles northwest of Quillayute River mouth, southwest Clallam County. The Quillayute name was *Ta-qwa-at,* meaning ''big curve in the bay.'' There appears to be no record designating which Johnson is responsible for the present name, but the name was extremely common in pioneer days.

Cape Labelle Creek *(T.36N;Rs.30,31E)*
The stream of the creek heads on Fir Mountain, east central Okanogan County; flows southwest for 10 miles to West Fork, San Poil River, on Colville National Forest. Kate Labelle, an old Indian woman, was the first settler on the creek. After it was named for her, the spelling was altered to that of the present name.

Cape Migley (Whatcom County) *see* Point Migley

Cape Saint Mary *(S.15;T.34N;R.1W)*
A southeast end headland of Lopez Island, elevation 188 ft., on Rosario Strait, between Shoal Bight and Telegraph Bay, southeast San Juan County. In 1855, it was named *Johnson Point* by U.S. Coast Survey. The present name was placed on British Admiralty charts a few years later, and has become official.

Cape Shoalwater *(T.14N;R.11W)*
Cape on the north side of the entrance to Willapa Harbor, northwest Pacific County. On July 5, 1788, the descriptive name was given by John Meares. The Indian name was *Quahtsum.* Other names used in the past were *Cape Foulweather* and *Point Lewis.*

Capitol Hill *(Ss.28,29;T.25N;R.4E)*
A residential area on one of Seattle's 12 ''official'' hills, central Seattle, north of Madison Avenue and east of Lake Union, King County. In 1901, it was named by James A. Moore, a real estate promoter, for Capitol Hill in Denver, Colorado.

Capitol Lake *(S.15;T.18N;R.2W)*
A 306-acre lake, maximum depth 30 ft., in Olympia, at the mouth of Deschutes River in Budd Inlet, Thurston County. It was formed when a dam was built at the river's mouth. The lake is located near the state capitol, from which it received its name.

Capitol Peak *(S.7;T.23N;R.6W)*
An Olympic National Forest peak, 1/2 mile east of Grays Harbor County boundary, northwest Mason County. It was named for a fancied resemblance to the dome of Washington state capitol building. (USBGN)

Capps, Capps Place (Lincoln, Spokane counties) *see* Reardan

Capsante (Skagit County) *see* Cap Sante

Carbon Glacier *(Mt. Rainier National Park)*
A north slope glacier of Mt. Rainier, 5-1/2 miles long and 10,600-ft. maximum elevation, extending from Willis Wall to the headwaters of Carbon River, north central area of the park. It is rated as the lowest perpetual ice field in the United States. The name is for the coal which was found in quantity along the upper reach of Carbon River. (see Carbon River) (USBGN)

Carbon River *(Mt. Rainier National Park)*

The stream of the river heads in Carbon Glacier, north slope of Mt. Rainier, and drains nearby Russell Glacier through Cataract Creek, a tributary, north central sector of the park; flows northwest to Puyallup River, 5 miles south of Sumner, Pierce County. Its flow is torrential in summer when glaciers are melting. In 1876, it was named for large coal deposits found along its upper course. In 1841, Cmdr. Charles Wilkes named it *Upthascap River*, but that name was evidently not used by subsequent map and chart makers.

Carbon River Entrance *(Mt. Rainier National Park)*

Ranger station location on Carbon River, extreme northwest corner of the park. Visitors register here, and are issued fire permits.

Carbonado *(S.4;T.18N;R.6E)*

Formerly a busy coal-mining town on Carbon River, 5-1/2 miles south of Buckley, north central Pierce County. It was one of the highest coal producers in the state. (*see* Carbon River)

Cardinal Peak *(T.30N;R.18E.uns)*

The highest point in Chelan Mountains ridge, elevation 8,800 ft., on the mountains' summit between Lake Chelan on the east, and North Fork, Entiat River on the west, between Okanogan and Wenatchee national forests, north central Chelan County. The name was chosen by U.S. Forest Supervisor A. H. Sylvester because of its supremacy among adjacent mountains.

Caribou Creek *(T.18N;R.20E)*

The stream of the creek rises in east central Kittitas County; flows about 22 miles southwest to Yakima River, near Thrall. In the 1860s, the name was applied when A. J. Splawn and other Yakima Valley stockmen drove herds of cattle northward along this creek to the Caribou Mining District of British Columbia. An earlier name was *Salahan*.

Carley *(S.3;T.4N;R.24E)*

A railroad station north of Columbia River, directly south of Canoe Ridge, extreme southwest Benton County. Not shown on recent maps, it was located on a site settled in 1904 by M. E. Carley. Spokane, Portland, & Seattle Railway officials named the station for him.

Carlisle *(S.12;T.19N;R.12W)*

A small settlement on Copalis River, 4 miles east of Pacific Ocean, southwest Grays Harbor County. When established in 1912 by Carlisle Lumber Company, it was a busy logging and sawmill center. It continued to be active until the company's timber supply was exhausted. It was named for the lumber company, which originated from Wisconsin and was founded by William Carlisle.

Carlisle (Whatcom County) *see* Village Point

Carlisle Lakes
(Ss.8,17,18;T.19N;R.11W)

Group of 5 small lakes 2-1/2 miles north of Copalis Crossing, west central Grays Harbor County. Located on a divide in a marshy area, their areas range from less than an acre to 4 acres. (*see* Carlisle)

Carlsborg *(S.15;T.30N;R.4W)*

A sawmill town 3-1/2 miles south of Dungeness Harbor, northeast Clallam County. It was established by and named for Carl J. Erickson, a Seattle contractor, who built the Port Angeles & Western Railway through the town; he was also president of Carlsborg Mill & Timber Company.

Carlson *(S.17;T.14N;R.5E)*

Once a busy sawmill town 2 miles south of Mineral, north central Lewis County. The only present industry is an electric power plant. The name is for the owner of the first sawmill.

Carlson Peak (Clallam County) *see* Snider Peak

Carnation (King County) *see* Tolt

Carne Mountain
(S.24;T.30N;R.16E.uns)

A Wenatchee National Forest peak, elevation 7,074 ft., on a ridge between Phelps and Ice creeks, near the headwaters of Entiat River, northwest Chelan County. It is used as a Forest Service lookout in season. In 1915, it was named by U.S. Forest Supervisor A. H. Sylvester for W. Stanley Carnes, an English clergyman.

Carp Lake *(S.2;T.31N;R.2E)*

A 7-acre lake on the north end of Camano Island, 3 miles south of Utsalady, central Island County. Local informants report that some misguided person planted carp in this lake many years ago.

Carpenter Creek *(T.38N;R.4E)*

The stream of the creek rises 2 miles northeast of Lake Whatcom, southwest Whatcom County; flows into the lake at Agate Bay on the east shore. On January 1, 1894, it was locally named for William Carpenter, an early settler and deputy sheriff.

Carr Inlet *(Ts.20-22N;Rs.1,2W)*

Inlet extending from McNeil Island on the south to Henderson Bay on the north, northwest Pierce County. A restricted area at the south end is used as a naval torpedo range. In 1841, the Wilkes Expedition named the inlet for Lieut. Overton Carr, a member of the exploring party. A conflicting record states that Wilkes named it *Brackenridge's Passage*, for William D. Brackenridge, a botanist with the expedition. The present name, however, is now accepted as official.

Carr Point *(S.36;T.30N;R.2W)*

A west shore point of Port Discovery Bay, 4 miles south of the entrance, northeast Jefferson County. In 1790, Manuel Quimper placed a cross here, but did not name the point; and, in 1792, Capt. George Vancouver refitted his ships at this place, but evidently did not apply a name either. In 1841, Cmdr. Charles Wilkes named it *Carr's Point* for Lieut. Overton Carr of his expedition. Capt. Henry Kellet named it *Vancouver Point* for Capt. George Vancouver, but his name failed to endure. *Contractors Point* is a local name. The present name is a shortened version of Wilkes' selection. Retention of placenames is difficult in a situation such as this, where any obscure map maker or surveyor may tamper with original names.

Carrolton *(S.19;T.7N;R.1W)*

A small community on Columbia River, 5 miles south of Kelso, southwest Cowlitz County. In 1873, it was named by Northern Pacific Railway officials for Maj. Carroll, a very early settler. They called it *Carrol's*, which was used until altered to the present form in 1915 by local residents.

Carp Lake (Clallam County) *see* Campbell Lake

Carrs Point (Jefferson County) *see* Carr Point

Carson *(S.29;T.3N;R.8E)*

Settlement on Carson Creek, 1 mile north of Columbia River, south central

Skamania County. It was named for Carson Creek, which is said to be a corruption of *Katsner*, the name of a pioneer. In 1805, Lewis and Clark called the place *Ash*, because they found ash trees (Oregon ash) here, the first they had seen in the west.

Carter Falls (*Mt. Rainier National Park*)

A Nisqually River falls at the confluence of Paradise Creek, 1-1/2 miles northeast of Longmire on Wonderland Trail, southwest sector of the park. The name, almost as old as the park, is for a guide, who built the first trail to Paradise Valley. At one time, the Longmires collected a 50-cent toll charge to use the trail.

Carter Point (Whatcom County) *see* Point Carter

Cascade Bay (*S.6;T.36N;R.1W*)

An east shore bay of East Sound, directly south of Rosario, Orcas Island, northeast San Juan County. In 1858, the name was charted by Capt. Henry Richards, British Admiralty Survey. He stated that the name derived from an elevated lake, which cascaded over a bank as it discharged into Cascade Bay, flowing west. The lake, known to be Cascade Lake, now drains into Buck Bay through Cascade Creek. An alternate name of this feature, not in present use, was *Rosario Bay*.

Cascade City (*S.1;T.16N;R.32E*)

A "paper town," platted in 1892 on 80 acres, 9 miles southwest of Lind, on Providence Coulee, south central Adams County. Although the lots were very small, they sold throughout the east and middle west at prices up to $250 each. Some, however, were given as a premium with the purchase of a $2.50 bottle of patent medicine. No buildings were ever constructed, contrary to claims made in the lurid literature distributed by promoters. In 1902, the county took the land for taxes, and, in 1917, sold it at public auction. This impressive name was chosen by promoters to impress possible buyers.

Cascade Creek (*Ts.36,37N;R.1W*)

The stream of the creek heads in Mountain Lake, eastern peninsula of Orcas Island, Moran State Park, San Juan County; flows south and west into Buck Bay, East Sound, and joined enroute by a short branch with cascades, or waterfalls. The creek was named for

the falls in the branch, which drains Cascade Lake. An early name was *Bowman's Creek*, for John H. Bowman, who, in 1879, filed a land claim along the stream.

Cascade Crest Trail

A developed foot and horse trail, elevations to over 8,000 ft., along Cascade Mountain Range summit, from the Canadian boundary to Columbia River, central Washington state; continues on the south side of Columbia River, extending into Mexico. The name is entirely descriptive.

Cascade Junction (Pierce County) *see* South Prairie

Cascade Lake (*Ss.31,32;T.37N;R.1W*)

A 171.6-acre lake, maximum depth 15 ft., on eastern peninsula of Orcas Island, 2 miles southwest of Mt. Constitution and 1/2 mile east of Rosario, northeast San Juan County. Originally, the site was a marshy area which was converted by a dam into a lake. The lake is used as a storage area for hydroelectric power generated for Rosario. (*see* Cascade Bay)

Cascade Mountain Range

A high mountain range in central Washington, dividing the state into 2 separate climatic zones, elevation about 8,000 ft. near the British Columbia boundary, averaging to 4,000 ft. approaching the Columbia River south of Mt. Adams, and including 5 volcanic peaks, ranging from 8,364 to 14,408 ft. high. It continues south of Columbia River through Oregon, and to a gap south of Lassen Peak, California.

Its 240-mile traverse through Washington state is almost entirely in national forest, national park and wilderness areas. In 1827, the name was applied to these mountains by the famous British botanist David Douglas, for the waterfalls which he saw in the lower Cascades along Columbia River. In 1841, Cmdr. Charles Wilkes used this name on his charts. The first naming by white men, however, was in 1790 by Manuel Quimper, who called the range *Sierra Madras de San Antonio*. Later names that did not become official were *Snowy Range, Snowy Mountains* and *Klannet Range*. In 1834, Hall J. Kelley, a fanatical Boston school teacher, tried to fix the name *Presidents' Range* on these mountains, but without success.

Cascade Mountain
(*Ss.21,28;T.25N;R.11E*)

A 5,500-ft. peak 5 miles southwest of Skykomish, between West Fork and East Fork, Miller River, northeast King County. It was named for the nearby Cascade Mountain Range. (USBGN)

Cascade River (*Ts.34,35N;Rs.11-14E*)

The stream of the river heads in 2 forks that originate on the west slope of Cascade Mountain summit, extreme east central Skagit County; flows 28 miles westerly to Skagit River at Marblemount. It was named for Cascade Mountains.

Cascade Tunnel, New
(*T.26N;Rs.13,14E*)

A Great Northern Railway tunnel, 7.79 miles long, through the Cascade Mountain summit near Stevens Pass. It replaces an older tunnel which was built in the 1890s. (*see* Cascade Tunnel, Old)

Cascade Tunnel, Old
(*Ss.10,11;T.26N;Rs.13,14E*)

An abandoned tunnel at Cascade Mountain summit, elevation 3,400 ft., in extreme northeast King and southwest Chelan counties. It was located in the early 1890s by John F. Stevens, chief engineer for Great Northern Railway Company, and was cut through the mountains for a distance of 13,873 ft. It has been replaced by a longer tunnel. Great Northern Railway officials named it for its mountain location.

Cascades (*T.2N;R.7E*)

Noted cascades in Columbia River, above Bonneville Dam, near the site of Bridge of the Gods, south central Skamania County. They have been altered by the dam, and were once a menace to river navigation until Cascade Locks were built. In 1805, Lewis and Clark applied the name *Great Shute* to the upper rapids. In 1825, John Work of Hudson's Bay Company was the first to apply the present descriptive name.

Cascades (town) (Skamania County) *see* North Bonneville

Case Inlet (Pierce, Mason counties) *see* Cases Inlet

Case Pond (*S.29;T.14N;R.8W*)

A 2-acre pond 1 mile east of Raymond, north central Pacific County. It was named for E. E. Case, a pioneer shingle manufacturer of Raymond and South Bend.

Case Shoal *(T.27N;R.1E)*

Shoal at the entrance to Suquamish Harbor, near north entrance to Hood Canal, Jefferson County. In 1841, it was named *Case's Bank* by Cmdr. Charles Wilkes for Lieut. A. L. Case of his command. On some maps it has appeared erroneously as *Cases's Shoal.* The present form is an unwarranted abbreviation of the original name.

Case's Bank (Jefferson County) *see* Case Shoal

Cases Inlet *(Ts.19-22N;R.1W)*

An 18-mile-long inlet, extending north from Nisqually Reach to North Bay in South Puget Sound; the boundary between northwest Pierce and southeast Mason counties follows the inlet in mid-channel. In 1841, this branch of Puget Sound was named *Case's Inlet* by Cmdr. Charles Wilkes. That form is used on some maps, while others use *Case Inlet.* (*see* Case Shoal)

Cashmere *(S.4;T.23N;R.19E)*

Town 12 miles northwest of Wenatchee, on Wenatchee River, Chelan County. It was established in 1889, and platted in 1895 as *Mission* by J. F. Woodring and I. W. Sherman. The name derives from a Jesuit mission which had been built here in 1863 to convert Indians to Christianity. In 1903, the present name was substituted, since another town in the state carried the name Mission. Responsible for the choice was Judge James H. Chase, who had visited the "Vale of Kashmir" in India, and liked the name.

Cashup *(S.15;T.18N;R.43E)*

Once an important wayside stop on Cottonwood Creek, 12 miles north of Colfax, north central Whitman County. In pioneer days, it was the stage line stop between Spokane and Colfax. It bears the nickname of James. H. Davis, the first settler and storekeeper. He extended no credit, and became known as "Cashup."

Casland *(S.6;T.20N;R.16E)*

Lumber camp 5 miles northeast of Cle Elum on Teanaway River, north central Kittitas County. The name was manufactured by Guthrie Construction Company by tacking "land" onto the first syllable of Cascade Lumber Company's title.

Castle Island *(S.21;T.34N;R.1W)*

Island in the Strait of Juan de Fuca,

1/2 mile off the southeast end of Lopez Island, southeast San Juan County. In 1855, it was named *Old Hundred Island* by the U.S. Coast Survey. In 1858, it was changed to the present name on British Admiralty charts by Capt. Henry Richards, R.N., for a fancied resemblance to a castle.

Castle Peak *(Mt. Rainier National Park)*

A 6,116-ft. peak at the headwaters of Ipsut Creek, directly northwest of Mother Mountain, northwest sector of the park. The name was given for a fancied resemblance to a castle. A former name was *Castle Rock.* (USBGN)

Castle Rock *(S.11;T.19N;R.2W)*

Town on the east bank of Cowlitz River, 10 miles north of Longview, northwest Cowlitz County. In 1853, it was named by William Huntington for a huge rock, 150-ft. high and covering an acre of ground directly south of town.

Castle Rock (Mt. Rainier National Park) *see* Castle Peak

Castle Rock (Skamania County) *see* Beacon Rock

Castlenook *(S.35;T.21N;R.1E)*

Once a commercial fishermen's town at the northeast end of Fox Island, near the present settlement of Sylvan, northwest Pierce County. The name of the person who chose this fancy name for a now-abandoned fishing settlement is not on record.

Casway *(S.3;T.19N;R.16E)*

A railway spur 5 miles southeast of Cle Elum, at the mouth of Teanaway River, on Yakima River, central Kittitas County. It was named by Guthrie Construction Company by combining the first syllable of "Cascade," for Cascade Lumber Company of Yakima, and the last syllable of "Teanaway."

Cat Creek *(T.28N;Rs.7,8W)*

The stream of the creek rises in mountains west of Bailey Range, south central Clallam County; flows northeast to Lake Mills in Elwha River basin. On March 1, 1890, it was named by Seattle Press Expedition, when one of its members killed a "cat" on the creek's bank. The record does not show whether it was a wildcat or cougar.

Cat Lake (Clallam County) *see* Campbell Lake

Cataract Falls *(Mt. Rainier National Park)*

Turbulent falls at the southeast base of Mother Mountain, in Cataract Creek near the confluence of Marmot Creek, northwest sector of the park. The falls create a cloud of mist, which covers the surrounding forest. The name, chosen by park officials, is definitely descriptive.

Catfish Lake (Clallam County) *see* Campbell Lake

Cathcart *(S.1;T.27N;R.5E)*

A small settlement 5 miles south of Snohomish, southwest Snohomish County. It was named for Isaac Cathcart, a pioneer hotelkeeper, logger, merchant, and county treasurer.

Cathedral Crag *(T.37N;R.7E.uns)*

Crag on the south slope of Mt. Baker, near Baker Pass, Mt. Baker National Forest, south central Whatcom County. In 1909, the name was chosen by the Mazamas, for the mountain's fancied resemblance to a cathedral.

Cathedral Rocks
(Mt. Rainier National Park)

A narrow rock island, 2-1/2 miles long, between Cowlitz and Ingraham glaciers, on the trail from Paradise Valley to Mt. Rainier summit on the southeast slope, central area of the park. The name was chosen by a very early party of climbers for a fancied resemblance to a cathedral at one trail point. (USBGN)

Catherine Creek *(T.40N;Rs.32,33E)*

The stream of the creek heads 3 miles south of the Canadian boundary, northeast Ferry County; flows west 5-1/2 miles to Kettle River, between Ferry and Toroda. It was named for the wife of a well-known Indian, Martin Alec.

Catherine Lake (Lewis County) *see* Chambers Lake

Cathlamah (Wahkiakum County) *see* Cathlamet

Cathlamet *(T.8N;R.6W)*

Town on the north bank of Columbia River, north of Little Island and Puget Island, on Cathlamet Channel, southeast Wahkiakum County. The name, which is also that of a small Indian band, means "stone," and relates to the rocky course of Columbia River through Cathlamet Channel. In the 1860s James Birnie, a former employee of Hudson's Bay Company, operated a trading post here. Alternate names include *Kathlamet, Katalamet, Cathlamah, Kahelamit, Birnie's Retreat* and *Birnie's Trading Post.*

Cathlamet Channel (*T.8N;Rs.5,6W*)

A 6-mile-long channel, 1/2 to 1 mile average width, between Little Island and Cathlamet in Columbia River, southeast Wahkiakum County. (*see* Cathlamet)

Cathlapootle River (Skamania, Cowlitz, Clark counties) *see* North Fork, Lewis River

Catlin (*T.8N;R.2W*)

Old town on Cowlitz River, across from Kelso, southwest Cowlitz County. It occupied part of the area which now is Longview. The present town of West Kelso is adjacent to the Donation Land Claim which was owned by Seth Catlin and his wife in the 1860s. In 1889, Catlin named the settlement *Marysville* for his wife. The name was already applied to a town in Snohomish County, so "Catlin" was chosen by popular vote. The Catlin claim was absorbed by Long-Bell Lumber Company when Longview was established.

Catt Creek (*T.14N;Rs.6,7E*)

The stream of the creek heads in Greenwood Lake, 9 miles north of Randle, east central Lewis County; flows 10 miles northwest to Big Creek, 2 miles southeast of National. It was locally named for a homesteader who had settled at the creek's mouth.

Cattle Point (*S.8;T.34N;R.2W*)

A southeast point of San Juan Island, on Middle Channel, south central San Juan County. It was the site of an early Hudson's Bay Company trading post, and of a U.S. military camp during the San Juan boundary dispute. In 1858, the name was first used on British Admiralty charts. Capt. Henry Richards chose the name because Hudson's Bay Company loaded and unloaded cattle here prior to the settlement of the San Juan Island boundary. The Lummi Indian name for the point was *Who-shung-ing.*

Cattle Point Narrows (San Juan County) *see* Middle Channel, Little Belt Passage

Cavanaugh Lake (*S.22;T.33N;R.6E*)

A 844-acre lake, 80 ft. deep and 2-3/4 miles long, elevation 1,008 ft., at the head of Lake Creek, 12 miles north-

east of Arlington, southwest Skagit County. It was named for a logger and lumberman who operated in this area.

Cave Creek (*S.28;T.6N;R.10E*)

The stream of the creek rises in Gifford Pinchot National Forest, in a region of ice and lava caves, extreme northwest Klickitat County; flows 8-1/2 miles northeast to White Salmon River. As reported in Pacific Railroad Survey of 1853, the stream was named for its course, which runs partly underground through the lava caves.

Cave Creek Butte (Skamania County) *see* Mann Butte

Cayuse Mountain (Ferry County) *see* Coyote Mountain

Cayuse Pass (*Mt. Rainier National Park*)

A 4,675-ft. pass at the junction of Mather Memorial Hwy. and the road to Ohanapecosh Hot Springs, between the heads of Cayuse and Klickitat creeks, 3.6 miles west of Chinook Pass, east central sector of the park. It is used in winter months as a ski area. The name derives from a warlike Indian tribe which formerly inhabited much of the Inland Empire. (USBGN)

Cebalop (*T.21N;R.3E*)

Once an Indian village of the Puyallup tribe, on the site of "Old Tacoma," which now includes Tacoma, northwest Pierce County. The tribe originally named the place *Ci-bal-ap,* meaning "shadow monster." Also spelled Chebaulip and Shubahlup.

Cecil Creek (*T.38N;Rs.24,25E*)

A stream with many tributaries that rises near Chickadee Ridge, north central Okanogan County; flows east 10 miles to Sinlahekin Creek, 2 miles south of Loomis. It was named for a part-Indian tribesman who owned an allotment at the creek's mouth.

Cedar Falls (*S.34;T.33N;R.8E*)

Small settlement on Rattlesnake Lake, 2-1/2 miles northwest of Cedar Lake, on Seattle's watershed, central King County. It was named for the nearby waterfalls in Cedar River, by Seattle officials when they established a hydro-electric plant here. The previous name had been *Moncton.*

Cedar Flat (*Mt. Rainier National Park*)

Flat between 2 branches of Ohanapecosh River, 1-1/2 miles north of Ohanapecosh Hot Springs, southeast

sector of the park. The name was well chosen, as the flat is covered with a growth of very old and very large western red cedar.

Cedar Lake (*T.22N;Rs.8,9E*)

Irregular, 7-mile-long lake, elevation 1,558 ft., in Cedar River, on Seattle's watershed, southeast King County. It was enlarged by a dam at its lower end, and is the source of a major part of Seattle's domestic water supply. In September 1853, this lake and the river were named by Catherine T. Maynard, wife of the famous Seattle pioneer Dr. D. S. Maynard, while on a canoe trip in the area. The name was very descriptive at the time, as the lower part of the river's course was lined with enormous, old-growth native cedars, up to 100 ft. in circumference. In 1955, the name *Chester Morse Lake,* for a former Seattle Water Department Superintendent, was placed on official City of Seattle maps.

Cedar River (*Ts.21,22N;Rs.5-11E*)

The stream of the river rises in 2 forks, on the west slope of Cascade Mountain summit, southeast King County; flows northwest through Seattle's watershed to Cedar Lake, then west and northwest by way of Renton to Duwamish River at Black River Junction. It is the principal source of Seattle's domestic water supply. Indian tribal names for the river were *Quab-quo* and *Nook-noo.* (*see* Cedar Lake)

Cedar River Watershed (*Ts.21-23N;Rs.7-11E*)

A 91,400-acre watershed, of which Seattle owns 63,926, extending 24 miles from Cascade Mountain summit to Landsburg, 22 miles from Seattle, King County. Developed and protected by Seattle as the main source of the city's domestic water supply, it contains 3 small lakes: Cedar, Rattlesnake, and Walsh. The name derives from the river on which it is located. (*see* Cedar River)

Cedar Valley (*Ts.6-8N;Rs.13-15E*)

A high valley within Yakima Indian Reservation, extending about 14 miles north from the south reservation boundary and 19 miles east from Klickitat River, with a total area of about 8 townships, southwest Yakima County. Once heavily populated by wheat farmers and sawmill operators, the valley is now virtually deserted except for minor logging operations. Much of the area is covered with second-growth pine timber.

The name source has been the cause of much speculation. Cedar is not an important timber species here, with only a few stunted trees among pines and firs. A pioneer tradition, colorful but of doubtful veracity, attributes the naming to a German, who was traveling through the valley on the old stage route. When the stage climbed into the foothills of Simcoe Mountains, the German is said to have exclaimed, ''Oh, see der walley!''

Cedarville *(S.22;T.16N;R.5W)*

Small settlement near Chehalis River, 11 miles southeast of Elma, southeast Grays Harbor County. In 1855, it was established when a blockhouse was built on the land claim of James L. Smith. It was named for nearby Cedar Creek.

Cedonia *(S.28;T.31N;R.37E)*

Settlement on Harvey Creek, 1/2 mile east of Columbia River, 32 miles south of Kettle Falls, southwest Stevens County. In 1889, a religious settlement was founded here on rented land by George Cornwall and Martin Scotan (Scotten), the first postmaster. The settlers, wanting a Biblical name for their post office, suggested *Macedonia*. Postal authorities shortened it to Cedonia. Alternate spelling on older maps include *Cidonia, Sedonia* and *Sadonia.*

Celilo Falls *(Ss.23,24;T.2N;R.14E)*

Once famous falls in Columbia River, directly downstream from Wishram, between south central Klickitat County and Oregon. Obliterated by The Dalles Dam in 1956-57, it was a very important fishing ground for several Indian tribes for as long as Indian tradition reaches into the past. In 1811, a Hudson's Bay Company official counted 3,000 Indians here. The main falls boiled in a sheer drop of 20 ft. over a basalt cliff in the river channel. Indians fished with spears and dipnets, drying most of the fish as soon as it was caught. The Indian word *Celilo* means ''floating sand cloud,'' which describes the sand storms which occurred here when high winds swept the Columbia Gorge.

Cement Basin
(S.29;T.17N;R.11E.uns)

A Snoqualmie National Forest basin, between Union Creek and Cement Creek, directly east of Cascade Mountain summit, extreme northwest Yakima County. The name is descriptive, as the basin is floored with a conglomerated mass of cemented pebbles.

Cement City (Skagit County) *see* Concrete

Cemetery Island *(S.34;T.37N;R.4W)*

One of the 3 Gossip Islands, with Gossip and Happy islands, at the entrance to Reid Harbor on Stuart Island, extreme northwest San Juan County. It was named because of numerous Indian burials here. After desecration of many graves, the bodies were moved by Indians to a Canadian island.

Center *(S.10;T.28N;R.10W)*

Community in Chimacum Valley, 5 miles west of Port Ludlow, northeast Jefferson County. In very early days, when western Jefferson County had few settlers, this small settlement was considered the center of Jefferson County, and so received its name.

Center Island *(T.35N;R.1W)*

A privately-owned island, about 200 heavily-wooded acres, in Reads Bay, directly southwest of Decatur, at the southwest tip of Decatur Island, San Juan County. It was named by a previous owner because of its location in the center of the bay.

Center Reef *(S.11;T.36N;R.4W)*

A bare, rocky reef in the center of Spieden Channel, 1 mile southwest of Spieden Island, northwest San Juan County. It was locally named because of its position in the channel.

Centerview (Spokane County) *see* Alpha.

Centerville *(S.11;T.3N;R.15E)*

Community 5 miles southwest of Goldendale, south central Klickitat County. This name was applied to many pioneer towns that hoped to be trade centers, although none could establish a post office under that name because of duplication. This ''center'' is overshadowed by nearby Goldendale.

Centerville, Centreville (Lewis County) *see* Centralia

Central Ferry *(S.9;T.13N;R.40E)*

Once a ferry terminal on the south bank of Snake River, directly east of the mouth of Meadow Creek, extreme northwest Garfield County. In early days, the place was named for the ferry. In 1881, when a post office was installed, postal authorities selected the unusual name *Reform*. After the post office was abandoned, the name reverted to the original.

Centralia *(T.14N;R.2W)*

City at the confluence of Chehalis and Skookumchuck rivers, 2 miles south of Thurston County boundary, northwest Lewis County. Once active in coal-mining, it is now an important trade center, served by several railroads. The first post office applied the name *Skookumchuck*. When the town was platted by George Washington, son of a black slave who acquired all or part of an 1850 Donation Land Claim, it was named *Centerville*. Because a town in Klickitat County had the same name, it was changed again in 1884 to its present name.

Ceres *(S.14;T.13N;R.4W)*

A small settlement in Chehalis River Valley, 11 miles west of Chehalis, west central Lewis County. The name was chosen by W. C. Albee, superintendent of South Bend branch of Northern Pacific Railway, when the branch was built. This name, in Roman mythology, denotes the goddess of agriculture. Evidently, Albee was quite impressed with the valley's fertile soil.

Cerro Nevado de Santa Rosalia (Jefferson County) *see* Mt. Olympus

Cha-Choo-Sen *(T.38N;R.1E)*

An ''island'' near the mouth of Lummi River, between the river's forks that flow into Lummi Bay and Bellingham Bay, west central Whatcom County. This Indian name, used by the Lummi Indians, appears to mean ''low, swampy island.''

Chadwick Hill *(S.21;T.34N;R.1W)*

A 448-ft. hill at the southeastern point of Lopez Island, immediately west of Watmough Bay, southeast San Juan County. It was locally named for an early settler. An alternate local name is *Mt. Chadwick.*

Chain Creek *(T.25N;Rs.14,15E)*

The stream of the creek rises in Chain Lakes on Icicle Ridge, 2 miles east of Cascade Mountain summit; flows about 2 miles southwest on Wenatchee National Forest, to Icicle Creek, southeast Chelan County. (*see* Chain Lakes, Chelan County)

Chain Lake *(S.19;T.10N;R.6E)*

A 3-acre lake, elevation 4,330 ft., 3 miles north of Spirit Lake, Gifford Pinchot National Forest, northwest Skamania County. The name was chosen because the lake appears to be chained to Obsurity Lake by a short channel, which aerially resembles links in a chain.

Chain Lakes *(S.5;T.25N;R.15E)*

Three lakes in a glacial cirque at slightly different levels, near the Icicle Ridge summit, at the head of Chain Creek, 2 miles east of Cascade Mountain summit on Wenatchee National Forest, southwest Chelan County. They were named by a U.S. Geological Survey topographer, who mapped the Skykomish Quadrangle. While not linked, the lakes do constitute a chain.

Chain Lakes *(S.20;T.24N;R.13E)*

A group of 6 small lakes joined by streams, totalling about 3-1/2 acres, on the west side of La Bohn Gap at Cascade Mountain summit, Snoqualmie National Forest, northeast King County. The name is descriptive, as the lakes are an actual chain.

Chain Lakes *(S.8;T.14N;R.11E)*

A group of 4 numbered lakes, elevation about 5,000 ft. and varying in size from 1/2 to 4 acres, 2 miles southwest of Cascade Mountain summit, extreme northeast Lewis County. These connected lakes, 3 of which are shallow, bear a name descriptive of their joined, chain-like pattern.

Chain Lakes *(S.8;T.31N;R.7E)*

A narrow, connected string of 4 small lakes, 7 miles northwest of Granite Falls, northwest Snohomish County. The lakes -- No. 1, No. 2, No. 3 and La Barge -- vary in size from 1 to 4 acres. The name is quite descriptive.

Chain Lakes (Whatcom County) *see* Galena Chain Lakes

Chain of Lakes *(T.9N;R.10E)*

A remarkable group of many small, glacial ponds and lakes, high in "blueberry country," between the headwaters of Adams and Sheep creeks, directly northwest of Mt. Adams, northeast Skamania County. The name is obviously and accurately descriptive.

Chambers Creek *(T.20N;R.2E)*

The stream of the creek heads in Leach and Flett creeks, in south Tacoma area; flows 4 miles southwest to Steilacoom Waterway, 1 mile northeast of Steilacoom. It was named for Thomas W. Chambers, a pioneer, who built the

first sawmill in the county on this creek. It was charted as *Chudley Creek* by Capt. R. N. Inskip, but his name did not persist.

Chambers Lake *(T.11N;R.10E.uns)*

Lake at the head of Chambers Creek, 5 miles west of Cascade Mountain summit, adjoining Goat Rocks Primitive Area, southeast Lewis County. Evidently, the name was applied by U.S. Forest Service personnel for a local Forest Service employee.

Chambers Lake *(T.18N;R.1W)*

Originally one lake, now divided into 2 segments by a 500-ft. ditch, covering less than a square mile, 1/2 mile east of Olympia, north central Thurston County. The segments are 49.1-acre Little Chambers Lake; and 72.5-acre Chambers Lake, or Russell Lake. It was named for Andrew and David Chambers, who, in 1845, claimed land on Chambers Prairie. The combined lake is shown on some older maps as *Lake Chambers*.

Chambers Prairie *(Ts.17,18N;R.1W)*

Prairie covering several square miles, 4 to 5 miles south of Olympia, central Thurston County. Settled since 1843, it was named for Andrew and David Chambers, who claimed land in 1845, and eventually owned 3,000 acres here and on a small prairie to the southeast. Before 1845, the name in use was *Eaton's Prarie* for Charles H. Eaton, who took a squatter's claim near Pattison Lake. The Indian name was *El-cu-men*.

Chamokane Creek
(Ts.27-29N;Rs.39,40E)

This watercourse rises near Lyons Hill, southwest of Springdale, south central Stevens County; flows east and southeast for about 24 miles to Spokane River, between Long Lake and Little Falls. The southern portion of its course constitutes the east boundary of the Spokane Indian Reservation.

The present name and an earlier version, *Tshimakain*, signify "plain of the springs" in the Spokane Indian dialect. Many creeks in this area disappear underground and then emerge as springs of considerable volume.

Chancellor *(S.30;T.38N;R.17E.uns)*

Once a mining camp on Ruby Creek, at the mouth of Slate Creek, 4 miles west of Cascade Mountain summit, southeast Whatcom County. It was named for the

Chancellor mine, which operated from 1890 to 1910. This "ghost town" now consists of a few deserted buildings.

Chandler *(S.17;T.9N;R.26E)*

Railroad stop on Yakima River, 10 miles northeast of Prosser, central Benton County. In 1890, Northern Pacific Railway officials named this station *Barnes* for a local landowner. In 1896, it was changed to the present name, evidently because the first name was confused with a similar station name in the state, probably Barneston in King County.

Chapman Cove *(S.15;T.20N;R.3W)*

Town on the east shore of Oakland Bay, 3 miles northeast of Shelton, southeast Mason County. An earlier name was *Swindall Cove*, for Calvin W. Swindall, who filed a Donation Land Claim here; he was the town's first storekeeper and postmaster. Source of the present name is unrecorded.

Chapman Creek *(Ts.3,4N;Rs.19,20E)*

The stream of the creek rises near Oak Grove district, east central Klickitat County; flows southeasterly 10 miles to Columbia River at Sundale. It was named for Eldon Chapman, postmaster of Six Prong in the early 1900s.

Chard *(S.7;T.12N;R.40E)*

Community on Pataha Creek, 15 miles west of Pomeroy, between Jackson and Dodge, northwest Garfield County. It was established as a railway station; in 1887, it supported a post office under the name *Tukannon*. The present name is from the postmaster, W. J. Chard.

Charles Island *(S.14;T.34N;R.2W)*

Island south of Lopez Island, between Davis Bay and Jones Bay, 1/2 mile southwest of Richardson, south central San Juan County. In 1858-59, this name was placed on British Admiralty charts by Capt. Henry Richards, R.N., for Capt. James Charles Prevost of the British ship *Satellite*. James Island, as well as nearby Charles Point and Prevost Harbor were named by Richards at the same time, for this same person.

Charles Lake *(S.1;T.25N;R.15E)*

A small, milky pond at the foot of Chiwaucum Glacier and headwaters of Glacier Creek, Wenatchee National Forest, south central Chelan County. The name was chosen by U.S. Forest Supervisor A. H. Sylvester for his friend, Charles Hayden.

Charles Lake *(S.34;T.32N;R.37E)*

A small lake 1 mile east of Columbia River, 6 miles south of Gifford, southwest Stevens County. Originally, it was named for James Clarke who had the lake surveyed in 1888; it was then known as *Clark Lake* or *Clarke Lake*. Who renamed it, and for whom, has not been ascertained.

Charles Point *(T.37N;R.4W)*

A north end point of Stuart Island, on the west entrance to Prevost Harbor, extreme northwest San Juan County. (*see* Charles Lake, San Juan County)

Charleston (Kitsap County) *see* West Bremerton

Charley Creek *(S.31;T.32N;R.12W)*

The stream of the creek heads 4 miles south of Strait of Juan de Fuca, northwest Clallam County; flows 5 miles north and northeast to Clallam River near Clallam. It was locally named for Charles Welker, the first homesteader in the vicinity.

Charlie Creek *(T.9N;Rs.43,44E)*

The stream of the creek rises on the south side of Tam Tam Ridge, northwest Asotin County; flows 8 miles east to Asotin Creek. In 1870, it was named for Charles Lyon, who settled at the creek's mouth. Because it is one of the forks of Asotin Creek, some maps show it as *Charlie Creek Fork*.

Charlie Knight Gulch *(T.8N;R.44E)*

Gulch 5-1/2 miles southwest of Cloverland, west central Asotin County. It was named for Charlie Knight, who was born in 1886 on a ranch here.

Charlie Lake No. 4 (King County) *see* Camp Robber Lake

Chatauqua (King County) *see* Ellisport

Chattaroy *(S.34;T.28N;R.43E)*

Village 18 miles north of Spokane, at the confluence of Little Spokane River and Deer Creek, north central Spokane County. It was established in the early 1880s by Robert P. Cowgill, who operated a store and carried the mail from Spokane. The original name was *Kidd*, selected by the postal authorities for an early homesteader. In 1889, the present Indian name was restored, at the insistence of Mrs. Robert Cowgill. Indian influence was strong in early days, as local tribes maintained a hunting and

fishing village here before white men arrived. Hudson's Bay Company used one of the area's trail crossings as a temporary trading center with the Indians.

Chatter Creek *(T.25N;R.16E)*

The stream of the creek heads in the "Lady Lake" area on Icicle Ridge, Wenatchee National Forest, central Chelan County; flows 3 miles southeast to Icicle Creek. It was named by U.S. Forest Supervisor A. H. Sylvester for the chattering sound of the creek's fast-flowing water.

Chauncy's Island (San Juan County) *see* Lopez Island

Chehalis *(T.14N;R.2W)*

An important trade and banking center, with substantial forest products industries, on Chehalis River, at the junction of Newaukum River, west central Lewis County. It was first named *Saundersville*, for S. S. Saunders, who, in 1873, owned a Donation Land Claim here. In 1874, it was changed to the present name by Northern Pacific Railway officials; in 1875, legislative action confirmed the change. This Indian name, altered from *Chi-ke-lis*, means "shifting sands," and refers to the sands at the mouth of the Chehalis River. An actual total of 32 spellings of Chehalis are on record.

Chehalis City *(T.16N;Rs.11,12W)*

A vanished settlement on Point Chehalis, at the south entrance of Grays Harbor, southwest Grays Harbor County. It was on the present site of Westport, and was founded during the 1850-51 winter by John Butler Chapman, who called it *Leo*. As the settlement developed, the name was changed to Chehalis City for Chehalis River, but no substantial town developed.

Chehalis Indian Reservation *(T.15N;R.4W)*

A 4,225-acre reservation 30 miles south of Olympia, on Chehalis River, extreme southwest Thurston and extreme southeast Grays Harbor counties. It was established by Federal Executive Orders on July 8, 1864, and October 1, 1886, with most of the land allotted to individual Indians. At last count, the population was 115. It was named for the Chehalis Indian tribe.

Chehalis River

The stream of the river rises in Wil-

lapa Hills, extreme southwest Lewis County; flows north and east through Doty and Chehalis, Thurston County, then westerly into Grays Harbor, Grays Harbor County. (*see* Chehalis)

Chelatchie Creek *(T.5N;R.3E)*

The stream of the creek heads south of Lake Merwin, northeast Clark County; flows 3-1/2 miles southwest to Cedar Creek at Amboy. In 1853, railroad surveyors applied the creek's original Indian name. On some maps, it appears as *Chilatch Creek*.

Chelatchie Prarie *(T.5N;R.3E)*

A 3-1/2-mile long prairie northeast of Amboy, 3 miles south of Lake Merwin, northeast Clark County. (*see* Chelatchie Creek)

Chelan *(S.13;T.27N;R.22E)*

A scenic town, which is a trade and tourist center, at the south end of Lake Chelan, 2 miles west of Columbia River, east central Chelan County. The name is a modification of *Tsill-anne*, the original Indian name for the lake, meaning "deep water."

Chelan County

This county in north central Washington is bounded on the north by Okanogan County; on the east by Douglas County; on the south by Kittitas County; and on the west by Skagit, Snohomish and King counties. It is the third largest county in the state, with 2,931 sq. miles, much of which is in mountainous and scenic country. On March 13, 1899, the county was formed by an act of the state legislature. The original plan was to call the county "Wenatchee" but legislators decided on the present name. It was formed from parts of Kittitas and Okanogan counties. (*see* Chelan)

Chelan Falls *(S.31;T.27N;R.23E)*

Falls located in a prosperous fruit-growing area on Columbia River, 3 miles south of Chelan, east central Chelan County. (*see* Chelan)

Chelan Mountains *(Ts.27-31N;Rs.17-20E)*

Range forming the boundary between Wenatchee National Forest and Chelan National Forest, trending northwest and southeast between Lake Chelan and Entiat River, north central Chelan County. It was named by U.S. Forest Supervisor A. H. Sylvester for Lake Chelan. (*see* Chelan)

Chelan Range, Chelan Ridge (Chelan County) *see* Chelan Mountains

Chelan River *(T.27N;Rs.22,23E)*

The short, rapid stream with one set of falls heads at the south end of Lake Chelan, southeast Chelan County; flows 3 miles southeast to Columbia River at Chelan Station. (*see* Chelan)

Cheney *(Ss.12,13;T.23N;R.41E)*

Town 10 miles southwest of Spokane, southwest Spokane County. In 1880, it was founded and named *Billings* for Frank Billings, president of Northern Pacific Railway, even though early railroad surveys had mapped the place as *Depot Springs*. Education-minded citizens wanted an academy, and appealed to Benjamin P. Cheney of Boston, a director of Northern Pacific Railway Company. Cheney donated $10,000, and the town was renamed for him. When Washington attained statehood, the academy became a Normal School; it now is the Eastern Washington University.

Chenuis Creek *(Mt. Rainier National Park)*

The stream of the creek rises between Independence Ridge and Chenuis Mountain, extreme north central zone of the park; flows north across the park boundary, then west and south to reenter the park in its northwest corner. It joins Carbon River just south of the park boundary. The name is very old, and evidently of Indian origin. The possibility exists that it was named for *Chinchin-no-wah*, an Indian tribal leader. (USBGN)

Chenuis Falls *(Mt. Rainier National Park)*

A low falls with sharp cascades, surrounded by timber, in Chenuis Creek near its junction with Carbon River, extreme northwest area of the park near the north boundary. (USBGN) (*see* Chenuis Creek)

Chenuis Lakes *(Mt. Rainier National Park)*

Three small lakes, elevation about 5,000 ft., on the east slope of Chenuis Mountain, 1-1/2 miles south of the park's north boundary, 8-1/2 miles north of Mt. Rainier summit, north central zone of the park. The lakes cover 2-1/2, 3 and 3-1/2 acres, respectively. (*see* Chenuis Creek)

Chenuis Mountain *(Mt. Rainier National Park)*

A long ridge extending from the north park boundary just east of Carbon River, 5 miles southeast to Yellowstone Cliffs, northwest quarter of the park. Maximum elevation is at Tyee Peak, elevation 6,030 ft., at the mountain's southeast extremity. (*see* Chenuis Creek)

Cherana (Cherakwa) River (Adams County) *see* Cow Creek

Cherbourg (Clallam County) *see* Port Angeles

Chesaw *(S.20;T.40N;R.30E)*

Village on Myers Creek, 7 miles southeast of Molson, northeast Okanogan County. It was one of many towns in the county that started as mining camps in the 1890s. In 1900, the townsite was platted; it was named for Chee Saw, a Chinese placer miner who acquired an Indian wife.

Chester Morse Lake (King County) *see* Cedar Lake

Chetlo *(S.8;T.11N;R.10W)*

Settlement on the north tip of a spit on the south side of Naselle River where it opens into Stanley Channel, facing Long Island, southwest Pacific County. The name applied by early settlers is Chinook jargon for "oyster," and is appropriate for the area.

Chetlo Harbor *(S.9;T.11N;R.10W)*

A wide river channel at salt water, on Willapa Bay, at the mouth of Naselle River, southwest Pacific County. (*see* Chetlo)

Chetwood Lake (King County) *see* Chetwoot Lake

Chetwoot Lake *(Ss.22,23;T.24N;R.12E)*

A 113.3-acre mountain basin lake, elevation 5,200 ft. and depth over 100 ft., on Snoqualmie National Forest, 3-1/2 miles west of Cascade Mountain summit, northeast King County. The name is Chinook for "black bear." It is shown on some maps and records, in error, as *Chetwood*.

Chevy Chase *(S.31;T.30N;R.1W)*

A large, private estate, used as a country club, on the east shore of Port Discovery Bay, directly northwest of Tukey, northeast Jefferson County. It includes several buildings built years ago by John F. Tukey, who established this place in the 1850s as a way station between Port Townsend and Port Discovery. An early name was *Saints Rest*; it caused so much ribald comment that the present name was substituted.

Chewelah *(S.14;T.32N;R.40E)*

Town 23 miles south of Colville, 58 miles north of Spokane, central Stevens County. In 1854, Thomas Brown filed a land claim that included the present townsite. In the 1860s, a military post was established, and, in 1873, an Indian agency. When the Spokane Falls & Northern Railway reached Chewelah in 1889, extensive mining operations began, including a smelter.

Now reported to be the largest magnesite operation on the American continent, Northwest Magnesite Company employs about 200 persons and manufactures a variety of mineral products. Dolomite is the most important rock in the area, although diatomite is also mined. Rock quarries are on Quartzite Mountain, about 1 mile distant.

The name, adopted by settlers in 1883, is the Indian name meaning *small, striped snake*. In the January 1892 issue of *The American Anthropologist*, Myron Eells stated that snakes were abundant at the creek which runs through Chewelah, but advanced the belief that the origin might have been in the serpentine appearance of the stream. Various spellings have included *Cha-we-lah*, *Chi-chel-awah*, *Che-we-lah* and *Chiel-Charle-Mous*; the latter was used on the 1897 U.S. Land Office map.

Chewelah Creek *(Ts.32-34N;Rs.40-42E)*

The stream of the creek heads near Saddle Mountain, east central Stevens County; flows 25 miles southwest in 2 forks, through Chewelah, to Colville River. In the 1853 Railroad Survey, Capt. George B. McClellan mapped the creek as *Kitsemawhere*. (*see* Chewelah)

Chewiliken Creek *(T.36N;R.27E)*

The stream of the creek rises on Tunk Mountain, Colville National Forest, east central Okanogan County; flows northwest 15 miles to Okanogan River, between Janis and Barker. The name is reported to be for the highly-respected chief of a local Colville Indian tribe.

Chibahdehl Rocks *(S.4;T.33N;R.15W)*

A group of rocky islets near the beach in the Strait of Juan de Fuca, 3 miles east of Cape Flattery, northwest Clallam County. The name is a greatly altered form of the Quillayute Indian name *Chi-chi-a-quil*, meaning "standing rocks." The Makah name, which had the same meaning, was *Kla-t-la-itc-koe*.

Chicken Rock *(S.8;T.34N;R.2W)*

A small rock near Cattle Point, off the southeast tip of San Juan Island, San Juan County. The name was applied by local residents when a small boat, loaded with chickens, was wrecked on the rock.

Chickerman Creek (Chelan County) *see* Chikamin Creek

Chico *(S.32;T.25N;R.1E)*

Settlement on Chico Bay, in Dyes Inlet, 3-1/2 miles northwest of Bremerton, central Kitsap County. In 1889, it was named by B. S. Sparks, a local resident, for Indian "Chief" Chico, who died in 1909 at the age of 105.

Chief Joseph Dam
(S.14;T.29N;R.25E)

A recently-built hydroelectric dam spanning Columbia River between south central Okanogan and north central Douglas counties; located 3-1/2 miles southeast of Bridgeport, Douglas County, at the mouth of Foster Creek from the south. On June 14, 1948, the name was changed from *Foster Creek Dam* to the present name by Senate Joint Resolution 229 of the 80th Congress. In 1950, when Wenatchee residents attempted to change the name to honor Rufus Woods, an outstanding newspaper publisher, local Indian tribesmen objected so vigorously that the name of this famous Nez Perce chief was retained.

Chikamin Creek
(Ts.28,29N;R.17E.uns)

The stream of the creek heads at McDonald Ridge in Entiat Mountains; flows 7-1/2 miles south to Chiwawa River, Wenatchee National Forest, central Chelan County. The name derives from a word in Chinook jargon or trade language that means "money" or "metal." In early days, fur traders came to an Indian village at the creek's mouth to buy pelts. The bargaining phrase was "Concha chikamin?" or "How much?"

Chikamin Creek

(S.3;T.23N;R.7W.uns)

The stream of the creek rises in Olympic Primitive Area, north of Klone Lakes, northeast Grays Harbor County; flows 2-1/2 miles northeast to Wynooche River. The creek, which runs through a mineralized area, is named for a Chinook jargon term with a generic meaning of "money," "metal," "gold," or "silver."

Chikamin Peak *(S.15;T.23N;R.12E)*

Peak at Cascade Mountain summit, at head of Gold Creek, in a heavily mineralized area 2 miles northwest of Spectacle Lake, northwest Kittitas County. (*see* Chikamin Creek, Grays Harbor County)

Chikamin Ridge *(T.23N;Rs.12,13E)*

Ridge between Spectacle Lake and Park Lakes, extending 7 miles southeast from Chikamin Peak at Cascade Mountain summit to Alta Pass, northwest Kittitas County. It was named by The Mountaineers. (*see* Chikamin Creek, Grays Harbor County)

Chilipis Pass *(T.26N;R.15E)*

A Wenatchee National Forest pass through Chiwaukum Mountains summit, north of Deadhorse Pass, southwest Chelan County. Lower than Deadhorse Pass, it is suitable only to passage by sheep. It was named for a sheepherder who used this range, and does not appear on most maps.

Chiliwist *(S.7;T.32N;R.25E)*

A Colville Indian Reservation settlement on Okanogan River, 4-1/2 miles southwest of Okanogan, central Okanogan County. It was named for "Indian Charley" Chiliwist, who once lived at the mouth of Chiliwist Creek.

Chiliwist Creek
(Ts.32,33N;Rs.23-25E)

The stream of the creek rises on Pole Pick Mountain, central Okanogan County; flows southeast 14 miles to Okanogan River, south of Malott. (*see* Chiliwist)

Chilliwack Creek
(Ts.39-41E;Rs.10,11E.uns)

The stream of the creek heads on the northeast slope of Ruth Mountain, 3 miles northeast of Mt. Shuksan, northeast Whatcom County; flows 13 miles northeast to the Canadian boundary, to Chilliwack Lake, British Columbia. It was named by the Boundary Survey party, for the Indian tribe of that name in

British Columbia. Other spellings are *Chilliwak, Chilliwhack, Chillukweyuk,* and *Chiloweyuck.* The Indian name for the stream was *Klabneh,* and a local name in early days was *Dolly Varden Creek.*

Chimacum *(S.14;T.29N;R.1W)*

A small town, once the site of an Indian village, in Chimacum Valley, 3 miles east of Port Discovery Bay, northeast Jefferson County. It was named for a now-extinct Indian tribe which once inhabited the valley. (USBGN)

Chimacum Creek *(Ts.28,29N;R.1W)*

The stream of this 10-mile-long creek heads 1 mile north of Browns Lake, northeast Jefferson County; flows north to Port Townsend Bay, directly north of Irondale. (USBGN) (*see* Chimacum)

Chimney Rock *(S.36;T.13N;R.10E)*

A locally-named rock in Goat Rocks Primitive Area, 3 miles east of Packwood Lake, east central Lewis County. The name reflects the fancied resemblance to a very tall chimney.

China Bend *(Ts.38,39N;R.38E)*

A river bend on Columbia River, several miles long, about 13 miles south of the Canadian boundary, northwest Stevens County. From the late 1860s through the 1890s, it was the scene of considerable placer mining for gold. The name, given by miners, relates to the many Chinese who washed gravel here in the 1860s.

China Creek *(T.37N;R.38E)*

The stream of this intermittent creek heads 1-1/2 miles east of Bossburg, northwest Stevens County; flows 3 miles southwest to Columbia River, north of Evans. In 1903, it was named for the Chinese who did extensive placer mining in early days at the creek's mouth and on a river bar near the mouth.

Chinaman's Bar *(S.10;T.39N;R.43E)*

A river bar 2 miles north of Metaline Falls on Pend Oreille River, north central Pend Oreille County. It was named for a Chinese crew, which placer-mined the bar in the 1870s.

Chinaman's Hat *(S.30;T.18N;R.21E)*

A small mountain 12 miles west of Columbia River, 1-1/2 miles west of Whiskey Dick Mountain, east central Kittitas County. It was named during the period of great mining excitement, when many Chinese were in this area, washing out placer gold along the rivers and creeks. Many of them wore the Chinese bowl-shaped hats. The name was chosen because of a fancied resemblance of this mountain to this Chinese male millinery.

Chinom Point *(S.35;T.24N;R.3W)*

An east shore point of Hood Canal, opposite Eldon, extreme southwest Kitsap County. In 1841, Cmdr. Charles Wilkes charted this feature as *Tchinom Point*, using the Indian name. The "T" has subsequently been dropped.

Chinook *(S.8;T.9N;R.10W)*

Village on the north bank of Columbia River, 5 miles southeast of Ilwaco, southwest Pacific County. When Pacific County was established on February 4, 1851, this important fishing center was the county seat, and was then called *Chinookville*. The name, chosen by the earliest settlers, is a distortion of the *sinuk or Chenoke*, the original name of an Indian tribe, which lived near the mouth of the Columbia River. The name also refers to the warm winds, originating in the Japan Current of Pacific Ocean, which often blow from the south and southwest up the Columbia River mouth; the warm air rapidly melts snow in spring at Cascade Mountains summit. A third name reference is to the jargon which developed between the local Indians and white men.

Chinook Creek *(Mt. Rainier National Park)*

The stream of the creek rises in Tipsoo Lake, near Cascade Mountains summit, southeast sector of the park; flows south to join Ohanapecosh River, 4-1/2 miles north of Ohanapecosh Hot Springs. *(see* Chinook)

Chinook Pass *(Mt. Rainier National Park)*

A Cascade Mountains summit pass at Mather Memorial Hwy. eastern terminus, east central boundary of the park. The Pacific Crest Trail extends north and south along the mountain summit at this pass. *(see* Chinook)

Chinook Pass
(Ss.13,14;T.16N;R.10E)

A Cascade Mountains summit pass, elevation 5,443 ft., at headwaters of American River, 20 miles south of Naches Pass, between northwest Yaki-

ma and southeast Pierce counties. (USBGN) *(see* Chinook)

Chinook Point *(S.21;T.9N;R.10W)*

A north shore point of Columbia River, now included in Ft. Columbia State Park, 2 miles south of Chinook, southwest Pacific County. Many names have been used, including the Indian name *Nose-to-Ilse*. In 1792, Broughton mapped it as *Village Point*; then, in 1811, David Douglas named it *Point Komkomle* for a famous Chenoke chief; and, in 1839, Belcher named it *Chenoke Point*. The present name honors the local Chenoke Indian nation. *(see* Chinook)

Chinook River *(Ts.9,10N;R.10W)*

This slough rises northeast of Ft. Columbia State Park, Pacific County; flows westerly 4 miles to a swampy bay at Chinook. The Indian name was *Wappalooche*, meaning "owl." *(see* Chinook)

Chinookville (Pacific County) see Chinook

Chipmunk Creek *(T.30N;R.16E)*

The stream of this small, glacier-fed creek heads in Ice Lakes, Entiat Mountains; flows 2-1/2 miles southwest to Phelps Creek, northwest Chelan County. It was named by Robert E. Nickles, former forest ranger, for the abundance of these lively little animals along the creek.

Chiwaukum Creek
(Ts.25,26N;Rs.16,17E)

The stream of the creek rises in Chiwaukum Mountains from Ewing Basin, Wenatchee National Forest, north central Chelan County; flows through Chiwaukum Lake, 10 miles east by south to Wenatchee River, at the head of Tumwater Canyon. The entire watershed is a huge, glacial cirque, with smaller cirques at the head of each tributary. This Wenatchee Indian word, meaning "many little creeks running into big one," was applied to the creek by U.S. Forest Supervisor A. H. Sylvester.

Chiwaukum Glacier
(Ts.25,26N;R.15E)

An east slope "cliff glacier" of Chiwaukum Mountains, 1-1/2 miles wide, at the head of Glacier Creek, which is a south fork of Chiwaukum Creek near its source, Wenatchee National Forest, central Chelan County. *(see* Chiwaukum Creek)

Chiwaukum Lake
(Ss.29,30;T.26N;R.16E)

A deep, rocky lake with timbered shores, about one mile long, occupying the pit of a hanging valley, Wenatchee National Forest, central Chelan County. It is in the course of Chiwaukum Creek near its head, between McCue Ridge and Glacier Creek. *(see* Chiwaukum Creek)

Chiwaukum Mountains
(T.26N;Rs.15,16E)

A Wenatchee National Forest mountain range, elevations over 8,100 ft., between Whitepine Creek and the headwaters of Chiwaukum Creek, with the crest running 8 miles north and northeast from Snowgrass Mountain to Nason Creek, southwest Chelan County. This ridge is higher than the main Cascade Mountains to the west. *(see* Chiwaukum Creek)

Chiwawa Mountain
(S.30;T.31N;R.16E.uns)

A very high mountain, towering to 8,300 ft., at Cascade Mountains summit, between Wenatchee and Okanogan national forests, on the boundary between Chelan and Snohomish counties. The name is an Indian word, which means "last canyon next to mountains."

Chiwawa Ridge
(Ts.28-30N;Rs.15,16E)

A very high ridge, elevations up to 8,400 ft., west of Chiwawa River, extending 20 miles southeast from Cascade Mountains summit to the vicinity of Wenatchee Lake, northwest Chelan County. It was named by U.S. Forest Supervisor A. H. Sylvester, following his method of naming ridges and ranges for adjacent streams. *(see* Chiwawa Mountain)

Chiwawa River
(Ts.27-31N;Rs.15-18E.partly uns)

The stream of the river rises on Cascade Mountains summit, Wenatchee National Forest, west central Chelan County; flows directly west of Glacier Peak, about 35 miles southeast, with many branches, to Wenatchee River, 5 miles southeast of Wenatchee Lake. It occupies a glacial valley, and drains a wide area of snow- and glacier-covered areas, which tower to altitudes up to 9,100 ft. *(see* Chiwawa Mountain)

Chocolate Creek
(Ts.30,31N;Rs.13,14E)

The stream of the creek rises on the east slope of Glacier Peak, directly north of Chocolate Glacier, northeast Snohomish County; flows 3 miles northeast to Suiattle River. It was named by The Mountaineers, for the chocolate-colored water discharged by the glacier during seasons of rapid melt.

Chocolate Glacier *(T.30N;Rs.13,14E)*

Glacier on the east slope of Glacier Peak, directly south of Chocolate Creek, northeast Snohomish County. (*see* Chocolate Creek)

Chopaka *(S.1;T.40N;R.24E)*

Settlement in Chopaka Valley, on Similkameen River, 21 miles northwest of Oroville, 1/4 mile south of the Canadian boundary, north central Okanogan County. On December 17, 1908, it was established as a post office. The settlement was almost obliterated on June 2, 1936, by a cloudburst. The name was adapted from the Indian word *Chopacca*, meaning "high mountain," which the Indians applied to Big Chopaka Mountain to the southwest.

Chopaka Creek *(Ts.39,40N;R.25E)*

The stream of the creek heads south of Little Chopaka Mountain; flows 9 miles southeast to Sinlahekin Creek, north central Okanogan County. In early days, it was the scene of mining activities. (*see* Chopaka)

Chopaka Lake
(S.33;T.40N;R.25E&S.4;T.39N;-R.25E)

A narrow, 1-1/2-mile-long lake, one mile west of Palmer Lake's west end, north central Okanogan County. It serves as an irrigation reservoir, and drains into Chopaka Creek. (*see* Chopaka)

Chopaka Valley *(T.40N;R.25E)*

A heavily-mineralized valley, extending 7 or 8 miles south and southeast along Similkameen River, from the Canadian boundary to Palmer Lake, north central Okanogan County. (*see* Chopaka)

Choral Creek *(T.30N;R.17E.uns)*

The stream of the creek rises on Gopher Mountain, Wenatchee National Forest, northwest Chelan County; flows between Snowbrushy Creek and Anthem Creek, 6 miles to Snowbrushy Creek, close to its confluence with Entiat River. It was named by U.S. Forest Supervisor A. H. Sylvester, who considered it a "singing stream."

Choral Lake *(S.18;T.30N;R.18E.uns)*

A very small, scenic mountain lake at head of Anthem Creek, directly south of Gopher Mountain, north central Chelan County. (*see* Choral Creek)

Chowder Ridge
(S.36;T.39N;R.7E&S.6;T.38N;-R.8E.uns)

A north slope ridge of Mt. Baker, on the southwest rim-wall of No Name Glacier, west central Whatcom County. In 1914, it was named by Charles F. Easton, when he conducted a party of politicians to the ridge and served them "mock chowder" from fossil shellfish.

Christine Falls *(Mt. Rainier National Park)*

A series of small, extremely scenic cataracts, elevation 3,367 ft., in Van Trump Creek, at the base of Cushman Crest, 11 miles east of Nisqually entrance, southwest area of the park. The name was selected by John Hayes of Yelm, Washington, to honor Christine Louise Van Trump, daughter of P. B. Van Trump, who made the first ascent of Mt. Rainier in 1870 with Hazard Stevens. (USBGN)

Christmas Creek (King County) *see* Boxley Creek

Christmas Lake *(S.34;T.23N;R.8E)*

An 8-acre lake near Cedar Falls, 1/2 mile east of Rattlesnake Lake, east central King County. It was named for the creek which drains it, locally known as Christmas Creek but officially named Boxley Creek. (*see* Boxley Creek)

Christopher *(S.1;T.21N;R.4E)*

A small settlement 1-1/2 miles north of Auburn, southwest King County. It was founded in 1863; and, when a post office was established in 1887, it was named for Thomas Christopher, a Norwegian who claimed 330 acres of land here.

Chromatic Moraine
(Ss.2,3;T.38N;R.7E.uns)

A northwest slope moraine of Mt. Baker, directly west of Bastile Ridge, Mt. Baker National Forest, east central Whatcom County. It actually consists of 2 terminal moraines from Roosevelt Glacier: one red and one gray-blue. It was named by mountain explorers because of its varied colors, which were in addition to the indigo-blue water in glacial potholes.

Chub Lake (King County) *see* Black Diamond Lake

Chuckanut Bay *(T.37N;R.2E)*

A crescent-shaped bay, about 3 miles long, directly south of Bellingham, at the southeast end of Bellingham Bay, southwest Whatcom County. Excellent oysters are produced in this bay. In 1791, it was named *Puerto del Socorro* by Lieut. Juan Francisco de Eliza. On December 1, 1852, the present name was chosen by Capt. Henry Roeder, who used the local Indian name meaning "long beach far from a narrow entrance."

Chuckanut Drive *(Ts.36,37N;Rs.2,3E)*

A 23-mile scenic drive skirting Bellingham Bay, from Bellingham, Whatcom County; extends south into Skagit County. (*see* Chuckanut Bay)

Chuckanut Lake *(S.19;T.37N;R.3E)*

A 2.4-acre lake 1/2 mile northeast of Chuckanut, southwest Whatcom County. (*see* Chuckanut Bay)

Chulta Peak (Mt. Rainier National Park) *see* Chutla Peak

Chumstick *(S.6;T.25N;R.18E)*

Camp site on Chumstick Creek, 7 miles north of Leavenworth, central Chelan County. The name, in use since pioneer days, is a Chinook jargon word, meaning "marked tree." Many old trails in this area may be followed by the "blazed" or marked trees along the original routes of travel.

Chumstick Creek *(Ts.24-26;R.18E)*

The stream of the creek heads 1-1/2 miles east of Plain, Wenatchee National Forest, central Chelan County; flows 12 miles south to Wenatchee River, east of Leavenworth. (*see* Chumstick)

Chumstick Mountain
(Ss.21,22;T.25N;R.19E)

A Wenatchee National Forest peak near the south extremity of Entiat Range, 8 miles west of Entiat, southeast Chelan County. It is used by U.S. Forest Service personnel for a forest fire lookout in season. In 1899, U.S. Forest Supervisor A. H. Sylvester established a triangulation station on the peak, and named the mountain for Chumstick Creek. (*see* Chumstick)

Church Creek *(T.23N;R.6W)*

The stream of the creek heads near Chapel Peak, Olympic National Forest, northwest Mason County; flows 3 miles northeast to South Fork, Skokomish River. (*see* Mt. Church)

Church Mountain (*T.40N;R.7E*)

One in a series of scenic mountain peaks with elevations up to 6,345 ft., 4 miles northeast of Glacier, 5 miles south of the Canadian boundary, north central Whatcom County. It was named by early settlers for a fancied resemblance to a cathedral.

Chute Creek (*T.34N;R.8E*)

The stream of the creek rises on Finney Peak, south central Skagit County; flows 2-1/2 miles north to Finney Creek, Mt. Baker National Forest. It was named by U.S. Forest Service personnel for an enormous quantity of supplies dropped here by parachute during a forest fire in 1938, when this creek was headquarters of the fire crew.

Chutes River (Thurston County) *see* Deschutes River

Chutla Peak (*Mt. Rainier National Park*)

Mountain south of Eagle Peak, 2-1/2 miles east of Longmire, south central zone of the park. The name is the original Nisqually Indian term for this peak, meaning "rock." It is erroneously listed in some records as *Chulta Peak*. (USBGN)

Cicero (*S.11;T.32N;R.6E*)

Once an important sawmill and shingle mill center, now a very small settlement surrounded by second-growth timber, 8 miles east of Arlington on North Fork, Stillaguamish River, north central Snohomish County. It was named by H. O. Siler, Newt Jones and C. D. Hills, for Mr. and Mrs. Stephen Cicero, pioneers, who operated a grocery and the local post office. When the first post office was established, it was named *Wana*, for John Wanamaker, postmaster. The community name had been *Hildebrand*, for Benton L. Hildebrand, operator of a ferry across Stillaguamish River. A later name was *Harmony*; no source for this name is on record.

Cinder Lake (*T.21N;R.6E*)

A small lake, covering 15 acres at high water and marshy at both ends, 1-1/2 miles north of Black Diamond, southwest King County. It was given its name by U.S. Geological Survey because it is in a large cinder bed, created by an old coal-mining operation. Local

people call it *Ginder Lake*, without any known reason.

Cinebar (*S.16;T.13N;R.3E*)

Settlement between Tilton River and Cinnabar Creek, 25 miles east of Chehalis, at the head of Shoestring Valley, central Lewis County. It was named for extensive *cinnabar* ore deposits, containing sulphide of mercury, which were mined here for many years.

Cinqpoil River (Ferry County) *see* Sanpoil River

Circle City (*S.28;T.40N;R.28E*)

Once a possible townsite on an abandoned railroad line, 4-1/2 miles south of the Canadian boundary, 5-1/2 miles east of Osoyoos Lake, north central Okanogan County. Local settlers state that the name was chosen because of the very wide circle in which the railroad was built in order to secure a reasonable grade in this rugged country.

Circle Creek (*T.32N;R.11E*)

The stream of the creek rises northwest of Crystal Lake, northwest Snohomish County; flows northwest in a wide, 6-mile semi-circle to Suiattle River. It was named by U.S. Forest Service personnel for its circular course.

Circle Peak (*S.36;T.32N;R.11E*)

Peak between Circle and Lime creeks, 2-1/2 miles south of Suiattle River, northeast Snohomish County. (*see* Circle Creek)

Circle Peak Lake (Snohomish County) *see* Indigo Lake

Cispus River (*Ts.10-12N;Rs.6-11E*)

The stream of the river rises in Goat Rocks Primitive Area, near Cascade Mountains summit, southeast Lewis County; flows southwest in a loop through northeast Skamania County, then northwest and west to Cowlitz River, 5 miles east of Kosmos.

Clallam Bay (*S.20;T.32N;R.12W*)

Village on the east shore of Clallam Bay, Strait of Juan de Fuca, northwest Clallam County. It was named for the bay, which was entered on British Admiralty Charts in 1846 by Capt. Henry Kellet as *Callam*, his Anglicized version of the Indian name. The name of the bay, as pronounced by Clallam Indians, might logically be *Kla-kla-wice*; however, Kellet attempted to reproduce the tribal name, which was S'klah-lam in Clallam dialect, or *Do-sklal-ob* in

Twana, meaning "big, strong nation."

Clallam Bay (*T.32N;R.12W*)

Bay at the mouth of Clallam River, on Strait of Juan de Fuca, northwest Clallam County. Sekiu, on the west shore, is a logging headquarters; Clallam, on the east shore, is a logging and fishing settlement. In 1790, it was named *Ensenada de Rojas* by Manuel Quimper, for Jose de Rojas, Conde de Casa Rojas, and a Rear Admiral in the Spanish navy. (USBGN) (*see* Clallam)

Clallam County

This county in northwest Washington is bounded on the north by the Strait of Juan de Fuca; on the east and south by Jefferson County; and on the west by Pacific Ocean. On April 26, 1854, it was created as *Clalm County* from part of Jefferson County by the Territorial Legislature. The major industries here are logging and fishing. (*see* Clallam)

Clallam Point (Clallam County) *see* Diamond Point

Clam Cove (King County) *see* Tahlequah

Claquato (*T.13N;R.3W*)

Community 3 miles southwest of Chehalis, on Skookumchuck River, west central Lewis County. It was one of the earliest settlements in this area, founded in 1852 by Louis H. Davis, who laid out the town and built a courthouse. A church, built in 1856, still stands. When bypassed by the railroad in 1873, the county seat, as well as most of the inhabitants, moved from here to Chehalis. The Indian name, chosen by the Davis family, means "open space at top of hill."

Clark County

This county in southwest Washington is bounded on the north by Cowlitz County; on the east by Skamania County; and on the south and west by Columbia River. It was the first county established in the state. On December 21, 1845, it was founded as the *County of Vancouver* by the Oregon Territorial Legislature. On September 3, 1849, the same body changed the name to *Clark*, to honor Capt. William Clark of the Lewis & Clark Expedition. In 1854, at the first session of Washington Territorial Legislature, the name of this county was entered in the record as *Clarke*. That spelling persisted in records and maps until corrected on December 23, 1925, by official act of Washington State Legislature.

Clark Island *(T.37N;R.1W)*

The largest of an island group, with Barnes Island and several islets, in Strait of Georgia, 1-1/2 miles northeast of the northeast shore of Orcas Island, northeast San Juan County. In 1791, the island group was named *Islas de Aguayo* by Lieut. Juan Francisco de Eliza, who used one the Viceroy of Mexico's many names. The name of this island, as presently recognized, was applied in 1841 by Cmdr. Charles Wilkes, for Midshipman John Clark, who was killed in the battle of Lake Erie in the War of 1812. Wilkes had actually named it *Clark's Island*, but the possessive form was dropped on subsequent charts.

Clark Lake (Stevens County) *see* Charles Lake

Clark Lock and Dam (Columbia, Whitman counties) *see* Little Goose Dam

Clark Mountain *(T.30N;R.15E.uns)*

A high, scenic mountain supporting 3 glaciers, elevation 8,520 ft., 3 miles southeast of Cascade Mountains summit, between the headwaters of White and Napeequa rivers, Wenatchee National Forest, northwest Chelan County. It was named by A. H. Sylvester for a lumberman from the state of Maine; Clark was the father-in-law of W. Stanley Carne, for whom Carne Mountain was named.

Clark Point *(S.26;T.36N;R.1E)*

A north end point of Guemes Island, in Samish Bay, northwest Skagit County. In 1841, this feature was named *Clark's Point* by Cmdr. Charles Wilkes, for Levin Clark, captain-of-the-top in one of the expedition's ships. The shortened form is now generally accepted.

Clark Reservoir *(S.26;T.2N;R.3E)*

A small 1-acre pond 3 miles north of Camas, southeast Clark County. It is used for irrigation, and drains into Lackamas Lake. (*see* Clark County)

Clarke Lake (Stevens County) *see* Charles Lake

Clarks Lake (Pierce County) *see* Herron Lake

Clarkston *(T.11N;R.46E)*

Town across Snake River from Lewiston, Idaho, extreme northeast Asotin County. In 1863, a ferry was es-tablished here by William Craig, a settler who had served in the Indian wars of 1855. In 1896, the town was platted under the name of Lewiston by Lewiston Water & Power Company; and, in 1897, the company built a bridge across Snake River. This name was frequently confused with Lewiston, Idaho, directly across the Snake River from the Washington town of the same name. Prior to 1900, the post office was called *Concord*, the choice of irrigation promoters, who came from Concord, Massachusetts. On January 1, 1900, the post office name was changed to *Clarkston* as a result of a citizen's petition, to end confusion, and to honor Capt. William Clark of the 1804-1806 Lewis & Clark Expedition. Uniformity was achieved in 1901, when the State Legislature enacted a bill which changed the town's name officially to Clarkston. In 1861, Clark's associate, Capt. Meriwether Lewis, was honored in the naming of Lewiston, Idaho, directly across the river.

Classet *(S.6;T.33N;R.15W)*

A fishing village on Makah Indian Reservation, Strait of Juan de Fuca, 3 miles east of Cape Flattery, extreme northwest Clallam County. The village retains its Indian name, which has also been spelled *Claaset* and *Clisseet* in historical journals.

Claxton, Claxten (Lincoln County) *see* Clasten

Clay Pit Pond (Whatcom County) *see* Brennan Pond

Clay River (Asotin County) *see* Grand Ronde River

Clayton *(S.19;T.29N;R.42E)*

Community 3 miles southeast of Loon Lake, 32 miles northwest of Spokane, southeast Stevens County. Founded in 1889, when the Spokane Falls & Northern Railway was built through the area, its excellent clay deposits supply the Washington Brick, Lime & Manufacturing Company plant. Many types of ceramic materials have been produced. At one time the brick plant here was the largest in the state. The name, chosen by local residents, indicates the great importance of clay to local industry.

Clealum (Kittitas County) *see* Cle Elum

Clear Creek *(Ts.26,27N;Rs.17,18E)*

The stream of the creek heads on the west slope of Entiat Mountain, south of Maverick Peak on Wenatchee National Forest, northwest Chelan County; flows 3 miles southwest to Chiwawa River. The name, used since pioneer days, is not an unusual title for mountain streams in the Pacific northwest; and in this case, it is quite appropriate.

Clear Creek *(Ts.30-32N;Rs.9,10E)*

The stream of the creek rises 10 miles south of Darrington, Mt. Baker National Forest, east central Snohomish County; flows 9 miles north by east to Sauk River. This very common name was used by early prospectors and has been adopted by the U.S. Forest Service.

Clear Lake (Thurston County) *see* McIntosh Lake

Clear Lake *(Ss.6,7;T.34N;R.5E;Ss.1,-12;T.34N;R.4E)*

A lake in west central Skagit County, 2 miles south of Sedro Woolley. (*see* Clear Lake -- town)

Clear Lake *(S.23;T.36N;R.9E)*

A 19-acre lake, elevation 4,057 ft., 8 miles northeast of Concrete, north central Skagit County. This lake should not be confused with one by the same name which is 2-1/2 miles south of Sedro-Woolley. Most mountain lakes are quite clear and this one is no exception.

Clear Lake *(Ss.1,2;T.34N;R.4E)*

Formerly an important sawmill town on the west side of Clear lake, 2 miles south of Sedro-Woolley. The town faded when Clear Lake Lumber Company sold its remaining timber to a paper and pulp corporation. The name is reasonably descriptive, now that it is no longer used for extensive storage of sawlogs. An early name was *Mountain View*.

Clear Lake *(Ss.30,31;T.24N;R.41E;-S.36;T.24N;R.40E)*

A narrow, 1-1/2-mile-long lake, 1-1/2 miles south of Medical Lake, west central Spokane County. It was named by W. F. Basset, a local resident, for the clarity of its water.

Clear Lake *(S.6;T.15N;S.31;T.16N;R.3E)*

A roughly triangular lake in the bald hills region, 10 miles southeast of Yelm, southeast Thurston County. It is 3/4 mile long and covers 172.8 acres. This lake should not be confused with a lake near McIntosh called Clear Lake as an alternative to McIntosh Lake.

Clear Lake (No. 1) *(S.31;T.16N;R.1W)*

A 3/4-mile-long, triangular lake, 7 miles west of Lagrande, southeast Thurston County. This lake, like many others in the state, has been saddled with a name so common that the feature loses its identity.

Clear Lake (No. 2) *(Ss.13,14,23;T.16N;R.1W)*

A lake directly north of McIntosh, south central Thurston County. Just another Clear Lake, of which there are a great many in this state.

Clearwater *(S.19;T.24N;R.12W)*

Settlement on Clearwater River, 1-1/2 miles north of Quinault Indian Reservation, southwest Jefferson County. It borrowed this name from the river on which it is located.

Clearwater Creek *(Ts.38,39N;Rs.6,7E)*

A north tributary of Middle Fork, Nooksack River, west of Mt. Baker, central Whatcom County. It was named *Clear Water Creek* on August 12, 1868, by Edmund T. Coleman, who evidently found the water not as milky as most streams that drained from Mt. Baker.

Cle Elum *(Ss.26,27;T.20N;R.15E)*

Settlement at the junction of Cle Elum and Yakima rivers, at the head of Yakima Valley and foot of Cascade Mountain range, west central Kittitas County. The first settlement here was in 1870 by Thomas Gambel, a prospector, who deferred making a land claim until 1883. Walter J. Reed and Thomas Johnson platted a 650 acre townsite after coal deposits had been discovered in 1886, when a railway came through. Northern Pacific Railway officials named the station *Clealum* after the Indian name of *Tle-el-Lum*, which means "swift water," and which refers to the Cle Elum River. In 1908, they altered the name to its present form. An earlier name, of which little record exists, was *Samahma*.

Cle Elum Lake *(Ts.20,21N;R.14E)*

An 8-mile-long lake, 1 mile average width, 9 miles northwest of Cle Elum, northwest Kittitas County. A dam at the southeast end controls the water level for irrigation purposes. In prehistoric times, a glacial moraine formed the lake by blocking the flow of a river. (*see* Cle Elum)

Cle Elum River *(Ts.20-24N;Rs.14,15E)*

The stream of the river rises in Hyak Lake, directly east of Cascade Mountain summit, extreme north end of Kittitas County; flows 28 miles southeast and south through Cle Elum Lake to Yakima River at South Cle Elum. (*see* Cle Elum)

Cleman Mountains *(Ts.15,16N;Rs.15-17E)*

This 15-1/2-mile-long ridge, elevation 4,944 ft., rises 2 miles northeast of Nile, north central Yakima County; extends southeast and east to point 4 miles north of Naches. The range was named in 1868 for a settler here, Auguston Cleman, who was an invalid, and who loaned money to stockmen. He also owned a large number of sheep.

Clements Reef *(T.38N;R.2W)*

A submerged reef in Strait of Georgia, less than 1 mile north of Sucia Island, extreme northern area of the San Juan Archipelago, San Juan County. It is a danger to local navigation. When charted by Capt. Henry Richards of the British Admiralty Survey in 1858, no name source was given in his records.

Cleveland *(S.30;T.6N;R.20E)*

Small settlement at head of Wood Gulch, 3 miles southwest of Bickleton, northeast Klickitat County. It was named for Grover Cleveland, 22nd and 24th president of the United States, when a post office was established shortly after Cleveland's first inauguration in 1885.

Cliff (Franklin County) *see* Cactus

Cliff Island *(S.34;T.36N;R.3W)*

A small island directly west of the northwest tip of Shaw Island, in Wasp Pass, central San Juan County. It has a lighthouse on the high point of its cliffs. In 1859, this descriptive name was charted by Capt. Henry Richards of British Admiralty Survey.

Cliff Lake *(Mt. Rainier National Park)*

A small, high lake near the west end of Tatoosh Range, 1/3 mile southwest of Lane Peak, south central area of the park. It drains into Butter Creek, about 3 miles east of Longmire and covers about 5-1/2 acres, elevation 5,100 ft. This descriptive name is said to have been applied by park packers in the early days of the park's establishment.

Cliff Point *(S.18;T.9N;R.9E)*

Village 1 mile northeast of Megler, on Columbia River, southwest Pacific county. It was named by early settlers because of a high, steep cliff at the Columbia River shore.

Cliffdell *(S.23;T.17N;R.14E)*

Town on north bank of Naches River, 39 miles northwest of Yakima, extreme southwest Kittitas County. The original name was *Spring Flats*. In 1923, when it was platted by Russell Davidson, the present name was chosen as a pleasant appellation for a somewhat exclusive river resort.

Cliffs *(S.30;T.3N;R.17E)*

Railroad station on north bank of Columbia River, 5 miles east of Maryhill, south central Klickitat County. The St. Paul & Spokane Railway named their station at this point for a series of cliffs along the river.

Cline *(S.27;T.30N;R.40E)*

This townsite, not shown on recent maps, was on Colville River, 1 mile north of Springdale, south central Stevens County. It was named for John James Orlando Cline, agent at Springdale for the Spokane Falls & Northern Railway for 20 years.

Clinton *(S.19;T.29N;R.4E)*

Community near the southeast point of Whidbey Island, directly north of Columbia Beach on Possession Sound, south Island County. It was named for Clinton County, Iowa, by Edward C. Hinman who came here from Iowa in 1883 and filed a timber claim. He built a hotel and a steamer landing, supplying steam vessels with wood and water. In the 1880s, a post office was established 2 miles from Clinton and was called *Phinney* for a Seattle land promoter. In the 1890s, it was moved to Clinton and assumed the name of this town.

Clipper *(S.20;T.38N;R.5E)*

Formerly a shingle-manufacturing center, now an area of small farms, 7 miles east of Lake Whatcom, north central Whatcom County. In 1900, the town was named for the Clipper Shingle Company which had a mill here, by James A. McDonald and James Peterson.

Clisseet (Clallam County) *see* Classe

Cloquallum *(S.16;T.19N;R.5W)*

Small settlement and school, 12 miles southwest of Shelton, southwest

Mason County. Local name is *Buck Prairie.* (see Cloquallum Creek)

Cloquallum Creek
(Ts.18,19N;Rs.5,6W)

The stream of the creek rises in Lystair Lake, southwest Mason county; flows 21 miles southwest through Grays Harbor County to Chehalis River, near Elma. In 1841, the Wilkes Expedition borrowed from the word *Klu-kwe-li-ub*, which was the Chehalis tribe's name for the Quillayute Indians. First 3 syllables refer to a dance performed by members of a secret society in order to gain magic power in war expeditions, and the last syllable means: "the people of." Literal translation might be: "the people of a dangerous Being, charged with magic." Wilkes charted the name as *Kluckullum.*

Cloudy Lake *(S.8;T.24N;R.13E)*

A glacier-fed lake on Snoqualmie National Forest, 2 miles west of Cascade Mountain summit, northeast King County. The name was applied because the lake is very turbid or cloudy.

Cloudy Pass *(S.18;T.31N;R.15E.uns)*

This pass, just east of the Cascade Mountain summit, is 3 miles south of Suiattle Pass, between northeast Snohomish and northwest Chelan County (although within Chelan County). The altitude is 6,500 ft., and the cloud cap here is the usual condition at most times of the year. Thus, the name is descriptive for this area, as well as for much of the adjacent high valley.

Clover Creek *(T.19N;R.2E)*

The stream of the creek rises near the north boundary of Ft. Lewis Army Post, northwest Pierce County; flows 2 miles northwest to Steilacoom Lake. It was named by Christopher Mahon, who took a Donation Land Claim here in the 1850s, because wild clover was abundant along the creek.

Cloverdale *(S.22;T.8N;R.27E)*

This post office was in the Horse Heaven Hills, 12 miles west by south of Kennewick, south central Benton County. Until 1903, it was operated by the family of Nathaniel Travis, who selected this flowery name.

Clover Lake *(Mt. Rainier National Park)*

A 9-acre lake, elevation 5,728 ft., in White River Park at the head of Sunrise Creek, northeast quarter of the park. In

1913, it was named by William O. Tufts, a topographic engineer, for a fancied resemblance of its shape to that of a clover leaf. (USBGN)

Cloverland *(S.13;T.9N;R.44E)*

Community 12-1/2 miles southwest of Clarkston, central Asotin County. In 1902, a townsite was platted and a post office established soon thereafter. The name of the post office was selected by local ranchers who expected to raise excellent crops of hay, grain, and fruit under irrigation.

Clugston Creek *(Ts.36-37N;R.39E)*

The stream of the creek rises on the west side of Gillette Mountain, Stevens County; flows southwest 9 miles, then sinks a short distance southeast of Echo. It was named for an early settler and prospector, William Clugston. Some early maps carry it as *Clagston Creek.* The Clugston Creek Mining District, including the Tenderfoot Mine, was a producer of silver-lead ore, and was also a prospect for iron ore.

Coal Bay *(Skagit County) see* Colby

Coal Canyon *(S.25;T.13N;R.4E)*

A ghost town, 4 miles northeast of Morton, central Lewis County. In 1911, the town was founded by Gustaf Lindberg of Tacoma, who installed a shingle mill, sawmill, and logging camp. In 1917, he added a store, schoolhouse, and 15 brick residences. In 1918, it was burned, rebuilt, and then named *Lindberg.* Lindberg lost his ownership through financial reverses and the name was changed to *Millberg* for the new owner whose name was Miller. Later the name was changed to the present designation by local influence. In addition to these 3 names, the place was called *Glenavon* originally by officials of Tacoma & Eastern Railway.

Coal Creek *(T.24N;R.5E)*

The head of this small creek rises 3 miles west of Issaquah, west central King County; flows 7 miles northeast to Lake Washington, south of Mercer Slough. It should not be confused with the Coal Creek located northeast of Enumclaw. The name is appropriate, as the creek flows through the famous Newcastle coal mining area which was once heavily productive.

Coal Creek *(Ts.20,21N;R.7E)*

The stream of the creek rises on the northwest slope of Grass Mountain,

south of Kanaskat, south central King County; flows 9 miles west into Fish Lake. It should not be confused with Coal Creek located west of Issaquah. The stream was named for extensive coal deposits along its course. An alternate name is *Cumberland Creek.*

Coal Creek *(S.28;T.39N;R.7E)*

The stream of the creek rises in an anthracite field, 4 miles southeast of Glacier, north central Whatcom County; flows 1 mile east to Glacier Creek. It was locally named for its origin in an area of low-grade anthracite coal. It should not be confused with 2 other creeks by the same name in this general area.

Coal Creek *(Ts.39,40N;R.5E)*

The stream of the creek rises in Paradise Valley on the southeast slope of Sumas Mountain, north central Whatcom County; flows 4 miles southeast to North Fork, Nooksack River. It was locally named because of outcroppings of anthracite coal along its course. It should not be confused with other creeks by this same name in Whatcom County.

Coal Creek *(T.40N;R.7E)*

The stream of the creek rises on Church Mountain, north central Whatcom County; flows 1-1/2 miles southwest to North Fork, Nooksack River, 2-1/2 miles northeast of Glacier. It was locally named for outcroppings of anthracite coal. This creek should not be confused with 2 others of the same name, one rising on Sumas Mountain, the other rising southeast of Glacier.

Coal Lake *(S.3;T.30N;R.10E)*

A 6.1-acre lake, elevation 3,420 ft., 4 miles northeast of Silverton, near the head of Coal Creek, Mt. Baker National Forest, central Snohomish County. The name developed by local usage, as the lake is at the head of one fork of Coal Creek.

Coal Mountain *(S.20;T.34N;R.7E)*

A Mt. Baker National Forest mountain, elevation 4,317 ft., 7 miles south of Hamilton, west central Skagit County. It is named because of heavy coal deposits, but little actual mining has been done.

Coat Mountain *(Chelan County) see* Crook Mountain

Cockeye Creek *(T.28N;R.15E.uns)*

The stream of this short creek rises near Irving Peak on Wenatchee Ridge, 7 miles east of Cascade Summit; flows

2-1/2 miles northwest and northeast to Panther Creek, Wenatchee National Forest, northwest Chelan County. In 1923, the name was applied by a U.S. Forest Service trail foreman, Carl Hardman, for what he termed a "cockeyed trip" to this area in order to control a forest fire.

Coco Mountain *(S.36;T.36N;R.31E)*

This 5,141-ft. peak is on Colville National Forest, on the outskirts of the Republic Mining district, on the border between east central Okanogan County and west central Ferry County, 6 miles east by north of Aeneas. It was named by Forest Service personnel as the result of a fire report by a lady lookout, Bernadine Moran. When Moran spotted the fire, she saw that its location on her map coincided with the county abbreviation symbols *Co.Co*, separated by the county line. She therefore reported the fire to be on Coco Mountain!

Coffin Rock *(T.8N;R.5W)*

A wooded promontory, formerly used for Indian burials, on the north bank of Columbia River, 18-1/2 miles west of Longview, southeast Wahkiakum County. This feature was locally named for many Indian burials, which were in dugout canoes, hung from cottonwood trees.

Cohasset *(S.13;T.16N;R.12W)*

An oceanside resort on Pacific Ocean, 1 mile west of South Bay, extreme southwest Grays Harbor County. In 1892, it was named by John Wooding, an Aberdeen banker, for a pleasant trip which he took to Cohasset, Massachusetts.

Cohasset *(S.29;T.16N;R.23E)*

Town 7 miles south of Vantage, near the west bank of Columbia River, extreme southeast Kittitas County. The first name of this town was *Ashby*. In the early 1920s, officials of Chicago, Milwaukee & St. Paul Railway changed the name to that of a resort town in Massachusetts. At the time there was a town with the same name on Grays Harbor, but it was not a railroad point and therefore not apt to cause confusion in rail shipments.

Cohassett Lake *(S.13;T.16N;R.12W)*

A shallow lake, slightly less than 1 acre, 1 mile south of Westport, southwest Grays Harbor County. It is named for Cohasset. An alternate name is *Westport Lake. (see* Cohassett)

Coke Creek *(Clallam County) see* Lamb Creek

Cokedale *(S.9;T.35N;R.5E)*

Community 4 miles northeast of Sedro-Woolley, west central Skagit County. The area has quantities of coking coal and iron ore; coal mines operated here from 1892 until 1902. It was named for coke production in the past.

Coker *(S.8;T.19N;R.36E)*

Railway station 3 miles northeast of Ritzville, northeast Adams County. In 1905, the Northern Pacific Railway Company called it *Moore*, but changed the station to the present name in 1909. Both names are reported to be for local ranchers.

Colbert *(S.23;T.27N;R.43E)*

Community on Little Spokane River, 8 miles north of Spokane's north city limits, north central Spokane County. It was named for a local sawmill owner and operator. In the early 1900s, it is reported to have had 5 sawmills, 3 livery stables, 2 saloons, and 2 blacksmith shops. The timber available was cut out rapidly, and the town declined to a few residents who farm.

Colbia *(Benton County) see* Berrian

Colby *(Ss.27,28;T.24N;R.2E)*

Settlement on Yukon Harbor, 2 miles west of Blake Island, east central Kitsap County. In 1884, it was named *Coal Bay*, when traces of coal were discovered near here. That name was later shortened to its present form.

Cold Basin *(Mt. Rainier National Park)*

Small mountain basin, elevation 5,100 ft., directly south of Grand Park at the foot of Sourdough Mountain, north central area of the park. This descriptive name was chosen by early campers according to local informants. The official name is not *Gold Basin*, as carried in some records. (USBGN)

Cold Spring *(Columbia County) see* Gilbreath Spring

Cold Spring Lake *(Cowlitz County) see* Blue Lake

Cole's Point *(San Juan County) see* Point Doughty

Cole Point *(S.9;T.19N;R.1E)*

A southeast point of Anderson Island, on Nisqually Reach, northwest

Pierce County. It was placed on British admiralty charts in 1846 by Capt. R. N. Inskip to honor Edmund P. Cole, master of *HMS Fisgard*.

Coleman *(S.31;T.24N;R.5E)*

Small community on the southeast shore of Lake Washington, 1-1/2 miles north of Renton, west central King County. It is shown on certain county maps, in error, as *Colman. (see* Coleman Point)

Coleman Creek
(Ts.17-20N;Rs.19,20E)

The stream of the creek heads at the south slope of Wenatchee Mountains; flows 24 miles south by west to Yakima River near Thrall, east central Kittitas County. The creek was named for the C. C. Coleman family who settled on the stream in 1870. *Altapus*, a name for the creek on very early maps, was evidently the Indian name for a portion of the stream.

Coleman Glacier *(T.38N;R.7E.uns)*

A large glacier which feeds Glacier Creek, on the slope of Mt. Baker, Mt. Baker National Forest, south central Whatcom County. (see Coleman Peak)

Coleman Peak
(Ss.34,35;T.39N;R.8E.uns)

A Mt. Baker National Forest peak on the northeast spur of Mt. Baker, on the divide between Wells and Swift creeks, Whatcom County. It was named for Edmund T. Coleman of the Mazamas, who first ascended the mountain to its summit.

Coleman Point *(S.31;T.24N;R.5E)*

A southeast shore point of Lake Washington, 1-1/2 miles north of Renton, west central King County. It was named for James E. Coleman, who settled here in early days, and who was shot in an ambush on February 6, 1886.

Colfax *(S.14;T.16N;R.43E)*

A wheat town in Palouse Valley, on both sides of Palouse River, 13 miles northwest of Pullman, Whitman County. It was a rough-and-tumble cattle center until the late 1880s. In 1870, the first settlement was established by J. A. Perkins under the name *Belleville*. In 1872, when the town was platted, the name was changed to honor Schuyler Colfax, vice-president of the U. S. during the first term of President U. S. Grant.

Colfax Peak *(T.38N;R.7E)*

A Mt. Baker National Forest peak (one of the Black Buttes group) on the southwest slope of Mt. Baker at the head of Middle Fork, Nooksack River, Whatcom County. In 1868, it was named by Edmund T. Coleman. (see Colfax)

College Place *(Ss.35,36;T.7N;R.35E)*

Town 3 miles west of Walla Walla, south central Walla Walla County. In 1892, the name was applied when a settlement grew around a college established by Seventh Day Adventists.

Collins Overland Telegraph *(Washington State Ref./Western Washington/Canada/Alaska) see* Telegraph Road

Colman (King County) *see* Coleman

Colonel Bob Mountain
(Ss.7,18;T.23N;R.8W.uns)

A snow-capped peak, elevation 4,500 ft., 8 miles east of Quinault on Olympic National Forest, northeast Grays Harbor County. It was named for Col. Robert G. Ingersoll by Joseph N. Locke on July 23, 1893. Locke actually named the peak *Mt. Ingersoll*, but the present form became official because it was universally used by local residents. Locke chose the name because the mountain "stood alone and high, like Col. Ingersoll." (USBGN)

Colonnade Cliff *(Mt. Rainier National Park)*

A columnar basalt cliff along the lower end of South Mowich Glacier, northwest quarter of the park. The name is for the columnar structure of the rock. (USBGN)

Colquhoun Mountain
(S.18;T.19N;R.11E)

A Huckleberry Mountain Ridge mountain, 3 miles northwest of Pyramid Peak, extreme southeast corner of King County. It was named by the owner of a summer home near the peak, for his son who drowned in a nearby pool.

Colton *(S.34;T.13N;R.45E)*

Town on Union Flat, 11 miles south of Pullman, southeast Whitman County. In 1879, a settlement started here and a town plat was filed by Gregor Koshir on November 7, 1881. The name on the plat was in honor of Dr. J. A. Cole, who helped the town secure a post office and a school.

Columbia Barracks (Clark County) *see* Ft. Vancouver

Columbia Beach *(S.30;T.29N;R.4E)*

A Whidbey Island beach near the southeast tip of the island, on Possession Sound, 5 miles north of Possession Point, south Island County. The name is reported to have been chosen by early settlers in the area, for an early nickname of the U.S., "Columbia, the gem of the ocean."

Columbia Center *(S.10;T.10N;R.42E)*

Community 8 miles south of Pomeroy, central Garfield County. On December 26, 1877, it was started when Thomas C. Bean and Andrew Blackman platted a townsite. At that time the townsite was in the center of Columbia County, which then comprised the present areas of Columbia, Garfield, and Asotin counties. Therefore, the descriptive name. It was also known as *Vernon.*

Columbia City *(T.24N;R.4E)*

Part of Seattle on the west shore of Lake Washington, in the Rainier Valley district, between The Uplands and Mt. Baker neighborhood, King County. In 1890, it was founded as a separate town, but with the southward expansion of Seattle, it has become part of the city. When Bowman & Rochester platted the town, they named it for the nickname of the U.S.

Columbia County

An 860-sq.-mile county in southeast Washington state; bounded on north by Whitman County, on east by Garfield County; on south by Oregon and on west by Walla Walla County. It is devoted principally to production of wheat, peas, and wool. On November 11, 1875, the county was established by the Territorial Legislature through the influence of delegate Elisha Ping. The Territorial governor had previously vetoed a bill which would have named the county for Ping. The name chosen was after that of Columbia River. The area had previously been part of Walla Walla County.

Concord (Asotin County) *see* Clarkston

Concrete *(S.10;T.35N;R.8E)*

Town on Skagit River at the mouth of Baker River, north central Skagit County. Since 1905, the town has produced very large amounts of Portland cement. In 1890, the place was named *Baker* for Baker River, by Magnus Miller. In 1905, when the cement plant was installed, the name used was *Cement City.* In 1909, when the town was incorporated, it chose the present name.

Cone Hill (Skagit County) *see* Eagle Cliff

Cone Islands *(S.21;T.36N;R.1E)*

A group of 3 small islands (the most westerly of which is called *Buttonhole Island*) in Bellingham Channel, off the northeast coast of Cypress Island, northwest Skagit County. In 1841, the name was applied by the Wilkes Expedition and is vaguely descriptive of the shapes of these islets.

Connell *(S.36;T.14N;R.31E)*

Railroad town, 36 miles northeast of Pasco, north central Franklin County. In 1883, when established by the Northern Pacific Railway Company, it was named *Palouse Junction.* In 1888, the name was changed to honor a former station agent at this point.

Connelly Creek *(T.13N;R.4E)*

The stream of the creek rises on Bergen Mountain, central Lewis County; flows 4-1/2 miles southeast to Tilton River near Morton. The stream was named locally for a bachelor homesteader.

Connor Gulch *(Ts.10,11N;Rs.43-45E)*

The gulch starts in northwest Asotin County, near the boundary of Garfield County; trends northeast to a point near the junction of Alpowa Creek with Snake River. It is a dry gulch, except that Page Creek follows its course and carries some water in season. It was named for a man who claimed land here in 1871 -- the first claimant along the gulch.

Connor Gulch (Asotin County) *see* Page Creek

Connors Prairie *(T.18N;R.1W)*

Prairie directly north of Chambers Prairie, north central Thurston County. The name was chosen by early settlers for the Joseph Conner family, owners of a Donation Land Claim on the prairie in 1851.

Conrad (Whatcom County) *see* Blaine

Conrad Creek *(T.12N;Rs.11,12E)*

The stream of the creek rises in Goat Rocks, east of Cascade Mountain summit, Snoqualmie National Forest, northwest Yakima County; flows 7-1/2 miles east to South Fork, Tieton River. The creek was named for a horse-and-cattle rancher who once used this range.

Conrad Creek *(T.32N;Rs.10,11E)*

The stream of the creek rises 6 miles east of Darington on Mt. Baker National Forest, north central Snohomish County; flows 4-1/2 miles northeast to Suiattle River. It was locally named for Jimmy Conrad, an Indian who had a government allotment of land at the creek's mouth in 1911.

Conrad Meadows *(S.27;T.12N;R.12E)*

A marshy, mountain meadow on Conrad Creek, Snoqualmie National Forest, 5 miles east of Goat Rocks summit, west central Yakima County. (*see* Conrad Creek)

Contractors Point (Jefferson County) *see* Carr Point

Conway *(S.18;T.33N;R.4E)*

Formerly a shingle manufacturing center, now a community of small farms on Skagit Delta, 4-1/2 miles south of Mt. Vernon, southwest Skagit County. The town was named for an early shingle mill operator.

Cook *(S.27;T.3N;R.9E)*

Community on north bank of Columbia River, 7 miles west of White Salmon, near the mouth of Little White Salmon River, southeast Skamania County. In the days of stern-wheelers on the river, this was a busy landing. The name is for Charles A. Cook, who homesteaded the ground on which the town was built. It was applied to the post office when suggested by the first postmaster, S. R. Harris.

Cook Creek *(Ts.18-20N;R.20E)*

The stream of the creek heads on east slope of Wenatchee Mountains, east central Kittitas County; flows 15 miles south by west to Caribou Creek. The first land claim on the creek was by the C. P. Cook family in 1870, for whom the creek was later named. Prior to settlement, the valley was a popular place for camas digging by Indians. The Indian name for the creek and valley was *Put-Chem-Nee* of *Pach-Un-Me*, meaning ''plenty'' as related to the supply of their favorite root food.

Cook Point *(T.20N;R.2W)*

An entrance point to Hammersley Inlet, southeast Mason County. In 1841, it was named by Cmdr. Charles Wilkes for a member of his crew. The name does not appear on recent maps or charts.

Cool Creek *(S.4;T.30N;R.17E.uns)*

This short stream rises in Entiat Meadows on Wenatchee National Forest, northwest Chelan County; flows 3 miles southeast to Entiat River. It was named by U.S. Forest Supervisor A. H. Sylvester, not for the water temperature, but for Tom Cool, a prospector who had claims along the creek.

Coolidge *(S.13;T.25N;R.26E)*

Projected town on north bank of Columbia River, 26 miles southwest of Kennewick, south central Benton County. In 1916, the town was launched by land promoters who selected the name. It might have been named for Calvin Coolidge, who at that time was Lieut. Governor of Massachusetts. This appears to be rather doubtful, however, as he had not then come into national prominence.

Coon Island *(T.36N;R.3W)*

A part of the Wasp Island group, directly west of McConnell Island, at the west entrance to Wasp Pass, central San Juan County. The name was locally chosen. Henry Tusler, Comm. of the Coon Island Yacht Club, calls it *Isle de Raton Laveur*. The latter name is unofficial, however.

Coon Lake *(S.24;T.22N;R.1W)*

An 18.4-acre private lake, quite shallow, 1-3/4 miles east of Allyn, east central Mason County. Racoons aren't as plentiful around the lake as they were in the past, but there are enough of them to make the name appropriate.

Cooper Point *(S.10;T.19N;R.2W)*

A long, sandy spit, pointing due north, on the north end of a peninsula separating Budd Inlet and Eld Inlet, extreme north Thurston County. In 1841, this feature was named *Point Cooper* for John Cooper, an armorer with the Wilkes Expedition. The reversal in the name is evidently a cartographer's error.

Cooper Point (San Juan County) *see* McCracken Point

Copalis *(S.27;T.19N;R.12W)*

A center of cranberrry culture on Pacific Ocean at the mouth of Copalis River, southwest Grays Harbor County. The name is from the Indian term for this place, *Che-pa-lis*, meaning ''opposite the rock.'' Copalis rock is offshore and 2 miles north of Copalis.

Copalis Crossing
(S.20;T.19N;R.11W)

A very small settlement, 12 miles northwest of Hoquiam at a highway intersection, west central Grays Harbor County. It was named for the Copalis tribe of Indians who frequented the area. (*see* Copalis)

Copalis Head *(S.16;T.19N;R.12W)*

A prominent headland on the Pacific Ocean coast, 2 miles north of Copalis River mouth, southwest Grays Harbor County. (*see* Copalis)

Copalis River *(Ts.19-21N;Rs.10-12W)*

The stream of the river rises near the south boundary of Quinault Indian Reservation, west central Grays Harbor County; flows 18 miles southwesterly to Pacific Ocean at Copalis. (*see* Copalis)

Copalis Rock *(S.9;T.19N;R.12W)*

A small rock island in Pacific Ocean, just offshore, between Iron Springs and Copalis Head, southwest Grays Harbor County. (*see* Copalis)

Copalus River (Pacific County) *see* Palix River

Cora Lake (Lewis County) *see* Lake Tannamus

Coppei *(S.36;T.9N;R.37E)*

A much-diminished settlement, 3-1/2 miles south of Waitsburg on Coppei Creek, southeast Walla Walla County. In 1861, it was started when Anderson Cox claimed land here. Others came and a post office was established in January, 1863. In 1865, the town faded when many of the settlers moved to Waitsburg. The name was adopted from that of the creek on which the town was located. The Indian name was *Kap-Y-O.*

Coppei Creek *(Ts.7-9N;Rs.37,38E)*

The stream of the creek rises in the foothills of Blue Mountains in extreme southeast Walla Walla County; flows north by west about 15 miles to Touchet River at Waitsburg. This stream was recorded by Lewis and Clark on May 2, 1806, and was called *Gamblers Creek*. The name did not come into general use and the Indian name was adopted. (*see* Coppei)

Copper City *(S.7;T.27N;R.3)*

A mining ghost town at headwaters of *Big Quilcene* and *Dungeness rivers*, near *Iron Mountain* in Olympic Primitive Area, east central Jefferson County. Some parts of the buildings now remain. In the early 1900s, it was built at the *Tubal*

Cain mine, but had no access except by pack trail along the *Big Quilcene River* It was named for the large quanity of copper ore in the adjacent mountain. But it was hardly a city.

Copper City *(S.19;T.15N;R.12E.uns)*

Ghost town on Deep Creek, southeast of Miners Ridge, 4 miles east of Cascade Mountain summit, northwest Yakima County. The name refers to a copper concentrator and smelter which at one time operated here during 9 months of each year.

Copper Lake *(S.3;T.24N;R.12E)*

Small 1/2-mile-long lake, 148 acres, at the head of West Fork, Foss River, 8 miles south of Skykomish, northeast King County. It was named because of the presence in its vicinity of copper ore, namely malachite.

Copper Lake *(S.36;T.40N;R.10E.uns)*

A Mt. Baker National Forest lake at the head of a tributary of Chilliwak Creek, north central Whatcom County. The lake was named for Copper Mountain, directly to the north.

Copper Mountain *(S.34;T.24N;R.5W)*

An Olympic National Park mountain, elevation 5,400 ft., 2-1/2 miles north of north end of Lake Cushman Reservoir, northwest Mason County. On July 7, 1890, the peak was named by Lieut. Joseph P. O'Neil, for copper ore pockets found that year on the mountain by prospectors.

Cora *(S.15;T.12N;R.8E)*

A community, rather than a town, on Cowlitz River, 8 miles east of Randle, east central Lewis County. The place was named for Cora Davis, wife of L. A. Davis, and the first married woman to settle in the "Big Bottom" country here. In 1886, the Davis family founded the community.

Corbaley Canyon
(T.25,26N;Rs.21,22E)

This 10 mile-long canyon starts 5 miles north of Waterville, west central Douglas County; extends southwesterly to Columbia River near Orondo. In 1885, the name was given by County Commissioners for Platt M. Corbaley who settled at the head of the canyon in 1883. It was the former route of a wagon road between Wenatchee and Waterville before 1916.

Cord Lake (Jefferson County) *see* Tarboo Lake

Corfu *(S.4;T.15N;R.27E)*

Railroad siding on Crab Creek, directly north of U.S. Atomic Energy Reservation, southeast Grant County. It was named for Corfu, largest of the Ionian Islands. The donor of this classical Grecian name was H. R. Williams, vice-president of Chicago, Milwaukee & St. Paul Railway, who bestowed many other interesting names on points in eastern Washington.

Cormorant Passage *(T.14N;R.1E)*

A passage between Ketron Island and the mainland, southwest of Steilacoom, northwest Pierce County. In 1846, it was named by Capt. R. N. Inskip, RN, and entered on British admiralty charts in 1847. It was to honor H.M. paddle-sloop *Cormorant* which was on this station from 1844 until 1850.

Cormorant Rock *(T.36N;R.3W)*

A rock in San Juan Channel, in the Wasp Island group between Crane Island and McConnell Island, central San Juan County. It is awash at high tides and usually covered with cormorants. This is one of many features in the San Juan Archipelago which is named for the abundance of sea birds of various species. An alternate name, used locally, is *Bird Rock.*

Cornet *(S.36;T.34N;R.1E)*

Settlement on the shore of Cornet Bay, south side of Deception Pass, extreme north end of Whidbey Island, Island County. It was locally named for John Cornet, who settled here with his Indian wife in the early 1860s.

Cornet Bay *(T.34N;R.1E)*

A sheltered bay on the south shore of Deception Pass, Whidbey Island, extreme north Island County. (*see* Cornet)

Corral Creek *(T.30N;R.18E.uns)*

The stream of the creek rises in Chelan Mountains, Wenatchee National Forest, north central Chelan County; flows slightly less than 2 miles southwesterly to South Pyramid Creek. The name was given by U.S. Forest Supervisor A. H. Sylvester because of a sheep corral near the creek's head.

Cosmopolis *(S.14;T.17N;R.9W)*

Town on Chehalis River, 3 miles from its mouth, southwest Grays Harbor County. Once, it was an important sawmill town, but when the largest sawmill closed, the town lost its payroll and be-

came a quiet, residential community. Recently it has been revived by the installation of a modern sawmill and a wood pulp plant. The name was given in pioneer days by a Frenchman named Brunn. It has the significance of "world city," which appears to be quite unsuited to this small town, even in its greatest period of prosperity. Local legend says the name is derived from an Indian headman who lived nearby.

Cosy Cove (King County) *see* *Anderson Bay*

Cottage Glen *(S.10;T.12N;R.16E)*

Community in Ahtanum Valley, 8 miles west of Wiley, central Yakima County. The former location of a trading post and post office on a post road from The Dalles to Ft. Simcoe and Okanogan. The fancy name, with no apparent significance, was chosen by James S. Imbrie (or Embree) in 1880, when a post office was established. This pioneer served as postmaster; the post office being located in his trade store.

Cotteral Rock *(S.10;T.12N;R.4E)*

A basaltic, andesite cliff, elevation 2,200 ft., 1 mile southwest of Morton, central Lewis County. It is a prominent landmark and viewpoint overlooking Morton. In 1888, it was named by Henry Temple and Thomas Hopgood for George Cotteral, who homesteaded an area including this rock in 1887. A local name is *Cutler's Rock.*

Cottonwood Creek/Cottonwood/Cottonwood Springs (Lincoln County) *see* Davenport

Cottonwood Island (Skagit County) *see* Sinclair Island

Cottonwood Island
(Ss.23,24;T.7N;R.2W)

An island in Columbia River channel, 5 miles northwest of Kalama, near mouth of Cowlitz River, south central Cowlitz County. In 1841, the Wilkes Expedition gave this island the original Indian name *Kanem,* meaning "canoe." It was changed to the present name by the U.S. Coast & Geodetic Survey for the abundant growth of cottonwood trees on the island.

Cottonwood Point *(S.21;T.1N;R.4E)*

A north bank point of Columbia River, north of the west end of Reed Island, southeast Clark County. This descriptive name was applied to the point by early river navigators. It had originally been named *Point Vancouver* for Capt. George Vancouver by Lieut. W. R. Broughton on October 30, 1792.

Cougar (*S.34;T.7N;R.4E*)

Village on the north bank of Lewis River, 24 miles northeast of Woodland, southeast Clark County. In 1906, when a post office was established here, settlers submitted a list of proposed names to postal authorities. This short and rather appropriate name was chosen from the list.

Cougar Creek (Chelan County) *see* Lion Creek

Cougar Creek (*Ts.27,28N;R.18E.partly uns*)

The stream of the creek heads 10 miles northwest of Wenatchee Lake, between Cougar Mountain and Signal Peak, Wenatchee National Forest, central Chelan County; flows 5-1/2 miles south to Mad River. It was named by Forest Service personnel for nearby Cougar Mountain.

Cougar Creek (*T.7N;R.4E*)

The stream of the creek heads northeast of Merrill Lake, southeast Cowlitz County; flows 7 miles south to Lewis River, 1/2 mile east of Cougar. One of several Cougar Creeks in the state, it is a local name which has become official. On a U.S.G.S. quadrangle dated 1953, it appears as *Panamaker Creek*. (USBGN)

Cougar Divide (*T.39N;R.8E.uns*)

A ridge directly north of Mt. Baker, between Deadhorse Creek and Wells Creek on Mt. Baker National Forest. It was named by C. C. Cornell, a pioneer settler, for his favorite hunting ground. An alternate name is *Cougar Ridge*.

Cougar Flat (*Ts.10,11N;R.3W*)

A farming area on the boundary between southwest Lewis County and northwest Cowlitz County, between Vader and Ryderwood. In 1875, the name originated when settlers, newly arrived from the east, treed an animal here. After long discussion, they decided that it was a cougar.

Cougar Lake (*S.24;T.30N;R.11E*)

This 4-acre, snow-fed lake, elevation 5,000 ft., is 2-1/2 miles east of Sauk River and 1/2 mile east of Bedal Peak, Mt. Baker National Forest, east central Snohomish County. In 1896, the name was applied by prospectors for abundance of cougars in this area. In 1898, surveyors adopted the name.

Cougar Mountain (*Ss.27,28;T.28N;R.18E.uns*)

A Wenatchee National Forest peak, 9 miles northeast of Wenatchee Lake, central Chelan County. Cougars inhabit much of the high country in Chelan County, and were very numerous in pioneer days. The name, common to many features in the state, was given by early stockmen to this mountain and to the adjoining creek. A wide view in all direction from the summit makes the peak valuable as a Forest Service lookout in season.

Cougar Mountain (*S.21;T.35N;R.33E*)

A Colville National Forest peak, elevation 4,085 ft., 9 miles south of Republic, west central Ferry County. This mountain was named by early settlers because it was crossed by a trail which cougars used in traveling from the Okanogan to the Kettle River range.

Cougar Ridge (Whatcom County) *see* Cougar Divide

Cougar Rock (*Mt. Rainier National Park*)

A massive rock outcroping below Rampart Ridge, on the west side of the main park highway, 7 miles east of Nisqually entrance. Park officials named this feature because cougars were in the habit of waiting on the rock to waylay deer which fed on a small meadow below the rock.

Cougar Smith Hill (*T.24N;R.1E*)

A hill northwest of the south end of Sinclair Inlet, west of Bremerton, central Kitsap County. It was named for John Andrew Smith, whose nickname was "Cougar," and who is reputed to have killed a cougar with his bare hands on the hill. This hardy pioneer, who logged in the Hood Canal country all of his life, died in Seattle in 1951 at the age of 109 years.

Coulee (Grant County) *see* Coulee City

Coulee City (*S.3;T.24N;R.28E*)

Town at the South Dam, 30 miles southwest of Grand Coulee Dam, northeast Grant County. It is the headquarters of the Grand Coulee Dam engineering staff. In 1889, the site was settled by Philip McEntee, who subsequently established a station for travelers at this junction point of railroad and stage travel. The first name was *McEntee's Crossing*. The post office name was operated as *McEntee* and later as *Coulee*. In 1937, the official name was changed to the present designation to conform with that of the town, which had been platted as *Coulee City* in 1890.

Coulee Creek (*T.26N;Rs.39-41E*)

The stream of the creek rises south of Horseshoe Lake, west central Spokane County; flows 18 miles eastward to Spokane River. At the forks of this creek, 3 miles west of Spokane river, is the site of Camp Washington, established in October 1853, by Gov. Isaac I. Stevens, when he arrived in Washington Territory to take office as the first territorial governor. Capt. George B. McClellan called this place *Helse-de-lite* in 1853, without explaining the meaning. The present name is for Coulee Township in which the creek is located.

Coulter Creek (*T.26N;R.16E*)

The stream of the creek rises on the north slope of McCue Ridge, 1 mile north of Chiwaukum Creek; flows 4 miles north to Nason Creek, Wenatchee National Forest, southwest Chelan County. It was named by U.S. Forest Supervisor A. H. Sylvester for Waldo Coulter, chief of a government party which surveyed the township.

County Creek (*T.18N;R.12E.uns*)

The stream of the creek rises 1 mile east of Cascade Mountain summit, extreme northwest Yakima County; flows east and northeast 3 miles along Yakima-Kittitas County boundary, to Naches River, Middle Fork. The name is because the stream flows, more or less, along the county boundary.

County Line Pond (*S.35;T.33N;R.6E*)

A 4-acre pond on the south side of Frailey Mountain, 3-1/2 miles northwest of Oso, at the Snohomish-Skagit County line. It received this name because of its location.

Coupeville (*Ss.33,34;T.32N;R.1E*)

The oldest town on Whidbey Island, south shore of Penn Cove, west central Island County. In 1852, it was founded by Capt. Thomas Coupe, who took a Donation Land Claim on the site. In early days the settlement was largely by retired sea captains and other seafaring men. It was named for the founder. The Indian name was *P't-sa-tl-y*, meaning "Snake Basket." An early nickname was *Port of Sea Captains*.

Couse Creek *(Ts. 7,8N;R.46E)*

The stream of the creek rises in Matheny Gully, southeast Asotin County; flows northeast 11 miles to Snake River south of Grahams Landing. The stream was named for the abundance here of Cous Biscuit-root *(Lomatium cous)*, which has globular tubers, is edible, and much used by Indians for making bread. The Indian name in common use was *Kowish*, a Nez Perce word.

Covada *(S.36;T.32N;R.36E)*

This almost-vanished settlement is on Borgeau Lake, 6 miles south of Inchelium, on the Colville Indian Reservation, east central Ferry County. During the hectic mining days of the 1890s, it was established by miners and had a post office and other town facilities which appealed to the mining profession. On January 31, 1954, the post office was closed. The name is reported to be a composite of the first letters of 6 nearby mining operations: *Columbia Camp, Orin Mine, Vernie Mine, Ada Mine, Dora Mine* and *Alice Mine*.

Coveland *(S.30;T.32N;R.1E)*

Settlement at the west end of Penn Cove on Whidbey Island, west central Island County. In 1850, the place was founded and was the commercial center of the island in 1854. Its name was borrowed from Penn Cove. In the 1850s, it was called *Barstow's Point*, for Capt. B. P. Barstow who operated a store here and owned a nearby Donation Land Claim.

Covello (Clark County) *see* Pioneer

Covello *(S.32;T.11N;R.40E)*

Settlement 8-1/2 miles northeast of Dayton, northeast Columbia County. In May 1883, the post office was established, this name having been chosen by postal officials from a list of 50 which was submitted. Prior to that selection the place was known as *Pioneer*. On February 2, 1889, the townsite was platted by John H. Putnam.

Covill *(S.6;T.30N;R.7W)*

One of the first farming communities in the county, 4 miles west of Port Angeles and 1 mile south of Freshwater Bay, north central Clallam County. The name was locally chosen for one of the pioneer homesteading families here.

Cow Creek (Yakima County) *see* Swamp Creek

Cow Creek *(Ts.15-19N;Rs.36,37E)*

The stream of the creek heads in Cow Lake, northeast Adams County; flows 33 miles in a southerly direction to Palouse River near Hooper Junction. In 1853, early railroad surveyors called this stream by Indian names which they picked up locally: *Cherana River, Cherakwa River*, and *Stkahp River*. Unfortunately, the name applied by ranchers in the vicinity, Cow Creek, continues in use.

Cow Creek *(T.29,30N;R.17E.uns)*

This short tributary of upper Entiat River rises on the northwest slope of Rampart Mountain, flows 2-1/2 miles northeast to Entiat River, Wenatchee National Forest, north central Chelan County. It was named by U.S. Forest Supervisor A. H. Sylvester because it was used as cattle range for a few years.

Cow Lake *(Ss.16,21;T.19N;R.37E)*

An "8-shaped" lake, 9 miles east of Ritzville at the head of Cow Creek, northeast Adams County. The lake has an area of 1/2 sq. mile and was named for Cow Creek.

Cow Lake (King County) *see* Lake Meridian

Cowap (Cowsap) Creek (Whatcom County) *see* Canyon Creek

Cowlitz Farms (Lewis County) *see* Cowlitz Prairie

Coweman Lake *(S.32;T.8N;R.3E)*

A 7-acre lake at the head of Coweman River, 21-1/2 miles east of Kelso, east central Cowlitz County. (*see* Coweman River)

Coweman River
(T.8N;Rs.1,2W&1,2E)

The stream of the river rises in the high country of Gifford Pinchot National Forest, central Cowlitz County; flows 26 miles west to Cowlitz River at Kelso. The original name was *Gobar's River* for Anton Gobar, a sheepherder for Hudson's Bay Company. It was renamed by local residents who borrowed the original Indian name of *Ko-wee-na*, meaning "short man." The name relates to a very short Indian who lived on the creek in pioneer days.

Cowiche *(Ss.28,32;T.14N;R.17E)*

Early farming community on Cowiche Creek, 10 miles northwest of Yakima, north central Yakima County. The name is a corruption of the Indian work *Kwai-Wy-Chess* or *Kwiwi-Chess*, meaning "good ford" or "crossing on." There are many alternate spellings of the name, including, *Cowecha, Cowitchee, Cowyche, Kah-Wi-Chi*, and *Kwi-Wy-Chas*.

Cowiche Basin *(T.13N;R.16E)*

A high valley, elevation 2,800 ft., 16 miles west of Yakima, between Cowiche Mountain on the south, and South Fork of Cowiche Creek on the north, northwest Yakima County. The valley contains an area of about 3 sections. (*see* Cowiche)

Cowiche Creek
(Ts.13,14N;Rs.15-18E)

The stream of the creek rises on south slope of Tieton Divide; flows southeast to join Naches River, just northwest of Yakima, north central Yakima County. The stream has 3 principal forks and many tributaries. (*see* Cowiche)

Cowiche Mountain *(T.13N;Rs.15-17E)*

A 12-mile-long mountain, elevation 4,300 ft., between Ahtanum Creek on south and South Fork of Cowiche Creek on north, with the eastern terminus 10 miles west of Yakima, north central Yakima County. (*see* Cowiche)

Cowlitz Bay *(T.37N;R.3W)*

A southwest shore bay of Waldron Island, in Georgia Strait, north central San Juan County. In 1859, this name was applied to British admiralty charts by Capt. Henry Richards, RN. It was named for the Hudson's Bay Company ship *Cowlitz*, which was a trading vessel in Puget Sound at the time.

Cowlitz Box Canyon *(Mt. Rainier National Park)*

A 3,040-ft. canyon in Muddy Fork, Cowlitz River, at the eastern foot of Stevens Ridge, southeast zone of the park. This name was given because it is truly a box canyon, with depth to 100 ft. and widths as narrow as 20 ft. Muddy waters from melting glaciers have worn this deep canyon over the years.

Cowlitz Chimneys *(Mt. Rainier National Park)*

A series of pointed, columnar, high rock towers on the divide between White River and Ohanapecosh River, across the east terminus of Sarvent Glacier. The elevation is 7,608 ft. and the name is for Cowlitz River. (*see* Cowlitz River) (USBGN)

Cowlitz Cleaver *(Mt. Rainier National Park)*

A narrow, rocky ridge which extends southeast from Gibraltar between Cowlitz and Nisqually glaciers, on the southeast slopes of Mt. Rainier. The name describes the function of this ridge, which divides ice flows, with part of the outflow reaching Puget Sound and part reaching Columbia River. (USBGN)

Cowlitz County

On April 21, 1854, the county was created by Washington Territorial Legislature. It contains 1,146 sq. miles. The development of Longview has created a very important center of forest products industries and other manufacturing plants. The name was taken from that of a local Indian tribe, the *Cow-e-lis-kee* or *Cow-e-lis-ke.*

Cowlitz Divide *(Mt. Rainier National Park)*

A rocky ridge, elevation 4,770 ft., extends about 5 miles north-south between the drainages of Ohanapecosh River and Muddy Fork, Cowlitz River, southeast area of the park. A southern expansion of the divide is called *Backbone Ridge*. The name is descriptive of the fact that it divides the drainage basins of 2 streams.

Cowlitz Glacier *(Mt. Rainier National Park)*

This ice river, on the southeast slope of Mt. Rainier, descends about 5 miles from a group of small glaciers near the summit, to the head of Muddy Fork, Cowlitz River. The large glacier, in the southeast part of the park, was named in 1870 by P. B. Van Trump and Gen. Hazard Stevens, when they found it to be the source of Cowlitz River via Muddy Fork. (USBGN)

Cowlitz Landing *(S.18;T.11N;R.1W)*

A very important early settlement, 15 miles south of Chehalis, southwest Lewis County. Founded in 1837, it was a River landing, a trading post, the site of a Roman Catholic Mission, and headquarters for a very large farm operated by Puget Sound Agricultural Company, a subsidiary of Hudson's Bay Company. The first name was *Plomondon's Landing*, for the owner of a Donation Land Claim at this place. Later the accepted name was *Cowlitz Landing*. A later name was *Warbassport*, and the present name is *Toledo*. (*see* Warbassport)

Cowlitz Park *(Mt. Rainier National Park)*

A peak northeast of the lower end of

Cowlitz Glacier, near the source of Muddy Fork, Cowlitz River, southeast sector of the Park. It was named by park officials for Cowlitz River. (*see* Cowlitz River) (USBGN)

Cowlitz Pass *(S.13;T.14N;R.11E.uns)*

A 5,191-ft. pass at Cascade Mountain Summit, located at the headwaters of Summit Creek on the west and the headwaters of Tieton River on the east, between northwest Yakima County and extreme northeast Lewis County. It is on the route of an early railroad survey and its name is from its location at the head of a Cowlitz River tributary. An alternate name, previously used, was *Packwood Pass*.

Cowlitz Prairie *(Ts.11,12N;R.1W)*

A 4,000-acre prairie north of Toledo, extending 4 miles up the Cowlitz River along the north bank, southwest Lewis County. In 1837 it was established as a very large farm by Puget Sound Agricultural Company, a subsidiary of Hudson's Bay Company. The original name was *Cowlitz Farms*, but was changed after Hudson's Bay Company ceased its operations in the state of Washington. (*see* Cowlitz Landing, Warbassport)

Cowlitz River

The stream of the river rises in 2 main forks on the south slope of Mt. Rainier and on the west slope of Cascade Mountain summit, respectively; flows to the west and south through central Lewis County, then south through Cowlitz County to Columbia River, 3 miles south of Kelso. It is an important river for navigation, fishing, and development of hydroelectric power. The Indian name was *Ta-wa-l-titch*, meaning "capturing the Medicine Spirit," and refers to Indian youths who were sent to prairies along the river to seek their guardian spirits. In 1792, Lieut. W. R. Broughton of the Vancouver Expedition, named the stream *Knight's River*. It appears as *Coweliskee River* in Lewis & Clark reports of 1805-1806. The present name is well established.

Cowlitz Rocks *(Mt. Rainier National Park)*

This short, sharp ridge, elevation 7,457 feet, divides Cowlitz and Paradise glaciers at a point 3-1/2 miles southeast of Mt. Rainier's summit. In 1907, the name was devised by Jules Stampfler, veteran park guide, in order to satisfy the

many questions asked by tourists regarding the feature. (USBGN)

Cowlitz Trail

A pioneer trail which extended northwest from Cowlitz Farm on the present site of Toledo to Tumwater Falls near Budd Inlet on Puget Sound, Lewis and Thurston counties. In pioneer days, thousands of settlers traveled afoot, by horse-drawn vehicles, and with ox teams. Traces of the trail may still be found and are visible on aerial photographs. It was named for its point of origin on Cowlitz River.

Coyle *(S.4;T.25N;R.1W)*

Settlement on the east entrance to Fisherman Harbor on Hood Canal, on the south tip of Toandos Peninsula, southeast Jefferson County. Until a post office was established in 1908, it was called *Fisherman's Bay*. The present name was selected for the post office to honor George Coyle, a pioneer resident.

Coyote Island (Benton County) *see* Blalock Island

Coyote Lake *(S.13;T.13N;R.10E)*

A very deep, 4-acre lake, elevation 5,100 ft., 5-1/2 miles southwest of White Pass, 4-1/2 miles west of Cascade Mountain summit, Lewis County. The lake is named for Coyote Creek, which drains it.

Coyote Mountain
(S.9;T.36N;R.36E.uns)

A 5,501-ft. ridge, 11 miles west of Columbia River, between Deadman and Sherman creeks, Colville National Forest, east central Ferry County. The name, used by early settlers, is typical of pioneer interest in wildlife. Scores of features throughout the state were named for native animals, birds, snakes, or fish. A local, unofficial name is *Cayuse Mountain* (USBGN)

Craige *(S.27;T.8N;R.46E)*

Town 13 miles south of Asotin, 4 miles west of Snake River, southeast Asotin County. In 1897, a mail route was started here by C. Thomas Craige. The post office was named for him.

Cranberry Lake *(S.35;T.34N;R.1E)*

A kidney-shaped lake, northwest corner of Whidbey Island, directly south of the west entrance to Deception Pass, Deception Pass State Park, north Island County. It covers 128 acres and was locally named for wild cranberries that originally grew along the marshy borders of the lake. It should not be confused with Cranberry Lake on Camano Island.

Cranberry Lake *(S.25;T.31N;R.2E)*

A lake which varies from 1 to 6 acres (average width 2 acres) on central Camano Island, 2-1/2 miles southeast of Camano, central Island County. The name is descriptive. This lake should not be confused with Cranberry Lake on the north end of Whidbey Island.

Cranberry Lake *(S.23;T.35N;R.1E)*

A small lake, surrounded by city-owned property, within the city limits of Anacortes, west central Skagit County. It was named in pioneer days for the abundance of wild cranberries around its shores.

Cranberry Lake
(Ss.28,29;T.21N;R.3W)

A 1-1/2-mile-long lake, with an area of 170.6 acres, 4-1/2 miles north of Shelton, central Mason County. Its swampy shores are surrounded by 96 acres of marshy land. The State Department of Fisheries uses this lake as a salmon-rearing pond and the lake itself is a natural cranberry bog.

Cranberry Slough *(S.3;T.21N;R.6E)*

A 1-acre lake in a 100-acre marsh area, 2 miles north of Black Diamond, south central King County. This is an early name which was applied by pioneers for abundant native cranberries. An alternate name is *Sawyer Lake Slough.*

Crane Island *(S.19;T.36N;R.2W)*

A small, 1-mile island between Pole and Wasp passes, directly south of the western peninsula of Orcas Island, central San Juan County. In 1858, the present name was applied on British admiralty charts by Capt. Henry Richards, RN. It is one of many features in the San Juan group which he named for native birds and mammals.

Crane Lake (Chelan County) *see* Domke Lake

Crane Point *(S.36;T.30N;R.1W)*

A west shore point of Indian Island, on Port Townsend Bay, extreme northeast Jefferson County. In 1841, the Wilkes Expedition named this feature *Middle Point.* The source of the present name is local and has been in use since the 1890s.

Crater *(S.9;T.20N;R.23E)*

Settlement 5 miles west of Quincy, 3 miles northeast of Columbia River, west central Grant County. The place was named for a nearby extinct volcanic crater.

Crater Creek *(Mt. Rainier National Park)*

A short, precipitous stream which rises in Mowich Lake, directly west of Mother Mountain; flows southward into North Mowich River. It was originally named for Crater Lake, now Mowich Lake. Prof. Bailey Willis, a geologist, used the name *Crater* in 1883, when he mistook glacier cirques for volcanic craters. The lake's name was changed, but the creek's name was not. (USBGN)

Crater Lake (Chelan County) *see* Lake Crater

Crater Lake (Mt. Rainier National Park) *see* Mowich Lake

Crater Lake *(S.7;T.33N;R.12E)*

A 63-acre lake, elevation 4,800 ft., at the head of Big Creek, 13-1/2 miles southeast of Marblemount, southeast Skagit County. The lake is 100 ft. deep and its name was given because the lake is in a deep crater, with towering cliffs to the north.

Craven Peninsula
(Ts.29,30N;Rs.1E,1W)

An area which includes both Marrowstone and Indian islands, east and southeast of Port Townsend, northeast Jefferson County. In 1841, this area was named *Craven's Peninsula,* by Cmdr. Charles Wilkes, for Lieut. Thomas T. Craven of his command. The name is a misnomer and never came into general use.

Crater Peak (Mt. Rainier National Park) *see* Columbia Crest

Craven's Peninsula (Jefferson County) *see* Marrowstone Island; Indian Island

Craven Rock *(S.21;T.30N;R.1E)*

An east shore rock off Marrowstone Island on Admiralty Inlet, 2 miles south of Marrowstone Point, northeast Jefferson County. This name was borrowed from *Craven's Peninsula,* a name given to Marrowstone and Indian island by Cmdr. Charles Wilkes in 1841. (see Craven Peninsula)

Crawford *(S.30;T.4N;R.3E)*

Settlement 14 miles northeast of Vancouver, central Clark County. It was named for the foreman of a construction

crew which built the Yacolt branch of Northern Pacific Railway through this place.

Crawford State Park
(S.4;T.40N;R.43E)

A 40-acre park, just west of Pend Oreille River, extreme northwest corner of Pend Oreille County. It surrounds Gardiner Cave and is intended to prevent vandalism in that unique limestone cavern. The park is named for W. H. Crawford, pioneer merchant of Metaline who donated the land to the state in 1921.

Crazy Creek (Jefferson County) *see* One Too Many Creek

Crazy Creek *(T.25N;R.5W)*

The stream of the creek heads in Hagen Lake on the north slope of Mt. Stone, Olympic National Park, southeast corner of Jefferson County; flows 4-1/2 miles north to Duckabush River. It was named by park employees because of many short and erratic tributaries, especially near its source. It should not be confused with One Too Many Creek, a short distance to the east. Some maps show the latter as a tributary to Crazy Creek, and label this creek as One Too Many. In this crazy, mixed-up jumble of mountains and streams, there may have been one too many creeks for the topographers. (USBGN)

Crego *(S.9;T.13N;R.3W)*

Settlement on Crego Hill, directly west of Adna, west Lewis County. It was named for Charles Crego, the first postmaster and a substantial local landowner.

Creosote *(S.35;T.25N;R.2E)*

Community on Bainbridge Island on the south shore of Eagle Harbor, east Kitsap County. It is the location of a large wood-treating plant, established in 1905. The name is for the large quantities of coal-tar creosote used in the treating plant.

Crescent *(S.10;T.36N;R.43E)*

Crescent on the east bank of Pend Oreille River, between Tiger and Blue Slide, central Pend Oreille County. In 1906, when a post office was established, postal authorities chose this name from a submitted list. It had been listed because of a crescent-shaped curve in nearby mountains.

Crescent Bay *(Ss.20,21;T.31N;R.8W)*

A bay on Strait of Juan de Fuca, 9

miles west of Port Angeles, north central Clallam County. In 1890, the bay area was platted as the townsite of Port Crescent. The boom was not successful. The shorelands are privately owned, but are used by local people as a public park. In 1790, the bay was named *Ensenada de Villarva* by Gonzalo Lopez de Haro. In 1791, Juan Francisco de Eliza charted it as *Ensenada de Villalba*. In 1846, the present name, based on the bay's countour, was placed on British Admiralty charts by Capt. Henry Kellett.

Crescent Creek *(Ts.26,27N;R.15E)*

This 3-mile creek rises on the steep south slope of Nason Ridge; flows southeast to Nason Creek, Wenatchee National Forest, southwest Chelan County. It was named by U.S. Forest Supervisor A. H. Sylvester because its short, rapid course is crescent-shaped, "like a strung bow," according to the namer. Because this word also named a popular brand of baking powder, Sylvester, in a whimsical moment, named the creeks to the west and east *Schilling* and *Royal*, respectively. The 3 streams are known locally as "the baking-powder creeks."

Crescent Harbor *(T.32N;Rs.1,2E)*

A large and distinctly crescent-shaped harbor, south shore of Whidbey Island's north lobe, Island County; it is bordered by a U.S. Naval Air Base, one of the fairly recent features of this county. In 1851, it was named by Dr. Richard H. Lansdale, and is quite descriptive. In 1841, the Wilkes Expedition named it *Duncan's Bay* for a naval officer who served on the *Saratoga* during the War of 1812. The Indian name was *Stole-sun*.

Crescent Lake *(Mt. Rainier National Park)*

A 5,452-ft. lake north of Crescent Mountain, at the head of South Fork, Spukwush Creek, northwest sector of the park. It was named for nearby Crescent Mountain. (USBGN)

Crescent Lake *(S.12;T.40N;R.43E)*

Small lake on the Kaniksu National Forest, 1/2 mile south of the Canadian boundary, extreme north central Pend Oreille County. The name is descriptive of its shape, which is roughly quarter-moon in outline.

Crescent Mountain *(Mt. Rainier National Park)*

A 6,703-ft. summit on the north slope of Mt. Rainier, 2 miles east of Mother Mountain, northwest area of the park. Its west slope adjoins the terminus of Carbon Glacier. In 1883, the name was applied by Prof Bailey Willis, a geologist, as descriptive of the mountain's general contour. (USBGN)

Crested Buttes *(S.36;T.29N;R.10E)*

Buttes 4 miles southwest of Monte Cristo, southeast Snohomish County. The descriptive name was chosen by the Lewis brothers, a pair of trappers and prospectors.

Creston *(Ss.10,15;T.26N;R.34E)*

Town 62 miles west of Spokane and 8 miles south of Columbia River, north central Lincoln County. In 1889, it was named by railroad locators, as its elevation of 2,462 ft. was the highest point or crest on the Central Washington Railroad. The original name, before the railroad came through, was *Benson*.

Crevice Creek *(T.33N;R.9E)*

The stream of the creek heads in mountains 10 miles north of Darrington, Mt. Baker National Forest, south central Skagit County; flows 4 miles south of North Fork, Stillaguamish River. The name is descriptive, because the creek flows through a narrow, deep canyon.

Crocker Lake *(Ss.1,12;T.28N;R.2W)*

A 65.3-acre lake, 3-1/2 miles south of the south end of Port Discovery Bay, 9 miles west of Port Ludlow, northeast Jefferson County. In 1870, this small lake was named for one of the earliest settlers in the area.

Crockett Lake *(T.31N;R.1E)*

A 10-acre lake on the west side of Whidbey Island, directly north of Admiralty Bay, west central Island County. Originally, it was 500 acres, parallel to the shore of Admiralty Bay, and separated from it by a narrow sand spit. Later it was drained to 250 acres, of which only 10 is actually lake. In the 1850s it was named for S. B. and W. Crockett, the first settlers here, who took Donation Land Claims directly north of the lake.

Cromwell *(S.25;T.21N;R.1E)*

Village 7 miles north of Steilacoom on the north shore of Hales Passage, northwest Pierce County. In 1902, it was named for J. B. Cromwell, who was postmaster at Tacoma.

Crook Mountain
(S.10;T.28N;R.16E.uns)

A Wenatchee National Forest peak, 1 mile north of north end of Twin Lakes, between Napeequa and Chiwawa rivers, northwest Chelan County. The name given by pioneers was *Goat Mountain*. U.S. Forest Supervisor A. H. Sylvester changed the name because "There are more Goat Mountains than goats in the Northwest." The name he substituted is for Lieut. George Crook, U.S. Army, who led cavalry troops against hostile Indians in this area during August 1858. He later became a general in the Civil War period.

Crosby *(S.12;T.24N;R.2E)*

Settlement 14 miles south of Bremerton, southwest Kitsap County. In 1891, the name was chosen by a local settler, Mrs. Graham, for a small hamlet in England where she was born and raised.

Crow Creek *(T.29N;R.18E.uns)*

The stream of the creek rises on Crow Hill, Chelan Mountain range, Wenatchee National Forest, north central Chelan County; flows 3 miles southwest to North Fork of Entiat River. The stream was named for Crow Hill by U.S. Forest Supervisor A. H. Sylvester.

Crow Lake (King County) *see* Walker Lake

Crow Hill *(T.29N;R.18E.uns)*

A 7,300-ft. peak in Chelan Mountains on the common boundary of Chelan and Wenatchee national forests, north central Chelan County. The peak is 4-1/2 miles southwest of Lake Chelan and crows are reported to be numerous in this country of high sheep ranges. This is one of the names placed on the land by sheepherders which may be used in polite circles.

Crown Creek *(Ts.39-40N;R.38E)*

The stream of the creek rises in Elbow Lake, 3-1/2 miles south of the Canadian boundary, northwest Stevens County; flows 9-1/2 miles southeast to the Columbia River opposite Marble. Local residents state that it was named for a settler, Crown, who lived on the creek in early days.

Crown Hill *(S.2;T.25N;R.3E)*

One of Seattle's 12 "official" hills, elevation 335 ft., northwest section of Seattle on 85th St. from 11th to 15th Avenue Northwest, King County. The name was chosen by local residents, evidently for the purpose of having a "high-sounding" title.

Crown Island (San Juan County) *see* Fortress Island

Crum Canyon *(T.26N;R.20E)*

A Wenatchee National Forest canyon, 5 miles west of Columbia River, 4-1/2 miles northeast of Entiat River, east central Chelan County. The canyon was named by local settlers for a homesteader by this name who lived and mined here for several years following 1908.

Cruzatte (Skamania County) *see* Prindle

Cruzatte River (Skamania County) *see* Wind River

Crystal City *(S.28;T.28N;R.26E)*

An abandoned mining town near Miles, which was on Spokane River, Lincoln County. In the early 1890s, it was established and called *Grayville*, for Capt. John Gray, a Spokane mining man who had an interest in the adjacent mine. The town faded away after being partly destroyed by fire on July 10, 1889. In 1903, a new town was platted, and was named Crystal City for the Crystal Mine, which was only 600 ft. from the town.

Crystal Creek *(Mt. Rainier National Park)*

The stream of the creek heads in Crystal Lake, west slope of Cascade Mountain summit, northeast sector of the park; flows northwest to White River at the foot of Sunrise Ridge. It was named for Crystal Lake. (*see* Crystal Lake)

Crystal Lake *(S.1;T.22N;R.10E)*

A very deep, 6.4-acre lake, 2-1/2 miles west of Snoqualmie Pass, 1/4 mile north of Granite Mountain peak, east central King County. It is one of 3 Granite Mountain lakes with Denny and Cad lakes. The name is descriptive, as the water is clear in all seasons.

Crystal Lake *(Mt. Rainier National Park)*

A 5,830-ft. lake on the west slope of Cascade Mountain summit, near the south end of Crystal Mountain, northeast sector of the park. This is a name which often is used for clear, mountain lakes at high altitude. The identity of the namer is not found in records. An alternate name is *Upper Crystal Lake*.

Crystal Lake *(S.36;T.27N;R.5E)*

A 39.1-acre lake near the King County boundary, 1-3/4 miles south of Maltby, Snohomish County. It has been artificially established by a dam. This rather fancy name for a man-made lake was chosen by owners of the land on which it is located.

Crystal Mountain *(Mt. Rainier National Park)*

A peak at Cascade Mountain summit, extending 5 miles along the summit, parallel to White River, with its southern extremity at Crystal Lake, northeast sector of the park. It was named for Crystal Lake and should not be confused with Crystal Mountain in the southwest part of the park. (*see* Crystal Lake)

Crystal Mountain *(Mt. Rainier National Park)*

A 6,306-ft. peak east of Indian Henrys Hunting Ground, between Pyramid Creek and Tahoma Creek, southwest sector of the park. It evidently was named by park officials because of its stark white appearance during winter snows and should not be confused with Crystal Mountain at Cascade Mountain summit, northeast sector of the park.

Crystal Springs *(S.33;T.25N;R.2E)*

Small settlement at the southwest extremity of Bainbridge Island, northwest of Pleasant Beach, Kitsap County. The name is reported to have been borrowed from nearby Crystal Springs Lake.

Crystal Springs Lake *(S.29;T.25N;R.2E)*

A Bainbridge island lake on the southwest sector of the island, 1/4 mile inland from Port Orchard Bay, east Kitsap County. An early name for this feature was *Gazzam Lake*, for a Seattle business executive who developed a summer home here. The present name is a poetic appellation devised by summer residents around the lake.

Cub Lake *(S.34;T.33N;R.13E.uns)*

Lake 2/1-2 miles southwest of Spire Peak at Cascade Mountain summit, extreme southeast Skagit County. The name was used by miners and prospectors to match with Big Bear lake, 600 ft. to the east, more recently designated as Itswoot Lake. That Chinook jargon word means *black bear*. (*see* Itswoot Lake)

Cuitan Creek *(T.11,12N;R.13E)*

The stream of the creek heads near

Darling Mountain on Yakima Indian Reservation, west central Yakima County; flows 3-1/2 miles south to Diamond Fork, Klickitat River. The name of this short stream comes from the Chinook jargon word, *Ku-I-Tan*, meaning "horse." It has been spelled both *Cuitan* and *Cuitin*

Cultus Bay *(T.23N;R.3E)*

An extreme southern end bay of Whidbey Island, between Scatchet Head and Possession Point, south Island County. It is a shallow bay, flooded only at high tides. It was named by George Davidson of U.S. Coast Survey, who used the Indian (Chinook jargon) name meaning "bad" or "worthless." He found the bay to be of no value for navigation, being dry at low tide levels. A local name, no longer in use, was *Bailey's Bay*.

Cultus Creek *(S.7;T.26N;R.11W)*

A tributary of Winfield Creek, between Hoh and Snahapish rivers, northwest Jefferson County. It was named after the Chinook jargon Indian name. (*see* Cultus Bay)

Cultus Lake *(S.2;T.6N;R.8E.uns)*

A 4-acre lake in Indian Heaven, at the head of Cultus Creek, central Skamania County. The lake is barren of fish and takes its name from the Chinook jargon. (*see* Cultus Bay)

Cultus Mountains *(T.34N;Rs.5,6E)*

Mountains extending 12 miles southeast and east to Day Lake, west central Skagit County, maximum elevation 4,100 ft. The locally applied name is from Chinook Indian dialect. (*see* Cultus Bay)

Cumberland *(S.28;T.21N;R.7E)*

Community in a former important coal mining area, 6 miles northeast of Enumclaw, south central King County. In 1893, the place was named by F. X. Schriner, for Cumberland Valley, Pennsylvania, which also is in a coal-mining belt. A typical pioneer jingle, which purports to explain the name was "Up in the hills is a cumb; under the cumb is a bear; under the bear is land." The pioneer poets did not explain the meaning of "cumb."

Cumberland Creek (King County) *see* Coal Creek

Cunningham *(S.4;T.15N;R.32E)*

Community 14 miles southwest of Lind, south central Adams County. In

1889, Northern Pacific Railway Company named the place *Scott*. In 1902, the company changed to Cunningham for Elder William R. Cunningham of Ritzville, who, in his youth, was one of the founders of Delta Tau Delta Fraternity and was reputed to have been one of Gen. John Hunt Morgan's Confederate "Raiders."

Cup Lake *(S.36;T.26N;R.15E)*

This small, muddy pond heads in Chiwaukum Creek on the east slope of Chiwaukum Mountains, Wenatchee National Forest, central Chelan County. It was so named by U.S. Forest Supervisor A. H. Sylvester because it nestles in a cup-shaped depression on the mountainside.

Cup Lake *(S.16;T.27N;R.13E)*

A 4,600-ft. lake on Snoqualmie National Forest, 1 mile southwest of Cascade Mountain summit, 6-1/4 miles north of Stevens Pass, extreme southeast Snohomish County. It covers 11.4 acres and was named to match nearby Saucer Lake. The lake is quite round and slightly smaller than Saucer, as it should be.

Curlew *(Ss.11,14;T.39N;R.33E)*

This weathered village is 8 miles south of the Canadian boundary, at the confluence of Curlew Creek and Kettle River, Ferry County. It is located among mountain peaks and is a former mining town which was established by prospectors during the 1890s. In 1896, it was named by Guy S. Helphrey, who used the name of the creek. Curlew Creek and Curlew Lake were named because very large numbers of curlews nested on benches in the vicinity, and to a distance of 8 miles southward. The Indian name for the lake was *Karanips,* which translates to curlew.

Curlew *(S.28;T.22N;R.45E)*

Early town 3-1/2 miles southeast of Fairfield, southeast Spokane County. It has almost disappeared and is reported to have been named by the first postmaster, Mr. Bibbee, for curlews which nested here in numbers in the tall prairie grass before it was disturbed by the plow.

Curlew Creek *(Ts.38,39N;R.33E)*

The stream of the creek rises in Curlew Lake, north central Ferry County; flows northward a distance of 9 miles through Malo to Kettle River at Curlew. (*see* Curlew, Ferry County)

Curlew Lake *(Ts.37,38N;R.33E)*

A deep, 6-mile-long lake, average width 1/2 mile, containing 4 islands, 5 miles northeast of Republic, 16 miles south of the Canadian boundary, Colville National Forest, northwest Ferry County. Curlew Creek drains the lake north into Kettle River. (*see* Curlew, Ferry County)

Curry Gap *(S.21;T.29N;R.12E)*

A gap at the head of Quartz Creek, 5-1/2 miles east of Monte Cristo, southeast Snohomish County. It was named for an early miner who used it for travel between Goat Lake Mines and Skykomish.

Curtis *(S.30;T.13N;R.3W)*

Community 11 miles southwest of Chehalis, west central Lewis County. It was named for Ben Curtis, the first postmaster and operator of a store in the early 1890s.

Curran's Flat (Yakima County) *see* Naches Flat

Curtis Glacier (Whatcom County) *see* Upper and Lower Curtis glaciers

Cushman Crest *(Mt. Rainier National Park)*

A long, rocky ridge between Nisqually River and Van Trump Creek, elevation 6,500 ft. at its north end; it extends southward from Van Trump Glacier and is rated as the most prominent feature on the south slope of Mt. Rainier. It was named for the late Congressman F. W. Cushman of Tacoma. (USBGN)

Cushman Falls (Mt. Rainier National Park) *see* Narada Falls

Cushman Reservoir No. 2 *(T.22N;R.4W)*

An artificial reservoir in Skokomish River, 2-3/4 miles west of Hoodsport, central Mason County. Built and used by the City of Tacoma, it covers 70.4 acres and has a maximum depth of 160 ft. The name is from that of Lake Cushman. Alternate names are *Lower Cushman Reservoir* and *Potlatch Reservoir.*

Cusick *(S.19;T.33N;R.44E)*

A sawmill town on Pend Oreille River, 19 miles northwest of Newport, south central Pend Oreille County. Its economy hinges on a large sawmill operated here by Diamond National Corporation. In the early 1890s, Capt. Joe W. Cusick settled here and platted

the town on May 24, 1902. He was a pioneer river skipper who ran the *Volunteer* and other early stern-wheelers on the river. The town took his name when platted.

Cypress Rock (Skagit County) *see* Towhead Island

Custer *(S.34;T.20N;R.2E)*

Community at the north end of Steilacoom Lake, 3 miles east of Steilacoom, west central Pierce County. The name originated by local use, and is for a settler who claimed land here in about 1890.

Custer *(S.36;T.40N;R.1E)*

Formerly a shingle-manufacturing town, now a scattered community with small farms in Whatcom County. Settlers named the place for A. W. Custer, a pioneer who operated a store and was the first postmaster in 1886.

Cutthroat Lakes *(S.16;T.29N;R.9E)*

A group of 7 small lakes, elevation 4,300 ft., total area of 8 acres, on the northeast slope of Bald Mountain, north of Sultan Basin, central Snohomish County. The group was named by the State Game Commission when cutthroat trout were planted in the 1930s. The name is now less appropriate, as the lakes are barren. An alternate name is *Bald Mountain Lakes.*

Cutts Island *(S.9;T.21N;R.1E)*

Very small island near the east shore of Henderson Bay, directly southwest of Raft Island, northwest Pierce County. In 1841, it was named by the Wilkes Expedition as *Scott Island.* The local name of *Deadman Island* is found on some recent maps as an alternative to the official name, as shown on U.S. Coast & Geodetic Survey charts. No source is given for *Cutts Island* in historical references or local records.

Cypress Island *(Ts.35,36N;R.1E)*

An irregular, 8-mile-long island on Rosario Strait, 3 miles northwest of Anacortes, northwest Skagit County. It was named *Isla de San Vincente* by Juan Francisco de Eliza in 1790, for one of the many names of the Viceroy of Mexico. On June 6, 1792, the present name was charted by Capt. George Vancouver, for the many juniper trees on the island which he believed to be cypress.

D

D Lake (*T.29N;R.16E.uns*)

A Wenatchee National Forest lake on the south branch of Y Creek, east slope of Chiwawa Ridge, northwest Chelan County. Both the lake and the creek which drains it, were named for their shapes by Forest Ranger Delmer S. Rice.

Dabob (*S.32;T.28N;R.1W*)

Small community on Tarboo Creek, 1/2 mile north of the head of Dabob Bay, east central Jefferson County. In the 1890s, it was called *Tarboo*. The present name is that used by local Indians when the first white explorers arrived. In 1841, Cmdr. Charles Wilkes interpreted the name as *Dabop*, and so charted it. (USBGN)

Dabob Bay (*Ts.25,26,27N;Rs.1,2W*)

A large bay extending 14 miles north from Brinnon as an arm of Hood Canal, east central Jefferson County. It is bounded on the east by Toandos Peninsula, and since 1949, it has been used by the U.S. Navy and University of Washington as an underwater acoustics and weapon-system laboratory. In 1841, it was named by Cmdr. Charles Wilkes as *Dabop Bay*, which was his translation of the Indian name. In 1846, Capt. Henry Kellett named it *Dahap Inlet*, also in an attempt to reproduce the Indian pronunciation. (USBGN)

Dabop (Jefferson County) *see* Dabob

Dabop Bay (Jefferson County) *see* Babob Bay

Daisy (*S.16;T.33N;R.37E*)

Small settlement on the east shore of Franklin D. Roosevelt Lake at the mouth of McGees Creek. When the lake was created back of Grand Coulee Dam, Daisy was safely above the 1,310-ft. elevation which was the deadline for towns and buildings. The site was claimed as a homestead in 1902 by Samuel L. and John H. Magee. While nearby mines were active, Daisy had a busy store, a hotel, a church, and a post office. Today the place is of less importance. The place was named by the Magee brothers for the nearby Daisy Mine.

Dakota Creek (*T.40N;Rs.1,2E*)

The stream of the creek rises 5 miles northeast of Custer, extreme northwest Whatcom County; flows 10 miles northwest to Drayton Harbor on Georgia Strait. It was named by a party of settlers from the Dakotas who established a community near the creek's mouth in 1872 and 1873.

Dalco Passage (*T.21N;Rs.2,3E*)

A Puget Sound passage between Point Defiance, northwest Pierce County, and the sound end of Vashon Island, southwest King County. In 1841, it was named by Cmdr. Charles Wilkes and is one of very few features named by him for which no name origin appears to be on record.

Dalkena (*Ss.27,28;T.32N;R.44E*)

A sawmill town, 11-1/2 miles north of Newport on the Pend Oreille River, south central Pend Oreille County. In 1902, it became a town when Dalton & Kennedy built a large sawmill here. A fire which destroyed the mill in 1935, coupled with timber depletion, badly crippled the local economy. The name is a combination of Dalton and Kennedy.

Dallas Bank (*T.31N;R.2W*)

Extensive shoals in Strait of Juan de Fuca, 2-1/2 miles north of Protection Island, northwest Jefferson County. In 1862, they were named by U.S. Coast Survey for Alexander Grant Dallas, representative for Hudson's Bay Company at Victoria, who supervised all Pacific coast interests.

Dalles Creek (Pierce County) *see* Minnehaha Creek

Dallesport (*S.33;T.2N;R.13E*)

Town on north bank of Columbia River, opposite The Dalles, Oregon, southwest Klickitat County. Once it was a town of considerable importance, and the county seat of Klickitat County. In 1891, it boomed under the hand of Rev. Orson D. Taylor, a Baptist missionary. In 1895, he was arrested for gross misrepresentation, but was released on a technicality. Several names were applied to the place in earlier days, including *Rockland*, *Grand Dalles*, and *North Dalles*. The present name is taken

from that of the Grand Dalles of the Columbia River. (*see* The Dalles)

Damnation Peak
(*S.28;T.37N;R.11E.uns*)

A Mt. Baker National Forest peak, 6 miles west of Newhalem, southeast Whatcom County. The name, applied by early prospectors, typifies the difficulty travelers encountered among these steep and rocky cliffs. Similar names in the area are *Desolation Peak*, *Devils Dome*, *Mt. Terror*, and *Mt. Fury*.

Damon (*S.26;T.18N;R.12W*)

Village on Oyhut Channel on the west side of North Bay, 5 miles north of Point Damon, southwest Grays Harbor County. It was named locally for C.A. Damon, who was the first settler here, and who claimed land in 1861. An alternate name, shown on some maps, is *Oyhut*. It is a modification of the Chinook *Weh-hut.*, meaning road, path, or trail.

Damon Lake (*S.16;T.19N;R.11W*)

A 15.7-acre lake on Damon Creek, 2 miles northeast of Copalis Crossing, west central Grays Harbor County. The name source is the same as that of Damon. On some maps it appears, in error, as *Diamond Lake*.

Damon's Point (Grays Harbor County) *see* Point Damon

Dana Passage (*T.19N;Rs.1,2W*)

A south Puget Sound passage between Hartsene Island, Mason County and the mainland, Thurston County. The inter-county boundary traverses the middle of the passage. In 1841, the Wilkes Expedition named it *Dana's Passage*, for James Dwight Dana, a mineralogist on the expedition. Since then, the name was shortened, evidently by cartographers.

Dan Creek (*T.32N;R.10E*)

The stream of the creek rises in the mountains, 8 miles east of Darrington, north central Snohomish County; flows 8 miles northwest to Sauk River, Mt. Baker National Forest. It was locally named for Dan Smyre, an early settler. An alternate name, in early use, was *Dan's Creek*.

Dan's Creek (Snohomish County) *see* Dan Creek

Danger Rock *(T.37N;R.3W)*

One of several rocks at the west entrance to President Channel, 1-1/2 miles southwest of Waldron Island, north central San Juan County. These rocks make navigation here difficult. In 1859, this descriptive name was placed on British admiralty charts by Capt. Henry Richards, R.N., who surveyed the San Juan Archipelago in 1858 and 1859.

Danger Shoal *(T.36N;R.4W)*

A very dangerous, submerged reef in Spieden Channel, between the western tip of Spieden Island and the northern tip of Henry Island, northwest San Juan County. In 1858, this descriptive name was placed on British admiralty charts by Capt. Henry Richards, R.N.

Danville *(S.4;T.40N;R.34E)*

A settlement, 1/2 mile south of the Canadian boundary, on Colville National Forest, north central Ferry County. The Kettle River runs nearby. In 1889, the site was claimed and platted by Peter B. Nelson and O. B. Nelson, and became a substantial town during the mining boom. It was called *Nelson* for the founders. To avoid confusion with Nelson, British Columbia, the name was later changed to that of the neighboring Danville Mining Company.

Daokoah Point *(S.12;T.33N;R.15W)*

Makah Indian Reservation point on Strait of Juan de Fuca, 8 miles east of Cape Flattery, northwest Clallam County. The original Makah Indian name has been retained, although in a greatly distorted form. As pronounced by Makahs and by Quillayutes, it should be spelled *Ta-qua.*

Darknell *(S.6;T.22N;R.45E)*

A railroad siding between Fairfield and Rockford, southeast Spokane County. It was named for a pioneer farmer, George Darknell, who settled here in 1880.

Daron Island (Pierce County) *see* Spanaway Lake

Darrington *(S.23;T.32N;R.9E)*

A logging and sawmill community on Sauk River, 29 miles east of Arlington, north central Snohomish County. It also was a meeting place for many Indian tribes in early days. From here there are 5 trails that lead into Glacier Peak Wilderness Area. Early names for this place were *Sauk Portage* and *The Burn.* The former related to a river portage here, and the latter to extensive burns in the forested area, which were caused by Indians who wanted better berry crops. In 1891, settlers decided on a name by flipping a card which carried the name *Portage* on one side and *Barrington,* the name of an early settler, on the other. Legend says that Barrington's name was on both sides of the card. That name won, but later became twisted to the present name when a post office was established in 1894.

Dartford *(S.6;T.26N;R.43E)*

Settlement on Little Spokane River, 4-1/2 miles north of Spokane, central Spokane County. It was named for the Dart family, founders of an early sawmill here. The first name was *Dart's Mill.*

Dartford Creek *(T.26N;R.43E)*

The stream of the creek heads on Half Moon Prairie, central Spokane County; flows south to Little Spokane River at Dartford, a distance of about 5 miles. Names which have been applied to this stream in the past are *Little Creek, Sheep Creek, Willow Creek,* and probably the original Indian name. The present title was made official by a petition signed by a majority of local residents. It was for the town of Dartford. (USGBN)

Dart's Mill (Spokane County) *see* Dartford

Davenport *(S.21;T.25N;R.37E)*

Town in the Big Bend country, 41 miles west of Spokane, north central Lincoln County. It is the county seat. In 1880, it was founded by a settler named Harker, who called it *Cottonwood Springs.* Other local names were Harker's Place, Cottonwood, and *Cottonwood Creek.* In 1881, J. C. Davenport of Cheney started a store close by, and called his place Davenport. In 1882, when that settlement was destroyed by fire, the citizens moved to Cottonwood Springs and changed the name to Davenport.

Davidson Rock *l(T.34N;R.1W)*

A rock in Strait of Juan de Fuca, 3/4 mile south of the southeastern tip of Lopez Island, southeast San Juan County. In 1854, it was named *Entrance Rock* by U.S. Coast Survey. The name was changed to the present title by Capt. Henry Richards, British admiralty sur-

veyor, in 1858 or 1859. It is named for George Davidson, who conducted much of the U.S. Coast Survey work in this area.

Davin *(Ss.17,20;T.13N;R.36E)*

Village on north bank of Snake River, 5-1/2 miles west of confluence with Palouse River, eastern Franklin County. Originally the place was given the descriptive name of *Sand.* In 1910, Northern Pacific Railway Company officials changed the station's name to Davin, for S. V. Davin, a local landowner from whom the right-of-way was acquired.

Davis *(S.34;T.14N;R.6W)*

Community on Elk Creek, 13 miles east of Raymond, northeast Pacific County. It was named for Frank Davis, who was logging foreman for Raymond Lumber Company.

Davis Bay *(Ss.9,10;T.34N;R.2W)*

A shallow bay at the southwest end of Lopez Island on Middle Channel, 3/4 mile west of Richardson, south central San Juan County. It is bordered by a low beach and a marsh, which offers anchorage to small craft only. In 1854, the bay was named *Shoal Bight* by the U.S. Coast Survey. In 1859, it was changed to the present name on British admiralty charts made by Capt. Henry Richards, R.N. Richards named it for Hezekiah Davis, an early settler on the bay. (USBGN)

Davis Creek *(T.32N;R.44E)*

The stream of the creek rises in Davis Lake, south central Pend Oreille County; flows 6 miles northeast to Pend Oreille River opposite Lenora. It was named for a pioneer who lived on the shore of Davis Lake.

Davis Lake *(S.31;T.32N;& S.6;T.31N;R.44E)*

A 1-1/2-mile-long lake, 3/4 mile average width, at the head of Davis Creek, 2 miles west of Dalkena, south central Pend Oreille County. (*see* Davis Creek)

Davis Mountain (Whatcom County) *see* Davis Peak

Davis Peak *(S.2;T.37N;R.12E.uns)*

A Mt. Baker National Forest peak, northeast of Mt. Rose and 3 miles northwest of Diablo Dam, southeast Whatcom County. The mountain was named for a homesteader, Davis, who took a land claim where Stetattle Creek enters Skagit River.

Davis Peak (Cowlitz County) *see* Mt. Davis

Davis Point (*T.34N;R.2W*)
An extreme southwest point of Lopez Island, at the west entrance to Davis Bay, south central San Juan County. It was named for Davis Bay. (USGBN)

Davisines (Lincoln County) *see* Almira

Dawn Lake (Clallam County) *see* Lake Dawn

Day City (*S.3;T.26N;R.5E*)
Small settlement, 1 mile northeast of Woodinville and 1 mile south of Snohomish County boundary, northwest King County. In 1889, it was named by Hans Anderson when he platted a townsite after Day's Sawmill, which operated here at the time. The area is now in pasture and farmland.

Day Creek (*Ts.34,35N;R.6E*)
The stream of the creek heads in Day Lake, 8 miles south of Hamilton in south central Skagit County; flows 10 miles north by west to Skagit River near Lyman. (*see* Day Lake)

Day Island (*Ss.4,9;T.20N;R.2E*)
A peninsula on the western limits of Tacoma at the south end of The Narrows, northwest Pierce County. It is connected to the mainland by a gravel spit which is flooded at extreme high tides. In 1841, it was named *Days Island* by Cmdr. Charles Wilkes, for Stephen W. Days, one of his hospital stewards. The ''s'' has been dropped by subsequent cartographers, in error. A local legend recounts a story that the gravel spit, which connects this feature with the mainland, is flooded on just one day of each year, at which time the peninsula becomes an island.

Day Lake
(*Ss.30,31;T.34N;R.7E;S.25;T.34N;-R.6E*)
A lake 8 miles south of Hamilton at the head of Day Creek, south central Skagit County. It was locally named in 1882 for John and Mike Day, who had operated a logging camp here for many years.

Day's Lake (San Juan County) *see* Killibrew Lake

Dayton (*S.18;T.20N;R.4W*)
Town 6 miles west of Shelton, near North Fork, Goldsborough Creek, south central Mason County. It is located at a railroad crossing on a logging railroad formerly operated by Simpson Timber Company. The present name is for an early settler. A former name was *Williamson,* for Frank Williamson, a pioneer logger.

Dayton (*Ss.19,30;T.10N;R.39E*)
Town at junction of Touchet River and Patit Creek, central Columbia County. The first settler here was Hm. M. Chase in 1855. On Nov. 23, 1871, a townsite plat was filed by Jesse N. and Elizabeth Day. In 1881, the town was incorporated by the storekeeper, Jesse Day. In early days, Dayton was a favored camping site of frieghters, as it had been of Indians. The name is for Jesse Day. In 1872, a post office, which was established at nearby Touchet in 1864, was moved to Dayton. On some early maps, the name of *Touchet* is found on the site of Dayton.

Dead Canyon (*Ts.5;5N;Rs.23,24E*)
The canyon heads in northeast Klickitat County, runs southeasterly through the southwest corner of Benton County; it terminates on the north bank of Columbia River near Castle Rock. The name of *Dead Horse Canyon* was applied to this feature by local residents in the winter of 1886-1887, when hundreds of dead horses and cattle starved or were frozen in the canyon. Within recent years, the ''Horse'' has been dropped by cartographers.

Dead Horse Canyon (Benton County) *see* Dead Canyon

Dead Mans Camp
(*S.8;T.39N;R.10E.uns*)
A Mt. Baker National Forest campground, at Hannegan Pass, north central Whatcom County. The campground was named for a wealthy eastern hunter who was lost in the area while hunting mountain goats. His body was never recovered.

Dead Man's Bar (Kitsap County) *see* Yoemalt Point

Dead Man's Eddy (*S.21;T.39N;R.43E*)

A dangerous pool in Pend Oreille River directly below Metaline Falls, north central Pend Oreille County. It was locally named in pioneer days for several bodies that were taken from the eddy. Sternwheel steamers were common on the river in that period, and navigation was perilous; if a person fell into the Pend Oreille, rescue was difficult.

Dead Man's Point (Snohomish County) *see* Skiou Point

Deadhorse Creek (*T.39N;R.8E.uns*)
The stream of the creek rises on the north slope of Mt. Baker, north central Whatcom County; flows 5-1/2 miles north to North Fork, Nooksack River. It was named for a packhorse which died here while cattle-drivers were looking for a pass to the east.

Deadhorse Pass
(*Ss.34,35;T.26N;R.15E*)
A Wenatchee National Forest pass, elevation 7,500 ft., through Chiwaukum Mountains, near the south end of that range, between Cup Lake and Wildhorse Creek, southwest Chelan County. It is the only suitable route across the summit for horse travel. A. H. Sylvester named this feature after the term applied by sheepmen who used the pass for pack strings and sheep

Deadman (Garfield County) *see* Deadman Creek

Deadman Bay (*S.24;T.35N;R.4W*)
A southwest shore bay of San Juan Island, on Haro Strait, 6 miles southwest of Friday Harbor, southwest San Juan County. It was locally named for a workman who was killed and buried here, and who, according to pioneer records, was the first white man to die in the San Juan Islands.

Deadman Creek (*T.37N;Rs.35-37E*)
The stream of the creek heads near King Mountain, central Ferry County, 14 miles east of Republic, on Colville National Forest; flows east and northeast for 16 miles, to enter Kettle River near Boyds. It has a large north fork and many tributaries. In local traditions, it was named for a person who was lost in this watershed, and who died of exposure. A name in use before this fatality was *Sherwood Creek,* which may be found on early maps.

Deadman Creek (*T.13N;Rs.40-42E*)
The stream of the creek rises in 2 branches, northeast Garfield County;

flows west by north 29 miles to Meadow Creek near its confluence with Snake River. It drains much of the north end of the county. The name was given by pioneers after the terribly cold winter of 1861-1862, when 2 miners and a great many cattle were frozen to death in Deadman Hollow along the creek. In 1880, a post office in the vicinity named Deadman was discontinued.

Deadman Island (Pierce County) *see* Cutts Island

Deadman Island *(S.9;T.34N;R.2W)*

A locally-named island directly west of Davis Bay on the southwest tip of Lopez Island, south central San Juan County. The origin of this name has not been located. However, it is quite common along Washington's seacoast where many shipwrecks happened before navigational aids were installed. (USGBN)

Deadmans Hollow *(S.5;T.9N;R.11W)*

A dangerous hollow on the Pacific Ocean, between North Head and Peacock Spit, southwest Pacific County. In 1853, when the bark *Vandalia* foundered at the mouth of Columbia River, all hands were lost and some of the bodies drifted into this hollow. Over a period of years, several drowned fishermen have also been found here.

Deadmans Island *(S.34;T.26N;R.2E)*

A cemetery island in Port Madison harbor on the north end of Bainbridge Island, northeast Kitsap County. In 1861, 6 men, who were killed in a boiler explosion at a Port Madison sawmill, were buried here. It continued to be a community cemetery until 1870, when another was established 1/2 mile east of Port Madison.

Deadman's Point (Whatcom County) *see* Commercial Point

Dean Creek *(T.29N;R.3W)*

The stream of the creek rises in hills southeast of Blyn, extreme east Clallam County; flows 4-1/2 miles northeast to Sequim Bay. It was named for a family of early homesteaders who lived near, or upon, the creek. A member of the family once was postmaster at Blyn.

Deans (King County) *see* Lester

Decatur (Kitsap County) *see* East Bremerton; Manette

Decatur *(S.21;T.35N;R.1W)*

Small settlement on the west shore of

Decatur Island on Reads Bay, southeast San Juan County. (*see* Decatur Island)

Decatur Head *(S.22;T.35N;R.1W)*

An east shore head of Decatur Island, directly west of James Island, southeast San Juan County. (*see* Decatur Island)

Decker Creek *(Ts.18-20N;R.6W)*

The stream of the creek heads directly south of Olympic National Forest boundary, extreme west central Mason County; flows 18 miles to East Fork, Satsop River. It was named for Lansing Deckeer, who settled on the creek in the early 1800s.

Decatur Island *(T.35N;R.1W)*

One of the medium-sized islands of the San Juan archipelago, between Blakely Island and Lopez Sound, southeast San Juan County. In 1841, it was named by Cmdr. Charles Wilkes for Capt. Stephen Dacatur, U.S. naval hero of the War of 1812. Wilkes actually named it *Decatur's Island*, but on subsequent charts, the possessive form was dropped. This happened to most of the names that Wilkes applied to features in Washington state.

Decatur Reef *(S.8;T.24N;R.3E)*

A southeastern reef at the end of Bainbridge Island, southeast of Restoration Point, Kitsap County. The name is for the U.S. sloop-of-war *Decatur*, which grounded here during the winter of 1855-1856. On January 25 and 26, 1856, this vessel was of material help to Seattle when attacked by Indians.

Deception Bay (Pacific County) *see* Baker Bay

Deception City (Skagit County) *see* Dewey

Deception Island *(S.27;T.34N;R.1E)*

A small, wooded island at the west entrance to Deception Pass, 1/2 mile southwest of Reservation Bay, northwest Skagit County. In 1854, it was named for Deception Pass by U.S. Coast Survey. In 1841, Cmdr. Charles Wilkes had named it *Ketslum Island* for a crew member, but his name did not persist.

Deception Lakes *(S.28;T.25N;R.13E)*

A group of 3 glacier-fed lakes, total 25-1/2 acres, on Snoqualmie National Forest, 5-1/2 miles south of Scenic and 1/2 mile to 1 mile west of Cascade Mountain summit, extreme southwest King County. They are numbered from 1

to 3, with no other known names. The group name is for Deception Creek which drains them. An alternate name, which is somewhat of a misnomer, is *Twin Lakes*. Why not Triplet?

Deception Pass *(T.34N;Rs.1,2E)*

A narrow, tidal passage between Fidalgo Island on the north and Whidbey Island on the south, Skagit and Island counties. It is subject to very strong tides and perilous to inexperienced navigators. On a strong ebb tide, 2-1/2 billion gallons of water boil through the rock-bound channel every hour. In 1790, this feature was named *Boca de Flon* by Manuel Quimper. The same name was charted by Juan Francisco de Eliza. In 1792, Capt. George Vancouver named it *Port Gardner*, not knowing that the channel was open at the west end. When Joseph Whidbey of his command found the western outlet, Vancouver renamed it *Deception Passage*, because he had been deceived as to its nature. In 1841, Cmdr. Charles Wilkes used Vancouver's name on his charts. The name has since been shortened to its present form.

Deception Pass State Park *(T.34N;R.2E)*

A 1,746-acre saltwater park on both shores of Deception Pass, south end of Fidalgo Island and the north end of Whidbey Island, Skagit and Island counties. It is the most popular of Washington's state-owned parks, offering camping, fishing, and swimming. It was named for Deception Pass, which it borders.

Deckerville *(Ss.8,17;T.20N;R.6W)*

Small settlement on Decker Creek, 3 miles southwest of Matlock, southwest Mason County. (*see* Decker Creek)

Deep Creek (Ferry County) *see* West Deer Creek

Deep Creek *(T.27N;R.18E)*

The stream of the creek heads on the west slope of Maverick Peak in Entiat Mountain range, and winds 2-1/2 miles southwest to Entiat River on Wenatchee National Forest, central Chelan County. It was named by U.S. Forest Supervisor A. H. Sylvester, not for its great depth, but because it flows through a very deep gorge.

Deep Creek *(T.18N;R.10E)*

The stream of the creek heads near Corvall Pass on Dalles Ridge, northeast Pierce County; flows 3 miles southwest to White River. This quite unexceptional name was evidently applied by personnel of Snoqualmie National Forest, on which the creek is located.

Deep Creek *(S.24;T.25N;R.40E)*

Village at the falls of Deep Creek, 5 miles north of Medical Lake, west central Spokane County. The first settlement here was in 1878. On May 14, 1883, the town was platted by Daniel, Alfred, Lucy, and Nancy Stroup. Its first name was *Deep Creek Falls*, which is descriptive of the location. When a post office was established, the name was shortened.

Deep Creek *(T.39N;R.7E)*

A 2-1/2-mile-long tributary of Glacier Creek, on Mt. Baker National Forest, north central Whatcom County. It was locally named for the deep canyon through which it flows.

Deep Creek Falls (Spokane County) *see* Deep Creek

Deep Lake (Grant County) see Sun Lakes State Park

Deep Lake (Jefferson County) *see* Twin Lakes

Deep Lake (Lincoln County/Spokane County) *see* Fishtrap Lake

Deep Lake *(S.29;T.21N;R.7E)*

A 39-acre lake, 76 ft. depth, 3/4 mile southwest of Cumberland, south central King County. The name is appropriate, because of the lake's depth.

Deep Lake *(S.3;T.16N;R.2W)*

A 17-ft. deep lake, 7 miles south of Olympia, adjoining Millersylvania State Park on the south, in a wooded area, central Thurston County.

Deep River *(T.10N;R.8W)*

The stream of the river rises in the northwest corner of Wahkiakum County; flows 7 miles south to Grays Bay on the north bank of Columbia River. *(see* Deep River -- town)

Deep River *(S.17;T.10N;R.8W)*

Community on Deep River, 55 miles west of Longview, southwest Wahkiakum County. It is essentially a logging community, with many Finns. The town is named for the river, of which the original name was *Ela-be-kail*, meaning ''deep river.''

Deepwater Bay *(S.4;T.35N;R.1E)*

A southeast shore bay of Cypress Island, on Bellingham Channel, north-

west Skagit County. The pointed terminus of the bay is called *Secret Harbor.* In 1858, the name was first used on British admiralty charts by Capt. Richards. He found from 15 to 21 fathoms here, which justified the name.

Deepwater Lake *(S.13;T.21N;R.3W)*

A 10.8-acre, narrow lake, 1,800 ft. long, 7-1/4 miles northeast of Shelton, southeast Mason County. The name is descriptive. No exact record of its depth is available, but local residents state that it is very deep.

Deer Creek (Ferry County) *see* East Deer Creek

Deer Creek (Snohomish County) *see* Pugh Creek

Deer Creek *(Mt. Rainier National Park)*

A small trout stream in the east central area of the park, rising on the west slope of Cascade Mountains near the summit. It flows west to Chinook Creek, southwest of Seymour Peak. It is one of many streams in the state that have been given this name because there are plenty of deer in the vicinity.

Deer Harbor *(S.7;T.36N;R.2W)*

A southwest point bay of Orcas Island, north of Pole Pass, central San Juan County. In 1858, the name was placed on British admiralty charts by Capt Henry Richards, RN, for excellent deer hunting found around this bay in the 1850s by Louis Cayou, hunter for Hudson's Bay Company. Lummi Indians, who lived in three long houses on the bay, called it *Tel-ki-each.*

Deer Harbor *(S.7;T.36N;R.2W)*

Town on the west shore of Deer Harbor bay, south end of the eastern peninsula of Orcas Island, central San Juan County. The town was locally named for the bay on which it is located.

Deer Lagoon *(S.18;T.29N;R.3E)*

A shallow, saltwater inlet at the head of Useless Bay, near the south end of Whidbey Island, south Island County. It is full of small marshy islands and it was named in 1856 by U.S. Coast Survey personnel for the prevalence of small, native deer in this vicinity.

Deer Lake *(S.26;T.29N;R.3E)*

An 82-acre lake in a populated area on the south end of Whidbey Island, 1-1/4 miles west of Clinton, Island County. The name was probably descriptive when applied in pioneer days, as nearly all Puget

Sound islands had deer populations.

Deer Lake *(S.15;T.24N;R.11E)*

A 45.8-acre lake between Bear Lake and Snoqualmie Lake, Snoqualmie National Forest, northeast King County. This locally-applied name is so commonly used in the Pacific Northwest that it fails to identify the features which bear it.

Deer Lake *(T.30N;R.41E)*

A 3-mile-long lake, elevation 2,380 ft., 5 miles east of Springdale, southeast Stevens County. It was named because deer, which swam across a narrow west arm of the lake in traveling from Deer Lake Mountain on the south, to Jump Off Joe Mountain on the west, could be easily killed from rowboats.

Deer Lake Mountain
(S.23;T.30N;R.41E)

A 3,735-ft. mountain, 1 mile south of Deer Lake, 6 miles east by north of Springdale, southeast Stevens County. (*see* Deer Lake, from which this name is borrowed.)

Deer Lake *(S.14;T.28N;R.9W.uns)*

Two Olympic National Park lakes, 3-1/2 miles southeast of Sol Duc Hot Springs, south central Clallam County. Located close together at the head of Canyon Creek, one lake is 8-1/2 acres, the other 1 acre. Scores of mountain lakes in the Pacific Northwest bear this name. In this case it is appropriate, as wildlife of many types is abundant in the Olympic National Park -- free from harvesting by the State Game Department.

Deer Park *(S.1;T.28N;R.5W.uns)*

An Olympic National Park mountain meadow, elevation 5,411 ft., south of Blue Mountain, 15 miles southeast of Port Angeles, northeast corner of the park. It is now part of a winter sports area. The name is descriptive and was given to the meadow, before 1900, by a part-Indian trapper and his partner.

Deer Park *(Ss.2,3;T.28N;R.42E)*

A sawmill town, 23 miles north of Spokane in a timbered area, northwest Spokane County. It was named for the many deer that wintered here in pioneer days.

Deer Point *(S.15;T.36N;R.1W)*

An extreme southeast point of the eastern peninsula of Orcas Island, on Obstruction Pass, northeast San Juan County. It was locally named in pioneer days for excellent deer hunting in this area.

Deer Trail *(S.11;T.29N;R.37E)*

Mining community on Alder Creek, 2 miles south of Turk, at head of Cedar Canyon Road, extreme southwest Stevens County. It was established prior to 1903, in a mineralized area, as a residence and supply point for the nearby Deer Trail Mine. It was named for the adjoining mine.

De Forest Creek *(T.34N;R.7E)*

A short tributary of Deer Creek, which originates 9 miles south of Birdsview, on Mt. Baker National Forest, south central Skagit County. It was locally named for William De Forest who homesteaded near the creek's mouth in 1902.

De Fuca (Clallam County) *see* Agnew

Dege Peak *(Mt. Rainier Natiional Park)*

A 7,006-ft. peak on the southeast rim of Sourdough Mountains, northeast sector of the park, 2 miles east of Sunrise Park (Yakima Park), at the west end of Sunrise Ridge. It offers an excellent view of Mt. Rainier and of the Cascade Mountains. In 1912, it was named for James Dege, a prominent Tacoman. (USBGN)

De Haro Archipelago (San Juan County) *see* San Juan Archipelago

Delacombe Point *(S.26;T.36N;R.4W)*

A northwest shore point of San Juan Island on Mosquito Pass, between Horseshoe Bay and Yacht Haven, west central San Juan County. This name was applied by Capt. Pender of the British Navy for Capt. William Addis Delacombe, RMLI, who commanded the British occupation camp near here from 1867 to 1872.

Delacy's Lake (Skagit County) *see* Big Lake

Delameter Valley *(T.19N;Rs.2,3W)*

The valley of Scantigrease Creek, 3 to 6 miles southwest of Castle Rock, northwest Cowlitz County. Originally it was called *Scantigrease Valley*, but later was renamed for Dan Delameter who settled here in 1871, and who operated a grist mill on Scantigrease Creek.

Delaney *(S.19;T.12N;R.39E)*

Small settlement on Pataha Creek, 13 miles north of Dayton, northwest Columbia County. It was named by officials of Union Pacific Railroad for a resident on whose land the station was located.

Delanty Lake *(S.30;T.29N;R.1W)*

A 13.1-acre lake, 1-1/2 miles south of the south end of Port Discovery Bay, at the head of Chimacum Creek, northeast Jefferson County. It was named for the pioneer Delanty family of Port Discovery -- Dick, a logger, and William, a sawmill operator.

Delcampo Peak *(S.23;T.29N;R.10E)*

A 5,780-ft. peak, 4 miles west of Monte Cristo, east central Snohomish County. It was named by early prospectors for the Del Campo Mine on the mountain slope. An alternate name, with no information on the source, is *Flag Peak*.

Dell Haven (Benton County) *see* Kennewick

Del Rosario La Marinera (Washington State Ref./northwest Washington) *see* Georgia Strait

Delta (Walla Walla County) *see* Waitsburg

Delrio *(S.13;T.29N;R.28E)*

Settlement 19 miles east of Bridgeport, 6-1/2 miles south of Columbia River, northeast Douglas County. The first name for this settlement was *Lella*, suggested by an early postmaster for his wife's name. The present name was applied to the post office by Violet Bailey, granddaughter of Postmistress A. C. Earl. Violet submitted the name as *Del Rio*, because of its location near the great river. Postal authorities ran the words together.

Delta *(S.2;T.40N;R.2E)*

Community 4 miles northwest of Lynden and 1-1/2 miles south of the Canadian boundary, in Nooksack River valley, northwest Whatcom County. In 1880, it was named by James Bremmer, a homesteader and the first postmaster, for the wide, level lands of Nooksack Valley.

Deming *(S.31;T.38N;R.5E)*

An old community on Nooksack River, 12 miles northeast of Bellingham, west central Whatcom County. It was platted before the turn of the century, and named for George Deming, first postmaster and owner of Deming Land Company. A local citizen, E. W. Owen, chose the name.

Deming Glacier *(T.38N;R.7E.uns)*

A southwest slope glacier of Mt. Baker, at the head of Middle Fork, Nooksack River, Mt. Baker National Forest, Whatcom County. In 1909, the glacier was named by Charles F. Eaton for George Deming. (*see* Deming)

Denison *(S.24;T.28N;R.42E)*

Community 3 miles southeast of Deer Park, northwest Spokane County. The name was *Hock Spur*, until changed to *Buckeye*, for Buckeye Lumber Company which operated here. Later it was called *Pratt*, for a local settler. The fourth name was given by F. H. Buell when he revived the town and secured a new post office. Denison was his wife's family name.

Denman Falls *(Mt. Rainier National Park)*

One of 3 closely associated waterfalls, in St. Andrews Creek, between North and South Forks, Puyallup River, southwest area of the park. It was named by Ben Longmire for A. H. Denman of Tacoma, mountaineer, photographer, and mountain lover.

Denman Peak *(Mr. Rainier National Park)*

A flat-topped mountain in Tatoosh Range, between Lane and Plummer peaks, south central area of the park. The first name of this peak was *That Mountain*. On June 21, 1931, The Mountaineers named it for A. H. Denman of Tacoma, mountaineer and photographer. The name was accepted by the National Park Service, but was not approved by USBGN.

Dennie Ahl Hill *(S.11,T.22N;R.5W)*

An Olympic National Forest hill, elevation 2,050 ft., 2 miles southwest of the south end of Lake Cushman Reservoir, central Mason County. It was named for Dennie Ahl, who worked for the U.S. Forest Service on Olympic National Forest for 30 years. He died on July 18, 1941. An incorrect name for this hill on some maps is *Gibbons Peak*. (USBGN)

Dennis Rock (Skagit County) *see Dennis Shoal*

Dennis Shoal *(T.34N;R.1E)*

A Rosario Strait shoal, 1/4 mile southwest of Allan Island, southwest Skagit County. The name was given in 1841, by Cmdr. Charles Wilkes, for a member of his crew. It was confirmed later by U.S. Coast Survey. The shoal is shown on some maps, in error, as *Dennis Rock* or *Denis Rock*.

Denny Creek *(Ts.22,23N;Rs.10,11E)*

The stream of the creek rises in Hemlock Pass 2-1/2 miles west of Cascade Mountain summit, east central King County; flows a short distance southward to South Fork, Snoqualmie River at Denny Creek Camp, established by U.S. Forest Service. The creek was named by The Mountaineers for David T. Denny, one of Seattle's original settlers, who located mining claims on the creek in the 1890s.

Denny Hill *(S.30;T.25N;R.4E)*

A hill which extended for several blocks north of Seattle's main business district until regraded in several operations. The hill was lowered from a 212-ft. elevation at Second Ave. and Stewart St., to 143 ft. At Second Ave. and Lenora, it was lowered from 225 ft. to 142 ft. It was named for the Denny family, one of several families who were the first settlers on Elliott Bay.

Denny Horn (King County) *see* The Tooth

Denny Lake *(S.1;T.22N;R.10E)*

A 14.3-acre lake, 2-1/2 miles west of Snoqualmie Pass, directly northeast of Granite Mountain, east central King County. It is one of 3 Granite Mountain lakes, along with Cad and Crystal lakes; and, it was named for Denny Creek, which drains it. An alternate name is *Evelyn Lake* or *Lake Evelyn*.

Denny Tooth (King County) *see* The Tooth

Depot Springs (Spokane County) *see* Cheney

Deschutes River
(Ts.15-18N;Rs.1-5E;1,2W)

The stream of the river rises in southeast Thurston County; flows 23 miles northwesterly to Puget Sound (Budd Inlet) at Olympia. Originally the river had names in several Indian dialects, including *Low-hum, Pu-kal-Bush, Pac-al-ups, To-war-na-hi-ooks* and *Dus-chut-wit.*. The present name is a French-Canadian translation of the latter name into *Des Chutes*, meaning "waterfall" or "cataract." It refers to the falls at Tumwater.

Des Moines *(S.17;T.22N;R.4E)*

Town on the east shore of Puget Sound, 10 miles northeast of Tacoma, southwest King County. In 1887, the name was given by F.A. Blasher, when he founded the town. He persuaded friends in his former home city, Des Moines, Iowa, to finance the venture if the town were named Des Moines. He operated under the name of Des Moines Improvement Company.

Destruction Island
(T.25N;R.14W;uns)

A grim, rocky 40-acre island, elevation 90 ft., in the Pacific Ocean, 4 miles offshore from west central Jefferson County, southwest of Hoh River mouth. It was named *Isla de Dolores* by Bodega y Quadra on July 14, 1775, after he lost 6 men of a boat crew to Indians who attacked them at Point Grenville. The men went ashore for water, but tried to take a boatload of Indian dried fish. The Indian name for the island was *hob-to-la-bish*.

Destruction River (Jefferson County) *see* Hoh River

Detroit *(S.5;T.21N;R.1W)*

Vanished town on a site near Grapeview, west shore of Cases Inlet, 5 miles east of Mason Lake, east central Mason County. It boomed in 1889 with Detroit Land & Improvement Company, backed by Ladd & Tilton Bank of Portland. There were plans to build a portage railroad between Cases Inlet and Hood Canal, but the town did not develop as anticipated. The post office name was changed to *Grapeview* when it moved a short distance to the south.

Devil Creek *(T.17N;R.14E)*

The stream of the creek rises north of Little Bald Mountain, northwest Yakima County on Snoqualmie National Forest, between Swamp Creek and Bumping River; flows 6 miles northeast to Naches River. It was named by local cattlemen when Barney Moore, on a cattle drive, branded the creek area as "A devil of a rough place."

Devil Lake *(T.28N;R.18E.uns)*

A small mountain lake directly south of Klone Peak, at the head of one branch of Tommy Creek, on Wenatchee National Forest, north central Chelan County. It was named by Forest Ranger John S. Brender, who called it "one of the Devil's many homes." (Many features in the state were named for His Satanic Majesty, but few carry the names of saints, other than those named by the Jesuits.)

Devilclub Creek *(T.28N;R.15E.uns)*

The stream of the creek rises on Wenatchee Ridge, west central Chelan County, on Wenatchee National Forest; flows 2 miles south to Little Wenatchee River. It was named by U.S. Forest Supervisor A. H. Sylvester, who encountered a large patch of Devil's Club (*Fatsia horrida*), while laying out a trail location along the creek.

Devil's Backbone
(T.28N;Rs.19,20.partly uns)

A 4-1/2-mile section of Chelan Mountain range, from Angle Peak to Stormy Mountain, east central Chelan County. It forms part of the boundary between Wenatchee and Okanogan national forests. This imaginative name was applied by settlers some time prior to 1908.

Devils Dome *(S.36;T.39N;R.14E.uns)*

A Mt. Baker National Forest peak, elevation 6,960 ft., 10 miles northeast of Ross Dam, east central Whatcom County. Local people chose this name for its rough, forbidding terrain. (It has been quite common with place namers to blame the Devil for the natural forces of erosion and of volcanic action.)

Devil's Dream Creek *(Mt. Rainier National Park)*

The stream of the creek -- a small tributary of Pyramid Creek -- heads in Squaw Lake on the east side of Indian Henry's Hunting Ground, on the southwest slope of Mt. Rainier. Records show that it was named by Ben Longmire "Because it is as crooked as a Devil's dream." The creek is an inferno on hot days when there is a heavy melt of glacial ice and snow at its head. (USBGN)

Devils Head *(S.2;T.19N;R.1W)*

A north shore point of Nisqually Reach at the entrance to Drayton Passage, northwest Pierce County. In 1841, it was named *Park Point*, for David P. Park, one of the sailmaker's mates on the Wilkes Expedition. In 1847, Capt. R. N. Inskip placed the name *Moore's Bluff* on British admiralty charts of this area. The present name was applied by George Davidson of the U.S. Coast Survey, with no explanation of his reason for the choice.

Devils Lake *(S.36;T.27N;R.2W)*

A 11.8-acre lake, 22 ft. maximum depth, 2 miles south of Quilcene, east central Jefferson County. It is surrounded by second-growth timber and is one of many features in the state that pioneers named for His Satanic Majesty. Washington has more places named for the Devil than for all of the angels mentioned in the scriptures. An alternate name, *Linger Longer Lake*, indicates that somebody had a higher opinion of this body of water in the forest.

Devil's Playground *(T.36N;R.1E)*

A group of reefs and shoals in Rosario Strait, directly north of Cypress Island, Skagit County. It includes Cypress Reef, Buckeye Shoal, and smaller hazards. This name, which does not appear on current maps, was used by early navigators to describe an area of considerable danger.

Devils Ridge

(Ss.17,19,20,30;T.8N;R.43E)

A 3-mile-long ridge in the Blue Mountains, Umatilla National Forest, extreme southeast Garfield County. The high, rugged ridge runs from southwest to northeast. Early stockmen gave it the fanciful name of *Devils Tailbone Ridge*. When it was included in Umatilla National Forest, Forest Service officers shortened the name.

Devils Tailbone Ridge (Garfield County) *see* Devils Ridge

Devils Thumb *(S.6;T.30N;R.10E)*

A peculiarly shaped mountain, 9 miles south of Darrington, north central Snohomish County. The name was given by prospectors in early mining days because the mountain has the appearance of a closed fist with the thumb protruding upward, as viewed from the 4-1/2- and 5-mile points along the trail which goes up Clear Creek.

Dewatto *(S.28;T.23N;R.3W)*

Community on the east shore of Hood Canal and the south side of Dewatto Bay, north central Mason County. The name is from the Indian designation *Du-a-ta*, meaning ''Place where the evil spirits come out of the earth.'' These spirits, called *Tub-ta-ba*, drove people crazy by entering their bodies. In 1847, Kellett placed the name *Dudah Point* on British admiralty charts. An intermediate name, used locally, was *Dewats*.

Dewatto Bay *(S.28;T.23N;R.3W)*

Shallow inlet on the east shore of Hood Canal, across from Lilliwaup Bay, north central Mason County. (*see* Dewatto)

Dewatto Creek *(Ts.23,24N;Rs.2,3W)*

The winding stream rises in Ludwick Lake, southwest Kitsap County; flows south and southwest into Dewatto Bay on the east shore of Hood Canal, north central Mason County. (*see* Dewatto)

Dewatto River *(Ts.23,24N;Rs.2,3W)*

The stream of the river rises in Ludvick Lake, southwest Kitsap County; flows 8 miles south and southwest to enter Dewatto Bay on the east shore of Hood Canal, north east Mason County. The former name was *Dewattoa Creek*. (USBGN)

Dewey *(S.24;T.34N;R.1E)*

Small settlement on the north shore of Deception Pass, adjoining Fidalgo on the south, southwest Skagit County. In 1889, the townsite was platted, but the settlement suffered in the financial panic of the early 1890s. In 1901, the post office was named Dewey, for Admiral George Dewey, hero of the naval Battle of Manila Bay in 1898. (*see* Fidalgo)

Diablo Canyon *(T.37N;R.13E.uns)*

A Mt. Baker National Forest canyon on the upper Skagit River, between Newhalem and Diablo Lake, Whatcom County. It is the site of a City of Seattle hydroelectric power development. This name was applied by early prospectors and miners because of the extreme difficulty in passing through the canyon.

Diablo Dam

(Ss.5,8;T.37N;R.13E.uns)

A City of Seattle hydroelectric dam, elevation 389 ft., on upper Skagit River in Diablo Canyon, 6 miles northeast of Newhalem on Mt. Baker National Forest, Whatcom County. It was built between 1927 and 1930 and named for Diablo Canyon.

Diablo Lake *(T.37N;R.13E)*

A large, irregular, artificial lake on upper Skagit River directly above Diablo Dam, on Mt. Baker National Forest, 7 miles east of Newhalem, Whatcom County. It was created by the building of Diablo Dam for hydroelectric power production. The lake was named for Diablo Canyon, downriver from it.

Diamond *(S.35;T.17N;R.42E)*

Town 9 miles northwest of Colfax, central Whitman County. It was platted when a railroad was built through Rebel Flat, on which the site is located, and named for the platter, Mr. Q. Diamond.

Diamond City *(S.25;T.12N;R.11W)*

Ghost town 2-1/2 miles east of Nahcotta, on the north tip of Long Island in Willapa Bay, west central Pacific County. In the late 1850s and early 1860s, it was once a busy oyster center. This alluring name was used when the town was platted in the 1850s. It appears to have no special significance.

Diamond Hill *(Ss.12,13;T.36N;R.2W)*

An Orcas Island peak, elevation 1,020 ft., in the southwest area of the middle peninsula, 1 mile inland from East Sound, northeast San Juan County. In 1859, this name was placed on British admiralty charts by Capt. Henry Richards, RN, who did not divulge his name source.

Diamond Lake *(Ss.1,2;T.30N;R.44E)*

A 1,000-acre, 1-mile-long, spring-fed lake, 9 miles southwest of Newport, south central Pend Oreille County. The name was given by a party of hunters, one of whom found an ace of diamonds in the forest adjoining the lake.

Diamond Point *(S.15;T.30N;R.2W)*

A west entrance point of Port Discovery Bay on Strait of Juan de Fuca, extreme northwest Clallam County. It was the site of an old U.S. quarantine station, with remains of old buildings and many graves. In July 1790, it was named *Punta de San Juan* by Manuel Quimper. In 1841, the Wilkes Expedition used the name *North Bluff*. In 1846, Capt. Henry Kellet charted it as Clallam Point, a name which was in general use until 1941, when the U.S. Board on Geographic Names ruled that the present name was official.

Diamond Point *(S.18;T.36N;R.1W)*

Southwest point of the middle peninsula of Orcas Island, at the west entrance to East Sound, northeastern San Juan County. It was named for Diamond Hill, 1-1/4 miles to the northwest.

Dick Creek *(Mt. Rainier National Park)*

The stream of the creek rises in Elysian Fields, northwest sector of the park, near the lower end of Carbon Glacier; flows west to Moraine Creek, a tributary of Carbon River. It was named by park officials for Dick Williams, formerly a park packer. (USBGN)

Dickenson Point (Thurston County) *see* Dickerson Point

Dickerman Mountain
(Ss.23,24;T.30N;R.10E)

A 5,766-ft. mountain at the site of Big Four Inn, 1-1/2 miles east of South Fork, Stillaguamish River, 5 miles east of Silverton, east central Snohomish County. It was named locally for William Dickerman, an early mining engineer.

Dickerson Peninsula (Jefferson County) *see* Quimper Peninsula

Dickerson Point *(S.6;T.19N;R.1W)*

A west entrance point to Henderson Inlet, on Dana Passage, 8 miles north of Olympia, central Thurston County. In 1841, the Wilkes Expedition named this point for Thomas Dickenson, carpenter's mate on one of Wilkes's ships. The subsequent error in spelling is probably due to careless cartography.

Dickey River *(Ts.28-30N;Rs.14,15W)*

The stream of the river rises in southwest Clallam County in 2 forks. The west fork rises in Lake Dickey; the east fork near Dickey Hoko Summit, 6 miles east of Lake Dickey. The forks join 3 miles north of Quillayute; flow southwesterly to Pacific Ocean near Mora. The name is a simplification and contraction of the Indian name which was *De-tho-date-t-doh*, which appears to have the meaning of "People who live on the dark water."

Dickodochteder River (Clallam County) *see* Dickey River

Dicks Creek *(Ts.32,33N;Rs.7,8E)*

The stream of the creek heads in Myrtle Lake, south central Skagit County; flows 5-1/2 miles southward to North Fork, Stillaguamish River, north central Snohomish County, 2-1/2 miles west of Hazel. It was named by pioneer settlers for "Indian Dick" Smith, whose favorite camp was near the creek's mouth.

Dieringer *(S.7;T.20N;R.5E)*

Site of a Puget Sound Power & Light Company hydroelectric plant, 1-1/2 miles west of Lake Tapps, north central Pierce County. In 1889, it was named by officials of Northern Pacific Railway Company, for J. C. Dieringer, from whom they acquired a right-of-way.

Dill Creek *(T.27N;R.19E)*

The stream of the creek heads on the lower southwest slope of Chelan Mountains, Wenatchee National Forest, central Chelan County; flows 2-1/2 miles

southwest to Entiat River. U.S. Forest Supervisor A. H. Sylvester named the creek for Bill Dill, who owned the land through which it runs.

Dilworth Point (King County) *see* Point Beals

Dinkelman Canyon *(T.25N;R.20E)*

The canyon heads 5 miles northwest of Chumstick Mountain and runs 2-1/2 miles east to Entiat River, 3 miles northeast of Entiat, southeast Chelan County. The name comes from local sources, and is for a pioneer settler who claimed land along the canyon.

Dinner Island *(S.25;T.35N;R.3W)*

An island at the entrance to North Bay on San Juan Channel, 2 miles south of Friday Harbor, south central San Juan County. In 1858, this name was applied to British admiralty charts by Capt. Henry Richards, RN, when seamen from his ship went ashore on this island to eat dinner.

Dirtyface Peak *(S.2;T.27N;R.16E.uns)*

A Wenatchee National Forest peak, 2 miles north of Wenatchee Lake and 12 miles east of Cascade Mountain summit, west central Chelan County. This is one of many whimsical names applied to features of Wenatchee National Forest by former U.S. Forest Supervisor A. H. Sylvester. Discolored snow banks, caused by rapid melting in the late spring months, prompted this title.

Disautel *(S.13;T.33N;R.28E)*

An almost-abandoned village on Colville Indian Reservation, southeast Okanogan County. It is on Omak Creek, 15 miles east of Omak and 17 miles north of Columbia River. Until the fall of 1958, the place was used by Biles-Coleman Lumber Company of Omak as a logging headquarters. When the shops and employees were moved to Omak, the town faded. The name origin has not been ascertained.

Discovery Creek (Clallam County, Jefferson County) *see* Port Discovery Bay

Discovery Creek (Clallam County) *see* Salmon Creek

Discovery Lake (Grays Harbor County) *see* Klone Lakes

Dishman *(S.17;T.25N;R.44E)*

Suburb 3 miles east of Spokane, east central Spokane County. The first installation here was a rock quarry estab-

lished by A. T. Dishman in 1889. The place was named for him.

Dishpan Gap *(S.32;T.29N;R.14E.uns)*

A high, grassy pass on Wenatchee National Forest, directly south of Meander Meadows, northwest Chelan County. It does not run through the main Cascade Ridge. Forest Supervisor A. H. Sylvester also named this place upon finding an old, rusty dishpan here.

Disque *(S.36;T.31N;R.9W)*

Former railroad depot 2 miles west of Joyce and 3 miles southwest of Crescent Bay, north central Clallam County. During World War I, this railroad point was a supply depot for the "Spruce Division," commanded by Col. Brice P. Disque. The railroad on which this depot was located was built by troops under Disque's command and later became the Port Angeles Western Railway. The place is named for Col. Disque.

Divide Lake *(S.17;T.22N;R.11E)*

A boundary lake between northwest Kittitas County and east central King County, on Cascade summit, at the head of Tunnel Creek, 1-1/2 miles south of Snoqualmie Pass. It was named by The Mountaineers because of its location. (USGBN)

Divide Lake (King County) *see* Olallie Lake

Division Rock *(Mt. Rainier National Park)*

A bold, rocky, isolated eminence, elevation 4,900 ft., at the northwest extremity of North Mowich Glacier, northwest of Mt. Rainier's summit, northwest area of the park. It was named by Prof. I. C. Russell, author of *Glaciers of Mount Rainier*, because the rock divides the glacier into 2 lobes. (USBGN)

Dixie *(S.26;T.8N;R.37E)*

Settlement on Dry Creek, 10 miles northeast of Walla Walla, Walla Walla County. In the 1860s, it was started with a land claim by Herman C. Actor. Many southerners came here after the Civil War; this name seemed to fit the majority of the population.

Dixie Crossing *(S.18;T.7N;R.35E)*

Village 6 miles northwest of Walla Walla, at confluence of Mud Creek and Dry Creek, south central Walla Walla County. The southerners who came here after the Civil War included 3 Kershaw Brothers who sang "Dixie" at frequent intervals while crossing the plains with an immigrant train. The name was applied to this town, as well as to a school, cemetery, and station on Dr. Dorsey S. Baker's ''Rawhide Railroad.''

Dixon's (Garfield County) *see* Gould City

Dockton (*S.30;T.22N;R.2E*)

A ghost town on the east shore of Quartermaster Harbor, Maury Island, southwest King County. In 1891, the name was applied by Puget Sound Dry Dock Company when the company started building a huge dry dock here. The place faded when competition from the mainland made operations unprofitable.

Dodge (*S.17;T.12N;R.40E*)

Town 11 miles northwest of Pomeroy on Pataha Creek, northwest Garfield County. Originally it was named *Buckley* for an early settler who owned much of the adjoining land. The name was dropped because of confusion with Buckley in Pierce County. The second name was chosen by the post office -- probably because it was short -- from a list of other early settlers.

Dodwell-Rison Pass (*T.26N;R.7W*)

An Olympic National Park pass between the headwaters of Elwha and Queets rivers, about 8 miles southeast of Mt. Olympus summit, central Jefferson County. It does not appear under this name on recent maps. It was named for Arthur Dodwell and Theodore F. Rixon, who surveyed almost 3,500 sq. miles of the Olympic Peninsula from 1898 to 1900 for U.S. Geological Survey.

Doe Bay Mountain (San Juan County) *see* Mt. Pickett

Doe Island (*S.2;T.36N;R.1W*)

A small island off the southeast shore of Orcas Island, directly southwest of Doe Bay, northeast San Juan County. It was named locally for nearby Doe Bay. (USBGN)

Doelle Lakes (*S.5;T.25N;R.15*)

Two Wenatchee National Forest lakes -- one of 30 acres and the other, 70 acres; they connect and drain through Doughgod Creek to Icicle Creek, southeast Chelan County. U.S. Forest Supervisor A. H. Sylvester named these lakes for William A. Doelle of Cashmere, a fisherman, sportsman, and mountain climber, who lost his life fighting a forest fire in this area.

Dofflemeyer Point (*S14;T.19N;R.2W*)

An east shore point of Budd Inlet, directly west of Boston Harbor, north central Thurston County. In 1841, the Wilkes Expedition called the feature *Brown's Point*, for James Brown, carpenter's mate on one of the expedition's ships. An early local name was *Pap's Point*. The present name is for James Dofflemeyer, who took a Donation Land Claim here in the 1850s.

Dogfish Bay (Kitsap County) *see* Liberty Bay

Dog Island (Skagit County) *see* Guemes Island

Dogwood Creek (Chelan County) *see* Doughgod Creek

Dolly Varden Creek (Whatcom County) *see* Chilliwack Creek

Dolphin (*S.1;T.36N;R.2W*)

Small settlement on the west shore of East Sound, southwest of Rosario, northeast San Juan County. (*see* Dolphin Bay)

Dolphin Bay (*S.1;T.36N;R.2W*)

A small bay on the west shore of East Sound, Orcas Island, 1 mile southwest of Rosario, across the sound. It was locally named, not for sea mammals, but for a group of capped piles, known by this name to mariners, installed for moorage in 1903.

Dolphin Point (*S.5;T.23N;R.3E*)

The northeast point of Vashon Island, 1/2 mile southeast of Vashon Heights, west central King County. The name was first used by George Davidson in the 1889 issue of *Pacific Coast Pilot*. It was named for porpoises that were abundant in Puget Sound at the time.

Domke Creek (*T.31N;R.18E.uns*) The stream of this short creek heads in Domke Lake, Wenatchee National Forest, north central Chelan County; flows 1-1/2 miles southeast to Lake Chelan via Domke Falls. (*see* Domke Lake)

Domke Falls (*T.31N;R.18E.uns*)

A Wenatchee National Forest falls at the entrance point of Domke Creek into Lake Chelan, north central Chelan County. (*see* Domke Lake)

Domke Lake (*T.31N;R.18E.uns*)

A large lake, 1-1/2 miles west of Lake Chelan at the head of Domke Creek, north central Chelan County. It was named for a millwright who estab-

lished a water-powered sawmill at Domke Falls, where Domke Creek discharges into Lake Chelan. An earlier name was Crane's Lake, and on an early map it is called *Round Lake*, which is inappropriate. Two misspellings of the present name, which are found in early records, are *Dumkie* and *Dumpky*.

Domke Mountain (*T.31N;R.18E.uns*)

A 4,000-ft. peak between Domke Lake and Lake Chelan, north central Chelan County. It is used in season as a forest fire lookout by personnel of Wenatchee National Forest. (*see* Domke Lake)

Donahue Spur (Lewis County) *see* Meskill

Donald (*S.2;T.11N;R.19E*)

Railway point directly north of Yakima River, 8 miles southeast of Yakima, central Yakima County. It was named by Northern Pacific Railway officials for George Donald, across whose property a local right-of-way was secured.

Donovan Creek (*T.27N;R.1W*)

The trickling stream of this creek heads 3 miles north of the head of Quilcene Bay; flows south to the bay in northeast Jefferson County. It was named locally for a very early settler who lived here with his Indian wife.

Donovan State Park (*T.36N;R.4E*)

A 3-acre picnic ground near Alger, 10 miles north of Burlington, northwest Skagit County. It was named for the donor, J. J. Donovan of Bellingham, a prominent lumberman and civil engineer.

Dooley Lake (Okanogan County) *see* Duley Lake

Doris Lake (Skamania County) *see* Forest Lake

Dosewallips River
(*T.26N;Rs.2-5W.part uns*)

The stream of the river heads north of Sentinel Peak in Olympic National Park; flows easterly to Hood Canal at Brinnon, southeast Jefferson County. The name is from the Twana or Clallam word *Dos-wail-opsh*, the title of a mythical Indian chief who was transformed by The Great Changer into a mountain near the head of this river. The stream was called *Sylopish Creek* on most maps published before 1889. (USBGN)

Dot (*S.32;T.5N;R.20E*)

Community 10 miles northwest of Roosevelt, east central Klickitat County. A settler named Hardison called the place *Dorothy* for his daughter. It later was shortened to the present name.

Dot Island (*S.10;T.35N;R.2E*)

An island between Saddlebag Island and Hat Island in Padilla Bay, 2-1/2 miles northeast of Anacortes, west central Skagit County. In 1790, Dionisio Galiano included this island with Huckleberry and Saddlebag islands as *Las Tres Hermanos*, because it is small and round. He called the 3-island group *Porpoise Rocks*. In 1904, Cmdr. Charles Wilkes's name of Dot Island was charted by U.S. Coast & Geodetic Survey.

Dot Rock (*S.27;T.35N;R.1W*)

A small, bare, rocky island in Rosario Strait, 1/4 mile off the southeast shore of Decatur Island, southeast San Juan County. In 1859, this descriptive name was placed on British admiralty charts by Capt. Henry Richards, RN, who named a majority of the prominent features in the San Juan Archipelago.

Doty (*S.2;T.13N;R.5W*)

A semi-abandoned town on Chehalis River, 19 miles west of Chehalis, west central Lewis County. Once it was a busy sawmill town, but has been inactive since the largest sawmill moved out in 1929. It was named for Chauncey Albert Doty, owner of Doty Lumber & Shingle Company, who built a sawmill and shingle mill here in the late 1890s.

Double Bluff (*T.29N;R.2E*)

Two bluffs, one above the other, elevations about 100 ft., between Mutiny Bay and Useless Bay on the southwest shore of Whidbey Island, south Island County. An immense slide in the glacial clay formation created this outstanding feature. In 1855, the name was given by George Davidson of U.S. Coast Survey. In 1841, Cmdr. Charles Wilkes had named the bluff *Ariels Point*, for a vessel in Perry's fleet on Lake Erie during the War of 1812. Another name for this feature, whose origin is obscure, was *Volcano Point*.

Double Hill (*Ss.14,15;T.37N;R.2W*)

Two small peaks, elevations about 500 ft., on north central Orcas Island, 1/2 mile west of the town of East Sound, north central San Juan County. In 1858, this descriptive name was placed on British admiralty charts by Capt. Henry Richards, RN.

Double Island (*S.17;T.36N;R.2W*)

Two small islands on the west side of the entrance to West Sound, Orcas Island, central San Juan County. They are connected at extreme low tides. (*see* Double Hill)

Double Peak (*Mt. Rainier National Park*)

A twin summit, with the taller peak's elevation 5,200 ft., 2 miles southeast of Cowlitz Chimneys, between Chinook Creek and Ohanapecosh River, southeast sector of the park. The name was given because of the double mountaintop.

Dougall Point (*S.19;T.21N;R.1W*)

A north end point on Cases Inlet, Hartstene Island, southeast Mason County. In 1841, the Wilkes Expedition named it *Point Dougall*, for W. H. Dougal, who engraved many plates for the expedition's printed reports.

Doughgod Creek (*T.25N;R.15E*)

The stream of the creek heads in Doelle Lakes on the western portion of Icicle Ridge; flows southeast and south 4-1/2 miles to Icicle Creek, Wenatchee National Forest, southeast Chelan County. In 1918 or 1919, it was named by Forest Supervisor A. H. Sylvester, for the camp bread which was cooked in frying pans by prospectors, sheepherders, and foresters.

Douglas (*S.31;T.25N;R.23E*)

Settlement 3 miles southeast of Waterville, southwest Douglas County. This small place was named after the county, which, in turn, was named for U.S. Senator Stephen A. Douglas.

Douglas Channel (San Juan County) *see* President Channel

Douglas County

County in east central Washington, 1,841 sq. miles; bounded on north by Okanogan County, on east by Adams and Lincoln counties, on south by Kittitas and Grant counties, and on the west by Chelan County. Wheat, apples, and livestock are the county's chief products. On November 28, 1883, Douglas County was created from a portion of Lincoln County by the Territorial Legislature only 4 days after Lincoln County had been established. It was named for Stephen A. Douglas, U.S. senator from

Illinois between 1847 and 1861, and twice a candidate for the presidency of the United States.

Douglas Mountain
(*Ss.28,29;T.38N;R.25E*)

A 5,420-ft. peak, 5-1/2 miles southwest of Loomis, north central Okanogan County. It is the source of 5 surrounding creeks and it was named for an old prospector, J. W. Douglas.

Downey Peak (*S.12;T.32N;R.12E*)

A locally-named peak, 11 miles north of Glacier Peak summit, between Sulphur Creek and Downey Creek, extreme northeast Snohomish County. It was named for an early settler on the lower Suiattle River.

Downs (*S.27;T.22N;R.35E*)

Community 11 miles southwest of Harrington, south central Lincoln County. On January 14, 1902, it was platted by Howard S. Amon, who named it for P. I. Downs, assistant general superintendent of the Great Northern Railway Company.

Dozer Lake (King County) *see* Skyline Lake.

Drayton (*S.14;T.40N;R.1W*)

Community on the southwest shore of Drayton Harbor, 3 miles south of the Canadian boundary, northwest Whatcom County. It was named for Drayton Harbor.

Drayton Harbor (*T.40N;Rs.1E,1W*)

Small bay immediately south of the Canadian boundary, partly enclosed by Semiahmoo Spit, northwest corner of Whatcom County. In July 1791, it was named *Puerto de San Jose* by Lieut. Narvaez of Eliza's expedition. In 1841, the present name was chosen by Cmdr. Charles Wilkes for Joseph Drayton, an artist on the ship *Vincennes* of his command.

Drayton Passage
(*Ts.19,20N;Rs.1W,1E*)

A passage between Anderson Island and the mainland to the northwest, 5-1/2 miles west of Steilacoom, northwest Pierce County. (*see* Drayton Harbor)

Drews Prairie (*S.15;T.11N;R.2W*)

A prairie 3 miles west of Toledo and west of LaCamas Creek, southwest Lewis County. In the 1850s, it was settled by French-Canadians who named it *Prairie de la Mousse*, meaning "Moss Prairie." The later name, now in use, is for George Drew, who owned a Donation Land Claim on the prairie.

Drewyers River (Spokane, Whitman, and Adams counties) *see* Palouse River

Drumheller *(S.26;T.12N;R.32E)*

A small wheat-growing town, 12 miles southeast of Connell, central Franklin County. It was named for Samuel Drumheller, a local farmer.

Drunken Charlie Lake
(S.5;T.26N;R.8E)

A small, 3-acre lake at the head of Cherry Creek, 8 miles northeast of Duvall, close to the Snohomish County boundary, north central King County. It was given this robust name by pioneer settlers, for a local character who camped on the lake shore, and who preferred a liquid diet. An alternate name is *Petit Lake*.

Drury Falls *(S.29;T.25N;R.17E)*

A Wenatchee National Forest falls in Fall Creek, 1-1/2 miles above the stream's mouth in Tumwater Canyon, central Chelan County. They were named for Drury Station on the Great Northern Railway, when that line ran through Tumwater Canyon.

Dry Creek *(Ts.7,8N;Rs.34-37E)*

The stream of the creek heads north of Dixie, southeast Walla Walla County; flows westerly 26 miles to Walla Walla River near Lowden. One of many "Dry Creeks" in the state, this deserves the name; its flow is quite seasonal, and it is listed as an intermittent stream.

Dry Creek *(S.5;T.7N;R.35E)*

Town on Dry Creek, 6 miles northwest of Walla Walla, south central Walla Walla County. It is named for the creek on which it is located.

Dry Creek *(T.9N;Rs.17-19E)*

The stream of the creek heads west of Vessie Springs, on Yakima Indian Reservation, south central Yakima County; flows east to join Satus Creek, 8 miles southwest of Toppenish. The name was applied because it is an intermittent stream. The Indian name was *Wee-tal-e-kee*, which means "moving up" or "leading up." An intermediate name was *North Creek*.

Dry Falls Dam
(Ss.32,33;T.25N;R.28E)

A dam directly west of Coulee City, at the south end of Grand Coulee's equalizing reservoir, northeast Grant County. It is so named because it is located at the prehistoric site of the famous Dry Falls of Columbia River. It is also called *South Dam*.

Dry Falls of Columbia River
(Ts.24,25N;Rs.27,28E)

A Sun Lakes State Park falls in Grand Coulee, directly west of Coulee City, north Grant County, adjoining Douglas County. These prehistoric falls were composed of 5 sweeping horseshoes, with a total perimeter of almost 3 miles. The basin was 417 ft. deep -- possibly the world's greatest waterfall. The name is obviously appropriate.

Dry Falls State Park (Grant County) *see* Sun Lakes State Park

Dry Gulch (Okanogan County) *see* Tonasket

Dry Lake *(S.3;T.26N;R.2W)*

A periodically dry lake, 1 acre average width, 4 miles southwest of Quilcene, east central Jefferson County. The name is descriptive.

Dryad *(S.1;T.13N;R.5W)*

Ghost town, 18 miles west of Chehalis, west central Lewis County. It is one of many abandoned lumber towns on the Chehalis-South Bend branch of Northern Pacific Railway. Originally the town was 2 miles south of the present location, and was called *Salal*. It moved when Leudinghaus Brothers of Chehalis built a sawmill at the present site. Its name -- applied by Northern Pacific Railway officials, at the suggestion of Supt. W. C. Albee, who bossed the South Bend branch -- is mythological. It is for the wood nymph or dryad, who lived in oak trees. Albee figured that the dryad might get used to living in fir trees in this region.

Dryden *(S.26;T.24N;R.18E)*

Village between Cashmere and Peshastin, 17 miles northwest of Wenatchee, south central Chelan County. In 1907, it was named by Great Northern Railway officials, for an eminent Canadian horticulturist who accompanied James Hill on a tour through this area. The place is noted for its fine fruits.

Dubor Creek *(T.31N;R.10E)*

The stream of the creek heads 3 miles south of Whitechuck Mountain, northeast Snohomish County; flows 2-1/2 miles north to Sauk River. It was locally named for the original home-steader in the area, who was also a land surveyor.

Duck Lake *(S.14;T.17N;R.12W)*

A privately-owned, 197-acre lake on the north side of entrance to Grays Harbor, 2-3/4 miles northeast of Point Brown, Grays Harbor County. This marshy body of water is descriptively named, as it harbors migrating wild ducks in season. An alternate name is *Oyhut Lake*.

Duckabush *(S.21;T.25N;R.2W)*

Community on the west shore of Hood Canal at mouth of Duckabush River, extreme southeast Jefferson County. (*see* Duckabush River)

Duckabush Mountain *(T.25N;R.6W)*

An Olympic National Park peak, elevation 6,230 ft., 1-1/2 miles southwest of Mt. Steel, south central Jefferson County. The mountain is near the head of Duckabush River and has the same name origin as the river. (USBGN)

Duckabush River *(T.25N;Rs.2-5W)*

The stream of the river rises in Marmot Lakes near O'Neil Pass, Olympic National Park; flows eastward to Hood Canal at Duckabush, southeast Jefferson County. The Indian name for a village at the river's mouth was *Do-he-a-bos* or *Do-hi-a-bos*, meaning "reddish face," as applied to a red bluff or escarpment on a nearby mountainside. Another legend states that the name came from the Twana word *Duk-a-boos*, a name for a chief of the mythical Salmon People, and applied specifically to the crooked-mouth salmon which were plentiful here.

Dudley *(S.33;T.19N;R.17E)*

Railroad point 11 miles northwest of Ellensburg, on Yakima River, central Kittitas County. In 1890, Northern Pacific Railway officials named their station at this point for F. M. Dudley, general land attorney for the railway.

Duley Lake *(Ss.24,25;T.31N;R.26E)*

A small lake on Colville Indian Reservation, 5-1/2 miles north of Columbia River, at the south end of a chain of many small lakes, southeast Okanogan County. Carried on some maps as *Dooley Lake*, it was named for W.M. Duley, an early cattleman, who used the lake area for roundups, and who later owned the Okanogan Hotel in Okanogan.

Dulwich (Ferry County) *see* Orient

Dumbbell Mountain
(S.23;T.31N;R.16E)

A double-topped peak, elevation 8,200 ft., on the summit of Chelan Mountains at the head of Phelps Creek, on the boundary between Okanogan and Wenatchee national forests, northwest Chelan County. It was named by U.S. Forest Supervisor A. H. Sylvester for a fancied resemblance to a dumbbell.

Dumkie (Dumpky) Lake (Chelan County) *see* Domke Lake

Duncan *(S.10;T.23N;R.43E)*

Settlement 5 miles north of Spangle, on Latah Creek at the mouth of Spangle Creek, south central Spokane County. In the 1890s, this was a rather important town, but it has faded. (*see* Duncan Canyon)

Duncan's Bay (Island County) *see* Crescent Harbor

Duncan Canyon
(Ss.2,3,11,12;T.23N;R.43E)

A scenic canyon, several hundred ft. deep, northwest of Mt. Hope, 4 to 5 miles north of Spangle, south central Spokane County. It was named for a settler who came here in the 1880s, and who lived near the canyon's mouth.

Duncan Creek *(Ts.29,30N;R.18E.uns)*

The stream of the creek runs from the north, between Entiat River and its North Fork, to join Entiat River 3 miles north of its junction with North Fork, Wenatchee National Forest, north central Chelan County. It was named by Forest Ranger James McKenzie for an early sheepman who used this range.

Duncan Hill *(Ts.29,30N;R.18E.uns)*

A 7-miles ridge which runs from Anthem Creek to the confluence of Entiat River with its North Fork, Wenatchee National Forest, north central Chelan County. (*see* Duncan Creek)

Duncan Rock *(T.33N;R.16W)*

A small, black rock with low visibility in Pacific Ocean, 1 mile northwest of Tatoosh Island, extreme northwest Clallam County. In 1792, it was named *Rock Duncan* by Capt. George Vancouver for Capt. Charles Duncan, RN, who charted the area in 1788 on the trading sloop *Princess Royal*, and who gave Vancouver valuable navigating information.

Dungeness *(S.30;T.31N;R.3W)*

Community on New Dungeness Bay on Strait of Juan de Fuca, 5 miles north of Sequim, northeast Clallam County. It was first called *New Dungeness*, from the name which Capt. George Vancouver applied to the bay and spit it faces, and which was for a promontory on Strait of Dover. It was later shortened to the present name, although Vancouver's nomenclature remains on the bay. An uncomplimentary nickname used by pioneer residents was *Whiskey Bend*. The original Indian name was *Tses-kut*. (USBGN)

Dungeness Harbor *(T.31N;R.4W)*

A harbor directly west of New Dungeness Bay, between Dungeness Spit and the mainland, northeast Clallam County. It is almost enclosed by a southern extension of the spit. (*see* Dungeness)

Duntze Island (Pierce County) *see* McNeil Island

Dungeness River
(Ts.27-31N;Rs.3,4W)

The stream of the river rises near Mt. Constance, northeast Jefferson County; flows 32 miles north through east Clallam County to Dungeness Bay on Strait of Juan de Fuca. (*see* Dungeness)

Dungeness Spit *(T.31N;R.4W)*

A low, sandy spit on Strait of Juan de Fuca, partially enclosing New Dungeness Bay and Dungeness Harbor, northeast Clallam County. It extends 5 miles northeast from the mainland, and has a branch to the south which almost encloses Dungeness Harbor. Early Spanish explorers charted the spit as *Punta de Santa Cruz.* Early pioneers called it *Graveyard Spit* because 30 British Columbia Indians were buried here following a massacre by Clallam Indians in 1875. The Clallam Indian name for the spit was *Tsi-tsa-kwich.*

Dunn *(S.35;T.33N;R.38E)*

Once a town 8 miles east of Columbia River, on upper Dunn Creek, southwest of Dunn Mountain range, southwest Stevens County. It had a post office and store, which have faded, and is not shown on recent maps. In 1889, Peter Dunn, a pioneer, settled on what is now known as Dunn Creek; the stream was named after him.

Dunn Creek *(Ts.32,33N;R.38E)*

The stream of the creek heads on the slopes of Dunn Mountains, 7 miles west of Addy, central Stevens County; flows 6 miles south and southeast to Mill Creek. It was named for Peter Dunn, who settled 2 miles above its mouth in 1889.

Dunn Mountains *(T.33N;R.38E)*

This range, with elevations from 4,730 ft. to 5,340 ft., is at the head of Dunn Creek, from 4 to 7 miles west of Addy, central Stevens County. Its length is about 3-1/2 miles from north to south. (*see* Dunn Creek)

Duntze Rock *(T.33N;R.16W)*

Promontory in Pacific Ocean at entrance of Strait of Juan de Fuca, 1-1/2 miles north of Tatoosh Island, extreme northwest Clallam County. In 1847, this name was charted by Capt. Henry Kellett, on *HMS Fisgard,* for Capt. John Alexander Duntze, RN, who served on this station between 1843 and 1847.

Dupont *(T.19N;R.1E)*

Town 6 miles southwest of Steilacoom, between Ft. Lewis and Nisqually Reach, northwest Pierce County. It is on the site of old Ft. Nisqually and was named for E. I. du Pont de Nemours Company, founder of an explosive-manufacturing industry here.

Durham *(S.2;T.21N;R.7E)*

Mining camp between Kangley and Kanaskat, 10 miles northeast of Enumclaw, southwest King County. It was founded as a coal mine by Moss Bay Iron & Steel Company, a British corporation. It was named by the founders for Durham, England, which also is in a coal-mining region.

Dusty Creek *(Ts.30,31N;Rs.14,15E)*

The stream of the creek heads on the high, eastern slope of Glacier Peak, extreme east central Snohomish County; flows in a wide curve north and east to Suiattle River. The name was applied by Forest Service personnel because of almost daily dust storms caused by the very light volcanic soil along the creek's banks.

Dutch Creek (Snohomish County) *see* Dubor Creek

Dutch Dave Creek (King County) *see* Tibbets Creek

Dutch Miller Gap *(S.29;T.24N;R.13E)*

A gap, elevation 4,900 ft., at the Cascade Mountain summit near Summit Lake, northeast King County. It is at the head of Middle Fork, Snoqualmie River. It was named for Andrew Jackson Miller, who was nicknamed "Dutch," and who located the Dutch Miller Mine nearby.

Duvall *(S.13;T.26N;R.6E)*

Small town on Snoqualmie River, 10 miles south of Monroe, north central King County. It was named for Francis M. Duvall, a farmer and sawmill operator, who located here in 1875. In October 1910, when the town was platted by John D. Bird, the name became official.

Duwamish, Dwamish (King County) *see* Georgetown

Duwamish Bay (King County) *see* Elliott Bay

Duwamish Head *(T.24N;R.3E)*

An abrupt headland at the north point of West Seattle, projecting north into Elliott Bay, King County. At tide level, the head has a sand spit. A park area is maintained on the headland, for which local citizens have suggested the name *Vancouver Park* or *George Vancouver Park*, for the famous British explorer. The head has had a variety of names over the years. Its Indian name was *Sqw-ed-qs*. Names given by early white settlers, and those who followed, are *Lamb's Point, Freeport, Dwamish Head,* and *Milltown,* which was modified to *Milton.* In 1856, the present name was charted by Capt. George Davidson of U.S. Coast Survey. (*see* Duwamish River)

Duwamish River *(Ts.23,24N;Rs.3,4E)*

The stream of the river originates at Black River junction, directly south of Renton, where Green River joins Cedar River to form the Duwamish; winds northward for 15 miles to the south end of Elliott Bay at Harbor Island in Seattle, King County. In 1859, Col. Isaac N. Ebey named this river *Dwams,* using his version of the Indian name. Lieut. James Alden of the U.S. Coast Survey charted the present name a few years later, and it has become official. A translation of the Indian word is "People living on the river." An interesting variety of spellings has been employed by historians, surveyors, cartographers, and land owners. Among these are: *Dux-u-duwa, Dewampsh, Dwamish, Duamish, Duwampsh, Sinowamish,* and *Sakpam.* (USBGN)

Dyes Inlet *(Ts.24,25N;R.1E)*

An inlet connected with Port Orchard Bay by Washington Narrows, directly north of Bremerton, 4 miles east of Hood Canal, central Kitsap County. The Indian name was *Squh-buck.* In 1841, its present name was chosen by the Wilkes Expedition, for John W. W. Dyes, assistant taxidermist on the ship *Vincennes.* (USBGN)

E

Eagle Cliff *(Mt. Rainier National Park)*

A 5,300-ft. cliff between Spray Creek and Crater Creek, 1/2 mile north of North Mowich River, northwest quarter of the park. This descriptive name was applied by park officials in the early days of the park. (USBGN)

Eagle Cliff *(S.17;T.36N;R.1E)*

A 752-ft. cliff on the northeast shore of Cypress Island on Rosario Strait, northwest Skagit County. In 1841, it was named *Cone Hill* by Cmdr. Charles Wilkes because of its shape. In 1854, the present name was chosen by U.S. Coast Survey, for eagles that nested on its slopes. The Indian name was *Sheh-ung-tlh,* meaning "Home of the Thunderbird." A local name, no longer used, was *Bald Peak.*

Eagle Cliff *(S.13;T.8N;R.5W)*

A high cliff on the north bank of Columbia River, 15 miles west of Longview, east Wahkiakum County. It was the site of the first salmon cannery in the Pacific Northwest, established in 1865. It was named by William Hume, one of the cannery owners, when he found eagles nesting here above the town.

Eagle Cove *(S.11;T.34N;R.3W)*

A south shore cove of San Juan Island, 5-1/2 miles south of Friday Harbor, directly east of Eagle Point, southwest San Juan County. The name source is the same as that of Eagle Point.

Eagle Gorge *(S.34;T.21N;R.8E)*

A Green River gorge, 11 miles northeast of Enumclaw, south central King County. In 1891, while building the Northern Pacific Railway over Stampede Pass, 40 laborers were killed by an earth slide. In 1886, it was named by Northern Pacific officials, adopting a local name. A pair of eagles had nested in the same tree near here for over 15 years.

Eagle Gorge Reservoir *(S.28;T.21N;R.8E)*

An artificial reservoir in Green River near Eagle Gorge, 6 miles southeast of Kanasket, south central King County. It was created for flood control, and named for Eagle Gorge. The accepted name is now Howard Hanson Reservoir.

Eagle Harbor *(T.25N;R.2E)*

On the east shore of Bainbridge Island, east central Kitsap County. It penetrates the island for 1/2 its width. In 1841, it was named by the Wilkes Expedition for Lieut. Henry Eagle, USN, naval hero of the War of 1812.

Eagle Island *(S.28;T.20N;R.1E)*

A Balch Passage island, between McNeil and Anderson Island, northwest Pierce County. In 1841, this name was placed on British admiralty charts by Capt. R. N. Inskip, RN, without reference to the name source.

Eagle Lake (Franklin County) *see* Scootenay Lake

Eagle Lakes *(S.14;T.30N;R.9W)*

Three small lakes in a row, 1-1/2 miles south of Fairholm, central Clallam County. They are about 500 ft. apart, and cover 5 acres each in the north and south lakes, and 8 acres in the middle one. The name is for Eagle Creek which drains them.

Eagle Peak *(Mt. Rainier National Park)*

A 5,995-ft. peak at the northwest end of Tatoosh Range, 2 miles east of Longmire, south central zone of the park. It may be reached by trail from Longmire. The name was chosen by The Mountaineers, for eagles that nested in trees on the mountain's slopes. (USBGN)

Eagle Point *(S.11;T.32N;R.13W)*

A point on Strait of Juan de Fuca, 2 miles west of Clallam Bay, northwest Clallam County. The name came into common use in pioneer days for a conspicuous eagle nest in a high tree on the point.

Eagle Point *(S.11;T.34N;R.3W)*

A south shore point of San Juan Island, 5-1/2 miles south of Friday Harbor, southwest San Juan County. In 1790, it was named *Punta de Herrera* by Lieut. Juan Francisco de Eliza. In 1858, it was charted under the present name by Capt. Henry Richards, British admiralty surveyor, for H. N. Eagle, a U.S. Naval officer.

Eagle Rock *(Ss.35,36;T.36N;R.33E)*

A Colville National Forest peak, elevation 4,600 ft., directly east of Refrigerator Canyon and 7 miles southeast of Republic, west central Ferry County. It was named by early settlers because it was the nesting place for a number of golden eagles.

Eagle Rock *(S.27;T.16N;R.15E)*

A Snoqualmie National Forest rock, near Nile, close to Naches River, northwest Yakima County. Local inhabitants applied the name for an eagle nest at the top of the rock.

Eagledale *(S.34;T.25N;R.2E)*

Community on the south shore of Eagle Harbor, Bainbridge Island, east central Kitsap County. The first name of the place was *Southside*, because of its location on the south side of Eagle Harbor. The present name was borrowed from Eagle Harbor.

Eagleton (Lewis County) *see* Bunker

Earl *(S.22;T.24N;R.35E)*

Community 8 miles northwest of Harrington, central Lincoln County. It was named for Robert Earl who came here in 1882 as the first white settler. In

1887, a post office was established here under Earl's name.

East Bluff (Jefferson County) *see* Cape George

East Bremerton *(S.18;T.24N;R.2E)*

Town consolidated with Bremerton, on the west shore of Port Orchard bay, directly east of Bremerton across Washington Narrows, east central Kitsap County. It was called *Manette* until incorporated with Bremerton. Older names are *String Town* and *Decatur*.

East Deer Creek *(T.39N;Rs.35,36E)*

The stream of this 11-mile-long creek rises on Rocky Mountain, Colville National Forest, northeast Ferry County; flows eastward into Kettle River, 1-1/2 miles south of Orient. It is one of many "Deer Creeks" throughout the state, named by early settlers when deer were important to their living economy.

East Farms *(S.1;T.25N;R.46E)*

A small town, 1/2 mile west of Idaho line in Spokane Valley, extreme east central Spokane County. In 1884, it was started by Louis Lee as *Halfway House* during the Coeur d'Alene mining boom. Its name was selected because it is at the east extremity of the Spokane Valley.

East Fork, Pataha Creek
(Garfield County) *see* Pataha Creek

East Marcus *(S.32;T.37N;R.38E)*

A small town, 1/2 mile west of miles east of Marcus and halfway between that town and Evans, northwest Stevens County. On August 5, 1890, it was platted during the period of many real estate promotions, by E. D. Morrison and O. B. Nelson. Development was meager, and the town ceased to exist when the area was flooded by Grand Coulee Dam in the 1939-40 years. The town borrowed its name from nearby Marcus, which was named for a pioneer, Marcus Oppenheimer.

East Peak, Mt. Olympus
(T.27N;R.8W.uns)

One of 2 major peaks of Mt. Olympus (with West Peak), Olympic National Park, north central Jefferson County. An alternative name, little used, is *Sphinx Head*. (*see* Mt. Olympus, West Peak)

East Point *(S.12;T.30N;R.2E)*

A southeast shore point of Whidbey Island, on Saratoga Passage near the entrance to Holmes Harbor, 4 miles east

of Greenbank, Island County. In 1841, it was named for its location on Whidbey Island, by Cmdr. Charles Wilkes.

East Rock *(S.28;T.25N;R.3W)*

One of 3 rocky peaks on the east wall of Cabin Creek cirque (with North and West rocks), Olympic National Forest, 5 miles west of Bellview, southeast Jefferson County. It is named for its position on the cirque's standing wall. (USBGN)

East Seattle *(T.24N;R.4E)*

The northwest portion of Mercer Island in Lake Washington, on the site of the old Proctor Ranch, west central King County. The name was chosen because it is directly east of Seattle's southern residential area. The Indian name was *Tsek-tsek*, meaning "Place where gooseberry bushes grow."

East Sound *(Ts.36,37N;Rs.1,2W)*

A 7-mile-long bay, average width 2-3 miles, in the central area of Orcas Island, extending north to almost bisect the island. It is named, in conjunction with West Sound, for its position on Orcas Island. In 1841, Charles Wilkes charted it as *Ironside Inlet*, for the nickname of the famous U.S. frigate *Constitution*. His name did not persist.

East Sound *(S.13;T.37N;R.2W)*

A small community -- though the largest on Orcas Island -- at the head of East Sound, San Juan County. It was named for the body of water on which it is located.

East Stanwood (Snohomish County) *see* Stanwood

East Wenatchee *(S.11;T.22N;R.20E)*

Town at the east end of an early steel bridge which spans Columbia River, between this town and Wenatchee, extreme southwest Douglas County. It derives its name, of course, from Wenatchee.

Eastman *(S.36;T.8N;R.37E)*

Railroad Station on Dry Creek, 9 miles east by north of Walla Walla, southeast Walla Walla County. Northern Pacific Railway officials named the place, when a station was established, for Thomas Eastman of Walla Walla.

Easton *(S.11;T.20N;R.13E)*

Village 12 miles west of Cle Elum, west central Kittitas County. Some settlers came here before 1886, but in that year the Northern Pacific Railway established Easton near the east end of the Stampede-Cascade tunnel. Weston was established near the west portal -- thus, the name of each of these railroad towns.

Eaton's Prarie (Thurston County) *see* Chambers Prarie

Eatonville *(S.14;T.16N;R.4E)*

Town on Mashel River, 33 miles southeast of Tacoma, south central Pierce County. In 1890, the name was applied when a post office was established. It was for Thomas C. Van Eaton, the first postmaster.

Ebey Landing (Island County) *see* Ebey's Landing

Ebey Slough *(Ts.29,30N;R.5E)*

A winding channel, the most northern branch of Snohomish River mouths, at Marysville, west central Snohomish County. It is used for log dumping and storage and was named for Ebey Logging Company which used the slough for log storage in early days. The slough was named for Col. Isaac N. Ebey, a famous pioneer of western Washington.

Ebey's Landing *(S.8;T.31N;R.1E)*

Early settlement on the west shore of Whidbey Island, facing Admiralty Inlet, 3 miles northwest of Admiralty Head, north Island County. It was named for Col. Isaac N. Ebey, a famous pioneer on whose Donation Land Claim the landing is located. On some recent maps the place is called *Ebey Landing*.

Ebey's Prairie *(T.31N;R.1E)*

A west shore prairie on Whidbey Island, 1 mile southwest of Coupeville, north Island County. The name is for Isaac N. Ebey, on whose Donation Land Claim the prairie is located.

Ebokwol River (Wahkiakum County) *see* Grays River

Echo *(S.6;T.36N;R.39E)*

Community 6-1/2 miles north of Colville, on Clugston (Clagston) Creek, at the south end of Echo Valley, west central Stevens County. It was named for Echo Valley in which it is located and which is noted for a pronounced echo of the slightest sounds.

Echo Bay *(T.38N;R.2W)*

A large bay, almost enclosed by Sucia Island, 3 miles north of Orcas Island, northeast San Juan County. It is a favorite cruising point for pleasure boats, with rocks and islands of fanciful

shapes, most of which are heavily fossilized. The local name is descriptive, as the high, rocky walls of the bay return strong echoes.

Echo Cliffs *(Mt. Rainier National Park)*

A very steep, rocky wall, about 4,000 ft. high, at the confluence of Cataract Creek with the headwaters of Carbon River. The cliffs are in the northwest sector of the park, just west of Carbon Glacier's terminal moraine. The name is said to be quite descriptive by those who are familiar with the cliffs. (USBGN)

Echo Lake *(S.2;T.23N;R.7E)*

A 19.8-acre lake at the head of Lake Creek, 2-1/4 miles southwest of Snoqualmie, central King County. The name is fairly descriptive, according to local residents. It should not be confused with Echo Lake in extreme northwest King County.

Echo Lake *(S.6;T.26N;R.4E)*

An 11.6-acre lake, 6 miles north of Seattle, 2 miles east of Puget Sound, directly south of Snohomish County boundary, extreme northwest King County. It is in a residential area, and should not be confused with Echo Lake near Snoqualmie. Formerly the lake was called *Lake Desire*.

Echo Rock *(Mt. Rainier National Park)*

A rock between Carbon Glacier and the lower terminus of Russell Glacier, northwest area of the park. It projects above fields west of Carbon River. The name is descriptive, according to park personnel. An alternate name, which is not official, is *Seattle Rock*. (USBGN)

Echo Valley *(Ts.36,37N;Rs.38,39E)*

A valley 3 to 5 miles east of Columbia River, 6 to 11 miles north of Colville, northwest Stevens County. It is so named because slight sounds echo clearly.

Eden *(S.29;T.18N;R.45E)*

Settlement 8 miles north of Palouse, northeast Whitman County. In February 1882, it was founded by George W. Hill, who developed a beautiful garden spot on land which he bought from Northern Pacific Railway Company. Railway officials named the place for his garden.

Edendale *(S.33;T.33N;R.37E)*

Once a town on Columbia River, 1 mile north of Gifford, west central Stevens County. In the 1890s, it was estab-

lished by land promoters and had a large cannery with many acres of surrounding orchards. Edendale declined, and was flooded out of existence by the creation of Franklin D. Roosevelt Lake when Grand Coulee Dam was built. The name, implying ideal living conditions, was bestowed by the promoters of the town.

Edgar Lake *(S.11;T.36N;R.9E)*

A Mt. Baker National Forest lake between Thunder Creek and Watson Creek, north central Skagit County. The name was applied by local settlers for a man who tried to establish a homestead here in very early days.

Edgar Rock *(S.26;T.17N;R.14E)*

A rock on the south bank of Naches River, 1 mile southeast of Clifdell, northwest Yakima County. It was named during the Indian wars of the 1850s, for John Edgar, a soldier from Ft. Steilacoom who was killed by Indians near Buckley on November 6, 1855. While acting as a scout for Lieut. W. A. Slaughter, he met Indians at this rock who warned of strong Indian forces under Qualchan, who were advancing to meet Slaughter's small detachment.

Edgecomb *(S.23;T.31N;R.5E)*

Town 2-1/2 miles south of Arlington, west central Snohomish County. Formerly it was an important logging center when the Seattle, Lake Shore & Eastern Railroad was built through here in 1889. It was named for John Edgecomb who operated extensive logging camps in this area in the early 1890s.

Edgewater *(S.18;T25N;R.4E)*

Town incorporated into Seattle on the north shore of Lake Union, directly east of Fremont Bridge, King County. It was outside the city limits of Seattle when platted in 1890 by Carliss R. Stone and William Ashworth and named by Stone for Edgewater Beach in Chicago, Illinois.

Edgewick *(S.25;T.23N;R.8E)*

Settlement 4 miles southeast of North Bend, near South Fork, Snoqualmie River, central King County. On December 23, 1918, it was the scene of a destructive flash flood caused by a breach in Cedar River Dam. In 1911, it was named by R. W. Vinnedge of North Bend, for lumberman W. C. Weeks. The name was pronounced *Wicks* and so used in the name of the settlement.

Edison *(S.33;T.36N;R.3E)*

Village on North Samish River at its entrance into Samish Slough and Samish Bay, about 8 miles northwest of Burlington, northwest Skagit County. The name is for the outstanding American inventor, Thomas A. Edison. It was suggested by Edward McTaggart, the first postmaster, when a post office was established in 1876. (USBGN)

Edison (Pierce County) *see* South Tacoma

Edison Slough *(S.33;T.36N;R.3E)*

A tidal slough at the mouth of North Samish River which discharged into Samish Bay, about 8 miles northwest of Burlington, northwest Skagit County. It was named for the nearby town of Edison. (USBGN)

Edith Creek *(Mt. Rainier National Park)*

A tributary of Paradise River, the stream of the creek rises in Paradise Glacier moraine, directly east of Paradise Park, central zone of the park. In 1907, it was named by the veteran park guide, Jules Stampfler, for a lady who was in one of his hiking parties. (USBGN)

Ediz Hook *(T.31N;R.6W)*

A narrow sandspit which projects 3 miles to the east into Strait of Juan de Fuca, and which protects Port Angeles harbor within the city of Port Angeles, north central Clallam County. It supports a Coast Guard base and a lighthouse, and is the former site of a fortified Clallam Indian village. In 1846, the spit was named by Capt. Henry Kellet when he placed the present name on British admiralty charts. *Ediz* was evidently his translation of the Indian name *Yennis*, which means "good place" in Clallam Indian dialect, and which was the name of a Clallam village on the spit. Other spellings of the Indian name are *Yenno-wis*, *Y-yenno-wis*, and *I-eh-nus*. For a period in the early 1850s it was called *False Dungeness*.

Edmiston Spring *(S.23;T.8N;R.40E)*

Spring 10 miles north of Oregon boundary on Umatilla National Forest, southeast Columbia County. It was named for James E. Edmiston, a pioneer attorney of Columbia County. An early and rather dismal name was *Mud Spring*. (USBGN)

Edmonds *(T.27N;R.3E)*

Prosperous commercial and residence city on Possession Sound, 2 miles north of King County boundary, southwest Snohomish County. It was incorporated in 1890. There is a persisting legend that in order to secure the number of names required for a petition to incorporate, the names of 2 oxen were added. In 1841, the point on which the town was built was named *Point Edmund* by the Wilkes Expedition. This evidently was altered to the present name when a post office was established in the 1880s. An alternate, but less authentic name source, is that of Sen. George Franklin Edmunds, who served Vermont in the U.S. Senate for 21 years. His name is presumed to have been applied to the town in 1876 by George Brackett, who is credited with having founded the original settlement as a logging camp.

Edmunds Glacier *(Mt. Rainier National Park)*

A small ice field on the northwest slope of Mt. Rainier, between North and South Mowich glaciers, in the central zone of the park. It is attached on the north to North Mowich Glacier. The name is for U.S. Sen. George F. Edmunds (see above) and was given when he visited the park in June 1883, with the vice president of Northern Pacific Railway, Mr. Oakes. This name originally was applied to South Mowich Glacier, but now is official for the smaller ice field. (USBGN)

Edmund's Group (San Juan County) *see* Matia Island

Edwall
(S.12;T.23N;R.38E.&S.7;T.23N;-R.39E)

Community in the Big Bend country, 16 miles east of Harrington, east central Lincoln County. It was named for Peter Edwall, a pioneer of 1881, who platted the town on May 19, 1892.

Edwards Island (King County) *see* Harbor Island

Edwards Point *(S.26;T.27N;R.3E)*

An Edmonds waterfront point in extreme southwest Snohomish County. The present name is evidently a misspelling of *Point Edmund* which was applied by Cmdr. Charles Wilkes in 1841, for a member of his expedition.

Egg Lake *(S.33;T.36N;R3W)*

A small, egg-shaped lake, elevation 155 ft., northeast San Juan Island, 3 miles northwest of Friday Harbor, west central San Juan County. Its area is 6.6 acres and the maximum depth is reported to be about 17 ft. It was locally named for its distinctive shape.

Egg Lake *(S.3;T.39N;R.10E.uns)*

A 2-acre Mt. Baker National Forest lake, elevation 5,260 ft., 8 miles north of Mt. Shuksan summit, north central Whatcom County.

Eglon *(S.35;T.28N;R.2E)*

Small settlement with a strong Scandinavian flavor, on Puget Sound between Kingston and Hansville, northeast Kitsap County. In 1904, it was named *Silver Creek* by local residents. On Oct. 20, 1906, when a post office was established, postal authorities objected to the name because of a Silver Creek in Lewis County. The present name was chosen by a committee of local settlers for Eglon in ancient Canaan, which had been named for the King of Moab.

Egypt *(S.13;T.27N;R.36E)*

Small settlement 4 miles west of Spokane River and 13 miles north of Davenport, northeast Lincoln County. It was named by John Inkster, a seafaring man, for a fancied resemblance to portions of Egypt. The surrounding area for several miles, but without distinct boundaries, is known locally as *The Egypt Country*.

Ehrlich *(S.17;T.33N;R.5E)*

Former mill town 7 miles southeast of Mt. Vernon, between Montborne and McMurray, southwest Skagit County. Residents named the place for F.O. Ehrlich, who operated a sawmill here when original, old-growth forest timber was available in quantity.

Eight Lake (Clallam County) *see* Lake No. 8

Eight Mile Creek
(Ss.22,23;T.31N;R.9E)

The stream of the creek rises in north central Snohomish County, 6 miles south of Darrington; flows 1-1/2 miles east to North Fork, Clear Creek. It was named for an 8-mile trail marker here in early days, on the trail from Bornite to Darrington.

Eighteenmile Island *(S.3;T.2N;R.11E)*

Rocky island in Columbia River near Oregon side, 4 miles east of Hood River (town), southwest Klickitat County. Federally owned, it was partially covered in the reservoir back of Bonneville Dam; and, it was named by rivermen in the days of steamboating on the Columbia, because it was believed to be 18 miles west of The Dalles (town). It actually was about 16 miles.

Elbe *(S.21;T.15N;R.5E)*

Settlement on Nisqually River, at the east end of Lake Alder, south central Pierce County. In the early 1880s, it was named by Henry C. Lutkens for the Elbe River in Germany. Lutkens was one of a number of German homesteaders who settled here, and many of whom came from the Elbe Valley. The name *Brown's Junction* was chosen by Northern Pacific Railway officials when they established a station here, but it never was applied to the settlement.

Elberton *(S.11;T.17N;R.44E)*

Community on Palouse River at mouth of Silver Creek, 12 miles northeast of Colfax, east central Whitman County. In 1877, an attempt was made to found a town around G. D. Wilbur's sawmill, using the name *Wilburville*. Sylvester M. Wait filed a townsite plat on August 19, 1886, using the given name, Elbert, of his deceased son. An intermediate name for the place was *Evergreen*.

Elbow Bend *(T.27N;R.35E)*

This abrupt bend in the Columbia River, from south to east, is less noticeable than before the river was flooded in the reservoir created by Grand Coulee Dam. It is between Lincoln County on the south, and Colville Indian Reservation on the north and northwest, Ferry County. During the mining boom of the 1890s, it is reported that considerable quantities of gold were extracted from river bars at Elbow Bend, by placer mining. The name is descriptive, as the rather sharp bend was elbow-shaped in the channel of the original river.

Elbow Lake *(S.9;T.37N;R.7E.uns)*

A 5-acre lake, elevation 3,400 ft., between Mt. Baker and Twin Sisters Range, at head of South Fork, Nooksack River, on Sisters Divide, south central Whatcom County. It was named by Carl Bell, U.S. Forest Service ranger, for the lake's peculiar shape.

Eld Inlet *(Ts.18,19N;Rs.2,3W)*

A 9-mile-long arm of Puget Sound, average width 1/2-1 mile, between Budd and Totten inlets, northwest Thurston and southeast Mason counties. The southwest portion is called *Mud Bay*. In 1841, the inlet was named by the Wilkes

Expedition, for Midshipman Henry Eld, a member of the Wilkes command.

Elder Creek *(Ts.27,28N;Rs.17,18E.partly uns)*

The stream of this creek rises on the west slope of Entiat Mountains; flows 2-1/2 miles southwest through Lost Lake into Alder Creek, Wenatchee National Forest, northwest Chelan County. It was named by U.S. Forest Supervisor A. H. Sylvester, who, in his imaginative way, changed one letter in the name of Alder Creek to christen this tributary.

Eldon *(S.27;T.24N;R.3W)*

Town on Eldon Bay, west shore of Hood Canal at the mouth of Hamma Hamma River, north central Mason County. The place is less important than in the logging days of the early 1900s. Local residents state that the name is for a logger who had a camp here at the turn of the century.

Eldorado (mountain) *(S.9;T.30N;R.13E.uns)*

An imposing peak, elevation 8,875 ft., Mt. Baker National Forest, northeast Skagit County. It is girdled with large glaciers on all sides. During the 1890s, the name was established by mining claims, including Skagit Queen mine.

Eld's Island *(T.17N;R.12W)*

Small island (obliterated by dredging or by jetty construction), once located at the mouth of Grays Harbor bay, between Brown and Chehalis points. In 1841, it was charted by Cmdr. Charles Wilkes for Passed Midshipman Henry Eld of his command. Eld commanded the party which surveyed Grays Harbor in July and August 1841. It does not appear on recent maps.

Electric City *(S.15;T.28N;R.30E)*

One of several communities built to house personnel needed for construction of the Grand Coulee Dam. It is 4 miles southwest of the dam near the upper end of the equalizing reservoir, northwest Grant County. At its peak, its population was about 1,500. The name is appropriate, as it was connected with one of the world's greatest hydroelectric projects.

Electron *(S.4;T.17N;R.5E)*

Town in Puyallup River valley, 1-1/2 miles northeast of Lake Kapowsin, central Pierce County. In 1904, it was named by Puget Sound Power & Light Company to describe the site of their hydroelectric power plant.

11 Mile Creek *(T.28N;R.15E.uns)*

The stream of the creek rises on the southeast side of Irving Peak, Wenatchee National Forest, west central Chelan County; flows 1-1/2 miles to Wenatchee River. It was named by Forest Ranger Delmer S. Rice because the mouth of the creek is 11 miles from Wenatchee Lake.

Elgin *(S.29;T.22N;R.1E)*

Site on the west shore of Carr Inlet, near the mouth of Miner Creek, northwest Pierce County. In 1882, a post office was established 1 mile south of this place and was named *Minter* for the first postmaster. When it was moved 1 mile north, the name was changed by a family of settlers from Elgin, Illinois.

Elip Creek *(Ts.24,25N;R.8W)*

The stream of the creek heads at Kurtz Lake, Olympic National Park, southwest Jefferson County; flows 3-1/2 miles east to North Fork, Quinault River. The name is from Chinook jargon, meaning "first" or "before." There appears to be some connection of names with nearby Kimta Creek, which means "behind" or "later."

Eliza Island *(S.32;T.37N;R.2E)*

A small, low, flat island at the entrance to Bellingham Bay, near the south end of Lummi Island, southwest Whatcom County. In 1841, it was named by Cmdr. Charles Wilkes for the Spanish mariner and explorer, Lieut. Juan Francisco de Eliza, as *Eliza's Island*. The name had been shortened to the present spelling.

Elk Creek *(Ts.23,24N;R.5W)*

The stream of the almost 3-mile-long creek on Olympic National Forest heads north of Lightning Peak, northwest Mason County; flows northeast to Olympic National Park and to North Fork, Skokomish River, 1-1/2 miles northwest of Lake Cushman. It was named locally for the bands of Roosevelt elk which feed here in season -- and is designated on some county maps, in error, as *Four Stream*. (USBGN)

Elk Lake (Clallam County) *see* Lake Crescent

Elk Lake *(S.12;T.31N;R.15W)*

A 59-acre lake, 11 miles south of Neah Bay and 5 miles east of Pacific Ocean, northwest Clallam County. It drains into Ozette Lake through Umbrella Creek. The name is appropriate, as many elk range this country in season, wandering as far west as the ocean beaches.

Elk Lake *(S.10;T.23N;R.8W)*

An 11-acre lake in Olympic Primitive Area, 6 miles east of Quinault Lake, northeast Grays Harbor County. The name is appropriate, as elk herds range this area in season.

Elk Lick Mountain *(T.25N;R.5W)*

A 6,517-ft. Olympic National Park peak, 2-1/2 miles east of Mt. Lacrosse, between Duckabush River and West Creek, central Jefferson County. It was named by early hunters and trappers for natural salt-licks in the area. (USBGN)

Elk Point (Clallam County) *see* Windy Arm

Ellensburg *(Ts.17,18N;R.18E)*

A city in Kittitas Valley, 1 mile east of Yakima River, east central Kittitas County. It started as a trading post in 1867, and now is a livestock and farming center. In 1880, when a post office was established, the name chosen was *Ellen's Burgh*, for the middle name of Mary Ellen Shoudy, wife of a pioneer settler. Postal officials changed that name to its present form. A nickname, widely used in early days, was *Robbers Roost*. It was invented in jest by A. J. Splawn, an outstanding pioneer cattle owner, for actions of an early trader who operated a post in the town.

Ellen's Burgh (Kittitas County) *see* Ellensburg

Ellen's Island (Pierce County) *see* Tanglewood Island

Ellice Point (Pacific County) *see* Point Ellice

Elliott Bay *(Ts.24,25N;Rs.3,4E)*

An arm of Puget Sound which constitutes Seattle's main harbor and the western boundary of the concentrated business area. It is bounded on the south by Alki Point and on the north by West Point, King County. Its main tributary stream is Duwamish River. In 1841, the bay was named by Cmdr. Charles Wilkes for Midshipman Samuel Elliott, who assisted in the survey of the promising harbor. Claims have been made that Wilkes named this feature for Rev. J. L. Elliott, chaplain of the flagship *Vincennes*. While Wilkes' records do not specifically state that the bay was named for Samuel Elliott, it seems certain that

this was the case, as the chaplain was in bad standing and had been suspended by Wilkes on April 3, 1841, for misconduct in the Sandwich Islands. Wilkes had prohibited him from performing any clerical duties.

Elliott Creek *(T.29N;R.11E)*

The stream of the creek rises in Goat Lake, 3-1/2 miles northeast of Monte Cristo, east central Snohomish County; flows 5 miles northwest to South Fork, Sauk River. The stream was named for an early miner who worked a claim on Goat Lake.

Ellisford *(S.14;T.28N;R.37E)*

A small place on the Okanogan River, 15 miles south of the Canadian boundary and 11 miles south of Oroville, north central Okanogan County. At one time, about 30 families of Dunkard Brethern lived in this irrigated, fruit-growing district. The name is a combination of the last names of George H. Ellis and James E. Forde, pioneer merchants and ranchers.

Ellisport *(S.4;T.22N;R.3E)*

Settlement at Tramp harbor, on the east central shore of Vashon Island, 3 miles southeast of Vashon, southwest King County. The first name of the settlement was *Chautauqua*, chosen when the Chautauqua Assembly selected this place as a permanent home. The present name is for a clergyman named Ellis, who came here in 1879 as a homesteader and founder of the settlement. It first was called *Elliston*, but was later altered to the present form.

Elliston (King County) *see* Ellisport

Ellsworth *(S.4;T.1N;R.2E)*

Community on the north bank of Columbia River, 6 miles east of Vancouver, south central Clark County. In 1886, the town was founded by a number of families from St. Paul and Minneapolis, Minnesota, and Omaha, Nebraska. It was named for Elmer Ellsworth, who organized the colonists but was killed before they moved to Clark County.

Elma *(Ss.34,35;T.18N;R.6W)*

Town on Chehalis River, 27 miles west of Olympia, southeast Grays Harbor County. Formerly it was an important logging center; now largely dependent on agriculture. It was named for Miss Elma Austin, whose family settled in the vicinity prior to 1860. Two other

name sources have been advanced by local persons. One is that the name is for Elmer E. Ellsworth, the first soldier to be killed in the Civil War, but with his given name shortened to the present form by post office officials. Another is that 2 residents of the town submitted the name *Elmira* when a post office was established, and that postal officials shortened the name to the present form because of another Almira in the state.

Eloika Lake *(Ts.29,30N;R.43E)*

A lake 5 miles northeast of Deer Park, north central Spokane County, extending a short distance into Pend Oreille County. Local inhabitants state that Eloika was the original name given the lake by Pend Oreille Indians, but disagree on its meaning.

Elokomin Lake *(S.20;T.10N;R.4W)*

A lake 12-1/2 miles northeast of Cathlamet, northwest Cowlitz County. It was named for Elokomin River which drains it. An alternate spelling, not now in common use, was *Elochoman*.

Elochoman Lake (Cowlitz County) *see* Elokomin Lake

Eltopa (Spokane County) *see* Marshall

Elokomin River *(Ts.9,10N;Rs.5,6W)*

The stream of the river rises in the northeast corner of Wahkiakum County; flows southwesterly to Columbia River, north of Cathlamet. The many names that have been applied to this river indicate the difficulty of translating Indian names into English. In 1841, Wilkes charted the stream as *Oluman Creek*. Other spellings that are of record include: *Alockaman, Alochaman, Alochoman, Alokomin, Elochoman, Elockaman,* and *Clokoman*. An early pioneer name was *Strong's River*.

Eltopai (Franklin County) *see* Eltopia

Eltopia *(S.11;T.11N;R.30E)*

A railroad wheat-shipping point, 15-1/2 miles north of Pasco, west central Franklin County. It was established as a station by Northern Pacific Railway Company in 1881. In 1902, a townsite was platted by Joseph McCabe, a railroad executive. Persisting legends relate that the name was given during railroad construction in 1880 when a Cockney laborer remarked that there would be Hell to pay, as a result of a heavy rain which wrecked a fill. A variation of the tale ascribes the naming to Harry

McCartney, a railroad locating engineer who also is said to have named Pascot. He is alleged to have made the same remark when a construction camp was wiped out by a cloudburst. A more credible origin is the Indian name for the place, *El-To-Pai*.

Elltopay (Franklin County) *see* Eltopia

Elwha *(S.29;T.30N;R.7W)*

Town on Strait of Juan de Fuca, 7 miles west of Port Angeles, north central Clallam County. The Indian name for this town has been retained. Originally it was a Quillayute word, *E-ilth-quatl*, meaning ''elk.'' When a post office was established, it was named *McDonald* for W. D. McDonald, the first settler and postmaster. His name is now on a mountain 3 miles to the southeast of this town.

Elwha Reservoir (Clallam County) *see* Lake Mills

Elwha River *(Ts.26-30N;Rs.6,7W)*

The stream of the river rises in Elwha Basin, Olympic National Park, 8 miles southeast of Mt. Olympus, north central Jefferson County; flows north through Lake Mills (Elwha Reservoir) and Lake Aldwell, to Strait of Juan de Fuca near Angeles Point. In 1847, this river was charted under the present Indian name by Capt. Henry Kellett. (*see* Elwha)

Elwha River Range *(T.29N;R.7W)*

A group of 4-mile-long peaks, average width 2-1/2 miles, east of Elwha River and 8 miles south of Strait of Juan de Fuca, central Clallam County. (*see* Elwha)

Elwood *(S.1;T.10N;R.34E)*

Railroad stop 23 miles north by west of Walla Walla, northwest Walla Walla County. When the Northern Pacific Railway built through this place, the station was named for Elwood E. Fall, former publisher of *The Statesman*.

Elysian Fields *(Mt. Rainier National Park)*

Beautiful mountain meadows between Moraine Park and Sluiskin Mountain, directly east of the terminus of Carbon Glacier, northwest sector of the park. These meadows were originally considered a part of Moraine Park, but now are officially named as a separate feature. In 1888, this name was given by Maj. E. S. Ingraham, because the delightful location and environment reminded him of a mythological region of paradise on earth. (USBGN)

Elysian Fields Lakes *(Mt. Rainier National Park)*

There normally are about 20 small, shallow lakes and ponds, elevation 5,700 ft., on Elysian Fields Flats, 64 miles north of Mt. Rainier summit. The lakes were named for Elysian Fields.

Emerald Lake *(S.7;T.24N;R.13E)*

One of 3 Necklace Valley Lakes (with Jade and Opal lakes), 2-1/2 miles west of Deception Pass at Cascade Mountain summit, northeast King County. It varies in acreage from 3-8 acres and is normally about 4 acres. Fed by Opal, Emerald Lake drains into Jade. The name is that of a fancied jewel in the necklace of lakes. An alternate name is *Necklace Valley Lake No. 2.*

Emerald lake (Whatcom County) *see* Toad Lake

Emerald Park *(T.31N;R.18E.uns)*

The stream of this creek rises on Emerald Peak, elevation 8,400 ft., Wenatchee National Forest, north central Chelan County; flows from Chelan Mountain range, 6 miles northeast to Domke Lake. It was named by Forest Supervisor A. H. Sylvester for the intense green coloration of the water in summer months.

Emerald Peak *(T.30N;R.18E.uns)*

A very high Wenatchee National Forest mountain, elevation 8,400 ft., on Chelan Mountain summit, between Saska Peak and Cardinal Peak, north central Chelan County. It was named for a creek which Forest Supervisor A. H. Sylvester called *Emerald Park*, and which has its source on the northeast slope of this mountain.

Emerald Ridge *(Mt. Rainier National Park)*

A short ridge, elevation 5,306 ft., at the terminus of Tahoma Glacier, between South Puyallup River and Tahoma Creek and Tahoma Ridge, southwest zone of the park. The name was applied for the greenish color of the rock which forms this divide. (USBGN)

Emery (Franklin County) *see* Emory

Emmons Glacier *(Mt. Rainier National Park)*

The largest glacier in the southern 48 states, on the northeast slope of Mt. Rainier, extending 5-1/2 miles northeast from the summit to headwaters of White River; it is part of an enormous glacial mass which is divided into Winthrop and Emmons glaciers by Steamboat Prow. It was named for Samuel F. Emmons, geologist and mountaineer, who made the second successful ascent of the mountain in 1870. Other names that have been used, unofficially, are *White, Blaine, Winthrop* and *White River Glaciers.* (USBGN)

Emory *(S.12;T.14N;R.31E)*

A railroad point, 4 miles north of Connell, north central Franklin County. In 1905, it was named by Northern Pacific Railway officials for Walter Emory, foreman of a crew that installed a rail siding here in that year. The place is listed as *Emery* on some maps, in error.

Empire *(S.33;T.9N;R.22E)*

Railroad stop 3 miles northwest of Mabton, southeast Yakima County. In 1905, the station at this place was named by Northern Pacific Railway officials, evidently for its location in the *Inland Empire.*

Empire Lake (Stevens County) *see* Franklin D. Roosevelt Lake

Empire Lake (Washington State Ref./northeast Washington) *see* Franklin D. Roosevelt Lake

Engineers' Town (Grant County) *see* Coulee City

Endicott *(S.31;T.17N;R.41E)*

Town on Rebel Flat Creek, 19 miles west of Colfax, central Whitman County. In January 1882, a town was founded by Oregon Improvement Company, which filed a townsite plat on May 18, 1882. The name chosen was that of William Endicott, Jr., a Boston banker who was a shareholder in Oregon Improvement Company. Prior to this naming, the place had been called *Rebel Flat* by southerners who settled here after the Civil War.

Endolyne *(S.2;T.23N;R.3E)*

The terminus of a former street railway from the center of Seattle, on the east shore of Puget Sound, directly south of Brace Point and 1 mile south of Lincoln Park, west central King County. The name was given by local residents because it was the end of the line -- as far as public transportation was concerned.

Enetai *(S.7;T.24N;R.2E)*

Community on the west shore of Port Orchard Bay, directly north of East Bremerton, east central Kitsap County. The Chinook Indian name which has been retained, means *"across," "opposite,"* or *"on the other side."*

Englewood, Engelwood (King County) *see* Issaquah

English *(S.19;T.31N;R.5E)*

Community 13 miles north of Everett, west central Snohomish County. Also shown as *Lakewood* on current maps; this place was named by the Great Northern Railway for Ed English of English Logging Company when a railway station was established here. The post office name of *Lakewood* was chosen by Fred Funk when he established Lakewood Garden Tracts in this area.

English Camp *(S.26;T.36N;R.4W)*

An abandoned British military camp on the east side of Garrison Bay, 2 miles south of Roche Harbor, northwest San Juan County. In 1859, it was established as a garrison point for British marines during the boundary dispute between Great Britain and the U.S., and in 1872, it was abandoned. The premises, including a log blockhouse and barracks, is now a national historical site. The name source is obvious.

Ennis Creek (Pierce County) *see* White Creek

Enriqueta Island (Pierce County) *see* Pitt Island

Ensenada de Bertodano (Clallam County) *see* Sequim Bay

Ensenada de Engano (Whatcom County) *see* Boundary Bay

Ensenada de Loera (Locra) (Whatcom County) *see* Lummi Bay

Ensenada de Nuestra/Senora del Rosario la Marinera (Washington State Ref./northwest Washington) *see* Georgia Strait

Ensenada de Villarva (Clallam County) *see* Crescent Bay

Ensenada de Davila (Clallam County) *see* Freshwater Bay.

Ensenada de Rojas (Clallam County) *see* Clallam Bay

Enterprise *(T.9N;R.28E)*

Town (now part of West Richland), 3 miles west of Richland on Benton City cutoff road, east central Benton County.

In 1949, it was founded as part of Greater Richland Community. A mass meeting of citizens at that time considered 18 names which were suggested. Mrs. Donald Deterick urged that the community adopt a name which implied growth and activity, such as *Enterprise.* Her motion prevailed. In 1953, Enterprise joined with Heminger City to become West Richland.

Enterprise *(S.15;T.29N;R.36E)*

Small community 5 miles east of Columbia River, in a river bend directly north of Spokane Indian Reservation, extreme southwest Stevens County. In 1895, it was founded as a stage station and post office by Allen A. Buck, and named *Buck's Station.* When it became quite a wild place during the early mining boom, local settlers nicknamed it *Robbers' Roost.* Somewhat later the place was dominated by very religious local people, and renamed *Jerusalem.* When the Enterprise Church was built here, the name was changed. The community now has a few residents, a store, a filling station, a nearby school, and a cemetery.

Enterprise *(S.8;T.39N;R.2E)*

Hamlet in the lower Nooksack Valley, 3 miles north of Ferndale, northwest Whatcom County. It was named by the 8 families who settled here in 1874, and who built a shingle mill, creamery, and a fine schoolhouse by their own enterprise.

Entiat *(S.17;T.25N;R.21E)*

Town at the confluence of Entiat River and Columbia River, 17 miles north of Wenatchee, east Chelan County. It is nicknamed *The Entry to a Sportsman's Paradise.* The town was moved 2 miles in 1961, before the site was flooded by Lake Entiat. (*see* Entiat River)

Entiat Glacier *(T.31N;R.16E.uns)*

A Glacier Peak Wilderness Area glacier, at the head of Entiat River, directly west of Entiat Meadows, northwest Chelan County. In the past several decades, it has been greatly reduced. Its name was given by U.S. Forest Supervisor A. H. Sylvester for the Entiat River, which drains its waters into Columbia River.

Entiat Meadows *(T.31N;R.16E.uns)*

Wenatchee National Forest meadows at the head of Entiat River Valley,

north central Chelan County. They were named by U.S. Forest Supervisor A. H. Sylvester for Entiat River.

Entiat Mountains *(Ts.27-31N;Rs.16-18E.partly uns)*

Wenatchee National Forest mountains between Entiat River and Chiwawa River, north central Chelan County; extending about 45 miles southeast from Cascade Mountain summit. They were named by U.S. Forest Supervisor A. H. Sylvestor for Entiat River.

Entiat River *(Ts.25-31N;Rs.17-21E.partly uns)*

A Wenatchee National Forest river, flows southeasterly through central Chelan County, from Entiat Meadows and Entiat Glacier, to Columbia River at Entiat. The name is a version of the Indian *En-ti-at-kwa,* meaning "rapid water." The stream banks were a favored living ground for Indians.

Entrance Mountain *(S.5;T.36N;R.1W)*

An eastern peninsula peak of Orcas Island, on the east side of the entrance to East Sound, northeast San Juan County. In 1858, it was placed on British admiralty charts by Capt. Henry Richards, RN, because of its position at the entrance to East Sound.

Entrance Rock (San Juan County) *see* Davidson Rock

Enumclaw *(Ss.23,24;T.20N;R.6E)*

Town at the Cascade foothills of south central King County, on a plateau between White River and Green River. It depends largely on logging and sawmilling. The early settlers were mostly Norwegians and Danes. In 1885, this Indian name was applied by Frank Stevenson, a resident of the town. The Indians used this word as the designation of a mountain about 6 miles north. The name has been variously translated as meaning "Place of the Evil Spirits" or "thunder and lighting." The local Indians believed that the Thunder Bird lived in a cave on this mountain, and had changed one of the tribesmen into thunder "for all time."

Ephrata *(Ss.14,15,16,21,22;T.21N;R.26E)*

Town at the extreme south end of Grand Coulee, north central Grant County. In 1882, it was founded by Egbert Brothers, a horse-breeding concern, and, in 1902, it was platted as a townsite by J. Cyrus. Before Grand Coulee Dam was built, irrigation was by use of local springs. The first name given this place by white men was *Indian Grave Springs*, as there were many Indian graves in nearby hills. Later the name was changed to *Beasley Springs*, for Frank Beasley, who located here before the Egberts, but moved on. In 1892, the present name was given by Great Northern Railway Company surveyors, reportedly for the Palestine village of Ephrata, mentioned in the Old Testament as Ephratah, the predecessor of Bethlehem, which also irrigated from wells.

Epley *(S.27;T.34N;R.26E)*

Settlement (now a part of Omak) in Okanogan County. In 1906, it was moved to another location. The name is for Mrs. Belle Epley, postmistress at the later location.

Equality *(S.26;T.36N;R.3E)*

A community founded as a socialist colony in the 1890s by Brotherhood of the Co-operative Commonwealth (broken up in 1904), on Colony Creek, 8 miles south of Bellingham, northwest Skagit County. The name was chosen by the colonists who believed in equal holdings and rights by all members. The colony also was called *Freeland Colony* and *Equality Colony*. It should not be confused with Freeland in Island County.

Equilibrium Rapids
(S.14;T.30N;R.30E)

Rapids in Columbia River, 3 miles above the mouth of Nespelem River, between northeast Douglas and southeast Okanogan counties. The rapids have been reduced by the waters of Rufus Woods Lake, back of Chief Joseph Dam. In 1881, they were named by Lieut. Thomas W. Symons. He wrote after his examination of the upper Columbia, "One of these immense rocks (in the stream) seemed to be nearly spherical, and to rest in an apparent state of very unstable equilibrium." This feature also was known as *Jumbo Rapids* because one of the rocks in the river had the appearance of an elephant when viewed at a certain angle.

Erie *(S.15;T.8N;R.28E)*

Train station 8 miles west of Kennewick and directly north of Horse Heaven Hills, southeast Benton County. In 1902, the name was applied by the Northern Pacific Railway Company of-

ficials. The selection, as near as can be determined, was simply in order to have a short name which did not conflict with other station names in the territory.

Erie Lake (Skagit County) *see* Lake Erie

Ernst Reservoir (King County) *see* Wildwood Pond

Eschbach *(S.29;T.14N;R.18E)*

Railroad stop directly north of Naches River and 5 miles northwest of Yakima, north central Yakima County. It was named by Northern Pacific Railway officials for Joseph E. Eschbach, a property owner at the point where a station was established.

Esjay (Yakima County) *see* Lichty

Espanola *(S.2;T.24N;R.40E)*

Town 2 miles northwest of Medical Lake, west central Spokane County. Its first name was *Manila*. In 1900, when a post office was established, postal authorities changed the name to Espanola because there was another Manila post office in the state.

Espy Lake *(S.16;T.12N;R.11W)*

A 20-acre, shallow lake, on North Beach Peninsula, 2 miles south of Oysterville, southwest Pacific County. It has a tendency to dry up in the late summer, and was named for R. H. Espey, a pioneer who founded Oysterville in 1854.

Estes Butte *(S.13;T.29N;R.16E.uns)*

A Wenatchee National Forest mountain on a ridge between Rock Creek and Chiwawa River, 3 miles above the confluence of these streams, northwest Chelan County. In 1910, it was named by U.S. Forest Supervisor A. H. Sylvester for an old settler who had mining claims in this area.

Estrada de Hezeta (Washington State Ref./Washington/Oregon) *see* Columbia River

Estrada de Nuestra/Senora Asuncion (Washington State Ref./Washington/Oregon) *see* Columbia River

Ethel *(S.13;T.12N;R.1W)*

Town 15 miles southeast of Chehalis, on LaCamas Creek, directly on the Willamette Meridian, south central Lewis County. Paul Lindeman, who was the first postmaster in 1886, suggested that the post office be called *LaCamas* for the creek on which the town is located. Postmaster General William F. Vilas ruled that there were "too many

Indian names in the state," and applied the present name, without an explanation of its origin.

Ethel Lake *(S.18;T.26N;R.16E)*

A Wenatchee National Forest lake on the east slope of Chiwaukum Mountains, at the head of Gill Creek, southwest Chelan County. This feature was named by U.S. Forest Supervisor A. H. Sylvester, for Ethel Lenzie, wife of Forest Ranger Frank Lenzie.

Etna *(S.7;T.5N;R.2E)*

Town 19 miles north of Vancouver on Lewis River, northwest Clark County. The name was chosen when a post office was established, at the suggestion of A. C. Reid and Nathan Davis, whose former home had been Etna Green, Indiana.

Etta Cartney Lake *(S.28;T.24N;R.5E)*

A 15-acre lake, 2 miles east of the south end of Lake Washington, 1/2 mile southwest of Newcastle, northwest King County. The earlier name of *Boren Lake* was changed to that of a popular local resident. An alternate name is *Etta Courtney Lake*.

Etta Courtney Lake (King County) *see* Etta Cartney Lake

Etta Lake (Clallam County) *see* Grand Lake

Eufaula *(S.3;T.8N;R.3W)*

A former logging town (now practically deserted), 2 miles north of Columbia River, 4 miles northwest of Longview, west Cowlitz County. In the late 1880s the town was named by Jefferson D. Brock, an employee of a logging company, for his home town in Alabama.

Eunice lake *(Mt. Rainier National Park)*

A small, 12-acre lake in a glacial cirque, west of Alki Crest, at the foot of Tolmie Peak and at the head of Meadow Creek, extreme northwest corner of the park. In 1883, the lake was named *Tolmie Lake*, by Prof. Bailey Willis, but was changed to the present name before it was officially mapped. The change was to honor Mrs. W. H. (Eunice) Gilstrap of Tacoma, a frequent visitor to the park. (USBGN)

Eureka *(S.36;T.10N;R.33E)*

Village 20 miles northwest of Walla Walla, northwest Walla Walla County. On June 6, 1904, the town was platted by Mrs. A. B. Blanchard, and named for

Eureka Flats on which it was located.

Eureka (Clark County) *see* Hockinson

Eureka (Ferry County) *see* Republic

Eureka Flats (Walla Walla County) *see* Eureka

Evans *(S.16;T.37N;R.38E)*

Community on the east bank of Columbia River, 8 miles north by east of the town of Kettle Falls, northwest Stevens County. The industry here is the American Gypsum Company plant, which uses vast quantities of the prevailing basic rock. A large power conveyor over the highway carries the rock from quarry to converting plant. The name, given in 1901, is for J. H. Evans, president of Idaho Lime Company, which established the original plant here.

Evans Lake *(S.26;T.35N;R.26E)*

A small lake, 3 miles west of Riverside, central Okanogan County. It is named for Berry Evans who was the first settler on the lake shore.

Eveline *(S.9;T.12N;R.2W)*

Railroad stop 8 miles south of Chehalis, west central Lewis County. It was named by Northern Pacific Railway officials as *Evaline A. Porter,* who was postmistress in 1911 when the railway built a spur to this place. The name was misspelled by postal officials, and the error has been perpetuated on maps and records.

Evelyn Lake (King County) *see* Denny Lake

Evergreen (Whitman County) *see* Elberton

Evergreen State, The (Washington State Ref./Washington) *see* Washington, State of

Everett *(T.29N;Rs.4,5E)*

A busy and prosperous industrial city on Port Gardner Bay at the mouth of Snohomish River, 30 miles north of Seattle, west central Snohomish County. Supported by many forest products industries, it was named for Everett Colby of New Jersey, son of Charles L. Colby, who invested heavily in Everett Land Company in 1890; he also established several of the town's first industries and was a member of the syndicate which built the Everett & Monte Cristo Railroad.

Evergreen Mountain
(Ss.9,10,16;T.27N;R.12E)

A 5,850-ft. peak, 5 miles southeast of Garland Mineral Springs, southeast Snohomish County. It was named for extensive meadows that remain green from the time the snow melts until fall.

Evergreen State, The *(Washington)*

A romantic but appropriate nickname for the state of Washington. In 1890, it was first used by Charles T. Conover, a pioneer realtor, who included this name in real estate advertisements. The Northern Pacific Railway Company included the name in its literature, and later the nickname came into fairly common use. It covers the entire state, but is more descriptive of western

Washington.

Everson *(S.25;T.40N;R.3E)*

Town on north bank of Nooksack River, 10 miles north by east of Bellingham. It was named for Ever Everson, a Norwegian who homesteaded here in 1871, and who was the first white settler north of Nooksack River.

Ewing Basin *(T.26N;R.15E)*

A glacial basin which occupies the upper 3 miles of Chiwaukum Creek valley, including Larch and Chiwaukum lakes, Wenatchee National Forest, southwest Chelan County. This beautiful, hidden Alpine valley was named by local usage for a miner named Ewing, who prospected here many years ago, and who built a log cabin in the valley.

Ewing Island *(T.38N;R.1W)*

A Strait of Georgia island, directly east of Sucia Island, northeast San Juan County. This name was placed on British admiralty charts in 1859 by Capt. Henry Richards, RN. It was for the schooner *Ewing* which was used by Lieut. James Alden of the U.S. Coast Survey in 1855.

Excelsior *(S.31;40N;R.8E)*

Mining camp on the west bank of Wells Creek near its juncture with North Fork, Nooksack River, north central Whatcom County. The first name was *Excelsior Camp* (later shortened to its present form), and it was the headquarters of Excelsior Gold Mining Company.

Eyakama River (Yakima County) *see* Yakima River

F

Faber (Skagit County) *see* Faber Ferry

Faber Ferry *(S.18;T.35N;R.9E)*

Community on the north bank of Skagit River, 3 miles east of Concrete, central Skagit County. The original name, which remains in general use, was for a man who operated a ferry across Skagit River in the days of mining excitement. Great Northern Railway officials called their station *Faber*.

Factoria *(S.9;T.24N;R.5E)*

An east suburb of Seattle, on the east shore of Lake Washington, 6 miles north of Renton, King County. In the 1890s, when established, its founders expected it to be a manufacturing center with many factories. The name was chosen in a contest. The winner, Richard R. Bird, was given one dollar as a prize.

Fairchild Air Force Base
(Ss.28,29,32,33;T.25N;R.41E)

An airfield 7-1/2 miles west of Spokane, west central Spokane County. On March 1, 1941, it was founded as Spokane Army Air Depot and became Spokane Air Force Base in February, 1948. The present name became effective on November 1, 1950, to honor Gen. Muir S. Fairchild, First Secretary of the Air Staff, and a WWI flier.

Fairfax *(S.35;T.18N;R.6E)*

Once a busy coal-mining and logging town (now a scattered settlement), 14 miles south of Enumclaw on Carbon River, central Pierce County. Sixty coke ovens operated here in 1902. It was named by W. A. McNeil, who came here from Fairfax, Iowa. The Iowa town had been named for Fairfax County, Virginia.

Fairfield *(S.24;T.22N;R.44E)*

Settlement in the wheat county, 5 miles southwest of Rockford, 6 miles west of the Idaho boundary, southeast Spokane County. In 1888, it was known as *Truax* when the Washington & Idaho Railroad came through here. In 1889, the name evidently was changed to *Regis* by Oregon Railway & Navigation Co. when that company purchased W.&I.R.R. On July 17, 1889, the present name was adopted when a post office

was established. It was for extensive grain fields which surrounded the town, and was suggested by Mrs. Edward H. Morrison. Her husband, Col. Morrison, platted the townsite of Fairfield in 1890.

Fairfield (Walla Walla County) *see* Adkins

Fair Harbor *(S.5;T.21N;R.1W)*

A narrow, shallow channel between Reach Island (Treasure Island) and the mainland, west shore of Case Inlet, extreme east central Mason County. Locally-chosen name seems appropriate because the channel affords only a fair harbor.

Fairhaven *(T.37N;Rs.2,3E)*

One of several old towns on Bellingham Bay which combined to make the present city of Bellingham. It was the southerly portion of the populated area on the bay, and still bears its original name with local old-timers. In the boom days of the 1890s, it was nicknamed *The Future Metropolis of Puget Sound*. Its founder, Daniel J. Harris, named it from a translation of the Indian name, *See-see-lich-em*, meaning "safe port" or "quiet place" -- hence fair haven.

Fairholm *(S.30;T.30N;R.9W)*

Small settlement, mostly summer camps, at the extreme west end of Lake Crescent, central Clallam County. In 1893, the name was coined as a poetic appellation by Mrs. George E. Machelle when the first post office needed a name.

Fairmont *(S.24:T.29N;R.2W)*

Village at the south end of Port Discovery Bay, northeast Jefferson County. In the 1870s, the place was named when it was a village of Indians who worked at the Moore & Smith sawmill at Port Discovery. The name was chosen locally for the post office name, and has no particular meaning, except that it is an ornamental word.

Fairweather (Lincoln County) *see* Reardan

Fallbridge (Klickitat County) *see* Wishram

Fall City *(S.15;T.24N;R.7E)*

Small settlement on Snoqualmie River, 6 miles northeast of Issaquah, north central King County. It was named for a man named Fall, who established a ferry and road house here at a point where a concrete bridge now stands. He formerly was a foreman on cattle drives over Snoqualmie Pass for Wadley & Phelps. Earlier names were *The Landing* and *Mountain View*.

Fall Creek *(T.25N;Rs.16,17E)*

The stream of the creek heads on the southeast slope of Big Jim Mountain, Wenatchee National Forest, central Chelan County; flows 4 miles east to Wenatchee River in Tumwater Canyon. It was named by Forest Service personnel for Drury Falls in the creek near the top of the canyon wall and should not be confused with a creek of the same name which is tributary to Little Wenatchee River.

Fall Creek *(T.28N;R.14E)*

The stream of this short, fast creek heads on the east slope of Fall Mountain, about 2 miles east of Cascade Mountain summit, Chelan County; flows 2 miles east to Little Wenatchee River. It was named by local people for the mountain on which it originates and it should not be confused with a creek of the same name which is tributary to Wenatchee River, and which rises on Big Jim Mountain.

Fall Mountain *(T.28N;R.14E.uns)*

A 5,595-ft. peak on Wenatchee National Forest, at the head of Fall Creek, 1 mile west of Cascade Mountain summit, west central Chelan County. It is 800 ft. higher than the nearby summit ridge, directly to the west. U.S. Forest Supervisor A. H. Sylvester stated that he named the mountain for the creek. Local people say that the creek was named for the mountain.

Fallen Rock *(Mt. Rainier National Park)*

A large rock mass in the southwest sector of the park, near the main highway, 2 miles east of Nisqually entrance. It was named because it once was part of

Tumtum Peak, but split away to its present position.

Fallon *(S.35;T.16N;R.45E)*

Town 5-1/2 miles southwest of Palouse, east central Whitman County. When a post office was established, citizens requested the name of W. M. Follis, a local rancher. The name was written *Fallons* in error, and later was shortened to its present form.

Falls Creek *(Ts.30,31N;Rs.10,11E)*

The stream of the creek rises in North Lake, 4-1/2 miles northeast of Silverton, northeast Snohomish County; flows easterly to South Fork, Sauk River. It was named for falls at its confluence with the Sauk. The Indian name was *Cheet-aligvas*, meaning "close throbbing heart" which refers to the sound of the falls.

Falls Lake (Grant County) *see* Sun Lakes State Park

Falls Lakes *(S.4;T.34N;R.11E)*

Two connected lakes, about 1,000 ft. apart, about 5 miles south of Marblemount, west central Skagit County. The lower lake, elevation 4,200 ft., covers 60.4 acres and is over 30 ft. deep. The upper lake, elevation 4,500 ft., covers 22.4 acres and is over 50 ft. deep. The name was chosen because there is a 300-ft. series of falls between the lakes, and cascading falls from the lower lake to Jordan Creek.

Falls of Saint Andrews *(Mt. Rainier National Park)*

A 4,000-ft. falls in St. Andrews Creek between North and South Puyallup rivers. The falls are on the west slope of Mt. Rainier, west central zone of the park. This name, which also applied to a nearby creek, a rock, and park, was chosen by a group of choirboys from St. Marks Episcopal Church of Seattle. They were among the first campers in this region.

Falk's Bay (Kitsap County) *see* Rolling Bay

Fallons (Whitman County) *see* Fallon

False Bay *(S.33;T.35N;R.3W)*

A shallow, sandy bay on the south shore of San Juan Island, 4 miles southwest of Friday Harbor, southwest San Juan County. At extreme low tides, the bay runs dry. In 1859, this descriptive name was charted by Capt. Henry Richards, British admiralty surveyor.

False Dungeness (Clallam County) *see* Ediz Hook; Port Angeles

False Scatchet (Island County) *see* Scatchet Head

Fan Lake (Mt. Rainier National Park) *see* The Fan

Fargher Lake *(S.25;T.5N;R.2E)*

Village 18 miles north of Vancouver, north central Clark County. It was named for Fargher Lake, which actually was a swamp on the homesteads of Fred and Horatio Farghuar, who came here from the Isle of Wight in the late 1860s. The change in spelling was due to local usage over the years.

Fargher Pond *(S.23;T.5N;R.2E)*

A 3-acre pond, 1 mile northwest of the town of Fargher Lake, north central Clark County. It should not be confused with the lake by this name, which now is dry, and which furnished the name for this pond.

Farmington *(S.31;T.19N:R.46E)*

Town on Idaho-Washington boundary, 11-1/2 miles north of Palouse, northeast Whitman County. It was founded on land claimed in 1878 by G. W. Truax. Northern Pacific Railway officials named the station for Farmington, Minnesota, at the request of Truax, who came to Washington Territory from the state.

Farrington *(S.9;T.12N;R.33E)*

Railroad station on Snake River, 6-1/2 miles south of Kahlotus, east central Franklin County. It was named by officials of Great Northern Railway Company for R. I. Farrington, its comptroller.

Fauntleroy Cove *(S.35;T.24N;R.3E)*

An east shore cove of Puget Sound at the south end of Lincoln Park, between Williams Point and Brace Point, west central King County. In 1857, the cove was named by George Davidson of U.S. Coast Survey, for the survey brig *R.H. Fauntleroy*, which he had named for Lieut. Robert H. Fauntleroy. The following year, he married Fauntleroy's daughter.

Favorsburg (Garfield County) *see* Pataha

Fawn Lake *(S.25;T.10N;R.4E)*

A 23.6-acre lake, 46 ft. maximum depth, 4 miles northwest of St. Helens Lake, northeast Cowlitz County. This name was given in earlier days when there were more deer than hunters.

Fawn Island *(S.18;T.36N;R.2W)*

An island at the southwest entrance to Deer Harbor, Orcas Island, central San Juan County. In 1858, the name was placed on British admiralty charts by Capt. Henry Richards. It is one of many San Juan Island features that he named for the animal or bird life abundant at the time of his surveys. An alternate local name, which does not appear on maps or charts, is *Fisherman Island*.

Fay-Bainbridge State Park *(T.26N;R.2E)*

A 16-acre public park on the northwest shore of Bainbridge Island, south of Point Monroe, east central Kitsap County. It offers camping, swimming, fishing, and clamming. The hyphenated name includes that of the donor and of the island on which the park is located.

Fay Peak *(Mt. Rainier National Park)*

A 6,500-ft. mountain between Spray Park and Mather Mountains, overlooking Mowich Lake, northwest part of the park. In 1890, it was named for Ms. Fay Fuller, who in that year became the first woman to reach the summit of Mt. Rainier. (USBGN)

Fayette *(T.13N;R.3W)*

A community of good farms directly west of Adna at the junction of Deep Creek and Bunker Creek, west central Lewis County. It was settled in 1864, but not shown on most recent maps and it was locally named for Joel H. Fay, who settled here in 1864.

Federation Forest State Park *(Ts.18-20N;Rs.6-11)*

A corridor of forested land on each side of the Naches Hwy., between Enumclaw and Cascade Mountain summit, King/Pierce counties. This land was purchased by the Washington Federation of Women's Clubs, wherever such land was in private ownership, in order to retain natural, old-growth forest along at least one stretch of state highway. The tract is supplemented on the eastern extremity by National Forest timber which has been left uncut. It has been turned over to Washington State Parks & Recreation Commission for administration. The park, which is in Sec. 6;Twp.19N;R.9E, has been developed with park facilities and will have a forest display building. Alternate names for the corridor are *Women's Federated Forest*, *Big-Tree Park*, and *Women's Federated State Park*.

Felster's Portage *(T.10N;R.11W)*

A portage trail extending from Columbia River to the south end of Willapa Bay, southwest Pacific County. Important in pioneer days, the trail is not shown on recent maps. It was named for an early resident, Harry Feister, who operated an ox-team transportation system in 1851 and for several years after.

Felida *(S.29;T.3N;R.1E)*

Village 5 miles northwest of Vancouver and directly east of Shillapoo Lake, southwest Clark County. In 1890, the name was established when a post office was installed. Marian E. McIrvin, the first postmaster, suggested *Lakeview* as the designation, but postal authorities refused his suggestion because there already was a post office by that name in the state. McIrvin's father-in-law suggested the present name, which had been refused as an Oregon post office name, but which postal authorities accepted for this settlement. A pioneer tradition, which appears to be unsupported by records, relates that the post office was named for a cat, using the Latin name for the cat family, *Felidae*, somewhat modified.

Fellows (Lincoln County) *see* Telford

Fence Creek *(S.18;T.40N;R.43E)*

The stream of the creek heads in the northwest corner of Pend Oreille County; flows 4-1/2 miles eastward to Pend Oreille River. It is reported to have been named by land surveyors for a stockman's fence across the stream at the time of the original land survey and it has been confused at times with Russian Creek or Peewee Creek. (USBGN)

Ferguson County (Yakima County) *see* Yakima County

Ferguson Lake *(S.34;T.18N;R.2W)*

A very small body of water on Bush Prairie on the southwest edge of Tumwater, central Thurston County. The name is for Jesse Ferguson, a Bush Prairie pioneer. an earlier name, also for a pioneer settler, was *Barnes Lake*.

Fern Cove *(S.18;T.23N;R.2E)*

Cove at the northwest end of Vashon Island, 3 miles northwest of Vashon on West Passage, west central King County. In 1857, it was named by U.S. Coast Survey. The name is quite descriptive, as the area has a heavy growth of native ferns of several species.

Fern Lake *(T.30N;R.18E.uns)*

A very small lake on Wenatchee National Forest, east slope of Duncan Hill, north central Chelan County. It drains eastward into North Fork, Entiat River, and was named by Forest Ranger Alfred McDonald for his daughter.

Fern Lake *(S.10;T.22N;R.1W)*

A lake 2 miles northeast of North Bay on Case's Inlet, extreme southwest Kitsap County. It is the location of a radiation biological laboratory maintained by University of Washington. This is a locally-given descriptive name, as several species of fern are plentiful around the lake.

Fern Prairie *(S.22;T.2N;R.3E)*

Farming community 5 miles north of Columbia River, 10 miles east of Vancouver, southeast Clark County. It was named by James Parker, an early settler, for the abundance of bracken fern which took over here wherever the timber was cut. The Indian name was *Illahee*, meaning "good land," as camas was found here in quantity.

Ferncliff *(S.23;T.25N;R.2E)*

Beach settlement on Murden Cove, east central Bainbridge Island, Kitsap County. The first name used for this place was *Pettit's Landing*, for a promoter who platted 180 acres and built a dock in 1910. The present, descriptive name was chosen by a local resident named Lowman.

Ferndale *(S.29;T.39N;R.2E)*

A country town on lower Nooksack River, 6 miles northwest of Bellingham, northwest Whatcom County. It grew rapidly during the 1950s, after the building of a large oil refinery in the vicinity. In 1876, it was named by Alice Eldrige, the first schoolteacher, for a heavy growth of ferns near the new log schoolhouse. Originally it was known as *Jam* for a log jam in the river at this point.

Fernow Mountain *(T.31N;R.16E.uns)*

A 9,100-ft. peak on Chelan Ridge summit at the divide between Railroad Creek and the headwaters of Entiat River, northwest Chelan County. It is on the boundary between the Okanogan and Wenatchee national forests. The naming, by U.S. Forest Supervisor A. H. Sylvester, was for Dr. Bernard E. Fernow, a German forester, who was chief of forestry in the U.S. Dept. of Agriculture in 1886, and who later taught forestry in the U.S. and wrote several textbooks.

Ferry *(S.4;T.40N;R.32E)*

Once a town on Kettle River, adjoining the Canadian boundary, opposite the town of Boundary on the Canadian side, north Ferry County. It was active in the early 1900s, but little now remains except a customs and immigration station. It was named for Ferry County, which in turn was named for Elisha P. Ferry, territorial governor of Washington from 1872 until 1880, and also the first governor of the state from 1889 until 1893.

Ferry County

This 2,241 sq. miles in northeast Washington is bounded on the west by Okanogan County, on the south by Columbia River, on the east by Columbia and Kettle rivers, and on the north by Canada. The northern half is largely on Colville National Forest and the south half is mainly occupied by Colville Indian Reservation. On January 12, 1899, it was created by a state legislative bill carrying the name of *Eureka* for the county, and Republic as the prospective county seat. The county name was changed by a legislative act on February 16, 1899, to honor Elisha P. Ferry. (*see* Ferry)

Fidalgo *(Ss.17,18;T.34N;R.22E)*

Community at the southeast end of Fidalgo Island's western sector, facing Similik Bay, about 5 miles south of Anacortes, southwest Skagit County. In 1889, a town of 341 blocks was platted here, but was killed as a growing townsite by the panic of the early 1890s. The first name used was *Deception*, for nearby Deception Pass. In its boom period it was called *Fidalgo City*. When Admr. George Dewey defeated the Spanish fleet at Manila Bay on May 1, 1898, patriotic citizens changed the name to *Dewey*. That name persists on the south end of Fidalgo townsite on Deception Pass. The present name is from the same source as Fidalgo Island. (*see* Fidalgo Island)

Fidalgo *(S.32;T.34N;R.32E)*

Old settlement on the east shore of Fidalgo Bay near the south end, 1-1/2 miles southeast of Anacortes, southwest Skagit County. The first name was *Munks' Landing*, for William Munks, who operated a trade store here in the

1860s. In 1890, when a post office was established, the name of the island was used for the town.

Fidalgo Bay *(T.35N;R.2E)*

A 4-mile-long bay on the northeast shore of Fidalgo Island, adjoining Anacortes, west central Skagit County. It is shallow at the south end. (*see* Fidalgo Island)

Fidalgo City (Skagit County) *see* Fidalgo

Fidalgo Cove (Clallam County) *see* Neah Bay

Fidalgo Island *(Ts.34,35N;Rs.1,2E)*

An island directly north of Whidbey Island, from Deception Pass on the south to Guemes Channel on the north, and eastward across Similik Bay to Swinomish Channel, southwest Skagit County. In 1791, Lieut. Juan Francisco de Eliza named the island *Isla de Fidalgo* for Lieut. Salvador Fidalgo of the Spanish Navy. In 1841, Cmdr. Charles Wilkes changed the name to *Perry's Island,* for Oliver Hazard Perry, hero of the Battle of Lake Erie in 1813. in 1847, Capt. Henry Kellett restored the original name on British admiralty charts, as he had a preference for original Spanish names.

Fidelity *(S.6;T.11N;R.17E.uns)*

Mining camp at Bear Gap on Cascade Mountain summit, 3-1/2 miles north of Chinook Pass, northwest Yakima County. It was the location of a former mining camp and post office, established in 1905 by Frank Ryerson. The name was chosen by Ryerson and others as one which would tend to promote the sale of mining stock.

Fields Spring (Asotin County *see* Fields Spring State Park

Fields Spring State Park *(T.7N;R.45E)*

A 253-acre park on a spur of Blue Mountains, 24 miles south of Asotin, south central Asotin County. Excellent springs are the chief feature of this park, which offers public camping grounds. It was named for an old cattleman named Fields who used the springs for his herds.

Fife *(S.6;T.20N;R.4E)*

Suburb of Tacoma in a fertile area which produces berries and garden truck, 2 miles east of Tacoma, north central Pierce County. The name is for Col. W. J. Fife of Tacoma.

Fife's Peak *(S.11;T.17N;R.12E.uns)*

A 6,954-ft. peak, 2 miles north of Naches Hwy., near American River, extreme northwest Yakima County. It is a remnant of an old volcano, and was the source of local lava flows. It was named for David Fife and his son, Tom, who were early prospectors here.

Fifth of July Mountain *(S.33;T.30N;R.17E.uns)*

A 7,000-ft. peak on Wenatchee National Forest, north central Chelan County. It is directly south of Larch Lakes, and 2 miles west of Entiat River. It was named by Forest Supervisor A. H. Sylvester, who first visited the mountain on July 5.

Fifth Plain *(T.3N;R.3E)*

A plain 10 miles northeast of Vancouver on upper Fifth Plain Creek, south central Clark County. This name was applied by Hudson's Bay Company, which used several plains for animal pasture, and numbered them consecutively from Ft. Vancouver.

Fifth Plain Creek *(Ts.2,3N;R.3E)*

This plain rises in central Clark County; flows 8 miles southwest to Lackamas Creek near Proebstel. (*see* Fifth Plain)

Filuce Bay (Pierce County) *see* Filucy Bay

Filucy Bay *(Ss.24,25;T.20N;R.1W)*

An inlet 1 mile west of McNeil Island, at the confluence of Pitt, Balch, and Drayton passages, northwest Pierce County. In 1841, it was named *Titusi Bay* by Cmdr. Charles Wilkes, using the original Indian name. In 1847, Capt. R. N. Inskip placed it on British admiralty charts as *Turnours Bay.* When the settlement of Longbranch developed on the bay, local settlers applied the same name to the bay. The present name -- which at one time was spelled *Filuce* -- may have been chosen by early seafaring men through a misspelling of *felucca,* a type of sailing vessel used on the Nile River. Some historians believe that it is a misspelling of the original Indian name, *Titusi.*

Finch Creek *(T.22N;R.4W)*

The stream of the creek heads south of Dow Mountain, 1-1/2 miles east of the south end of Lake Cushman Reservoir; flows southeast and east 3-1/2 miles to Hood Canal at Hoodsport, Mason County. It was named for Mrs.

Ida Finch, daughter of Capt. George K. Robbins, who was the first settler at Hoodsport and the original owner of Finch Creek Valley. Until 1950, the local name for the creek's course was *Venture Valley.* Settlers wanted a better name and held a contest for it in July 1950. Mrs. Christine Ahl of Belfair won the award with the name *Legend Valley.* The background for this name was a legend that the valley served as a prison for Indian slaves who had been captured by local tribes.

Findley Lakes *(S.7;T.21N;R.10E)*

Three lakes, 14-1/2 miles east of Kanasket, southeast King County. They are 22.3 acres, 1.7 acres, and 1.6 acres respectively. The group name is reported to be that of an early settler in the area.

Finley *(S.26;T.18N;R.30E)*

Railroad station 1-1/2 miles west of Columbia River, 5 miles southeast of Kennewick, southeast Benton County. It was named for George E. Finley, whose land adjoined the town, and who was one of the first settlers under the Northern Pacific Irrigation Canal.

Finn Creek *(T.12N;R.9W)*

The stream of the creek rises in central Pacific County, 7 miles east of Willapa Bay; flows 5 miles west and south to Nehmah River, 4 miles from its mouth. In the early 1890s, local settlers named the creek for the large number of Finns who came into the region at that time.

Finney Creek *(Ts.34,35N;Rs.8,9E)*

The stream of the creek rises in high mountains, 3 miles east of Little Deer Park, south central Skagit County; flows northerly about 19 miles to Skagit River between Birdsview and Concrete. It was named for an early settler who claimed land at the mouth of the creek.

Fir *(S.24;T.33N;R.4E)*

Once an important landing, now a scattered settlement on one of several delta outlets of Skagit River, directly southwest of Conway, southwest Skagit County. It was locally named for the stands of large, old-growth fir trees in the area. When originally settled, it was called *Mann's Landing.*

Fire Creek *(T.31N;Rs.12,13E)*

The stream of the creek rises near a high peak on the northwest slope of Glacier Peak, elevation 6,874 ft., northwest Snohomish County; flows west 4 miles to Whitechuck River. It was named by Forest Service officials for a big fire along the creek which burned in 1916.

Fire Mountain *(S.13;T.31N;R.12E)*

A peak 5 miles northwest of Glacier Peak summit, between the headwaters of Fire Creek and Lime Creek, northeast Snohomish County. It was named by Forest Service fire crews for its proximity to Fire Creek.

First Creek *(T.39N;R.34E)*

The stream of this short creek rises on Colville National Forest, north central Ferry County; flows about 2 miles from the northeast to join West Deer Creek, 5-1/2 miles east of Curlew. The name describes the creek as the first tributary of West Deer Creek from its mouth. Second Creek and Third Creek were named similarly.

First Creek *(T.20N;R.17E)*

The stream of the creek heads south of Tenaway Ridge, north central Kittitas County; flows southwest and west 5 miles to Tenaway River west of Swauk Prairie. Its name derives from the fact that it is the first stream to enter the river, as counted upstream from the mouth.

First Hill *(Ss.29,32;T.25N;R.4E)*

One of Seattle's 12 "official" hills, directly east of the main business district, King County. The elevation is 322 ft. at Boren and Madison and 339 feet a few blocks to the east. Once the site of many of the city's finest homes, it is now occupied mostly by apartment houses and hospitals. It was named for its relation to the center of Seattle. The next hill to the east was called *Second Hill* or *Renton Hill*.

First Lake (King County) *see* Jade Lake

First Lake *(S.28;T.20N;R.7E)*

A 2-1/2-acre lake, 3/4 mile east of Enumclaw in White River drainage, southwest King County. It is one of 3 numbered lakes in the same area. An alternate name is *One Lake*.

First Thought Mountain *(S.7;T.39N;R.37E)*

A 3,968-ft. peak in Colville National Forest, 2 miles east of Kettle River and 2 miles northeast of Orient, extreme northwest Stevens County. This mountain is topped by a Forest Service fire

lookout station. It is located in a mineralized area, and the name is borrowed from that of an early mine in the immediate vicinity.

Fisgard Island (Pierce County) *see* Anderson Island

Fish Creek *(Mt. Rainier National Park)*

A very short stream which rises in Lake George on Mt. Wow, southwest sector of the park; flows southeast to Tahoma Creek, 1 mile east of Lake George. It has many beaver dams and offers fair fishing. This descriptive name, used over and over for mountain streams in this state, seems barely applicable to this creek.

Fish Creek *(S.8;T.34N;R.2W)*

A narrow inlet, rather than a creek, on the north side of Cattle Point at the southeast tip of San Juan Island, south central San Juan County. The name was locally applied, and relates to a very small tidal stream which enters the inlet at its upper end. A name which has not been recorded or mapped, and which is therefore unofficial, is *Illinois Inlet*. It was applied by Prof. L. C. Muenscher when he attended summer sessions at the Puget Sound Marine Station near Friday Harbor; and it was in honor of many Illinois students and faculty who were in attendance at the time.

Fish Lake *(S.3;T.23N;R.14E)*

A high mountain lake on Wenatchee National Forest, in the Middle Fork of the Cle Elum River, 40 miles north of Roslyn, Kittitas County. Many lakes in the state bear this rather unimaginative name because they contain fish. This one has a more distinguished alternative name, inherited from local Indians -- *Tucquala*.

Fish Lake *(S.7;T.10N;R.12E.uns)*

A 4,042-ft. lake near Cascade Mountain summit, 4 miles east of Two Lakes, southwest Yakima County. It is accessible only by trail, and is closed to the public, as are all places in the western portion of Yakima Indian Reservation. It drains to the southeast through Fish Lake Stream. Many Indian families camp here during summer months, fishing, and drying most of the catch for winter food. Planting by Indian Service personnel has maintained the yield of fish.

Fish Lake (Clallam County) *see* Lake Sutherland

Fish Lake (King County) *see* Retreat Lake

Fish Lake (Lincoln County/Spokane County) *see* Fishtrap Lake

Fish Lake (Whatcom County) *see* Silver Lake

Fish Lake Stream *(Ts.9,10N;R.12E.uns)*

The stream of the creek heads in Fish Lake, on Yakima Indian Reservation, 2-1/2 miles southeast of Cascade Mountain summit, southwest Yakima County; flows 8 miles through wild country to Clearwater Creek. The name is borrowed from Fish Lake. On some maps this creek is shown, in error, as *Lake Stream*.

Fish River (Clallam County) *see* Pysht River

Fisher *(S.12;T.1N;R.2E)*

Settlement on the north bank of Columbia River, 8 miles east of Vancouver in south central Clark County. It was named for Solomon W. Fisher who filed a Donation Land Claim here in the early 1850s -- 160 acres on the mainland and 160 acres on Government Island. The first name was *Fisher*, and later was modified to *Fishers Landing*. The present name came into use as a simplification by popular usage.

Fishers (Clark County) *see* Fisher

Fisher Island *(S.21;T.8N;R.3W)*

A narrow 1-1/2-mile-long island in Columbia River, 2-1/2 miles south of Eufaula in southwest Cowlitz County. In 1841, the Wilkes Expedition named this feature *Plomondon Island*. The present name was borrowed from that of an adjoining channel to the north.

Fisherman Bay *(Ss.22-27;T.35N;R.2W)*

A west shore bay of Lopez Island on San Juan Channel, in south central San Juan County. It is almost entirely landlocked by a long spit. In 1858, this feature was first charted by Capt. Henry Richards of the British admiralty survey. He charted it simply as *Lagoon*. In January, 1912, the present name was applied by the U.S. Coast & Geodetic Survey. It is a moorage for many commercial fishing craft.

Fisherman Harbor *(S.4;T.25N;R.1W)*

A south tip bay of Toandos Peninsula on Hood Canal, 1/2 mile east of

Oak Head, southeast Jefferson County. Much used by fisherman, it was named locally. Other names that have been used include *Fisherman's Harbor* and *Fisherman's Bay.*

Fisherman Island (San Juan County) *see* Fawn Island

Fisherman's Bay (Jefferson County) *see* Coyle

Fishers Hornpipe Creek (*Mt. Rainier National Park*)

The stream of this small, noisy stream (a tributary of Pyramid Creek), rises on the southwest slope of Mt. Rainier, south of Pyramid Glacier, the southwest sector of the park. It was named by Ben Longmire while he was building the Longmire-Indian Henry Trail, "Because it sang a regular 'Fisher's Hornpipe' to us at our camp." (USBGN)

Fishing Bay (*Ss.14,23;T.37N;R.2W*)

A northwest shore bay of East Sound, directly southwest of the town of East Sound, northeast San Juan County. In 1851, this name was charted by Capt. Henry Richards of the British admiralty survey, because of good fishing encountered here by members of his crew.

Fishtrap (*S.24;T.22N;R.39E*)

A scattered community with a railroad siding, 9 miles northeast of Sprague, extreme southeast Lincoln County. In 1902, the place was founded as a railway station. Northern Pacific Railway Company officials named it *Vista.* It was renamed Fishtrap in 1906, at the urgent suggestion of John W. Lawton, a local landowner. The present name is for fishtraps that Indians formerly operated in Fishtrap Lake, 2-1/2 miles south. A former post office under this name has been discontinued.

Fishtrap Creek (*Ts.40,41N;Rs.2,3E*)

The stream of the creek rises near the Canadian boundary west of Sumas, northwest Whatcom County; flows 5 miles southwest to Nooksack River. In the 1860s, it was named by John Cornelius, a surveyor, for a large Indian fish trap and drying house on the creek.

Fishtrap Lake (*Ts.21,22N;Rs.39,40E*)

A 3-mile-long lake, average width 1/2 mile, 7 miles northeast of Sprague, southeast Lincoln and southwest Spokane counties. It was named for fishtraps that Indians operated here in the early

days. Local names which have been used are *Fish Lake* and *Deep Lake.*

Five-Mile Rapids (Klickitat County) *see* The Dalles

Five-Mile Rock (King County) *see* Four-Mile Rock

Five Stream (*T.24N;R.6W*)

The 4-1/2-mile-long stream of the creek heads 1 mile northwest of Wonder Mountain on Olympic National Forest, northwest Mason County; flows northeast into Olympic National Park, to North Fork, Skokomish River. It was named in the same numerical sequence as 8 other creeks that enter the river from south and west. Often confused with McKay Creek and Four Stream on certain county maps. (USBGN)

Flag Peak (Snohomish County) *see* Delcampo Peak

Flag River (Spokane, Whitman, Adams counties) *see* Palouse River

Flat Creek (*Ts.39,40N;R.38E*)

The stream of this 12-mile-long watercourse rises on Colville National Forest, northwest corner of Stevens County; flows southeasterly to Columbia River at China Bend. The name was given by local settlers because the creek flows through flat land for several miles before entering the river.

Flat Point (*S.10;T.35N;R.2W*)

A northwest point of Lopez Island, on Upright Channel, 2 miles north of Lopez. In 1859, this descriptive name was placed on British admiralty charts by Capt. Henry Richards, RN.

Flat Point Lake (*S.10;T.35N;R.2W*)

A 2-1/2-acre, privately-owned lake in a game preserve on the northwest area of Lopez Island, near Flat Point, central San Juan County. The lake was named for Flat Point.

Flattery Creek (*Ss.1,12;T.33N;R.16W*)

The stream of this very short creek rises on Cape Flattery, on Makah Indian Reservation, extreme northwest Clallam County; flows 1-1/2 miles northwest to Hole-in-the-Wall on Pacific Ocean.

Flattery Rocks (*S.11;T.33N;R.16W*)

Makah Indian Reservation rocks in Pacific Ocean, south of Cape Flattery and about 1/2 mile offshore, extreme northwest Clallam County. On October 16, 1792, they were named by Capt. George Vancouver for nearby Cape

Flattery. In 1793, Martinez y Zayas named them *Las Islas Deseadas.* The name "Flattery" had been applied to the cape by Capt. James Cook on March 22, 1778.

Flattop Island (*T.36N;R.3W*)

A rather flat island in New Channel, between Spieden Island and Orcas Island, northwest San Juan County. It slopes to the southeast and has sparse vegetation, thus the descriptive name which was applied by Cmdr. Charles Wilkes in 1841.

Flatwoods (Clark County) *see* Manor

Fletcher (*S.20;T.16N;R.36E*)

A small settlement and early post office, 8 miles north of Washtucna, southeast Adams County. It was named for Postmaster James F. Fletcher, an early settler in the area.

Fletcher (*S.19;T.19N;R.45E*)

Railroad station 2 miles east of Oakesdale, northeast Whitman County. In 1889, it was named by railroad officials for James F. Fletcher, the farmer who owned the land on which the station was built.

Fletcher Bay (*S.20;T.25N;R.2E*)

A west shore bay of Bainbridge Island on Port Orchard bay, east central Kitsap County. The name was applied locally for William C. Fletcher, who took a land claim here on July 17, 1869. A local name which has not persisted was *Greek George's Bay.*

Flett Creek (Pierce County) *see* Gale Creek

Flett Glacier (*Mt. Rainier National Park*)

The northwest lobe of Russell Glacier in the northwest area of the park, on the northwest slope of Mt. Rainier. It is between Ptarmigan Ridge and Spray Falls Park and drains through Spray Creek into North Mowich River. The glacier was named for Prof. J. B. Flett, who made the first collection and scientific description of Mt. Rainier's flora. (USBGN)

Florence (*S.31;T.32N;R.4E*)

Town 2-1/2 miles southeast of Stanwood on lower Stillaguamish River, northwest Snohomish County. (*see* Florence Island)

Florence Island (*Ts.31,32N;Rs.3,4E*)

No longer an island, this 2,000 acres

of delta land is on Port Susan Bay, directly south of Stanwood, northwest Snohomish County. Hat Slough, which used to separate it from the mainland, no longer carries water. Farmers use electric pumps to drain the land. It was named for the daughter of F. S. Norton, a pioneer of 1883.

Flounder Bay *(Ss.27-28;T.35N;R.1E)*

A bay at the north extremity of Burrows Bay on the northwest end of Fidalgo Island, west central Skagit County. In 1841, it was named *Boxer Cove* by Cmdr. Charles Wilkes for the British brig *Boxer*, captured on September 5, 1813, by Lieut. William Burroughs. This association of ship and commander was common in Wilkes's nomenclature. In this case he linked a captured ship with the capturer, as the bay now known as *Burrows Bay* was named in honor of Lieut. Burroughs. The present name came into local use when Fidalgo Island was settled, and supplanted Wilkes's name.

Flower Dome *(Ss.27,34;T.31N;R.14E)*

A round-topped hill between Glacier Peak and Buck Creek Pass, on Mt. Baker National Forest, extreme east Snohomish County. It provides an excellent view of Glacier Peak and was named by U.S. Forest Supervisor A. H. Sylvester for its shape and for the array of wild flowers in grassy meadows in season.

Foam Creek *(T.29N;R.14E.uns)*

The stream of the creek heads at Cascade Mountain summit on Wenatchee National Forest, 2 miles north of White Mountain, northwest Chelan County; flows 2 miles southeast to White River. It was named by U.S. Forest Supervisor A. H. Sylvester, because it is creamy and foaming during the warm months when the glaciers are grinding at its head.

Foggy Peak *(S.13;T.29N;R.11E)*

A 6,000-ft. peak, 3 miles east by north of Monte Cristo, east central Snohomish County. It is in a heavily mineralized area. The descriptive name was applied by early miners because there are nearly always banks or shreds of fog on the northwest slopes.

Foolhen Creek *(T.25N;Rs.16,17E)*

The stream of the creek rises on a broad-topped ridge of Wenatchee National Forest, southwest Chelan County;

flows 2-1/2 miles northeast to Chiwaukum Creek. It was named by early sheepmen for the many "foolhens" in the area.

Fools Prairie *(T.31N;R.40E)*

This prairie includes a wide area in Colville River Valley, near the town of Valley, central Stevens County. The original name was given by French Canadians in the employ of the North West Company, fur-traders, and was *Prairie du Fou*. The present name is simply an English translation. There are 2 traditions regarding the source of this name. One, which is somewhat simpler and slightly more plausible, is that it was named for an old Indian who lived here when the white occupancy started, and who was nicknamed *le Fou* or "the fool." The other tradition, mentioned by several early historians, is that the landscape fooled travelers coming from the north. On rounding a big bend in the river, north of the present town of Valley, the landscape strongly resembled that of the area directly south of Chewelah, leading the traveler to believe that he was many miles from his destination.

Fonte Bank (San Juan County) *see* Hein Bank

Forbes Point *(S.12;T.32N;R.1E)*

A Saratoga Passage point directly east of Maylor Point, between Oak Harbor and Crescent Harbor on Whidbey Island, north Island County. It occupies part of the original Donation Land Claim of S. Maylor. This name appears on the 1792 charts of Capt. George Vancouver, with no reference to the name source.

Ford *(Ss.19,20;T.28N;R.40E)*

Small community located near the eastern boundary of Spokane Indian Reservation, 11 miles south of Springdale, southeast Stevens County. During earlier years the name used for this place was *Walkers Prairie*. Recently Ford has become increasingly important because of the discovery of uranium ore on adjoining Indian lands, including portions of 3 allotments.

Fords Point (Island County) *see* Blowers Bluff

Fords Prairie *(S.31;T.15N;R.2W)*

Village 1 mile northwest of Centralia on Chehalis River, northwest Lewis County. It was named for Judge Sidney Ford, known locally as "Uncle Sid," who operated a public house here on

Cowlitz Road, on the mail route between Olympia and Columbia River.

Forest *(S.19;T.13N;R.1W)*

Small settlement on Newaukum River, 8 miles southeast of Chehalis on the Julien Bernier Donation Land Claim, west central Lewis County. In the 1890s, it was established and named for an early schoolteacher, John T. Forrest. A local name is *Newaukum Prairie*.

Forest City *(S.34;T.24N;R.1E)*

Community on south shore of Sinclair Inlet, near its head, central Kitsap County. In 1946, the name was chosen by residents when the town was incorporated because it was surrounded by a vigorous stand of second-growth coniferous trees. In April, 1949, the town disincorporated, possibly the only incorporated town in the state to vote itself out of existence.

Forest Lake *(S.19;T.10N;R.5E)*

An 8-acre lake, elevation 3,900 ft., on the Skamania-Cowlitz County boundary, extreme northwest Skamania and northeast Cowlitz counties. The name is descriptive, as the lake is surrounded by heavy timber stands. An alternate name is *Doris Lake*.

Forest Mountain *(S.13;T.27N;R.20E)*

A 5,100-ft. peak on the boundary between Okanogan and Wenatchee national forests, east central Chelan County. It is the last prominent peak near the southeast end of Chelan Ridge and was named by Forest Service personnel because it is heavily timbered.

Fork Creek *(T.12N;Rs.6,7W)*

The stream of the creek rises in southeast Pacific County; flows 9 miles northwest to Willapa River between Nalpee and Lebam. Local settlers chose this name because the stream has a great many forks and branches.

Forks *(S.9;T.28N;R.13W)*

A logging town between Bogachiel and Calawah rivers, 12 miles east of Pacific Ocean, southwest Clallam County. It has many small, independent logging operators, commonly called *gyppos*. The town is named for Forks Prarie. (*see* Forks Prarie)

Forks Lake (Okanogan County) *see* Osoyoos Lake

Forks Prairie *(Ts,28,29N;R.13W)*

An extensive prairie (on which is located the town of Forks), over 4 miles long, between the Calawah and Boga-chiel rivers, southwest Clallam County. It was named because it is located in the forks formed by 2 rivers.

Forlorn Lakes
(Ss.1,2;T.5N;&Ss.35,36;
T.6N;R.8E.uns)
Twelve unnamed lakes, 1-1/2 miles north of Big Lava Bed on Gifford Pin-chot National Forest, central Skamania County. The lakes, of which 10 cover areas of 1 or more acres, are located in a heavily-forested area. There appears to be little justification for this gloomy name, said to have been chosen by For-est Service personnel.

Forsell *(S.16;T.9N;R.23E)*
A produce-shipping point, 2-1/2 miles west of Grandview, southeast Ya-kima County. It was named by the local railway superintendent for Jim Forsell, a pioneer resident, because Forsell was the only person who ever called on him without registering a complaint.

Forresterville (Okanogan County) *see* Conconully

Forsyth Glacier *(T.9N;R.5E)*
Once a north slope glacier of Mt. St. Helens, northwest quarter of Skamania County. In 1912, it was named by Washington state legislature at the sug-gestion of The Mazamas, for Charles E. Forsyth of Castle Rock. In 1908, For-syth had led a life-saving party on the glacier. The name was not approved by the U.S. Board on Geographic names, because Forsyth was living at the time. The unofficial name continues in use.

Forsythe Creek (King County) *see* Syl-vester Creek

Fort Alden (King County) *see* Fort Alder

Fort Alder *(S.32;T.24N;R.8E)*
An historic fort above Snoqualmie Falls, on the site of the small community of Meadowbrook, near the town of Snoqualmie, central King County. In February and March 1856, it was built by the Northern Battalion, Washington Territorial Volunteers, under Capt. J. J. H. Van Bokkelin. Its purpose, with sever-al nearby forts, was to prevent Indians of eastern Washington from joining forces with Puget Sound Indians. The name was for abundant growths of native alder on Rangers Prairie, where the fort was located. Some maps and records have altered this name to *Fort Alden*.

Fort Arkansas *(T.9N;R.2W)*
A blockhouse and palisade on Cow-litz River near Castle Rock, at southeast end of Arkansas Valley, Cowlitz Coun-ty. It was erected during the Indian wars of the late 1850s; nothing remains today. The name was given by the volunteer troops who built and manned the fort.

Fort Bellingham *(S.16;T.38N;R.2E)*
This old fort, built in 1856 and abandoned in 1860, was on a bluff overlooking Bellingham Bay, 3-1/2 miles west of the mouth of Whatcom Creek, southwest Whatcom County. It was named for Bellingham Bay.

Fort Bennett *(S.4;T.6N;R.35E)*
An historic, stockaded fort on north bank Walla Walla River, 2 miles above Whitman Station, south central Walla Walla County. On December 10, 1855, it was started by troops of Oregon Mounted Volunteers under Lieut. Col. James J. Kelly. It was named for Capt. Bennett of Company F of this command, who died shortly before the fort was built.

Fort Borst *(S.6;T.14N;R.2W)*
An old blockhouse adjoining Cen-tralia on the west, on Chehalis River and the Old Military Road, northeast Lewis County. In 1856, it was built during the Indian wars on the claim of Joseph Borst, and is named for him. The fort has also been called *Borst Blockhouse* and *Borst's Fort*.

Fort Canby *(S.4;T.9N;R.11W)*
An inactive fort (now a state park site) on Cape Disappointment east of North Head, southwest Pacific County. On April 5, 1864, it was established as Fort Cape Disappointment. On January 28, 1875, it was renamed to honor Maj. Gen. Edward Richard Sprigg Canby, who was killed in the Modoc war. While active, it maintained 2 full batteries of coast artillery weapons, and with Fort Columbia and Fort Stevens constituted the defense organization of Columbia River.

Fort Canby Lake *(S.9;T.9N;R.11W)*
A small, shallow lake (which is full of stumps), at Fort Canby, 1-3/4 miles southwest of Ilwaco, extreme southwest Pacific County. The name is for Fort Canby. An alternate name is *O'Neil Lake*. (*see* Fort Canby)

Fort Cascades *(S.11;T.2N;R.7E)*
This rather large fort was built on a hill above the old town of Cascade City, on Columbia River near the present Cas-cade Locks, Skamania County. On Sep-tember 30, 1855, it was completed and was abandoned on November 6, 1861. It was named by Washington Territorial Volunteers for the Cascades of Colum-bia River, which it adjoined.

Fort Casey *(S.22;T.31N;R.1E)*
An old coast defense fort on the west shore of Whidbey Island at Admiralty Head, directly west of Admiralty Bay, west Island County. In 1897, when es-tablished, it boasted 10 batteries of coast artillery; in 1950, it was inactivated. Now it is under the jurisdiction of Wash-ington State Parks & Recreation Com-mission, with 2 restored batteries. It was named by army officials for Brig. Gen. Thomas Lincoln Casey, once Chief of Engineers, U.S. Army. At one period he was in command of the Puget Sound District. His son, Lieut. Col. Silas Casey, later commanded the same dis-trict.

Fort Chehalis *(T.16N;Rs.11,12W)*
An abandoned fort on Point Cheha-lis, south of the entrance to Grays Har-bor, southwest Grays Harbor County. On February 11, 1860, a U.S. military post was established here and a fort built to protect settlers against the imagined hostility of Chehalis Indians. There seems to have been no logical reason for the fort, which was abandoned on June 19, 1861. It was named for the point on which it was located.

Fort Collins *(S.21;T.20N;R.2W)*
An old, vanished fort opposite Ar-cadia, near Hungerford Point, southeast Mason County. It was built during the Indian troubles of the 1850s. Local set-tlers stockaded in the fort whenever there was an Indian scare.

Fort Columbia
(Ss.15,16,21;T.9N;R.10W)
A coast defense fort (now a state park) at Chinook Point on the north bank of Columbia River, 2 miles east of Chinook, Pacific County. Established on November 30, 1899, it originally had 3 full batteries of coast artillery located on 720 acres of ground. On July, 1899, it was named by army officers for the river which it guarded. (*see* Fort Co-lumbia State Park)

Fort Columbia State Park
(T.9N;R.10W)
A 293-acre historical area on Chin-

ook Point, 2 miles east of Chinook, southwest Pacific County. It was once the site of Fort Columbia, an active coast defense unit; now this state park offers a museum and a partial restoration of the buildings and defenses. In 1899, the name was chosen by U.S. Army officers when the fort was established. It was named for the river which it guarded. (*see* Fort Columbia)

Fort Colville (*T.36N;R.37E*)

An historic post located on extensive flats along the southeast bank of Columbia River, 1 mile above the Kettle Falls cascades, and 3/4 mile above the portage trail around these falls. On April 14, 1825, it was established by Hudson's Bay Company as a trading post, farm, defensive station, and supply depot for other company posts in Columbia River basin. It was completed during 1826 by moving company property and equipment from old Spokane House, which Hudson's Bay Company had acquired by merger with North West Company in 1821. On the day this post was established, George Simpson noted in his journal that he had "lined out the site of the establish't, 150 ft. square on a bank facing and commanding a view of the River, and I have taken the liberty of naming it Fort Colvile as both the establishments that bore that Gentleman's name were abandoned at the Coalition. of Hudson's Bay Company and Northwest Company." The area on which the fort was established was flooded by Franklin D. Roosevelt Lake when Grand Coulee Dam was completed in 1939-1940. It was named for Andrew W. Colvile, one-time governor of the Company of Adventurers of England Trading into Hudson's Bay, commonly known as Hudson's Bay Company. Fort Colvile should not be confused with Fort Colville.

Fort Colville (*Ss.35-45;T.36N;R.39E*)

A 1,070-acre Army post, 3 miles northeast of Colville, on a flat skirted by Mill Creek, directly south of old Pinckney City, west central Spokane County. This fort was also called *Harney Military Depot* and was first occupied by the 9th U.S. Infantry Regiment, on June 21, 1859, commanded by Maj. Pinckney Lugenbeel. The regular troops were withdrawn that year for active duty in the Civil War. They were replaced by a lot of jailbirds from San Francisco who had been given the alternative of prison

or enlistment. All troops were withdrawn in 1881 and the fort was abandoned in 1882. It was given the name of an adjoining town and river, which derived from that of Andrew W. Colvile, once governor of Hudson's Bay Company. This installation should not be cofused with old Fort Colvile, on Columbia River, 14 miles to the northwest.

Fort Decatur (*S.32;T.25N;R.4E*)

This old fort, built in 1855 during the Indian wars, was located in Seattle at the corner of Cherry St. and Front St. (which now is First Ave.), King County. It was a blockhouse of heavy timbers and roofed with split cedar shakes, 25 by 40 ft. in area, first called *North Blockhouse*. It was built by Seattle residents and reinforced in January 1856 by marines from the *U.S.S. Decatur*. After the town of Seattle was saved from hostile Indian bands with the help of the ship, the fort was named after it.

Fort Duwamish (*S.20;T.24N;R.4E*)

A two-story structure south of Seattle on Duwamish River, directly north of the old town of Duwamish on the L. M. Collins land claim, King County. It is 22 ft. square, with a gable roof and the second story has an overhang. In September 1855, it was built during the Indian wars and named for the Duwamish River, near which it stood.

Fort Eaton (*T.18N;R.1W*)

An old fort, 4 miles southwest of Nisqually Flats, on the Eaton land claim, northeast Thurston County. It consisted of 16 log buildings, built in a square and erected during the winter of 1855-1856 by local settlers during the Indian troubles. It was named for the owner of the land on which the fort was built.

Fort Ebey (*S.4;T.28N;R.5E*)

An abandoned fort on Ebey Island in Snohomish River, 1 mile upstream from Lowell, east central Snohomish County. In 1855, it was established by Washington Territorial Volunteers during the Indian wars and was named for Isaac Neff Ebey.

Fort Flagler (*S.17;T.30N;R.1E*)

This coast defense fort was located on Marrowstone Point, on the north end of Marrowstone Island, northeast Jefferson County. In 1897-1900, the fort was built and abandoned in 1937. It was located in a triangular pattern with Fort Casey and Fort Worden. In 1899, it was

named by U.S. Army officials for Brig. Gen. Daniel Webster Flagler, Chief of Ordnance, U.S. Army, at the time the fort was completed.

Fort George Wright (*T.25N;R.42E*)

A once active military base along Spokane River, adjoining the northwest part of Spokane, Spokane County. This 1,022-acre site was acquired by the U.S. Army on October 31, 1895. It was named for Col. George Wright, 9th Infantry, USA, who took command of Columbia River district in January 1856, during the Indian wars.

Fort Hayden (Clallam County) *see* Camp Hayden

Fort Henderson (*T.24N;R.7E*)

This old fort, built during the Indian wars of the 1850s, was at the mouth of a small stream which enters Snoqualmie River just below Falls City, King County. It was built by the Northern Battalion, Washington Territorial Volunteers, which was on duty at nearby Fort Tilton. The fort was named for Capt. Henderson, an officer of the Volunteers. It evidently was later renamed *Fort Patterson*.

Fort Henness (*T.15N;R.3W*)

A large stockade (with block houses at alternate corners) on Mound Prarie, directly north of the town of Mt. Prarie, southwest Thurston County. In 1856, it was built by a local settlers during the Indian scare and was named for Capt. Benjamin Henness, of Washington Territorial Volunteers, who owned a nearby Donation Land Claim.

Fort Lander (*T.24N;R.4E*)

This old fort was located on a site which is now within the city limits of Seattle, on Duwamish River, 1/2 mile north of the administration building at King County airports (Boeing Field), King County. In 1856, it was built by Washington Territorial Volunteers during the Indian wars. Materials were assembled in Seattle and barged upriver for erection. The stockade was 98 ft. long and 58 ft. wide. It was named for Capt. Edward Lander of the W.T.V..

Fort Lawton (*T.25N;R.3E*)

A 701-acre military reservation on the west end of Lawton Peninsula, between Elliott Bay and Shilshole Bay in Seattle, excluding the tip of West Point, King County. It includes 2 dock sites. The land was donated by Seattle citizens between October 14, 1896, and February 17, 1898, and the military installations were built in 1898. In 1900, the name was given by U.S. Army officials for Maj. Gen. Henry Ware Lawton, who was killed during the Philippine Insurrection in 1899, in the battle of San Mateo on December 19. It has modern facilities and equipment. A portion of the land will revert to the estates of original donors if used for other than military purposes.

Fort Lewis *(Ts. 17-19N;Rs. 1-3W)*

An army post, east of Nisqually River, west central Pierce County. In 1917, it was established as *Camp Lewis* at the start of WWI and covered about 62,000 acres. It has since been increased to about 94,000 acres. The name is for Capt. Meriwether Lewis, one of 2 leaders of the famous Lewis & Clark Expedition of 1804-1806 to the mouth of Columbia River.

Fort Maloney *(S.21;T.20N;R.4E)*

A log blockhouse on the north bank of Puyallup River, near the present bridge on East Meridian, north central Pierce County. In 1856, it was built during the Indian troubles by regular army troops to protect a river ferry from Indians. It was named for Capt. Maurice Maloney, USA, who was then stationed at Fort Steilacoom.

Fort Mason *(T.31N;R.1W)*

An abandoned fort on Wilson Point, adjoining the city of Port Townsend, on Strait of Juan de Fuca, northeast Jefferson County. During the Indian troubles of the 1850s, a log blockhouse was built here, but never was actively garrisoned. In 1900, the site was occupied by Fort Worden, which now has been abandoned. In 1857, the fort was named for Acting Gov. Charles H. Mason, 1st Secretary of Washington Territory.

Fort McAllister *(T.19N;R.6E)*

A blockhouse, long since vanished, on South Prairie, 4 miles southwest of Buckley, north central Pierce County. In April 1856, it was built by troops under the command of Capt. C. W. Swindal, during the Indian troubles. The fort was named for James McAllister, a pioneer settler of 1846.

Fort Miller *(T.16N;R..1E)*

A blockhouse and corral (of which no signs now remain), on Tenalquot Prairie, 12 miles southeast of Olympia, south central Thurston County. Governor Stevens ordered it built as a Quartermaster Depot. The name used was

evidently that of one of the W.T.V. officers.

Fort Naches *(XXXXXXX)*

An old fort on the south bank of Naches River, 5 miles west of Painted Rocks, northwest Yakima County. In June 1856, it was established by troops under Col. George Wright. This was a large, rectangular structure of *Basket Fort* type, made of gabions. (*see* Naches Pass)

Fort Nez Perce *(Walla Walla County) see* Fort Walla Walla (trade post)

Fort Nisqually *(S.22;T.19N;R.1E)*

Two forts by this name were built by Hudson's Bay Company on different sites, 2 miles apart. They were near the present town of Steilacoom, northwest Pierce County. The first, built in 1833, was on Nisqually Reach near the water's edge, directly south of Sequalitchew Creek, and was usually referred to as *Fort Nesqually*. In 1843, it was moved northeast about 2 miles, and was referred to as *Nisqually House* by Puget Sound Agricultural Company, a Hudson's Bay Company subsidiary, which operated it as a trading post and fort. The name source is the same as that of Nisqually River.

Fort Patterson *(King County) see* Fort Henderson

Fort Preston *(T.16N;R.4E)*

Nothing now remains of this stockade near Mashel River, on Mashel Prairie, south central Pierce County. In 1857, it was built by Capt. Miller's company of Washington Territorial Volunteers. It is reported to have been named for the person on whose Donation Claim the fort was located.

Fort Rains Blockhouse *(T.2N;R.7E)*

An early fort built in 1856 during the Indian wars, was on the north bank of Columbia River at the Middle Cascades, 40 miles east of Vancouver, south central Skamania County. In 1927, it was restored by Skamania County Historical Society. It was named for Maj. Gabriel Rains, under whose orders the fort was built.

Fort Riggs *(S.17;T.1N;R.4E)*

A blockhouse and palisade on the north bank of Columbia River, directly south of Washougal, southeast Clark County. In April 1856, defense structures were built here during the Indian wars by Clark County Rangers, a volunteer military company. It was named Col. Reuben

Riggs who had a land claim on the fort site.

Fort Simcoe *(T.10N;Rs. 15,16E)*

A restored fort on Agency Creek, 38 miles southwest of Yakima, central Yakima County. On August 8, 1856, a U.S. Army post and fort were established here by Maj. Robert S. Garnett and 2 garrison companies. It was maintained as an army post until May 22, 1859. From that year until 1923, Fort Simcoe housed the Yakima Indian Agency and an Indian school. A restoration of the premises was started in 1953 by Washington State Parks & Recreation Commission, assisted by Fort Simcoe and Mool-Mool Restoration Society. for this purpose, the Yakima Indian nation gave a 99-year lease on 200 acres. The name is from the Yakima word *Simku-wee* or *Simkwee*, meaning *a saddle*. It refers to a saddle on a ridge north of the fort. The original Indian name for the place was *Mool-mool* meaning *bubbling springs*, and referred to gurgling, cold springs at a trail crossing here.

Fort Slaughter *(S.20;T.21N;R.5E)*

A vanished fort on Muckleshoot Prairie, directly east of Auburn, southeast of the intersection of Ray Road with old McClellan Military Road, southwest King County. In July 1856, it was built during the Indian wars, by regular army troops. It was named for Lieut. W.A. Slaughter, who was killed near this point by Indians on December 4, 1855.

Fort Spokane *(S.29;T.28N;R.32E)*

An abandoned U.S. Army post, 1/2 mile from Spokane River, 3/4 mile from the junction with Columbia River, Lincoln County. The 640-acre fort, elevation 400 ft., was founded by U.S. Army General Order No. 2, February 11, 1882. On April 17, 1898, troops were withdrawn from this post and the fort was abandoned on August 28, 1899, as it proved to be an inconvenient site with no practical purpose. The name is for that of a local Indian tribe. It should not be confused with Fort Spokane in Spokane County.

Fort Spokane *(S6;T.26N;R.42E)*

An historic fort site, 6 miles northwest of Spokane city limits, near the confluence of Spokane and Little Spokane rivers, northwest Spokane County. A combined trading post and fort was erected on this site in 1812 by John Clarke for John Jacob Astor's Pacific Fur Company. It was called *Fort Jacob*, for the company's owner. On October 6, 1813, the establishment was acquired by the Northwest Company and the name changed to *Spokane House*. In 1821, Hudson's Bay Company took over the place and operated here until 1826. Remains of the post, partially excavated, are reserved as an historic site by the state. The name stems from the Indian word *Spehkumne*. A name often used to distinguish it from a U.S. Army post in Lincoln County is *Old Fort Spokane*. The Indian name for the site of this old fort was *Lantou*.

Fort Steilacoom *S.33;T.20N;T.2E)*

An old fort on the site of Western Washington State Hospital, 1-1/2 miles east of Steilacoom, northwest Pierce County. It had 15 buildings, and was the first U.S. Army post of Puget Sound, having been established in 1849. The name is from Steilacoom.

Fort Stevens *(T.17N;R.2E)*

A vanished stockaded blockhouse on Yelm Prairie in east central Thurston County, directly northeast of Yelm. In spring, 1856, it was built by Washington Territorial Volunteers during the Indian scare and named for Gov. I. I. Stevens.

Fort Taylor *(S.36;T.22N;R.4E)*

A vanished fort on the south bank of Green River, 260 ft. east of the Auburn-Kent highway, on the Thomas donation claim near the community of Thomas, King County. It was built by regular army troops during the Indian wars of the 1850s and was 26 ft. square, built of logs and cedar shakes. It was named for John M. Thomas, on whose land it stood.

Fort Tilton *(T.30N;R.1W)*

An abandoned fort on Port Townsend Bay, 2-1/2 miles south of Port Townsend, northeast Jefferson County. Established on October 26, 1856, it was abandoned in 1893. Of its 615.1 acres, 421 acres are now in Old Fort Townsend State Park. It was named for Port Townsend, which had been named for the Marquis of Townshend.

Fort Vancouver *(T.2N;R.1E)*

A Hudson's Bay Company establishment on the north bank of Columbia River at the present site of Vancouver, southwest Clark County. On March 19, 1825, development was started when the company moved here from Fort George at Astoria. The name was given by Chief Factor John McLoughlin and was to honor Capt. George Vancouver who ex-

plored Columbia River in 1792. In 1849, following the settlement of the boundary dispute between Great Britain and the U.S., the site was used by American troops and was named *Columbia Barracks*. On July 31, 1853, the name reverted to the original designation.

Fort Walla Walla *(S.28;T.17N;R.31E)*

This combined fort and fur-trading post in Walla Walla County should not be confused with 3 military forts in the Walla Walla vicinity. The original establishment, in the southeast part of the county, 1/2 mile north of the mouth of Walla Walla River, fronting on Columbia River, was built by Northwest Company in 1818. It was purchased by Hudson's Bay Company in 1821, and continued in operation until 1857, although twice rebuilt. The original river town of Wallula was later built on the site. The fur traders first called the post *Fort Nez Perce*, through an error in tribal identification. The later name was for the river near which it was located, and which brought a great deal of trade to the post. It is often referred to as *Old Fort Walla Walla*, to distinguish it from later fort bearing the same name.

Fort Walla Walla *(S.18;T.7N;R.37E)*

This was the first of 3 forts built by U.S. regular troops in this vicinity during 1856 and 1857 on Mill Creek, directly west of Kibler and 5 miles northeast of Walla Walla, southeast Walla Walla County. Col. Edward J. Steptoe supervised the building, which consisted of a blockhouse and stockade. It was named for the Walla Walla Valley in which it was located.

Fort Walla Walla *(S.28;T.7N;R.36E)*

The second U.S. Army fort on north side of Mill Creek, 6 miles east of junction of Walla Walla River with Mill Creek, Walla Walla County. It was built in October and November, 1856, by U.S. regular army troops as protection against hostile Indians.

Fort Walla Walla *(S.28;T.7N;R.36E)*

This third of U.S. posts was built in 1857 on 13th Ave. and Rose St., adjoining the city of Walla Walla, Walla Walla County. It was more extensive than the first 2 forts, covering 613 acres. In 1889, it was deactivated and abandoned in 1911. Its name, like those of the other 2 forts nearby, was for the valley in which it was located.

Fort Ward *(T.24N;R.2E)*

A 375-acre abandoned military reservation on Beans Point at the south end of Bainbridge Island, on Rich Passage, east central Kitsap County. Its numerous buildings have been abandoned for protective and military purposes. It was one of 4 coastal defense forts in the Artillery District of Puget Sound and it was named for Col. George Hull Ward, 15th Massachusetts Volunteer Infantry, who died at Gettysburg on July 3, 1863.

Fort Waters *(S.32;T.7N;R.35E)*

A rather makeshift fort on the site of Whitman Mission, 4 miles west of Walla Walla, south central Walla Walla County. Built as protection against Indian aggression, it was put together in March 1848, by Oregon Riflemen under Col. Cornelius Gilliam. Materials used were from the ruins of the mission, which had been partially burned by Cayuse Indians in 1847. It was named for Col. Waters of the Oregon Riflemen.

Fortress Mountain
(S.25;T.31N;R.15E)

A 7,700-ft. peak at Cascade Mountain summit, between Helmet Butte and Chiwawa Mountain, facing Snohomish County to the west, northwest Chelan County. In 1908, it was named by U.S. Forest Supervisor A. H. Sylvester for its fancied resemblance to a fortress.

Fortson *(S.11;T.32N;R.3E)*

Town 21 miles east of Arlington, north central Snohomish County. Established in 1896, it was named for Capt. George H. Fortson 3 years later. On March 26, 1899, he was killed at Passig Bridge in the Philippines during the Philippine Insurrection.

Fortune Mountain
(Ss.30,31;T.28N;R.13E.uns)

A 5,905-ft. peak, 1-1/2 miles west of Wenatchee Pass at Cascade Mountain summit, extreme southeast Snohomish County. The original name was *5900 Mountain*, because of the elevation. In 1935, it was changed to the present name for nearby Fortune Pass. (*see* Fortune Pass)

Fortune Pass *(S.36;T.28N;R.12E)*

A west slope pass of Cascade Mountain summit, directly east of Fortune Mountain, southeast Snohomish County. It was named because the pass was a boon to travelers passing from Evergreen to Benchmark Mountain.

Fortune Ponds *(S.30;T.28N;R.13E)*

Two shallow, connected lakes, 1/2 mile west of Cascade Mountain summit on Snoqualmie National Forest, extreme southeast Snohomish County. No. 1, elevation 4,700 ft., covers 1 acre; No. 2 has an area of 8 acres, elevation 4,600 ft. The small lakes were named for nearby Fortune Pass. (*see* Fortune Pass)

Fosdick Point (Pierce County) *see* Point Fosdick

Fossil Bay *(T.38N;R.2W)*

The southernmost bay on Sucia Island, extreme north central San Juan County. This narrow bay, much used by owners of pleasure craft, was locally named because the rock structure surrounding it is very heavily fossilized, and has been eroded into fanciful shapes.

Foster *(S.15;T.23N;R.4E)*

Small settlement on Duwamish River, 3 miles west of Renton, west central King County. It was named for Joseph Foster, who came here from Wisconsin in 1852 as the first settler. He served in the Territorial Legislature for 22 years.

Foster Creek Dam (Okanogan County/Douglas County) *see* Chief Joseph Dam

Foster Island *(Ss.21,22;T.25N;R.4E)*

A small island in Seattle, on Union Bay of Lake Washington, on the west shore of the lake adjoining the University of Washington, King County. Used by local Indians for tree burials before white settlers took over the land, it was named for an early settler whose claim included the island.

Foster Point *(T.36N;R.2W)*

An extreme south point of the middle peninsula of Orcas Island, on the north side of Harney Channel, central San Juan County. In 1859, this name was first charted by Capt. Henry Richards, British admiralty surveyor. Evidently he named it for a Hudson's Bay Company official who served at Victoria in early days.

Foulweather Bluff *(T.28N;R.1E)*

An extreme north end bluff at the east side of Hood Canal entrance, Kitsap County. In May 1792, the name was charted by the Vancouver expedition for violent weather changes which they encountered here. In 1841, the Wilkes

party applied the name *Suquamish Head*, which failed to endure. The original Indian name was *Pitch-pol.*

Found Lake (Skagit County) *see* Found Lakes

Found Lakes *(S.16;T.34N;R.12E)*

Four lakes at the head of Found Creek, 11 miles southeast of Marblemount, east central Skagit County. They are connected in a chain by Found Creek, which covers 70.9 acres and is 75 ft. deep; Neori Lake has a surface area of 13 acres and a depth of 40 ft.; Skaro Lake is 75 ft. deep and covers 12 acres. Snowking Lake, fed by glacial water, has an area of 36.3 acres and is 75 ft. deep. The group is named for Found Creek which drains the lakes.

Fountain Lake *(S.4;T.39N;R.3E)*

A 140-acre lake, 3 miles southeast of Lynden in lower Nooksack River drainage, northwest Whatcom County. The lake was named for Reuben Fountain, a pioneer of the 1870s, who owned several nearby tracts of land. An earlier name was *Trede Lake.*

Four Lakes *(S.23;T.24N;R.41E)*

Village 4 miles north of Cheney, north central Spokane County. In 1879, the town was founded by Col. G. H. Morgan, who started a store. On September 1, 1858, it was the site of an important battle with Indians when Col. George Wright's troops defeated an allied Indian force in the Battle of Four Lakes. It was named by W. F. Bassett, a pioneer of 1871, for the group of 4 lakes here -- Meadow, Granite, Willow, and Silver.

Four-Mile Ridge *(T.28N;R.19E)*

This spur of Chelan Ridge extends 4 miles northwest from Angle Peak in Chelan Mountains, central Chelan County; it forms the watershed between Lake Creek and several small creeks to the south. This descriptive name was applied by U.S. Forest Supervisor A. H. Sylvester.

Four-Mile Rock *(S.22;T.25N;R.3E)*

A very large boulder in tidal water (now marked with a beacon), near the north shore of Elliott Bay in Seattle harbor, 1-1/2 miles southeast of West Point, King County. The name was given by mariners because it is 4 miles from the central waterfront of Seattle at Colman Dock. On maps published in 1894, it appears as *Five-Mile Rock*. Evidently

the city has crept up on the rock during the past 60 years. The Indian name was *Le-ple-pl.*

Four Mound Prarie *(Ts.26,27N;R.41E)*

A farming district on a prairie about 4-1/2 to 5 miles long, northwest to southeast, 6-1/2 to 11 miles northwest of Spokane and parallel to Spokane River, 3 miles to the north, northwest Spokane County. It was named for a series of rather large, low mounds, evidently of glacial origin.

Four Stream *(T.32N;R.5W)*

The almost 5-1/2-mile-long watercourse heads 1-1/2 miles north of Mt. Tebo on Olympic National Forest, northwest Mason County; flows northeast into Olympic National Park to North Fork, Skokomish River. This is the fourth of 9 streams that enter the river from south and west, and are numerically designated from Lake Cushman toward the river's source. It should not be confused with Five Stream or Elk Creek, as found on certain county maps. (USBGN)

Fourche de Glace (Asotin County) *see* Grand Ronde River

Fourth Plain (Clark County) *see* Orchards

Fowler's Lake (Cowlitz County) *see* Lake Sacajawea

Fox Creek *(T.28N;R.19E)*

The stream of the creek rises on Four-Mile Ridge, Wenatchee National Forest, central Chelan County; flows 3 miles southwest to Entiat River. The name was applied by Forest Ranger James McKenzie for foxes he sighted in this area.

Fox Island *(Ts.20,21N;Rs.1,)*

An island between Carr Inlet and Hales Passage, 2 miles northeast of McNeil Island, northwest Pierce County. In 1841, Cmdr. Charles Wilkes named it for Dr. J. L. Fox, assistant surgeon of the Wilkes Expedition.

Foy *(S.20;T.26N;R.4E)*

Station on the interurban electric railway between Seattle and Everett, 1 mile north of Haller Lake, near the north city limits of Seattle, northwest King County. It was named for David and Henrietta Foy, who settled here in 1904.

Fragaria *(S.22;T.23N;R.2E)*

Village on the west shore of West

(Colvos) Passage, 4 miles south of Harper, southeast Kitsap County. On February 15, 1912, it was named by Ferdinand Schmitz of Seattle for the excellent early strawberries that grew there, using the generic name of strawberries.

Frailey Mountain (*T.33N;R.6E*)

A 5-mile-long chain of peaks, up to 2,795 ft. elevation, south of Lake Cavanaugh and parallel to the lake, on the south central boundary of Skagit County; also extending over the county boundary into Snohomish County. It was locally named for Henry Frailey, who claimed land southeast of the mountain in early days.

Frailey Mountain Ponds (Skagit County) *see* Frailey Ponds

Frailey Ponds (*S.29;T.33N;R.6E*)

A very small, 1-acre lake at the north end of Frailey Mountain, 1-1/2 miles west of Cavanaugh Lake. It was named for Frailey Mountain. An alternate name is *Frailey Mountain Ponds*.

Frances (*S.2;T.12N;R.7W*)

Once a sawmill center, now a scattered settlement, in Willapa River valley, 14 miles southeast of Raymond, east central Pacific County. E. H. McHenry, a prominent logger, used his wife's middle name when he named the town.

Francis (Benton County) *see* Longview

Frankfort (*S.11;T.9N;R.9W*)

Small settlement on the west side of Grays Bay on Columbia River, 5 miles east of Knappton, southwest Pacific County. In 1890, it was founded by Frank Bourn and Frank Scott. The 2 promoters perpetuated their first names in naming the place.

Franklin (Pierce County) *see* Puyallup

Franklin (*S.18;T.21N;R.7E*)

Formerly a coal mining town, on Green River, 2 miles east of Black Diamond, south central King County. It has the deepest coal mine in the state and the second largest production. In 1902, it was named by Pacific Coast company for Benjamin Franklin, American patriot and statesman.

Franklin County

In southeast Washington, encircled except on the north by Palouse, Snake, and Columbia rivers; bounded on north by Adams County; on east by Whitman County; on south by Benton and Walla Walla counties; on west by Grant, Yakima and Benton counties. Wheat, livestock, and wool are the leading products of Franklin County's 1,262 sq. miles. On November 28, 1883, the county was established by the Territorial Legislature and was named for the revered statesman Benjamin Franklin. The name was proposed by Samuel A. Wells.

Franklin D. Roosevelt Lake

A 151-mile-long artificial lake, formed in Columbia River by the backwaters of Grand Coulee Dam; it extends from that dam east and north, between Okanogan, Lincoln, Ferry, and Stevens counties to the boundary of British Columbia, and for varying distances up each of the tributary streams. It is normally 1,290 ft. elevation and acts as a storage basin for hydroelectric power and for irrigation of lands in the Inland Empire. The planning for this lake by the U.S. Bureau of Reclamation started in 1936. Most of the water had been impounded by 1940. All of the timber and man made structures below an elevation of 1,310 ft. were removed, including the towns of Keller, Peach, Lincoln, Gerome, Inchelium, Gifford, Daisy, Hunters, Kettle Falls, Boyds, and Marcus. Some of these towns were moved to higher elevations retaining their identities, or some citizens moved to other towns. On April 17, 1945, the lake was named by Harold Ickes, Secretary of the Interior, for Franklin Delano Roosevelt, 32nd president of the U.S. (1933-1945). Other names suggested were *Lake Columbia, Columbia River Reservoir, Empire Lake, Lake O'Sullivan, Lake Spokane* and *Swa-Nekt-ohu.* (approved USBGN, 1945)

Fraser Creek (*Clallam County*) *see* Tumwater Creek

Fravel (*Skagit County*) *see* Blanchard

Freeland (*S.10;T.29N;R.2E*)

Town on the south shore of Holmes Harbor, Whidbey Island, south Island County. The name is for the Free Land Association, a cooperative and somewhat socialistic organization which founded the town in 1900. The site had been platted previously by real estate promoters as *St. Louis*, but no town resulted. At one brief period the place was called *Newell*, which was a post office name only.

Freeman (*S.2;T.23N;R.44E*)

10 miles southeast of Spokane, east central Spokane County. The place was named by railroad officials for Truman W. Freeman, telegraph operator, when the C.M.&ST.P. established a station.

Freeman Island (*S.16;T.37N; R.2W*)

A small island at the northeast end of Orcas Island, 1-1/2 miles south of Point Doughty, north central San Juan County. In 1841, Cmdr. Charles Wilkes charted it as *Freeman's Island* for J. D. Freeman, sailmaker on the expedition's ship *Peacock*. The possessive form was dropped on later charts, as in the case of many other features.

Freeport (*T.8N;R.2W*)

An old town (which now is included in Longview), southwest Cowlitz County. It later was called *Catlin*. The name was established by Nathaniel Stone who owned a Donation Land Claim on this site, and was in honor of Freeport, Indiana, his former home.

Freeport (*S.2;T.24N;R.3E*)

Small settlement in west Seattle, on Duwamish Head at the south shore of Elliott Bay, King County. In 1865, it was founded and was named by Capt. John R. Williamson when he came here from Seabeck. The name was changed to *Milltown* when a sawmill was built here a year later, but local use altered that name to *Milton*. A substantial shipyard operated here until 1872.

Fremont (*S.18;T.25N;R.4E*)

Once a town (now part of Seattle) in the central area of the city, northwest end of Lake Union, where the lake meets the ship canal, King County. After the area was logged by oxen in the early 1880s, it was platted as a town by David Denny and Judge John P. Hoyt. In 1892, the name was applied by L. H. Griffith when he laid out a subdivision here. It was for his original home in Fremont, Nebraska.

French Creek (*T.25N;R.15E*)

The stream of the creek heads at Sprite Lake in Wenatchee Mountains, southwest Chelan County; joins Icicle Creek. It is also known as the South Fork of Icicle Creek. Presumably it was named by local usage, for a prospector who worked here for several years in early days.

French Creek (*T.32N;R.8E*)

The stream of the creek rises 2 miles east of Hazel, north central Snohomish

County; it joins North Fork, Stilleguamish River, Mt. Baker National Forest. It was named because the first 3 settlers were of French origin — Peter Voisard, Peter Ladebush, and John Richards. An alternate name is *French Slough*.

French Creek Pond
(S.17;T.32N;R.8E)

A 6-acre lake in French Creek, 1-1/2 miles south of Hazel, northwest Snohomish County. It was named for French Creek. *(see French Creek)*

French Lake *(King County) see* Mirror Lake

Frenchtown *(Walla Walla County) see* Whitman

Frenzelspitz *(S.7;T.38N;R.12E)*

A Mt. Baker National Forest peak in the southern Picket Range, at the head of Crescent Creek, east central Whatcom County. This sharp, snow-covered pinnacle is known as one of the Crescent Creek Spires. *(see Ottohorn)*

Freshwater Bay *(T.31N;Rs.7,8W)*

A Strait of Juan de Fuca bay between Angeles Point and Observatory Point, 3 miles west of Port Angeles, north central Clallam County. In 1790, Lopez de Haro named this bay *Ensenada de Davila* for Capt. Juan Herrera Davila of the Spanish navy. In the same year, Manuel Quimper, in *Princessa Real*, secured a supply of fresh water in this bay. However, the present name first appeared in 1847, on British admiralty charts prepared by Capt. Henry Kellett.

Freshwater Lake *(S.22;T.11N;R.11W)*

A 5-acre lake on North Beach Peninsula, 5 miles north of Long Beach, southwest Pacific County. The name is descriptive, as some of the lakes on the peninsula tend to be brackish, due to underground infiltration of ocean water.

Friday Harbor *(T.35N; R.3W)*

An east side by of San Juan Island, on San Juan Channel, southwest San Juan County. It is an excellent harbor, protected at its entrance by Brown Island, which has good docks and several industries. At the north entrance, on Dash Point, is the 484-acre institution operated by the University of Washington as Friday Harbor Laboratories for the study of marine life and oceanography. The Lummi Indian name for the bay was *Sta-l-quith*, meaning *Where the first-run sockeye salmon come*.

Friday Harbor *(S.14;T.35N;R.3W)*

Town on Friday Harbor bay, east central San Juan Island, southwest San Juan County. It is the commercial center of the San Juan Archipelago, originally established as a farming center by Hudson's Bay Company. The original name, when established, was *Bellvue* or *Bellvue Farm*. An alternate name in early days was *Friday's Place*, or *Kanaka's Place*, for an Hawaiian islander who herded sheep here for Hudson's Bay Company, and whose name was John Friday. In 1858, it was charted under the present name by Capt. Henry Richards, RN. A typical pioneer legend ascribes the name to an incident in which a small trading ship entered the harbor and hailed a sheepherder ashore, asking *What bay is this?* The sheepherder thought what they wanted to know was the day of the week, and he replied, *Friday*. So the traders inscribed *Friday Harbor* on their chart. Other legends regarding the name are also interesting and fantastic.

Friendly Reach *(T.2N;Rs.1W&1E)*

An 8-mile stretch of Columbia River extending upstream from the mouth of Willamette River in Oregon, Clark County. In December 1792, William Broughton of Capt. Vancouver's expedition chose the name because of the friendly attitude of the local Indians, and the favors extended to him by their chief. For many years the name was dropped, but was approved by USBGN in 1927 at the request of Oregon Camp Fire Girls. However, it does not show on current maps.

Fritz Point *(S.12;T.36N;R.3W)*

A southwest point of Orcas Island, 1-1/2 miles northeast of Jones Island, central San Juan County. It is not shown on recent maps, but was charted under the present name by Cmdr. Charles Wilkes.

Frog Heaven *(Mt. Rainier National Park)*

A marshy flat 1-1/2 miles northeast of the junction of Paradise and Nisqually rivers, 1 mile below Narada Falls in Paradise River drainage, southwest sector of the park. The name was selected because the marsh houses a multitude of frogs. (USBGN)

Frolic Straits *(San Juan County) see* Upright Channel

Frontier *(S.3;T.40N;R.39E)*

Settlement on Sheep Creek, 1 mile south of the Canadian boundary, northwest Stevens County. In 1902, both settlement and post office came into existence when the Spokane Falls & Northern Railway branch line was built through here from Northport. This short line was originally called the Columbia & Red Mountain Railroad. The rail facilities here were called *Velvet Station* by the railroad since this was the shipping point for the Velvet Mine. The name is not carried on recent maps, though *Velvet* is still used by local people. Original settlers chose this name for the post office because of its location on the north border of the U.S.

Frost Island *(T.35N;R.1W)*

A Lopez Sound island off the northeast end of Lopez Island, 1-1/2 miles east of Port Stanley, east central San Juan County. In 1841, the present name was charted by Cmdr. Charles Wilkes for John Frost, boatswain of the expedition's ship *Porpoise*. It was listed at one time, in error, as *Foost Island*.

Frosty Creek *(T.25N;R.15E)*

The stream of the creek rises on Wenatchee National Forest, runs through a canyon with 2 small lakes at the head, west Chelan County; flows from Lake Mary through Lake Margaret, then 2 miles southwest to Icicle Creek. On September 23, 1910, it was named by Forest Supervisor A. H. Sylvester when his camp on this creek turned frosty overnight.

Frosty Creek *(Ts.35,36N;4.31E)*

The stream of the creek heads on Fir Mountain, east central Okanogan County; flows 7 miles south to the West Fork of San Poil River, 1-1/2 miles west of Aeneas. The name is descriptive, as the creek flows through a mountainous area with elevations from 4,000 to 4,800 ft., which is said to be frost-free only in summer months.

Frozen Lake *(S.23;T.23N;R.10E)*

A 1.5-acre lake on Snoqualmie National Forest, 4 miles northwest of Snoqualmie Pass, east central King County. It is within 300 ft. of Ice Lake and both are in a glacial area. The name is descriptive, as the lake is frozen most of the year.

Frozen Lake *(Mt. Rainier National Park)*

A small 2-1/2-acre lake, elevation 6,700 ft., 1-1/2 miles north of the lower end of Emmons Glacier. The lake lies 1.3 miles west of Sunset Park at the southwest foot of Sourdough Mountains. Its banks are covered with perpetual snow and it furnishes the water supply for Sunset Park (Yakima Park). (USBGN)

Fruitland (*S.30;T.30N;R.37E*)

Small settlement, 1-1/2 miles east of Franklin D. Roosevelt Lake, 39 miles north of Davenport, on Alder Creek. The first occupancy by white settlers was in 1880, when A. N. Washburn and a Mr. Price took pre-emption claims, followed by J. N. Allison. They planted orchards, which produced excellent fruit. In 1886, Moses Peltier, who peddled supplies in this area with a covered wagon, established a trade shop in a tent, and later built a store and blacksmith shop. In 1887, when a post office was set up with Peltier as postmaster, 3 names were submitted. Fruitland was chosen by the postal authorities. Previous names for the place had been *Spring Valley* and *Robbers Roost*. The latter name was used during a period when the Old Queen Mine was active, and

this was a rather tough town.

Fryingpan Creek (*Mt. Rainier National Park*)

The stream of the creek heads at the lower east lobe of Fryingpan Glacier, east central area of the park; flows northeast to White River, at the northern base of Tamanos Mountain. In 1894, the stream was named by Arthur French, Guy F. Evans, and W. M. Bosworth. When they threw their packs across this creek, a frying pan fell from Bosworth's pack and was carried away. An alternate name source, which seems less credible, is that the name was borrowed from Fryingpan Glacier, which had been named by Prof. I. C. Russell for a fancied resemblance to a frying pan. If this is factual, it seems that the professor had a powerful imagination. (USBGN)

Fryingpan Glacier *Mr. Rainier National Park*)

This ice mass is on the east slope of Mt. Rainier, in the central zone of the park. It heads in a triangular rock wedge, and extends over 3 miles eastward, faning broadly to the northeast where it joins the lower part of Emmons Glacier. Its head at Little Tahoma Peak has an elevation of 10,700 ft. (*see* Fryingpan Creek) (USBGN)

Fuca Pillar (*S.2;T.33N; R. 16W*)

A conspicuous, rocky crag near the beach, south of Flattery Creek's mouth, on Makah Indian Reservation, extreme northwest corner of Clallam County. In 1788, it was named for Juan de Fuca by John Meares as *Fuca's Pillar*. Later fur traders called it *Pinnacle Rock* and *Pinnacle Island*. The Makah Indian name was *Tsar-tsar-dark*, meaning *Tall, tall, leaning rock*.

Fulton (*Lewis County*) *see* Kosmos

G

Gale Creek (*T.19N;R.6E*)

The stream of the creek rises west of Wilkeson, north central Pierce County; flows into South Prairie Creek at South Prairie. The name was applied locally for a miner who prospected for coal along the creek in 1874. An earlier name was *Flett Creek* for 2 part-Indian brothers who assisted Gale.

Galena (*S.19;T.28N;R.11E*)

Town on North Fork, Skykomish River, 8 miles northeast of Index, Snoqualmie National Forest, southeast Snohomish County. It was a "boom town" during the Monte Cristo gold rush. The name was given by miners because there was evidence of valuable lead ore.

Galena (*S.29;T.25N;R.41E*)

Railroad station on the west boundary of Fairchild Air Force Base, west central Spokane County. The name was evidently chosen at random by railroad officials. The post office, formerly called *Bong*, is now called Fairchild Air Force Base.

Galena Chain Lakes
(*S.24;T.39N;R.8E.uns*)

Four small, mountain lakes which

drain into North Fork, Nooksack River, on Mt. Baker's northeast slope, 2-1/2 miles southwest of Mt. Baker Lodge, north central Whatcom County. In early mining days, they were called *Galena Lakes* by prospectors. In 1906, The Mazamas named them *Chain Lakes*. The present name is a compromise by USBGN. Individual lake names are Iceberg, Mazama, Hayes and Arbuthnot.

Galena Lakes (*Whatcom County*) *see* Galena Chain Lakes

Galer Hill (*King County*) *see* Queen Anne Hill

Gallopp Creek (*T.39N;R.7E*)

The stream of this short creek rises 2-1/2 miles south of Glacier, north central Whatcom County; flows north to North Fork, Nooksack River, at Glacier. It was named for a very early settler, George B. *Gallup*.

Galvin (*S.35;T.15N;R.3W*)

Town 4 miles northwest of Centralia, near Lincoln Creek, northwest Lewis County. On June 3, 1910, it was platted by Galvin, Teal Company. In 1911, it was named for John Galvin, the

town's founder. Before platting, it had been called *Lincoln*.

Gamblers Creek, Gamblers River (*Walla Walla County*) *see* Coppei Creek

Garda Falls (*Mt. Rainier National Park*)

Falls in Granite Creek, at foot of Winthrop Glacier, north slope of Mt. Rainier, north central zone of the park. The name was chosen by C. A. Barnes of Tacoma, a photographer who specialized in park subjects for many years; his selection honors Miss Garda Fogg of Tacoma. (USBGN)

Garden Island (*S.15;T.30N;R.15W*)

Very small, timbered island near the northeast end of Lake Ozette, west central Clallam County. The name is ascribed to Judge James G. Swan, who explored here in 1887. The nomenclature hardly seems appropriate for an island which was covered with timber.

Garden Point (*Kitsap County*) *see* Restoration Point

Garden (Garde) Station (*King County*) *see* Tukwila

Gardena (*S.10;T.6N;R.33E*)

Farming community 1-1/2 miles south

of Touchet, south central Walla Walla County. The name was chosen to offer promise of irrigated garden crops when a plat of the area was filed by Walla Walla Irrigation Company.

Gardiner *(S.34;T.30N;R.2W)*

Community on Port Discovery Bay west shore, 3 miles south of the entrance, northeast Jefferson County. In 1792, it was the landing site of Capt. Vancouver's *Discovery*. The name is for Herbert B. *Gardner*, who founded the community in 1911, and who logged about 4,000 acres of timber on the Olympic Peninsula. When a post office was established in 1916, Mrs. Gardner had the ''i'' inserted in the name, as the family name had originally been Gardiner.

Gardiner Cave *(S.4;T.40N;R.43E)*

A rather isolated, 850-ft.-long cave 1 mile west of Pend Oreille River and 1/2 mile south of the Canadian boundary, extreme north central Pend Oreille County. The site, now a state park, contains a rare display of stalactites and stalagmites, and is rated the largest limestone cavern in the state. It was named for Ed Gardiner, a nearby homesteader who discovered the cave in 1900.

Gardner *(S.27;T.10N;R.2W)*

An old settlement on the north bank of Toutle River at its junction with Cowlitz River, 2-1/2 miles north of Castle Rock, northwest Cowlitz County. In 1857, it was carried on maps of the surveyor general of Washington Territory, but does not appear on recent maps. The name is for a settler who took a land claim here in the 1850s.

Garfield *(S.38;T.18N;R.45E)*

Town 18 miles northeast of Colfax, east central Whitman County. Samuel J. Tant, who owned the plat on which the town is located, had a townsite surveyed by C. A. Grimes in 1881, although the plat was not filed until May 27, 1887. Tant named the town for James A. Garfield, twentieth President of the United States.

Garfield County

This county in extreme southeast Washington is bounded on the north by Whitman County; on the east by Whitman and Asotin counties; on the south by Asotin and Columbia counties, and Oregon; and on the west by Columbia County. The southern portion of the

county's 714 sq. miles is in Blue Mountains, and mostly within Umatilla National Forest. Much of the northern sector is devoted to livestock raising, and to wheat and fruit culture. On November 29, 1881, it was created by legislative action from Columbia County. It was named for James A. Garfield, twentieth President of the United States.

Garfield Mountain Lakes
(S.24;T.24N;R.10E)

Two lakes, 1,300 ft. apart and connected by a stream, 15 miles east of North Bend, Snoqualmie National Forest, east central King County. The lower lake covers 8 acres; the upper about 7 acres. They were named for nearby Garfield Mountain.

Garland Creek *(T.29N;R.17E.uns)*

The stream of this short creek rises on Wenatchee National Forest, north central Chelan County; flows from the east side of Garland Peak into Entiat River. It was named by U.S. Forest Supervisor A. H. Sylvester for a man who grazed sheep on Garland Peak in early days.

Garland Mineral Springs
(S.25;T.28N;R.11E)

Springs 12 miles northeast of Index, Snoqualmie National Forest, southeast Snohomish County. They were named for A. H. ''Bert'' Garland of Wenatchee, who prospected here in 1894, and who purchased property from Mr. and Mrs. J. N. Starr. Previous names were *Soda Springs* and *Starr Hot Springs*.

Garland Peak *(S.15;T.29N;R.17E.uns)*

A Wenatchee National Forest peak, elevation 7,545 ft., 1 mile southeast of Entiat Mountains, north central Chelan County. It is also known as *Garland Mountain*. The name was applied before 1908, by U.S. Forest Supervisor A. H. Sylvester. (*see* Garland Creek)

Garner (Clark County) *see* Yacolt

Garrard Creek *(T.15N;Rs.4,5W)*

The stream of the creek rises in extreme southeast Grays Harbor County; flows 8-1/2 miles east to Chehalis River near Balch. It was first called *Barber Creek* for Henry Barber, who settled near the stream's mouth in 1870. The present name is for James Garrard, who took a land claim on the creek in 1872. Some maps carry it, in error, as *Garrod* or *Garrad*.

Garrison Bay *(S.26;T.36N;R.4W)*

Small bay almost entirely land-locked, 2 miles south of Roche Harbor, northwest end of San Juan Island, west central San Juan County. The name derives from a garrison of British troops, mostly marines, which was retained here in the English Camp from 1860 until 1872, during the boundary dispute between the United States and Great Britain.

Garrod (Garrad) Creek (Grays Harbor County) *see* Garrard Creek

Gaston Bay (Whatcom County) *see* Bellingham Bay

Gate City n.(S.25;T.16N;R.4W)

Small settlement on Black River, 22 miles south of Olympia, southwest Thurston County. In 1890, it was boomed as a railroad center. The settlement was so named because it was expected to be the gateway between Puget Sound and the Grays Harbor area. Also, the town expected to have the railroad shops, which were built in South Tacoma instead. The original name applied by Northern Pacific Railway officials was *Harlowe Junction*.

Gate Creek *(T.28N;R.17E)*

The stream of this very short creek rises on the west slope of Entiat Mountains, Wenatchee National Forest, northwest Chelan County; flows 1-1/2 miles to Chiwawa River. Early residents built a gate at a bridge over the creek on Chiwawa Road, and marked it with a sign, ''Gate Creek.''

Gatton Creek *(T.23N;R.9W)*

The stream of the creek rises 3 miles southeast of Lake Quinault, north central Grays Harbor County; flows northwest into the lake, 1-1/2 miles southwest of Quinault. It was named for an original homesteader through whose land the creek ran.

Gaynor *(S.2;T.26N;R.15E)*

Railroad station on Nason Creek, 8 miles east by north of Stevens Pass, west Chelan County. It was named by Great Northern Railway officials for a company employee.

Gedney Island *(T.29N;R.4E)*

A 1-1/2-mile-long island, 3/4 mile wide, at Port Gardner Bay west entrance, Possession Sound, extreme west central Snohomish County. The original Indian name was *Chuh-chuh-sul-lay*, and an early alternate name was *Hat Island.* In 1841, the recognized name was given by Cmdr. Charles Wilkes, for Jonathan H. Gedney, a New York inventor and friend of Wilkes.

Gee Creek *(T.4N;Rs.1E&1W)*

The stream of the creek rises south of Pioneer, northwest Clark County; flows northwest 9 miles to Columbia River, directly south of Lewis River mouth. It was named for a settler who took a Donation Land Claim here in the 1850s. It should not be confused with Gee Creek, Skagit County.

Gee Creek *(T.34N;R.8E)*

The stream of the creek rises at Gee Point, 7-1/2 miles southwest of Concrete, Mt. Baker National Forest, central Skagit County; flows 4 miles east to Finney Creek. It was locally named for William Gee, who filed timber claims along the creek in 1904. It should not be confused with Gee Creek, Clark County.

Gee Point Lake *(S.19;T.34N;R.8E)*

A 4-acre lake, elevation 4,100 ft., on the southeast side of Gee Point, at the headwaters of Gee Creek, 8-1/2 miles south of Concrete, Skagit County. (*see* Gee Creek, Skagit County)

Geese Islets *(T.34N;R.2W)*

Group of 11 small- to medium-sized islands and rocks directly southwest of Davis Bay, south Lopez Island, in Middle Channel, southeast San Juan County. They include Buck, Long, Charles, Goose, Iceberg and Deadman islands; Secar Rock; Richardson Rock; Whale Rocks; Mummy Rocks; and Hall Islands. In 1841, the group was named and charted by Cmdr. Charles Wilkes; his group name has not persisted on maps and charts.

Geiger Field
(Ss.28,29,31-33;T.25N;R.42E)

Municipal airport 2 miles west of Spokane city limits, central Spokane County. It was originally an Army air base. In 1941, it was named by Secretary of War Stimson for Maj. Harold Geiger, a veteran of World War I, who was killed in an air crash in 1927.

Geiger Municipal Airport (Spokane County) *see* Geiger Field

Gem Lake *(S.13;T.23N;R.10E)*

A 14.9-acre lake 5 miles northwest of Snoqualmie Pass and 1/2 mile north of Snow Lake, east central King County. The small lake was given an ornamental name by the Mountaineers on one of their early expeditions.

Geneva *(Ss.27,34;T.38N;R.3E)*

Town on the west shore of Lake Whatcom, adjoining Bellingham, southwest Whatcom County. When platted in 1887, it was named by David C. Jenkins, one of the platters, for a fancied resemblance of Lake Whatcom to Lake Geneva in Switzerland.

George *(Ss.5,6;T.18N;R.24E)*

Town 32 miles west of Moses Lake, extreme west central Grant County. In February 1961, it was founded when Charles Brown requested incorporation as a fourth-class town. The name was chosen so that the address would be ''George, Washington.''

George Creek *(Ts.8,9N;Rs.44,45E)*

The stream of the creek rises at Arnold Spring, southwest Asotin County; flows 16 miles northeast to Asotin Creek, 2-1/2 miles west of Asotin. Records carry 2 accounts of the name origin. One states that the creek bears the name of an early tribesman, ''Indian George,'' who trapped and fished here in early days. The other indicates that it carries the first name of George Penny, the first settler on the stream. If Penny was nicknamed ''Indian George,'' both stories may be correct.

Georgetown *(T.23N;R.4E)*

Industrial area in southern part of Seattle, north of Boeing Air Field, King County. It was formerly a separate town with streetcar service to Seattle's business district. In 1890, the town was platted and named by Julius Horton for his son, George M. Horton. The senior Horton took a Donation Land Claim of 160 acres here, and raised hops on a large scale. His son later became a popular Seattle surgeon. The original name of the place was *Duwamish.*

Georgia Strait

Broad strait bordering Whatcom County on the east, San Juan County on the west, and continuing north between Vancouver Island and British Columbia mainland. It is an essential element of the inside channel of northwest Washington and southwest British Columbia. In 1791, it was named *Gran Canal de Nuestra Senora del Rosario la Marinera* by Juan Francisco de Eliza. In 1792, it

acquired the name *Gulf of Georgia* from Capt. George Vancouver, who honored King George III of England; in 1841, Cmdr. Charles Wilkes confirmed that name. The present variation has been approved by USBGN.

German Lake (Snohomish County) *see* Lake Riley

Germania (Stevens County) *see* Wellpinit

Gertrude *(S.15;T.20N;R.1E)*

Settlement on Still Harbor, northeast shore of McNeil Island, northwest Pierce County. When established in 1882, it was named *Sunne* by Charles Julin from Sweden, who was the first postmaster. Later, it was changed by local choice to the present name, which is for Gertrude Island.

Gertrude Island *(S.15;T.20N;R.1E)*

Island in Still Harbor, northeast end of McNeil Island, northwest Pierce County. In 1846, the name *Gertrudis* was charted by Capt. R. N. Inskip. In 1911, that name also appeared on U.S. Coast & Geodetic Survey charts. Since then, cartographers have evidently distorted the name, without official authority.

Gertrudis Island (Pierce County) *see* Gertrude Island

Getchell *(S.24;T.30N;R.5E)*

Small community 12 miles north of Snohomish, west central Snohomish County. Its importance decreased when the Everett & Monte Cristo Railroad ceased operating. In 1894, the original name *Springfield* was changed to the present name because there was another post office town in the state by that name. The name is for M. L. *Getschell,* who purchased the townsite in expectation that it would become valuable with the traffic created by the railroad. Postal officials evidently missed the ''s'' in the name.

Gettysburg *(S.22;T.31N;R.9W)*

A logging center in the 1890s near Strait of Juan de Fuca at Low Point, 4-1/2 miles west of Crescent Bay, north central Clallam County. In 1897, the place was named for Bob Getty, a local logger. It does not appear on recent maps.

Geyser Basin (Clallam County) *see* Geyser Valley

Geyser Valley *(T.28N;R.7W.uns)*

Valley along Elwha River basin, slightly over 2 miles long, 3 miles south of Elwha Reservoir, Olympic National Park, central Clallam County. On March 29, 1890, the name was applied by members of Seattle Press Expedition, who thought they heard a geyser, but could not locate it. The sound was probably the drumming of one or more ruffed grouse. A previous, unofficial name was *Geyser Basin.* (USBGN)

Ghost Lake *(Mt. Rainier National Park)*

A 2-acre lake, elevation 4,400 ft., at the head of Klickitat Creek, between Governors' Ridge and Chinook Pass, near the east central boundary of the park. Evidently, the name was chosen by early park personnel for the lake's ghostly appearance under certain atmospheric conditions. (USBGN)

Gib Creek *(Ts.29,30N;Rs.16,17E.uns)*

The stream of the creek rises on the east slope of Old Gib Mountain, Wenatchee National Forest, northwest Chelan County; flows 3-1/2 miles to Rock Creek. It was named by U.S. Forest Supervisor A. H. Sylvester for Old Gib Mountain.

Gibb Point (Jefferson County) *see* Kalset Point

Gibbon *(S.26;T.9N;R.25E)*

Railroad station 7 miles northeast of Prosser, directly north of Horse Heaven Hills, west central Benton County. In 1885, the station was named *Bender* by Northern Pacific Railway Company. In 1896, it was changed to the present name, honoring Gen. John Gibbon, U.S.A.

Gibbon Range *(Ts.25-27N;Rs.4-8W)*

Group of Olympic National Park mountains, central Jefferson County. Although designated a ''range,'' they have not been recognized as such. Establishment of these mountains as a group was the idea of Lieut. Joseph P. O'Neil, U.S.A., who headed exploration and mapping groups here in 1885 and 1890. The name he proposed was that of his commanding general. The mountains include Anderson, McMillan, Olympus, Lee and The Brothers.

Gibraltar *(Mt.Rainier National Park)*

Massive, square rock cliff, elevation 12,679 ft., directly southeast of Mt. Rainier's summit, in a saddle at the head of Ingraham Glacier. In 1888, it was named by Maj. E. S. Ingraham and members of his exploring party, for its resemblance to Gibraltar at the west entrance to Mediterranean Sea. (USBGN)

Gibraltar (Skagit County) *see* Dewey

Gibraltar Rock (Mt. Rainier National Park) *see* Gibraltar

Gibson Point *(S.18;T.20N;R.2E)*

A south end point of Fox Island, 3 miles north of Steilacoom, northwest Pierce County. In 1841, it was named *Point Gibson* by Cmdr. Charles Wilkes, for James H. Gibson, coxswain in one of the expedition's ships. In 1846, it was charted as *Patterson Point* by Capt. R. N. Inskip, R.N., for Lieut. George Y. Patterson of *HMS Fisgard.* Inskip's name on British Admiralty charts did not displace the name given by Wilkes.

Giesy *(T.14N;R.8W)*

Settlement on Willapa River, adjoining the town of Willapa, northwest Pacific County. In 1853, it was established by a Christian Socialist colony from Missouri. It was named for the settlement founders, Sebastian and Christian Giesy, who were the colony's leaders until the group moved to Oregon in 1856.

Gifford *(S.3;T.32N;R.37E)*

Once a small town 57 miles north of Davenport, on the east bank of Columbia River across from Inchelium, southwest Stevens County. The place was named for James O. Gifford, who founded the settlement in 1890. It had an active ferry, operated by cable, as well as a post office and other town facilities. With the creation of a lake behind Grand Coulee Dam, the site was covered by almost 90 ft. of water.

Gifford Pinchot National Forest

A 1,421,080-acre forest in the south Cascade Mountain area, west of Cascade Mountain summit; Skamania, Lewis, Klickitat and Cowlitz counties. Forest headquarters are in Vancouver, Washington. It is one of 18 national forests in Region 6 of the Forest Service, with headquarters in Portland, Oregon. In 1908, it was established as *Columbia National Forest*, from a portion of Rainier National Forest. On June 15, 1949, the name was changed to that of a forester and conservationist, who was the leading influence in the establishment of national forests in the United States.

Gig Harbor *(T.21N;R.2E)*

Small, well-protected bay 2 miles northwest of Point Defiance, northwest Pierce County. It is the home port of a large fishing fleet, and the location of a town by the same name. In 1841, the bay was named by Cmdr. Charles Wilkes, when his gig found safe water here.

Gig Harbor *(T.21N;R.2E)*

Town surrounding Gig Harbor bay, 2 miles northwest of Point Defiance, northwest Pierce County. It consists of an ''old town'' and a more recently built ''new town,'' which are both principally fishing villages. (*see* Gig Harbor bay)

Gilbert Peak *(S.35;T.12N;R.11E.uns)*

An 8,200-ft. peak at the northwest corner of Yakima Indian Reservation, in Goat Rocks Primitive Area, west central Yakima County. It was named for Curtis Gilbert, a Yakima mountaineer.

Gilbreath Spring *(S.26;T.9N;R.40E)*

Spring 12 miles southeast of Dayton, northwest corner of Umatilla National Forest, central Columbia County. It was named for Mrs. Margaret H. Gilbreath, the first white woman settler in the county. On some maps it is called *Cold Spring.* (USBGN)

Gill Creek *(T.26N;R.16E)*

The stream of the creek rises in Lake Ethel, east slope of Chiwaukum Mountains; flows northeast to Nason Creek, 1/2 mile below Marritt Station, southwest Chelan County. It was named by U.S. Forest Supervisor A. H. Sylvester for Justus A. Gill, who had a homestead at the creek's mouth.

Gillespie (Adams County) *see* Marengo

Gilliam *(S.34;T.8N;R.37E)*

Railroad station 8 miles northeast of Walla Walla, southeast Walla Walla County. Northern Pacific Railway officials named their station here for W. S. Gilliam, from whom they acquired a right-of-way.

Gilman (King County) *see* Issaquah

Gilman City, Gilman Park (King County) *see* Ballard

Gilmer *(S.32;T.5N;R.11E)*

Community on Gilmer Creek, 10 miles north of White Salmon, west central Klickitat County. It was named for George W. Gilmer, who served as postmaster here for 37 years.

Gilmer Creek (*Ts.4,5N;Rs.10,11E*)

The stream of the creek heads in west central Klickitat County; flows southwest 6 miles to White Salmon River, 4 miles above Husum. (*see* Gilmer)

Ginder Lake (King County) *see* Cinder Lake

Gingerless Lake (Kittitas County) *see* Alaska Lake

Ginkgo Petrified Forest
(*T.17N;Rs.22,23E*)

Claimed to be the largest petrified forest discovered in the world, on Columbia River, 30 miles east of Ellensburg, near Vantage, Kittitas County. It is a state archeological site, with a museum exhibiting numerous types of petrified wood. The name was chosen because many of the petrifacts are of Ginkgo, a genus of tree which must have grown here many thousands of years ago, but which has not grown naturally on this continent for ages.

Glacier (*S.7;T.39N;R.7E*)

Town 44 miles northeast of Bellingham, near the confluence of Glacier Creek and North Fork, Nooksack River, north central Whatcom County. On September 7, 1909, it was platted and named for nearby Glacier Creek.

Glacier Basin (*Mt. Rainier National Park*)

Meadow area on the northeast slope of Mt. Rainier, between Winthrop and Emmons glaciers, at the foot of Inter Glacier. It was a site of mining activity at the turn of the century. The name, applied by park officers, is quite descriptive.

Glacier Bridge (*Mt.Rainier National Park*)

Bridge 11 miles east of Nisqually entrance, on Paradise Road where it crosses Nisqually River, 1 mile beyond Christine Falls, southwest zone of the park. When named, an excellent view of Nisqually Glacier was found at the bridge. Since 1910, however, the glacier has receded almost 1 mile.

Glacier Creek (*Ts.25,26N;Rs.15,16E*)

The stream of the creek heads in Chiwaukum Glacier; flows 4 miles to Chiwaukum Creek, through a typical, U-shaped, glacial valley on Wenatchee National Forest, central Chelan County. The descriptive name was applied by U.S. Forest Supervisor A. H. Sylvester.

Glacier Creek (*T.12N;R.10E.uns*)

The stream of the creek rises in Lily Basin, 3-1/2 miles west of Cascade Mountain summit, Gifford Pinchot National Forest, east central Lewis County; flows 6 miles west to Johnson Creek. The name was given because the creek's head is in a glaciated area.

Glacier Creek (*Mt. Rainier National Park*) *see* Paradise River

Glacier Creek (Whatcom County) *see* Little Beaver Creek

Glacier Island (*Mt. Rainier National Park*)

"Island" of towering rock cliffs with a dome worn smooth by centuries of ice action, north of Pyramid Peak, between Tahoma and South Tahoma glaciers, southwest slope of Mt. Rainier, southwest zone of the park. It is about 1 mile square, elevation 7,651 ft. The name is quite descriptive, as the cliffs actually constitute a rock island among glaciers. (USBGN)

Glacier Lake (*S.16;T.25N;R.13E*)

A 60.4-acre lake in a glacial area 1 mile west of Cascade Mountain summit, 3-1/2 miles south of Scenic, Snoqualmie National Forest, extreme northeast King County. It is one of 2 Scenic Lakes, the other being Surprise Lake. The name is appropriate, as the lake is glacier-fed. Alternate names are *Upper Scenic Lake* and *Upper Surprise Lake.*

Glacier Lake (*S.8;T.12N;R.10E*)

A 19.8-acre lake in the course of Glacier Creek, 5-1/2 miles southeast of Packwood, east central Lewis County. It was named for the creek. (*see* Glacier Creek, Lewis County)

Glacier Peak (*Ts.30,31N;Rs.12-14E*)

Famous volcanic peak, elevation 10,568 ft., northeast Snohomish County. It is the central point of a Wilderness Area, and the hub of numerous, live glaciers. The original Indian name was *Dahkobed, Takomed,* or *Takobud,* the generic term for "white mountain." The present name was applied by early prospectors, and was adopted by government surveyors.

Glacier Peak (Whatcom County) *see* Spickard Peak

Glacier Peak Wilderness Area

Primitive mountain area covering 458,505 acres, in Cascade Mountains on both sides of the summit, within Mt. Baker and Wenatchee national forests; Skagit, Snohomish, and Chelan counties. It contains 38 peaks over 8,000 ft. elevation, including 10,528-ft. Glacier Peak. Most of the major peaks support live glaciers. On September 8, 1960, this primitive expanse was set aside as a Wilderness Area by the Secretary of Agriculture. It is the subject of a strong controversy promoted by forest industries, which claim that some commercial timber is being "locked up" for a single use, and not available for logging. The name is for the highest peak in the area, a vast, glacier-studded mountain. (*see* Glacier Peak, Snohomish County)

Glade (*S.19;T.10N;R.30E*)

Railroad station 6 miles north of Pasco in Esquatzel Coulee, southwest Franklin County. In 1883, it was named by Northern Pacific Railway officials, who thought the label was descriptive of local topographic features.

Glass Canyon (Klickitat County) *see* Glass Creek

Glass Creek (*T.4N;R.19E*)

The stream of this short creek rises near Dot, east central Klickitat County; flows west and southwest 7 miles to Harrison Creek. It was named for Jim Glass, who settled here in 1876. The creek is locally known as *Glass Canyon.*

Glasses Lake (*S.10;T.27N;R.13E*)

Wenatchee National Forest lake, elevation 5,630 ft., directly east of Cascade Mountain summit, 1 mile south of Heather Lake into which it drains, northwest Chelan County. The name was applied by U.S. Forest Supervisor A. H. Sylvester, who noted that the lake's 2 lobes gave the general appearance of a pair of spectacles.

Gleed (*S.32;T.14N;R.18E*)

Railroad stop directly north of Naches River, 4 miles northwest of Yakima, north central Yakima County. It was named by Northern Pacific Railway officials for James Gleed, a pioneer of 1870, on whose land a railway station was located.

Glen Cove (*S.6;T.21N;R.1E*)

A west shore cove of Carr Inlet, 1 mile east of Key Center, northwest Pierce County. In 1890, it was named *Balch's Cove,* for Capt. Lafayette Balch, a ship owner who founded Steilacoom and who was a pioneer legislator. The present name was substituted by local residents, who evidently wanted a more poetic name.

Glenavon (Lewis County) *see* Coal Canyon

Glencove (*S.36;T.22N;R.1W*)
Settlement on Glen Cove, off Carr Inlet, directly north of Key Center, northwes Pierce County. It was named for the cove on which it is located (*see* Glen Cove)

Glendale (*S.1;T.28N;R.3E*)
Town on the southeast tip of Whidbey Island, on Possession Sound, 2-1/2 miles north of Possession Point, south Island County. In 1907, it was named by Mrs. E. M. Peck, who believed that the name expressed "the beauty of the locality."

Glendale (Snohomish County) *see* Trafton

Glenoma (*S.14;T.12N;R.5E*)
An area of marginal farms and abandoned tie mills 8 miles southeast of Morton, on Uden Frost Creek in Rainey (Rene) Valley, south central Lewis County. The mills devastated the young, growing timber in the area. The name was composed by Mrs. Beverly W. Coiner, a settler, who used "glen" for the valley, and the Greek word "oma" for "fruitful"; hence, "fruitful valley." Earlier names, for which no source has been found, were *Vern* and *Verndale*.

Glenwood (*S.10;T.6N;R.12E*)
Small mountain community in Klickitat River valley, northwest Klickitat County. Located in a heavily-timbered county south of Mt. Adams, it was given a fairly descriptive name by those who settled the town in the 1880s.

Glenwood (*S.32;T.17N;R.44E*)
Town 5 miles northeast of Colfax, on Palouse River, east central Whitman County. The name was chosen by local residents because it is in a wooded glen or valley.

Gletty Creek (*S.2;T.32N;R.42E*)
The stream of the creek rises 8 miles west of Cusick, southwest Pend Oreille County; flows 3 miles southeast to Calispell Creek. It was named for George Gletty, who homesteaded the land through which the creek runs. (USBGN)

Glines Canyon Reservoir (Clallam County) *see* Lake Mills, Ilwha Reservoir

Gloverville (Okanogan County) *see* Twisp

Gloyd (*S.34;T.21N;R.28E*)
Railroad station 12 miles southeast of Ephrata, central Grant County. When Northern Pacific Railway Company established a station here in 1910, officials named it for F. H. Gloyd, a Ritzville banker.

Goat Butte (*S.3;T.8N;R.11E.uns*)
A 7,407-ft. peak on the east slope of Mt. Adams, west boundary of Yakima Indian Reservation, southwest Yakima County. It is one of Mt. Adams' subsidiary volcanic cones, long extinct. The crater walls have largely disintegrated. The U.S. Indian Service operates a fire lookout on the summit during fire season. The name is for the herds of mountain goats which inhabit the mountainside and peaks. Earlier names were *Rainbow Butte* and *Sheepherder's Butte*.

Goat Creek (*Ts.17,18N;Rs.10,11E*)
The stream of the creek rises on the west slope of Cascade Mountain summit, 8 miles northeast of Chinook Pass, Snoqualmie National Forest, extreme east central Pierce County; flows 4-1/2 miles northwest to Silver Creek. It was named by Forest Service personnel because it flows down the west side of Castle Mountain through a wild goat range.

Goat Creek (*T.33N;R.13E.uns*)
The stream of the creek rises in a small glacier, east slope of Mt. Buckindy, Mt. Baker National Forest, southeast Skagit County; flows 3 miles southeast to Downey Creek, a tributary of Suiattle River. It was named for a large herd of wild goats which used this range each summer. A previous name was *North Fork, Downey Creek*.

Goat Creek (Okanogan County) *see* Mazama

Goat Island (*S.11;T.33N;R.2E*)
Small island on Skagit Bay, near the south entrance to Swinomish Channel, 2 miles southwest of LaConner, southwest Skagit County. It was a military reservation from 1909 until 1947, when Ft. Whitman was abandoned and the island transferred to the State Department of Game. The name is reported to have originated locally, for a herd of goats which a settler established on the island.

Goat Island Mountain (*Mt. Rainier National Park*)
Extensive, round-topped peak, elevation 7,301 ft., on the northeast slope of Mt. Rainier, bounded on the northeast by White River, on the southeast by Fryingpan Creek, on the southwest by Fryingpan Glacier, and on the northwest by Emmons Glacier. The name was chosen for the abundance of mountain goats on the mountain. In season, elk also inhabit the area.

Goat Island Rock (*Mt. Rainier National Park*)
Long, narrow rock splitting the lower flow of Carbon Glacier, northwest zone of the park. The naming is obscure, although there are many mountain goats on slopes adjoining the glacier.

Goat Lake (*S.28;T.24N;R.11E*)
Small, 24.5-acre lake, less than 1/4 mile long, 12 miles south-southwest of Skykomish, Snoqualmie National Forest, northeast King County. It was named by prospectors several years ago, for the mountain goats which inhabited nearby mountain slopes. (USBGN)

Goat Lake (*S.18;T.12N;R.11E*)
A 10-acre lake, elevation 6,900 ft., at Goat Creek headwaters, 1-1/2 miles west of Cascade Mountain summit, in Goat Rocks Primitive Area, extreme east central Lewis County. It was named for Goat Creek, which drains the lake.

Goat Lake (*S.7;T.17N;R.11E*)
Lake at Cascade Mountain summit, 7-1/2 miles north of Chinook Pass, Pierce County. It is named for Goat Creek, which drains the lake. An alternate name is *Broadhead Lake*. (*see* Goat Creek, Pierce County)

Goat Lake (*T.29N;R.11E*)
A 64-acre lake, about 1/2 mile long and over 100 ft. deep, elevation 3,154 ft., 3 miles northeast of Monte Cristo, Mt. Baker National Forest, east central Snohomish County. It was locally named for mountain goats which frequent the steep slopes around the lake.

Goat Marsh Lakes (*S.23;T.8N;R.4E*)
Two connected lakes, 750 ft. apart, in Goat Marsh, southeast slope of Goat Mountain, east central Cowlitz County. The larger lake covers 13 acres; the smaller covers 5 acres. The lakes and marsh are named for Goat Mountain.

Goat Mountain (Mt. Rainier National Park) *see* Mt. Wow

Goat Mountain (Okanogan County) *see* Old Goat Mountain, McLeod Peak

Goat Peak *(S.27;T.20N;R.13E)*

A 5,100-ft. peak on the boundary of Wenatchee National Forest, 3 miles south of Easton in Big Creek drainage area, west central Kittitas County. It is used as a fire lookout in season. Many mountain goats are visible from the peak from time to time; hence, the name.

Goat Rocks *(T.12N;R.11E.uns)*

Rocks rising to an 8,201-ft. elevation, east of Cascade Mountain crest, Goat Rocks Primitive Area, extreme west central Yakima County. An old Indian legend tells that *La-Con-Nie* was God of the Goat Rocks, and herded wild goats in the area. This wild, rugged country is inhabited by many of these animals.

Goat Rocks Primitive Area
(Ts.11-13N;Rs.10,11E.uns)

High, rugged, and scenic reservation, elevations to 8,200 ft. or more, extending along Cascade Mountain summit, from Lakeview Mountain on the south to White Pass area, about 18 miles north; reaches 8 miles west into Lewis County, 6 miles east into Yakima County. It is replete with snowfields and mountain meadows, and abounds in wild game and bird life, including many herds of wild goats. The name derives from these mountain-loving animals.

Goats Pass *(Mt. Rainier National Park)*

High pass, elevation 5,300 ft., at the western foot of Barrier Peak, 1/2 mile south of Owyhigh Lakes and directly east of Kotsuck Creek, east central zone of the park. It is located among the glacial ridges and pinnacles of Cascade Mountain range. The name origin is not recorded, but the pass was undoubtedly named for the mountain goats which inhabit nearby mountains.

Gobar's River (Cowlitz County) *see* Coweman River

Gobbler's Knob *(Mt. Rainier Park)*

A bald promontory at the northwest extremity of Mt. Wow summit, overlooking Lake George, southwest corner of the park. The National Park Service uses the peak as a forest fire lookout in season. In 1930, it was named by a

Tennessee native, who worked here on a trail crew; it reminded him of wild turkey country in his home state. (USBGN)

Goblin Peak (Snohomish County) *see* Kyes Peak

Go-Devil Canyon
(Ss.29,32;T.7N;R.43E)

Short canyon 1-1/2 miles north of Grouse, Umatilla National Forest, terminating at Grouse Creek, extreme southwest Asotin County. It reportedly was named by pioneer settlers because one side of the canyon was extremely steep, causing rock slides.

Godfrey *(S.16;T.37N;R.37E)*

Small sawmill town on Kettle River east bank, 4 miles west of Evans, northwest Stevens County. In 1909, it was named for the Godfrey brothers, who operated a sawmill here at the time. The town does not appear on recent maps.

Godkin Creek *(Ts.25,26N;R.6W)*

The stream of the creek rises north of Quinault River, south central Olympic National Park, Jefferson County; flows north to Elwha River, 1-1/2 miles east of Mt. Wilder. In 1890, it was named by members of Seattle Press Expedition, for E.L. Godkin, editor of *New York Post*.

God's Pocket (San Juan County) *see* Fish Creek

Gold Bar *(S.6;T.27N;R.9E)*

River bar on Skykomish River, 13 miles east of Monroe, south central Snohomish County. It was named by Alonzo Low and a partner named Hooverson, who had a prospector's camp on the river bar in 1879. The prospect was a placer mine, where they worked for some time.

Gold Basin *(T.30N;R.8E)*

Mining town 2 miles north of Mt. Pilchuck on the old Everett & Monte Cristo Railroad grade, central Snohomish County. The name reflects the area's past as a busy mining center.

Gold Basin (Mt. Rainier National Park) *see* Cold Basin

Gold Hill (Snohomish County) *see* Gold Mountain

Gold Mountain *(T.32N;R.10E)*

Mt. Baker National Forest mountain 2-1/2 miles east of Darrington, northeast Snohomish County. The Indian name

was *Tel-kaiaks*, meaning "the mountain that came down to water." The present name was chosen by Charles Burns, an early prospector, in order to boost interest in mining in the locality. Alternate names have been *Gold Hill* and *Deer Mountain*.

Gold Ridge *(T.26N;Rs.18,19E)*

Wenatchee National Forest ridge extending east from Sugarloaf Peak to the junction of Mad River with Tillicum Creek, central Chelan County. Origin of the name appears to be unrecorded, but persons familiar with the area state that there are no known gold indications on the ridge or nearby.

Golden *(S.11;T.39N;R.26E)*

Town on a flat north of Wannicut Lake, east slope of Palmer Mountain, north central Okanogan County. In 1886, it was named for nearby gold mines, long since deserted. In 1892-94, it was a lively town, but faded when ores proved difficult to refine.

Golden Harvest Creek *(T.36N;R.32E)*

The stream of the creek rises on the east slope of Cornell Butte, 7 miles southwest of Republic, close to the Okanogan-Ferry county line, Ferry County; flows 9 miles east to San Poil River, Colville National Forest. It was named for Golden Harvest Consolidated Mining Company, which produced gold as late as 1937-38.

Golden Lakes *(Mt. Rainier National Park)*

Group of 15 small lakes in a richly flowering area, totaling 43 acres, elevation 4,556 ft., in Sunset Park, between North Puyallup River and Rushingwater Creek, near the west park boundary, west central zone of the park. The name was chosen by park officials because "at sundown the lakes glow like molten gold." (USBGN)

Goldendale *(T.14N;R.16E)*

Town on Little Klickitat River, 9 miles north of Columbia River, central Klickitat County. In 1863, a settlement was started by John J. Golden, who filed a homestead claim in 1872. He platted a townsite under the present name, and gave each of his friends a town lot.

Goldie River *(Ts.26,27N;Rs.6,7W)*

The stream of the river rises north of Elwha Basin, Olympic National Park, 3 miles east of Mt. Queets; flows north and northeast to Elwha River at Press

Valley, north central Jefferson County. In 1890, it was named by Charles A. Barnes, historian of Seattle Press Expedition, for R. H. Goldie of Seattle.

Goldmeyer Hot Springs
(S.15;T.23N;R.11E)

Springs 4 miles northeast of Snoqualmie Pass, 2 miles west of Cascade Mountain summit, east central King County. They were named for William Goldmeyer, a Virginian who came to Washington Territory in 1863, and who claimed land near the springs.

Goldsboro Lake (Lewis County) *see* Mineral Lake

Goldsborough Creek
(T.20N;Rs.3,4W)

The stream of the creek rises 4-1/2 miles west of Shelton, south central Mason County; flows east to Oakland Bay. It was named for Maj. Hugh A. Goldsborough, who filed a Donation Land Claim on the creek in 1853, but returned east before proving up.

Goodalls Landing *(S.11;T.36N;R.11E)*

A river-boat landing in the days of Skagit River steamboating, on the river's south bank, just below Diablo Gorge, northeast Skagit County. Little now remains of the place, which does not appear on recent maps. The name was for a local logger and landowner, who settled here at the upper limit of steamboat navigation.

Goodman Creek *(S.21;T.27N;R.14W)*

The stream of the creek rises 10 miles east of Pacific Ocean, extreme northwest Jefferson County; flows west to the ocean, 10 miles north of Destruction Island. In 1890, it was named for one of the surveyors on a township survey. The original Indian name, *Tsa-dis-qualth*, had the meaning "narrow mouth overhung with brush."

Goodman Creek *(T.31N;R.10E)*

The stream of the creek rises 10 miles southeast of Darrington, Mt. Baker National Forest, northeast Snohomish County; flows north by west 5 miles to Sauk River. It was named for A. E. Goodman, a homesteader on a nearby Sauk River tract.

Goodnoe *(S.26;T.3N;R.18E)*

Small settlement near the north bank of Columbia River, 17 miles southeast of Goldendale, south central Klickitat County. It was named for an early

stock-raising family. The railway station was first called *Harbin*, but was changed to the present name in order to agree with the post office name.

Goodnoe Hills *(S.18;T.3N;R.19E)*

Village 4 miles north of Columbia River and 17 miles southeast of Goldendale, south central Klickitat County. (*see* Goodnoe)

Goodwin (Stevens County) *see* Ward, St. Francis Regis Mission

Goose Creek (Lincoln County) *see* Wilbur

Goose Heaven *(S.11;T.33N;R.37E)*

Swampy area on a mountainside near Waterloo, 3 miles east of Columbia River, west central Stevens County. The name, in local use, was originally applied by "Grandma" Tipton, first postmistress of Waterloo, for the multitudes of wild geese which stopped here to feed and rest during migrations. It does not appear on recent maps.

Goose Island *(S.8;T.34N;R.2W)*

Island directly east of the southeast point of San Juan Island, 1/2 mile north of Cattle Point, south central San Juan County. In 1859, it was charted under the present name by Capt. Henry Richards, British Admiralty surveyor. It is one of many features in the San Juan Islands which was named for wildfowl. The abundance of native seabirds here is notable.

Goose Lake *(Ss.12,11;T.5N;R.8E.uns)*

A 58-acre lake, maximum depth 25 ft., at the north end of Big Lava Beds, Gifford Pinchot National Forest, southeast Skamania County. At one time, the lake was almost completely drained by fracture of the lake bed from earthquakes. It was restored by U.S. Forest Service personnel, who filled the cracks with brush, rock and soil. The name was given because the lake was a stop-over for many wild geese in pioneer days.

Goose Point *(S.8;T.13N;R.10W)*

Point at the mouth of Palix River on Willapa Bay, west central Pacific County. The name was given by local residents because the point was a feeding and resting place for migrating flocks of wild geese.

Goose Point (Clallam County) *see* Spak Point

Gooseberry Point *(S.34;T.38N;R.1E)*

A south entrance point to Lummi

Bay, Lummi Indian Reservation, across Hale Passage from Lummi Island, Whatcom County. The name was given for the abundance of wild gooseberries here in early days, which were a Lummi Indian food source. The original Indian name was *T-ham-gli-hi-xem*.

Goosmus Creek *(T.40N;Rs.33-34E)*

The stream of the creek rises in Canada, directly north of central Ferry County; flows through Colville National Forest, 5 miles southeast to Kettle River. It was named for an Indian sub-chief, who died of smallpox in the early days. Within one month, his 12 sons also died of the same disease.

Gopher Mountain *(T.30N;R.18E.uns)*

A Wenatchee National Forest peak on the divide between the headwaters of Snowbrushy Creek and North Fork, Entiat River, northwest Chelan County. It was named by U.S. Forest Supervisor A. H. Sylvester, for the striped pattern of rock formations which resemble the stripes of the native gophers.

Gordon Lake (Pierce County) *see* American Lake

Gordon Point *(S.1;T.19N;R.1E)*

A north end point of Cormorant Passage, directly west of Steilacoom, northwest Pierce County. In 1841, it was named *Qulam Point* by Cmdr. Charles Wilkes, using his version of the Indian name. In 1846, the present name was charted by Capt. R. N. Inskip, R.N., for Capt. George Thomas Gordon, commander of *HMS Cormorant*, who was on this station between 1846 and 1850. It is one of few names in the region retained from British Admiralty charts. A local name, no longer used, was *Salter's Point*, for Capt. John Salter, a local landowner.

Gorge Dam *(S.14;T.37N;R.12E)*

Hydroelectric dam in Skagit River, between Newhalem and Diablo Dam, Mt. Baker National Forest, southeast Skagit County. It was built by the City of Seattle, and named for the deep, rugged gorge in which the Skagit River runs at this point.

Gorge Lake *(S.14;T.37N;R.12E)*

An artificial, hydroelectric reservoir behind Gorge Dam in Skagit River, 2-1/2 miles northeast of Newhalem, southeast Skagit County. It is about 3 miles long, covers 210 acres, and has a maximum depth of 125 ft. (*see* Gorge Dam)

Gorst (*S.32;T.24N;R.1E*)

Settlement at the head of Sinclair Inlet, 4 miles southwest of Bremerton, central Kitsap County. It was named for Samuel and Mary Gorst, who settled here in 1897, and who purchased extensive acreage from Port Blakely Mill Company. Other names which have been used are *Gorst Creek, Head of the Bay,* and *Butler.*

Gorst Creek (*T.24N;Rs1W, 1E*)

The stream of the creek rises 8 miles southeast of Bremerton, south central Kitsap County; flows 4-1/2 miles east to the head of Sinclair Inlet. On county maps published by a Seattle firm, the creek is named *Goest Creek* in error.

Gosnell Creek (*Ts.19,20N;Rs.3,4W*)

The stream of the 28-mile-long creek rises 7 miles southwest of Shelton; flows northeast through Isabella Valley into Isabella Lake. From the lake, it runs northeast and east into Hammersley Inlet, between Arcadia and Shelton, Mason County. The name is for Wesley B. Gosnell, an associate of Michael Simmons and Orrington Cushman, who built the first sawmill in Mason County. These pioneers selected a site at the mouth of the creek in Hammersley Inlet; hence, the lower stretch of the creek was called *Mill Creek* in early days.

Gossip Island (*S.34;T.37N;R.4W*)

One of 3 islands in the Gossip Islands group, with Cemetery and Happy islands, at the entrance to Reid Harbor, Stuart Island, northwest San Juan County. Along with Cemetery Island, it was used for Indian burials in early years. Most of the remains were moved to Canadian islands by Indians after white men desecrated the graves. An alternate name appearing on some maps is *George Island.* (*see* Gossip Islands)

Gossip Islands (*S.34;T.37N;R.4W*) a group of 3 small islands at the entrance to Reid Harbor, Stuart Island, northwest San Juan County. The islands include Cemetery, Gossip, and George islands, and were previously the site of Indian burials. Individual islands appear on more detailed maps and charts, but the group name does not, except on British Admiralty charts made in 1858-59 by Capt. Henry Richards. The name Richards used was for an old Indian cus-

tom of feasting, drinking, and gossiping here during sockeye salmon seasons. An alternate name for the group, in early use, was *Cemetery Islands,* relating to the many Indian burials.

Gothic Peak (*S.24;T.29N;R.10E*)

A 5,560-ft. peak 3-1/2 miles west of Monte Cristo, east central Snohomish County. In 1896, it was named not for its shape but for a local settler named William Gothic.

Goudy (*T.35N;R.37E*)

Place now under the flood basin of Grand Coulee Dam, east bank of Columbia River, directly south of Colville River mouth, west central Stevens County. In 1826, it was built at the falls in Colville River, for Hudson's Bay Company, and named for a man who built the first grist mill on the upper Columbia River. Goudy and his crew lived here during construction of the mill, and for some time thereafter.

Gouge Eye (*Ts.33,34N;Rs.36-38E*)

A range extending from Rice on the north, to Daisy on the south, east to the foothills of Huckleberry Range, west central Stevens County. The name is not on maps, but was used by local settlers. In some old records it is written as *Gouji.* It was named for a one-eyed, old horse which was turned loose on the range by "Grandma" Tipton, first postmistress of Waterloo, and wandered here for several years.

Gould City (*S.19;T.13N;R.42E*)

Former town 8 miles north of Pomeroy on Deadman Creek, 6 miles south of Snake River, north central Garfield County. In 1887, a post office was established as *Dixon's* or *Dixon,* with Sarah Dixon as postmistress. It later acquired the present name, evidently for a local landowner, who owned part of the townsite area before it was platted in 1891.

Gourd Island (San Juan County) *see* Patos Island

Govan (*S.20;T.26N;R.32E*)

Small farm community 76 miles west of Spokane, northwest Lincoln County. In 1889, it was established as a railroad station; on June 24, 1899, it was platted as a townsite by Carrie Hesseltine. The name is for R. B. Govan, a civil engineer employed by Washington Central Railroad on construction in the area.

Government Locks (King County) *see* Hiram M. Chittenden Locks

Governors Ridge (*Mt. Rainier National Park*)

Ridge between Shaw and Kotsuck creeks on the west, Chinook and Klickitat creeks on the east, east central zone of the park. Maximum elevation is 6,400 ft. It was named by former Park Superintendent Ethan Allen, for the governor of the state of Washington, and applied to all men who have held that office or may hold it in the future. (USBGN)

Graham Point (*S.4;T.20N;R.2W*)

A west shore point on Peale Passage, 8 miles northeast of Shelton, southeast Mason County. In 1841, Cmdr. Charles Wilkes named this feature *Kopo Point,* evidently using the Indian designation. The present name is of local origin, for a pioneer family.

Gran Canal de Nuestra Senora del Rosario la Marinera (Northwest Washington) *see* Georgia Strait

Grand Coulee (*T.22-28N;Rs.26-30E*)

This great coulee heads at Grand Coulee Dam, extreme northeast Grant County; extends over 50 miles southwest to Ephrata, between Grant and Douglas counties. It was the bed of Columbia River when diverted in the glacial period. In 1853, the first recorded use of the present name, in print, was by Lieut. Arnold in *Pacific Railroad Reports.* In 1841, Cmdr. Charles Wilkes called it *Grand Coulee;* in 1825, John Work of Hudson's Bay Company called it *Grand Coolley.*

Grand Coulee (*T.28N;R.30E*)

Town on slopes above Columbia River, northeast corner of Grant County. It is a merger of 3 construction towns which were used during the building of Grand Coulee Dam: Coulee Heights, Coulee Center, and Grand Coulee. In 1933 and a few years following, the place resembled a western frontier town. It was, of course, named for Grand Coulee itself.

Grand Dalles (Klickitat County) *see* Dallesport

Grand Junction (Asotin County) *see* Jerry

Grand Lake (*T.28N;R.5W.uns*)

Lake in Grand Valley, Olympic National Park, between Gladys and Moose lakes, southeast Clallam County. Records indicate that the name was applied because the lake is larger than several adjoining lakes in Grand Valley. The name *Etta Lake*, shown on some recent maps, is unofficial. (USBGN)

Grand Mound *(T.15N;R.3W)*

A scattered settlement 25 miles south of Olympia, southwest Thurston County. Washington State School for Delinquent Girls, often called Grand Mound, is one mile west. An early name for the place was *Mt. Vernon*. The present name is for a tree-covered hillock, 125 ft. above the prairie, and the highest of the Mima Mounds. (*see* Mima Mounds)

Grand Park *(Mt. Rainier National Park)*

High plateau 3-1/2 miles long and about 1 mile wide, with elevations to 5,700 ft., southwest of Lake Eleanor, between West Fork, White River, and Huckleberry Creek, north central area of the park. It is the largest natural park area on the north side of Mt. Rainier, with many alpine firs and hemlocks, and visited by many deer. The descriptive name, chosen by park officials, is well deserved. (USBGN)

Grand Rapids *(Stevens, Ferry counties)* *see* Rickey Rapids

Grand Valley *(T.28N;R.5W.uns)*

A series of mountain meadows, surrounded by peaks towering to 6,000 ft., near the head of Grand Creek, Olympic National Park, southeast Clallam County. This very descriptive name for a scenic valley was chosen by a homesteader named Cameron, who settled here in 1899, and was a rancher, hunter, and packer.

Grande Ronde River
(Ts.6,7N;Rs.43-46E)

The stream of the river rises in northeast Oregon; flows northeast into southwest Asotin County at Horseshoe Bend, to Snake River at Rogersburg, in a very crooked course. It was named for Grande Ronde Valley, Oregon. French-Canadian employees of fur-trading companies applied the name for the elliptical contour of the valley. A literal translation would be "great round." They called the stream *Riviere de Grand Ronde*. The Indian name was *Way-lu-wa*, meaning "ice river," which corresponds with another French name, *Fourche de Glace*. It is possible that this

French term was actually *Fourche de Glaise*, meaning *clay fork* or *clay branch*, as American miners called the stream *Clay Creek* for its yellow color. This explains the name *Glaise River* used in certain old records and maps.

Grandma Creek *(T.28N;R.19E)*

The stream of the creek rises on Entiat Ridge south of Signal Peak, Wenatchee National Forest, central Chelan County; flows 3 miles northeast to Entiat River. The unusual name was given by Forest Ranger James McKenzie, for "Grandma," a life-sized figure of a woman which was erected at the summit of Signal Peak opposite the head of this stream. It was carved from a tree trunk by Harvey Reed, whose family settled here in 1869. Reed herded sheep along the creek and in the general area, when he wasn't creating wooden statuary.

Grandview *(S.23;T.9N;R.23E)*

Town 44 miles southeast of Yakima, southeast Yakima County. When it was platted in 1906, the name was applied to the townsite. Elza Dean and F. L. Pittman, members of the townsite company, agreed that the place offered a magnificent view of Mt. Adams, Mt. Rainier, and other features in the Cascade Range.

Grandy Creek *(Ts.35,36N;Rs.7,8E)*

The stream of the creek heads in Grandy Lake, 3 miles northwest of Concrete, north central Skagit County; flows 7 miles southwest ot Skagit River, near Birdsview. The creek and lake were named for John Grandy, who claimed land at the creek's mouth in 1878.

Grandy Lake *(S.32;T.36N;R.8E)*

Lake at the head of Grandy Creek, 2-1/2 miles northwest of Concrete, north central Skagit County. The lake appears on certain county maps, in error, as *Grundy Lake*. (*see* Grandy Creek)

Grange City *(S.3;T.12N;R.37E)*

Abandoned town at the junction of Tucannon and Snake rivers, near Tucannon, northwest Columbia County. The name originated in the 1870s when Grange Warehouse Company established a shipping point for wheat by river steamers. The town vanished when railroads displaced river shipments.

Granger *(S.21;T.10N;R.21E)*

Produce-packing and rail-shipping center on the north bank of Yakima River, 21 miles southeast of Yakima,

southeast Yakima County. It was founded in 1902; in 1909, it was platted as a townsite by Granger Land Company, and named for Walter N. Granger, president of the company and manager of Washington Irrigation Company.

Granite Creek *(Ts.36,37N;Rs.32,33E)*

The stream of the creek rises on the south side of Granite Mountain, northwest Ferry County; flows south and east 10 miles to San Poil River, directly south of Republic. The name describes the rock formation along part of the creek's course.

Granite Creek *(Mt. Rainier National Park)*

The stream of the creek rises on Burroughs Mountain, north central sector of the park; flows northwest to Winthrop Creek at the terminus of Winthrop Glacier. It was named by park officials for nearby granite outcroppings. (USBGN)

Granite Falls *(T.30N;Rs.6,7E)*

Formerly an important forest products center, now an area of excellent, young-growth timber 16 miles east of Marysville near Pilchuck River, west central Snohomish County. It was originally called *Portage* by an early Indian trader. The present name was given when the Everett & Monte Cristo Railroad was built, and is for a large falls in Stillaguamish River nearby, which cascades over granite ledges and boulders.

Granite Lake
(Ss.21,22,27,28;T.24N;R.41E)

One of a group of 4 lakes, with Meadow, Silver and Willow, 3 miles east of Soap Lake, southwest Spokane County. These lakes, and an adjoining town, are called *Four Lakes*. The name was applied by W. F. Bassett, a pioneer of 1871, for granite outcroppings around the lake.

Granite Lake No. 1
(S.36;T.35N;R.11E)

Smallest of a group of 4 Granite Lakes, covering 4.5 acres, about 7 miles southeast of Marblemount, east central Skagit County. (*see* Granite Lakes, Skagit County)

Granite Lake No. 2
(S.36;T.35N;R.11E)

A 7-acre lake about 7 miles southeast of Marblemount, east central Skagit County. It is one of 4 in the Granite Lakes group, all of which are numbered and connected. (*see* Granite Lakes, Skagit County)

Granite Lake No. 3
(S.36;T.35N;R.11E)
One of 4 connected and numbered lakes in the Granite Lakes group, about 7 miles southeast of Marblemount, east central Skagit County. Locally called *Lower Granite Lake*, it covers 38.4 acres and is 3,300 ft. long. (*see* Granite Lakes, Skagit County)

Granite Lake No. 4 *(S.1;T.34N;R.11E)*
Largest of 4 connected and numbered Granite Lakes, at the head of Boulder Creek, about 7 miles southeast of Marblemount, east central Skagit County. It is the deepest of the group of lakes, and covers 144 acres. Local names for this feature are *Upper Granite Lake* and *Big Granite Lake*. (*see* Granite Lakes, Skagit County)

Granite Lakes *(Ss.23,25;T.23N;R.9E)*
Two lakes 1,200 ft. apart, at the head of Granite Creek, 8-3/4 miles southeast of North Bend, east central King County. The upper lake covers 14.8 acres; the lower lake extends over 9 acres. The name is for Granite Creek which drains them.

Granite Lakes
(S.36;T.35N&S.1;T.34N;R.11E)
A group of 4 connected and numbered lakes at the head of Boulder Creek, about 7 miles southeast of Marblemount, east central Skagit County. The name is appropriate, as the lakes are located in an area of previous volcanic activity, with massive, granite formations. (*see* Granite Lake No. 1, No. 2, No. 3, No. 4)

Granite Mountain Lakes
(S.1;T.22N;R.10E)
A group of 3 lakes 2-1/2 miles west of Snoqualmie Pass, Snoqualmie National Forest, east central King County. It includes Crystal, Denny, and Cad lakes. The name is for nearby Granite Mountain. (*see* Crystal, Denny, Cad lakes)

Granite Pass *(Ss.3,10;T.30N;R.9E)*
Mt. Baker National Forest pass at the head of North Fork, Clear Creek, east central Snohomish County. It is located in a heavily-mineralized area, and locally named for a very large granite outcropping in the pass.

Grant *(S.4;T.20N;R.2W)*
Ferry landing on the west shore of

Pickering Passage, 6 miles northeast of Shelton, southeast Mason County. There is a post office and a school. In 1900, the name was chosen locally for Miss Mary Grant, who was school teacher and postmistress.

Grant County
This county in east central Washington is circled by Columbia River on the south and west; bounded on the north by Douglas County; on the east by Lincoln and Adams counties; on the south by Benton County; and on the east by Douglas, Yakima, and Kittitas counties. It is an agricultural county covering 2,777 sq. miles, and producing wheat, fruit, potatoes, and livestock. On February 24, 1909, it was established by an act of the State Legislature. At that time, the county was named for Ulysses S. Grant, eighteenth president of the United States, and leader of Union forces in the Civil War.

Grant Creek *(T.32N;R.6E)*
Stream entering North Fork, Stillaguamish River, near Cicero, northwest Snohomish County. Like many features in the area, it was named for a very early settler.

Grant Island (Pierce County) *see* Tanglewood Island

Grant Orchards *(S.32;T.22N;R.27E)*
Town 2 miles east of Soap Lake, 5 miles northwest of Ephrata, central Grant County. The name was chosen by residents because the town is in the principal tree-fruit area of the county.

Grant Peak *(T.38N;R.8E.uns)*
Main summit peak of Mt. Baker, elevation 10,778 ft., on the north rim of the crater, Mt. Baker National Forest, central Whatcom County. In August 1868, it was named by Edmund T. Coleman for President Ulysses S. Grant.

Grapeview *(S.8;T.21N;R.1W)*
Town on the west shore of North Bay near its northern extremity, 3 miles east of Hood Canal, east central Mason County. It is an important grape-growing center, with wineries and juice plants. The Island Belle grape is the favorite. The original post office name was *Detroit*, chosen in 1889 by Detroit Land & Improvement Company which helped make the boom town. In 1890, the present name was substituted by order of Postmaster Walter O. Eckert. The name was very appropriate, as grape

culture had proven successful.

Grass Bay (Wahkiakum County) *see* Grays Bay

Grass Lake *(S.12;T.25N;R.13E)*
A 20-acre pond midway in the course of Trapper Creek, 1 mile southeast of Cascade Mountain summit, Wenatchee National Forest, southwest Chelan County. The name was given by local fishermen because of the lake's reedy shores.

Grass Lake *(S.32;T.28N;R.13E)*
A 2-acre lake, elevation about 4,700 ft., at Cascade Mountain summit near Wenatchee Pass, extreme southeast Snohomish County. Two other names which have been applied to this feature, in error, are *Apple Lake* and *Plum Lake*.

Grassmere *(S.9;T.35N;R.8E)*
Former mill town 1 mile west of Concrete, central Skagit County. The first name was *Ponto*, chosen by Great Northern Railway officials. Residents disliked the name, and changed it to the name of a town in Michigan.

Grave Island (Pierce County) *see* Tanglewood Island

Gravel (Benton County) *see* Longview

Gravelle *(S.34;T.25N;R.38E)*
Grain shipping point 7 miles southeast of Davenport, east central Lincoln County. It was named for Alphonse Gravelle, who, with A. M. Cannon, platted the townsite on May 18, 1889.

Gravelly Lake *(S.11;T.19N;R.2E)*
A 147.8-acre lake, 65 ft. deep, in a residential area 2 miles southwest of Lakewood Center, directly northeast of American Lake, west central Pierce County. The locally-chosen name is quite descriptive. The original Indian name was *Cook-alls-shy*, meaning "pond lilies."

Graveyard Point (Whatcom County) *see* Commercial Point

Graveyard Spit (Clallam County) *see* Dungeness Spit

Gray *(S.10;T.30N;R.40E)*
Railroad stop on Colville River, 4 miles north of Springdale, south central Stevens County. The place was settled by William C. Gray, who owned a 700-acre timothy hay ranch here when Spokane Falls & Northern Railway built through the area in 1889, and established a station. Railway officials named it for the first settler,

as *Gray's Siding*. By 1901, a sawmill, post office, store, and a few houses were established. Local people shortened the name to *Gray's*, and later to Gray.

Gray Wolf River *(Ts.27-29N;Rs.4,5W)*
The stream of the river rises on the north slope of Deception Mountain, Olympic National Park, northeast Jefferson County; flows 15 miles northeast to Dungeness River, 6-1/2 miles south of Sequim, Olympic National Forest, Clallam County. Former names were *Greywolf River, Gray Wolf River, Graywolf River* and *West Fork, Dungeness River*. (USBGN)

Grayland *(S.6;T.15N;R.11W)*
Community on Pacific Ocean, 7 miles south of Grays Harbor entrance, extreme southwest point of Grays Harbor County. It has numerous cultivated cranberry bogs, many owned by Finns. The name is a combination of the name of Robert Gray, who discovered Grays Harbor, with ''land,'' for poetic effect.

Grays Bay *(Ts.9,10N;Rs.8,9W)*
North bank bay of Columbia River, at the mouths of Deep and Grays rivers, south Pacific and southwest Wahkiakum counties. In 1792, the name was applied by Lieut. Broughton to honor Robert Gray, who discovered and named Columbia River in the same year. In 1805, Lewis and Clark called the bay *Shallow Nitch*. In 1841, Cmdr. Charles Wilkes charted it as *Kutzule Bay*. It has appeared on some maps, in error, as *Grass Bay*.

Grays Harbor *(Ts.16-18N;Rs.9-12W)*
A protected saltwater harbor on Pacific Ocean, at the mouth of Chehalis River, southwest Grays Harbor County. This large, important harbor is fed by many rivers and creeks from the north, south, and east. It is navigable by ocean-going ships in dredged channels. It was named for Robert Gray, who discovered the harbor on May 7, 1792; he named it *Bullfinch's Harbor*. It had been named *Puerto Grek* by Martinez y Zayas, and, in 1825, was called *Whitbey Harbour* by David Douglas. However, the original name has been retained.

Grays Harbor City *(S.5;T.17N;R.10W)*
Railroad station 3 miles west of Hoquiam, on Grays Harbor, southwest Grays Harbor County. In 1889, it was boomed by eastern capitalists, but failed

to develop. The name was borrowed from Grays Harbor. (*see* Grays Harbor)

Grays Harbor County
This county in west central Washington is bounded on the north by Mason and Jefferson counties; on the east by Mason and Thurston counties; on the south by Lewis and Pacific counties; and on the west by Pacific Ocean. On April 14, 1854, the Territorial Legislature created Chehalis County, which included the present area of Grays Harbor County. In February 1907, the State Legislature created this 1,905-sq.-mile county from the wester portion of Chehalis County. (*see* Grays Harbor)

Grays Point *(Ss.10,11;T.9N;R.9W)*
Point on Columbia River, 2 miles east of Knappton, south central Pacific County. In 1841, it was named by Cmdr. Charles Wilkes for Robert Gray, who discovered Columbia River. An earlier name applied by Sir Edward Belcher in 1839 was *Cape Broughton*, for Lieut. W. R. Broughton.

Grays River *(S.13;T.10N;R.8W)*
Town on Grays River, 46-1/2 miles west of Longview, northwest Wahkiakum County. This Finnish community of loggers, fishermen, and dairymen is named for the river on which it is located. (*see* Grays River (river))

Grays River *(T.10N;R.8W)*
The stream of the river rises on the boundary ridge between Lewis and Wahkiakum counties; flows 20 miles to Columbia River at Grays Bay. The Indian name was *Moolhool* or *Moohool*. In 1841, Cmdr. Charles Wilkes charted the stream as *Ebokwol River*. The present name is for Robert Gray, who discovered and named Columbia River.

Grayville (Lincoln County) *see* Crystal City

Great Bend (Douglas, Lincoln, Grant counties) *see* Big Bend

Great Falls of the Columbia (Klickitat County) *see* The Dalles

Great Peninsula (Kitsap, Mason counties) *see* Indian Peninsula

Great Plains of the Columbia (Eastern Washington and Oregon, Western Idaho) *see* Inland Empire

Great Shute (Skamania County) *see* Cascades

Greek George's Bay (Kitsap County) *see* Fletcher Bay

Green Island (Clallam County) *see* Tatoosh Island

Green Island (Jefferson County) *see* Destruction Island

Green Lake *(Ss.5-8;T.25N;R.4E)*
A shallow, 255-acre lake adjoining a residential area in Woodland Park, 2 miles north of Lake Union, north central Seattle, King County. It is used extensively for recreation. The name, which was applied by early Seattle settlers, describes the coloration of the lake's water. In 1946, William F. Devin, mayor of Seattle at one time, tried to have the lake officially named for Seattle banker Joshua Green. It is called *Lake Green* on an 1857 Washington Territorial map, published by the surveyor-general of the Territory. The Indian name was *Du-tlec*.

Green Lake *(Mt. Rainier National Park)*
A small lake surrounded by heavy forest, elevation 3,000 ft., in the course of Ranger Creek, 1-1/2 miles south of the north park boundary, northwest corner of the park. The name given by park officials is appropriate, as the lake appears to be emerald green in the shade of the heavy forest cover.

Green Lake *(S.15;T.37N;R.10E.uns)*
Mt. Baker National Forest lake 11-1/2 miles north of Marblemount, south central Whatcom County. It should not be confused with another Green Lake, in the northwest part of the county. Reports indicate that it was named by U.S. Forest Service officers for its dark green color.

Green Lake *(Ss.9,10;T.39N;R.3E)*
A small lake 3-1/2 miles south of Lynden, in lower Nooksack River drainage, west central Whatcom County. It was locally named for James Green, a very early settler.

Green Mountain *(S.20;T.10N;R.10E)*
A Gifford Pinchot National Forest peak, elevation 5,007 ft., 11 miles northwest of Mt. Adams summit in Cispus River drainage, extreme northeast Skamania County. The name was chosen because of heavy forest cover on most of the mountain's slope.

Green Mountain *(Ts.30,31N;R.8E)*
A Mt. Baker National Forest peak, elevation 4,441 ft. and 9 miles long,

between South Fork, Canyon Creek, and South Fork, Stillaguamish River, central Snohomish County. It was locally named because it is covered with an unbroken canopy of green forest.

Green Mountain Lake
(S.29;T.10N;R.10E)

A 4-acre lake, elevation 4,000 ft., on the south slope of Green Mountain, Gifford Pinchot National Forest, northeast Skamania County. (*see* Green Mountain, Skamania County)

Green Point *(S.2;T.30N;R.5W)*

Heavily-wooded point on Strait of Juan de Fuca, 5-1/2 miles east of Port Angeles, northeast Clallam County. In 1854, the U.S. Coast Survey gave the point its descriptive name.

Green Point *(S.28;T.21N;R.1E)*

An east shore point of Carr Inlet, 9 miles northwest of Steilacoom, northwest Pierce County. In 1841, Cmdr. Charles Wilkes named the point for Daniel Green, a gunner's mate on the Wilkes Expedition.

Green Point *(S.7;T.36N;R.3W)*

Point at the southeast end of Spieden Island, in Spieden Channel, northwest San Juan County. In 1858, the descriptive name was placed on British Admiralty charts by Capt. Henry Richards, R.N.

Green Point *(S.28;T.35N;R.1E)*

A northwest shore point of Fidalgo Island, 1-1/2 miles west of Anacortes, northwest Skagit County. In 1858, the name was first applied to British Admiralty charts by Capt. Richards, R.N., because of heavy vegetation on the point.

Green River *(Ts.19-23N;Rs.4-12E)*

The stream of the river heads on the west slope of Cascade Mountain summit, near Green Pass, southeast King County; flows west through Auburn, then north through Kent to join Cedar River at Black River Junction, forming Duwamish River. Green River Gorge, a 5-mile canyon which is deep and scenic, is intermediate in its course. The river is an important source of domestic water for Tacoma. It was named in pioneer days because both the water and much of the canyon's rock formation is green. Indian dialect names for the river included *Noo-sco-pe* and *Nook-han-noo.*

Green River Gorge *(T.21N;R.7E)*

A deep, scenic gorge running

through a sandstone and shale canyon for 5 to 6 miles in Green River, 6 miles east of Enumclaw, south central King County. The water is green, and the rock has been eroded into fanciful patterns. (*see* Green River, King County)

Green River Siding (King County) *see* Palmer

Greenacres *(S.18;T.25N;R.45E)*

An area of garden tracts, once abundantly irrigated, but later unable to secure enough water, 3 miles northwest of Liberty Lake, east central Spokane County. The name was quite appropriate when selected by local farmers.

Greenbank *(S.8;T.30N;R.2E)*

Town on the east shore of Whidbey Island, west entrance to Holmes Harbor, south Island County. In 1906, the name was chosen by Calvin Phillips of Seattle, for his boyhood home on the eastern seaboard.

Greens Spur (Whatcom County) *see* Standard

Greenwater *(S.10;T.19N;R.9E)*

A camp ground and public lodge at the confluence of White and Greenwater rivers, 20-1/2 miles east of Enumclaw, northeast Pierce County. It was named for Greenwater River, on which it is located. (*see* Greenwater River)

Greenwater Lakes (Pierce County) *see* Meeker Lakes

Greenwater River
(Ts.18,19N;Rs.9-11E)

The stream of the river rises in several branches at Cascade Mountain summit, north and south of Government Meadows; flows 17 miles east to White River at Greenwater, forming part of the boundary between King and Pierce counties. The name is for the color of the water during winter and late fall months when snow is not melting at the higher elevations.

Greenwood *(S.6;T.17N;R.5W)*

2-1/2 miles southeast of Elma, southeast Grays Harbor County. It was named by John Landers, oldest settler in the area, for Greenwood Timber Company, which logged here in the early 1900s.

Greenwood Lake *(S.34;T.14N;R.7E)*

7-1/2-acre lake, elevation 4,450 ft., 9 miles northeast of Randle, Gifford Pinchot National Forest, northeast Lewis County. The name is appropriate, as the lake is surrounded by heavy old-growth,

coniferous timber.

Gregor *(Adams County) see* McGregor

Greider Lakes *(S.36;T.29N;R.9E)*

Two lakes 9 miles north of Index, Snoqualmie National Forest, east central Snohomish County. The smaller lake, elevation 2,900 ft., is called Lower or Little Greider, and covers 8-1/2 acres; Upper or Big Greider, elevation 2,935 ft., covers 58.4 acres. The lakes are 1,200 ft. apart. They were named by Forest Service personnel for Claude E. Greider, a former Forest Service employee.

Grenville Arch *(S.24;T.21N;R.13W)*

A rock arch on one of 3 small, adjacent islands in Pacific Ocean, 3/4 miles southwest of Point Grenville, northwest Grays Harbor County. (*see* Point Grenville)

Grenville Bay *(T.21N;Rs.12,13W)*

Bay extending 3 miles south from Point Grenville to the mouth of Wreck River, northwest Grays Harbor County. (*see* Point Grenville)

Greywolf Ridge *(T.28N;R.4W)*

A series of very high peaks 18 miles southeast of Port Angeles, northeast Olympic National Park, southeast Clallam County. Evidently, the ridge was named in 1890 by Lieut. Joseph O'Neil, on his second exploration of the Olympics. More than likely, there were wolves in the area at that time, as others reported wolves throughout the high Olympics.

Greywolf River *(Clallam County) see* Gray Wolf River

Griffin Bay *(Ts.34,35N;Rs.2,3W)*

A large, crescent-shaped bay, rocky in the southern portions, at the southeast end of San Juan Island, on San Juan Channel, at the southeast end of San Juan County. In 1841, the bay was named *Ontario Roads* by Cmdr. Charles Wilkes, for *USS Ontario*, a ship which fought in the War of 1812 and was named for Lake Ontario. His name was replaced when Capt. Henry Richards of the British Admiralty survey charted the harbor as presently named, for Charles John Griffin, farm overseer for Hudson's Bay Company on San Juan Island, in charge of Bellvue Farm. It was Griffin's pig which raided a potato patch owned by a U.S. citizen. When the irate potato-grower shot the British pig, the famous *Pig War* started. An early name for the bay, which did not persist, was *Man of War Harbor.*

Griffith *(Adams County) see* Marcellus

Griffiths Corners *(T.20N;R.35E)*

Once a town and post office between Ritzville and Marcellus, north central Adams County. It was named for William C. Griffith, an early settler, farmer, postmaster, and townsite proprietor.

Grindstone *(S.29;T.17N;R.7E)*

An early-day miners' camp prior to establishment of the park, 1-1/2 miles west of Mt. Rainier National Park, directly north of North Mowich River, southeast Pierce County. It was named by miners for a grindstone which was left here for general use, on the trail to Tahoma Mining District near North Mowich Glacier.

Grindstone Creek *(T.25N;R.15E)*

The stream of the creek rises in a basin on the southwest slope of Grindstone Mountain, 1 mile south of Cape Horn, Wenatchee National Forest, west central Chelan County; flows 2 miles southwest to Icicle Creek. It was named by U.S. Forest Supervisor A.H. Sylvester and Forest Ranger John Brender, for a small gridstone which was lost from the load of pack horse at this crossing years ago.

Grindstone Harbor
(S.23;T.36N;R.2W)

Harbor on Harney Channel, at the south end of Orcas Island's middle peninsula, central San Juan County. In 1869, it was given the present name when the only grindstone in San Juan Islands was brought here by Paul K. Hubbs. Hubbs started the first trade store on Orcas Island when settlers came here from all parts of the islands to sharpen tools. The harbor is also called *Grindstone Bay.*

Grindstone Mountain
(S.30;T.25N;R.16E)

A Wenatchee National Forest peak at the head of Grindstone Creek, 1 mile south by east of Cape Horn, southwest Chelan County. It is part of Icicle Ridge, but somewhat south of the main axis. The mountain was named by Forest Supervisor A. H. Sylvester for Grindstone Creek.

Grisdale Pond *(S.25;T.21N;R.8W)*

A 13-acre lake 5-1/4 miles south of Camp Grisdale, draining to Wynoochee River, northeast Grays Harbor County. (*see* Camp Grisdale)

Grizzly Bear Ridge *(T.7N;R.41E)*

A Umatilla National Forest ridge in Blue Mountains, 7 miles north of the Oregon boundary, southeast Columbia County. In the 1880s, it was named by cattlemen and sheepmen for the abundance of large bears in the area.

Grizzly Peak *(Ss.8,9;T.27N;R.13E)*

A 5,593-ft. peak 2 miles south of Wenatchee Pass at Cascade Mountain summit, between Okanogan and Snoqualmie national forests, on the boundary between Chelan and Snohomish counties. It was named by U.S. Forest Supervisor A. H. Sylvester, not because of bears, but for its hoary and grizzly appearance from a distance.

Goat Point *(S.31;T.24N;R.5E)*

An east shore point of Lake Washington, southeast of Medina, King County. This promontory points to the south and forms the west boundary of Meydenbauer Bay. It was named by local residents for an early landowner here. The Indian name was *Ct-ce-gwus.*

Grossoup *(S.2;T.9N;R.27E)*

Small settlement 4-1/2 miles west of Richland, east central Benton County. It was named for Benton S. Grossoup, who was active in the separation of Benton County from Yakima and Klickitat counties in 1905, and who owned land in the vicinity.

Grotto *(S.17;T.26N;R.11E)*

Settlement 4 miles northwest of Skykomish, on South Fork, Skykomish River, northeast King County. The name was chosen because the deep ravines and gorges of nearby Grotto Mountain resemble caves.

Grotto Lake *(S.9;T.26N;R.11E)*

A deep, 4-acre lake on the northeast side of Grotto Mountain, 2 miles northeast of Grotto, northeast King County. It was named for Grotto Mountain. An alternate name is *Baring Lake.* (*see* Grotto)

Grouse *(S.9;T.6N;R.43E)*

An abandoned settlement on Grouse Creek, 1-1/2 miles north of the Oregon boundary, southwest Asotin County. This name also applies to a post office in northeast Oregon, in a locality known as Grouse Flats. (*see* Grouse Creek, Asotin County)

Grouse Creek *(Ts.6,7N;R.43E)*

The stream of the creek rises near Garfield County boundary, extreme southwest Asotin County; flows southeast 8 miles into Oregon. It was named by early settlers because of the abundance of native grouse in thickets along the creek.

Grouse Creek *(T.30N;R.18E.uns)*

The stream of the creek rises in Chelan Mountains, Wenatchee National Forest, north central Chelan County; flows 3 miles southwest to North Fork, Entiat River, near its source. The name was applied by sheepmen because the brush and timber along the creek make a haven for native grouse. (*see* Grouse Creek, tributary of Chiwawa River)

Grouse Creek *(T.28N;R.17E)*

The stream of the creek rises on the west slope of Entiat Mountains; flows 3 miles southwest to Chiwawa River, between Twin and Gate creeks, Wenatchee National Forest, northwest Chelan County. In 1908, it was named by hunters in the creek valley. (*see* Grouse Creek, tributary of Entiat River)

Grouse Creek *(T.38N;R.7E.uns)*

The stream of the creek rises on the north slope of Grouse Ridge, Mt. Baker National Forest, central Whatcom County; flows 2-1/2 miles northeast to Glacier Creek. (*see* Grouse Ridge)

Grouse Ridge *(T.38N;R.7E.uns)*

Mt. Baker National Park ridge, maximum elevation 5,858 ft., extending 4-1/2 miles west from the west slope of Mt. Baker, central Whatcom County. The local name is for the abundance of native grouse on the ridge and in adjacent areas.

Grub Canyon *(Ss.21-23;T.9N;R.41E)*

A Umatilla National Forest canyon in Blue Mountains, 17 miles north of the Oregon boundary, terminating at Tucannon River, southeast Columbia County. In 1880, the name was given by settlers, for the Grubb family, which lived on Tucannon River near the mouth of the canyon.

Grundy Lake *(Skagit County)* see Grandy Lake

Guemes Channel *(T.35N;Rs.1,2E)*

A narrow channel, 4 to 5 miles long, connecting Padilla Bay with Rosario Strait, between Guemes and Fidalgo Islands, west central Skagit County. In 1841, it was named *Hornet's Harbor* by Cmdr. Charles Wilkes, for the Sloop-of-War *Hornet*, which fought in the War of 1813 under command of Capt. James Lawrence. The original Spanish name has persisted, however.

Guemes Island *(Ts.35,36N;Rs.1,2E)*

A triangular island about 8 sq. miles, directly north of Anacortes, across Guemes Channel, northwest Skagit county. In 1791, the name was applied by Lieut. Juan Fancisco de Eliza, for the Viceroy of Mexico, Senor Don Juan Vincente de Guemes Pacheco y Padillo Orcasitas y Aguayo, Conde de Revilla Gigedo. Various portions of the Count's name were appended to other features of Pacific Northwest scenery in the days of early Spanish exploration. In 1841, Cmdr. Charles Wilkes charted the feature as *Lawrence Island*, for Capt. James Lawrence, USN, who commanded the Sloop-of-War *Hornet* in the War of 1812; however, Eliza's name persisted. Applied in 1853, a local name was *Dog Island*, for an episode in which wild dogs raided the camp of Russell Peabody and Capt. Roeder, and ate all their food.

Guerriere Bay *(San Juan County) see* West Sound

Guide Meridian *(Western Washington)*

This true north-south meridian, established by U.S. Public Land Survey, runs 12 miles east of Willamette Meridian through western Washington. It was used to guide surveys in the northwest area of the state, as Willamette Meridian entered Puget Sound in the vicinity of Chimacum, Jefferson County. It is located between ranges 2 and 3 east of Willamette Meridian. The name, in common use by surveyors, indicates that it was used as a guide line in surveying the public lands of the United States.

Guler *(S.15;T.6N;R.10E)*

A small mountain community 1/4 miles south of Trout Lake, Klickitat County. It is located in an area of ice caves, which are an interesting natural phenomenon of the state. Few Washingtonians know about these caves because they are relatively isolated.

Gulf of Georgia *(San Juan County) see* Georgia Strait

Gull Reef *(S.36;T.37N;R.4W)*

A small, low reef 1/2 mile north of the west end of Spieden Island, in New Channel, northwest San Juan County. It is a feeding ground for seagulls at low tides. In 1859, the name was placed on British Admiralty charts by Capt. Henry Richards, R.N. The name would be descriptive of practically all reefs in San Juan Islands.

Gull Rock *(Ss.4,5;T.36N;R.3W)*

A small, low island, maximum elevation 30 ft., in New Channel, 1-1/2 miles northeast of Spieden Island, northwest San Juan County. It was locally named because it is a favorite nesting place for seagulls.

Guss Island *(S.26;T.36N;R.4W)*

Island in Garrison Bay, northwest end of San Juan Island, west central San Juan County. It was locally named for Guss Hoffmaster, who operated a store for the British camp during the period of joint occupancy of San Juan Islands by British and U.S. forces.

Guye Peak *(S.33;T.23N;R.11E)*

A 5,200-ft. peak 1-1/2 miles west of Cascade Mountain summit, 1-1/2 miles north of Snoqualmie Pass, east central King County. It was named for Francis M. Guye, a partner of David T. Denny in locating mining claims in this vicinity in pioneer days. One of their locations was the Industry Mine. Alternate names are *Guye Mountain* and *Guye's Mountain*.

H

Hackney Island *(S.11;T.30N;R.2E)*

Island at the east entrance to Holmes Harbor, southern Whidbey Island, 1/4 mile northwest of Rocky Point, to which it connects at extreme low tides, south central Island County. The name source is unclear, but evidently was for an early trader in the area. A name for the island used by sports fishermen is *Baby Island*.

Hadlock *(S.2;T.29N;R.1W)*

Very small settlement on the southwest shore of Port Townsend bay, northeast Jefferson County. It was formerly an important sawmill center. In 1886, it was named *Port Hadlock* by Capt. Samuel Hadlock when he platted the town. Later, postal authorities shortened the name for convenience.

Haidah Point *(S.8;T.36N;R.2W)*

An east shore point of West Sound, Orcas Island, at the north point of White Beach Bay, central San Juan County. In 1859, the name was placed on British Admiralty charts by Capt. Henry Richards, R.N., for attacks here on local Indians in early days by the fierce Haidah Indians from British Columbia.

Hahamish Harbor (Kitsap County) *see* Seabeck

Haig Creek *(T.40N;R.22E.uns)*

The stream of the creek rises on the west slope of Haig Mountain, North Cascade Primitive Area, 1-1/2 miles south of the Canadian boundary, extreme north central Okanogan County; flows north into East Fork, Ashnola River, British Columbia. Both the creek and mountain were named for Capt. R. W. Haig, R.A., astronomer on the British Boundary Commission, 1858-62. (USBGN)

Haig Mountain *(S.7;T.40N;R.23E)*

Peak directly adjoining North Cascade Primitive Area to the west, 1-1/2 miles south of the Canadian boundary, extreme north central Okanogan County. (USBGN) *(see* Haig Creek*)*

Haipwil Lake (Okanogan County) *see* Palmer Lake

Hale Passage *(Ts.37,38N;R.1E)*

Passage between Lummi Island and the mainland, opening on the east into Bellingham Bay, southwest Whatcom County. In 1841, it was named by Cmdr. Charles Wilkes for Horatio Hale, the Wilkes Expedition's philologist and ethnographer, who compiled the first publication on Chinook jargon. In 1791, Juan Francisco de Eliza named this feature *El Canal de Pacheco;* that name did not persist. A name carried on some marine charts is *Hale's Passage.*

Hales Passage *(Ts.20,21N;Rs.1,2E)*

Passage between Fox Island and the mainland, directly west of Tacoma, northwest Pierce County. In 1841, Cmdr. Charles Wilkes named the passage for Horatio Hale. *(see* Hale Passage*)*

Haley's Bay (Pacific County) *see* Baker Bay

Half Moon (Pacific County) *see* Lebam

Half Moon Creek *(T.13N;Rs.6,7W)*

The stream of the creek rises in east central Pacific County; flows west in a wide curve to Willapa River at Lebam. Local residents applied the name because the creek's pattern is a distinct loop, which roughly resembles a half moon.

Halftide Rock *(S.36;T.35N;R.3W)*

Bare rock in Griffin Bay, San Juan Channel, southeast end of San Juan Island, southwest San Juan County. It was locally named because the rock is awash at low tide. An alternate name is *Halftide Reef.*

Halfway Flat *(S.9;T.17N;R.14E)*

Snoqualmie National Forest camping site near the confluence of Naches and Bumping rivers, northwest Yakima County. This place received its name because it is roughly half way between Naches and Bumping Lake by road distance.

Hall Creek *(Ts.33-35N;Rs.34-36E)*

The stream of this rather extensive creek rises in high mountains, central Ferry County; flows 29 miles southeast to Columbia River, near Inchelium. It has 2 main forks and many tributaries. The creek was named for an early family of miners and stockmen who lived on the stream.

Hall Island *(S.14;T.34N;R.2W)*

Island on the south shore of Lopez Island, 1 mile southwest of Richardson, south central San Juan County. In 1859, the name was placed on British Admiralty charts by Capt. Henry Richards, R.N., with no reference to name source.

Haller City *(T.13N;R.5E)*

Town 12 miles north of Everett, at the junction of North and South forks, Stillaguamish River, west central Snohomish County. On April 4, 1890, it was platted under the present name, in honor of Maj. Granville O. Haller, who fought in the Indian wars and later became a prominent Seattle citizen. When it was joined to the town of Arlington in 1903, the latter name was selected by popular vote.

Haller Lake *(S.19;T.26N;R.4E)*

A 15.2-acre lake in the north suburban area of Seattle, between Puget Sound and the north end of Lake Washington, King County. A residential and recreation environment has been built around the lake. It was named for Col. Granville O. Haller, a pioneer army officer and land investor, by his son Theodore N. Haller, when he platted property here in 1905.

Halls Pass (Mt. Rainier National Park) *see* Round Pass

Hamilton *(S.14;T.35N;R.6E)*

Logging community on the north bank of Skagit River, 10 miles east of Sedro Woolley, central Skagit County. It was once "boomed" as "The Pittsburgh of the West," because of iron and coal deposits in the vicinity. The town was named for William Hamilton, who homesteaded the land on which the town was built. His land claim was in 1877; the town was incorporated in 1891, and the name was applied at that time.

Hamilton Creek *(Ts.2,3N;Rs.6,7E)*

The stream of the creek heads at Three Corner Rock, southwest Skamania County; flows 9 miles south by east to Columbia River at Hamilton Island near Greenleaf. It was named for Samuel M. Hamilton of Lower Cascades, who took a Donation Land Claim on the creek in

1850, and survived the 1856 Indian attack at the Cascades.

Hamilton Island *(Ss.29,30;T.2N;R.7E)*
Island in Columbia River, 3 miles below Boonneville Dam, southwest Skamania County. (*see* Hamilton Creek)

Hamilton Mountain
(Ss.13,24;T.2N;R.6E)
A small peak, previously volcanic, elevation 2,432 ft., 3 miles north of Columbia River at Beacon Rock, southwest Skamania County. (*see* Hamilton Creek)

Hamilton Slough *(S.14;T.35N;R.6E)*
A crescent-shaped lake with 3 segments totaling 9 acres, adjoining Hamilton, central Skagit County. It was named for Hamilton. An alternate name is *Alder Creek Slough.* (*see* Hamilton)

Hamlet *(S.32;T.16N;R.30E)*
Site of a former post office and school, 5 miles east of Othello, southwest Adams County. Both post office and school originally carried the name *Billington*. That name remains on the school, but the post office was renamed Hamlet because of confusion with Bellingham, Whatcom County. Local tradition relates that the name was chosen "in keeping with the Shakespearean atmosphere already introduced by the nearby town of Othello."

Hamma Hamma *(S.34;T.24N;R.3W)*
Small settlement on the west shore of Hood Canal, 1 mile south of Hamma Hamma River's mouth, northeast Mason County. (*see* Hamma Hamma River)

Hamma Hamma River
(T.24N;Rs.3-5W)
The stream of the river rises in high country on the northwest side of Mt. Elinor, Olympic Primitive Area, Mason County; flows east and southeast to Hood Canal at Eldon. The name is a greatly altered version of the Twana Indian name, *Du-hub-hub-bai*, which referred to a small rush called *Hub-hub* that was very plentiful along the river. (USBGN)

Hammersley Inlet *(T.20N;Rs.2,3W)*
An 8-mile-long inlet, 1/4 mile average width, extending 8 miles east from Shelton to Totten Inlet and joining Oakland Bay at Shelton, southeast Mason County. In 1841, it was named by Cmdr. Charles Wilkes for Midshipman

George W. *Hammersly*. Wilkes applied the name to also include Oakland Bay. The original Indian name was *Sa-ha-wamsh*. A local name, *Bog Skookum*, means "strong" in Chinook jargon, and refers to the tidal currents at the inlet's mouth. (USBGN)

Hammond (Douglas County) *see* Rock Island (town)

Hanaford Creek *(S.33;T.15N;R.2W)*
The stream of the creek heads south of Blue Ridge, north central Lewis County; flows east to Chehalis River, 1 mile north of Centralia. It was named in an early period of settlement for the Theophilus Hanaford family, settlers at the head of this stream.

Hanbury Point *(S.34;T.36N;R.4W)*
A northwest shore point of San Juan Island on Mosquito Pass, west central San Juan County. In 1869, it was named by Cmdr. Pender, R.N., for Ingham Henry Hanbury, R.N., assistant surgeon on British warships which were on this station during the boundary dispute over San Juan Islands.

Hancock Brook *(T.31N;R.8W)*
A very short brook entering the Strait of Juan de Fuca at Angeles Point, 3 miles northwest of Port Angeles, north central Clallam County. It was named in very early pioneer days for Samuel Hancock, who operated a trading post at Neah Bay in 1854.

Hanford *(T.13N;Rs.27,28E)*
Town on the south bank of Columbia River, 18 miles north of Richland, in the federal A.E.C. Reservation, northeast Benton County. In 1906, it was established by Hanford Irrigation & Power Company. The name is for Judge Cornelius H. Hanford, who owned a ranch within the neighborhood, and was the first U.S. district judge. The entire state was his district.

Hanging Glacier
(S.26;T.39N;R.9E.uns)
A north slope glacier of Mt. Shuksan, at the terminus of Crystal Glacier, central Whatcom County. The name was given by the earliest explorers of Mt. Shuksan, and is definitely descriptive.

Hangman Creek (Spokane County) *see* Latah Creek

Hangman's Creek *(Spokane County)* *see* Alpha

Hannaford Creek *(Lewis County) see* Hanaford Creek

Hannegan Pass
(S.8;T.39N;R.10E.uns)
Pass between the headwaters of North Fork, Nooksack River, and Chilliwack Creek; 5 miles northeast of Mt. Shuksan, Mt. Baker National Forest, north central Whatcom County. It was named for Tom Hannegan, county commissioner, who found the pass while searching for a route to herd cattle from east of Cascade Mountains.

Hanson *(S.25;T.26N;R.30E)*
Railroad station 15 miles northeast of Coulee City, northeast Grant County. In 1910, it was established by Northern Pacific Railway Company as a siding for the Farmers' Union. It was named by railroad officials for H. M. Hanson, owner of the land on which the siding was built, and builder of the first warehouse here.

Hanson Ferry *(S.5;T.6N;R.44E)*
Post Office on Grande Ronde River, 2-1/2 miles north of the Oregon boundary, southwest Asotin County. In 1882, the place was settled by John Hansen, with his wife and sons Frank and Henry. When the post office was established in 1890, it was named for Hansen, although postal authorities misspelled his name. His son Henry was the first postmaster.

Hansville *(S.16;T.28N;R.2E)*
Small settlement on Norwegian Point, between Point No Point and Foulweather Bluff, extreme north Kitsap County. Consisting largely of Norwegians, the settlement was locally named for Hans Zachariasen, an early settler.

Happy Island *(San Juan County) see* Gossip Islands

Happy Lake *(S.15;T.29N;R.8W.uns)*
Lake at the head of Happy Lake Creek, 6 miles southeast of Lake Crescent, central Clallam County. (*see* Happy Valley, Clallam County)

Happy Lake Creek *(T.29N;R.8W.uns)*
The stream of the creek heads in Happy Lake, central Clallam County; flows 3 miles northwest to Barnes Creek. (*see* Happy Valley, Clallam County)

Happy Valley *(T.29N;R.8W.uns)*
Valley of Happy Lake Creek, 6 miles southeast of Lake Crescent, cen-

tral Clallam County. It was named in early pioneer days by 3 bachelors who were among the earliest settlers; they were Andrew Abernathy, Arthur Sinclair, and Charley Hyde. The men agreed that a valley without women was a happy one, and named their valley accordingly.

Happy Valley *(Yakima County) see* Bird Creek Meadows

Harin *(Klickitat County) see* Goodnoe

Hardan *(Whatcom County) see* Maple Falls

Hardersburg *(Franklin County) see* Kahlotus

Harbor Island *(T24N;R.4E)*
An artificial island made by dredging Duwamish River channel, in the industrialized south area of Seattle, at Duwamish River mouth, south shore of Elliott Bay, King County. The East and West waterways, into which the channel is divided, furnish deep water for sea-going ships, and an excellent harbor. The descriptive name was chosen by city and county officials when the island was created. The Indian name for the river's mouth was *Ts-ekas*, meaning "muddy." A low, muddy island, which existed here before the extensive dredging, was called *Edwards Island*.

Harbor Rock *(S.5;T.34N;R.2W)*
Rock at the south entrance to Griffin Bay, near the southeast end of San Juan Island, on San Juan Channel, south central San Juan County. In 1858, the name was placed on British Admiralty charts by Capt. Henry Richards, R.N., because the rock stands at the entrance to a harbor. This feature should not be confused with Harbor Rock in West Sound, Orcas Island.

Harbor Rock *(S.8;T.36N;R.2W)*
A submerged rock at the entrance to Massacre Bay in West Sound, Orcas Island, central San Juan County. In 1859, the name was placed on British Admiralty charts, presumably because it is at the entrance to a bay which is a harbor for small craft. It should not be confused with Harbor Rock at the entrance to Griffin Bay, San Juan Island.

Hard-To-Get-To Ridge
(Ss.12,14,23;T.8N;R.42E)
A 3-mile-long ridge on Umatilla National Forest, southeast of Simpson Ridge, south central Garfield County.

The name had once been applied to Simpson Ridge because it offered difficult access. When U.S. Board on Geographic Names restored the original name to Simpson Ridge, they transferred the name to this ridge. It is shown on some maps, in error, as *Hardy Ridge*. (USBGN)

Hardscrabble Lakes
(S.36;T.24N;R.11E)
Two lakes in a mineralized area in Hardscrabble Creek, 3 miles west of Cascade Mountain summit, Snoqualmie National Forest, east central King County. The lower lake is larger and covers 10 acres; the upper lake covers 8 acres. The name is for Hardscrabble Creek.

Hardwick Point; Hardwick Spit *(Clallam County) see* Takup Point; Travis Spit

Hardy Ridge *(Garfield County) see* Simpson Ridge

Harker's Place *(Lincoln County) see* Davenport

Harlinda *(Ferry County) see* Keller

Harlowe Junction *(Thurston County) see* Gate; Gate City

Harmony *(Snohomish County) see* Cicero

Harney Channel *(T.36N;R.2W)*
Narrow channel between east end of Shaw Island and central peninsula of Orcas Island, central San Juan County. It is one of the chief navigation routes in San Juan Islands. The name was placed on British Admiralty charts by Capt. Henry Richards, R.N., for Brig. Gen. W. S. Harney, USA, who took possession of the San Juan Islands on July 7, 1859, in the name of the United States.

Haro Strait *(Ts.34-37N;Rs.4,5W)*
An irregular channel between San Juan Archipelago, and Vancouver Island and smaller adjacent Canadian islands, San Juan County. It marks the international boundary between British Columbia and San Juan County, United States. In 1790, the strait was named *Canal de Haro* or *Canal de Arro* by Lieut. Manual Quimper, for his first mate, Gonzalo Lopez de Haro. In 1847, the name was altered to its present form by Capt. Henry Kellett, R.N.

Harold Lake *(Snohomish County) see* Cadet Lake

Harrah *(S.34;T.11N;R.18E)*
Town in Toppenish Valley, 12 miles west of Toppenish, central Yakima County. In 1910, the land at this point was claimed by Julius T. Harrah, for whom the town is named.

Harriman *(Thurston County) see* Boston Harbor

Harrington *(S.15;T.23N;R.36E)*
A typical wheat town in Big Bend country, 14 miles southwest of Davenport, on Coal Creek, southeast Lincoln County. In 1879, the site was claimed as a homestead by Adam Luby. It was named for W. P. Harrington of Colusa County, California. He was a banker and land speculator, who, in 1882, purchased 1,500 acres here. In 1883, the town was platted by Horace and Emily Cutter.

Harrison *(Adams County) see* Keystone

Harrison Lake *(Jefferson County) see* Twin Lakes (near Quilcene)

Harriston *(Adams County) see* Keystone

Hart Creek
(S.2;T.13N;&S.34;T.14N;R.13E.uns)
The stream of the creek rises on the south slope of Russell Ridge, Snoqualmie National Forest, northwest Yakima County; flows 2 miles southeast to Tieton Reservoir. It was named for Elmer Hart, who ran cattle on Russell Ridge many years ago.

Hart Lake *(S.3;T.31N;R.16E.uns)*
Lake in heavily-mineralized country, elevation 3,890 ft., 4 miles northeast of Cascade Mountain summit, near the head of Railroad Creek, northwest Chelan County. It was named by miners for George Hart, who located the nearby Crown Point Mines.

Hart Lake *(S.18;T.25N;R.5W.uns)*
A 16-acre lake near the head of Duckabush River, 2 miles northwest of Mt. Steel, Olympic National Park, southeast Jefferson County. In 1890, it was named by Joseph P. O'Neil for William Hart, a pioneer who died during the year the lake was named for him. Some county maps show this lake as *Heart Lake*, but it should not be confused with the officially-named Heart Lake in Jefferson County. (USBGN)

Hart Lake *(Skagit County) see* Heart Lake

Hartford *(S.4;T.29N;R.6E)*

Town on Little Pilchuck River, 10 miles east of Everett, west central Snohomish County. On June 23, 1891, James V.VanHorn and his wife, Kate, platted the town and named it for Mrs.VanHorn's former home in Hartford, South Dakota.

Hartline
(S.1;T.25N;R.29E&S.6;T.25N;R.30E)

Town 10 miles northeast of Coulee City, northeast Grant County. In 1889, an earlier town named Parnell (Parnall), 4-1/2 miles north, was abandoned when bypassed by railroad construction. It moved to the present site, and was renamed for a pioneer, John Hartline, who owned the land on which the townsite and post office were located.

Harts Pass *(S.7;T.37N;R.18E)*

A high, pass, 30 miles northwest of Winthrop, elevation 6,197 ft., through Cascade Mountain summit; leads west through Slate Creek country, Whatcom County, and east to Methow Valley, Okanogan County. It was named for Capt. Hart, who operated the Bonita Mine in Whatcom County, and who built a narrow-gauge road up Robinson Creek through the pass to his mine.

Harts Pass *(S.12;T.37N;R.17E)*

A 6,197-ft. pass in a mineralized area at Cascade Mountain summit, Mt. Baker National Forest, southeast Whatcom County. It was named for W. R. Hart, a miner who opened a pack route across the summit from Winthrop to Slate Creek in the 1890s.

Hartstene *(S.24;T.21N;R.2W)*

A grape-growing center with several vineyards at the north end of Hartstene Island, on Jarrell Cove off Pickering Passage, southeast Mason County. *(see* Hartstene Island)

Hartstene Island *(Ts.19-21N;Rs.1,2W)*

A large, 10-mile-long island, 2 to 2-1/2 miles in average width, on the west side of Cases Inlet, east of Peale Passage and Pickering Passage, southeast Mason County. In 1841, it was named by Cmdr. Charles Wilkes for Lieut. Henry J. Hartstene. An error in the muster roll of the ship *Porpoise* shows the name as *Hartstein* and has resulted in some confusion regarding the proper spelling. Incorrect names that

have been used for this island include *Hartstein, Hartstine, Harstine,* and *Hartstone.* (USBGN)

Harvey *(S.7;T.34N;R.36E)*

Once a town on the east bank of Columbia River, 12 miles south of Kettle Falls on Quillascut Creek, northwest Stevens County. In 1884, it was founded by and named for George W. Harvey, who owned the land, having reportedly purchased it from an Indian in 1880. He was a pioneer surveyor, miner, builder, and storekeeper. He planted the first orchard on the upper Columbia River here, and built a ferry to cross the river. In 1884, a post office was secured, with Mrs. Harvey as first postmistress. Harvey later built a water-powered sawmill and grist mill on Quillascut Creek. The place was largely abandoned some time prior to 1922.

Harvey Creek *(T.38N;R.44E)*

The stream of the creek rises at Monumental Mountain, north Pend Oreille County; flows 10-1/2 miles northwest to Maitlen Creek, near Sullivan Lake. It was named for an early prospector, Carl C. Harvey, who came here in 1868, and who placer-mined for almost 40 years at Harvey's Bar.

Harvey Creek *(Ts.31,32N;Rs.37,38E)*

The stream of this 13-mile-long creek rises in 2 forks on the west slope of Huckleberry Mountains, southwest Stevens County; flows southwest to Columbia River at Cedonia. It was named for George W. Harvey. (*see* Harvey)

Hat Island *(T.35N;R.2E)*

A small, rounded mountain 1 mile east of the east end of Guemes Island in Padilla Bay, 2 miles east of Anacortes, west central Skagit County. In 1841, it was named *Peacock Island* by Cmdr. Charles Wilkes, for one of the Wilkes Expedition's ships. It was renamed by U.S. Coast Survey, and given the present name for the island's oval shape. It should not be confused with Gedney Island, Snohomish County, which has an alternate name of Hat Island.

Hat Island (Snohomish County) *see* Gedney Island

Hatchery Creek *(T.25N;R.17E)*

The stream of the creek rises at the east end of The Badlands, Wenatchee National Forest, central Chelan County; flows 2 miles east to Wenatchee River,

at the north end of Tumwater Canyon. It was named for an early fish hatchery at the creek's mouth, which was abandoned in 1907.

Hatchery Creek *(Ts.34,35N;R.8E)*

The stream of the creek rises in a mountainous area 4-1/2 miles south of Concrete, Mt. Baker National Forest, central Skagit County; flows 3-1/2 miles northeast to Finney Creek. It was named by local settlers for a trout hatchery established on the creek in 1904 by U.S. Bureau of Fisheries.

Hatchet Lake *(S.10;T.23N;R.10E)*

A 6.8-acre lake directly southeast of Preacher Mountain, Snoqualmie National Forest, east central King County. The name describes the lake's shape.

Hathaway Creek *(T.22N;Rs.9,10W)*

The stream of the creek rises 2 miles southeast of Neilton, north central Grays Harbor County; flows northwest into lower Quinault River. It was named for a homesteader, through whose land the stream runs.

Hatton *(s.20;T.15N;R.23E)*

Town 17 miles southwest of Lind, south central Adams County. In 1881, Northern Pacific Railway Company established a station here as *Twin Wells.* When a post office was installed in 1888, it was given the present name, which was also adopted by the railway for its station. The name is a combination of the last name of John D. Hackett, first postmaster, and the family name of his wife, who was Miss Ida Belle Sutton.

Haulwater *(S.19;T.4N;R.21E)*

Pioneer settlement, long since vanished, 6-1/2 miles north of Columbia River on Wood Creek (Wood Gulch), at the junction with Big Horn Canyon, southeast Klickitat County. The name is peculiarly descriptive.

Hause Creek *(T.14N;R.14E.uns)*

The stream of the creek heads on the south slope of Bethel Ridge, Snoqualmie National Forest, northwest Yakima County; flows south 2-1/2 miles to Tieton River, northeast of Tieton Reservoir. It was named for Roscoe Hause, a cattleman who lived in the Tieton area.

Hautboy Island (Skagit County) *see* Strawberry Island

Haven (*S.34;T.14N;R.25E*)

Railroad station on the north bank of Columbia River, 2 miles above Coyote Rapids in U.S. Atomic Energy Reservation, southwest Grant County. In 1908, it was named for Henry H. Haven, an early settler.

Havermale Island (*S.17;T.25N;R.43E*)

Island in Spokane River, just above Spokane Falls in Spokane, Spokane County. It was named for Rev. Samuel G. Havermale, first resident preacher in the Spokane Falls area.

Hawk Creek (*Ts.25-27N;Rs.36,37E*)

The stream of the creek rises near Davenport, central Lincoln County; flows northwest and north 29 miles to Columbia River at the site of Peach, a former town. The mouth of the creek was flooded for 3 miles when the reservoir was created behind Grand Coulee Dam. The name is an abbreviation of Hawkins, the name of an early settler on the creek.

Hawks Point (*Ss.3,4;T.14N;R.10W*)

A west shore point of Shoalwater Bay on Willapa Harbor, northwest Pacific County. It was named for the Hawk family of Chinook Indians, who lived here when the first settlers arrived.

Hawks Prairie (*T.18N;R.1W*)

Prairie 5 miles east of Olympia near St. Martins College, northeast Thurston County. The original name was *Tyrrell Prairie*, for Freeman W. Tyrrell, who was the first settler here in 1851. The present name is for a later settler, J. M. Hawk, who arrived in 1858.

Hawley (*S.25;T.25N;R.2E*)

Site on the northshore of Eagle Harbor, east central Bainbridge Island, Kitsap County. It was named for a man who purchased the site in 1924 to plat for summerhomes, but who died shortly afterward.

Hawthorne Creek (*T.30N;R.8E*)

The stream of the creek rises on Pilchuck Mountain, central Snohomish County; flows 2-1/2 miles northwest to South Fork, Stillaguamish River. It was locally named for the prevalence of native *hawthorn* along the creek bank. Evidently, the "e" was added for poetic value.

Hayes Lake (Whatcom County) *see* Galena Chain Lakes

Hayes River (*Ts.26,27N;Rs.5,6W*)

The stream of the river rises west of Mt. Anderson, Olympic National Park, 16 miles southeast of Mt. Olympus, Jefferson County; flows north to Elwha River, 2 miles south of Press Valley. In 1890, it was named by Seattle Press Expedition for Christopher O'Connell Hayes, the expedition's youngest member.

Haynie (*S.12;T.40N;R.1E*)

Place 5 miles east by south of Blaine, 2 miles south of the Canadian boundary, northwest Whatcom County. Not shown on recent maps, it was never much more than a post office for the surrounding area, as it never developed into a town. It was to have been the first station east of Blaine on the projected Blaine & Eastern Railway. The name was for Michael J. *Heney*, who planned and surveyed the railway route. When a post office was established in 1891, officials misspelled Heney's name.

Hazard (*S.33;T.28N;R.42E*)

Village 4-1/2 miles southwest of Deer Park, 1 mile east of Stevens County boundary, northwest Spokane County. It was named for R.R. Hazard, who founded the place in 1886 by erecting and operating a store.

Hazel (*S.8;T.32N;R.8E*)

Town 18 miles east of Arlington, near North Fork, Stillaguamish River, north central Snohomish County. It was formerly the site of important logging and milling industries. The original name was *Packard*, for Clayton Packard, a timberman. When the town was platted and named by Peter D. McMartin in 1903, he used the name of his first child.

Hazel Point (*S.35;T.26N;R.1W*)

A southeast tip point of Toandos Peninsula on Hood Canal, southeast Jefferson County. On May 11, 1792, Capt. George Vancouver applied the name because of "many hazel trees." However, he placed the name on the southwest point of the peninsula, which now is called Tskutsko Point. In 1841, Cmdr. Charles Wilkes charted the southeast point as *Squalus Point*. In 1847, Capt. Henry Kellet restored Vancouver's name, this time applying it to this area.

Hazelmere (*SW1/4 of T.32N;R.36E*)

Once a town on the west bank of Columbia River near Rogers Bar, east central Ferry County. When the river was flooded by Grand Coulee Dam, this town was classified as being in a "slide area," and the place was vacated. The name remains on a nearby school. The post office was given this name for Hazel Dana, who taught here at the time

Hazelwood (*S.20;T.24N;R.5E*)

Community on the east shore of Lake Washington, 3-1/2 miles north of Renton, west central King County. The place was established as "Hillman's Garden of Eden Addition to Seattle." The garden, however, did not flourish. In 1907, when a post office was established, residents were invited to propose names. A public drawing from this list resulted in the present name. It is quite appropriate, as there is a considerable amount of native hazel in the neighborhood.

He He Mountain (*S.34;T.40N;R.29E*)

A Chelan National Forest peak 6 miles west of Chesaw, on the state road to Oro, northeast Okanogan County. It was named by pioneers for nearby Hee Hee Stone. Map makers altered the spelling. (*see* Hee Hee Stone)

Head of the Bay (Kitsap County) *see* Gorst

Heart Lake (*T.28N;R.8W.uns*)

Small, heart-shaped lake on the north slope of High Divide, at the head of Bridge Creek, Olympic National Forest, south central Clallam County. It is located in an area with many other small lakes. This lake should not be confused with Hart Lake, Jefferson County, which is shown on certain county maps as Heart Lake. In 1890, Lieut. Joseph P. O'Neil named the lake for its shape.

Heart Lake (*S.18;T.25N;R.5W*)

Lake at the head of Duckabush River, Olympic National Park, south central Jefferson County. The descriptive name was applied by Lieut. Joseph P. O'Neil on his 1890 expedition, for the lake's shape.

Heart Lake (*S.14;T.12N;R.10E*)

A 4-acre lake, elevation about 5,700 ft., 9-1/4 miles southeast of Packwood, east central Lewis County. It was named for the strong resemblance of its shape to a human heart.

Heart Lake (*S.36;T.35N;R.1E*)

A 60.8-acre lake on Fidalgo Island,

2-1/2 miles south of Anacortes, west central Skagit County. The name is fairly descriptive of the lake's contour. An alternate name is *Hart Lake*. This lake should not be confused with a smaller lake by the same name north of Hamilton.

Heart Lake *(S.5;T.36N;R.7E)*

A 15-acre lake 8-3/4 miles north of Hamilton, north central Skagit County. The name is quite descriptive of the lake's shape. This lake should not be confused with a much larger lake of the same name south of Anacortes.

Heart Lake *(S.27;T.10N;R.5E)*

A 5-acre lake, elevation 4,645 ft., 3-1/2 miles north of Spirit Lake, Gifford Pinchot National Forest, extreme northwest Skamania County. The lake was named for its shape, which has a fair resemblance to a heart.

Heart Lake *(S.32;T.37N;R.7E.uns)*

Lake almost on the north boundary of Skagit County, Mt. Baker National Forest, south central Whatcom County. Its shape resembles that of a heart. The name became fixed through long, local usage.

Heath Bay (Pierce County) *see* Steilacoom Waterway

Heather Lake
(Ss.3,4;T.27N;R.13E.uns)

A beautiful, 200-acre lake at the head of Lake Creek, 1/2 mile east of Cascade Mountain summit, Wenatchee National Forest, northwest Chelan County. It occupies the lower end of a hanging, glacial valley or cirque, under the steep east slope of Grizzly Peak. The lake is bordered on 3 sides by dense forest and on the west by a talus slope. U.S. Forest Supervisor A. H. Sylvester named the lake from a map, assuming that it would be bordered by heather, like most lakes in the area. It is probably the forester's only misnomer in naming places on Wenatchee National Forest.

Hedley Spit *(S.26;T.26N;R.2E)*

A hook-shaped spit with Point Monroe on the north extremity, 1 mile east of Port Madison (town), northeast tip of Bainbridge Island, east central Kitsap County. It was named for an early settler and land claimant. A local name, still used by old-timers, is *Jack Spit*.

Hee Haw Creek *(T.26N;R.8W)*

The stream of the creek heads in Lake Beauty, west of Mt. Seattle, Olympic National Park, central Jefferson County; flows 4-1/2 miles west to Queets River. The name was evidently applied by some unrecorded humorist to harmonize with nearby Hee Hee Creek, which has an Indian origin.

Hee Hee Creek *(T.26N;R.8W)*

The stream of the creek rises 6 miles south of Mt. Olympus summit, Olympic National Park, central Jefferson County; flows 3-1/2 miles east to Queets River. In Chinook jargon, "hee hee" means "to laugh" or "laughter." The name might therefore be interpreted as "laughing creek."

Hee Hee Stone *(S.34;T.40N;R.29E)*

An historic, large boulder adjacent to He He Mountain, about 6 miles west of Chesaw, Chelan National Forest, northeast Okanogan County. Shaped somewhat like a human body, it was worshipped by local Indians. Before it was dynamited and destroyed by vandals, the rock was usually covered with trinkets deposited by Indians: leather straps, arrow points, handkerchiefs, old clothes, and small coins. The name is from Chinook jargon, meaning "laugh," "mirth" or "joy." Evidently, it was connected with one of the legends which related to the stone.

Hegler Creek *(T.26N;R.17E)*

The stream of this small, intermittent creek rises between Nason Creek and Wenatchee River, 3 miles southeast of Wenatchee Lake, Wenatchee National Forest, south central Chelan County; flows 2 miles east to Wenatchee River at Plain. It was named for William Hegler, an employee of Great Northern Railway Company, who owned land here, and who lived in Leavenworth.

Hein Bank *(T.33N;R.3W)*

A dangerous, off-shore shoal, 2-1/4 to 5 fathoms deep, in Strait of Juan de Fuca, 7 miles south of the south shore of San Juan Island, 8 miles west by north of Smith Island, San Juan County. In 1854, it was named by A. D. Bache, superintendent of U.S. Coast Survey, for Samuel Hein, his general disbursing agent.

Heisen *(S.19;T.4N;R.3E)*

Community 15 miles northeast of Vancouver, north central Clark County. It was named for Alexander Heisen, who

crossed the plains with an ox team in 1852. It is shown on some current maps, in error, as *Heisson*.

Heisson (Clark County) *see* Heisen

Heislers Creek *(T.38N;Rs.5,6E)*

The stream of the creek heads 3 miles south of Canyon Lake, west central Whatcom County; flows southwest 2-1/2 miles to Middle Fork, Nooksack River. It was named for Charles and Albert Heisler, who homesteaded near the creek's mouth in 1909.

Helena Creek *(T.31N;R.10E)*

The stream of the creek rises in Helena Lake, 8-1/2 miles south of Darrington, northeast Snohomish County; flows 5 miles north to North Fork, Clear Creek, Mt. Baker National Forest. (*see* Helena Peak)

Helena Lake *(S.31;T.31N;R.10E)*

A small, mountain lake in Helena Creek, 4 miles north of Silverton, north central Snohomish County. It covers 27-1/2 acres, and is over 100 ft. deep. (*see* Helena Peak)

Helena Peak
(Ss.31,36;T.31N;Rs.9,10E)

Peak at the head of Helena Creek, 8-1/2 miles south of Darrington, north central Snohomish County. It was named by a party of early prospectors from Helena Montana, who came in through Coal Creek Pass.

Heliotrope Ridge
(Ss.10,14,15;T.38N;R.7E.uns)

Ridge on the northwest slope of Mt. Baker, between Bastile and Grouse ridges, central Whatcom County. In 1911, it was named by H. C. Engberg and C. C. Wright for the profusion of blooming valerian on the ridge and slopes. The blue flowers of valerian somewhat resemble heliotrope.

Helix Point (Jefferson County) *see* Mill Point

Hell Gate *(T.28N;R.33E)*

Once a narrow, turbulent gorge in Columbia River, 3 miles east of San Poil River's mouth, Ferry and Lincoln counties. It was flooded out by the reservoir created by Grand Coulee Dam. The name was applied by pioneers because of its rough waters, caused by a crooked channel, jutting point, and several rock islands. It certainly wasn't heaven for early river navigators.

Hell-roaring Creek *(T.7N;R.11E.uns)*

The stream of the creek rises in Mazama Glacier, southeast slope of Mt. Adams, southwest Yakima County; flows a precipitous 5 miles east to Big Muddy Creek, a few miles from Klickitat River. The very descriptive name, applied by early settlers, will be understood by any person who witnesses the violent turbulence of this glacial stream during periods of hot summer weather when Mazama Glacier is rapidly melting.

Hell-roaring Glacier (Yakima County) *see* Mazama Glacier

Hellgate *(S.36;T.28N;R.33E)*

Post Office 3-1/2 miles south of Columbia River, northwest Lincoln County. When a post office was established, it carried the name *Layton* Because it was confused with Dayton in Columbia County, postal officials changed the nam, in 1894, to Hellgate. The series of rapids in Columbia River for which the place was named has since been flooded out by Grand Coulee Dam.

Helmet Butte *(T.31N;R.15E.uns)*

A 6,900-ft. peak directly north of Buck Creek Pass at Cascade Mountain summit, between northwest Chelan and northeast Snohomish counties. In 1908, it was named by U.S. Forest Supervisor A. H. Sylvester for its resemblance to a helmet.

Helsing *(S.6;T.15N;R.4W)*

Town near Chehalis River, 2 miles southwest of Rochester, extreme southwest Thurston County. Members of a Finnish settlement here wanted the placed called *Helsingfors*. The railway named its station *Helsoning Junction*, and the postal authorities called the post office *Helsing*. The post office name became commonly accepted as the town's proper name.

Helsoning Junction (Thurston County) *see* Helsing; Helsing Junction

Heminger City *(T.9N;R.28E)*

Town in Hanford Atomic Energy Commission project area, Greater Richland Community, west of Enterprise, on either side of Van Giesen Road, east central Benton County. It was named for Carl Heminger, a local landowner and builder. In December 1953, it joined with Enterprise to form West Richland.

Hemlock Pass *(S.25;T.23N;R.10E)*

A 4,800-ft. pass extending from the head of Denny Creek to Melakwa Lake, about 3 miles northwest of Snoqualmie Pass, east central King County. On June 15, 1916, it was named by The Mountaineers for an abundance of mountain hemlock growing around the pass.

Hemlock Peak (King County) *see* Bryant Peak

Henderson Bay *(Ts.21,22N;R.1E)*

Bay extending 6 miles northeast from Carr Inlet to Burley Lagoon, northwest Pierce County. (see Henderson Inlet)

Henderson Inlet *(T.19,20N;R.1W)*

A narrow inlet, 5-1/2 miles long, extending south from Danas Passage to a point 3 miles northeast of Olympia, north central Thurston County. In 1841, it was named by Cmdr. Charles Wilkes for Quartermaster James Henderson, a member of the Wilkes Expedition.

Henry Creek *(T.26N;R.15E)*

The stream of this small, steep creek heads on the northeast slope of Jim Hill Mountain, Wenatchee National Forest, southwest Chelan County; plunges 2 miles north to Nason Creek, opposite Berne Station on Great Northern Railway. It was named by U.S. Forest Supervisor A. H. Sylvester with the first name of one of his forest rangers.

Henry Island *(T.36N;R.4W)*

A fairly large, H-shaped island in Haro Strait, northwest of San Juan Island, 1-1/2 miles west of Roche Harbor, San Juan County. In 1841, the island was named by Cmdr. Charles Wilkes for Midshipman Wilkes Henry, who was killed by natives in the Fiji Islands on July 18, 1840.

Hen's Nest (Lewis County) *see* Pleasant Valley

Herman Peak (Whatcom County) *see* Mt. Herman

Herrin Creek *(T.37N;R.33E)*

The stream of the creek heads on the west slope of Cooke Mountain, central Ferry County; flows west for 5 miles through Colville National Forest, to the south end of Curlew Lake. It was named for George Herrin, a blind Indian whose allotment bordered the south end of Curlew Lake. The name is spelled *Herron Creek* on some maps and records.

Herron Creek (Ferry County) *see* Herrin Creek

Herron Island *(S.32;T.21N;R.1W)*

A 350-acre island in Case Inlet, 1-1/2 miles east of Hartstene Island, northwest Pierce County. In 1841, Cmdr. Charles Wilkes named the island for Lewis Herron, a petty officer on one of the Wilkes Expedition ships.

Herron Lake *(S.33;T.21N;R.1W)*

A 9.9-acre lake 1 mile south of Herron and 2-1/2 miles west of Lake Bay, northwest Pierce County. It was named for nearby Herron Island. An alternate name, now in limited use, was *Clarks Lake*. (see Herron Island)

Herzog's Lake (Clark County) *see* Steigerwald Lake

Hessong Rock *(Mt. Rainier National Park)*

A 6,149-ft. rock on the northwest slope of Mt. Rainier, midway between Mother Mountain and Ptarmigan Ridge, west of Spray Park, northwest area of the park. It was named for a Lake Kapowsin photographer who took many excellent photographs in the park. (USBGN)

Hewitt Lake (Thurston County) *see* Hewitts Lake

Hewitts Lake *(S.36;T.18N;R.2W)*

A 26.6-acre lake in an area of other small lakes 2 miles southeast of Olympia, Thurston County. Located in a kettle-like depression, it is 60 ft. deep. The name honors Judge C. C. Hewitt, who purchased the John N. Low land claim here. An earlier name was *Lowe Lake*, a misspelling of Low's name.

Heyer's Point (King County) *see* Point Heyer

Hidden *(S.12;T.2N;R.1E)*

Community 2 miles north of Vancouver, southwest Clark County. The original name was *St. John*. When Northern Pacific Railway built a branch here in 1905, railway officials changed it to the present name because there already was a St. John railway point in Oregon. The name was for L. M. Hidden, who built the branch line to this place on contract, at the suggestion of Trainmaster John T. Foster of Vancouver.

Hidden Lake *(S.23;T.27N;R.16E)*

Small lake, popular with fishermen, on a bench 500 ft. above the southwest shore of Wenatchee Lake, in the course of Plainview Creek, west central Chelan County. U.S. Forest Supervisor A. H. Sylvester placed this name on the map, using a name which had been in use for years. It evidently relates to the fact that the lake is not seen until the viewer is close to its shores.

Hidden Lake *(S. 11;T. 28N;R. 9W. uns)*

A 5-acre lake, elevation 2,825 ft., 2 miles southeast of Sol Duc Hot Springs, Olympic National Park, south central Clallam County. The name is descriptive, as the lake can only be seen at close range, unless viewed from the air.

Hidden Lake *(Mt. Rainier National Park)*

A 7-acre lake, elevation 5,926 ft., between Sunrise and Prospector creeks, White River Park, northeast sector of the park. In 1913, the descriptive name was chosen by Wm. F Tufts, topographic engineer, because the lake is rather concealed by forest and terrain. (USBGN)

Hidden Lake *(S. 25;T. 35N;R. 12E. uns)*

A small, secluded lake 3-1/2 miles southwest of Eldorado mountain summit, Mt. Baker National Forest, northeast Skagit County. Together with a creek and several high peaks, the lake was named for seclusion among towering mountain ranges in the area.

Hidden Lake (Whatcom County) *see* Ipsoot Lake

Hidden Lake Creek *(T. 35N;R. 13E. uns)*

The stream of the creek rises in Hidden Lake, Mt. Baker National Forest, northeast Skagit County; flows 2-1/2 miles southeast to North Fork, Cascade River. It is named for the secluded lake in which its waters originate.

Hidden Lake Peaks
(Ss. 23-26;T. 35N;R. 12E. uns)

Rugged peaks, elevations to 7,000 ft., 4 miles southwest of Eldorado mountain summit, Mt. Baker National Forest, northeast Skagit County. They were named by early miners because of their seclusion among other towering mountains, and for Hidden Lake in their midst.

Hidden Lakes *(S. 36;T. 7N;R. 8E. uns)*

Three small lakes spaced at 400 ft. and 900 ft. with elevations from 4,050 ft. to 4,100 ft., 7-1/2 miles north of Big Lava Bed, Gifford Pinchot National Forest, central Skamania County. No. 1, or Upper Hidden Lake, covers 10 acres;

No. 2, or Lower Hidden Lake, has an area of 5 acres; and No. 3, or Little Hidden Lake, is only 2.4 acres in extent. The name is descriptive, as the lakes are concealed in heavy timber stands.

Higgins Creek *(T. 33N;R. 8E)*

The stream of the creek heads on Mt. Higgins, Mt. Baker National Forest, south central Skagit County; flows 4-1/2 miles north and northwest to Deer Creek. (*see* Mt. Higgins)

Higgins Mountain (Skagit County) *see* Mt. Higgins

High Box Mountain (Kittitas County) *see* Box Ridge

High Pass *(S. 11;T. 30N;R. 15E. uns)*

A 6,800-ft. pass at Cascade Mountain summit, 2-1/2 miles south of Buck Creek Pass, in Glacier Peak Wilderness Area, between northeast Snohomish and northwest Chelan counties. It was named by U.S. Forest Supervisor A. H. Sylvester, because it is very high for a pass over Cascade Mountain summit.

High Point *(S. 25;T. 24N;R. 6E)*

Small town 2 miles east of Issaquah, west central King County. In 1905, it was established as a sawmill center and named by John Lovegren. The name is descriptive, as the place was at the top of a steep grade on the Snoqualmie branch of Northern Pacific Railway. It was nicknamed *Little Sweden*, and Swedish was the prevailing language.

Highlands (Lewis County) *see* Jackson Prarie

Highwood Lake *(S. 17;T. 39N;R. 9E)*

A 2-acre, mountain lake, elevation 4,100 ft., 3-1/2 miles northwest of Mt. Shuksan summit, 1-1/2 miles southwest of Mt. Baker Lodge, north central Whatcom County. It is joined by a stream with Picture Lake; both lakes are drained by Bagley Creek, and are often referred to as *Bagley Lakes*. Reportedly, this poetic name was applied to the lake by a party of mountain climbers some years ago.

Hilda *(S. 35;T. 31N;R. 9W)*

Railroad point 12 miles west of Port Angeles and 1-1/2 miles south of Strait of Juan de Fuca, north central Clallam County. It was not a permanent community, and does not appear on most maps. The locally-applied name was for Hilda Hulgerson, a popular waitress in a nearby logging camp.

Hildebrand (Snohomish County) *see* Cicero

Hillhurst *(s. 36;T. 19N;R. 2E)*

A Northern Pacific Railway station on Ft. Lewis Army Post, 4 miles east of Army Headquarters, central Pierce County. When the railroad was built in 1873, the place was named for a hill on the line which caused train delays. Even after the stretch was eliminated by rerouting, the name was retained. An alternate version explaining the name source states that the word is a combination using the name of a part-owner of the townsite -- Hillsdale -- with "hurst" for adjacent woodlands.

Hillhurst Lake *(S. 36;T. 19N;R. 2E)*

A 6-acre, marshy and shallow lake on Ft. Lewis Army Post, directly south of McChord Field, west central Pierce County. (*see* Hillhurst)

Hillman (Thurston County) *see* Boston Harbor

Hillman City *(T. 24N;R. 4E)*

Originally an organized town between Columbia City and Seward Park, south of Seattle, west central King County. In 1921, it was annexed to Seattle under a state law which compelled a community entirely surrounded by an incorporated city to become a part thereof. It was named for C. D. Hillman, a prominent Seattle realtor, who was instrumental in organizing the town.

Hillsdale *(t. 20N;R. 2E)*

A southeast suburb of Tacoma, northwest Pierce County. When settled in 1886, mostly by German families, it was named for Prince von Bismarck-Schonhausen of Germany, "The Iron Chancellor." It retained this name when annexed to Tacoma. At the start of World War I, the German name surrendered to the present one. A 4-block street in the area still bears the original name.

Hillside *(S. 33;T. 15N;R. 19E)*

Railroad station 10 miles north of Yakima, on Yakima River, extreme southeast Kittitas County. In 1905, it was named by railroad officials with a compound word which suited the landscape.

Hillyard *(S. 27;T. 26N;R. 43E)*

A northeast suburb of Spokane, central Spokane County. On October 25, 1892, a townsite was platted here by Leland D. and Kate C. Westfall. It was named to honor James J. Hill of Great Northern Railway Company, through whose influence a very large set of railroad shops was built here when Hillyard was an independent town. In 1825, John Work of Hudson's Bay Company named the site *Horse Plains*.

Himes *(S.21;T.19N;R.10E)*

Campground on Greenwater River, 3-1/2 miles east of the river's confluence with White River, southeast King County. The place was named for George H. Himes, and was dedicated to him on August 31, 1934, by Prof. Edmond S. Meany at a public ceremony. At that time, Himes was the sole survivor of the party that brought the first wagon train through Naches Pass in October 1853. (USBGN)

Himmelgeisterhorn
(S.7;T.38N;R.12E.uns)

A sharp, snow-covered pinnacle in the southern Picket Range, at the head of Crescent Creek, Mt. Baker National Park, east central Whatcom County. It is one of a group of mountains known as Crescent Creek Spires. Prior to 1961, it was possibly the last unclimbed, major peak in the Cascade Range. (*see* Ottohorn)

Hindoo Creek *(T.15N;R.13E.uns)*

The stream of the creek rises on Nelson Ridge, Snoqualmie National Forest, northwest Yakima County; flows 7 miles east to Rattlesnake Creek, 9 miles north of Tieton Reservoir. With its tributary, Little Hindoo Creek, it drains several sections south and southeast of Mt. Aix. Both the creek and its tributary are named for a Hindoo sheepherder who was killed in this area in 1897 when he tried to stop a stampede of 2,000 sheep.

Hintzville Beaver Ponds
(S.23;T.24N;R.2W)

Several small beaver ponds in Stavis Creek, with a total area of about 3 acres, 1/4 mile south of Hintsville, west central Kitsap County. The local name is obviously descriptive.

Hiram M. Chittenden Locks
(T.25N;R3E)

Locks in the northwest area of Seattle, at the junction of Shilshole Bay with Lake Washington Ship Canal, King County. They are operated by government employees, and, until recently, were known as *Government Locks*. Large ships and other crafts enter Seat-

tle's lakes through these locks. In 1917, they started operating, raising ships as much as 26 ft. above tide levels on Shilshole Bay. The large lock is 825 ft. long and 80 ft. wide; the small lock is 150 ft. long and 30 ft. wide. The structure was named for Gen. Hiram M. Chittenden, USA, Corps of Engineers, who was a strong advocate of the present location and prompt construction of the locks. Largely as a result of his efforts, Congress passed a Rivers & Harbor Act on June 25, 1910, which included federal participation with the city and county in this project.

Hoch Spur (Spokane County) *see* Denison

Hockinson *(S.19;T.3N;R.3E)*

Settlement 10 miles north of Columbia River, 3 miles east of Bush Prairie, south central Clark County. The original name was *Eureka*, which was used by a Norwegian Lutheran congregation for Martin Luther's exclamation when he discovered the nucleus of the religious doctrine which he founded. Old-time Norwegian residents still adhere to that name. When a post office was installed in 1890, the present name was applied, honoring the first postmaster, Ambrosius Hockinson.

Hoffstedt Creek *(T.10N;Rs.2-4E)*

The stream of the creek heads in extreme northwest Cowlitz county; flows 15 miles west to North Fork, Toutle River, near St. Helens. It was named through local usage for an early homesteader.

Hog Island (Skagit County) *see* Vendovi Island

Hogback Ridge
(Ss.24-26;T.8N;R.43E)

Umatilla National Forest ridge 9 miles southwest of Cloverland, southwest Asotin County. It was named by pioneer settlers for a fancied resemblance to a hog's back.

Hogeye Hollow *(T.9N;R.38E)*

Canyon 3 to 7 miles east of Waitsburg, running west to Touchet River, southwest Columbia County. In 1880, it was named by settlers for ''Hogeye'' Davis, who raised hogs and whose eyes are reported to have resembled those of his livestock.

Hogum Bay *(T.19N;Rs1,2W)*

A shallow bay in southwest Nisqually Flats on Nisqually Reach, north

central Thurston County. It was locally named when Northern Pacific Railway started to build through the area. A few people who quickly acquired all the land along the right-of-way were called ''hogs'' by those who tried to make land purchases later.

Hoh *(S.21;T.26N;R.13W)*

Small community on Hoh River, 2 miles from the river's mouth, on Pacific Ocean, west central Jefferson County. The name is a much-simplified form of the Indian name, which was *Oh-la-qu-hoh* or *Hooh-oh-ah-lat*, meaning ''can speak Quinault at that place.''

Hoh Creek *(T.28N;R.9W)*

The stream of this short creek heads in Hoh Lake, Olympic National Park, south central Clallam County; flows southeast through north central Jefferson County to Hoh River, 4 miles southeast of Bogachiel Peak, a distance of about 3 miles. It was named for Hoh River. A former name, *Lake Creek*, appears on some rather recent maps. (USBGN) (*see* Hoh River)

Hoh Head *(S.11;T.26N;R.14W)*

Point on Pacific Ocean, 2-1/2 miles north of Hoh River mouth, west central Jefferson County. (*see* Hoh)

Hoh Indian Reservation
(t.26N;R.13W)

A small, 443-acre reservation on the south bank of Hoh River at its mouth, on Pacific Ocean, 40 miles south of Cape Flattery, northwest Jefferson County. It has a small resident population with no tribal organization. On September 11, 1893, it was established by an Executive Order, and given the tribal name. (*see* Hoh)

Hoh Lake *(S.30;T.28N;R.8W.uns)*

An Olympic National Park lake covering almost 19 acres, maximum depth 44 ft., 1/2 mile southwest of Bogachiel Peak, south central Clallam County. It was named for Hoh River into which it drains. (*see* Hoh River)

Hoh River *(Ts.26,27N;Rs.7-13W)*

The stream of the river rises at the base of Hoh Glacier, east slope of Mt. Olympus, Olympic National Park; flows west to Pacific Ocean at Hoh Indian Reservation, northwest Jefferson County. In 1787, Capt. Charles W. Barkley named the stream *Destruction River* when members of a boat crew were killed by Indians while securing fresh water. On

July 14, 1775, Bodega y Quadra had a similar experience here, losing 6 men from the crew of the schooner *Sonora;* he called the river *Rio de los Martires.* Another early name, source unknown, was *Chablat River.* (*see* Hoh)

Holpus Point (Island County) *see* Hoypus Point

Hoko River *(Ts.30-32N;Rs.13,14W)*
The stream of the river rises northwest of Lake Pleasant, west central Clallam County; flows north to Strait of Juan de Fuca at Kydaku Point, 4 miles west of Clallam Bay. The Indian name is for a tribe which lived along the river called *Ho-qwol-th,* meaning "projecting." The term referred to a very large rock at the canyon's mouth, near the Indian village. In 1846, Capt. Henry Kellett interpreted the name as *Okho,* and so placed it on British Admiralty charts.

Holcomb *(S.36;T.13N;R.8W)*
Once an active sawmill town, now a scattered settlement on Willapa River, 8-1/2 miles southeast of Raymond, central Pacific County. The name was chosen by Northern Pacific Railway officials for Judge George J. Holcomb, who was active in the operations of South Bend Land Company in the 1890s.

Holden *(S.7;T.31N;R.17E.uns)*
Famous mining town on Railroad Creek, 11 miles west of Lake Chelan, northwest Chelan County. In 1937, it was founded by Howe Sound Mining Company; in 1958, it ceased operations. The land is on Okanogan National Forest and therefore federally owned, but the complete town facilities have been donated by owners to Seattle Lutheran Bible Institute. It was named for J. H. Holden, a miner from Colorado, who made a big strike at nearby Copper Peak on July 20, 1890.

Holden Creek *(T.32N;R.16E.uns)*
The stream of the creek heads in Holden Lake, 5 miles east of Cascade Mountain summit, Okanogan National Forest, northwest Chelan County; drains 2 miles eastward into Railroad Creek. (*see* Holden)

Holden Lake *(T.32N;R.16E.uns)*
Lake at the head of Holden Creek, 5 miles east of Cascade Mountain summit, Okanogan National Forest, northwest Chelan County. (*see* Holden)

Hole-in-the-Wall *(S.2;T.33N;R.16W)*
Rock cave at the mouth of Flattery Creek, Pacific Ocean, Makah Indian Reservation, extreme northwest Clallam County. The name is very descriptive of this spectacular, wave-worn rock cave. At high tides it is occupied by seals and other sea animals. It also is the hideout for many octopi.

Holgate and Hanford Hill (King County) *see* Beacon Hill

Holly *(S19;T.24N;R.2E)*
Community on the east shore of Hood Canal, directly south of Anderson Cove, extreme southwest Kitsap County. The name was chosen by Robert Wyatt, who homesteaded here in 1890. In 1895, he named the place when he introduced the first holly tree to the Pacific northwest with a planting near the post office. The species is not native.

Holman Pass *(S.33;T.39N;R.17E.uns)*
A 5,150-ft. pass over Cascade Mountain summit leading from the headwaters of West Fork, Pasayten River, Okanogan County; over the divide into the headwaters of Ruby Creek, Whatcom County. It was named for the Holman brothers, engineers who made a reconnaisance here for Northern Pacific and Canadian Pacific railroads in 1907. Their name is also on a mountain to the north and a creek to the east.

Holmes *(S.13;T.17N;R.18E)*
Industrial railway spur 1-1/2 miles south of Ellensburg, central Kittitas County. It was installed to load ice for shipment to Portland, Oregon. Railway officials named the spur for R. J. Holmes, owner of the ice plant.

Holmes Harbor *(Ts.29,30N;R.2E)*
A branch of Saratoga Passage, extending south into Whidbey Island for 6 miles, south Island County. This bay is noted for excellent salmon fishing. In 1841, it was named for Silas Holmes, assistant surgeon of the Wilkes Expedition.

Holy City (Yakima County) *see* Sunnyside

Homan *(S.32;T.3N;R.2E)*
Town 5 miles northeast of Vancouver, southwest Clark County. The original name was *Thornton,* for Al Thornton, who settled here in 1897. In 1903, it was changed to *Glenwood* for nearby Glenwood Valley. In May 1909, the present

name was applied by Northern Pacific Railway officials for a pioneer family.

Home *(Ss.25,26,35;T.21N;R.1W)*
Community on Von Geldern Cove (Joe's Bay), 10 miles northwest of Steilacoom, northwest Pierce County. In 1896, Mutual Home Association, formed by socialists and political dissenters, established a colony here. The name is for the association. An alternate name was *Home Colony.*

Home Colony (Pierce County) *see* Home

Home Valley *(S.26;T.3N;R.8E)*
Farm community on the north bank of Columbia River, at the mouth of Wind River, 5-1/2 miles east of Stevenson, south central Skamania County. It was settled in early days by Norwegians. In 1893, the name *Heim Dal* was applied by John Kanekberg. When a post office was established, postal authorities translated the name to Home Valley.

Hompegg Falls *(S.16;T.8N;R.40E)*
Falls in East Fork, Touchet River, 13 miles southeast of Dayton, south central Columbia County. In 1875, it was developed as a summer resort, but, in 1931, was largely destroyed by a heavy flood. Hompegg is a composite word which includes the first letter of 7 family names: Hexter, Oppenheimer, Myers, Pietryzcki, Eckler, and Dennis and Frank Guernsey. These 7 families were the original developers of the resort at the falls.

Hongking *(S.31;T.22N;R.3E)*
A "ghosted" community on the east shore of Quartermaster Harbor, southwest end of Maury Island near Manzanita, southwest King County. In the early 1880s, the community was established by and named for Chinese fishermen. At its peak, the Chinese population was estimated at almost 3,000. In 1885, the place was abandoned at the time of the "Chinese Riots" in western Washington.

Honor Lake (Chelan County) *see* Honour Lake

Honour Lake *(S.29;T.26N;R.16E)*
Lake adjoining Chiwaukum Lake at the southeast end, connected by a narrow channel, Wenatchee National Forest, central Chelan County. It is one of several small lakes adjoining Chiwaukum Lake on the south. The lake was

named for a party of fishermen who avoided excellent fishing in this lake after Chiwaukum Lake had been planted and closed. However, they did realize that the State Game Commission had overlooked the connecting stream with Chiwaukum Lake.

Hoo Hoo Lake *(S.15;T.8N;R.6E.uns)*

A 5-acre lake, elevation 1,600 ft., 6-1/2 miles east of Mt. St. Helens, Gifford Pinchot National Forest, northwest Skamania County. The lake is reported to have been named by local lumbermen for the lumbermen's social society, Concatenated Order of Hoo Hoo.

Hood *(S.28;T.3N;R.10E)*

Railroad station 2 miles east of White Salmon, north bank of Columbia River, southeast Skamania County. It was named by Spokane, Portland & Seattle Railway Company for Mt. Hood, across the river in Oregon.

Hood Canal *(Ts.22-27N;Rs.1-3W&1E)*

An 80-mile-long, inland, salt-water channel extending southwest from the vicinity of Port Ludlow, Jefferson County, between Kitsap and Mason counties to the "Great Bend" at Union; then northeast to Belfair, Mason County. It is subject to tidal influence, and is noted for shellfish. On May 13, 1792, it was named *Hood's Channel* by Capt. George Vancouver for the Right Honourable Lord Hood, member of the British Board of Admiralty; however, it was entered on Vancouver's charts as *Hood's Canal*. A 1947 bill in the State Legislature (H.J.M..10) would have petitioned the President to change the name to *Hood Inlet*, but it died in the House. The channel was called *Hoods Canal* quite generally until the USBGN made the present form official.

Hood Head (Jefferson County) *see* Hood's Head

Hood Point *(S.23;T.25N;R.2W)*

An east shore point of Hood Canal across from Belleview, southwest Kitsap County. In 1841, the descriptive name *Sandy Point* was chosen by Cmdr. Charles Wilkes. Because too many features were given that name, the present designation was borrowed from Hood Canal.

Hoodlum Mike Lake *(T.20N;R.3E)*

Formerly a lake in Tacoma, near 12th and Union, Pierce County. Now filled, it once was about 1 block wide and 6 blocks

long. The lake was so named because it was a hangout for tough boys.

Hoodooville (Lincoln County) *see* Sprague

Hood's Head *(T.28N;R.1E)*

A triangular head, joined to the mainland by a narrow spit, west shore of Hood Canal, 4 miles southeast of Port Ludlow, east central Jefferson County. In 1856, the name was applied by U.S. Coast Survey. It was named for Hood Canal, which then was known as Hood's Canal. The possessive form is not shown on recent maps.

Hoodsport *(S.11;T.22N;R.4W)*

Town on the west side of Hood Canal, 3-1/2 miles east of the south end of Lake Cushman Reservoir, central Mason County. Once a busy logging center, it is now largely reliant on revenue from tourists and fishermen. The Twana Indian name for this place was *Slal-atl-atl-tul-hu*. The present name was chosen by local residents because of the town's position on the shore of Hood Canal. The use of "Hoods" rather than "Hood" harks back to the years when this body of water was called Hoods Canal.

Hooper *(S.27;T.15N;R.37E)*

Railroad station on the east bank of Palouse River, 2-1/2 miles northeast of Palouse Falls (town), southwest Whitman County. In 1883, it was named by Oregon Railway & Navigation Company officials for Albert J. Hooper, an early settler.

Hope Island *(Ss.27,28;T.20N;R.2W)*

Small island east of Squaxin Island, between it and the mainland, extreme southeast Mason County. In 1841, it was named by Cmdr. Charles Wilkes. There appears to be no record of the name source. A local name for the island, which continues in use by older residents, is *Johns Island*, for John Gilmore, an early settler.

Hope Island *(S.28;T.34N;R.2E)*

Island in the north end of Skagit Bay, 3-1/2 miles west of LaConner, southwest Skagit County. In 1841, it was named by Cmdr. Charles Wilkes. Contrary to his usual careful charting, he evidently left no record of his reason for the name.

Hopewell (Clark County) *see* Rock Creek (town)

Hopgood *(S.27;T.13N;R.4E)*

A prominent, sandstone rock and cliff

1 mile northwest of Morton, central Lewis County. It is a landmark in these foothills. The name is for Thomas Hopgood, an 1889 pioneer, on whose homestead the rock is located. Hopgood was one of the founders of Morton.

Hopkins Pass *(S.32;T40N;R.17E.uns)*

A 6,050-ft. pass over Cascade Mountain summit, leading from Chuchuwanteen Creek headwaters, northwest Okanogan County, west to Castle Fork, Three Fools Creek, northeast Whatcom County. It was named for an early stockman who lived in Methow Valley, and who used the range on both sides of the pass.

Hoquiam *(Ts.1-3,11,12N;R.9W)*

Manufacturing center for forest products, including pulp and paper, on Hoquiam River, north side of Grays Harbor, 12 miles from Pacific Ocean, Grays Harbor County. (see Hoquiam River)

Hoquiam Range

A series of mountain peaks, south central Jefferson County. In 1890, Lieut. Joseph P. O'Neil named the range. His classification was not used by later geographers or map makers.

Hoquiam River *(Ts.17-19N;Rs.9,10W)*

The stream of this 20-mile-long river rises in 2 forks, central Grays Harbor County; the forks flow south to join directly north of Hoquiam, then flows into the east end of Grays Harbor. The river takes its name from a local Indian band, the *Ho-qui-umpts*, meaning "hungry for wood," which relates to the Indian custom of using driftwood from this river for fuel.

Hornbeck's Spit *(S.26;T.25N;R.2E)*

Former ship-building site on the north shore of Eagle Harbor, directly east of Winslow, east central Bainbridge Island, Kitsap County. the place was named in the days of sailing ships for a ship-builder who built many vessels, including *Tolo* and *Alta*.

Hornet Creek *(T.26N;R.19E)*

The stream of the creek heads at the south end of Miners Ridge, north of Sugarloaf Peak, Wenatchee National Forest, central Chelan County; flows 3-1/2 miles east by south to Mad River at Pine Flat. It was named by U.S. Forest Ranger John Brender, for an encounter on the creek with stinging insects which he thought were hornets, but probably were yellow jackets.

Hornets Harbor (Skagit County) *see* Guemes Channel

Horse Creek (*T.33N;R.12E*)

The stream of the creek rises on the south slope of Mt. Buckindy, Mt. Baker National Forest, southeast Skagit County; flows 5 miles south to Buck Creek, near Snohomish County boundary. The name was given because local Indians trapped a number of wild horses here, which almost died of starvation.

Horse Heaven (*S.11;T.7N;R.26E*)

Small settlement on Carter Canyon, 14 miles southeast of Prosser, south central Benton County. It is in the center of Horse Heaven country, south of Horse Heaven Hills. Many wild-horse roundups were made here in the past, and some more recently. The name is quite appropriate, as in its native state the region was a perfect sea of the finest bunch-grass. It is said to have been named by James Gordon Kinney, of Kinneyville near Prosser. An early name for the settlement was *Bedrock Springs*.

Horse Heaven Hills
(*Ts.6-8N;Rs18-28E*)

Extensive area of low, rolling hills east of Satus Creek, southeast Yakima County; east of Goldendale, Klickitat County; and between Columbia and Yakima rivers, south Benton County. In 1881, it was aptly named by James Kinney, a Yakima pioneer, because the area offers excellent forage and comparative isolation. In the past, numerous bands of wild horses roamed this range.

Horse Plains (Spokane County) *see* Hillyard

Horse Slaughter Camp
(*S.2;T.25N;R.46E*)

Area 1/2 mile west of Spokane Bridge, extreme east central Spokane County. In September 1858, 700 Indian horses were shot, on orders from Col. George Wright, who justified the carnage as a military precaution against Indian raids. The place was named for that incident.

Horseshoe Bend (Benton County) *see* Kiona

Horseshoe Lake (*S.19;T.5N;R.1E*)

A shallow, 90-acre lake directly southeast of Woodland and adjacent to Lewis River, extreme south central Cowlitz County. Formerly part of Lewis

River channel, it was cut off from the river in 1940, when U.S. Hwy. 99 was built through the area. The name is quite descriptive, as the lake was formed by a wide loop in the old channel, creating three-quarters of a circle.

Horseshoe Lake (*S.6;T.15N;R.11W*)

Small lake near Pacific Ocean, northeast of Grayland, southwest Grays Harbor County. It has a tendency to dry up in season, and may not be permanent. This name has been applied to many lakes which are more or less curved. In this case, the name rather strains the imagination.

Horseshoe Lake (*S.24;T.28N;R.1W*)

A 13-acre lake 3-3/4 miles southwest of Port Ludlow, northeast Jefferson County. Ox Shoe would be a much more appropriate name, as indicated by a contour sketch of the lake. Perhaps the namer went around the lake twice!

Horseshoe Lake (*S.28;T.24N;R.11E*)

Crescent-shaped, 24-1/2-acre lake, less than 1/2 mile long, 12-1/2 miles south-southwest of Skykomish, Snoqualmie National Forest, northeast King County. The name, applied by early prospectors, was for a fancied similarity in shape to a horseshoe. It should not be confused with nearby Goat Lake. (USBGN)

Horseshoe Lake (*S.18;T.14N;R.2W*)

A 4-acre lake 1-1/2 miles southwest of Centralia, adjacent to the west side of Chehalis River, northwest Lewis County. It obviously occupies a portion of an old river channel. The locally-applied name describes the lake's shape, which at best is an "elbow-type" horseshoe.

Horseshoe Lake (*S.33;T.36N;R.1W*)

A privately-owned lake covering 84 acres, maximum depth 92 ft., northwest of Blakely Island, east San Juan County. The name might be termed descriptive by using some imagination. Alternate names are *Luna Lake* and *Blakely Lake*.

Horseshoe Lake (*S.33;T.10N;R.10E*)

A 24-acre lake, elevation 4,150 ft., 8-1/2 miles northwest of Mt. Adams summit, Gifford Pinchot National Forest, northeast Skamania County. One of many Horseshoe Lakes in the state, this one might look like a horseshoe if an observer closed one eye -- or both.

Horseshoe Lake (Cowlitz County) *see* Lake Sacajawea

Horsethief Canyon (*S.36;T.9N;R.43E*)

A dark, steep, brushy canyon extending 1 mile north from Iron Ridge to North Fork, Asotin Creek, west central Asotin County. The name comes from the tradition that this dead-end canyon was used in early days by horse thieves to corral horses. The tradition also states that the thieves were caught in one early episode.

Hoska Island (Pierce County) *see* Tanglewood Island

Hostak Lake (King County) *see* Shady Lake

Hot Springs (*S.21;T.20N;R.10E*)

Hot springs on upper Green River at its confluence with Champion Creek, southeast King County. In 1886, the railway station here was named *Kendon* by Northern Pacific Railway officials. In 1888, a bathhouse and hotel were built here to make the springs available to the public. The present, descriptive name was substituted for the earlier name when the springs were developed.

Houghton (*S.17;T.25N;R.5E*)

Community on the northeast shore of Lake Washington, 2 miles south of Kirkland, northwest King County. It was named for James Leland and Willard Houghton, early loggers in the area, who started timber operations in 1889.

Hover (*S.5;T.7N;R.31E*)

Town on the west bank of Columbia River, 8 miles southeast of Kennewick, southeast Benton County. In 1907, the settlement was started during a local land boom caused by an irrigation system. When the McNary Dam was built, all property here was condemned by U.S. Army engineers, and subsequently was flooded in Lake Wallula. The town was named for Herbert A. Hover, president of Kennewick Land Company. A flowery nickname for Hover during its period of growth was "The California of the Northwest."

Howard A. Hanson Reservoir (King County) *see* Eagle Gorge Reservoir

Howard Peak (*Mt. Rainier National Park*)

A 5,700-ft. peak 2-1/2 miles northwest of Mother Mountain, at the head of Ranger Creek, northwest sector of the park. It was named for Howard Rust, a prominent Tacoma citizen. (USBGN)

Hoxsey Creek *(T.25N;R.16E)*

The stream of the creek heads on the south slope of Icicle Ridge, Wenatchee National Forest, central Chelan County; flows 1-1/2 miles south to Icicle Creek, between Ida and Chatter creeks. It was named by local residents for Dr. Hoxsey of Leavenworth, a Great Northern Railway physician and general practitioner, who built a fishing cabin near the mouth of the stream.

Hoydus Point (Island County) *see* Hoypus Point

Hoypus Point *(S.30;T.34N;R.2E)*

A northeast shore point of Whidbey Island, east entrance to Deception Pass, extreme north Island County. In 1841, Cmdr. Charles Wilkes named the feature *Hoipus Point*, with no explanation of the source. Over the years, the ''y'' in the present name has been subsituted for the ''i'' which Wilkes used.

Hozamen Mountain (Whatcom County) *see* Hozomeen Mountain

Hozomeen Lake
(S.18;T.40N;R.14E.uns)

Lake 1-1/2 miles east of Ross Lake, 3 miles south of the Canadian boundary, northeast Whatcom County. (*see* Hozomeen Mountain)

Hozomeen Mountain
(S.5;T.40N;R.14E.uns)

A black slate peak, elevation 9,080 ft., Mt. Baker National Forest, 3-1/2 miles east of Ross Lake, northeast Whatcom County. In the old days, this mountain was off-limits to all Indians except the Skagits. The name is from Fraser River Indian dialect, meaning ''twin peaks with a rocky depression between.'' The same name has been applied to nearby features, including a pass, ridge, and lake.

Hubbard (King County) *see* Juanita

Hubbard Canyon *(T.28N;R.30E)*

Canyon in Grand Coulee, northeast Grant County. Most of the canyon was inundated in the equalizing reservoir created below Grand Coulee Dam. It was named for the man who first claimed land here in 1887.

Hubner *(S.9;T.20N;R.13E)*

Junction point of a spur to Cabin Creek Lumber Company and a sawmill owned by Cascade Lumber Company of Yakima, 2-1/2 miles southeast of Kachess Lake, northwest Kittitas Coun-

ty. It was named by Northern Pacific Railway officials for A. H. *Huebner* of Cascade Lumber Company.

Huckleberry Creek *(Mt.Rainier National Park)*

The stream of the creek rises in several branches in Huckleberry Park, north side of Sourdough Mountain, northeast area of the park; flows north and northeast to White River, 6 miles north of the park boundary. (*see* Huckleberry Park)

Huckleberry Island*(T.35N;R.2E)*

Island at the north entrance to Padilla Bay, between Guemes and Saddlebag islands, northwest Skagit County. In 1790, it was included with Dot and Saddlebag islands as *Los Tres Hermanos* by Dionisio Galiano. In 1841, Cmdr. Charles Wilkes called the group *Porpoise Rocks*. The present name was given by local residents because abundant, native huckleberries grow on the island.

Huckleberry Mountain
(Ts.19,20N;Rs.9,10E)

A long ridge with several peaks, maximum elevation 4,770 ft., between Green and Greenwater rivers, running parallel to both rivers for about 9 miles, southeast King County. It was named for an abundance of mountain huckleberries which have been harvested by Indians and white men for many years. An early name applied in 1841 by Lieut. Robert E. Johnson of the Wilkes Expedition was *La Tete*. This French phrase, meaning ''the head,'' was obviously applied to one of the several high, rounded peaks along the ridge. It is not carried on recent maps. The Indian name was *Sxa-yus*. This mountain should not be confused with another with the same name northeast of Snoqualmie Pass.

Huckleberry Mountain
(S.18;T.23N;R.12E)

Peak at Cascade Mountain summit, 6 miles northeast of Snoqualmie Pass, between Chikamin Peak and Mt. Thompson, east central King County. The name was locally applied because of abundant native huckleberries on the mountain slopes, which are popular in season with bears and humans alike. This mountain should not be confused with a ridge by the same name in southeast King County.

Huckleberry Mountain (Chelan County) *see* McCall Mountain

Hudson Point *(S.1;T.30N;R.1W)*

A northwest point at the entrance to Port Townsend bay, within city limits of Port Townsend, extreme northeast Jefferson County. In 1841, it was named by Cmdr. Charles Wilkes as *Hudson's Point*, for Lieut. William F. Hudson of Wilkes Expedition. As in many similar names, the possessive form has been dropped for simplification. On a few early maps, this feature was identified as *Point Hudson*.

Hugo Peak *(S.27;T.16N;R.4E)*

Highest point in Pack Demonstration Forest, 2 miles east of LaGrande, south central Pierce County. In 1924, the peak was named by faculty of the College of Forestry, University of Washington, for Dean Hugo A. Winkenwerder, now deceased.

Hull's Island (San Juan County) *see* Orcas Island

Humes Glacier
(Ss.1,2;T.26N;R.8W.uns)

Glacier on the southeast slope of Mt. Olympus, northwest of Queets Basin, north central Jefferson County. In 1907, it was named by members of The Mountaineers for Grant and Will Humes, who were guides, explorers, and pack-train operators.

Hummel Lake
(Ss.14,23,24;T.35N;R.2W)

Lake in a peat bog area, elevation 97 ft., emptying into Swifts Bay at the northeast end of Lopez Island, 1 mile east of Lopez, central San Juan County. Normally it covers 36 acres, but may decrease in size to 5 acres during dry spells. The lake was locally named for a family of settlers called *Hummel* or *Hummil*. An alternate name, in local use, is *Lopez Lake*.

Hummil Lake (San Juan County) *see* Hummel Lake

Humorist *(S.10;T.8N;R.31E)*

Railroad station 7 miles east of Pasco, southwest Walla Walla County. When Oregon-Washington Railway & Navigation Company built through here, someone erected directional signs which read ''Wallula 9 miles, and ''Hell 1 mile.'' An arrow affixed to the latter sign pointed straight down. A railroad officials remarked, ''There must be a humorist here,'' and his phrase was shortened to one word as the station name.

Humpback Creek
(Ss.13,24,25;T.22N;R.10E)

The stream of the creek rises in Annette Lake, west of Silver Peak at Cascade Mountain summit, 3 miles south of Rockdale; flows 2-1/2 miles north to South Fork, Snoqualmie River, east central King County. It was named by The Mountaineers for nearby Humpback Mountain. (*see* Humpback Mountain)

Humpback Mountain
(S.23;T.22N;R.10E)

A Snoqualmie National Forest peak, elevation 4,839 ft., 2 miles west of Cascade Mountain summit and 2 miles southwest of Rockdale, east central King County. It was named by The Mountaineers for the shape of its profile.

Humphrey *(S.7;T.20N;R.9E)*

Railroad station on upper Green River, 17 miles west of Cascade Mountain summit, southeast King County. In 1891, the place was named *Canton* by Northern Pacific Railway officials, for hundreds of Cantonese laborers who were employed to build the Stampede switchbacks, and later the Cascade tunnel at Cascade Mountain summit to the east. In July 1908, the railway changed the name to its present form, for William E. Humphrey of Seattle, a U.S. congressman.

Humphrey Head *(S.1;T.35N;R.2W)*

Point at the north entrance to Swifts Bay, northeast end of Lopez Island, central San Juan County. This feature was locally named for a pioneer settler who came here in 1877.

Humphries (King County) *see* Youngstown

Humptulips *(S.8;T.20N;R.10W)*

Once a great logging center, now an area of scattered, small ranches on Humptulips River, 17 miles north of Aberdeen, west central Grays Harbor County. The name is from the Quinault word *Ho-to-la-bixh*, meaning "hard to pole." The phrase relates to Humptulips River, on which Indians used to propel their canoes with poles. (USBGN)

Humptulips River
(Ts.18-23N;Rs.8-10W)

The stream of the river rises in 2 forks on the south edge of Olympic National Forest, flowing southwest to join near Humptulips; the combined stream flows south in a winding course to North

Bay on Grays Harbor, southwest Grays Harbor County. (USBGN) (*see* Humptulips)

Hungry Harbor *(S.13;T.9N;R.10W)*

Harbor on Columbia River, 1/2 mile northeast of Megler, southwest Pacific County. The name derives from a legend, stating that 7 men drifted into this harbor in a disabled boat and starved to death. An alternative version of the name source is based on the habit of fishermen who found the harbor ideal for anchoring at mealtime.

Hunt *(S.23;T.7N;R.31E)*

Railroad station 2 miles south of Attalia, extreme southwest Walla Walla County. When Northern Pacific Railway established a station here in 1883, it was known as *Hunts Junction*, named for G. W. Hunt, a pioneer road builder. In 1909, it was shortened to the present name.

Hunt Point (King County) *see* Hunts Point

Hunter Bay *(S.7;T.34N;R.1W)*

Bay on southeast Lopez Island, 3-1/2 miles northeast of Richardson, southeast San Juan County. In 1912, a "ghost village" was established on the shores of the bay by a religious colony; in 1922, the place was abandoned. The name was reportedly given because the last elk on Lopez Island was killed here by Indians. An alternate name is *Hunter's Bay*.

Hunters *(S.7;T.30N;R.37E)*

Town 41 miles north of Davenport, southwest Stevens County. It was originally located on the east bank of Columbia River, but was moved about 1-1/2 miles east when the site was flooded by Grand Coulee Dam in 1939-40. In 1880, it was founded by and named for James Hunter, who was reputed to be the first settler between Rickey Rapids on the north and Spokane River mouth on the south. On April 15, 1901, H. W. Latta platted it as a townsite. Hunter built a ferry across Columbia River from the mouth of Hunters Creek, and established a water-powered sawmill and feed-mill on the creek. The place became a distributing center for mines to the east and south, with 3 stores, a cheese factory, hotel, church, and stage line to Kettle Falls.

Hunters Creek *(Ts.30,31N;Rs.3738E)*

The stream of the creek rises in 2

branches in Huckleberry Mountain, southwest Stevens County; flows west 15 miles to Columbia River, west of Hunters. (*see* Hunters)

Huntoon Point *(S.25;T.39N;R.8E)*

An inspirational viewpoint at the terminus of Mt. Baker Hwy., Mt. Baker National Forest, west central Whatcom County. It was locally named for Bert Huntoon of Bellingham. (USBGN)

Hunts (Walla Walla County) *see* Hunt

Hunts Bluff *(S.28;T.32N;R.18E)*

East shore bluff of Lake Chelan, 2-1/2 miles north of Lucerne, north central Chelan County. It was named for Harry Hunt, who came here to recover from tuberculosis. He did, and lived to the age of 80!

Hunts Junction (Walla Walla County) *see* Hunt

Hunts Point *(T.25N;R.4E)*

A residential area on a long, east shore point of Lake Washington, between 2 narrow coves, 2 miles south of Kirkland, northwest King County. It was named for Leigh S. J. Hunt, who purchased the *Seattle Post-Intelligencer* on November 1, 1886, and who once owned this point and nearby Yarrow Point. It is shown on some maps as *Hunt Point*.

Huntsville *(S.6;T.9N;R.38E)*

Once a settlement 24 miles northeast of Walla Walla, west central Columbia County. In 1878-79, it was founded by United Brethren Society, with the establishment of a flouring mill and Washington Institute. The settlement failed before the turn of the century. The name was for B. J. Hunt, who, with John Fudge, donated 90 acres for the townsite.

Hurd Creek (Lewis County) *see* Mill Creek

Hurricane Creek *(T.29N;R.7W.uns)*

The stream of the creek rises on Hurricane Hill, Olympic National Park, east central Clallam County; flows 2 miles west to Elwha Reservoir. (*see* Hurricane Hill)

Hurricane Hill *(T.29N;R.7W.uns)*

An Olympic National Park peak, elevation 5,757-ft., near the head of Hurricane Creek, 3 miles east of Elwha Reservoir, east central Clallam County. It is used as a forest fire lookout in season by National Park Service. The name was given by early prospectors for the frequent, violent winds in the vicinity. Prior to 1916, the name *Old Hurricane* was in local use.

Hurricane Ridge *(T.28N;R.6W.uns)*

Olympic National Park ridge extending from Hurricane Hill to Obstruction Point, 10 miles south of Port Angeles, east central Clallam County. (*see* Hurricane Hill)

Huston Creek *(T.27;R.16E)*

The stream of the creek heads on Wenatchee Ridge, west central Chelan County; flows 2 miles southeast to Little Wenatchee River, 3 miles west of Wenatchee Lake. It was named for Forest Ranger Rush J. Huston, whose homestead adjoined the creek on the west.

Hutchinson Creek
(Ts.37,38N;Rs.5,6E)

The stream of the creek rises near Bowman Mountain, 12 miles west of Mt. Baker, south central Whatcom County; flows 8 miles southwest to North Fork, Nooksack River. It was named for the widow of the first settler, John Hutchinson, who died before making his final proof of homestead.

Hyak *(S.15;T.22N;R.11E)*

A mountain resort at the north end of Keechelus Lake, east portal of abandoned Chicago, Milwaukee & St. Paul Railway tunnel, northwest Kittitas County. The station was named by railroad officials for the nearby creek and lake of the same name. (*see* Hyak Creek)

Hyak Creek *(S.23;T.28N;R.10W)*

The stream of the creek rises between Bogachiel River and its North Fork, Olympic National Park, south central Clallam County; flows 2-1/2 miles north to North Fork, Bogachiel River, dropping 1,500 ft. enroute. The Chinook jargon name is quite appropriate, as it means "swift," "fast," or "hurry."

Hyak Creek *(T.22N;R.11E)*

The stream of this short, high-altitude creek rises in Hyak Lake, 2-1/2 miles south of Snoqualmie Pass, northwest Kittitas County; plunges 1-1/2 miles to Coal Creek, Snoqualmie National Forest. The Indian word, meaning "swift" or "fast," was applied to the creek by The Mountaineers, who invariably used colorful and appropriate names for geographic features. (USBGN)

Hyak Lake *(S.16;T.22N;R.11E)*

A very small lake directly east of Cascade Mountain summit, 2-1/2 miles south of Snoqualmie Pass, extreme west Kittitas County. (USBGN) (*see* Hyak Creek, Kittitas County)

Hyas Creek *(S.4;T.29N;R.12W)*

The stream of the creek heads near Hyas Mountain, Olympic National Forest, southwest Clallam County; flows 6-1/2 miles southwest to Sitkum River. The Chinook jargon name means "large," "great," or "wide."

Hyas Lake *(S.10;T.33N;R.11E)*

A 4-acre lake, elevation 4,000 ft., 13 miles northeast of Darrington, Mt. Baker National Forest, southeast Skagit County. An alternate name is *Big Lake*. (*see* Hyas Creek)

Hyde Point *(S.23;T.20N;R.1E)*

An east shore point of McNeil Island, 2-3/4 miles northwest of Steilacoom, northwest Pierce County. In 1841, it was named by Cmdr. Charles Wilkes, for William Hyde, a ship's carpenter on the Wilkes Expedition. In 1846, the same point was named *Dyke Point* by Capt. R. N. Inskip, for Lieut. Charles Dyke of *HMS Fisgard*. The name given by Wilkes has persisted, as Inskip's name was on a British Admiralty chart.

Hylebos *(S.36;T.21N;R.3E)*

A former post office at St. George School for Indian Boys on Puyallup Indian Reservation, Pierce County. Now discontinued. (*see* Hylebos Creek)

Hylebos Creek *(T.20N;Rs.3,4E)*

The stream of the creek heads 3 miles north of Milton, southwest King County; flows south, then northwest to Hylebos Waterway on Tacoma waterfront. It was named for Rev. Peter F. Hylebos, a Catholic priest who came to Tacoma about 1880.

I

Ibex Creek *(T.28N;R.15E.uns)*

The stream of the creek heads on Whittier Creek, Wenatchee National Forest, northwest Chelan County; flows 3 miles east and south to Panther Creek. It was named by Forest Supervisor A. H. Sylvester, for the abundance of wild goats.

Ice Creek *(T.30N;R.17E.uns)*

The stream of the creek heads in Ice Lakes, north central Chelan County; flows 5 miles southeast to Entiat River, Wenatchee National Forest. It was named by Forest Supervisor A. H. Sylvester, because it drains Ice Lakes.

Ice Harbor Dam *(S.8;T.9N;R.32E)*

A hydroelectric dam in Snake River, 10.2 river miles above the the river's mouth, between Walla Walla and Franklin counties. Generally, it has been known as *Ice Harbor* for a tiny bay in the river, where small craft formerly tied up to await the break-up and passage of upstream ice-jams. A Senate Joint Memorial, dated February 11, 1949, recommended that the structure be named in honor of Dr. Marcus Whitman.

Ice Lake *(S.23;T.23N;R.10E)*

A 1.9-acre lake, 300 ft. from Frozen Lake, 4 miles northwest of Snoqualmie Pass, Snoqualmie National Forest, east central King County. The name is quite descriptive, as the lake is frozen most of the year.

Ice Lakes.
(S.36;T.31N&S.1;T.30N;R.16E.uns)

Two lakes between Mt. Maude and Spectacle Buttes, Wenatchee National Forest, northwest Chelan County. They were named by Forest Supervisor A. H. Sylvester, because they are ice-covered during most of the year.

Ice River (Asotin County) *see* Grand Ronde River

Iceberg Lake *(S.11;T.23N;R.12E)*

A 21.1-acre alpine lake in a glaciated area near Cascade Mountain summit, 7-1/2 miles northeast of Snoqualmie Pass, northeast King County. The name is quite descriptive. An alternate name is *Upper Burnt Boot Lake.*

Iceberg Lake *(S.24;T.39N;R.8E)*

The largest of 3 mountain lakes in the Galena Chain, on the northeast slope of Mt. Baker, 2-1/2 miles southwest of Mt. Baker Lodge, central Whatcom County. Ice floats on the lake the year around; in 1906, it was named by The Mazamas for its ice-studded water.

Iceberg Lakes *(S.18;T.26N;R.5W)*

Two lakes directly northwest of Eel Glacier, adjoining the glacier at an elevation of 6,100 ft., covering 1-1/2 and 2 acres respectively, at the head of Silt Creek, Olympic National Park, central Jefferson County. The name is descriptive, as both lakes receive glacial ice.

Iceberg Point *(S.23;T.34N;R.2W)*

A south end point of Lopez Island, at the south entrance of Outer Bay, south central San Juan County. In 1854, it was named by George Davidson of U.S. Coast Survey. As recorded in *Pacific Coast Pilot*, his reason for the name was that "On part of its southern cliff we discovered . . . remarkably deep and smooth marks of glacial action." An alternate name, evidently never used on maps and charts, was *Jennis Point.* (USBGN)

Icicle (Chelan County) *see* Leavenworth

Icicle Creek *(Ts.24,25N;Rs.13-17E)*

The stream of the creek rises from Lake Josephine, at Cascade Mountain summit, southwest Chelan County; flows southeast to Wenatchee River, near Leavenworth, south central Chelan County. The creek's 30-mile course traverses a spectacular canyon for 7 or 8 miles. The name is a distortion of the Wenatchee Indian word *Na-sik-elt*, meaning "narrow-bottom canyon."

Icicle Ridge *(Ts.24-26N;Rs.15-17E)*

A Wenatchee National Forest ridge, extending from Cascade Mountain summit, 2 miles south of Stevens Pass in an irregular southeast course, to the junction of Icicle Creek and Wenatchee River, at Leavenworth, central Chelan County. It was named for Icicle Creek by Forest Supervisor A. H. Sylvester. (*see* Icicle Creek)

Ida Creek *(T.25N;R.16E)*

The stream of the creek heads on the south slope of Icicle Ridge, in Lake Ida; flows south 2 miles to Icicle Creek, Wenatchee National Forest, central Chelan County. It was named by Forest Supervisor A. H. Sylvester, for its source in Lake Ida. (*see* Lake Ida)

Idlewild *(S.9;T.37N;R.4E)*

Resort on the east shore of Lake Whatcom, northwest Whatcom County. In 1889, it was named by Frederick K. Hughes of Fairhaven, when he platted the townsite. The poetic name has no particular relevance.

Idlewild (San Juan County) *see* Newhall's Point

Illabot Creek *(Ts.34,35N;Rs.10-12E)*

The stream of the creek heads on the south slope of Snowking Mountain, Mt. Baker National Forest, southeast Skagit County; flows 14 miles northwest to Skagit River, between Rockport and Marblemount. This Sauk Indian name means "painted"; it applies to the vivid green water in Illabot Lake, at the creek's head.

Illabot Lake *(S.22;T.34N;R.11E)*

A small, irregular lake at the confluence of Otter and Illabot creeks, Mt. Baker National Forest, southeast Skagit County. (*see* Illabot Creek)

Illahee *(S.31;T.25N;R.2E)*

Post Office on the west shore of Port Orchard bay, 3 miles north of Bremerton, central Kitsap County. The Chinook jargon name has been retained, and means "country," "land," or "place where one lives."

Illahee State Park *(S.31;T.25N;R.2E)*

A 70-acre public campground on the west shore of Port Orchard bay, 3 miles northeast of Bremerton, central Kitsap County. Park activities include swimming, fishing and clamming. (*see* Illahee)

Illinois Inlet (San Juan County) *see* Fish Creek

Iltkoyape (Stevens County) *see* Kettle Falls

Ilwaco *(T.10N;R.11W)*

Town on the northwest shore of

Baker Bay, at the mouth of Columbia River, southwest Pacific County. At one time, it was a southern terminus of a narrow-gauge railroad, which extended north to Nahcotta. The town was named for *El-wa-co* Jim, a very intelligent Indian, who married a daughter of Chief Comcomly of the Chinook nation.

Image *(Ss.32,33;T.2N;R.2E)*

Suburb on the north bank of Columbia River, 4 miles east of Vancouver, south central Clark County. The name is a shortened version of *Image Canoe Island*, which was the name applied to a nearby island in 1905 by Lewis and Clark. An earlier name for the town was *Russell Landing*.

Image Lake *(S.8;T.31N;R.15E)*

A small, vivid green lake in an alpine meadow, elevation 6,050 ft., at the head of Miners Creek, on the upper Suiattle River drainage, extreme northeast Snohomish County. It was named by early mountain climbers for its mirror-like qualities; an alternate name is *Mirror Lake*.

Impach *(S.10;T.32N;R.36E)*

Community on Colville Indian Reservation, 3 miles west of Inchelium, at the mouth of a long coulee called Butler Flats, east central Ferry County. On January 31, 1954, the post office, which also served the town of Meteor 3 miles southwest, was discontinued. The Indian name is said to mean "white lake" in the San Poil language.

Inatl Bay *(S.25;T.37N;R.1E)*

An east shore bay of Lummi Island, Bellingham Bay, across Hale Passage from Point Francis, southwest Whatcom County. The meaning of this Indian name is "across," "beyond," or "opposite to"; it relates to the position of the bay with regard to Point Francis. Other spellings of this name are *En-a-ti* and *E-nat-it*.

Inchelium *(S.7;T.32N;R.36E)*

Town on Colville Indian Reservation, about 1-1/2 miles west of Franklin D. Roosevelt Lake's west shore, across Columbia River from Gifford, east central Ferry County. The Inchelium subagency is about a mile to the north. Before the lake was created in the reservoir behind Grand Coulee Dam, the town was 1-1/2 miles east of its present site on the river bank, and was connected with Gifford by cable ferry. It was moved to a

higher bench, and retained its name; the previous location is under deep water.

Two early names were *Buffalo* and *Troy*. The present name was applied by government surveyors when they mapped the town; it is their interpretive spelling of the San Poil Indian name *En-char-lay-um* or *En-ch'lay-um*, which is said to mean "where big water meets little water," or "a meeting place among three waters." It refers to the confluences of nearby Hall and Stranger creeks with Columbia River.

Independence *(S.11;T.15N;R.4W)*

Post Office 3 miles southwest of Rochester, extreme southwest Thurston County. It was named for Independence Day by government land surveyors, who arrived here on July 4 to make the first official survey.

Independence (Snohomish County) *see* Silverton

Index *(Ss.17,20;T.27N;R.10E)*

Once a brisk mining community north of Mt. Index, at Skykomish River forks, 38 miles east of Everett, south central Snohomish County. In 1890, it was named for Mt. Index by Amos D. Gunn, who, in that year, purchased land here and established a tavern. (USBGN)

Index Creek *(Ts.25,26N;R.16E)*

The stream of the creek rises on the east side of Cape Horn, upper Chiwaukum drainage area, central Chelan County; flows 4 miles northeast to South Fork, Chiwaukum Creek, Wenatchee National Forest. The creek traverses a glacial canyon, with a hanging valley at its head. It was named for Forest Supervisor A. H. Sylvester's index finger! He described the drainage area of Chiwaukum Creek by the fingers of his left hand, held with the palm upward.

Index Mountain (King, Snohomish counties) *see* Mt. Index

Indian Addition (Pierce County) *see* Reservation; Puyallup Indian Reservation

Indian Bar *(Mt. Rainier National Park)*

A river bar, elevation 4,150 ft., near the head of Ohanapecosh River, on the southeast slope of Mt. Rainier, southeast quarter of the park. It consists of a large, gravel bank, surrounded by cliffs and glaciers. On September 21, 1929, it was named by Park Superintendent O. A. Tomlinson, at the suggestion of Prof.

Edmund S. Meany. In early days, before the park was established, this was a favorite Indian camp, surrounded by good hunting grounds and berry patches.

Indian Cove *(S.34;T.36N;R.2W)*

A southeast shore cove of Shaw Island, directly northwest of Canoe Island, central San Juan County. It was locally named to harmonize with nearby Canoe Island. In early days, a somewhat permanent Indian village was located here.

Indian Creek *(T.26N;R.19E)*

The stream of the creek rises on Sugarloaf Mountain, central Chelan County; flows southeast and northeast to Mad River, 2 miles north of Ardenvoir. It was mapped by Forest Supervisor A. H. Sylvester under this pioneer name, for an old Indian campsite at the creek's mouth, which was a wintering place for deer. This creek should not be confused with another of the same name in the same county, which is a tributary to White River.

Indian Creek *(T.29N;Rs.14,15E.uns)*

The stream of the creek rises in Indian Pass, at Cascade Mountain summit, between the headwaters of White and Little Wenatchee rivers, west central Chelan County; flows 9 miles east to White River, Wenatchee National Forest. It was named for Indian Pass by Forest Supervisor A. H. Sylvester. This creek should not be confused with another of the same name in the same county, which is a tributary to Mad River. *(see* Indian Pass)

Indian Creek *(Ts.26,27N;Rs.36,37E)*

The stream of the creek heads near Larene, 6 miles north of Davenport, northeast Lincoln County; flows 9-1/2 miles northwest to Hawk Creek, near its confluence with Columbia River. It was given its name because, in early days, an Indian village was located on the creek.

Indian Grave Springs (Grant County) *see* Ephrata

Indian Head *(S.15;T.29N;R.14E.uns)*

An isolated Wenatchee National Forest peak, with 3 small glaciers on its northwest slope, 2 miles northeast of Indian Pass, near Cascade Mountain summit, between Indian Creek and White River, northwest Chelan County. It was named by Forest Supervisor A. H. Sylvester, for a fancied resemblance to an Indian's headdress.

Indian Head (Island County) *see* Indian Point

Indian Heaven *(T.6N;R.8E.uns)*

A secluded area at the headwaters of Lewis and Wind rivers, 4 to 5 miles north of Big Lava Bed, Gifford Pinchot National Forest, central Skamania County. The name is well chosen, as the place has many small lakes and ponds, plentiful berries, and fairly abundant game. The Indian name was *Sahalee-Tyee*, meaning "the diety" or "chief above."

Indian Heaven Lake (Skamania County) *see* Lake Sahalee-Tyee

Indian Heaven Lakes *(T.6N;R.8E.uns)*

A large number of small lakes and ponds in Indian Heaven, at the headwaters of Lewis and Wind rivers, 5 to 6 miles north of Big Lava Bed, Skamania County. The individual lakes have no official names; the group name is for the area in which they are located. An alternate name is *Sahalee-Tyee Lakes*. (*see* Indian Heaven)

Indian Henrys Hunting Ground *(Mt. Rainier National Park)*

An outstanding mountain meadow, extending from the south slope of Pyramid Peak to Satulick Mountain, between Kautz Creek and South Tahoma Glacier, southwest sector of the park. Mirror Lakes, at the north end, give a spectacular reflection of Mt. Rainier, under certain light conditions. This meadow was named by Henry Winsor, pioneer mail carrier, for a Cowlitz Indian goat hunter, who camped here. His name was *Satulick* or *Sotolick*; white men gave him the nickname *Indian Henry*. (USBGN)

Indian Island *(Ts.29,30N;Rs.1W,1E)*

Island directly west of Marrowstone Island, between Port Townsend bay and Kilisut Harbor, northeast Jefferson County. In 1841, Cmdr. Charles Wilkes included it with Marrowstone Island as *Craven's Peninsula*, which was a misnomer, and was never in common use. The island was inhabited by local Indians when the first explorers arrived. The present name evidently came into local use during the early 1900s, although it did not appear on some maps until about 1915.

Indian Creek *(T.29N;Rs.14,15E.uns)*

The stream of the creek rises in Indian Pass, at Cascade Mountain summit, between headwaters of White and Little Wenatchee rivers, west central Chelan County; flows 9 miles east to White River, Wenatchee National Forest. It was named by Forest Supervisor A. H. Sylvester, for Indian Pass. It should not be confused with another creek of the same name, which is tributary to Mad River, Chelan County.

Indian Pass *(S.21;T.29N;R.14E.uns)*

A 5,026 ft. pass through Cascade Mountain summit, at the head of Indian Creek, Chelan County; and North Fork, Sauk River, Snohomish County. It was a favored route of Sauk and Wenatchee Indians, before white men took over the area. Forest Supervisor A. H. Sylvester named the pass appropriately.

Indian Peninsula
(Ts.22-28N;Rs.1-4W;1,2E)

An area no longer so designated, extending from Hood Canal on the west to Puget Sound and its inlets on the south and east, then north to the junction of Hood Canal with Puget Sound, northeast Mason and North Kitsap counties. In 1841, Cmdr. Charles Wilkes charted the area; his records show it as both *Great Peninsula* and Indian Peninsula. The Indian name was *Ah-ches-tul-boo*.

Indian Point *(S.8;T.23N;R.3E)*

A southwest point of Whidbey Island, directly south of Maxwelton, near the east entrance to Useless Bay, south Island County. In 1841, it was named by Cmdr. Charles Wilkes, at a time when the south end of Whidbey Island supported several Indian villages because of the abundant seafood. A local name for the point is *Indian Head*.

Indian Ponds *(S.14;T.28N;R.15E.uns)*

Two small ponds, dry at intervals, on Wenatchee National Forest, 1-1/2 miles west of White River, northwest Chelan County. They were named by Forest Supervisor A. H. Sylvester, because a well-used Indian trail led to the ponds from White River valley.

Indian Reserve Siding (Pierce County) *see* Reservation; Puyallup Indian Reservation

Indian Rock Paintings *(T.26N;R.42E)*

The name describes a number of prehistoric Indian pictographs 5 miles northwest of Spokane, on Little Spokane River near its confluence with Spokane River, west central Spokane County.

Indian Rock Paintings
(S.9;T.13N;R.18E)

An 18.8-acre state historical site directly west of Yakima, on U.S. Hwy. 410, central Yakima County. The reserve contains prehistoric Indian pictographs on a 70-ft. rock cliff.

Indianola *(S.15;T.26N;R.2E)*

A residential settlement on the north shore of Port Madison bay, 2 miles northeast of Suquamish, northeast Kitsap County. It was named by Ole Hanson, former Seattle mayor, who purchased it from an old settler named Lockrey. Hanson named the townsite for Lockrey's Indian wife, and for himself by adding his first name in a slightly altered form for euphony.

Indigo Lake *(S.31;T.32N;R.12E)*

A 21.7-acre lake, elevation about 4,500 ft., on the east side of Circle Peak, Mt. Baker National Forest, northeast Snohomish County. Forest Service personnel report that the name is for the lake's intense blue color. Alternate names are *Circle Peak Lake* and *Blue Lake*.

Inglewood (King County) *see* Issaquah

Ingraham Glacier *(Mt. Rainier National Park)*

One of the 6 largest glaciers on Mt. Rainier, heading at the mountain summit, and extending 6-1/2 miles southeast, between Whitman and Paradise glaciers, to the headwaters of Muddy Fork, Cowlitz River. It joins Cowlitz Glacier in its lower reaches, below Cathedral Rocks. In 1889, it was named by Prof. I. C. Russell for Maj. E. S. Ingraham of Seattle, an explorer and mountain climber in early days on Mt. Rainier. (USBGN)

Inland Empire

This very large area, without specific boundaries, lies between the Rocky Mountains and the Cascades in the Pacific northwest, including eastern Washington, eastern Oregon, and western Idaho. It is similar geographically, with mostly volcanic origin. The climate, common throughout the area, is more extreme than that of western Washington and Oregon, with less precipitation. This general term is not found on most maps, and has no political identity.

Inspiration Point *(Mt. Rainier National Park)*

A vantage point above Narada Falls, offering an impressive view of Mt. Rainier, 16-1/2 highway miles east of Nisqually entrance, south central zone of the park. Park officials gave the point this descriptive name because of its "inspirational" view.

Inter Fork, White River *(Mt. Rainier National Park)*

The stream of the river fork rises at the terminus of Inter Glacier, on the northeast slope of Mt. Rainier, northeast sector of the park; flows 4-1/2 miles east, skirting Emmons Glacier base, to White River, north of Goat Island Mountain. It is named for the glacier at its source. (*see* Inter Glacier) (USBGN)

Inter Glacier *(Mt. Rainier National Park)*

A northeast slope glacier of Mt. Rainier, directly northeast of The Wedge and Steamboat Prow, between Emmons and Winthrop glaciers. It is small and not very active, since it is fed only by snow which falls on lower slopes. In 1866, it was named by Maj. E. S. Ingraham of Seattle. He used the term, properly spelled *Interglacier*, because the glacier is hemmed in by rock rims, does not head on upper slopes, and is tributary to no other glacier. (USBGN)

Interbay *(S.14;T.25N;R.3E)*

A low area between Elliot Bay and Salmon Bay, northwest sector of Seattle, King County. When the first settlers came here, this area was a tule swamp, navigable by small boats at high tides. Now it is an industrial area, with many small manufacturing plants, and a roundhouse and freight yard operated by Great Northern Railway Company. The Seattle, Lake Shore & Eastern Railroad established the first station north of Seattle at this point, and named it *Boulevard* for Grand Boulevard, now Dravus Street. The present name was chosen because the area is between 2 bays.

Interior *(S.34;T.14N;R.43E)*

Grain storage point on north bank of Snake River, 6 miles southeast of Almota, southeast Whitman County. It was named for Interior Warehouse Company, which established a grain tramway and warehouse here.

Iona *(Adams County) see* Tokio

Ione *(S.6;T.37N;R.42E)*

Town on the west side of Pend Oreille River, 51-1/2 miles northwest of Newport, northwest Pend Oreille County. Its economy is largely dependent on one sawmill. In 1906, a cement plant was installed near here, but was unsuccessful. The place was named for Ione Stecker, daughter of an early settler.

Iowa Rock *(T.35N;R.2W)*

Obstructions in San Juan Channel, off the southwest shore of Lopez Island, south central San Juan County. In 1909, it was named for the state of Iowa by Dr. R. B. Wylie of the University of Iowa, while he was attending a summer session at Puget Sound Marine Station near Friday Harbor. This unofficial name is not mapped or recorded.

Ipsoot Creek *(Mt. Rainier National Park) see* Ipsut Creek

Ipsoot Lake *(S.8;T.37N;R.10E.uns)*

A small lake 3 miles east of Baker Lake, in Hidden Creek drainage area, Mt. Baker National Forest, south central Whatcom County. Originally, it was called *Hidden Lake* , but was changed to avoid confusion with another Mt. Baker National Forest lake with the same name. The present name, taken from Chinook Indian jargon, and having an alternate spelling *Ipsut*, means hide, or keep secret; it is well named, as the lake is quite concealed in its topography.

Ipsoot Pass *(Mt. Rainier National Park) see* Ipsut Pass

Ipsut Creek *(Mt. Rainier National Park)*

The stream of the creek rises in Ipsut Pass, 1 mile north of Mowich Lake, northwest corner of the park; flows 3 miles northeast to Carbon River, near the park's Carbon River entrance. Its approved name is an alternative spelling to *Ipsoot*. (*see* Ipsoot Lake) (USBGN)

Ipsut Creek Campground *(Mt. Rainier National Park)*

One of the park's best campgrounds, 5 miles southeast of Carbon River entrance, northwest corner of the park. (*see* Ipsoot Lake)

Ipsut Pass *(Mt. Rainier National Park)*

A 5,646-ft. pass on the southeast slope of Tolmie Peak, between the headwaters of Ipsut and Meadow creeks, northwest sector of the park. (*see* Ipsoot Lake) (USBGN)

Ipsut Saddle *(Mt. Rainier National Park)*

Ridge in Ipsut Creek drainage basin, northwest of Castle Peak (Castle Rock), northwest sector of the park. (*see* Ipsoot Lake (USBGN)

Irby *(S.25;T.22N;R.31E)*

Railroad station on Crab Creek, 7 miles west of Odessa, southwest Lincoln County. In 1878, it was established as a ranch by John Irby, and was locally called *Irby's Ranch*. Later, it was sold to a company, which set up warehouse facilities. The name is for the original owner.

Irby Ranch *(Lincoln County) see* Irby

Iron Mountain *(Mt. Rainier National Park)*

A 6,200-ft. peak, 5-1/2 miles southwest of Mt. Rainier's summit, directly east of Indian Henrys Hunting Ground, southwest area of the park. It was named for the extensive reddish stain, assumed to be iron or iron oxide, which appears on the mountain's slopes. (USBGN)

Iron Mountain *(Ss.31,32;T.35N;R.7E)*

Mountain 4 miles southeast of Hamilton, central Skagit County. The descriptive name is for the mountain's heavy deposits of iron ore, which have not been developed to any extent.

Iron Mountain *(Ss.5,6;T.27N;R.11E)*

A 5,241-ft. peak 2-1/2 miles from Galena, southeast Snohomish County. The mounain and its adjacent area are heavily mineralized, providing the source for this descriptive name.

Iron Springs *(S.9;T.19;R.12W)*

A resort area on Pacific Ocean, 3 miles north of Copalis, west central Grays Harbor County. It has a splendid beach and several mineral springs. The name is for the iron content in the springs, which gives a rusty color to the ground.

Ironsides Inlet *(San Juan County) see* East Sound

Irvin *(S.3;T.25N;R.44E)*

Small community 5 miles east of Spokane, east central Spokane County. The name was chosen by Northern Pacific Railway Company officials for Charles Irvin, manager of International Portland Cement Company at this location.

Irving Peak *(S.k30;T.28N;R.15E.uns)*

A Wenatchee National Forest peak, elevation 5,847 ft., at the head of Cockeye Creek, 7 miles east of Cascade Mountain summit, northwest Chelan County. It is one of 5 peaks in the area which Forest Supervisor A. H. Sylvester named for early American authors; this one was for Washington Irving.

Irwin *(Spokane County) see* Irvin

Isabella Lake *(Ts.19,20N;Rs.3,4W*
Lake in the course of Gosnell Creek, 2 miles south of Shelton, south central Mason County. In 1852, it was named by John Campbell, who took a Donation Land Claim on the lake for a member of his family.

Isla de Carrasco *(Jefferson County) see* Protection Island

Isla de Dolores *(Jefferson County) see* Destruction Island

Isla de Mata *(San Juan County) see* Matia Island

Isla de Macheco *(Whatcom County) see* Lummi Island

Isla de San Vincente *(Skagit County) see* Cypress Island

Isla de Suemes *(Skagit County) see* Guemes Island

Isla Lemos *(San Juan County) see* Waldron Island

Island Center *(S.21;T.25N;R.2E)*
Settlement on the west shore of Bainbridge Island, 1/2 mile southeast of Fletcher Bay, east central Kitsap County. The descriptive name, rather exaggerated, was chosen by Ida Anderson, who settled here with her husband in 1878.

Island County.
This county in western Washington is bounded on the north by Deception Pass; on the east by Skagit Bay, Port Susan, and Possession Sound; on the south by Possession Sound and Admiralty Inlet; and on the west by Admiralty Inlet and the Strait of Juan de Fuca. It consists entirely of islands. The largest are Whidbey and Camano islands; Smith and Minor islands, to the west, are quite small; and many very small islands are in the Deception Pass area, including Deception Island. On January 6, 1853, the county was created from a portion of King County, by Oregon Territorial Legislature. The name chosen is most appropriate.

Island Crest Park *(T.24N;R.5E)*
A 40-acre, undeveloped parksite on central Mercer Island, Lake Washington, west central King County. It was purchased by King County from the University of Washington. The descriptive name was chosen in a contest conducted by

Mercer Island residents.

Island Lake *(S.4;T.22N;R.10E)*
A 17.4-acre lake, 5-1/2 miles west of Snoqualmie Pass, Snoqualmie National Forest, east central King County. It is one of the 3 Island Lakes, with Rainbow and Blazer Lakes. The name derives from several small, rock islands within the lake's perimeter.

Island Lake *(S.3;T.25N;R.1E)*
A 42.7-acre lake, maximum depth 35 ft., 2 miles southwest of Keyport, north central Kitsap County. It was named for a one-acre island near the lake's south end.

Island Lake *(S.6;T.20N;R.3W)*
A 109-acre lake, 2-1/2 miles north of Shelton, south central Mason County. The name is for a small island in the lake's center.

Island Lake *(S.21;T.11N;R.11W)*
A 6,500-ft.-long lake, covering only 55.8 acres, 4 miles south of Ocean Park, North Beach Peninsula, southwest Pacific County. Two small islands near the lake's south end account for the name.

Island Lake *(S.35;T.30N;R.8E)*
A 2-1/2-acre lake, elevation 3,500 ft., on the southeast side of Pilchuck Mountain, 3 miles south of Gold Basin, central Snohomish County. It contains several very small islands, for which it is named.

Island Lakes *(S.4;T.22N;R.10E)*
A group of 3 lakes, totalling nearly 30 acres, directly east of Mason Lake, Snoqualmie National Forest, east central King County. The group, which includes Rainbow, Island, and Blazer Lakes, was named for small rock islands in at least one of the lakes. *(see Rainbow Lake, Island Lake, Blazer Lake; King County)*

Islandale *(Ss.7,18;T.34N;R.1W)*
A settlement on the southeast end of Lopez Island, east of Richardson, southeast San Juan County. The town's 2 divisions are about 1/2 mile apart. Division 1 is on the north shore of Mud Bay; Division 2 extends from Mackay Harbor to Mud Bay's south tip. The descriptive name was coined by local residents.

Islas Aguallos (de Aguayo) *(San Juan County) see* Barnes Island; Clark Island

Islas de Bonilla *(Island County) see* Smith Island; Minor Island

Islas de Moraleja *(San Juan County) see* Stuart and Waldron Island

Isle de Raton Laveur *(San Juan County) see* Coon Island

Isles de Pierres *(Douglas County) see* Rock Island (Rocks)

Isquah, Isquowh *(King County) see* Issaquah

Isssaquah *(T.24N;R.6E)*
Town 12 miles east of Seattle, 1-1/2 miles southeast of the south end of Lake Sammamish, central King County. Originally a coal mining and hops-growing community, this industrial town is now growing with Seattle, extending to the east. It has had a variety of names since pioneer days. The first was *Squak*, the white man's pronunciation of the Indian name *Is-qu-ah*, meaning *snake*. Ingebright Wold, who settled here in 1867, disliked the name, and changed it to *Englewood*, a modification of his own name. Then, when a post office was established, 1892, Daniel H. Gilman, promoter of Seattle, Lake Shore & Eastern Railroad, incorporated the town as *Gilman*. Finally, in the 1890s, the present name was adopted, and came into general use; it derives from the original Indian name.

Itsami Ledge *(S.32;T.20N;R.1W)*
Ledge at the mouth of Henderson Inlet in Dana Passage, extreme north Thurston County. In 1841, it was named by Cmdr. Charles Wilkes, and is one of few names he applied with no source recorded. Another name is *Itsami Shoal*.

Itsami Shoal *(Thurston County) see* Itsami Ledge

Itswoot Creek
(S.36;T.26N;Rs.10-1/2,11W)
The stream of the creek rises 17 miles east of Pacific Ocean, in Clearwater River valley, west central Jefferson County; flows 2-1/2 miles west to Clearwater River. This original Indian name, which has an alternate spelling *Itchwoot*, means *black bear* in Chinook jargon.

Itswoot Lake *(S.34;T.33N;R.13E.uns)*
A very small lake, 2-1/2 miles southwest of Spire Peak, at Cascade Mountain summit, Mt. Baker National Forest, extreme southeast Skagit County. *(see Itswoot Creek)*

Ives; Ives Landing *(Okanogan County) see* Pateros

J

Jack Island *(S.25;T.36N;R.1E)*

Island 3/4 mile northeast of Guemes Island, at the north entrance to Padilla Bay, northwest Skagit County. In 1841, Cmdr. Charles Wilkes named it *Jack's Island*. The person responsible for later abbreviating Wilkes's choice is not on record.

Jack Spit (Kitsap County) *see* Hedley Spit

Jack Splawn Mountain *(S.15;T.13N;R.13E.uns)*

A Snoqualmie National Forest peak, south of Tieton Reservoir, northwest Yakima County. It was named for A. J. Splawn, early cattleman and author of *Ka-mi-akin, The Last Hero of the Yakimas.*

Jackman Creek *(Ts.35,36N;Rs.8-10E)*

The stream of the creek rises 8 miles north of Rockport, Mt. Baker National Forest, north central Skagit County; flows 11 miles southwest to Skagit River at Van Horn. It was locally named for Jack Jackman, a Scotsman who took a land claim at the creek's mouth in the 1880s, and extensively logged the area.

Jack's Island (Skagit County) *see* Jack Island

Jackson *(S.10;T.12N;R.39E)*

Railroad station on Pataha Creek, 2-1/2 miles south of Snake River, central Columbia County. Railroad officials named the station at this point for a pioneer resident.

Jackson Courthouse *(S.9;T.12N;R.1W)*

A state historical site on Jackson Prairie, 9 miles south of Chehalis, near Marys Corner, west central Lewis County. Built in 1845, it was the first home in western Washington north of Columbia River, and belonged to John R. and Matilda N. Jackson. In October 1851, the first court session in Lewis County was held here. In 1917, it was deeded to the state of Washington by heirs of the Jackson estate. The DAR was responsible for reconstruction of this historical site.

Jackson Cove *(T.26N;R.2W)*

A locally named cove on Dabob Bay, 6 miles south of Quilcene, southeast Jefferson County. It was named for R. E. DeJackson, who homesteaded here in early days. In 1841, Cmdr. Wilkes charted the cove as *Hoo-etzen Harbor*, using the original Indian name; this name, however, did not come into common use.

Jackson Creek *(T.36N;R.5E)*

The stream of the creek rises 2-1/2 miles southeast of Wickersham, northwest Skagit County; flows 2 miles west to Samish River. It was locally named for John W. Jackson, who settled here in 1888, and lived in the Samish Valley for 15 years.

Jackson Prairie *(T.12N;R.1W)*

Prairie covering several square miles, 10 miles south of Chehalis, 4 miles southeast of Napavine, central Lewis County. It includes the original land claim of John R. Jackson, taken in 1845. That same year, it was named for this noted pioneer, whose home was the first courthouse in Lewis County. A local name for part of this prairie was *Highlands.*

Jacksons Island *(Ss.18,19;T.8N;R.5W)*

A Columbia River island in Cathlamet Channel, northwest of Puget Island, southeast Wahkiakum County. In 1841, it was mapped by Cmdr. Wilkes as *Stutzi Island*. The present name is for a pioneer settler on the island.

Jade Lake *(S.2;T.24N;R.13E)*

A Snoqualmie National Forest lake in a glacial area, 2 miles west of Deception Pass, at Cascade Mountain summit, northeast King County. The name was chosen to harmonize with several lakes in the area, which are named for jewels. It should not be confused with Jade Lake in Section 7 of this township and range.

Jade Lake *(S.7;T.24N;R.13E)*

A Snoqualmie National Forest lake in Necklace Valley, 2-1/2 miles west of Cascade Mountain summit, northeast King County. It is one of the 3 Necklace Valley Lakes, totaling about 7 acres; the other 2 are Emerald and Opal lakes. This lake is named for one of the "jewels" in the "necklace." It should not be con-fused with Jade Lake in Section 2 of this township and range.

Jahnvan Creek (Kitsap, Mason counties) *see* Tahuya River

James Creek *(T.30N;R.16E.uns)*

The stream of this short creek rises on the east slope of Chiwawa Ridge, northwest Chelan County; flows 2 miles northeast to Chiwawa River, Wenatchee National Forest. In 1925, it was named for James Naughton, president of Royal Development Company, by Jay Lonergan, who was a mining engineer for that corporation.

James Island *(T.28N;R.15W)*

A small, U-shaped island in Pacific Ocean, directly south of Quillayute River mouth, southwest Clallam County. It connects with the beach at low tide. In 1775, this island was included with Quillayute Needle and possibly with Huntington Rock under the name of *Los Frayles*, given by Bruno Heceta. The present name is for Francis W. James of Port Townsend. In 1855, while guarding the wreck of *S.S. Southerner* for the U.S. Customs Service, he became the first white man to scale this rocky island to the peak.

James Island *(S.23;T.35N;R.1W)*

A dumbbell-shaped island directly east of Decatur Island, in Rosario Strait, 1/4 mile east of Decatur Head, southeast San Juan County. In 1841, it was named by Cmdr. Wilkes for Reuben James, a U.S. sailor, who saved Stephen Decatur's life in the Tripoli campaign. It should not be confused with Satellite Island, also called James Island, in Prevost Harbor.

James Island (San Juan County) *see* Satellite Island

James River (Pacific County) *see* Wallacut River

James Rock *(Grays Harbor County)* *see* Ned's Rock

Jameson *(S.26;T.26N;R.25E)*

Small settlement 6 miles south of Mansfield, 3 miles northwest of Jameson Lake, central Douglas County. It was named for an old settler, who lived near a lake 3 miles southeast, which also bears his name. The place is not shown on some recent maps.

Jameson Lake *(Ss.1,12;T.25N;R.25E)*
Lake in Moses Coulee, 8 miles south of Mansfield, central Douglas County. (*see* Jameson)

Jamestown *(S.5;T.30N;R.3W)*
A beach settlement on Strait of Juan de Fuca, 3-1/2 miles north of Sequim, northeast Clallam County. It consists of a long, single row of houses, mostly occupied by local Indians. In 1875, the community was named for "Lord" James Balch, head chief of the Clallam tribe, who established this village in imitation of white settlements. An alternate name source is believed by some old-timers to be "Chief" Billie James, an Indian Shaker preacher, who lived at the south end of the village for many years. Indian names for the place were *Hui-au-ulch* and *St-tee-tlum.*

Jared *(S.6;T.34N;R.44E)*
Landing on the west bank of Pend Oreille River, between Ruby and Locke, central Pend Oreille County. It was named for Robert W. Jared, who settled in the valley in 1886. He operated a small store and was also Justice of the Peace; in 1908, when a post office was established, he also served as postmaster.

Jarrell Cove *(Ss.25,26;T.21N;R.2W)*
A small, irregular cove at the north end of Hartstene Island, southeast Mason County. It was named locally for a logger, who had a camp at the head of the cove in the early 1890s. His wife, Mrs. Phileura Jarrell, was the first postmistress.

Jasper Lake (Lewis County) *see* Backbone Lake

Jasper Mountain *(S.7;T.39N;R.36E)*
A Colville National Forest peak, elevation 4,780 ft., 4 miles northwest of Orient, northeast Ferry County. As was the case for many Colville National Forest features, this peak was named for a former U.S. Forest Service employee, Jasper Taylor.

Jawbone Flat *(T.11N;R.46E)*
Flat, originally a barren waste near the site of Vineland, between Clarkston and Clarkston Heights, northeast Asotin County. In early days, it was named for an old western term, which meant "on credit, rather than cash payment"; it was quite appropriate to this land area before

irrigation was installed. An alternate name source suggested by old-timers is for the remains of many horses, which died here when forage was scarce. Other pioneers aver that the name was for the contour of the river shore at this point.

Jay Creek *(Ts.24,25N;R.16E)*
The stream of the creek rises on the southwest slope of Icicle Ridge, central Chelan County; flows 2 miles southwest to Icicle Creek, Wenatchee National Forest. It was named by Forest Ranger John S. Brender, for the first name of an early employee on Chelan National Forest, now Okanogan National Forest.

Jeffers Glacier *(T.27N;R.8E)*
A southeast slope glacier of Mt. Olympus, Olympic National Park, north central Jefferson County. It was named for Joseph C. Jeffers, an Olympia photographer, who fell to his death at the head of the ice field on August 24, 1924. (USBGN)

Jefferson County
This county in northwestern Washington, on the Olympic Peninsula, is bounded on the north by Clallam County and Strait of Juan de Fuca; on the east by Admiralty Inlet and Hood Canal; on the south by Mason and Grays Harbor counties; and on the west by Pacific Ocean.

It contains 1,812 square miles, a major part of which is in Olympic National Forest and Olympic National Park.

The county was created on December 23, 1852, by Oregon Territorial Legislature, from a portion of Lewis County. It was named for Thomas Jefferson of Virginia, third president of the United States, who greatly assisted in the development of the Pacific Northwest.

Jefferson Point (Kitsap County) *see* Point Jefferson

Jennie Creek (Ferry County) *see* Jenny Creek

Jenny Creek *(Ts.39,40N;R.36E)*
The stream of this short, intermittent creek heads southeast of Grouse Mountain, Colville National Forest, extreme northeast Ferry County; flows 2-1/2 miles southeast into Little Boulder Creek, near its confluence with Kettle River. Based on information from a Colville National Forest officer, it is believed that the creek was named for the daughter of an early settler near the creek's mouth. The name is sometimes

erroneously spelled "Jennie." (USBGN)

Jennis Point (San Juan County) *see* Iceberg Point

Jensen Bay *(S.36;T.35N;R.3W)*
Small cove in the southwest area of San Juan Island, west side of Griffin Bay, 4 miles south of Friday Harbor, San Juan County. It was named by government surveyors while they were mapping San Juan Island, for a Norwegian settler, who came here in 1881, and in whose home the surveyors lived for some time.

Jericho *(S.35;T.16N;R.24E)*
Railroad point 7 miles east of Columbia River, on Crab Creek, southwest Grant County. Many towns along the Chicago, Milwaukee & St. Paul Railway in the Inland Empire, such as this one, were pleasingly named for old-world places. H. R. Williams, vice president of the Milwaukee line, selected this biblical name of a town in Palestine, 15 miles north of Jerusalem.

Jerry *(S.23;T.10N;R.45E)*
Community on Asotin Creek, 4-1/2 miles southwest of Clarkston, northeast Asotin County. In 1868, it was founded by Jerry McGuire, a rancher, packer and landowner; according to local stories, he raised horses, and had hundreds of them at one time. On August 8, 1906, the place was named for him by John Knight. Previously, it has been known as *Grand Junction,* because Asotin and George creeks meet here.

Jerusalem (Stevens County) *see* Enterprise

Jessie Slough *(S.16;T.16N;R.11W)*
A salt-water slough on the east side of South Bay, southwest Grays Harbor County. It was named for an Indian, who rafted logs on the slough, and whose nickname was "Humptulips Jesse."

Jim Creek *(Ts.31,32N;Rs.6,7E)*
The stream of this very crooked creek with many tributaries heads on the south slope of Wheeler Mountain, northwest Snohomish County; flows 16 miles southwest to South Fork, Stillaguamish River, near Arlington. It was named for Jim Garney, an Indian born near the creek's mouth, who guided prospectors in the 1880s.

Jim Crow Creek *(Ts.9,10N;R.7W)*

The stream of the creek heads on Elk Mountain, west central Wahkiakum County; flows 4-1/2 miles south to Columbia River, at Brookfield. On the point at the creek's mouth was a very tall tree, which could be seen for miles along the river; it was a favorite roost for multitudes of crows, and was called the "crow tree." Both the creek and the point were named for the crows.

Jim Crow Point *(S.16;T.9N;R.7W)*

Point at the mouth of Jim Crow Creek, Columbia River, southwest Wahkiakum County. (*see* Jim Crow Creek)

Jim Hill Mountain
(Ss.19,20;T.26N;R.15E)

A Wenatchee National Forest peak, elevation 6,175 ft., 3-1/2 miles east of Cascade Mountain summit, at the head of Lanham and Henry creeks, southwest Chelan County. It was named by Forest Supervisor A. H. Sylvester, for James J. Hill, the strong man of Great Northern Railway Company, who said, "Give me enough Swedes and enough whiskey, and I'll build a railroad through hell!"

Jim Town *(S.30;T.17N;R.11E.uns)*

A deserted mining camp at the Cascade Mountain summit, on Silver Creek trail, Snoqualmie National Forest, extreme northwest Yakima County. The name source is found in a pioneer legend, which avers that the camp once was occupied by 7 miners, each of whom had the given name "Jim."

Jimmy Creek *(Ts.27,28N;R.18E)*

The stream of this short creek rises on Cougar Mountain, 9 miles east of Wenatchee Lake, central Chelan County; flows 3 miles southwest to Mad River, Wenatchee National Forest. It was named by Forest Ranger James McKenzie, for his son.

Jimmycomelately Creek
(T.29N;R.3W)

The stream of the creek rises near Bear Mountain, Olympic National Forest, northeast Clallam County; flows east and north to Sequim Bay. It was named by early Portuguese settlers, who used this nickname for Jimmy Whilker, or Whittier, because they could not pronounce his last name. Jimmy was a jovial Sequim watchmaker, who lived in a small cabin near the creek.

Joe Brown Spit, Joe Brown's Point (Island County) *see* Sandy Point

Joe Creek *(T.20N;Rs.11,12W)*

The stream of the creek rises south of Quinault Indian Reservation, west central Grays Harbor County; flows south and west 13 miles to Beaver Creek, near its mouth on Pacific Ocean. It was named for a member of the Campbell family, which operated a shingle mill on the creek for a number of years.

Joe's Bank *(T.17N;R.11W)*

Grays Harbor bank, just inside the north entrance, southwest Grays Harbor County. It is not shown on recent maps, as tidal currents have caused the bank to vanish. In 1841, it was named by Cmdr. Wilkes for a half-breed interpreter, whom Wilkes used throughout the Pacific northwest, and who was on the Grays Harbor survey party under Henry Eld.

Joe's Bay (Pierce County) *see* Von Geldern (Von Gelden) Cove

Joes Lake (Clallam County) *see* Big Joes Lake

Johansons Corner *(S.27;T.25N;R.1E)*

A small community 2-1/2 miles north of Bremerton, north central Kitsap County. It was named for Mr. and Mrs. John Johanson, long-time operators of a local bus line.

John Burroughs Mountain (Mt. Rainier National Park) *see* Burroughs Mountain

John Day Pool (Benton County) *see* Lake Umatilla

John Day Rapids *(T.3N;R.17E)*

Once hazardous rapids in Columbia River, flooded in a hydroelectric reservoir, 9 miles southeast of Goldendale, between south central Klickitat County and Oregon. They were so named because the Upper Rapids were opposite the mouth of John Day River. That Oregon river was named for a Kentuckian on Hunt's Astoria Expedition during the winter of 1811-12; he became insane from hardships, and subsequently died at Astoria.

Johnny Creek *(T.24N;R.16E)*

The stream of the creek heads on the southwest slope of Icicle Ridge, central Chelan County; flows 1-1/4 miles south by west to Icicle Creek, Wenatchee National Forest. It was named by Forest Ranger John S. Brender, for an early

Forest Service employee on Chelan National Forest.

Johns Creek *(Ts.20,21N;Rs.3,4W)*

The stream of the creek heads on Johns Lake, south central Mason County; flows east into Oakland Bay. A water-powered sawmill, established on the creek in 1867 by Enoch Willey, cut lumber for the early homes in Shelton. The creek was locally named for "Uncle" John Gilmore, a very early settler. (USBGN)

Johns Island *(T.37N;R.4W)*

A 1-1/2-mile-long island, average width 1/4 mile, directly east of Stuart Island, 1-1/2 miles north of Spieden Island, northwest San Juan County. In 1841, it was named by Cmdr. Wilkes, presumably for a member of his expedition.

Johns Lake *(Ss.1,2;T.20N;R.4W)*

Small lake 3 miles northwest of Shelton, directly north of Munson Lake, south central Mason County. (*see* Johns Creek)

Johns Prairie *(S.9;T.20N;R.3W)*

A northwest shore prairie of Oakland Bay, 2 miles northeast of Shelton, south central Mason County. It was part of an 1852 Donation Land Claim by John Gilmore, for whom it was named.

Johns River *(Ts.16,17N;Rs.9-11W)*

The stream of this winding river with many tributaries rises north of North River divide, southwest Grays Harbor County; flows northwest to Grays Harbor, at Markham. It was named for "Uncle" John Hale, who located a land claim on its banks in pioneer days. In 1841, Cmdr. Wilkes mapped it as *Dinsmas River*, but that name never came into popular use.

Johnson *(Ss.3,10;T.13N;R.45E)*

Town 7 miles south of Pullman, southeast Whitman County. When a post office was established, the place was named for Jonathan Johnson, who purchased the site and, in 1877, platted a town.

Johnson Bay (Pierce County) *see* Still Harbor

Johnson Creek *(Ts.11-13N;Rs.9,10E)*

The stream of the creek rises near Hugo and Chambers lakes in 2 forks, extreme southeast Lewis County; flows northwest to Cowlitz River, 2 miles southwest of Packwood, east central

Lewis County. It was locally named for Andrew Johnson, a settler who came here from Tennessee.

Johnson Creek *Ts.34,35N;R.26E)*

The stream of the creek rises in a lake region west of Okanogan River, central Okanogan County; flows east in a wide circle to join Okanogan River at Riverside. It was named for Jake Johnson, who drove cattle to the Cariboo country in British Columbia during the 1860s, and who kept the weaker animals at the mouth of this creek.

Johnson Lake
(Ss.28,33;T.10N;R.11W)

A 30-acre lake near the mouth of Columbia River, 1/2 mile north of Ilwaco, extreme southwest Pacific County. It is used as a domestic water source by Ilwaco. The original name was *Black Lake*, for its dark water. The present name is evidently for a local family.

Johnson Mountain
(Ss.17,18;T.29N;R.13E.uns)

A 6,680-ft. peak 9 miles south by west of Glacier Peak summit, extreme east central Snohomish County. It is used as a fire lookout in season by the Forest Service. The mountain was locally named for "Mackinaw Johnson," who lived and prospected in this area in early days.

Johnson Point *(T.38N;R.2W)*

Southeast point of Sucia Island, in Gulf of Georgia, north central San Juan County. In 1855, it was named by the U.S. Coast Survey, for P. C. Johnson, passed midshipman with Lieut. Alden in *Active* and *Ewing*.

Johnson Point *(T.20N;R.1W)*

East entrance point of Henderson Inlet, on Dana Passage, 9 miles north of Olympia, extreme north Thurston County. In 1841, this feature was charted by Cmdr. Wilkes as *Point Moody*, for Quartermaster William Moody of his command. In 1853, the present name was applied by Ezra Meeker, for J. R. Johnson, M.D., who lived in a cabin near the point. The doctor called his log cabin "Johnson's Hospital."

Johnsons Landing
(S.13;T.11N;R.10W)

Landing on Naselle River, at junction of Hwys. 830 and 101, southwest Pacific County. It was named for Capt. James Johnson, the first Columbia River

bar pilot, who drowned in 1854 when his sloop foundered.

Johnstone Island (Clark County) *see* Lady Island

Johnstone's Decoy (Jefferson County) *see* Kilisut Harbor

Jones Island *(Ss.11,14;T.36N;R.3W)*

Island in San Juan Channel, 1/2 mile west of the southwest tip of Orcas Island, central San Juan County. In 1841, it was named by Cmdr. Wilkes for Capt. Jacob Jones, USN, a War of 1812 hero.

Jones Reservoir (San Juan County) *see* Sportsman Lake

Jonesville (Grays Harbor County) *see* Neilton

Jordan *(S.27;T.31N;R.6E)*

Post Office 5 miles southeast of Arlington, on South Fork, Stillaguamish River, northwest Snohomish County. When a post office was established, the name was applied by Mrs. Charles Lundberg, for her previous home in Jordan, Scott County, Minnesota.

Jordan Lakes *(Ss.10,11;T.34N;R.11E)*

Two connected lakes 7 miles southeast of Marblemount, in an area with many mountain lakes, east central Skagit County. The upper lake covers 64.9 acres, elevation 4,550 ft., and is over 50 ft. deep; the lower lake covers 58.7 acres, elevation 4,150 ft., and is very deep. They were named for Jordan Creek, which drains them through the lower lake.

Joseph Creek *(Ts.6,7N;R.46E)*

The stream of the creek rises in extreme northeast Oregon; flows 8 miles northeast to Grande Ronde River, 2-1/2 miles southwest of Rogersburg, southeast Asotin County. It was named for Chief Joseph, famous Nez Perce Indian, who lived on this creek for many years prior to the Nez Perce War of 1877.

Josephine Lake *(S.26;T.26N;R.14E)*

Mountain lake on Icicle Ridge, near its junction' with Cascade Mountain summit, at the head of Icicle Creek, Wenatchee National Forest, southwest Chelan County. It was named by Forest Supervisor A. H. Sylvester for Josephine Williams, wife of Forest Ranger Jason P. Williams.

Jove Peak *(Ss.13,24;T.27N;R.13E)*

Wenatchee National Forest peak, elevation 5,900 ft., at the head of Rainy

Creek, Cascade Mountain summit, west central Chelan County. It was named by Forest Supervisor A. H. Sylvester for the head deity of Roman mythology.

Jovita Lake (King County) *see* Trout Lake

Joy Creek (Chelan County) *see* Jay Creek

Joyce *(S.33;T.31N;R.8W)*

A very small settlement 1-1/2 miles south of Crescent Bay and 16 miles west of Port Angeles, north central Clallam County. It was locally named for J. M. Joyce, who operated a store and shingle mill here when Port Angeles Western Railroad was completed to this point.

Juan de Fuca Strait (Clallam, Jefferson, San Juan counties) *see* Strait of Juan de Fuca

Juanita *(S.31;T.26N;R.5E)*

Town on the east shore of Lake Washington, near the lake's north end on Juanita Bay, 1-1/2 miles north of Kirkland, King County. When the community was founded in 1870, it was named *Hubbard*, for an early settler. In 1921, the present name was applied when a townsite was platted, borrowing the name of Juanita Bay.

Juanita (Yakima County) *see* Waneta

Judd Creek *(T.32N;R.3E)*

The stream of the creek rises in central Vashon Island, southwest King County; flows 3-1/2 miles southeast into Quartermaster Harbor, north of Burton. It was locally named for A. W. Judd, a farmer and retired Methodist minister, who lived on Quartermaster Harbor, north of the creek.

Judson (Franklin County) *see* Mesa

Judson Lake
(S.36;T.41N;R.3E;&S.31;T.41N;R.4E)

Shallow lake 2-1/2 miles west of Sumas, directly on the Canadian boundary, northwest Whatcom County and British Columbia. It covers 112 acres: 82 in Whatcom County; 30 in British Columbia. The lake was named for George H. Judson, a pioneer surveyor.

Julia *(S.8;T.14N;R.27E)*

A post office on Columbia River, opposite Wahluke (now White Bluffs), north central Benton County. It was named for Julia Craig, the postmaster's daughter.

Julin's Bay (Pierce County) *see* Still Harbor

Julius Lake *(S.20;T.26N;R.16E)*

A Wenatchee National Forest lake near the head of Roaring Creek, on the east slope of Chiwaukum Mountain, southwest Chelan County. It was named by Forest Supervisor A. H. Sylvester, for Julius Kummel of the regional office of U.S. Forest Service. Kummel accompanied Sylvester on his first trip to the lake.

Jumbo Mountain
(Ss.1,2,11,12;T.31N;R.9E)

A 5,806-ft. peak, 3-1/2 miles south of Darrington, north central Snohomish County. It was named by early prospectors Charles Burns, Knute Nester, and George and John Knutson, for a fancied resemblance to an elephant.

Jumbo Rapids (Douglas County) *see* Equilibrium Rapids

Jump Off Creek
(Ss.25,35,36;T.31N;R.40E)

The stream of the creek heads in Jump Off Lake, 9 miles south of Chewelah, central Stevens County; flows 2-1/2 miles northwest to Colville River. The creek, the lake in which it heads, and a nearby peak were named in pioneer days for an episode which occurred on the Walla Walla-Spokane-Colville stage route. The stage started to tip on a muddy, rutted road at this point. Passengers tried to keep the vehicle from tipping over, and shouted "Jump off, Joe!" when they lost control. The driver, taking their advice, landed on his face in the mud.

Jump Off Lake *(Ts.30,31N;Rs.40,41E)*

Small lake at the head of Jump Off Creek, 5 miles northeast of Springdale, central Stevens County. An alternate name, shown on some maps, is *Jump Off Joe Lake*. (*see* Jump Off Creek)

Jump Off Mountain *(S.8;T.30N;R.41E)*

A 3,472-ft. peak 6 miles northeast of Springdale, 3 miles west of Deer Lake, central Stevens County. (*see* Jump Off Creek)

Jumper's Flat (Douglas County) *see* Waterville

Juno *(S.30;T.19N;R.42E)*

Railroad station on Cottonwood Creek, 1-1/2 miles north of St. John, northwest Whitman County. It was named by railroad officials, who wanted to give the place a short, classical name.

Jupiter Hills *(T.26N;R.3W)*

Hills between Duckabush and Dosewallips rivers, 12 miles southwest of Quilcene, southeast Jefferson County. In 1841, Cmdr. Wilkes charted the name, possibly to continue the Greco-Roman mythology references started in the area with the earlier naming of Mt. Olympus, "Home of the Gods."

Jupiter Lakes *(S.27;T.26N;R.3W)*

A group of 4 lakes, varying in size from 1/2 to 6 acres, on the northeast slope of Mt. Jupiter on Olympic National Forest, 11 miles southwest of Quilcene, southeast Jefferson County. (*see* Jupiter Hills)

K

Kachess Lake *(Ts.21,22N;R.13E)*

A 12-mile-long lake, elevation 2,222 ft., between Cle Elum Lake and Keechelus Lake, 5 miles east of Cascade Mountain summit, northwest Kittitas County. It was formed by the dam which a glacial moraine left across a prehistoric river. The Indian name means "many fish." In September 1858, it was mapped by Capt. George B. McClellan as *Kahchess Lake*.

Kahelamit (Wahkiakum County) *see* Cathlamet

Kahkwa Creek
(Ss.27,34;T.28N;R.12W)

The stream of this short creek heads southeast of Mountain 3, Olympic National Park, southwest Clallam County; flows 2 miles south to Bogachiel River. This Chinook jargon word means "similar" or "alike," and usually is used in word combinations. The meaning of its application here is somewhat obscure.

Kahlotus *(S.4;T.13N;R.34E)*

Town on west shore of Washtucna Lake, 40 miles northeast of Pasco, northeast Franklin County. In the 1890s, the first settler, Jon Harder, arrived. In June 1901, the town was platted by Hardersburg Townsite & Improvement Company as *Hardersburg*. The name was later changed to the original Indian name, which means "hole in the ground," and refers to nearby deep springs. Another translation of the Indian name is said to be "coyote water," which relates to an Indian legend of these springs.

Kahlotus Lake (Franklin County) *see* Lake Kahlotus

Kala Point *(S.35;T.30N;R.1W)*

A southwest shore point of Port Townsend bay, 1/2 mile north of the mouth of Chimacum Creek, northeast Jefferson County. In 1841, Cmdr. Wilkes named this feature *Kula Point*, evidently using the Indian name. His name probably relates to the Chinook jargon term for "bird," which is *Kala-kala*, or *Kalakula*, for "goose."

Kalaloch *(S.10;T.24N;R.13W)*

A small, sheltered beach on Pacific Ocean, 4-1/2 miles north of Queets River mouth, southwest Jefferson County. The name is the Quinault Indian term for "good place to land," which would be more logically spelled *K-e-le-ok*. This area is the only safe landing for canoes between the Hoh and Queets rivers.

Kalaloch Creek *(Ts.24,25N;R.13W)*

The stream of the creek heads between Clearwater and Hoh rivers, 6 miles from Pacific Ocean, southwest Jefferson County; flows southwest to the ocean, 1/2 mile above Kalaloch. (USBGN) (*see* Kalaloch)

Kalaloch Rocks *(T.24N;R.13W)*

Rocks in Pacific Ocean, 1/4 mile off

the mouth of Kalaloch Creek, southwest Jefferson County. (USBGN) (*see* Kalaloch)

Kalama *(T.6N;R.1W)*

Once an important railroad town on the east bank of Columbia River, at Kalama River mouth, southwest Cowlitz County. Trains were ferried here from Goble, Oregon. In 1871, the name was applied to the town and river by Gen. J. W. Sprague of Northern Pacific Railway Company. The name is from the Indian word *Calama*, meaning "pretty maiden."

Kalama River *(Ts.6-8N;Rs.1-4E)*

The stream of the river heads near the west boundary of Skamania County; flows 35 miles west by south to Columbia River, north of Kalama, Cowlitz County. (*see* Kalama)

Kalamut Island *(T.32N;R.1E)*

Almost an island at extreme high tides, but actually a peninsula, separating Oak Harbor and Crescent Harbor, on the east shore of Whidbey Island, Island County. It is now part of the U.S. Naval Air Base. In 1841, it was named by Cmdr. Wilkes, who believed it to be separated from Whidbey Island. The name is a modification of the Indian word *Cal-a-met*, meaning "a stone" or "rocky ground."

Kaleetan Lake *(S.23;T.23N;R.10E)*

A 3-acre lake, among many other mountain lakes, 4-1/2 miles northwest of Snoqualmie Pass, and 1 mile northwest of Kaleetan Peak, Snoqualmie National Forest, east central King County. It was named for Kaleetan Peak. In 1916, the peak's original Indian name was suggested to the USBGN by The Mountaineers. In Chinook jargon, *Ka-lee-tan* means "arrow."

Kaleetan Peak
(Ss.23,24;T.23N;R.10E)

A Snoqualmie National Forest peak, elevation 5,500 ft., in a region of many small lakes, 4 miles northwest of Snoqualmie Pass, east central King County. (USBGN) (*see* Kaleetan Lake)

Kalispel Indian Reservation
(Ts.33,34N;R.44E)

A relatively small reservation along the east bank of Pend Oreille River, covering 4,629 acres, 12 miles northwest of Newport, south central Pend Oreille County. It was established by a Congressional Act of February 8, 1887, and by

an Executive Order, dated March 23, 1914. In 1961, the Indian population numbered 165. The reservation was named for a branch or sub-tribe of the Pend Oreilles. An alternate spelling on many maps is *Calispel* or *Callispel*. According to its pronunciation by Indians, the original name would have been spelled *Kalispelus*.

Kalispell Creek *(T.36N;R.45E)*

The stream of the creek rises at Kalispell Rock, east central Pend Oreille County; flows east to the Idaho boundary, then through Idaho to Priest Lake. (USBGN) (*see* Calispell Creek)

Kalispell Falls *(S.20;T.36N;R.45E)*

Falls in Kalispell Creek, 1-1/2 miles below the stream's source, east central Pend Oreille County. (USBGN) (*see* Calispell Creek)

Kalispell Rock *(S.16;T.36N;R.45E)*

A Kaniksu National Forest peak, elevation 5,290 ft., 31 miles north of Newport, east central Pend Oreille County. It is used by the Forest Service as a fire lookout in season. (USBGN) (*see* Calispell Creek)

Kalispellem River (Pend Oreille County) *see* Pend Oreille River

Kalowa River (Clallam County) *see* Calawah River

Kalset Point *(S.1;T.29N;R.2W)*

A west shore point of Port Discovery Bay, 1-1/2 miles north of Port Discovery, northeast Jefferson County. In 1846, it was named and entered on British Admiralty charts as *Calset Point* by Capt. Henry Kellet. That name is now official, with the spelling change, which appears to have been in error. Later names were *Quiney Point* and *Gibb Point* or *Gibbs Point*. (USBGN)

Kamas Prairie Creek (Spokane County) *see* Latah Creek

Kamiack Butte *(S.20;T.16N;R.45E)*

An isolated mountain, elevation 3,650 ft., 10 miles east of Colfax, east central Whitman County. Many names have been applied to this feature, including *Kamiak Mountain, Kamiak Butte, Kamiakin Butte* and *Kamiakin Mountain*. A request for a ruling has been made to the USBGN, suggesting that the mountain be named for Kamiakin, war chief of the Yakimas in 1858.

Kamilche *(S.18;T.19N;R.3W)*

Small settlement at the southwest extremity of Skookum Inlet, 6 miles south

of Shelton, southeast Mason County. It was formerly an important logging center. The Indian name, in Twana dialect, means "valley." It evidently has developed by local usage. Kamilche is a modification of the original word *Ka-bel-chi*.

Kanaskat *(S.10;T.21N;R.7E)*

Community on the north bank of Green River, 8 miles northeast of Enumclaw, south central King County. It is reported to have been named for a Yakima Indian sub-chief, who had a wife here, as well as 2 wives in the Yakima country.

Kanem Island (Cowlitz County) *see* Cottonwood Island

Kanem Point *(S.4;T.30N;R.2W)*

Southwest point of Protection Island, in Strait of Juan de Fuca, 6 miles west of Port Townsend, northeast Jefferson County. In 1841, it was named by Cmdr. Wilkes as *Canim Point*, which remains in use, with the unexplained change in spelling. Wilkes called the base of the point *Daisy Bluff*, but that name did not persist. The word *canim* is Chinook jargon for "canoe."

Kaner Flat *(S.32;T.18N;R.14E)*

A north bank flat of Naches River, 14 miles east of Cascade Mountain summit, Snoqualmie National Forest, extreme southwest Kittitas County. It was named for a trapper and sheepherder who lived here in pioneer days.

Kangaroo Point *(T.37N;R.1W)*

East shore point of San Juan Island, northwest of Point Lawrence, northeast San Juan County. It was named by a local resident, George Burke, "who had happy memories of Australia." The name is not shown on recent maps.

Kangley *(S.26;T.22N;R.7E)*

Railroad station on a small tributary of Green River, 11 miles northeast of Issaquah, southwest King County. It was named by Northern Pacific Railway officials, for John Kangley, general manager of Northern Pacific Coal Company. An alternate name is *Kangley Junction*.

Kangley Junction (King County) *see* Kangley

Kaniksu National Forest

This forest occupies 258,766 acres in northeast Washington, and extends into northern Idaho, with headquarters in Sandpoint, Idaho. It is one of many forests under the jurisdiction of Region 1, U.S. Forest Service, with offices in Missoula, Montana. The name, chosen by Forest Service officials, is one given by Pend Oreille Indians to Father John Roothan, a Jesuit missionary, who ministered to Indians in this area.

Kansas Cove *(S.17;T.35N;R.2W)*

Cove on the eastern tip of San Juan Island, in San Juan Channel, inside Turn Island, San Juan County. The name was applied by Prof. Walter L. C. Muenscher of the University of Kansas, while attending a summer session at Puget Sound Marine Station near Friday Harbor. It was in honor of his native state, but was never recorded and is unofficial.

Kapowsin *(S.6;T.17N;R.5E)*

Logging and recreational area on northwest side of Lake Kapowsin, 9 miles north of Eatonville, south central Pierce County. This original Indian name means ''shallow,'' which is an inappropriate reference to the lake. Other spellings previously used include *Kipowsin* and *Kapousen*.

Kapowsin Lake *(T.17N;Rs.4,5E)*

Northernmost of an extensive group of lakes, itself covering 512 acres with maximum depth 58 ft., 7 miles north of Eatonville, in the ''Blue Water Lakes District'' of south central Pierce County. (*see* Kapowsin)

Karamin *(S.21;T.38N;R.33E)*

Small settlement on Curlew Creek, directly north of Curlew Lake, Colville National Forest, northeast Ferry County. It was named for the Karamin Lumber Company, which operated here.

Karanips (Ferry County) *see* Curlew Lake

Karnes Lake (Jefferson County) *see* Twin Lakes (near Quilcene)

Katalamet (Wahkiakum County) *see* Cathlamet

Kate Labelle Creek (Okanogan County) *see* Cape Labelle Creek

Kathlamet (Wahkiakum County) *see* Cathlamet

Kautz Creek *(Mt. Rainier National Park)*

The stream of the creek rises on the southwest slope of Mt. Rainier, in several branches which drain Kautz and Pyramid glaciers; flows southwest to Nis-

qually River in two branches, 3 miles east of Nisqually entrance. On October 1 and 2, 1947, a severe flood caused a huge landslide along the creek, which moved at least 50 million cubic yards of rock and debris into the lower valley. An immense area of forest was destroyed. The creek was named for Lieut. A. V. Kautz of Ft. Steilacoom, who made the first attempt to reach Mt. Rainier's summit. In 1857, he climbed to 12,000 ft. before admitting defeat.

Kautz Glacier *(Mt. Rainier National Park)*

One of Mt. Rainier's smaller ice rivers on the south slope, between Van Trump and Pyramid glaciers; heads at Peak Success, the southern summit of the mountain, and extends to the head of Kautz Creek, south central area of the park. (USBGN) (*see* Kautz Creek)

Keechelus *(S.2;T.21N;R.11E)*

Post Office on the west shore of Keechelus Lake, 3 miles east of Cascade Mountain summit, extreme northwest Kittitas County. This Indian name means ''few fish'' or ''less fish,'' in contrast with Kachess, which means ''many fish.''

Keechelus Lake *(Ts.21,22N;R.11E)*

Extensive and valuable 5-1/2-mile-long lake, average width less than one mile and elevation 2,454 ft., at head of Yakima River, 3 to 4 miles east of Cascade Mountain summit, extreme northwest Kittitas County. On some maps it is shown, in error, as *Lake Keechelus*. (*see* Keechelus)

Keekwulee Falls *(S.6;T.22N;R.11E)*

Lowest waterfalls in Denny Creek, 2-1/2 miles west of Cascade Mountain summit, east central King County. In 1916, The Mountaineers gave the falls this Indian name, a Chinook jargon word meaning ''to fall down.'' (USBGN)

Keelog's Point (Island County) *see* Admiralty Head

Keller *(S.33;T.30N;R.33E)*

Community on the west bank of San Poil River, 9 miles from the river's present mouth, on Franklin D. Roosevelt Lake, Ferry County. In 1940, when the Grand Coulee Dam flooded the river mouth to a distance of 8 miles, the town was moved about 7 miles upstream, then 3 miles back because of differing factions. The old site is under approximately 80 ft. of water. In 1898, Keller was

founded when the south half of Colville Indian Reservation was opened for mining. It was named for J. C. Keller, who started the first store in a tent here at that time. The town was a wide-open mining camp, with a cable ferry across Columbia River, which was operated by James Novotney. In the early days, Keller moved a mile up-river, and platted the town's first location as *Harlinda*.

Keese (Whatcom County) *see* Kendall

Keeslingville (Whatcom County) *see* Bellingham

Kellett Bluff *(S.28;T.36N;R.4W)*

A very high bluff, elevation 305 ft., at the south end of Henry Island in Haro Strait, 2-1/2 miles southwest of Roche Harbor, west central San Juan County. In 1847, it was charted by Lieut. Cmdr. Wood of *HMS Pandora*, for Capt. Henry Kellett, R.N., who surveyed this area in 1846-47 for the British Admiralty as commander of the survey vessel *Herald*.

Kellett Ledge *(S.10;T.34N;R.1W)*

Ledge off the southeast point of Lopez Island in Rosario Strait, 1/2 mile east of Cape St. Mary, southeast San Juan County. In 1854, it was named by the U.S. Coast Survey for Capt. Henry Kellett, R.N. (*see* Kellet Bluff)

Kelley Mountain *(S.15;T.37N;R.37E)*

A 2,730-ft. mountain directly north of a fork between Kettle and Columbia rivers, across Columbia River from Bossburg, northwest Stevens County. It was named for an early prospector, whose mineral location on this mountain was found to contain tungsten ore. On some maps it is shown as *Kelley Hill*.

Kellum's Lake Isthmus *(Ts.21,22N;Rs.2,3W)*

Narrow isthmus, not named on recent maps, between Cases Inlet and Hood Canal, east central Mason County. It was named for Kellum's Lake, which has been renamed Mason Lake. In 1841, the original name was chosen by Cmdr. Charles Wilkes for John Kellum, quartermaster in one of Wilkes's crews. An alternate name, not in present use, was *Wilkes' Portage*.

Kellyville (Skagit County) *see* Sedro Wooley

Kelp Rock (San Juan County) *see* Harbor Rock

Kelso *(T.8N;R.2W)*

Small city on the east bank of Cowlitz River, and including West Kelso on the river's west bank, opposite Longview, southwest Cowlitz County. It was named for Kelso, Scotland, by Peter Crawford, who claimed land here on December 25, 1847. In 1882, the railway station was called *Wallace's* by Northern Pacific Railway Company.

Kendall *(S.25;T.40N;R.5E)*
Community 18 miles northeast of Bellingham, in the valley of North Fork, Nooksack River, north central Whatcom County. The first post office was named *Keese*. Some time after 1887, the name was changed to Kendall, for Carthage Kendall, who homesteaded here in 1884.

Kendall Lake *(S.27;T.40N;R.5E)*
A 12-acre lake at the head of Kendall Creek, 1-1/4 miles north of Kendall, 4-1/2 miles south of the British Columbia boundary, northwest Whatcom County. (*see* Kendall)

Kendon (King County) *see* Hot Springs

Ken Lake (Thurston County) *see* Simmons Lake

Kenmore *(T.26N;R.4E)*
Suburb of Seattle at the extreme north end of Lake Washington, northwest King County. In 1890, John McMaster of Kenmore, Ontario, established a shingle mill here; he became known as "the dean of the shingle industry." On January 10, 1901, McMaster named the town for his home. The site had been a meeting place for local Indians, who called it *Sta-tab-eh*, meaning "lots of people talking."

Kennebee River (Pacific County) *see* Naselle River

Kennedy *(S.9;T.20N;R.11E)*
Railroad point at the headwaters of Green River, 3 miles west of Cascade Mountain summit, extreme southeast King County. In 1906, it was named by Northern Pacific Railway officials, for one of the partners of Klement-Kennedy Lumber Company, which operated logging and sawmill activities here.

Kennewick *(Ts.8,9N;Rs.29,30E)*
City on the south bank of Columbia River, directly across from Pasco, southeast Benton County. In 1883, a railroad town was located here by Northern Pacific Railway Company, during construction of a bridge across the river. In 1892, a townsite was platted

by Northern Pacific Irrigation Company. Irrigation canals were in operation by 1903, causing a spectacular land boom. The first name applied to the town was *Dell Haven*. The Indian name was later restored by Col. H. S. Huson of Northern Pacific Irrigation Company. It has been translated as "grassy place," "winter paradise" and "dried acorns."

Kenova *(S.29;T.20N;R.42E)*
A platted but undeveloped townsite 3 miles southwest of Malden, on Pine Creek, north central Whitman County. It was named by officials of Chicago, Milwaukee & St. Paul Railway, who stated that it was "a chance selection." Their name choice may have been for towns in Arkansas and West Virginia with this same name.

Kent *(T.22N;Rs.4,5E)*
City between Auburn and Renton, 4 miles east of Puget Sound, west central King County. In the 1880s and '90s, this area was a very important hop-growing center. In 1886, it was named *Titusville*, for James Henry Titus, a pioneer homesteader. When platted in 1888, Ezra Meeker, who had extensive hop fields here, named the town Kent, for a famous hop-growing center in England. An adjoining community, platted by Henry Yesler of Seattle as Yesler's First Addition to Kent, was called Yesler.

Kent Creek *(Ts.31,32N;R.44E)*
The stream of this short creek rises in Kent Meadows, south central Pend Oreille County; flows 3 miles north to Pend Oreille River, 2 miles southeast of Dalkena. It was named for Fred Kent, who owned Kent Meadows.

Kerriston *(S.25;T.23N;R.7E)*
Once an important logging center on upper Raging River, 4 miles west of Cedar Falls, central King County. It was named for A. S. Kerry, president of Kerry Timber Company, which logged here for some years in the very early 1900s.

Kessiso Rocks *(S.2;T.33N;R.16W)*
Rocks at the far west point of Cape Flattery, Makah Indian Reservation, on Pacific Ocean, between Fuca Pillar and Hole-in-the-wall, extreme northwest Clallam County. This Makah Indian name should be spelled *Ke-sis-so*, according to Indian pronunciation.

Ketron *(S.12;T.19N;R.1E)*
Railway station on Cormorant Pass,

2 miles southwest of Steilacoom, northwest Pierce County. It was named by Northern Pacific Railway Company officials for nearby Ketron Island, which, in 1841, was named by Cmdr. Wilkes for William *Kittson* of Hudson's Bay Company. Wilkes' incorrect spelling persisted. Other spellings which have been used include *Kitron's Island, Kitson Island* and *Kittson Island*.

Ketron Island *(T.19N;R.1E)*
An island separated from the mainland by Cormorant Passage, in Nisqually Reach, west central Pierce County. (*see* Ketron)

Ketslum Island (Skagit County) *see* Deception Island

Kettle Falls *(T.36N;R.37E)*
Historical Columbia River falls 2 miles below the mouth of Kettle River, on the boundary between Stevens and Ferry counties. It was an important salmon-fishing place for local Indian tribes until 1939-40, when the falls were flooded out by Grand Coulee Dam. French-Canadian employees of early fur traders called the falls *Les Chaudieres* (The Kettles); boulders revolving in the current had worn huge, kettle-shaped holes in the stream bed below the falls. Yankee traders and settlers changed the name to English. The original Indian name was reported as *Ilth-koy-ape*, a Salish phrase meaning "net of tightly-woven baskets," devices which were used to catch salmon below the falls. An Indian name more often given, and somewhat more plausible, is *Schwan-ate-ku*, meaning "the place of the deep-sounding water."

Kettle Falls *(S.20;T.36N;R.38E)*
Town on the old townsite of Meyers Falls, north of Colville River, northwest Stevens County. In 1888, Marcy H. Randall filed a homestead claim on land located one mile below the famous Kettle Falls and rapids, on the east bank of Columbia River, north of Colville River mouth. Randall intended to develop this water power, but could not locate closer because of land ownership by St. Paul's Mission. On August 14, 1889, a townsite was platted. The town boomed in the 1890s, but slumped badly in the early 1900s. When the site was flooded by Grand Coulee Dam in 1939-40, many buildings and most of the population found a new home in Meyers Falls, 3 miles east. At a town meeting, in which

Kettle Falls migrants outnumbered Meyers Falls voters 4 to 1, the name was changed to Kettle Falls.

Kettle River

The stream of the river heads near Monashee Pass, in southeast British Columbia; and flows south 85 miles, to the extreme corner of northwest Ferry County. It continues south, east and north in a wide semi-circle, re-entering British Columbia at Danville; then re-enters the United States 13 miles east at Laurier, and flows 25 miles to Columbia River near Marcus, between Ferry and Stevens counties. In 1939-40, the river's lower 8 miles were flooded in the basin created by Grand Coulee Dam. As late as 1882, the Indian name *Ne-hoi-al-pit-kwa* was used on maps, with spelling variations. (*see* Kettle Falls)

Kewa *(S.9;T.31N;R.36E)*

Settlement on Colville Indian Reservation, near Nez Perce Creek, 4 miles west of Franklin D. Roosevelt Lake, southeast Ferry County. The town was originally given its Indian name, *Kewah*, which means "yes" in San Poil language. When a post office was established, postal authorities refused Kewah, but accepted the present, shortened version.

Key *(Thurston County) see* Rochester

Keyport *(S.36;T.26N;R.1E)*

Location of a Naval torpedo station on the south shore of Liberty Bay at its east entrance, 8 miles north of Bremerton, Kitsap County. In 1896, the site was settled by Pete Hagen, O. A. Kuppler and H. B. Kuppler. They chose the present name from an atlas, for a small town on the New Jersey coast. A local name, no longer used, was *School Point*.

Keyport Lagoon *(S.36;T.26N;R.1E)*

A 22.4-acre lake near tide water, 1/2 mile south of Keyport, north central Kitsap County. Is is used by State Department of Fisheries for rearing salmon. (*see* Keyport)

Keystone *(S.9;T.20N;R.37E)*

Community 13 miles northeast of Ritzville, 2 miles west of Lake Colville, northeast Adams County. In 1900, it was named by John W. Smith, owner of the townsite and first postmaster, for his native state of Pennsylvania, which is nicknamed Keystone. That state was the seventh of the 13 original states, hence

in the middle of the union, and reason for the name. Originally, this Northern Pacific Railway station was called *Harriston*.

Keystone *(S.24;T.31N;R.1E)*

Ferry terminal on the north shore of Admiralty Bay, at the east end of Crocketts Lake, Island County. Ft. Casey, an old coast defense fort 2 miles east, has been rehabilitated by Washington State Parks & Recreation Commission as one of Whidbey Island's scenic attractions. The terminal's present name, without particular significance, was chosen locally when the boom town of *New Chicago* faded away in the 1893 panic. That town, on the site of Keystone, was to have been the western terminus of Chicago & Skagit Valley Railroad, with an eastern terminus at Sedro Wooley.

Kiapot Point *(Clallam County) see* Long Spit

Kickerville *(S.9;T.39N;R.1E)*

Very small community on Terrell Creek, 1 mile north of Lake Terrell, northwest Whatcom County. It was named by Hon. Edward Brown, state legislator, who later was named county commissioner because so many petitions to the county board originated here.

Kicket Point *(Skagit County) see* Kiket Island

Kidd *(Spokane County) see* Chattaroy

Kiddekubbut Point *(Clallam County) see* Kydikabbit Point

Kidd's Peak *(King County) see* Bryant Peak

Killkelly Creek *(Jefferson County) see* Kilkelly Creek

Kiket Island *(S.21;T.34N;R.2E)*

An island only at high tide, extending west from the west shore of Swinomish Indian Reservation, between Similk and Skagit bays, Skagit County. In 1841, Cmdr. Wilkes applied the name, evidently using the Indian term for the place. On some local maps, it is shown as *Kicket Point*.

Kilisut Harbor *(Ts.29,30N;R.1E)*

Channel between Indian and Marrowstone islands, northeast Jefferson County. It connects Port Townsend Bay on the north with Oak Bay on the south; the latter is only open at high tide. Few features in the state have such a variety

of names. On May 5, 1792, Capt. George Vancouver named it *Johnstone's Decoy*, for the master of his armed tender *Chatham*. In 1841, Cmdr. Wilkes named it *Kilisut Harbour*. Pioneers called it *Scow Bay*, after Alberg Briggs brought 30 head of cattle here in 1852 on a scow, which used no power other than tides; he made the trip from Tumwater in 15 days. Other early names used by U.S. Coast Survey in 1889 were *Long Bay* and *Long Harbor*.

Kilkelly Creek *(Ss.20,29;T.26N;R.8W.uns)*

A 2-mile-long tributary of Queets River, entering the river 5 miles south of Mt. Olympus, Olympic National Park, central Jefferson County. It was named by Park Service officials for a pioneer settler. A common misspelling is *Killkelly*. (USBGN)

Killibrew Lake *(S.14;T.36N;R.2W)*

Privately-owned, 13-acre lake near south end of Orcas Island's middle peninsula, 6-1/4 miles south of East Sound (town), central San Juan County. It was named *Killibrew's Lake* by local settlers, for an early landowner in the area. An alternate name, evidently not found on maps, was *Day's Lake*.

Kimooenim Creek *(Columbia County) see* Tucannon River

Kimta Creek *(T.25N;R.8W)*

The stream of the creek heads in 3 forks, southeast of Kimta Peak, Olympic National Park, southwest Jefferson County; the forks combine and flow southeast to North Fork, Quinault River. It is somewhat smaller than other North Fork tributaries. The Indian name has survived, and, in Chinook jargon, means "the last," "behind" or "weaker."

Kimta Lake *(S.11;T.25N;R.5W.uns)*

A 2-acre lake on North Fork, Kimta Creek, southeast of Kimta Peak on Olympic National Park, southeast Jefferson County. (*see* Kimta Creek)

Kimta Peak *(Ss.3,4,9,10;T.25N;R.8W)*

An Olympic National Park mountain, elevation 5,399 ft., 8 miles south of Mt. Olympus summit, central Jefferson County. Although named for Kimta Creek, the meaning is not appropriate to this peak, which is higher than most in the vicinity. (*see* Kimta Creek)

King County

This county in western Washington

is bounded on the west by Puget Sound; on the north by Snohomish County; on the east by Cascade Mountain summit; and on the south by Pierce County.

Covering 2,136 square miles, it has diversified industries and the heaviest population of any county in the state.

On December 22, 1852, the county was established from a portion of Thurston County, by the Oregon Territorial Legislature. On March 5, 1853, county functions started, with so many offices and so few qualified citizens that some men held as many as 6 positions.

It was named for William Rufus King of Alabama, vice president of the United States, 1853-57, in the Pierce Administration; he had served 29 years in the Senate, and had been Minister to France.

King Lake *(S.18;T.30N;R.16E.uns)*

Lake in a rock cup at the foot of a small, receding glacier; drains into Buck Creek from its high position near Cascade Mountain summit, on the northeast slope of Buck Mountain, northwest Chelan County. In 1928, it was named by Forest Supervisor A. H. Sylvester, for Harry King of Cashmere. King had accompanied Sylvester on an inspection trip, during which they sighted this lake from a high pass in Entiat Mountains.

Kings Lake *(Ss.1,2;T.33N;R.44E)*

One of a group of small- to medium-sized lakes east of Pend Oreille River, Kaniksu National Forest, south central Pend Oreille County. It was named for John King, an early homesteader in the area.

Kingston *(S.25;T.27N;R.2E)*

Western terminus of a state ferry from Edmonds, on the north shore of Appletree Cove, north Kitsap County. It was named for William P. Kingston, a lumberman, who started operations here in 1888.

Kinneyville *(S.3;T.8N;R.24E)*

Formerly a community about one mile west of Prosser, west central Benton County. The founder was James Gordon Kinney, stage stationmaster here in early days, when Prosser was called Prosser Falls. It bore his name until the community merged with Prosser.

Kinnooenim Creek (Columbia Creek) *see* Tucannon River

Kioma *(S.19;T.9N;R.27E)*

Small settlement on Yakima River, 20 miles west of Pasco, central Benton County. In 1885, it was established as a way-point by Northern Pacific Railway, when it built through here. The first name used was *Horseshoe Bend*, because of the sharp bend in Yakima River, 4 miles across. The present name is said to be derived from the Indian word for "brown hills," and is very descriptive of the surrounding landscape.

Kiona Creek *(Ts.12,13N;Rs.6,7E)*

The stream of the creek rises in high country north of Kiona Peak, central Lewis County; flows southeast to Cowlitz River, 1-1/2 miles south of Randle. It is located in "Big Bottom" country, populated largely by mountain people from southern states. In 1854, the creek was named by pioneer J. T. Chilcoat, for Columbia Kionee, an Indian who lived near here in a native village.

Kiona Peak *(S.35;T.13N;R.6E)*

A 4,860-ft. peak at the headwaters of Kiona Creek, 4 miles northwest of Randle, Lewis County. It is used as a forest fire lookout in season, since it offers an excellent view of eastern Gifford Pinchot National Forest. *(see* Kiona Creek)

Kirkland *(T.25N;R.5E)*

City on the east shore of Lake Washington, near the lake's north end, northwest King County. It was named for Peter Kirk, a Scottish millionaire, who purchased a promising iron mine from the pioneer Denny family in 1886; he planned to establish a large steel plant here. Kirk and L.S.J. Hunt, owner of Seattle's *Post-Intelligencer,* organized Kirkland Land & Improvement Company and Great Western Iron & Steel Company. The industries failed in the financial panic of 1893, and Kirkland was a deserted place for several years. The Indian name for the site was *Sta-lal.*

Kitron's Island (Pierce County) *see* Ketron Island

Kitsap County

This county in western Washington is bounded on the north and east by Puget Sound; on the south by Thurston and Mason counties; and on the west by Hood Canal.

It was created from portions of King and Jefferson counties, by acts of the Teritorial Legislature, passed on January 16 and 27, 1857. At that time it was named

for Lieut. W. A. Slaughter, who was killed in the Indian wars of 1855. On July 13, 1857, the present name was officially substituted. It was for Chief Kitsap, who assisted white men, and was friendly to them until, on April 8, 1860, he was killed by his own tribesmen.

Kitsap Lake (Kitsap County) *see* Lake Kitsap

Kitsap Memorial State Park *(T.27N;R.1E)*

A 45-acre public campground near Lofall on Hood Canal, 6 miles nortof Poulsbo, northwest Kitsap County. Park activities include swimming, fishing and clamming. *(see* Kitsap County)

Kittitas *(S.11;T.17N;R.19E)*

Town near Caribou Creek, 6 miles east of Ellensburg, east central Kittitas County. The name is from the Indian word *K-tatus,* meaning "gray gravel bank"; it refers to an extensive gravel bank on a river shoal near Ellensburg.

Kittitas County

This county in central Washington is bounded on the north by Chelan County; on the east by Grant County; on the south by Yakima County; and on the west by Yakima and King counties. It contains 2,315 sq. miles. Coal, potatoes, livestock and forest products are the principal items produced. On November 2, 1883, the county was established by Washington Territorial Legislature, from a portion of Yakima County. *(see* Kittitas)

Kitzmiller *(S.29;T.15N;R.45E)*

Community on Missouri Flat Creek, 1-1/2 miles north of Pullman, southeast Whitman County. It was named for E. D. Kitzmiller, a local farmer.

Klaber *(S.1;T.12N;R.4W)*

Village on South Fork, Chehalis River, 13 miles southwest of Chehalis, west central Lewis County. It was named for Herman Klaber, who once owned extensive hop yards here on rich, river-bottom soil. At one time, they were reputed to be the largest hop yards in the world.

Klachopis Point *(S.12;T.33N;R.15W)*

A rocky ledge on Strait of Juan de Fuca, east of Neah Bay, on Makah Indian Reservation, northwest Clallam County. The original Makah Indian name has been retained, although in 1841 Cmdr. Wilkes named it *Sail Rock Point,* and, in 1846, Capt. Kellett charted the ledge as *Scarborough Point.*

Klahanee Ridge *(T.29N;R.6W.uns)*

A 2-1/2-mile-long ridge on Olympic National Park, between Mt. Angeles on the west and Rocky Peak on the east, east central Clallam County. This Chinook Indian jargon name, usually spelled Klahanie, means "out" or "out of doors." (USBGN)

Klahanee Gardens *(T.29N;R.6W)*

Mountain meadow near the foot of Mt. Angeles, 8-1/2 miles south of Port Angeles, northeast Clallam County. Olympic National Park officials retained its Indian name. (*see* Klahanee Ridge)

Klaholah Rock *(Clallam County) see* Seal Rock

Klannet Range *(Central Washington) see* Cascade Mountain Range

Klapatche Lake *(Mt. Rainier National Park)*

A 1-acre lake in an open meadow, 5-3/4 miles west of Mt. Rainier summit, at the east end of Klapatche Ridge. The name, taken from Klapatche Ridge, was suggested on May 7, 1912, by Jerry Meeker, an Indian who lived in Tacoma. It was for an Indian whom Meeker called "the greatest of the Puyallup chiefs."

Klapatche Park *(Mt. Rainier National Park)*

Park at the east end of Klapatche Ridge, elevation 5,500 ft., in North Puyallup River drainage, west central zone of the park. It includes several small lakes. (USBGN) (*see* Klapatche Lake)

Klapatche Ridge *(Mt. Rainier National Park)*

A 2-mile-long ridge, maximum elevation 5,500 ft., between North Puyallup River and St. Andrew's Creek, extending west from Klapatche Peak to the western park boundary. (USBGN) (*see* Klapatche Lake)

Klas Rock *(T.29N;R.1E)*

Rock directly off Basalt Point on Admiralty Inlet, at the mouth of Mats Mats Bay, northeast Jefferson County. Evidently, the Indian name was retained by Cmdr. Wilkes when he named this rock in 1841. Its meaning has not ben determined.

Klasset *(Clallam County) see* Cape Flattery

Klaxta *(T.28N;R.36E)*

Abandoned townsite on the south bank of Spokane River, close to Old Ft. Spokane, north central Lincoln County. It was platted as a rendezvous for soldiers, who were stationed at the fort. The name is a Chinook jargon word, more commonly spelled *Kla-sta* or "who." It is not clear why it was considered appropriate to this place.

Klickitat *(S.23;T.4N;R.13E)*

Railroad station on Klickitat River, 14 miles north of Dallesport, west central Klickitat County. In 1890, it was established by L. C. Wright, and called *Wright's*. In 1910, the post office changed to the present name, an, in 1913, so did the railroad station. The name is for an Indian nation, which lived in the vicinity, and was called *Hladachut* by Chinooks on the lower Columbia; a translation is "beyond," meaning Indians who lived beyond thmountains. The present name is a corruption of that Indian nation's name. Past renditions of the name were recorded as *Klackatat, Clickitat* and *Klikatat*.

Klickitat County

This county in south central Washington is bounded on the north by Yakima and Skamania counties; on the east by Benton County; on the south by Columbia River; and on the west by Skamania County. It was established on December 20, 1859, by Washington Territorial Legislature as *Clickitat County*. Livestock, wheat, hay and pears are primary products of the county's 1,825 square miles, although forest products are of growing importance. (*see* Klickitat)

Klickitat Creek *(T.12N;Rs.2,3E)*

The stream of the creek rises near Swoffort, south central Lewis County; flows west to Cowlitz River, 2-1/2 miles north of Mayfield. (*see* Klickitat)

Klickitat Creek *(Mt. Rainier National Park)*

The stream of the creek heads in Ghost Lake, 1-1/2 miles west of Chinook Pass, east central zone of the park; flows north to White River, near the park's White River entrance. It was named by Park Ranger Thomas E. O'Farrell for many Klickitat Indians, who visited the park area regularly in early days. (USBGN)

Klickitat Glacier *(T.8N;R.11E.uns)*

One of 8 live glaciers on Mt. Adams, on the mountain's southeast slope, southwest Yakima County. (*see* Klickitat)

Klickitat Landing *(Klickitat County) see* Lyle

Klickitat Prairie *(T.12N;R.3E)*

Prairie south of Mossyrock, south central Lewis County. The Indian ame, used by pioneer settlers, was *Coulph*. The present name was adopted during the Indian wars, when Klickitat Indians drove white settlers out of this area.

Klickitat River *(Ts.3-12N;Rs.11-14E)*

The stream of the river rises in Goat Rocks, on the east slope of high Cascades, near Cisput Pass, with its Diamond Fork rising 15 miles to the east, Yakima County; winds through deep, rocky canyons for about 60 miles to Columbia River, near Lyle, Yakima County. (*see* Klickitat)

Kline *(S.34;T.22N;R.39E)*

Station 6 miles northeast of Sprague, southeast Lincoln County. The source of the name, applied by Northern Pacific Railway Company officials in 1888, is obscure.

Klipsan Beach *(Ts.11,12;R.11W)*

Ocean beach south of Ocean Park, on North Beach Peninsula, southwest Pacific County. A life-saving station operated here for some years, under command of Coast Guard officers. This Indian name, meaning *sunset*, was chosen by Capt. Theodore Conic, of the U.S. Coast Guard.

Klonaqua Lakes
(Ss.3,4,10;T.24N;R.14E)

Three lakes, one which is very small, with a common outlet, between French and Leland creeks, one mile east of Cascade Mountain summit, Wenatchee National Forest, southwest Chelan County. The name derives from 2 Indian languages; *Klone* is Chinook jargon for *three*; *Qua* means *three* in Wenatchee dialect. Forest Supervisor A. H. Sylvester coupled the two words into one for an appropriate name.

Klone Creek *(T.29N;R.18E)*

The stream of the creek rises on Klone Peak, Wenatchee National Forest, north central Chelan County; flows 3 miles northeast to Three Creek. Forest Supervisor A. H. Sylvester named this creek and the peak for his dog, Klone, which means *three* in Chinook Indian jargon; it was appropriate since he paid $3 for the animal. He later added the word *pesitkin* to the dog's name, when he paid 50 cents for a chicken the dog had killed. *Klone-pesitkin* means *three* and *one half* in Chinook.

Klone Lake *(Grays Harbor County) see* Klone Lakes

Klone Lakes *(S.14;T.23N;R.7W)*

Three lakes, including 2-acre Klone, 5-acre Discovery and 9-acre Bone, in upper Wynooche River drainage area, on Olympic National Forest, extreme northeast Grays Harbor County. The name is the Chinook Indian word for *three*.

Klone Peak *(S.32;T.29N;R.18E.uns)*

A Wenatchee National Forest peak, 2 miles north of Two Little Lakes, north central Chelan County. A wide view from this high mountain makes it valuable as a forest fire lookout in season. (*see* Klone Creek)

Kloochman Creek
(T.25,26N;R.19E)

The stream of the creek heads on the east slope of Entiat Mountains, east central Chelan County; flows 4 miles northeast to Tillicum Creek, Wenatchee National Forest. Forest Supervisor A. H. Sylvester named it with the Chinook jargon word for *wife* or *woman*. Another stream, which he named Indian Creek, also joins Tillicum Creek in this area. Figuring that an Indian should have both a wife and a friend, or *tillicum*, Sylvester made this name part of a three-way combination.

Kloochman Peak *(S.14;T.25N;R.10W)*

An Olympic National Park mountain, on the park's west boundary, 15 miles southwest of Mt. Olympus, southwest Jefferson County. The person responsible for the name appears to be unrecorded. Earlier names were *Boulder Hill* and *Kloochman Rock*. (*see* Kloochman Creek)

Kloochman Rock *(Jefferson County) see* Kloochman Peak

Kloontz Flat *(Franklin County) see* Ringold

Kloshe Creek *(T.28N;R.11W)*

The stream of the creek rises on Olympic National Park, south central Clallam County; flows 2 miles south to Bogachiel River, 1 mile below Cultus

Creek mouth, extreme north Jefferson County. The original Indian name has been retained, which is Chinook jargon for *good* or *pleasant*. It was probably selected to contrast with Cultus Creek, which has an opposite meaning.

Kloshe Nanich *(S.23;T.30N;R.11W)*

An Olympic National Forest peak, 8 miles southeast of Pysht, north central Clallam County. Because of the excellent view of surrounding countryside, it is maintained as a forest fire lookout in season. The Indian name is a combination of Chinook jargon words: *Kloshe* means *pleasant* or *beautiful*; *Nanich* means *look* or *see*.

Knapp *(S.19;T.3N;R.1E)*

Railroad station 7 miles north of Vancouver and 1 mile east of Columbia River, west central Clark County. When a station was established here in 1908, Northern Pacific Railway officials named it for a local farmer from whom the railway secured property for a right-of-way.

Knapp Coulee *(Ts.26,27N;R.21E)*

Coulee extending from Maple Creek on Columbia River, north to Lake Chelan, east central Chelan County. It was named for Frank Knapp, who established the first ferry across Columbia River at this point.

Knappton *(S.8;T.9N;R.9W)*

A village on the north bank of Columbia River, 3 miles northeast of Megler, southwest Pacific County. It was originally named *Cementville*, but was renamed in 1871 to honor J. B. Knapp, who had built a sawmill and cement plant here in 1868. Other names were *Todd Bay* and *Centerville*.

Knapsack Pass *(Mt. Rainier National Park)*

Pass near the southwest end of Mather Mountain, less than a mile east of Mowich Lake, northwest quarter of the park. The name was chosen by Park Ranger Thomas E. O'Farrell while on a hiking trip, which included his small daughter, Ethel. When she could walk no farther, O'Farrell carried her in his large knapsack. (USBGN)

Knotgrass Ridge *(S.10;T.10N;R.43E)*

Ridge extending east from Garfield County, through extreme northwest Asotin County, northwest of Pow-Wah-Kee Gulch. In the late 1870s, this feature was named for Kelly Knotgrass, who settled here at that time.

Knowlton *(S.7;T.31N;R.24E)*

Post Office 8 miles northwest of Brewster, on Swamp Creek, south central Okanogan County. It was named for Arthur R. Knowlton, who started a ranch here on land he claimed April 21, 1902. He was also the first postmaster.

Knowlton Knob *(S.25;T.31N;R.23E)*

Peak in Buckhorn Mountains, 7 miles northwest of Brewster, south central Okanogan County. It serves as a fire lookout in season. (*see* Knowlton)

Knox Lake *(S.5;T.25N;R.16E)*

Very small lake at the head of a south branch of Glacier Creek, Wenatchee National Forest, southwest Chelan County. It was named for William Knox, a sheepman, who used this range for many years.

Kodak Peak *(T.29N;R.14E.uns)*

A Wenatchee National Forest Peak, directly south of Indian Pass, at Cascade Mountain summit, northwest Chelan County. It was named by Forest Supervisor A. H. Sylvester, for a Kodak camera which was lost here by Forest Assistant Willett Ramsdell.

Koitlah Point *(S.3;T.33N;R.15W)*

A rocky cliff at Neah Bay's west entrance, on Makah Indian Reservation, northwest Clallam County. In competition with many names applied to this point by early explorers and coast surveyors, the original Indian name has been retained. As pronounced by Makah Indians, it should be spelled *Quo-eet-la*. On August 3, 1790, Manuel Quimper named it *Punta de Rada*; in 1841, Cmdr. Wilkes applied the name *Point Hilcomb*; and, in 1846, Capt. Henry Kellett placed it on British Admiralty charts as *Koikla Point*. This is one case in which Indians prevailed over Spanish, British and American influences.

Kool-aid Lake *(S.18;T.34N;R.14E)*

Small lake 2-1/2 miles south of Cascade Pass, on the west side of Cascade Mountain summit, east central Skagit County. It is a favorite campsite for hikers, and reportedly was named for a popular soft drink by a group of mountaineers who camped here.

Kopachuck State Park
(Ts.21,22N;R.1E)

An 84-acre park on Horsehead Bay, 16 miles west of Tacoma, northwest Pierce County. Fishing, clamming and picnic facilities are open to the public.

The Chinook Indian name for this area means *near the water.* An alternate name is *Horsehead Bay State Park.*

Kosmos *(S.28;T.12N;R.5E)*

Headquarters for extensive logging operations of U.S. Plywood Corp., on Cowlitz River, 8 miles southeast of Morton, south central Lewis County. In pioneer days, it was named by Charles Hopkinson, who operated a water-powered sawmill at the mouth of Rainey (Rene) Creek, which enters Cowlitz River here. There appears to be no record of the name origin. At one time, the place was locally called *Fulton.*

Kowish Creek *(Asotin County) see* Couse Creek

Kruger Mountain *(T.40N;R.25E)*

Turtle-shaped hill east of Similkameen River, directly south of the Canadian boundary, north central Okanogan County. It was named for Theodore Kruger, a huge German, who was employed by Hudson's Bay Company in the 1860s to run a store at Osoyoos.

Krupp *(Grant County) see* Marlin

Kula Point *(Jefferson County) see* Kala Point

Kulakala Point *(S.4;T.30N;R.3W)*

Small headland on Strait of Juan de Fuca, 3 miles southeast of Dungeness, northeast Clallam County. At one time, it was a duck refuge on the Alfred H. Anderson estate. In 1841, Cmdr. Wilkes applied the name as *Kulo Kala Point.* This Indian name is a combination of Chinook jargon words for bird *(Kula)* and goose *(Kala),* and refers to the great abundance

of waterfowl at this place in early days.

Kulshan Ridge *(S.19;T.39N;R.9E)*

A Mt. Baker National Forest ridge, average elevation 5,000 ft., extending 1-1/2 miles east from the east end of Ptarmigan Ridge on Mt. Baker, central Whatcom County. The Skagit Indian name means *foot that has been frozen,* and appears to be appropriate.

Kultus Mountain *(Skagit County) see* Cultus Mountains

Kummer *(S.26;T.21N;R.6E)*

Site of a former clay mine on Green River, 2 miles south of Black Diamond, south central King County. It was named for George Kummer, former general manager of Denny-Renton Clay Company, which mined clay here and at Taylor.

Kumtux *(S.35;T.4N;R.2E)*

Community near Battleground, central Clark County. It was named for an Indian chief, who was killed by soldiers of the 21st Infantry here during the Indian wars. The meaning of this Indian word is *to know* or *to understand.*

Kurtz Lake *(S.34;T.25N;R.8W.uns)*

A 1-1/2-acre lake at the head of a north branch of Three Prune Creek, Olympic National Park, southeast Jefferson County. It was named for David A. Kurtz of Aloha, Grays Harbor County.

Kutuzle Bay *(Wahkiakum County) see* Grays Bay

Kwad-dis Lake *(S.20;T.6N;R.8E.uns)*

A 3-1/2-acre lake, elevation 4,300 ft., 4 miles northwest of Big Lava Bed, in Indian Heaven area of central Skamania

County. The Chinook Indian name means *whale;* the reason for applying this name appears to be lost in Indian traditions.

Kydaku Point *(S.10;T.32N;R.13W)*

Point on Strait of Juan de Fuca, 2-1/2 miles west of Clallam Bay, at Hoko River mouth, northwest Clallam County. In 1847, it was placed on British Admiralty charts under its original Indian name by Capt. Henry Kellet.

Kydikabbit Point *(S.4;T.33N;R.15W)*

Point on Strait of Juan de Fuca, 1 mile west of Neah Bay entrance, on Makah Indian Reservation near Classet Indian village, extreme northwest Clallam County. This Indian name, sometimes spelled *Kiddekubbut,* has been retained on most charts and maps of the area.

Kyes Peak *(S.32;T.29N;R.12E.uns)*

A 7,239-ft. peak, on the boundary between Mt. Baker and Snoqualmie national forests, 4-1/2 miles southeast of Monte Cristo, east central Snohomish County. The original name was *Goblin Peak* or *Goblin Mountain.* In 1944, it was changed to honor Cmdr. James E. Kyes, USN, who died when the destroyer *Leary* was torpedoed in the North Atlantic on Christmas Eve, 1943; on August 15, 1920, he had made the first recorded ascent of the peak.

Kyro *(S.36;T.18N;R.1W)*

Railway station 6 miles east of Olympia, northeast Thurston County. It was named by Northern pacific Railway Company officials at the request of J.D. McIntyre, president of Planters Nursery Company of Seattle; the origin of the name has not been discovered.

L

La Barge Lake *(S.8;T.31N;R.7E)*

A 3-acre lake, maximum depth 20 ft., 7 miles north of Granite Falls, northwest Snohomish County. One of 4 in the Chain Lakes group, it is reported to have been named after the Alaska lake which Robert Service brought to attention in one of his best-known poems.

Labyrinth Mountain
(S.12;T.27N;R.14E.uns)

A Wenatchee National Forest peak, elevation 6,360 ft., 3 miles northeast of Cascade Mountain summit, between Lake and Rainy creeks, northwest Chelan County. It was named by Forest Supervisor A. H. Sylvester, when he discovered that the contour lines of this mountain on a topographic map appeared to make a labyrinth. (*see* Minotaur Lake, Theseus Lake)

La Center *(S.3;T.4N;R.1E)*

Town on East Fork, Lewis River, 15 miles north of Vancouver, west Clark County. The name originated when the town was head of navigation on the river here, and the center of shipping and travel in this area.

Lacey *(S.21;T.18N;R.1W)*

Town 5 miles east of Olympia, adjoining St. Martin's College on the south, central Thurston County. Once a sawmill town, it later became a horse racing center. Its original name was *Woodland*, but was changed to the present name because another Woodland existed in Cowlitz County. It was named by and for O. C. Lacey, a realtor and attorney who owned much local property.

La Du (Cowlitz County) *see* Mt. Coffin

La Fleur Creek *(Ts.39,40N;R.33E)*

The stream of the creek rises south of Vulcan Mountain, northwest Ferry County; flows 7 miles through Colville National Forest, to Kettle River near Curlew. This creek, and another with the same name 30 miles southeast, were named for the same Indian family. When the north half of Colville Indian Reser-

vation was restored to public domain on July 1, 1892, the La Fleurs moved to the south half. A creek was named for them near each of their homes.

La Fleur Creek *(T.35N;R.36E)*

The stream of the creek rises on the east slope of Huckleberry Mountain, east central Ferry County; flows south about 5 miles, where it goes underground near Columbia River. (*see* La Fleur Creek, northwest Ferry County)

La Grande *(S.32;T.15N;R.4E)*

A 400-ft. cliff above Nisqually River, 2 miles north of Alder Dam on Lake Alder, south central Pierce County. It is the site of a city of Tacoma hydroelectric plant. This rather poetic and grandiloquent name appears to have been locally chosen.

La Monte (Whitman County) *see* Almota

La Push Indian Reservation (Clallam County) *see* Quillayute Indian Reservation

La Tete (King County) *see* Huckleberry Mountain

La Point (Thurston County) *see* Nisqually Head

LaCamas *(S.34;T.13N;R.1E)*

Small settlement at the head of LaCamas Creek, 3 miles east of Oanalaska, west central Lewis County. It was named for the edible root *Camassia* or *camas*, called *La Camas.* by French-Canadians employed by Hudson's Bay Company in the area. This plant flourished on the prairies along the creek, and was a stable food in the Indian diet during pioneer days.

LaCamas Creek
(Ts.11,12N;Rs.1E&1,2W)

The stream of the creek rises near LaCamas (town), southwest Lewis County; flows 23 miles southwest to Cowlitz River, east of Vader. (*see* LaCamas)

LaCamas Creek *(Ts.17,18N;Rs.2,3E)*

The stream of the creek rises 4 miles east of McKenna, southwest Pierce County; flows 10 miles north and northwest to Muck Creek at Roy. (*see* LaCamas)

Lackamas Creek *(Ts.1-3N;Rs.1-3W)*

The stream of the creek rises west of Larch Mountain, southeast Clark County; flows southwest and southeast 21 miles to Columbia River via Lackamas Lake. (*see* Camas)

Lackamas Lake *(Ts.1,2N;R.3E)*

A narrow lake, 2 miles long, on Lackamas Creek, directly north of Camas (town), southeast Clark County. It was formed by building 2 dams in the creek at Round Lake, which adjoins it on the south. The lake is used for fresh water supply by Crown-Zellerbach Corp.'s pulp and papermills at Camas. (*see*Camas)

Laconia *(T.22N;R.11E)*

Railroad station at Snoqualmie Pass, near east portal of Chicago, Milwaukee & St. Paul Railway tunnel, Kittitas County. It was used as a station before the Cascade tunnel was completed. H. R. Williams, vice president of the railway, named this place for a village which he thought was in the Swiss Alps, but wasn't. Williams placed a great number of pleasing names on Washington state landscape.

La Conner *(S.36;T.34N;R.2E)*

Trade center for much of Skagit Delta country, on Swinomish Channel, adjacent to Skagit Bay, southwest Skagit County. In 1867, it started as a trading post; a year later a post office was established, using the name *Swinomish*. In 1869, when John S. Conner purchased the trade store here, he secured a name change to the present form, which is his last name preceded by his wife Louisa Ann's initials.

La Conner Flats *(T.33N;Rs.2,3E)*

Area of marshes and sloughs, popular with wildfowl hunters, at the mouth of Swinomish Channel, southeast of

La Conner, southwest Skagit County. (*see* La Conner)

La-cos-tum (Kittitas County) *see* Saddle Mountain

Lacrosse Lake (Jefferson County) *see* Lake Lacrosse

Ladd Mountain (*S.2;T.14N;R.4E*)
Mountain at the head of Wildcat Creek, 3-1/2 miles west of Mineral, north central Lewis County. It was named for W. M. Ladd, part owner of a coal mine located directly south.

Ladder Creek (*T.37N;Rs.12,13E.uns*)
The stream of the creek heads in Neve Glacier, southeast Whatcom County; flows 5-1/2 miles northwest to Skagit River at Newhalem. It was named for the ladder-like effect of several waterfalls in the creek.

Ladder Creek Falls
(*S.21;T.37N;R.12E.uns*)
Waterfalls 400 ft. up Ladder Creek from New Halem Power House on Skagit River, Mt. Baker National Forest, southeast Whatcom County. It is a showplace for Seattle City Light, with illumination and music. (*see* Ladder Creek)

Ladies Pass (*S.18;T.25N;R.16E*)
Basin on the north slope of Cape Horn, Icicle Ridge, Wenatchee National Forest, southwest Chelan County. It was named by Forest Supervisor A. H. Sylvester for a party he conducted through here, which included women.

Lady Island (*T.10N;R.3E*)
Island in Columbia River near its north bank, directly south of Camas, southeast Clark County. In 1792, Lieut. W. R. Broughton of the Vancouver Expedition named it *Johnstone Island*; and, in 1805, it was called *White Brant Island* by Lewis and Clark. The present name is for Joseph Lady, who came here in 1853 from Missouri; at one time he had a land claim on the island. Now it is the property of Crown-Zellerbach Corp.

Laguna del Garzon (Whatcom County) *see* Drayton Harbor

Lahtoo (Spokane County) *see* Latah Creek

Lake (Franklin County) *see* Mesa

Lake Alder (*T.15N;Rs.4,5E*)
A city of Tacoma artificial reservoir in Nisqually River, 5 miles south of Eatonville, at the junction of Pierce, Lewis and Thurston counties. Used to generate hydroelectirc power, it is 7 miles long and covers 2,931 acres. (*see* Alder)

Lake Aldwell (*T.30N;R.7W*)
Lake 3 miles southwest of Port Angeles, on Elwha River, north central Clallam County. It was named for Thomas T. Aldwell, a Clallam County pioneer, who promoted the power dam which created this lake in 1911.

Lake Alice (*S.24;T.25N;R.15E*)
Scenic lake at the head of Spanish Camp Creek's south branch, on the north slope of Grindstone Mountain, Icicle Ridge, Wenatchee National Forest, west central Chelan County. During an exploration in Septmeber 1910, Forest Supervisor A. H. Sylvester named the lake for his wife.

Lake Allen (*Mt. Rainier National Park*)
Small lake, elevation 4,596 ft., on Mt. Wow near its southern extremity, 1 mile west of Tahoma Creek, southwest corner of the park. It was named for O. D. Allen, veteran professor of botany at Yale University; during 1913-14, he lived just outside the park.

Lake Angeles (*T.29N;R.6W*)
Small mountain lake in a glaciated area, at the head of Lake Creek in Heather Park, northeast corner of Olympic National Park, east central Clallam County. It was named for Port Angeles, through the influence of citizens of that city.

Lake Ann (*S.33;T.39N;R.9E.uns*)
Mountain lake, elevation 4,700 ft., with a fine view of Mt. Shuksan 2 miles west, at the head of Shuksan Creek, Mt. Baker National Forest, central Whatcom County. At normal water stages the lake covers slightly over 6 acres. It was named by The Mountaineers for Ann Howard Price, one of its members.

Lake Annette (*S.25;T.22N;R.10E*)
Very small mountain lake at the head of Humpback Creek, west slope of Silver Peak, 1/2 mile west of Cascade Mountains summit, east central King County. It was named by George E. Wright of The Mountaineers, for Annette Wiestling, also a member of that

organization. An alternate name is *Annette Lake*.

Lake Armstrong (*S.26;T.32N;R.5E*)
Small, ham-shaped lake 2 miles north of Arlington, northwest Snohomish County. It was named for John Armstrong, Stanwood pioneer, who located a land claim on the lake shore.

Lake Augusta (*S.22;T.25N;R.16E*)
A Wenatchee National Forest lake on the south slope of Big Jim Mountain, central Chelan County. In 1910, Forest Supervisor A. H. Sylvester and Forest Ranger Ganby "went on a lake-naming spree." Sylvester described this feature as "a lovely tarn," and named it for his mother.

Lake Ballinger (*S.32;T.27N;R.4E*)
Lake directly north of King County line, draining south into Lake Washington via McAleer Creek, southeast Snohomish County. The original name was *McAleer Lake*, for Hugh McAleer, who patented the surrounding land. When the land was sold to R. A. Ballinger, Secretary of the Interior under President Taft, the name was changed to honor Col. R. H. Ballinger, father of the secretary. The creek, however, retained its original name.

Lake Bay (*Ss.25,36;T.20N;R.1W*)
A west shore bay of Carr Inlet, 1/2 mile north of Bay Lake, northwest Pierce County. The proximity of lake and bay, and the fact that the bay drains into the lake were reasons for the local residents' naming of these features.

Lake Bay (*S.1;T.20N:R.1W*)
Town on the shores of Lake Bay, Carr Inlet, 1/2 mile northeast of Bay Lake, northwest Pierce County. (*see* Lake Bay (bay))

Lake Blethen (*Ss.13,14;T.24N;R.9E*)
Mountain lake 2-1/2 miles west of Lake Hancock, at the head of Quartz Creek, central King County. It actually consists of 2 connected lakes, 1,500 ft. apart. The upper lake covers 3.2 acres; the lower lake 8.4 acres. The name is reportedly for Col. Alden J. Blethen, publisher of *The Seattle Times*.

Lake Burien (*S.19;T.23N;R.4E*)
A 43.7-acre lake 1-1/2 miles northeast of Point Pully (Three Tree Point), west central King County. Local informants state that the name was that of an early landowner, Gottlieb *Burian*, who homesteaded on the lake shore in 1884,

and sold his holdings when they became valuable for residential property.

Lake Byrne *(Ss.11,12;T.30N;R.12E)*

A west slope lake of Glacier Peak, at the head of Lost Creek, northeast Snohomish County. It was named for a member of an early survey party.

Lake Carter *(S.21;T.25N;R.16E)*

Very small lake on Wenatchee National Forest, 2 miles north of Icicle Creek, southwest Chelan County. It was named by Forest Supervisor A. H. Sylvester for a sheepherder whom he met here during a camping trip. The lake is shown on some maps, in error, as *Crater Lake.*

Lake Celilo

A name suggested for the reservoir created above The Dalles Dam, Klickitat County, and Gilliam County, Oregon. It commemorates the famous Celilo Falls, ancient fishing ground of many local Indian tribes.

Lake Chambers (Thurston County) *see* Chambers Lake

Lake Chelan *(Ts.27-33N;Rs.17-23E)*

A spectacular lake, 60 miles long, occupying a U-shaped valley which extends northwest to southeast through Chelan County. One of Washington state's scenic wonderlands, this glacier-made body of water has a maximum depth of 1,419 ft., 340 ft. below sea level. It is relatively narrow, averaging slightly over a mile in width. *(see* Chelan)

Lake Chelan State Park
(T.27N;R.21E)

A 140-acre park on Lake Chelan, 9 miles west of Chelan (town), east Chelan County. It offers swimming, fishing and camping. The park was named for the lake by state officials. *(see* Chelan)

Lake Christine *(S.16;T.15N;R.7E)*

Small lake 4 miles northeast of Ashford, 1 mile west of Mt. Rainier National Park boundary, southeast Pierce County. It was named for Christine Lutkens, daughter of a pioneer family which settled at Elbe.

Lake Columbia (Stevens County) *see* Franklin D. Roosevelt Lake

Lake Constance
(S.13;T.26N;R.4W.uns)

An 11-acre, clear lake surrounded by mountain meadows, 1-1/2 miles south of Mt. Constance summit, Olympic National Park, east central Jefferson County. *(see* Mt. Constance)

Lake Creek *(Ts.28,29N;Rs.18,19E)*

The stream of the creek rises in Chelan Mountains in many branches; flows to Entiat River in a winding course of about 12 miles through central Chelan County. It was named before 1908 by local settlers. The name was chosen because the stream heads in one lake and runs through 3 others. It should not be confused with a tributary of Little Wenatchee River, also called Lake Creek.

Lake Creek *(Ts.27,28N;Rs.13,14E)*

The stream of the creek heads in Heather Lake, 1 mile east of Cascade Mountains summit, Wenatchee National Forest, northwest Chelan County; flows 6 miles east by north to Little Wenatchee River. It was named for its origin in Heather Lake, and should not be confused with Lake Creek, a tributary of Entiat River.

Lake Creek (Clallam County) *see* Hoh Creek

Lake Crescent *(T.30N;Rs.8,9W)*

Scenic lake, 10 miles long and over 1 mile average width, with depths to 600 ft., 6 miles south of Strait of Juan de Fuca, extreme northern Olympic National Park, north central Clallam County. In 1856, it was named *Lake Everett* when John Everett and John J. Sutherland trapped and hunted on this lake and on Lake Sutherland. In 1890, it was changed to the present name through agitation by citizens of Port Crescent, and assisted by a local newspaper. Local names, used prior to this change, were *Big Lake* and *Elk Lake.*

Lake Crescent (town) (Clallam County) *see* Fairholm

Lake Cushman Reservoir
(Ts.22,23N;Rs.4,5W)

This approximately 10-mile-long reservoir, 1 mile average width, is in the course of Skokomish River, 4 miles from Hood Canal at the lower end of the reservoir, northwest Mason County. It was converted from a small lake, 1-1/2 miles long, by building 2 dams in North Fork, Skokomish River. It now furnishes part of Tacoma's water supply. In 1852, the original lake was named by B. F. Shaw, for Orrington Cushman, a remarkable character who was nicknamed "Devil Cush." He was a woodsman from Maine, who served Gov. Stevens as an interpreter in dealing with Indians. He also was the first treasurer of Mason County.

Lake Dawn *(S.3;T.29N;R.6W)*

An 8-acre reservoir at the head of Little River, Olympic National Park, 5-1/4 miles south of Port Angeles, central Clallam County. It furnishes a water reserve for Port Angeles. City officials evidently chose this romantic name for their little lake.

Lake Dawn (Clallam County) *see* Dawn Lake

Lake Desire (King County) *see* Echo Lake

Lake Devereaux
(Ss.7,18;T.22N;R.1W)

A 1-mile-long lake, with an area of 100.4 acres, between Hood Canal and the north end of North Bay, 1-1/2 miles northwest of Allyn, east central Mason County. The name origin of this lake is elusive. Local informants are of the opinion that the name is for a very early settler who also was a hand-logger. *Lake Deborah*, an alternate name, is said to have been given for a young daughter of an early homesteader. Other alternate names are *Trout Lake* and *Lakewood Lake.*

Lake Donald *(S.19;T.26N;R.16E)*

Small lake on Wenatchee National Forest, in a little rock pocket 750 ft. above Loch Eileen, southwest Chelan County. It heads one branch of Roaring Creek. The lake was named for a son of Jason P. Williams, an early forest ranger on Wenatchee National Forest.

Lake Dorreen *(S.9;T.37N;R.7E.uns)*

Small lake in a group of several small lakes covering only 1 acre, elevation 3,380 ft., 7 miles southwest of Mt. Baker summit, at the head of South Fork, Nooksack River, Mt. Baker National Forest, south central Whatcom County. It was named by early settlers for the daughter of a local timber owner.

Lake Edna *(S.19;T.25N;R.16E)*

Small, clear lake surrounded by bare rock in a hanging valley, on the east slope of Cape Horn, at the head of Index Creek, Wenatchee National Forest, west central Chelan County. In 1909, it was named by Forest Supervisor A. H. Sylvester, for the sweetheart of a forest ranger. At that time, Sylvester started naming lakes on this forest for ladies connected with the Forest Service.

Lake Ellen *(Ss.26,27;T.35N;R.36E)*

Small lake on Colville National Forest, 3 miles west of Columbia River, 14 miles north of Inchelium, east central Ferry County. Although not verified, a local resident states that the lake was named for an early school teacher in this area, whose first name was Ellen.

Lake Elsey *(S.24;T.29N;R.15E.uns)*

An east slope lake of White Mountain, in a glacial cirque, at the head of a short branch of Napeequa River, Wenatchee National Forest, northwest Chelan County. It was named by Assistant Forest Supervisor C. J. Conover, for Elsey Smith, a Forest Service stenographer.

Lake Entiat *(Ts.24-30N;Rs.20-25E)*

A 42-mile, artificial lake, covering about 9,000 acres, in Columbia River, extending upstream from Rocky Reach Dam to Wells Dam, between Chelan and Douglas counties. Impounding of the lake was completed in late 1961. On July 2, 1958, the name was chosen by Chelan County Public Utility District. (*see* Entiat)

Lake Erie *(S.11;T.34N;R.1E)*

A Fidalgo Island lake directly west of Mt. Erie, 2-1/2 miles south of Anacortes, west central Skagit County. (*see* Mt. Erie)

Lake Ethel *(Mt. Rainier National Park)*

Lake directly north of Lake James, elevation 4,287 ft., in a mountain lake area between Independence Ridge and West Fork, White River, north central sector of the park. In 1912, it was named by The Mountaineers, for Ethel O'Farrell, daughter of Park Ranger Thomas E. O'Farrell. (USBGN)

Lake Evelyn *(King County) see* Denny Lake

Lake Everett *(Clallam County) see* Lake Crescent

Lake Flora *(S.18;T.25N;R.16E)*

One of two small lakes at the head of South Fork, Chiwaukum Creek, Wenatchee National Forest, central Chelan County. It was named by Forest Supervisor A. H. Sylvester, for Mrs. Flora Green, wife of Forest Ranger Otto Green. This lake, bright green in color, is one of many Wenatchee National Forest lakes Sylvester named for ladies.

Lake Florence
(Ss.23,24;T.25N;R.15E)

A Wenatchee National Forest lake at the head of a Spanish Camp Creek fork, on Icicle Ridge, west central Chelan County. On September 25, 1910, it was named by Forest Supervisor A. H. Sylvester, for Florence Payne, a teacher in Leavenworth schools.

Lake Forest Park *(T.26N;R.4E)*

Residential suburb of Seattle, on the west shore of Lake Washington, near the lake's north end, King County. The name was applied when the area was platted, and is reasonably descriptive, as the site is mostly covered with second-growth coniferous trees.

Lake Geneva *(S.22;T.21N;R.4E)*

Small lake 2 miles southwest of Auburn, southwest King County. It was originally named for a pioneer settler named *Beede*. Local residents, desiring a romantic name, changed it to that of a famous Swiss lake, which has a reputation for supreme beauty.

Lake George *(Mt. Rainier National Park)*

A pestle-shaped lake, elevation 4,232 ft., in a deep basin on the north slope of Mt. Wow, southwest quarter of the park. It drains through Fish Creek, and covers 33 acres. The lake was named for George Caesar, son of Philip Caesar of Tacoma. (USBGN)

Lake Goodwin *(T.31N;R.4E)*

Largest of a group of 10 lakes 3 miles inland from Port Susan and 10 miles north of Everett, northwest Snohomish County. It is named for a family of very early developers in this area.

Lake Grace *(S.2;T.25N;R.15E)*

A west slope lake of Chiwaukum Mountains, 1 mile northwest of Snowgrass Mountain, Wenatchee National Forest, southwest Chelan County. It was named by Forest Supervisor A. H. Sylvester, for the wife of Charles Haydon, with whom he was exploring when he found the lake.

Lake Green *(King County) see* Green Lake

Lake Holy Cross *(Jefferson County) see* Lake Lacrosse

Lake Hooker *(T.28N;R.2W)*

A 99.3-acre lake 4-1/2 miles north of Quilcene, 6 miles south of Port Discovery Bay, east central Jefferson County.

It was named for Otis Hooker, a pioneer homesteader of 1870. Other locally-used names are *Leland Lake* and *Lake Leland*.

Lake Ida *(S.28;T.25N;R.16E)*

An unmapped, 60-acre lake at the head of Ida Creek, on Icicle Ridge and draining into Icicle Creek, Wenatchee National Forest, southeast Chelan County. It was named by Forest Supervisor A. H. Sylvester, for his wife's sister, Ida Peirce.

Lake Ilswoot *(S.8;T.24N;R.13E)*

A 48-acre mountain lake in a glacial area on Snoqualmie National Forest, 2-1/2 miles west of Cascade Mountain summit. The name is a distortion of the Chinook word *itswoot*, meaning "black bear."

Lake James *(Mt. Rainier National Park)*

Southernmost of a group of 5 mountain lakes, between Independence Ridge and West Fork, White River, north central zone of the park. In 1912, it was named by The Mountaineers, for James O'Farrell, son of Park Ranger Thomas E. O'Farrell. (USBGN)

Lake Janus *(S.14;T.27N;R.13E)*

Lake directly west of Cascade Mountain summit, at the head of South Branch, Rapid River, extreme east Snohomish County. It was named by Forest Supervisor A. H. Sylvester, for the Roman god who looked in both directions. Misled by an existing map, Sylvester thought that the lake drained both east and west.

Lake Jason *(S.29;T.26N;R.16E)*

One of 3 small lakes draining into Chiwaukum Lake, on a side hill south of that lake but about 500 ft. higher, Wenatchee National Forest, central Chelan County. It was named by Forest Supervisor A. H. Sylvester, for Forest Ranger Jason P. Williams.

Lake Judson *(Whatcom County) see* Judson Lake

Lake Kahlotus
(Ss.2-4;Ts.13,14N;R.34E)

A 2-mile-long, spring-fed lake in a coulee, average width 1/2 mile, 2 miles east of Kahlotus, northeast Franklin County. A former name was *Washtucna Lake*. (USBGN) (*see* Kahlotus)

Lake Kanim *(S.11;T.25N;R.10E)*

A very deep, 18-acre lake 6-1/2

miles southwest of Skykomish, Snoqualmie National Forest, northeast King County. It carries the Chinook Indian name for "canoe."

Lake Keechelus (*Kittitas County*) *see* Keechelus Lake

Lake Ki (*T.31N;R.4E*)

Lake in the Lakewood Garden Tracts, 5 miles east of Port Susan, northwest Snohomish County. The name appears to be a distortion of the original Indian name for the lake, *Kah.*

Lake Kitchelus (Nicheless) (*Kittitas County*) *see* Keechelus Lake

Lake Kitsap (*Ss.8,17;T.24N;R.1E*)

A 238.4-acre lake, about a mile long and less than 1/2 mile wide, 2-1/2 miles west of Bremerton, central Kitsap County. The level is stabilized by a 5-ft. dam. On some maps the lake is called *Kitsap Lake*. The Indian name was *K'l-loot.* (*see* Kitsap)

Lake Kulla Kulla (*S.32;T.23N;R.10E*)

A high lake, covering 60.1 acres on the east side of Mt. Defiance, Snoqualmie National Forest, 11-1/2 miles southeast of North Bend, east central King County. The name is from Chinook Indian jargon, meaning "enclosed."

Lake Lacrosse (*S.8;T.25N;R.5W*)

An Olympic National Park lake, 19 miles southeast of Mt. Olympus summit, southeast Jefferson County. In 1890, it appears the lake was named *Lake Holy Cross* by Lieut. Joseph P. O'Neil. How and when it was changed is not recorded.

Lake Leland (*Jefferson County*) *see* Lake Hooker

Lake Lillian (*S.1;T.27N;R.6W*)

An 8-acre lake at the headwaters of Lillian River, 17-1/2 miles south of Port Angeles, Olympic National Park, north central Jefferson County. (*see* Lillian River)

Lake Lorraine (*S.13;T.25N;R.13E*)

A Wenatchee National Forest lake 2 miles south of Grass Lake, 2-1/2 miles east of Cascade Mountain summit, southwest Chelan County. It drains 2 miles north to Trapper Creek. The lake was named by Forest Supervisor A. H. Sylvester, for the wife of Assistant Supervisor C. J. Conover.

Lake Louis (*Ts.27,28N;R.13E*)

A real "lake of the woods" on a bench in dense forest, 1 mile east of Cascade Mountain summit, directly north of Heather Lake, Wenatchee National Forest, northwest Chelan County. In 1934, it was named by Forest Supervisor A. H. Sylvester, for Louis Crollard of Wenatchee, who was with Sylvester when he found the lake.

Lake Lucerne (*S.28;T.22N;R.6E*)

A 16.1-acre lake 4-1/2 miles northwest of Black Diamond, southwest King County. It was named by an unrecorded person for a famous lake in Switzerland.

Lake Margaret (*S.11;T.25N;R.15E*)

A Wenatchee National Forest lake on Icicle Ridge, directly west of Frosty Pass, west central Chelan County. On September 25, 1910, Forest Supervisor A. H. Sylvester named the lake for a sister of Forest Ranger Burn Canby.

Lake Margaret (*S.27;T.26N;R.7W*)

An Olympic National Park lake in Marmot Pass, on a low divide between headwaters of Elwha and Quinault rivers, central Jefferson County. On July 16, 1890, this feature was named by Seattle Press Expedition. The person whom they honored is not of record. Evidently, expedition members were in a romantic mood, as they named a nearby small lake Lake Mary, and one farther west Lake Beauty.

Lake Mary (*S.14;T.25N;R.15E*)

A Wenatchee National Forest lake on Icicle Ridge, directly west of Frosty Pass, near Lake Margaret, west central Chelan County. As with Lake Margaret, this lake was named by Forest Supervisor A. H. Sylvester for a sister of Forest Ranger Burn Canby.

Lake Mary (*S.27;T.26N:R.7W*)

An Olympic National Park lake in Marmot Pass, on a low divide between headwaters of Elwha and Quinault rivers, central Jefferson County. On July 16, 1890, it was named by Seattle Press Expedition. (*see* Lake Margaret, Jefferson County)

Lake McMurray (*Skagit County*) *see* McMurray Lake

Lake Meredian (*King County*) *see* Lake Meridian

Lake Meridian (*S.27;T.22N;R.5E*)

A small lake, not over a mile long and about 1/4 mile wide, 3 miles south-

east of Kent, southwest King County. The original name was *Cow Lake*. The present name is for Meridian Prairie, 1-1/2 miles east, which is located on a guide meridian of the U.S. Public Land Survey. It is shown on some maps as *Meridian Lake*, and on certain county maps, in error, as *Lake Meredian.*

Lake Merrill (*Cowlitz County*) *see* Merrill Lake

Lake Merwin (*Ts.5,6N;Rs.2,3E*)

A 12-1/2-mile-long, artificial lake 14 miles east of Kalama, in North Fork, Lewis River, southeast Cowlitz County. It was created by Northwestern Electric Company when Ariel Dam was built. The lake was named by H. J. Campbell, publisher of *Vancouver Columbian*, for L. T. Merwin of Northwestern Electric Company. An earlier name was *Yale Lake.*

Lake Mills (*T.29N;R.7W.uns*)

An artificial, mountain lake fed by 7 creeks, occupying Glines Canyon in Elwha River, Olympic National Park, central Clallam County. Also called *Elwha Reservoir*, it was created by a hydroelectric power dam which was built in 1926-27 by Washington Pulp & Paper Corp. The reservoir was named for E. M. Mills, who promoted pulp and paper plants on the Olympic Peninsula and at other points in the Pacific Northwest.

Lake Moolock (*S.22;T.24N;R.9E*)

A 45.4-acre lake 7-1/4 miles east of North Bend, east central King County. It is one of 3 Moolock Lakes, with Nadeau and SMC lakes. The Indian name means "elk" in Chinook jargon.

Lake Mountains (*T.36N;R.1E*)

Mountains in the central area of Cypress Island, elevations to 1,514 ft., northwest Skagit County. In 1854, they were named by U.S. Coast Survey for "two large sheets of fresh water" among the peaks.

Lake Nadeau (*S.22;T.24N;R.9E*)

An 18.9-acre lake 7 miles east of North Bend, directly west of Bessemer Mountain, east central King County. It is one of 3 Moolock Lakes, with Moolock and SMC lakes. In the early 1900s, the name was chosen for Ira A. Nadeau, Seattle attorney, director-general of A.Y.P. Exposition, and railroad official. An alternate name, *No Ketchum Lake*, indicates the absence of fish; it was obviously applied before 1951-52, when the lake was planted to trout.

Lake No. 8 *(S.19;T.28N;R.8W.uns)*

An Olympic National Park lake in Seven Lakes Basin, south central Clallam County. It was so named because it is the eighth of 7 lakes in the basin. An alternate name is *Eight Lake*.

Lake of the Angels *(S.1;T.24N;R.5W)*

A 1-1/2-acre lake in Olympic Primitive Area, at the head of Whitehorse Creek, extreme northwest Mason County. It earned its name for its location in the Valley of Heaven.

Lake of the Sun (Clallam County) *see* Ozette Lake

Lake Osett (Clallam County) *see* Ozette Lake

Lake O'Sullivan (Stevens County) *see* Franklin D. Roosevelt Lake

Lake Ozette (Clallam County) *see* Ozette Lake

Lake Padden *(Ss.8,17;T.37N;R.3E)*

A 152-acre lake in the southeast area of Bellingham, southwest Whatcom County. It is a natural lake, stabilized by a dam and a Whatcom County park. The lake was named for Michael Padden, who filed a homestead claim in 1873 that included the lake and its outlet. On some records it is shown as *Padden Lake*.

Lake Pierre (Stevens County) *see* Pierre Lake

Lake Pillwaltas (Kittitas County) *see* Little Kachess Lake

Lake Pleasant *(T.30N;R.13W)*

Lake in Soleduck Valley, 19 miles east of Pacific Ocean, west central Clallam County. The original name was *Lake Tyee*, meaning "chief" in Chinook jargon. The present, innocuous name was evidently substituted by land promoters, who thought that it might assist them in selling lots around the lake.

Lake Plehnam (Yakima County) *see* Bumping Lake

Lake Quinault (Grays Harbor County) *see* Quinault Lake

Lake Retreat *(S.32;T.22N;R.7E)*

A 53-acre resort lake 2 miles east of Ravensdale, southwest King County. The fairly descriptive name was given to this rather secluded lake by a resort owner. A former name was *Lake 32*, referring to the lake's location in Section

32 of the U.S. Public Land Survey. Like hundreds of other lakes in the west, it once was locally known as *Fish Lake*.

Lake Riley *(Ss.19,20;T.32N;R.7E)*

A 30-acre lake with its shores in a peat bog, maximum depth 45 ft., 2 miles south of Oso at the head of Jim Creek, northwest Snohomish County. In 1890, it was named for an axeman on a land surveyor's crew, who first sighted the lake when employed by George James, a contract surveyor. A name in use for some years was *German Lake*, as most of the early settlers in the area were from Germany.

Lake River *(Ts.3,4N;Rs.1W&1E)*

The stream of the river rises in Vancouver Lake, southwest Clark County; flows 12 miles north to Columbia River, north of Ridgefield. It parallels Columbia River for most of its course. In 1841, Cmdr. Charles Wilkes mapped this stream as *Callepuya River*, using the Indian name. It was subsequently changed to the present name because of its origin in Vancouver Lake.

Lake Roosevelt (Stevens County) *see* Franklin D. Roosevelt Lake

Lake Sacajawea *(Ts.32-34N;Rs.9-13E)*

An artificial reservoir in Snake River, from a point 9.7 miles above the mouth, at Ice Harbor Dam, 32 miles upstream to a point directly downstream from Lower Monumental Dam, Walla Walla and Franklin counties. The reservoir was created to impound water for hydroelectric power and irrigation.

Lake Sacajawea (Sacagawea) *(T.8N;R.2W)*

A curving lagoon, stretching from near Cowlitz River to the highlands north of Longview, southwest Cowlitz County. The name was applied when the town of Longview was founded. Prior to that time, it had been called *Horseshoe Lake* and *Fowler's Lake*. The former name related to the lake's shape; the latter was for Jessie Fowler, whose 1852 Donation Land Claim included the lake.

Lake Sahalee-Tyee *(Ss.22,27;T.6N;R.8E.uns)*

A 7-acre lake, elevation 4,700 ft., located in a region of many small lakes and ponds called Indian Heaven, at the headwaters of Lewis and Wind rivers, central Skamania County. The meaning of this Chinook Indian jargon name is "Heaven Lake" or "Chief-Above

Lake." Alternate names are *Indian Heaven Lake* and *Round Lake*.

Lake Sally Ann *(S.5;T.28N;R.14E)*

A small, scenic lake 2 miles north of Cady Pass, directly east of Cascade Mountain summit, Wenatchee National Forest, northwest Chelan County. It was named by Forest Supervisor A. H. Sylvester "for nobody in particular, but because the name seemed to fit like the hand in the glove."

Lake Samish (Whatcom County) *see* Samish Lake

Lake Sammamish *(Ts.24,25N;Rs.5,6E)*

A 4,897-acre, "S"-shaped lake, about 8 miles long and 1-2 mile wide, 4-5 miles east of Lake Washington and roughly parallel to that lake, north central King County. It drains northward into Lake Washington through Sammamish River. This original Indian name comes from *samma*, meaning "the sound of the blue crane," and *mish*, meaning "river." Other tribal names were *Xa-tcx-atcu*, meaning "small lake" (as compared to Lake Washington), and *Sts-apa-bc*, which has about the same meaning.

Lake Sammamish State Park *(T.24N;R.6E)*

A 253-acre public park at the south end of Lake Sammamish, 2 miles north of Issaquah, west central King County. It offers swimming, fishing and small-boat launching. The name was chosen by State Parks & Recreation Commission, for the name of the lake on which it is located. (*see* Lake Sammamish)

Lake Sawyer *(S.4;T.21N;R.6E)*

A 279-acre lake with 4 small islands, 2 miles northwest of Black Diamond, south central King County. It is reported to have been named for an early settler on the lake's shore.

Lake Serene *(S.31;T.27N;R.10E)*

A deep, snow-fed, 53-acre lake directly northeast of Mt. Index, 3 miles south of Index, south central Snohomish County. The name is appropriate, as the lake is secluded in a deep mountain pocket, surrounded by talus slopes. It should not be confused with another lake with the same name, 6 miles southwest of Everett.

Lake Serene *(S.34;T.28N;R.4E)*

A very small lake 6 miles southwest

of Everett, 2 miles east of Possession Sound, southwest Snohomish County. It carried the humble name of *Mud Lake*, until changed by demand of local residents. This lake should not be confused with Lake Serene, 3 miles south of Index.

Lake Shannon *(Ts.35,36N;R.8E)*

An artificial lake, impounded for hydroelectric power development, at the lower stretch of Baker River, extending 7-1/2 miles from the south boundary of Whatcom County, to the north limits of Concrete, north central Skagit County. It was named by Stone & Webster Corp., for W. D. Shannon, construction engineer on this project. The lake is carried on some maps as *Shannon Lake.*

Lake Sixteen *(S.16;T.33N;R.4E)*

A 41.6-acre lake 2-1/2 miles east of Conway, southwest Skagit County. As with several other geographic features in the Pacific Northwest, it was named for the legal section in which it is located.

Lake Stevens *(T.29N;R.6E)*

A rather large lake 4 miles east of Everett, west central Snohomish County. It was formerly a center of lumber and shingle manufacture. On September 1, 1859, the present name first appeared on the surveyor general's map of Washington Territory, and honored Gov. I. I. Stevens. On some early maps, it was shown as *Stevens Lake.*

Lake Stevens *(S.8;T.29N;R.6E)*

Town on Lake Stevens, 9 miles east of Everett, Snohomish County. *(see* Lake Stevens (lake)

Lake Stickney *(S.15;T.28N;R.9E)*

Lake 6 miles northeast of Gold Bar, drained by a branch of Olney Creek, south central Snohomish County. It was named for a local prospector. *(see* Mt. Stickney)

Lake Stream (Yakima County) *see* Fish Lake Stream

Lake Sutherland *(T.30N;R.8W)*

Lake at the foot of Storm King Mountain, 1 mile east of Lake Crescent, north central Clallam County. It was named for John J. Sutherland, who came here from Victoria with John Everett in 1856 to hunt and trap, selling furs to Hudson's Bay Company post at Victoria. They also trapped on Lake Crescent, which originally was named for Everett. On a map made by the surveyor

general of Washington Territory dated 1886, it is called *Shuecraft Lake.*

Lake Tannamus *(S.23;T.14N;R.7E)*

A deep, 28-acre lake, elevation about 3,900 ft., at the east end of Sawtooth Ridge, 9-1/4 miles southeast of National, Snoqualmie National Forest, northeast Lewis County. The name is a version of the Chinook Indian jargon *Tamahnous,* meaning ''magic'' or ''spirits''; Indians had many superstitions regarding lakes. An alternate name is *Cora Lake.*

Lake Tannum, Taneium, Tanum (Yakima County) *see* Bumping Lake

Lake Tapps *(T.26N;R.5E)*

A 2,296-acre, artificial lake with a 45-mile shoreline, 4 miles south of Auburn, north central Pierce County. This irregularly-shaped lake was impounded by Puget Sound Power & Light Company as water storage for White River power plant.

Lake Ten *(S.10;T.33N;R.4E)*

A low-level, 16.4-acre lake 3-1/2 miles northeast of Canway, southwest Skagit County. It was named for the legal section in which it is located.

Lake Terrell *(T.39N;R.1E)*

Marsh and bird sanctuary, varying in size from 400 to 700 acres, 9 miles northwest of Bellingham, 2 miles east of Georgia Strait, northwest Whatcom County. The lake bed is reported to have been partially drained to reclaim farmland at one time. Before it was drained, the lake was named for a member of the first government survey party in this area. It is now county park. In 1791, Juan Francisco de Eliza had named the lake *Laguna del Garzon.*

Lake 32 (King County) *see* Lake Retreat

Lake Toke-Tie *(S.22;T.6N;R.8E.uns)*

A 3-1/2-acre lake, elevation 4,700 ft., 4 miles north of Big Lava Bed in Indian Heaven area, central Skamania County. The Chinook Indian name means ''pretty.'' It is unusual to find any comment on scenic beauty by Indians.

Lake Tolmie (Pierce County) *see* American Lake

Lake Tucker (San Juan County) *see* Sportsman Lake

Lake Tyee (Clallam County) *see* Lake Pleasant

Lake Umatilla

Artificial lake formed in Columbia River by impounding water behind John Day Dam, extending about 110 river miles upstream, almost to McNary Dam, Benton and Klickitat counties, and Oregon. Generally, it is called *John Day Pool* by engineers involved with development of water resources in Columbia River basin. *(see* Umatilla Rapids)

Lake Union *(T.25N;R.4E)*

A 598-acre, navigable lake linking Lake Washington on the east with Salmon Bay on the west through Lake Washington Ship Canal, central Seattle, King County. It is bordered by boathouses, house boats, boat-building plants and industries. On July 4, 1854, the name was adopted at a pioneer picnic on the lake, at the suggestion of Thomas Mercer; he stated that the lake would some day unite Lake Washington with Puget Sound. The Duwamish Indian name was *Ka-chug,* meaning ''small body of fresh water''; other Indian tribes called it *Xa-tcu,* meaning ''little lake.'' Both names were in comparison to Lake Washington.

Lake Valhalla *(S.35;T.27N;R.13E)*

Lake on the northwest slope of Lichtenberg Mountain, at the head of an upper fork of Nason Creek, directly east of Cascade Mountain summit, Wenatchee National Forest, southwest Chelan County. In 1910, it was named by Forest Supervisor A. H. Sylvester ''on an inspiration,'' as he stated.

Lake Vancouver (Clark County) *see* Vancouver Lake

Lake Victoria *(S.16;T.24N;R.16E)*

Lake at the head of Victoria Creek, 1 mile north of Cashmere Mountain, Wenatchee National Forest, southeast Chelan County. On September 27, 1910, it was named by Forest Supervisor A. H. Sylvester, for Victoria Creek which drains it.

Lake Wallula *(Ts.5-8N;Rs.28-31E)*

A 64-mile-long, 32,000-acre, artificial lake in Columbia River, impounded by McNary Dam, and extending from the dam to the vicinity of Pasco, between southeast Benton and southwest Walla Walla counties, and northern Oregon. In 1955, Washington State Legislature adopted House Joint Memorial No. 2., petitioning Congress to adopt the name *Lake Wallula.* The name memorialized the old town of Wallula, in Walla Walla County, which was inundated in the lake. (USBGN)

Lake Washington
(Ts.23-26N;Rs.4,5E)

The state's 2nd largest natural lake, covering 22,138 acres with 58 miles of shoreline, bordering Seattle on the west shore, and extending 19-1/2 miles north from Renton to Kenmore, King County. The lake's south end is largely industrial; the north, mostly residential. It came into existence during the glacial period, when a prehistoric stream was dammed by a glacial moraine. In 1851, it was named *Lake Geneva* by Isaac N. Ebey, for the Swiss lake. On July 4, 1854, the lake was given its present name at a pioneer picnic, when Thomas Mercer suggested the name of the first president of the United States. In 1856, it appeared on Preston's Map as *Duwamish*. The Duwamish Indian name was *It-kow-chug*, meaning "large body of fresh water"; other tribes called it *At-sar-kal*, with about the same general meaning.

Lake Washington Ship Canal
(T.25N;Rs.3,4E)

Navigable waterway in Seattle, between Lake Washington and Shilshole Bay, passing through Lake Union and Salmon Bay, King County. On July 4, 1854, such a canal was suggested at a pioneer picnic on Lake Union. Private companies, Washington state, and the federal government assisted in building the canal until its completion in 1917, when the locks between Salmon and Shilshole bays were opened.

Lake Webster *(Clallam County) see* Ozette Lake

Lake Wenatchee *(Chelan County) see* Wenatchee Lake

Lake Wenatchee State Park
(T.27N;R.17E)

A 358-acre park on Lake Wenatchee, 22 miles north of Leavenworth, central Chelan County. It offers camping, swimming and fishing. State officials named it for the lake. (*see* Wenatchee Lake)

Lake Whatcom *(Ts.37,38N;Rs.3,4E)*

A 12-mile-long, 5,003-acre lake, maximum depth about 311 ft., 3 miles east of Bellingham and adjoining the city at the north end, southwest Whatcom County. It drains into Bellingham Bay through Whatcom Creek. Many small settlements are scattered along its shores; some had been industrial communities before timber was depleted. In 1853, the lake appeared on maps of U.S. Pacific Railroad Surveys as *Whatcom Lake*. Sometime prior to 1890, the name was reversed. (*see* Whatcom Falls)

Lake Wilderness *(S.22;T.22N;R.6E)*

Resort lake 2 miles south of Maple Valley, west central King County. A resort owner chose the descriptive name because the lake is surrounded by dense forest.

Lake Wilson *(King County) see* Langlois Lake

Lake Wiseman *(S.8;T.37N;R.7E.uns)*

Small lake in Mt. Baker foothills, 8 miles southwest of Mt. Baker summit, at the head of Green Creek, which is a tributary of Middle Fork, Nooksack River, Mt. Baker National Forest, south central Whatcom County. It was named by early settlers for Mrs. Wiseman, a pioneer of Minkler Lake area.

Lake Youngs *(T.22N;R.5E)*

A 790-acre storage basin for City of Seattle Water Dept., 5 miles southeast of Renton, west central King County. In 1867, the original name *Swan Lake* was applied by government surveyors, when they found wild swans on the lake. It was renamed by Seattle Water Dept. officials, for L. B. Youngs, who was a department superintendent for many years, and who died on June 10, 1923. (USBGN)

Lakedale *(Kittitas County) see* Lakeview

Lakeside *(S.15;T.24N;R.22E)*

Suburb of Chelan on the south shore of Lake Chelan, 1 mile west of the lake's outlet, east central Chelan County. The descriptive name was applied by local residents.

Lakeside *(S.25;T.24N;R.41E)*

Railroad station 5 miles east of Medical Lake, west central Spokane County. In 1906, it was named by Northern Pacific Railway Company officials, for its proximity to Meadow Lake.

Lakeview *(S.2;T.20N;R.14E)*

Once a town at the south end of Cle Elum Lake, northwest Kittitas County. It was abandoned when the lake level was raised by a higher dam. The name is descriptive. On some maps and records, it is given as *Lakedale*.

Lakeview *(S.1;T.19N;R.2E)*

A south suburb of Tacoma, directly northwest of McChord Field, Pierce County. When Northern Pacific Railway Company established a station here in 1873, the name was chosen by Charles Prosch, for a small lake in the vicinity.

Lakeview Mountain
(S.35;T.11N;R.11E.uns)

A high peak, elevation 6,661 ft., at Cascade Mountain summit, between southwest Yakima County and the southeast corner of Lewis County. It is used by Yakima Indian Reservation personnel as a fire lookout in season. The name is appropriate, as the mountain offers a view of a number of small lakes to the south and east, and of Walupt Lake to the west.

Lakeview Peak *(Ss.23,26;T.7N;R.3E)*

A Gifford Pinchot National Forest peak, elevation 3,700 ft., 5 miles north of Yale, southeast Cowlitz County. It apparently was named because it offers a fine view of Lakeview Peak Lake; the lake, in turn, is said to have been named for the peak. Those who travel through this isolated area can get a good peek at the lake from the peak, as well as a peek at the peak from the lake.

Lakeview Peak Lake *(S.26;T.7N;R.3E)*

A 3-acre lake, elevation 2,950 ft., directly east of Lakeview Peak, 4-1/2 miles north of Yale, southeast Cowlitz County. (*see* Lakeview Peak)

Lakewood *(S.19;T.31N;R.5E)*

Settlement 13 miles north of Everett, west central Snohomish County. The nearby railroad station was named *English* by the Great Northern Railway, for English Logging Company, which shipped many logs over this line. The present name was coined by Fred Funk as the name of the settlement and of Lakewood Garden Tracts. Both names are carried on some county maps.

Lamar *(S.2;T.9N;R.34E)*

Settlement on Touchet River, 17 miles northwest of Walla Walla, central Walla Walla County. The original name was *Riverside*, but was changed in 1902 by Northern Pacific Railway official to honor Joseph Lamar, from whom the right-of-way had been acquired.

Lamb Creek *(Ts.31,32N;R.13W)*

The stream of the creek heads 6 miles southwest of Clallam, northwest Clallam County; flows 5 miles north to

Hoko River. Local residents state that the stream was named for an early homesteader, whose land was adjacent to the creek. (USBGN)

Lambert Creek *(Ts.37,38N;Rs.33,34E)*

The stream of the creek heads on the west slope of Lambert Mountain, central Ferry County; flows west and northwest to Curlew Creek, 1 mile northeast of Curlew Lake, Colville National Forest. It has a number of tributaries. The name is for an Indian family, which had an early-day allotment at the mouth of the creek.

Lambert Mountain *(S.2;T.37N;R.34E)*

A Colville National Forest peak, elevation 6,529 ft., 14 miles northeast of Republic, central Ferry County. *(see* Lambert Creek)

Lamb's Point (King County) *see* Duwamish Head

Lamoine *(S.25;T.26N;R.23E)*

Community 9 miles northeast of Waterville, west central Douglas County. After a good start in pioneer days, the town diminished in importance, and lost its post office when bypassed by Great Northern Railway Company. The original name was *Arupp*. According to local reports, the present name was given by a resident named Bragg, for the name on a sardine can label in the general store.

Lamona *(S.36;T.22N;R.34E)*

Settlement 10 miles east of Odessa, south central Lincoln County. In 1890-91, J. M. Newland established the settlement when he set up a store here. It was named for J. H. Lamona, who bought Newland's store in 1892, and operated it for some years.

Lamont *(S.28;T.20N;R.39E)*

Town in an area of small lakes, 11 miles west of Rock Lake (lake), extreme northwest Whitman County. It was named by Northern Pacific Railway Company officials, for Daniel Lamont, then company vice president.

Landes Cleaver *(T.38N;R.8E.uns)*

A glacial cleaver on Mt. Baker, Mt. Baker National Forest, central Whatcom County. It was named by The Mountaineers, for Prof. Henry Landes of the University of Washington, a past president of the group.

Landsburg *(S.19;T.22N;R.7E)*

Site of Cedar River Dam and Seattle's water department intake on Cedar River, 4 miles southeast of Maple Valley, southwest King County. It was named for David E. Landsburg, a Nova Scotian, who came to Seattle in 1886; he was in charge of the dam and water intake here for some time. The name is shown on some county maps, in error, as *Landsberg*.

Lane Creek *(T.36N;R.36E)*

The stream of this short creek heads on the south slope of Cayuse Mountain, Colville National Forest, east central Ferry County; flows 3 miles south to North Fork, Sherman Creek. It was named for a man who operated a stage station near here during the early mining boom.

Lane Peak *(Mt. Rainier National Park)*

A 3-point peak, elevation 6,000 ft., at the west end of Tatoosh Range, 1 mile west of Pinnacle Peak, south central area of the park. In 1910, it was named by The Mountaineers, for Franklin K. Lane, former secretary of the Department of the Interior. (USBGN)

Lange (Skamania County) *see* Spirit Lake (town)

Langley *(Ts.29,30N;R.3E)*

Town on the southeast shore of Whidbey Island, on Saratoga Passage, south Island County. It was named for Judge J. W. Langley of Seattle, a member of a company which platted the townsite in 1890.

Langley Bay *(S.10;T.34N;R.1E)*

Southern stretch of Burrows Bay, on the west shore of Fidalgo Island, southwest Skagit County. The name is for a pioneer settler who lived on the bay.

Langley Point *(S.10;T.34N;R.1E)*

A southwest shore point of Fidalgo Island, at the south entrance to Burrows Bay on Rosario Strait, southwest Skagit County. In 1841, it was charted by Cmdr. Charles Wilkes as *Point Sares*, for Henry Sares, captain-of-the-top in one of the expedition's ships. That name was later transferred as Sares Head to a point 1 mile south. *(see* Langley Bay)

Langlois Lake *(S.22;T.25N;R.7E)*

A 40-acre lake, maximum depth 98 ft., 1-1/2 miles southeast of Tolt (Carnation), near Tolt River, north central King County. The Girl Scouts have a 160-acre campsite here. The lake was named for Mr. and Mrs. Joe Langlois, who, in 1890, filed a claim on a home-

stead here. An alternate name is *Lake Wilson*.

Lanham Creek *(T.26N;R.15E)*

The stream of the creek rises from Lanham Lake, on the northwest slope of Jim Hill Mountain, Wenatchee National Forest, southwest Chelan County; flows 3-1/2 miles east of Cascade Mountain summit to join Nason Creek. The name, as in the case of Lanham Lake, was in use prior to 1902, and evidently is for an early-day prospector.

Lanham Lake *(S.19;T.26N;R.15E)*

Lake at the head of Lanham Creek, on the northwest slope of Jim Hill Mountain, Wenatchee National Forest, 3-1/2 miles east of Cascade Mountain summit, southwest Chelan County. *(see* Lanham Creek)

Lantz *(S.4;T.17N;R.38E)*

Community 18 miles southeast of Ritzville, east central Adams County. It was named by postal authorities, for the son of John O. Robinson, first postmaster, who was appointed on May 28, 1904, when the post office was installed. The name was also adopted by Spokane, Portland & Seattle Railway when a siding was built here.

LaPoel Point *(S.32;T.30N;R.9W)*

Location of a camp and guard station on the southwest shore of Lake Crescent, Olympic National Park, central Clallam County. The name is French for frying pan or stove. The French spelling, *La poele*, was altered to *La-po-el* when it was adopted into Chinook jargon. A local name, not in common use, is *Pancake Point*. (USBGN)

La Push *(S.22;T.28N;R.15W)*

Indian fishing village, in the only sheltered cove between Cape Flattery and Grays Harbor, at the mouth of Quillayute River, Quillayute Indian Reservation, extreme southwest Clallam County. The name is a Chinook jargon distortion of the French *la bouche*, meaning "the mouth," which refers to the mouth of the river. Other suggested origins of the name, which appear to be less logical or authentic, include the French term *la peche*, referring to the act of fishing, and the French word *perche*, meaning "a pole." (USBGN)

Larch Lake *(S.36;T.26N;R.15E)*

A 40-acre lake at the headwaters of Chiwaukum Creek, on the southeast slope of Chiwaukum Mountains, Wenatchee National Forest, central Chelan County. The lake basin supports a stand of alpine larch. The person who applied this well-suited name is not identified.

Larch Lakes *(S.28;T.30N;R.17E)*

Two small lakes directly north of Fifth of July Mountain, near the headwaters of Entiat River, Wenatchee National Forest, north central Chelan County. The name was applied by Forest Ranger James McKenzie, for the stands of alpine larch around the lakes.

Larrabee State Park *(S.36;T.37N;R.2E)*

A 1,362-acre public park on Chuckanut Bay and Drive, 7 miles south of Bellingham, southwest corner of Whatcom County. It offers camping, swimming and fishing. The park was named for Charles Xavier Larrabee, a Fairhaven pioneer in 1890; land for the park was donated from his estate to the state.

Larsen Lake *(S.35;T.25N;R.5E)*

A 7.3-acre lake 3 miles east of Bellevue, northwest King County. It is said to have been named for a very early settler. Alternate names, in local use, are *Green Lake* and *Blueberry Lake.*

Larson *(S.27;T.38N;R.3E)*

An area of Bellingham, now called "Silver Beach," on the west shore of Lake Whatcom, joining northeast Bellingham at this town's north end, southwest Whatcom County. It was named for Peter Larson of Montana, a famous railroad builder and principal stockholder in Larson Lumber Company, Lake Whatcom Logging Company, and other corporations operated by J. J. Donovan and J. H. Bloedel.

Larson Air Force Base *(S.32;T.20N;R.28E)*

A WWII air base 3 miles northwest of Moses Lake (town), central Grant County. Used largely for testing air equipment, it was named for Maj. Donald A. Larson of Yakima, who, in 1944, was killed in a flight over Germany. Now the Moses Lake Airport.

Las Islas Morros (Skagit County) *see* Allan Island, Burrows Island

Las Tres Hermonos (Skagit County) *see* Dot, Huckleberry and Saddlebag islands

Last Crossing *(S.25;T.19N;R.10E)*

Historic place in Greenwater River, at the river's confluence with Pyramid Creek, southeast Pierce County. It is on Old Naches Trail, over which many early pioneers reached Washington Territory. In October 1853, it was named by the Longmire Party, which consisted of 149 people and 53 wagons. They made their last crossing of the Greenwater River at this point.

Latah *(Ss.29,30;T.21N;R.45E)*

Once a busy town 9 miles south of Fairfield, extreme southeast Spokane County. Where it previously had 4 stores, it now has one, and a greatly reduced population. (*see* Latah Creek)

Latah Creek *(Ts.21-25N;Rs.42-46E)*

The stream of the creek rises near Tensed, Idaho; flows through the northeast tip of Whitman County, and continues about 50 miles northwest to join Spokane River in a deep canyon just below Spokane Falls, in Spokane, Spokane County. The Indian name was *Sin-sin-too-ooley* or *Sin-sin-too-aley,* meaning "the place where the little fish are caught." A very early name given by white men was *Ned-Wauld River.* Railroad surveyors had named it *Camas (Kamas) Prairie Creek.* Late in 1858, the creek acquired the dismal name of *Hangman Creek;* it was on a council ground near the creek that Col. George Wright hanged 7 Indians in reprisal for recent Indian victories over white troops. The name was later changed to its present form by act of the legislature.

Lathrop Drive *(T.16N;R.4E)*

A 7-mile loop road on Charles Lathrop Pack Demonstration Forest, directly northeast of LaGrande, south central Pierce County. It circles the forest for fire protection, forest utilization and administration. The name is for Charles Lathrop Pack, a conservationist and philanthropist, who gave this forest tract to the University of Washington.

Latona *(S.17;T.25N;R.4E)*

Once a booming, small town, now included in Seattle city limits, on the north shore of Lake Union, a short distance east of the University of Washington campus, King County. It was locally named for a 30-ft. steam launch, *Latona,* built as a pleasure craft by J. M. Colman, and later sold to realtor James A. Moore for use as a passenger boat on Lake Washington. The Duwamish Indian name for the place was *Squaltzquilth.*

Laughing Jacobs Lake *(S.10;T.24N;R.6E)*

A very small lake 3 miles north of Issaquah, 3 miles east of Lake Washington, central King County. It was reportedly named by 2 early settlers, William Bush and Wilford Stewart, when they heard another settler, named Jacobs, trying to imitate a loon's cry on the lake. Other names used in the past were *Sutter Lake.* and *Sutter Mill Pond.*

Laughingwater Creek *(Mt. Rainier National Park)*

The stream of the creek rises near Cascade Mountain summit, southeast park boundary; flows southwest to Ohanapecosh River, less than a mile north of Ohanapecosh Hot Springs. It is used as the domestic water supply for buildings and camps at the hot springs. There appears to be no record of the person who named this lively stream, but the name is certainly picturesque and well deserved.

Laurel Point (King County) *see* Webster Point

Laurier *(S.3;T.40N;R.36E)*

Small village on tthe Canadian boundary, close to Kettle River, extreme northeast Ferry County. Town business is mostly concerned with the operation of a U.S. Customs and Immigration Station. During the 1890s mining boom, it had a population of about 2,000; the present population is about 35. The name is reported to have been given in honor of the "Liberal" Sir Wilfred Laurier, prime minister of the Dominion of Canada from 1896 to 1911.

Lava Glacier *(T.9N;R.11E.uns)*

A major glacier on the north slope of Mt. Adams, one of 8 ice rivers on the mountain, southwest Yakima County. It is in a deep niche with lava rock sides, and extends down the slopes into the drainage areas of Clearwater and Little Muddy creeks. In August 1901, it was aptly named by Prof. Harry Fielding Reid of Johns Hopkins University, an eminent glaciologist.

Lavender *(S.21;T.20N;R.14E)*
Railroad spur on Yakima River, 2-1/2 miles south of Cle Elum Lake's south end, west central Kittitas County. It was established as a loading spur for wood and livestock by Chicago, Milwaukee & St. Paul Railway. H. R. Williams, the railway's vice president, stated that the choice was a "chance selection." The place is carried on some maps as *Lavendar.*

Lawrence *(S.21;T.39N;R.4E)*
Formerly a shingle manufacturing center, now a scattered settlement, near Nooksack River, 8 miles northeast of Bellingham, northwest Whatcom County. In the 1890s, the name was coined to honor Laura Blankenship, daughter of the owner of Lawrence Shingle Company.

Lawrence Island (Skagit County) *see* Guemes Island

Lawrence Point *(S.30;T.37N;R.1E)*
An extreme eastern point of Orcas Island, in Georgia Strait, northeast San Juan County. In 1841, it was charted by Cmdr. Charles Wilkes as *Point Lawrence,* for Capt. James Lawrence, a U.S. naval hero killed in the War of 1812. The name was reversed on subsequent charts. The Lummi Indian name was *Mat-tel-les,* which means "the point."

Lawson Reef *(T.34N;R.1E.uns)*
A series of submerged shoals in Strait of Juan de Fuca, 2-1/2 miles west of Deception Pass, extreme northwest Island County. The reef was named for Lieut. James S. Lawson of U.S. Coast Survey; in 1870-71, he discovered it while exploring in the brig *Fauntleroy.*

Lawson Rock *(S.10;T.35N;R.1W)*
Island in Thatcher Pass, between Blakely and Decatur islands, southeast San Juan County. It is one of 3 islands called *The Pointers,* with Pointer Island

and Black Rock. In the 1870-71 survey of the San Juans by U.S. Coast Survey, it was named for Lieut. James S. Lawson of the Coast Survey.

Lawton Wood *(S.10;T.25N;R.3E)*
Small residence community, 149-1/2 acres, on the north shore of Lawton Peninsula, between Ft. Lawton and Shilshole Bay, northwest Seattle, King County. In 1925, it was named by members of Lawton Wood Improvement Club; they combined the name Ft. Lawton with the wooded nature of the area. A previous name, applied by Mrs. H.K. Owen in early days, was *Shilsholia,* for its location on Shilshole Bay. That name was not used after the Owen family left the area.

Layton (Lincoln County) *see* Hellgate

Le Conte Lake (Skagit County) *see* South Cascade Lake

Le Roi's (Ferry County) *see* West Fork

Leadbetter Lake *(S.34;T.40N;R.43E)*
Small lake 1 mile west of Pend Oreille River, 4 miles north of Metaline, Falls, Kaniksu National Forest, northwest Pend Oreille County. It was named for John Leadbetter, an early settler.

Leadbetter Point *(T.13N;R.11W)*
A low, sandy point at the north end of North Beach Peninsula, northwest Pacific County. On July 5, 1788, it was named *Low Point* by Capt. John Meares. In 1852, Lieut. James Alden of U.S. Coast Survey changed the name to honor Lieut. Danville Leadbetter, an associate in the survey.

Leahy *(S.14;T.28N;R.27E)*
Settlement 21 miles northeast of Mansfield, 8 miles south of Columbia River, north central Douglas County. In 1884, it was founded by Michael Richard Leahy, an early cattleman, and was named for him or for his brother, James B. Leahy, who served as postmaster at the Leahy post office.

Leavenworth *(S.11;T.24N;R.17E)*
Town on Wenatchee River, 20 miles northwest of Wenatchee, south central Chelan County. Prehistorically, it was the site of an Indian village. In 1891, a

settlement was established under the name *Icicle.* In 1892, the townsite was platted by and named for Capt. C. F. Leavenworth, who operated Leavenworth Townsite Company.

Lebam *(S.4;T.12N;R.7W)*
Community on Half Moon Prarie, 11 miles southeast of Raymond, central Pacific County. The original name was *Half Moon.* When a post office was established, postal officials objected to the two-word name. They accepted the present name, offered by the town's founder, Joe W. Goodell, which was his daughter Mabel's name spelled backward.

Leber *(S.20;T.17N;R.4E)*
Small settlement 1 mile west of Trout Lake, 6 miles northwest of Eatonville, southwest Pierce County. It was named for the first postmaster, Peter Leber.

LeClerc Creek *(Ts.35-37N;Rs.44,45E)*
The stream of the creek rises east of Pend Oreille River, in West, East and Middle branches, east central Pend Oreille County; flows south and southwest 15 miles to Pend Oreille River, opposite Ruby. It was named for the LeClerc brothers, early settlers.

Lee *(S.16;T.10N;R.34E)*
Railroad station 22 miles northwest of Walla Walla, northwest Walla Walla County. When Northern Pacific Railway built the Pleasant View branch into this part of the county, the station at this place was named for Henry Lee, a rancher, who owned the land on which the station was erected.

Lees Creek *(T.30N;R.5W)*
The stream of the creek heads 1 mile north of Mt. Pleasant, northeast Clallam County; flows 4 miles north to Port Angeles Harbor. It was locally named for Alfred Lee, who purchased the Goodwain farm on the creek.

Legoe Bay *(Ss.7,8;T.37N;R.1E)*
A northwest shore bay of Lummi Island, east of Village Point, southwest Whatcom County. It is headquarters for reef-netting craft. The name appears to have been distorted since first used; records reveal no pioneers or explorers by this name, and it bears no similarity to Indian dialect nomenclature. The name probably was chosen by Christian Tuttle, who settled on the bay in 1871.

Legrow (*S.17;T.8N;R.32E*)

Railway station 12 miles east by south of Pasco, southwest Walla Walla County. In 1899, it was established as a station on Northern Pacific Railway. Railway officials named the station for Asa Legrow, a prominent sheepman, whose camp was nearby.

Leitchville (*S.19;T.13N;R.45E*)

Former town on Union Flat Creek, 14 miles northwest of Clarkston, southwest Whitman County. In 1871, it was founded by and named for M. H. Leitch, who settled here from Idaho. It no longer appears on recent maps.

Leland (*S.25;T.28N;R.2W*)

Small settlement on Lake Hooker (Leland), 7 miles south of Port Discovery Bay, northeast Jefferson County. Residents chose the name *Lealand* for the first post office. The first 3 letters were the initials of Laura E. Andrews, the first white woman settler. Postal authorities misspelled the word, but it remained in use.

Leland Lake (Jefferson County) *see* Lake Hooker

Lella (Douglas County) *see* Del Rio

Lemolo (*S.28;T.21N;R.8E*)

Railway siding on Green River, 18 miles west of Cascade Mountain summit, south central King County. In 1914, the railway station at this place was given the present name by officials of Northern Pacific Railway. Their records contain no information regarding the name origin.

Lemolo (*S.25;T.26N;R.1E*)

Settlement on the east shore of Liberty Bay, 1-1/2 miles southeast of Poulsbo, north central Kitsap County. The Chinook Indian name has been retained, and means *wild, untamed* or *barbarous.*

Lenora (*S.4;T.32N;R.44E*)

Village on the east bank of Pend Oreille River, at the mouth of Skookum Creek, 12 miles northwest of Newport, south central Pend Oreille County. In 1902, it was named for Lenora Lucas, daughter of a partner in the local Lucas & Sutton sawmill.

Leon (*S.39;T.12N;R.46E*)

Small settlement 7-1/2 miles north of Clarkston, directly west of Idaho boundary, extreme southeast Whitman County. It was named by Northern Pacific Railway officials for Leon Kinser, a prominent, local resident.

Leroy Creek (*Ts.30,31N;R.16E*)

This small glacier-fed stream rises directly south of the north boundary of Wenatchee National Forest, northwestern Chelan County; flows from the north end of Entiat Mountains, 3 miles southwest to Phelps Creek. The name has been in local use for many years and is believed to be for an early prospector.

Les Dalles (Klickitat County) *see* The Dalles

Les Grand Dalles de la Columbia (Klickitat County) *see* The Dalles

Leschi Park (*S.3;T.24N;R.4E*)

Park on the west shore of Lake Washington, directly north of the west terminus of the floating bridge crossing the lake, Seattle, King County. It was named for an outstanding Nisqually Indian chief, who was hanged in 1858 by white settlers, for an alleged murder. He is said to have met Indians from east of the Cascades at this point, just prior to the 1856 Indian attack on Seattle.

Lester (*S.23;T.20N;R.10E*)

Small mountain village on upper Green River, in the Tacoma watershed, southeast King County. In 1890, it was named *Deans* by Northern Pacific officials. The following year, it was changed to the present name, for Lester Hansacker, the railway's telegraph operator here.

Levant Passage (*T.35N;R.2E*)

Short passage between Saddlebag and Huckleberry islands, in Padilla Bay, northwest Skagit County. In 1841, it was charted under the present name by Cmdr. Charles Wilkes, for the British ship *Levant*, captured by the *Constitution* in the War of 1812. It no longer appears by this name on recent maps.

Levey (*S.8;T.9N;R.32E*)

Railroad station on the north bank of Columbia River, near the site of Ice Harbor Dam, 11 miles east of Pasco, south Franklin County. The railroad station was named by Northern Pacific Railway Company officials, for C. M. Levey, vice president.

Lewis (Lewis County) *see* Packwood

Lewis County

This county in southwest Washington is bounded on the west by Pacific County; on the north by Grays Harbor, Thurston and Pierce counties; on the east by Yakima County; and on the south by Yakima, Skamania, Cowlitz and Wahkiakum counties. It is the largest county in the state, with 2,447 sq. miles. On December 21, 1845, it was established by the Provisional Government of Oregon Territory, with an area taken from Vancouver District. The name is in honor of Capt. Meriwether Lewis, of the Lewis and Clark Expedition.

Lewis & Clark State Park (*S.16;T.12N;R.1W*)

A 530-acre remnant of the original forest directly south of Marys Corner, 12 miles south of Chehalis, west central Lewis County. It was named for the 2 famous explorers Capt. William Clark and Meriwether Lewis. The park is traversed by visible portions of the old Cowlitz Trail, which extended from Cowlitz Landing to Tumwater. It offers public camping facilities.

Lewis & Clark Trail State Park (*T.9N;R.38E*)

A 35-acre park on Touchet River, 5 miles southwest of Dayton, extreme west central Columbia County. It offers public camping and fishing. The name is for Lewis & Clark Expedition, which used the site for a one-night camp.

Lewis Lock and Dam (Franklin, Walla Walla counties) *see* Lower Monumental Dam

Lewis Peak (*S.13;T.29N;R.10E*)

Peak 3-1/2 miles northwest of Monte Cristo, 2 miles southwest of Barlow Pass, east central Snohomish County. It was named by The Mountaineers, for the Lewis brothers, local trappers and prospectors. (USBGN)

Lewis River (*Ts.4-9N;Rs.1W-10E*)

The main branch, or North Fork, rises on the northwest slope of Mt. Adams, northeast Skamania County;

flows southwest and west through Skamania County, between Clark and Cowlitz counties via Lake Merwin, to Columbia River at Woodland. The East Fork rises near Cougar Mountain, southwest Skamania County; flows east through Skamania and Clark counties, joining the main branch 3-1/2 miles above its junction with Columbia River. It was named for Adolphus Lee Lewis, who claimed land on the river's west bank in 1845, and operated a store here for many years. His English father had been factor of a Hudson's Bay Company trading post on Hudson's Bay. In 1853, railroad surveyors mapped the North Fork as *Cathlapootle River,* using the Indian name. Another early name was *Washington River.*

Lewis River, Lewis and Clark River (Walla Walla, Franklin, Columbia, Whitman, Garfield, Asotin counties) *see* Snake River

Liars Creek (Okanogan County) *see* Thompson Creek

Liberty *(S.1;T.20N;R.17E)*
Settlement on Williams Creek, near Sauk Creek junction, 1-1/2 miles west of Meaghersville, north central Kittitas County. The area once yielded large amounts of placer gold; an arrastra near here operated until recently. The patriotic name was chosen by the first permanent resident, Gus Nelson, when he started the settlement. In 1891, he built a cabin, which was later used for a school, and then for a post office.

Liberty Bay *(T.26N;R.1E)*
A northwest arm of Port Orchard bay, 3 miles long and 1/2 mile wide, 4 miles east of Hood Canal, north central Kitsap County. Settlements around the bay have a very strong Norwegian flavor. It was once the winter headquarters of the codfish fleet, which is now almost nonexistent. In 1841, the bay was named *May's Inlet* by Cmdr. Charles Wilkes, for Past Midshipman William May. The first white settlers called it by its appropriate name, *Dogfish Bay,* for the bay's tremendous population of dogfish. State Legislature disliked that name, and renamed it *Patterson,* which did not persist. The present name was chosen by local inhabitants.

Liberty Cap *(S.35;T.31N;R.15E.uns)*
Peak at Cascade Mountain summit,

1/2 mile south of Buck Creek Pass, northwest Chelan County. In 1908, it was named by Forest Supervisor A. H. Sylvester, for its resemblance to the cap usually depicted in drawings of the Goddess of Liberty.

Liberty Cap *(Mt. Rainier National Park)*
Sharp, 14,112-ft. peak, the northernmost of 3 peaks at Mt. Rainier summit. It is eternally snow-covered with a pure white, glittering cap. In 1883, it was named by Prof. Bailey Willis, for its shape and color. An unofficial, alternate name is *Tahoma Peak.* (USBGN)

Liberty Creek *(Ts.24,25N;Rs.45,46E)*
The stream of the creek rises in west central Idaho; flows northwest into Liberty Lake, 13 miles east of Spokane, Spokane County. It was named for the lake into which it flows. (*see* Liberty Lake (lake))

Liberty Lake *(Ss.23-26;T.25N;R.45E)*
Lake 13 miles east of Spokane, near the Idaho boundary, east central Spokane County. It was named for Stephen *Liberte,* who came here from Quebec in 1866, and, in 1869, settled on the lake. He acted as a guide and also carried mail for some years.

Liberty Lake *(S.22;T.25N;R.45E)*
Resort Community on the west shore of Liberty Lake, 12 miles east of Spokane, extreme east central Spokane County. (*see* Liberty Lake (lake)

Liberty Mountain *(S.32;T.31N;R.9E)*
A Mt.Baker National Forest peak, elevation 5,678-ft., 5 miles northeast of Gold Basin, at the head of South Fork, Canyon Creek, north central Snohomish County. Prior to World War I, it reputedly had a local German name. The present name was a substitution. (USBGN)

Liberty Ridge *(Mt. Rainier National Park)*
A 10,775-ft. ridge dividing the head of Carbon Glacier into 2 feeders, 1-1/2 miles northwest of Mt. Rainier summit, on the west border of Willis Wall, central area of the park. This patriotic name was suggested by John H. Williams, author of *The Mountain That Was God.* In 1914, his name was adopted by U.S.

Geological Survey engineers, who made an official map of the park. (USBGN)

Lichtenberg Mountain
(S.35;T.27N;R.13E)
A Wenatchee National Forest peak, elevation 5,920-ft., 3 miles north of Stevens Pass, 1 mile southeast of Cascade Mountain summit, southwest Chelan County. Prior to 1902, it was called *Lightning Mountain.* There is evidence that the present name was applied by Forest Supervisor A. H. Sylvester of Wenatchee National Forest, although his choice of name is obscure.

Lichtenwasser Lake
(S.36;T.27N;R.13E)
A Wenatchee National Forest lake, 3 miles north of Stevens Pass, northeast slope of Lichtenberg Mountain, southwest Chelan County. In 1910, it was named by Forest Supervisor A. H. Sylvester, to harmonize with Lichtenberg Mountain.

Lichty *(S.4;T.9N;R.23E)*
Railroad station 3 miles southeast of Sunnyside, southeast Yakima County. It was named by Northern Pacific Railway officials, when the Sunnyside branch was completed. It was for the H. M. Lichty family, from whom the railway acquired a local right-of-way. An earlier name was *Esjay.*

Lick Creek *(T.9N;Rs.43,44E)*
The stream of the creek rises in east Garfield County; flows 7-1/2 miles east to South Fork, Asotin Creek, Asotin County. The local name relates to alkaline deer licks along the creek.

Licked Skillet *(T.33N;Rs.37-38E)*
Stock range on the east bank of Columbia River, extending from Gifford to Daisy, then inland several miles to the vicinity of Maud, west central Stevens County. Most of the area was later occupied by the Slingsby Ranch. The name, given by early settlers, was for a bachelor who lived here, and who had extremely unsanitary habits. He is reported to have allowed his dogs to lick the dishes after a meal, rather than waste his time washing them. Presently, the area has no specific name, but is traversed from north to south by Bachelor Creek Road.

Licking *(S.6;T.39N;R.4E)*
Long-vanished pioneer settlement 2

miles south of Nooksack, on the east bank of Nooksack River, northwest Whatcom County. It was named by J. V. Smith, who claimed the first homestead in this area in the 1870s. The name is for Smith's former home in Licking Township, Ohio.

Lighthouse Tower *(T.20N;R.16E)*

Granite mountain, elevation 8,400 ft., in Stuart Range, 7 miles southwest of Leavenworth, southwest Chelan County. Evidently, it was named by local mountain climbers, although the first recorded ascent to the peak was as late as August 30, 1948.

Lightning Creek *(Ts.25,30N;R.14E)*

The stream of this glacial creek rises near the Cascade Mountain summit, on the northeast slope of White River Glacier, Wenatchee National Forest, northwest Chelan County; flows 2-1/2 miles south to the headwaters of White River. It drains a large part of the glacier. Forest Supervisor A. H. Sylvester named the creek because of its location in an area of severe electrical storms.

Lightning Creek *(Ss.4-6;T.18N;R.10E)*

The stream of the creek rises on Dallas Ridge, Snoqualmie National Forest, east central Pierce County; flows 2-1/2 miles west to White River. It was named by Forest Service personnel, because lightning strikes quite often along the stream.

Lightning Mountain (Chelan County) *see* Lichtenberg Mountain

Lillian River *(Ts.27,28N;Rs.5-7W)*

The stream of the river rises in Lillian Glacier and Lillian Lake, north central Jefferson County; flows northwest to Elwha River, south central Clallam County. In 1890, it was named by Seattle Press Expedition for Lake Lillian. (*see* Lake Lillian)

Lilliwaup *(S.30;T.23N;R.3W)*

Village on Lilliwaup Bay, west side of Hood Canal, 3 miles north of Hoodsport, north central Mason County. The name is a modification of the Twana dialect word *Lil-la-wop*, meaning "inlet."

Lilliwaup Bay *(Ss.19,30;T.23N;R.3W)*

A west shore bay of Hood Canal, at the mouth of Lilliwaup Creek, opposite Dewatto, north central Mason County. (*see* Lilliwaup)

Lilliwaup Creek *(T.23N;Rs.3,4W)*

The stream of the creek rises 3-1/2 miles northeast of Lake Cushman Reservoir; flows 7 miles southeast to Lilliwaup, west shore of Hood Canal, north central Mason County. (*see* Lilliwaup)

Lilliwaup Falls *(S.19;T.23N;R.3W)*

A scenic falls, with a 150-ft. drop, in Lilliwaup Creek, 1/2 mile above its mouth on the west shore of Hood Canal, Mason County. The water, from swampy, forest pools, is quite dark. (*see* Lilliwaup)

Lilliwaup Swamp *(Ss.10,11,15;T.23N;R.4W)*

A swampy, 225-acre lake, maximum depth 10 ft., 6 miles north of Hoodsport, north central Mason County. (*see* Lilliwaup)

Lily Pond *(S.22;T.21N;R.3W)*

A shallow, 8.6-acre lake 6-1/4 miles north of Shelton, southeast Mason County. The name appears to be descriptive, as native waterlillies are reported to grow along the lake's margin.

Lime Kiln (Pierce County) *see* McMillan

Lime Lake *(S.14;T.39N;R.43E)*

A very small lake 2 miles northeast of Metaline Falls (town), north central Pend Oreille County. It was named for a heavy deposit of lime on the bottom of this very clear body of water.

Lime Mountain (Snohomish County) *see* Lime Ridge

Lime Point Rapids (Asotin County) *see* Limekiln Rapids

Lime Ridge *(S.35;T.32N;R.12E)*

Ridge between Lime Creek and Suiattle River, maximum elevation 6,744 ft., at the northwest extremity of Glacier Peak slopes, northeast Snohomish County. It was named for Lime Creek by early surveyors, and the name has been adopted by U.S. Forest Service on their maps. An alternate name is *Lime Mountain*.

Limekiln Rapids *(S.7;T.7N;R.47E)*

Rapids in Snake River, 1 mile below the mouth of Grande Ronde River, between southeast Asotin County and western Idaho. The name was applied locally before 1890, when the lime deposits on both banks of Snake River

were being worked. An alternate name is *Lime Point Rapids*.

Lincoln

A proposed new state which caused agitation in 1907. It was to have included all of The Inland Empire east of Cascade Mountain summit -- specifically, eastern Washington, eastern Oregon, and parts of western Idaho. The reason given for forming this state was that the area had common interests in agriculture and other pursuits, which differed greatly from other parts of the 3 states involved.

Lincoln *(S.36;T.28N;R.35E)*

Small town, one of 12 flooded by Grand Coulee Dam, on Columbia River south bank, near the confluence of Spokane River, north central Lincoln County. In 1939, most of its small population moved to nearby Miles. It was named for Lincoln County.

Lincoln (Lewis County) *see* Galvin

Lincoln County

This county in east central Washington is bounded on the west by Grant County; on the north by Okanogan, Ferry and Stevens counties; on the east by Spokane County; and, on the south by Whitman and Adams counties. It contains 2,317 square miles, and was established by an act of the Territorial Legislature on November, 24, 1883, from a portion of Spokane County. It was named in the act for Abraham Lincoln, 16th president of the United States. The proposed name had been *Sprague*, to honor John W. Sprague, general superintendent of Northern Pacific Railway Company. The legislative bill was altered to carry the present name, as a political move to gain support for its passage.

Lincoln Creek *(Ts.14,15N;Rs.3-5W)*

The stream of the creek heads in extreme northwest Lewis County; flows east to Chehalis River near Fords Prarie. The first name was the Indian designation *Nat-che-les*, meaning "place where camas grows." The change to the present name came from efforts of homesteader Frank M. Rhodes, who wanted the creek named for Abraham Lincoln. On some records, the Indian name has been distorted to *Natural Creek*, an obvious error.

Lincoln Memorial (Chelan County) *see* Lincoln Rock

Lincoln Peak *(T.38N;R.7E.uns)*

A sheer, black butte on the southwest slope of Mt. Baker, between Thunder and Deming glaciers, south central Whatcom County. In 1868, it was named by E. T. Coleman, for President Abraham Lincoln.

Lincoln Rock *(S.26;T.24N;R.20E)*

A massive rock formation on the north bank of Columbia River, at Swakane Creek mouth, southeast Chelan County. The rock's profile is assumed to resemble that of Abraham Lincoln. In 1898, it was named by Wenatchee pioneers when they viewed it from a river packet. An alternate name is *Lincoln Memorial.*

Lind *(Ss.11-14;T.17N;R.33E)*

Town 87 miles southwest of Spokane, in central Adams County wheat belt. In 1888, it was founded by an Icelandic family named Nielson, who established a store and developed an excellent well from a natural spring. In 1890, the name chosen by Northern Pacific Railway officials is said to be the Icelandic word for spring or small watercourse. Three local explanations for the town's name state that it was for a woman cook who accompanied railroad construction crews; for Jenny Lind, the "Swedish nightingale"; and, for a woman who alighted from a train to take a look at the town!

Lindberg (Lewis County) *see* Coal Canyon

Line Creek *(T.27N;Rs.15,16E)*

The stream of the creek rises on Wenatchee Ridge, Wenatchee National Forest, west central Chelan County; flows 1-1/2 miles south to Little Wenatchee River. It was named by Forest Ranger R. J. Huston, because it follows quite closely the line between Range 15 East and Range 16 East.

Lingerlonger Lake (Jefferson County) *see* Devils Lake

Lion Creek *(T.24N;R.17E)*

The stream of this spring branch rises on Wenatchee National Forest, central Chelan County; flows 2 miles south from Icicle Ridge to Icicle Creek. The present name was applied by Forest Ranger John Brender; he changed it from *Cougar Creek* to avoid repetition of the latter name.

Lion Gulch *(T.21N;Rs.17,18E)*

Gulch originating in northeast Kittitas County, near Chelan County boundary; extending about 8 miles south and southwest to Williams Creek at Liberty. It is reported that the name was given by G. D. Virden, an early miner, who shot a cougar in the gulch.

Liplip Point *(S.9;T.29N;R.1E)*

A southeast point of Marrowstone Island on Admiralty Inlet, northeast Jefferson County. In 1841, the name was applied by Cmdr. Charles Wilkes, using the original Indian name. In Chinook jargon, it means "boiling" or "the sound of boiling." It is quite descriptive, as there are turbulent tide rips around the point.

Lisabeula *(S.11;T.22N;R.2E)*

Small settlement on the west shore of Vashon Island, 2 miles west of Burton on West Passage, southwest King County. Founded in 1890, records indicate that the name was conceived by a postal official in the office of the Postmaster General, Washington, D.C., who combined the names of 2 office girls: Eliza and Beulah. It is shown on some county maps, in error, as *Lisabuella.*

Lisabuella (King County) *see* Lisabeula

Littel *(S.3;T.13N;R.3W)*

Small settlement 3 miles southwest of Chehalis, west central Lewis County. Once a sawmill and shingle mill town, it was named in 1898 by Northern Pacific Railway officials for C. R. Littel, a sawmill operator.

Little Baldy (Spokane County) *see* Mt. Spokane

Little Beaver Creek
(T.39N;Rs.11-13E.uns)

The stream of the creek heads in glaciers of Pocket Range, near Whatcom Peak, Mt. Baker National Forest, east central Whatcom County; flows 15 miles east by north to Ross Lake, 5-1/2 miles south of Canadian boundary. It was named by U.S. Forest Service personnel, for the beaver which were plentiful near the mouth of the creek, and on several other creeks in the area, before the flooding on upper Skagit River by Ross Dam.

Little Belt Passage (San Juan County) *see* Middle Channel, Cattle Point Narrows

Little Big Chief *(S.31;T.24N;R.13E)*

Peak at Cascade Mountain summit, directly south of Dutch Miller Gap, extreme east central King County and Kittitas County. In 1925, the name was chosen by The Mountaineers, for L. A. "Shorty" Nelson, a diminutive mountaineer and hiker, who could out-walk and out-climb almost anyone who ever traveled with him.

Little Boston *(S.5;T.27N;R.2E)*

An Indian village at Point Julia, on the east shore of Port Gamble bay, north end of Kitsap County. It was created when local Indians were moved by a lumber company from their home in Teekalet, now Port Gamble. Lumber company officials wanted the site of Teekalet for a sawmill. Local white men christened the new Indian village, influenced by derision and lusty pioneer humor.

Little Calispell Peak
(Ss.2,11;T.33N;R.42E)

Peak 8-1/2 miles northwest of Cusick, west central Pend Oreille County. (USBGN) (*see* Calispell Creek)

Little Chambers Lake (Thurston County) *see* Chambers Lake

Little Chetwoot Lake
(S.23;T.24N;R.12E)

A 1-acre lake, 300 ft. north of Chetwoot Lake in an outlet stream draining into Angeline Lake, 3-1/2 miles west of Cascade Mountain summit, Snoqualmie National Forest, northeast King County. (*see* Chetwoot Lake)

Little Chief Peak *(S.10;T.29N;R.10E)*

Snoqualmie National Forest peak, 4 miles south of Silverton, east central Snohomish County. The name was applied by The Mountaineers for mountain climber and forester L. A. Nelson, who was known to his friends as "Shorty," a well-deserved nickname.

Little Chopaka Mountain
(S.30;T.40N;R.25E)

A 7,390-ft. pinnacle, one of 2 very high peaks in Chopaka Mountains, 4-1/2 miles south of the Canadian boundary, 4 miles northwest of Palmer Lake, north central Okanogan County. (*see* Chopaka)

Little Coulee (Douglas County) *see* Moses Coulee

Little Cowlitz Creek (Mt. Rainier National Park) *see* Williwakas Creek

Little Cranberry Lake (Skagit County) *see* Cranberry Lake

Little Creek (Spokane County) *see* Dartford Creek

Little Dalles *(S.21;T.39N;R.39E)*

Vanished town on the east bank of Columbia River, 15 miles south of the Canadian boundary by river and 9 miles by air, northwest Stevens County. The settlement was established sometime before 1881, in which year it suffered a disastrous fire. In 1900, it again came to life during the building of Spokane Falls & Northern Railway, and had a more or less fixed population of 63. When mail service came, in the form of a combination box car, saloon and post office, postal authorities accepted the name of the nearby rapids.

Little Dalles *(S.20;T.39N;R.39E)*

Columbia River rapids flooded by Grand Coulee Dam, 737 miles from the river's mouth, 15 miles by river from the Canadian border, northwest Stevens County. These rapids, between massive stone cliffs and Kettle Falls, 26 miles down river, were the chief hazards to navigation during the period when river boats furnished transportation to the entire upper river area. The first official use of the name appears to be in a report by Lieut. Thomas W. Symons, U.S. Army Corps of Engineers, based on field work done in the fall of 1881. Published in 1882, the report is titled ''An Examination of the Upper Columbia River.'' The use of the word ''dalles'' for rocky rapids was common with French-Canadian voyageurs, who worked along Columbia River for early fur traders. Its French meaning is ''flagstones'' or ''slabs.'' The smooth, polished rock surfaces in these rapids evidently reminded these boatsmen of flagstones, which were used for paving in eastern Canada. They applied the same term to rapids further down the river. (*see* The Dalles)

Little Devil's Table (Yakima County) *see* Meek's Table

Little Falls (Lewis County) *see* Vader

Little Gee Lake *(S.19;T.34N;R.8E)*

A 1.5-acre lake, elevation 4,240 ft., 8 miles southwest of Concrete, south central Skagit County. It was named for Gee Creek, which drains the lake. (*see* Gee Creek)

Little Giant Creek *(T.29N;R.16E.uns)*

The stream of the creek rises on the east side of Chiwawa Ridge, Wenatchee National Forest, northwest Chelan County; flows 2 miles east to Chiwawa River. This old name was applied by early prospectors, because the creek plunges down a steep slope and carries a heavy burden of detritus, like the ''giants'' used in placer mining.

Little Goose Dam *(T.13N;R.39E)*

Dam in Snake River, 6 miles above Riparia, 70.3 miles above the river's mouth, between north central Columbia and southwest Whitman counties. In 1949, Congressional resolutions suggested the name *Clark Lock & Dam*, honoring Capt. William Clark of Lewis & Clark Expedition. The present name, given by the U.S. Army engineers, is for the Little Goose Island in Columbia River.

Little Goosmus Creek *(T.40N;Rs.33-34E)*

The stream of the creek rises on the southeast slope of Vulcan Mountain, elevation 4,500 ft., Colville National Forest, northeast Ferry County; flows 5 miles southeast to Kettle River. (*see* Goosmus Creek)

Little Hidden Lake (Skamania County) *see* Hidden Lakes

Little Hindoo Creek (Yakima County) *see* Hinder Creek

Little Hoko River *(S.15;T.31N;R.13W)*

The stream of the river rises in Lizard Lake, 6-1/2 miles southwest of Sekiu, northwest Clallam County; flows 3 miles north to Lamb Creek, a tributary of Hoko River. (*see* Hoko River)

Little Island *(T.8N;Rs.5,6E)*

A 2-1/2-mile-long island, about 1/2 mile wide at center, in Columbia River, Cathlamet Channel, directly northeast of Puget Island, southeast Wahkiakum County. The locally-applied name refers to the island's size when compared to adjoining Puget Island, not the size of the island itself.

Little Kachess Lake *(T.22N;R.13E)*

Narrow, 3-1/2-mile-long extension of extreme north Kachess Lake, joining it by a narrow channel, Wenatchee National Forest, northwest Kittitas County. On 1853 Railroad Survey maps, the Indian name *Pilwaltas* was used. (*see* Kachess Lake)

Little Klickitat River *(Ts.4,5N;Rs.14-16E)*

The stream of the river rises 2-1/2 miles north of Goldendale, central Klickitat County; flows south and west 17 miles to Klickitat River, 5-1/2 miles northeast of Klickitat. (*see* Klickitat)

Little Kulla Lake *(S.32;T.23N;R.10E)*

A 2.6-acre lake 400 ft. south of Kulla Kulla Lake, Snoqualmie National Forest, east central King County. (*see* Kulla Kulla Lake)

Little Loup Loup Creek *(Ts.33,34N;R.25E)*

The stream of the creek heads near the old townsite of Loop Loop, 8 miles northwest of Okanogan, central Okanogan County; flows 7 miles south to Loup Loup Creek. It is the smaller of two streams named Loup Loup. (*see* Loup Loup)

Little Mt. Adams *(S.23;T.8N;R.11E.uns)*

''Parasitic'' volcanic cone, elevation 6,815 ft., between Big Muddy and Hell-Roaring creeks, southeast slope of Mt. Adams, southwest Yakima County. In August 1901, it was named by glaciologist Harry Fielding Reid of Johns Hopkins University. This child of a mighty mountain appears to have been aptly named.

Little Mountain *(S.29;T.35N;R.3W)*

A 475-ft. mountain on San Juan Island, 4 miles southwest of Friday Harbor, southwest San Juan County. In 1858, it was charted as *Mt. Little* by British Admiralty Surveyor Richards. The name was changed to the present form by U.S. Coast & Geodetic Survey.

Little Muddy Creek *(T.9N;Rs.11,12E.uns)*

The stream of the creek rises at Rusk Glacier, northeast slope of Mt. Adams; flows 9 miles northeast to Clearwater Creek, southwest Yakima County. During periods of hot weather, when the glacier is melting rapidly, the stream carries an extraordinary volume of rocks, mud and glacial flour. However, the volume is considerably less than the detritus carried by Big Muddy Creek on Mt. Adams' east slope. From that difference, the well-earned name was derived.

Little Nespelem River *(Ts.30-32N;Rs.30,31E)*

The stream of the river rises in 2

branches: one in Lake Owhi, southeast Okanogan County, the other in southwest Ferry County; flows southwest and west 19 miles to Nespelem River, near the confluence of that river with Columbia River. (*see* Nespelem)

Little Nisqually Glacier (Mt. Rainier National Park) *see* Paradise Glacier

Little Pend Oreille River
(Ts.34-36N;Rs.39-42E)

The stream of the river rises in several small branches, in Lake Sherry, northeast Stevens County; flows southwest and west 28 miles to Colville River, at Arden. Its name is borrowed from the larger Pend Oreille River to the east, Pend Oreille County. Evidently, French-Canadians, employed by fur trading companies, gave the name to Indians who wore ear ornaments that caused the earlobes to hang rather low. *Oreilles pendates* is French for "hanging ears."

Little Pete Lake *(S.21;T.27N;R.13E)*

A 2-acre lake, elevation 4,900 ft., 2 miles southwest of Cascade Mountain summit, Snoqualmie National Forest, extreme southwest Snohomish County. It was named for Pete Lake, located slightly over 1,000 ft. southeast.

Little Pierre Lake *(S.17;T.39N;R.37E)*

Small, narrow lake 3 miles east of Orient on Toulou Creek, Colville National Forest, northwest Stevens County. As with Pierre Lake, it was named for Peter Arcasa, also called "Peter Pierre." He was the son of a Hudson's Bay Company express man, and worked as a trapper, guide, hunter, prospector, and, finally, as a successful stockman.

Little Pratt Lake *(S.35;T.23N;R.10E)*

A 4.3-acre lake at the head of Pratt River, 1/2 mile east of Pratt Lake, Snoqualmie National Forest, east central King County. The lake's name is in contrast to the larger 43.5-acre Pratt Lake. (*see* Pratt Lake)

Little Quilcene River
(Ts.27,28N;Rs.2,3W)

The stream of the river heads on the northeast slope of Mt. Townsend, southeast Clallam County; flows east and south to Big Quilcene River. (*see* Quilcene)

Little Rattlesnake Lake (King County) *see* Rainbow Lake

Little Retreat Lake *(S.32;T.22N;R.7E)*

Lake 1/4 mile southwest of Lake Retreat, southwest King County. Its area has a seasonal variation, averaging 3.4 acres. (*see* Lake Retreat)

Little Rock *(S.2;T.16N;R.3W)*

Small place between Bordeaux and Mayton, 5-1/2 miles south of Black Lake, southwest Thurston County. It was named by a pioneer settler named Shumach, for a natural stone which he found here, that was perfectly shaped for a "mounting stone."

Little Sheep Creek *(T.40N;R.39E)*

The stream of this short creek heads just north of the Canadian Border, Colville National Forest, extreme north central Stevens County; flows south for 3 miles to join Big Sheep Creek, a tributary of Columbia River. Its name, like that of Big Sheep Creek, was evidently applied by early settlers because of extensive use of the area for sheep range.

Little Si Lake *(S.2;T.23N;R.8E)*

A 2-acre lake 1-1/2 miles east of North Bend, between Mt. Si and Little Si Mountain, east central King County. The name is for Little Si Mountain, which was named for Mt. Si. (*see* Mt. Si)

Little Sweden (King County) *see* High Point

Little Tahoma Peak *(Mt. Rainier National Park)*

Peak at a wedge formed by the upper reaches of Whitman, Ohanapecosh and Fryingpan glaciers, 2-1/2 miles east of Mt. Rainier summit; includes the highest point on the east flank of Mt. Rainier, elevation 11,117 ft. The name is from the Indian word *Tahoma*, meaning "snow-covered mountain." It is quite appropriate for this peak. (USBGN)

Little Twin Lakes (Snohomish County) *see* Twin Lakes

Little Wapato Lake *(S.29;T.20N;R.3E)*

A shallow, marshy lake covering 22 acres in Wapato Park, connected with nearby Wapato Lake, directly east of South Tacoma business district, Pierce County. (*see* Wapato)

Little Wenatchee River
(T.27N;Rs.16,17E)

The stream of the river heads on Wenatchee National Forest, northwest Chelan County; flows 22 miles southeast by east from Cascade Mountain summit

to the west end of Wenatchee Lake. In 1908, it was named by U.S. Forest Supervisor A. H. Sylvester to indicate that it was separated from Wenatchee River by Wenatchee Lake.

Little White Salmon River
(Ts.3-5N;Rs.9,10E)

The stream of the river rises on Gifford Pinchot National Forest, extreme west Klickitat County; flows southwest and south 24 miles to Columbia River at Cook. (*see* White Salmon River)

Littlers Lake (King County) *see* Lizard Lake

Livingston *(S.4;T.2N;R.3E)*

Mountain community and school district on Shanghai Creek, 10 miles northeast of Vancouver, south central Clark County. It was named for John Livingston, who homesteaded here in the late 1870s, and who is reputed to have made apple brandy under a government license.

Lizard Lake *(S.15;T.31N;R.13W)*

Lake at the head of Little Hoko River, 6 miles west of Sekiu, west central Clallam County. The name is reported to have been a local choice, because the swampy shores harbor many small lizards.

Lizard Lake *(S.25;T.21N;R.11E)*

A 4.6-acre lake, elevation 3,540 ft., in Stampede Pass, Cascade Mountain summit, southeast King County. On many rather shallow lakes like this one, especially those with swampy margins, lizards are apt to prey on insects along the shore. Alternate names are *Mona Lake* and *Littlers Lake*.

Lizard Lakes (King County) *see* Stink Lakes

Lizzard Lake (Kitsap County) *see* Ludvick Lake

Loa Point (Thurston County) *see* Nisqually Head

Loch Eileen *(S.19;T.26N;R.16E)*

Beautiful mountain tarn in a glacial cirque at the head of Roaring Creek, east slope of Chiwaukum Mountains, Wenatchee National Forest, southwest Chelan County. It was named by U.S. Forest Supervisor A. H. Sylvester, for the daughter of Forest Ranger Jason P. Williams.

Locke *(S.24;T.34N;R.43E)*

Once a settlement between Jared and

Cusick, 1 mile west of Pend Oreille River, south central Pend Oreille County. When Chicago, Milwaukee & St. Paul Railway built through here and established a station, officials named the place for a local landowner, David Locke Smith. He dropped the "Smith" becuase there were too many settlers with that name in the area.

Locket Lake *(S.7;T.24N;R.13E)*

A 56-acre lake on the west side of Necklace Valley, 3-1/2 miles west of Cascade Mountain summit, Snoqualmie National Forest, northeast King County. It was given a jewelry name to harmonize with Necklace Valley.

Lockwood *(Cor. of Ss.5-8;T.23N;R.45E)*

Vanished town 5 miles north of Rockford, southeast Spokane County. In 1890, a post office was established, then discontinued in 1903. The town was named by Chicago, Milwaukee & St. Paul Railway officials, for a local settler on whose land the station was built.

Lodge Creek *(S.8;T.22N;R.11E)*

The stream of the creek rises in Lodge Lake, 1 mile southwest of Snoqualmie Pass, east central King County; flows 1 mile west to Snoqualmie River. In 1916, it was named by The Mountaineers for Lodge Lake. They had submitted the name *Mountaineer Creek* to USBGN, but it was not accepted. (USBGN) (*see* Lodge Lake)

Lodge Lake *(S.8;T.22N;R.11E)*

A 9.3-acre lake directly west of Cascade Mountain summit, 1 mile southwest of Snoqualmie Pass, at the head of Lodge Creek, east central King County. It was named by The Mountaineers when they built a lodge here. An earlier name was *Big Lake*, which was a locally-applied name chosen to contrast with nearby Little Lake. (USBGN)

Lodi Creek *(Mt. Rainier National Park)*

The stream of the creek rises west of Mt. Fremont, north central sector of the park; flows northwest through Affi Falls to West Fork, White River, 2-1/2 miles south of the park's north boundary. It has a very steep gradient until it enters White River valley. The creek was named by early-day prospectors, for Lodi, California. (USBGN)

Lofall *(S.22;T.27N;R.1E)*

Settlement on the east shore of Hood Canal, 6 miles north of Poulsbo, north-

west Kitsap County. When a post office was established, it was named for Helge Lofall, an early logger and settler.

Lofgren Mountain *(S.21;T.37N;R.4W)*

A 305-ft. peak west of Charles Point, northwest area of Stuart Island, northwest San Juan County. It was named for Svante Lofgren, who bought a farm on the island in 1927, which included the mountain. He was a well-known historian, specializing in the history of Swedish people in the Pacific northwest.

Lonesome Lake *(S.18;T.10N;R.5E)*

A 6-acre lake, elevation 3,895 ft., Gifford Pinchot National Forest, at the head of a Miners Creek tributary, extreme northwest Skamania County. It may be lonesome now, but it wasn't 70 or 75 years ago, when prospectors and miners swarmed the area.

Lone Tree *(S.24;T.17N;R.12W)*

Point of land on the south end of Armstrong Bay, near Grays Harbor north entrance, southwest Grays Harbor County. The name is for a very famous Douglas fir tree which stood alone on this point until it was blown down in 1935. In May 1792, Robert Gray mentioned the tree as a landmark. Mariners used the tree as a guide, and surveyors used it for a triangulation point.

Lone Tree (Benton County) *see* Prosser

Lone Tree Creek *(Ts.37,38N;R.14E.uns)*

The stream of the creek rises 4 miles east of Ross Dam, Mt. Baker National Forest, southeast Whatcom County; flows 2-1/2 miles southwest to Ruby Creek. It was named by U.S. Forest Service personnel for a single, large tree on the creek's bank, which was the lone survivor of a forest fire some time prior to 1884.

Lone Tree Island *(T.37N;R.1W)*

Largest and most northerly of a group of very small islands called *The Sisters* or *Sisters Islands*, in Strait of Georgia, directly south of Clark Island and 2 miles northeast of Orcas Island, northeast San Juan County. It was locally named because it bore a single, coniferous tree, while the associated islands were entirely bare.

Long (Columbia County) *see* Longs

Long Alec Creek *(Ts.38,39N;Rs.33-35E)*

The stream of the creek heads on Taylor Ridge, Colville National Forest, north central Ferry County; flows 10 miles northwest to join Kettle River at Curlew. The name, incorrectly called *Long Alex Creek* on some maps, is for "Long Alec," a Colville Indian, who was over 6 feet tall.

Long Alex Creek (Ferry County) *see* Long Alec Creek

Long Bay (Jefferson County) *see* Kilisut Harbor

Long Beach *(T.10N;R.11W)*

Hard, sandy beach facing Pacific Ocean, 300 ft. wide at low tide, near south end of North Beach Peninsula, southwest Pacific County. It is an ideal summer resort town. In 1881, H. H. Tinker named the place when he built a large hotel here.

Long Branch *(S.24;T.20N;R.1W)*

Settlement of country homes on Filucy Bay, 2 miles west of McNeil Island, northwest Pierce County. It was named by an early resident for Long Branch, New Jersey.

Long Branch Bay (Pierce County) *see* Filucy Bay

Long Harbor (Jefferson County) *see* Kilisut Harbor

Long Island *(Ts.11,12N;Rs.10,11W)*

Very irregular island, 7 miles long, in Willapa Bay west of Naselle River mouth, southwest Pacific County. In 1857, the descriptive name was applied by James G. Swan.

Long Island *(S.15;T.34N;R.2W)*

Island directly south of Davis Bay, southwest end of Lopez Island, south central San Juan County. In 1858, the name was placed on British Admiralty charts by Capt. Henry Richards, R.N. The name is not especially descriptive, although the island's length exceeds its width. It is one of the *Geese Islets*, with Buck Island, Whale Rocks and Mummy Rocks.

Long Island (Benton County) *see* Blalock Island

Long Lake *(Ss.5-8;T.29N;R.3E)*

A 92-acre lake, roughly heart-shaped, on Whidbey Island, 2-1/2 miles southwest of Langley, south central Island County. The locally-chosen name seems inappropriate, as there are other lakes in the vicinity, one within a mile.

Long Lake *(S.19;T.28N;R.8W.uns)*

A 15-acre lake, second largest of 8 lakes in Seven Lakes basin, Olympic National Park, south central Clallam County. The descriptive name refers to the lake's elongated shape due to its location in a long, narrow valley.

Long Lake *(T.23N;R.28E)*

A 5-1/2-mile-long lake, width about 1/2 mile, 7 miles west of Wilson Creek (town), northeast Grant County. The name is fairly descriptive for this irrigation reservoir.

Long Lake *(T.23N;R.3E)*

Locally-named lake 3-1/2 miles southeast of Port Orchard, southeast Kitsap County. It was named for its shape, being 2 miles long and quite narrow.

Long Lake *(S.36;T.27N;R.6E)*

A 1-1/2-acre lake, about 700 ft. long and narrow, in Snoqualmie River, 4-1/2 miles south of Monroe, just north of King County boundary, southwest Snohomish County. The descriptive name is for the lake's shape.

Long Lake *(S.26;T.18N;R.1W)*

Two connected lakes, covering 311 acres, 5-1/2 miles east of Olympia, directly south of Union Mills, northeast Thurston County. It contains 2 islands, Holmes and Kirby. In 1853, the fairly descriptive name was placed on official maps by Tilden Sheats, a government contract surveyor.

Long Lake (King County) *see* Rainbow Lake

Long Mountain *(S.13;T.30N;R.9E)*

Mt. Baker National Forest peak, elevation 5,109 ft., 1-1/2 miles northwest of Silverton, north central Snohomish County. The name is from local usage, describing this long, fairly level ridge that has no prominent points.

Long Narrows (Klickitat County) *see* The Dalles

Long Point *(S.35;T.32N;R.1E)*

East shore point of Whidbey Island, near south entrance to Penn Cove, 1-1/2 miles east of Coupeville and 1 mile west of Snatelum Point, west central Island County. The fairly descriptive name was a local choice. The Indian name was *Bla-satts*. Another name, *Snakelum*, is used by Whidbey residents.

Long Spit *(S.23;T.30N;R.3W)*

Narrow sand spit, about 3/4 mile long, at Sequim Bay entrance, extending almost across the mouth of the bay from Miller Peninsula, northeast Clallam County. The descriptive name developed through local usage. An earlier name, evidently applied in 1841 by Cmdr. Charles Wilkes, was *Kiapot*, which may have been a distortion of *la pote*, Chinook jargon for "door" or "entrance." The name *Travis Spit* has been used on USGS charts.

Longfellow Creek *(T.24N;R.3E)*

The stream of the creek rises in South Park, Seattle, west of Duwamish River, King County; flows 3 miles north through West Seattle Municipal Golf Links to Elliott Bay. Its course has been altered with commercial developments along its original traverse. In early days, there was a heavy salmon run in the creek, and excellent trout fishing. It was named by pioneers for Charles Longfellow, who homesteaded land near the creek's mouth in the 1870s. The Indian name was *Tua-wt*, meaning "trout."

Longfellow Mountain
(S.11;T.28N;R.14E.uns)

Wenatchee National Forest peak, elevation 6,563 ft., 5 miles east of Cascade Mountain summit, in Little Wenatchee River drainage, northwest Chelan County. It was named by Forest Supervisor A. H. Sylvester, for Henry Wadsworth Longfellow, and is one of 5 nearby peaks which he named for early American authors.

Longmire *(Mt. Rainier National Park)*

Area including National Park Service administrative offices, a museum, post office and campgrounds, 6-1/2 miles east of Nisqually entrance, southwest zone of the park. Many trails begin at this point. It was named for James Longmire and other members of the Longmire family, who were leaders of the first immigrant train over Naches Pass in 1853; in 1883, they claimed land here. (USBGN)

Longmire Meadows *(Mt. Rainier National Park)*

Meadows 1/2 mile south of Longmire, across Nisqually River, southwest area of the park. They were named for James Longmire, who discovered mineral springs here in 1883. From that time, the site was owned by the Longmire family, until 1915, when Elcaine Longmire died.

Longmire Springs *(Mt. Rainier National Park)*

Warm mineral springs in Longmire Meadows, 1/2 mile south of Longmire, across Nisqually River, southwest area of the park. Water temperature reaches 76 degrees, and has a high iron content. (*see* Longmire)

Longs *(Ss.2,3;T.9N;R.38E)*

Railroad station on Touchet River, 3 miles southwest of Dayton, central Columbia County. When Northern Pacific Railway was established in the 1860s, this place was an important shipping point for wheat and flour. The original name was *Milton Mills*, applied in 1866, as the first flouring mill began operation. The present name was given to the station by railway officials for an early citizen. On some recent maps, it is called *Long*, for Garret Long.

Longs Lake *(S.22;T.18N;R.1W)*

Lake 1/2 mile east of Lacey, north central Thurston County. It normally has an area of about 10 acres, but may diminish to 6 acres in dry periods. The name is reportedly for an early settler on the lake's shore. This lake should not be confused with Long Lake, 2,600 ft. to the southeast.

Longview *(S.11;T.5N;R.27E)*

Community just above Devil's Bend Rapids, north bank of Columbia River, north central Benton County. The town has enjoyed 4 names. The first was *Gravel*, for the abundance of that commodity in the area. The railroad changed the station name to *Francis*, and then to *Tuton*. When the latter name was confused with Luzon in Benton County, it was changed to the present name, which is descriptive of the extensive view of Columbia River from this place. Since the establishment of Longview in Cowlitz County, there still exists a chance for confusion.

Longview *(Ts.7,8N;R.2W)*

First planned city in Pacific northwest, on a delta at the confluence of Cowlitz and Columbia rivers, southwest Cowlitz County. Planned and built in the 1920s, it was named for the founder, R. A. Long of Long-Bell Lumber Company.

Looking Glass Lake
(S.21;T.8N;R.10E.uns)

A 1-1/2-acre lake in Mt. Adams Wild Area of Gifford Pinchot National

Forest, elevation 5,600 ft., in Madcat Meadows, southwest slope of Mt. Adams, east central Skamania County. The name is appropriate, as the lake surface mirrors the majestic slopes of Mt. Adams. An alternate name is *Mirror Lake.*

Lookout *(S.8;T.11N;R.24E)*

Highest point on Rattlesnake Hills, elevation 3,627 ft., 2-1/2 miles northwest of Bennett Springs, northwest Benton County. The name was given to this hilltop because it had been a signal station for Indians.

Lookout Mountain
(Ts.19,20N;Rs.16,17E)

Extensive, horseshoe-shaped ridge with an opening to the south, elevation 3,440 ft., 5 miles east of Cle Elum, central Kittitas County. This name ordinarily indicates the use of a peak for fire lookout, but in this case derives from the Indian name *Lo-kout.* The name is that of an Indian who was a vigorous participant in the 1850s Indian wars, and was the son of a Yakima war chief.

Lookout Mountain
(Ss.15,22;T.37N;R.2W)

A 690-ft. mountain at the head of East Sound, north end of Orcas Island, 1/2 mile west of Fishing Bay, northeast San Juan County. The local name is descriptive of the wide range of vision from the mountain.

Loomis *(S.1;T.38N;R.25E)*

Small town on Sinlahekin Creek, 13 miles south of the Canadian boundary, north central Okanogan County. In the 1890s gold rush, it was a booming mining camp; now the town is largely supported by cattle-raising. The name is for Julius A. Loomis, first merchant to permanently establish a store here.

Loomis *(S.16;T.11N;R.11W)*

Summer resort area on the ocean side of North Beach Peninsula, 8 miles north of Ilwaco, southwest Pacific County. The place was named for Louis Alfred Loomis, an 1852 pioneer, who lived here until his death in 1913.

Loomis Lake
(Ss.9,16,21;T.11N;R.11W)

Long, narrow lake, parallel to Pacific Ocean beach, on North Beach Peninsula facing the ocean, 7 miles north of Ilwaco, southwest Pacific County. (*see* Loomis)

Loomis Mountain
(S.24;T.37N;R.7E)

A 5,521-ft. peak 7 miles south of Mt. Baker summit, south central Whatcom County. In 1909, it was named by The Mazamas, for a Swiss mountaineer, who was on one of their exploring parties.

Loon Island (Skagit County) *see* Strawberry Island

Loon Lake *(Ts.29,30N;R.41E)*

A 3-mile-long lake, average width 1 mile, 38 miles northwest of Spokane and 7 miles east of Springdale, southeast Stevens County. A public recreation center at the north end was previously a private park. In July 1881, the lake was named by John U. Hofstetter, a Colville valley pioneer, because it was a favored nesting place for loons.

Loon Lake *(Ss.28,33;T.30N;R.41E)*

Resort at north end of Loon Lake, northeast Stevens County. In 1889-90, it was established as a private park by D. C. Corbin, a railroad builder and banker. In 1897, it was sold to Evan Morgan, who made it a public recreation center. The name is borrowed from Loon Lake, on which the town is located. (*see* Loon Lake (lake)

Loop Loop *(S.17;T.34N;R.25E)*

Deserted mining camp 4 miles south of Ruby, on Little Loup Loup Creek, central Okanogan County. It was boomed in the 1890s, but faded rapidly when the price of silver dropped. The original spelling *Loup Loup* was evidently changed by some map makers to the present form. The name was first applied to Loup Loup Creek by French-Canadian employees of fur-trading companies. A literal French translation is ''wolf wolf.''

Lopez Hill *(S.36;T.35N;R.2W)*

A 553-ft. hill 1-1/4 miles west of Lopez Sound, south central Lopez Island, south central San Juan County. It was named for the island on which it is located. Local, unofficial names used are *Lopez Peak* and *Mt. Lopez.* (USBGN) (*see* Lopez Island)

Lopez Island *(Ts.34-36N;Rs.1,2W)*

Southernmost and third largest island of the San Juan group, between San Juan Island on the west and Decatur Island on the east, San Juan County. In 1790, it was named by Lieut. Juan Francisco de

Eliza, for Gonzalo Lopez de Haro, who discovered the island that year. In 1841, Cmdr. Charles Wilkes renamed the island *Chancy's Island*, for Capt. Isaac Chauncey, commander of U.S.S. *Washington* at the action in Algiers in 1815. In 1847, Capt. Henry Kellett changed the name back to that given by Eliza. The Lummi Indian name was *Swa-la-tch.*

Lopez Lake (San Juan County) *see* Hummel Lake

Lopez Pass *(Ts.34,35N;R.1W)*

Pass between Decatur Island and east shore of Lopez Island, southeast San Juan County. In 1854, it was charted under the present name by U.S. Coast Survey, for Spanish explorer Gonzalo Lopez de Haro, who was here in 1789. An unofficial name not on recent maps was *Maury Pass.*

Lopez Sound *(T. 35N;R.1W)*

Body of water between Lopez and Decatur islands, southeast San Juan County. In 1841, it was charted by Cmdr. Charles Wilkes as *Macedonian Crescent*, honoring Capt. Stephen Decatur, who captured the British frigate *Macedonian* on October 25, 1812, while commanding the U.S. frigate *United States*. In 1854, that name was disregarded by U.S. Coast Survey, when they named it for Lopez Island. (*see* Lopez Island)

Lord Lake *(Ss.28,33;T.28N;R.2W)*

Small mountain lake 2-1/2 miles west of Leland, directly east of Olympic National Forest and Little Quilcene River, northwest Jefferson County. It was named for a homesteader, who took a claim east of the lake.

Los Frayles *(T.28;R.15W)*

Rocks in Pacific Ocean, 1/4 to 1/2 mile offshore, southwest of LaPush, extreme southwest Clallam County. On July 12, 1775, the name was applied by Bruno Heceta to Quillayute Needle, James Island, and probably Huntington Rock. The name never came into common use, and is not found on recent maps. The name may indicate Heceta's observation that these rocks resembled a group of monks or friars.

Los Islas Deseadas (Clallam County) *see* Flattery Rocks

Lost Creek *(T.36N;Rs.42,43E)*

The stream of this intermittent creek rises in Miles Lake, central Pend Oreille

County; flows 8 miles southeast to Pend Oreille River. It has a south branch of almost equal length, which flows east to join the main creek near its mouth. The name signifies that the creek "gets lost" underground during a part of its course.

Lost Creek *(S.22;T.36N;R.43E)*

Settlement on Pend Oreille River, at the mouth of Lost Creek, central Pend Oreille County. (*see* Lost Creek (creek))

Lost Creek *(T.30N;R.12E)*

The stream of the creek rises near Lake Byrne, west slope of Glacier Peak, Glacier Peak Wilderness Area; flows 5-1/2 miles west to North Fork, Sauk River, east central Snohomish County. The name was applied by an early survey party, which lost its way in swamps along the creek.

Lost Lake *(S.31;T.28N;R.18E)*

Wenatchee National Forest lake in the course of Elder Creek, Entiat Mountains, 2 miles west of Cougar Mountain, northwest Chelan County. It was named by early sheepmen because it is in dense timber, and not visible from a distance. It should not be confused with Lost Lake on Nason Ridge, Chelan County.

Lost Lake *(S.24;T.27N;R.15E)*

Wenatchee National Forest lake on the north slope of Nason Ridge near the summit, 1-1/4 miles east of Mastiff Mountain, northwest Chelan County. The seemingly inappropriate name was given by early sheepmen. It should not be confused with Lost Lake in Entiat Mountains, Chelan County.

Lost Lake *(S.11;T.5N;R.4E)*

A 2-acre, natural lake, elevation 1,500 ft., 7-1/2 miles northeast of Yacolt, 2-1/2 miles east of Tumtum Mountain, northeast Clark County. Any lake in the Pacific northwest which cannot be seen for miles appears to bear this name. A slight variation in this type of name is Hidden Lake, which is much more descriptive.

Lost Lake *(S.24;T.31N;R.2E)*

A 1-1/2-acre lake 2 miles southeast of Camano, central Camano Island, Island County. The name was evidently chosen because the lake appears to be concealed in a 12-acre marsh.

Lost Lake *(S.7;T.27N;R.1E)*

A 7.1-acre lake 2 miles southwest of Squamish Harbor, east central Jefferson County. When fishermen or hikers cannot find a lake, they call it "Lost Lake." It isn't the *lake* that's lost.

Lost Lake *(Ss.3,4;T.1N;R.11E)*

Lake 1 mile west of Keechelus Lake, 1-1/2 miles east of Cascade Mountain summit, northwest Kittitas County. The Indian name was *Wee-Ly-Let-Sars*, and the first name used by white miners was *Guetes Lake*. The present name was chosen because the lake, although large for a mountain lake, is difficult to locate.

Lost Lake *(S.1;T.28N;R.7E)*

A 17.8-acre lake, maximum depth 25 ft., 6 miles north of Sultan, southwest Snohomish County. This is a common name local residents seem to use for any lake which is at all difficult to locate. The lake should not be confused with Lost Lake in Monte Cristo area.

Lost Lake *(Ss.29,32;T.30N;R.11E)*

Lake southeast of Monte Cristo Lake, near South Fork, Sauk River, east central Snohomish County. It was named by early travelers on Sauk-Monte Cristo Road, because no trail existed to this difficult-to-locate lake.

Lost Lake *(S.31;T.40N;R.5E)*

A 4.4-acre lake, elevation 2,850 ft., on Sumas Mountain, 3 miles west of Kendall, northwest Whatcom County. Washington state has at least 30 Lost Lakes; this is one of 5 in Whatcom County, in addition to several Hidden Lakes. Incidentally, this lake's alternate name is *Hidden Lake*.

Lost Lake (Lewis County) *see* Buesch Lake

Lost Meadows *(Ss.9,16;T.18N;R.13E)*

Mountain meadow on Naches River, 9 miles east of Cascade Mountain summit, extreme northwest Yakima County. It was named by pioneer settler C. M. Longmire, because it was very difficult to locate.

Lost Point Ridge *(S.26;T.9N;R.42E)*

Blue Mountains ridge 2 miles south of Horseshoe Springs, Umatilla National Forest, south central Garfield County. The name is reported to have been given by Forest Service personnel, for a peak in the ridge called Lost Point. (USBGN)

Lost River *(S.3;T.27N;R.6W)*

The stream of the river rises at Lost Peak, north central Jefferson County; flows 9 miles northwest to Elwha River, near Clallam County boundary. There are 3 "lost" features in Jefferson County, and dozens in the state.

Lott *(T.28N;R.36E)*

Long-abandoned settlement on Spokane River, near the old DeTillion Bridge, north central Lincoln County. It consisted primarily of a stage station and roadhouse on the route between Davenport and Hunters. The name is for a well-known, local Indian resident.

Louis Creek *(T.30N;R.15E)*

The stream of the creek heads west of Buck Mountain, 1-1/2 miles from Cascade Mountain summit, Wenatchee National Forest, northwest Chelan County; flows 2-1/2 miles south to Napeequa River. It is glacier-fed, with many waterfalls. On July 24, 1924, Forest Supervisor A. H. Sylvester applied the name, for Louis Lauzier, a sheepman who had a grazing allotment on the creek.

Louise Lake *(S.4;T.19N;R.2E)*

A small, 39.1-acre lake 2 miles southeast of Steilacoom, 1-1/2 miles north of American Lake, northwest Pierce County. It was originally named for Capt. Lafayette Balch, a famous pioneer who founded Steilacoom. The substitution of an obscure person's name is unfortunate, but typical of similar changes made for other features.

Loup Loup Creek *(Ts.32,33N;Rs.24,25E)*

The stream of this twice-named creek rises in high country 10 miles west of Okanogan, central Okanogan County; flows 11 miles southeast to Okanogan River at Malott. (*see* Loop Loop)

Louse Rocks *(T.11N;R.10W)*

Two rocks in Willapa Bay, near the south end of Long Island, southwest Pacific County. The name comes from an Indian legend regarding these rocks, which tells of an Indian chief and his wife who were turned to stone by a magician after they had introduced lice among members of the local tribe; these rocks are the result.

Love Creek *(Ts.1,2N;R.2E)*

The stream of the creek rises in Biddle Lake, south central Clark County; flows south to Columbia River, between

Vancouver and Camas. In 1827, the first sawmill in the state was built at the mouth of the creek on Columbia River, and operated by Hudson's Bay Company. In 1862, Capt. Lewis Love purchased the site, and founded a flouring mill on Love's Pond, in the course of the creek. The creek was named for him.

Lovegren *(S.22;T.24N;R.7E)*

Former Northern Pacific Railway station 9 miles east of Issaquah, central King County. Railway officials named it for John Lovegren, who came to this area from Sweden in 1889, and operated sawmills in Preston and other nearby points for many years.

Lovejoy *(S.34;T.32N;R.1E)*

East shore point of Whidbey Island, near Penn Cove south entrance, west Island County. The name is for a seafaring captain, who settled here in early years. The Indian name was *Duck-a-sats.* A local name is *Lovejoy's Point.*

Lovejoy's Point (Island County) *see* Lovejoy

Low Island *(S.11;T.35N;R.4W)*

Small rock in Andrews Bay, Haro Strait, off the west coast of San Juan Island, San Juan County. Local settlers applied the descriptive name to this island that rises only about 5 ft. above high tides. It should not be confused with Low Island in San Juan Channel.

Low Island *(T.36N;R.3W)*

Very small, flat, rocky island, emerging only a few feet above high tide levels, in San Juan Channel, northwest of Shaw Island's west point, San Juan County. It is the most southerly of the Wasp Island group. In 1858, the descriptive name was placed on British Admiralty charts by Capt. Henry Richards, R.N. It should not be confused with Low Island in Haro Strait, west of San Juan Island.

Low Lake (Thurston County) *see* Hewitts Lake

Low Mountain *(S.36;T.23N;R.10E)*

Snoqualmie National Forest peak, elevation 5,357-ft., south of Hemlock Pass, between Denny and Granite mountains, 3 miles west of Cascade Mountain summit, extreme east central King County. It was named by The Mountaineers, not for its lack of height, but for John and Alonzo Low, original Seattle settlers who prospected the area

with the Dennys. (USBGN)

Low Point *(S.22;T.31N;R.9W)*

Point on Strait of Juan de Fuca, 4-1/2 miles west of Crescent Bay, north central Clallam County. In 1846, the descriptive name was placed on British Admiralty charts by Capt. Henry Kellett.

Low Point (Pacific County) *see* Leadbetter Point

Lowe Lake (Thurston County) *see* Hewitts Lake

Lowell *(S.5;T.28N;R.5E)*

South suburb of Everett on Snohomish River, west central Snohomish County. This industrial town is based on a large pulp and paper plant. When a post office was established in 1871, Reuben Lowe suggested the name of his home town, Lowell, Massachusetts. At that time, the place consisted of a store and logging camp.

Lower Baker Reservoir (Skagit County) *see* Lake Shannon

Lower Burnt Boot Lake (King County) *see* Avalanche Lake

Lower Curtis Glacier *(s.34;T.39N;R.9E.uns)*

West slope glacier of Mt. Shuksan, directly west of the summit, central Whatcom County. It was named by The Mountaineers, for Asahel Curtis, famous photographer and mountaineer.

Lower Elwha Indian Reservation *(T.30N;R.5W)*

A 372-acre reservation at Elwha River mouth, on Strait of Juan de Fuca, directly west of Port Angeles, Clallam County. Under the Indian Reorganization Act of 1934, it was purchased by the federal government for several Indian bands. There is no tribal organization. (*see* Elwha River)

Lower Elwha Reservoir (Clallam County) *see* Lake Aldwell

Lower Granite Dam *(T.13N;R.43E)*

Hydroelectric dam in Snake River, 107-1/2 river miles from the river's mouth, Lower Granite Canyon, 12 miles southwest of Pullman, between north Garfield and south Whitman counties. It was named by U.S. Army Engineers for Lower Granite Canyon, which is 2,000 ft. deep in some places. In 1949, a bill was introduced in Congress proposing the name *Spalding Lock & Dam,* for the

early missionary Henry H. Spalding; it died in committee.

Lower Granite Lake (Skagit County) *see* Granite Lake .3

Lower Monumental Lock & Dam *(S.35;T.13N;R.35E)*

Multi-purpose dam, 41.6 river miles above Snake River mouth, 32 river miles above Ice Harbor Dam, between Franklin and Walla Walla counties. A February 11, 1949, Senate memorial suggested the name *Lewis Lock & Dam,* in honor of Capt. Meriwether Lewis. The present name derives from nearby Monumental Rapids in Snake River.

Lower Scenic Lake *(S.16;T.25N;R.13E)*

Lake 2 miles west of Cascade Mountain summit, 3 miles south of Scenic, northeast King County. It was named for the nearby town, which is an entry point into this mountain area. (USBGN)

Lower Scenic Lake (King County) *see* Surprise Lake

Lowgap *(S.10;T.17N;R.24E)*

Area on north slope of Frenchman Hills, 16 miles south of Quincy, southwest Grant County. In 1905, it was named by George Grant for a gap in the nearby hills.

Lucas *(S.11;T.6N;R.14E)*

Once a town in Cedar Valley, Yakima Indian Reservation, 17 miles northwest of Goldendale, extreme north central Klickitat County. In the early 1880s, it was established by settlers from Missouri, and was once the trade center for heavily-populated Cedar Valley. Destructive frosts, and defoliating butterflies which killed the pine timber, ruined the valley commercially. The now-vanished town was named for Samuel Lucas, first postmaster.

Lucas Creek *(Ts.13,14N;Rs.1E,1W)*

The stream of the creek rises 4 miles northwest of Alpha, central Lewis County; flows west to North Fork, Newaukum River, 6 miles below Chehalis water system intake. It was named for Henry Lucas, an 1861 pioneer.

Lucerne *(T.31N;R.18E.uns)*

Boat landing on the west shore of Lake Chelan, at the mouth of Railroad Creek north central Chelan County. It was named in 1903 for Lake Lucerne in Switzerland by a Mrs. Shear from that country.

Ludlow Head (Jefferson County) *see* Point Tala

Ludlow Lake *(S.14;T.28N;R.1W)*
A 15.6-acre lake 4-1/2 miles west of Port Ludlow, east central Jefferson County. (*see* Port Ludlow)

Ludvich Lake (Kitsap County) *see* Ludvick Lake

Ludvick Lake *(S.31;T.24N;R.2W)*
A 2-acre lake 2 miles south of Holly, 2 miles southeast of Port Orchard, south central Kitsap County. It was locally named for an early settler. Alternate, unofficial names include *Ludvich Lake*, *Lizard Lake*, and *Lizzard Lake*. (USBGN)

Lummi *(S.7;T.38N;R.2E)*
Indian village on Lummi Indian Reservation, 4 miles northwest of Bellingham, between the mouths of Lummi and Nooksack rivers, southwest Whatcom County. It was named for the Lummi Indian tribe. An older name, in Lummi dialect, was *N'wh-ah-tk-hm*, which was also the Lummi name for Whatcom Falls.

Lummi Bay *(T.38N;R.1E)*
Shallow bay on Georgia Strait, at the mouth of Lummi River, southwest Whatcom County. Until diverted by high waters over a century ago, the Nooksack River emptied into this bay. It was named for the Lummi Indian tribe. Spanish explorers named the bay *Ensenada de Loera* or *Ensenada de Locra*. Spanish charts of Galliano and Valdes, dated 1792, use the latter name. (USBGN)

Lummi Indian Reservation *(T.38N;Rs.1,2E)*
An 8,338-acre Indian reservation, mostly on the peninsula between Lummi and Bellingham bays, Whatcom County. It was established by the Point Elliott Treaty of 1855, and enlarged by an Executive Order dated November 22, 1873. Originally assigned to Lummi, Nooksack, Samish and Semiamhoo Indians, all except Lummis were relocated because of incompatibility. It was named for the Lummi tribe.

Lummi Island *(Ts.37,38N;Rs.1,2E)*
A 9-mile-long island, average width 1 to 1-1/2 miles, between Hale Passage and Rosario Strait, west entrance to Bellingham Bay, southwest Whatcom County. The original, heavy stand of timber has been destroyed by "cut-out-and-get-out" logging. In 1791, Juan Francisco de Eliza named it *Isla de Pacheco*, for the Viceroy of Mexico. Charts of 1792 by Valdes and Galliano used the same name. In 1841, Cmdr. Charles Wilkes called it *McLaughlan's Island*, to honor Dr. John *McLoughlin*, chief factor of Hudson's Bay Company on Columbia River. In 1853, it was named by U.S. Coast Survey, for the Lummi Indian tribe, which once controlled the island, as well as Lopez, Shaw and Orcas islands in San Juan County. Indian names for the island, in 2 dialects, were *Skall-a-ham* and *Smemma-uk*.

Lummi Peak *(S.26;T.37N;R.1E)*
A 1,740-ft. peak near the south end of Lummi Island, southwest Whatcom County. It is the high point of a 3-mile ridge through the center of the island. It was named for the Lummi Indian tribe.

Lummi River *(Ts.38,39N;R.1E)*
The stream of the river heads in a branch outlet of Nooksack River, Lummi Indian Reservation, northwest of Bellingham Bay, west central Whatcom County; flows 5 miles into Georgia Strait. It is in the original channel of Nooksack River, before that river was diverted into Bellingham Bay by high waters, over a century ago. It was named for the Lummi Indian tribe.

Lummi Rocks *(S.27;T.37N;R.1E)*
Group of offshore rocks, 2 of which are quite large, in Rosario Strait, directly west of Lummi Island's west central shore, southwest Whatcom County. In 1854, the rocks were named by U.S. Coast Survey, for the Lummi Indian tribe. An alternate name, used by early navigators, was *Race Rocks*.

Luna Lake (San Juan County) *see* Horseshoe Lake

Lunch Creek *(T.23N;R.11W)*
The stream of the creek rises 6 miles west of Quinault Lake, Quinault Indian Reservation; flows west by south to Raft River, northwest Grays Harbor County. When the mail was carried by horseback from Quinault to Queets, the carrier planned to arrive at this creek at a proper time for lunch; the name has persisted since that time.

Lundin Peak *(S.22;T.23N;R.11E)*

Snoqualmie National Forest peak 1 mile west of Cascade Mountain summit, 2-1/2 miles northeast of Snoqualmie Pass, extreme west central King County. It was named by The Mountaineers, for John Lundin, a district ranger on Snoqualmie National Forest. A previous name was *Snoqualmie Little Sister*. (USBGN)

Lunker Lake *(S.29;T.24N;R.11E)*
A 3-1/2-acre lake, one of 5 Nordrum Basin Lakes, 7-1/2 miles north of Snoqualmie Pass, Snoqualmie National Forest, northeast King County. It is reputed to yield large rainbow trout, which fishermen often call "lunkers."

Luzon (Benton County) *see* Whitcomb

Lyle *(S.3;T.2N;R.12E)*
Town on Columbia River's north bank, near Klickitat River mouth, southwest Klickitat County. The original name was *Klickitat Landing*. In 1880, it was changed to the present name when James O. Lyle purchased the claim of J. M. Williamson, and platted a townsite.

Lyman *(S.17;T.35N;R.6E)*
Small town on north bank of Skagit River, 5 miles east of Sedro Woolley, northwest Skagit County. At one time, it had a large sawmilling operation. In 1880, it was locally named for B. L. Lyman, first postmaster. In the period of Skagit River steamboating, it was called *Williamson's Landing*, for A. R. Williamson, a local settler.

Lyman Glacier *(T.31N;R.16E.uns)*
Glacier near Cascade Mountain summit, at the head of Railroad Creek, northwest Chelan County. In 1909, it was named by The Mountaineers, for Prof. William Denison Lyman of Whitman College. It should not be confused with Lyman Glacier, Yakima County.

Lyman Glacier *(Ts.8,9N;R.11E.uns)*
Live glacier, on the northeast slope of Mt. Adams, one of 8 on the mountain, southwest Yakima County. In August 1901, it was named by C. E. Rusk and Prof. Harry Fielding Reid of Johns Hopkins University, for Prof. William Denison Lyman of Whitman College.

Lyman Lake *(T.31N;R.16E.uns)*
Lake at the foot of Lyman Glacier, elevation 5,525 ft., at the head of Railroad Creek, northwest Chelan County. (*see* Lyman Glacier, Chelan County)

Lynch Cove *(Ts.22,23N;Rs.1,2W)*

An eastern extremity cove of Hood Canal, northeast Mason County. In 1841, it was named by Cmdr. Charles Wilkes, for Lieut. William Francis Lynch, U.S. Navy, who explored Jordan and the Dead Sea.

Lynden *(S.20;T.40N;R.3E)*

Town on Nooksack River, 12 miles north of Bellingham, northwest Whatcom County. It was a lively pioneer town in the days when river boats traveled the Nooksack River. When a post office was established in 1874, the name was chosen from a poem, which Eason Ebey read to Mr. and Mrs. H. A. Judson. Mrs. Judson was impressed by the passage, ''On *Linden* when the sun was low.'' She changed the ''i'' to ''y'' because she thought it more poetic, and the name was adopted. The Indian name was *Squ-o-hal-itch*.

Lynnwood *(T.27N;R.4E)*

Residential city 3 miles east of Edmonds, southwest Snohomish County. Part of the community developed on land purchased by I.M. O'Biern. He honored his wife, Lynn, in naming the townsite.

Lyre River *(Ts.30,31N;R.9W)*

The stream of the river rises on the north slope of Pyramid Peak, north central Clallam County; flows 5-1/2 miles north to Strait of Juan de Fuca, near Low Point. In 1790, it was named *Rio de Cuesta* by Lopez de Haro; in 1791, Juan Francisco de Eliza applied the same name. In 1847, Capt. Henry Kellett charted the river as *River Lyre*. The present, reversed form of that name is generally accepted.

M

M.J.B. Creek *(T.38N;R.36E)*

The name of both a spring and a very short creek which rises on Colville National Forest, 9 miles northwest of Boyds, northeast Ferry County; the creek then flows 2 miles to Boulder Creek. The creek and spring were named for a brand of coffee by Mike Moran, a Forest Service trail construction foreman. A vast amount of coffee was used in Moran's camp at this spring.

Mabana *(S.10;T.30N;R.3E)*

Small settlement on the southwest shore of Camano island, on Saratoga Passage, 4 miles north of Langley, southeast Island County. On May 15, 1912, the place was named by J. A. Woodard for Nils Anderson's daughter, Mabel. He combined the first syllables of her first and last names, and added an *a* for euphony.

Mabton *(S.1;T.8N;R.22E)*

Town on east boundary of Yakima Indian Reservation, 33 miles southeast of Yakima, southeast Yakima County. In 1885, the town was named by Northern Pacific Railway officials when a station was established here. The word is a combination which uses the first half of the given name of Mabel Baker Anderson of Walla Walla, daughter of Dr. Dorsey S. Baker, who built the famous "rawhide railroad" between Walla Walla and Wallula.

Mac Creek *(T.24N;R.16E)*

The stream of the creek rises on Wenatchee National Forest, central Chelan County; flows from the southwest slope of Icicle Ridge, 1-1/2 miles southwest to Icicle Creek, 2 miles west of Icicle Lookout. It was named by Forest Ranger John S. Brender for the first name of an early employee on Okanogan National Forest.

Macall *(S.10;T.18N;R.38E)*

Railroad station 18 miles east of Ritzville, east central Adams County. *Waukee* was the original name of the railroad station at this place, being the last two syllables of *Milwaukee* (C.M.&St.P. Railway). In 1916, it was changed to Macall to conform to the post office name. The town is shown on some maps as *McCall*.

Macedonian Crescent (San Juan County) *see* Lopez Sound

Machias *(S.21;T.29N;R.6E)*

Settlement 5 miles north of Snohomish, west central Snohomish County. In 1877, it was started under the name of *Rudd*. In 1890, the townsite was purchased by M. L. Getschell, who renamed it for his home town in Maine. The same man purchased the townsite of Getchell, which carried his name, but with the elimination of one letter. The alteration in spelling is presumed to have been made by postal authorities at the time a post office was established.

Mack Mountain *(S.27;T.37N;R.35E)*

A 6,278-ft. Colville National Forest mountain, 17 miles east of Republic, central Ferry County. It was named for Hugh McIntosh, using his common nickname. "Mack" was a Forest Service ranger on the Orient District.

Mackaye Harbor *(T.34N;Rs.1,2W)*

Area directly east of Richardson on the Strait of Juan de Fuca, south central Lopez Island, southeast San Juan County. In 1859, the name was placed on British admiralty charts by Capt. Henry Richards, RN. The name evidently was that of a local factor of Hudson's Bay Company.

Mac's Cove *(S.26;T.34N;R.1E)*

A very small cove (not shown on most maps) on the northwest tip of Whidbey Island, on Deception Pass, directly west of Deception Pass bridge, north Island County. It was named for A. O. McCormick of Seattle, who used this for a point of departure on over 45 annual trips by rowboat through the San Juan Islands.

Mad Lake *(T.28N;R.17E)*

Small mountain lake, Wenatchee National Forest, at the head of Mad River between Entiat and Chiwawa rivers, central Chelan County. It was named for Mad River by Forest Service personnel. (*see* Mad River)

Mad River *(Ts.26-28N;Rs.17-20E)*

The stream of this largest tributary of Entiat River, rises on Wenatchee National Forest, central Chelan County; flows 23 miles from Mad Lake to Entiat River near Ardenvoir, with many tributaries. This is an old name used by early settlers. The river hardly seems to deserve such a designation.

Maddocksville *(S.23;T.22N;R.4E)*

A vanished settlement on the bank of White River, 17 miles south of Seattle, King County. Once the place boasted 2 churches, a school, a general store, and "almost daily" steamboat service from Seattle. It was named for M. B. Maddocks, who acquired land here in 1878 and sold a number of town lots.

Madison Park *(S.22;T.25N;R.4E)*

A city park, with a beach, dock, and other facilities in Seattle, west shore of Lake Washington, at the foot of Madison St., directly south of Union Bay, King County. It was named for Madison Ave., which was named for James Madison, fourth president of the U.S. The Indian name was Xe-xt-l, meaning "Where one chops." Cedar dugout canoes were made here by local Indians.

Madrona Point
(Ss.13,14;T.37N;R.2W)

An extreme north end point of East Sound on Orcas Island, between Ship Bay and Fishing Bay, northeast San Juan County. The name was applied by local residents because of abundant native madrona trees (*Arbutus menziesii*) on the point. There also are 24 other species of trees and shrubs, including some which were imported from England.

Madrone (Kitsap County) *see* Winslow

Mae *(S.23;T.19N;R.27E)*

Community 4 miles west of Moses Lake (town), directly north of Potholes Reservoir, central Grant County. On February 1, 1907, it was named for the first postmistress, Mrs. Mae Shoemaker, by J. B. Lee when the post office was established.

Magee Creek *(T.33N;R.37E)*

This intermittent stream heads in southwest Stevens County; flows west 4 miles to the Columbia River at Daisy. Formerly it was known as *Gods Creek*. It was named for Samuel L. and John H. Magee, who homesteaded at the mouth of the creek in 1902.

Maggie Creek *(Ss.2-5;T.18BN;R.11E)*

The stream of the creek rises on the west side of Cascade Mountain summit south of Naches Pass, Pierce County; flows 3 miles west to Greenwater River. It was named by Charlie Jackson, an early Forest Service patrolman stationed at Last Crossing, for his girl-friend.

Magic City, The (Skagit County) *see* Anacortes

Magnolia Beach *(S.24;T.22N;R.2E)*

A west shore beach of Quartermaster Harbor, Vashon Island, southwest King County. It was named by Silas Cook, who homesteaded here in 1878, for his home town, Magnolia, Iowa.

Magnolia Bluff *(T.25N;R.3E)*

A steep bluff on the north shore of Elliott Bay, northwest area of Seattle. The name has also been applied to a residential district which extends northward from the bluff. Also it is often used, in error, as the name of the entire Lawton Peninsula which includes 9 named communities in addition to Fort Lawton and the Salmon Bay industrial area. The bluff, with an elevation of about 200 ft., is one of Seattles 12 "official" hills. In 1856, it waas named by Capt. George Davidson of U. S. Coast Survey, who confused the many native madrona trees (*Arbutus Menziesii*) with magnolias.

Mahar Creek *(T.27N;R.16E)*

The stream of the creek heads in Merritt Lake on Nason Ridge, Wenatchee National Forest, southwest Chelan County; flows 3 miles southeast to Nason Creek. It was named by Forest Supervisor A. H. Sylvester for G. D. Mahar who homesteaded near the creek's mouth.

Mahler State Park *(T.20N;R.6E)*

A park 1 mile northwest of Enumclaw, directly north of the National Park Highway, south central King County. It was named by the State Parks & Recreation Commission for the donor, J. H. Mahler. Since acquiring the 31-acre site in 1923, little development work has been accomplished by the state.

Maiden Peak *(T.28N;R.5W;uns)*

A 6,434-ft. Olympic National Park peak, 1/2 mile south-southwest of Maiden Lake, 1-1/2 miles west of Green Mountain, east central Clallam County. This glamorous name is reported to have been chosen by an early party of hikers who came through this area from Lake Cushman.

Makah Indian Reservation *(Ts.32,33N;Rs.15,16W)*

A 27,979-acre Indian reservation, including Cape Flattery and Neah Bay, extreme northwest corner of Clallam County. It is bounded on the west by Pacific Ocean and on the north by Strait of Juan de Fuca. On January 31, 1855, the reservation was created by the Neah Bay Treaty and was enlarged in 1872 and 1873. The Indian name has the meaning of "People who live on point projecting into the sea." The Makahs have common blood ties with the Nootkas on Vancouver Island.

Mal Abrigo (San Juan County) *see* Matia Island

Malachite Falls *(S.34;T.24-1/2N;R.12E)*

A north end falls of Copper Lake, 8 miles south of Skykomish, in a tributary of West Fork, Foss River, northeast King County. It was locally named for the presence of malachite ore, a carbonate of copper.

Malden *(S.14;T.20N;R.42E)*

Town 25 miles north of Colfax, north central Whitman County. It was named by H. R. Williams, vice-president of C.M.&St.P. Railway, for Malden, Massachusetts.

Mallardy Creek *(T.30N;R.9E)*

The stream of this short creek rises 1-1/2 miles north of Bald Mountain, Mt. Baker National Forest, central Snohomish County; flows 4 miles north and west to South Fork, Stillaguamish River. It was named for a miner who worked a claim at the creek's mouth on which he never filed.

Malo *(S.2;T.38N;R.33E)*

Small settlement on the Colville National Forest, on Curlew Creek, 13 miles north by east of Republic, north central Ferry County. The name, evidently bestowed by a discontented early-day prospector, is a Spanish word meaning "bad, evil, unhealthy." The name of the donor is not of record.

Malone *(S.17;T.17N;R.5W)*

Community on Moxie Creek, 15 miles east of Montesano, southeast Grays Harbor County. Once it was a busy sawmill and shingle mill town, but now it has no important industry. The name is for Hector J. Malone, who established the first shingle mill here in 1897. For many years, Malone was a company town, owned by one forest products industrialist.

Maloney Lakes *(Ss.12,13;T.25N;R.11E)*

A group of 3, joined lakes on Snoqualmie National Forest, 3 miles south of Skykomish, near the head of Maloney Creek, northeast King County. One lake covers 1 acre, the second 1.5 acres, and the third has an expanse of 3 acres. The lake system was named for nearby Maloney Mountain. (*see* Maloney Mountain)

Maloney Meadow Lake *(S.13;T.25N;R.11E)*

A 5.5-acre lake at the head of Maloney Creek, 3-1/4 miles south of Skykomish, Snoqualmie National Forest, King County. It is in a meadow on Maloney Mountain, for which it is named. (*see* Maloney Mountain)

Maloney Mountain *(T.25N;R.11E)*

A peak in the Skykomish Valley, 2 miles south of Skykomish, northeast King County. It is the site of a large limestone quarry, which formerly sent its product by cable tramway to a cement plant at Grotto. It was named for John Maloney of Skykomish, who discovered limestone deposits near the peak's summit many years ago.

Malott *(S.9;T.32N;R.25E)*

Small town at the confluence of Loup Loup Creek and the Okanogan River, 9 miles southwest of Okanogan, 18 miles north of Brewster, south central Okanogan County. In 1890, it was granted a post office and platted as a townsite in 1909. On April 19, 1938, it was practically destroyed by a severe flood, caused by a broken dam on Loup Loup Creek. It was named for a pioneer settler, L. C. Malott, who settled here in August, 1886, and who was postmaster for 20 years.

Maltby *(S.24;T.27N;R.5E)*

Small settlement 8 miles south of Snohomish, southwest Snohomish County. Once it was an important lumber and shingle center. In 1888, a post office was established as *Yew*. It later was changed to the present name by railroad influence, for Robert Maltby, a landowner and real estate operator.

Manashtash Creek
(Ts.17,18N;Rs.15-18E)

The stream of the creek heads near Frost Mountain, south central Kittitas County; flows 25 miles east to Yakima River west of Ellensburg. The present name is a corruption of "Mnas-A-Tas," under which title the creek was mapped by A. W. Tinkham in 1854. Early railroad surveyors mapped it as *Ptehnum River*. This is an example of the divergent naming of various portions of rivers and creeks by Indians, and the consequent difficulty encountered in placing a single name on streams by early surveyors and mappers.

Mandon Creek (Clallam County) *see* Blackwood Creek

Manette (Kitsap County) *see* East Bremerton

Manette Peninsula
(Ts.25-28N;Rs.1,2;1.W)

The northern portion of Kitsap County mainland, north from Bremerton to Foulweather Bluff. It was locally named for the first steamer which used a new wharf at Manette, now East Bremerton.

Manitou Park *(S.13;T.25N;R.2E)*

A Bainbridge Island park on Skiff Point, between Rolling Bay and Ferncliff, on the east central shore of the island, Kitsap County. In 1907, it was named by W. E. Parker when he platted the town. The Indian name refers to The Great Spirit.

Mann Butte *(Ss.2,11;T.5N;R.9E)*

A Gifford Pinchot National Forest butte, 17 miles north of Columbia River, 2 miles west of Klickitat County boundary, southeast Skamania County. The naming of this feature was for Jesse M. Mann, a former officer on Gifford Pinchot National Forest. A previous name was *Cave Creek Butte*.

Mann's Landing (Skagit County) *see* Fir

Man of War Harbor (San Juan County) *see* Griffin Bay

Manor *(Ss.7,8;T.3N;R.2E)*

Community 8 miles north of Vancouver, between Mill and Salmon creeks, west central Clark County. Between 1861 and 1863, the name of this place was *Flatwoods* for the flat lands covered by native tree species. In 1863, Capt. Ira Patterson prevailed upon the county commissioners to change the name to that of a ship which he had commanded, *Manor*.

Manor Lake (Snohomish County) *see* Martha Lake

Mansfield *(S.25;T.27N;R.25E)*

Town 13 miles south of Bridgeport, north central Douglas County. In 1905, it was named by R. E. Darling, when a post office was established for his home town in Ohio. That town, in turn was named for Col. Jared Mansfield, once surveyor-general of the United States. Great Northern Railway Company officials state that the station here was originally called *Appledale*, but that this name was shifted to a town in lower Moses Coulee.

Mansford *(s.33;T.33N;R.10E)*

Village on Sauk Prairie, 6 miles northeast of Darrington, Mt. Baker National Forest, southeast Skagit County. The name was taken from Mansford Grange, a post office established a short distance to the northwest in 1890.

Manson *(S.35;T.28N;R.21E)*

Small town on the east shore of Lake Chelan, 8 miles northwest of Chelan, east central Chelan County. In 1912, it was named by Lake Chelan Land Company for Manson F. Backus, president of the company.

Manzanita *(S.8;T.25N;R.2E)*

Community on the northwest side of Bainbridge Island, 4 miles southeast of Keyport, east Kitsap County. Records show that the place was named by Margaret A. Wheeler, postmistress, who believed that madrona trees in this area were manzanitas. There might well have been manzanitas here, however, as it is abundant in the vicinity of Chico, 8 miles to the southwest.

Maple Cove *(S.1;T.29N;R.3E)*

An east shore cove of Whidbey Island at the east extremity of Saratoga Passage, directly southeast of Langley, south island County. The local name is for many large maples along the shore, although the cove is very indistinct, almost imaginary.

Maple Creek *(T.29N;R.16E)*

The stream of the creek rises on Wenatchee National Forest, northwest Chelan County; flows 2-1/2 miles east to Chiwawa River from the east slope of Chiwawa Ridge. It was named by Forest Ranger Delmer S. Rice for a fine grove of maples at its mouth.

Maple Falls *(S.30;T.40N;R.6E)*

Settlement on Maple Creek, near North Fork, Nooksack River, 5-1/2 miles south of Canadian boundary, north central Whatcom County. The first post office name of this rough sawmilling and mining town was *Hardan*. In 1901, the post office was moved and the name changed to Maple Falls. The name was devised by G. A. King, who combined the nearby 35-ft. falls in Maple Creek with the abundance of native maples along the creek.

Maple Valley *(S.10;T.22N;R.6E)*

Small town 10 miles south of Renton, near Cedar River, central King County. In 1879, the town was founded by George W. Ames of Seattle, and was platted in 1890. In 1888, the name was chosen by George Ames, when a post office was established. It was not for the abundant native maple trees in the area, but for the Maple family (Jacob and Samuel), who settled on the Duwamish River before the Denny party arrived at Alki Point. (USBGN)

Maplecreek *(S.1;T.26N;R.21E)*

Settlement on the north bank of Columbia River, 8 miles southwest of Chelan at the mouth of Knapp Coulee, southeast Chelan County. The name is of local origin and has been used for many years.

Marble *(S.28;T.39N;R.39E)*

Settlement on the east bank of Franklin D. Roosevelt Lake, between Evans and Northport, northwest Stevens County. In 1898, it was started after the Spokane Falls & Northern Railway came through. At that time, it was believed that there was an unlimited amount of fine marble in the surrounding area. Investigation proved that the rock was dolomite, which has much less architectural value than true marble. In 1910, a Kansas City corporation reported to have been White & Company, made a boomtown of Marble, evidently with an idea of seed growing. A very large acreage was planted to orchard, which were interplanted with vegetables for seed production. About 2 million dollars is reported to have been spent for an irrigation system. Residences were built on 3 sides of an extensive central square, in which there was a schoolhouse, a post office, and what might be called a residence hotel for unmarried workers. In 1917, the project was evidently abandoned. There is evidence that failure was due to smelter fumes which had permeated the valley from Trail, British Columbia. The place was almost deserted, the orchards died, and the buildings were looted. At one time, Marble had a sawmill, a general store, a blacksmith shop, and a rowboat ferry across the river. It might be termed a ghost town today, although not entirely deserted. The post office was abandoned in 1945.

Marble Creek *(T.28N;R.17E)*

The stream of the creek heads near the summit of McDonald Ridge, Wenatchee National Forest, northwest Chelan County; flows southwest 5 miles to Chikamin Creek, near the confluence of that stream with Chiwawa River. It was named by Forest Supervisor A. H. Sylvester for a marble ledge, 100 ft. thick, which the creek crosses.

Marble Creek *(Ss.19,30;T.30N;R.10E)*

The stream of the creek rises at Marble Pass, 1 mile south of Silverton, Mt. Baker National forest, central Snohomish County; flows 1-1/2 miles northwest through a heavily mineralized area to South Fork, Stillaguamish River. The creek was named by prospectors for deposits of crystalline limestone along the creek.

Marble Peak *(S.30;T.30N;R.10E)*

A 5,156-ft. peak, 1-1/2 miles south of Silverton, Mt. Baker National Forest, east central Snohomish County. It is in a heavily mineralized area and the name was given by early prospectors for deposits of crystalline limestone on the peak.

Marblemount *(S.7;T.35N;R.11E)*

Community on north bank of Skagit River, 1/2 mile upstream from Cascade River's mouth, Mt. Baker National Forest, north central Skagit County. In the 1890s, over 1,500 miners and prospectors worked in this area, and river steamers came within 2 miles of the town. In 1890, the place was named by the first hotel-keeper, Mrs. Buller, for a mountain of marble across the river.

March Point *(S.28;T.35N;R.2E)*

A west entrance point to Padilla Bay, 2 miles east of Anacortes, west central Skagit County. In 1841, the Wilkes Expedition charted it as *Sachem Point*, with

no reference to its meaning. When the Skagit Delta was diked and cultivated, the name chosen locally for this feature was to honor Hiram H. March, who first started the intensive growing of vegetable seeds. It was called *Marches Point* until shortened by cartographers.

Marcellus *(S.15;T.20N;R.35E)*

Village 7 miles north of Ritzville, north central Adams County. The original name was *Griffith*, for an early settler. Officials of the Chicago, Milwaukee & St. Paul Railway Company changed the name to Marcellus when a rail station was established. H. R. Williams, the Milwaukee's vice-president at the time Marcellus was given its name, borrowed many of his titles from ancient and medieval history. This one is probably from Roman history, as Marcellus was the adopted son of Emperor Augustus, and a Roman favorite in the year 23 B.C.

Marches Point (Skagit County) *see* March Point

Marcus *(S.31;T.37N;R.37E)*

Town now located 3 miles north of Kettle Falls on the east bank of Franklin D. Roosevelt Lake, west central Stevens County. Formerly it was on Marcus Flat, 1-1/2 miles southwest of its present location. The town was moved when its original location was flooded by the lake created by Grand Coulee Dam, in 1939-40, to a depth of 50-60 ft. In 1860, the British Boundary Survey Commission built barracks here on Garrison Flat, which they occupied until 1862. Marcus Oppenheimer and W. V. Brown moved into these log structures in 1863, with a stock of trade merchandise, and remained until the buildings were removed in 1881. In 1890, a townsite was platted here by Oppenheimer, Brown, and Joseph Monaghan, using Oppenheimer's first name for the designation. In 1896, the place boomed into a lively town as a result of the opening of the north half of the Colville Indian Reservation to mineral entry by white miners. Marcus was the termination suggested for a cross-state wagon road which was considered by the Washington State Legislature in the 1890s. When the Columbia River was an important arterial, Marcus was the southern terminus for river steamboats which navigated for some distance into British Columbia. Several stern-wheelers were built here.

Marcus Peak *(Mt. Rainier National Park)*

A 6,968-ft. peak near the north end of Sourdough Mountain, between the headwaters of Huckleberry and Sunrise Creeks, northeast area of the park. It was named for Marcus Whitman, an early missionary in the Walla Walla Valley. (USBGN)

Marengo (Adams County) *see* Marengo Junction

Marengo *(S.13;T.11N;R.40E)*

Community on Tucannon River, 14 miles northeast of Dayton, northeast Columbia County. In 1853, the settlement was started by Louis Raboin, a French-Canadian who married a Flathead Indian woman. Because he was small and lively, local Indians nicknamed him ''Maringouin,'' a French slang term for mosquito. White men twisted the name to marengo and applied it to the settlement. On May 29, 1876, the townsite was platted by John Silcott, but was not recorded until February 23, 1878. For a period this place was served by Burksville post office, 1/2 mile to the southwest, which carried the name of Marshall B. Burk. The place should not be confused with Marengo Junction in Adams County, which often is referred to as Marengo.

Marengo Junction
(S.29;T.18N;R.37E)

A railroad point, 13 miles southeast of Ritzville, east central Adams County. It is reported to have been named by H. R. Williams, vice president of Chicago, Milwaukee & St. Paul Railway, to commemorate the famous battle of Marengo which took place in Italy on June 14, 1800. An earlier name for the place was *Gillespie*. It should not be confused with Marengo in Columbia County.

Margaret Falls *(Mt. Rainier National park)*

Waterfall on the southeast slope of Mt. Rainier, in a short, unnamed tributary of Muddy Fork, Cowlitz River, between Cowlitz Park and Cowlitz Glacier. The falls were named for Margaret Hall, daughter of E. S. Hall, former park superintendent. (USBGN)

Marhoo River (Pacific County) *see* Newmah River

Marie Falls (Mt. Rainier National Park) *see* Nahunta Falls

Marietta *(S.17;T.38N;R.2E)*

Village at the mouth of Nooksack River, north shore of Bellingham Bay, southwest Whatcom County. Formerly it was a town of considerable importance when river boats ran the river to Ferndale and Lynden. Until 1892, the name of this riverside town was *Lummi.* In that year the post office name was changed to Marietta. It was for a deceased daughter of homesteaders Solomon and Mary Allen, whose name was Mary Etta.

Marjorie Lake *(Mt. Rainier National Park)*

A triangular lake, close to Oliver Lake, east of the south end of Independence Ridge, between Chenius Creek and West Fork, White River. This feature was named by Oliver Taylor, one of a survey party that worked here in 1911. He used the name of his sweetheart, Marjorie McDougal and linked his name with hers by naming nearby Oliver Lake for himself. (USBGN)

Marjorie Lakes (Mt. Rainier National Park) *see* Marjorie Lake, Oliver Lake

Markham *(S.2;T.16N;R.11W)*

Community on the south shore of Grays Harbor at mouth of Johnson River, southwest Grays Harbor County. The name is for Simon S. Markham, a pioneer dairyman and cattle breeder who settled here in 1870.

Marlin */(S.12;T.22N;R.30E)*

Community on Crab Creek, 69 miles southwest of Davenport, on the east central boundary of Grant County. In 1871, this wheat town was settled by John Marlin, who is reputed to have been the first permanent white resident of the Big Bend country. In 1909 and 1914, the town was burned and rebuilt. It was named *Krupp* by Great Northern Railway officials to please a very influential farmer called Eckhart, whom they presumed to be German. He turned out to be a Scot named Urquhart. When the U.S. became involved in the WWI, the place was renamed Marlin, for the first settler.

Marmot Creek *(Mt. Rainier National Park)*

The stream of the creek rises on the northwest slope of Mt. Rainier at the foot of Russell Glacier; flows north to Cataract Creek, at the southeast slope of Mother Mountain, a distance of about 2 miles. This creek, as well as many other features in such rocky terrain at high altitude, was named for the many whistling marmots which are native to this area. (USBGN)

Marmot Lake *(S.31;T.25N;R.13E)*

A 135-acre, glacier-fed lake, 6-3/4 miles south of Scenic, 2 miles northeast of Cascade Mountain summit, Snoqualmie National forest, extreme northeast King County. (*see* Marmot Creek)

Marmot Lakes
(S.20;T.25N;R.5W.uns)

Three small mountain lakes, at the head of Duckabush River, Olympic National Park, southeast Jefferson County. The largest lake covers 4 acres; the other two cover 1/2 acre each. In 1890, the lakes were named by Lieut. Joseph P. O'Neil's expedition. (*see* Marmot Creek)

Marmot Pass *(S.27;T.26N;R.7W)*

An Olympic National Park pass at the headwaters of Elwha River, 1-1/2 miles east of Mt. Seattle, central Jefferson County. This pass is on the divide between the Elwha and North Fork, Quinault River. (*see* Marmot Lakes)

Marmot Point *(Mt. Rainier National Park)*

An entrance point to Paradise Valley, 17 miles by highway from Nisqually Entrance and 2 miles beyond Narada Falls, south central zone of the park. (*see* Marmot Creek)

Marriage Peak *(Mt. Rainier National Park)*

A peak between Huckleberry and Sunrise creeks, Sourdough Range, northeast portion of the park. This name was applied to the peak by horse guides stationed at Sunrise Park (Yakima Park0, "Because it is smooth on one side and rough on the other."

Marrowstone Island
(Ts.29,30N;R.1E)

A 7-mile-long island, 1/2 mile average width, between Kilisut Harbor and Admiralty Inlet, directly east of Indian Island, northeast Jefferson County. Fort Flagler once occupied part of the north end, but has been abandoned. On May 8, 1792, Capt. George Vancouver named the north extremity *Marrowstone Point.* Eventually the name came into use for the entire island. The Wilkes Expedition named this island, together with nearby Indian Island, as *Craven's Peninsula,* for Lieut Thomas T. Craven of his expedition. His name never came into common use. (*see* Marrowstone Point)

Marrowstone Point *(T.30N;R.1E)*

A north end point of Marrowstone Island in Port Townsend bay, northeast Jefferson County. It was the former site of Fort Flagler. On May 8, 1792, it was named by Capt. George Vancouver, who charted the fact that the cliff appeared to be entirely of marrowstone. In 1841, Cmdr. Charles Wilkes named the same feature *Point Ringgold,* for Lieut Cadwalader Ringgold of his command. This name did not persist. (*see* Marrowstone Island)

Marsh Creek *(Ss.5,-8;T.30N;R.8E)*

This short, marshy stream rises 2 miles northeast of Robe, central Snohomish County; flows 1-1/2 miles southwest to South Fork, Stillaguamish River, Snohomish County. It was named by settlers because its course is mostly through a wild cranberry marsh.

Marshall *(S.21;T.24N;R.42E)*

Village 9 miles southwest of Spokane on Lake Creek, central Spokane County. In March, 1880, the town was named for William H. Marshall who filed a homestead here on January 9, 1880. He started a sawmill company, Marshall & Smith, which originally cut timbers and ties for the Northern Pacific Railway Company. The town grew around the sawmill. Earlier names for the place were Marshalltown and Marshall Junction.

Marshall Junction (Spokane County) *see* Marshall

Marshalltown (Spokane County) *see* Marshall

Marshfield (Thurston County) *see* Olympia

Marshville *(T.18N;R.2W)*

An old settlement on the west side of Budd Inlet, on the site of a portion of present-day Olympia, Thurston County. It was named for Edwin Marsh, on whose claim the settlement was established. (*see* Olympia)

Marten Lake *(Ss.2,3;T.24N;R.10E)*

A 40.4-acre lake, 14 miles northeast of North Bend, east central King County. Originally there were many native pine martens in this area. There are still a few, according to reports, but they are heavily trapped.

Marten Lake *(S.5;T.34N;R.11E)*

A 10-acre lake, 30 ft. average depth, altitude 4,650 ft., 5 miles south of Marblemount, east central Skagit County. It was named for Marten Creek which drains the lake.

Marten Lake *(S.23;T.38N;R.8E)*

A 5-acre, 3,650-ft. lake on the northeast side of Lava Divide, 16 miles north of Concrete, south central Whatcom County. It appears that this name was used by pioneer settlers for the many native pine martens which were here in early days.

Martha Falls *(Mt. Rainier National Park)*

A 3,110-ft. waterfall on the southeast slope of Mt. Rainier, north of Bench Lake, in Unicorn Creek, at the midway point of Stevens Canyon, south central zone of the park. The fall was named for the deceased wife of Elcaine Longmire, by Ben Longmire, Elcaine's son. (USBGN)

Martha Lake *(S.1;T.27N;R.4E)*

A small lake, 7 miles south of Everett, southwest corner of Snohomish County. In 1912 and 1913, extensive logging operations flourished around here. The lake's name was chosen by officials of Merril & Ring who logged the area. The same name applied to a station on the electric line between Seattle and Everett. It now also applies to a small community near the lake. It should not be confused with another lake which bears the same name and which is 12 miles northwest of Everett.

Martha Lake *(Ss.18,19;T.31N;R.4E)*

A banana-shaped body of water, 5 miles south of Stanwood, 12 miles northwest of Everett, northwest Snohomish County. The lake is 1 mile long, with a surface area of 58.4 acres, and 70 ft. deep. Older maps indicate that the name was originally *Marthen's Lake*, and named for an early settler; but the present name was applied to later maps and records. It should not be confused with a lake by the same name in southwest Snohomish County, 7 miles south of Everett. On some rather old maps, this lake is shown as *Warm Beach Lake*.

Marthen's Lake *(Snohomish County) see* Martha Lake

Martin *(S.36;T.21N;R.12E)*

Railway station on Yakima River, 4-1/2 miles west of south end Kachess Lake, near Stampede Tunnel, northwest Kittitas County. It was named by Judge Conkle for the abundant pine martens which he hunted here. Somewhere in railroad procedure, the name was twisted to *Martin.*

Martin Island *(S.3;T.5N;R.1W)*

An island in Columbia River, directly south of Martins Bluff, south central Cowlitz County. It was named for a pioneer who settled on the adjacent mainland in 1872. In 1841, the Wilkes Expedition charted this feature as *Smoke Island.* (*see* Martins Bluff)

Martin Lake *(Snohomish County) see* Martha Lake

Martindale *(S.20;T.9N;R.31E)*

Community on north bank of Snake River, 5 miles east of Pasco, south Franklin County. It was named by the S.P.&S. Railway Company for M. P. Martin, comptroller of that company and of Northern Pacific Railway Company.

Martins Bluff *(S.34;T.6N;R.1W)*

This settlement is 4 miles southeast of Kalama on the Columbia River, extreme southwest Cowlitz County. It was named by Northern Pacific Railway officials for William S. Martin who settled here in 1872.

Mary Belle Falls *(Mt. Rainier National Park)*

Waterfall in Nickel Creek, a tributary of Muddy Fork, Cowlitz River, directly west of Cowlitz Divide, southeast area of the park. It was named by park officials for the daughter of E. S. Hall, formerly superintendant of the park. (USBGN)

Maryhill *(S.33;T.3N;R.16E)*

A museum of fine arts, this estate is on the north bank of Columbia River, 8 miles south of Goldendale, south central Klickitat County. In the early 1900s, very extensive acreage was purchased in this area by Samuel J. Hill, good-roads advocate, for the purpose of growing European wine grapes. He built an enormous concrete structure on a cliff overlooking the Columbia, copying the design of a European castle, and intended for the entertainment of European royalty. In 1926, it was dedicated by Queen Marie of Roumania. The ''castle'' is now used as a museum and the land

holdings are devoted to cattle grazing. At the suggestion of M. Jean Adrien Antoine Jules Jusserand, French ambassador, Sam Hill called this estate for the given name of his mother, his wife, and his daughter, all of whom bore the name *Mary.* An earlier name for the area was *Columbia.*

Marys Corner *(S.9;T.12N;R.1W)*

A corner at the junction of National Park Highway and old Pacific Highway, 10 miles southeast of Chehalis, west central Lewis County. Built in 1845, the old Jackson courthouse is nearby. The corner is named for Mary Loftus, who built and operated a store here in 1924.

Marysville *(Cowlitz County) see* Catlin

Marysville *(T.30N;R.5E)*

An early community (established in 1877 as a trading post) on Snohomish River, 3 miles north of Everett, west central Snohomish County. The town was named for Mary Comeford, wife of J. P. Comeford, original owner of the townsite, and a trader on the Tulalip Indian Reservation. An alternate version of the name origin is a legend that the place was named for the Virgin Mary by Father Casimir Chirouse at the suggestion of J. P. Comeford. A further version is that the place was named for Marysville, California, by two settlers who came to this Washington town from California -- Thomas Lloyd and James Johnson. The original Indian name was *Slup-puks.*

Mashel Prairie *(T.16N;R.4E)*

A beautiful expanse of 100-acre meadow, between Ohop Creek(2) and Mashel River, 3 miles west of Eatonville, south central Pierce County. The prairie was named for Mashel River. (*see* Mashel River)

Mashel River *(T.16N;Rs.4,5,6E)*

The stream of the river heads in the hills 5 miles west of Mt. Rainier National Park, south central Pierce County; flows west to Nisqually River, 1 mile north of LaGrande. The name is from the Indian designation meaning, ''Place of dark shadows in the water,'' and has been variously spelled as *Mi-shawl, Mi-chel, Mish-ell, Mishall,* and *Mashel.* In pioneer days, it was known as *Michel's Fork, Nisqually River.*

Mason City *(S.6;T.28N;R.31E)*

Construction town at the site of the Grand Coulee Dam, on the east side of the Columbia River, extreme southeast corner of Okanogan County. In September, 1934, it was named at the suggestion of George H. Atkinson, for Silas B. Mason, chairman of the board of the contracting firm of Mason-Mason-Atkinson-Kier Company. This firm was a prime contractor in building the dam.

Mason Lake *(S.5;T.22N;R.10E)*

A 32.6-acre lake, 6 miles west of Snoqualmie Pass, Snoqualmie National Forest, east central King County. It is reported to have been named in territorial days or soon after, for Charles H. Mason, first secretary of Washington Territory. Alternate names are *Short Lake* and *Big Mason*.

Mason's Creek (Grays Harbor County) *see* Workman Creek

Massacre Bay *(Ss.5,6;T.36N;R.2W)*

An Orcas Island bay at the head of West Sound, central San Juan County. In 1859, the name was applied to British admiralty charts by Capt. Henry Richards, RN, for the evidence of massacre of local Indians by northern Haidah Indians. A mass burial of Lummi Indian corpses was obvious.

Massie Lake *(S.6;T.30N;R.16E)*

A water-filled glacial cirque, near the north boundary of Wenatchee National Forest; it is 2-1/2 miles east of Cascade Mountain summit on the east side of a ridge between Chiwawa River and Buck Creek. It was named by early prospectors for Joe Massie, who prospected here between 1906 and 1912.

Mastiff Mountain *(S.26;T.27N;R.15E)*

A Wenatchee National Forest peak on Nason Ridge, 1 mile east of Mt. Howard, between Little Wenatchee River and Nason Creek, northwest Chelan County. It was named by Forest Supervisor A. H. Sylvester, who saw a resemblance to the head of a mastiff when the mountain was viewed from Wenatchee Lake.

Mather Memorial Parkway (Yakima/Pierce counties)

This highway border, established by congressional action in 1931, extends from Naches Ranger Station, 10 miles northwest of Yakima, along State Highway 5 through Chinook Pass to the northeast corner of Mt. Rainier National Park. It is 56 miles long, and extends on each side of the highway for a distance of 1/2 mile. It is named for Stephen T.

Mather, first director of the National Park Service.

Mathew Meadow *(S.10;T.18N;R.13E)*

A meadow directly north of Naches River, between Mathew and Pileup creeks, extreme southwest Kittitas County. The name is for an old squatter, who built a cabin here in early days.

Matia East (San Juan County) *see* Puffin island

Matia Island *(T.37N;R.1W)*

The largest island of a small group in Strait of Georgia, 3 miles north of Orcas Island, northeast San Juan County. In 1790, Lieut. Juan Francisco de Eliza charted this island as *Isla de Mata*, using the Spanish word for bush or shrub. An alternate name used by early Spanish explorers was *Mal abrigo*, with a meaning of "Poor shelter," In 1841, Cmdr. Charles Wilkes charted this island in a grouping with Puffin Island and adjacent rocks as *Edmunds Group*, for a member of his crew. In 1854, the U.S. Coast Survey recognized Eliza's name, but used it on their charts with the added "i." The Lummi Indian name was *Punna-whing*, for an edible bulb which they harvested on the island. (USBGN)

Mats Mats Bay
(S.4;T.28N;&S.33;T.29N;R.1E)

A small inlet with a rock quarry on Admiralty Inlet, 2 miles north of Port Ludlow, northeast Jefferson County. The original Indian name of the bay and of an Indian village here was used by the U.S. Coast Survey in 1856. It has become official. A local name at one time was *Boat Harbor*.

Mattawa (Yakima County) *see* Priest Rapids (town)

Matterhorn (King County) *see* Kaleetan Peak

Matthews Beach *(T.26N;R.4E)*

A city park and bathing beach on the west shore of Lake Washington in Seattle, directly north of Sand Point, King County. It was named for the late John G. Matthews, Seattle attorney and timber investor, who owned the beach before it became city property.

Maud. *(S.30;T.33N;R.38E)*

Small settlement, 3-1/2 miles east of the Columbia River on Stranger Creek, 20 miles south of Kettle Falls, west central Stevens County. At one time, the place had a post office; it has a school

and some residences. It was named for Maude Morgan, daughter of an 1885 settler, S. C. Morgan. She was the first and only postmistress.

Maude Mountain (Chelan County) *see* Mount Maude

Mauden Creek (Clallam County) *see* Blackwood Creek

Maury Island *(Ts.21,22N;R.3E)*

The "island" is actually a peninsula of Vashon Island (connected to that island by a narrow sand spit), between East Passage and Quartermaster Harbor in Puget Sound, southwest King County. In 1841, it was named by Cmdr. Charles Wilkes for Lieut. William L. Maury, who was an astronomer and hydrographer on Wilkes' ship *Vincennes*. (USBGN)

Maury Pass (San Juan County) *see* Lopez Pass

Maverick Peak *(S.16;T.27N;R.18E)*

A 5,308-ft. Wenatchee National Forest peak, on Entiat Ridge, 6 miles northeast of Wenatchee Lake, central Chelan County. The name was applied by personnel of the Old Chicago Mine, which operated here in early days. The reason for this choice is not of record.

Maxfield Creek *(T.29N;R.13W)*

The stream of the creek rises near Calawah Ridge, Olympic National Forest, southwest Clallam County; flows 5 miles west to Soleduck River. This stream, as in the case of Maxfields Creek, 9 miles to the southwest, was named for W. H. "Jesse" Maxfield, a pioneer settler. Why two creeks were named for one person is a riddle.

Maxfields Creek *(T.28;Rs.13,14W)*

The stream of the creek rises on the west slope of Anderson Ridge, extreme southwest Clallam County; flows west to Bogachiel River. (*see* Maxfield Creek)

Maxwelton *(S.4;T.28N;R.3E)*

An island community near the southwest tip of Whidbey Island, south entrance to Useless Bay, south Island County. The place was named by two Scottish residents, the McKee brothers, for the *bonnie bra'es of Maxwellton*. Either the McKees or the cartographers did not know how to spell the Scottish name.

May Creek *(Ts.23,24N;R.5E)*

The stream of the creek rises in Meadow Lake, 4 miles east of Renton; flows 7 miles northwest to Lake Washington opposite the south end of Mercer Island. It was named for a pioneer homesteader who evidently failed to prove up on his land. The Indian name was *Cbaltu*, meaning "Place where things are dried." It referred to the many redfish that they caught and dried near the creek's mouth.

May's Inlet (Kitsap County) *see* Liberty Bay

Mayfield *(S.21;T.12N;R.2E)*

Village on Cowlitz River, 20 miles east of Winlock, south central Lewis County. It is the site of a City of Tacoma hydroelectric dam. Platted as a large town, it did not develop. The name is for the first postmaster, H. T. Mayfield, who installed postal facilities in 1891.

Mayfield Reservoir *(T.12N;R.2E)*

A hydroelectric pool in Cowlitz River back of Mayfield Dam, 13 miles east of Toledo, south central Lewis County. This pool covers about 2,200 acres in a length of 10 miles, and has a maximum depth of 185 ft. It was built by the City of Tacoma and named for the town of Mayfield.

Maylor Point *(S.11;T.32N;R.1E)*

An east entrance point to Oak Harbor on Whidbey Island, on the U.S. Navy Air Base, north Island County. It was locally named for Alfred S. Maylor, owner of a Donation Land Claim on the point. An alternate name is *Navy Point*. *(USBGN)*

Maynard *(S.14;T.29N;R.2W)*

Settlement on west shore of Port Discovery Bay near the bay's head, northeast Jefferson County. The place was named for Mrs. S. P. Maynard, who operated a rustic hotel here while the passenger train service was in effect.

Mays *(S.3;T.13N;R.4W)*

Logging campsite 15 miles west of Chehalis on Chehalis River, west central Lewis County. The place was named for one of the principals of Baker-May Lumber Company, which operated a sawmill here for several years until it burned in 1912.

Maytown *(S.4;T.16N;R.2W)*

Town 9 miles northeast of Rochester, central Thurston County. In 1911, it

was originally founded by Taylor Lumber & Shingle Company as a sawmill town. The name was given by Isaam Noe, sawmill owner, for his former home town in Kentucky.

Mayview *(S.7;T.13N;R.43E)*

Community 12 miles northeast of Pomeroy, 2 miles southwest of Snake River, extreme northeast Garfield County. Before 1880, it was founded by Henry Victory and other settlers. Henry Victor chose this decorative name for the post office in 1880.

Maywood *(S.11;T.20N;R.9E)*

Railroad point on the upper Green River, 13 miles west of Cascade Mountain summit, southeast King County. In 1886, this name was given by Northern Pacific Railway officials, "because it was euphonious."

Mazama *(S.30;T.36N;R.20E)*

Old mining camp on the upper Methow River, Chelan National Forest, west central Okanogan County. This place marks the end of paved roads as one drives northwestward through the Methow Valley; the road leads northwest to Harts Pass at the Cascade Summit, making this the entry point for miners headed for the high Cascade range. The name is the Spanish name for "mountain goat." Prior to this nomenclature, the place was known as *Goat Creek*. Plenty of mountain goats inhabit the high mountains to the west and northwest of Mazama.

Mazama Falls *(S.26;T.39N;R.8E.uns)*

A series of falls which total 600 ft., with one drop of 90 ft., on the northeast slope of Mt. Baker, in Wells Creek near the terminus of Mazama Glacier, central Whatcom County. The falls were named for The Mazamas, an Oregon mountaineering organization, by four Mazamas who "discovered" them.

Mazama Glacier *(Ts.38,39N;R.8E.uns)*

This very large glacier extends 4 miles northeast of the Mt. Baker summit, Mt. Baker National Forest, central Whatcom County. It feeds several creeks that drain north into North Fork, Nooksack River. The Mazamas used the name of their organization when they named this glacier in the early 1900s.

Mazama Glacier
(Ss.8,17;T.8N;R.11E.uns)

This vast, fan-shaped glacier on the southeast slope of Mt. Adams, descends

into the head of Hell-Roaring Creek Canyon, southwestern Yakima County. The original name was *Hell-Roaring Glacier*. In 1895, the Mazamas renamed it for their organization, thereby forfeiting one of the lusty pioneer names of this region.

Mazama Lake *(S.2;T.37N;R.7E.uns)*

A small 5-acre lake, elevation 5,150 ft., southwest slope of Mt. Baker, Mazama Park, directly east of Meadow Point, south central Whatcom County. In 1900, the lake waas named for and by The Mazamas. It is one of four Galena Chain Lakes, with Iceberg, Hayes, and Arbuthnot Lakes.

Mazama Park *(S.2;T.37N;R.7E.uns)*

Mountain meadow on the southwest slope of Mt. Baker, near the foot of Deming Glacier, south central Whatcom County. In 1909, this place was named by and for The Mazamas.

Mazama Ridge *(Mt. Rainier National Park)*

This ridge heads near Sluiskin Falls, south of Paradise Glacier; it is between Paradise Valley and Stevens Canyon. With an unobstructed view, this elevation in the south central zone of the park, is a favorite spot for summer hikers. It was named by and for The Mazamas, when they camped on the ridge near Sluiskin Falls in 1905.

McAdam *(S.15;T.14N;R.35E)*

Railroad point 8 miles northeast of Kahlotus, northeast Franklin County. It was named by Spokane, Portland & Seattle Railway officials for Owen McAdam, an old settler who owned land at this place. It appears on some maps, in error, as *McAdams*.

McAdams (Franklin County) *see* McAdam

McAleer Creek *(T.26N;R.4E)*

The stream of the creek rises in Lake Ballinger, extreme southwest Snohomish County; flows south about 4 miles to the north end of Lake Washington, King County. The stream was named for Hugh McAleer, who patented the land around Lake Ballinger, formerly called *Lake McAleer*, and who sold out to R. A. Ballinger.

McAleer Lake (Snohomish County) *see* Lake Ballinger

McAllister Creek *(Ts.18,19N;R.1E)*

The stream of this small, but historic

creek rises in McAllister Springs, 2 miles east of Long Lake, northeast Thurston County; flows north to Nisqually Reach of Puget Sound. On December 26, 1854, a treaty with Nisqually Indians and other western Washington tribes, was signed at a campground on this stream. It was called the *Medicine Creek Treaty* because Indians used that name for the lower portion of the creek. The name is for James McAllister, who built a water-powered sawmill on the creek in 1851, and who shipped the first sawed lumber from Puget Sound in the following year. The Indian name was *She-nah-Nam...*

McAllister Meadow
(S.1;T.13N;R.13E.uns)

Mountain meadow on Snoqualmie National Forest, northwest Yakima County. It was innundated in the reservoir which was created back of Rimrock Dam, namely Tieton Reservoir. The meadow was named by and for a man who purchased the land, living there for his health in the late 1880s.

McBride Lake *(S.36;T.8N;R.4E)*

A marshy, 9-acre lake, 4 miles northeast of Merrill Lake, east central Cowlitz County. It appears on some maps, in error, at the location of Goat Marsh Lakes. The lake is named for a local pioneer; an alternate name, little used nowadays, was *Snowshoe Lake*.

McCain Creek *(T.20N;R.10E)*

The stream of the creek rises on Bald Mountain, Snoqualmie National Forest, extreme southeast King County; flows 4 miles southwest to Green River at Hot Springs. The creek was named for a man who built the first hotel and bath house at Hot Springs in 1888.

McCall (Adams County) *see* Macall

McCall Mountain *(S.23;T.28N;R.16E)*

A Wenatchee National Forest peak, between White and Chiwawa rivers, 1 mile east of the south end of Twin Lakes, northwest Chelan County. Originally it was called *Hucklelberry Mountain*. Because this name was too common, it was re-named by Forest Supervisor A. H. Sylvester for Lieut. J. K. McCall, U.S. Army, who fought here during the Indian Wars in 1858.

McCarty's Portage *(Ts.9,10N;R.10W)*

A fur-trading trail built in the early 1800s, which extended north from Columbia River to Shoalwater Bay via Bear River. It was named for one of the first settlers in southwest Pacific County, who lived on the portage trail.

McCauley Creek *(T.39N;Rs.4,5E)*

The stream of this short creek heads in high country, 2-1/2 miles north of Deming, west central Whatcom County; flows 3 miles southwest to Nooksack River. The creek was named for Hugh MacCaulay, who homesteaded here in 1883 when the area was a trackless wilderness.

McCay Mountain
(S.23;T.36N;R.23E.uns)

A 7,628-ft. Chelan National Forest peak, 8-1/2 miles northwest of Conconully, central Okanogan County. Three Tiffany brothers of a wealthy New York family, with other affluent young men, camped for 2 years at the foot of Tiffany Mountain, 4 miles to the north of this peak. They named this mountain for one of their associates. The spelling was changed, probably by cartographers.

McChord Air Force Base
(T.19N;R.3E)

A U. S. Army airport at the northeast corner of Fort Lewis Army Post, northwest Pierce County. The field was named for Col. William C. McChord, Army Air Corps, who was killed in flight during 1937. Prior to that the strip was called *Tacoma Airport*. It was changed to *McChord Field*, and later to the present designation.

McCleary *(S.11,T.18N;R.5W)*

Town on Wildcat Creek, 19 miles west of Olympia, southeast Grays Harbor County. This forest products manufacturing town is based on the sustained yield forest of Simpson Timber Company. The name is for Henry McCleary who once operated a very large door manufacturing plant in this town and provided practically all of the employment.

McClellan Butte *(S.11;T.22N;R.9E)*

A 5,175-ft. butte, 10 miles west of Cascade Mountain summit, between Cedar Lake and South Fork, Snoqualmie River, east central King County. The mountain was named for Capt. George B. McClellan, USA, who attempted to locate a road over Snoqualmie Pass in 1853, but who failed in 2 expeditions.

McClure Rock *(Mt. Rainier National Park)*

A rocky platform, elevation 7,384-ft., overlooking Paradise Glacier, near the west moraine of that ice river, northeast of Panorama Point, southeast sector of the park. The peak allows an extensive panoramic view. The rock was named for Prof. Edgar McClure of the University of Oregon, who took barometric measurements at the summit in 1897, and who was killed here during his descent. An alternate name of this feature, which is unofficial, is *The Sphinx*. (USBGN)

McConnell Island *(T.36N;R.3W)*

The largest of a group of 7 islands between the west ends of Orcas and Shaw islands, San Juan Channel, central San Juan County. These islands carried the early name of *Wasp Islands*. Another name, *Brown Island*, was replaced by the present name, which was for the first settler on the island in the 1880s, Victor McConnell.

McCormick *(S.5;T.12N;R.5W)*

Community on Rock Creek, 26 miles southwest of Chehalis, southwest Lewis County. This town depended on one large sawmill for its industry and when the mill cut the available timber, the place was almost abandoned. In 1898, it was named for H. McCormick, owner of McCormick Lumber Company.

McCoy *(S.32;T.20N;R.44E)*

A railway and highway point, 4 miles north of Oakesdale, northeast Whitman County. The name was originally applied to Oakesdale, but in 1886, the name was shifted to this place by the Northern Pacific Land Company. It is for James McCoy, who settled on land in this vicinity in 1886.

McCracken Point *(T.36N;R.4W)*

A north end point of Henry Island, near Roche Harbor, west central San Juan County. The original name of this feature was *Cooper Point*, for Lieut. Henry Towry Miles Cooper, Royal Marines, who was on the San Juan station in *HMS Sutlej* in 1863-1866, during the San Juan boundary dispute between Great Britain and the U.S. That name remains on British charts, but has been replaced with the present name on charts and maps published in this country.

McCrea Creek (Chelan County) *see* McCree Branch

McCredie *(S.24;T.4N;R.22E)*

Railroad siding on north bank of Columbia River, 39 miles east of Goldendale, southeast Klickitat County. It was named by S.P.&S. Railway officials for Judge W. W. McCredie of Vancouver, Washington.

McCree Branch *(T.28N;R.19E)*

The stream of this creek rises on Wenatchee National Forest, central Chelan County; flows 3 miles southwest to Entiat River from Angle Peak. It was named by Forest Service personnel for an early squatter at the mouth of the stream. An alternate name is *McCrea Creek.*

McCue Ridge *(T.26N;Rs.16,17E)*

A Wenatchee National Forest ridge, which extends 9-1/2 miles east-by-south from Chiwaukum Mountains to Skinney Creek, central Chelan County. It is used in season as a forest fire lookout by Forest Service personnel. The naming was by early sheepmen for William McCue who used this fine pasturage for summer sheep range.

McDonald (Clallam County) *see* Elwha

McDonald's Island (Island County) *see* Camano Island

McDonald Mountain *(S.34;T.30N;R.7W)*

A peak 1-1/2 miles southeast of Elwha, 7 miles south of Strait of Juan de Fuca, north central Clallam County. It was named for W. D. McDonald, first settler in this area, and former postmaster of Elwha.

McDonald Ridge *(Ts.28,29N;R.17E.uns)*

A Wenatchee National Forest ridge, between Entiat and Chiwawa rivers, north central Chelan County. It is the part of Entiat Mountains which extends south from Garland Peak to the head of Three Creek. The name is local, and is for an early sheepman who used the range. It was the upper limit of sheep grazing in early days.

McDonough's Island (Island County) *see* Camano Island

McEntee's Crossing (Grant County) *see* Coulee City

McGahee Creek *(S.15;T.36N;R.35E)*

The stream of this 2-mile-long creek heads on Colville National Forest, 15 miles east of Republic, central Ferry County; flows south into the North Fork of Sherman Creek. It is named for a pioneer who operated a stage section in this locality during the mining boom of the 1890s. The name was McGahee, not McGanee or McGauhee, as carried on some maps. (USBGN)

McGanee Creek (Ferry County) *see* McGahee Creek

McGauhee Creek (Ferry County) *see* McGahee Creek

McGees *(S.19;T.30N;R.1W)*

Early settlement on the east shore of Port Discovery Bay, 1-1/2 miles southeast of Beckett Point, northeast Jefferson County. In September, 1905, this place, which does not appear on recent maps, was named by A. Loasby for Samuel McGee, who settled here in earlier days.

McGinnis Creek *(Ss.7,18;T.36N;R.7E)*

The stream of the creek heads 1 mile south of Whatcom County boundary; flows south into South Fork, Nooksack River. The stream was named for Emery McGinnis, a pioneer and customs collector in the 1890s, who was shot while hunting in the Mt. Baker foothills.

McGlinn Island *(S.1;T.33N;R.2E)*

A Skagit Bay island at the mouth of Swinomish Passage, 1 mile south of LaConner, southwest Skagit County. The island was named for an early hotel-keeper at LaConner.

McGowan *(S.22,T.9N;R.10W)*

Community on the north bank of Columbia River, 1 mile east of Fort Columbia, southwest Pacific County. It was named for J. P. McGowan, who settled here in 1852, and who operated a salmon saltery and cannery on a 320-acre tract which he purchased from Father Leonette. Because it was bought from a missionary, the land was called *Old Mission Grant.*

McGowan Pond *(S.21;T.9N;R.10W)*

A 2-acre lake in Fort Columbia State Park, 7-1/4 miles southeast of Ilwaco, southwest Pacific County. (*see* McGowan)

McGregor *(S.36;T.15N;R.36E)*

Railroad station north of Palouse River, 1-1/2 miles west of Palouse Falls, southeast Adams County. The name is for that of a local landowner. The railroad station was altered to *Gregor*, to avoid possible confusion with McAdam on the same division.

McGregor Mountain *(T.34N;R.16E.uns)*

A 8,140-ft. mountain, 8 miles north of the head of Lake Chelan, 2 miles north of Stehekin River, north end of Chelan County. The name was applied by local settlers for Billie McGregor, a trapper who died on this mountain while hunting goats.

McInnis Mills *(S.24;T.34N;R.43E)*

A ghost town on the Pend Oreille River opposite Jared, central Pend Oreille County. In 1902, it was established and in 1907, it was abandoned. The name is for John McInnis and his 2 sons, who built a sawmill here in 1902.

McIntosh *(S.23;T.16N;R.1W)*

Town on Clare lake, 12 miles southeast of Olympia, southwestern Thurston County. In 1889, the name was placed on the railway station here by Northern Pacific officials, and is that of a landowner from whom right-of-way was acquired.

McIntosh Lake *(Ss.13,14,23;T.16N;R.1W)*

A narrow, 115.8-acre lake directly north of McIntosh, south central Thurston County. The lake is about 1-1/2 miles long and is bordered by timber. It was named for the town of McIntosh which it adjoins. An older name is *Clear Lake.* (*see* McIntosh)

McKenna *(S.28;T.17N;R.2E)*

Early town 2 miles south of Fort Lewis Army Post, 1-1/2 miles east of Yelm, southwest Pierce County. This former lumber town faded when local timber was cut off. It was named for E. W. McKenna of Chicago, a vice-president of Chicago, Milwaukee & St. Paul Railroad.

McKenzie Canyon *(Ts.26,27N;R.20E)*

A Wenatchee National Forest canyon on the southwest slope of Chelan Mountains, extending 3-1/2 miles southwest to Entiat River, east central Chelan County. The name is from local usage and is for a family which lived at the mouth of the canyon in early days.

McKenzie Head *(S.8;T.9N;R.11W)*

A southwest shore head of Cape Disappointment, on Pacific Ocean, southwest Pacific County. The feature was named in fur trading days for Donald McKenzie, partner in Pacific Fur Company and leader of the first overland party to reach Astoria, in 1811.

McKenzie Head Lagoon *(S.8;T.9N;R.11W)*

A marshy, 6-1/2-acre lake on Fort Canby Military Reservation, 2 miles southwest of Ilwaco, southwest Pacific County. The lake is named for McKenzie Head. (*see* McKenzie Head)

McLaughlans Island (Whatcom County) *see* Lummi Island

McLeod Lake (Whatcom County) *see* Green Lake

McLeod Mountain (Okanogan County) *see* McLeod Peak

McLeod Peak *(S.17;T.37N;R.20E.uns)*

A 8,123-ft. North Cascade Primitive Area peak, 10 miles north of Mazama, northwest Okanogan County. It is designated on some maps as *Goat Mountain* or *McLeod Mountain* and was named for Angus McLeod, an early pioneer of the Methow Valley.

McLoughlin Canyon *(Ss.2,3,10;T.36N;R.27E)*

A canyon 4 miles south of Tonasket, extending southwest 2-1/2 miles to Okanogan River, central Okanogan County. It was named for David McLoughlin, son of Hudson's Bay Company's Dr. John McLoughlin, who led a party of miners through the canyon in 1858, headed for Fraser River gold fields. Six were killed and several wounded when attacked by Indians here.

McMillan *(S.18;T.19N;R.5E)*

Community 5 miles south of Sumner, 15 miles southeast of Tacoma, central Pierce County. In 1877, and for many years later, Roche Harbor Lime Company made lime here. In 1891, the town was named for John S. McMillan, president of Roche Harbor Lime Company. Until 1877, the accepted name was *Lime Kiln*.

McMillan Lake(s) 2 (Skagit County(*see* Texas Pond(s)

McMurray *(S.25;T.33N;R.4E)*

Scattered community of small farms and homes on the west shore of Lake McMurray, 7 miles southeast of Mount Vernon, southwest Skagit County. Once it was an important lumber and shingle manufacturing town. The station here

was named by Northern Pacific Railway officials for Dr. McMurray, a physician who homesteaded the site of the town.

McMurray Lake *(S.30;T.33N;R.5E;S.25;T.33N;R.4E)*

Lake 7 miles southeast of Mount Vernon, 1 mile north of Snohomish County boundary, southwest Skagit County. (*see* McMurray)

McNary Dam *(T.5N;R.28E)*

A Columbia River dam between Washington and Oregon, directly below Umatilla Rapids, extreme south central Benton County. Dedicated on September 23, 1954, the dam is 7,300 ft. long and contains 32,000 acres in its impounded reservoir. It was named for the late U.S. Senator, Charles L. McNary of Oregon, who was the author of important conservation legislation.

McNary Reservoir (Benton and Walla Walla counties/Oregon) *see Lake Wallula*

McNeil Island *(T.20N;R.1E)*

The site of a state penitentiary, south end of Carr Inlet, 3 miles northwest of Steilacoom, northwest Pierce County. It was named by Cmdr. Charles Wilkes for Capt. William Henry McNeill (sic), who was captain of Hudson's Bay Company's steamship *Beaver*. For years he competed with Hudson's Bay Company in his tradeship, the brig *Llama*, until bought out by them in 1832. In 1846, Capt. R. N. Inskip named the feature *Duntze Island* for Capt. John A. Duntze of *HMS Fisgard*. The name failed to supplant the name which Wilkes used.

McNeil Peak (Yakima County) *see* Russell Ridge

Mead *(S.10;T.26N;R.43E)*

Suburb 3-1/2 miles north of Spokane, central Spokane County. It is the site of a large aluminum reduction plant. In the 1870s, the town was founded and was named by James Berridge for Gen. George Gordon Meade, a Civil War leader of Union forces.

Meadow Creek *(T.21N;R.11E)*

The stream of the creek heads in Stirrup Lake near Meadow Pass, east of the Cascade Mountain summit, Wenatchee National Forest, west central Kittitas County; flows 4 miles east to Keechelus Lake. It is named for its origin in a mountain meadow, near Meadow Pass.

Meadow Creek *(S.13;T.21N;R.11E)*

Settlement at the south end of Keechelus Lake, at the mouth of Meadow Creek, northwest Kittitas County. The town is named for the creek. (*see* Meadow Creek)

Meadow Creek *(Mt. Rainier National Park)*

The stream of the creek rises in Mountain Meadows, near its west boundary, northwest area of the park; flows southwest to Mowich River, 1-1/2 miles west of the park in Pierce County. In 1883, the creek was named for the meadow in which it rises by Prof. Bailey Willis. (USBGN)

Meadow Lake (lake) (Spokane County) *see* Four Lakes

Meadow Lake *(S.4;T.7N;R.8E.uns)*

A shallow, 2-1/2-acre lake, elevation 3,900 ft., Gifford Pinchot National Forest, northwest side of Squaw Butte, central Skamania County. The name appears to have been chosen because the lake drains through a marshy meadow. An alternate name is *Squaw Butte Lake*.

Meadow Lake *((S.14;T.24N;R.41E)*

Town in the Four Lakes area, 1 mile north of Meadow Lake (lake), west central Spokane County. It was named for the lake near which it is located.

Meadow Mountain *(Ss.9,10,15,16;T.31N;R.8E.uns)*

A Mt. Baker National Forest peak, 7 miles south of Hazel, between Boulder and Canyon creeks, north central Snohomish County. The name was given by early settlers because of extensive alpine meadows, and has been adopted by the Forest Service. It should not be confused with another Meadow Mountain which is 24 miles to the east.

Meadow Mountain *(Ss.9,16;T.31N;R.12E)*

A 6,360-ft. Mt. Baker National Forest peak, between Lime Creek and Whitechuck River, northeast Snohomish County. The peak was named by early surveyors for extensive mountain meadows on its slope and the Forest Service uses this name. It should not be confused with another mountain by the same name, 24 miles to the west.

Meadow Point *(T.26N;R.3E)*

A sandy promontory on the east shore of Puget Sound, directly north of Golden Gardens, near Seattle's north city limits, northwest King County. This is a descriptive name applied by the U. S. Coast Survey.

Meadow Point *(S.35;T.38N;R.7E)*

A high mountain meadow on the southwest slope of Mt. Baker near the foot of Deming Glacier, south central Whatcom County. It is near Mazama Park and Lake. The name, applied by the Mazamas, is descriptive as this high mountain meadow is on a rocky point near Deming Glacier.

Meadowdale N.(S.8;T.27N;R.4E)

Community 3 miles northeast of Edmonds on Possession Sound, southwest Snohomish County. On April 2, 1904, the name was applied by Robert Maltby because of an extensive area which might be converted into meadow if cleared and grassed.

Meaghersville *(S.1;T.20N;R.17E)*

Old mining town on Williams Creek, near its junction with Swauk Creek, 1-1/2 miles east of the original site of Liberty, central Kittitas County. The town was named for Thomas F. Meagher, an early miner.

Meander Meadow *(T.29N;R.13E.uns)*

A 100-acre meadow directly east of Cascade Mountain summit, at the head of Little Wenatchee River, northeast of Wards Pass, Wenatchee National Forest, northwest Chelan County. The name came from the fact that the headwaters of Little Wenatchee River meander back and forth through the meadow. In 1912, the name was applied by Forest Supervisor A. H. Sylvester.

Meany Crest *(Mt. Rainier National Park)*

A small, 7,200-ft. peak on the east slope of Mt. Rainier near the north margin of Fryingpan Glacier, central zone of the park. It was named for Prof. Edmond S. Meany of the University of Washington, who had a personal attachment to this area. The naming was at the suggestion of L. A. (''Shorty'') Nelson of Portland, Oregon, during a summer outing of The Mountaineers in 1930. (USBGN)

Mecena Point (Clallam County) *see* Baada Point

Media (Pierce County) *see* Roy

Medical Lake *(T.24N;Rs.40,41E)*

Town 15 miles southwest of Spokane, on Medical Lake (lake), west

central Spokane County. In 1859, the settlement was started by Andrew Lefevre, a prospector. It became a resort center for Spokane citizens, and in 1889, it was chosen as the site of Eastern Washington State Hospital. In 1887, it was named by Stanley Hallett, a local settler, for the lake on which it is located. (*see* Medical Lake)

Medical Lake *(Ss.18,19;T.24N;R.41E)*

A lake 15 miles southwest of Spokane, west central Spokane County. Indians had used the lake long before as a cure for rheumatism. In 1877, it was named by a settler, Stanley Hallett, for its medicinal properties because the lake is heavily impregnated with salts of various types.

Medicine Creek (Thurston County) *see* McAllister Creek

Medicine Creek *(T.21N;R.17E)*

The stream of the creek rises on Teanaway Ridge, Wenatchee National Forest, central Kittitas County; flows 4 miles east to Swauk Creek. The name was given by early miners because of the strong taste of sulphur in the water.

Medicine Creek Park *(S.6;T.18N;R.1E)*

A park on the west side of Nisqually River, 1 mile south of its mouth on Nisqually Flats, northwest Pierce County. The site has not been improved for park purposes. On December 26, 1854, it was named for an Indian treaty which Gov. I. I. Stevens concluded with Nisqually, Puyallup, and Squaxon Indians. A sign in the park indicates the actual treaty site.

Medicine Ridge *(T.26N;R.19E)*

A Wenatchee National Forest ridge extending from the south end of Sugarloaf Peak, 5 miles southeast to Indian and Talamook creeks, central Chelan County. It was named by an early sheepherder who registered no reason for his choice.

Medina *(T.25N;R.4E)*

A residential suburb of Seattle, directly north of Bellevue, on the east shore of Lake Washington, northwest King County. In 1914, when the town was platted, it was named by Mrs. S. A. Belote as *Medina Heights*, for the Oriental city of Medina which is the second holiest city to those of the Moslem faith. The ''heights'' had been known by this name, however, since 1892. It has now

been simplified to the present form.

Meeker *(S.36;T.20N;R.4E)*

Settlement 1-1/2 miles east of Puyallup, north central Pierce County. In 1882, it was named by Northern Pacific Railway Company personnel. In 1889, the same agency changed the name to *Meeker Junction*, for the famous pioneer and hop-grower, Ezra Meeker. The ''junction'' has been sidetracked in later years.

Meeker Lakes *(S.31;T.19N;R.11E)*

Two connected lakes, 1,300 ft. apart, in Greenwater River, 26-1/2 miles east of Enumclaw, between southeast King County and northeast Pierce County. The upper lake covers 6.2 acres and the lower, 3.9 acres. The name is reported to be in honor of Ezra Meeker. (*see* Meeker)

Meekersville (Pierce County) *see* Puyallup

Meeks Table *(S.5;T.15N;R.14E)*

A 4,000-ft. plateau on Snoqualmie National Forest, 8 miles west of Nile, northwest Yakima County. This feature was locally named for Clarence Meeks, a packer for the sheep camps of Augustan Cleman. An alternate name is *Little Devils Table*.

Megler *(S.24;T.9N;R.10W)*

Village 12 miles from the mouth of Columbia River, on its north bank, southwest Pacific County. It was named for Joseph G. Megler, a pioneer legislator, who operated a fish cannery up the river at Brookfield.

Melakwa Lake *(S.25;T.23N;R.10E)*

A lake (actually 2, small, connected lakes) directly northwest of Denny Mountain, at the head of Tuscohatchie Creek, east central King County. In 1916, the lake was named by The Mountaineers, using the same name source as that for Melakwa Pass. (*see* Melakwa Pass) (USBGN)

Melakwa Pass *(S.24;T.23N;R.10E)*

A pass between Kaleetan and Chair peaks, directly west of Snow Lake, east central King County. In 1916, it was named by The Mountaineers, using the Indian term for ''Mosquito.'' The name is quite appropriate. (USBGN)

Melbourne *(S.24;T.17N;R.8W)*

An early logging center and booming ground on Chehalis River, 7-1/2 miles east of Aberdeen, south central

Grays Harbor County. In the late 1850s, it was named for Melbourne, Australia, by Reuben Redmond when he platted the town. Redmond was a brother-in-law of Samuel Benn who founded Aberdeen in the same period.

Melrose (King County) *see* Redmond

Memaloose Island
(Ss.31,32;T.3N;R.12E)

A basalt island in Columbia River, 8 miles upstream from White Salmon, between Klickitat County and Oregon. The island was used for centuries by Indians as a cemetery and was then flooded by Bonneville Dam; most of the graves were removed beforehand. The name translates into "Place of the Dead."

Memaloose Rock *(T.8N;R.4W)*

Rock at the mouth of Abernethy Creek, on Columbia River, near Oak Point, southwest Cowlitz County. It was named by Capt. Rockwell, who triangulated the Columbia River in this area. Indians buried their dead here in former days. (*see*. Memaloose Island)

Menatchee Creek *(Ts.6,7N;R.43E)*

The stream of the creek heads north of Mt. Horrible, southwest Asotin County; flows 11 miles southeast and south to Grande Ronde River, southwest quarter of the county. The name probably derives from an Indian word which is said to mean "Water coming from a canyon." It is not *Wenatchee* or *Venatchee*, as shown on some maps. (USBGN)

Mendem Creek *(T.30N;R.16E)*

The stream of this small creek rises on Wenatchee National forest, northwest Chelan County; flows 1-1/2 miles to Phelps Creek from the west side of Entiat Mountain. The creek (not shown on most maps) was named by Forest Supervisor A. H. Sylvester in 1936. He camped here with Gilbert Brown who had to mend his trousers.

Mendota *(S.3;T.14N;R.1W)*

Small settlement 7 miles east of Chehalis, near the head of Packwood Creek, northwest Lewis County. In 1908, it was named by owners of Mendota Coal & Coke Company, which had an operation here. Their first plant had been located at Mendota, Missouri.

Menlo *(S.10;T.13N;r.8W)*

Community on the Willapa River, 4-1/2 miles southeast of Raymond, central Pacific County. It was established when the Northern Pacific Railway built through the Willapa Valley. When John Brophy, a pioneer settler, platted this townsite, he erected a large sign on the property which read "Menlo Park," in memory of his former home in Menlo Park, California. Railway employees cut the sign in half, leaving only *Menlo*. The original name applied to this station by Northern Pacific officials was *Preston*. That name was dropped in favor of Menlo when it was found that another town by the same name had been in existence for some time in King County.

Mentor *(S.6;T.11N;R.43E)*

Community 3 miles southeast of Pataha, on Pataha Creek, north central Garfield County. Although it is not shown on recent maps, Mentor was once a contender for the county seat. The first name was *Rafferty's Ranch*. Later it was changed to Belfast, and again in 1881, to the present name, for the Ohio town which President James A. Garfield considered his home.

Mercer Island *(T.24;Rs.4,5E)*

A popular suburban residence area, 5 miles long, average width 1 mile, in the southern stretch of Lake Washington, directly east of Seattle, west central King County. The island was named for Thomas Mercer, a pioneer, who was a brother of Asa and Aaron Mercer. In October, 1852, he settled on the island which the Indians called *Klut-use*.

Mercer Slough *(T.25N;R.5E)*

A slough and stream which extend about 5 miles northward from the east shore of Lake Washington, opposite the north end of Mercer Island, west central King County. It was named for Aaron Mercer, a brother of the Seattle pioneers. In 1862, Aaron came here from Oregon and settled on 80-1/2 acres on the slough. (*see* Mercer Island)

Merchant Peak *(S.29;T.27N;R.11E)*

A high peak, elevation 6,100 ft., directly west of Eagle Lake, at the east end of Jump Off Ridge, southeast Snohomish County. The peak was named by The Mountaineers, but the reason for their choice of name appears to be unrecorded. (USBGN)

Meredith *(S.1;T.21N;R.4E)*

Small settlement between Kent and Auburn, 5 miles east of Puget Sound, southwest King County. In 1905, it was named by an official of Puget Sound Electric Railway Company, for his former home, Meredithville, Virginia.

Meridian Lake (King County) *see* Lake Meridian

Merrifield Cove *(S.25;T.35N;R.3W)*

A southeast coast cove of San Juan Island, in Griffin Bay, directly south of North Bay, south central San Juan County. It was named for Stafford Merrifield, a very early settler.

Merrill Lake *(T.17N;R.4E)*

A lake near the headwaters of Kalama River, 2 miles northwest of Lewis River, extreme southeast Cowlitz County. In 1890, the name was applied by James McBride and Frank Vandever for a pioneer family who settled here.

Merritt *(S.3;T.26N;R.16E)*

Recreation point on Wenatchee National Forest, 4 miles southwest of Wenatchee Lake on Nason Creek, southwest Chelan County. It was named by Great Northern officials for a local railroad agent.

.Merritt Lake *(S.25;T.27N;R.15E)*

A small pond in Wenatchee National Forest, on the steep south slope of Nason Ridge, at the head of Mahar Creek, southwest Chelan County. It was named by local usage for the nearby town of Merritt.

Mesa *(S.26;T.13N;R.30E)*

A railroad point, 24 miles north of Pasco, west central Franklin County. In 1883, it was named *Lake* by Northern-Pacific officials. In 1903, the railroad changed the station's name to the present form, which appears to be more appropriate in its Spanish meaning of "tableland." No lake appears in the vicinity on current maps. An intermediate name of this place was *Judson*.

Mesatchee Creek *(T.16N;R.11E.uns)*

The stream of the creek rises 2 miles northwest of Bumping Lake, northwest Yakima County; flows 3 miles north to American River, 5 miles northeast of Chinook Pass. The name is from Chinook Jargon, with a meaning of "wicked" or"cruel." Evidently this short, turbulent stream did not please the aborigines.

Meskill *(S.10;T.13N;R.4W)*

A railroad station, 14 miles west of Chehalis, on Chehalis River, west central Lewis County. In 1902, the first name of the place, given by Northern

Pacific Railway officials, was *Donahue Spur*, for W. J. and Thomas Donahue, from whom right-of-way was acquired. Some years later the Northern Pacific re-named their station for D. W. Meskill, president of Meskill & McNaughton Lumber Company.

Metaline *(S.28;T.39N;R.43E)*

Town on the west bank of Pend Oreille River, above Metaline Falls (falls), northwest Pend Oreille County. The name is taken from the adjacent falls in the Pend Oreille River.

Metaline Falls *(S.21;T.39N;R.43E)*

This 19-ft. drop in the Pend Oreille River is 9 miles south of the Canadian boundary, in north central Pend Oreille County. The historic Dewdney Trail, over which early fur traders traveled, crosses the foot of the falls. The name was given by very early miners and prospectors, who estimated that the area was completely covered with valuable minerals.

Metaline Falls *(S.21,T.39N;R.43E)*

A mineral-minded town on the east bank of Pend Oreille River, 9-1/2 miles south of the Canadian boundary, north central Pend Oreille County. In 1910, it was founded as an industrial town by the influence of the Mammoth and Morning mines. Some years later it was a stronghold of the Industrial Workers of the World (I.W.W.). Operating corporations were American Lead & Zinc Co., Metaline Mining & Smelting Co., Pend Oreille Mines & Metal Co., and Lehigh Cement Co. The name is borrowed from nearby Metaline Falls. (*see* Metaline Falls)

Meteor *(S.21;T.32N;R.36E)*

Small settlement, with few inhabitants and little activity, on the Colville Indian Reservation, 5 miles southwest of Inchelium, on Stranger Creek, east central Ferry County. Reputed to have been the first settlement in southeast Ferry County, Meteor was a lively mining camp when founded in 1898. It had a post office which was discontinued in 1953, and the town secured mail service at Impach, 3 miles to the northeast. The name is for the nearby Meteor Mine.

Meteor *(T.23N;R.16E)*

A 8,400-ft. granite mountain in the Stuart Range, 7 miles southwest of Leavenworth, southwest Chelan County. It was named by mountain climbers who devised this rather imaginative name

when they completed the first ascent of the lofty peak.

Methow *(S.s6;T.30N;R.23E)*

Settlement on the Methow River, 7 miles northwest of Pateros, south central Okanogan County. The name is a white man's version of an Indian tribal designation, *Smeetheowe*, and is said to mean ''sun.'' In 1811, David Thompson used this designation.

Methow River *(Ts.30-37N;Rs.18-23E)*

This mountain stream rises at Methow Pass, which traverses the Cascade summit between Skagit and Okanogan counties, 15 miles west of Mazama; flows south and east some 80 miles to join the Columbia River near Pateros. The name is for an Indian tribe which formerly lived between the Methow River and Lake Chelan. This tribe called the river *Buttle-mule-emauch*. In 1841, Wilkes called the stream *Barrier River*. (*see* Methow)

Methow Valley *(Ts.30-37N;Rs.18-23E)*

A popular resort area, the ''valley'' is usually considered as the lands adjoining the Methow River from Mazama to the Columbia River at Pateros, Okanogan County. It is narrow and there are few large farms. Livestock raising and a limited amount of mining and logging occupy most of the population. (*see* Methow River and Methow Valley)

Meydenbauer Bay *(S.31;T.25N;R.5E)*

A popular bay on the east shore of Lake Washington, directly north of the east end of Mercer Island, in the Bellevue area, northwest King County. The bay is popular with pleasure boat owners. In 1869, it was named for William Meydenbauer, who homesteaded here and who was the first permanent settler on the east shore of Lake Washington.

Meyers Falls *(ss.29-30;T.36N;R.37E)*

Waterfall in the Colville River, about 3 miles above the river's mouth and 2 miles south of the present site of Kettle Falls, west central Stevens County. Previously the town of Kettle Falls was the location of the town of Meyers Falls. In 1826, a grist mill was built here by an artisan named Goudy, employed by Hudson's Bay Company. It was the first grist mill on the upper Columbia River. In 1830, the mill was rebuilt. In 1866, when Hudson's Bay Company had sold out their local holdings, the mill was taken over by Louther Walden Meyers, who came here from eastern

Canada in 1862 and rebuilt the mill in 1871. In 1889, operations were discontinued. The falls were named for Louther Walden Meyers, who operated grist mills here for 23 years.

Meyers Falls *(S.20;T.36N;R.38E)*

One of the few towns in the state which might be classified as having a double identity, Meyers Falls is actually now Kettle Falls, Stevens County. In 1939-1940, when the town of Kettle Falls was flooded by Grand Coulee Dam backwaters, much of its population and many of the better buildings moved to Meyers Falls; then the name of the town was changed to Kettle Falls, as there were more of the newcomers than of the original citizens. The first permanent resident of the original Meyers Falls was Louther Walden Meyers, who filed a homestead on adjoining land. A close examination of the buildings will usually identify those which were moved from Kettle Falls. (*see* Meyers Falls)

Meyers Ridge *(T.7N;R.46E)*

A ridge between Meyers Creek and its West Fork, southeast Asotin County. It was locally named for the first settler, Charles Meyers. **Mia Chin Rocks** (Pacific County) *see* Louse Rocks

Mica Lake *(S.29;T.31N;R.14E.uns)*

A 13.4-acre lake, elevation 5,450 ft., Mt. Baker National Forest, on the northwest slope of Glacier Peak, east central Snohomish County. It was named for a quantity of mica which is visible in the sand and gravel on the lake's bottom. **Michel River** (Pierce County) *see* Mashel River

Mica Peak *(S.15;T.24N;R.45E)*

A rather isolated peak, elevation 5,225 ft., 10 miles south of Liberty Lake, east central Spokane County. Mica schist found on the mountain by Spokane Mica Company when the only access was by trail from Liberty Lake, explains the name.

Michel's Fork, Nisqually River (Pierce County) *see* Mashel River

Mick Creek *(T.37N;Rs.34-35E)*

The stream of the creek heads on the east slope of Midnight Mountain, Colville National Forest, north central Ferry County; flows 5 miles northeast and north to Boulder Creek. It was named by U.S. Forest Service personnel for Harry (''Mickey'') Elliot, a former employee of the Colville National forest.

Midchannel Bank (Kitsap County) *see* Allen Bank

Middle Channel *(T.34N;R.2W)*

A narrow passage between the southeast points of San Juan and Lopez islands. It connects San Juan Channel with the Strait of Juan de Fuca, San Juan County. In 1841, Cmdr. Charles Wilkes charted this channel as *Little Belt Passage*, to honor Comm. Rodgers, USN, who fought the British ship *Little Belt* on May 16, 1811, prior to the War of 1812. Coast surveyors did not accept his name, but applied the present descriptive name to the passage. A local name, which does not appear on maps, is *Cattle Point Narrows*.

Middle Fork Calispell Creek *(T.31N;R.42E)*

The stream of the creek rises 12 miles west of Dalkena, southwest Pend Oreille County; flows 7 miles northeast to Calispell Creek. (*see* Calispell Creek) (USBGN)

Middle Oregon

A name applied to the area now occupied by Okanogan County and adjacent land before counties were established.

Middle Point (Jefferson County) *see* Crane Point

Middle Point *(S.32;T.31N;R.1W)*

A north end point of Quimper Peninsula, 1 mile west of Port Townsend, on the Strait of Juan de Fuca, northeast Jefferson County. In 1854, the name was chosen by Capt. George Davidson of U.S. Coast Survey, because the point is midway between Wilson Point and Cape George. A local name for this point, no longer used, was *Rocky Point*.

Middle River (Clallam County) *see* Calawah River

Mid Lake (King County) *see* Sturtevant Lake

Midland *(S.3;T.19N;R.3E)*

A southeast suburb of Tacoma, on the Mountain Highway, northwest Pierce County. In 1855, this community was named for a farm and hop ranch established here by pioneer Ezra Meeker.

Midvale *(S.12;T.9N;R.22E)*

A railroad junction point in southeast Yakima Valley, 2-1/2 miles south of Sunnyside, Yakima County. It was named by officials of O.W.R.&N. railroad because it is in a middle valley between Mabton and Sunnyside.

Midway *(S.26;T.24N;R.41E)*

Community 3-1/2 miles north of Cheney, on Meadow Lake in Four Lake Township, southwest Spokane County. In 1906, the name was chosen, evidently by officials of an electric railroad which passed through the place, and who may have considered it a midway point between Cheney and the terminus.

Midway *(S.13;T.10N;R.11E.uns)*

A low pass, elevation 4,420 ft., over Cascade Mountain summit, between northeast Skamania County and Yakima Indian Reservation, 5 miles south of Walupt Lake, southwest Yakima County. An unimproved road leads into the Yakima Indian Reservation, but is not open to the public. It is used by Yakima Indians during the huckleberry season. The Indian name is *Wal-kva-veet*, meaning "the place where the trail goes over," or "up and down trail." The name now used was devised by U.S. Indian Service officials, and indicates that this gap is midway between very high mountain elevations to the south and north.

Miles *(S.20;T.28N;R.36E)*

Settlement on Spokane River, 2 miles from its confluence with the Columbia, north central Lincoln County. In 1939, when the nearby town of Lincoln was flooded by Grand Coulee Dam, most of its population moved to Miles. It was named for Gen. Nelson A. Miles, Indian fighter and Spanish-American war hero. On October 4, 1877, he accepted the surrender of Chief Joseph, Nez Perce warrior, at Bear Paw, Montana, terminating the Nez Perce War. Gen. Miles, at one time also commanded the Department of the Columbia.

Miles Range *(Ts.26-29N;Rs.4-6W)*

A 22-mile-long mountain grouping extending north from Mt. Constance, Jefferson County to Mt. Angeles (Mt. Sherman), Clallam County, following a northwesterly direction. In 1890, this grouping was conceived by Lieut. Joseph P. O'Neil as a distinct range. It is one of three "ranges" which he described, but which were not recognized as such. The name was also chosen by Lieut. O'Neil, and was for Maj. Gen. Nelson A Miles. (*see* Miles)

Milham Pass *(T.30N;Rs.17,18E.uns)*

A pass on Chelan Ridge at the head of Snowbrushy Creek, getween Pinnacle Mt. and Saska Peak, on the boundary between Chelan and Wenatchee National Forests, north central Chelan County. It was named by Forest Supervisor A. H. Sylvester for George W. Milham, former supervisor of Chelan National Forest.

Military Road

The coastal route from Fort Steilacoom to Bellingham Bay, Pierce, King, Snohomish, Skagit, and Whatcom counties. In 1856, it was built by local military and civilian personnel, with an assisting appropriation of $10,000 from Congress. The purpose was to allow movement of military forces during the Indian troubles. Parts of the route are still used in the present road system of Pierce and King counties.

Military Road

A military wagon road which crossed the Cascades at Naches Pass and which terminated at Steilacoom to the west, Walla Walla to the east, Pierce and Walla Walla counties. In 1855, it was built by "the people of northern Oregon." The road was discontinued after the Indian troubles subsided, and when better roads were built.

Milk Creek *(T.17N;Rs.14,15E)*

The stream of the creek rises in Milk Lake, extreme southwest Klickitat County; flows 7 miles west to Naches River at Little Naches Camp, Snoqualmie National Forest. The name is for a strong discoloration of the water by a heavy burden of fine clay which the stream carries in flood season.

Milk Creek *(Ts.31,32N;R.14E.uns)*

The stream of the creek rises in Mica Lake, northwest slope of Glacier Peak in a heavily glaciated area, Snohomish County; flows 6 miles northwest to Suiattle River. The name was given because of the milky color of the stream, due to a heavy burden of glacial flour.

Milk Shakes *(T.6N;R.39E)*

Twin buttes in the Blue Mountains, close to the Oregon boundary, near Table Rock, Umatilla National Forest, southwest Columbia County. In the 1880s, this feature was named by male settlers because the formation resembled breasts in their imaginations. An alternate name is *Twin Tits*.

Millberg (Lewis County) *see* Coal Canyon

Mill Creek *(T. 10N;R.46E)*

The stream of this small creek enters Snake River from the west, about 4 miles above Asotin, Asotin County. This name was used because the firm of Starr & Atwood built a sawmill on the creek in the winter of 1862-1863.

Mill Creek *(T.26N;Rs.14,15E)*

The stream of the creek rises on the east slope of Cascade Mountain summit, 1-1/2 miles southeast of Stevens Pass, Wenatchee National Forest, southwest Chelan County; flows 4 miles northeast to Nason Creek west of Berne. Since before 1908, the name has been in local usage, with an indication that there was a water-powered sawmill on the creek in early days.

Mill Creek *(T.20N;R.17E)*

The stream of the creek rises on Teanaway Ridge; flows 2-1/2 miles east to Swauk Creek, near Liberty Ranger Station, central Kittitas County. Most of the ''Mill Creeks'' in the state were named because they powered sawmills or grist mills. This one is different -- it powered a miner's stamp mill in very early days.

Mill Creek *(T.12N;R.1E)*

The stream of the creek rises in high country on the west boundary of Snoqualmie National Forest, south central Lewis County; flows southwest to Cowlitz River, 3 miles west of Mayfield. Early names were *Hurd Creek* and *Salkum Creek*. The present name came into use when a sawmill was built near the creek's mouth, and a grist mill at the falls in the lower course of the stream.

Mill Creek *(T.13N;Rs.6,7,8W)*

The stream of the creek rises near Walville, central Pacific County; flows west by north to Willapa River, 3 miles southeast of Raymond. In 1856, the creek was named for a water-powered sawmill built near the creek's mouth by Daniel Wilson.

Mill Creek *(Ts.34,35N;R.7E)*

The stream of the creek rises in mountains south of Birdsview, central Skagit County; flows 5 miles north to Skagit River near Birdsview. In 1878, it was named for Minkler-Savage water-powered sawmill which was the first in that district.

Mill Creek *(Ts.36-37N;Rs.39-41E)*

The stream of the creek heads north of Little Round Top Mountain, north central Stevens County; flows southwest via Pinkney City, 20 miles to the Colville River near Palmers. It draws a sweeping semi-circle around Mt. Colville, north of Colville. This was an important source of water power in early days, furnishing the thrust for at least one grist mill and two sawmills. Earlier names for this creek were *Pe-Tah-Shin, Riviere du Cedrier, Cedar Creek* and *Morgeau's Creek.*

Mill Creek *(T.8N;Rs.4,5W)*

The stream of the creek rises north of Waterford, southeast Wahkiakum County; flows east to Columbia River at Oak Point, Cowlitz County. It was named for a water-powered mill which was built at the mouth of the creek in 1848 by Alexander S. Abernethy.

Mill Creek *(Ts.6,7N;Rs.35,36,37E)*

The stream of the creek rises in the Blue Mountains, extreme northeast Oregon; flows north near Kookskooskie, then northwest, west, and southwest through Walla Walla to Walla Walla River, west of that city, Walla Walla County. Thirteen Washington counties have ''Mill Creeks,'' named after the large number of water-powered sawmills and gristmills established in pioneer days. Perhaps one of the most historic of these mills was the one which Marcus Whitman established on this Mill Creek, about 20 miles east of his mission. There he sawed most of the lumber which was used in buildings at Waiilatpu.

Mill Creek (Cowlitz County) *see* Abernethy Creek

Mill Creek (Grays Harbor County) *see* Beaver Creek

Mill Plain *(T.2N;R.2E)*

A plain 5 miles east of Vancouver, southwest Clark County. In 1824, this name was applied by Hudson's Bay Company. Until 1859, that company used this area for growing grain and operated a grist mill and sawmill between this place and the Columbia River.

Mill Point *(S.7;T.29N;R.1W)*

A west shore point of Port Discovery Bay, at the site of old Port Discovery, northeast Jefferson County. In 1854, a very large rock at this point, inscribed by members of the Vancouver Expedition in 1792, was blasted to provide foundation material for a sawmill. The name is for a large sawmill erected here by S. L. Mastick of San Francisco in 1854. Remains of the mill foundations may be found on the beach at low tides. In 1841, Cmdr. Charles Wilkes named this feature *Helix Point,* but his name did not become official. A name found on certain recent maps, in error, is *Nill Point* or *Point Nill.* These are distortions by cartographers.

Miller Bay *(Ss.9,16;T.26N;R.2E)*

A north extension of Port Madison Bay, north of Suquamish, north central Kitsap County. An early name for the bay was *Squaib.* The present name is reported to be for an early Indian trader.

Miller Creek *(T.25;R.12W)*

This tributary of Clearwater River rises between that stream and Hoh River, southwest Jefferson County; flows 9 miles southeast to the Clearwater. It was locally named for Loomis A. Miller, who homesteaded here in 1902.

Miller Creek *(T.38N;R.13E)*

This small tributary of Stetattle Creek rises 3 miles northwest of Diablo Dam, Mt. Baker National Forest, southeast Whatcom County. It was named for Peter H. Miller, who prospected and mined here from 1895 until 1898.

Miller Peninsula *(Ts.29,30N;Rs.2,3W)*

A 4-6 mile-long area between Port Discovery and Sequim bays, northeast Clallam County, northwest Jefferson County. There is little population here. It was named for an early settler and logger.

Miller (Millers) Point (Island County) *see* Point Polnell

Miller River *(S.28;T.26N;R.11E)*

Settlement at the confluence of Miller and Skykomish rivers, 2-1/2 miles northwest of Skykomish, northeast King County. At the turn of the century, this town boomed, but it is now almost abandoned. Originally it was a center for mining and prospecting. The first name was *Berlin,* as applied by Great Northern Railway officials for German assistance in building the railway westward to Puget Sound. When the U.S. declared war on Germany in WWI, the name was changed to that of the river on which it is located.

Millersylvania State Park
(Ss.26,27,34,25;T.17N;R.2W)

An 833-public park on Deep lake, 11 miles south of Olympia, central Thurstona County. The park offers camping, swimming, fishing, and boating. It is named for Frederich Miller, an Austrian who built a fine estate on Deep Lake, and who donated 720 acres to the state for park purposes.

Millerton .(S.1;T.39N;R.3E)

Small settlement 1/1-2 miles southwest of Nooksack, 1/2 mile west of Nooksack River, northwest Whatcom County. It was named for W. L. Miller, who platted the townsite, and who was mayor of New Whatcom in 1892.

Millington (Stevens County) *see* Bossburg

Mills Canyon *(T.25N;R.20E)*

This canyon heads 7 miles southwest of Entiat; runs 4-1/2 miles northeast to Entiat River, southwest Chelan County. It carries a stream which is the last large tributary of Entiat River. Local residents state that it was named for an early settler, although there is a record of a sawmill in the canyon which ran from 1911 to 1920.

Milltown *(S.31;T.31N;R.4E)*

Originally a steamboat landing on Douglas Slough (until that waterway dried up), on the Skagit Delta, extreme southwest Skagit County. The place is between several sloughs which are outlets of Skagit River. In the 1890s, it was locally named because there were 4 sawmills and shingle mills, one of which operated until 1920.

Millwood *(Ss.5-8;T.25N;R.44E)*

Suburban community in Spokane Valley, 4 miles east of Spokane, central Spokane County. In 1900, it was chosen as a station by Spokane-Coeur d'Alene Electric Railway, and was named *Woodward's* for the family who owned the land along this part of the railway route. When Inland Empire Paper Company built a paper mill here, they requested a name change to *Milltown*. Railway officials refused the change unless the Woodward family agreed. A compromise resulted, using the word *mill* combined with the first four letters of Woodward.

Milton (Milltown) (King County) *see*

West Seattle

Milton Mills (Columbia County) *see* Longs

Mima *(S.16;T.16N;R.3W)*

Small settlement 10 miles west of Tenino, on Mima Prairie, southwest Thurston County. It takes its name from Mima Prairie. That Indian name has the meaning of *A little farther along.*

Mima Creek *(T.16N;R.3W)*

The stream of the creek heads 1-1/2 miles northeast of Bordeaux; flows 5 miles southwest to Black River, southwest Thurston County. (*see* Mima)

Mima Mounds *(T.16N;R.3W)*

A geological puzzle, consisting of spaced, rounded mounds of gravel and silt, 7-70 ft. in diameter, on an old glacial moraine, on Mima Prairie, southwest of Bordeaux, southwest Thurston County. The mounds are not confined to this prairie, but extend for miles to the south and east. (*see* Mima)

Mima Prairie *(T.16N;R.3W)*

A flat prairie covered with mysterious, post-glacial Mima Mounds, west of Mima Creek, 10 miles west of Tenino, southwest Thurston County. (*see* Mima; Mima Mounds)

Mineral *(S.9;T.14N;R.5E)*

A small logging and shingle mill village on Mineral Lake, 14 miles north of Morton, north central Lewis County. Once it had several producing mines in the vicinity; the ore was used for production of arsenic. It was named for mineral deposits along Mineral Creek, and producing mines 6 miles from the town.

Mineral Creek *(Ts.13,14N;Rs.5,6E)*

The stream of the creek rises 5 miles north of Randle; flows northwest to Nisqually River, 2 miles east of Lake Alder, north central Lewis County. It was named for mineral deposits along the creek, some of which were worked before the turn of the century.

Mineral Hill *(S.34;T.36N;R.24E)*

A 6,500-ft. peak between Salmon Creek and the South Fork of that stream, 2-1/2 miles northwest of Conconully, central Okanogan County. Its name stems back to prospectors who combed this heavily-mineralized country in the late 1880s.

Mineral Lake *(Ss.3,4;T.14N;R.5E)*

A 1-mile-long lake, 2 miles south of

Elbe, north central Lewis County. It is used for log dump and storage. In 1857, it was charted by the surveyor general of Washington Territory as *Goldsboro Lake*. In the late 1890s, the present name was substituted when mineral deposits were discovered along Mineral Creek.

Mineral Mountain (Mt. Rainier National Park)

A north slope peak of Mt. Rainier, overlooking Mystic Lake, north central area of the park. The peak is located at the head of West Fork, White River, between Carbon and Winthrop glaciers. The name chosen by Park officials is appropriate, because prospectors found much evidence of mineral deposits before the park was established. (USBGN)

Miner's Creek (Skagit County) *see* Suiattle River

Miners Creek *(T.27N;R.18E)*

The stream of the creek heads on Miners Ridge, 9 miles east of Wenatchee Lake; flows northwest and north to Mad River, 1 mile southeast of Maverick Peak, Wenatchee National Forest, central Chelan County. It was named by sheepmen for many early prospectors who were in this area in early days.

Miners Ridge *(T.27N;R.18E)*

A 4-1/2-mile-long ridge which parallels Miners Creek on the northeast, 7-1/2 miles east of Wenatchee Lake, central Chelan County. This ridge forms the watershed between Miners Creek and Mad River. (*see* Miners Creek)

Miners Ridge
(Ss.5,6;T.31N;R.14E;S.1;
T.31N;R.13E.uns)

A high ridge on the northeast slope of Glacier Peak, 2 miles west of Cascade Mountain summit, Mt. Baker National Forest, northeast Snohomish County. It is used as a forest fire lookout in season. In pioneer days, it was locally named when there was a great deal of prospecting in this area and on the ridge itself.

Mink Lake *(S9;T.28N;R.9W.uns)*

A 10-acre, Olympic National Park lake, 1-1/2 miles south of Sol Duc Hot Springs, south central Clallam County. The lake is named for Mink Creek, which both feeds and drains it.

Minkler *(S.13;T.35N;R.5E)*

Small settlement directly north of Skagit River, between Lyman and Sedro

Woolley, west central Skagit County. In 1897, the place was named for an early sawmill operator on the upper Skagit River, Birdsley D. Minkler, by his family.

Minkler Lake *(Ss.13,14;T.35N;R.5E)*

A lake on the north side of Skagit River, between Lyman and Sedro Woolley, west central Skagit County. (*see* Minkler)

Minnehaha Creek *(T.18N;R.10E)*

The stream of the creek rises on Dalles Ridge, near the northeast corner of Mt. Rainier National Park, northeast Pierce County; flows 4 miles northwest to White River. The first name of this stream was *Dalles Creek.* It later was changed by local residents to the present name, which was taken from the heroine of Longfellow's *The Song of Hiawatha.*

Minnesota Reef *(T.35N;R.2W)*

A rock ledge, partly uncovered at low tide, on the east shore of San Juan Island, east end of Madrona Peninsula, near Turn Island, San Juan County. It was named by Prof. Josephine E. Tilden of the University of Minnesota, while attending sessions at the Puget Sound Marine Station near Friday Harbor. She named it for her home state, although the name is unofficial and is not shown on any maps or charts.

Minnick *(S.13;T.8N;R.37E)*

Railroad station 11 miles northeast of Walla Walla, southeast Walla Walla County. The name was applied by Northern Pacific officials in honor of 2 brothers who were prominent local farmers.

Minnow Creek *(T.28N;R.17E)*

The stream of the creek rises on the south slope of Basalt Peak; flows 4 miles southeast to Chiwawa River, Wenatchee National Forest, northwest Chelan County. It was so named by Forest Ranger Rush J. Huston because fish in the creek are very small.

Minor Island *(unsurveyed)*

A very small, low island in the Strait of Juan de Fuca, near Smith Island, 7 miles west of Whidbey Island, extreme western Island County. At low tide the island is connected with Smith Island by a rocky ridge. In 1854, it was named by U.S. Coast Survey. The name chosen was for the minor value and appearance of the islet. In 1791, Lieut. Francisco de Eliza called this feature, together with Smith Island, *Islas de Bonilla.*

Minotaur Lake
(Ss.12,13;T.27N;R.14E)

A Wenatchee National Forest lake on the southeast side of Labyrinth Mountain, between Lake and Rainy creeks, directly west of Theseus Lake, northwest Chelan County. It was named by Forest Supervisor A. H. Sylvester in conjunction with Theseus Lake and Labyrinth Mountain, following the Greek mythology of Minotaur slain by Theseus in a labyrinth.

Minter *(S.28;T.22N;R.1E)*

Settlement on the west shore of Carr Inlet, 8 miles northwest of Point Defiance. In 1882, this small place was named for the first permanent settler.

Minter River (Cowlitz County) *see* Owl Creek

Mirror Lake (Skamania County) *see* Looking Glass Lake

Mirror Lake (Snohomish County) *see* Image Lake

Mirror Lake *(T.31N;R.18E.uns)*

An Okanogan National Forest lake in Tumble Creek, 5 miles southwest of Lucerne, north central Chelan County. It was named by A. L. Cool, a local resident, as a descriptive term for the clear body of water.

Mirror Lake *(S.7;T.21N;R.4E)*

A lake 1-1/2 miles east of Puget Sound, 5-1/2 miles south of Des Moines, southwest King County. This descriptive name was applied by early settlers around the lake. An earlier name was *French Lake*

Mirror Lakes *(Mt. Rainier National Park)*

A group of 4 small lakes on the southwest slope of Mt. Rainier, west of Indian Henrys Hunting Ground, 1/2 mile south of the foot of South Tahoma Glacier, 5-1/4 miles southwest of the summit. The lakes were given this name because they offer the most perfect mountain reflections of any found in the park.

Misery Point *(S.17;T.25N;R.1W)*

An entrance point to Seabeck Bay on Hood Canal, southwest Kitsap County. In 1841, it was charted as *Scabock Point* by the Wilkes Expedition in an attempt to imitate the Indian name *L-ka-buk-hu.* The present name is locally applied, and one of many such names in the state which reflect pioneer hardships.

Misery Spring *(S.35;T.8N;R.42E)*

An Umatilla National Forest spring in Blue Mountains, at the head of Tucannon River, south Garfield County. The name comes from nearby Mt. Misery, and reflects the hardships of early stockmen in the high Blue Mountain country.

Mishall Creek (Pierce County) *see* Mashel River

Mission (Chelan County) *see* Cashmere

Mission (Okanogan County) *see* St. Marys Farm

Mission Beach *(S.27;T.30N;R.4E)*

A popular fishing resort on Tulalip Bay, Tulalip Indian Reservation, 4 miles west of Marysville, Snohomish County. In 1858, the name was for the Tulalip Catholic Mission established at nearby Priest Point by Father E. C. Chirouse.

Mission Prairie (Pierce County) *see* American Prairie

Mission Lake *(S.32;T.24N;R.1W)*

One of a group of 3 lakes which drain to Hood Canal via Mission Creek, 9 miles west of Bremerton, west central Kitsap County. Mission Lake totals 87.7 acres in area. Panther and Tiger lakes are partly in Mason County. This lake is named for Mission Creek, which drains it.

Mist Park *(Mt. Rainier National Park)*

A flowering meadow which extends northwest toward Mother Mountain, at the headwaters of Cataract Creek, 1-1/4 miles east of Mowich Lake, northwest sector of the park. The name is descriptive, as brawling Cataract Creek creates a continuous cloud of mist along its channel.

Mitchell's Peak (Skamania County) *see* Mt. Mitchell)

Mitchell Point *(S.34;T.30N;R.35E)*

A high point of land which gives an excellent panorama of the Columbia River, on the west side of Franklin D. Roosevelt Lake, 5 miles north of the mouth of the Spokane River, southeast Ferry County., It is reported to have been named for an early settler in this neighborhood.

Mock *(S.16;T.22N;R.41E)*

Small village, 5-1/2 miles southwest of Cheney, southwest Spokane County. It was named by railroad officials for W.

C. Mock, chief draftsman in the engineers' office of S.P.&S. Railway Company.

Moclips *(S.8;T.20N;R.12W)*

Community on Pacific Ocean, at the mouth of Moclips River, 28 miles northwest of Hoquiam, west central Grays Harbor County. It is a center of cedar shingle and shake manufacturing. The name is a variation of the Quinault *No-mo-Klopish*, meaning "people of the turbulent water." (USBGN)

Moclips River *(Ts.20,21N;Rs.11,12W)*

A Quinault Indian Reservation river, heading in swamps and flowing southwest 12 miles to Pacific Ocean at Moclips, west central Grays Harbor County. (*see* Moclips) (USBGN)

Moe Canyon *(T.26N;Rs.19,20E)*

The canyon heads 7 miles southwest of Ardenvoir, central Chelan County; runs 3-1/2 miles northeast to Entiat River, Chelan County. It was named by local usage for a family who once lived at the mouth of the canyon.

Mohler *(S.18;T.22N;R.36E)*

Community 6 miles southwest of Harrington, south Lincoln County. It was named for Morgan Mohler, an early-day stage driver before the railroads came into this region.

Mohr Canyon *(T.23N;R.23E)*

A canyon 6 miles north of Palisades, southwest Douglas County. It was probably named for John Mohr, who homesteaded in this region in the early 1880s.

Mold *(S.7;T.26N;R.28E)*

Community 9 miles north of Coulee City, east Douglas County. On April 11, 1899, it was named by Marshall McLean, the first postmaster when the post office was established. The name is descriptive of the rich soil in this area, as well as being a short name for postal purposes.

Molson *(S.8;T.40N;R.29E)*

This place, scarcely classifying as a town since the mining boom faded, is 25 miles east of Oroville, 2 miles south of the Canadian boundary, northeast Okanogan County. In 1900, it was founded by the manager of a mining company, George B. Mechem. It was named for the president of this company, John W. Molson. The company's business name was Colville Reservation Syndicate.

Monaghan Rapids *(Ts.30-33N;Rs.30,31E)*

Rapids 12-14 miles downstream from the site of Grand Coulee Dam, near the mouth of Nespelem River, southeast Okanogan County. These rapids, like many similar features along the Columbia River, have been modifed by higher water levels created by hydroelectric dams. In 1881, the name was applied by Lieut. Thomas W. Symons, USA, to honor James Monaghan of Chewelah, who encountered trouble in these rapids in 1879-1880, when he brought rafts of lumber and supplies to a military camp near the mouth of the Okanogan River.

Mona Lake (King County) *see* Lizard Lake

Mondovi *(S.9;T.25N;R.38E)*

Small community 8 miles east of Davenport, northeast Lincoln County. In 1881, the name was chosen by Elihu B. Gifford when a post office was established. In May, 1878, Gifford had traveled overland in a wagon train to Spokane with about 40 others from the village of Mondovi, Wisconsin. He later moved to this new settlement in Lincoln County. Gifford was a scholarly man for his time and evidently had been instrumental in naming the Wisconsin town for a town in northwest Italy where Napoleon defeated Sardinian forces on April 22, 1796.

Money Creek *(T.26N;Rs.10,11E)*

The stream of the creek rises in Elizabeth Lake, Snoqualmie National Forest, 5 miles south of Baring, northeast King County; flows 6-1/2 miles east to South Fork, Skykomish River. It was named in early mining days by local miners because of the large sums of money spent by eastern interests in developing a mine on the creek.

Monitor *(S.14;T.23N;R.19E)*

Community 6-1/2 miles northwest of Wenatchee on Wenatchee River, southeast Chelan County. The name was chosen by townsite platters for reasons which are not of record, and which appear to have no local significance. Prior to platting, the place was known as *Brown's Flats*.

Monohan *(S.7;T.24N;R.6E)*

Area 4 miles north of Issaquah, on the east shore of Lake Sammamish, northwest King County. The place was locally named for Martin Monohon, who settled here in 1871 and who farmed here in 1871, and for the rest of his life. The error in spelling has been repeated by cartographers for many years, although it is entirely incorrect.

Monohon (King County) *see* Monohan

Monroe (Island County) *see* Monroe Landing

Monroe *(S.1;T.27N;R.6E)*

Town 13 miles southeast of Everett on Skykomish River, southwest Snohomish County. Located here is the Washington State Reformatory. In 1873, it was called *Park Place* by Salem Wood when he founded the settlement. In 1889, it was re-named *Monroe* by John Vanasdlen when he filed a townsite plat, and that name applied to the post office. Park Place continues to exist as a suburb. The post office name, and name of the first plat was for James Monroe, 5th president of the U.S. Adjacent areas, associated with Monroe, were named *Wales* and *Tyre* or *Tyre City*.

Monroe Landing *(S.21;T.32N;R.1E)*

Beach on the north shore of Penn Cove, directly opposite Coupeville, east side of Whidbey Island, central Island County. It was locally named for A. W. Monroe, who owned land here, and who built a substantial dock which no longer exists. On modern maps the place is shown as *Monroe*

Monse *(S.34;T.31N;R.25E)*

Hamlet 7 miles northeast of Brewster, 3-1/2 miles north of the Columbia River, south central Okanogan County. Its first name was *Swanson*, which later was altered to *Swansea*. On October 24, 1916, during WWI, citizens changed it to the present name in commemoration of a valiant defeat suffered by British forces at the Battle of Mons in Belgium. The final *e* was added in error, but persists.

Montborne *(S.6;T.33N;R.5E)*

Small community on the east side of Big Lake (lake), 8 miles south of Sedro Woolley, southwest Skagit County. It was named locally for Dr. H. P. Montborne, who established himself here in 1884. The Seattle, Lake Shore & Eastern Railway used the name for their station when it was built in 1890.

Monte *(S.30;T.11N;R.20E)*

A siding between Toppenish and

Yakima, east central Yakima County. It is reported to have been named by Northern Pacific Railway construction engineers, because the section gang which built the siding at this place played three-card monte in off hours.

Monte Celle (Cowlitz County) *see* Monticello

Monte Cristo *(S.21;T.29N;R.11E)*

Old mining town at the head of South Fork, Sauk River, Mt. Baker National Forest, east central Snohomish County. It is in a heavily mineralized area and is most widely known as a ghost town in western Washington. In 1889, the name was applied by J. Bishop and Fred and Mack Williams when they discovered a wide vein of galena ore. Their name was in comparison with the fabled wealth of the Count of Monte Cristo.

Monte Cristo Lake
(S.29;T.30N;R.11E)

A 14-acre lake, elevation 1,970 ft., 5 miles north of Monte Cristo, east central Snohomish County. (*see* Monte Cristo)

Monte Cristo Peak
(S.26;T.29N;R.11E)

A 7,100-ft., glaciated peak, Snoqualmie National Forest, 2 miles east-by-south of Monte Cristo, southeast Snohomish County. It was named by The Mountaineers for the nearby Monte Cristo mines. An alternate name, used on certain maps, is *Wilmon Peaks.(see* Monte Cristo)

Montesano *(T.17N;R.7W)*

Town 8 miles east of Aberdeen, on Chehalis River near the mouth of Wynooche River, central Grays Harbor County. In 1862, the name *Mount Zion* was suggested by the religious wife of the first settler, J. L. Scammon. Another pioneer, Samuel James, suggested the present name from the Spanish *monte* or "mountain," and *sano* or "health." Local authorities thought Sam's name had more meaning.

Montgomery Ridge *(S.25;T.8N;R.46E)*

This ridge parallels Montgomery Gulch, 3-4 miles west of Snake River, southeast Asotin County. It bears the name of B. C. Montgomery, one of the first settlers in this area.

Monticello *(T.8N;R.2W)*

This vanished town was on the Cowlitz River, on the present site of

Longview, south Cowtliz County. It was the first town in the county and an important place. It was named by H. D. ("Uncle" Darby) Huntington who lived here in 1852, for his home town in Indiana. An alternate name was *Mount Solo.*

Monument *(S.16;T.13N;R.34E)*

Area in Devils Canyon, 2-1/2 miles south of Kahlotus, southeast Franklin County. It was named for a distinctive rock formation in Devils Canyon called *Devils Pulpit and Monument.*

Monument Butte *(S.12;T.32N;R.37E0*

A bald hill, elevation 2,098 ft., on the Colville Indian Reservation, 2 miles south-by-west of Inchelium, east central Ferry County. The name origin traces back to early miners who used it as a landmark, and who built stone pillars on the summit to make it distinctly visible.

Monument Mountain (Ferry County) *see* Monument Butte

Moody Point (Pierce County) *see* Johnson Point

Moody's Camp (Skagit County) *see* Belfast

Moohool (Wahkiakum County) *see* Grays River

Moolock Lakes *(S.22;T.24N;R.9E)*

Three lakes, 7-1/2 miles northeast of North Bend, central King County. The lakes are called *Lake Moolock, Lake Nadeau,* and *SMC Lake. Moolock* is the Chinook Indian term for "elk."

Moon Mountain *(T.32;Rs.35-36E)*

A 3,888-ft. peak on the Colville Indian Reservation, directly south of Round Lake, east central Ferry County. It is used as a fire lookout in season and named for a man who homesteaded land at the foot of the mountain, near Round Lake.

Moonax *(S.31;T.24N;R.22E)*

Hamlet on north bank of Columbia River, 34 miles east of Goldendale, southeast Klickitat County. The name evidently traces back to the Lewis and Clark expedition, which found a pet woodchuck in an Indian camp here. The Indian name for woodchuck is *Moonax.*

Moore (Adams County) *see* Coker

Moore *(S.28;T.32N;R.18E.uns)*

Resort on the east shore of Lake Chelan, 5-1/2 miles south of Stehekin,

north central Chelan County. It was named for J. Robert Moore who homesteaded the land and who built and operated a summer hotel here.

Moores Bluff (Pierce County) *see* Devils Head

Moose Creek *(T.32N;Rs.8,9E)*

The stream of the creek heads 2 miles southeast of Fortson, Mt. Baker National Forest, north central Snohomish County; flows northeast and north 3 miles to North Fork, Stillaguamish River near Shomer. The creek was named for the Bull Moose limestone claims at its head.

Moose Lake *(S.32;T.28N;R.5W)*

An Olympic National Park lake at the head of Grand Creek, 15 miles south of Port Angeles, southeast Clallam County. The lake was named by an early settler for his hunting partner, Frank Moose.

Mora *(S.22;T.28N;R.15W)*

A fishing village, with many resident Indians, on Quillayute River, 1-1/2 miles from the river's mouth, extreme southwest Clallam County. The first name of the settlement was *Boston,* as applied to the post office by Mr. and Mrs. Frank T. Balch, pioneers. It was changed to the present name because of postal confusion with Boston, Massachusetts. The present name was suggested by K. O. Erickson, a Clallam County pioneer, for Mora Parish, Dalarna, Sweden.

Moraine Lake *(S.11;T.35N;R.13E)*

A 52-acre, glacier-fed lake, elevation 4,500 ft., 2-1/4 miles southeast of Eldorado, east central Skagit County. It was aptly named, as it lies in a moraine at the foot of Inspiration Glacier.

Moraine Park *(Mt. Rainier National Park)*

A north slope park of Mt. Rainier, east of Moraine Creek, between Carbon Glacier and Old Desolate (mountain), north central zone of the park. This descriptive name was chosen by Prof. I. C. Russell. The park is a succession of glacial moraines along the east side of lower Carbon Glacier. (USBGN)

Moran Prarie *(T.24N;R.43E)*

A prairie and small town directly south of the southeast limits of Spokane, central Spokane County. Both were named for a pioneer settler, Joseph Moran.

Moran State Park *(T.37N;R.1W)*

A 4,804-acre area on the east peninsula of Orcas Island, including Mt. Constitution, Mountain Lake, and Cascade Lake, San Juan County. It was donated to the state by the famous ship builder, Robert Moran, who also served as mayor of Seattle for 2 terms. The park offers both fresh and saltwater recreational facilities. It was named for the donor.

Morgan (Ferry County) *see* Orient

Morganrath Lake (Clallam County) *see* Soleduck Lake

Morganroth Lake
(S.19;T.28N;R.8W.uns)

In Seven Lakes Basin, a 10-acre, Olympic National Park lake (one of 8 in the basin -- not 7, as the name indicates), northeast of Bogachiel Peak, south central Clallam County. The name is reported to be for a pioneer who trapped and prospected here.

Morgenroth Lake (Clallam County) *see* Soleduck Lake

Morical Canyon *(T.26N;R.20E)*

A Wenatchee National Forest canyon, extending 3-1/2 miles northeast from Entiat River, 7 miles west of Columbia River, east central Chelan County. The name developed by local usage, and is for the Morical family who lived at the canyon's mouth.

Morocco (Lincoln County) *see* Mohler

Morovitz Creek *(Ts.37,38N;Rs.8,9E)*

The stream of the creek rises at the foot of Park Glacier, east slope of Mt. Baker, Mt. Baker National Forest, south central Whatcom County; flows 4-1/2 miles southeast to Swift Creek. It was named for Joe Morovitz, a Swiss rancher, hunter, and prospector who was called "The Hermit of Baker Lake." In some records the name is spelled *Morovits.*

Morovitz Lake *(S.30;T.38N;R.9E)*

A 2-acre beaver pond, elevation 1,200 ft., in Beaver Creek, near the east slope of Mt. Baker, south central Whatcom County. It was named for Morovitz Creek. *(see* Morovitz Creek)

Morristown (Pierce County) *see* Spiketown

Morse Creek *(Ts.29,30N;R.5W)*

The stream of the creek rises in Olympic National Park, east central Clallam County; flows east and north to Strait of Juan de Fuca, 2 miles east of Port Angeles. The stream was named for David Waterman Morse, a pioneer storekeeper, who was born on Morse Creek on April 19,1863.

Morse (Morses) Island (San Juan County) *see* Battleship island

Morton (S.35;T.13N;R.0E)

A logging and sawmill town on Tilton River, 33 miles east of Chehalis, central Lewis County6 It holds an annual celebration based on logging contests. The town was named by pioneer H. G. Temple for Levi P. Morton, vice-president of the U.S. from 1889 until 1893. In 1891, the name was applied when a post office was established.

Moscow (Lincoln County) *see* Bluestem

Moses Coulee *(Ts.20-27N;Rs.22-26E)*

This coulee heads in central Douglas County; runs southwest about 50 miles through center of county to Columbia River, extreme south tip of the county. It is a large coulee with intermittent streams, formed in prehistorical times by glacial action. It is named for Chief Moses, a famous Indian warrior and diplomat, who favored the coulee as a winter camp, usually at the mouth of Douglas Canyon. An alternate name was *Little Coulee.*

Moses Coulee *(S.13;T.21N;R.22E)*

Hamlet 1-1/2 miles east of Columbia River, in Moses Coulee, at the extreme south tip of Douglas County. It derives its name from the coulee in which it is located.

Moses Lake
(Ts.18,19,20N;Rs.27,28E)

An irregular body of water, with many channels, directly north of Potholes Reservoir, southeast Grant County. It is shallow, with a maximum depth of 30 ft., average width between 1/2 and 1/4 mile. A former name was *Salt Lake.* *(see* Moses Lake)

Moses Lake
(Ss.14-16,21-23;T.19N;R.28E)

City on east shore of Moses Lake (lake), east central Grant County. The town is thriving due to local prosperity based on many thousands of acres of irrigated land. It was named for the lake, which was named for Chief Moses,

warrior and diplomat. His tribe used the shores of the lake as campgrounds for many generations. An earlier name was *Neppel.*

Moses Lake Air Force Base (Grant County) *see* Larson Air Force Base

Moses Lake State Park *(T.18N;R.28E)*

A 15-acre park, 4 miles south of Moses lake, south central Grant County. It offers swimming, fishing, and general recreation and is named for Moses Lake. *(see* Moses Lake)

Mosquito Bay (Kitsap County) *see* Manzanita Bay

Mosquito Flat *(Mt. Rainier National Park)*

A stretch of level ground, elevation 4,400 ft., east of Natural Bridge, directly south of Lakes Ethel and James, north central area of the park. The name was chosen by park officials and is sadly descriptive, at least during warmer periods. (USBGN)

Mosquito Island (Pierce County) *see* Pitt Island

Mosquito Lake *(S.23;T.38N;R.5E)*

A lake 10 miles west of Mt. Baker, 1 mile west of Middle Fork, Nooksack River, west central Whatcom County. In 1885, the lake was named by Charles M. Park, the original surveyor of the area, when his crew ws driven frantic by mosquitoes.

Mosquito Lake (King County) *see* Summit Lake

Mosquito Lakes *(S.2;T.7N;R.8E.uns)*

Two small lakes in a marshy area, 14 miles north of Trout Lake, central Skamania County. Big Mosquito Lake covers 24. 6 acres; Little Mosquito Lake has an area of 5 acres. The name is said to be quite descriptive, as mosquitoes breed heavily in stagnant marshes here.

Mosquito Ridge *(T.26N;R.19E)*

A Wenatchee National Forest ridge between Tillicum and Kloochman creeks, directly west of Ardenvoir, central Chelan County. The name, applied by sheepherders, appears to be quite descriptive.

Moss Lake (Lewis County) *see* Newukum Lakes

Mossyrock *(S.18;T.12N;R.3E)*

Town on Cowlitz River, 12 miles west of Morton, south central Lewis County. It is the site of a City of Tacoma hydroelectric dam. In 1852, it was named by an early settler, William Halland, for a mossy crag which rises 200 ft. above the east end of Klickitat Prairie.

Mossyrock Reservoir *(T.12N;R.3E)*

A planned hydroelectric pool in Cowlitz River, 21 miles east of Toledo, near the town of Mossyrock, central Lewis County. As designed by the City of Tacoma, this pool covers 10,200 acres, maximum depth 325 ft. It is named for Mossyrock. (*see* Mossyrock)

Mother Mountain *(Mt. Rainier National Park)*

A 6,540-ft. peak between Carbon and Mowich rivers, northwest of Cataract Creek, northwest area of the park. This extensive ridge is 2-1/2 miles long and was named in the distant past by Indians for the figure of a woman in rock on the northeast summit. It may be so recognized against the sky from Carbon River Trail, or by imaginative persons. (USBGN)

Mott Creek *(T.28N;R.19E)*

The stream of the creek runs 3 miles northeast from Tyee Mountain to Entiat River, Wenatchee National forest, central Chelan County. It was named by Forest Ranger James McKenzie for C. P. Mott who homesteaded at the creek's mouth.

Mottinger *(S.2;T.25N;R.29E)*

Railroad point on north bank of Columbia River, 21 miles south of Kennewick, extreme southeast Benton County. In 1906, it was named by officials of S.P.&S. Railway for the early homesteaders, G. H. and Martha Morttinger.

Mouat Reef (San Juan County) *see* Mouatt Reef

Mouatt Reef *(S.23;T.37N;R.3W)*

A southwest shore reef of Waldron Island, in Cowlitz Bay, north central San Juan County. In 1858, the reef was named by Capt. Henry Richards, British admiralty surveyor. It was in honor of Capt. William Alexander Mouatt, a famous ships' captain for Hudson's Bay Company in Pacific northwest waters. It is shown on some local maps, in error, as *Mouat Reef.*

Mound Prairie *(Ts.15,16N;Rs.2,3W)*

A flat prairie covered with conical "Mima Mounds," 6-7 ft. high, 30 ft. diameters, extending 6 miles northeast to southwest, north of Grand Mound, extreme southwest Thurston County. It was named for the great number of these mysterious earth mounds. Cmdr. Wilkes, who explored these mounds in 1841, called this feature *Bute Prairies.*

Mt. Abercrombie *(S.35;T.40N;R.42E)*

A Colville National Forest peak, elevation 7,308 ft., 17-1/2 miles west of the Pend Oreille River, extreme northeast Stevens County. This mountain is part of the watershed between the Columbia and Pend Oreille rivers and it is in a heavily mineralized area. It was named for Col. W. R. Abercrombie, who served in the Indian wars of 1877, and as a lieutenant in the U.S. Army, surveyed the Pend Oreille River in 1879 and 1883. In 1931, the naming was by act of the state legislature, one of the few features in Washington so named. Formerly it was called *Mt. Baldy.* (USBGN)

Mt. Adams *(Ts.8,9N;Rs.10,11E.uns)*

A 12,307-ft. volcanic peak in the Cascade Mountain range, northeast Skamania and southwest Yakima counties. The mountain has a central dome and 4 summits; it supports 8 major glaciers which feed a number of glacial streams. The Indian name was *Pah-too,* meaning "High sloping Mountain." In 1841, the present name was given by the Wilkes Expedition for John Adams, second president of the U.S.

Mt. Adams Lake *(S.20;T.9N;R.12E.uns)*

A 120-acre lake in a shallow crater of a mountain plateau, northeast slope of Mt. Adams, southwest Yakima County. This high mountain lake drains into Klickitat River through a branch of Clearwater Creek. It is accessible only by trail and is closed to public use by the Yakima Tribal Council. It was named for the nearby mountain. (*see* Mt. Adams)

Mt. Aix *(S.18;T.15N;R.13E.uns)*

A Snoqualmie National forest peak, elevation 7,805 ft., 5 miles southeast of Bumping Lake, northwest Yakima County. This high peak is reported to have been named for the town of Aix in southern France by The Mountaineers. (USBGN)

Mt. Anderson *(S.28;T.26N;R.5W)*

An Olympic National Park peak at the headwaters of Quinault River and West Creek, east central Jefferson County. The mountain is in a heavily-glaciated area and supports 4 live glaciers; it also has a double peak, East Anderson and West Anderson. In 1890, the mountain was named by a U.S. Army mapping party under Lieut. Joseph P. O'Neil of the 14th U.S. Infantry. He gave it the name of Maj. General T. M. Anderson, who was then the commandant at Vancouver Barracks, and O'Neil's commanding officer.

Mt. Angeles *(S.21;T.29N;R.6W.uns)*

An Olympic National Park peak, 8 miles south of Port Angeles, east central Clallam County. In 1885, this peak was named *Mt. Sherman* by Lieut. Joseph P. O'Neil on his first exploration of the Olympics. In 1890, on his second expedition, he reported that businessmen in Port Angeles had secured a change to the present name in order to advertise their city.

Mt. Ararat *(Mt. Rainier National Park)*

A 5,996-ft. peak west of Indian Henrys Hunting Ground, 5 miles northeast of Nisqually entrance, southwest corner of the park. The mountain lies between drainages of Tahoma and Pyramid creeks. The name was applied by Ben Longmire when he found pieces of petrified wood and a tree stump circled by an iron ring. Ben opined that the stump "Might have been used by Noah for mooring the Ark." (USBGN)

Mt. Baker *(Ts.37,38N;Rs.7,8E)*

A 10,778-ft., snow-covered peak, 27 miles east of Bellingham at the headwaters of Nooksack and Baker rivers, central Whatcom County. The mountain supports 12 glaciers and 44 sq. miles of ice fields. On April 30, 1792, the name was chosen by Capt. George Vancouver for one of his officers who discovered the peak, 3rd Lieut. Joseph Baker. A number of other names had been previously used by Indians and explorers. Nooksack Indians called it *Koma-Kulshan,* meaning "White, shining, steep mountain." Clallam Indians used the name "P-kowitz", meaning "White mountain." In 1790, Manuel Quimper charted it as *Gran Montana de Carmelo,* for a resemblance to the white robes of Carmelite monks. Other names were *Ko-ma-el,* used by Skagit Indians, *White Friar, Great White Watcher,* and the suggested names of Presidents Polk and Tyler.

Mt. Baker Lodge
(S.17;T.39N;R.9E.uns)

A chalet-type inn, a ski area, and a ski school, 4 miles west of Mt. Shuksan, near Austin Pass, central Whatcom County. (*see* Mt. Baker)

Mt. Baker Lodge Lakes (Whatcom County) *see* Picture Lake, Highwood Lake

Mt. Baker-Snoqualmie National Forest

This great federal forest stretches from the Canadian boundary for a distance of about 60 miles south through Whatcom, Skagit, and a part of Snohomish counties. It is joined to the Snoqualmie National Forest which meets it at the south extremity, and the Chelan and Wenatchee National forests on the east, just across the Cascade Mountain summit. This forest's 818,237 acres can produce about 140 million board feet of commercial timber annually on a sustained-yield basis. One-quarter of the values received from timber sales goes to the county in which these sales are made for school support and other public purposes. The forest was originally called *Washington National Forest*. When changed by Forest Service officials, it took the name from Mt. Baker. It is under the jurisdiction of Region 6 of the National Forest system, with headquarters in Portland, Oregon. (*see* Mt. Baker)

Mt. Baldy (Cowlitz County) *see* Mt. Davis

Mt. Baldy (Spokane County) *see* Mt. Spokane

Mt. Baring *(S.6;T.26N;R.11E)*

A 6,125-ft. peak at the head of Barclay Creek, 2-1/2 miles east of Baring, northeast King and southeast Snohomish counties. This mountain was named by The Mountaineers on a summer expedition, for one of the party. It is carried on some maps, in error, as *Baring Mt.*. (USBGN)

Mt. Barnes *(Ts.26,27N;R.7W)*

A peak at the head of Queets and Elwha rivers, 5-1/2 miles east of Mt. Olympus summit, north central Jefferson County. In 1890, it was named by Seattle Press Expedition for Capt. Charles Adams Barnes, topographer of the expedition, who made the first good map of the Olympic Mountain area.

Mt. Beljica *(S.17;T.15N;R.7E)*

A 5,486-ft. peak, 1 mile west of Mt. Rainier National Park boundary, 5 miles northeast of Ashford, southeast Pierce County. The first name was *Beljacka Mt.*, and is said to have been named by a pioneer settler named Messler, who used portions of the first names of his 2 daughters. A later name was *Baljica Peak*, and it is shown as *Mt. Beljica* on recent maps. Another name source which has been presented is reported to be a combination of the initials of a party of hikers who climbed the mountain in July, 1897.

Mt. Beljacka (Pierce County) *see* Mt. Beljicka

Mt. Bell (Clark County) *see* Bells Mountain

Mt. Blum *(Ss.26,27;T.38N;R.10E.uns)*

A Mt. Baker National Forest peak, 12 miles east of Mt. Baker, in the Baker River drainage area, east central Whatcom County. The peak was named for John Blum, a Forest Service airplane pilot on fire patrol in this area in 1930-1931. In 1931, he was killed in a crash near Snoqualmie Pass. On some maps, this peak is recorded as *Bald Mountain* in error.

Mt. Bonaparte
(Ss.13,14;T.38N;R.29E)

A Colville National Forest peak, elevation 7,280-ft., 3 miles west of Bonaparte lake, northeast Okanogan County. (*see* Bonaparte Lake)

Mt. Booker (Chelan County) *see Booker Mountain*

Mt. Bretherton
(Ss.29,32;T.25N;R.4W)

An Olympic National Park peak at the head of Delta Creek, southeast Jefferson County. In 1890, it was named by B. J. Bretherton, naturalist of Olympic Mountains Exploring Expedition. On some maps it is shown as *Mt. Brotherton* in error.

Mt. Brotherton (Jefferson County) *see* Mt. Bretherton

Mt. Bullen (Snohomish County) *see* Bullen Mountain

Mt. Carleton (Spokane County) *see* Mt. Spokane

Mt. Carrie *(T.28N;R.7W)*

The highest peak in the Bailey Range, elevation 7,020 ft., 8 miles

northeast of Mt. Olympus, south central Clallam County. It was named by Theodore Rixon of Dodwell-Rixon Survey, for Caroline Jones of Lake Crescent, whom he later married.

Mt. Challenger
(S.27;T.39N;R.11E.uns)

A Mt. Baker National Forest peak, elevation 8,296 ft., in the Picket Range, 12 miles east of Mt. Shuksan summit, east central Whatcom County. This is a steep, rugged, and highly glaciated peak. (*see* Mt. Terror)

Mt. Chatham *(S.3;T.28N;R.2W)*

A 2,250-ft. peak, 3 miles southwest of the south end of Port Discovery Bay, northeast Jefferson County. In 1855, it was named by the U.S. Coast Survey for Capt. George Vancouver's armed tender, *Chatham*. The Indian name of this mountain was ''O-oo-quah'', meaning ''crying baby,'' because of constant rainfall on the peak.

Mt. Christie
(Ss.34,35;T.26N;R.7W.uns)

An Olympic National Park peak, 10 miles southeast of Mt. Olympus, at the headwaters of North Fork, Quinault River, central Jefferson County. In 1890, it was named by the Seattle Press Expedition for their leader, James H. Christie.

Mt. Clay Wood (Jefferson County) *see* Mt. Claywood

Mt. Claywood *(S.30;T.27N;R.5W)*

An Olympic National Park peak at the head of Lost River, 15 miles east of Mt. Olympus summit, north central Jefferson County. In 1885, the peak was named by Lieut. Joseph P. O'Neil as *Mt. Clay Wood*, for Col. H. Clay Wood, assistant adjutant general, Department of the Columbia, who signed the orders for O'Neil's 1885 exploration of the Olympics. Since that time, the clay has evidently adhered to the wood.

Mt. Cleveland *(S.7;T.25N;R.11E)*

A 5,301-ft. peak, 4 miles south of Grotto, between Kimball Creek and West Fork, Miller River, northeast King County. It was named for Grover Cleveland when he was first elected president of the U.S. in 1891. The peak is called *Cleveland Mountain* on certain county maps.

Mt. Coffin *(T.8N;R.3W)*

A hill on the north bank of Columbia River, 5 miles below the mouth of

Cowlitz River, southwest Cowlitz County. It was a place for Indian burials before white men came to the vicinity and as recently as the late 1880s -- hence, the name.

Mt. Constance *(S.1;T.26N;R.4W.uns)*

An Olympic National Park peak, elevation 7,735 ft., at the headwaters of Tunnel Creek, east central Jefferson County. In 1856, this prominent peak was named by Capt. George Davidson of U.S. Coast Survey, for Constance Fauntleroy, a sister of Davidsons' fiancee, Ellinor.

Mt. Constitution *(T.37N;R.1W)*

A Moran State Park peak, elevation 2,454-ft., on the east peninsula of Orcas Island, northeast San Juan County. It is a noted lookout point, with a 52-ft. granite tower on the summit. In 1841, the mountain was named by Cmdr. Wilkes for the *U.S.S. Constitution* (*Old Ironsides*), famous in the War of 1812. The Indian name for the mountain was *Sweh-lagh*.

Mt. Colonel Bob (Grays Harbor County) *see* Colonel Bob Mountain

Mt. Dalles *(Ss.13,24;T.35N;R.4W)*

A San Juan Island peak, elevation 1,936 ft., 6 miles west of Friday Harbor, southwest part of the island, southwest San Juan County. The highest point of the island, this mountain was named by Capt. Henry Richards, RN, in 1858, for Alexander Grant Dallas, a director of Hudson's Bay Company and president of the Hudson's Bay Company Council in North America. Between May, 1857 and May 1862, he served at Victoria.

Mt. Dana *(S.31;T.27N;R.6W)*

An Olympic National Park peak, elevation, 6,209 ft., 10 miles east of Mt. Olympus, central Jefferson County. In 1890, it was named by Charles A. Barnes, historian for Seattle Press Expedition. He named it for Charles A. Dana, editor of the *New York Sun*, ''Because it stands out prominently and independently.''

Mt. David *(S.33;T.29N;R.15E.uns)*

A Wenatchee National Forest peak, on a ridge south of Indian Creek, 7-1/2 miles east of Cascade Mountain summit, northwest Chelan County. The name was applied by Forest Supervisor A. H. Sylvester. He also named Mt. Jonathan, 1 mile to the west, linking the 2 peaks

through Biblical history in his imaginative style.

Mt. Davis *(S.17;T.6N;R.2E)*

A peak between Kalama River and Lake Merwin, 10 miles northeast of Woodland, south central Cowlitz County. It was named for ''Uncle'' Nathan Davis who lived at Reno, south of the mountain.

Mt. Degenhardt *(T.38N;R.11E)*

A Mt. Baker National Forest peak in the Picket Range, west of Ross Lake, east central Whatcom County. It was named for William A. Degenhardt, former president of The Mountaineers and a member of the party which made the first ascent of the peak. He died in 1956. Alternate names are *Peak 8200* and *The Pyramid*.

Mt. Ditney *(Ss.5,6;T.31N;R.8E)*

A Mt. Baker National Forest peak, 5 miles south of Hazel at the head of Jim Creek, north central Snohomish County. The mountain and adjacent creek are reported to have been named in pioneer days for an early homesteading family.

Mt. Erie *(Ss.1,12;T.34N;R.1E)*

A 1,270-ft. peak, central Fidalgo Island, between Lakes Erie and Whistle. In 1841, the mountain was named by Cmdr. Charles Wilkes for Comm. Perry's victory in the Battle of Lake Erie during the War of 1812.

Mt. Fernox (Chelan County) *see* Fernow Mountain

Mt. Fernow *(S.11;T.26N;R.12E)*

A 6,190-ft. peak, 7 miles west of Stevens Pass, extreme northwest King County. It was named by Forest Service personnel for Dr. Bernhard E. Fernow, a German forester who was chief of the U.S. Division of Forestry from 1886-1898, and who initiated legislation to create ''Forest Reserves,'' the foundation of our national forests.

Mt. Fernow Potholes *(Ss.2,11;T.26N;R.12E)*

A group of 5 small lakes or potholes, average size 3 acres, directly north of Mt. Fernow, Snoqualmie National Forest, extreme northeast King County.(*see* Mt.Fernow)

Mt. Ferry *(T.27N;R.7W.uns)*

An Olympic National Park peak, 7 miles northeast of Mt. Olympus, north central Jefferson County. In April 27, 1899, the peak was named by members

of Seattle Press Expedition for Elisha P. Ferry, first governor of the state of Washington. A former name was *Mt. Henry*.

Mt. Finlayson *(S.7;T.34N;R.2W)*

A San Juan Island peak on the southeast tip of the island, northwest of Cattle Point, south central San Juan County. In 1858, it was charted under the present name by Capt. Henry Richards, RN. It was named for either Duncan or Roderick Finlayson of Hudson's Bay Company, both of whom were outstanding pioneers in the Pacific Northwest.

Mt. Fitzhenry *(T.28N;R.7W.uns)*

A 7,000-ft. peak between the headwaters of Elwha and Hoh Rivers, south central Clallam County; this is the most northerly peak of the Bailey Range and was named for E. A. Fitzhenry, who served as the state's surveyor general, county engineer of Clallam County, and in many similar capacities.

Mt. Forgotten *(Ss.7,18;T.30N;R.11E)*

A Mt. Baker National Forest peak, elevation 5,700 ft., 6 miles northeast of Silverton in Sauk River Valley, east central Snohomish County. In 1919, the name was chosen by a Forest Service trail-building crew, although it would seem difficult to forget this high mountain in a wide river valley.

Mt. Fromme *(S.30;T.27N;R.5W)*

An Olympic National Park peak, elevation 6,655 ft., 1 mile north of Hayden Pass and southeast of Mt. Claywood, central Jefferson County. The peak was named for R. L. Fromme, a former assistant supervisor of the U.S. Forest Service. (USBGN)

Mt. Fury *(Ss.1,2;T.38N;R.11E)*

A Mt. Baker National Forest peak, 10 miles northwest of Newhalem, in the Picket Range, east central Whatcom County. (*see* Mt. Terror)

Mt. Harrison (Mt. Rainier National Park) *see* Mt. Rainier

Mt. Henry (Jefferson County) *see* Mt. Ferry

Mt. Herman *(S.13;T.39N;R.8E)*

A Mt. Baker National Forest peak, 1-1/2 miles west of Mt. Baker Lodge, central Whatcom County. It was named for Binger Herman, a federal officer connected with the National Park Service. On some maps this mountain is shown as *Herman Peak*.

Mt. Higgins *(T.33N;R.8E)*

A Mt. Baker National Forest peak, elevation 5,202 ft., 1 mile north of Snohomish County boundary, 2-1/2 miles north of Hazel, extreme south central Skagit County. The peak is used as a forest fire lookout in season by Forest Service personnel. IN 1890, it was named by Maliky Ryan for Walter D. Higgins, who homesteaded south of the mountain in 1887.

Mt. Hoquiam *(S.32;T.24N;R.7W)*

An Olympic National Park peak, 3 miles south of Quinault River near Grays Harbor County boundary, extreme south central Jefferson County. In 1890, the peak was named by Lieut. Joseph O'Neil for hospitality shown to his crew by Hoquiam citizens at the end of his trip through the Olympic Mountains. Among other items of assistance, Hoquiam people cut 30 miles of trail to meet O'Neil's trail in the mountains.

Mt. Horrible *(S.9;T.7N;R.43E)*

A 6,000-ft. peak, 2 miles from the summit of northern Blue Mountains, 7 miles north of Oregon boundary, southwest corner of Asotin County. In the 1889s, it was named by stockmen, the same group who named Mt. Misery in Garfield County, and for the same reason. Sweeping blizzards in the fall and winter make the difficult trail over this mountain almost impossible to negotiate.

Mt. Howard *(S.27;T.27N;R.15E)*

A Wenatchee National Forest peak, elevation 7,520 ft., on Nason Ridge between Rock Mountain and Mt. Mastiff, northwest Chelan County. It was named prior to 1897 by local residents and evidently for a mine owner in the vicinity.

Mt. Hozomeen (Whatcom County) *see* Hozomeen Mountain

Mt. Index *(Ts.26,27N;Rs.9,10E)*

A series of leaning rock needles which point northward, Snoqualmie National Forest, 3 miles south of Index, King-Snohomish County boundary. In 1890, the mountain was named by A. D. Gunn when he bought out a nearby squatter's rights. It was for sharp spires, like index fingers. (USBGN)

Mt. Jonathan *(S.32;T.29N;R.15E.uns)*

A Wenatchee National Forest peak,

6-1/2 miles east of Cascade Mountain summit, on a ridge south of Indian Creek, northwest Chelan County. It ws named by Forest Supervisor A. H. Sylvester in conjunction with Mt. David, 1 mile to the east, following Biblical history -- "The soul of Jonathan was knit with the soul of David."

Mt. Jupiter *(S.33;T.26N;R.3W)*

An Olympic National Forest peak, 8 miles west of Dabob Bay, southeast corner of Jefferson County. This name is reputed to have been applied by the Seattle Press Expedition, to tie this mountain with Mt. Olympus in Greco-Roman mythology.

Mt. Kent Lakes *(S.14;T.22N;R.8E)*

Two lakes, 600 ft. apart, on the west side of Mt. Kent, 10-1/2 miles southeast of North Bend, east central King County. One lake covers 1.8 acres, the other 1 acre. They were named for Mt. Kent; an alternative name is *Alice Lakes*.

Mt. Kit Carson *(S.17;T.28N;R.45E)*

A Mt. Spokane State Park peak, 33 miles northeast of Spokane, northeast Spokane County. It was named for Christopher ("Kit") Carson, of Kentucky, famous frontiersman, scout, and trapper.

Mt. Lawson *(S.16;T.25N;R.7W)*

An Olympic National Park peak, 11 miles southeast of Mt. Olympus, central Jefferson County. In 1890, the peak was named by Seattle Press Expedition, for Victor F. Lawson, editor of *Chicago News*.

Mt. Little (San Juan County) *see* Little Mountain

Mt. Mathias *(S.23;T.27N;R.8W)*

A 7,169-ft. peak, 1-1/2 miles northeast of Mt. Olympus, between Hoh and Blue Glaciers, north central Jefferson County. The name is for F. W. Mathias of Hoquiam, who died in 1959 and who climbed Mt. Olympus 14 times.

Mt. Maude *(S.36;T.31N;R.16E.uns)*

A Wenatchee National Forest peak, elevation 9,100 ft., directly south of Entiat Glacier, adjoining Glacier Peak Recreation Area, northwest Chelan County. This is the second highest peak on Wenatchee National Forest and was named by Forest Supervisor A. H. Sylvester for Sir Frederick Stanley Maude, a British General in WWI.

Mt. McKay (Okanogan County) *see* McCay Mountain

Mt. Meany *(S.18;T.26N;R.7W.uns)*

An Olympic National Park peak, elevation 7,150 ft. 6 miles southeast of Mt. Olympus, central Jefferson County. The mountain has a glacier on the east slope. In 1890, it was named by Seattle Press Expedition for Edmond S. Meany, then city editor of *Seattle Press*, later U. of Washington professor. The name has been endorsed by The Mountaineers.

Mt. Minot *(S.10;T.16N;R.6W)*

A low, 1,711-ft. peak, 8 miles south of Elma, 1-1/2 miles east of Weikswood, southeast Grays Harbor County. The mountain was named for Minot Davis, president of Clemons Logging Company which operated in this area.

Mt. Misery *(S.35;T.8N;R.42E)*

A Umatilla National Forest peak, elevation 6,309 ft., near the summit of northern range of Blue Mountains, 9 miles north of the Oregon boundary, extreme south extension of Garfield County. In the 1880s, it was graphically named by stockmen because of a difficult trail over the summit and howling blizzards during each fall at this high altitude. The same group of cattlemen named Mt. Horrible in Asotin County for the same reason.

Mt. Mitchell *(S.4;T.6N;R.5E)*

A peak 10 miles south of Mt. St. Helens, at head of North Sioux Creek, west central Skamania County. Used by Cowlitz Volunteers during the Indian wars as a lookout station to guard Chelatchie Pass against invasion from the east, this mountain was named for a pioneer who lived on Chelatchie Prairie, in Clark County to the west. An alternate name was *Mitchell's Peak*.

Mt. Noyes *(S.19;T.26N;R.7W.uns)*

An Olympic National Park peak, 6 miles southeast of Mt. Olympus, central Jefferson County. In 1890, it was named by Seattle Press Expedition for Crosby S. Noyes of *Washington Star* (D.C.).

Mt. Olympus *(T.27N;R.8W.uns)*

An Olympic National Park peak, elevation 9,965 ft., at the summit of Olympic Mountains, north central area of Jefferson County. This is the highest elevation in the Olympic Range; there are 2 peaks, East and West, both heavily glaciated and surrounded by the Mt. Olympus National Park, consisting of 896,000 acres, established first as a national monument by presidential proclamation in 1909. On

August 11, 1774, it was first named *El Cerro Nevada de Santa Rosalia* by Juan Perez. On July 4, 1774, the present name was applied by Capt. John Meares who said at the time, "For truly it must be the home of the Gods." The Indian name was *Sunh-a-do*.

Mt. O'Neil *(Ss.12,13;T.23N;R.9W)*

An Olympic National Park peak, 3-1/2 miles east of Lake Quinault, 2 miles south of Olympic National Park boundary, north central Grays Harbor County. The peak was named for Lieut. Joseph P. O'Neil who led exploring expeditions into the Olympic Range in 1885 and 1890. He was the first to suggest that a national park be established in these mountains.

Mt. Persis *(S.35;T.27N;R.9E)*

A peak 2-1/2 miles southwest of Index, 1-1/2 miles south of Stevens Pass Highway, southeast Snohomish County. The mountain was locally named for Mrs. Persis Gunn, a member of a local pioneer family.

Mt. Pickett *(S.27;T.37N;R.1W)*

A Moran State Park peak, elevation 1,765 ft., near the eastern end of Orcas Island, between Mountain Lake and the east shore of the island, San Juan County. It was named for Capt. George Edward Pickett, USA, who commanded the U.S. garrison on the San Juan Islands in 1859, during the early part of the boundary dispute with Great Britain, and who later became a Confederate officer in the Civil War. It is shown on some maps and records, in error, as *Doe Bay Mountain*.

Mt. Pilchuck *(Ss.29,30;T.30N;R.8E)*

A 5,334-ft. peak, 8 miles east of Granite Falls, in Pilchuck River drainage, central Snohomish County. The peak is used as a Forest Service fire lookout in season and was named for Pilchuck River. (*see* Pilchuck River)

Mt. Purcell (Lewis County) *see Purcell Mountain*

Mt. Queets *(Ss.7,8;T.26N;R.7W)*

A heavily-glaciated peak at the headwaters of Elwha River, 5-1/2 miles southeast of Mt. Olympus, central Jefferson County. (*see* Queets River)

Mt. Rainier

At 14,408 ft., the highest elevation in the state, this volcanic peak is in the center or Mt. Rainier National Park, west central Washington state, bordered on the north and west by Pierce County, on the south by Lewis County, and on the east by

Cascade Mountain summit. Mt. Rainier boasts 28 named glaciers, which constitute the most extensive glacier system in the U.S., except Alaska. The mountain and surrounding park area attract visitors world-wide. The park is ably administrated by the National Park Service, with headquarters at Longmire. More names have been used or suggested for this lofty mountain than for any other geographical feature in the state. The present official, federally-approved name was applied in 1792 by Capt. George Vancouver, to honor Rear-Admr. Peter Rainier, RN, Admiral of the Blue. The City of Tacoma fought vigorously for years to change the name to *Tacoma* or *Tahoma*, and many staunch Tacoma citizens call it *The Mountain*. Indian names include *Tu-ah-ku*, *Puak-coke*, *Ta-co-be* and *Ta-co-pe*. Hall J. Kelley tried to have it included in his President's Range as *Mt. William Henry Harrison*. In 1920, the Grand Army of the Republic wanted it renamed *Mt. Lincoln*. The present name was approved by the U.S. Board on Geographic Names, following a public hearing in 1917.

Mt. Rainier National Park

An outstanding, 377.78-sq. mile park, bounded on the north and west by Pierce County, on the east by Cascade Mountain summit, and on the south by Lewis County, west central Washington. This park is rated as the most superb landmark in the Pacific Northwest. On March 2, 1899, it was established by congressional action. It contains 62 major lakes, 34 waterfalls, and 700 species of flowering plants. Practically all of the indigenous land animals and birds of the region are found within the park boundaries. The park was named for Mt. Rainier which is in the center of the area and towers above it all.

Mt. Rena (Okanogan Counties) *see* Old Goat Mountain

Mt. Roosevelt Lake *((S.10;T.23N;R.10E)*

A 3.8-acre lake on the northwest side of Mt. Roosevelt, Snoqualmie National Forest, east central King County. It was named for Mt. Roosevelt which carries the name of Theodore Roosevelt, 26th president of the U.S.

Mt. Ross *(S.9;T.37;R.12E.uns)*

A Mt. Baker National Forest peak, elevation 7,300 ft., 2-1/2 miles north of Newhalem, southeast Whatcom County.

It was named for James Delmage Ross, the man who planned and started the hydroelectric development of upper Skagit River while superintendent of Seattle City Lighting Department. In 1930, the name was placed on Forest Service maps, but it had been in common use for some previous years. Some maps show a peak with an identical name in Section 16, and 1-1/2 miles south, in error.

Mt. Ruth *(Mt. Rainier National Park)*

A peak of The Wedge, elevation 8,700 ft., 2-1/2 miles northeast of Mt. Rainier's summit, overlooking Emmons and Inter glaciers, central confines of the park. Two versions of the name origin are recorded. One relates that it was named for a daughter of Ethan Allen, an early superintendent of the park. Another states that it was named for Ruth Knapp, daughter of a prospector who built Knapp's Cabin, a tourist landmark in Glacier Basin. (USBGN)

Mt. St. Helens *(Ts.8,9N;Rs.4,5,6E)*

A nationally known active volcanic peak, elevation 8,634 ft., northwest Skamania and northeast Cowlitz County. On May 18, 1980, the mountain violently erupted, devastating the surrounding landscape, killing 61 people, and causing millions of dollars worth of damage. The peak is monitored carefully nowdays and periodically spews lava from its dome; but it has not yet erupted again with such force as the May tragedy. In October, 1792, the name was given this mountain by Capt. George Vancouver and was in honor of the British ambassador to Spain at that time, and a personal friend. In 1834, Hall J. Kelley suggested the name *Mt. Washington* for this peak, as one name in his President's Range. The Indian name was *Low-We-Not-Thlat* or *Low-We-Lat-Klah*, meaning *Throwing Up Smoke* or *The Smoking Mountain*.

Mt. St. Pierre *(Douglas County) see* Badger Mountain

Mt. Sauk *(Skagit County) see* Sauk Mountain

Mt. Saul *(Ss.19,20;T.29N;R.15E.uns)*

A Wenatchee National Forest peak on a ridge between White River and Indian Creek, 4-1/2 miles east of Cascade Mountain summit, northwest Chelan County. The peak was named by Forest Supervisor A. H. Sylvester in conjunction with Mt. David and Mt. Jonathan in the immediate vicinity. In Biblical history Saul was close to David and Jonathan, *but forever separated them.*

Mt. Scott *(S.11;T.27N;R.7W.uns)*

An Olympic National Park peak, 8 miles northeast of Mt. Olympus, 2-1/2 miles west of Press Valley, north central Jefferson County. On April 26, 1890, this peak was named by members of Seattle Press Expedition, for James W. Scott of *Chicago Herald.*

Mt. Seattle *(T.26N;R.7W.uns)*

An Olympic National Park peak, 7 miles southeast of Mt. Olympus, central Jefferson County. On April 29, 1890, this peak was named by Seattle Press Expedition for the City of Seattle.

Mt. Sefrit *(S.20;T.39N;R.10E.uns)*

A 6,300-ft. sharp peak at the west end of Ruth Range, 4 miles northeast of Mt. Shuksan summit, north central Whatcom County. This peak, surrounded by other giant mountains on Mt. Baker National Forest, was named for one of the influential men of the Pacific Northwest, who died in 1950. He was Frank I. Sefrit, editor and general manager of *Bellingham Herald.* This nationally-known editor and scholar owned one of the finest libraries in the state. (USBGN)

Mt. Shuksan *(Ts.38,39N:R.9E.uns)*

A Mt. Baker National Forest peak, elevation 9,127 ft., 12 miles northeast of Mt. Baker, central Whatcom County. Although close to Mt. Baker, this mountain is entirely different, being more rugged and rocky, and with many *hanging* glaciers. The name is a Skagit Indian word meaning *Roaring Mountain.* It is well named, as noisy snow and ice avalanches are common.

Mt. Si *(Ss.2,11;T.23N;R.8E)*

A Snoqualmie National Forest peak, elevation 4,190 ft., 2-1/2 miles northeast of North Bend, east central King County. The peak was named for Josiah Merritt, who settled near the mountain slopes in 1862, and whose affectionate nickname was *Uncle Si.* The name *Si Mountain* which appears on some maps, is incorrect.

Mt. Sherman *(Clallam County) see* Mt. Angeles

Mt. Solo *(Cowlitz County) see* Monticello

Mt. Spokane *(T.28N;R.45E)*

A Mt. Spokane State Park peak, elevation 5,808 ft., southeast Spokane County. Francis H. Cook, an early Spokane editor, bought land on the mountain, built a cabin, and boosted the area as a recreation center. It is now a ski resort with camping and fishing in summer months. On August 23, 1912, it was named in a ceremony by Governor Hay and W. J. Hindley, mayor of Spokane. The name source is the same as for Spokane. A number of names were formerly used, including *Mt. Baldy, Bald Peak, Mt. Carleton, Mt. Carlton, Old Baldy, Baldy Mount,* and *Little Baldy.* (see Spokane)

Mt. Spokane State Park *(Ts.27,28,29N;Rs.44,45E)*

A 24,240-acre area, including Mt. Spokane and Mt. Kit Carson, also a number of sections and part-sections of land, northeast Spokane County. (*see* Spokane)

Mt. Steel *(S.30;T.25N;R.5W)*

An Olympic National Park peak at the headwaters of North Fork, Skokomish River, southeast Jefferson County. In 1890, the mountain was named by Lieut. Joseph P. O'Neil for William Gladstone Steel of Portland, Oregon, a mountaineer and author who helped in organizing the Olympic Mountain Exploring expeditions of 1885 and 1890. The peak is shown as *Steel Mountain* on some maps, and on others as *Mt. Stone.* Both are unofficial. (USBGN)

Mt. Stickney *(Ss.14,23;T.28N;R.9E)*

A peak 6 miles northeast of Gold Bar, directly north of Wallace River, south central Snohomish County. The peak was named for a prospector who spent many years of hard labor building trails and developing prospects here. He was reported to have been killed by wolves in Alaska in the winter of 1898-1899.

Mt. Stone *(Jefferson County) see* Mt. Steel

Mt. Storm King *(T.30N;R.8W)*

A 4,534-ft. peak, 6 miles south of Lake Crescent and immediately south of Lake Sutherland, central Clallam County. The name chosen is descriptive, as storm clouds are prevalent around its summit.

Mt. Stuart *(S.19;T.23N;R.16E)*

A 9,470-ft. peak, 14 miles southwest of Leavenworth at the head of Mountaineer Creek, southwest Chelan County. On September 23, 1853, the peak was named by Capt. George B. McClellan, U.S. Army, for an army friend, Jimmy Stuart.

Mt. Stuart *(S.28;T.37N;R.4W)*

A Stuart Island hill, elevation 420 ft., between Tiptop Hill and Lofgren Mountain, extreme northwest San Juan County. It was locally named for the island on which it is located.

Mt. Terror *(Ss.17,20;T.38N;R.12E)*

A Mt. Baker National Forest peak, elevation 8,151 ft., 6-1/2 miles north of Newhalem at the head of Terror Creek, southeast Whatcom County. The name of this mountain, together with several others in the Picket Range, reflect their rugged character, and the success or failure of mountain climbers. Some of these in the glaciated area are: Challenger, Fury, Triumph, Despair, and Damnation. This peak would be a terror to the amateur mountaineer.

Mt. Tacoma (Tacobe, Tacope) *(Mt. Rainier National Park) see* Mt. Rainier.

Mt. Tahoma (Tahome) *(Mt. Rainier National Park) see* Mt. Rainier

Mt. Thompson *(King County) see* Mt. Thomson

Mt.Thomson *(Ss.13,24;T.23N;R.11E)*

A 6,500-ft. peak at Cascade Mountain summit, 4 miles northeast of Snoqualmie Pass, extreme east central King County. This imposing mountain was named by Northern Pacific Railway surveyors for R. H. Thomson, an outstanding Seattle city engineer. On recent county maps it appears, in error, as *Mt. Thompson..*

Mt. Triumph *(S.10;T.37N;R.11E.uns)*

A Mt. Baker National Forest peak, elevation 7,270 ft., at the head of Triumph Creek, 5 miles northwest of Newhalem, southeast Whatcom County. The mountain appears to have been named by those who mapped and surveyed this area in the first federal land survey. No record of the reason for their name choice appears to exist. (*see* Mt. Terror)

Mt. Turner *(S.22;T.26N;R.2W)*

A peak 4 miles north of Brinnon, 1-1/2 miles west of Dabob Bay, southeast Jefferson County. The mountain was named for Ben Turner, who built a logging chute on the mountain. The logs split at the terminus of the chute, which was too steep and Ben went bankrupt.

Mt. Van Buren *(Jefferson County) see* Mt. Olympus

Mt. Vernon *(Thurston County) see* Grand Mound

Mt. Walker *(S.35;T.27N;R.2W)*

A 2,769-ft. peak, 3 miles south of Quilcene, east central Jefferson County. The peak is used for a forest fire lookout, and for a sweeping view of Hood Canal, the Olympics, and the strait of Juan de Fuca. A good roadway allows motorists to reach the summit. It was named for a local logger who built the first log chute on Puget Sound on the side of this mountain.

Mt. Washington *(Skamania County) see* Mt. St. Helens

Mt. William Henry Harrison *(Mt. Rainier National Park) see* Mt. Rainier

Mt. Woodward *(San Juan County) see* Mt. Woolard

Mt. Woolard *(S.11;T.36N;R.2E)*

A 1,200-ft. mountain on the middle peninsula of Orcas Island, 2-1/2 miles east of the town of West Sound, central San Juan Island. This mountain was named for a family of early settlers. On some recent maps it is shown in error as *Mt. Woodward.* (USBGN)

Mt. Wow *(Mt. Rainier National Park)*

A 6,030-ft. peak, 2 miles northeast of Nisqually entrance, between Tahoma and Goat creeks, extreme southwest corner of the park. Numerous mountain goats may be seen on its cliffs at high elevations. *Wow* is the Indian name for mountain goat, and was applied because this was a favorite hunting ground for Indian tribesmen who relished goat meat. (USBGN)

Mt. Wright *(S.13;T.23N;R.10E)*

A 5,400-ft. peak, 6-1/2 miles west of Cascade Mountain summit, between Wildcat and Gem lakes, 4 miles northwest of Snoqualmie Pass, northeast King County. In July, 1925, this mountain was named by The Mountaineers for George E. Wright of Seattle, a member of their group, an attorney, and conservationist. (USBGN)

Mt. Young *f(S.25;T.36N;R.4W)*

A 650-ft. hill, 1/2 mile east of Garrison Bay, northwest part of San Juan Island, west central San Juan County. In 1858, it was named by Capt. Henry Richards, RN, and placed on British admiralty charts. The name is for a British naval officer who served on this section in the 1850s. An alternate name, carried on county maps, is *Young Hill.*

Mount Hope *(S.34;T.23N;R.44E)*

A declining settlement, 3-1/2 miles west of Rockford, southeast Spokane County. In the early part of the present century, this place flourished. In 1884, it was named by ''Grandpa'' Cyrus Bankson, because ''It took a mountain of hope to come out here and carve homes and farms out of the wilderness.''

Mount Pleasant *.(S.24;T.1N;R.4E)*

Settlement 1/2 mile north of Columbia River, 6 miles east of Camas, southeast Clark County. When this place grew up around the S.P.&S. Railway station, the name was selected because of a sweeping view of nearby hills and mountains.

Mount Vernon *(T.34N;R.4E)*

The main trade center for the rich Skagit Delta area, on Skagit River and Delta, 25 miles south of Bellingham, west central Skagit County. In March, 1877, the town was named by E. C. English and Harrison Clothier, for George Washington's home on the Potomac River in Virginia.

Mountain Lake *(T.37N;R.1W)*

A large, 198-acre lake, maximum depth over 100 ft., on the east peninsula of Orcas Island, directly southeast of Mt. Constitution, northeast San Juan County. This lake offers recreational facilities and supplies domestic water to Olga and Doe Bay. It was locally named for Mt. Constitution.

Mountain Meadows *(Mt. Rainier National Park)*

Meadows 1 mile south of Tolmie Peak, at the head of Meadow Creek, northwest confines of the park. In 1883, this very descriptive name was chosen by Prof. Bailey Willis, geologist. (USBGN)

Mountain View *(Skagit County) see* Clear Lake (town)

Mountain View *(King County) see* North Bend

Mountain View *(S.22;T.3N;R.3E)*

Farming community 13 miles east of Hockinson, central Clark County. In 1888, the name was adopted at the suggestion of Miss Lizzie Dolan, local school teacher, who was impressed by the excellent view of distant mountains. This place should not be confused with View in the north part of the county, which was also once called Mountain View.

Mountain View *(S.27;T.39N;R.1E)*

Small community on a hill, 3-1/2 miles west of Ferndale, west central Whatcom County. In 1877, it was named by an early settler, Mrs. A. H. Smith, for the excellent view of the mountains to the east.

Mountaineer Camp *(T.37N;R.9E)*

A permanent camp of The Mountaineers, 2-1/2 miles west of Baker lake on Concrete Trail, between Park and Boulder creeks, south central Whatcom County.

Mountaineer Creek *(King County) see* Lodge Creek

Mouse River *(Pacific County) see* Bone River, Querquelin River

Mowich Glacier *(Mt. Rainier National Park) see* N. Mowich, S. Mowich glaciers

Mowitch Lake *(S.4;T.24N;R.10E)*

A 15.8-acre lake, 13 miles northeast of North Bend, east central King County. The lake carries the Chinook Indian jargon name, meaning ''deer'' or ''venison.''

Mowich Lake *(Mt. Rainier National Park)*

A fairly large, 122.6-acre lake, elevation 4,929 ft., at the head of Crater Creek, west of Mother Mountain, northwest corner of the park. This round lake is a glacial cirque. In 1883, it was named *Crater Lake* by geologist Bailey Willis with the belief that it was located in a volcanic crater. When Willis discovered his mistake many years later, the name was changed. The name of the creek which drains it was not changed, however. (USBGN)

Mowich River *(Mt. Rainier National Park)*

The stream of the creek rises in 2 forks, in North Mowich and South Mowich glaciers respectively, northwest confines of the park; the branches join in the park and flow westward 11 miles through Pierce County to Puyallup River. (*see* Mowich)

Mox La Push *(T.21N;R.5E)*

The site of an abandoned Indian village near Auburn, at the confluence of White and Green rivers, southwest King County. This Indian name, shown on some older maps as *Moxt-la-poosh*, has the meaning of ''The forks'' or ''Two forks.'' It referred to the river junction.

Moxee *(S.1;T.12N;R.19E)*

Town 5 miles southeast of Yakima, northeast Yakima County. In 1867, it was settled by Mortimer Thorp and a number of French-Canadian farmers who specialized in hop growing. In 1921, the town was incorporated. The Indian name, which was *Mooxee*, translates to ''Smoke on the water,'' and refers to a spring on the Thorpe ranch which emitted vapor, even in the coldest weather, and which never froze.

Moxlie Creek *(S.23;T.18N;R.2W)*

The stream of this short tributary of Budd Inlet, rises in Olympia, north central Thurston County. It was named for R. W. Moxlie, a pioneer of very early days, who died in 1869.

Muck *(S.32;T.18N;R.2E)*

Abandoned settlement at the south end of Fort Lewis Army Post, 2 miles west of Roy, Pierce County. Once an important agricultural unit of Hudson's Bay Company during their tenacy in this area, the place was used to raise much of the company's food for its local posts. The name was applied by employees of Hudson's Bay Company. It is evidently from the Chinook jargon word *Muck-a-muck*, meaning ''food.''

Muck Creek *(T.18N;Rs.1,2E)*

The stream of the creek rises in a group of small lakes on the south border of Fort Lewis Army Post; flows south and west through Muck Lake and Roy to Nisqually River. The original Indian name was *Yee-whaltz*. It was named *Douglas River* by Puget Sound Agricultural Company, a subsidiary of Hudson's Bay Company, when these fur traders farmed and ran livestock in this area. It was changed to the present name by American settlers. *(see Muck)*

Muck Lake *(S.34;T.18N;R.2E)*

A 25.7-acre lake, 1/2 mile northeast of Roy in the course of Muck Creek, southwest Pierce County. *(see Muck)*

Muckamuck Creek *(Ts.35,36N;R.24E)*

The stream of this rather short creek rises on Muckamuck Mountain, west central Okanogan County; flows 4-1/2 miles to the South Fork of Salmon Creek. A Chinook jargon word meaning ''food'' or ''to eat,'' *Muckamuck* was the name applied to this creek and the adjacent area because there was an abundance of game here.

Muckamuck Hill *(S.22;T.36N;R.24E)*

A 5,600-ft. hill, 1 mile west of Salmon Creek, 4 miles northwest of Conconully, Okanogan County. *(see Muckamuck Creek)*

Muckamuck Mountain *(S.20;T.36N;R.24E.uns)*

A 6,390-ft. peak at the head of Muckamuck Creek, 6 miles northwest of Conconully, west central Okanogan County. *(see Muckamuck Creek)*

Muckamuck Pass *(S.27;T.36N;R.24E)*

A 5,500-ft. pass between Mineral Hill on the south and Muckamuck Hill on the north, near the east boundary of Chelan National Forest, 3 miles northwest of Conconully, west central Okanogan County. *(see Muckamuck Creek)*

Muckleshoot Indian Reservation *(Ts.20,21;R.5E)*

A 1,959-acre reservation, scattered over five sections of land in a diagonal pattern southeast of Auburn, along White River, southwest King County. Established on December 26, 1854 by the Medicine Creek Treaty, this reservation is for the Muckleshoot band, a branch of Duwamish tribe. In the Point Elliott Treaty of 1855, these Indians were referred to as the *Skopamish*. *(see Muckleshoot Prairie)*

Muckleshoot Prairie *(T.21N;R.5E)*

A swampy area, alternating with second-growth forests, partly on Muckleshoot Indian Reservation, 7 miles southeast of Auburn, between the Green and White rivers, southwest King County. The name is from the Muckleshoot Indian band. In the Sahaptin dialect, this word was pronounced as *O-kul-schoo-el* with a meaning of ''Green prairie.''

Mud Bay *(Ss.7,8,17,18;T.34N;R.1W)*

A south end bay of Lopez Sound, Lopez Island, southeast San Juan County. It was locally named because it is shoal and foul, and offers poor anchorage.

Mud Bay *(Ts.18,19N;Rs.2,3W)*

A bay at the head of Eld Inlet, 4 miles west of Olympia, northwest Thurston County. Oyster beds here produce the famous Olympia oysters. At low tides the name is very descriptive.

Mud Bay Spit *(Thurston County) see* Point Cooper; Coopers Point

Mud Creek *(Ts.26,27N;R.20E)*

The stream of the creek rises on the south slope of Baldy Mountain, Chelan Mountains; flows southwesterly to Entiat River, Wenatchee National Forest, east central Chelan County. This very common name was applied by early residents. The stream carries a large amount of detritus in warmer months when snow is melting at its headwaters.

Mud Creek *(T.7N;Rs.35,36E.&Ts.6,7N;- Rs.34,35E)*

Two creeks in the county, each tributary to Walla Walla River, bear the same dismal, unimaginative name. One, previously called *Wild Horse Creek*, rises 2 miles northeast of Walla Walla; flows 9 miles west to Dry Creek at Sudbury. The other rises southwest of Walla Walla near the Oregon boundary; flows 10 miles west-by-north to Walla Walla River west of Lowden. Pioneers and more recent settlers must have been fond of mud or very allergic thereto, judging by the many streams which they named in its honor.

Mud Flat *(Thurston County) see* Nisqually Flats

Mud Lake *(Clallam County) see* Campbell Lake

Mud Lake *(King County) see* Alice Lake

Mud Lake *(Snohomish County) see* Lake Serene

Mud Lake *(S.6;T.4N;R.1E)*

A 92-acre lake which stretches along lower Allen Canyon for a distance of 6,200 ft., 2-1/2 miles west of La Center, northwest Clark County. This is a handy name for any lake which isn't crystal clear during the entire year.

Mud Lake *(S.12;T.21N;R.6E)*

A 24-acre lake, 1 mile northeast of Black Diamond, south central King County. This name was applied by local residents because the lake dries up periodically, leaving a muddy bottom.

Mud Lake *(S.33;T.20N;R.2E)*

A shallow, 21.7-acre lake, 1-1/2 miles east of Steilacoom, northwest Pierce County. The lake has a very marshy area on the west side. This is one of the many Mud Lakes in the state that really deserves the name. An alternate name is *Waughop Lake*.

Mud Mountain *(S.8;T.19N;R.7E)*

A peak on the north side of White River, west end of Mud Mountain Reservoir, south central King County. In May, 1857, this descriptive name was applied by the surveyor general of Washington Territory.

Mud Mountain Dam
(S.17;T.19N;R.7E)

A flood-control dam which is claimed to be the highest earthen dam in the world, in White River, 7-1/2 miles southeast of Enumclaw, on the boundary between King and Pierce counties. It was named for nearby Mud Mountain, a name which has been proposed, but is not in general use is *Howard Hanson Dam*, for a Seattle attorney and project planner. A previous suggestion. which did not mature, was to name it for Governor Issac I. Stevens. (*see* Mud Mountain)

Mud Mountain Reservoir
(S.17;T.19N;R.7E)

This 1,200-acre, flood-control reservoir, impounded by Mud Mountain Dam, is in White River, 7 miles southeast of Enumclaw; White River forms the boundary between King and Pierce counties at this point. In 1948, it came into existence following the completion of the dam. (*see* Mud Mountain)

Mud Spring (Columbia County) *see* Edmiston Spring

Muddy Creek (Chelan County) *see* Mud Creek

Muddy Fork, Cowlitz River
(Ts.14,15N;R.9E)

The stream of the fork rises on Cowlitz Glacier, southeast slope of Mt. Rainier; flows 15 miles south to Cowlitz River, 5 miles northeast of Packwood. The upper reach of the river runs through a rocky box canyon, over 100 ft. deep in places. The name is descriptive because the stream carries a heavy load of glacial rock sediment.

Mukilteo *(S.4;T.28N;R.4E)*

Town 4 miles south of Everett on Possession Sound, southwest Snohomish County. Originally it was a trading center for Indians and the site of the signing of an important Indian treaty called the "Point Elliott Treaty." Until 1862 when a post office was established, the place was called *Point Elliott*. The present name, suggested by J. D. Fowler, the first postmaster, is from the Indian name of the place, *Muckl-te-oh*, as revised to suit the postal service. Spellings on older maps include *Muck-*

ilteo, Muckleteo and *Muckiltoe.*

Mukkaw Bay *(Ts.32,33N;R.15W)*

A shallow bay, 4 miles long, open to the Pacific Ocean, 5 miles south of Cape Flattery, northwest Clallam County. The name of this bay is spelled as the Makah Indians pronounce their tribal name. It should not be considered a misspelling.

Mule Creek *(Ts.25,26N;R.15E)*

The stream of the creek heads on the north slope of Icicle Ridge; flows 2-1/2 miles north to White Pine Creek, Wenatchee National Forest, southwest Chelan County. The stream was named by Forest Supervisor A. H. Sylvester for the many pack mules used in this area.

Mule Lake *((S.27;T.33N;R.13E)*

A Mt. Baker National Forest lake, 2 miles west of Cascade Mountain summit, at the head of Bachelor Creek, extreme southeast Skagit County. It was named by Forest Ranger Hugh Ritter, for huge mule deer which he saw on the lake's bank.

Mullan Road

A pioneer road, built from Wallula, Washington to Fort Benton, Montana, crossed through Walla Walla to Whitman County, and northeasterly through Spokane County into Idaho and Montana. Between 1858 and 1862 it was built by military and civilian labor for a distance of 624 miles. Traces of the old road are visible at some points, and several historical markers indicate the exact route. It was named for Lieut. John Mullan, USA, who had charge of the entire project.

Mulano Cove *(S.26;T.35N;R.3W)*

A small cove on the southeast shore of San Juan Island, west side of Griffin Bay, south central San Juan County. It was locally named for a family who settled here in 1905.

Mummy Rocks *(S.15;T.34N;R.2W)*

Indian burial rocks south of Davis Bay, in Middle Channel, on the southwest end of Lopez Island, south central San Juan County. In 1841, these rocks were named by Cmdr. Wilkes and they were included with Buck Island, Long Island, and Whale Rocks as *Geese Islets* by Wilkes.

Muncaster Mountain
(S.24;T.25N;R.7W.uns.)

An Olympic National Park peak, 3 miles southeast of Mt. Lawson, south central Jefferson County. The peak was

named for Roy Muncaster, a forester who was employed on the forest. He was drowned when the *S.S. Tuscania* was torpedoed during WWI, at which time he was enroute to France with the 20th Engineers, a forestry regiment. Forest Service officials chose his name for this mountain. On some maps there is another mountain by the same name in Sections 2 and 3; Township 24 North; Range 7 West, unsurveyed; 2-1/2 miles southwest of the mountain described herein. There has been an error of double-naming or of location, as National Park records show that there should be only one peak by that name.

Munden Creek (Clallam County) *see* Blackwood Creek

Munks Landing (Skagit County) *see* Fidalgo

Murden Cove *(T.25N;R.2E)*

A proposed western terminus for a cross-sound bridge from West Point in Seattle between Ferncliff and Manitou Beach, on the east shore of Bainbridge Island. In 1856, it was named by the U.S. Coast Survey for a beach dweller in the cove. It appears on some older maps as *Murden's Cove*, Murders Cove, or *Rolling Bay*.

Murden's Cove (Kitsap County) *see* Murden Cove

Murders Cove (Kitsap County) *see* Murden Cove

Murdock Creek
(Ss.29,31;T.31N;R.9W)

The stream of the creek rises 22 miles west of Port Angeles, entering the Strait of Juan de Fuca between Twin and Low Point, north central Clallam County. It has an excellent beach at its mouth. It was named for a homesteader who filed on land near the creek's mouth in 1880, and whose name was Mohrdick.

Murdock Gulch *(Ts.26,27N;R.20E)*

The gulch heads on the south slope of Baldy Mountain in Chelan Mountains; extends 3 miles south to Mud Creek, Wenatchee National Forest, east central Chelan County. It was named by local usage for a settler in the gulch in early days.

Mutiny Bay *(T.29N;R.2E)*

A southwest shore bay of Whidbey Island, between Bush Point and Double Bluff, south Island County. In 1855, the bay was named by U.S. Coast Survey for a number of British sailors who deserted their ship here to become settlers. A legend which recounts a different name source is that of mutiny by the Indian crew of a trading post. They conspired with local Indians to kill the white master and mate, and to steal the cargo, which consisted largely of whiskey. According to the story, the ship was then ransacked and abandoned.

Muscleshell Rapids (Benton County) *see* Umatilla Rapids

Mutton Mountain *(S.24;T.18N;R.10E)*

A Snoqualmie National Forest peak, elevation 6,142 ft., 4 miles northeast of the northeast corner of Mt. Rainier National Park, southeast Pierce County. The mountain was so named because it is the center of an extensive sheep range.

Myrtle Falls *(Mt. Rainier National Park)*

These falls are in Edith Creek, a tributary of Paradise River, on the south slope of Mt. Rainier, south central zone of the park. In 1907, they were named by Julius Stampfler, a park guide, for a woman whom he met on a guided tour. It is to be hoped that Julius guided her in the right paths.

Myrtle Lake *(S.34;T.30N;R.17E)*

A small lake directly west of upper Entiat River, 1-1/2 miles east of 5th of July Mountain, Wenatchee National Forest, north central Chelan County. The lake drains into Entiat River by a small stream. Prior to 1908, the name was applied by early residents. The shrubs around the lake, however, are of varieties other than myrtle.

Myrtle Lake *(Ss.31,32;T.33N;R.8E)*

A Mt. Baker National Forest lake, 1 mile west of Mt. Higgins, 1 mile north of Snohomish County boundary, extreme south central Skagit County. In 1904, the lake was named by Fritz Stolzenberg, for Myrtle Pierson, a local 7-year-old girl who was the first of her sex to climb Mt. Higgins.

Mystery Bay *(S.32;T.30N;R.1E)*

A west shore bay of Marrowstone Island, Kilisut Harbor, northeast Jefferson County. It was named by the crews of sealing vessels which operated out of Neah Bay, and which wintered in this small bay. The reason for their choice of name is not known.

Mystic Lake *(Mt. Rainier National Park)*

A 7-acre, irregular lake at the head of West Fork, White River, north central precincts of the park. It nestles at the foot of Mineral Mountain, between Carbon and Winthrop glaciers, elevation 5,700 ft. The lake is a favorite camp for parties who attempt to scale Mt. Rainier's north slopes. It was named by Prof. J. B. Flett and H. H. Garretson, who saw a mysterious temporary whirlpool near the lake's outlet. (USBGN)

N

Naches *(S.3;T.14N;R.17E)*

Substantial town on north bank of Naches River, 15 miles northwest of Yakima, north central Yakima County. In 1908, it was started when farmers in the valley began irrigating. The name is from Naches River. Indians combined the word *Naugh*, meaning "rough or turbulent" with *Chez*, meaning "water," to describe the river. (USBGN)

Naches Flat *(S.1;T.16N;R.14E)*

A flat stretch in Snoqualmie National Forest, 30 miles northwest of Yakima, northwest Yakima County. The original name was *Curran's Flat*, for a squatter who lived here. (see Naches)

Naches Pass *(S.35;T.19N;R.11E)*

A 4,923-ft. pass at Cascade Mountain summit, at the common corner of 4 counties, near the head of Naches River, 1-1/2 miles south of Pyramid Creek, Yakima, Pierce, Kittitas, King counties. On the east, the pass meets the headwaters of Greenwater River. (see Naches)

Naches Peak *(S.24;T.16N;R.10E.uns)*

A peak on Cascade Mountain summit, directly southeast of Chinook Pass, between northwest Yakima and southeast Pierce counties. (see Naches)

Naches River *(Ts.13-19N;Rs.11-18E)*

The stream of the river rises at Naches Pass area, Cascade Mountain summit, in 3 forks, near Pyramid Peak; flows southeast between Yakima and Kittitas counties, then through Yakima to Yakima River, 1 mile north of Yakima. (see Naches) (USBGN)

Naco *(S.33;T.21N;R.7E)*

Railroad point 5 miles northeast of Enumclaw, at the site of Sunset Mine, an abandoned coal mining operation, south central King County. The original name was *Sunset*, from the name of the mine. In 1908, this was changed to *Navy*, and in 1916, the present name was given by officials of Northern Pacific Railway. It is a coined name.

Nagrom *(S.13;T.20N;R.9E)*

Small community 11 miles west of Cascade Mountain summit, on upper Green River, southeast King County. This is the site of extensive sawmill and logging operations which started in 1911. The name was devised by the division superintendent of Northern Pacific Railway, and is *Morgan*, spelled in reverse. It was for E. G. Morgan, president of the Morgan Lumber Company which operated a sawmill here for many years.

Naha Lake *(S.21;T.6N;R.8E.uns)*

A little lake, elevation 4,740 ft., in the Indian Heaven area, 4-1/2 miles northwest of Big Lava Bed, central Skamania County. The significance of this Chinook Indian name is not quite clear, as applied to the lake, the translation being "mother."

Nachotta *(S.28;T.12N;R.11W)*

Community on the west shore of Willapa Bay, west central Pacific County. Formerly it was the terminus of a narrow gauge railroad from Ilwaco, and an important center of the oyster industry. At one time there were 2 adjoining towns on this site; the south side being platted as *Nachotta* and the north side as

Sealand. In 1881, after the oyster industry declined and in the following years, the town diminished and *Sealand* was dropped. The present name is for Chief Nachotte who guided early settlers to the oyster beds.

Nachotta Channel *(Ts.11,12N;R.11W)*

A Willapa Bay channel, between North Beach Peninsula and Long Island, southwest Pacific County. (*see* Nachotta)

Nahwatzel Lake
(Ss.4,5,8,9;T.20N;R.5W)

A 1-mile-long, roughly rectangular lake, 3-1/2 miles east of Matlock at the head of Outlet Creek, southwest Mason County. The name is the Quinault word *Nah-watl,* considerably altered, which means "true." In 1841, the Wilkes Expedition construed the Indian name as *Nauvitz* and applied it to the lake. There have been 5 other spellings of the word on charts and maps. (USBGN)

Nahunta Falls *(Mt. Rainier National Park)*

A small, delicate waterfall east of Cushman Crest, 1/2 mile east of Christine Falls, in Van Trump Creek, south central zone of the park. This feature was originally called *Marie Falls.* It was changed to the present name by Josephus Daniels, former secretary of the Navy, for that of a river in North Carolina which had been named by Tuscarora Indians. It means "Tall trees" or "Tall timber."

Nalpee *(S.1;T.12N;R.8W)*

Once a lumber town, now a scattered settlement on Willapa River, 9 miles southeast of Raymond, central Pacific County. It was named by the owner of a lumber mill when the Northern Pacific Railway was built through here. The lumberman wanted to name the station for W. C. Albee, division superintendent of the railway. When Mr. Albee objected, a composite name was made by using the initials "N.P." and Albee's name.

Nanum Creek (Kittitas County) *see* Wilson Creek

Napavine *(T.13N;R.2W)*

Town 7 miles southeast of Chehalis, on Newaukum River, west central Lewis County. It is on John Urquhart's Donation Land Claim, dating back to 1855. On December 17,1863, it was named by James Urquhart, using the Indian name

which means "small prairie." In 1873, Northern Pacific Railway officials accepted this name for their station. According to Indian pronunciation, the name should be spelled *Napavoon.*

Napeequa River
(Ts.28-30N;Rs.15,16E.uns)

The stream of the river heads at High Pass on the east side of Cascade Mountain summit, Wenatchee National Forest, northwest Chelan County; flows 15 miles southeast to White River near Twin Lakes. The stream was originally called the North Fork of White River. Forest Supervisor A. H. Sylvester changed the name to the Indian word for "white water," as the water is milk-white in late spring and summer when it carries a burden of glacial rock-flour.

Napoleon *(S.8;T.11N;R.10W)*

Settlement at the north end of a point between Long Island Slough and the mouth of Naselle River, southwest Pacific County. In 1910, this place was the scene of a great land promotion with 2,000 lots platted and 1,696 sold. Within a few years the owners stopped tax payments and the land reverted to the county. This impressive name was chosen by Willapa Trust Company which financed the promotion.

Napoleon *(S.33;T.37N;R.37E)*

Settlement on the east bank of Kettle River, Colville Indian Reservation, 2 miles north of Boyds, northwest Stevens County. It is in a highly mineralized area, and was founded during the mining boom of the 1890s to serve as a supply base for the nearby Napoleon Mine. The name of this town is missing from most current maps, although the name of the Napoleon School and Napoleon Mine persist. The town was named for the mine.

Narada Falls *(Mt. Rainier National Park)*

A 168-ft. waterfall, one of the park's most impressive sights, on the south central slope of Mt. Rainier, in Paradise River, 15 miles by highway from Nisqually entrance, southwest quarter of the park. Rainbows are seen under favorable light conditions, and rare water ousels flit along the nearby river. On August 24, 1893, the falls were given this name by Arthur F. Knight of Tacoma, for the Narada branch of the Theosophical Society of Tacoma. This Hindu word has the meaning of "uncontaminated" or

"pure." An alternate name, which is unofficial, was *Cushman Falls.* (USBGN)

Narrows (Pierce County) *see* The Narrows

Naselle *(S.8;T.10N;R.9W)*

Small settlement, dependent on logging, at the confluence of Naselle River with its South Fork, southwest Pacific County. The name, considerably altered from the original, is that of a division of the Chinook nation, the *Nisal.* The alteration was made by postal authorities when a post office was created here.

Naselle River *(Ts.10,11N;Rs.9,10W)*

The stream of the river rises in high country at a divide, south central Pacific County; flows westerly to Willapa Bay at Stanley Channel. Various names which have been used for this stream include *Nisal, Nisel, Nasal,* and *Kennebec.* (*see* Naselle)

Nason Creek *(Ts.25,26N;Rs.13-17E)*

The stream of the creek heads near Stevens Pass in several branches on the east slope of Cascade Mountain summit, southwest Chelan County; flows 20 miles east, then 5 miles north to Wenatchee River, 1 mile from Wenatchee Lake. In 1890, it was named by local residents for a Wenatchee Indian, *Mow-mo-nash-et,* whose "white" name was Charley Nasen, and who owned a rancheria on the lower course of the creek. The original Indian name, *Natopac,* has been applied to a nearby mountain. (*see* Natopac Mountain)

Nason Ridge *(T.27N;Rs.14-17E)*

A Wenatchee National Forest ridge, extending from the Cascade Mountain summit to the junction of Nason Creek with Wenatchee River, southwest Chelan County. It is over 20 miles long, average width 3-5 miles. It was named by Forest Supervisor A. H. Sylvester for Nason Creek. (*see* Nason Creek)

Natches, Natchess, Natchez, Nathess, Nah-Cheeze, Nachese, Naugh-Chez (Yakima County) *see* Naches

National *(S.28;T.15N;R.6E)*

Community on Mt. Rainier Hwy., 7 miles west of Mt. Rainier National Park at Nisqually entrance, extreme south Pierce County. The name was chosen because of the town's proximity to the national park.

Natopac Mountain
(S.15;T.26N;R.17E)

A low, 8-mile-long sandstone ridge, average width 1-3 mile, between Nason Creek and Wenatchee River, Wenatchee National Forest, central Chelan County. The name was given by Forest Supervisor A. H. Sylvester in order to preserve an old Indian term for Nason Creek.

Natural Bridge *(Mt. Rainier National Park)*

A 200-ft. stone arch which spans a gorge along the west border of Mosquito Flat, 1/2 mile southwest of Lake James, near the south end of Independence Ridge, northwest part of the park. The very descriptive name was chosen by park officials.

Natural Creek (Lewis County) *see* Lincoln Creek

Navarre Coulee *(Ts.26,27N;R.21E)*

A coulee extending from Columbia River near Winesap, 5 miles north toward Lake Chelan, southeast Chelan County. It was named for Judge Navarre, a pioneer in this area, who also was a civil engineer and surveyor.

Navarre Peaks *(T.31N;R.20E.uns)*

Two peaks, with north and south designations, on Sawtooth Ridge, 8 miles east of Lake Chelan, on the boundary of Okanogan County, east central Chelan County. They were named for Judge Navarre. (*see* Navarre Coulee)

Navy (King County) *see* Naco

Navy Archipelago

This is not a geographical feature, but a name for the San Juan Archipelago which is used because Cmdr. Charles Wilkes during his explorations in 1841, named a large number of the features for U.S. Naval officers and for ships which participated in the War of 1812. A few were named for other naval engagements.

Neah Bay *(T.33N;R.15W)*

A Strait of Juan de Fuca bay, within Makah Indian Reservation, extreme northwest Clallam County. This small bay is protected from the north by an artificial breakwater and is a popular rendezvous for saltwater sports fishing. In 1792, a Spanish fort was built here -- the first building erected by white men in the state. In 1790, the Spanish Captains Manuel Quimper and Juan Francisco de Eliza took possession of the bay for Spain and named it *Bahia de Nunez*

Gaona. In 1841, the Wilkes Expedition mapped the bay and called it *Scarborough Harbor* for Capt. James Scarborough of Hudson's Bay Company. In 1847, Capt. Henry Kellett named it *Neah Bay*, using the name of a Makah chief whose actual name was *Dee-ah*. The present name is a slight simplification.

Neah Bay *(T.33N;R.15W)*

Village on the shore of Neah Bay, Makah Indian Reservation, northwest Clallam County. The village extends along the bay for 1/2 mile, and inland for several city blocks. It is headquarters of Makah Indian Reservation and of its tribal council. (*see* Neah Bay)

Neah Creek (Clallam County) *see* Village Creek

Neah Island (Clallam County) *see* Waada Island

Nebraska Springs *(T.35N;R.3W)*

A group of small springs on a steep, rocky shore on San Juan Island, at the foot of South Hill near Friday Harbor, central San Juan County. The name was given by Nebraska students who took summer course work at Puget Sound Marine Station near Friday Harbor. It is unofficial and does not appear on local maps.

Neck Point *(S.8;T.34N;R.2W)*

An extreme south point of San Juan Island in Middle Channel, south central San Juan County. In 1859, the name was charted by British admiralty surveyor Richards. The point is joined to the island by a narrow neck of land. It should not be confused with a point by the same name which is on the northwest point of Shaw Island, and which is shown on recent maps and charts. The point named by Richards is found only on British admiralty charts.

Neck Point *(S.25;T.36N;R.3W)*

A northwest point of Shaw Island at the west end of Wasp Pass, central San Juan County. The point was locally named for its shape and should not be confused with another point of the same name on San Juan Island.

Necklace Valley Lakes
(Ss.7,17;T.24N;R.13E)

A group of 3 lakes -- Jade, Emerald, and Opal -- which are in a glaciated area directly northeast of Cascade Mountain summit, Snoqualmie National Forest, northeast King County. The group name is quite descriptive, as the lakes are

connected by short streams.

Necklace Valley Lake No. 1 (King County) *see* Jade Lake

Necklace Valley Lake No. 2 (King County) *see* Emerald lake

Necklace Valley Lake No. 3 (King County) *see* Opal Lake

Neclim Point *(S.28;T.20N;R.2W)*

A small, south side point on the east entrance to Hammersley Inlet, opposite Ayres Point, southeast Mason County. In 1841, it was named by the Wilkes Expedition and the name was retained by Capt. Kellett in his 1847 chartings. In 1854, it was recognized by the U.S. Coast Survey. Although not shown on recent maps, the point may be found directly south of Potlatch.

Necomanchee River (Pacific County) *see* North River

Neds Rock *(S.2;T.17N;R.11W)*

A rock directly offshore from Point New at the east entrance to North Bay, southwest Grays Harbor County. In 1841, the name was charted by the Wilkes Expedition and is official. A local name which is not official is *James Rock* for a family who settled here in 1857. (USBGN)

Needle Creek *(Mt. Rainier National Park)*

The stream of the creek rises near the sharp cliffs of Cowlitz Chimneys, east central zone of the park; flows 3 miles east to Kotsuck Creek, south of Barrier Peak. It was named for very sharp rock spires at its point of origin. (USBGN)

Ned-Waulk River (Spokane County) *see* Latah Creek

Needle Rock *(Mt. Rainier National Park)*

This sharp rock, elevation 7,575 ft., projects through the center of North Mowich Glacier on the northwest slope of Mt. Rainier, west central confines of the park. This pinnacle was named by Prof. J. B. Flett for a presumed resemblance to Cleopatra's Needle. (USBGN)

Negisticook Creek (Cowlitz County) *see* Abernethy Creek

Neguamos Island (Skagit County) *see* Reservation Head

Neill Point *(S.1;T.21N;R.2E)*

A southeast tip point of Vashon Island, on Dalco Passage, southwest King County. In 1841, the point was named by Cmdr. Charles Wilkes, for one of his quartermasters, William Neill.

Neilton *(S.12;T.22N;R.10W)*

Settlement 3 miles south of Quinault Lake, on McCalla Creek, north central Grays Harbor County. It is in a large, burned-over area, resulting from a forest fire. In 1910, when a post office was established, the settlement had been called *Jonesville* for Neil A. Jones, an early settler who established the first store in the area. Postal authorities rejected that name because of a town by the same name in Klickitat County. The applicants switched to the storekeeper's first name, which was accepted. A local name for the settlement is *The Burn* or *Quinault Burn*.

Nellita *(S.10;T.24N;R.2W)*

Settlement on the east shore of Hood Canal, 2 miles northeast of Holly, southwest Kitsap County. On July 23, 1900, the settlement was named by Ralph Brueger for his wife, Nellie. An earlier name was *Brown's Cove*, for Arthur Brown, a pioneer logger.

Nelson *(S.35;T.28N;R.26E)*

Small settlement 7 miles northeast of Mansfield, north central Douglas County. In the 1890s, it was named when a post office was established for a town in Nebraska which had been the home of nearby settlers.

Nelly's Run (Clallam County) *see* Tumwater Creek

Nels Lake (Snohomish County) *see* Bedal Lake

Nelson (Ferry County) *see* Danville

Nelson *(S.26;T.20N;R.14E)*

A railway station 5 miles west of Cle Elum, west central Kittitas County. In 1886, it was named by Northern Pacific Railway officials for a landowner on whose property the station was built. The first name ws *Nelson's*.

Nelson Butte *(T.15N;R.12E.uns)*

A Snoqualmie National Forest ridge, elevation 7,200 ft., 3-1/2 miles west of Mt. Aix, northwest Yakima County. The ridge is bounded on the northeast and northwest by North Fork of Rattlesnake Creek. It was named by The Mountaineers for L. A. Nelson of Portland -- aptly nicknamed "Shorty" by his many friends -- who was a great mountain explorer during his vigorous years.

Nelson Creek *(T.16N;R.13E.uns)*

A short and very steep stream which rises on Nelson Butte; flows 1-1/2 miles to North Fork of Rattlesnake Creek, Snoqualmie National Forest. (*see* Nelson Butte)

Nelson Peaks (Yakima County) *see* Fifes Peaks

Nelson Point *(S.31;T.26N;R.5E)*

An east shore point of Lake Washington at the south side of Juanita Bay, northwest King County. This small point jutts into Juanita Bay and was named for an early settler, J. T. Nelson. The Indian name, *Leqa-bt*, evidently related to red ochre which Indians found here, and which they used for coloring.

Nelson Ridge (Yakima County) *see* Nelson Butte

Nelson's (Kittitas County) *see* Nelson

Nemah *(S.22;T.12N;R.10W)*

Settlement at the mouth of Nemah River on Willapa Bay, west central Pacific County. It is on the site of a very old Indian village which carried this name. The meaning of the word has been lost, as the Indian band which lived here became extinct in the early years of white settlement.

Nemah River *(Ts.11,12N;Rs.9,10W)*

The stream of the river rises north of Naselle River, southwest Pacific County; flows northwest into Willapa Bay. Actually there are 3 rivers with a single name. The northern branch is separate from the middle and south streams which join near the outlet.

Neori Lake (Skagit County) *see* Found Lakes

Neppel (Grant County) *see* Moses Lake (town)

Nequally Creek (Cowlitz County) *see* Abernethy Creek

Nesika *(S.2;T.11N;R.4E)*

Community 1 mile south of Cowlitz River, near Steel Canyon, south central Lewis County. The name was chosen by an early settler, Mrs. J.T. Chilcoat, and the source is reported to be the Indian name of the place, but the Chinook designation was *We-our-ours-us*. The word means "mine."

Nesika Bridge *(S.35;T.12N;R.4E)*

A bridge spanning the Cowlitz River, 4 miles west of Kosmos, central Lewis County. (*see* Nesika)

Nespelem *(S.19;T.31N;R.31E)*

Town on Colville Indian Reservation, 3 miles northeast of Columbia River, extreme southeast corner of Okanogan County. This is a tribal name, and has the meaning of "large, open meadow," or "big, flat land." It aptly describes a large meadow adjoining this important town. In 1841, the word evidently sounded like Spillnin to members of the Wilkes Expedition who so charted it. Another early spelling was *Nspilich*.

Nespelem River
(Ts.30-33N;Rs.30,31E)

The source of the river is directly east of San Poil Divide, east central Okanogan County; flows south and southwest 26 miles to Columbia River, 4 miles southwest of Nespelem. (*see* Nespelem)

Nesqually House (Pierce/Thurston counties) *see* Fort Nisqually

Nesqually River (Pierce County) *see* Nisqually River

Nestos *(S.24;T.35N;R.8E)*

A small place which is mostly a logging camp, north bank of Skagit River, directly south of Van Horn, central Skagit County. It was named for Robert Reginald Nestos, who logged from these headquarters and who built a bridge across the Skagit River.

New Boston (Kitsap County) *see* Little Boston

New Boundary (Stevens County) *see* Boundary

New Channel *(T.36N;R.3W)*

A channel between Spieden and Flattop islands, north of Spieden Channel, northwest San Juan County. In 1858, the name was placed on British admiralty charts, without reference to its origin, by Capt. Henry Richards, RN.

New Chicago (Island County) *see* Keystone

New Chicago *(S.23;T.31N;R.1E)*

Abandoned town on the north shore of Admiralty Bay, on Whidbey Island, west central Island County. Once this was a boom town on the narrow strip of land between Admiralty Bay and Crocketts Lake. In 1890, the town was platted, its ambitious name chosen by real estate promoters. It was to be the western terminus of Chicago & Skagit Valley Railroad, with the eastern terminus at Sedro-Woolley.

New Dungeness *(T.31N;Rs.3,4W)*

Village enclosed by Dungeness Spit, on the Strait of Juan de Fuca, northeast Clallam County. In 1791, it was charted by Capt. George Vancouver because it resembled somewhat a promontory by that name in the Strait of Dover. The name was later used for the town, but has been shortened to *Dungeness*. It remains on the bay. (*see* New Dungeness Bay)

New Dungeness Bay *(T.31N;Rs.3,4W)*

A Strait of Juan de Fuca bay, partially enclosed by Dungeness Spit, northeast Clallam County. On July 8, 1790, Sub-Lieut. Manuel Quimper landed here and took possession in the name of the Spanish crown. He named it *Puerto y Bahia de Quimper*. On April 30, 1792, Capt. George Vancouver explored the bay and applied the present name for an English promontory on the Strait of Dover. The Indian name for the bay and surrounding area was *Tsescut*.(USBGN)

New Georgia

These coastal areas of Washington, north Oregon, and south British Columbia were claimed for the British Empire on June 4, 1792, by Capt. George Vancouver. Vancouver, anchored near the present site of Everett, chose this date because it was the birth date of H. M. George III, and the King's name was placed on the newly discovered land. Boundaries were not exact, but extended south from Desolation Sound to 45 degrees north latitude, as claimed by Vancouver for the British crown.

New Jerusalem *(T.19N;R.1W)*

Town (platted but never developed) on Henderson Inlet, 6 miles northeast of Olympia, north central Thurston County. Government officials and other prominent persons who pushed this embryo town, chose the resounding name, evidently hoping to interest religious citizens. *Harpers Magazine* featured the boom town in its September, 1870 issue. The name is not on recent maps.

New Kamilche *(S.29;T.19N;R.3W)*

Small hamlet in Skookum Creek Valley, west side of Oyster Bay, southeast Mason County. It is quite active during summer months, and was once a lively logging center. A post office, installed on Skookum Inlet, bore the name *Kamilche*. When it moved to the north side of Oyster Bay, its name was changed to the present form. *Kamilche*, the Indian name for this general area, has the meaning of ''valley.''

New Market (Thurston County) *see* Tumwater

New Utsaladdy *(S.19;T.32N;R.3E)*

Fairly recent settlement on the east shore of Utsaladdy Bay, Camano Island, east Island County. It is 1-1/2 miles east of the very old site of Utsalady. (*see* Utsalady)

New Whatcom *(Ts.37,38N;Rs.2,3E)*

An early town of Bellingham Bay, formed by the merger of Whatcom and Sehome in 1891, assisted by the coming of a large number of settlers from Kansas. This town later combined with Fairhaven to form the city of Bellingham. (*see* Whatcom Falls)

New York, New York Alki (King County) *see* Alki

New York Bar *(S.32;T.13N;R.38E)*

An important wheat-shipping point before railroads came to the area, on Snake River at Texas Ferry, directly above present-day Riparia. The name was given by a pioneer wheat shipper for his home state.

New York Point (King County) *see* Alki Point

Newaukum *(S.8;T.13N;R.2W)*

Small community 3 miles south of Chehalis, west central Lewis County. The Puget Sound Agricultural Company, a Hudson's Bay Company subsidiary, maintained a farm here in the early pioneer years of the state. It was named by Northern Pacific Railway Company officials for Newaukum River. *Newaukum* is an Indian name, locally applied, and means ''gently flowing water.''

Newaukum Creek *(Ts.20,21N;Rs.6,7E)*

The stream of the creek rises in a swamp 4-1/2 miles northeast of Enumclaw in several branches, south central King County; flows 16 miles west and northwest to Green River, 3 miles southwest of Black Diamond.

Newaukum Lake (Lewis County) *see* Newaukum Lakes

Newaukum Lakes *(Ss.30,31;T.14N;R.3E)*

Three connected lakes, elevation 3,000 ft., at the head of South Fork, Newaukum River, Snoqualmie National Forest, north central Lewis County. Newaukum Lake covers 17 acres; Spud Lake has an area of 3 acres; Moss Lake measures about 3-1/2 acres. (*see* Newaukum)

Newaukum Prairie (Lewis County) *see* Forest

Newaukum River *(Ts.13,14N;R.2W)*

The stream of the river rises 8 miles southeast of Chehalis, west central Lewis County; flows northwest to Chehalis River at the south city limits of Chehalis. (*see* Newaukum)

Newcastle *(S.27;T.24N;R.5E)*

Community on Coal Creek, 2 miles east of the south shore of Lake Washington, west central King County. In 1863, excellent coal seams were discovered here. One of the first coal mines in the state was developed, which became a very heavy producer. In August 1869, the name was applied by F. H. Whitworth, J. E. Whitworth, and Rev. George F. Whitworth, when they uncovered an excellent coal vein. Their choice of name was based on the old adage relating to the carrying of coals to Newcastle, which related to the famous English coal mining town of Newcastle-On-Tyne.

Newell (Island County) *see* Freeland

Newhalem *(S.21;T.37N;R.12E)*

Community on Skagit River, 6 miles southwest of Diablo Dam, Mt. Baker National Forest, southeast Whatcom County. It is the headquarters for Seattle City Light operations on the upper Skagit River. The name appears to have been originated by officials of Seattle City Lighting Department, as no town existed here before the City of Seattle moved in.

Newhalem Creek *(T.37N;R.12E.uns)*

The stream of the creek heads in northeast Skagit County; flows northwest to Skagit River at Newhalem power house, southeast Whatcom County. (*see* Newhalem)

Newhall (San Juan County) *see* Rosario

Newhall's Point *(T.35N;R.2W)*

A south end point of Friday Harbor, east shore of San Juan Island, central

San Juan County. The point was named for Andrew Newhall, who operated shingle, stave, and bolt mills in the San Juan Islands. Judge E. D. Warbass, who lived here for some years, called the point *Idlewild.* It is not shown on most maps and charts.

Newman Creek *(T.27N;R.45E)*

The stream of the creek heads in northeast Spokane County, near the Idaho boundary; flows 5 miles south and southwest to Newman Lake. (*see* Newman Lake)

Newman Lake *(Ts.26,27N;R.45E)*

A 2-1/2-mile-long lake, average width 1/2 to 1-1/2 miles wide, 13 miles northeast of Spokane, 2 miles west of the Idaho boundary, east central Spokane County. It was named for William Newman who settled on the lake in 1865 after serving in the escort of the American surveyors who worked with Canadian surveyors in determining the boundary between the 2 countries. The lake has many bays.

Newport *(T.31N;R.45E)*

A leading town on the west bank of Pend Oreille River, 50 miles north of Spokane, southeast Pend Oreille County. Directly west of the Idaho line, part of the town is in Idaho, and is known as *Old Town.* In the 1860s, the place was a miners' camp and became a real town on the Idaho side in the 1880s. In 1901, the post office was moved from Idaho, a distance of 3,175 ft., to Newport, Washington, bringing the name with the post office. The name was suggested by an early resident, M. C. Kelly, when a new river landing was built on the Pend Oreille to accommodate the first sternwheelers.

Newport Beach *(S.18;T.22N;R.3E)*

A northeast shore beach of Quartermaster Harbor, Vashon Island, 1/2 mile north of Burton, southwest King County. In 1906, it was named by Dr. A. L. Goff, an early resident, for his former home in Newport, Rhode Island.

Newskah Creek *(Ts.16,17N;R.9W)*

The stream of the creek heads west of Artic, south central Grays Harbor County; flows northwest to Grays Harbor directly west of South Aberdeen. The name is a variation of the Indian designation *Noos-koh,* meaning "good water to drink." A post office was established here under the name *Neush-*

kah, but was discontinued before 1915. The name had been shortened to the present form by local usage. (USBGN)

Nez Perce Creek *(T.31N;Rs.35,36E)*

The stream of the creek rises on Colville Indian Reservation, south central Ferry County; flows east and south 11 miles to Columbia River, 4-1/2 miles south of Kewa. It was named for a legendary ambush and massacre of Nez Perce Indians by Colville Indians (*Skoyelpi*) near the mouth of this creek.

Niawiakum River *(T.13N;R.10W)*

The stream of this short river rises south of South Bend, west central Pacific County; flows 4 miles to Willapa Bay between Bone River and Palix River. The Indian name, which has been retained, has the meaning of "tidelands." Previous names have been *Mouse River* and *Querquellin River.*

Nibbyville *(Kitsap County) see* Point White

Nickel Creek *(Mt. Rainier National Park)*

The stream of the creek rises near the foot of Ohanapecosh Glacier, on the southwest slope of Mt. Rainier, southwest zone of the park; flows 4-1/2 miles to Muddy Fork, Cowlitz River, 1/2 mile north of the park's south boundary. This name was once applied to a small stream which enters the Muddy Fork from the east, near the park boundary, and along which there was some prospecting for nickel ore. For some reason which is not on record, the name was shifted to the present Nickel Creek. (USBGN)

Nickomin River *(Grays Harbor County) see* North River

Nigger Bar *(T.38N;R.38E)*

A Columbia River bar at China Bend, between Marble and Ryan, northwest Stevens County. A considerable amount of placer gold is reputed to have been recovered here. A clue to the origin of this name may be found in the great diversity of racial strains among the early placer miners along the upper Columbia. Names applied by these adventurers were often lusty.

Nigger Creek *(T.22N;R.17E)*

The stream of the creek heads on the north slope of Wenatchee Mountains, 6 miles west of Blewett, southwest Chelan County; flows 7 miles east into Peshastin Creek, 1 mile north of Blewett. The

name was applied in early mining days, based on a legend that a black man took a fortune in placer gold from the creek.

Nigger Head Rapids *(S.4;T.6N;R.47E)*

Snake River rapids, 5 miles upstream from the mouth of Grande Ronde River, between southeast Asotin County and west Idaho. In 1880, this feature was named by pioneers, for several large, black rocks which protruded above the water near the center of the rapids.

Niggerhead Pond *(S.33;T.11N;R.8E)*

A 6-acre lake which is drained by Niggerhead Creek, 11-1/2 miles southeast of Randle, southeast Lewis County.

Nighthawk *(S.13;T.40N;R.25E)*

A former mining boom town, 11 miles northwest of Oroville, 2-1/2 miles south of the Canadian boundary, north central Okanogan County. In 1899, when it secured a post office, the name of the nearby Nighthawk Mine was proposed and accepted. The mine was named for the many birds of that species in the vicinity.

Nikepun River *(Klickitat County) see* White Salmon River

Nikepun River *(Skamania County) see* White Salmon River

Nile *(S.33;T.16N;R.15E)*

Settlement on south bank of Naches River, in Nile Valley, at the mouth of Rattlesnake Creek, northwest Yakima County. In the middle 1890s, it was established by the families of Henry Sedge, James Beck, and William Markle. (*see* Nile Creek)

Nile Creek *(T.16N;Rs.13-15E)*

The stream of the creek rises in Clover Spring, 5 miles east of Bumping Lake; flows 15 miles east to Naches River at Nile, northwest Yakima County. The creek, valley, and town were named by early settlers for its fertility, resembling that of Nile Valley in Egypt.

Nill Point *(Jefferson County) see* Mill Point

Nine Pins *(T.6N;R.35E)*

A group of rocks of fantastic shapes, west of Walla Walla, in the valley of Walla Walla River, Walla Walla County. In 1841, this name was applied by the Wilkes Expedition when they first approached the rocks.

Ninemile Creek
(Ts.29-32N;Rs.34-35E)

The stream of the creek rises in the mountains back of Twin Lakes, Colville Indian Reservation, southeast Ferry County; flows 25 miles southeast to the Columbia River, 9 miles above the mouth of Spokane River. The name registers the fact that the mouth of the creek is 9 miles above the mouth of Spokane River. Threemile and Sixmile creeks are similarly named.

Nippon (King County) *see* Alpine

Nisqually *(S.4;T.18N;R.1E)*

Small settlement on Nisqually River delta, 20 miles southwest of Tacoma on the west boundary of Fort Lewis Army Post, southwest Pierce County. It borrowed the name from the river on which it is located. The name is for a local Indian tribe whose name has been variously interpreted as *Nasqually, Nezqually, Niskwalli, N'skwali,,* and *Si-gwal-it-chie.* A suggested name origin, which has no authentication, is from the French, *Nez Quarrees,* meaning ''square noses.'' (USBGN)

Nisqually Entrance *(Mt. Rainier National Park)*

This heavily-traveled entrance to the park is near Nisqually River, extreme southwest corner of the park. Car and fire permits are issued at the entrance gate and a public campsite is nearby. The name was taken from Nisqually River. (*see* Nisqually)

Nisqually Flats *(T.19N;R.1E)*

The delta of Nisqually River, on Nisqually Reach at the mouth of Nisqually River, northeast Thurston and northwest Pierce counties. This is an extensive alluvial deposit named for the river. An earlier name was *Inskip Bank,* shown only on very old maps. A local name, which has persisted to some extent, is *Mud Flat.* (*see* Nisqually)

Nisqually Glacier *(Mt. Rainier National Park)*

A receding ice river on the south slope of Mt. Rainier, extending from the summit to headwaters of Nisqually River, a distance of about 5 miles. This is one of the 6 largest glaciers in the park and its terminus was about 1,500 ft. lower in the middle 1880s. In 1870, it was named for Nisqually River by Gen. Hazard Stevens and P. B. Van Trump, when they found it to be the source of

that stream. (*see* Nisqually) (USBGN)

Nisqually Head
(Ss.29,32;T.19N;R.1E)

An east side head of Nisqually River mouth, on Nisqually Reach, extreme northeast Thurston County. In 1841, this head was named *Loa Point* by the Wilkes Expedition's exploration of Mauna Loa in Hawaii. On some older charts this was distorted into *Laa Point.* (*see* Nisqually)

Nisqually House (Pierce/Thurston counties) *see* Fort Nisqually

Nisqually Indian Reservation
(T.18N;R.1E)

A 1,364-acre reservation along Nisqually River, directly southwest of Fort Lewis Army Post, southwest Pierce County. On December 26, 1854, it was established by the Medicine Creek Treaty which was made with several tribes at this site. (*see* Nisqually)

Nisqually Lake *(Ss.24,25;T.18N;R.1E)*

A lake directly southwest of Fort Lewis Army Post, along Nisqually River near its mouth on Nisqually Flats, Pierce County. (*see* Nisqually)

Nisqually Reach *(T.19N;Rs.1W;1E)*

A crescent-shaped channel of Puget Sound, between Anderson Island and the mainland, average width 2 miles, 12 miles long; it is on the boundary between southwest Pierce and east Thurston counties. (*see* Nisqually)

Nisqually Reservoir (Pierce County) *see* Lake Alder

Nisqually River *(Ts.14-19N;Rs.1-7E)*

The stream of the river rises in Nisqually Glacier on the south slope of Mt. Rainier; flows west to Alder Lake, then northwest between Pierce and Thurston counties to Puget Sound at Nisqually Reach. (*see* Nisqually)

Nisson *(S.21;T.19N;R.9W)*

Settlement near Hoquiam River, 9 miles north of Aberdeen, central Grays Harbor County. In 1896, the name was applied when a post office was established. It is for the first man to log in the East Hoquiam Valley, about 1894 or 1895.

No Name Lake *(S.2;T.24N;R.13E)*

Shallow, glaciated 8-acre lake, 2 miles west of Deception Pass at Cascade Mountain summit, northeast King County. The namer is also anonymous, but he

did a better job of naming than those who saddled *Mud, Fish, Deer,* and *Clear* onto scores of lakes in the state.

No Name Mountain (Chelan County) *see* Booker Mountain

Nob Island *(S.24;T.36N;R.3W)*

One of the smallest of 8 islands in the Wasp Island group, directly west of Wasp Pass, central San Juan County. In 1858, it was charted by Capt. Henry Richards of British admiralty survey. The name reflects its very small size.

Nob Point (San Juan County) *see* Point Doughty

Noble Nob *(S.14;T.18N;R.10E)*

A high point on a ridge between Lost and Twenty-Eight-Mile creeks, Snoqualmie National Forest, 6 miles southwest of Naches Pass, southeast Pierce County. It is used as a fire lookout in season and was named for Noble Firs which were supposed to be here -- but are not.

Nocktosh (Yakima County) *see* Yakima River

Nodule Point *(S.4;T.29N;R.1E)*

A southeast shore point of Marrowstone Island, on Admiralty Inlet, northeast Jefferson County. In 1792, the present name was applied by Capt. George Vancouver because of peculiar geological formations which he found here. In 1841, it was named *Ariel Point* by the Wilkes Expedition. In 1868, the U.S. Coast Survey ruled that Vancouver's name was official.

Noisy Creek *(T.37N;R.9,10E)*

The stream of the creek rises on south slope of Bacon Peak, south central Whatcom County; flows 6 miles north-by-west to Baker Lake. It is locally known as ''a boisterous creek.'' The descriptive name was applied by government surveyors. A previous name was *Bacon Creek.*

Noname Creek *(T.39N;R.13E.uns)*

The stream of the creek rises in Noname Lake, 3 miles west of Ross Lake, Mt. Baker National Forest, east central Whatcom County; flows 5 miles northeast to Ross Lake. The donor of the name appears to be as anonymous as the creek.

Noname Glacier *(T.38N;R.8E.uns)*

A north slope glacier of Mt. Baker, between Mazama and Bastille glaciers, central Whatcom County. In 1886, the glacier was discovered by W. H. Dorr, and was further explored in 1892 by B. B. Dobbs, neither of whom recorded any naming. In 1911, the present anonymous name was chosen by Henry C. Engberg. It does not appear on USGS and other standard maps.

Noname Lake *(S.33;T.39N;R.13E.uns)*

A 10-acre, Mt. Baker National Forest lake, elevation 3,900 ft., 8-1/2 miles northwest of Ross Dam, 3 miles west of Ross Lake, at the head of Noname Creek, east central Whatcom County. It was named for Noname Creek.

Nooksack *(S.29;T.40N;R.4E)*

Town 12 miles northeast of Bellingham, 1 mile east of Nooksack River, northwest Whatcom County. On September 16, 1885, the town was named for the Nooksack Indian tribe when the townsite plat was filed by W. R. Moultray. The first use of the name *Nooksack* appears to have been on an 1857 map compiled by the surveyor general of Washington Territory. It is for a local Indian tribe, the *Neuk-sack* or *Noot-saak*, meaning "fern-eating people." (*Noot* -- "people;" *Saak* -- "bracken fern.") This word has been found in many spellings on maps and records, including *Nootsack, Nooksak, Nook-sahk*, and others.

Nooksack Community

A number of individual Indian allotments in the Nooksack Valley, total 2,906 acres. This small community of allottees resides south of Everson. Tribal affairs are governed by a community tribal council and it is named for the Nooksack Indian tribe. (*see* Nooksack)

Nooksack Falls *(S.31;T.40N;R.8E)*

A 100-ft. waterfall on Nooksack River, 9 miles directly north of Mt. Baker summit, north central Whatcom County. (*see* Nooksack)

Nooksack River *(Ts.38-40N;Rs.2-7E)*

The stream of this important river rises in 3 forks which unite near Deming, flows from the west and south slopes of Mt. Baker to Bellingham Bay near Marietta, through west central Whatcom County. It originally emptied into Lummi Bay, but was diverted into Bellingham Bay by immense log jams in very early days. (*see* Nooksack)

Noon *(S.2;T.38N;R.3E)*

Small farming community, 4 miles southeast of Bellingham, between Wahl and Van Wyck, west central Whatcom County. On April 16, 1890, it was locally named for A. F. Noon, a successful farmer in this area.

No-Outlet Sand Hills *(T.18N;R.28E)*

Sandy hills which cover several sq. miles, directly south of Moses Lake (lake), south central Grant County. Many of these hills have been submerged in Potholes Reservoir. The name, given by pioneer settlers, was intended to be descriptive, indicating that Moses Lake had no apparent southern outlet.

Nordland *(S.32;T.30N;R.1E)*

Townsite near the center of Marrowstone Island, extreme northeast Jefferson County. In 1890, it was named for Peter F. Nordby, who owned land here and who platted the townsite in 1892.

Nordrum *(S.16;T.24;R.10E)*

The site of a mountain camp, with cabins, Snoqualmie National Forest, 14 miles west of Cascade Mountain summit, at the confluence of Quartz Creek and Taylor River, northeast King County. It was locally named for Martin Nordrum of North Bend, who homesteaded near Taylor River, and who was employed by the U.S. Forest Service. An alternate name is *Nordrum Cabins*.

Nordrum Basin Lakes
(Ss.19,20;T.24N;R.11E)

A group of 5 mountain lakes in Nordrum Basin, Snoqualmie National Forest, 8 miles north of Snoqualmie Pass, northeast King County. The lakes are: 10-acre *Judy*; 11-acre *Caroline*; 60-acre *Nordrum*; 9-acre *Rock*; 3-1/2-acre *Lunker*. These lakes are individually described under their proper headings. (*see* Nordrum)

Nordrum Lake *(S.20;T.24N;R.11E)*

One of 5 Nordrum Lakes, located 8-1/2 miles north of Snoqualmie Pass, 16-1/2 miles northeast of North Bend, northeast King County. This lake is 60 acres, the largest of the group. (*see* Nordrum)

Norman *(S.35;T.32N;R.4E)*

Former post office 19 miles north of Everett, near Stillaguamish River, northwest Snohomish County. It was locally named for P. O. Norman, the first settler in that part of Stillaguamish valley.

Norse Peak *(S.19;T.17N;R.11E)*

A Snoqualmie National Forest peak, elevation 6,862 ft., at the head of North Fork, Union Creek, southeast Pierce County. Originally it was named *Swede Butte* for the nickname of U.S. Forest Ranger Lind. It later was changed to the present designation, as the first name was considered undignified by Forest Service officials.

North Bay *(Ts.17,18N;Rs.11,12W)*

A north entrance bay of Grays Harbor, 5 miles west of Hoquiam, at the mouth of Humptulips River, southwest Grays Harbor County. It is a locally applied descriptive name, matched by South Bay at the south entrance. In 1841, the Wilkes Expedition charted it as *Useless Bay* because it is shallow and has many silt bars and winding channels.

North Bay (Pacific County) *see* Willapa Harbor

North Bay *(T.22N;R.1W)*

A 3-1/2-mile-long bay, 1/2 mile average width, 3 miles southeast of the east extremity of Hood Canal, east central Mason County. The Indian name for the bay was *Skwak-sin*. In 1841, the Wilkes Expedition named it *Paun Cove*. Present name came into local use because the bay is a northern extension of Cases Inlet.

North Bay *(S.24;T.35N;R.3W)*

A southeast shore bay of San Juan Island, 1 mile south of Friday Harbor, northeast portion of Griffin Bay, San Juan County. It was locally named because of its position in Griffin Bay.

North Beach *(T.37N;R.2W)*

A seaside resort at the north end of Orcas Island, facing the Strait of Georgia, northeast San Juan County. The resort offers good saltwater fishing and was locally named because it is the most northerly of beaches on Orcas Island.

North Beach Peninsula
(Ts.10-13N;R.11W)

An extraordinary ocean beach peninsula extending 28 miles north from Columbia River to Willapa Harbor, Pacific County. It offers the finest ocean beach in the state and is a summer resort area. There was once a railroad from Ilwaco to Nahcotta. Originally it was called *North Peninsula*, but the name was changed by popular consent to the more descriptive name which is now official.

North Bend (S.9;T.23N;R.8E)

A highway town 11 miles east of Issaquah on South Fork, Snoqualmie River, central King County. The town was named because of a sharp bend here in Snoqualmie River before it flows over Snoqualmie Falls. Other names that were used for this place in the past were *Mountain View, South Fork,* and *Snoqualmie.*

North Bluff (S.4;T.30N;R.2E)

A Whidbey Island bluff at the northwest entrance to Holmes Harbor, on Saratoga Passage, south central Island County. In 1841, the bluff was named by the Wilkes Expedition for James North, acting master of the *U.S.S. Vincennes,* one of Wilkes' ships.

North Blockhouse (King County) *see* Fort Decatur

North Bluff (Clallam County) *see* Diamond Point

North Bonneville (S.16;T.2N;R.7E)

Town on north bank of Columbia River, 39-1/2 miles east of Vancouver, on the Washington state side of Bonneville Dam, Skamania County. In the early 1930s, it was established by workers on the dam and was named after the dam. The dam was named for Capt. Benjamin Louis Eulalie Bonneville -- soldier, explorer, and adventurer.

North Cascade Primitive Area

An extensive 801,000-acre area in Whatcom and Okanogan counties, reserved for public recreation and exempted from commercial use in general, on July 19, 1935, by the secretary of agriculture. On Chelan National Forest there are 366,800 acres; on Mt. Baker National Forest, 434,200 acres. The site is almost entirely high, mountainous country, with many glaciers and few access roads or trails. It extends for about 65 miles along the Canadian boundary and about 20 miles southward. Elevations of over 9,000 ft. are found among the higher peaks. It is handled by the Forest Service as a Wilderness Area, with regulations against uses which might destroy its primitive nature.

North Cove (S.10;T.14N;R.11W)

Fishing village (with beach recreation facilities) on Dibkey Slough at the north entrance of Willapa Harbor, northwest Pacific County. The name was chosen by local residents because the town borders on a small cove at the north entrance to the harbor.

North Creek (Yakima County) *see* Dry Creek

North Dalles (Klickitat County) *see* Dallesport

North Fork, Calispell Creek (T.32N;R.42E)

The stream of the creek rises 11 miles west-by-north of Dalkena, southwest Pend Oreille County; flows 5 miles southeast to Calispell Creek. (*see* Calispell Creek) (USBGN)

North Fork, Downey Creek (Skagit County) *see* Goat Creek

North Fork, Entiat River (Ts.29,30N;R.18E.uns)

The stream of the creek heads near Emerald Peak, between Chelan Mountains and Entiat River, north central Chelan County; flows 10 miles southeast to Entiat River at North Fork Camp. Since 1897, this descriptive name has been in use, having been applied by local prospectors.

North Fork, Nason Creek (Chelan County) *see* Smith Brook

North Fork, Salmon Creek (T.37N;Rs.23,24E)

The stream of the creek heads near Tiffany Lake, central Okanogan County; flows southeast 10-1/2 miles to Salmon Creek, near the junction of Pelican Creek. On some maps, it is called *North Salmon Creek* (USBGN)

North-Half (Ferry County) *see* North portion of Ferry County

North Head (S.5;T.9N;R.11W)

A north entrance head to Columbia River, 1-1/2 miles west of Ilwaco, extreme southwest corner of Pacific County. A lighthouse on the head is 260 ft. high. The name, applied by Davidson in 1889, is quite descriptive. Another name, *Point Lewis,* used by the Lewis & Clark Expedition in 1905, did not persist.

North Lake (S.33;T.31N;R.10E)

A 10.6-acre, Mt. Baker National Forest lake, elevation 4,100 ft., 9 miles southeast of Darrington, north central Snohomish County. The name developed from local usage, and is descriptive because the lake is at the head of North Fork, Falls Creek.

North McNary (S.9;T.5N;R.28E)

Railroad station on north bank of Columbia River, near site of McNary Dam, extreme south central Benton County. In 1947, this delivery point for construction materials was established when work on McNary Dam started. It was named by railroad officials for McNary Dam, which was named for the late Sen. Charles L. McNary of Oregon, a statesman and a conservationist.

North Mountain (Ss.23,26,35;T.33N;R.9E)

A peak 4 miles north of Darrington, between Sauk River and North Fork, Stillaguamish River, extreme south central Skagit County. It is reported to have been named by government surveyors because of its position directly north of the Snohomish County boundary.

North Mowich Glacier (*Mt. Rainier National Park*)

A northwest slope glacier on Mt. Rainier, between Russell and Edmunds glaciers, northwest quarter of the park. Other names that have been used are *Willis, Tyler,* and *North Puyallup.* (*see* Mowich River) (USBGN)

North Mowich River (*Mt. Rainier National Park*)

The stream of the river rises at the foot of North Mowich Glacier, northwest zone of the park; flows 3 miles westward to join South Mowich River, 1 mile east of the park's west boundary. (*see* Mowich River) (USBGN)

North Pass (S.13;T.36N;R.3W)

A short passage between Reef Island and Steep Point, at the southwest tip of Orcas Island, San Juan County. In 1858, it was named by Capt. Henry Richards, British admiralty surveyor. He chose the name because it is the most northerly of the passes between Shaw and Orcas islands.

North Pine (S.28;T.21N;R.43E)

Settlement on North Pine Creek, 22-1/2 miles south of Spokane, extreme south central Spokane County. It was named for the creek on which it is located.

North Point (S.14;T.26N;R.4E)

An east shore point of Lake Washington, 1 mile south of mouth of Sammamish River, northwest King County.

The name chosen by local residents is descriptive, as this is the most northerly distinct point on Lake Washington's shores. The Indian name was *U-as,* meaning "gravel rattling down."

Northport *(S.36;T.40N;R.39E)*

A former smelter town on Columbia River, 6 miles south of the Canadian border, north central Stevens County. Early miners had camped at this place for several years before the Spokane Falls & Northern Railway reached it on September 18, 1892. Also 3 homesteads had been filed by A. V. Downs, Fred Farquhar, and Frank George. In that year, a townsite was platted on parts of these 3 homesteads by Northport Townsite Company, owned by the railroad magnate D. C. Corbin. The name was given by officials of Spokane Falls & Northern Railway Company, because Northport was destined to be the most northerly town on the railroad, south of the Canadian border. A previous town name was *Terminal City.*

North Puyallup Glacier (Mt. Rainier National Park) *see* North Mowich Glacier

Northrup (King County) *see* Northup

North Puyallup River *(T.15N;R.6,7E)*

The stream of the river rises at the foot of Puyallup Glacier, in many branches, Mt. Rainier National Park; flows 12 miles west-by-north to join South Puyallup River in Pierce County, 2 miles west of the park boundary. (*see* Puyallup River)

North River *(Ts.15,16N;Rs.6-10W)*

The stream of the river heads in the extreme northeast corner of Pacific County; flows west through Grays Harbor and Pacific counties to Shoalwater Bay on Willapa Harbor. The Indian name was *Nic-o-man-chie,* meaning "Shadowy waters." In Tilton's map of Washington Territory, published in 1859, the stream is designated as *North Channel.* In the following years, the name was altered to the present form by local usage.

North Rock *(S.21;T.25N;R.3W.uns)*

One of 3 rocky peaks on the east wall of Cabin Creek Cirque, Olympic National Forest, 5 miles west of Bellview, extreme southeast corner of Jefferson County. The other peaks are East Rock and West Rock. All are named with reference to their position around the cirque. (USBGN)

North Samish River *(T.35N;R.3E)*

The stream of the river heads north of Allen, northwest Skagit County; flows 6 miles northwest to Edison Slough on Samish Bay. (*see* Samish)

North Salmon Creek (Okanogan County) *see* North Fork Salmon Creek

No. 32 Lake (King County) *see* Retreat Lake

North Skookum Lake *(S.36;T.34N;R.44E)*

A small lake, 5 miles east of Pend Oreille River, just inside the boundary of Kaniksu National Forest, south central Pend Oreille County. It is connected by a stream with South Skookum Lake, 1/2 mile to the south. About 1901, this Chinook jargon word was placed on both lakes by early settlers. It has 2 meanings, either of which may have been in the minds of the namers. One meaning is "strong" or "solid." The other refers to ghosts or spirits. As there appears to be nothing very strong or powerful connected with the lakes, the later meaning might be more logical. However, the name might have been borrowed from Skookum Creek which drains South Skookum, and which is fairly "skookum" at certain seasons.

North Twin Lake *(T.32N;R.35E)*

A 2-mile-long, Colville Indian Reservation lake, 8 miles west of Inchelium, east central Ferry County. It is fed by several creeks, and drains east into Columbia River through Stranger Creek. The name is descriptive, as it is directly north of South Twin Lake, which has about the same shape and is only slightly larger.

North Twin Mountain (Whatcom County) *see* Twin Sisters Range

Northport *(S.36;T.40N;R.39E)*

Almost a ghost town on Columbia River, 6 miles south of the Canadian border, north central Stevens County. Early miners had camped at this place for several years before the Spokane Falls & Northern Railway reached it on September 18, 1892. Also 3 homesteads had been filed by A. V. Downs, Fred

Farquhar, and Frank George. In that year, a townsite was platted on parts of these 3 homesteads by Northport Townsite Company, owned by the railroad magnate D. C. Corbin. The name was given by officials of Spokane Falls & Northern Railway Company, because Northport was destined to be the most northerly town on the railroad, south of the Canadian border. A previous town name was *Terminal City.*

Northup *(S.21;T.25N;R.5E)*

Small community, 1-1/2 miles east of Lake Washington, 2-1/2 miles south of Kirkland, northwest King County. It was named for Benson L. Northup, who owned land here and who published Seattle's first city directory. It appears on certain recent maps as *Northrup,* in error. An older name, not used now, was *Northup Landing.*

Northup Landing (King County) *see* Northup

Norwegian Point *(S.16;T.28N;R.2E)*

An Admiralty Inlet point, between Point No Point and Foulweather Bluff, directly east of Hansville, extreme north Kitsap County. This rounded, rather indistinct point was named by U.S. Coast & Geodetic Survey in 1855, for the preponderance of Norwegian settlers in this area.

Nova Albion

This is the name applied to the west coast of the U.S. by the British Capt. Francis Drake in 1578. He possibly reached a latitude of about 48 degrees north, which was off the Washington coast. The name means "New England," using the Roman name for England. It was applied long before that name was used on the east coast of the U.S.

North Yakima (Yakima County) *see* Yakima

N-Soy-Akin (Spokane County) *see* Spangle

Nuisance Creek *(T.36N;R.45E)*

The stream of this very small creek rises south of Diamond Peak, Kaniksu National Forest, east central Pend Oreille County; flows 1 mile east to Kalispel Creek, almost at the Idaho state boundary. No records have been found to indicate why this little stream was an annoyance.

O

Oak Bay *(T.29;R.1E)*

An Admiralty Inlet bay, south of Marrowstone Island, northeast Jefferson County. In 1841, Cmdr. Charles Wilkes named this bay *Port Lawrence* for Capt. James Lawrence, who was killed in 1813 during the battle between *Shannon* and *Chesapeake*. On May 9, 1792, Capt. George Vancouver had named the bay *Oak Cove* for the abundance of native oak trees in the vicinity. In 1846, Capt. Henry Kellett restored Vancouver's name, but with a change from *Oak Cove* to the present name.

Oak Harbor *(T.32N;R.1E)*

East shore harbor of Whidbey Island, between Penn Cove and Crescent Harbor, northwest Island County. This semi-circular harbor, almost bisected by a narrow sand spit, is directly southwest of a U.S. Naval air base. The harbor was named by settlers for the many large oak trees in the vicinity, quite an unusual feature in this part of the state.

Oak Harbor *(S.32;T.32N;R.1E)*

City on Oak Harbor bay, east shore of Whidbey Island, northwest Island County. Founded in 1849, this is a very old Puget Sound community. The Indian name for the place was *Kla-tole-tsche*. (*see* Oak Harbor)

Oak Head *(S.4;T.25N;R.1W)*

An extreme south end head of Toandos Peninsula on Hood Canal, southeast Jefferson County. In 1841, this point was charted by Wilkes, using the original Indian name, *Nukolowap*. In 1847, Capt. Henry Kellett charted the point under the present name.

Oak Island *(S.16;T.36N;R.2W)*

A very small island on the east shore of West Sound, opposite Double Island on the west shore, central San Juan County. In 1859, this name was charted by Capt. Henry Richards, British Admiralty surveyor, because of a few native oak trees on the island.

Oak Point *(S.9;T.18N;R.4W)*

A north bank point of Columbia River, 14 miles west of Longview, southwest Cowlitz County. It was named for very large oak trees, up to 13 ft. circumference, which grow on the point.

In 1792, these were noted by Lieut. W. R. Broughton of Capt. George Vancouver's expedition.

Oakesdale *(S.22;T.19N;R.44E)*

Town 18 miles northwest of Palouse, northeast Whitman County. On July 19, 1886, this town was platted under the name of *McCoy*. Later in the same year, Northern Pacific Railway Company officials used the present name for their station. It is for Thomas F. Oakes, who at the time was vice president and general manager of the railroad. The name also was used by Northern Pacific Land Company. McCoy's name was transferred to a smaller place 4 miles to the northwest.

Oakinacken (Okanogan County) *see* Okanogan

Oakland *(S.9;T.20N;R.3W)*

Community on Oakland Bay, 1-1/2 miles northeast of Shelton, southeast Mason County. In 1864, it was the largest town in this area. It was named for numerous scattered oak trees in the vicinity, by William T. Morrow, the first settler and owner of a Donation Land Claim here in 1855.

Oakland Bay *(T.20N;R.3W)*

A 5-mile-long bay, 1/2 mile average width, directly northeast of Shelton, southeast Mason County. In 1841, when Cmdr. Charles Wilkes discovered the bay, he applied the name *Hammersley Inlet* as a common name for both the bay and the present Hammersley Inlet. Oakland Bay was named by William T. Morrow. (*see* Oakland)

Oakville *(S.30;T.16N;R.4W)*

Once a Chehalis Indian campsite, now a farm center, 1/2 mile east of Chehalis River, 1 mile north of Chehalis Indian Reservation, extreme southeast corner of Grays Harbor County. It was named for the prevalance of rather scrubby White Oak, *Guercus garryana*.

O'Brien *(S.12;T.22N;R.4E)*

Small settlement, populated largely by Irish settlers in the 1860s, 2-1/2 miles north of Kent, west central King County. It was named for the founders, Morgan and Terence O'Brien, who homesteaded here in 1868. The post office was called *White River*.

O'Brien Creek *(T.36N;Rs.33,34E)*

The stream of the creek, with many tributaries, rises on the west slope of Snow Peak, Colville Indian Reservation, central Ferry County; flows west and northwest 15 miles to the San Poil River east of Republic. The creek is reported to be named for an early settler, Frank O'Brien, who became a prosperous rancher and stockman.

Observation Point (Mt. Rainier National Park) *see* Observation Rock

Observation Rock *(Mt. Rainier National Park)*

An 8,364-ft. pinnacle on the northwest slope of Mt. Rainier, topping a ridge which separates Russell and Flett glaciers, northwest quarter of the park. In 1885, it was named *Observation Point* by L. F. Henderson, for its excellent view. The name was changed to its present form at a later date by park mappers. (USBGN)

Observatory Point *(S.25;T.31N;R.8W)*

A west entrance point on Freshwater Bay, Strait of Juan de Fuca, 3 miles east of Crescent Bay, north central Clallam County. On July 4, 1790, this feature was named *Punta de Salvi* by Manual Quimper. In 1847, Capt. Henry Kellett used this point for observations and entered the present name on British Admiralty charts.

Obstruction Island *(T.36N;R.1W)*

A triangular island which almost closes the passage in which it is located, between north end of Blakely Island, southeast end of Orcas Island, east central San Juan County. Obstruction Pass is on its north; Peavine Pass on its south. In 1841, Cmdr. Charles Wilkes named the island because it offers an obstruction to passage of larger ships.

Obstruction Pass *(T.36N;R.1W)*

A short and very narrow passage between Orcas and Obstruction islands, east central San Juan County. It was named by the U.S. Coast & Geodetic Survey for Obstruction Island. (*see* Obstruction Island)

Obstruction Point *(T.28N;R.5W)*

A 6,448-ft. point northwest of Badger

Valley, 13 miles south of Port Angeles, southeast Clallam County. In 1889, it was named by a rancher, hunter, and packer named Cameron, because the point obstructed the building of a trail along the ridge on which it is located.

Ocean City *(S.3;T.18N;R.12W)*

Settlement of small homes along Pacific Ocean beach, 13 miles northwest of Hoquiam, west Grays Harbor County. In 1890s, this descriptive name was applied by local residents.

Ocean City State Park (Grays Harbor County) *see* Oceanside State Park

Ocean Park *(T.12N;R.11W)*

Resort center on Pacific Ocean, midway between the north and south ends of North Beach Peninsula, southwest Pacific County. In 1888, the center was founded by Ocean Park Camp Meeting Association as a Christian summer resort for members. It was named by Rev. William R. Osborn for Ocean Park, New Jersey, which he also founded and named.

Oceanside State Park *(T.18N;R.12W)*

A public park on Ocean Beach near Ocean City, 13 miles northwest of Hoquiam, west Grays Harbor County. It offers swimming, clamming, and picnic facilities. On November 6, 1961, the previous name of *Ocean City State Park* was changed to the present form by State Parks & Recreation Commission. It is quite descriptive.

Oceanview *(S.28;T.10N;R.11W)*

A popular summer resort area on Pacific Ocean, 1 mile south of Seaview, southwest Pacific County. It was named by resort owners when the place first developed as a summer playground.

Ocosta *(T.6N;R.11W)*

A boom town, established in 1892, and quite deserted by 1930, on the south shore of Grays Harbor, across South Bay from Westport, southwest Grays Harbor County. In 1892, it was named by Judge William H. Calkins of Tacoma and Mrs. George E. Filley of Olympia. They used the Spanish *La Costa*, but substituted *O* for *La*, to make a one-word name acceptable to postal authorities. A poetic variation, used in advertising the embryo town, was *Ocosta By The Sea*. The Indian name was *Nu-shis-tska*.

Odair *(S.35;T.25N;R.28E)*

Small settlement 1-1/2 miles north-

east of Coulee City, northeast Grant County. It was named for W. H. Adair, who owned a ranch here and who operated a restaurant in Coulee City. The name was changed from *Adair* because of its resemblance to Adrian in central Grant County.

Odessa *(Ss.5,8;T.21N;R.33E)*

Settlement 40 miles southwest of Davenport, southwest Lincoln County. Founded in 1886 by German immigrants from southern Russia, German was the second language in this area. It was named by railroad officials for Odessa on the Black Sea, because of many settlers from Russia.

Offut *(S.32;T.17N;R.1W)*

Small settlement on Offuts Lake, 9 miles southeast of Olympia, south central Thurston County. The name is from the same source as that of Offuts Lake.

Offut Lake (Thurston County) *see* Offuts Lake

Offuts Lake *(Ss.32,33;T.17N;R.1W)*

A 192-acre lake, maximum depth 25 ft., 9 miles south of Olympia, central Thurston County. On some maps it is shown as *Offut Lake*.

Ohanapecosh Entrance, Mt. Rainier National Park *(T.14N;R.10E)*

A guard station and registration unit for those entering or leaving the park, 15 miles northeast of Packwood, southeast corner of the park. The road north of here through the park is often closed in the winter by very heavy snowfall. (*see* Ohanapecosh Hot Springs)

Ohanapecosh Glacier *(Mt. Rainier National Park)*

An interglacier with Fryingpan Glacier and one of the smaller ice rivers in the park, on southeast slope of Mt. Rainier, extending 2 miles southeast from the middle reach of Fryingpan Glacier to the Cowlitz Park area. (*see* Ohanapecosh Hot Springs) (USBGN)

Ohanapecosh Hot Springs *(Mt. Rainier National Park)*

These developed springs are near Ohanapecosh Entrance, on Ohanapecosh River, extreme southwest corner of the park. Facilities include a lodge, cabins, campgrounds, and mineralized springs which emerge at temperatures of from 105-124 degrees F. The original Indian name used, which actually applied to Ohanapecosh River, means *"look down*

on something beautiful." Some students of local Indian languages state that it means "deep blue stream" or "deep blue pool." Many Indian legends attach to this river, especially in the area just south of the park.

Ohanapecosh Park *(Mt. Rainier National Park)*

An east slope park of Mt. Rainier, elevation 5,500 ft., at the headwaters of Boulder Creek, east central portion of the park. It is surrounded by Ohanapecosh Glacier on the west, Fryingpan Glacier on the northwest, and Sarvent Glacier on the north. (*see* Ohanapecosh Hot Springs)

Ohanapecosh River *(Mt. Rainier National Park)*

The stream of the river rises in Ohanapecosh Park, at the foot of Ohanapecosh Glacier, southeast slope of Mt. Rainier; flows south and southeast into Lewis County and to Cowlitz River near La Wis Wis forest camp, 7 miles northeast of Packwood. (*see* Ohanapecosh Hot Springs) (USBGN)

O'Hare Cove (San Juan County) *see* Squaw Bay

Oh My Point *(Mt. Rainier National Park)*

A very popular scenic observation point above the Paradise River canyon, below Narada Falls, 15 miles east of Nisqually Entrance, southwest zone of the park. The name was used because of the exclamation of tourists when they took their first look from here.

Ohop *(Ss.20,21;T.17N;R.5E)*

Small settlement in the Ohop Valley, 12 miles west of Mt. Rainier, central Pierce County. It was first called *Stringtown* because the residents lived along a single road in Ohop Valley. It also was called by the original Indian name for the valley. The name is an adaption of the original Indian word, *Ow-hap*, meaning "pleasant."

Ohop Bob *(S.17;T.16N;R.4E)*

Settlement at the head of Ohop Valley, 3-1/2 miles northwest of Eatonville, south central Pierce County. The name is a combination of the Indian name for Ohop Valley, *Ow-hap*, and the Scottish name for hill. The place is on a 790-ft. hill. (*see* Ohop)

Ohop Creek (1) *(T.17N;Rs.5,6E)*

The stream of the creek rises in Ohop

Valley, 5 miles east of Ohop; flows west and north into south end of Lake Kapowsin. IN 1857, this stream was mapped as *Ow-hap Creek* by the surveyor general of Washington Territory. This creek is not to be confused with one of the same name near LaGrande. (*see* Ohop)

Ohop Creek (2) *(T.16N;Rs.3,4E)*

The stream of the creek rises at the south end of Ohop Lake; flows southwest to Nisqually River, west of Mashel Prairie. It is not to be confused with Ohop Creek, a tributary of Lake Kapowsin. (*see* Ohop)

Ohop Creek Ponds *(S.30;T.17N;R.6E)*

Two connected ponds at the head of Ohop Creek, 7-1/2 miles southeast of Kapowsin, Pierce County. Located in a marshy area, one pond covers 2 acres, the other 2-1/2 acres. The ponds were named for Ohop Creek. (*see* Ohop)

Ohop Lake *(T.16N;R.4E)*

A narrow, crescent-shaped lake, 2-1/2 miles long, with an area of 235.6 acres, in Ohop Valley, 2-1/2 miles northwest of Eatonville, south central Pierce County. In 1857, this feature was mapped as *Ow-hap Lake* by the surveyor general of Washington Territory. (*see* Ohop)

Ohop Valley *(T.17N;R.5E)*

A valley 2-3 miles south of Puyallup River, in the valley of Ohop Creek, south central Pierce County. (*see* Ohop)

Okanogan (Douglas County) *see* Okanogan City

Okanogan *(S.17;T.33N;R.26E)*

An important town at the junction of Okanogan River with Salmon Creek, south central Okanogan County. In 1886, the town was founded by F. J. (''Pard'') Cummings as a trading post. In those days, sternwheel steamers reached Okanogan in the high waters of May and June. The neighboring settlements of Pogue and Alma have been combined into the present town. The name is Salish, *Okinagen*; it has been translated as ''meeting place of water,'' because 2 streams meet, and ''rendezvous,'' because Indians met here for their annual potlaches. Other spellings are *Okinakane, Okanagen,* and ''O-Kan-Okan.''

Okanogan City *(S.28;T.25N;R.23E)*

A vanished town, once the county seat, 6 miles east of Waterville, southeast Douglas County. It lost out to Waterville when its well ran dry. The town's first name was *Okanogan* which, together with the present name, was taken from the same source as Okanogan River. (*see* Okanogan)

Okanogan County

A north central Washington county, containing 5,295 sq. miles. It is bounded on the west by Whatcom, Skagit, and Chelan counties; on the south by Douglas and Lincoln; on the east by Ferry; and on the north by British Columbia. On February 2, 1888, it was established by an act of the Territorial Legislature from a portion of Stevens County. Before the establishment of counties, Okanogan and adjacent areas carried the name of *Middle Oregon* on some early maps. (*see* Okanogan)

Okanogan National Forest

A 2,090,632-acre national forest, east of Cascade Mountain summit, in the zone directly south of the Canadian boundary, Okanogan and Chelan counties. In 1911, this forest was created partly from land in Chelan National Forest. In 1920, it was entirely transferred to that forest. In 1955, the name was changed from *Chelan* to the present name. Forest Service officials in Washington, D.C., chose the name of *Okanogan River* in naming the original forest. Forest headquarters are in Okanogan. It is under the general jurisdiction of Region 6, U.S. Forest Service, with headquarters in Portland, Oregon.

Okanogan River
(Ts.30-40N;Rs.25-27E)

The largest river in the county heads at Osoyoos Lake, 3-1/2 miles south of the Canadian boundary, northeast Okanogan County; flows south and southwest to Columbia River, 2 miles east of Brewster, a distance of 73 miles. A name in limited use was *Wantana*. (*see* Okanogan)

Okho River (Clallam County) *see* Hoke River; Sail River

Olalla *(Ss.3,4;T.22N;R.2E)*

Settlement on West (Colvos) Passage, 7-1/2 miles north of Tacoma, southeast Kitsap County. It inherited the Chinook jargon name, *Olallie*, meaning ''salmon berry'' or berries, in general. The slight change evidently was made when a post office was established.

Olalla Bay *(Ss.3,4;T.22N;R.2E)*

A bay on West (Colvos) Passage, 7-1/2 miles north of Tacoma, southeast Kitsap County. (*see* Olalla)

Olallie Creek *(T.27N;R.12W)*

The stream of the creek heads in Olympic National Park between Hoh and Bogachiel rivers, northwest Jefferson County; flows 2 miles northwest to Bogachiel River, southwest Clallam County. This Indian name from Chinook jargon is used for many features in the state. (*see* Olalla)

Olallie Creek *(T.22N;Rs.10,11E)*

This short stream rises at the Cascade Mountain summit, Snoqualmie National Forest, extreme east central King County; flows 2 miles northwest to South Fork, Snoqualmie River. On June 15, 1916, it was named by The Mountaineers, using the Chinook jargon word for berries. (USBGN)

Olallie Creek *(Mt. Rainier National Park)*

Olallie Creek *(Mt. Rainier National Park)*

The stream of the creek rises on the east side of Cowlitz Divide, near the Wonderland Trail crossing, southeast sector of the park; flows south and southeast to Ohanapecosh River at Cedar Flat. The original Indian name for this creek has been retained. During an untold number of years in the past, Indians camped along this stream in season to pick and dry mountain huckleberries. (*see* Olallie)

Olallie Lake *(S.3;T.22N;R.10E)*

A 13.4-acre lake, 4-1/2 miles west of Snoqualmie Pass, Snoqualmie National Forest, east central King County. An alternate name is *Divide Lake*. (*see* Olallie)

Olallie Lake *(S.1;T.9N;R.9E.uns)*

A 15.6-acre lake, elevation 4,250 ft., Gifford Pinchot National Forest, 23-1/2 miles southeast of Randle, northeast Skamania County. The lake is in high, huckleberry country; thus the name. An alternate name is *Sheep Lake*. (*see* Olallie)

Olallie Meadow *(T.22N;Rs.10,11E)*

A meadow at the head of Ollalie Creek, 3 miles west of Cascade Mountain summit, 3-1/2 miles southwest of Snoqualmie Pass, east central King County. On June 15, 1916, this name was chosen by The Mountaineers. (*see* Olallie)

Old Desolate *(Mt. Rainier National Park)*

A large, barren mountain on the north slope of Mt. Rainier, between Carbon Glacier and the foot of Winthrop Glacier; the peak is 5 miles due north of Mt. Rainier's summit, between Moraine and Vernal peaks, north central zone of the park. The name given is descriptive, as the dome is bald and desolate. (USBGN)

Old Baldy (Spokane County) *see* Mt. Spokane

Old Dominion Mountain
(Ss.27,34;T.36N;R.40E)

A Colville National Forest peak, elevation 5,774 ft., 8 miles east-by-north of Colville, east central Stevens County. It takes its name from the famous Old Dominion Mine nearby. Prior to 1885, it had been called *Colville Mountain.*

Old Fort Klickitat (Klickitat County) *see* Blockhouse

Old Fort Spokane (Lincoln County) *see* Fort Spokane

Old Fort Townsend State Park
(T.30N;R.1W)

A 241-acre state park on the site of an old fort (which once had 642 acres), on Quimper Peninsula, 3 miles south of Port Townsend, facing east on Port Townsend bay, Jefferson County. In 1856, the fort was built and in 1893, abandoned. The park offers camping, fishing, and clamming.

Old Fort Walla Walla (Walla Walla County) *see* Fort Walla Walla (trade post)

Old Goat Mountain
(S.17;T.29N;R.23E)

A 5,290-ft. peak on the south end of a ridge, 5 miles southwest of Pateros, 5 miles west of Columbia River, extreme southwest Okanogan County. In 1890, the name *Mt. Rena* was applied by local climbers. Another former name was *Goat Mountain.* The origin is probably due to the presence of mountain goats, as it adjoins Sawtooth Ridge -- a rough, unsurveyed area of high peaks.

Old Hurricane (Clallam County) *see* Hurricane Hill

Old Maid Coulee *(T.13N;Rs.31-33E)*

A 17-mile-long coulee, extending from Vale to Estes, south of Connell, north central Franklin County. In 1901, it was named by local residents for two "old maids" who are said to have taken adjoining homesteads, and who built a cabin on their mutual boundary, with separate rooms for each.

Old Man House *(S.29;T.26N;R.2E)*

A very old Indian village (long since vanished) on the west side of Agate Passage, on the beach 1 mile south of Suquamish, northeast Kitsap County. Once it boasted a cedar "long house," 520 ft. long and 60 ft. wide. The Indian name, *Tsu-suc-cub*, had the meaning of the present name. The structure was capable of housing as many as 700 Indians in 40 separate compartments.

Old Tacoma *(Ss.30,31;T.21N;R.3E)*

This is a local term for the original town of Tacoma, on Commencement Bay, between Ruston and Tacoma Stadium, north of the present business district. The Indian name was *Shi-bal-up*.

Old Telegraph Road (Washington State Ref./ Western Washington, Canada, Alaska) *see* Telegraph Road

Old Toroda *(S.21;T.38N;R.31E)*

One of many mining ghost towns, 16 miles south of the Canadian boundary, 5 miles northeast of Wauconda, on Toroda Creek, northeast Okanogan County. It should not be confused with the town of Toroda, also on Toroda Creek, 15 miles to the northeast, in Ferry County. (*see* Toroda)

Old Wauconda *(S.7;T.37N;R.31E)*

Town, formerly a mining camp, on Granite Creek, 20 miles south of the Canadian boundary, northeast Okanogan County. It should not be confused with the town of Wauconda, 2-1/2 miles to the northwest. (*see* Wauconda)

Old Women's Gulch
(S.32;T.21N;R.3E)

Once a wooded gulch, now the site of Tacoma Stadium, overlooking Commencement Bay, north Tacoma. Fishermen once built shacks here for the widows of other fishermen who had drowned, thus the name. It is no longer used and is now almost forgotten.

Olds *(S.15;T.23N;R.20E)*

Railroad point on Columbia River, 3 miles north of Wenatchee, southeast Chelan County. It was named for A. H. Olds, a pioneer orchardist.

O'Leary Creek
(Ss.32,33,34;T.17N;R.10W)

The stream of the creek heads on the south side of Grays Harbor, 4-1/2 miles east of Markham; flows west and north, 3-1/2 miles to South Channel of Grays Harbor, Grays Harbor County. In 1848, it was named for William O'Leary, who settled near the creek's mouth. In July 1841, the Wilkes survey party applied the name *Rogers Creek*, for one of the marines on the survey party. That name was evidently never used by local residents.

Olele Point *(S.28;T.29N;R.1E)*

A south entrance point to Oak Bay on Admiralty Inlet, directly north of Mats Mats Bay, northeast Jefferson County. In 1841, it was named by Cmdr. Charles Wilkes, who applied the Indian name. The words means "berries" in Chinook jargon, although the usual spelling is *Olallie*. The name, *Point Kanawi*, charted by U.S. Coast Survey in 1854, did not persist.

Olema *(S.11;T.32N;R.24E)*

Small settlement, 4-1/2 miles west of Malott, Chilliwist Creek valley, south central Okanogan County. In 1897, it was named by Mrs. L. C. Malott for some person or location which appears to be unrecorded.

Olequa *(S9;T.10N;R.2W)*

Community on Olequa Creek, 6 miles north of Castle Rock, northwest Cowlitz County. It was named for a local Indian chief called *Old Laquash*, who lived here in the 1850s.

Olequa Creek *(T.10N;R.2W)*

The stream of the creek heads near Ryderwood, northwest Cowlitz County; flows east into Cowlitz River near Olequa. (*see* Olequa)

Olga *(S.8;T.36N;R.1W)*

Community on the east shore of East Sound, at the head of Buck Bay, southwest Orcas Island, east central San Juan County. On March 3, 1890, this name was adopted when a post office was established. Petitioners for the post office requested the name *Rosario*, but it was refused because of another post office by that name in the state. John Ohlert, owner of a local store and dance hall, suggested the name of his mother in

Germany, Olga Ohlert, and his idea met with post office approval.

Olive Lake (Mt. Rainier National Park) *see* Oliver Lake

Oliver Lake *(Mt. Rainier National Park)*

A lake east of the south end of Independence Ridge, between Chenius Creek and West Fork, White River, north central area of the park. It is one of 2 adjacent, triangular lakes; the other is Marjorie Lake. It was named for Oliver Taylor, a member of an official survey party that worked here in 1911. (USBGN)

Olivine Hill *(S.4;T.35N;R.1E)*

A dome-shaped hill, elevation 600 ft., southeast tip of Cypress Island, 3 miles northwest of Anacortes, northwest Skagit County. The hill is mostly dunite with a high olivine content.

Ollala Canyon *(T.24N;Rs.18,19E)*

A canyon extending from near Blag Mountain, 6 miles south to Columbia River, between Cashmere and Peshastin, south central Chelan County. Local informants state that it was named for a Wenatchee Indian who lived in the canyon in early days. An alternate name in local use is *Williams Canyon*.

Ollie Lake (King County) *see* Pratt Lake

Olney (King County) *see* Issaquah

Olney Creek *(T.28N;R.8E)*

The stream of the creek rises 4-1/2 miles north of Sultan, south central Snohomish County; flows south to Wallace River near Sultan. It was locally named for a very early pioneer settler.

Olsen Creek *(T.38N;R.4E)*

This small creek heads 4-1/2 miles east of Lake Whatcom, southwest Whatcom County; flows west and southwest to the northeast shore of the lake. On December 3, 1885, it was locally named for Olaf Olsen, a pioneer settler.

Oluman Creek (Wakkiakum County) *see* Elokomin River

Olympia *(T.18N;R.2W)*

The capital of the state, this city is at the head of Budd Inlet, north central Thurston County. The site of Olympia was called *Schiet-woot*, meaning "place of the bear." In 1846, when Edmund Sylvester and Levi Smith took 320-acre land claims, they combined parts of their names to create the name of *Smither*.

The name was later altered to *Smithfield*. When several adjoining settlements combined, the name *Marshville* was chosen, and was in use for a short time. In 1851, Col. Isaac N. Ebey persuaded the inhabitants to adopt the present name, which he took from a book titled *Life of Olympia*.

Olympic Mountains

This stupendous group of peaks occupies a large part of the Olympic Peninsula, northwest Washington, Clallam, Jefferson, Grays Harbor, and Mason counties. Heavily glaciated in the interior portions, these peaks have elevations to 9,965 ft. The more scenic mountains are contained within Olympic National Park, with a perimeter of lower peaks and heavy forest protected by inclusion in Olympia National Forest. Mt. Olympus National Monument, surrounding Mt. Olympus, contains 608,640 acres. Other names are *Olympus Range*, *Olympian Mountains*, and *Coast Range*. Classification as a range is contested by some geographers because the mountains have no central axis. The name is for Mt. Olympus. (*see* Mt. Olympus)

Olympic National Forest

A 689,883-acre federal forest on the Olympic Peninsula, almost surrounding Olympic National Park, west central Washington state, Grays Harbor, Mason, Jefferson, Clallam counties. Headquarters of the forest are in Olympia, functioning under the jurisdiction of Region 6, U.S. Forest Service in Portland, Oregon. In 1897, the forest was created; since then there have been extensive withdrawals and additions. A considerable area was transferred to Olympic National Park in 1940, 1943, and 1953. The name chosen by Forest Service officials is that of the Olympic Mountain range.

Olympic National Park

A federal park on the Olympic Peninsula, surrounded in part by Olympic National Forest, and with a 50-mile strip along Pacific Ocean from Cape Alava to Quinault Indian Reservation, northwest corner of the state, Clallam, Jefferson, Grays Harbor, and Mason counties. In 1938, the park was created by an act of Congress, which reserved about 1,000 sq. miles. Additions were made in 1940, 1943, and 1953. It contains about 50 glaciers and also a rain forest which is one of the world's natural wonders. The

highest peak, Mt. Olympus, is 9,965. It was named after that mountain.

Olympic Ocean Strip
(Ts.24-31N;Rs.13-16W)

This strip of Olympic National Park stretches along Pacific Ocean coast from Cape Alava south to the Quinault Indian Reservation. On January 6, 1953, it was reserved by presidential proclamation, together with the Queets Corridor. Its purpose is to preserve about 50 miles of primitive ocean beach for public enjoyment.

Olympic Peninsula

A beautiful peninsula in northwest Washington, west of Hood Canal and north of Grays Harbor; it is bounded on the west by Pacific Ocean; on the north by Strait of Juan de Fuca, in Clallam, Jefferson, Grays Harbor, and Mason counties. Mostly mountainous, the Olympic Peninsula has a high proportion of its area in Olympic National Forest and Olympic National Park. (*see* Mt. Olympus)

Omak *(S.35;T.34N;R.26E)*

A busy sawmill and logging center on Okanogan River, 4 miles north of Okanogan, central Okanogan County. In 1906 and 1907, the name of the first post office was *Epley*. In 1907, when Omak was platted, the post office name was changed to its current designation. The name origin is from the Indian word *Omache*, meaning "good medicine" or "plenty," which was applied to a nearby creek and lake. This was altered to Omak at the suggestion of postal authorities, who prefer brevity to history.

Omak Lake *(Ts.32,33N;Rs.27,28E)*

An 8-mile-long lake, 3/4 mile average width, on Colville Indian Reservation, 9 miles north of Columbia River, southeast Okanogan County. This lake has a white band of alkaline deposit at the water level and has no fish in its waters. (*see* Omak)

Onalaska *(S.30;T.13N;R.1E)*

Community on South Fork, Newaukum River, 9 miles east of Napavine, west central Lewis County. In 1914, the town was founded when Carlisle Lumber Company built the largest sawmill in the county; in 1938, it closed. It was named for *Onalaska* in the Aleutian Islands, as described by a Scottish poet, Thomas Campbell. William Carlisle had previously applied the same name to towns in Wisconsin, Arkansas, and Texas which had been established as sawmill centers by Carlisle Lumber Company. Thus, this Aleut Indian name has made almost a complete circuit of the U.S. In Alaska it has been modified to *Unalaska*.

One Acre Lake *(S.14;T.28N;R.9E)*
A small, 1-1/2-acre lake, 7 ,miles northwest of Sultan, south central Snohomish County. The name is descriptive.

One Hundred Island (San Juan County) *see* Castle Island

One Lake (King County) *see* First Lake

One Too Many Creek
(T.25N;R.5W.uns)
The stream of the creek heads in Scout Lake, 1-1/2 miles north of Mason County boundary, southeast Jefferson County; flows 3 miles north to Duckabush River, Olympic National Park. The donor of this interesting name is anonymous, but might well have been a packer. The Duckabush has 11 tributaries in 4 miles through this rugged stretch of mountains, each of which crosses the pack trail. An alternate name for this creek is *Crazy Creek*, but this should not be another creek of the same name which is directly to the west. (USBGN)

O'Neal Island *(S.20;T.36N;R.3W)*
A Rocky Bay island off the northeast shore of San Juan Island, west central San Juan County. In 1841, it was named by the Wilkes Expedition for a U.S. Naval hero of the War of 1812.

O'Neil Creek *(Ts.24,25N;R.6W)*
The stream of the creek heads in a small lake, 1-1/2 miles east of O'Neil Peak, Olympic National Park, southeast Jefferson County; flows west-by-south through north Mason County and back into Jefferson County to join Quinault River. It was named for 2nd Lieut. Joseph P. O'Neil, 14th U.S. Inf., who led Olympic Mountains exploring expeditions in 1885 and 1890. He named a great many features in Clallam and Jefferson counties.

O'Neil Creek *(S.33;T.25N;R.6W)*
The stream of the creek heads in a small, mountain lake near O'Neil Pass, Olympic National Park, south central Jefferson County; flows 6-1/2 miles west to Quinault River. (*see* O'Neil Creek)

ferson County. (*see* O'Neil Creek)

O'Neil Lake (Pacific County) *see* Fort Canby Lake

O'Neil Pass *(S.19;T.25N;R.5W)*
An Olympic National Park pass at the head of Duckabush River, directly south of Marmot Lakes, southeast Jefferson County.

O'Neil Peak *(S.26;T.25N;R.6W)*
An Olympic National Park peak, elevation 5,757-ft., 1-1/2 miles southeast of Quinault River, southeast Jefferson County. The peak is between the headwaters of O'Neil and Upper O'Neil creeks. (*see* O'Neil Creek)

Onion Creek *(Ts.37-39N;Rs.39,40E)*
The stream of the creek heads on Gillette Mountain, north central Stevens County; flows north-by-west 14 miles to the Columbia River, north of Marble. There are 2 name origins on this feature: It was named by early settlers because of toothsome wild onions (Allium) which grew here. Also, in the 1870s and 1880s, Chinese miners raised onions near the mouth of the creek.

Onslow *(S.1;T.19N;R.12W)*
Settlement directly north of Copalis River, 4 miles east of Pacific Ocean, southwest Grays Harbor County. The place was named by Robert Polson of Polson Logging Company, for his former home in Onslow County, Nova Scotia.

Ontario Roads (San Juan County) *see* San Juan Channel

Opal Lake *(S.17;T.24N;R.13E)*
A snow-fed lake in Necklace Valley, 1 mile northwest of Cascade Mountain summit, northeast King County. One of 3 Necklace Valley Lakes (with Jade and Emerald lakes), Opal Lake varies in size from 3-5 acres in season. It is one of the "jewels" in the string. An alternate name is *Necklace Valley Lake No. 3*.

Open Bay *(Ss.22,27,28;T.36N;R.4W)*
A southeast side bay of Henry Island, in Haro Strait, directly north of San Juan Island, west central San Juan County. It was locally named; and because the bay is open to south winds, the name is quite descriptive.

Ophir *(S.5;T.31N;R.25E)*
A mining ghost town, 9 miles northeast of Brewster on Okanogan River, south central Okanogan County. It was located on the old Conconully stage route, but does not appear on re-

cent maps. It was named for Biblical references in the Old Testament to a mysterious seaport from which King Solomon's ships brought fine gold in great quantities.

Opportunity *(S.14;T.25N;R.44E)*
Settlement in Spokane Valley, 6-1/2 miles east of Spokane, east central Spokane County. It is largely dependent on truck gardening. This inspirational name was selected when the town was platted.

Orcas *(S.22;T.36N;R.2W)*
A small community 2 miles south of the town of West Sound, on the middle lobe of Orcas Island, central San Juan County. In 1873, the place was named *Orcas Island* for the island on which it is located. On November 2, 1898, the name was shortened to its present form. Both the original name and the change were of local origin.

Orcas Island *(Ts.36,37N;Rs.1,2W)*
A saddle-bag-shaped island, almost bisected by East Sound which penetrates to within 1-1/2 miles of the north shore, northeast San Juan County. This is one of the 2 largest islands in the San Juan group. On charts prepared by Lieut. Juan Francisco de Eliza in 1791, the name is shown as *Orcasitas*. It was named by Jose Maria Narvaez for the schooner *Horcasitas* which he commanded under Eliza. The Spanish "h" is often mute, which probably explains the chart's spelling. In 1841, the Wilkes Expedition named it *Hulls Island* for Comm. Isaac Hull, hero of the War of 1812. In 1847, Capt. Henry Kellett, British Admiralty surveyor, changed the island's name back to *Orcas* on his charts. The present name has become official.

Orchard Prairie *(S.18;T.26N;R.43E)*
Community 2-1/2 miles north of Spokane city limits, central Spokane County. In 1879, it was founded by Thomas Howard Doak and Harold Dart, and so named because these founders planted many fruit trees.

Orchard Valley (Lincoln County) *see* Peach

Orchards *(S.9;T.2N;R.2E)*
Suburban area 3-1/2 miles northeast of Vancouver, southwest Clark County. When Hudson's Bay Company first occupied Fort Vancouver, they numbered their grazing plains or pastures consecutively, 1-6, from their headquarters. The

area was called *Fourth Plain*. The present name was suggested by D. H. Stearns Realty Company when a post office was established in 1885, and was accepted by postal officials.

Ordway Creek (Cowlitz County) *see* Abernethy Creek

Orient *(S.23;T.39N;R.36E)*

Mining settlement 10 miles south of the Canadian boundary on Kettle River, northeast Ferry County. In 1902, it was founded by Orient Improvement Company and platted by that corporation in 1903. It is on Colville National Forest in the Kettle River & Pierce Lake Mining District. Named for the Orient Mine, 2-1/2 miles distance, Orient was originally known as *Noto*, and later as *Morgan*. The railroad station, which consisted only of a signboard 1-1/2 miles to the south, was called *Dulwich*.

Orient *(T.30N;R.11E)*

A mining ghost town near Bedal Camp on Sauk River, near the confluence of North Fork, northeast Snohomish County. In 1895, this town had a trade store and some population. It was named by Mrs. Moorehouse, when she and her husband founded the settlement. She exclaimed, ''I can't go any farther; this must be China!'' Hence, the Oriental name.

Orillia *(S.36;T.23N;R.4E)*

Community on Duwamish River, 12 miles south of Seattle, west central King County. In 1887, the place was named by Malcolm McDougall, a settler, for his home town in Simcoe County, Ontario, Canada.

Orin *(S.33;T.35N;R.39E)*

Once a town in Stevens County, this place flourished when Winslow Lumber Company established a sawmill in 1903. When bypassed by the main north-south highway, the town slumped, and the post office was discontinued. The name is for Orin S. Winslow, one of the founders of the Winslow Lumber Company.

Oro Bay *(T.19N;R.1E)*

A southeast shore bay of Anderson Island, on Nisqually Reach, west central Pierce County. In 1841, Cmdr. Charles Wilkes applied this name. Five years later, the name *Rodd Bay* was charted by Inskip in making British Admiralty charts. It was for Lieut. John R. Rodd of *H.M.S. Fisgard*, but the name did not displace that of Wilkes.

Orondo *(S.32;T.25N;R.21E)*

Community at the mouth of Pine, or Corbaley Canyon, 14 miles north of Wenatchee, west Douglas County. In 1886, this place was named by its founder, J. B. Smith, for Orondo, an Indian whose tribe worked ancient Lake Superior copper mines. Smith explained that ''Orondo was the superintendent of the ancient Lake Superior copper mines, who had about 1,000 miners under his charge when their native continent (Atlantis) sunk beneath the ocean. They took native wives and were the progenitors of the Mound Builders...'' According to Smith, these early miners are presumed to have escaped from their sinking continent by way of an isthmus which joined it to the North American continent.

Oroville *(S.28;T.40N;R.27E)*

Town 4-1/2 miles south of the Canadian boundary, 1 mile south of Osoyoos Lake, near the confluence of Okanogan and Similkameen rivers. Originally it was called *Oro*, grafted to ''ville'' at the suggestion of postal authorities who anticipated confusion with Oso in Snohomish County. In 1873, the town was founded by Alexander McCauley on land claimed by his friend, Chief Moses. The name is from the Spanish, *oro*, meaning ''gold.'' A considerable amount of gold deposits were located nearby.

Orr's Pond *(S.25;T.29N;R.3E)*

A 1-acre lake on the south end of Whidbey Island, 1/2 mile southwest of Columbia Beach. It was named for a local resident, Martin Orr. An alternate name is *Martin Orr Pond*.

Orting *(T.19N;R.5E)*

Town 15 miles south of Tacoma, between Puyallup and Carbon rivers, central Pierce County. The Indian name was retained when Col. S. A. Black, superintendent of Pacific division, Northern Pacific Railway Company, chose this Indian word meaning ''town on the prairie.'' A prior name was *Gunson's Prairie*.

Osborn Mountain *(Ss.7,8;T.14N;R.7E)*

A Snoqualmie National Forest peak, elevation 5,119 ft., 2 miles southwest of Nisqually Entrance to Mt. Rainier National Park, northeast Lewis County. It was named for J. W. Osborn, an early settler and homesteader.

Osborne *(S.20;T.28N;R.30E)*

Settlement 5 miles southwest of Grand Coulee Dam, extreme northeast Grant County. In 1883, the site was claimed by Oscar Osborne. In 1932, a town was established in Grand Coulee on Hubbard Canyon, before the existence of the equalizing reservoir in the coulee. (*see* Osborne Lake)

Osborne Lake *(T.28N;R.30E)*

This lake, now drowned in the equalizing reservoir of Grand Coulee Dam, was below Electric City, northeast Grant County. It was a swampy lake with open water only in the wet season. It was named for the first settler here, Oscar Osborne.

Oso *(S.8;T.32N;R.7E)*

Community 12 miles east of Arlington, directly north of Stillaguamish River, north central Snohomish County. The name is reported to have been chosen by J. P. Britzius for a town in Fayette County, Texas. No such town now appears on the Texas map, however. A previous name was *Allen*, for John B. Allen, a territorial delegate to Congress. It was changed to Oso because of confusion with the town of Allyn in Mason County.

Osoyoos Lake *(T.40N;R.27E)*

A 10-mile-long, international lake, drained by Okanogan River, extending north into British Columbia, northeast Okanogan County. The lake has an average width of 1 mile and its shores are flat and sandy. A former name was *Forks Lake*. A favorite folktale related that the lake was originally known as *Soyoos*, but that an Irish surveyor added the ''O'' as a prefix, mapping it as *O'Soyoos Lake*. The authentic origin of this name is from the Salish Indian word, *Soyoos*, meaning ''narrow,'' or ''the water cut in half by land.'' The lake is greatly constricted and quite narrow at 2 points in British Columbia.

Osoyoos Lake State Park *(T.40N;R.27E)*

A 20-acre park on Osoyoos Lake, 1 mile north of Oroville, 4 miles south of the Canadian boundary. It offers camping, swimming, and fishing to the public. (*see* Osoyoos)

Ostrander *(S.11;T.8N;R.2W)*

Community on Cowlitz River, 3 miles northeast of Longview, at the mouth of Ostrander Creek, central

Cowlitz County. Once it was a thriving sawmill town, but is now of little importance. In 1898, the name was applied by Northern Pacific Railway for Dr. Nathaniel Ostrander who filed a Donation Land Claim here in 1852.

Ostrander Creek
(Ts.8,9N;Rs.1,2W)

The stream of the creek heads 4 miles south of Silver Lake, west central Cowlitz County; flows west and southwest 10 miles to Cowlitz River at Ostrander. *(see* Ostrander)

Ostrich Bay *(T.24N;R.1E)*

A south extension bay of Dyes Inlet, directly northwest of Bremerton, central Kitsap County. In 1841, it was named by Cmdr. Charles Wilkes, because the bay's outline on his detailed chart had a certain resemblance to an ostrich.

O'Sullivan Dam *(T.17N;R.28E)*

An irrigation dam at the southeast end of Potholes Reservoir, 9 miles south of Moses Lake (town), southeast Grant County. This dam forms a retaining wall for water impounded in Potholes Reservoir, in the middle of Columbia Basin agricultural acreage. It is also called *Potholes Dam* and *South Coulee Dam*. It was named for James O'Sullivan of Ephrata and Spokane, through Senate Joint Resolution 202 (Public Law 814), which was passed on June 29, 1948. O'Sullivan worked for many years on projects dealing with eastern Washington irrigation. He had been administrative assistant of Columbia Basin Commission, and was largely responsible for the construction of the dam which now bears his name.

Othello *(S.3;T.15N;R.29E)*

Town 6 miles northeast of the east termination of Saddle Mountains, southwest Adams County. In 1907-1908, the name was accepted by H. R. Williams, vice president of Chicago, Milwaukee & St. Paul Railway, for its western division headquarters site. In 1904, it had originally been applied to the local post office by an early homesteader in memory of the Roane County, Tennessee post office of her youth. In 1910, the town was incorporated.

Otis (Spokane County) *see* Otis Orchards

Otis Orchards
(Ss.3,4;T.25N;R.45E)

Community 11 miles east of Spokane near the Idaho boundary, east central Spokane County. The first name was for an early settler. In 1912, when fruit culture boomed here, the second name was added.

O'Toole Creek *(Ts.34,35N;R.7E)*

The stream of the creek rises 6 miles southeast of Hamilton, central Skagit County; flows 4-1/2 miles north to Skagit River between Hamilton and Birdsview. In 1888, the creek was named for Capt. W. D. O'Toole, a miner who located iron ore at the creek's mouth.

Otso Point *(S.32;T.20N;R.1E)*

A north end point of Anderson Island, on Balch Passage, northwest Pierce County. In 1841, the name was charted by Cmdr. Charles Wilkes. It is a modification of the Puyallup Indian word *Ot-sl,* a type of war canoe, and the largest canoe that could be landed at this point.

Ottohorn *(S.7;T.38N;R.12E.uns)*

A Mt. Baker National Forest peak in the south Picket Range, at the head of Crescent Creek, east central Whatcom County. This sharp, snow-covered pinnacle is one of a group known as *Crescent Creek Spires.* In the fall of 1961, this was one of 3 *Mustard Peaks* named by J. C. Firey, Joan Firey, and party, when they made the first recorded ascents of Ottohorn, Frenzelspitz, and Himmelgeisterhorn. The names were taken from a label on a container of German mustard which the party carried. Otto Frenzel was the manufacturer of the mustard; his factory is located on Himmelsgeisterstrasse in Dusseldorf, Germany.

Outlook *(S.20;T.10N;R.22E)*

Settlement 4 miles west of Sunnyside, east central Yakima County. In 1900, it was started by John Dempsey, who established a store. It is reported to have been named by Dempsey "because of an excellent distance view."

Overcoat Lake *(S.2;T.23N;R.12E)*

A 14-acre lake on the northwest side of Overcoat Peak, Cascade Mountain summit, 8-1/4 miles northeast of Snoqualmie Pass, extreme east central King County. *(see* Overcoat Peak)

Overcoat Peak *(S.4;T.23N;R.12E)*

A mountain 8-1/2 miles northeast of

Snoqualmie Pass, at Cascade Mountain summit, extreme east central King and west Kittitas counties. It was named by A. H. Sylvester, once a forest supervisor of Wenatchee National Forest, when he left his overcoat on the mountain during a surveying trip. On some maps the peak is shown as *Overcoat Mountain.*

Owl Creek *(T.7N;R.1W)*

The stream of the creek heads 2 miles east of Carrolton, southwest Cowlitz County; flows 3-1/2 miles northwest to Columbia River. The name is of local origin, and is shown on very early maps. On some intermediate maps it appears as *Minter River.*

Owyhigh Lakes *(Mt. Rainier National Park)*

A group of 5 small lakes in a flat mountain meadow at the head of Shaw Creek, south foot of Government Ridge, east central zone of the park. Together, the lakes cover 6-1/2 acres. The name is for a former Yakima Indian chief, *Owyhigh* or *Ow-hi,* who was an outstanding fighter in the Indian wars of the 1850s. (USBGN)

Ox Bow (King County) *see* South Park Junction

Oyhut (Grays Harbor County) *see* Damon

Oyhut Channel *(Ts.17,18N;R.12W)*

A tidal channel in shallow North Bay, near the west shore and extending north past Damon, southwest Grays Harbor County. The name is a modification of the Indian designation which was *Oo-e-hut,* meaning "a road, path, or trail."

Oyhut Lake (Grays Harbor County) *see* Duck Lake

Oyhut Lake (Snohomish County) *see* Wayhut Lake

Oyster Bay *(S.16;T.24N;R.1E)*

The extension of Ostrich Bay, Dyes Inlet, 1/2 mile west of Bremerton, central Kitsap County. In the 1880s and 1890s, the name was locally chosen because the bay was full of good oysters.

Oyster Bay *(T.19N;R.3W)*

A south end bay of Totten Inlet, between northwest Thurston and southeast Mason counties. The bay is 5 miles long, average width 3/4 mile. It produces Olympia oysters in its shallow, protected waters and was named for these small, choice oysters.

Oyster Bay *(S.27;T.19N;R.3W)*

Community on Burns Cove, Oyster Bay, at the southwest end of Totten Inlet, northwest Thurston County. It was locally named for the Olympia oysters which flourish in adjacent waters. (*see* Oyster Bay)

Oysterville *(S.3;T.12N;R.11W)*

Settlement on Willapa Bay, 15 miles north of Columbia River, 3 miles north of Nahcotta, southwest Pacific County. In the 1850s, this town was an important center for oyster harvesting and shipping, and was the county seat. In 1893, the county records were kidnapped by South Bend. The town has greatly diminished since that time. In 1852, it was named by I. A. Clark, an oysterman, for the abundance of native oysters in Willapa Bay.

Ozette *(S.32;T.31N;R.15W)*

A small resort settlement, 2-1/2 miles east of Pacific Ocean, north end of Ozette Lake (where Ozette River meets the lake), west central Clallam County. The name is that used by Makah Indians for the lake and those who lived along its shores. *O-se-ilth* or *O-se-elth* means "middle tribe." (USBGN)

Ozette Indian Reservation *(Ss.23-26;T.31N;R.16W)*

An abandoned reservation on Cape Alava, facing Pacific Ocean, 2 miles northwest of Ozette Lake, west central Clallam County. In 1893, the reservation was established for the Ozette band of Makah Indians. The last Ozette died in 1953. (*see* Ozette)

Ozette Island *(S.27;T.31N;R.16W)*

A 1/2-mile-long island, elevation 240 ft., 1/2 mile offshore from Cape Alava, in Pacific Ocean, northwest Clallam County. (*see* Ozette) (USBGN)

Ozette Lake *(Ts.29-31N;R.15W)*

A very irregular, 8-mile-long lake, maximum width 2-1/2 miles, 2 miles inland from Pacific Ocean, at the head of Ozette River, west central Clallam County. The shoreline measures 57 miles. There are 2 small islands, Tivoli and Garden, which bear heavy stands of timber, as does the surrounding area. The Ozette Indian name was *Ka-houk*, meaning "fresh water lake." Makah tribesmen called it *O-se-ilth*. Other names that have been used include *Osette Lake*, *Swan Lake*, *Lake of the Sun*, and *Lake Webster*. (*see* Ozette) (USBGN)

Ozette River *(T.31N;Rs.15,16W)*

A 4-mile-long, winding river which rises near Cape Alava, adjacent to Ozette Indian Reservation, west central Clallam County; flows northwest from the north and from Ozette Lake to the Pacific Ocean. (*see* Ozette) (USBGN)

P

Pacific Beach *(S.20;T.20N;R.12W)*

A resort town, popular since the first settlement of the Grays Harbor area, Grays Harbor County. In the 1890s, this descriptive name was applied when the first hotel was built.

Pacific City *(S.35;T.21N;R.4E)*

A suburb of Auburn, 2-1/2 miles southwest of Auburn, 18 miles south of Seattle's south city limits, southwest King County. This is an ornamental name devised by C. D. Hillman, an early land promoter. In 1906, he platted this "city," and advertised it as "An addition to Seattle."

Pacific City *(Ts.9,10N;R.11W)*

A vanished town on Baker Bay, near the mouth of Columbia River, extreme southwest Pacific County. The short-lived town was based on dishonest promotion by Dr. Elijah White. In 1862, it was included in Fort Canby Military Reservation. The name was chosen by Dr. White when the townsite was platted.

Pacific County

An extreme southwest Washington county, consisting of 925 sq. miles. It is bounded on the north by Grays Harbor County; on the east by Lewis County; on the south by Wahkiakum County, and Columbia River; and on the west by Pacific Ocean. On February 4, 1851, it was established as a county of Oregon Territory with Chinook as the county seat. The name was chosen because of its frontage on the Pacific Ocean.

Pack Demonstration Forest *(T.16N;R.4E)*

A forested, 2,000-acre area directly northeast of La Grande, 1 mile southwest of Eatonville, south central Pierce County. Owned by University of Washington, it is used for the training of forestry students and for scientific experiments in forest management. In 1924, the forest was given to the college of forestry, University of Washington. It was named for the donor, Charles Lathrop Pack, a distinguished conservationist and philanthropist.

Packard (Snohomish County) *see* Hazel

Packtrain Ridge *(Mt. Rainier National Park)*

A ridge between Burrough and Skyscraper mountains, above Berkeley Park, north central area of the park. It is crossed by Wonderland Trail in a series of switchbacks. In 1932, the name was chosen by District Park Ranger Oscar Sedegrin, because the ridge is crossed by many pack trains in the open season.

Packwood *(S.22;T.13N;R.9E)*

A trade center and outfitting headquarters, 35 miles east of Morton, in the "Big Bottom" country on Cowlitz River, west central Lewis County. The headquarters arranges trips to Goat Rocks Primitive Area. From 1890 until 1897, the original settlement here was called *Sulpher Springs* to honor John Lewis, president of Valley Development Company; this firm developed the Packwood Power Project. More recently, the name of Lewis has been replaced by the present name for William Packwood, who came to this area from Virginia in the 1840s, and who was a famous guide and explorer.

Packwood Lake *(T.13N;R.10E.uns)*

A 1-1/2-mile-long lake, elevation 2,800 ft., 6 miles east of Packwood, 8 miles west of Cascade Mountain summit, extreme east Lewis County. It was named for William Packwood, who discovered the lake and who acted as a guide in this area from 1844 until 1899. (*see* Packwood)

Packwood Pass (Yakima County) *see* Cowlitz Pass

Packwood Saddle *(T.12N;R.11E)*

A Goat Rocks Primitive Area saddle, 1 mile west of Cascade Mountain summit, east central Lewis County. A trail through the saddle connects with Cascade Crest Trail. (*see* Packwood)

Padden Lake (Whatcom County) *see* Lake Padden

Paddock *(S.17;T.9N;R.35E)*

Settlement 13 miles north-by-west of Walla Walla, central Walla Walla County. The name was given when stock raising predominated, because of extensive corrals established here for securing horses after roundups.

Paddy-Go-Easy Pass *(S.27;T.24N;R.14E)*

A very rough pass over the divide between northwest Kittitas and southwest Chelan counties, Wenatchee National Forest. It is between the drainage areas of Cle Elum River and French Creek. The name was locally applied for a miner who had a burro named Paddy. At rough spots, the miner warned the animal to go easy.

Padilla (Skagit County) *see* Whitney

Padilla Bay *(Ts.34-36N;Rs.2,3E)*

A bay between Samish Island and Swinomish Channel, directly east of Anacortes, west central Skagit County. In 1791, the bay was named *Seno de Padilla* by Juan Francisco de Eliza, for Count Revilla Gigedo y Padilla, viceroy of Mexico. In 1847, the name was changed to its present form by Capt. Henry Kellett, as entered by him on British Admiralty charts.

Page *(S.23;T.10N;R.32E)*

Hamlet on the west bank of Snake River, 16-1/2 miles northeast of Pasco, south Franklin County. It was established as a ferry landing, and named by St. Paul & Spokane Railway officials for Danville W. Page, a local stockman and operator of the Fishook Ferry.

Page *(S.22;T.21N;R.8E)*

Small community on North Fork, Green River, 1-1/2 miles north of Eagle George, southeast King County. It is also known as *Page Sawmill*, and was named locally for Page Lumber Company which operated a sawmill here some years ago.

Page Creek *(Ts.10,11N;Rs.44,45E)*

A watercourse, dry most of the year, which follows Connor Gulch in its lower reach; (Asotin County). trends northeast 16 miles to Alpowa Creek, which sinks in its lower stretch. It was named for an 1871 land claimant.

Page Sawmill (King County) *see* Page

Paha *(S.25;T.18N;R.34E)*

Railway station 7 miles northeast of Lind, central Adams County. Indians called this place *Paha* or ''big water,'' for an abundance of water supplied from the underground source which white men named Providence Spring. In 1883, the Northern Pacific Railway Company applied the Indian name when they installed the station here.

Pah-Too (Yakima County) *see* Mt. Adams

Paia Island (Cowlitz County) *see* Burke Island

Paine Field *(Ss.15,22,23;T.28N;R.4E)*

A Snohomish County airfield, 3 miles southwest of Everett, between Possession Sound and Pacific Hwy., southwest Snohomish County. It was named for Lieut. Topliff Paine, who died in 1922 while preparing to make a flight for the Post Office Department with airmail.

Painter Creek *(T.25N;R.16E)*

The stream of the creek rises on the north slope of Icicle Ridge, Wenatchee National Forest, central Chelan County; flows 6-1/2 miles northeast and northwest to South Fork, Chiwaukum Creek. The name was applied by Asst. Forest Supervisor C. J. Conover as a change from the commonplace *Cougar Creek*.

Palat Creek (Columbia County) *see* Patit Creek

Palmer Junction (King County) *see* Palmer

Palisade *(S.27;T.20N;R.41E)*

Rock structure near north end of Rock Lake, 13 miles west of Rosalia, north central Whitman County. This name was given because the rocks around the lake looked to settlers from New York like the Palisades of Hudson River. The name is misspelled as *Pallisade* on some maps.

Palisades *(S.11;T.22N;R.23E)*

Village in Moses Coulee, 11 miles south of Waterville, southwest Douglas County. Once known as *Beulah Land,* the town was given its present name by George A. Virtue of Seattle in 1906. Sharp-pointed basaltic rocks along Moses Coulee give the effect of palisades.

Palix River *(Ts.12,13;Rs.9,10W)*

The stream of the river rises in high country south of South Bend, west central Pacific County; flows west to Willapa Harbor at Bay Center. Three forks of the river join here in a wide tidal estuary. The name is Chinook Indian, meaning ''slough covered with trees.'' The middle fork is known locally as *Tomhays River,* for a notorious Indian who lived at the river forks in the 1850s. The middle fork appears on some old maps as *Canyon River.* In 1857, James G. Swan called this stream *Palux River* in his journals. Another early version of the name is *Copalux River.*

Palmer *(S.15;T.21N;R.7E)*

Community on Green River, above Green River Gorge, 8 miles northeast of Enumclaw, south central King County. In 1885, this place was named *Green River Siding* by officials of Northern Pacific Railway Company. In 1888, they changed the station to the present name for George L. Palmer, a timber cruiser for Northern Pacific Land Company, and later superintendent of a coal mine at nearby Durham. Palmer Junction, 1 mile to the east, has the same name origin.

Palmer Lake *(T.39N;Rs.25,26E)*

A crescent-shaped, 3-1/2-mile-long lake, at the southwest extremity of Chopaka Valley, 9 miles west of Oroville, north central Okanogan County. Once called *Haipwil Lake,* its average width approximates 1 mile. It is named for James Palmer, a Forty-Niner who came here from California in the 1870s, and is reported to have made a fortune in cattle in 1888.

Palmer Mountain *(T.39N;Rs.25,26E)*

A 4,267-ft. peak directly south of Palmer Lake, north central Okanogan County; it is bounded on the west by Sinlahekin Creek. (*see* Palmer Lake)

Palouse
(S.6;T.16N;R.46&S.1;T.16N;R.45E)

Town in upper valley of South Fork, Palouse River, east central Whitman County. In 1875, the settlement started here when homesteads were claimed by Modoc Smith and W. P. Breeding; by the 1890s, it had become a farming and trade center for the area. In 1805, Lewis & Clark used the Indian name, *Palloat-pallah*. In 1812, Astorians used the same spelling for the Indian name, *Pallatapalla*. The present name is from *La Pelouse*, applied by French-Canadian fur traders, which translated to "grassland country."

Palouse City *(S.19;T.13N;R.37E)*

An old ferry point on the road to Colville, at the confluence of Palouse and Snake rivers, extreme southwest Whitman County. In the 1860s, this name was applied by a ferry operator named McWhirk. It does not appear on standard maps of the period, and should not be confused with Palouse.

Palouse Falls *(S.30;T.14N;R.37E)*

Waterfalls in Palouse River, 6 miles above confluence with Snake River, between extreme northeast Franklin and extreme southwest Whitman counties. These falls are now the site of a state park. The Indian name, as recorded by Cmdr. Charles Wilkes in 1841, was *Aputaput*. The present name was taken from that of Palouse River.

Palouse Falls State Park
(S.30;T.14N;R.37E)

A 95-acre picnic area on Palouse River, 6 miles above its confluence with Snake River, Franklin County. The park is administered by Washington State Parks & Recreation Commission. (*see* Palouse)

Palouse Hills

A system of rolling and rounded hills which extends from south of Spokane along the east boundary of the state to Snake River and Blue Mountains. This is one of Washington's most fertile farmlands, originally covered with tall bunchgrass, but a heavy producer of wheat and field peas since the 1870s. Between 1809 and 1815, this area was explored by David Thompson and by French-Canadian voyageurs and trappers. In 1868, homesteading started and in 1877, wheat farming began. (*see* Palouse)

Palouse Junction *(Franklin County)*
see Connell

Palouse River

The stream of the river rises in west central Idaho, northwest of Moscow; flows westward into Whitman County, and through Palouse and Colfax. Then it continues southwest, bordering Adams and Franklin counties, to enter Snake River at extreme southwest corner of Whitman County. This gentle, winding stream drains much of the Palouse Hills region of Whitman, Adams, and Spokane counties. In 1824, the river was called *Pavilion River* by Alexander Ross; *Peluse River* by the Wilkes Expedition in 1841; and, it has been described as *Pavion River* by Astorians in 1812. In 1825, John Work of Hudson's Bay Company called it *Flag River*. In 1806, Lewis and Clark named it *Drewyers River* for an expedition member, George Drewyer. The Indian name most used appears to have been *Moh-Ha-Na-She*. (*see* Palouse)

Palux River *(Pacific County)* see *Naselle, Palix rivers*

Panama Reef *(Skagit County)* see Boulder Reef

Panamaker Creek *(T.7N;R.4E)*

The stream of the creek heads northeast of Merrill Lake, southeast Cowlitz County; flows 6 miles south to Lewis River. On USGS maps, this creek is reversed with Cougar Creek. It was named by residents for an early settler.

Pancake Point *(Clallam County)* see Lapoel Point

Pandora *(S.16;T.20N;R.44E)*

Railway station in Pine Creek Valley, 7-1/2 miles north of Oakesdale, northeast Whitman County. The name is reported to have been devised by officials of Chicago, Milwaukee & St. Paul Railway when they named the station here. Pandora failed to live up to its Greek meaning of "all gifted," as no town developed from the platted townsite. If the reference was to Pandora's famous box, it evidently remained unopened.

Pandora Reef *(T.30N;R.4W)*

A small reef in Strait of Juan de Fuca, 3 miles east of Green Point, northeast Clallam County. It is not shown on current charts. The reef was named by Capt. Henry Richards, RN,

who surveyed these waters from 1857 until 1863 in *H.M.S. Pandora*. He named it for this survey vessel.

Pangborn Lake *(S.1;T.40N;R.3E)*

A lake 3-1/2 miles west of Sumas, 1-1/2 miles south of the Canadian boundary, northwest Whatcom County. The lake was locally named for Lorenzo Dow Pangborn, a pioneer.

Panhandle Gap *(Mt. Rainier National Park)*

This high gap, elevation 6,900 ft., lies between Sarvent Glacier and the foot of Fryingpan Glacier, east slope of Mt. Rainier. It connects Ohanapecosh Peak with Summer Land, east central zone of the park. The name describes the gap's contour, and evidently was chosen by members of an early exploring party. (USBGN)

Panhandle Lake *(S.24;T.10N;R.5E)*

A 15.1-acre mountain lake, elevation 4,520 ft., Gifford Pinchot National Forest, 3 miles north of Spirit Lake, extreme northwest Skamania County. The lake has a long "handle" but appears to have very little "pan." Air photos of these high lakes often show entirely different contours from those visible from the lake shores.

Panjab Creek *(T.8N;R.41E)*

The stream of the creek rises at Grizzly Bear Ridge, Blue Mountains, southeast Columbia County; flows 4 miles north to Meadow Creek. A pioneer legend dating back to the 1880s states that the creek was named for a frying pan that was jabbed into the ground at the creek's mouth.

Panorama Point *(Mt. Rainier National Park)*

A south slope point of Mt. Rainier, between Paradise and Nisqually glaciers, 1-1/2 miles north of Paradise Valley. It affords an excellent panoramic view of Nisqually watershed and Paradise Valley. The name chosen by park officials is very descriptive.

Panther Creek *(T.28N;Rs.14,15E)*

The stream of the creek heads on the southeast slope of Longfellow Mountain, 5 miles east of Cascade Mountain summit; flows 7 miles east to White River at Rocky Ford, Wenatchee National Forest, northwest Chelan County. The original name was *Cougar Creek*. Because of duplication of names, it was changed to the present designation by

Asst. Forest Supervisor C. J. Conover.

Panther Creek *(Mt. Rainier National Park)*

The stream of the creek rises near Cascade Mountain summit, southeast area of the park; flows west to Ohanapecosh River, 3-1/2 miles north of Ohanapecosh Hot Springs. The name is extremely common for creeks throughout most of the state. In this case, there still are panthers in the high mountain areas around the stream's source. An alternate name is *Cougar Creek*, which is just as commonly used.

Panther Creek *(Ts.3-5N;Rs.7-1/2,8E)*

The stream of the creek heads near Race Track, south central Skamania County; flows 17 miles south to Wind River north of Carson. It was named by an early settler, B. Tillotson, for a panther which he saw crossing a log over this creek.

Panther Lake *(S.6;T.23N;S.31;T.24N;R.1W)*

A 104-acre lake about 10 miles west of Bremerton, west central Kitsap and northeast Mason counties. About 74 acres of the lake's area are in Kitsap County, 30 acres in Mason County. A small island is included in this lake; and the lake is one of a group of 3, with Mission and Tiger Lakes. It was named for Panther Creek which drains it. An alternate name, which is most descriptive, is *No Fish Lake.*

Papoose Creek *(Ts.28,29N;R.14E)*

The stream of the creek heads on Longfellow Mountain, 4-1/2 miles east of Cascade Mountain summit; flows 2-1/2 miles north to Indian Creek, Wenatchee National Forest, northwest Chelan County. It was so named "because the parent stream is Indian" by the imaginative forest supervisor A. H. Sylvester.

Parachute Meadow *(S.16;T.37N;R.23E)*

This very high, 1/2-mile-long mountain meadow, average width 100 yds., is on the Chelan National Forest, 2 miles northwest of Tiffany Lake, central Okanogan County. The name is well earned, as the Forest Service used the meadow to develop methods of forest fire control by dropping men and supplies via parachute.

Paradise Glacier *(Mt. Rainier National Park)*

This ice river, elevation 9,000 ft., originates in snowfields on the southeast slope of Mt. Rainier, south central area of the park; it extends between Cowlitz and Nisqually glaciers. This is the source of Paradise River, and is an interglacier, rather than a primary. It melts rapidly in summer months, and has many caverns near its terminus. In 1870, it was named *Little Nisqually Glacier* by Gen. Hazard Stevens and P. B. Van Trump. The present name, which was substituted, has been declared official by USBGN.

Paradise River *(Mt. Rainier National Park)*

The stream of the river rises at the foot of Paradise Glacier, southeast slope of Mt. Rainier; flows southwest to Nisqually River, 2 miles northeast of Longmire, south central zone of the park. Its valley once was occupied by an extension of Paradise Glacier. In 1870, this river was named *Glacier Creek* by P. B. Van Trump and Gen. Hazard Stevens. The present name was substituted by Mrs. Elaine Longmire on her first trip to the locality in 1885, as she considered the entire Paradise Valley to be a heavenly sight. (USBGN)

Paradise Valley *(Ss.5,6;T.24N;R.8W)*

An area of small lakes and mountain meadows, Olympic National Park, at the head of Tshletshy Creek, southwest Jefferson County. Few mountainous parks and recreation areas escape this name at some appropriate place. This valley is probably as close to Heaven as many of us will get.

Paradise Valley *(Mt. Rainier National Park)*

A flat mountain valley at the foot of Mt. Rainier, in Paradise River Valley, 20 miles east of Nisqually Entrance, south central area of the park. This is the most often visited location in the park. Abundant alpine flowers bloom here in summer; in winter months the snow is usually about 20 ft. deep. Here is located a large inn, a district ranger station, and the hub of many trails leading to points in the park. In 1885, it was named by Mrs. Elcain Longmire when she first saw the valley and exclaimed, "Oh, it looks just like Paradise!" (USBGN)

Park *(S.23;T.37N;R.4E)*

Small settlement at the southeast end of Lake Whatcom, 3/4 mile south of Blue Canyon, southwest Whatcom County. It was locally named for Charles Park, a pioneer settler and owner of timber claims. The name was suggested for the post office when it was established in 1884, by Hon. Michael Anderson.

Park *(S.18;T.14N;R.37E)*

Community on east bank of Palouse River, 2 miles north of Palouse Falls (waterfall), southwest Whitman County. Reports indicate that the place was named by O.W.R.&N. Company officials for Charles Park, a local pioneer.

Park Cliffs *(T.38N;R.8E.uns)*

A sheer, 2-mile-long precipice on the east slope of Mt. Baker at Park Glacier, central Whatcom County. This precipice splits Park Glacier and its ice blocks fall over into the valley below. The name was chosen by The Mazamas.

Park Creek *(Ts.17,18N;Rs.19,20E)*

The stream of the creek rises in east central Kittitas County; flows 20 miles southwest to Yakima River near Thrall. The name comes from an early nickname for the east Kittitas Valley -- *The Park.*

Park Lake *(Grant County) see* Sun Lakes State Park

Park Place *(Snohomish County) see* Monroe

Park Point *(Pierce County) see* Devils Head

Parker *(S.29;T.12N;R.19E)*

Railway station 5 miles south of Yakima, central Yakima County. In 1890, it was named by Northern Pacific Railway officials for William Parker, who settled here in 1864.

Parker Reef *(S.1;T.37N;R.2W)*

A bare, rock island 1 mile north of the north end of Orcas Island, in Strait of Georgia, northeast San Juan County. In 1841, it was named *Parker's Rock* by the Wilkes Expedition for George Parker, a petty officer with the expedition. The name was altered to the present form on subsequent charts.

Parker's Landing *(Clark County) see* Washougal

Parkland *(S.8;T.19N;R.3E)*

Flat, prairie area directly east of McChord Field, U.S. Army airfield west central Pierce County. The name was a local choice. Throughout this area scattered clumps of coniferous trees and small lakes lend a park-like appearance to the landscape.

Parkwater *(S.11;T.25N;R.43E)*

Suburb directly east of Spokane city limits, central Spokane County. The name resulted from the inclusion of UpRiver Park in the Spokane City Waterworks which are located here.

Parnell (Parnall) (Grant County) *see* Hartline

Parragon Lake (Okanogan County) *see* Pearrygin Lake

Partridge Point (Island County) *see* Point Partridge

Pasco *(T.9N;Rs.29,30E)*

City at confluence of Snake and Columbia rivers, southeast Franklin County. In 1884, it was established by Northern Pacific Railway Company, and originally it was a railroad town. In 1891, it was incorporated. The name comes from Cerro de Pasco in Peru, 4,000 meters high in the Andes Mountains. Henry M. McCartney, a location engineer for the Northern Pacific, was greeted by a heavy sandstorm on his first day in this eastern Washington town. He also suffered from excessive heat. Recently he had surveyed a railroad in an Andean mining district, the Oroya Railway, highest in the world and the coldest place he had ever been. He named this town *Pasco*, for the mining town of Cerro de Pasco, because of a complete contrast in climate between the places.

Pass Creek *(T.28N;Rs.12,13.uns)*

The stream of the creek rises at Cady Pass, Cascade Mountain summit, Snoqualmie National Forest, southeast Snohomish County; flows 5 miles west to North Fork, Skykomish River. The creek was named by The Mountaineers because of its origin at Cady Pass.

Pass Island *(S.26;T.34N;R.1E)*

A small, cone-shaped rock which has been used as a natural pier for Deception Pass Bridge. It divides Deception and Canoe passes, extreme southwest Skagit County. The name is descriptive, because of its position between the 2 passes. An alternate name, used locally, is *Canoe Island*.

Pass Lake *(S.23;T.34N;R.1E)*

A 98.6-acre lake on Fidalgo Island, 6 miles south of Anacortes, less than 1 mile north of Deception Pass. Part of the lake is in Deception Pass State Park. The

lake was named after the pass.

Pass-No-Pass *(S.26;T.31N;R.15E)*

A primitive pass between Helmet Butte and Fortress Mountain, at Cascade Mountain summit, northwest Chelan County, facing Snohomish County. It was named by U.S. Forest Supervisor A. H. Sylvester because the pass has neither road nor trail, and is suited only to trailing of sheep.

Pataha *(S.32;T.13N;R.37E)*

Community on the south bank of Snake River, 4-1/2 miles northwest of Starbuck, northwest corner of Columbia County. The site was included in an 1861 land claim by James Bowers, and was platted as a townsite by A. J. Favor on August 21, 1882. This Nez Perce Indian name means ''brushy creek,'' and refers to dense growths of bushes and small trees along Pataha Creek. The town should not be confused with Pataha in Garfield County, 33 miles to the east. (USBGN)

Pataha *(S.34;T.12N;R.42E)*

Town on Pataha Creek, 2 miles east of Pomeroy, north central Garfield County. In 1861, the place was established by James Bowers, who sold it to his brother-in-law, J. Benjamin Norton. In 1867, Norton sold out to A. J. (''Vine'') Favor, a stage driver. On August 21, 1882, a townsite was platted by the owner under his full name of Angevine J. T. Favor, and was called *Favorsburg*. It later reverted to the original name used by local Indians. Intermediate names were *Watertown*, *Waterstown*, and *Pataha City*. (see Pataha)

Pataha City (Garfield County) *see* Pataha

Pataha Creek *(Ts.9-12;Rs.38-42)*

The stream of the creek heads at Clearwater, Umatilla National Forest, southwest Garfield County; flows north to Pataha, then west through Houser, Dodge, and Jackson to Tucannon River, 2 miles northwest of Tucannon in Columbia County. Prior to recognition of this name by USBGN in 1947, the stream was sometimes called *East Fork, Pataha Creek*. (see Pataha) (USBGN)

Pataha Stage Station (Garfield County) *see* Pomeroy

Pateros *(S.36;T.30N;R.23E)*

Town at the confluence of Methow and Columbia rivers, 6 miles southwest

of Brewster, south central Okanogan County. It is often referred to as the ''Gateway to Methow Valley.'' In 1886, a settlement was established here by Lee Ives and was called *Ives* or *Ives Landing*. It was named for a town in south central Luzon, Philippine Islands, by Lieut. Nosler, USA, who campaigned in the Philippines during the Spanish-American War.

Paterson *(S.8;T.5N;R.26E)*

Settlement on the north bank of Columbia River, south slope of Paterson Ridge, directly upstream from Blalock Island, southwest Benton County. The name of Henry Paterson, a pioneer settler, was applied to the settlement, the ridge, and to nearby springs. (USBGN)

Patit Creek *(T.10N;Rs.39-41E)*

The stream of the creek rises at the north boundary of Umatilla National Forest, east central Columbia County; flows northwest and west 18 miles to Touchet River at Dayton. The name is a corruption of the original Indian name, *Pa-At-Te-Tah* or *Pat-It-Ta*, meaning ''Bark Creek'' in translation from the Nez Perce language. A garbled version, *Palat Creek*, has been used in the past. One informant offers the less valid origin as the French word, *petite*, explaining that the creek carries little water in autumn months.

Pato (Kittias County) *see* Roza

Patos Island *(T.38N;R.2W)*

A rather small, whale-shaped island, 5 miles north of Orcas Island in Strait of Georgia, extreme north central San Juan County. In 1792, the island was named by Lieut. Dionisio Galiano as *Isla de Patos* which translates to ''Island of Ducks.'' In 1841, the Wilkes Expedition charted it as *Gourd Island*, but Capt. Henry Kellett of the British Admiralty survey changed it back to the Spanish name in 1847. In 1854, the U.S. Coast Survey adopted the present name. The Lummi Indian name was *Klu-whit-eton*, which means ''abundant native oysters.''

Patterson Lake (Thurston County) *see* Pattison Lake

Patterson Lake
(Ss.8,17;T.34N;R.21E)

A 1-1/2-mile-long lake, 2 miles south of Methow River, 3 miles southwest of Winthrop, southwest Okanogan County. The average width is 1/3 mile.

The lake was named for the first local settler, Sam Patterson.

Pattison Lake *(Ts.17,18N;R.1W)*

A 2-1/2-mile-long lake, 5 miles southeast of Olympia, east central Thurston County. In April 1852, a Donation Land Claim was taken on the southwest shore of this lake by William Pattison. His 3 sons took similar claims soon afterward. The lake is named for this pioneer family. On some recent maps it is incorrectly noted as *Patterson Lake*.

Patterson Point (Pierce County) *see* Gibson Point

Pattison Creek (Thurston County) *see* Woodward Creek

Pattles Point *(S.36;T.38N;R.2E)*

A Bellingham Bay point, southwest Whatcom County. Not shown on recent maps, this point was called *Point Clatawa* in pioneer days. A nickname during the period of Indian unrest was *Point Runaway*, because both whites and Indians retreated during an armed skirmish. It was named for Capt. William R. Pattle, who directed the first settlers to the bay and who mined coal here in 1853.

Pawn Lakes *(T.29N;R.19E)*

Three small lakes in a group, 1 mile west of Chelan Mountains summit, Wenatchee National Forest, central Chelan County. The lakes were named *Fawn Lakes* by Forest Ranger James McKenzie. An error was made in applying his name to the maps.

Pavilion (Pavion) River (Whitman/Franklin/Adams counties) *see* Palouse River

Paxton *(S.15;T.18N;R.38E)*

Railway point 18 miles southeast of Ritzville, east central Adams County. It was named by officials of Chicago, Milwaukee & St. Paul Railway. H. R. Williams, who was vice president of that railroad, stated that it was "a chance selection."

Pe Ell *(S.34;T.13N;R.5W)*

Small town, once a busy sawmill center, on Chehalis River, 24 miles south of Chehalis, southwest Lewis County. The name is a distortion of the first name of Pierre Charles, who took a Donation Land Claim in the 1850s on what is now known as Pe Ell Prairie, south of Boisfort. Local Indians, unable to pronounce the name *Pierre*, called this pioneer *Pe Ell*, and the name became attached to the place.

Pe Ell Prairie (Lewis County) *see* Pe Ell

Peace Arch State Park *(S.31;T.41N;R.1E)*

A 10-acre, landscaped area on the international boundary at Blaine, northwest Whatcom County. Here is the Peace Arch which celebrates 100 years of peace between the U.S. and Canada. An alternate name is *Sam Hill Memorial State Park*, for Sam Hill, philanthropist and peace advocate, who prompted the Peace Arch idea.

Peach *(S.28;T.27N;R.35E)*

One of 12 towns drowned out by the reservoir created in back of Grand Coulee Dam, on Columbia River, at the mouth of Hawk Creek, north central Lincoln County. It was named for peach orchards in the vicinity. An earlier name was *Orchard Valley*.

Peach Lake *(S.32;T.28N;R.13E)*

A 17-acre lake, elevation 4,800 ft., on Snoqualmie National Forest, near Wenatchee Pass, Cascade Mountain summit, extreme southeast Snohomish County. This lake is 1,000 ft. south of Pear Lake. In 1936, the name was chosen by Elmer Buss to match nearby Plum, Pear, and Apple lakes.

Peaches Ridge *(Ss.27,28,33,34; T.19N;R.14E)*

A Wenatchee National Forest ridge, 9 miles south of Cle Elum, southwest Kittitas County. The name hinges on an incident in 1910, when a district ranger of the Wenatchee National Forest took a group of boys for a camping trip on the ridge. They ate canned peaches, which did not bother the boys, but which made the ranger sick. The boys named the ridge.

Peacock Island (Skagit County) *see* Hat Island

Peacock Mountain *(S.19;T.35N;R.25E)*

A 4,520-ft. peak, 1-1/2 miles south of Conconully Reservoir, central Okanogan County. The name is for a mine near the summit started in 1885 by John Picard.

Peacock Spit *(T.9N;R.11W)*

A large, dangerous sand spit at the North Jetty, near Columbia River's entrance into Pacific Ocean, extreme southwest corner of Pacific County. This spit has been called the "Graveyard of the Pacific" for the many ships that have been wrecked here. The name is for *U.S.S. Peacock*, a ship of the Wilkes Expedition which foundered here in 1841.

Peak 8200 (Whatcom County) *see* Mt. Degenhardt

Peak Success (Mt. Rainier National Park) *see* Columbia Crest

Peale Passage *(T.20N;R.2W)*

A passage between Hartstene and Squaxin islands, southeast Mason County. In 1841, this feature was named *Peale's Passage* by the Wilkes Expedition for Titian R. Peale, a naturalist with the expedition.

Peapod Rocks *(S.1;T.36N;R.1W)*

Two islands 1-1/2 miles south of Lawrence Point, near the east extremity of Orcas Island, northeast San Juan County. The islands are called *North* and *South Peapod*, respectively. The northern island is larger and has a beacon. In 1841, the islands were named for their shape by Cmdr. Charles Wilkes. An alternate name on some maps is *The Peapods*.

Pear Lake *(S.32;T.28N;R.13E)*

A 33-acre lake on Snoqualmie National Forest, elevation 4,800 ft., at Wenatchee Pass, Cascade Mountain summit, southeast Snohomish County. It is one of 4 lakes in this area that are named for fruits, the others being, *Peach, Plum,* and *Apple lakes*. The name is fairly descriptive of the lake's contour, especially when viewed from nearby high peaks or from the air. It was named by A. H. Sylvester, once supervisor of Wenatchee National Forest, after he had seen it from a local, high elevation.

Pearl Falls *(Mt. Rainier National Park)*

Waterfalls in Pearl Creek, a branch of Pyramid Creek, southwest zone of the park. The water falls from lava cliffs below Pyramid Peak, making one of the highest waterfalls in the park. In 1912, they were named by A. H. Barnes, a Tacoma photographer who spent many years photographing points in the park. Droplets from the cascade resemble pearls under the proper light conditions. (USBGN)

Pearl Island *(S.14;T.36N;R.4W)*

A north entrance island at Roche

Harbor, northwest San Juan Island, west central San Juan County. The island covers about 3/4 of the harbor entrance. In 1841, it was named by Cmdr. Charles Wilkes who stated that the name was ''for its shape and position,'' which is not entirely clear.

Pearrygin Creek (*T.35N;Rs.21,22E*)

The stream of the creek rises on the south side of Tripod Peak, Chelan National Forest, west central Okanogan County; flows 7-1/2 miles southwest to Pearrygin Lake. (*see Pearrygin Lake*)

Pearrygin Lake (*S.36;T.35N;R.21E*)

A 1-1/2-mile-long lake, average width 1/2 mile, 1-1/2 miles northeast of Winthrop, west central Okanogan County, It was named for the third person to settle here, Benjamin Franklin Pearrygin, who had a claim on the lake shore. An early version of the name was *Parragon*.

Pearson (*S.26;T.26N;R.1E*)

Community on the south shore of Liberty Bay, north central Kitsap County. It was locally named for Per Johan Pearson, a homesteader of 1886, who opened the first store on the bay, and who helped to secure a post office.

Pearson Creek (Snohomish County) *see* Canyon Creek

Peavine Creek (*T.27N;R.15E*)

The stream of this short creek rises on Wenatchee Ridge, 7 miles west of Wenatchee Lake; flows 2 miles southwest to Little Wenatchee River, Wenatchee National Forest, west central Chelan County. It was named by U.S. Forest Supervisor A. H. Sylvester because of wild peavine along the creek which furnished horse feed during trail construction.

Peavine Pass (*S.28;T.36N;R.1W*)

A pass between Obstruction Island and the north end of Blakely Island, east central San Juan County. The name was chosen locally because of extensive growths of native peavine (*Lathyrus*) on the Blakely Island side of the pass. The Lummi Indian name for the passage was *Sch-wa-ugen*.

Pedigo (*S.21;T.7N;R.35E*)

Railway station 3 miles northwest of Walla Walla, south central Walla Walla County. The naming was by Northern Pacific Railway officials for John H.

Pedigo, owner of a large farm adjacent to the station.

Peekaboo Lake (*S.35;T.31N;R.10E*)

A 22.4-acre lake, elevation 4,000 ft., 6 miles northeast of Silverton, Mt. Baker National Forest, north central Snohomish County. The lake was given this bashful name by Blanche Wrage of Arlington, on a trip to Mt. Pugh in 1923.

Pe Ell (*S.34;T.13N;R.5W*)

Small town, once a busy sawmill center, on Chehalis River, 24 miles south of Chehalis, southwest Lewis County. The name is a distortion of the first name of Pierre Charles, who took a Donation Land Claim in the 1850s on what is now known as Pe Ell Prairie, south of Boisfort. Local Indians, unable to pronounce the name *Pierre*, called this pioneer *Pe Ell*, and the name became attached to the place.

Pe Ell Prairie (Lewis County) *see* Pe Ell

Peewee Creek (Pend Oreille County) *see* Fence Creek

Peewee Falls (Pend Oreille County) *see* Periwee Falls

Peloose River (Whitman/Franklin/Adams counties) *see* Palouse River

Pelouse (Peluse) River (Whitman County) *see* Palouse River

Pelton Creek (*T.25N;R.8W*)

The stream of the creek heads 10 miles southwest of Mt. Olympus summit, south central Jefferson County; flows 3-1/2 miles northwest to Queets River. In Chinook jargon, the word *pelton* or *pehlten* means ''a fool'' or ''insane.'' A logical translation might be ''Crazy Creek.'' (USBGN)

Penawawa (*S.17;T.14N;R.41E*)

Village 12 miles west of Almota, at confluence of Snake River and Penawawa Creek, extreme south central Whitman County. In 1872, C. C. Cram built a ferry across Snake River at this point, and on November 23, 1877, Cram and Emsley Fincher platted a townsite. In the late 1870s and early 1880s, it was an important wheat-shipping point, but it declined when railroads came to haul the grain. The Indian name indicates that this place might have been a council place or general meeting ground of Indian bands.

Pend Oreille County

The most northeastern county in Washington state. It is bounded on the west by Stevens County; on the south by Spokane County; on the east by Idaho; and on the north by Canada. On March 1, 1911, the state legislature created this county, separating it from Stevens County. The name is that which was given to the local Indians by French-Canadians who worked for early fur traders in this area. A literal translation would be ''hanging ears.'' Many natives wore ear ornaments in earlier periods, so it is probable that their ear lobes were quite distended.

Pend Oreille River

The stream of the river heads in Pend Oreille Lake, northwest Idaho, enters Washington at Newport; flows north through the central part of Pend Oreille County into British Columbia. Then the river turns west and joins Columbia River just north of the Canadian boundary. On some maps it is called *Clarks Fork* or *Clarks Fork, Pend Oreille River*. Other names which do not correctly apply but which are found on very early maps are *Missoula*, *Hells Gate*, *Deer Lodge*, *Silver Bow*, and *Flathead*. (*see* Pend Oreille County)

Pend Oreille State Park (*S.13;T.30N;R.43E*)

A 393-acre state park, 15 miles west of Newport, southwest Pend Oreille County. (*see* Pend Oreille County)

Penguin Harbor (*T.36N;R.2E*)

A channel between Samish and Guemes islands, northwest Skagit County. In 1841, this name was applied by Cmdr. Charles Wilkes. It was for a British brig-sloop captured during the War of 1812 by Capt. Lawrence in *Hornet*. Following his often-used method of nomenclature by association, Wilkes named nearby Guemes Channel *Hornet's Harbor*. The present name is not shown on recent maps and charts.

Penguin Island (San Juan County) *see* Bare and Skipjack Islands

Penn Cove (*T.32N;R.1E*)

An east shore harbor of Whidbey Island, off Saratoga Passage, west Island County. This commodious harbor was very important in pioneer days, and the home of many retired sea captains. In 1792, it was named by Capt. George Vancouver, ''in honor of a particular friend.'' The person honored was evidently either John or Richard Penn, both of whom were grandsons of William Penn, famous American statesman. In 1841, the harbor was charted by Cmdr. Charles Wilkes in 1841 as *Penn's Cove*.

Penner Lake (Ferry County) *see* Renner Lake

Penns Cove (Island County) *see* Penn Cove

Penrose Point State Park *(S.31;T.21N;R.1E)*
A 125-acre public park on the west shore of Carr Inlet, 3 miles north of Longbranch, northwest Pierce County. It offers camping, boating, swimming, fishing, and clamming; the park was named for the point on which it is located.

Peone *(S.8;T.26N;R.44E)*
Settlement in Peone Township, 5 miles northeast of Spokane city limits, east central Spokane County. It was named for the prairie which was named for Louis Peone, an employee of Hudson's Bay Company, who is said to have homesteaded on the present site of Colville before settling here.

Peone Creek *(T.26N;R.44E)*
The stream of the creek rises in 2 forks in Foothills township, east central Spokane County; flows northwest 6 miles to Deadman Creek. (*see* Peone)

Peone Prairie *(T.26N;Rs.43,44E)*
A prairie south of Deadman Creek, 4-6 miles northeast of Spokane city limits, central Spokane County. In 1866, Father Cataldo founded on this prairie the original St. Michaels Mission, which later was moved to a site north of Hillyard. (*see* Peone)

Perch Lake (Grant County) *see* Sun Lakes State Park

Percival Cove Lake (Thurston County) *see* Percival Lake

Percival Creek *(S.33;T.18N;R.2W)*
The stream of this short creek rises south of Simmons Lake, directly west of Olympia, northwest Thurston County; flows 2 miles south to the north end of Black Lake. It was named for a pioneer sea captain who also was interested in logging operations along the creek.

Percival Group (San Juan County) *see* Sucia Islands

Percival Lake *(S.22;T.18N;R.2W)*
A 22-acre lake at the mouth of Per-

cival Creek, in Olympia, north central Thurston County. It was named for Percival Creek, which feeds it. An alternate name is *Percival Cove Lake*. (*see* Percival Creek)

Periwee Falls *(S.16;T.40N;R.43E)*
Waterfall in Pewee Creek, 2-1/2 miles south of the Canadian boundary, north central Pend Oreille County. In 1895, it was named by a French-Canadian who hunted and prospected in this area. The name origin has not been determined. An alternate name in local use is *Pewee Falls*.

Perkins Landing (Pierce County) *see* Buckley

Perrinville *(S.7;T.27N;R.4E)*
Small settlement on Snake Trail Road, 3 miles northeast of Edmonds, southwest Snohomish County. It was named for Mrs. Gertrude Perrin, owner and operator of an antique shop here.

Perry *(S.19;T.13N;R.36E)*
Village on north bank of Columbia River, at junction of Palouse River, extreme east Franklin County. Perry was a son of Daniel Lyons who was the first postmaster here in 1881. The post office was named for him when established. Lyons also operated a ferry across Snake River.

Perry's Island (Skagit County) *see* Fidalgo Island

Peshastin *(S.17;T.24N;R.18E)*
Community on Wenatchee River, 4 miles southeast of Leavenworth, south central Chelan County. When founded in 1892, the Indian name of the place was retained. It means "broad-bottom canyon." Indian pronunciation of the name was *Pish-pish-astin*.

Pete Lake *(S.17;T.27N;R.13E)*
A 2.8-acre lake, elevation 4,900 ft., Snoqualmie National Forest, 2 miles southwest of Cascade Mountain summit, extreme Snohomish County. The very small lake was named by U.S. Forest Service employees for a faithful old packhorse that worked for years in this area.

Peters Creek *(T.12N;R.7E)*
The stream of the creek rises south of Watch Mountain, 2-1/2 miles north of Randle, east central Lewis County; flows south to Kiona Creek near its confluence with Cowlitz River. This is a rich farm area in the "Big Bottom Coun-

ty." It was named for Thomas Martin Peters who settled on the creek in 1890, by his son, John W. Peters.

Peterson Park (King County) *see* Brace Point

Peterson's Point (Grays Harbor County) *see* Point Chehalis

Petit lake (King County) *see* Drunken Charlie Lake

Pettit's Landing (Kitsap County) *see* Ferncliff

Pheasant Lake (Jefferson County) *see* Twin Lakes (near Port Ludlow)

Phelps Creek *(Ts.30,31;R.16E)*
The stream of this 6-mile-long creek heads in Spider Glacier on Red Mountain; flows south to Chiwawa River, near the north boundary of Wenatchee National Forest, northwest Chelan County. The name was in use prior to 1908 and is presumed to be that of an early prospector who worked along this creek.

Phelps Ridge *(T.30N;R.16E)*
This ore-filled ridge is between Chiwawa River and Phelps Creek, at the extreme north end of Wenatchee National Forest, northwest Chelan County. A mine tunnel is at the south end. It was named for Phelps Creek by U.S. Forest Supervisor A. H. Sylvester. (*see* Phelps Creek)

Philleo Lake *(Ss.10,11,12;T.22N;R.42E)*
A narrow lake, slightly over 1 mile long, 3 miles west of Spangle, south central Spokane County. It was named by, and for, T. A. E. Philleo, who owned land adjoining the lake.

Phinney (Island County) *see* Clinton

Phinney Ridge *(Ss.1,12;T.25N;R.3E)*
This is one of Seattle's 12 "official" hills, in north central Seattle, along Phinney and Greenwood Avenues, west of Green Lake, King County. Its highest elevation of 350 ft. is at N. 55th St. and its lowest of 340 ft. is at N. 60th St. The ridge was named for John G. Phinney, a pioneer of Whidbey Island and Seattle, who owned a considerable amount of real estate here.

Pialschie, Pialchie (King County) *see* Thomas

Pickard *(S.22;T.11N;R.35E)*
Railway point 24 miles north of Walla Walla, north central Walla Walla

County. It was named by Northern Pacific Railway officials for a prominent local wheat rancher who was killed by a runaway team.

Pickering Passage *(Ts.20,21;R.2W)*

An 8-mile-long passage, 1/2 mile average width, between the north end of Hartstene Island and the mainland, east central Mason County. In 1841, it was named by the Wilkes Expedition for naturalist Charles Pickering, who was one of several civilian scientists with Wilkes. Each of the other scientists has a Pacific Northwest feature named for him.

Picnic Point *(S.29;T.28N;R.4E)*

A flat, sandy point with a long tidal run, on Possession Sound, 5-1/2 miles north of Edmonds, southwest Snohomish County. It was named because it has an excellent beach for camping and picnics.

Picnic Point Lake *(S.29;T.28N;R.4E)*

A 4.3-acre lake, 5-3/4 miles north of Edmonds, 800 ft. north of Picnic Point, southwest Snohomish County. It was named for Picnic Point. An alternate name, which is quite romantic but not commonly used, is *Windantide Lake.*

Picture Lake *(S.17;T.39N;R.9E)*

A 3-acre lake, elevation 4,100 ft., 4 miles northwest of Mt. Shuksan summit, near Mt. Baker Lodge, north central Whatcom County. This is one of 2 Mt. Baker Lodge lakes. Local informants state that the name was applied because of the clear reflection of nearby mountains in the lake.

Piedmont *(S.14;T.30N;R.9W)*

Small settlement on the north shore of Lake Crescent, near the east end, central Clallam County. In 1893, it was named by a local resident, William Dawson, for its position at the foot of a mountain.

Pierce County

This county is in west central Washington state. It is bounded on the north by Kitsap and King counties; on the east by Yakima County; on the south by Lewis and Thurston counties; and on the west by Thurston and Mason counties. This important county contains 1,680 sq. miles and was created from a portion of Lewis County on December 22, 1852, by Oregon Territorial Legislature. It was named for Franklin Pierce, 14th president of the U.S., 1853-1857. At the time

of naming, he was president-elect.

Pierce's River (Chelan County) *see* Stehekin River

Pierre Lake *(Ss.5,8;T.39N;R.37E)*

A 1-mile-long lake, average width 1/4 mile, on Colville National Forest, 4 miles northeast of Orient on Toulou Creek, northwest Stevens County. It was named for Peter Arcasa. (*see* Little Pierre Lake)

Pifer *(S.1;T.20N;R.37E)*

Settlement on the west shore of Lake Colville, northeast Adams County. In 1915, it was founded as a railroad spur and siding to serve Pifer's ice plant. It was named by officials of Northern Pacific Railway Company for J. H. Pifer, who had contracts to furnish ice to the railroad at a number of places along the system.

Pigeon Creek (Clark County) *see* Bachelor Island Slough

Pigeon Peak *(Mt. Rainier National Park)*

This peak is located just inside the park, at the north central portion of the boundary, west of West Fork, White River. The name was chosen by an early party of climbers for the many band-tailed pigeons on the mountain slopes and meadows.

Pigeon Point *(S.13;T.24N;R.3E)*

A west side point of Duwamish River, where the river discharges into Elliott Bay, West Seattle, King County. This name, not found on recent maps, was applied by early settlers who hunted wild pigeons here. Some of these birds were seen as recently as 1907 in this vicinity. It now is entirely altered into large industrial installations.

Pigeon Springs *(Mt. Rainier National Park)*

A group of warm springs in Longmire Meadows near Nisqually River, southwest corner of the park. The springs were named by the original landowner, James Longmire, for great numbers of band-tailed pigeons which lived here in early days.

Pilchuck *(S.10;T.29N;R.7E)*

Settlement on Pilchuck River, 12 miles north of Monroe, west central Snohomish County. This place should not be confused with one of the same name on Pilchuck Creek, northwest Snohomish County. The name is from

Chinook jargon and has the meaning of "red water." The same name has been applied to other streams in the state which have dark water from mineral or vegetable infiltrations.

Pilchuck *(S.16;T.32N;R.5E)*

Community on Pilchuck Creek, 5 miles northwest of Arlington, northwest Snohomish County. It should not be confused with another place of the same name on Pilchuck River, west central Snohomish County. (*see* Pilchuck)

Pilchuck Creek *(Ts.31,32N;R.15W)*

The stream of the creek heads 3-1/2 miles north of Lake Ozette, northwest Clallam County; flows 6-1/2 miles north to Sooes River. (*see* Pilchuck)

Pilchuck Creek *(Ts.31-34N;Rs.4-6E)*

The stream of the creek rises on the south side of Cultus Mountain range, southwest Skagit County; flows southwest through Pilchuck, northwest Snohomish County to Stillaguamish River near Silvana. (*see* Pilchuck)

Pilchuck Mountain *(S.28;T.30N;R.8E)*

A 5,334-ft. peak at the headwaters of Pilchuck River, 18 miles east-by-north of Everett, central Snohomish County. The mountain drains north into Stillaguamish River and south into Pilchuck River. (*see* Pilchuck)

Pilchuck River *(Ts.28,29N;Rs.7-9E)*

The stream of the river heads on the west side of Bald Mountain, near Sultan Basin, central Snohomish County; flows 32 miles west and south to Snohomish River at Snohomish. (*see* Pilchuck)

Pildish Point (Jefferson County) *see* Broad Spit

Pile Point *(S.32;T.35N;R.3W)*

A southwest shore point of San Juan Island, at the west entrance to Kanaka Bay, on Strait of Juan de Fuca, southwest San Juan County. In 1858, the name was first applied to British admiralty charts by Capt. Henry Richards, RN, who surveyed these waters in 1858-1860. The name origin is not of record.

Pillar Point *(S.3;T.31N;R.11W)*

A south shore point on Strait of Juan de Fuca, 1-1/2 miles north of Pysht, north central Clallam County. In 1847, the name was placed on British Admiralty charts by Capt. Kellett; in 1858, it was approved by U.S. Coast Survey. The name is quite descriptive.

Pillar Rock (*S.17;T.9N;R.7W*)

A detached point of conglomerate rock, elevation 100 ft., on the north bank of lower Columbia River, 15 miles from the mouth, southwest Wahkiakum County. This very descriptive name was charted by Cmdr. Charles Wilkes. The Chinook Indian name was *Taluaptea* .

Pilot Point (*S.35;T.28N;R.2E*)

A west shore point of Admiralty Inlet, south of Point No Point, northeast Kitsap County. (*see* Pilots Cove)

Pilots Cove (*S.35;T.28N;R.2E*)

A cove on Admiralty Inlet, between Point No Point and Eglon, northeast Kitsap County. In 1841, the cove was named by George W. Colvocoresses of the Wilkes Expedition for Capt. William Henry McNeill, captain of Hudson's Bay Company steamer *Beaver*, who gave pilotage to Fort Nisqually for Wilkes' squadron.

Pinckney City (*S.35;T.36N;R.39E*)

This long-abandoned town was on Mill Creek, 3 miles north of the present town of Colville, central Stevens County. At one time it was the most important settlement in the entire area. It came into being concurrently with the establishment of Fort Colville, for which Pinckney City was a trading post, post office, and recreation center. The fort adjoined this ''city'' on the south and was occupied on June 21, 1859, by several companies of the 9th, U.S. Infantry, a regular army regiment, commanded by Maj. Pinckney Lougenbeel. In 1860, the settlement became the county seat of Spokane County and of Stevens County in 1864 when the 2 counties were separated. The name was for the commanding officer of the fort. In 1868, it was changed to *Fort Colville* by act of the Territorial Legislature. It is shown on older maps a *Pinkney City, Fort Colville* and *Old Colville*. Small evidence exists today to indicate the site of this pioneer town, and none to indicate the site of the 1,070-acre military post, except a roadside monument. The last of the fort's log structures were burned several years ago to add ground for wheat growing.

Pine City (*S.28;T.20N;R.42E*)

Community in Pine Creek Valley, 2-1/2 miles southwest of Malden, north central Whitman County. In the 1870s and later, this place was a trading post and way station on the stage road between Walla Walla and Cheney. The name was taken from Pine Creek Valley in which the town is located and which was so named because of commercial pine timber in the valley used in early-day construction.

Pine Creek (*T.6N;R.33E*)

The stream of the creek rises in northeast Oregon; flows into Walla Walla County, 4 miles southeast of Touchet, thence 4-1/2 miles northwest to Walla Walla River just southeast of Touchet. The Walla Walla Indian name was *Te-Hoto-Nim-Me*. The present name, chosen by settlers, was because the principal timber species along the creek was western yellow pine (*Pinus ponderosa*).

Pine Grove (Spokane County) *see* Spangle

Pine Island (*T.14N;R.10W*)

A small, sandy islet, south of the entrance to Willapa Harbor, 1-1/4 miles west of Stony Point, northwest Pacific County. The islet is covered with beach grass and low, stunted conifers. The island was named for its trees by oystermen who formerly camped here.

Pine Lake (*Ss.4,9;T.24N;R.6E*)

An 88-acre lake, 1-1/2 miles east of Lake Sammamish, 4 miles north of Issaquah, west central King County. It was locally named for a few native white pine trees that grew here in earlier days.

Ping (*S.28;T.14N;R.41E*)

Settlement 13 miles north of Pomeroy and 2-1/2 miles south of Snake River, north central Garfield County. It was named for Robert and Frank Ping, early settlers.

Ping County (Columbia County) *see* Columbia County

Pingston Creek (Stevens County) *see* Pingstone Creek

Pingstone Creek (*Ss.2-6;T.36N;R.38E*)

The stream of the creek rises 6 miles east of Columbia River, northwest Stevens County; flows west to the river directly south of old Marcus. The creek was named in the era of Columbia River sternwheelers for Capt. Alfred T. Pingstone, who had a homestead on the stream, and who was the second navigator to captain the famous sternwheeler *Forty Nine*, built above Little Dalles for the upper Columbia route.

Pinhook Country (*T.34N;R.37E*)

This is a pioneer name for the country in west central Stevens County, along the east bank of Columbia River, south from from Kettle Falls, including the towns of Harvey, Rice, Waterloo, and Arzina. There were no roads and no stores for these early settlers, and they had no money. There were fish to be caught, however, so legends persist that these people made fish hooks from bent pins.

Pinksten Creek (Stevens County) *see* Pingstone Creek

Pinnacle Glacier (*T.8N;R.10E.uns*)

A west slope glacier of Mt. Adams, between Adams and White Salmon glaciers, Gifford Pinchot National Forest, Skamania County and southwest Yakima County. On August 2, 1901, it was named by C. E. Rusk and Prof. Harry Fielding Reid, a noted glaciologist associated with Johns Hopkins University. It is small as compared with surrounding glaciers, but has a peaked or pinnacled effect.

Pinnacle Island (Clallam County) *see* Fuca Pillar

Pinnacle Mountain
(*S.1;T.30N;R.17E.uns*)

A peak in Chelan Mountains chain at the heads of Candy and Tumble creeks, on the boundary of Okanogan and Wenatchee national forests, north central Chelan County. This descriptive name was applied by Forest Supervisor A. H. Sylvester.

Pinnacle Peak (*Mt. Rainier National Park*)

A 6,562-ft. peak in Tatoosh Range, 1 mile south of Reflection Lakes, south central zone of the park. The peak has a small glacier on its north slope. This descriptive name was chosen by park officials. (USBGN)

Pinnacle Rock (Clallam County) *see* Fuca Pillar

Pinnea Creek (Wahkiakum County) *see* Skamokawa Creek

Pins (*T.26N;R.12W*)

An abandoned pioneer settlement on Hoh River, between Hoh and Spruce, northwest Jefferson County. It has been deserted since the early 1900s, but was first named for an early settler and homesteader.

Pinus Lake *(S.4;T.39N;R.8E)*

A shallow, 1-1/2 acre lake, elevation 2,450 ft., Mt. Baker National Forest, 7 miles east of Glacier, north central Whatcom County. It is reported to have been named by U.S. Forest Service personnel who used the generic name for all species of pines.

Pioneer *(S.26;T.4N;R.1E)*

Settlement 4 miles east of Ridgefield, west central Clark County. In 1871, the name was applied when a post office was established. The name was chosen from a list supplied to postal officials by local settlers. Prior to that the name was *Covellow.*

Pioneer (Columbia County) *see* Covello

Pipestem Canyon (Okanogan County) *see* Pipestone Canyon

Pipestone Canyon *(Ts.33,34N;R.22E)*

A canyon in the Methow Valley drainage basin, southwest Okanogan County; extends from Campbell Lake, 3-1/2 miles south to Beaver Creek, 3 miles northeast of Twisp. It was named for soft, blue slate-clay deposits from which Indians made smoking pipes. An alternate name in early days was *Pipe-Stem Canyon.*

Pisco (Pisko) River (Yakima County) *see* Toppenish Creek

Pit Island (Pierce County) *see* Pitt Island

Pitcher Canyon *(T.22N;R.20E)*

This canyon and creek are 4 miles west of Wenatchee, southeast Chelan County. The creek, which runs through the canyon, rises near Beehive Mountain; flows east and north to Squillchuck Creek. Both are named for George A. Pitcher who filed on a quarter-section of land here in 1888.

Pitcher Creek (Chelan County) *see* Pitcher Canyon

Pitch-Pol (Kitsap County) *see* Foulweather Bluff

Pitship Point *(S.22;T.30N;R.3W)*

A west shore point of Sequim Bay, 2-1/2 miles southeast of Sequim, northeast Clallam County. In 1841, the point was named by Cmdr. Charles Wilkes. The name was that of one of his crew members on the expedition, although the available records do not indicate which one was honored.

Pitt *(S.22;T.4N;R.13E)*

Railway point on west side of Klickitat River, 2-1/2 miles southwest of Klickitat, southwest Klickitat County. The name was given by St. Paul & Spokane Railway for a gravel pit from which they secured ballast material while building grade.

Pitt Island *(S.17;T.20N;R.1E)*

A Pitt Passage island, west of McNeil Island, northwest Pierce County. In 1841, the name *Pit Island* was charted by Cmdr. Charles Wilkes. Later the U.S. Coast & Geodetic Survey altered this name to the present form. In 1846, the name *Enriqueta Island* was placed on British Admiralty charts by Inskip. A local name, used by early settlers and loggers, was *Mosquito Island.*

Pitt Passage *(T.20N;R.1E)*

A narrow passage between McNeil Island and the mainland to the west, northwest Pierce County. In 1846, Inskip placed the name *Crauford Channel* on British Admiralty charts, but this nomenclature was not used on later maps.

P. J. Lake *(T.28N;R.6W.uns)*

A very small Olympic National Park lake, at the head of South Branch, Morse Creek, 1/2 mile northwest of Eagle Point, east central Clallam County. The lake was locally named for P. J. Williams, an early Port Angeles jeweler and an ardent fisherman. (USBGN)

Placid Lake *(S.4;T.6N;R.8E.uns)*

A 19.2-acre lake, elevation 5,000 ft., 7 miles north of Big Lava Bed, central Skamania County. Ths lake is in a secluded part of the county and bears quite a descriptive name. It is in the Indian Heaven region, which is not heavily traveled or well known outside of the county.

Plain *(S.12;T.26N;R.17E)*

Settlement on east side of Wenatchee River at the mouth of Beaver Creek, Wenatchee National Forest, southwest Chelan County. In 1910, the place was settled by Dunkards (Church of the Brethren), who asked postal authorites for a "plain name" for the post office. They got it.

Plainview *(S.23;T.7N;R.22E)*

Community in Coyote Canyon, 2 miles south of Horse Heaven Hills, extreme southeast corner of Yakima County. In 1898, the name is reported to have been given by Mr. and Mrs. James L.

Keith, "for the clear air and distant view."

Plainview Creek *(T.27N;R.16E)*

The stream of the creek heads on Wenatchee National Forest, west central Chelan County; flows north-by-east 2 miles through Hidden Lake to Wenatchee Lake. The stream falls 2,300 ft. in its 2-mile course. It was named by Forest Supervisor A. H. Sylvester because it is in plain view as a "narrow tape of white water" from a nearby highway.

Plante's Ferry *(S.3;T.25N;R.44E)*

This famous ferry across Spokane River, abandoned in 1878, was 9 miles east of Spokane Falls (falls), near the present site of Trent. It is marked by a monument. In 1851, the ferry was built by Antoine Plante, a French-Indian trapper, stockman, and guide. He moved when bridges were built and his ferry business vanished.

Plaza *(S.9;T.21N;R.43E)*

Village 27-1/2 miles south of Spokane, south central Spokane County. In 1879, the town was founded and named *Rock Creek.* When a post office was established in the home of an early homesteader, Robert Patterson, he suggested this Spanish name which carries the meaning of "open valley."

Pleasant Beach *(S.3;T.24N;R.2E)*

A popular recreation beach, with scattered residences at the south end of Bainbridge Island, on the north shore of Rich Passage, east central Kitsap County. A previous name was *Sylvan Grove.*

Pleasant Harbor *(T.25N;R.2W)*

A Hood Canal harbor, 2 miles southwest of Brinnon, southeast Jefferson County. In 1841, the Wilkes Expedition applied the Indian name *Tzee-sated,* adding *Cove* for good measure. Pioneer settlers, usually allergic to Indians and Indian names, substituted the present conventional and rather meaningless cognomen.

Pleasant Prairie *((T.26N;R.44E)*

A prairie in Pleasant Prairie Township directly east of Hillyard, central Spokane County. This pastoral title was devised by Henry Eilenfelt, who first settled on this prairie and claimed land on June 1, 1878.

Pleasant Valley
(Ss.25,36;T.15N;R.4E)

A valley directly south of Alder

Lake, extreme north central Lewis County. This flattering name was chosen by a group of early settlers, most of whom were married. The bachelors among the settlers called the valley *Hen's Nest.*

Pleasant View *(S.29;T.12N;R.36E)*

Railroad station 13 miles north of Prescott, northeast Walla Walla County. The name, possibly more decorative than descriptive, was chosen by W. C. Painter when he filed a townsite plat on November 26, 1894. The town was at that time the terminus of a branch line of Northern Pacific Railway Company. The name was applied to that branch.

Plomondoe's Landing (Lewis County) *see Warbassport; Plomondon Landing*

Plomondon Island *(Cowlitz County) see Fisher Island*

Plum Lake (Snohomish County) *see* Grass Lake

Plummer Peak *(Mt. Rainier National Park)*

A peak in the Tatoosh Range, directly west of Pinnacle Peak, near the south-central portion of the park boundary. The peak was named by Park Superintendent Ethan Allen, for Fred G. Plummer, a geographer employed by the U.S. Forest Service. In 1910, the name was recommended for official approval by The Mountaineers. (USBGN)

Plummer Peak *(S.3;T.31N;R.14E.uns)*

A 7,800 ft. peak at Cascade Mountain summit, 1-1/2 miles northwest of Suiattle Pass, northeast Snohomish County. It was named by an early surveying party, without recording the reason for the choice of name. It is probably that there was a Plummer with the party.

Plumper's Reef (San Juan County) *see* West Bank

Pluvius *(S.3;T.12N;R.6W)*

The highest point between Chehalis and South Bend, at the crest of a divide, 28 miles southeast of South Bend, east central Pacific County. W. C. Albee, when superintendent of South Bend branch of Northern Pacific Railway, devised this name because of the extremely heavy rainfall. It is an alteration of the Latin word *Pluviosus* which has the significance of heavy rains or precipitation.

Plymouth *(S.8;T.5N;R.28E)*

Hamlet near Columbia River, opposite Umatilla, Oregon, extreme south

central Benton County. The name was chosen because a huge basaltic rock projects into the river at this point; it is so extensive that it was drilled for an 800-ft. railroad tunnel. The name suggested by the railroad was *Gibraltar,* but patriotic settlers settled for the present American name. The original Indian name for the locality is said to have been *So-loo-sa.*

Pocket Lake *(S.11;T.37N;R.7E)*

A lower south slope lake of Mt. Baker, south of Mazama Park, south central Whatcom County. It is a descriptive name, applied by early mountain climbers. This lake should not be confused with one of the same name near the Canadian boundary, northeast of Mt. Baker.

Pocket Lake (No. 2) *(S.5;T.40;R.10E)*

A very small lake, 1 mile south of the Canadian boundary, 12 miles north of Mt. Shuksan, extreme north central Whatcom County. The lake is in a deep pocket and drains north into Canada by Ensawkwatch Creek. It was given this name because of its location in the distinct pocket.

Pocket Lake (No. 3)
(S.5;T.40N;R.10E)

A 2-acre Mt. Baker National Forest lake, elevation 4,500 ft., which is a tributary to Ensawkwatch Creek; it's located 1 mile south of the British Columbia boundary, north central Whatcom County. The name is descriptive as this is one of 3 Pocket Lakes which nestle in deep depressions.

Poe Mountain *(S.24;T.28N;R.14E)*

A Wenatchee National Forest peak at the headwaters of Cougar Creek, 5-1/2 miles east of Cascade Mountain summit, northwest Chelan County. It is used as a forest fire lookout in season and is one of 5 nearby peaks named for early American authors by Forest Supervisor A. H. Sylvester. This one is for Edgar Allen Poe.

Poe's Point *(T.27N;R.2E)*

The present site of a Pacific-American Fisheries plant, in south Bellingham near the foot of McKenzie Ave., southwest Whatcom County. The point was named for Alonzo M. Poe, whose Donation Land Claim included this place in the 1850s, and who surveyed the original townsite of Whatcom in 1858.

Pogue (Douglas County) *see* Okanogan

Pogue (Okanogan County) *see* Okanogan

Pogue Flat *(T.36N;R.26E)*

A flat agricultural area directly northwest of Omak, central Okanogan County. Cultivation was started here by Joseph I. Pogue, a pioneer physician who first came to the country in 1888 and established orchards and an irrigation system. The name is in his honor. On some maps it is listed incorrectly as *Pogue Flats.*

Point Alan (Island County) *see* Point Allen

Point Allen *(T.30N;R.3E)*

An extreme south end point of Camano Island, at the south extremity of Camano Head, southeast Island County. In 1792, the point was named by Capt. George Vancouver for Rear Admr. Sir Alan Gardner, RN. The error in spelling Gardner's given name was continued by Wilkes in 1841. Vancouver intended the name to be *Alan Point.*

Point Angeles (Clallam County) *see* Angeles Point

Point Armstrong (Grays Harbor County) *see* Point Chehalis

Point Beals *(S.21;T.23N;R.3E)*

A northeast shore point of Vashon Island, 3 miles south of Vashon Heights, southwest King County. In 1841, this point was named by Cmdr. Charles Wilkes for Artimus W. Beals, captain of the hold in one of the expedition's ships. It appears on some maps incorrectly as *Dilworth Point.* The name was once used locally for Rev. R. B. Dilworth, who purchased a squatter's rights here in 1884 and established a residence.

Point Bolin *(S.6;T.25N;R.2E)*

A north end point of Port Orchard bay, 1-1/2 miles southeast of Keyport, north central Kitsap County. In 1841, the point was named by the Wilkes Expedition for Jacob Bolin, captain of the forecastle in one of the expedition's ships.

Point Carter *(S.6;T.36N;R.2E)*

An extreme south end point of Lummi Island, 1 mile west of Eliza Island, southwest Whatcom County. In 1841, the point was named by the Wilkes Expedition for William Carter, captain of the top in one of the expedition's ships. The name *Carter Point* found on some maps is incorrect.

Point Caution *(S.1;T.35N;R.3W)*

An east shore point of San Juan Island, on San Juan Channel, 2 miles north of Friday Harbor. In 1858, the name was chosen by Capt. Richards, RN, British Admiralty surveyor, and placed on his charts of that year. There are strong tide rips off this point.

Point Chehalis *(T.16N;Rs.11,12W)*

A south entrance point to Grays Harbor bay, 2 miles north of Westport, southwest Grays Harbor County. This point is at the terminus of a 4-mile sand spit which projects to the north. In 1841, the the name was charted by Cmdr. Charles Wilkes. The official name is a modification of *Chickeeles*, which in the Chehalis Indian language means "sand." It had been named *Point Hanson* by Lieut. Joseph Whidbey of the Vancouver Expedition in 1792, for Lieut. James Hanson who commanded the store-ship *Daedalus*. in 1857, it was named *Peterson's Point* for Glenn Peterson, a settler. Some years later the name was changed to *Armstrong's Point* by local residents, for a sawmill owner on Chehalis River. (USBGN)

Point Clatawa (Whatcom County) *see* Pattles Point

Point Colville *(S.21;T.34N;R.1W)*

A southeast extremity of Lopez Island, on Rosario Strait, southeast San Juan County. In 1847, the point was named by Capt. Kellett, RN, for Andrew Colvile, governor of Hudson's Bay Company. In 1859, the name was placed on British Admiralty charts by Capt. Richard, RN.

Point Cooper (Thurston County) *see* Cooper Point

Point Crowlie *(S.31;T.22N;R.3W)*

A southeast point of Annas Bay in Great Bend of Hood Canal, at Union, central Mason County. In 1841, it was named by the Wilkes Expedition for Lieut. Charles E. Crowley, USN, a hero of the battle of New Orleans in 1812. This name has not survived.

Point Cummings *(S.26;T.24N;R.3W)*

The north point of Eldon Bay, at the mouth of Hama Hama River, west shore of Hood Canal, northeast Mason County. In 1841, it was named by the Wilkes Expedition for W. H. Cummings, boatswain's mate on one of the expedition's ships.

Point Dalco *(S.2;T.21N;R.2E)*

A south end point of Vashon Island, on Dalco Passage, extreme southwest King County. The U.S. Coast Survey Report of 1858 states that this point was named by Cmdr. Charles Wilkes in 1841, but does not give the name source used by Wilkes.

Point Damon *(Ss.23,24;T.17N;R.12W)*

A point which forms part of the north entrance to Grays Harbor, southeast of the North Jetty, southwest Grays Harbor County. It was named for a pioneer, C. A. Damon, who settled at Oyhut, now called Damon. An alternate, unofficial name is *Damon's Point*.

Point Defiance *(S.10;T.21N;R.2E)*

A north entrance point to The Narrows on Dalco Passage, at the north extremity of Tacoma, northwest Pierce County. In 1841, the point was named by Cmdr. Charles Wilkes, who stated that "This narrow pass was intended by nature for the defence of Puget Sound." The name he selected reflects this idea. While Hudson's Bay Company maintained posts and operations in this area, they referred to this feature as *Point Ryan*. Their name did not persist.

Point Demock *(S.22;T.32N;R.2E)*

A northwest shore point of Camano Island, on Saratoga Passage, central Island County. In 1841, the point was named by Cmdr. Wilkes for John Demock, captain of the top in one of Wilkes ships. An alternate name which is shown on some maps is *Rocky Point*.

Point Disney *(S.23;T.37N;R.3W)*

A south tip point of Waldron Island, northwest San Juan County. In 1841, this feature was named by the Wilkes Expedition for Solomon Disney, sailmaker's mate in one of the expedition's ships.

Point Doughty *(S.9;T.37N;R.2W)*

A northwest tip of Orcas Island, in President Channel, north central San Juan County. In 1841, the point was named by the Wilkes Expedition for John Doughty, captain of the top in Wilkes' ship *Peacock*. Names that have been applied, but are no longer used, are *Cole's Point*, *Bill of Orcas*, and *Nob Point*.

Point Edmund (Snohomish County) *see* Point Edwards

Point Edwards *(S.26;T.27N;R.3E)*

A point on Edmonds waterfront, on

Possession Sound, extreme southwest Snohomish County. In 1841, this feature was named *Point Edmund* by Cmdr. Charles Wilkes. It was later changed on government charts, without explanation, to *Edwards Point* or to the present name.

Point Ellice *(S.23;T.9N;R.10W)*

A Columbia River point, 1 mile southwest of Megler, extreme southwest Pacific County. It was named by officials of the North West Company, fur traders, for Edward Ellice, their London agent. He was quite instrumental in combining North West Company with Hudson's Bay Company in 1821. The Indian name was *No-wehtl-kai-ilse*. Sgt. Patrick Gass of the Lewis & Clark Expedition named this feature *Blustery Point* when the party camped here in 1805. On April 11, 1825, David Douglas mapped it as *Point Ellis*.

Point Elliott *(S.4;T.28N;R.4E)*

A Possession Sound point, 3 miles southwest of Everett, southwest Snohomish County. This is on the site of Mukilteo, and is the scene of the signing of a famous Indian treaty on January 22, 1855. In 1841, the name was given by Cmdr. Charles Wilkes for Midshipman Samuel Elliott of his command. A local name, no longer used, was *Rose Point*.

Point Fosdick *(S.5;T.20N;R.2E)*

A north shore point of Hale Passage, at the south entrance of The Narrows, northwest Pierce County. In 1841, the name was charted by Cmdr. Charles Wilkes for Stephen Fosdick, one of his gunner's mates.

Point Frances (Whatcom County) *see* Point Francis

Point Francis *(T.37N;Rs.1,2E)*

A west entrance point to Bellingham Bay, on Hale Passage, across Hale Passage from Lummi Island, Whatcom County. In 1792, it was given the present name by Capt. George Vancouver. In 1841, Cmdr. Charles Wilkes charted the feature as *Point Frances*. The U.S. Coast & Geodetic Survey changed the name back to the spelling used by Vancouver.

Point Gibson (Pierce County) *see* Gibson Point

Point Glover *(S.9;T.24N;R.2E)*

A south side point of Rich Passage, opposite the south end of Bainbridge Island, east central Kitsap County. The point was once fortified to protect the

Bremerton area, especially Puget Sound Navy Yard. In 1841, the name was given by the Wilkes Expedition for John Glover, captain of the top on one of the expedition's ships.

Point Gordon (Kitsap County) *see* Restoration Point

Point Grenville *(S.24;T.21N;R.13W)*

A Pacific Ocean point, 5 miles northwest of Moclips, northwest Grays Harbor County. On April 28, 1792, this point was named by Capt. George Vancouver to honor Lord William Wyndham Grenville, who was the British secretary of state at the time. In the same year it had been labeled *Punta de la Bastida* by Galiano, for its fort-like appearance. In 1775, an earlier name of *Punta de los Martires* was applied by the Heceta Expedition. This name was based on the killing of several crew members by Indians near this point on July 14.

Point Hammond *(S.1;T.37N;R.3W)*

A northeast tip of Waldron Island, in President Channel, northwest San Juan County. In 1841, the point was named by the Wilkes Expedition for Henry Hammond, a quartermaster in one of the expedition's ships.

Point Hancock (Pacific County) *see* Cape Disappointment

Point Hannon *(S.25;T.28N;R.1E)*

An extreme east point of Hoods Head, Hood Canal, 4-1/2 miles southeast of Port Ludlow, east Jefferson County. In 1841, the point was named by Cmdr. Charles Wilkes for an unidentified member of his crew.

Point Hanson (Grays Harbor County) *see* Point Chehalis

Point Harmon *(S.31;T.21N;R.3E)*

A Tacoma waterfront point, near Stadium High School and the Washington State Historical Society Museum, northwest Pierce County. Now the point is covered with wharves and the name almost forgotten. In 1841, it was named by the Wilkes Expedition for John Harmon, captain of the forecastle in one of the expedition's ships.

Point Herron *(S.13;T.24N;R.1E)*

A Port Orchard bay point, directly east of Bremerton, east central Kitsap County. It is occupied by the town of Manette. In 1841, it was named by the Wilkes Expedition for Lewis Herron, a cooper who

was attached to the expedition.

Point Harris *(Pierce County) see* Browns Point

Point Heyer *(S.4;T.22N;R.3E)*

An east shore point of Vashon Island, directly north of Ellisport, southwest King County. In 1841, this feature was named *Hyer's Point* by Cmdr. Charles Wilkes for one of his quartermasters, Henry R. Heyer. His name has been modified on subsequent maps.

Point Hilcome *(Clallam County) see* Koitlah Point

Point Hudson *(Jefferson County) see* Hudson Point

Point Island *(S.11;T.35N;R.1W)*

A Rosario Strait island, 1/2 mile off the southeast coast of Blakely Island, east central San Juan County. This is one of 3 small islands that were named *The Pointers* by the Wilkes Expedition in 1841, as they pointed the route through Thatcher Pass. This island was originally called *White Rock*. The others in the group were named *Black Rock* and *Lawson Rock*, and remain so named on recent maps.

Point Jefferson *(S.13;T.26N;R.2E)*

A north entrance point to Port Madison Bay, 4 miles south of Kingston, northeast Kitsap County. In 1841, the point was named for President Thomas Jefferson, 3rd president of the U.S., by the Wilkes Expedition.

Point Julia (Kitsap County) *see* Port-Gamble Indian Reservation

Point Kanawi *(Jefferson County) see* Basalt Point, Olele Point

Point Komkomle *(Pacific County) see* Chinook Point

Point Lawrence *(San Juan County) see* Lawrence Point

Point Leadbetter *(Pacific County) see* Leadbetter Point

Point Leavett *(Island County) see* Bush Point

Point Lewis *(Pacific County) see* Cape Shoalwater, North Head

Point Lloyd *(San Juan County) see* Upright Head

Point Lowell *(S.1;T.30N;R.2E)*

A west shore point of Camano Island, 4 miles south of Camano, on Saratoga Passage, central Island County. In 1841, the point was named by Cmdr. Wilkes for

James Lowell, captain of the forecastle on one of Wilkes's ships.

Point Migley *(Snohomish County) see* Priest Point

Point Migley *(S.32;T.38N;R.1E)*

A south entrance point to Lummi Bay, at the north end of Lummi Island, southwest Whatcom County. In 1841, the point was named by the Wilkes Expedition for William Migley, quarter-gunner on one of the expedition's crews.

Point Mill *(Jefferson County) see* Mill Point

Point Monroe *(S.26;T.26N;R.2E)*

A northwest point of Bainbridge Island, at the north extremity of Hedley Spit, 1 mile east of Port Madison (town), northeast Kitsap County. In 1841, the point was named by the Wilkes Expedition for President James Monroe, 5th president of the U.S. Wilkes charted this name as *Munroe*, an error which has since been corrected.

Point Moody *(Pierce County) see* Johnson Point

Point Moody *(Thurston County) see* Johnson Point

Point New *(S.2;T.17N;R.11W)*

An east entrance point to North Bay on Grays Harbor, 5 miles west of Hoquiam, southwest Grays Harbor County. On October 20, 1792, the point was named by Joseph Whidbey of the Vancouver Expedition, for Thomas New who was master of the store-ship *Daedalus*.

Point Nill *(Jefferson County) see* Mill point

Point No Point *(S.27;T.28N;R.2E)*

A northeast point of Kitsap County, 1 mile east of Hansville. This is the site of the Point No Point Treaty between Governor I. I. Stevens and the Clallams, Snohomish, and Chimacums. The Indian name was *Hahd-skus*, meaning *long nose*. In 1841, it was named by Cmdr. Charles Wilkes for Point No Point of the Hudson River, also known as Dietrick's Hook. This point appeared and disappeared when viewed from the decks of passing ships.

Point of the Arches
(Ss.25,36;T.32N;R.16W)

A Pacific Ocean point, 10 miles south of Cape Flattery, northwest Clallam County. This is an exremely rough stretch of coastal area with many huge rocks, some of which have been eroded into arched forms by wave action.

Point Partridge *(S.36;T.32N;R.1W)*

The most westerly point of Whidbey Island, on Strait of Juan de Fuca, 4 miles west of Coupeville, west Island County. In 1790, the point was named *Punta de Menendez* by Manuel Quimper, for Salvador Menendez Valdes, a close friend. On June 6, 1792, Capt. George Vancouver charted it under the present name for an English family into which his brother, John, had married. An unofficial local name is *Red Bluff.*

Point Piner *(S.5;T.21N;R.3E)*

A southeastern tip point of Maury Island, on East Passage, southwest King County. In 1841, the place was named by Cmdr. Charles Wilkes for one of his quartermasters, Thomas Piner.

Point Polnell *(S.9;T.32N;R.2E)*

A point on the southwest extremity of the U.S. Naval Air Base on Crescent Harbor, north Whidbey Island, Island County. In 1841, the point was named by the Wilkes Expedition for John Polnell quarter-gunner in one of Wilkes's crews. A local, unofficial name is *Miller Point* or *Millers Point.* The Indian name was *Tscha-tup.*

Point Pully *(S.26;T.23N;R.3E)*

An east shore point of Puget Sound, directly south of Seahurst Park, southwest King County. This is a very popular beach residence area on a sharp-pointed, low sand spit. In 1841, the name was given by Cmdr. Charles Wilkes for one of his quartermasters, Robert Pully. This name is used by navigators, but local residents call it *Three Tree Point,* for 3 isolated trees which stood on a grassy knoll.

Point Richmond *(S.22;T.22N;R.2E)*

A west shore point of Colvos Passage, 4 miles north of Point Defiance, northwest Pierce County. In 1841, the point was named by Cmdr. Wilkes for William Richmond, a boatswain's mate in one of his crews. On some maps and records this place is shown as *Richmond Point.*

Point Ringgold *(Jefferson County) see* Marrowstone Point

Point Roberts *(King County) see* Alki Point

Point Roberts *(Ts.40,41N;R.3W)*

This is the name for both a town and cape in an isolated area, 6 miles between Georgia Strait and Boundary Bay, adjoining British Columbia across the International Boundary. The only access to U.S. territory by land is through Canada. The southwest cape, directly south of the town, bears the same name, which was chosen by Capt. George Vancouver on June 12, 1792. It was for Capt. Henry Roberts, RN, who had previously commanded Vancouver's flagship *Discovery.* Several Spanish names which were charted for this point in about the same period, never came into common use. In 1792, Galiano used the name *Punta de Zapeda.* One year earlier, Narvaez had christened the point *Punta de Cepeda.* In 1791, Francisco de Eliza thought the point was an island, and charted it as *Isla de Zapeda.* The Lummi Indian name was *Sma-gu-ach.*

Point Robinson *(King County) see* Robinson Point

Point Runaway *(Whatcom County) see* Pattles Point

Point Ryan *(Pierce County) see* Point Defiance

Point Salsbury *(Kitsap County) see* Salsbury Point

Point Sanford, Sandford *(King County) see* Sandford Point

Point Sares *(Skagit County) see* Sares Head; Langley Point

Point Scabock *(Kitscap County) see* Seabeck

Point Southworth *(S.1;T.23N;R.2E)*

A north entrance point to West (Colvos) Passage, 1 mile west of the north tip of Vashon Island, southeast Kitsap County. In 1841, the point was named by the Wilkes Expedition for Edward Southworth, one of Wilkes's quartermasters.

Point Success *(Mt. Rainier National Park)*

The most southerly of 3 peaks at the summit of Mt. Rainier, elevation 14,150 ft., located on the southwest side of the summit platform. This sharp, snow-covered crest ws named by Gen. Hazard Stevens and P. B. Van Trump, for their success in making the first recorded ascent of Mt. Rainier in 1870. (USBGN)

Point Tala *Jefferson County) see* Tala Point

Point Termination *(Jefferson County) see* Termination Point

Point Thompson *(S.7;T.37N;R.1W)*

A north end point of Orcas Island, 1-1/2 miles northeast of the town of East Sound, north San Juan County. In 1841, it was named by the Wilkes Expedition for Matthew Thompson, captain of the top in one of the expedition's ships.

Point Treble *(S.12;T.19N;R.1W)*

The west cape point of Anderson Island, on Nisqually Reach, northwest Pierce County. In 1841, the point was named by Cmdr. Wilkes for one of his seamen, George Treble, In 1846, it was placed on British admiralty charts by Inskip as *Richard Point.* This re-naming, for Fleetwood J. Richards, Lieut. of marines in *Fisgard,* failed to supersede Wilkes' nomenclature. This feature is found on some maps under the name of *Treble Point.*

Point Turner *(S.13;T.24N;R.1E)*

A west entrance point to Washington Narrows, on the east side of Bremerton, central Kitsap County. In 1841, the Wilkes Expedition named this point for Henry Turner, captain of the forecastle in one of Wilkes' ships.

Point Totten *(Kitsap County) see* Port Gamble

Point Vancouver *(Clark County) see* Cottonwood Point

Point Vashon *(King County) see* Vashon Point

Point Wells *(S.35;T.27N;R.3E)*

A Possession Sound point, 2 miles south of Edmonds, extreme southwest corner Snohomish County. Here are very extensive tanks and a dock for the unloading and storage of petroleum oils. In 1841, the point was named by Cmdr. Charles Wilkes for Yeoman William Wells, a member of his expedition. On some maps it appears as *Wells Point.*

Point White *(S.5;T.24N;R.2E)*

An east shore point of Port Orchard bay, at the southwest end of Bainbridge Island, east central Kitsap County. In 1841, the Wilkes Expedition named the point for James White, captain of the forecastle on one of the expedition's ships. A local name, which did not endure, was *Nibbyville.* In 1885, it was applied for Jack Nibby, who had an Indian trade store and was postmaster.

Point Whitehorn *(S.2;T.39N;R.1W)*

A south entrance point to Birch Bay, on Georgia Strait, northwest Whatcom County. In July 1791, the point was named *Punta del Garzon* by Marcos Garzon, a Spanish army officer. In 1841, the present name was charted by the Wilkes Expedition for Daniel Whitehorn, quarter-gunner on one of the expedition's ships. On some maps the place has been named *Whitehorn Point* in error.

Point Whitney *(Jefferson County) see* Whitney Point

Point Williams *(Skagit County) see* William Point

Point Williams *(T.24N;R.3E)*

An east shore point of Puget Sound in Seattle, at Lincoln Park, 3 miles south of Alki Point, King County. In 1841, the feature was named *William's Point* by Cmdr. Charles Wilkes for one of his gunner's mates, Samuel Williams. As in the case of most of Wilkes's possessive titles, it has been altered on subsequent maps. The Indian name was *Tcix-ha*, meaning *tight*.

Point Wilson *(T.31N;R.1W)*

A point north of Port Townsend on Strait of Juan de Fuca, extreme northeast Jefferson County. It is part of the site of Fort Worden, now abandoned. These are 2 distinct versions of the name source: One related that the point was named on June 6, 1792, by Capt. George Vancouver for Capt. George Wilson, RN; the other version states that it was named by Cmdr. Charles Wilkes in 1841, for Thomas Wilson, a sailmaker's mate with the expedition. The Clallam Indian name for the point was *Kam-kun*; the Chimacum name was *Kam-kam-ho*.

Polack Mill *(S.30;T.8N;R.15E)*

A long-abandoned sawmill on Yakima Indian Reservation, 7 miles north of Lucas on Brush Creek, southwest Yakima County. This was the center of a Polish colony that settled in Cedar Valley in the early 1890s. These people are gone, as are all others who settled this high mountain valley.

Poland Butte *(S.34;T.8N;R.14E.uns)*

A small, isolated peak, elevation 3,143 ft., on Yakima Indian Reservation, southeast Yakima County. (*see* Polack Mill)

Pole Pass *((T.36N;R.2W)*

A very narrow passage, 1-1/2 miles south of Deer Harbor, between Crane and Orcas islands, central San Juan County. This passage is only 120 ft. wide at high tide, but is much used by all types of vessels. The name was locally given because Indians in early days suspended nets from poles on each side of the passage to catch ducks as they flew through the pass.

Pollalie Point *(Jefferson County) see* Pulali Point

Pol Nell (Polnell) Point *(Island County) see* Point Polnell

Polson Creek *(T.18N;R.10W)*

The stream of the creek rises 5 miles northwest of Hoquiam, southwest Grays Harbor County; flows east to West Fork, Hoquiam River, 4 miles north of Hoquiam. The name is for Alex and Robert Polson who came here from Nova Scotia in the early 1900s, forming Polson Brothers Logging Company. They logged timber along this creek with ox teams and splash dams.

Polson State Park *(T.17N;R.10W)*

This small public park is just outside the city limits of Hoquiam, southwest Grays Harbor County. It was donated by Alex and Robert Polson. (*see* Polson Creek)

Pomas Creek *(T.30N;R.17E)*

The stream of this short creek rises 1 mile north of Larch Lakes, north central Chelan County; flows north into Ice Creek on Wenatchee National Forest. It was named by Forest Ranger James McKenzie for the huge fields of pumice that were blown into this area from Glacier Peak. Jim evidently was better at ranging than spelling.

Pomeroy *(Ss.30,31;T.12N;R.42E)*

Town on Pataha Creek, 32 miles west of Clarkston, north central Garfield County. Prior to 1864, the land was claimed by Walter Sunderland, who established a stock ranch. On December 8, 1864, he sold out to Joseph M. Pomeroy, who had been a mechanic for Wells, Fargo & Company and was a Civil War veteran. On May 28, 1878, Pomeroy platted the area as a townsite. It was named for him. Pomeroy was on the old stage route to Lewiston, Idaho. Old-timers insist that at one time the place supported 20 saloons. While the capacity of early-day miners was prodigious, this number of oases appears to have been somewhat more than one

small roadside town could maintain.

Pomona (Lewis County) *see* Adna

Pomona *(S.20;T.14N;R.19E)*

Railway station 6 miles north of Yakima, on east bank of Yakima River, northeast Yakima County. In 1885, the station was named *Selah* by Northern Pacific Railway officials. In 1908, the name was changed to the present one because Wenas station was quite generally called Selah. The name was suggested by the local Northern Pacific agent, Edmund Stevens, for the patroness of gardens and fruits in Roman mythology.

Pontiac Bay *(T.25N;R.4E)*

A small west shore cove of Lake Washington, Seattle, directly north of Sand Point, south of Matthews Beach, King County. It is reported to have been named for Pontiac Shingle Company which had a mill here in early days. The Indian name was *Sla-gwel-ag-wets*, meaning "cedar bark; where it grows." Puget Sound Indians used the inner bark of native cedar for basketry and other weaving.

Ponto (Skagit County) *see* Grassmere

Poodle Dog Pass *(S.28;T.29N;R.11E.uns)*

A pass on the boundary between Mt. Baker and Snoqualmie national forests, 1 mile south of Monte Cristo, east central Snohomish County. This name was suggested for verification to the USBGN by The Mountaineers, but was not accepted. It remains in common use, however.

Porpoise Rocks (Skagit County) *see* Huckleberry, Saddlebag, Dot islands

Port Angeles *(Ts.30,31N;Rs.6,7W)*

The largest city in Clallam County, on Strait of Juan de Fuca, 17 miles south of Victoria, B.C., northeast Clallam County. It has an excellent harbor and substantial industries. In 1791, the bay was named *Puerto de Neustra Senora de Los Angeles* by Juan Francisco de Eliza, through his lieutenant, Juan Pantoja y Arriago, who mapped the harbor. In 1792, Capt. George Vancouver altered the long Spanish name to the present form. In 1861, a post office was established here as *Cherbourg*, but was changed to Port Angeles the following year. The Indian name of the bay was *I-en-nis*. Victor Smith, a special treasury agent appointed by President Abraham Lincoln, persuaded Lincoln to issue an order which reserved 3,520 acres on the bay for lighthouse and military purposes. Smith had most of this platted as a townsite and had the custom house removed from Port Townsend to Port Angeles. He called his platted town *The Second National City* of the U.S., after Washington, D.C., only.

Port Arthur *(T.32N;R.1E)*

Town that never developed on the south shore of Penn Cove, Whidbey Island, west of Coupeville, central Island County. In 1895, it was named by John Phinney when he platted the town, for his brother, Arthur.

Port Blakely *(S.2;T.24N;R.2E)*

Scattered community on the north shore of Blakely Harbor, southeast Bainbridge Island, east central Kitsap County. This was once a very active sawmilling town which, for a time, boasted the largest sawmill in the world. Ships loaded here for world-wide markets. In 1841, it was named for Blakely Harbor which was named by Cmdr. Charles Wilkes for Capt. Johnson Blakely, USN, hero of the War of 1812. Blakely was lost at sea with his ship, *Wasp*. The Indian name of the harbor and locality was *Kol-lus-um*.

Port Columbia *(S.20;T.30N;R.25E)*

Town on Columbia River, 5 miles northwest of Bridgeport, northwest Douglas County. On July 24, 1891, the town was platted and used as a steamboat landing and stage station. Local informants state that the name was given by a salesman from Chicago, Illinois, "who enjoyed his vacation here." His tastes must have differed widely from those of most Chicago salesmen, who generally are not fascinated by wide open spaces.

Port Crescent *(T.31N;R.8W)*

Town which never developed on Crescent Bay, 9 miles west of Port Angeles, north central Clallam County. In the 1890s, the town was platted and "boomed." In 1891, it was named by Port Crescent Improvement Company, for the bay on which it was located.

Port Discovery *(S.13;T.29N;R.2W)*

Abandoned town on the west shore of Port Discovery Bay, at Mill Point, northeast Jefferson County. Once this was the location of a large sawmill and town, but all that remains now is a cemetery and some remains of the sawmill on the beach at low tide. (*see* Port Discovery Bay)

Port Discovery (Jefferson, Clallam counties) *see* Port Discovery Bay

Port Discovery Bay
(Ts.29,30N;Rs.1,2W)

An "S"-shaped bay, extending 9 miles south from Strait of Juan de Fuca, northeast Jefferson and Clallam counties. This bay was important in the early development of the state. In 1790, it was explored by Manuel Quimper and used as a base by Juan Francisco de Eliza in 1791. In 1792, Capt. George Vancouver also used it as a base for exploration of adjacent water areas. he re-fitted his ships here. On May 2, 1792, he named it for his flagship *Discovery*. On July 11, 1790, a previously applied name was *Puerto de Bodega y Quadra*, chosen by Gonzalo Lopez de Haro in honor of the famous Spanish navigator, Juan Francisco de Bodega y Quadra. This name evidently was used only on Spanish charts. The commonly used name for the bay among local Indians was *Cha-ya-mat*.

Port Gamble (Bay) *(T.27N;R.2E)*

An arm of Hood Canal, on its east shore, 7 miles from its entrance to Puget Sound, 7 miles southeast of Port Ludlow, north Kitsap County. The Indian name of the bay was *Kel-up-kwa*. (*see* Port Gamble/town)

Port Gamble (Town) *(S.6;T.27N;R.2E)*

Town at the northwest entrance to Port Gamble bay, east shore of Hood Canal, north Kitsap County. One of very few pioneer lumber towns which has not been deserted, this sawmilling center has been in continuous operation by Pope & Talbot, Inc. since 1853. The town borrows its name from Port Gamble bay, which was named by the Wilkes Expedition in 1841. The name is for Lieut. Robert Gamble, USN, a hero of the War of 1812. The Indian name was *Teekalet*.

Port Gamble Indian Reservation
(T.27N;R.2E)

A 1,301-acre reservation at Point Julia on Port Gamble bay, opposite Port Gamble (town), north Kitsap County. On March 12, 1936, the site was purchased by the federal government under authority of a congressional act dated June 18, 1894. The purpose of the reservation was to furnish an official home for the descendants of Indians who were evicted from Teekalet village in 1853. The name is borrowed from the bay on which the reservation is located. (*see* Port Gamble; Teekalet)

Port Gardner (Island County) *see* Saratoga Passage

Port Gardner Bay
(Ts.29,30N;Rs.4,5E)

The harbor of the City of Everett, at the north end of Possession Sound, west central Snohomish County. In 1792, the bay was named by Capt. George Vancouver for Rear Admr. Sir Alan Gardner, RN, who had recommended Vancouver for the exploration of the Pacific Northwest by British naval units.

Port Hadlock (Jefferson County) *see* Hadlock

Port Ludlow (Bay) *(T.28N;R.1E)*

A bay off Admiralty Inlet, 6 miles south of Marrowstone Island, northeast Jefferson County. This is the site of a former large sawmill and a substantial settlement. In 1841, the bay was named by Cmdr. Charles Wilkes for Lieut. Augustus C. Ludlow, USN, who was killed in 1813 during the battle between *Shannon* and *Chesapeake*.

Port Ludlow (Town)
(S.16;T.28N;R.1E)

Settlement on Port Ludlow bay, 12 miles south of Port Townsend, northeast Jefferson County. For many decades after 1852, this was an important sawmill center, and was a fully organized town. As timber supply diminished, many of the facilities were moved to Port Gamble. The Chimacum Indian name of the place was *Sna-nul-kwo*. Skokomish Indians called it *Dos-la-latl*.

Port Madison *(Bay)* *(T.26N;R.2E)*

West shore bay of Puget Sound, directly east of Suquamish, northeast Kitsap County. The Indian name was *Tu-che-kup*. In 1824, John Work, of Hudson's Bay Company, named this feature *Soquamic Bay*, while investigating sites for a trading post. In 1841, the Wilkes Expedition named the bay for James Madison, 4th president of the U.S. It should not be confused with a smaller bay, directly to the south, which often is referred to as *Port Madison* or *Port Madison Bay*.

Port Madison (Town)
(S.34;T.26N;R.2E)

Once a ghost town, now the site of a residential area of country homes on a narrow arm of Port Madison bay, north end of Bainbridge Island, east Kitsap County. In 1841, it was named by the Wilkes Expedition for President James Madison. (*see* Port Madison)

Port Madison Indian Reservation
(T.26N;R.2E)

A 7,284-acre reservation from President and Jefferson points, west to Suquamish, south to the vicinity of Keyport, northeast Kitsap County. The acreage is interspersed with non-Indian ownership. The reservation was established by the Point Elliott Treaty of January 22, 1855, and was enlarged by an executive order, dated October 21, 1864. (*see* Port Madison)

Port of Sea Captains (Island County) *see* Coupeville

Port Orchard *(Ts.24,25N;Rs.1,2E)*

A bay between Bainbridge Island and Kitsap County mainland, with Sinclair Inlet to the south and Agate Passage to the north, central Kitsap County. In 1792, the place was named by Capt. George Vancouver for H. M. Orchard of the ship *Discovery*; he was a clerk who first sighted the bay.

Port Orchard *(T.24N;R.1E)*

Town on the south shore of Sinclair Inlet, directly across from Bremerton, central Kitsap County. In 1792, the place was named for Port Orchard bay. The first post office here was called *Sidney*. In 1903, the name of the town was officially changed to the present designation by the state legislature. The original Indian name was *Ter-cha-duk*.

Port Susan *(Ts.30,31N;Rs.3,4E)*

A saltwater channel of Puget Sound between Camano Island in Island County and the mainland in Snohomish County. On June 4, 1792, the channel was named by Capt. George Vancouver for Susanna, wife of Rear Admr. Sir Alan Gardner, RN. Admr. Gardner had recommended Capt. Vancouver for exploration of the Pacific Northwest by British naval units.

Port Townsend (Bay)
(Ts.29,30N;Rs.1E,1W)

A 7-mile-long bay between Quimper

Peninsula on the west and Indian and Marrowstone islands on the east, extending from Hadlock north to Admiralty Inlet, northeast Jefferson County. On May 8, 1792, the bay was named by Capt. George Vancouver as *Port Townshend*, for the Marquis of Townshend. In 1841, Cmdr. Charles Wilkes charted the bay, dropping the ''h'' from the name. This misspelling has persisted. Clallam Indians had called the bay *Ka-tal* or *Kah-tai*; the Chimacum name was *Tsu-tlat-u-kwat*.

Port Townsend (City)
(Ts.30,31N;Rs.1E,1W)

City on Quimper Peninsula, on Port Townsend bay, extreme northeast Jefferson County. The northern suburbs extend to Strait of Juan de Fuca. This city is over a century old and has retained much of the original flavor of the sea and of pioneer building. (*see* Port Townsend bay)

Port Washington (Kitsap County) *see* Dyes Inlet

Port Washington Narrows
(T.24N;R.1E)

Narrows extending southeast from Dyes Inlet to Port Orchard bay, between Bremerton and East Bremerton, central Kitsap County. The name was adopted from the previous name of Dyes Inlet -- *Port Washington*.

Port Williams *(S.15;T.30N;R.3W)*

Town which never developed on Strait of Juan de Fuca, 4-1/2 miles southeast of Dungeness, northeast Clallam County. This unsuccessful town was named for a contractor who tried to promote the townsite in the 1890s.

Portage *(S.28;T.22N;R.3E)*

A narrow spit of land which connects Maury and Vashon Island, on Tramp Harbor, southwest King County. This place was named by early settlers who carried small boats across the spit from Quartermaster to Tramp Harbor. An alternate name, used on some recent maps, is *Portage Landing*.

Portage *(S.29;T.36N;R.11E)*

Old river town, now a small community on Skagit River, 5 miles above the mouth of Cascade River, north central Skagit County. This was once a landing for sternwheel steamboats which ceased to run in the upper Skagit in 1894. It was named in very early pioneer days because it was necessary to portage car-

goes of deep draft steamboats at this point. Much of the cargo was hay for oxen used in logging camps. Like many ambitious pioneer towns, it once appended the term ''City'' to its name.

Portage Bay *(Ss.20,21;T.25N;R.4E)*

A west entrance bay to lake Washington Canal, in Seattle, at the extreme east end of Lake Union, King County. It covers 148-acres which are mostly occupied by Seattle and Queen City yacht clubs. It was the west end of a very old portage route between Lakes Union and Washington. It was named by Seattle Port Commission, because coal cargoes were portaged over a narrow neck of land near this point in early days of coal mining in the state. The Indian name was *Sxwa-tsug-wil*, meaning ''Where one lifts up his canoe.''

Portage City (Skagit County) *see* Portage

Portage Slough *(T.38N;R.2E)*

A 2-mile-long slough on Lummi Indian Reservation, directly north of Bellingham Bay, Whatcom County; there is an entrance into Nooksack River about 1/2 mile from its discharge into Bellingham Bay. The name is explained by the use of this very swampy slough for a portage in early days by local Indians, traveling in ''shovel-nose'' canoes.

Portal Peak *(S.36;T.30N;R.12E)*

A Mt. Baker National Forest peak, southwest slope of Glacier Peak, at the headwaters of Whitechuck River, east central Snohomish County. It was named by a party of mountain climbers because it is at the entrance to Red Pass. It has been shown on some maps, in error, as *Porthole Peak*.

Porter *(S.21;T.17N;R.5W)*

Settlement near the confluence of Chehalis River and Porter Creek, southeast corner of Grays Harbor County. It was named for Fairchild Porter, a pioneer of 1860, when a post office was established in 1890. The namer was C. P. Boyer, the first postmaster.

Porter Creek *(Ts.17,18N;Rs.4,5W)*

The stream of the creek rises in west Thurston County; flows west to Chehalis River at Porter, southeast Grays Harbor County. (*see* Porter)

Porthole Peak (Snohomish County) *see* Portal Peak

Portugese Point *(S.11;T.9N;R.9W)*

A west entrance point of Grays Bay, north bank of Columbia River, south central Pacific County. It was named by early Columbia River navigators, with some evidence that the name ties in with a shipwreck.

Possession Point *(T.38N;R.3E)*

An extreme southern tip of Whidbey Island, at the entrance to Possession Sound, south Island County. On June 4, 1792, it was named by Capt. George Vancouver. An unofficial local name is *Skagit Head.* (*see* Possession Sound)

Possession Sound
(Ts.27-30N;Rs.3,4W)

A Puget Sound passage between southeast Whidbey Island and the adjacent mainland in Snohomish County. On June 4, 1792 (the birthday of King George III of England), this feature was named by Capt. George Vancouver. On that occasion, Vancouver took formal possession of *New Albion*, renaming it *New Georgia* in the king's honor. In 1841, Cmdr. Charles Wilkes followed Vancouver's nomenclature.

Potato Hill *(S.24;T.10N;R.10E.uns)*

A 5,450-ft. peak, 2 miles south of Midway (pass), at Cascade Mountain summit, between Yakima Indian Reservation, southwest Yakima County, and Gifford Pinchot National Forest, northeast Skamania County. This mountain has a rounded top, thus the name was given in mapping Cascade summit, for a fancied resemblance to a potato. The mapper evidently had a powerful imagination.

Potholes *(Ts.16-19N;Rs.25-28E)*

Irregular, scattered bodies of water which are south, southwest, and west of Moses Lake, south Grant and southwest Adams counties. The potholes are a result of glaciation; they are shallow and vary greatly in size. Extensive, high, rounded sand dunes are interspersed between the potholes. During a soils survey of 1905-1911, the name was given by U.S. Bureau of Soils.

Potholes Dam (Grant County) *see* O'Sullivan Dam

Potholes Reservoir
(Ts.17-19N;Rs.27,28E)

A 12-mile-long body of water, directly south of Moses Lake (lake), connected thereto, southeast Grant County. This irregular reservoir, aver-

age width 3 miles, was impounded for irrigation purposes by O'Sullivan Dam. The name is appropriate, as the reservoir is in an area of extensive potholes. (*see* Potholes)

Potlatch *(S.23;T.22N;R.4W)*

Town on the west side of Hood Canal at the Great Bend, central Mason County. The name is a Nootka word that passed into the Chinook jargon and has the meaning of "to give" or "a gift." A potlatch house which stood here is reported to have been "50 fathoms long and 25 fathoms wide." Many famous potlatches were held in this building. In 1841, the Wilkes Expedition called the place *Neclim Point*, using the original Indian name. The name seems not to have been used on any subsequent maps in its correct spelling. Altered to *Neelim Point*, it is now applied to a headland immediately south of Potlatch.

Potlatch Point *(S.28;T.20N;R.2W)*

A south entrance point to Hammersley Inlet, near Arcadia, southeast Mason County. In 1841, the Wilkes Expedition named this feature *Cook Point* for John Cook, boatswain's mate on one of the expedition's ships. The present name derives from the potlatch house at Potlatch. (*see* Potlatch)

Potter White Hill *(S.19;T.10N;R.44E)*

A hill directly west of Pleasant Ridge, 6 miles northwest of Cloverland, northwest Asotin County. It was named for 2 families of settlers in this area, Potter and White.

Poulsbo *(S.23;T.26N;R.1E)*

Fishing town on the east shore of Liberty Bay, north central Kitsap County. Originally the village had a 90 percent Scandinavian population, mostly Norwegian. It was headquarters for the codfish fleet. The town was named by Iver Brynildsen, a pioneer resident, for the town of Poulsbomoen in Enning Valley, Halden, Norway.

Poverty Bay (King County) *see* Redondo

Pow Wah Kee Gulch
(Ts.10,11N;Rs.43,44E)

This gulch heads south of Knotgrass Ridge, northwest Asotin County; trends 11 miles northeast to Alpowa Creek. The name applies both to the gulch and to a stream which follows it. The name is for Lucy Powaukie, a Nez Perce Indian who lived with her brother Henry

on a land claim at the mouth of the gulch. She was a handsome woman who was locally known as "The Princess." The Powaukies were related to Chief Joseph and to Chief Red Wolf, and were respected by white settlers. Alternate names for the gulch and creek are *Powaukie Canyon* and *Powahkee Creek*, indicating the difficulty of translating Indian names into the English spellings.

Pow Wow Creek (Spokane County) *see* Alder Creek

Power Creek *(T.24N;R.17E)*

The stream of the creek heads in a small unnamed lake, northeast slope of Icicle Ridge, Wenatchee National Forest, central Chelan County; flows northeast to Wenatchee River in Tumwater Canyon. It was named by Forest Supervisor A. H. Sylvester to describe the swift drop of the stream from mountain to river.

Prairie *(S.18;T.36N;R.5E)*

Settlement on Samish River, 6 miles north of Sedro Woolley, northwest Skagit County. In 1890, it was named when a post office was established, for its location on an extensive, natural prairie.

Prairie Center *(S.35;T.32N;R.1E)*

Community directly south of Penn Cove, on central Whidbey Island, central Island County. This very descriptive name became official through local use over many years.

Prairie De Fou (Stevens County) *see* Fools Prairie

Prairie Mountain
(Ss.11,14;T.32N;R.10E.uns)

A Mt. Baker National Forest peak, 6 miles east-by-north of Darrington, northeast Snohomish County. The name was chosen by Sauk Prairie settlers because of the beautiful prairie at the mountain's base.

Pratt (Spokane County) *see* Denison

Pratt Lake *(S.34;T.23N;R.10E)*

A 43-1/2-acre lake, 4 miles west of Snoqualmie Pass, at the head of Pratt River, east central King County. This feature was named by The Mountaineers for one of their members -- John W. Pratt of the Seattle *Post-Intelligencer*. An earlier name was *Ollie Lake*.

Pratt Mountain *(S.33;T.23N;R.10E)*

A Snoqualmie National Forest peak, elevation 5,105 ft., 5 miles west of

Snoqualmie Pass, east central King County. The mountain is located in an area of many small, glacial lakes. (*see* Pratt Lake)

Pratt River (*Ts.33,34N;R.10E*)

The stream of the river heads in Tuscohatchie Lake, 3 miles west of Cascade Mountain summit, Snoqualmie National Forest, east central King County; flows 10 miles northwest to Middle Fork, Snoqualmie River at Halfway House. (*see* Pratt Lake)

Preachers Slough (*T.17N;R.8W*)

This tidal stream is in Chehalis River drainage area, 3 miles east of Cosmopolis, south central Grays Harbor County. It was named for Rev. J. S. Douglass, a Methodist Episcopal minister who navigated his boat up this slough in the belief that it was the main Chehalis River. The episode dates back to 1859 when local settlers first used the name.

Prescott (Pierce County) *see* Tidewater

Prescott (*S.33;T.10N;R.36E*)

Community on Touchet River, 15 miles north-by-east of Walla Walla, east central Walla Walla County. Rev. Henry H. Spalding, an early Protestant missionary, established a home here in 1859. On May 12, 1882, Oregon Improvement Company platted a townsite. The place was named by officials of Oregon Railway & Navigation Company for C. H. Prescott, its general superintendent.

President Channel (*T.37N;Rs.2,3W*)

A wide, 7-mile-long channel between Waldron and Orcas islands, north central San Juan County. In 1841, the name was applied by the Wilkes Expedition to the channel which is now called *San Juan Channel*. It was named for Comm. John Rodgers, a hero of the War of 1812, who later became president of U.S. Naval Commissioners. It later was changed to apply to the present location. In 1859, British admiralty surveyor Richards named this feature *Douglas Channel* for Sir James Douglas, governor of Vancouver Island. That name did not persist. (USBGN)

President Point (*S.1;T.26N;R.2E*)

A west shore point of Puget Sound, 2 miles southeast of Kingston, northwest Kitsap County. In 1856, it was named by U.S. Coast Survey and refers to the fact that Wilkes, in 1841, had named 3 nearby points for Presidents Jefferson,

Monroe, and Madison.

Press Valley (*T.27N;R.6W*)

An Olympic National Park valley, 20 miles south of Port Angeles, in the Elwha River valley, north central Jefferson County. On April 14, 1890, the valley was named by members of the Seattle Press Expedition for *The Seattle Press*, a newspaper which fitted out and promoted the expedition.

Pressentin Creek (*Ts.34,35N;Rs.7,8E*)

The stream of the creek heads in mountains 6 miles south of Birdsview, central Skagit County; flows 7-1/2 miles to the north and enters Skagit River 1 mile east of Birdsview. In 1877, it was locally named for Charles von Pressentin, the first settler in this area.

Preston (*S.33;T.24N;R.7E*)

Village 5 miles east of Issaquah, on Raging River, central King County. The town has a sawmill and some logging of young-growth timber. It was named by Daniel H. Gilman, for his associate in building the Seattle, Lake Shore & Eastern Railway, William T. Preston. That road, now the Northern Pacific's line to Sumas, was built through Preston.

Preston Creek (*T.28N;R.19E*)

The stream of the creek heads on Devil's Backbone, Chelan Mountains, Wenatchee National Forest, central Chelan County; flows 3 miles southwest to Entiat River. It is a locally applied name for an early settler.

Preston Point (*S.7;T.29N;R.5E*)

A Port Gardner Bay point, at the mouth of Snohomish River, opposite Priest Point, west central Snohomish County. It was named for a pioneer operator of a trading post here. The Indian name was *Hay-bohl-ub*.

Prevost (*S.21;T.37N;R.4W*)

A very small place on a thinly-inhabited island, on Stuart Island, west shore of Prevost Harbor, extreme northwest San Juan County. (*see* Prevost Harbor)

Prevost Harbor (*T.37N;R.4W*)

A good haven for small craft on Haro Strait, north side of Stuart Island, northwest San Juan County. In 1859, the harbor was named by the British Admiralty surveyor, Capt. Richards, RN, for Capt. James Charles Prevost. Capt. Prevost had commanded *H.M.S. Satellite* on this station in the 1850s.

Price Glacier (*T.39N;Rs.9,10E*)

One of Mt. Shuksan's large glaciers, on the north slope of Mt. Shuksan, Mt. Baker National Forest, southeast of Price Lake, Whatcom County. (*see* Price Lake)

Price Lake (*S.23;T.39N;R.9E*)

A 40-acre glacial lake at the northwest terminus of Price Glacier, north slope of Mt. Shuksan, Mt. Baker National Forest, Whatcom County. It was named by The Mountaineers for W. Montelius Price, who made the first ascent of Mt. Shuksan, accompanied by Asahel Curtis.

Price's Valley (Stevens County) *see* Fruitland

Priest Point (*S.1;T.29N;R.4E*)

A Port Gardner Bay point at the north entrance to Snohomish River, directly north of Everett, west central Snohomish County. In 1841, this feature was named *Point Migley* by the Wilkes Expedition for an expedition member. The Indian name was *Schuh-tlahks*, meaning "stony nose." The present name was chosen to honor Father Chirouse, a Catholic mission founder and administrator, who was very active at Tulalip in pioneer days.

Priest Point (*S.2;T.18N;R.2W*)

This point is the location of Priest Point Park, near the northern limits of Olympia, east shore of Budd Inlet, north central Thurston County. The name was for Father Pascal Ricard, who established St. Joseph's Mission near here in 1848.

Priest Point Park (*S.2;T.18N;R.2W*)

A 30-acre city park near the north limits of Olympia, on Priest Point, north central Thurston County. It was named by Elias J. Payne for Priest Point. (*see* Priest Point)

Priest Rapids (*Ts.13-15N;R.23E*)

Rapids in Columbia River, 27 miles east of Yakima, adjoining southwest Grant County, extreme northeast tip of Yakima County. This is the site of a recently built power dam and reservoir which is operated by Grant County Public Utilities District. For centuries it was the homeland of the Wanapum tribe, which now has dwindled to a few individuals. Their name applies to the dam. On August 18, 1811, the name of the rapids was given by Alexander Ross for an Indian priest whom he met here, and whose name was *Haqui-laugh.*

Priest Rapids *(S.3;T.13N;R.23E)*

Community on Columbia River at south end of Priest Rapids Reservoir, extreme northeast Yakima County. The original name of this place was *Mattawa.* The name was changed to the present designation when the townsite was purchased by 3 speculators in 1955. The name is for Priest Rapids near the town. (*see* Priest Rapids)

Prince Creek *(Ts.31,32N;Rs.19,20E)*

The stream of the creek rises on a divide 10 miles east of Lake Chelan, northeast Chelan County; flows southwest to Lake Chelan, 15 miles from the lake's head, a distance of about 10 miles. In 1866, the name was applied by William Sanders and Henry Dumpke when their packhorse, Prince, was killed on this stream.

Prindle *(S.11,T.1N;R.5E)*

Railroad point on north bank of Columbia River, 28 miles east of Vancouver, southwest Skamania County. This place was named by officials of St. Paul & Spokane Railway for the first settler, Ernest Hinsdale Prindle. In 1806, the first name, *Cruzatt,* was applied by Lewis and Clark for one of their party, Peter Cruzatte.

Proebstel *(S.7;T.2N;R.3E)*

Settlement on Lacamas Creek, 7-1/2 miles northeast of Vancouver, south central Clark County. In 1887, this name was used when a post office was established. It was for John Proebstel, one of 6 brothers who came here in 1852 to settle on Donation Land Claims.

Profanity Hill *(S.33;T.25N;R.4E)*

A hill of glacial clay in south central Seattle, north of Jackson Street, King County. When wet the clay has a strong tendency to slide. The city tries to prevent slides by bulkheading. In the 1890s, the King County courthouse was built on this hill. About this time the name was applied by Seattle citizens for the language used by attorneys and others when they climbed this steep, slippery hill to the courthouse. Other methods of reaching the courthouse were by hack or cable car -- and the cable cars often broke down during the climb. An alternate name, used by conservatives, was *Yesler Hill.*

Prospect Mountain (Snohomish County) *see* Mt. Stickney

Prosser *(Ss.1,2;T.8N;R.24E)*

Town on Yakima River, 34 miles west of Pasco, west central Benton County. The site was an Indian camp during seasons when salmon ran in the river. The first settler was James Kinney, who homesteaded in 1880. Several names have been applied to this location, including *Yakima Falls,* and later, *Prosser Falls.* At one time it was known as *Cook's* or *Colonel Cook's Ferry.* In 1884, the first post office was named *Lone Tree,* from Lone Tree landing on the south side of the river, where a single, old cottonwood tree stood. On January 26, 1885, a townsite plat was filed by Col. William F. Prosser and Flora T. Prosser. In the same year the present name was applied by Northern Pacific Railway officials when their line was built through here, naming the station for the Prossers and the town which they had platted.

Prosser Falls (Benton County) *see* Prosser

Protection Island *(T.10N;R.2W)*

A rocky island, with little habitation or culture, in Strait of Juan de Fuca, 2 miles north of the entrance to Port Discovery Bay, northeast Jefferson County. On May 27, 1792, the island was named by Capt. George Vancouver because it sheltered Port Discovery Bay from north and northwest winds, and also because it could be fortified for military protection. On July 11, 1790, 2 years earlier, Juan Carrasco, second pilot for Manuel Quimper, named this island *Isla de Carrasco* for himself. His name did not persist. The Indian name was *Cha-cha-ne-cuk* or *Cha-cha-nu-cah.*

Prouty Peak *(S.9;T.39N;R.45E)*

A Kaniksu National Forest peak, elevation 6,268 ft., 4 miles west of the Idaho line, 1 mile north of Sullivan Creek, northeast Pend Oreille County. The peak was named for Harry Prouty, an early settler and prospector, who located mining claims on this mountain. (USBGN)

Providence *(S.36;T.17N;R.32E)*

Railway point on Providence Coulee, 7 miles southwest of Lind, central Adams County. In 1883, it was named by Northern Pacific Railway Company officials for the coulee on which it is located. (*see* Providence Coulee)

Providence Coulee *(Ts.14-16N;Rs.31,32E)*

The coulee starts in north central Franklin County, extends north-by-east for about 20 miles to the vicinity of Providence, 6 miles southwest of Lind. It was named for Providence Springs at Paha.

Prune Hill *(Ss.7,8;T.1N;R.3E)*

Community directly east of Fisher, extending north from Columbia River to Grass Valley, south central Clark County. The first name of this area was *Rock Quarry District,* for a large quarry on Columbia River near Fisher. In 1900, when extensive prune orchards were planted here and several following years, the present name was adopted.

Ptarmigan Glacier *(T.31N;R.13E)*

A Mt. Baker National Forest glacier which covers part of the north slope of Glacier Peak, at the head of Milk Creek, northeast Snohomish County. This is a large, live glacier and the name is reported to have been applied by Forest Service personnel some years ago for a species of native grouse which is quite abundant in the area.

Ptarmigan Ridge *(Mt. Rainier National Park)*

This ridge is on the northwest slope of Mt. Rainier, north of North Mowich Glacier, south of Flett and Russell glaciers, northwest quarter of the park. It was named by Prof. J. B. Flett and H. H. Garrison for the abundance of ptarmigan here during summer months. (USBGN)

Ptarmigan Ridge *(T.39N;R.8E)*

A Mt. Baker National Forest ridge between Coleman Peak and Table Mountain, on the northeast slope of Mt. Baker, central Whatcom County. The ridge was named by C. F. Eaton for the abundance here of this species of native grouse.

Ptenum Creek (Kittitas County) *see* Taneum Creek

Puerto de Alava (Clallam County) *see* Cape Alava

Puerto de Bodega y Quadra (Jefferson County) *see* Port Discovery Bay

Puerto de Garzon (Whatcom County) *see* Birch Bay; Semiahmoo Bay

Puerto De San Jose (Whatcom County) *see* Semiahmoo Bay

Puerto Del Socorro (Whatcom County) *see* Chuckanut Bay

Puffin Island *(T.38N;R.1W)*

An island in Strait of Georgia, directly east of Matia Island, 3 miles north of Orcas Island, extreme northeast San Juan County. In 1859, the island was named on British Admiralty charts by Capt. Richards for crested puffins which nested here in large numbers. The U.S. Coast Survey later changed the name to *Matia East*. More recently the U.S. Coast & Geodetic Survey restored Richards's name.

Puget City *(S.10;T.19N;R.1W)*

Area on Hogum Bay, Nisqually Reach, north central Thurston County. This name, borrowed from Puget Sound, was chosen for the place when promoters "boomed" it in the 1890s, claiming that it was bound to be the metropolis of Puget Sound. The city did not take.

Puget Island *(T.8N;Rs.5,6W)*

A heavily-diked island in the center of Columbia River channel, southeast Wahkiakum County. The island is 5 miles long, average width 2 miles. On October 26, 1792, it was named by W. R. Broughton of the Vancouver Expedition for Lieut. Peter Puget, RN, who also was a member of the expedition. In 1805, Lewis and Clark named it *Sturgeon Island*, but their name did not persist.

Puget Sound

This inland, saltwater sound extends about 53 miles south from Point Wilson near Port Townsend, western Washington; then extends southwesterly some 30 miles to Budd Inlet and other branches in Thurston and Mason counties. It does not include Hood Canal, Port Susan, Bellingham Bay, or the San Juan waterways. It was named by Capt. George Vancouver for Lieut. Peter Puget, RN, who examined the southern part of the sound in May, 1792. His name originally applied to waters south of Vashon Island, but has since been extended to northern waters. Cmdr. Charles Wilkes charted the name only on waterways south of The Narrows and Point Defiance. Indian names for parts of the sound included *Whulch*, *Whulge*, *Whole-itch*, *K'u-k'luts* and others which related only to a single bay or passage.

Puget Sound Falls (Thurston County) *see* Tumwater Falls

Puget Sound Naval Shipyard *(T.24N;R.1E)*

A 285-acre naval installation, in the city of Bremerton, central Kitsap County. It was founded on September 16, 1891. The name source is obvious.

Puget Sound Navy Yard Lake *(S.8;T.24N;R.1E)*

A 3-acre lake on U.S. Naval Depot reservation, directly west of Bremerton, central Kitsap County. The name is descriptive of its location.

Pugh Creek *(Ts.30,31N;R.11E)*

The stream of the creek rises in Round Lake, Mt. Baker National Forest, between Whitechuck and South Fork, Sauk rivers, northeast Snohomish County; flows 4-1/2 miles northerly to Whitechuck River. An alternate name for this stream, found on some maps, is *Deer Creek*. It was locally named for William Pugh, an early homesteader who packed mail and supplies in the Sauk valley in the 1890s.

Pugh Mountain *(S.27;T.31N;R.11E)*

A Mt. Baker National Forest peak, elevation 7,150 ft., on the divide between Sauk and Lower Whitechuck rivers, northeast Snohomish County. A forest fire lookout is operated here, in season, by the Forest Service. It was locally named for William Pugh. (*see* Pugh Creek)

Pugh Ridge *(Ts.29,30N;R.18E.uns)*

A Wenatchee National Forest ridge between South Pyramid Creek and North Fork, Entiat River, north central Chelan County. The ridge runs 5 miles north-south. In the 1890s, it was named for William Pugh. (*see* Pugh Creek)

Pulali Point *(Ss.18,19;T.26N;R.1W)*

A west shore point of Dabob Bay, on the east side of Jackson Cove, southeast Jefferson County. In 1841, the point was named by the Wilkes Expedition, using the Chinook jargon for the feature. The meaning is "powder, dust," or "sand" -- in this case, probably the latter. A more common spelling of the word is *Pollalie*.

Pullman *(Ss.31,32;T.15N;Ss.5,6;T.14N;R.45E)*

Town on south fork of Palouse River, southeast Whitman County. In the late 1870s, this place was settled by Bolin Farr and 2 other cattlemen who homesteaded. In 1882, a townsite was platted as *Three Forks*. In 1884, railroad influence caused a change of name to *Pullman*, to honor George M. Pullman, president of Pullman Car Company and an associate of railroad builder Henry Villard. This "college town" is the location of Washington State University, founded in 1892 as a land grant school, Washington Agricultural College. In 1917, the name was changed to Washington State College, and in 1960 to Washington State University.

Pully Point (King County) *see* Point Pully

Pumice Creek *(T.31N;Rs.12,13E)*

The stream of the creek heads in a glacial field on the west slope of Glacier Peak, northeast Snohomish County; flows 3-1/2 miles west to Whitechuck River at the base of Glacier Peak. It was named for extensive pumice deposits along the creek, by Nels Bruseth, a Forest Service employee and local historian.

Pumpkin Mountain *(Ss.13,14;T.38N;R.13E)*

A Mt. Baker National Forest peak, in the fork of Beaver Creek and Ross Lake, east central Whatcom County. In 1910, the name was chosen by U.S. Forest Ranger Joe Ridley, for the shape of the mountain.

Punta De Davila (Clallam County) *see* Angeles Point

Punta De Errera (Herrera) (San Juan County) *see* Eagle Point

Punta De Hijosa (Clallam County) *see* Cape Alava

Punta De La Bastida (Grays Harbor County) *see* Point Grenville

Punta De Loera (Whatcom County) *see* Sandy Point

Punta De Los Martires (Grays Harbor County) *see* Point Grenville

Punta De Martinez (Clallam County) *see* Cape Flattery

Punta De Mendendez (Island County) *see* Point Partridge

Punta De Rada (Clallam County) *see* Koitlah Point

Punta De Rojas (Clallam County) *see* Sekiu Point; Slip Point

Punta De Salvi (Clallam County) *see* Observatory Point; Striped Peak

Punta De San Juan (Clallam County) *see* Diamond Point

Punta De Santa Cruz (Clallam County) *see* Dungeness Spit

Punta De Solano (Skagit County) *see* William Point

Punta De Zepeda (Whatcom County) *see* Point Roberts

Punta Del Garzon (Whatcom County) *see* Point Whitehorn

Pyramid Butte (Whitman County) *see* Steptoe Butte

Purcell Mountain *(S.20;T.13N;R.8E)*

A 4,600-ft. peak, 7-1/2 miles northeast of Randle, east central Lewis County. It was named by J. T. Chilcoat for one of the earliest settlers. It appears on some maps as *Mt. Purcell.*

Purdy *(Ss.13,24;T.22N;R.1E)*

Community at the east entrance to Burley Lagoon, 4 miles north of Gig Harbor, northwest Pierce County. The town was named for F. C. Purdy, who operated a trading post at Union in Mason County in the 1860s, and who furnished lumber for the first schoolhouse in Purdy. He also had a ranch in Purdy Canyon.

Purdy Canyon *(T.21N;R.4W)*

A canyon along the lower reach of Purdy Creek, before the creek enters Skokomish River valley, central Mason County. (*see* Purdy)

Purdy Creek *(T.21N;R.4W)*

The stream of the creek heads in Kent Lake, 4 miles northwest of Shelton, central Mason County; flows 5-1/2 miles north in a winding course to Skokomish River. (*see* Purdy)

Puyallup *(T.20N;R.4E)*

The oldest town in Puyallup Valley, on Puyallup River, 7 miles east of Tacoma, north central Pierce County. The first name used by white men was *Meekersville,* for Ezra Meeker, who platted the town in February 1877. When a post office was established, postal authorities chose the name *Franklin.* When incorporated in 1890, the original Indian name was used. Although spelled in many ways, the best version of Indian meaning and pronunciation appears to be *Pough-allup,* or ''generous people.'' The word *pough* means ''to add more,'' and *allup* means ''people.'' Indians living along Puyallup River had a reputation for generosity in dealing with travelers.

Puyallup Cleaver *(Mt. Rainier National Park)*

A very narrow rock ledge, elevation 11,562 ft., between Puyallup and Tahoma glaciers, extending 2 miles southwest from Saint Andress Rock to Tokaloo Rock, west central zone of the park. It was named by park officials for Puyallup Glacier. (USBGN) (*see* Puyallup)

Puyallup (Glacier) *(Mt. Rainier National Park)*

This glacier heads in Sunset Amphitheater, a large cirque whose perpendicular walls form the south base of Liberty Cap at Mt. Rainier's summit; extends west-by-south for about 4 miles to headwaters of Puyallup River, west central precincts of the park. The canyon in which it flows has sheer basalt walls. It was named by park officials for Puyallup River. (USBGN) (*see* Puyallup)

Puyallup Indian Reservation *(T.20N;R.3E)*

A 33-acre stretch of tribal land at the mouth of Puyallup River, Tacoma, Pierce County. It was established as a larger reservation by the Medicine Creek Treaty of December 26, 1854, and enlarged by an executive order dated September 6, 1873. At its largest the reservation was 17,645 acres. For many years the Cushman General Hospital on this site, administered to Indian needs throughout the state. The remaining fragment of this reservation is carried on Tacoma maps as *Indian Addition.* (*see* Puyallup)

Puyallup River *(Ts.16-21N;Rs.3-7E)*

The stream of the river rises at the foot of Puyallup and Tahoma glaciers, on the west and southwest slopes of Mt. Rainier; flows northwesterly through Puyallup Valley to Commencement Bay at Tacoma, Pierce County. The lower reaches are diked to prevent flooding. (*see* Puyallup)

Pyramid Creek *(Mt. Rainier National Park)*

The stream of the creek rises at the foot of Pyramid Glacier and Pyramid Peak in several branches, southwest slope of Mt. Rainier; flows southwest in an inter-branched pattern, to Kautz Creek, southwest quarter of the park. It was named for Pyramid Peak, near its point of origin. This name, descriptive of its shape, was applied by surveyors who used it as a triangulation station in 1897.

Pyramid Glacier *(Mt. Rainier National Park)*

This relatively short glacier heads in a glacial cirque at the very steep southwest cliff of Success Cleaver; extends 1-1/2 miles southwest to the headwaters of Pearl Creek. It was named for Pyramid Peak. (USBGN) (*see* Pyramid Creek)

Pyramid Mountain *(S.23;T.30N;R.18E.uns)*

A 8,240-ft. peak between Pyramid Creek and Lake Chelan, on the boundary between Okanogan and Wenatchee national forests, Chelan Mountains, Chelan County.

Pyramid Mountain *(T.30N;R.9W)*

A sharp, pyramidal peak, elevation 3,140 ft., on the north slope of Lake Crescent, in a wide band of the lake, north central Clallam County. It was locally named for its pyramidal contour. Once it was called *Sugarloaf.*

Pyramid Peak *(S.28;T.19N;R.11E)*

A 5,723-ft. peak at Cascade Mountain summit, 1-1/2 miles north of Naches Pass, extreme southeast King County. The U.S. Forest Service has used this peak as a forest fire lookout, in season, since 1923. It was named by Forest Service personnel for its pyramidal shape.

Pyramid Peak *(Mt. Rainier National Park)*

A 6,937-ft. peak on the southwest slope of Mt. Rainier, at the east end of Indian Henrys Hunting Ground, southwest of Pyramid Glacier. This descriptive name was chosen by James L. Mosman of Yelm. The mountain resembles an almost perfect pyramid. (USBGN)

Pyramid Peak *(S.20;T.37N;R.13E.uns)*

A Mt. Baker National Forest peak, elevation 7,800 ft., 3 miles south of Diablo Dam on Skagit River, southeast Whatcom County. This glaciated peak was named by Forest Service personnel for its shape.

Pysht *(S.10;T.31N;R.11W)*

Village on a small inlet at the wide mouth of Pysht River, on Strait of Juan de Fuca, north central Clallam County. Formerly it was the headquarters for the Merrill & Ring Tree Farms. It is an example of scientific forest management of extensive acreage, which was logged out several decades ago. This Indian name, meaning ''fish,'' has been spelled in almost every possible form, including *Pisht, Pyscht, Pisth, P-he-slth,* and *Postch-et.* A colorful pioneer legend states that the place was named for the ship *Psyche,* whose name-board floated ashore here when that vessel was wrecked in Strait of Juan de Fuca. (USBGN)

Pysht River *(T.31N;Rs.11,12W)*

The stream of the river rises in high country, 8 miles south of Clallam Bay, north central Clallam County; flows northeast and east to Strait of Juan de Fuca at Pysht. Early explorers named the stream *Rio Canil* and *Canel River.* The present name is the original designation used by Indians who fished and hunted in this area. (*see* Pysht)

Q

Qualam Point (Pierce County) *see* Gordon Point

Qualla Creek (Whatcom County) *see* Squalicum Creek

Quartermaster Cove (King County) *see* Smith Cove

Quartermaster Harbor
(Ts.21,22N;Rs.2,3E)

A long, narrow bay between Maury Island and the south end of Vashon Island, on Dalco Passage, southwest King County. Once an important ship-building and drydock center, it is hook-shaped at the north end. In 1841, it was named by Cmdr. Charles Wilkes as a fancied haven for the spirits of his petty officers.

Quartz Creek *(S.26;T.40N;R.19E)*

The stream of this very short mountain creek rises on the south slope of Quartz Mountain, North Cascade Primitive Area, northwest Okanogan County; flows 1-1/2 miles southwest to the East Fork, Pasayten River. It was named by The Mountaineers for a mine which operated here in 1886. The mountain at its source was similarly named.

Quatsap Point *(S.22;T.25N;R.2W)*

A west shore point of Hood Canal, near the mouth of Duckabush River, 2-1/2 miles south of Brinnon, southeast Jefferson County. In 1841, this original Indian name was charted by the Wilkes Expedition.

Queen Anne Hill *(T.25N;Rs.3,4E)*

One of Seattle's 12 "official" hills, elevation 456 ft., in the central Seattle residential district, north of the main business district, between Elliott Bay and the Ship Canal, King County. In the 1880s, the name was coined by Rev. Daniel Bagley, after a number of influential citizens built homes on the hill which followed the Queen Anne style of architecture. Bagley called it *Queen Anne Town,* but the name became official as applied to the entire hill. An earlier name was *Galer Hill* for Jacob Galer, a pioneer resident of the hill.

Queen City *(Ts.24-26N;Rs.3-5E)*

This is a poetic name for Seattle. In 1869, a Portland, Oregon, realtor published a circular lauding Seattle as an excellent place for investments in property. It was titled *The Future Queen City of the Pacific.* The same title for Seattle was used on Northern Pacific time schedules published in 1882. The nickname has been used ever since.

Queets *(S.35;T.24N;R.13W)*

Community near the mouth of Queets River, Quinault Indian Reservation, extreme southwest corner of Jefferson County. It was named for the once-powerful Quiatso Indian tribe which inhabited this place when the first white explorers came to this coast. The name is from a tribal legend in which The Great Spirit waded across a river and rubbed his legs to restore circulation. He then threw the rolls of dirt which came from his legs, and they landed in the river. Out came a man and a woman to form the *Qu-itz-qu* or *Qu-ai-tso* tribe. The name literally means "out of the dirt of the skin."

Queets Corridor
(Ts.24,25N;Rs.10-1/2,11,12,13W)

A 14-mile strip of land along the lower Queets River, added to Olympic National Park by presidential proclamation on January 6, 1953, in order to join the main area of the park with a 50-mile strip along the ocean, which was added to the park by the same proclamation. The Queets Corridor contains about 30 square miles. (*see* Queets)

Queets Glacier *(Ss.6,7;T.26N;R.7W)*

A northwest slope glacier of Mt. Queets, 5 miles southeast of Mt. Olympus, central Jefferson County. This is a rather small glacier, about 3/4 mile long. (*see* Queets)

Queets River *(Ts.24-26N;Rs.7-12W)*

The stream of the river rises in Queets Basin, southeast slope of Mt. Olympus, Olympic National Park, north central Jefferson County; flows southwesterly to Pacific Ocean through the Queets Corridor, with one loop into northwest Grays Harbor County near Queets. (*see* Queets)

Querquelin River (Pacific County) *see* Bone River, Niawiakum River

Quilceda Creek *(Ts.29-31N;R.5E)*

The stream of the creek rises 5-1/2 miles north of Marysville, on Tulalip Indian Reservation and the adjoining area to the east, west central Snohomish County; flows south 7-1/2 miles to Ebey Slough. The name is an adaptation of the Indian name, *Kwilt-seh-da* or *Kkul-see-dah,* meaning "saltwater people," and referring to the Indians who lived along this creek.

Quilcene *(T.27N;R.2W)*

Small town at the head of Quilcene Bay, at the mouth of Quilcene River, east central Jefferson County. The name is for the Indian tribe which lived here before white settlement, the *Quil-ceed-a-bish.* In 1841, the Wilkes Expedition charted the place as *Kwil-sid.* Other spellings that have been used are *Kol-sids, Col-cene, Col-see-ed,* and *Cul-ah-seen.* The tribal name means *saltwater people."*

Quilcene Bay *(Ts.26,27N;R.1W)*

An arm of Dabob Bay, between Bolton Peninsula and the mainland, east central Jefferson County. The bay supports a moderate oyster industry and was charted as *Kwil-sid Harbor* by the Wilkes Expedition in 1841. (*see* Quilcene)

Quilcene River
(Ss.22-24;T.27N;R.2W)

This river is formed by the Big and Little Quilcene rivers; the former rises in east central Jefferson County and the latter rises in southeast Clallam County. They merge 2-1/2 miles from their discharge into Quilcene Bay. (*see* Quilcene)

Quillayute *(S.8;T.28N;R.14W)*

A small Indian settlement north of Soleduck River, 5 miles east of Pacific Ocean, extreme southwest Clallam County. The Indian name means ''joining together of rivers.'' It also is the official name of the tribe which lives in this area. The name has been variously spelled as *Quillehute, Quillyhuyte, Kwilleute, Quallayute* and *Quelaiault.*

Quillayute Indian Reservation
(Ss.27,34;T.28N;R.15W)

A 595-acre reservation on Pacific Ocean at mouth of Quillayute River, southwest Clallam County. This reservation is listed as *Quileute* in some government publications. About 150 members of the tribe live here. It was designated in the Quinault River Treaty of July 1, 1855, and was established by an executive order dated February 19, 1889. (*see* Quillayute)

Quillayute Needle *(T.28N;R.15W)*

An offshore, needle-shaped rock, 80 ft. above the water on average tides, in Pacific Ocean, 3 miles south of Quillayute River mouth, southwest Clallam County. This rock is in a group with Huntington Rock and James Island. On July 12, 1775, it was named, together with James Island, as *Los Frayles* by

Bruno Heceta. The present name is descriptive of the sharply-pointed peak and its location near the mouth of Quillayute River. (*see* Quillayute)

Quillayute Prairie *(T.28N;R.15W)*

A prairie bordering on Pacific Ocean, near the mouth of Quillayute River, southwest Clallam County. It was the scene of an early white settlement which faded away when the Indian reservation was officially established. (*see* Quillayute)

Quillayute River *(T.28N;Rs.14,15W)*

A short, 5-mile-long river, formed by the confluence of Soleduck and Bogachiel rivers, extreme southwest Clallam County. The combined stream flows west to Pacific Ocean at La Push.(*see* Quillayute)

Quimper *(T.30N;R.1W)*

A peninsula between Port Townsend bay and Port Discovery Bay, northeast Jefferson County. This ''S''-shaped peninsula is bounded on the north by Strait of Juan de Fuca. In 1862, it was named by Capt. George Davidson of U.S. Coast Survey, to honor Sub-Lieut. Manuel Quimper, who explored Strait of Juan de Fuca in 1790. It had previously been named *Dickerson Peninsula* in 1841 by the Wilkes Expedition, for Hon. Mahlon Dickerson, who had been secretary of the U.S. Navy when orders were issued for the Wilkes Expedition on March 20, 1838.

Quinault *(S.9;T.23N;R.9W)*

Community on Quinault River, near its entrance to Quinault Lake, north central Grays Harbor County. This town is on Quinault Indian Reservation and is the tribal headquarters of the Quinaults. The name of the town is the tribal designation, *Kwle-ni-lth* or *Wi-ni-nlth.* In 1787, the river was named by Capt. Charles William Barkley for the Quin-

ault Indian nation which lived along the river and its mouth. (USBGN)

Quinault Burn (Grays Harbor County)
see Neilton

Quinault Indian Reservation
(Ts.20-24N;Rs.9-13W)

A 189,621-acre reservation in northwest Grays Harbor and southwest Jefferson counties. The reservation includes over 25 miles of frontage on Pacific Ocean, and tapers to a wedge shape at Quinault Lake, 20 miles east of the ocean. The Quinault River flows west through the reservation to Taholah, on the ocean, which is Indian Agency headquarters for tribal affairs. The reservation has material assets in salmon fishing and timber. On July 1, 1855, it was created by the Quinault River Treaty and was enlarged by an executive order dated November 4, 1873. The name is for the Quinault Indian nation.

Quinault Lake *(T.23N;Rs.9,10W)*

A 3,729-acre lake in the course of Quinault River, 20 miles east of Pacific Ocean, Quinault Indian Reservation, north central Grays Harbor County. This lake is Indian-owned and is 4 miles long, average width 1-1/2 miles. It is valuable as a salmon-spawning ground, as well as for fishing and recreation. (USBGN) (*see* Quinault)

Quinault River *(Ts.21-25N;Rs.5-13W)*

The stream of the river rises in Anderson Glacier, south slope of Mt. Anderson, south central Jefferson County; flows 35 miles southwest to Quinault Lake, northwest Grays Harbor County, then 29 miles southwest in a winding course to Pacific Ocean at Taholah. (USBGN) (*see* Quinault)

R

Race Lagoon *(S.7;T.31N;R.2E)*

Lagoon on east central Whidbey Island, 4-1/2 miles south of Coupeville on Saratoga Passage, Island County. It was named for Henry Race, who came to Kitsap County from Australia in 1856, and moved in 1876 to Whidbey Island.

Race Rocks (Whatcom County) *see* Lummi Rocks

Race Track *(Ss.5,6;T.5N;R.8E)*

A rather deep depression marking the location of an oval race track on a high mountain meadow 2-1/2 miles west of Goose Lake, Gifford Pinchot National Forest, central Skamania County. This fascinating reminder of old Indian activities is where Yakima and Klickitat tribesmen raced horses while their women picked huckleberries each summer. The Klickitat name was *Cal-La-Met* or *Cal-U-Mut*.

Race Track Lakes *(S.5;T.5N;R.8E.uns)*

Two small lakes, covering a total of 2-1/2 acres, 1 mile north of Red Mountain, 15-1/4 miles north of Carson, south central Skamania County. The lakes are at the southeast side of a very old Indian race track. (*see* Race Track)

Races Cove *(T.28N;R.2E)*

An east entrance cove of Hood Canal, extreme north Kitsap County. It was named for Henry Race, who settled here in 1856, and who worked at Port Gamble. The cove does not appear on recent maps. (*see* Race Lagoon)

Racoon Point *(S.16;T.37N;R.1W)*

An indistinct point on the northeast coast of Orcas Island, 3-1/2 miles east of East Sound (town), northeast San Juan County. In 1855, it was named *Racoon Bluff* by the U.S. Coast Survey. The present name, which appeared on later charts, is not as descriptive as the original name for this feature, which is more bluff than point.

Raeco *(S.22;T.22N;R.3E)*

Small settlement on the southeast shore of Maury Island, on East Passage, southwest King County. In 1908, it was named when the place was founded by Rhodes, Appel & Earnest Company, a real estate organization. The name consists of the first letter in each name with the abbreviation for "company" appended.

Rafferty's Ranch (Garfield County) *see* Mentor

Raft Island *(S.10;T.21N;R.1E)*

Island in Lay Inlet, Henderson Bay, 4 miles west of Gig Harbor, northwest Pierce County. The local name is based on an imaginary resemblance of the island to a raft; the namers must have had powerful imaginations. In 1841, Cmdr. Charles Wilkes charted this feature as *Allshouse Island*, for Joseph Allshouse, a crew member. Wilkes's name never came into general use.

Raft River *(T.23N;Rs.11-13W)*

The stream of the river rises on Quinault Indian Reservation, northwest Grays Harbor County; flows west to Pacific Ocean, 5 miles south of Queets. It drains most of the north half of the Indian reservation. The name is of very early origin, based on the fact that this river could only be crossed on rafts when there were no bridges. In 1857, the name was placed on this river by the surveyor general of Washington Territory. The Indian name, in Makah language, was *Loh-whilse*.

Raft Rock *(T.23N;R.13W)*

Rock at the mouth of Raft River, 5 miles south of Queets, northwest Grays Harbor County. (*see* Raft River)

Raft Rock (Grays Harbor County) *see* Tunnel Island

Raging Creek *(T.28N;Rs.16,17E)*

The stream of the creek heads directly south of Schaefer Lake, Wenatchee National Forest, northwest Chelan County; flows southeast and east 5 miles to Chiwawa River. Charles Allen, a pioneer settler, verifies the fact that this name was in use in very early days. In 1908, the name became twisted to *Roaring Creek*, but was not mapped as such. It is shown as *Williams Creek* on U.S.G.S. quadrangles.

Ragnar *(S.36;T.23N;R.8E)*

A Milwaukee Railroad station 3 miles east of Cedar Falls, 2 miles north of Cedar Lake, east central King County. It was named by Harry W. Higman, Seattle naturalist and writer, for Ragnar Stone, a thoroughbred English bulldog. In 1908, the dog was left in Higman's care by the owner, H. R. Williams, then president of Milwaukee Railroad.

Rahms *(S.18;T.21N;R.45E)*

Railroad siding with grain elevator and warehouse, rather than an organized community, 2 miles northeast of Latah, southeast Spokane County. It was named for Juan *Ramm*, a pioneer sugar beet raiser. An alternate name is *Rahms Siding*.

Rail Creek *(T.28N;R.40E)*

The stream of the creek rises 6 miles northeast of Ford, south central Stevens County; flows 5-1/2 miles west to Chamokane Creek. It was named by early settlers for the tall, straight, small timber along the creek, which was excellent for splitting into fence rails.

Rail Creek *(Ts.28,29N;R.37E)*

The stream of this short creek rises south of Boundary Butte, on Spokane Indian Reservation, southwest Stevens County; flows 3 miles southeast to Sand Creek. The name is probably from the same source as Rail Creek, a tributary of Chamokane Creek located to the east. (*see* Rail Creek)

Railroad Creek *(T.31N;Rs.16-18E.uns)*

The stream of the creek rises directly east of Cascade Mountain summit, near Suiattle Pass, north central Chelan County; flows almost due east to Lake Chelan at Lucerne. In 1890, it was named for a railroad which was surveyed over Suiattle Pass by Great Northern Railway, but never built; its destination was to have been Bellingham Bay. In 1910, there were piles of rails for miles along the creek.

Railroad Grade *(S.13;T.37N;R.7E.uns)*

A natural ridge northwest of Schrieber's Meadows area, directly south of Mt. Baker, Mt. Baker National Forest, south central Whatcom County. It was named by U.S. Forest Service personnel for its level top and steep slopes, resembling a railroad grade.

Rainbow Butte (Yakima County) *see* Goat Butte

Rainbow Falls (Lewis County) *see* Rainbow Falls State Park

Rainbow Falls State Park *(S.7;T.13N;R.4W)*

A timbered, 116-acre recreation area with camping and fishing facilities, at Rainbow Falls on Chehalis River, 16 miles west of Chehalis, west central Lewis County. Evidently, it was named for rainbows which form in the falls under certain light conditions. A local legend states that it was named by George Onn of Dryad, for the Rainbow Division, which participated in World War I.

Rainbow Lake *(S.26;T.23N;R.8E)*

A 3-1/2-acre lake 1-3/4 miles northeast of Cedar Falls, east central King County. It was named for the small rainbow trout prevalent in this area. An alternate name is *Little Rattlesnake Lake.* This lake should not be confused with another Rainbow Lake located 6 miles west of Snoqualmie Pass.

Rainbow Lake *(S.4;T.22N;R.10E)*

A 6-acre lake 6 miles west of Snoqualmie Pass, Snoqualmie National Forest, east central King County. It is one of 3 Island Lakes, with Island and Blazer lakes. This lake should not be confused with another of the same name located northeast of Cedar Falls, and also named for small rainbow trout prevalent in this area. Alternate names are *Trail Lake, Long Lake* and *Camp Lake.*

Rainbow Lake (Grant County) *see* Sun Lakes State Park

Rainey Creek *(Ts.12,13N;Rs.5,6E)*

The stream of the creek rises in Coleman Weed Patch, east central Lewis County; flows southwest through Rainey Valley, to Cowlitz River at Kosmos. The creek and its valley were named by J. T. Chilcoat for Dave *Rene,* who drowned, or nearly drowned, in the creek while crossing with a party of government surveyors. The original name has been distorted over the years so that maps and records generally carry it as *Rainey* for both creek and valley.

Rainier *(S.9;T.16N;R.1E)*

Formerly a sawmill town, ghosted by timber depletion, on Telequot Prairie, 12 miles southeast of Olympia, southeast Thurston County. In 1884, it was named by Northern Pacific Railway officials for Mt. Rainier, which is quite visible from this point.

Rainier Creek (Mt. Rainier National Park) *see* Tahoma Creek

Rainy Creek *(T.27N;Rs.13-15E)*

The stream of the creek heads on the east slope of Cascade Mountain summit, at Joyce and Union peaks, southwest Chelan County; flows east and northeast 8 miles to Little Wenatchee River, of which it is the largest tributary. The name, applied by very early inhabitants, is appropriate in this area of high precipitation.

Rainy Lake *(S.4;T.23N;R.10E)*

A 4.8-acre mountain lake 12 miles east of North Bend, 1 mile northwest of Preacher Mountain, east central King County. It was named for its location in an area of high and constant precipitation.

Ralston *(Ss.6,7;T.17N;R.36E)*

Railroad shipping point 13 miles east of Lind, central Adams County. Located in the eastern Washington wheat belt, it was reportedly named for a brand of health food by an official of the Chicago, Milwaukee & St. Paul Railway. In 1907, a townsite was platted, and the population once approximated 250. Grain elevators now constitute the most important feature of Ralston's landscape.

Rampart Mountain *(S.4;T.29N;R.17E)*

Peak 2 miles west of Entiat River, between Entiat and 5th of July mountains, north central Chelan County. The name was applied by Forest Supervisor A. H. Sylvester because the east side is a huge, almost vertical rock.

Rampart Ridge (Mt. Rainier National Park)

Long group of prominent crags, elevation 4,080 ft., forming the east wall of Gold Creek Valley, on the south slope of Mt. Rainier, west of Longmire Divide, between Kautz Creek and Nisqually River. It dominates the skyline west of Longmire and harbors many mountain goats. The descriptive name was chosen by The Mountaineers on one of their expeditions in the park. (USBGN)

Rams Head (Douglas County) *see* Rock Island (rocks)

Randle *(S.8;T.12N;R.7E)*

Community on Cowlitz River in the "Big Bottom" country, 18 miles east of Morton, east central Lewis County. It was named for James Randle of Randle Lumber Company, who founded the town in 1886 by establishing a sawmill.

Ranger Creek (Mt. Rainier National Park)

The stream of the creek rises on North Tolmie Peak, northwest corner of the park; flows north by east 3 miles, through Green Lake to Carbon River, at the north park boundary. In 1911, when park names were being standardized, this name was suggested by a committee of The Mountaineers in recognition of the efficient rangers, the backbone of park administration.

Rankin Creek *(T.38N;R.7E.uns)*

The stream of the creek heads at Black Buttes, southwest slope of Mt. Baker; flows southwest to Middle Fork, Nooksack River, south central Whatcom County. In 1909, it was named by C. H. Sholes of The Mazamas, for Miss A. L. Rankin, a member of the organization.

Rapids City *(S.3;T.5N;R.28E)*

Once a "boom town" at Umatilla Rapids, north bank of Columbia River, southeast Benton County. In 1925, the boom was started by real estate promoters, offering small lots in the sagebrush for $400; the boom busted.

Rattlesnake Hills *(Ts.10,11N;Rs.23-26E)*

A 16-mile-long range, elevations over 3,500 ft., rising 3 miles west of Yakima-Benton county line, and continuing east by south through west central Benton County. It was named by early settlers for the numerous rattlesnakes in the lower portions of the hills.

Rattlesnake Lake *(S.34;T.23N;R.8E)*

A 112-acre lake, 1/2 mile southwest of Cedar Falls, 5 miles south of North Bend, central King County. It takes its name from Rattlesnake Prairie, which was named by Seattle pioneer Arthur A. Denny, when a member of a road survey crew on the prairie was frightened by the rattling of dry seed pods, thinking that he was being attacked by a rattlesnake. An alternate name is *Big Rattlesnake Lake.*

Rattlesnake Mountain (Benton County) *see* Rattlesnake Hills

Rattlesnake Prairie *(T.23N;R.8E)*

Prairie directly west of Cedar Falls,

north of Cedar River, central King County. (*see* Rattlesnake Lake)

Rattlesnake Spring *(S.4;T.24N;R.20E)*

Locally-named spring at the head of a tributary to Tenas George Canyon, Wenatchee National Forest, 8-1/2 miles northeast of Cashmere, southeast Chelan County. It was named for the prevalence of rattlesnakes in this area during summer months. (USBGN)

Ravenna Park *(S.9;T.25N;R.4E)*

Residential area 2 miles northwest of the University of Washington, northeast Seattle, King County. In 1887, it was named for Ravenna, Italy, by W. W. Beck, owner of this site. Originally, it was a city park of several hundred acres, with sulphur springs and old-growth timber. Because of the mineral springs, it was locally known as *Ravenna Springs Park*. After the death of President Theodore Roosevelt, the park was renamed *Roosevelt Park*; that name, however, never came into common use. A local tradition recounts that the original name was *Ravina*, because the park was located in a ravine. The name was altered to the present form by Italian residents who were less interested in ravines than in a well-known city in their homeland.

Ravens Roost
(S.24;T.18N;R.11E.uns)

A 6,227-ft. mountain at the head of Crow Creek, 4-1/2 miles southeast of Naches Pass, 3 miles east of Cascade Mountain summit, extreme northwest Yakima County. The name was given to harmonize with that of Crow Creek at the base of the peak.

Ravensdale *(S.36;T.22N;R.6E)*

Coal mining community 3 miles north of Black Diamond, south central King County. Because of the mines, it suffered disasters from fire and mine explosions. In 1902, residents named the town for a large colony of ravens nesting in the vicinity.

Ravensdale Lake *(S.36;T.22N;R.6E)*

Lake covering 18 acres at normal stages, 1/4 mile west of Ravensdale, southwest King County. On some maps it appears as *Beaver Lake*. (*see* Ravensdale)

Ray (Spokane County) *see* Rodna

Raymond *(T.14N;Rs.8,9W)*

Town on the estuary of Willapa River, 1 mile east of South Bend, north central Pacific County. In early days, it was developed on lumber and shingle manufacturing. The name is for Leslie V. Raymond, who platted the town in 1904, and who was the first postmaster.

Rayville *(S.15;T.18N;R.5W)*

Settlement between Whites and McCleary, 6 miles northeast of Elma, southeast Grays Harbor County. The place was named for Joe Ray, a local sawmill operator.

Razorhead *(T.23N;R.16E)*

An 8,400-ft. peak with a sharp, granite crest, 7 miles southwest of Leavenworth, in Stuart Range, southwest Chelan County. This descriptive name was applied by mountain climbers in early days.

Razorhone Creek *(T.39N;R.9E)*

The stream of the creek heads 2 miles northwest of Mt. Shuksan, Mt. Baker National Forest, central Whatcom County; joins Bagley Creek, and flows 4 miles north to North Fork, Nooksack River. It was named for a fine rock formation, without grit, found along the creek, and once tried for commercial purposes.

Reach Island *(S.5;T.21N;R.1W)*

A west shore island of Cases Inlet, near the entrance to North Bay, east central Mason County. In the early 1890s, it was given this name, probably in a play of words between this island and Stretch Island, directly to the south.

Reardan *(S.15;T.25N;R.39E)*

Town 15 miles east of Davenport, northeast Lincoln County. The original name of the settlement was *Capps* or *Capp's Place*, for J. S. Capps, on whose land the post office was located. On September 23, 1882, a town named *Fairweather* was platted here by John W. Still and William F. Hooker. Assisted by other settlers, they dug a well to show railroad engineers that water was available. Evidently the name was for H. W. Fairweather, who had been associated with Northern Pacific Railway Company during construction of the Pend Oreille division. Fairweather did not prosper, and, on June 13, 1889, Mr. and Mrs. George A. Fellows platted the town of Reardan. The name honored C. F. Reardon, a civil engineer, who was in charge of construction on Central Washington Railway.

Rebel Flat *(Ts.15-17N;Rs.40-43E)*

Valley without exact boundaries, along the course of Rebel Flat Creek, from about 6 miles south of Colfax; continues west through Endicott (formerly the town of Rebel Flat), to the vicinity of Winona, west central Whitman County. Together with a town and creek, it was named by Confederate sympathizers, who settled here soon after the Civil War.

Rebel Flat (town) (Whitman County) *see* Endicott

Rebel Flat Creek *(Ts.16-17; Rs.40-43E)*

The stream of the creek heads 5 miles south of Colfax, Whitman County; flows west 32 miles through Diamond and Endicott, to Palouse River at Winona. (*see* Rebel Flat, Union Flat, Union Flat Creek)

Red Bluff (Island County) *see Admiralty Head, Point Partridge*

Red Butte *(S.20;T.9N;R.11E.uns)*

Rounded, volcanic butte, elevation 7,203 ft., at Cascade Mountain summit, on southeast slope of Mt. Adams, southwest Yakima County. It is covered with talus slopes of dark red rock, which make ascent difficult. In August 1901, the descriptive name was applied by C. E. Rusk and Prof. Harry Fielding Reid, a glaciologist associated with Johns Hopkins University.

Red Cedar Grove *(Mt. Rainier National Park)*

Forest grove along the main highway, 3 miles north of Ohanapecosh Hot Springs, southeast quarter of the park. It consists largely of old, western red cedar trees with diameters to 10 ft., as well as western white pine, Douglas fir, and black cottonwood. The descriptive name was applied by early park personnel.

Red Creek *(T.30N;R.12E)*

The stream of the creek rises on Red Mountain, 7 miles southwest of Glacier Peak summit, Mt. Baker National Forest, east central Snohomish County; flows 3 miles southeast to North Fork, Sauk River. It was named for Red Mountain, which received its name from early prospectors Sam Strom and W. Brillmeyer, for the mountain's distinctive coloration.

Red Harbor (San Juan County) *see* Reid Harbor

Red Mountain *(S.27;T.31N;R.16E)*

A Wenatchee National Forest peak on a ridge between Chiwawa River and Phelps Creek, northwest Chelan County. It was named by early miners because of dark red rock on the east face.

Red Mountain
(Ss.21,22;T.30N;R.12E)

A 6,930-ft. peak at the head of Red Creek, 7 miles southwest of Glacier Peak, east central Snohomish County. The Indian name was *Ska-hal-a-bats,* meaning "painted mountain." (*see* Red Creek)

Red Pass *(S.36;T.30N;R.13E.uns)*

Pass between Portal Peak and White Peak, directly southwest ofWhitechuck Glacier, Mt. Baker National Forest, west central Snohomish County. The name was applied by U.S. Forest Service personnel because of the red color of soil and rocks in the vicinity.

Redmond *(S.1;T.25N;R.5E)*

City on Sammamish River, 3 miles east of Kirkland, 1-1/2 miles north of the north end of Lake Sammamish, northwest King County. It was named for Luke McRedmond, the town's founder and first postmaster. An early name was *Melrose;* another was *Salmonberg,* for the quantities of dog salmon which ran in the Sammamish River.

Redondo *(S.32;T.22N;R.4E)*

Beach resort with many summer cottages on the east shore of East Passage, extreme southwest King County. It was reportedly named by a settler from California for Redondo Beach in that state. A previously-used nickname was *Poverty Bay.*

Redrock Coulee
(Ts.16,17N;Rs.25,26E)

Coulee starting in Frenchman Hills, southeast Grant County; extends 12 miles southeast to Crab Creek. In 1896, it was named by local settlers because of the abundance of red rock exposed along its course.

Redstone Peak *(Mt. Rainier National Park)*

A 5,700-ft. peak between White River and the head of Van Horn Creek, north central zone of the park. The descriptive name was chosen by an early exploring party, for the definitely red coloration of the mountain's slopes. (USBGN)

Reed Lake (Whatcom County) *see* Reid Lake

Reef Island *(S.13;T.36N;R.3W)*

One of the 7 Wasp Islands, at the entrance to Deer Harbor, Orcas Island, central San Juan County. It was locally named because of a surrounding reef at low tide.

Reef Point *(S.8;T.35N;R.1E)*

A southwest point of Cypress Island, on Rosario Strait, northwest Skagit County. In 1858, the name was charted by a British survey ship, commanded by Capt. Richards; the name has persisted.

Reese's Camp *(Mt. Rainier National Park)*

A 5,557-ft. camp on the south central slope of Mt. Rainier, in Paradise Park, south central zone of the park. The site was named for John L. Reese, who operated a log-and-canvas hotel here prior to 1916. An earlier name was *Theosophy Ridge.*

Reflection Lake *(S.4;T.24N;R.8W)*

A one-acre lake at the head of Big Creek, in Paradise Valley, Olympic National Park, south central Jefferson County. It was named because the image of mountains reflected in the lake appears sharper than the view of the mountains themselves.

Reflection Lake (Grant County) *see* Sun Lakes State Park

Reflection Lakes *(Mt. Rainier National Park)*

Group of 2 large and several smaller lakes at the foot of Mazama Ridge, elevation 4,592 ft., 1 mile south of Paradise Valley, south central area of the park. The 2 large lakes are Reflection and Louise. In this saddle north of Tatoosh Ridge, the glacial lakes offer striking reflections of Mt. Rainier, providing a reason for the descriptive name. (USBGN)

Reflector Bay *(S.8;T.37N;R.13E.uns)*

Bar at the confluence of Stetattle Creek with Skagit River, just below Diablo Dam, southeast Whatcom County. Seattle City Light buildings now occupy part of the bar. The name origin has not been traced, but in pioneer days this was a "spirit boundary" for upper Skagit River Indians; above this br was "the country of the ghosts."

Reflexion Lakes *Mt. Rainier National Park) see* Reflection Lakes

Reform (Garfield County) *see* Central Ferry

Refuge Display Pool
(S.29;T.11N;R.10W)

Willapa National Wildlife Refuge display pool of tidewater sealifeon Long Island, 9 miles northeast of Ilwaco, southwest Pacific County. It was established by U.S. Fish & Wildlife Service.

Regal *(S.6;T.17N;R.19E)*

Railway loading sput 1 mile east of Ellensburg, south central Kitttas County. It was named by officials of Chicago, Milwaukee & St. Paul Railway, for the owner of the land on which the spur was built.

Regis (Spokane County) *see* Fairfield

Register Rock *(Mt. Rainier National Park)*

A 14,161-ft. rock less than 1/2 mile northeast of Mt. Rainier's summit at Columbia Crest, central area of the park. The name refers to a registry point established on the rock, where successful climbers by the Giraltar route sign their names.

Reid Glacier (Yakima County) *see* Adams Glacier

Reid Harbor *(T.37N;R.4W)*

A southeast shore harbor of Stuart Island, northwest San Juan County. In 1860, it was named on British Admiralty charts, for Capt. James Murray Reid of Hudson's Bay Company.

Reid Lake *(S.29;T.37N;R.4E)*

Lake directly southwest of the upper end of Lake Whatcom, 1 mile north of Cain Lake, southwest Whatcom County. The name is for Frank H. Reid a civil engineer, who came here to homestead on this lake in 1883. In 1897, he joined the Alaska Gold Rush, and, on July 12, 1898, shot and killed the infamous outlaw "Soapy Smith" in a gun battle at Sylvester's Wharf in Skagway. Reid died of wounds 9 days later. The lake is incorrectly shown on some maps as *Reed Lake.*

Reid Rock *(S.6;T.35N;R.2W)*

Rock in San Juan Channel, between Shaw and San Juan islands, central San Juan County. (*see* Reid Harbor)

Reil Harbor *(S.25;T.37N;R.1E)*

A southeast shore harbor of Lummi Island, Bellingham Bay, southwest

Whatcom County. The name is reputed to have been for an early steamboat navigator on Puget Sound. The original Indian name was *Hiks-pe-slak-en*.

Reiter *(S.10;T.27N;R.9E)*

Early settlement on the north bank of Skykomish River, 9 miles east of Sultan, south central Snohomish County. It was the scene of early mining activity. In July 1906, the place was named by V.V. Clark, for Charles G. Reiter of East Orange, New Jersey, who was president of Bunker Hill Mining & Smelting Company.

Relief *(S.20;T.9N;R.29E)*

Railroad point on Columbia River, 5 miles west of Pasco, extreme southwest Franklin County. In 1889, it was named by Northern Pacific Railway Comany officials, for the helper-engine system which was used here at the time.

Rena *(S.15;T.30N;R.4W)*

Village south of Dungeness and directly west of Carlsborg, northeast Clallam County. It was established in the railroad boom of 1892, and ao named in that year by Maj. Hooker, in memory of his daughter. The village does not appear on recent maps.

Rendsland Creek *(S.17;T.22N;R.3W)*

The stream of the creek rises on the peninsula enclosed by Great Bend of Hood Canal, central Mason County; flows 3-1/2 miles southwest to Hood Canal, near Musqueti Point. The name is for a pioneer settler on the creek. An elier name, since discarded, was *Dry Creek.* USBGN)

Rene Creek (Lewis County) *see* Rainey Creek

Rene Valley (Lewis County) *see* Rainey Valley

Renner Lake *(S.24;T.38N;R.36E)*

Small lake 2-1/2 miles west of Columbia River at Barstow, Colville National Forest, northeast Ferry County. It was named for Gilbert Renne, a local homesteader, and is shown on some maps, in error, as *Penner Lake.* (USBGN)

Rennie Island *(T.17N;R.10W)*

A low, swampy, 300-acre island in Grays Harbor, between North and iddle channels, off the mouth of Hoquiam River, southwest Grays Harbor County. It was named for an early settler, who lived on the mainland to the south.

Renslow *(S.15;T.17N;R.20E)*

Railway station 10 miles east of Ellensburg, southeast Kittitas County. The name was "a chance selection," according to H. R. Williams, vice president of Chicago, Milwaukee & St. Paul Railway, who applied it in 1908.

Renton *(T.23N;R.5E)*

Once a coal-mining town, now an industrialized city, at the southeast end of Lake Washington, on flats formed by Cedar River and the former Black River, west central King County. In 1876, it was platted by Erasmus M. Smithers, and named for Capt. William Renton, a pioneer of 1853, who founded sawmills and coal mines in King and Kitsap counties. A very early name was *Black River Bridge.*

Renton Hill *(S.32;T.24N;R.4E)*

Hill directly southeast of Seattle's main business district, with the summit at 17th and East Madison streets, King County. It was named for Capt. William Renton, who owned much of the land on the hill, and founded Port Blakely Mill Company and Renton Coal Company. The hill has been called *Second Hill,* referring to Seattle's 12 "official" hills.

Republic *(S.6;T.36N;R.33E)*

Town in the old Eureka Gulch mining district, near the head of San Poil River at the confluence of Granite Creek, 25 miles south of the Canadian border, Ferry County. This town, the most important in the county, was once called *Republic Camp*; the area on Eureka Creek is sometimes called *Old Town* or *North Republic.* The dramatic history of Republic hinges around early-day mining. After a rich gold strike on Eureka Creek, the town was established by a group of 60 miners as *The Mining District of Eureka,* and platted by Philip Creasor. At about the same time, another rich strike was made on Granite Creek. By 1900, it had become the sixth city in eastern Washington, with the usual town facilities, including 28 saloons and 2 dance halls. The high producer was the Great Republic claim, discovered on March 5, 1896, by Thomas Ryan and Creasor. Postal authorities refused the name of Eureka for the post office because a town existed with that name in Clark County. The present name, proposed by citizens to

honor the Great Republic mining claim, was accepted.

Reser *(S.14;T.11N;R.35E)*

Railroad station 25 miles north of Walla Walla, north central Walla Walla County. It was named by Northern Pacific officials, for William P. Reser, a rancher who settled here in 1863.

Reservation *(S.10;T.20N;R.3E)*

A 33-acre reservation, once much larger, near Puyallup River in the eastern suburbs of Tacoma, northwest Pierce County. It was established on December 26, 1854. In 1886, the name *Indian Reserve Siding* was applied by Northern Pacific Railway officials. In 1890, they shortened it to the present form. (*see* Puyallup Indian Reservation)

Reservation Bay *(S.23;T.34N;R.1E)*

A southwest tip bay of Fidalgo Island, directly north of the west entrance to Deception Pass, extreme southwest Skagit County. The locally-applied name was reportedly chosen because of the bay's proximity to Swinomish Indian Reservation, although it is not actually on the reservation. An earlier name was *Bowman's Bay,* for an early settler.

Reservation Head *(S.26;T.34N;R.1E)*

South side head of Reservation Bay, Fidalgo Island, at the west end of Deception Pass, extreme southwest Skagit County. It is almost separated from the mainland at extreme high tides. This feature, not on most maps, borrowed its name from nearby Reservation Bay. In 1841, Cmdr. Charles Wilkes charted it as *Neguamos Island,* evidently having sighted it at very high tide. (*see* Reservation Bay)

Restoration Point *(S.11;T.24N;R.3E)*

A southeast point of Bainbridge Island, at the south entrance of Blakely Harbor, east Kitsap County. In 1792, it was named *Village Point* by Capt. George Vancouver. He altered his chart to the present name when he celebrated Restoration Day here on May 25, 1792, the 132nd anniversary of the restoration of the Stuart dynasty after Oliver Cromwell's death. In 1841, Cmdr. Charles Wilkes charted this feature as *Gorden Point,* for John Gorden, a quartermaster with the expedition. On some older maps it appears, in error, as *Garden Point.* A local name, no longer used, was *Bean's Point.*

Retreat Lake *(S.32;T.22N;R.7E)*

A small, isolated lake 2 miles east of Ravensdale, south central King County. In June 1923, the name was chosen by local residents, and sent to USBGN for approval. Previous names were *Fish Lake* and *Number 32 Lake*. (USBGN)

Retsil *(S.25;T.24N;R.1E)*

Community on the south shore of Sinclair Inlet, south of Bremerton and directly east of Port Orchard, east central Kitsap County. It was named by state officials when a veteran's home and hospital were established. The name is that of Gov. Ernest Lister, spelled in reverse.

Revere *(S.5;T.18N;R.39E)*

Town on Rock Creek, 30 miles northwest of Colfax, northwest Whitman County. It was named by H. R. Williams, vice president of Chicago, Milwaukee & St. Paul Railway, for the famous American patriot Paul Revere.

Rex *(S.11;T.29N;R.29E)*

Community 9 miles northwest of Grand Coulee Dam, northeast Douglas County. The name was chosen by the post office when postal facilities were installed, and apparently for no reason other than to have a short name.

Reynolds *(T.12N;R.5/*

An early sawmill town on Rock Creek, near Walville and Pacific County boundary, extreme west Lewis County. It was established before Walville and McCormick, and faded as a result of timber depletion. The town was named for J. W. Reynolds, who had a sawmill here in early settlement days.

Rhodesia Beach *(T.13N;R.10W)*

Beach extending from Goose Point on the north to Sandy Point on the south, on Willapa Bay, west central Pacific County. It was locally named for Leonard *Rhoades*, a Bay Center pioneer.

Rice *(S.22;T.34N;R.37E)*

Village on Cheweka Creek, 3/4 mile east of Columbia River, 13 miles southwest of Kettle Falls, west central Stevens County. In 1903, it was named for and founded by William Rice, who homesteaded here; the place had previously been a water-powered sawmill on Cheweka Creek. A general store and post office were established. In 1950, Rice had a destructive fire, after which some of the buildings were restored.

Rich Passage *(T.24N;R.2E)*

A V-shaped channel, 1/2 mile wide, with strong tidal currents, between Pt. Glover and the south end of Bainbridge Island, Kitsap County mainland. In 1841, Cmdr. Charles Wilkes named it *Rich's Passage*, for William Rich, a botanist with the expedition. On some older maps, it is shown as *Rich Pass* in error.

Richard Point (Pierce County) *see* Treble Point

Richardson *(S.14;T.34N;R.2W)*

A small rendezvous location for commercial fisherman on Jones Bay, at the south end of Lopez Island, southeast San Juan County. It was named for the first settler, George Richardson.

Richland *(Ts.9,10N;R.28E)*

City on the west bank of Columbia River, 10 miles northwest of Pasco, east central Benton County. In 1900, it was founded by Benjamin Rosencrance, a homesteader who bought land from Northern Pacific Railway Company. In 1905, a townsite was platted by H. M. Amon, and an irrigation canal was built, which watered 3,500 acres. An authoritative source states that, in 1904, the place was named for Nelson Rich, a landowner. Certain local residents claim that the name was applied because of the rich soil, with $6,000 realized from hops grown on 32 acres. A nickname is *The Atomic City*.

Richmond Beach *(S.2;T.26N;R.3E)*

Suburban waterfront on Puget Sound, near Snohomish County boundary, extreme northwest King County. On October 4, 1889, the place was named by E. W. Mills and John Pappendick, at the suggestion of local landowner John Spencer, who had formerly lived in Richmond, England.

Richmond Highlands
(S.6;T.26N;R.4E)

Residential community 2 miles east of Richmond Beach, 1 mile south of Snohomish County boundary, extreme northwest King County. In 1912, when a post office was established, the name was borrowed from nearby Richmond Beach. (*see* Richmond Beach)

Richmond Lake (Pierce County) *see* American Lake

Richmond Point (Pierce County) *see* Pt. Richmond

Rickey Canyon *(T.35N;R.37E)*

Canyon followed by a stream that heads on the west slope of Mingo Mountain, west central Stevens County; flows 7 miles northwest to join Columbia River at the site of an old town called Rickey, 7 miles north of Harvey. The name is for John Rickey, a well-known, early pioneer, who ran a trading post at the mouth of the canyon. A former name was *Rickey Creek*.

Rickey Creek (Stevens County) *see* Rickey Canyon

Rickey Rapids *(S.10;T.35N;R.37E)*

Once hazardous rapids 3 miles downstream from the mouth of Colville River, Stevens and Ferry counties. The rapids were tamed by flooding Columbia River to an elevation of 1,290 ft. by Grand Coulee Dam. When the Columbia was the arterial highway of the Inland Empire, small craft often portaged around these rapids. On April 21, 1826, they were named by David Douglas, a famous early-day botanist, for David Thompson of North West Company. Thompson was an outstanding geographer, surveyor and explorer, who charted much of northeast Washington for the fur traders, and, as Douglas records, "was the first person who ever descended the whole chain of the river from its source to the ocean." The present name was given by pioneers, for John Rickey, who lived at the rapids and had a trade store. Another name, found on maps dated as late as 1882, was *Grand Rapids*.

Ricksecker Point *(Mt. Rainier National Park)*

A flat-topped, arrow-shaped point between Paradise and Nisqually rivers, 1-1/2 miles beyond Glacier Bridge on Paradise Hwy., southwest corner of the park. Five glaciers are visible from this point. The feature was named for Eugene Ricksecker, a civil engineer, who made the original survey of Paradise Hwy. in 1904, and who was in charge of building the road for the Park Service. (USBGN)

Ridgefield *(S.19;T.4N;R.1E)*

Town on Willamette Meridian, 2 miles east of Columbia River, 12 miles north of Vancouver, east central Clark County. It was called *Union Ridge* until changed by postal officials in 1890 to the present name. It appropriately describes this town on a large field that covers a beautiful ridge.

Ridley Creek *(T.37N;R.7E.uns)*

The stream of the creek heads at Mazama Park, on southwest slope of Mt.Baker, central Whatcom County; flows west as the headwater of Middle Fork, Nooksack River. In 1905, it was named by Forest Supervisor C. H. Park of Mt. Baker National Forest, for Ranger Joseph Ridley, who worked in this district from 1910 to 1916, and almost drowned in this creek.

Ridley Lake *(S.18;T.40N;R.14E.uns)*

A 14-acre lake, elevation about 3,000 ft., between Ross Lake and Lightning Creek, Mt. Baker National Forest, northeast Whatcom County. (*see* Ridley Creek)

Riffe *(S.24;T.12N;R.3E)*

Town on Cowlitz River, 8 miles southwest of Morton, south central Lewis County. It is included in the flood basin of Mossyrock Dam. The town was named for Floyd L. Riffe, founder of the Primitive Baptist Church here in 1896; when a post office was established in 1897, he became the first postmaster. An earlier name, source unknown, was *Baugh.*

Riffle *(S.12;T.7N;R.36E)*

Settlement and railroad station 3 miles northeast of Walla Walla, southeast Walla Walla County. The place was named by officials of Oregon & Washington Territory Railroad, for the corporation's chief engineer, Frank Riffle.

Right Smart Cove *(S.24;T.26N;R.2W)*

A west shore cove of Dabob Bay, 6-1/2 miles south of Quilcene, southeast Jefferson County. The locally-applied name resulted from a conversation in pioneer days between a timber owner and Ed Brown, a logger, who was looking for a good log dump. The timber owner used the term "right smart" in reference to this cove for the purpose.

Riley Lake (Snohomish County) *see* Lake Riley

Rimrock Lake (Yakima County) *see* Tieton Reservoir

Ringgolds Channel (Skagit, San Juan counties) *see* Rosario Strait

Ringold *(S.36;T.12N;R.28E)*

Settlement on east bank of Columbia River, 25 miles northwest of Pasco, extreme west central Franklin County. The

name reportedly honors an early stockman, whose animals ranged in the adjoining country. An earlier name was *Koontz Flat.*

Ringold Point (Jefferson County) *see* Marrowstone Point

Rinker Point *(Ss.22,27;T.34N;R.9E)*

Point 5 miles south of Rockport, Mt. Baker National Forest, south central Skagit County. It was named by local settlers for nearby Rinker Creek, which was named for an 1880s homesteader at the creek's mouth.

Rio Canil (Clallam County) *see* Pysht River

Rio de Canel (Clallam County) *see* Twin River

Rio de Cuesta (Clallam County) *see* Lyre River

Rio de la Cruz *(T.29N;R.2W)*

The stream of the river heads on southeast Miller Peninsula, northwest Jefferson County; flows 3 miles northeast into Port Discovery Bay, south of Carr Point. In 1789, this name was used by Gonzalo Lopez de Haro when he placed a cross at the mouth of the stream. It does not appear on recent maps.

Rio de los Martires (Jefferson County) *see* Hoh River

Riparia *(S.30;T.30N;R.38E)*

Settlement in two parts, joined by a bridge over Columbia River, 18 miles north of Dayton, extreme southwest Whitman and Columbia counties. The post office is in Whitman County, the town's north side. Before the bridge was built, early names were *Texas City* and *Texas Ferry.* The present name was chosen by officials of Northern Pacific Railway Company for the station; it is from the Latin *Riparius*, meaning "river bank."

Ripple Island *(T.37N;R.4W)*

Small island surrounded by a reef in New Channel, between Spieden and Johns islands, northwest San Juan County. In 1859, the fairly descriptive name was placed on British Admiralty charts by Capt. Richards, R.N.

Ritzville *(S.23;T.19N;R.35E)*

Town 70 miles southwest of Spokane, in the center of a rich wheat-growing area, north central Adams County. In 1878, the site was home-

steaded by Philip Ritz, a wheat and fruit grower, who acquired 8,000 acres of agricultural land, and was a sub-contractor in railroad building. On December 22, 1880, the town was platted by affiliates of Northern Pacific Railway Company, and named for Ritz. Between 1891 and 1900, a large contingent of German-Russian farmers settled here.

River Homes *(S.29;T.27N;R.37E)*

Community consisting mostly of orchard tracts along Spokane River, opposite the mouth of Sand Creek, northeast Lincoln County. Not shown on recent maps, the name refers to the community's physical location. At one time, it had a post office under this name.

River Lyre (Clallam County) *see* Lyre River

Riverside *(S.25;T.35N;R.26E)*

Pioneer town on Okanogan River, 8 miles north of Omak, central Okanogan County. It was an important trading center during the days of extensive river navigation. The name is descriptive of the location.

Riverside State Park *(Ts.25,26N;R.42E)*

A 5,380-acre park on Spokane River, 3 miles northwest of Spokane, adjoining old Ft. George Wright, central Spokane County. It was once a favorite Indian fishing place before white men took it over. The name is descriptive of the park's location along the river.

Roaring Creek (No. 1) *(T.26N;R.16E)*

The stream of the creek rises in 3 lakes on east slope of Chiwaukum Mountains, southwest Chelan County; flows north 5-1/2 miles to Nason Creek, 2 miles east of Merritt Station. The locally-applied name appears to be unjustified, although the same name is appropriate for another creek with the same name, which is tributary to Entiat River, Chelan County.

Roaring Creek (No. 2) *(T.25N;Rs.19,20E)*

The stream of the creek rises in several branches in Entiat Mountains, southeast Chelan County; flows east to Entiat River, 5-1/2 miles northwest of Entiat. This local name seems appropriate, as the drainage area is subject to heavy rains and washouts. It should not be confused with a creek by the same name, which is tributary to Nason Creek, Chelan County.

Robber's Roost (Kittitas County) *see* Ellensburg

Robber's Roost (Stevens County) *see* Fruitland

Robe *(S.7;T.30N;R.7E)*

Small settlement 23 miles east of Marysville, near Stillaguamish River, central Snohomish County. It was once a lumber and shingle manufacturing center, and was named for the operator of one of the mills in the 1890s.

Robinson *(S.36;T.37N;R.18E.uns)*

Former mining camp on the road to Harts Pass through Chelan National Forest, 8-1/2 miles northwest of Mazama, northwest Okanogan County. It was named, along with a mountain, creek and pass in the vicinity, for James Robinson, who trapped here in the 1890s.

Robinson Mountain
(S.2;T.37N;R.18E)

A 8,738-ft. peak in North Cascade Primitive Area, 3-1/2 miles east of Cascade Mountain summit, 4-1/2 miles northwest of Robinson, northwest Okanogan County. (*see* Robinson)

Robinson Point
(Ss.14,23;T.22N;R.3E)

An east tip point of Maury Island, on East Passage, southwest King County. In 1841, it was named *Point Robinson* by Cmdr. Charles Wilkes, for R. P. Robinson, purser's steward on *Vincennes*. The name was reversed in subsequent mapping.

Roche Harbor (Bay) *(T.36N;R.4W)*

A northwest tip bay of San Juan Island, between Henry and San Juan islands, west central San Juan County. It is an excellent harbor for small craft. In 1858, the bay was named by British Admiralty Surveyor Capt. Richards, for Richard Roche, R.N., 3rd Lieut. in *HMS Satellite*, stationed here from 1857 to 1860. The Lummi Indian name was *Whal-lalk.*

Roche Harbor (Town)
(S.14;T.36N;R.4W)

Resort on the northwest tip of San Juan Island, on Roche Harbor bay, west central San Juan County. Once a very important center for lime and cement manufacture, it is now a haven for pleasure craft. (*see* Roche Harbor (bay))

Rochester *(S.32;T.16N;R.3W)*

Railroad junction and trade center 24

miles south of Olympia, on the edge of Bakers Prairie, southwest Thurston County. When a post office was established in 1890, the name chosen was *Key*, possibly referring to nearby Gate City. At one time, the town boasted a hotel, large store and 3 sawmills. In 1904, the present name was substituted at the suggestion of John L. Nye, who wanted to honor his home town in England.

Rock Creek *(Ts.29,30N;Rs.16,17E)*

The stream of the creek heads on the west slope of Entiat Mountains, northwest Chelan County; flows 11 miles south where it joins Chiwawa River as its largest tributary. This local name, applied to several streams in the state, refers to the many rocks in the creek's course.

Rock Creek *(S.12;T.4N;R.2E)*

Settlement 15 miles northeast of Vancouver, north central Clark County. In 1887, a post office was established as *Hopewell*; in 1903, however, it was abandoned. Before and after the operation of the post office, the accepted name of the settlement was its present form, referring to the creek on which it is located.

Rock Creek *(Ts.4,5N;Rs.2,3E)*

The stream of the creek heads north of Yacolt, north central Clark County; flows 7-1/2 miles southwest to East Fork, Lewis River. This locally-applied name, used for many streams in the state, is probably appropriate to most of the creeks in the Pacific northwest. The original Indian name, *Now-wow-ee*, would have been more distinctive.

Rock Creek *(Ts.3-6N;Rs.18,19E)*

The stream of the creek heads in Simcoe Mountains, southeast of Satus Pass, Klickitat County; flows southeast 25 miles to Columbia River near Fountain. This creek, like most streams in the state, has rocks in its course.

Rock Creek *(T.22N;R.42E)*

The stream of the creek rises in a fertile valley near Rockford, southeast Spokane County; flows 12 miles northwest to Latah Creek, near Duncan. The name is reasonably descriptive, as most of the creek bed is strewn with boulders. It should not be confused with a smaller Rock Creek in south central Spokane County.

Rock Creek *(T.23N;R.44E)*

The stream of the creek rises west of Freedom, south central Spokane County; flows 6-1/2 miles west to a small lake or pothole. The name could probably be justified for nearly any stream in the Pacific northwest.

Rock Creek (Lewis County) *see* Walville

Rock Creek (Spokane County) *see* Plaza

Rock Crusher Point *(Mt. Rainier National Park)*

Point on Sunset Park Hwy., 3-1/2 miles below Sunrise Point, northeast quarter of the park. From a parking area at the point, a wide view of the Cascades and of White River valley may be seen. Park officials state that several places in the park bear this unofficial name, applied here by a mapping crew when a rock crusher was in operation.

Rock Duncan (Clallam County) *see* Duncan Rock

Rock Island *(S.5;T.21N;R.22E)*

A very large rock island in Columbia River, 9 miles southeast of Wenatchee, between Douglas and Chelan counties. The name was applied long before the construction of Rock Island Dam. In 1881, Lieut. Thomas W. Symons named the adjoining rough waters *Rock Island Rapids*. This feature should not be confused with Rock Island in northwest Skagit County.

Rock Island (Town)
(S.29;T.22N;R.21E)

Community on the east bank of Columbia River, 2 miles upstream from Rock Island Dam, near the mouth of Rock Island Creek, southwest Douglas County. The original name was *Hammond*. It was renamed for Rock Island in Columbia River. (*see* Rock Island (island))

Rock Island (Skagit County) *see* Towhead Island

Rock Island Dam *(S.4;T.21N;R.22E)*

Hydroelectric dam in Columbia River, 10-1/2 miles southeast of Wenatchee, between Douglas and Chelan counties. Completed in 1931, it was built by Puget Sound Power & Light Company at the site of Rock Island Rapids and Rock Island (island), for which it was named. (*see* Rock Island)

Rock Island Rapids *(T.21N;R.22E)*

Scenic rapids, over 2 miles long, in

Columbia River, 12 miles below Wenatchee, between Douglas and Chelan counties. Local Indians called them *Squah-ah-shee*. In 1881, Lieut Thomas W. Symons applied the present name, for the nearby rock island in the river. (*see* Rock Island (island))

Rock Island Station (Douglas County) *see* Rock Island (town)

Rock Lake (*S.34;T.27N;R.15E*)

Lake at the head of Schilling Creek, Wenatchee National Forest, southwest Chelan County. It nestles in a rocky basin on the south slope of Rock Mountain, which prompted the name by Forest Supervisor A. H. Sylvester.

Rock Lake (*Ts.19,20N;Rs.40,41E*)

A 10-mile-long lake, average width 1/2 mile, 25 miles northwest of Colfax, north central Whitman County. It is the largest of a 3-lake chain which extends north into Spokane County. The south end is marshy, but the rest of the lake's perimeter consists of steep, rocky cliffs. Kamiakin, famous war chief of the Yakimas, spent his last days here, following the termination of the Indian wars. The name is descriptive of the lake's rocky terrain.

Rock Lake (*Ss.13,24;T.19N;R.40E*)

Platted but undeveloped townsite on Rock Creek, at the southwest end of Rock Lake (lake), northwest Whitman County. The name is for the lake which the plat adjoined. (*see* Rock Lake, Whitman County)

Rock Mountain (*S.27;T.27N;R.15E*)

A Wenatchee National Forest peak, elevation 7300-ft., on Nason Ridge, 5 miles east of Cascade Mountain crest, northwest Chelan County. In 1931, it was named by Forest Supervisor A. H. Sylvester, for Rock Lake which nestles in a rocky basin on its south slope. The peak is used as a forest fire lookout.

Rock Point (*S.28;T.35N;R.2W*)

A rather indistinct, rocky point in San Juan Channel, on the west shore of Lopez Island, 1/2 mile south of Fisherman Bay, south central San Juan County. In 1858, the descriptive name was placed on British Admiralty charts by Capt. Henry Richards, R.N.

Rock Quarry District (Clark County) *see* Prune Hill

Rock Quarry Lake (*S.5;T.19N;R.7E*)

A 1.4-acre lake in an abandoned

rock quarry, 3-1/2 miles southeast of Enumclaw, south central King County.

Rockcut (*S.2;T.39N;R.36E*)

Once a railroad station on Kettle River, 6 miles south of the Canadian boundary, extreme northeast Ferry County. In 1902, the station was established by Spokane Falls & Northern Railway, when they built northward up Kettle River. It was named by the railroad for an extensive rock cut made here along the right-of-way. At one time, it included a store, post office, and a few other town facilities; today it is little more than a name.

Rockdale (*S.18;T.22N;R.11E*)

Railroad station at the west portal of Milwaukee Railroad's Cascade 11,894-ft.-long tunnel, elevation 2,520 ft., 1-1/2 miles west of Cascade Mountain summit, east central King County. It was named by Milwaukee Railroad officials for the station's immediate surroundings which consist entirely of rock.

Rockdale Creek (*T.22N;R.11E*)

The stream of the creek heads in Rockdale Lake, at Cascade Mountain summit, 3 miles south of Snoqualmie Pass, King County; flows 1-1/4 mile west to South Fork, Snoqualmie River, near the west portal of Milwaukee Railroad's tunnel. It was named by The Mountaineers for nearby Rockdale. (USBGN) (*see* Rockdale)

Rockdale Lake (*T.22N;R.11E*)

Lake in Rockdale Creek, 3 miles south of Snoqualmie Pass, 1/2 mile west of Cascade Mountain summit, east central King County. It was named by The Mountaineers for Rockdale Creek and nearby Rockdale. (USBGN) (*see* Rockdale)

Rockford
(*Ss.28,29,32,33;T.23N;R.45E*)

Town on Rock Creek, 4 miles west of the Idaho boundary, southeast Spokane County. D. C. Farnsworth, who settled here in 1879, named it for several fords across Rock Creek in the town's vicinity. In 1900, the population was about 1,000, but now has diminished to about 1/2 its former size.

Rockland (Klickitat County) *see* Dallesport

Rocklyn (*S.28;T.25N;R.36E*)

Small community 5-1/2 miles west

of Davenport, central Lincoln County. It is on the edge of a rough, rocky area which extends 15 miles northwest to Creston. The name is for the town's physical location.

Rockpile Creek (*T.9N;Rs.44,45E*)

The stream of the creek rises directly west of Cloverland, central Asotin County; flows 6-1/2 miles northeast and east to George Creek. In the 1870s, it reportedly was named by pioneers. The creek has a very rocky bed, but no actual rock piles.

Rockport (*S.26;T.35N;R.9E*)

Community on the north bank of Skagit River, directly upstream from Sauk River's mouth, 32 miles east of Sedro-Woolley, central Skagit County. Near the turn of the century, the name was suggested by town residents for the post office, but has no particular significance.

Rockwell (*S.15;T.19N;R.38E*)

Railroad point 17 miles east of Ritzville, directly south of Mud Lake, northeast Adams County. The descriptive name refers to a well drilled here through solid rock for railroad water supply.

Rocky Bay (*S.20;T.36N;R.3W*)

A northeast shore bay of San Juan Island, on San Juan Channel, 5 miles northwest of Friday Harbor. In 1859, the descriptive name was placed on British Admiralty charts by Capt. Richards, R.N.

Rocky Creek (*T.29N;R.6W.part uns*)

The stream of the creek heads on the northeast slope of Rocky Peak, Olympic National Park, 6 miles southeast of Port Angeles, east central Clallam County; flows northeast about 3 miles to Lake Creek. The descriptive name was applied by local residents. (USBGN)

Rocky Creek (*T.37N;R.8E.uns*)

The stream of the creek rises at Baker Pass, on the south slope of Mt. Baker, south central Whatcom County; flows southeast to Lake Shannon, with a slight dip into north Skagit County. The descriptive name was locally chosen.

Rocky Peak (*T.29N;R.6W.uns*)

An Olympic National Park peak, elevation 6,218 ft., 8 miles south of Port Angeles, 2 miles east of Mt. Angeles, east central Clallam County. Evidently of local origin, this rather ordinary name would apply to almost any mountain in Olympic National Park. (USBGN)

Rocky Point *(S.11;T.30N;R.2E)*

An east entrance point to Holmes Harbor, in Saratoga Passage on south Whidbey Island, Island County. In 1841, the descriptive name, used frequently in the Pacific northwest, was chosen by Cmdr. Wilkes.

Rocky Point (Island County) *see* Point Demock

Rocky Point (Jefferson County) *see* Middle Point

Rocky Reach Dam *(T.24N;R.20E)*

An L-shaped, 1-mile-long dam in Columbia River, 7 miles north of Wenatchee, between Chelan and Douglas counties. Built by Chelan County PUD, it impounds a storage basin, called Lake Entiat, in Columbia River, to a distance of about 42 miles. The name, in use before the dam was built, was chosen as a descriptive term for the portion of Columbia River occupied by the dam.

Rodd Bay (Pierce County) *see* Oro Bay

Rodgers Island (San Juan County) *see* San Juan Island

Rodna *(S.20;T.21N;R.40E)*

Railroad station in Graves Township, 1 mile north of Downs Lake, extreme southwest Spokane County. It was first called *Ray* by railroad officials, for E. W. Ray, assistant engineer of the Spokane, Portland & Seattle Railway. The name was reported to have been changed to avoid confusion with Roy on the Northern Pacific Railway; the choice was apparently a chance selection.

Roesiger Lake *(Ss.16,21,28;T.29N;R.7E)*

A 352.2-acre lake, about 2 miles long and 15 ft. deep at the north end, 8-1/2 miles north of Monroe, west central Snohomish County. It was named for an early settler and timber operator.

Rogers Bar *(T.27N;R.35E)*

Gold-bearing river bar in Columbia River before flooding of the upper river by Grand Coulee Dam, at the west end of Elbow Bend, bordering southeast Ferry County. In the 1880s, it was heavily placer-mined for gold by Chinese, and again by local inhabitants during the 1930s great depression. It was named for an early prospector and homesteader.

Rogersburg *(S.13;T.7N;R.46E)*

Village at the junction of Snake and Grande Ronde rivers, 22-1/2 miles south of Clarkston, southeast Asotin County. In 1860s gold-rush days, this place became a way point when a ferry was installed to cross Grande Ronde River. In 1904, it was platted and named for G. A. Rogers, who owned the entire townsite.

Rolling Bay *(S.11;T.25N;R.2E)*

A scattered settlement of beach homes and small farms on the northeast shore of Bainbridge Island, east central Kitsap County. The first name was *Falk's Bay*, for Dona Falk, who claimed land here in 1876. On April 6, 1892, a post office was established and named *Rollins Bay*, for a local beach squatter. Inhabitants objected on the grounds that Rollins' character and habits were off-color, and changed the name to its present form. This pleasant name has no particular significance.

Rolling Bay City (Kitsap County) *see* Ferncliff

Rollins Bay (Kitsap County) *see* Rolling Bay

Rome *(S.27;T.9N;R.27E)*

Railroad station on the north slope of Horse Heaven Hills, 14 miles west of Kennewick, east central Benton County. In 1907, it was named by Northern Pacific Railway officials, evidently choosing a short name without any serious comparison between the place and the capitol of the Roman Empire.

Ronald *(S.7;T.26N;R.4E)*

Small community directly south of Richmond Highlands, on Pacific Hwy., extreme northwest King County. It was named for Judge J. T. Ronald of Seattle, a local landowner.

Ronald *(S.7;T.20N;R.15E)*

A coal-mining town on Roslyn field, 5 miles northwest of Cle Elum, northwest Kittitas County. It was named for Alexander Ronald, a Scot, who was superintendent of mines.

Roosevelt *(S.16;T.3N;R.21E)*

Village on Columbia River, southeast Klickitat County, opposite Arlington, Oregon. When platted, the town was named by T. B. Montgomery to honor Theodore Roosevelt, 26th president of the United States. Montgomery built stores, hotels and other structures, which he offered rent-free for one year to tenants.

Roosevelt Glacier *(T.38N;Rs.7,8E.uns)*

A northwest slope glacier of Mt. Baker, Mt. Baker National Forest, central Whatcom County. In 1906, it was named by The Mazamas, for President Theodore Roosevelt.

Roosevelt Lake (Stevens, Lincoln, Grant & Ferry Counties) *see* Franklin D. Roosevelt Lake

Roosevelt Park (King County) *see* Ravenna Park

Rosalia *(S.14;T.20N;R.43E)*

Town in Pine Creek Valley, 25 miles north of Colfax, north central Whitman County. By the early 1870s, the place was settled, and, on August 28, 1886, was platted as a townsite by John M. Whitman. When a post office was established, it was named for the wife of Rosalia's first postmaster, T. J. Favorite. About a mile south of Rosalia in Steptoe Memorial Park, a high monument, which is a state historical site, commemorates the May 17, 1858 defeat of military forces under Lieut. Col. Edward J. Steptoe by Palouse Indians.

Rosario *(S.31;T.37N;R.1W)*

Resort on the east shore of East Sound, at the head of Cascade Bay, northeast San Juan County. In 1890, it was founded by Andrew Newhall as a shingle, bolt and stave mill operation, which operated under the name Cascade Lumber Company. At that time, the post office was named *Newhall*. In 1905, Robert Moran, a prominent ship builder, bought Newhall's interest; on June 15, 1906, he changed the name to its present form. Moran built a remarkable estate, which has been a showplace for over a half-century. The name was taken from Rosario Strait. (*see* Rosario Strait)

Rosario Bay (San Juan County) *see* Cascade Bay

Rosario Head *(S.22;T.34N;R.1E)*

A small peninsula on the west side of Reservation Bay, southwest Fidalgo Island, on Rosario Strait, southwest Skagit County. It was named for Rosario Strait. A local name, which was a misnomer, was *Watsok Island*. (*see* Rosario Strait)

Rosario Hill *(S.31;T.37N;R.1W)*

Rocky hill, elevation 806 ft., on the east shore of East Sound, 1 mile north of Cascade Bay, northwest San Juan County. In 1858, the feature was charted as

Stony Hill by Capt. Richards, R.N. That name was changed by U.S. Coast Survey to the present, official designation, using the name of Rosario Strait. On older maps, it appears as *Mt. Rosario*. (USBGN) (*see* Rosario Strait)

Rosario Island (Pierce or San Juan County) *see* Fox Island

Rosario Strait (*Ts.34-36N;Rs.1W,1E*)

Strait extending north and south between the San Juan group, San Juan County, and the inland waters of Whatcom and Skagit counties; north from Strait of Juan de Fuca to Georgia Strait. (Note: check placement of San Juan County in description above.) In 1791, this body of water was named *Canal de Fidalgo* by Lieut. Eliza, for Lieut. Salvador Fidalgo. In 1847, Capt. Kellet applied the present name, which is a simplification of the name *Canal de Nuestra Senora del Rosario la Marinara*, given in 1790 by Manuel Quimper, for the patroness of the Spanish exploring ship *San Carlos*. In 1841, Cmdr. Wilkes applied the name *Ringgolds Channel*, for Cadwalader Ringgold, one of the expedition's officers. Other unofficial names were *Vancouver's Straits* and *Boca de Flon*. (USBGN)

Rosburg (*S.23;T.10N;R.8W*)

Hamlet on Grays River, 10 miles northwest of Skamokawa, west central Wahkiakum County. It was named for Christian Rosburg, the first postmaster.

Rose Creek (*Ts.15,16N;Rs.44,45E*)

The stream of the creek rises near Fallon, east central Whitman County; flows west 5 miles to Four Mile Creek, near Shawnee. It was named by the first settlers, for an abundance of wild roses growing along the creek.

Rose Point (Snohomish County) *see* Point Elliott

Rosedale (*S.2;T.21N;R.1E*)

Community on Lay Inlet, Henderson Bay, 3 miles west of Gig Harbor, northwest Pierce County. In 1883, it was named by W. E. White, a local resident, for the abundance of wild roses around the inlet.

Roslyn (*S.17;T.20N;R.15E*)

Town 3 miles northwest of Cle Elum, in the soft-coal belt of northwest Kittitas County. In 1880, the first settler, "Cayuse" Johnson, came here. In 1886, Northern Pacific Coal Company installed extensive mining operations; 6

years later, Roslyn produced 1,039,870 tons of coal, the largest output of any mine in the state. The name is said to have been chosen by Logan M. Bullitt, general manager of Northern Pacific Coal Company, for Roslyn, New York, the hometown of his sweetheart.

Ross (*S.13;T.25N;R.3E*)

Community and railroad station no longer in existence, in central Seattle, on the Ship Canal, present site of Seattle Pacific University, King County. It was named for John Ross, owner of the land, who patented his 1877 land claim. He had been a sergeant in Company A, Washington Territorial Volunteers, during the Indian wars.

Ross Dam (*S.35;T.38N;R.13E.uns*)

Huge hydroelectric dam in Skagit River, at the confluence of the river with Ruby Creek, southeast Whatcom County. It is the largest unit in the City of Seattle's development on the river. The original name was *Ruby Dam*, for Ruby Creek. The present name is for James Delmage Ross, who planned hydroelectric development of the Skagit River for Seattle City Lighting Dept.

Ross Lake (*Ts.37-40N;Rs.13,14E;& 1-1/2 m. in B.C.*)

An artificial lake, impounded for hydroelectric power development, in Skagit River above Ross Dam, extending 24 miles up Ruby and Beaver creeks, tributaries of Skagit River, northeast Whatcom County; and 1-1/2 miles into British Columbia. The flood area included 17,000 acres, of which 11,678 were in Whatcom County. The original name was *Ruby Lake*. (*see* Ross Dam)

Ross Mountain (Whatcom County) *see* Mt. Ross

Ross Pass (*S.8;T.32N;R.14E.uns*)

A 6,400-ft. pass at Cascade Mountain summit, at the head of Spruce Creek to the east, and the head of Sulphur Creek to the west, extreme northeast Snohomish County. It was named for Alexander Ross, a fur trader employed by North West Company in 1814, when he was reputed to be the first white man to cross the pass.

Round Island (*S.31;T.11N;R.10W*)

A 2-acre island 1 mile south of Long Island in Willapa Bay, southwest Pacific County. Most of the island is covered with spruce trees and brush, and was once an Indian burial ground. In 1858,

the descriptive name was applied by U.S. Coast Survey. It appears on some recent maps as *Baby Island*.

Round Lake (*S.19;T.28N;R.8W.uns*)

One of 8 lakes in Seven Lakes Basin, covering less than 3 acres, Olympic National Park, south central Clallam County. The name is reasonably descriptive of this almost-round lake.

Round Lake (*S.24;T.3N;R.1W*)

A 16-acre lake between Lake River and Columbia River's main channel, 8 miles northwest of Vancouver, southwest Clark County. Viewed from either end, the lake might appear round, but is actually oblong. This lake should not be confused with a large lake by the same name, 1 mile north of Camas.

Round Lake (*S.2;T.1N;R.3E*)

A 32-acre lake comprising the southeast part of Lacamas Lake, separated from the larger lake by a narrow neck of land, 1 mile north of Camas, southeast Clark County. Evidently, the name was a pioneer term for any lake which wasn't square. It should not be confused with Round Lake, 8 miles northwest of Vancouver.

Round Lake (*S.7;T.32N;R.36E*)

Small, round lake 6 miles west of Inchelium, Colville Indian Reservation, east central Ferry County.

Round Lake (*S.31;T.25N;R.8W.uns*)

A 2-1/2-acre lake near the head of Tshletshy Creek, Olympic National Park, southeast Jefferson County. The name is descriptive of the lake's shape.

Round Lake (Chelan County) *see* Domke Lake

Round Lake (Skamania County) *see* Lake Sahalee-Tyee

Round Mountain (*S.35;T.27N;R.16E*)

A Wenatchee National Forest peak between Wenatchee Lake and Nason Creek, at the head of Plainview Creek, west central Chelan County. It has a broad, round top, which accounts for the name applied by Forest Supervisor A. H. Sylvester.

Round Pass (*Mt.Rainier National Park*)

A 3,879-ft. pass near the west end of Emerald Ridge, at the head of Fish Creek, 1 mile north of Lake George, southwest quarter of the park. A superb view of Puyallup Glacier may be seen from the pass, which is used as a forest fire lookout in season. The name, applied by park packers, describes the contour of the pass at a central point. (USBGN)

Roundup Park *(T.33N;R.26E)*

Community park on Woody Island in Okanogan River, directly south of Okanogan, Okanogan County. The name reflects the nature of county-wide celebrations held in the park, which feature rodeos, horse racing and riding.

Roundy Creek *(T.26N;R.19E)*

The stream of the creek rises on Wenatchee National Forest, central Chelan County; flows from the west to Entiat River, 3 miles north of Ardenvoir. It was named for an early settler at the creek's mouth.

Rowles Bay (Kitsap County) *see* Rolling Bay

Rowley Chasm *(T.37N;R.16E.uns)*

A series of rough, precipitous creek canyons south of Canyon Creek, northwest of McKay Ridge, southeast Whatcom County. It was named for Jack Rowley, who, in 1872, prospected here and on Ruby Creek.

Roxboro *(S.24;T.17N;R.31E)*

Station 12 miles west of Lind, on Lind Coulee, west central Adams County. It was named by Milwaukee Railway officials, presumably for a town of that name in another part of the country, possibly North Carolina.

Roy *(S.34;T.18N;R.2E)*

Small town on Lacamas Creek, directly south of Ft. Lewis Army Post, west Pierce County. When a railway station was established in 1884, Northern Pacific Railway officials called the town *Media*. In 1889, it was changed to the present name, for the son of James McNaught, general counsel for Northern Pacific.

Roy Lake (Pierce County) *see* Muck Lake

Royal Basin *(T.27N;R.4W)*

Basin at the head of Royal Creek, south of Greywold Ridge, Olympic National Park, north central Jefferson County. In 1890, the name was given by the O'Neil Expedition, according to reports. The reason for the name is not evident.

Royal City *(S.3;T.16N;R.25E)*

Town 3 miles north of Smyrna, 15 miles southwest of Potholes Reservoir, southwest Grant County. It was platted by Albert Widmer, J. C. Freeman, and A. Schott, all of Worden. The name was chosen as a high-sounding title for a new townsite.

Royal Creek *(Ts.26,27N;R.15E)*

The stream of the creek heads on the south slope of Mt. Mastiff, Wenatchee National Forest, southwest Chelan County; flows 2-1/2 miles southeast to Nason Creek. This creek, and adjacent Schilling and Crescent creeks, were named for popular brands of baking powder by Forest Supervisor A. H. Sylvester.

Royal Lake *(S.17;T.27N;R.4W)*

Lake in Royal Basin, at the head of Royal Creek, 15-1/2 miles west of Quilcene, Olympic National Park, east Jefferson County. (*see* Royal Basin)

Roza *(S.16;T.15N;R.19E)*

Community 20 miles north of Yakima, at the junction of Roza Creek and Yakima River, southeast Kittitas County. It is the site of a diversion dam in Roza Irrigation Project, which waters 72,000 acres. The first name applied to this town was *Pato*, by Northern Pacific Railway officials. In 1887, it was changed to the present name, for one of the official's daughters.

Ruby *(S.29;T.35N;R.25E)*

Ghost town in the old Salmon River mining district, on lower Salmon Creek, 3 miles south of Conconully Reservoir, central Okanogan County. In 1885, it was founded by prospectors and miners, and named for nearby Ruby Mine, by Thomas D. Fuller, part owner of the mine. The mine, in turn, was named for a small creek in which miners found rubies. The town was formerly called *Ruby City*. Famous author Owen Wister referred to the place as "The Babylon of the West," because of its wild activities during mining boom days. In 1900, the town was almost destroyed by fire.

Ruby *(S.19;T.35N;R.44E)*

Settlement on the west bank of Pend Oreille River, 26 miles northwest of Newport, central Pend Oreille County. For many years, a ferry crossed the river from this place. When the post office was established in 1905, it was named for a number of rubies found in Ruby Creek, 2-1/2 miles west.

Ruby *(S.36;T.38N;R.13E)*

Once a mining town and supply point, now under water in Ross Lake, on upper Skagit River, at the mouth of Ruby Creek, near the present location of Ross Dam, Whatcom County. In the days of mining excitement, it was called *Ruby City*. (*see* Ruby Creek)

Ruby City (Whatcom County) *see* Ruby

Ruby City (Okanogan County) *see* Ruby

Ruby Creek *(T.37N;R.14E.uns)*

The stream of the creek is formed by Granite Creek, which flows northwest from Skagit County, and Canyon Creek, rising at Cascade Mountain summit, Whatcom County; flows 6-1/2 miles to Ross Lake, through the old Ruby Creek mining district. In 1872, it was named by 3 prospectors, who were placer mining on the creek, and found what they thought was a ruby. The stone was identified as a garnet, but the creek kept the name of Ruby. In 1879-80, the creek was a famous gold producer.

Ruby Dam Reservoir (Whatcom County) *see* Ross Lake

Ruby Lake (Whatcom County) *see* Ross Lake

Rudd (Snohomish County) *see* Machias

Ruff *(S.1;T.19N;R.30E)*

Townsite on Rocky Coulee, 12 miles east of Moses Lake, extreme east central Grant County. It was named for Cottlieb Ruff, a pioneer homesteader, on whose property the town was platted. It never became much of a settlement.

Rufus Woods Lake *(T.29N;Rs.25-28E)*

A 72,000-acre lake behind Chief Joseph Dam in Columbia River, between Okanogan County to the north and Douglas County to the south. On July 9, 1952, it was officially named by act of Congress, for Rufus Woods of Wenatchee, a dynamic newspaper publisher, who was called "the father of Grand Coulee Dam."

Rush Ridge (Mt. Rainier National Park) *see* Rust Ridge

Rusk Creek *(T.8N;R.11E)*

The stream of the creek rises in Rusk Glacier, on east slope of Mt. Adams, southwest Yakima County; flows east by south 4-1/2 miles to Big Muddy Creek. In August 1901, it was named by Prof. Harry Fielding Reid of Johns Hopkins University, for C. E. Rusk, who helped him explore Mt. Adams. In 1890, Rusk had explored the mountain with his mother and sister, and had written *Tales of a Western Mountaineer.* An earlier name was *Rusk River.*

Rusk Glacier *(T.8N;R.11E.uns)*

An east slope glacier of Mt. Adams, at the head of Rusk Creek, southwest Yakima County. In 1890, it was explored by C. E. Rusk. (*see* Rusk Creek)

Rusk River (Yakima County) *see* Rusk Creek

Russell *(S.32;T.8N;R.36E)*

Settlement 4 miles north of Walla Walla, southeast Walla Walla County. It was first called *Russell's Station,* for Patrick Russell, an early settler. Later, it was shortened to its present form.

Russell Cliff *(Mt. Rainier National Park)*

A 13,000-ft. cliff east of Liberty Cap, 3/4 mile north of Mt. Rainier summit, central area of the park. During a 1909 ascent to the summit, it was named by The Mountaineers, for Prof. I. C. Russell, a mountaineer and scientist. (USBGN)

Russell Creek *(Ts.6,7N;Rs.36,37E)*

The stream of the creek rises near Kooskooskie, extreme southeast Walla Walla County; flows northwest and west 16 miles to Yellowhawk Creek, southeast of College Place. It was named for Charles Russell, who, in 1889, settled here.

Russell Glacier *(Mt. Rainier National Park)*

A north slope glacier of Mt. Rainier, adjoining Carbon Glacier on the west as a short tributary, northwest zone of the park. The ice river was named by The Mountaineers, for Prof. I. C. Russell, a mountaineer and scientist. (USBGN)

Russell Lake (Thurston County) *see* Chambers Lake

Russell Landing (Clark County) *see* Image

Russell Ridge *(T.14N;Rs.12,13E.uns)*

Curved ridge, approximately 8 miles long, with maximum elevation 6,788 ft. at McNeil Peak, north and west of Tieton Reservoir, Snoqualmie National Forest, northwest Yakima County. It was named for John Russell, a school teacher who homesteaded in the Tieton Basin in early years. It is reported that he shot himself because his own children were too retarded to enter school.

Russell's Station (Walla Walla County)

see Russell

Russian Creek *(Ss.4-7;T.40N;R.43E)*

The stream of the creek flows through the northwest corner of Pend Oreille County, from Stevens County into British Columbia. It was locally named for Russians who mined here in early days. (USBGN)

Rust Ridge *(Mt. Rainier National Park)*

A 5,000-ft. ridge extending north from Arthur Peak, between Ranger and Fall creeks, northwest corner of the park, just south of the park boundary. The feature was named for W. R. Rust, a prominent Tacoma citizen. (USBGN)

Rustler Creek (Jefferson County) *see* Rustler River

Rustler River *(T.25N;Rs.6,7W)*

The stream of the river rises in Olympic National Park, south central Jefferson County; flows southwest to North Fork, Quinault River. The source of this pioneer name has not been located. On some maps it appears as *Rustler Creek.*

Ruston *(S.23;T.21N;R.2E)*

"City within a city" in the northwest extremity of Tacoma, directly southeast of Point Defiance Park, Pierce County. In 1890, W. R. Rust established Tacoma Smelting & Refining Company, and named the place *Smelter.* On October 22, 1906, residents voted to change to the present name, honoring Rust.

Ruth Creek *(S.20;T.39N;R.10E.uns)*

The stream of the creek heads at Hannegan Pass, north central Whatcom County; flows 8 miles west to North Fork, Nooksack River, Mt. Baker National Forest. In 1893, the creek and a nearby mountain were named by Banning Austin, for Ruth Cleveland, newborn daughter of President Grover Cleveland.

Ruth Mountain *(Ts.39,40N;Rs.9,10E.uns.)*

A 7,500-ft. peak, extending from Hannegan Pass to North Fork, Nooksack River, northeast Whatcom County. In 1893, the peak was named by Banning Austin for Ruth Cleveland, daughter of President Grover Cleveland, at her birth.

Ruth Prairie *(S.21;T.16N;R.1E)*

Prairie 1-1/2 miles south of Rainier, south central Thurston County. In pioneer days, it was named for B. F. Ruth,

one of the first settlers in the vicinity.

Ruud Canyon *(T.24N;R.22E)*

Draw 3 to 4 miles south of Waterville, southwest Douglas County. It was locally named for Ole Ruud, who settled here in May 1883, and established a prosperous ranch.

Ryan *(S.10;T.38N;R.38E)*

Station on the east bank of Columbia River, between Bossburg and Marble, northwest Stevens County. When a Spokane Falls & Northern Railway line was built through this area in 1896, a post office and station were established. A cable ferry ran across the river to the mouth of Flat Creek. The name was applied by local settlers, for Daniel Ryan, the original homesteader. The railroad used the same name for its station.

Ryan Hill *(S.25;T.38N;R.34E)*

A 5,692-ft. mountain 16 miles northeast of Republic, Colville Indian Reservation, north central Ferry County. It was named for an early-day trapper, who built a cabin on the mountain and lived here for many years.

Ryan Point *(T.2N;R.1E)*

A north bank point of Columbia River, 1-1/2 miles above Columbia River, southwest Clark County. It was locally named for William Ryan, who took a Donation Land Claim here in the early 1850s.

Ryder Channel (Pierce County) *see* Balch Passage

Ryderwood *(S.3;T.10N;R.3W)*

Community in logged-off foothills on Campbell Creek, extreme northwest Cowlitz County. It was formerly a logging headquarters camp for Long-Bell Lumber Company, housing about 700 men; now it is a a town of retired persons, whose homes are remodeled camp buildings. It was named by officials of the lumber company, for W. F. Ryder, a company employee for 35 years.

Ryderwood Pond *(S.3;T.10N;R.3W)*

Artificial lake in a branch of Campbell Creek, east Ryderwood, northwest Cowlitz County. It is used for local water supply. (*see* Ryderwood)

Rye*(S.19;T.16N;R.22E)*

Station 21 miles southeast of Ellensburg, near Johnson Creek, southeast Kittitas County. It was named by Chicago, Milwaukee & St. Paul Railway officials, for Rye, New York, although the resemblance is not striking.

Rye Grass Coulee
(Ss.17,18;T.11N;R.31E)

Coulee 5 miles north of Sagemoor, 2 miles southeast of Eltopia, central Franklin County. The name is descriptive, as native rye grass maintains a successful growth in this area, wherever sufficient soil depth is present.

Rye Grass Flat *(T.12N;Rs.32,33)*

Prairie extending about 7 miles from Connell Road east to Ray Road, north central Franklin County. (*see* Rye Grass Coulee)

S

Sacajawea Lake (Cowlitz County) *see* Lake Sacajawea

Sacajawea State Park
(S.3;T.8N;R.30E)

A 19-acre state park, 6 miles southeast of Pasco, directly north of the confluence of Snake and Columbia rivers, extreme south central Franklin County. The City of Pasco donated the acreage to establish this park which offers, among other attractions, an excellent museum specializing in Indian artifacts. The name is for a Shoshone Indian woman who accompanied the Lewis and Clark Expedition as the wife of Touissaint Charbonneau, a French-Canadian interpreter and guide. Her name has been spelled *Sacajawea* in most of the histories and other publications which refer to this famous expedition. Although the USBGN has ruled that the correct spelling should be *Sacagawea,* the more popular version is used for this park.

Sachal (Thurston County) *see* Black River; Black Lake

Sachap (Satchap) River (Grays Harbor County) *see* Satsop River

Sachem Point (Skagit County) *see* March Point

Saddle Butte *(Ss.19,20;T.7N;R.43E)*

An Umatilla National Forest butte, elevation 5,873 ft., 1 mile east of Garfield County boundary, extreme southwest Asotin County. It was named by local stockmen for a fancied resemblance to a saddle. Henry Hansen, a local resident, calls this feature *Saddlehorn Mountain,* and has made a careful sketch to prove that the mountain's outline resembles a saddle horn.

Saddle Mountains
(Ts.15,16N;Rs.21-27E)

This relatively low mountain range, with peaks less than 3,000 ft. high, extends east-west 26 miles across the southwest portion of Grant County to the Columbia River. It resumes westward 13 miles across the southeast corner of Kittitas County to within 10 miles of the Yakima River. The maximum elevation -- Wahatis Peak, southwest Grant County -- is 2,696 ft. The Indian name for the range was *Swalla-la-Hoost* The name *La-cos-tum* was applied to the mountains near Priest Rapids, south of Crab Creek. This present name derives from the saddle-like shape of many of the elevations.

Saddlebag Island *(S.9;T.35N;R.2E)*

An island directly north of Hat Island, at the entrance to Padilla Bay, northwest Skagit County. This island, with nearby Dot and Huckleberry Islands, was charted as *Las Tres Hermanas* by Dionisio Galiana in 1790. In 1841, the same island group was called *Porpoise Rocks* by Cmdr. Charles Wilkes. This present name was charted by U.S. Coast & Geodetic Survey for a vague resemblance to saddlebags.

Saddlehorn Mountain (Asotin County) *see* Saddle Butte

Sage *(S.22;T.5N;R.25E)*

Railroad point on north bank of Columbia River, opposite Blalock Island, southwest Benton County. It was named by local ranchers and railroad officials for the prevailing type of vegetation.

Sage Valley (Yakima County) *see* Waneta

Sagemoor *(S.33;T.11N;R.30E)*

Station 11 miles north of Pasco, southwest Franklin County. The original name was *Sagewood,* but this was changed in 1902, by officials of Northern Pacific Railway Company to the present name. Either name appears quite appropriate, as Artemisia, commonly known as sagebrush, covers many miles of the landscape.

Sagewood (Franklin County) *see* Sagemoor

Saghalie *(T.26N;R.8E)*

The stream of the creek rises on the west slope of Mt. Meany, Olympic National Park, central Jefferson County; flows 5 miles west to Queets River. This Chinook Indian name has the meaning of "top, highest," or "upper." An alternate, unofficial name is *Sahale Creek.* (USBGN)

Saginaw *(S.13;T.17N;R.6W)*

Area on Chehalis River, 3 miles southeast of Elma, southeast Grays Harbor County. The name is for Saginaw Timber Company of Aberdeen, who used this area for logging headquarters. The company originated in Saginaw, Michigan.

Sahale Mountain *(T.35N;R.15E)*

A 8,850-ft. peak on the Cascade Mountain summit, between Chelan and Skagit counties, 2 miles northeast of Cascade Pass, at the head of Stehekin River. This high peak was named by the Mazamas with the Chinook word which means "away up high." A former name was *Boston Peak.*

Sahaptin River (Whitman, Franklin, Walla Walla, Columbia, Garfield, and Asotin counties) *see* Snake River

Sah-da-ped-thl *(S.5;T.33N;R.15W)*

A group of rocks along the south shore of the Strait of Juan de Fuca, directly west of Kydikabbit (Kiddekubbut) Point, on Makah Indian Reservation, northwest Clallam County. Evidently no name other than the original Indian designation has been applied to these dangerous rocks.

Sahpenis (Yakima County) *see* Toppenish Creek

Sail River *(T.33N;R.15W)*

The stream of the river rises near the east boundary of Makah Indian Reservation, northwest Clallam County; flows 5-1/2 miles north to the Strait of Juan de Fuca near Sail and Seal rocks. It was named for Sail Rock, 1 mile east of its mouth. Former names are *Okho River*, charted by Capt. Henry Kellett in 1847, and *Tocosos River*, as mapped by U.S.C.&G.S. in later years.

Sail Rock *(S.17;T.33N;R.14W)*

A sharp-pointed rock, elevation less than 100 ft., in the Strait of Juan de Fuca, 2-3/4 miles east of Waada Island, 1/4 miles southeast of Seal Rock, northwest Clallam County. In 1841, this rock was named by the Wilkes Expedition because of its sail-like shape and light color. George Davidson of the U.S. Coast Survey charted it, some years later, as *Inner Rock*, referring to its position with relation to nearby Seal Rock. A name used on some early maps was *Klaholah*. The Makah Indians called this rock *Kaithl-ka-ject*. (USBGN)

St. Andrews *(S.33;T.26N;R.27E)*

Settlement 7 miles north of Sun Lakes State Park, at Dry Falls, east central Douglas County. In 1890, it was named for Capt. James St. Andrews, an early settler and the first postmaster.

St. Andrews Creek *(Mt. Rainier National Park)*

The stream of the creek rises in Saint Andrews Park, between North and South Puyallup rivers, west slope of Mt. Rainier, west central park area.(see Falls of Saint Andrews)

St. Andrews Park *(Mt. Rainier National Park)*

A park at the headwaters of Saint Andrews Creek, between the headwaters of North and South Puyallup Rivers, southwest zone of the park. (USBGN) (*see* Falls of Saint Andrews)

St. Andrews Park Lake *(Mt. Rainier National Park)*

Less than 1 acre lake, at the head of St. Andrews Creek, 5 miles southwest of Mt. Rainier summit. (*see* Saint Andrews Park)

St. Andrews Rock *(Mt. Rainier National Park)*

A 11,562-ft. rock, west slope of Mt. Rainier, at the entrance to Sunset Amphitheatre, between Puyallup and Tahoma glacier, directly southwest of Liberty Cap, central area of the park. (USBGN) (*see* Falls of Saint Andrews)

St. Clair Island (Skagit County) *see* Sinclair Island

St. Elmo Pass *(Mt. Rainier National Park)*

A 7,415-ft. pass through the ridge *which divides Winthrop and Inter Glaciers*, north slope of Mt. Rainier, central zone of the park. In 1887, this pass was named by Maj. E. S. Ingraham, when he camped on the ridge with a party of climbers. During an electrical storm, ''St. Elmo's Fire'' appeared on alpenstocks, ice axes, cooking utensils, and even around the heads of the campers. (USBGN)

St. Francis Regis Mission *(S.21;T.36N;R.38E)*

This early Jesuit mission is 2 miles east of Kettle Falls, northwest Stevens County. In 1870, it was established by Fathers Grassi, Menetrey, and Bandini. By 1902, the mission had 9 teachers and 150 scholars. When the post office was established, the name of *Goodwin* was used, which later was changed to *Ward*, both names being for local settlers. The Spokane Falls & Northern Railway used the same name for its station. Therefore, the name of the place has appeared on various maps as *Goodwin Mission*, *Goodwin Station*, and *Ward P.O.*. The name chosen by the Jesuit fathers still applies to the mission.

St. Francis Xavier Mission *(Ts.11, 12N;R.1W)*

An active mission on a Donation Land Claim, 6 miles south of Marys Corner, southeast Lewis County. This is the site of the first Roman Catholic Church in Washington. Here also is St. Marys Academy. It was named for a Catholic saint by Father Francis Norbert Blanchet when he established the mission in 1838, assisted by missionaries from Canada. It is called *Cowlitz Mission* by some local residents.

St. Helens *(S.23;T.10N;R.2E)*

Small community near North Fork, Toutle River, 19 miles, northeast of Castle Rock, northeast Cowlitz County. It was named for Mt. St. Helens, 20 miles to the southeast.

St. Helens Lake *(S.34N;T.10N;R.5E)*

A Gifford Pinchot National Forest peak, elevation 4, 567 ft., 7 miles north of Mt. St. Helens summit, extreme northwest Skamania County. This scenic lake covers 79 acres and was named for the mountain. The area is badly damaged by the May, 1980 eruption.

St. Helens Reach *(T.8N;R.5W)*

A portion of Columbia River along its north bank, east and west of Cape Horn, adjoining the southeast corner of Wahkiakum County. This name is not carried on recent maps, but in 1841, it was charted by Cmdr. Charles Wilkes. (*see* Mt. St. Helens)

St. Ignatius Mission *(S.17;T.33N;R.44E)*

Once a Catholic mission, long since destroyed by flood, on the Kalispel Indian Reservation, east side of Pend Oreille River, 2 miles northeast of Cusick, Pend Oreille County. In 1845, it was established by Fathers Pierre Jean DeSmet and Adrien Hoecken.

St. John (Clark County) *see* Hidden

St. John *(S.1;T.18N;R.41E)*

Town on Pleasant Valley Creek, 18 miles northwest of Colfax, north central Whitman County. In 1888, the name was chosen by officials of O.R.&N. Company, for E. T. St. John, an early settler and landowner.

St. Joseph's Mission *(T.18N;R.2W)*

This old mission, long since vanished, was established on Budd Inlet, 1 mile north of Olympia, by Rev. Pascal Ricard, O.M.I. in 1848. He chose the name of a Roman Catholic saint.

St. Joseph's Mission *(S.14;T.12N;R.16E)*

An Indian mission in Ahtanum Valley, 16-1/2 miles southwest of Yakima, central Yakima County. In 1847, this mission was established and named by the Oblate Fathers. In 1855, Oregon Volunteers destroyed the buildings during the Indian wars, because they found a keg of powder which had been buried to conceal it from Indians. In 1870, the buildings were replaced.

St. Louis (Island County) *see* Freeland

St. Louis *(S.10;T.29N;R.2E)*

This boom town of the early 1890s existed mostly on paper, and was on the site of Freeland, at the south end of Holmes Harbor, Whidbey Island, Island County. The impressive name was chosen by Nathaniel Hilton and George B.

Morrison, who platted the town in 1890.

St. Martin Hot Springs
(S.22;T.3N;R.8E)

Hot springs on west bank of Wind River, opposite the mouth of Little Wind River, south central Skamania County. The St. Martin family, of Indian and Hawaiian blood, settled about 1880 and developed the springs as a health resort. Descendants still reside here.

St. Martin Lake *(S.30;T.3N;R.9E.uns)*

A 1-acre lake, 4-1/2 miles east of Carson, southeast Skamania County. (*see* St. Martin Hot Springs)

St. Marys Farm *(S.7;T.33N;R.27E)*

Farm settlement on the Colville Indian Reservation, 2-1/2 miles to the east of St. Marys Mission, 5 miles east of Okanogan, Okanogan County. The settlement was established in connection with the mission and the post office was called *Mission*.

St. Marys Mission *(S.9;T.33N;R.27E)*

A Colville Indian Reservation mission, on Omak Creek, 5 miles southeast of Omak, central Okanogan County. In 1889, it was founded by Father Etienne Stephen de Rouge, a French Jesuit missionary. The name source is obvious.

St. Michaels Mission *(T.26N;R.43E)*

Catholic mission first established on Peone Prairie in 1877 by Father Cataldo; later moved to a site near Hillyard, directly northeast of Spokane. The name chosen was that of a Catholic saint.

St. Pauls Chapel *(S.11;T.36N;R.37E)*

A very early Jesuit chapel on a high plateau, close to the site of Kettle Falls, in the Columbia River, east bank of that river, northwest Stevens County. This chapel is the second established in the state. The falls were drowned in the basin created by Grand Coulee Dam, but the chapel is above the 1,290-ft. flood line. In 1845, it was built by Father Anthony Ravalli at the request of Colville tribal leaders, who had appealed to Father De Smet. In 1865, it was restored and reopened by Father Louis Vercruysse. The chapel has also undergone recent restoration as an historical site, and is so marked, although it is no longer used as a chapel. In early pioneer days, when Fort Colvile was operating nearby, and when several eastern Washington tribes fished annually at Kettle Falls, the chapel was an important point of worship.

St. Peter Creek *(T.38N;Rs.33-34E)*

The stream of this north fork of the creek heads on the west slope of Profanity Mountain, southwest of Taylor Ridge, north central Ferry County; the south fork heads on west slope of Stickpin Hill, 3-1/2 miles to the southwest. Each fork flows west to join 2 miles south of Malo; the combined stream then flows 2 miles northwest to Curlew Creek at St. Peter Flat. The name, like that of the flat, is for an Indian family that was prominent here in the early days.

St. Peter Flat *(Ss.11-12;T.38N;R.33E)*

This rather extensive flat is on the east side of Curlew Creek, at the mouth of St. Peter Creek, directly south of Malo, north central Ferry County. It is on the Colville Indian Reservation. (*see* St. Peter Creek)

Saints Rest (Jefferson County) *see* Chevy Chase, Tukey

Sakpam River (King County) *see* Duwamish River

Salal Prairie *(Ss.18,19;T.23N;R.9E)*

A large prairie 4 miles southeast of North Bend, north bank of South Fork, Snoqualmie River, central King County. The prairie was once largely planted to hops. A very small settlement by the same name is located west of the prairie. The name is for very abundant growths of salal brush.

Saleesh (Pend Oreille County) *see* Pend Oreille River

Salkum *(S.13;T.12N;R.1E)*

Community 12 miles northeast of Toledo, near Mill Creek, central Lewis County. At one time Salkum had 2 sawmills and was a lively town, but timber depletion closed the mill and crippled the settlement. The Indian name means ''boiling,'' and refers to the turbulent waters at the falls of nearby Mill Creek.

Salkum Creek (Lewis County) *see* Mill Creek)

Sallie's Lake (Whatcom County) *see* Rock Lake

Salmon Bank *(T.34N;R.2W)*

Almost a mile of shoals, as shallow as 1-2 fathoms, 1/2 mile south of the southeast tip of San Juan Island, Strait of Juan de Fuca, extreme south central San Juan County. In 1854, the name was given by U.S. Coast Survey. It is quite appropriate, as migrating salmon pass this point in large numbers each year.

Salmon Bay *(T.25N;R.3E)*

A west end bay of Lake Washington Ship Canal in Seattle, extending west to the Hiram Chittenden Locks from Ballard Bridge, King County. The bay was named by Arthur A. and David T. Denny, for the heavy salmon run in Salmon Creek, now included in the Lake Washington Ship Canal and in Salmon Bay. This bay should not be confused wiht Shilshole Bay, which is outside the locks to the west. (USBGN)

Salmon Bay City (King County) *see* Ballard

Salmon City (Okanogan County) *see* Conconully

Salmon Creek *(Ts.28-29N;R.2W)*

The stream of the creek heads on Olympic National Forest, 5 miles south of Sequim Bay, east Clallam County; flows 6 miles northeast to Discovery Bay, northeast Jefferson County. In 1847, the stream was charted as *Salmon River* by Capt. Henry Kellett. His name has been altered by cartographers or by local usage. A local name, once in use, was *Discovery Creek*.

Salmon Creek *(Ts.33-37N;Rs.23-26E)*

This stream, with many tributaries, heads on the east slope of Rock Mountain, central Okanogan County; flows 15 miles southeast to a reservoir south of Conconully, then 15 miles southeast to the Okanogan River at Okanogan. The Indian name for this stream was *Con-con-ulps*. Later names were *Conconully Creek, White Salmon Creek,* and *Salmon River*. The name has been applied to many rivers, creeks, and lakes in Washington. Before the advent of hydroelectric dams in Washington state, spawning salmon ran to the headwaters of most of those streams that offered access from the Pacific Ocean. (USBGN)

Salmon Creek Pond *(S.15;T.3N;R.2E)*

A 6-acre artificial lake, 1/2 mile north of Brush Prairie, central Clark County. This lake is used by the Department of Fisheries for rearing salmon. The pond is named for Salmon Creek on which it is located.

Salmon-Fall River (Okanogan County) *see* Methow River

Salmon La Sac *(S.9;T.22N;R.14E)*

A big pothole in Cle Elum River, at the mouth of Salmon La Sac Creek, 3-1/2 miles north of Cle Elum Lake, northwest Kittitas County. This is a prehistoric Indian fishing place and was named in very early days by French-Canadian fur traders who found Indians fishing salmon in the pothole with woven cedar-bark baskets. The latter portion of the name is the French term for "bar" or "pouch."

Salmon Lake (Okanogan County) *see* Conconully Lake

Salmon River (Okanogan County) *see* Salmon Creek

Salsbury Point *(S.1;T.27N;R.1E)*

An east shore point of Hood Canal, 1 mile west of Port Gamble, north Kitsap County. This is the southeast terminus of Hood Canal Floating Bridge. In 1841, the name was given by Cmdr. Charles Wilkes to honor Francis Salsbury, captain of the top in one of his ships.

Salmonberg (King County) *see* Redmond

Salt Lake (Grant County) *see* Moses Lake

Salter's Point (Pierce County) *see* Gordon Point

Saltese Creek *(Ts.24-25N;Rs.44,45E)*

The stream of the creek rises on the north slope of Mica Peak, east central Spokane County; flows 12 miles northwest through the drained bed of Saltese Lake to Spokane River near Carders. (*see* Saltese Lake)

Saltese Lake *(T.25N;R.45E)*

A lake in the course of Saltese Creek, 2 miles west of Liberty Lake, in Greenacres Township, east central Spokane County. This lake was named for Andrew Saltese (Seltis, Seltice), a Coeur d'Alene chief who is credited by some historians as having remained friendly to whites during the Nez Perce War of 1877.

Saltwater State Park *(S.20;T.22N;R.4E)*

A 90-acre recreational area on Puget Sound, 18 miles south of Seattle, between Zenith and Redondo, King County. The park offers camping, swimming, fishing, and trailer accommodations. The name was chosen by the State Parks & Recreation Committee and is descriptive.

Salzer Valley *(T.14N;R.2W)*

A valley in the lower course of Salzer Creek, directly southeast of Centralia, northwest Lewis County. It was named for the first local homesteaders, Joseph and Gottlieb Salzer.

Sam Hill Memorial State Park (Whatcom County) *see* Peace Arch State Park

Samahma (Kittitas County) *see* Cle Elum

Samego Point *(S.8;T.20N;R.1E)*

The northwest point of McNeil Island, on Pitt Passage, northwest Pierce County. In 1841, this name (which has not persisted), was charted by the Wilkes Expedition. It is one of few names applied by Wilkes for which no record of source is found. In 1846, it was charted as *McCarthy Point* by Inskip, another name which is no longer used.

Samis River *(T.24N;Rs.9,10W)*

The stream of the river rises in Round Lake, Olympic National Park, southwest of Paradise Valley; flows west to Queets River, 22 miles, southwest Jefferson County. This Indian name is an abbreviated form of *Samms-mish*, which was the name of Quinault tribal group whose home was on this stream. It is shown on certain recent maps as *Sams River*.

Samish *(S.27;T.36N;R.2E)*

Abandoned town in the center of Samish Island, northwest Skagit County. It was established in the days of steamboat navigation on Samish Bay, but is no longer an organized settlement. It was named, together with an island, bay, and river, for a local Indian leader named *Samens*. He is buried in an abandoned cemetery on Samish Island. (*see* Atlanta)

Samish Bay *(T.36N;Rs.2,3E)*

A bay between Samish Island and Bellingham Bay, northwest Skagit County. It is bordered on the south and east by extensive, shallow tidelands that have been filled by deposits from Samish River. (*see* Samish)

Samish Island *(T.36N;R.2E)*

Originally an island at high tide, being separated from the mainland by a tidal slough, now it is filled for a highway connection with the *island*, located between Samish Bay on the north and Padilla Bay on the south, northwest Skagit County. It is famous for filbert orchards. (*see* Samish)

Samish Lake *(T.37N;R.3E)*

An 814-acre lake, maximum depth 145 ft., 6-1/2 miles southeast of Bellingham, extreme southwest Whatcom County. The lake is crescent-shaped, about 3 miles long. The name is from an Indian word, *Samena*, meaning *hunter*, which was the name of a tribe that lived around this lake and on Samish Island. On some maps this feature is called *Lake Samish*.

Samish River *(Ts.35-37N;R.3-5E)*

The stream of the river rises near Saxon, southwest Whatcom County; flows south and west to Samish Bay, 1 mile west of Edison, northwest Skagit County. (*see* Samish)

Sammamish Lake (King County) *see* Lake Sammamish

Sammamish River *(Ts.25,26N;Rs.4,5E)*

This slow, swampy stream rises at the north end of Lake Sammamish; flows north and west through Woodinville to the north end of Lake Washington near Kenmore. The stream's course has been dredged where it passes through agricultural bottomlands. Alternate names for this stream which have been in use previously are *Squak Slough* and *Sammamish Slough*. The latter is still used to some extent. The original Indian name was *T-sab* or *Sts-ap*, meaning *crooked*. That name was well applied.

San de Fuca *(Ss.20,29;T.32N;R.1E)*

Village on Penn Cove, Whidbey Island, 2-1/2 miles northwest of Coupeville, west central Island County. In 1889, the town was named by a real estate syndicate composed of H. S. Power, L. H. Griffiths, and J. W. Gillespie. These promoters used a shortened version of *San Juan de Fuca*. The town was *boomed* as the east entrance of a cross-island canal.

San Juan Archipelago *(Ts.34-38N;Rs.1-4W)*

An island group which extends from the Canadian boundary on the west and north, from the boundaries of Whatcom and Skagit counties on the east, and to the center of the Strait of Juan de Fuca on the south. There are 25 major islands and many smaller islands and reefs; classed as habitable are 172 units of this group. The original name of the archipelago was for Lopez de Haro, who discovered the group in 1789. On June 24, 1791, the birthdate of San Juan Bautista, Lieut. Eliza renamed the group using the name of that saint. His name has become official. In 1841, the name *Navy Archipelago*, was applied by the Wilkes Expedition, but it never came into common use.

San Juan Channel
(Ts.34-36N;Rs.2,3W)

A channel between San Juan Island to the west, and Lopez, Shaw, and Orcas islands to the east, central San Juan County. In 1791, this channel was named *Boca de Horcasitas* by Lieut. Juan Francisco de Eliza, for a Spanish schooner under command of Jose Maria Narvaez. It appeared on Eliza's charts as *Orcasitas*, the Spanish *"h"* being mute in many cases. In 1841, the Wilkes Expedition charted it as *President's Channel* for Comm. John Rodgers, USN, who was president of U.S. Naval Commissioners. Other names that have been used in the past are *Ontario Roads, Middle Channel* and *Washington Channel.*

San Juan County

A 172-sq. mile county in the extreme northwest corner of Washington state. It is bounded on the west and northwest by Haro Strait; on the north and northeast by Georgia Strait; on the east by Rosario Strait; and on the south by the Strait of Juan de Fuca. On October 31, 1873, the county was formed by the Territorial Legislature after Emperor William of Germany had decided the San Juan dispute on October 21, 1872, awarding the San Juan Archipelago to the U.S. The county was named for the largest island in the group.

San Juan Island *(Ts.34-36N;Rs.2-4W)*

The most southwesterly island of the San Juan group, bordered by the Strait of Juan de Fuca on the south, Haro Strait on the west, Spieden Channel on the north, and San Juan Channel on the east. In 1770, the island was named *Isla y Archipelago de San Juan* by Lieut. Juan Francisco de Eliza. It was not in honor of Jaun de Fuca, but for the Catholic Saint, Juan Bautista. Hudson's Bay Company personnel called it *Bellevue Island* during their tenancy. In 1841, Cmdr. Wilkes charted it as *Rodgers Island* for Comm. John Rodgers, USN. In 1847, Capt. Kellett, RN, restored the present name, which is recognized by all official agencies.

San Juan Islands *(San Juan County) see* San Juan Archipelago

Sand *(Franklin County) see* Davin

Sand Island *(T.9N;R.11W)*

This low sand island extends across the mouth of Baker Bay, near the mouth of Columbia River, southwest Pacific County. It has been used for many years as a spot for beach-seining by salmon fishermen, as it is very low and clear of obstacles. The name is of local origin and quite descriptive.

Sand Point *(Ss.1,2;T.25N;R.4E)*

A level, sandy promontory in Seattle, west shore of Lake Washington, opposite Kirkland on the east shore, King County. It was formerly occupied by a U.S. Navy air base. In the 1860s, this descriptive name was applied by Seattle pioneers. The Indian name for the point was *Sqw-seb.*

Sandy Beach *(Island County) see* Sandy Point

Sandy Lake *Jefferson County) see* Sandy Shore Lake

Sandy Point *(Jefferson County) see* Beckett Point

Sandy Point *(King County) see* West Point

Sandy Point *(S.2;T.29N;R.3E)*

A southeast shore point of Whidbey Island, 2 miles southwest of Camano Head, south Island County. This is a long, low sandy spit and its very descriptive name was applied by Cmdr. Charles Wilkes in 1841. A local name for this feature is *Sandy Beach*. Other local names, for a settler named Joseph F. Brown, are *Brown's Point, Joe Brown's Point,* and *Joe Brown Spit.*

Sandy Point *(S.20;T.13N;R.10W)*

A south end point of Rhodesia Beach, on Willapa Bay, west central Pacific County. In the 1890s, a town called *Seaport* was platted here, but the plat was vacated when the town failed to develop. This descriptive name is of local origin and is quite suited to the place.

Sandy Point *(S.33;T.20N;R.2W)*

A point at the junction of Totten Inlet and Squaxin Pass, directly south of Steamboat Island, extreme west central Thurston County. In 1841, this descriptive name was chosen by the Wilkes Expedition.

Sandy Point *(S.17;T.38N;R.1E)*

A north point entrance to Lummi Bay, on Lummi Indian Reservation, east central Whatcom County. In 1841, this descriptive name was charted by the Wilkes Expedition. In 1791, Juan Francisco de Eliza called this feature *Punta de Loera,* for Nicholas de Loera, chaplain of the San Blas Fleet of Spain. On older maps this may show as *Punta Lara* or *Punta Loera.*

Sandy Shore Lake *(S.26;T.28N;R.1W)*

A 36.2-acre lake, 5 miles southwest of Port Ludlow, northeast Jefferson County. The name is quite descriptive. An alternate name is *Sandy Lake.*

Sanderson *(S.3;T.28N;R.29E)*

Settlement 8-1/2 miles west of Grand Coulee Dam, northeast Douglas County. It was named for Thomas Sanderson, the first postmaster.

Sandford Point *(S.14;T.22N;R.2E)*

A west shore point of Vashon Island, on West Passage (Colvos Passage), southwest King County. In 1841, this point was named *Point Sandford* by Cmdr. Charles Wilkes, for Thomas Sandford, quartermaster in one of the expedition's ships. It appears on some maps, in error, as *Point Sanford.*

Sanitarium Lake *(Grant County) see* Soap Lake

Sanpoil Lake *(S.32;T.37N;R.33E)*

Small lake 2-1/2 miles northeast of Republic, Colville Indian Reservation, on an east tributary of the upper Sanpoil River, west central Ferry County. The name origin can be traced back to an original name of an Indian band. A popular belief is that the name was given to the area by French-Canadian employees of early fur traders as *san-poil,* or *without hair,* because of a scarcity of fur-bearing animals. However, David Thompson, who explored here in 1811, before other fur traders came, referred in his journal to *Simpoil* Indians. As a further argument against the French-Canadian origin, records show that this region produced quite a lot of furs. A logical conclusion is that the French-Canadians, in a pessimistic mood, distorted the original Indian word to a term in their own language. The same inversion was common among early settlers, as a criticism of untamed areas from which they tried to extract a meager living. Other spellings of this name on early maps were: *Cinqpoil, Sans Poil, Lampolle, San Poel, San Poele, San Puell,* and *Sin Pui.*

Sanpoil River *(Ts.28-37N;Rs.32-34E)*

This historic stream heads in the high mountains of the Colville Indian Reservation, north central Ferry County; flows 65 miles to the south and west to join the Columbia River, 7 miles south of Keller. This stream was extremely important in the fur-trapping and trading period of this region. The mouth of the river was flooded for 8 miles in the reservoir created by

Grand Coulee Dam, forcing the town of Keller to be moved to higher ground. (*see* Sanpoil Lake)

Santa Rosalia (*Jefferson County*) *see* Mt. Olympus

Sapolil (*S.1;T.7N;R.36E*)

Settlement 5 miles northeast of Walla Walla, southeast Walla Walla County. This word means *wheat* in Walla Walla Indian language, which makes the name most appropriate for a town in this area.

Sappho (*S.29;T.30N;R.12W*)

A former logging-railway headquarters and camp, 2 miles west of Lake Pleasant, on Beaver Creek, west central Clallam County. In the early 1920s, reports indicate that it was named by Joe Meeley, a construction worker of Greek origin, who became logging superintendent for the company which logged here. The name given is that of a Greek poetess who lived a colorful life in about 580 B.C. She would not have enjoyed life in Sappho.

Sara (*S.17;T.3N;R.1E*)

Community 2 miles east of Columbia River, 7 miles north of Vancouver, east central Clark County. It was named by Postmaster Emmons for one of his daughters when the original petition was made for establishment of postal service.

Saratoga (*S.19;T.30N;R.3E*)

Community on the southeast shore of Whidbey Island, 4 miles northwest of Langley, Island County. (*see* Saratoga Passage)

Saratoga Passage (*Ts.30-32N;Rs.2,3E*)

A passage between Camano and Whidbey islands, in Puget Sound, central Island County. On June 4, 1792, the pass was named *Port Gardner*, by Capt. George Vancouver, for Vice-Admr. Sir Alan Gardner, RN. In 1841, Cmdr. Wilkes charted the passage under the present name in honor of the U.S. flagship in the battle of Lake Champlain during the War of 1812. Capt. Kellett tried to restore Vancouver's name in 1847, but was unsuccessful. Gardner's name, however, is on a bay in Snohomish County.

Sares Head (*S.22;T.34N;R.1E*)

A high, precipitous cliff, 2-3 miles long, 1 mile northwest of Reservation Bay, on the southwest coast of Fidalgo Island, southwest Skagit County. In 1841, the Wilkes Expedition applied the

name *Point Sares* to Langley Point, 1 mile to the north. The name was later shifted to this cliff, and altered to the present spelling. It is named after Henry Sares, captain of the top on one of Wilkes's expedition ships.

Sarvent Glaciers (*Mt. Rainier National Park*)

Two small glaciers which head in cirques, elevation 6,600 ft. and 7,000 ft., between Fryingpan Glacier and Cowlitz Chimneys, at the headwaters of Fryingpan Creek, east central park area. They were named for Henry M. Sarvent, a civil engineer who made the first detailed map of Mt. Rainier. (USBGN)

Saska Peak (*S.7;T.30N;R.18E.uns*)

A Wenatchee National Forest peak on Chelan Ridge summit, between Emerald Peak and Milham Pass, north central Chelan County. It was named for a former chief of the Entiat tribe by Forest Supervisor A. H. Sylvester.

Satellite Island (*Ss.22,27;T.37N;R.4W*)

An island in Prevost Harbor, north shore of Stuart Island, northwest San Juan County. In 1858, Capt. Richards, RN, placed this island on British Admiralty Charts as *James Island*, for Capt. James Charles Prevost, who was on the Pacific station in *H.M.S. Satellite* between 1857 and 1860. The present name was substituted later because of another James Island in the San Juan Group. (USBGN)

Satsop (*S.31;T.18N;R.6W*)

Formerly headquarters for the Schafer logging interests, and the head of navigation on Chehalis River, 6 miles east of Montesano, southeast Grays Harbor County. It was named for a local Indian band, the *Sats-a-pish*.

Satsop Lakes (*Ss.1,2,11;T.22N;R.7W*)

Five lakes in a group, at the head of West Fork, Satsop River, 6 miles northeast of Camp Grisdale, northeast Grays Harbor County. The lakes are identified by consecutive numbers, and their areas range from 1-1/2 to 4 acres. (*see* Satsop)

Satulick Mountain (*Mt. Rainier National Park*)

A 5,574-ft. peak south of Indian Henrys Hunting Ground, overlooking Kautz Creek, 6-1/2 miles southwest of Mt. Rainier's summit, southwest zone of the park. The mountain was named by

P. B. Van Trump for a local Indian named Sotolick. His nickname was "Indian Henry," which is the official name for the meadows and lakes which he used as a hunting ground. The proper name has been distorted in later mapping. (USBGN)

Satulick Point (Mt. Rainier National Park) *see* Satulick Mountain

Satus (*S.14;T.9N;R.21E*)

Community on Satus Creek, 10 miles southeast of Toppenish, southeast Yakima County. The Yakima Indian name means "rich land," and refers to an abundance of camas and other edible roots that grew in the vicinity. The present name is a corruption of the Indian form, which is closer to *Setass*, and means "rich grazing land," or the word *Settasslema*, meaning "people of the rye prairie or of the bunch-grass range." The name also identified a sub-tribe or group of the Yakima nation.

Satus Creek (*T.9N;Rs.17-22E*)

The stream of the creek rises east of Satus Peak, south central Yakima County; flows 36 miles east to Yakima River, 2 miles east of Satus. The upper reaches are heavily timbered, and were once a refuge for herds of wild horses. (*see* Satus)

Satus Creek (*Ts.6-9N;Rs.16-21E*)

The stream of the creek rises 3 miles north of Indian Rock, Yakima Indian Reservation, in Simcoe Mountains, north central Klickitat County; flows east and northeast into Yakima County, then northeast to Yakima River near Satus -- a total distance of about 41 miles. (*see* Satus)

Satus Pass (*Ss.14,23,26;T.6N;R.17E*)

A 1,610-ft. pass at the summit of Simcoe Mountains, between drainage areas of Satus Creek, north and Little Klickitat River on the south, extreme north central Klickitat County. The pass was much used by Indians in early periods, and by white troops during the Indian wars. It now is an important state highway pass. (*see* Satus Creek)

Satus Pass State Park (Klickitat County) *see* Brooks Memorial Park

Saucer Lake (*S.16;T.27N;R.13E*)

A 13.8-acre lake, elevation 4,500 ft., directly west of Cascade Mountain summit, 6-1/4 miles north of Stevens Pass, extreme southeast Snohomish

County. It was named to match nearby Cup Lake; it is quite round and slightly larger than Cup Lake.

Sauk *(S.34;T.35N;R.9E)*

Once a lively mining town, now practically deserted, on Skagit River, at the mouth of Sauk River, central Skagit County. It should not be confused with Sauk City, 2 miles downstream on the Skagit River, also an abandoned town. The name is from an Indian band who lived along the river, the *Sah-kee-me-hue.*

Sauk City *(S.21;T.35N;R.9E)*

Abandoned town on Skagit River, 2 miles below the mouth of Sauk River, central Skagit County. In the 1890s, it was used as a landing for river boats that brought supplies for Monte Cristo, to go over the *Sauk River Tote Road.* (see Sauk)

Sauk Lake *(S.13;T.35N;R.9E)*

A 10-acre lake, average depth 30 ft., on the east side of Sauk Mountain, 7 miles east of Concrete, central Skagit County. Alternate names are *Sauk Mountain Lake* and *Baldy Lake.* (see Sauk)

Sauk Mountain *(S.14;T.35N;R.9E)*

A Mt. Baker National Forest peak, elevation 5,510 ft., 2-1/2 miles northwest of Rockport, central Skagit County. The peak is used as a fire lookout in season by Forest Service personnel. (see Sauk)

Sauk Mountain Lake (Skagit County) *see* Sauk Lake

Sauk Portage (Snohomish County) *see* Darrington

Sauk Prairie
(S.33;T.33N;R.4;T.32N;R.10E)

A prairie directly east of Sauk River and south of Mansford, on the boundary between south central Skagit County and north central Snohomish County. (see Sauk)

Sauk River *(Ts.29-35N;Rs.9-11E)*

The stream of the river heads in 2 forks, one at Indian Pass in Cascade Mountain summit, the other at Monte Cristo, east Snohomish County; these forks join at Bedal Camp and flow north and northwest through Darrington and Skagit County to Skagit River near Rockport. (see Sauk)

Sauk River Tote Road
(Ts.29-35N;Rs.9,10,11E)

An old wagon and sled road (in use until 1899), which started at Sauk City on Skagit River, Skagit County, and terminated at Monte Cristo, Snohomish County. The road followed the Sauk River grade. In 1890, this 55-mile road was built and was the only access to the Monte Cristo mining district until a railroad was built from Everett in 1893. (see Sauk)

Saundersonville (Lewis County) *see* Chehalis

Savage Island *(Ss.4,10;T.12N;R.28E)*

A 2-mile-long island in Columbia River, 23 miles northwest of Pasco, northwest Franklin County; its length is bordered by Columbia River on the west and a slough on the east. It is reported to have been named for Gibson Savage, who owned a large ranch in this vicinity.

Sawmill Creek *(Ts.19-20N;R.11E)*

The stream of the creek heads on the north side of Huckleberry Mountain, Snoqualmie National Forest, southeast King County; flows 6 miles north to Green River, 1 mile east of Lester. It was named for the sawmilling operations of Morgan Lumber Company, some years ago and is now included in the City of Tacoma watershed.

Sawmill Flat *(S.10;T.17N;R.14E)*

A river flat in Snoqualmie National Forest, on Naches River, 2-1/2 miles northwest of Cliffdell, northwest Yakima County. It was named by early cattlemen who found a prospector whipsawing lumber for placer sluice boxes.

Sawyer *(S.7;T.11N;R.20E)*

Railroad point on north bank of Yakima River, 11 miles southeast of Yakima, east central Yakima County. This is an important point for rail shipments of fruit and was named by Northern Pacific officials for William P. Sawyer, from whom they acquired a local right-of-way.

Sawyer Lake Slough (King County) *see* Cranberry Slough

Saxon *(S.17;T.37N;R.5E)*

Town on Samish River between Acme and Wickersham, southwest Whatcom County. In 1887, the name was applied when a post office was established. It was named for Mrs. Elizabeth Lyle Saxon, who homesteaded here in 1855.

Scabock Harbor (Kitsap County) *see* Seabeck Bay

Scabock Point (Kitsap County) *see* Misery Point

Scadget Head (Island County) *see* Scatchet Head

Scaffold Camp Creek
(T.33N;R.20E.uns)

The stream of the creek rises north of Scaffold Peak, southwest Okanogan County; flows 4 miles north to Twisp River, Chelan National Forest. On September 30, 1853, the name was given by Capt. George B. McClellan during his exploring trip in this region. The most logical assumption is that his party found tepee poles at a deserted Indian camp on the creek. Local Indians called the creek *Nai-hai-ul-ix-on.*

Scaffold Peak *(S.6;T.32N;R.20E.uns)*

A Chelan National Forest peak, elevation 7,600 ft., 5 miles north of Sawtooth Ridge summit, southwest Okanogan County. (see Scaffold Camp Creek)

Scandia *(S.27;T.26N;R.1E)*

Settlement on the west side of Liberty Bay, opposite Poulsbo, north central Kitsap County. It consists almost entirely of Norwegians or persons of Norwegian descent. The first name chosen by early Norwegian settlers was *Frykholm.* In 1914, when they changed to the present name, they retained the town's Scandinavian flavor.

Scantigrease Creek *(T.9N;Rs.2,3W)*

The stream of the creek heads in Scantigrease Valley, 7 miles west of Castle Rock; flows east to Monahan Creek, 3 miles west of Castle Rock. It was named by Willard Johnson, a pioneer settler, for a woman in the valley who always complained of a shortage of cooking grease (scant of grease), and who "greased" her skillet with a turnip. This name originally applied to the creek's valley and to a school. A spelling of the name on some older maps is *Scanty Grease.*

Scantigrease Valley *(T.9N;Rs.2,3W)*

A valley along Scantigrease Creek, southwest of Castle Rock, northwest Cowlitz County. An alternate name is *Delameter Valley.* (see Delameter Valley, Scantigrease Creek)

Scarboro Shoals (Pierce County) *see* Toliva Shoal

Scarborough Harbor (Clallam County) *see* Neah Bay

Scarborough Hill (*T.9N;R.10W*)

Hill northeast of Fort Columbia, near Chinook, southwest Pacific County. It was once the home of Chief Comcomly of the Chinook nation, and was named for Capt. James Scarborough, a sea captain in the employ of Hudson's Bay Company, who owned a land claim here in 1848. In 1813, the hill was named *Chinook Hill* by Alexander Henry and so charted by Wilkes in 1841. On some older maps the feature is called *Scarboro Head.*

Scarborough Point (Clallam County) *see* Klatchopis Point

Scarface (*Mt. Rainier National Park*)

A 6,100-ft. mountain, within a mile of the park's north boundary, between Huckleberry Creek and White River. The name applied by park officials is descriptive, as the face of the mountain has been scarred by erosion and landslides, which might be more aptly termed "rock slides." (USBGN)

Scatchet Head (*Ss.15,16;T.23N;R.3E*)

High cliffs of glacial clay on the south tip of Whidbey Island, west of Possession Point, extreme south Island County. In 1841, these cliffs were named *Skadg-it Head* by Cmdr. Wilkes for a local Indian tribe. Early steamship and sailing ship navigators on Puget Sound called them *False Skatchet* and called Possession Point *Scatchet Head.* The present name, a modified version of *Skagit*, has been officially recognized. (USBGN)

Scenic (*S.29;T.26N;R.13E*)

Highest community west of the Cascade range, in western Washington, 8 miles east of Skykomish, 4 miles west of Cascade Mountain summit, extreme northeast King County. It is near the west portal of the Burlington Northern Railway's Cascade tunnel, elevation 2,106 ft. The name is descriptive and was applied by officials of Great Northern Railway Company. It has a wide vista of snow-clad mountains.

Scenic Lakes (*S.16;T.25N;R.13E*)

Two glacier-fed lakes, 1 mile west of Cascade Mountain summit, 3 miles south of Scenic, extreme northeast King County. The lakes are in deep pockets and called *Surprise Lake* and *Glacier Lake.* (*see* Scenic)

Schafer (*S.27;T.22N;R.7W*)

An area of active logging on the upper West Fork, Satsop River, 2-1/2 miles northeast of Camp Grisdale, northeast Grays Harbor County. The place is named for the Schafer family who logged in this area for many years and whose history is recorded in the book *Fifty Years in the Timber.*

School Point (Kitsap County) *see* Keyport

Scheuerman Creek (*S.10;T.25N;R.3E*)

The stream of the creek rises on the north area of Fort Lawton, northwest Seattle, north side of Lawton Peninsula; flows 1-1/2 miles northeast and north to Shilshole Bay at Lawton Wood, opposite Shilshole Breakwater, King County. The creek was used extensively by Indians as a source of fresh water while traveling in this part of Puget Sound. It was locally named for Christian Scheuerman, who owned a land claim at the creek's mouth from 1870 until his death in 1907.

Schilling Creek (*Ts.26,27E;R.15E*)

The stream of the creek heads in Rock Lake on the steep south slope of Nason Ridge, Wenatchee National Forest, southwest Chelan County; flows 2 miles southeast to Nason Creek. This creek, with nearby Royal and Crescent creeks, was named for a popular brand of baking powder by Forest Supervisor A. H. Sylvester.

Schmid Meadows (*Ss.22,27;T.32N;R.38E*)

A 2,800-ft. mountain valley, on Smith Creek, 5-1/2 miles east of the Columbia River, west central Stevens County. The meadows are less than 1/2 mile wide and about 2 miles long. Formerly there was a settlement here named *Schmidt* which does not appear on recent maps. It is reported to have been named for an early settler called Schmid or Schmidt.

Schmidt (*S.14;T.32N;R.38E*)

Vanished town 7-1/2 miles east of the Columbia River, on Smith Creek, west central Stevens County. This old town in the Colville River Drainage is one of many early settlements which flourished, supported a post office and store, then was abandoned when modern highways and fast transportation brought the mail by Rural Free Delivery and enabled the inhabitants to shop in larger

towns. The name was applied to the post office for the town's first settler. (*see* Schmid)

Schrag (*S.7;T.18N;R.32E*)

Settlement on Weber Coulee, 13 miles northwest of Lind, west central Adams County. It was named for J. R. Schrag, an early resident, by officials of Northern Pacific Railway Company when that line was built through here.

Schrieber's Meadows (*S.13;T.37N;R.7E*)

Mountain meadow in the valley of Sulphur Creek, directly south of Mt. Baker, south central Whatcom County. It is named for one of the earliest settlers in this area.

Schwock River (Kittitas County) *see* Swauk Creek

Scootenay Lake (*Ss.12,13;T.14N;R.29E*)

A narrow, 1-mile-long lake, 15 miles northwest of Connell, northwest Franklin County. The name is for an Indian band who lived in the Inland Empire. An alternate name, used locally, is *Eagle Lake.*

Scott (Adams County) *see* Cunningham

Scott Island (Pierce County) *see* Cutts Island

Scott Point (*S.21;T.21N;R.1E*)

A sharp, sandy point at the south entrance to Horsehead Bay, on Carr Inlet, northwest Pierce County. In 1841, it was named by Cmdr. Wilkes for one of his quartermasters, Thomas Scott.

Scottys Lakes (King County) *see* Tsuga Lakes

Scout Lake (*S.30;T.25N;R.4W*)

A 1/2-mile-long lake at the head of a tributary to One Too Many Creek, Olympic National Park, southeast Jefferson County. The lake covers 25-1/2 acres and was evidently named by a troop of Boy Scouts who visited the lake on a hiking trip. (USBGN)

Scow Bay (Jefferson County) *see* Kilisut Harbor

Scrabble Lake (*S.20;T.27N;R.13E*)

A 3-acre lake on the west side of Scrabble Mountain, elevation 5,000 ft., Snoqualmie National Forest, extreme southeast Snohomish County. It was named for Scrabble Mountain.

Scriber Lake (*S.16;T.27N;R.4E*)

A lake in Alderwood Manor district, 4 miles east of Edmonds, southwest Snohomish County. It was named for **Peter Schriber, a Dane, whose 1890** homestead here included the entire lake.

Scribner (*S.21;T.24N;R.42E*)

Railroad point 5 miles southwest of Spokane city limits, in Marshall Township, central Spokane County. It was named by W. P. Kenney, vice president of Great Northern Railway Company, for a personal friend, Peter Scribner.

Scribner Lake (Snohomish County) *see* Scriber Lake

Sea Lion Rock (*T.23N;R.12W*)

A Pacific Ocean rock, 3 miles off the shore of Quinault Indian Reservation, 9 miles northwest of Taholah, northwest Grays Harbor County. In 1869, it was named by Davidson of U.S. Coast Survey for the number of sea lions in the vicinity.

Seabeck (*T.25N;R.1W*)

The former site of a very large sawmill on the east shore of Hood Canal, 10 miles northwest of Bremerton, at the head of Seabeck Bay, northwest Kitsap County. In 1856, the sawmill was established. In 1841, the place was called *Scabock Harbor* by the Wilkes Expedition, using a modificatioin of the Indian name, *L-ka-buk-hu*. In 1847, Capt. Kellett charted it as *Hahamish Harbor*, using another Indian term. Marshall Blinn, owner of the first sawmill altered *Scabock* to *Seabeck*.

Seabeck Bay (*T.25N;R.1W*)

A tongue-shaped, 2-mile-long bay on the east shore of Hood Canal, across from Duckabush, northwest Kitsap County. It is the site of a very large sawmill in pioneer days. (*see* Seabeck)

Seabold (*S.33;T.26N;R.2E*)

Area on the east shore of Agate Passage, northwest Bainbridge Island, east central Kitsap County. The first name was *Bull Town*, for William Bull, who settled here in 1880. In 1892, when a post office was established, Bill Bull suggested the present name for the town's proximity to tidewater.

Seabury (*S.36;T.20N;R.44E*)

Railroad point 6 miles southwest of Tekoa, northeast Whitman County. The name was given by H. R. Williams, vice president of C.M.&St.P. Railway Company, presumably for a place in the state of Maine.

Seafield Lake (*S.18;T.31N;R.15W*)

A 22-acre lake, 12-1/4 miles south of Neah Bay, 1/2 mile or less from the ocean, west central Clallam County. The name is descriptive, as it is on the fairly flat, marshy prairie near the ocean shore.

Seahaven (*S.20;T.14N;R.9W*)

Abandoned town on the south side of Willapa River at its mouth, on Potter Slough, Pacific County. In 1889, the name was chosen by Herman Trott of St. **Paul, Minnesota, when he platted and** "boomed" this town with the aid of local investors. In 1890, the town had a bank, newspaper, hotel, and several other buildings. The venture failed and the buildings were moved to South Bend.

Seal River (Clark County) *see* Washougal River

Seal Rock (*S.17;T.33N;R.14W*)

Strait of Juan de Fuca rock, 22-1/2 miles east of Waada Island, 660 yards offshore, northwest Clallam County. The rock is 1/4 mile northwest of Sail Rock, with which it sometimes is confused. In 1841, the Wilkes Expedition called it *Sail Rock*; and the rock to the southeast, which is now Sail Rock, he named *Bird Rock*. In 1846, Capt. Kellett charted it as *Klaholah Rock*. The reason for the present name, which ws applied in pioneer days, is the multitude of seals around the rock that were noted on charts by early navigators.

Sealand (Pacific County) *see* Nahcotta

Seaport (*S.20;T.13N;R.10W*)

Vanished town at Sandy Point, on the east side of Willapa Bay, west central Pacific County. In the early 1890s, Lewis Henry Rhoades chose this name when he platted a townsite here. The plat was vacated when the venture failed and the place is not shown on recent maps.

Sears Creek (*T.28N;Rs.15,16E*)

The stream of the creek heads on the northeast slope of Wenatchee Ridge, Wenatchee National Forest, northwest Chelan County; flows 2 miles east to White River. It was named by Forest Ranger Robert E. Nickles for Ross Sears, through whose homestead the creek ran.

Seatco (Thurston County) *see* Bucoda

Seattle (*Ts.24-26N;Rs.3-5E*)

The largest city in Washington state, on Puget Sound, northwest King County; it extends 15 miles north-south, and about 9 miles east-west, with the main business section centering around Elliott Bay. The city has diversified industries and businesses. It was named for Noah Sealth, chief of Suquamps and allied tribes when Seattle was established in 1851. He was very friendly to white settlers. The Indian name of the site of this city was *Tzee-tzee-lal-itc*, meaning "little place where one crosses over." The reference was to an Indian trail which started at the foot of Yesler Way and ran over the hills to the east, terminating on Lake Washington.

Seattle Harbor (King County) *see* Elliott Bay

Seattle Park (*Mt. Rainier National Park*)

A small, beautiful park area between Russell and Carbon glaciers, near the terminus of Russell Glacier, northwest quarter of the park. It was named for the City of Seattle by a party of Seattle climbers in the early days of park development. (USBGN)

Seattle Rock (Mt. Rainier National Park) *see* Echo Rock

Seaview (*S.21;T.10N;R.11W*)

A summer resort area on the ocean side of North Beach Peninsula, near its south end, southwest Pacific County. J. L. Stout, founder of Ilwaco, purchased **400 acres here and built a resort hotel** which he called *Seaview*. The name spread to the surrounding settlement.

Second Creek (*T.39;R.34E*)

The stream of this very short creek rises on the Colville National Forest, 6 miles east of Curlew, north central Ferry County; flows 2 miles from the northeast to West Deer Creek. It was named because it is the second stream of any size which enters Deer Creek above the mouth of that creek. Similarly named, and of about the same size, are First and Third creeks.

Second Hill (King County) *see* Renton Hill

Second Lake (*S.21;T.20N;R.7E*)

A small, 2-1/2-acre lake, in White River drainage basin, 3 miles east of Enumclaw, southwest King County. It is the second of 3 numbered lakes in fairly close proximity and has been called *Boise Lake*, in error, on some maps.

Sedge Ridge *(T.12N;Rs.14,15E)*

A 4,263-ft. ridge between South and North forks, Ahtanum Creek, west central Yakima County. The ridge extends about 8 miles southwest to northeast and was named for Henry Sedge, a former U.S. Forest Service ranger in this district.

Segelson Creek (Snohomish County) *see* Segalson Creek

Sedro-Woolley *(T.35N;R.4E)*

Town on Skagit River, 6 miles northeast of Mount Vernon, west central Skagit County. This town was founded on forest products industries and is the only place in the world with this name. It was called *Kellyville* by Norman P. Kelley, who platted land here prior to 1890. Before that it had been facetiously named *Bug* by local citizens, at the suggestion of Mortimer H. Cook in 1884; this last name met with general disapproval. Cook then tried to have his own name established as that of the post office, but failed. He then offered the name *Cedro*, Spanish for "cedar," because of extensive manufacture of red cedar shingles in the area. Postal authorities accepted the name, but altered it to *Sedro* for some unknown reason. Meanwhile, Phillip A. Woolley had started a rival town which directly adjoined, and he chose his own name for the place. The rivalry was intense until the towns were combined by popular vote on December 19, 1898, using the present hyphenated name. On November 10, 1936, an attempt to change the name to *Sedro* failed by an overwhelming vote.

Segalson Creek *(Ts.32-33N;R.8E—*

The stream of the creek rises at Covey Pass, 3 miles northeast of Fortson, south central Skagit County; flows 2-1/2 miles south to North Fork, Stillaguamish River, Snohomish County. The name is that of an early homesteader on this creek which settlers called *Swede Heaven*.

Sehome *(T.38N;R.3E)*

Once a town on Bellingham Bay (now combined with 3 other towns to form the present city of Bellingham), Whatcom County. This was the first town on Bellingham Bay, platted on May 8, 1858. It was named when platted for Sehome, a sub-chief of Clallam In-

dians, who married a Samish woman.

Seigleman Creek (Snohomish County) *see* Segalson Creek

Sekiu *(S.18;T.32N;R.12W)*

Small community on the west shore of Clallam Bay, Strait of Juan de Fuca, northwest Clallam County. The place is based on a log dump and rafting ground in the bay. Capt. Henry Kellett chose the present name, using the original Indian designation. Captain George Davidson of U.S. Coast Survey, confirmed Kellett's naming, but spelled the name *Sikke-u,* which corresponds more closely to the Indian pronunciation. (USBGN)

Sekiu Point *(S.18;T.32N;R.12W)*

A west entrance point to Clallam Bay, Strait of Juan de Fuca, northwest Clallam County. In 1791, the point was named by Manuel Quimper at the same time he named a point at the east entrance to the bay. One of these he charted as *Punta de Rojax*, but it could have been either one. (*see* Sekiu)

Sekiu River *(T.32N;Rs.13,14W)*

The river rises near the southeast corner of Makah Indian Reservation, northwest Clallam County; flows east to the Strait of Juan de Fuca, 2 miles west of Kydaku Point. (*see* Sekiu)

Sekou Point *(Clallam County) see* Sekiu Point

Sekou River (Clallam County) *see* Sekiu River

Selah *(S.36;T.14N;R.18E)*

Town on Yakima River, 3 miles north of Yakima, north central Yakima County. In 1907, it was started by Almin Swanson and other Swedish settlers from Tacoma. This Indian name, meaning "still" or "smooth" water, was applied by Yakima tribesmen to about 1-1/2 miles of Yakima River where it emerges from Kittitas Canyon. Settlers extended the name to a town, creek, and valley. Until 1909, the station here was called *Wenas*; Northern Pacific Railway officials changed the name to its present form.

Selah Creek *(Ts.13-14N;Rs.19-22E)*

The stream of the creek rises in northeast Yakima County; flows west and northwest 23 miles throughout Yakima Fishing Center to Yakima River near Pomona. It has numerous small tributaries. (*see* Selah)

Selkirk Mountains

Most of the Selkirk Range is located in Canada, with south extensions into northeast Washington, and into Idaho and Montana. The portion in Washington is in east Pend Oreille County, east of Pend Oreille River. It is heavily mineralized in some areas. The range was named by Canadians for Sir Thomas Douglas, Fifth Earl of Selkirk, a heavy shareholder in Hudson's Bay Company, and founder of the Red River Colony in Canada. He has a magnificent monument to his memory, with peaks towering to 11,100 ft. (USBGN)

Selleck *(S.24;T.22N;R.7E)*

Settlement 12 miles northeast of Enumclaw, central King County. It was formerly an important logging center, based on timber purchased from City of Seattle watershed. It was named by Pacific States Lumber Company for their resident superintendent, F. L. Selleck.

Seltice *(S.12;T.19N;R.45E)*

Village 5 miles south of Tekoa, on Willow Creek, northeast corner of Whitman County. It is named for Andrew Seltice (Saltice, Saltese), a friendly Coeur d'Alene Indian of influence, who remained friendly to whites during the Nez Perce War of 1877.

Semiahmoo (Whatcom County) *see* Blaine

Semiahmoo *(S.2;T.40N;R.1W)*

Once a community, now owned by a development corporation, on a long spit, directly west of Blaine, between Drayton Harbor and Semiahmoo Bay, extreme northwest Whatcom County. This was formerly an important trading center and the first station in U.S.-Canadian Boundary Survey. This name, which once applied also to Blaine, is for an Indian tribe, the *Sem-mi-an-mas*. In 1841, the Wilkes Expedition applied the name *Tongue Point*, which did not persist. A local name is *The Spit*.

Semiahmoo Bay *(T.40N;R.1W)*

A stretch of shoreland, rather than an indented bay from Birch Point to Semiahmoo, on Georgia Strait, northwest Whatcom County. The "bay" has borne a long list of names from the earliest exploration until recently, many of which confuse Drayton Harbor and Birch Bay with this feature. (*see* Semiahmoo)

Seno de Gaston (Whatcom County) *see* Bellingham Bay

Seno de Padilla (Skagit County) *see* Padilla Bay

Seno de Santa Rosa (Clallam/Jefferson counties) *see* Strait of Juan de Fuca

Sentinel Island *(S.2;T.36N;R.4W)*

A small, rocky island, elevation 140 ft., in Spieden Channel directly south of Spieden Island, northwest San Juan County. In 1841, this island, and nearby Sentinel Rocks, were named by Cmdr. Wilkes. Their position in the channel evidently gave Wilkes the impression of sentinels guarding the passage between Spieden and San Juan islands.

Sentinel Rock *(S.2;T.36N;R.4W)*

Rock 1/2 mile west of Sentinel Island, directly south of the west end of Spieden Island, northwest San Juan County. On some charts this feature is called *Sentinel Rocks*. In 1841, the name was applied by Cmdr. Wilkes at the same time he named Sentinel Island. (*see* Sentinel Island)

Sepulchre Island (Klickitat County) *see* Memaloose Island

Sequalitchew Creek *(T.19N;R.2E)*

The stream of the creek heads in Sequalitchew Lake, west of American Lake, west central Pierce County; flows west to Nisqually Reach at the east end of Nisqually Flats. In 1841, the name was charted by members of the Wilkes Expedition and is the original Indian designation. The meaning is *The face is marked,'' and refers to dark markings on the faces of fish in the lake, possibly Dolly Varden trout.*

Sequalitchew Lake *(Ss.19,30;T.19N;R.2E)*

An 80.9-acre lake on Fort Lewis Military Reservation, directly west of American Lake, 1-1/2 miles northeast of Dupont, west central Pierce County. The lake is 3/4 mile long and 1/4 mile wide. (*see* Sequalitchew Creek)

Sequim *(S.19;T.30N;R.3W)*

Town 3 miles west of Sequim Bay, northeast Clallam County. This is an interesting area; it has a dry, sunny climate, with low precipitation and irrigated farms. The name is from the Clallam Indian dialect, and means ''quiet waters.'' As pronounced by Indians, it should be spelled *Such-e-kwai-ing* or *Such-i-kwe-ing.*

Sequim Bay *(Ts.29,30N;R.3W)*

A Strait of Juan de Fuca bay, 3 miles east of Sequim, northeast Clallam County. The bay is almost closed by a long, narrow sand spit from the northwest tip of Miller Peninsula. In 1791, the bay was named *Ensenada de Bertodano* by Juan Francisco de Eliza. In 1841, the Wilkes Expedition applied the name *Budd's Harbor*, for Thomas A. Budd, acting master of *Peacock*. In 1847, Capt. Kellett used the name *Washington Harbor* on British Admiralty Charts. In 1858, Capt. George Davidson of U.S. Coast Survey adopted Kellett's name. The USBGN ruled that Washington's name could not be officially used for minor features that had nothing to do with ''The Father of His Country.'' They have approved the present name. (USBGN) (*see* Sequim)

Sequim Bay State Park *(Ts.29,30N;R.3W)*

A 73-acre public park on the west shore of Sequim Bay, 3 miles east of Sequim, northeast Clallam County. The park offers camping, swimming, fishing, and clamming. (*see* Sequim)

Servia *(S.35;T.17N;R.32E)*

Railway station on Lind Coulee, 1 mile northwest of Providence, west central Adams County. When the Milwaukee Railway was built through this area, the station was named by its officials for the Kingdom of Servia, now a part of Yugoslavia.

Serviss Glacier (Mt. Rainier National Park) *see* Ingraham Glacier

Setass (Yakima County) *see* Satus

Setass Creek (Yakima County) *see* Satus Creek

Seven Fingered Jack *(T.31N;R.16E.uns)*

A mountain at the junction of Chelan Ridge and Entiat Mountains, at the headwaters of Big Fork Creek, northwest Chelan County. It is on the boundary of Chelan and Wenatchee national forests and was named by A. H. Sylvester for the 7 spires or fingers which top the peak.

Seven Lakes *(Ss.18,19;T.28N;R.8W.uns)*

Actually, this is a group of 8 lakes in Olympic National Park, at the head of Soleduck River, northeast of Bogachiel Peak, south central Clallam County. Each lake has its own name and except

for the slight error in mathematics, the name is descriptive.

Sevenmile Creek *(T.13N;R.17E.uns)*

The stream of the creek rises near Tinpan Mountain, north central Chelan County; flows north to Railroad Creek, 7 miles west of Lucerne. The local name describes the creek's approximate length.

Seventeen Mile Creek *(T.34N;Rs.32-34E)*

The stream of the creek rises on the east slope of the Columbia Mountain Range, central Ferry County; flows west 11 miles to join the Sanpoil River, 1-1/2 miles south of West Fork. The name indicates the distance of its mouth from Republic, as measured along the Sanpoil River.

Seventeen Mile Mountain *(S.32;T.35N;R.34E)*

A Colville National Forest peak, elevation 4,886 ft., 13 miles southeast of Republic, at the head of Seventeen Mile Creek, west central Ferry County. The peak is used as a fire lookout. (*see* Seventeen Mile Creek)

Seventy Six Gulch *(T.29N;R.11E)*

The gulch runs north from a pass above Twin Lakes, southeast Snohomish County; runs 3 miles to Monte Cristo. On July 14, 1889, the gulch was named by James Pearsall when he discovered galena ore here. He called the gulch and his claim ''Independence of 1776.'' The name of the gulch was later shortened to the present form.

Seward Peak *(T.38N;R.7E)*

A peak on the southwest slope of Mt. Baker, between Thunder and Deming glaciers, central Whatcom County. It was named by John A. Lee for William H. Seward, secretary of state from 1861 until 1869.

Seylor Valley *(S.28;T.33N;R.36E)*

This valley is several miles in length and runs in a general north-south direction, from 3 miles north of Impach, Colville Indian Reservation, east central Ferry County. It was named for an early white settler, Mike Seylor.

Seymour Peak *(Mt. Rainier National Park)*

A 6,351-ft. peak south of Chinook Peak and Naches Pass, between Chinook Creek and the park's east boundary, east central zone of the park. It was named by The Mountaineers for W. W.

Seymour, mountaineer and ex-mayor of Tacoma. (USBGN)

Shadow Lake *(S.7;T.22N;R.6E)*

A 50-acre lake, 2-1/4 miles west of Maple Valley, 2 miles east of Lake Youngs, southwest King County. It was locally named many years ago when it was heavily shaded by old-growth virgin timber on its shores. An early name, which has not appeared on recent maps, was *Spoon Lake.*

Shadow Lake *(Mt. Rainier National Park)*

A large campground and picnic area, elevation 6,200 ft., 1 mile by trail from Sunrise (Yakima) Park, northeast quarter of the park. On April 24, 1914, this name was recommended by Park Ranger Thomas E. O'Farrell to a 7-man committee on park names, because it had been a well-established name for many years, and had become semi-official. (USBGN)

Shady Lake (King County) *see* Mud Lake

Shady Lake *(S.1;T.22N;R.5E)*

A 21.1-acre lake, 3-1/2 miles northwest of Maple Valley, west central King County. The lake is located in a heavy, second-growth of timber. This romantic name is supported by the shade cast on the lake by surrounding forests. Alternate names are *Hostak Lake* and, of course, *Mud Lake.*

Shag Reef *(T.37N;R.4W)*

A New Channel reef, near Cactus Island, northwest Island County. In 1860, this name was placed on British Admiralty Charts by Capt. Richards, RN. The name is not carried on recent maps or charts, although it is in local use in the adjoining islands.

Shag Rock *(S.19;T.36N;R.1W)*

Small rock or reef in Harney Channel, directly south of the middle peninsula of Orcas Island, central San Juan County. The name is locally applied for this reef which has a rather ragged appearance at low tides.

Shake Creek (Snohomish County) *see* Shaup Creek

Shallow Bay *(S.23;T.38N;R.2W)*

A west end bay of Sucia Island, extreme north central San Juan County. This descriptive name was locally applied, but it is not shown on many maps or charts.

Shallow Nitch (Pacific County) *see* Grays Bay

Shallow Nitch (Wahkiakum County) *see* Grays Bay

Shamel Creek *(T.27N;R.19E)*

The stream of the creek rises between Windy and Tyree creeks, Wenatchee National Forest, central Chelan County; flows 2 miles east to Entiat River. It was named by local usage for an early settler on the creek.

Shanghai *(T.2N;R.3E)*

Small settlement, 9 miles northeast of Vancouver, south central Clark County. The name derives from the large number of Chinese laborers in this area, digging the Eureka Ditch drainage system under a Chinese boss, Au Sue.

Shanghai Creek *(Ts.2,3N;R.3E)*

A tributary of Fifth Plain Creek which flows 5 miles to that creek through the Shanghai District, south central Clark County. (*see* Shanghai)

Shannon Lake (Skagit County) *see* Lake Shannon

Shannon Point *(S.21;T.35N;R.1E)*

Northwest point at the tip of Fidalgo Island, Guemes Channel, west central Skagit County. In 1858, Capt. Richards placed this point on British Admiralty charts as *Ship Point*. Later it appeared on U.S.C.&G. Survey charts under the present name, without explanation.

Shano *(S.25;T.15N;R.30E)*

Railway station 10 miles southeast of Othello, southwest Adams County. It was named by railroad officials for J. Shannon, trainmaster of Northern Pacific Railway Company at Pasco in 1912. At one time it was listed as *Shano Spur.*

Shano Spur (Adams County) *see* Shano

Shanwappum (Yakima County) *see* Tieton River

Shark Reef *(S.4;T.34N;R.2W)*

Small, bare island off the southwest shore of Lopez Island, San Juan Channel, south central San Juan County. In 1859, it was named by Capt. Richards, British Admiralty surveyor. While the record does not so indicate, it is quite possible that Richards found basking sharks in the area, because they are still seen in these waters.

Shaup Creek *(T.30N;R.10E)*

The stream of the creek rises on Stillaguamish Peak, east central Snoho-

mish County; flows 2 miles north to Falls Creek, Mt. Baker National Forest. This Indian name means "rock slide," which is fairly descriptive. It is carried on some maps, in error, as *Shake Creek.*

Shaw Creek *(Mt. Rainier National Park)*

The stream of the creek rises in Owyhigh Lakes, east slope of Mt. Rainier; flows north and northeast to White River, near White River Entrance, circling Tamanos Mountain on the west and north. The creek was named by The Mountaineers for Carrie Shaw of Tacoma.

Shaw Island *(Ts.35,36N;R.2W)*

An island between Orcas and Lopez islands, central San Juan County. In 1841, it was named *Shaws Island* by the Wilkes Expedition for Capt. John D. Shaw, USN, a hero of the War of 1812, who also fought at Algiers in 1815. The Lummi indian name for the island was *Scom-em-ana*, which was their name for a small, oily fish found here in quantity.

Shawpatin Mountains (Columbia, Asotin, Garfield counties) *see* Blue Mountains

Shawpatin (Saptin) River (Walla Walla, Franklin, Columbia, Whitman, Garfield, and Asotin counties) *see* Snake River

Sheep Creek (Spokane County) *see* Dartford Creek

Sheep Creek *(T.29N;R.18E.uns)*

The stream of the creek rises in Chelan Mountains, north central Chelan County; flows 3-1/2 miles west to Pyramid Creek. The name was applied by Forest Supervisor A. H. Sylvester because the area had been used for a sheep range.

Sheep Creek *(T.30N;Rs.40-41E)*

The stream of the creek rises in Loon Lake, southeast Stevens County; flows west and north through Springdale, a distance of 14 miles, to Colville River, near Gray. In pioneer days, it was called *Spring Creek*. The origin of the present name appears to be unrecorded, although it is a common name in areas where sheep raising was prevalent.

Sheep Island *(S.9;T.36N;R.2W)*

A very small island near the east shore of West Sound, Orcas Island, north central San Juan County. In 1858, this name was charted by Capt. Richards, RN, at which time Hudson's Bay Company grazed a small band of sheep here.

Sheep Lake (Skamania County) *see* Olallie Lake

Sheep Lake (Mt. Rainier National Park)

Shallow, 3-acre lake, elevation 4,881 ft., in the Cascade Mountain Range, 6-1/2 miles south of Chinook Pass, 1 mile east of Ohanapecosh River, southeast sector of the park. Local information indicates that this area was used as a sheep range before the park was extended to the Cascade Mountain summit. (USBGN)

Sheep Mountain
(Ss.5,8;T.29N;R.11E)

Peak 2-1/2 miles northwest of Monte Cristo, east central Snohomish County. Records show that the mountain was named by early prospectors, probably for mountain sheep that were rather plentiful in these high mountains in pioneer days.

Sheepherders' Butte (Yakima County) *see* Goat Butte

Sheepskull Gap (*Mt. Rainier National Park*)

Gap between ridges which are located west of Klickitat Creek's headwaters, 1-1/2 miles west of Chinook Pass, east central zone of the park. This is one of many places in wild areas of the state which were named by early trappers and prospectors. The namer, in this case, is unidentified. (USBGN)

Shepherds Lake (Clark County) *see* Steigerwald Lake

Sheridan *(S.2;T.24N;R.1E)*

Small residential settlement on Port Washington Narrows, directly north of Bremerton, central Kitsap County. It was named by residents in the early days of occupancy for Gen. Philip H. Sheridan. U.S. Army.

Sheridan Point *(S.14;T.2N;R.7E)*

A north bank point of Columbia River, 3 miles southwest of Stevenson, directly downstream from Cascade Locks. The name came into disuse, but was revived by actions of pupils of Ainsworth School in Portland, Oregon. (*see* Sheridan)

Sherman *(S.24;T.27N;R.33E)*

Community 6 miles northeast of Wilbur, on Goose Creek, northwest Lincoln County. It was named for

George W. Sherman, first postmaster, on whose land the town was located.

Sherman Creek
(Ts.35-36N;Rs.35-37E)

The north fork stream of this rather historic creek rises at Jungle Hill, 11 miles east of Republic, then flows 12 miles southeast to join the south fork. The south fork rises 13 miles southeast of Republic and flows east and northeast for 12 miles to join the north fork. Their combined stream flows 7 miles east to Franklin D. Roosevelt Lake. The creek is on Colville National Forest, east central Ferry County. These two forks drain a wide area. An old Hudson's Bay Company trail once followed Sherman Creek, continuing through Republic to the Okanogan River. In 1883, Gen. William T. Sherman made an inspection trip along this trail, "viewing out the road enroute." The creek was named for him.

Sherman Creek Pass
(S.24;T.36N;Rs.34-35E)

High pass, elevation 5,596 ft., through the central mountain range of Ferry County, which extends between Columbia Mountain on the north and Sherman Peak on the south, 12 miles east of Republic. Today the pass is on the route of a secondary highway. (*see* Sherman Creek)

Sherman Peak
(Ss.24-25;T.36N;R.34E)

A Colville National Forest peak, elevation 7,008 ft., directly west of Sherman Creek Pass, 12 miles east-by-south of Republic, central Ferry County. (*see* Sherman Creek)

Sherman Peak *(T.38N;R.8E)*

A Mt. Baker peak, 10,613 ft., on the south rim of Summit Crater, Mt. Baker, central Whatcom County. In August, 1868, the peak was named by Edmund T. Coleman, for Gen. William T. Sherman, Commander-in-Chief of the U.S. Army.

Sherwood *(S.35;T.34N;R.39E)*

Settlement 10 miles south of Colville on the Colville River, central Stevens County. In 1867, it was settled by S. F. (Fred) Sherwood, for whom it was named. This name is not on recent maps.

Shi Shi Beach *(T.32N;R.15E)*

Stretch of Pacific Ocean beach, between Point of Arches and Portage Head, northwest Clallam County. The

meaning of this Indian name has not been determined.

Shillapoo Lake *(T.3N;Rs.1E,1W)*

A drained lake on the flood plain of Columbia River, 6 miles northeast of Vancouver, southwest Clark County. Originally this old lake covered about 1,000 acres and was quite shallow. Pioneers adopted the Indian name.

Shilshole Bay *(T.25N;R.3E)*

An open bay which leads to Hiram Chittenden Locks and Salmon Bay, north and west of the north shore of Lawton Peninsula, west of Golden Gardens, Shilshole Breakwater, and Yacht Basin, in northwest Seattle, King County. This bay was the outlet of Salmon Creek before the locks were built. The name is from the Duwamish Indian word *Cil-col*, which means "threading" or "inserting," as a thread through a bead. The reference was to the bay's narrow entrance into Salmon Creek. White pioneers translated the word as *Shil-shale*, and used it to designate the Indians who lived around Salmon Bay and north along the Puget Sound shore to Everett. That band is now extinct.

Shilsholia (King County) *see* Lawton Wood

Shine *(S.33;T.28N;R.1E)*

Community on the west shore of Hood Canal, 4 miles south of Port Ludlow, on Squamish Harbor, east central Jefferson County. When a post office was established here, local residents suggested the name *Sunshine*. Postal authorities rejected that name, but accepted the abbreviated form.

Ship Bay *(T.37N;R.2W)*

Small, shallow bay at the head of East Sound on Orcas Island, 1/2 mile east of the town of East Sound, northeast San Juan County. The bay is surrounded by resorts and homes. This name is of local origin, based on the fact that the bay offers abundant anchorage for small ships.

Ship Harbor *(S.22;T.35N;R.1E)*

A Fidalgo Island harbor on the north tip of the island, Guemes Channel, west central Skagit County. The name was applied in the early days of whaling along the coast, because many whaling ships were careened here for cleaning of hulls. It also was a haven for early merchant ships and patrol boats. Whaling crews called the bay *Squaw Harbor*, because of many Indian women in the vicinity.

Ship Point (Skagit County) *see* Shannon Point

Shoal Bight (San Juan County) *see* Davis Bay

Shoalwater Bay (Pacific County) *see* Willapa Bay

Shoalwater Indian Reservation (*T.14N;R.11W*)

Very small reservation of 335 timbered acres, on the north side of Willapa Harbor, 3 miles north of Tokeland, northwest Pacific County. The few Indians who own the reservation have no tribal organization. This name was borrowed from adjacent Shoalwater Bay when the reservation was established by executive order on September 22, 1866.

Shoestring (Lewis County) *see* Alpha

Shoestring Valley (*T.13N;R.2E*)

Valley between Alpha and Bear Canyon Road, north central Lewis County. It was named for the tough, wiry, stringy roots of a yellow-flowering Delphinium or larkspur which grows abundantly here, and which locally is called *shoestring.*

Shoofly Mountain (*S.35;T.28N;R.13E*)

A Wenatchee National Forest peak, on Cascade Mountain summit, 3-1/2 miles east of Wenatchee Pass, northwest Chelan County. It was named by Carl Hardman, a Forest Service trail foreman, while building Lake Creek trail. In a meadow near the ridge, he encountered many big horse flies, little deer flies, and swarms of mosquitoes.

Short and Dirty Creek (*Ts.12-13N;R.13E.uns*)

The stream of the creek rises on a divide between South Fork, Tieton River and North Fork, Ahtanum Creek, northwest Yakima County; flows 6 miles northeast to South Fork, Tieton River near Tieton Reservoir. The name was applied by local stockmen in honor of a sheepherder who ranged sheep here, and whose physical characteristics were so described.

Short and Dirty Ridge (*T.13N;R.13E.uns*)

A Snoqualmie National Forest ridge on the forest's south boundary, extending 4 miles north between Short and Dirty Creek and South Fork, Tieton

River, Yakima County. The ridge connects several minor peaks south of Tieton Reservoir. It borrows the name of the creek which flows along its east flank. (*see* Short and Dirty Creek)

Short Lake (King County) *see* Mason Lake

Shovel Creek (*S.8;T.6N;R.47E*)

The stream of this short creek rises north of Mt. Wilson, extreme southeast Asotin County; flows 2-1/2 miles east to Snake River. It was named by prospectors who told tales of taking gold by the shovelful from a bar where the creek flows into Snake River. This triggered a stampede into the area in 1865. Little gold was found, but the name stuck.

Shriner Lake (*Mt. Rainier National Park*)

Small lake, elevation 5,000 ft., 2-1/2 miles west of Cascade Mountain summit, directly southeast of Shriner Peak, southeast quarter of the park. It is in a beautiful setting, 900 ft. lower than the peak. (USBGN) (*see* Shriner Peak)

Shriner Peak (*Mt. Rainier National Park*)

A 5,846-ft. peak, 3 miles west of Cascade Mountain summit, 1-1/2 miles east of Chinook Creek, southeast quarter of the park. It is used by the park as a forest fire lookout in season. The name was chosen by park officials when a fire lookout tower was established. Evidently, it has Masonic significance. (USBGN)

Shuecraft Lake (Clallam County) *see* Lake Sutherland

Shuksan Creek (*T.38N;R.9E.uns*)

The stream of the creek heads on the west slope of Mt. Shuksan, central Whatcom County; flows 4-1/2 miles southwest to Swift Creek. On a recent county map the name is misspelled as *Shukson.* (*see* Mt. Shuksan)

Shuksan Lake (*S.13;T.38N;R.9E*)

Very deep, 28-acre lake, elevation 3,700 ft., at the head of Lake Creek, 4 miles south of Mt. Shuksan summit, on Mt. Baker National Forest, south central Whatcom County. (*see* Mt. Shuksan)

Shushuskin Canyon (*T.17N;R.18E*)

Canyon 2-4 miles south of Ellensburg, running parallel to Yakima River, south central Kittitas County. The canyon carries a small, intermittent stream bearing the same name. It was named for

an Indian who became a farmer and who was highly respected by early settlers. He fed and assisted many prospectors and travelers. In some records the name is spelled *Shoskin* in error.

Shutes River Falls (Thurston County) *see* Tumwater Falls

Shuwah Creek (*T.29N;Rs.12,13W*)

The stream of the creek rises on Calawah Ridge, northwest corner of Olympic National Forest; flows west to Soleduck River, 4 miles north of Forks, southwest Clallam County. It was named for an Indian village which stood at the mouth of Shuwah Creek on Soleduck River. The Quillayute villagers were called *Sho-wh-quok.*

Si Mountain (King County) *see* Mt. Si

Sidney (Kitsap County) *see* Port Orchard

Sieclode River (Snohomish County) *see* Stillaguamish River

Sierras Nevadas De San Antonio (Wash. State Ref./Central Wash.) *see* Cascade Mountain Range

Sifton (*S.11;T.2N;R.2E*)

Settlement 5-1/2 miles northeast of Vancouver, south central Clark County. In 1908, it was named for a Dr. Sifton of Portland who was an important stockholder in a local power company.

Signal Peak (*T.28N;R.18E*)

A Wenatchee National Forest peak, elevation 6,918 ft., 3 miles west of Entiat River, 2-1/2 miles east of Cougar Mountain, central Chelan County. The peak was named with this rather common designation for high peaks by Forest Ranger James McKenzie.

Signal Peak (*S.36;T.9N;R.13E*)

A Yakima Indian Reservation peak, elevation 5,111 ft., 17 miles east of Mt. Adams, southwest Yakima County. The mountain is used in season as a fire lookout by Indian Service personnel. Quantities of marine fossils are embedded in the soil at the summit. The name was given because the peak was used as a signal point by Indians in the past. It has a wide range of visibility in all directions.

Silcott (*S.20;T.11N;R.45E*)

An abandoned town on the south bank of Snake River at its junction with Alpowa Creek, 5 miles west of Clarkston, north central Asotin County. In

1861, a trading post was established here by Sam Smith. The place was named for John Silcott, an early sheriff who operated the Clearwater ferry across the river. In 1882, William S. Newland platted a townsite as *Alpowa City*. The name did not take and Silcott was restored. This was a stage stop and ferry landing on the Lewiston-Pomeroy route.

Silcott's Landing (Asotin County) *see* Silcott

Silent Lake *(S.35;T.27N;R.1W)*

An 11.9-acre lake, 5-1/2 miles southeast of Quilcene, in the center of Toandos Peninsula, east central Jefferson County. The name of this lake is well chosen because there is little to disturb the peace in this sparsely settled area.

Siler Creek *(S.21;T.12N;R.7E)*

The stream of the creek rises east of Vance, southeast Lewis County; flows about 5-1/2 miles westward to Cowlitz River. It was named by pioneer settlers for Judson S. Siler, an early homesteader.

Silesia Creek
(Ts.39-41N;Rs.9,10E.uns)

The stream of the creek heads in Egg and Copper lakes, north central Whatcom County; flows northwest through the town of Boundary to Chilliwack River in British Columbia. The name is a distortion of the Indian word *Se-neh-sey*, as applied by the British Boundary Survey in 1846. Other spellings of the Indian name include, *Slesse, Selacee, Silecia, Silicia, Selacee,* and *Sen-eh-say.*

Silica Peak *(T.38N;R.8E)*

A Mt. Baker National Forest peak, between Coleman Peak and Mt. Baker, central Whatcom County. In 1915, it was named by a party of mountain climbers for a name found in a monument on the summit.

Silvan Island *(Mt. Rainier National Park)*

Area on the northeast slope of Mt. Rainier, south side of Emmons Glacier, northeast sector of the park. This descriptive name was chosen by Prof. J. B. Flett, a botanist who made the first collection and description of Mt. Rainier's flora.

Silvana *(S.2;T.31N;R.4E)*

Community 6 miles west of Arling-

ton on Stillaguamish River delta, northwest Snohomish County. Scandinavian influence is strong here. In 1892, when a post office was established, the name used was *Stillaguamish* The change to the present name was suggested by C. Jorgenson, who filed a plat for the townsite. It was for Silvanus, the god of forests and guardian deity of homesteads in Roman mythology.

Silver Beach *(S.23;T.38N;R.3E)*

A lakeshore hamlet and resort on the northwest shore of Lake Whatcom, directly east of Bellingham, southwest Whatcom County. On July 11, 1889, it was named by E. F. G. Carlyon, when he platted the townsite. It is now joined to Bellingham.

Silver Creek (Kitsap County) *see* Eglon

Silver Creek *(T.27N;R.2E)*

The stream of this small creek rises in extreme northeast Kitsap County; flows to Puget Sound between Apple Cove Point and Hansville. It was locally named for a man who homesteaded here in 1870.

Silver Creek *(Ts.12,13N;R.7E)*

The stream of the creek rises on the south slope of Allen Mountain, Snoqualmie National forest, northeast Lewis County; flows south to Cowlitz River, 1-1/2 miles southwest of Randle. It was so named because early settlers found small, bright particles in the creek which they mistook for silver.

Silver Creek *(S.16;T.12N;R.1E)*

Settlement 22 miles southeast of Chehalis, 1 mile north of Mayfield Dam, south central Lewis County. This is one of the older Lewis County communities, established in 1868 by John Tucker. On April 28, 1868, it was named for the creek on which it is located. The creek should not be confused with one of the same name in northeast Lewis County.

Silver Creek *(T.17N;R.10E)*

The stream of the creek rises near Bear Gap, close to the northeast corner of Mt. Rainier National Park; flows 9 miles north and northwest to White River near Silver Spring Camp. It is probable that the stream was locally named for silver mines at the creek's head near Cascade Mountain summit. At least this is the opinion of older residents in the area.

Silver Creek
(Ts.28,29N;R.11E.part.uns)

The stream of the creek rises in Silver Lake, 1 mile southwest of Monte Cristo, southeast Snohomish County; flows south and southwest to Skykomish River at Galena. (see Silver Gulch)

Silver Creek *(T.17N;R.44E)*

The stream of the creek rises east of Garfield, east central Whitman County; flows southwest 9 miles to Palouse River near Elberton. The name is taken from silvery sands at Silver Springs on the creek, where Colfax has developed a supply system for domestic water.

Silver Creek *(T.29N;R.18E)*

The stream of this short creek rises 20 miles northwest of Entiat, Wenatchee National Forest, Chelan County.

Silver Creek Ponds *(S.4;T.12N;R.2E)*

A 7-acre lake on upper Silver Creek, 3 miles northeast of Salkum, central Lewis County. The lake was the result of beaver dams in Silver Creek. (see Silver Creek)

Silver Falls *(T.29N;R.18E.uns)*

Waterfall in Silver Creek, a tributary of Entiat River, Wenatchee National Forest, north central Chelan County. The falls were named for Silver Creek by Forest Supervisor A. H. Sylvester.

Silver Falls *(Mt. Rainier National Park)*

Falls in Ohanapecosh River, 1-1/2 miles north of Ohanapecosh Hot Springs, southeast quarter of the park. The falls are very scenic and may be reached by trail through a heavily forested area. The name was chosen by early campers at the hog springs and is quite descriptive because the water is clear, silvery under a bright sun.

Silver Forest *(Mt. Rainier National Park)*

Large area of fire-killed, standing timber in Paradise River drainage, extending from Ricksecker Point to Narada Falls, south central zone of the park. This spectacular "ghost forest" was the result of a forest fire in 1885. Alaska yellow cedar and alpine firs constituted the stand. After almost 100 years, the cedar remains sufficiently sound to be used for buildings. The name is entirely descriptive because the bark has fallen from the trees and the bleached trunks have a delicate silvery color.

273

Silver Gulch *(T.30N;R.10E)*

Gulch extending from Marble Pass to South Fork, Stillaguamish River at Silverton, central Snohomish County. This name was applied to several features in the area by early miners because there were indications of silver-lead deposits over a wide range of country.

Silver Lake (lake) (Spokane County) *see* Four Lakes

Silver Lake *(Ts.9,10N;R.1W)*

A 4-pronged lake with 3 islands, 6 miles long and 1-1/2 miles wide, 4-1/2 miles east of Castle Rock, north central Cowlitz County. This common name was applied by local residents. At one time the lake was called *Toutle Lake* which is certainly more distinctive a name.

Silver Lake *(S.4;T.9N;R.1W)*

Community on the shore of Silver Lake, 5 miles northeast of Castle Rock, north central Cowlitz County. The town was named for the lake on which it is located.

Silver Lake *(S.12;T.16N;R.3E)*

A 138-acre lake, maximim depth 25 ft., 4-1/2 miles west of Eatonville, in Ohop Valley, southeast Pierce County.

Silver Lake *(S.30;T.28N;R.5E)*

A 102.3-acre lake, 5-1/2 miles south of Everett, southwest Snohomish County. This lake should not be confused with one of the same name near Monte Cristo. The name developed by local usage in the early days of settlement here.

Silver Lake *(S.29;T.29N;R.11E)*

Lake at the head of Silver Creek, 1 mile southwest of Monte Cristo, east central Snohomish County. This lake is one of many features in the Monte Cristo mining district that were named for promising silver-lead deposits.

Silver Lake *(S.21;T.24N;R.41E)*

Town on the east shore of Silver Lake (lake), 2 miles east of Medical Lake, west central Spokane County. It was named for the lake on which it is located.

Silver Lake *(T.40N;R.6E)*

Small lake 4 miles north of Maple Falls, north central Whatcom County. An alternate name, which is even more commonplace, is *Fish Lake*.

Silver Lakes *(S.9;T.27N;R.3W)*

Two small lakes, one covering 2 acres and the smaller barely 1 acre, on Olympic Primitive Area, 9 miles west of Quilcene at the head of Silver Creek, east central Jefferson County. They are named for Silver Creek.

Silver Ridge *(T.29N;R.18E)*

A Wenatchee National Forest ridge, extending about 5 miles between Pope and Silver creeks, from Chelan Mountains to Entiat River, north central Chelan County. It was named for Silver Creek by Forest Supervisor A. H. Sylvester.

Silverdale *(S.20;T.25N;R.1E)*

Settlement at the head of Dyes Inlet, 5 miles north of Bremerton, northwest Kitsap County. In 1880, it was given the flattering name of *Goldendale* by a local resident named Munson. When he found the same name on a town in Klickitat County, he switched to the present, and rather similar, designation.

Silvertip Mountain (Snohomish County) *see* Silvertip Peak

Silvertip Peak *(S.29;T.29N;R.11E)*

A heavily-mineralized area 2 miles southwest of Monte Cristo, on the boundary between Mt. Baker and Snoqualmie national forests, east central Snohomish County. It was named for silver-lead prospects found here during early mining days.

Silverton *(S.19;T.30N;R.10E)*

Ghost town of the 1890s, on Stillaguamish River, 29 miles east of Hartford, central Snohomish County. On August 26, 1891, at a mass meeting of miners here the name was suggested by James W. Hall because of silver-bearing ore discovered by Hall in 1890. A previous name for the place has been *Independence*.

Simcoe (Yakima County) *see* Wapato

Simcoe Creek *(Ts.10,11N;Rs.14-17E)*

The stream of the creek rises on Yakima Indian Reservation in branches on both north and south sides of Rattlesnake Ridge, west central Yakima County; flows east and southeast to Toppenish Creek, 2 miles south of Brownstown. On August 16, 1853, Capt. George B. McClellan mapped this stream as *Simkwe Creek*. (see Fort Simcoe)

Similk Bay *(T.34N;R.2E)*

North extension of Skagit Bay, between southeast Fidalgo Island and the mainland, northeast of Deception Pass, west central Skagit County. In 1841, this Indian name for the bay was charted by the Wilkes Expedition. It was retained on U.S.C.& G. Survey charts.

Similkameigh River (Okanogan County) *see* Similkameen River

Similkameen River *(T.40N;Rs.25-27E)*

The stream of this meandering creek enters Washington from British Columbia at Chopaka, north central Okanogan County; flows east to join the Okanogan River, 2 miles south of Osoyoos Lake near Oroville. This was the local name for several bands of the Okinagan on a river of the same name. The river was named for the Similkameigh tribe of Indians. A literal translation of the word is "treacherous waters."

Simkwe Creek (Yakima County) *see* Simcoe Creek

Simlayshe (Mt. Rainier National Park) *see* Eagle Peak

Simmons Lake *(S.20;T.18N;R.2W)*

Small lake 1 mile west of Olympia, north central Thurston County. It was named for Col. Michael Troutman Simmons, who lead a party of Kentuckians to Tumwater, and thus established the first American settlement on Puget Sound in 1845.

Simpson Ridge
(Ss.1,11-12;T.8N;R.42E)

A 2-mile-long Umatilla National Forest ridge, directly east of Cougar Canyon, west of Frying Pan Spring, south central Garfield County. The ridge has had several name changes over the years. Originally it was *Simpson Ridge*, for a pioneer stockman. Because it offered difficult access, other stockmen nicknamed it *Hard-to-get-to-Ridge*. When it was included in Umatilla National Forest, Forest Service officials shortened the name to *Hardy Ridge*. When a ruling was requested, the USBGN approved the original name and applied *Hard-to-get-to* as the name of a ridge to the east. (USBGN)

Sinclair Inlet *(T.24N;Rs.1,2E)*

Southwest extension of Port Orchard Bay, adjoining Bremerton on the south, south central Kitsap County. In 1841, the inlet was mapped by the Wilkes Expedition as *Sinclair's Inlet*, for George T. Sinclair, who had been Acting Master in 3 of the expedition's ships.

Sinclair Island *(T.36N;R.1E)*

Triangular island between Cypress and Lummi islands, in Rosario Strait, extreme northwest corner of Skagit County. Once the island was heavily wooded with cottonwood trees. Spanish explorers charted it as *Isla de Ignacio* or *Isla de Aguayo*. Pioneers called it *Cottonwood Island* or *Urban Island* for the small settlement of Urban. The Indian name was *Scut-las* in Lummi dialect. In 1841, the present name was chosen by the Wilkes Expedition for Capt. Arthur Sinclair, a prominent officer in the U.S. Navy during the War of 1812. The name used was *Sinclair's Island*.

Sine *(S.24;T.18N;R.5W)*

Small settlement on Chehalis Creek, 1 mile south of McCleary, southeast Grays Harbor County. The place is now without a post office, but when the first post office was established in 1905, it was named for Jackson Sine, a pioneer.

Sink Hole Lake *(S.35;T.21N;R.6E)*

A 3-acre lake, 3 miles south of Black Diamond, south central King County. The name was chosen because the lake drains underground to Cristy Creek, a tributary of Green River.

Sink Lake *(S.2;T.27N;R.3W)*

Small lake at the headwaters of Townsend Creek, Olympic National Forest, 7-1/2 miles west of Quilcene, east central Jefferson County. The lake varies in size from 1/2 acre to a dry condition -- hence the name.

Sinlahekin Valley *(Ts.37-39N;R.25E)*

Valley adjoining Sinlahekin Creek from Blue Lake Reservoir on the south to Palmer Lake on the north, a distance of about 14 miles, north central Okanogan County.

Sisco *(S.35;T.31N;R.5E)*

Area 5 miles north of Marysville near the source of Quilceda Creek, northwest Snohomish County. It was named for a pioneer of 1890 by officials of Stimson Mill Company when that company logged in this area.

Si-Si-Ah Creek (Pend Oreille County) *see* CCA Creek

Sister Islands (San Juan County) *see* The Sisters

Sisters Rock *(S.2;T.27N;R.1E)*

Two rocks on the west shore of Hood Canal, 1-1/2 miles east of Shine, extreme east Jefferson. In 1841, the

Wilkes Expedition called these rocks *The Sisters*. The name alteration has occurred subsequently and appears to be less descriptive than Wilkes's choice.

Sit Down Creek *(T.34N;R.35E)*

The stream of the creek heads to the south of Seventeen Mile Mountain, on the Colville Indian Reservation, 10 miles northwest of Inchelium, central Ferry County; flows east 10 miles to Hall Creek. A translation of the Indian name indicates that Indians could sit down on the mountain slopes and have everything they most desired at hand, including berries, deer, bear, fish, water, edible roots, and also spruce roots and birch bark for making baskets; a primitive paradise!

Sit Down Mountain *(Ss.28-29;T.34N;R.35E)*

A Colville Indian Reservation peak, elevation 4,871 ft., between Grizzly Creek to the north and Sit Down Creek to the south, 13 miles northwest of Inchelium, east central Ferry County. (*see* Sit Down Creek)

Sitkum River *(T.28N;Rs.10-12W)*

The stream of the river rises 7 miles west of Sol Duc Hot Springs, central Clallam County; flows 12 miles west to Calawah River, 6-1/2 miles east of Forks. *Sitkum* is Chinook jargon for "half, a part, middle." This stream actually is the middle fork of Calawah River.

Siwash Slough *(S.36;T.36N;R.2E)*

Tidal slough (now bridged) between Samish Island and the mainland, northwest Skagit County. This pioneer name was used because of the large number of local Indians on the slough for fishing and hunting in early days. Early settlers called all local Indians *Siwashes* as a generic term. The name was a distortion of the French *sauvage*, which French-Canadian employees of fur traders applied to northwest natives.

Six Mile Bar *(T.37N;R.38E)*

A Columbia River bar now flooded in the reservoir created by Grand Coulee Dam. It was once located 6 miles north of the Kettle Falls, at the mouth of China Creek, east side of Columbia River, northwest Stevens County. Like several other bars that were worked for placer gold in the early days, it is named for its river distance above the Kettle Falls.

Six Prong Creek *(T.5N;Rs.21-23E)*

The stream of the creek rises southeast of Bickleton, east Klickitat County; flows east 14 miles to join Alder Creek, 2-1/2 miles north of Columbia River. The name origin appears to be in the Indian term, *Sick Prong*, meaning "dead man," relating to an Indian group that died near here in an epidemic. Another suggested origin, which seems less valid, is that the place was named for the six branches of Alder Creek, several miles to the north.

Six Mile Creek *(T.29N;R.34-35E)*

The stream of this creek rises on the west bank of the Columbia River, 6 miles above the mouth of Spokane River, southeast Ferry County; flows 6 miles east from Whitestone Mountain to the Columbia River. The creek was of some importance during the early mining excitement. It was named for its distance above the mouth of Spokane River, as were Threemile and Ninemile creeks.

Six Prong *(S.3;T.4N;R.22E)*

Settlement on Six Prong Creek, 8 miles northwest of Alderdale, extreme southeast Klickitat County. In 1903, settlement started here with a homestead claim by Jacob King. (*see* Six Prong Creek)

Skagit Bay *(Ts.32-34N;Rs.2,3E)*

Large bay between Skagit Delta and Whidbey Island, northwest of Stanwood, southwestern *Skagit,* southeastern Island, and northwestern Snohomish counties. The bay was important in the days of steamboating on the Skagit River. The name is from the powerful Skagit Indian tribe. As pronounced by Indians, the word might logically be spelled *Sca-ad-chet*. The name has been variously spelled as *Scaadchet, Scatchet,* and *Skagit*.

Skagit City *(S.1;T.33N;R.3E)*

River town (now faded) on the old channel of South Fork, Skagit River, on the Skagit Delta, southwest Skagit County. Once a very important river landing and an organized town, it slumped when the river channel changed and left the town 100 yds. from the river. (*see* Skagit)

Skagit County

A county of 1,735-sq. miles in northwest Washington state. It is bounded on the north by Whatcom County; on the east by Chelan County;

on the south by Snohomish County, and on the west by Rosario Strait. On November 28, 1883, the county was created from a portion of Whatcom County by Washington Territorial Legislature. (*see* Skagit)

Skagit Delta *(Ts.32-34N;Rs.2-4E)*

Rich delta of very fertile land covering several townships at the wide-spread mouth of Skagit River, Skagit County. The several river branches discharge into Skagit Bay, from LaConner to Milltown. The trade center is at Mount Vernon. (*see* Skagit)

Skagit Head (Island County) *see* Scatchet Head, Possession Point

Skagit Island *(S.20;T.34N;R.2E)*

Small Islet, 1 mile southeast of Fidalgo, in Skagit Bay directly east of Deception Pass, southwest Skagit County. It was named for the Skagit Indian tribe. (*see* Skagit)

Skagit River

A 125-mile-long river, the largest stream of which enters Puget Sound and heads in Beaver Lake, 20 miles north of the U.S.-Canadian boundary, southeast of Hope; flows south and west through Whatcom and Skagit Counties to Skagit Bay. This is a most important river for the generation of hydroelectric power and for sports and commercial fishing. (*see* Skagit)

Skait Island (Skagit County) *see* Skagit Island

Skalawag Ridge *(T.36N;R.35E)*

High ridge on Colville National Forest, 15 miles east of Republic, between north and south forks of Sherman Creek, east central Ferry County. In an east-west line of about 3 miles, there are 4 peaks in line, with elevations of from 5,800 ft. to 5,833 ft. One is used as a fire lookout. A local tradition regarding the name source reports that a homesteader named Nueske, who packed supplies to a Forest Service fire crew on this mountain, cached part of the supplies on each trip for his winter's grubstake. *Pack Rat Mountain* might have been appropriate.

Skamania *(S.34;T.2N;R.6E)*

Settlement on north bank of Columbia River, 33 miles east of Vancouver, southwest Skamania County. An early name for this settlement, no longer used, was *Butler*. The Indian name, which applies to parts of the Columbia River, means *swift water* or *swift river*.

Skamania County

A southwest Washington county on Columbia River. It is bounded on the north by Lewis County; on the east by Yakima and Klickitat counties; on the south by Columbia River; and on the west by Clark and Cowlitz counties. Most of this country is in national forest. On March 9, 1854, it was created from the east part of Clark County by the Washington Territorial Legislature. (*see* Skamania)

Skamokawa *(S.17;T.9N;R.6W)*

Community on the north bank of Columbia River, at the mouth of Skamokawa Creek, south central Wahkiakum County. This is an original Chinook Indian name meaning "Smoke on the water." It indicates the prevailing fog on the waters at the mouth of the creek. One early map shows it as *Pinnea Creek*.

Skamokawa Creek *(Ts.9,10N;R.6W)*

The stream of the creek rises on Grays River Divide, north central Wahkiakum County; flows 14 miles south to Columbia River at Skamokawa. (*see* Skamokawa)

Skaro Lake (Skagit County) *see* Found Lakes

Skate Creek *(Ts.13,14N;Rs.8,9E)*

The stream of the creek rises on the west slope of Skate Mountain on Snoqualmie National Forest; flows east to Cowlitz River near Packwood. It was named for Skate Mountain on which it rises.

Skeeney Creek (Chelan County) *see* Skinney Creek

Skidmore Slough
(Ss.23,26;T.14N;R.9W)

Slough extending along the south side of Willapa Bay, between Raymond and South Bend, northwest Pacific County. The name is for J. N. Skidmore who settled near the slough in 1872.

Skiff Point *(T.25N;R.2E)*

An east shore point of Bainbridge Island, directly south of Rolling Bay, east central Kitsap County. In 1856, it was named by George Davidson of U.S. Coast Survey for a fancied resemblance to an overturned skiff at low tide.

Skinney Creek *(Ts.25,26N;R.17E)*

The stream of the creek heads 2 miles south of Nason Creek, Wenatchee National Forest, central Chelan County; flows south 8-1/2 miles to Chiwaukum Creek near its confluence with Wenat-

chee River. Since 1908, this name has been in local use. Local residents of long-standing state that it is a corruption of the original name *Skeeney Creek*, which they say was for an early settler.

Skiou Point *(S.34;T.30N;R.4E)*

Southeast entrance point to Tulalip Bay, Tulalip Indian Reservation, west central Snohomish County. The name is from the Indian word *Skyu*, meaning "dead body," because the point was an Indian burial ground when the first settlers arrived. Pioneers called it *Dead Man's Point*.

Skipjack Island *(T.37N;R.3W)*

Small, tree-covered island, 1 mile north of the north end of Waldron Island, northwest San Juan County. In 1841, the name was applied by the Wilkes Expedition, with an inclusion of Bare Island to the east. In 1853, this name was changed to *Wooded Island* by the U.S. Coast Survey, but it reverted to *Skipjack* on later charts. The smaller of the two islands was charted as *Penguin Island* by Captain Richards, RN, in 1858. The U.S. Coast & Geodetic Survey rejected Richards's name and charted it as *Bare Island*. The Lummi Indian name was *Che-stone-gewth*.

Skookum Canyon *(S.21;T.13N;R.35E)*

Canyon 2 miles west of Harder, directly north of Snake River, northeast Franklin County. This Indian name means "strong, tough, solid, powerful, violent" in Chinook jargon. It probably may be considered appropriate for this rocky canyon.

Skookum Creek *(Ts.32-34N;R.44E)*

This creek, with 3 branches, drains a large area in southeast Pend Oreille County. The main creek heads in Halfmoon Lake; the north fork heads in South Skookum Lake; and the south fork heads in the area directly west of Bead Lake. The branches join near Lenora to flow into Pend Oreille River. (*see* Skookum Canyon)

Skookum Creek *(T.37N;Rs.5,6E)*

Four creeks which combine to form Skookum Creek, extreme south central Whatcom County. This torrential stream flows west-by-south to South Fork, Nooksack River, 3 miles northeast of Wickersham. In 1885, the creek was named by I. M. Galbraith, a land surveyor. (*see* Skookum Canyon)

Skookumchuck (town) (Lewis County) *see* Centralia

Skookumchuck Creek
(T.18N;Rs.21,22E)

The stream of the creek rises 10 miles west of Columbia River, east central Kittitas County; flows east and southeast to Columbia River, 6 miles north of Vantage. The creek is intermittent. The Indian name is composed of the Chehalis word *Sku-kum*, meaning "strong," and the Chinook word for water, *tl-tsuk* or *chuck*.

Skookumchuck River
(Ts.14,15N;Rs.1,2W;1,2,3E)

The stream of the river rises near Huckleberry Mountain, north central Lewis County; flows northwest into Thurston County, then west and southwest to Chehalis River at Centralia, Lewis County. Its total length is about 33 miles. (*see* Skookumchuck Creek)

Skootenay Springs (Franklin County) *see* Scootennay Lake

Skopamish (King County) *see* Muckleshoot Prairie and Indian Reservation

Skull Island *(S.5;T.36N;R.2W)*

Island in Massacre Bay, at the north end of West Sound, Orcas Island, north central San Juan County. It was named for many skulls and bones left here after a massacre of local Indians by northern Haidahs in 1858.

Skull Point *(S.2;T.29N;R.3W)*

Southwest shore point of Sequim Bay, adjoining Sequim Bay State Park, northeast Clallam County. The point was originally named *Schoolhouse Spit* or *School Point*, because the first schoolhouse in the Blyn District was placed here. The name became twisted into the present one, possibly through mispronunciation by pioneers or Indians.

Skull Rock *(S.5;T.36N;R.2W)*

Massacre Bay rock, West Sound, on the southwest lobe of Orcas Island, north central San Juan County. (*see* Skull Island)

Skullcap Peak
(Ss.25,36;T.30N;R.12E)

A Mt. Baker National Forest peak, 3 miles northwest of White Pass, east central Snohomish County. The shape of the mountain's top and its coloration caused this name to be chosen by Forest Service personnel. (USBGN)

Sky Pilot Pass *(S.33;T.39N;R.17E)*

A Mt. Baker National Forest pass at Cascade Mountain summit, 1 mile south of Holman Pass, northeast Whatcom County. In 1918, it was named by sheepmen for a character who wrote Biblical quotations on rocks, logs, and cliffs in this area.

Skykomish *(Ss.26,35;T.26N;R.11E)*

Originally a railroad construction town, later a sawmill center on South Fork, Skykomish River, 13 miles east of Stevens Pass, northeast King County. The name was taken from that of an Indian tribe that lived along the river, *Skaikmish*, or *"Inland people."* Capt. George B. McClellan translated the verbal pronunciation of the tribal name as *Skywhamish*. Coastal tribes pronounced the name as *Sq-o-xwabc*.

Skykomish River
(Ts.25-29N;Rs.6-13E)

The stream of the river rises in 2 forks on the west slope of the Cascade Mountain summit. The North Fork originates in southeast Snohomish County; the South Fork in northeast King County. These 2 branches flow west to join near Index, southeast Snohomish County, then continue westward to Snoqualmie River, 3 miles southwest of Monroe. (*see* Skykomish)

Skyline Divide *(T.39N;R.7E)*

Divide extending north from the north slope of Mt. Baker, between Deadhorse and Glacier creeks, to North Fork, Nooksack River, Whatcom County. In 1908, this feature was explored and named by the Easton-Sprague Research Expedition.

Skyline Lake *(S.11;T.26N;R.13E)*

A 2-acre, glacial lake 1 mile north of Stevens Pass at Cascade Mountain summit, extreme northeast King County. The name is descriptive, because this small lake is on the summit of the Cascade range. An alternate name, much less romantic, is *Dozer Lake*.

Skyo Mountain *(T.13N;R.9E)*

A 2,470-ft. peak, 1 mile north of Cowlitz River, 4 miles southwest of Packwood, northeast Lewis County. The U.S. Forest Service maintains a fire lookout here in season. While serving as lookout on this mountain, Martha Hardy collected material for her book, *Skyo*. The name is the Indian word for "skunk."

Skyscraper Mountain *(Mt. Rainier National Park)*

A 7,065-ft. peak between Lodi and Winthrop creeks at the west limit of Sourdough Mountain, north central area of the park. An early camping party in nearby Berkeley Park chose this name for a fancied resemblance to a tall building. (USBGN)

Slate (Walla Walla County) *see* Slater

Slater *(S.10;T.8N;R.32E)*

Station 13 miles east of Pasco, southwest Walla Walla County. It was named by Northern Pacific Railway officials for a local homesteader, C. C. Slater. It appears on some maps, in error, as *Slate*.

Slaughter (King County) *see* Auburn

Slesse Creek (Whatcom County) *see* Silesia Creek

Slick Ear Creek *(T.6N;R.40E)*

The stream of the creek rises in the Table Rock area of Blue Mountains, Umatilla National Forest, extreme southeast Columbia County; flows south into Oregon, a distance of 1-1/2 miles to the boundary. In the 1880s, the name was given by stockmen when they found stolen cattle corralled here.

Slide Creek *(T.24N;R.17E)*

The stream of the creek heads on the northeast slope of Icicle Ridge, Wenatchee National Forest, central Chelan County; flows 3 miles east-by-north to Wenatchee River at the south end of Tumwater Canyon. It was named by Forest Supervisor A. H. Sylvester to describe the steep course of the stream from mountain to river.

Slide Mountain *(Mt. Rainier National Park)*

A 6,630-ft. peak between Lost Creek and White River, 2 miles south of the park's north boundary, northeast corner of the park. The name, which has been used for many years, is descriptive because frost action and other erosive elements cause frequent rock slides. (USBGN)

Slim Lake *(S.10;T.33N;R.13E)*

Very narrow, 7-acre lake, elevation 4,700 ft., 4 miles west of Cascade Mountain summit, extreme southeast Skagit County. It was named by Forest Service personnel because it is quite long compared with its width.

Slip Point *(S.16;T.32N;R.12W)*

East entrance point to Clallam Bay on the Strait of Juan de Fuca, northwest

Clallam County. The point has a broken formation and is subject to frequent slides, hence the name. In 1791, Manuel Quimper named this place *Punta de Rojas*, but like most Spanish names in this state, it did not persist.

Sloan Creek *(T.29N;Rs.12,13E)*

The stream of the creek rises in Blue Lake, 2 miles west of Cascade Mountain summit, Mt. Baker National Forest, east central Snohomish County; flows 8 miles northwest to Cadet Creek. It was named for James Sloan, miner-prospector of the 1890s.

Sloan Peak

(Ss.35,36;T.30N;Ss.1,2;T.29N;-R.11E.part uns)

A Mt. Baker National Forest peak, elevation 7,790 ft., 1-1/2 miles north of Goat Lake, east central Snohomish County.

Sluiskin Falls *(Mt. Rainier National Park)*

Waterfall in Paradise River, at the convergence of 3 upper branches, near the foot of Paradise Glacier, south central zone of the park. The stream falls 300 ft. over basalt crags to the lower river bed, elevation 5,900 ft. The waterfall was named by Gen. Hazard Stevens and P. B. Van Trump for an Indian who guided them on the first successful ascent of Mt. Baker on August 17, 1870. Sluiskin camped here while the two white men completed the climb, because the upper peak was sacred to Indians and not to be invaded. (USBGN)

Sluiskin Mountain *(Mt. Rainier National Park)*

A 7,015-ft. peak between West Fork, White River and Elysian Fields, overlooking Vernal Park, north central zone of the park. (USBGN) (*see* Sluiskin Falls)

Smallpox Bay *(S.11;T.35N;R.4W)*

West coast bay of San Juan Island on Haro Strait, directly south of Andrews Bay, San Juan County. The name is of local derivation and used because many Indians died here after becoming infected with smallpox at Victoria. The bodies were burned by U.S. officials to prevent spreading of the disease.

SMC Lake *(S.22;T.24N;R.9E)*

One of 3 Moolock Lakes, with Lakes Nadeau and Moolock, 6-3/4 miles east of North Bend, east central King County. This lake has an area of 40.7 acres. It

is an old name which evidently is formed by the initials of a pioneer settler. Local information as to his identity is conflicting.

Smith Brook *(T.27N;Rs.13,14E)*

The stream of the brook heads in Lichtenwasser Lake, 3 miles north of Stevens Pass, southwest Chelan County; flows 3 miles southeast to Nason Creek. This stream was previously mapped as North Fork, Nason Creek; it was re-mapped by Forest Supervisor A. H. Sylvester with the name of H. B. Smith, an early settler in Nason Creek Valley.

Smith Cove *(Ts.23,24N;R.3E)*

An area in Seattle at Interbay, north shore of Elliott Bay, King County. It contains large docks. Once it extended north to Salmon Bay, as a slough which was navigable by small craft at high tides. It was named for Dr. Henry A. Smith who settled here in 1852 with his mother and sister. In 1841, Cmdr. Charles Wilkes named this cove *Quartermaster Cove* but his name did not persist.

Smith Creek *(Ts.14,15N;Rs.7,8W)*

The stream of the creek rises near Brooklyn, northeast corner of Pacific County; flows southwest to Shoalwater Bay near the mouth of North River. It was named for Almon Smith who settled near the creek's mouth in 1853.

Smith Creek *(T.29N;R.4E)*

The stream of the creek rises at Sumas Mountain, 5 miles southeast of Nooksack, northwest Whatcom County; flows 4-1/2 miles south-by-east to Nooksack River. It should not be confused with Smith Creek which is a short tributary of Lake Whatcom. It was locally named for Thomas J. Smith, a homesteader of 1884, who was a pioneer hardware merchant on Bellingham Bay.

Smith Creek *(Ts.37,38N;R.4E)*

The stream of the creek rises 3 miles east of Lake Whatcom, southwest Whatcom County; flows southwest to the lake. It should not be confused with Smith Creek, a tributary of Nooksack River. It was named for William Smith, who came here from England in 1882, and who introduced successful English farming methods in the vicinity.

Smith Island *(uns)*

Lighthouse and bird refuge reservation in the east reach of the Strait of Juan de Fuca, 7 miles west of Whidbey Is-

land, extreme west Island County. In 1841, this isolated feature was charted by Cmdr. Wilkes as *Blunt's Island*, for one of his midshipmen, Simon F. Blunt. An earlier explorer, Lieut. Francisco de Eliza, named this island and nearby Minor Island as *Islas de Bonilla* in 1791. In 1847, the present name first appeared on British Admiralty charts and in 1858, on U.S. Coast Survey charts. Records indicate that the name had been used prior to these dates by Hudson's Bay Company, and was for a member of the H.B.C. staff.

Smith Prairie *(T.31N;Rs.1,2E)*

Whidbey Island prairie on the east central part of the island, 3 miles southeast of Coupeville, central Island County. It was locally named for Joseph S. Smith, who took a Donation Land Claim on the prairie, south of Snatelum Point in 1853.

Smiths Island *(Ss.5,8;T.29N;R.5E)*

An alluvial, 600-acre island, surrounded by tidal sloughs, at the mouth of Snohomish River, directly north of Everett, west central Snohomish County. It was named for Dr. Henry A. Smith, who tried to drain and reclaim the island. He succeeded in draining about 75 acres by diking.

Smith's Prairie (Island County) *see* Smith Prairie

Smoke Island (Cowlitz County) *see* Martin Island

Smoothing Iron Ridge

(Ts.8,9N;Rs.43,44E)

Ridge extending about 45 miles northeast from the Garfield County boundary, west central Asotin County. It was named by the earliest pioneers for a fancied resemblance to an old-fashioned sad iron.

Smugglers Cove (San Juan County) *see* Smallpox Bay

Smyrna *(S.35;T.16N;R.25E)*

Railroad point on Crab Creek, directly north of Saddle Mountains, southwest Grant County. It was named by H. R. Williams, vice-president of Chicago, Milwaukee & St. Paul Railway, who bestowed European and historical names on many places along his railroad. This one is for a famous ancient port on the Aegean Sea.

Snagtooth Ridge
(S.15;T.35N;R.18E.uns)

Area of sharp, glacial peaks between headwaters of Cedar and Willow creeks, Chelan National Forest, 4 miles east of Cascade Mountain summit, west central Okanogan County. The name is appropriate because of the sharp silhouette of broken mountain tops.

Snahapish *(Ts.25,26N;R.11W)*

The stream of the river rises in a marshy area northeast of Mt. Octopus, northwest Jefferson County; flows 10 miles south to Clearwater River, southwest Jefferson County. It was named for a tribal group of the Quinault nation that lived near the mouth of the river.

Snake River *(Franklin, Walla Walla, Whitman, Columbia, Garfield, and Asotin counties)*

This largest tributary of the Columbia River forms part of the boundaries of 6 counties in the state. The great river heads in a lake region of Yellowstone National Park and flows through Wyoming and Idaho; then, it flows along the northeast border of Oregon and enters Washington at Clarkston. From that point it flows northwest, west, and southwest to Columbia River at Pasco, skirting the 6 southeast counties. A vast program of hydroelectric development in Snake River is operated by federal agencies and private corporations. The Nez Perce name was *Shawpatin, Sahaptin* or *Saptin*, as spoken in several dialects, and as heard by many early traders and explorers. A less known Indian name for the river was *Kimooenim*. In 1805, Capt. William Clark named it *Lewis River*, for his associate Capt. Meriwether Lewis. The present name is for the Snake Indians who once eked out a poor existence along the stream. Other names that have been applied from time to time are *Lewis Fork* of the Columbia River, and *Lewis & Clark's River*.

Snake Rock *(S.4;T.28N;R.1E)*

Admiralty Inlet rock directly south of Mats Mats Bay, east central Jefferson County. In 1841, it was named by the Wilkes Expedition. The name was confirmed and used by U.S. Coast Survey in 1856 and charted accordingly.

Snakeland Point (Island County) *see* Snatelum Point

Snakelum Point (Island County) *see* Snatelum Point

Snatelum Point *(S.36;T.32N;R.1E)*

South entrance point to Penn Cove, east shore of Whidbey Island, central Island County. In 1841, this feature was named *Watsak Point* by Cmdr. Wilkes, but the name did not endure. The present name, locally chosen, was for an Indian, *Snatelum*, whose nickname was "Long Charlie." (USBGN)

Snee-oosh *(S.27;T.34N;R.2E)*

Swinomish Indian village at the north end of Skagit Bay on the east shore, 2-1/2 miles west of La Conner on Swinomish Indian Reservation. The name is an old tribal name for the place.

Snider Peak *(S.21;T.30N;R.11W.uns)*

An Olympic National Forest peak, elevation 3,174 ft., 8 miles south of Pysht, 1-1/2 miles north of Soleduck River, west central Clallam County. The peak was named for Snider Ranger Station at its foot, by U.S. Forest Service personnel. (USBGN)

Snipes Creek *(Ts.9,10N;R.25E)*

The stream of this intermittent creek rises in Rattlesnake Hills, northwest Benton County; flows 13 miles south to join Yakima River, 5 miles below Prosser. It was named for Ben Snipes, a famous early "cattle king" in the Yakima-Ellensburg-Kittitas area.

Snipes Mountain
(Ts.9,10N;Rs.21,22E)

A 1,290-ft. peak with a 7-mile-long ridge, north of Yakima River between Granger and Sunnyside, east central Yakima County. (*see* Snipes Creek)

Snohomish *(T.28N;Rs.5,6E)*

Town 5 miles southeast of Everett at the confluence of Snohomish and Pilchuck rivers, southwest Snohomish County. An early name was *Cadyville* for Capt. Cady who built a military trail over the Cascade Mountain summit, known as Cady Pass. In the late 1850s, the growing town was called *Snohomish City*. The present name is a variation of the Indian nomenclature which has been spelled *Sda-hob-bish* by certain linguists. The meaning evidently is "Tidewater people."

Snohomish County

A northwest Washington county. It is bounded on the north by Skagit County; on the east by Chelan County; on the south by King County; and on the west by Puget Sound. It contains over 60 peaks with altitudes more than 5,000 ft., 8 of which are over 7,000 ft. The area is 2,100 sq. miles. On January 14, 1861, the county was formed by act of the Territorial Legislature from a portion of Island County. (*see* Snohomish)

Snohomish River
(Ts.27-29N;Rs.5,6E)

River formed by the confluence of Skykomish and Snoqualmie rivers, 4 miles southwest of Monroe, southwest Snohomish County; flows 24 miles northwest to Port Gardner Bay, directly north of Everett. In 1841, it was named *Tuxpam* by the Wilkes Expedition. In 1847, Capt. Kellett and in 1854, U.S. Coast Survey used the Indian name *Sin-a-ho-mis*. The present name is a variation of the Indian name. (*see* Snohomish)

Snoqualmie *(S.32;T.24N;R.8E)*

Town on Snoqualmie River, directly above Snoqualmie Falls, 3 miles northwest of North Bend, central King County. The small community is based on farming and forest products. The name is from an Indian tribe that was powerful when white men came here. The tribal name, as Indians pronounced it, was *Sdoh-kwahlb-bhuh*. The Snoqualmies abused and ridiculed other tribes in the region, and the name given them by other Indians reflects fear and dislike. The most logical translation of the name appears to be "not of much account, but strong." Other spellings of the tribal name are *Sdo-Kwal-Bix* and *Sno-Kwal-Mis*. On some early maps this place was shown as *Snoqualme, Snowaulmie* or *Snoqualmoo*. (USBGN)

Snoqualmie Falls *(S.30;T.24N;R.8E)*

Impressive waterfall, with a vertical drop of 268 ft., in Snoqualmie River, below the junction of the river's 3 forks, central King County. The Snoqualmie Indian name for the top of the falls was *Sk-al-dal*, meaning "Lip." Their name for the pool below the falls was *Sq-wud*, meaning "underneath." (*see* Snoqualmie)

Snoqualmie Falls *(S.29;T.24N;R.8E)*

Community between Fall City and North Bend, near Snoqualmie River, central King County. This is a forest products manufacturing center. (*see* Snoqualmie

Snoqualmie Lake *(S.16;T.24N;R.11E)*

A 126.4-acre lake on Snoqualmie National Forest, 9-1/2 miles north of Snoqualmie Pass, northeast King County. (*see* Snoqualmie)

Snoqualmie Mountain
(Ss.21,22;T.23N;R.11E)

A 6,270-ft. peak, 2-1/2 miles north of Snoqualmie Pass, 2 miles west of Cascade Mountain summit, extreme east central King County. The mountain is in a heavily mineralized area. (*see* Snoqualmie)

Snoqualmie National Forest (King, Snohomish, Lewis, Yakima, Kittitas counties)

Extensive forest in the central Cascade Mountain area, both east and west of the summit, but with the majority of its 1,538,142 acres on the western slopes. Forest headquarters are at Seattle, Washington. Higher administrative functions are performed in the offices of Region 6, at Portland, Oregon. Most of its area was included in Washington National Forest, established in 1897. In 1908, the Snoqualmie was created from part of the Washington National Forest. In 1911 and 1933, more acreage was added from Rainier National Forest, making a total of 5 counties in the state which have substantial areas with this forest. The name, chosen by Forest Service officials in Washington, D.C., is from that of the Indian tribe. (*see* Snoqualmie)

Snoqualmie Pass *(S.4;T.22N;R.11E)*

A 3,004-ft. pass at Cascade Mountain summit, at the head of Snoqualmie River drainage to the west, and Yakima River drainage to the east, between east King County and northwest Kittitas County. This pass carries more highway traffic than any other pass over the Cascade Mountains. In 1865, the first wagon road was built through here by A. A. Denny and other early settlers. In 1914, the road was transformed into a modern highway.

Snoqualmie River
(Ts.22-27N;Rs.6-11E)

The stream of the river rises in 3 branches. The South Fork rises near Snoqualmie pass; the Middle Fork near Summit Lake at the Cascade Mountain summit; the North Fork in Lake Kanim

-- all in northeast King County. The branches merge 2 miles east of Snoqualmie Falls. The river flows north and northwest in a winding pattern into Snohomish County where it joins Skykomish River, 4 miles southwest of Monroe, forming the Snohomish River. This drainage area is very extensive. (*see* Snoqualmie)

Snoqualmie Little Sister (King County) *see* Lundin Peak

Snow Brushy Creek
(T.30N;R.17E.uns)

The stream of the creek rises in Milham Pass, Chelan Mountains, south of Borealis Ridge, north central Chelan County; flows 5 miles to enter Entiat River from the northeast. It evidently was named by sheepmen for an abundance of snow plant which is common in the Cascade mountain region.

Snow Creek *(T.28N;R.2W)*

The stream of the creek rises on the east slope of Mt. Zion, Olympic National Forest, southeast Clallam County; flows 6-1/2 miles east to Lake Crocker, northeast Jefferson County. The stream was named for a settler who homesteaded just below Lake Crocker.

Snow Creek *(Ss.17,20;T.33N;R.14W)*

The stream of the creek rises directly east of Makah Indian Reservation, 3 miles southeast of Neah Bay, northwest Clallam County; flows north to Strait of Juan de Fuca. This very short stream was locally named, but the name appears to have little relation to snowfall or run-off from snowfields. The Indian name was *To-kwak-sose.*

Snow Grass Flat *(T.12N;R.11E)*

A 6,400-ft. flat, 1 mile west of Cascade Mountain summit, Goat Rocks Primitive Area, extreme east central Lewis County. The flat is reputed to be the highest good camp site in the state. It was named for the prevalence of the type of vegetation which stockmen call *snow grass*, not uncommon in the Cascade Mountains.

Snow King Lake (Skagit County) *see* Found Lakes

Snow Lake *(S.19;T.23N;R.11E)*

Deep, 160-acre lake in the high Cascades, elevation 5,000 ft., 4 miles northwest of Snoqualmie Pass, east central King County. The name, given by government surveyors, is descriptive, because the lake's elevation is condu-

cive to heavy snowfall which persists into early summer. The Indian name was *Enum-klah-pah*, which means "Place of thunder."

Snow Lake *(S.23;T.10N;R.5E)*

A 4.8-acre lake on Gifford Pinchot National Forest, elevation 4,700 ft., 3-1/2 miles north of Spirit Lake, in extreme northwest Skamania County. It is snow-fed during most of the year, which accounts for the locally chosen name. An alternate name is *Burgoyne Lake.*

Snowgrass Mountain
(S.12;T.25N;R.15E)

A Wenatchee National Forest peak at the junction of Icicle Ridge and Chiwaukum Mountains, directly north of Frosty Pass, west central Chelan County. Local residents state that it was named by sheepmen for a common type of vegetation on the mountain which they considered good feed.

Snowshoe Creek *(Ts.35-36N;R.35E)*

The stream of this short creek rises on the south side of Skalawag Ridge, Colville National Forest, central Ferry County; flows south 2 miles to the South Fork, Sherman Creek, 16 miles east of Republic. The creek takes its name from Snowshoe Camp at the mouth, which was so labeled because the caretaker of the first telephone line in this area followed the line on snowshoes in the winter, all the way from Marcus to Republic.

Snowshoe Falls *(T.22N;R.10E)*

Highest falls in Denny Creek, elevation 3,600 ft., 2-1/2 miles west of Snoqualmie Pass, east central King County. This name was devised by The Mountaineers and was recommended for approval to USBGN on June 15, 1916. The creek was named in honor of Arthur A. Denny, Seattle pioneer, who had mining claims in this area. (USBGN)

Snowshoe Lake (Cowlitz County) *see* McBride Lake

Snowy Creek *(T.27N;R.15E)*

The stream of the creek heads on a divide between Nason and Rainy creeks, Wenatchee National Forest, northwest Chelan County; flows north-by-east 2 miles to Rainy Creek. This descriptive name was applied by Forest Supervisor A. H. Sylvester.

Snowy Lakes *(S.27;T.36N;R.17E)*

Two connected lakes at Snowy Pass, Cascade Mountain summit, 19 miles southeast of Ross Dam, extreme northeast Skagit County. The upper of the lakes is 3 acres, elevation 6,600 ft.; the lower lake is 1 acre, elevation 6,400 ft. The lakes appear to have been named for Snowy Pass. They are snow-fed and snowbound much of each year.

Snowy Range (Snowy Mountains) (Wash. state ref./central Wash.) *see* Cascade Mountain Range

Soap Lake (lake) *(T.22N;Rs.26,27E)*

Heavily mineralized lake, of volcanic origin, 7 miles northeast of Ephrata, north central Grant County. This lake is the southernmost of a string of lakes in Grand Coulee. It is strongly alkaline and soapy to the touch; it foams readily when exposed to high winds. This 2-mile-long lake is a popular bathing lake. Claims that it contains 21 chemicals and is useful for medicinal purposes are strengthened by the Indian name, which meant "witch doctor." A previous name, *Sanitarium Lake*, was given because a number of these establishments were sprinkled along the shores.

Soap Lake (town) *(S.19;T.22N;R.27E&S.24;T.22N;- R.26E)*

Town on south shore of Soap Lake (lake), at the south end of Grand Coulee, 4-1/2 miles north of Ephrata, north central Grant County. The town formerly depended on visitors with real or imaginary ailments which might be cured by the medicinal content of Soap Lake water. More recently it has flourished on increased farming as a result of irrigation from Grand Coulee Dam.

Sobey *(S.22;T.30N;R.6E)*

Settlement on Little Pilchuck River, 2 miles southwest of Granite Falls, east central Snohomish County. It was named for James Sobey who operated a shingle mill here and who later had a larger mill in Ballard.

Soda Creek *(Ts.27,28N;R.15E)*

The stream of the creek heads on Wenatchee Ridge, Wenatchee National Forest, west central Chelan County; flows 3 miles south to Little Wenatchee River. It was named by Forest Supervisor A. H. Sylvester for a fine, cold soda spring close to the creek which has been included in a public campground.

Soda Spring *(S.35;T.9N;R.12E.uns)*

Mineralized springs on Yakima In-dian Reservation, west bank of Klickitat River, 4 miles southeast of Mt. Adams Lake near confluence of Soda Springs Creek and Klickitat River, southwest Klickitat County. This is one of many similar springs along the Klickitat, from McCormick Meadows near the river's head to the lower reaches north of Columbia River. As it emerges from these underground sources, the water is effervescent and has enough sulphur content to stain adjoining rocks and soil. It is quite potable and was sold in bottled form at one time.

Soda Springs (Snohomish County) *see* Garland Mineral Springs

Sol Duc Falls *(S.3;T.28N;R.9W.uns)*

Falls in Soleduck River, 2 miles above Sol Duc Hot Springs, south central Clallam County. This Indian name means "magic waters." A legend tells of 2 dragons, Sol Duc and Elwha, who fought to a draw, then sealed themselves up in caverns. They wept hot tears, which furnishes the water for the springs.

Sol Duc Hot Springs *(S.32;T.29N;R.9W)*

Mineralized, natural hot springs, elevation 1,200 ft., on Olympic National Forest, near the headwaters of Soleduck River, south central Clallam County. (*see* Sol Duc Falls)

Soldiers Pond *(S.6;T.18N;R.5E)*

Short lake, 700 ft. south of State Soldiers Home at Orting, central Pierce County. A longer name for the lake is *State Soldiers Home Pond*.

Soleduck Lake *(T.28N;R.9W.uns)*

Small lake, not over 1/4 mile in width, 5 miles southeast of Sol Duc Hot Springs, Olympic National Park, south central Clallam County. An unofficial local name is *Morganrath Lake* or *Morgenroth Lake*. (*see* Sol Duck Falls)

Soleduck Park *(T.28N;R.8W.uns)*

Mountain meadow, 1/2 mile-long, near the head of Bridge Creek, 7-1/2 miles north-northwest of Mt. Olympus, Olympic National Park, south central Clallam County. (*see* Sol Duc Falls)

Soleduck River *(Ts.28-30N;Rs.8-13W)*

The stream of the river rises in Soleduck Park near High Divide, south central Clallam County; flows west to join Bogechiel River, 5 miles east of La Push, the 2 streams forming Quillayute River. (USBGN) (*see* Sol Duc Falls)

Soleduck Valley *(Ts.29,30N;Rs.12,13E)*

Valley which includes several sections at the northwest end of Olympic National Park, in a wide bend of Soleduck River, west central Clallam County. (*see* Sol Duc Falls)

Solleks River *(T.25N;Rs.10,10-1/2,11W)*

The stream of the river rises on the west boundary of Olympic National Park; flows 10-1/2 miles west to Clearwater River. This original Indian name means "angry" in Chinook jargon.

Soloosa (Benton County) *see* Plymouth

Sonora Reef *(T.21N;R.13W)*

Pacific Ocean reef, 1 mile off the coast of Quinault Indian Reservation, directly north of Cape Grenville, northwest Grays Harbor County. The reef, partly bare at low water, was named by Davidson of the U.S. Coast Survey in 1889 for the Spanish schooner *Sonora*, which passed over this reef unscathed in 1775.

Sooes *(S.6;T.32N;R.15W.)*

Village on Makah Indian Reservation, Mukkaw Bay, 1 mile south of mouth of Sooes River, northwest Clallam County. The Indian name is *Tsooess* or *Tsooyes,* as pronounced by Makahs.

Sooes River *(Ts.32,33N;Rs.14,15W)* miles northeast of Lake Ozette, northwest Clallam County; flows west and northwest through Makah Indian Reservation to Mukkaw Bay on Pacific Ocean. (*see* Sooes)

Sopenah (Lewis County) *see* Vader

Sopun Inlet *(T.16N;R.11W)*

Inlet extending from the mouth of Elk River to South Bay, southwest Grays Harbor County. In 1841, it was named by the Wilkes Expedition without recording for whom. Recent maps do not show the Wilkes name.

Soquamic Bay (Kitsap County) *see* Port Madison (Bay)

Sorenson Creek *(Ts.34,35N;Rs.5,6E)*

The stream of the creek rises at Haystack Mountain, 8 miles southwest of Hamilton, central Skagit County; flows 4 miles northwest to Skagit River between Hamilton and Sedro-Woolley. The creek was locally named for Peter Sorenson who settled at the mouth of the creek in 1880.

Sotolick Point Mount Rainier National Park) *see* Satulick Point, Mountain

Source Lake (*S.30;T.23N;R.11E*)

Very small lake, 1/2 mile south of Snow Lake, 3-1/2 miles west of Cascade Mountain Summit, at the head of South Fork, Snoqualmie River, east central King County. It was named by The Mountaineers because it is the source of a river.

Sourdough Creek (*T.25N;R.19E*)

The stream of the creek rises on the north side of Chumstick Mountain, Wenatchee National Forest, central Chelan County; flows 3-1/2 miles northeast to Roaring Creek. This common pioneer name was placed on the stream by Forest Ranger James McKenzie.

Sourdough Lake (*S.21;T.38N;R.13E*)

A 33.4-acre lake, elevation 4,400 ft., at the head of Pierce Creek, 3-1/2 miles northwest of Ross Dam, southeast Whatcom County. The lake is reported to have been named by early-day prospectors for the "frying pan" which was a staple article of the diet.

Sourdough Mountain (Mount Rainier National Park)

Very extensive mountain ridge, elevation 7,062 ft., north of Sunrise Park and Sunrise Ridge, northeast sector of park. It extends in a wide, 9-mile-curve from Berkeley Park to The Palisades. The name originated during the days of heav prospecting for minerals, before the park was established. It is for the sourdough bread and pancakes that wandering miners made over campfires.

South Bay (*S.7;T.19N;R.1W*)

West shore bay of Henderson Inlet, 5-1/2 miles north of Olympia, north centralThurston County. It is locally applied.

South Bay (*S.28;T.37N;R.4E*)

Southwest end bay of Lake Whatcom, southwest Whatcom County. For many years there was a logging camp and log dump here; now it's a scattered community. The first name applied to this bay was *Austin's Landing,* for Harry Austin who homesteaded here in 1883. At that time it was a landing for lake steamers, before there were adequate roads. The present name is locally applied and is descriptive, as this is the most southerly bay on the

lake. The hamlet of South Bay is on its eastern shore.

South Bend (*Ss.27,28;T.14N;R.9W*)

Town on Willapa River, 3 miles from entrance of Willapa River into Willapa Harbor, north central Pacific County. In 1860, the nucleus of this town was a sawmill. The South Bend Land Company boomed the town and it developed rapidly in the 1890s. The name indicated the distinct bend to the south in Willapa River at this point. This name was chosen by local settlers. John B. Woods, the first postmaster, used it for the post office.

South Cascade Lake
(*S.1;T.33N;F.13E*)

A 40-acre lake, elevation 5,200 ft., directly west of Cascade Mountain Summit, southwest side of Le Conte Mountain, at the foot of South Cascade Glacier. It is a turbid lake, maximum depth 181 ft. It was named for South Cascae Glacier.

South Dam (*Ss.32,33;T.25N;R.28E*)

Dam at the south end of Banks Lake, Grand Coulee's equalizing reservoir. This dam is directly west of Coulee City, northeast Grant County. It is named after its location at the prehistoric site of the famous Dry Falls of the Columbia River. (*see* Dry Falls Dam)

South Fork Calispell Creek
(*Ts.31,32;R.43E*)

The stream of the creek rises at Boyer Mountain, 18 miles west of Newport, southwest Pend Oreille County; flows 5-1/2 miles northeast to Calispell Creek. (*see* Calispell Creek) (USBGN)

South Fork Chiwaukum Creek
(*Ts.25,26N;R.16E*)

The stream of the creek rises at the south end of Chiwaukum Mountains, Wenatchee National Forest, central Chelan County; flows 6-1/2 miles t Chiwaukum Creek. The name was applied by Forest Supervisor A. H. Sylvester. (*see* Chiwaukum Creek)

South Fork Salmon Creek
(*Ts.35,26N;Rs.23,24E*)

The stream of the creek rises near Old Baldy Mountain, central Okanogan County; flows 14-1/2 miles east to Salmon Creek, south of Conconully. (USBGN) (*see* Salmon Creek)

South Mowich Glacier (*Mt. Rainier National Park*)

Glacier on the northwest slope of Mt. Rainier, between Edmunds and Puyallup Glaciers, west central zone of the park. It

drains into South Mowich River. (USBGN) (*see* Mowich River)

South Mowich River (*Mt. Rainier National Park*)

The stream of the river rises at the foot of South Mowich Glacier, west slope of Mt. Rainier, flows northwest to join North Mowich River, northwest area of the park. (USBGN) (*see* Mowich River)

South Park (*T.23N;R.4E*)

Suburban area in West Seattle, east of White Center, west central King County. The original name was Ox Bow, for a distinctive curve in Duwamish River. An alternate name is *South Park Junction.* At the time the name was applied, this area was in the extreme south end of Seattle, so the name was easonably descriptive.

South Point (*S.6;T.27N;R.1E*)

South entrance point to Squamish Harbor, on Hood Canal, east central Jefferson County. In 1841, the point was named by the Wilkes Expedition. Their coice was due to the point's location at the most southerly extreme of Squamish Harbor.

South Point (*S.36:t.24N;R.4E*)

Southernmost promontory on Mercer Island, Lake Washington, west central King Cunty. This locally-chosen name is quite descriptive. The Indian name was *La-gwit-sa-teb,* which means "Stripping bark from logs." Puget Sound Indian women stripped a great deal of cedar bark for basketry and other weaving.

South Prairie (*S.7;T.19N;R.6E*)

Prairie on South Prairier Creek 3 miles southwest of Buckley, north central Pierce County. In the early 1850s, it was named by Paul Emery, who filed a Donation Land Claim here. Northern-Pacific Railway personnel adopted the name foa station on the prairie in 1881, but changed it to *Cascade Junction* in 1885. Local residents later reverted to the use of the original name.

South Prairie Creek
(*Ts.18,19N;Rs.5-7E*)

The stream of the creek rises in Snoqualmie National Forest, 2 miles north of Mt. Rainier National Park, north central Pierce County; flows east and northeast to Carbon River at Crocker. It was named for South Prairie, through which it flows. (*see* South Prairie)

South Ainsworth (Walla Walla County) *see* Burbank

South Bay (community) (Whatcom County) *see* South Bay (bay)

South Bluff (Whatcom County) *see* Birch Point

South Boistfort (Lewis County) *see* Wildwood

South Coulee Dam (Grant County) *see* O'Sullivan Dam

South Dam (Grant County) *see* Dry Falls Dam

South Fork (King County) *see* North Bend

South Fork Icicle Creek (Chelan County) *see* French Creek

South Fork Salmo River (Pend Oreille County) *see* South Salmo River

South-Half (Ferry County) *see* Ferry City

South Prairie Junction (Pierce County) *see* Cascade Junction

South Puyallup River (*Mt. Rainier Park*)

The stream of the river rises on the southwest slope of Mt. Rainier, at the foot of Tahoma Glacier; flows west to join North Puyallup River, Pierce County, 1-1/2 miles west of the west park boundary. (*see* Puyallup River)

South Skookum Lake
(*S.1;T.33N;R.44E*)

Small lake at the head of North Fork, Skookum Creek, just outside Kaniksu National Forest, south central Pend Oreille County. The lake is drained by Skookum Creek and is connected by a small stream with North Skookum Lake, directly to the north. (*see* North Skookum Lake)

South Tacoma (*T.20N;Rs.2,3E*)

Suburb adjoining Tacoma on the south, northwest Pierce County. In 1890, a railway station here was called *Edison* by officials of Northern Pacific Railway Company. In 1895, local residents chose the present name.

South Tahoma Glacier (*Mt. Rainier National Park*)

A 10,900-ft. glacier on southwest slope of Mt. Rainier, 1-1/2 miles southwest of the summit, in a glacial cirque; it extends 4 miles southwest to the headwaters of Tahoma Creek, southwest quarter of the park. This glacier is medium-sized compared with other glaciers in the park. (*see* Tahoma Creek)

South Twin Lake (*T.32N;R.35E*)

A 2-mile-long lake, elevation 2,572 ft., on Colville Indian Reservation, 8 miles west of Inchelium, east central Ferry County. The lake is directly south of North Twin Lake and drains into that body of water through a swampy stream. The name is descriptive as the 2 lakes are of almost the same size.

South Twin Mountain (Whatcom County) *see* Twin Sisters Range

Southside (Kitsap County) *see* Eagledale

Southwest Island (San Juan County) *see* Colville Island

Soyoss Lake (Okanogan County) *see* Osoyoos Lake

Spak Point (*S.36;T.30N;R.3W*)

Small, pointed spit on east side of Sequim Bay, east central Clallam County. In 1841, it was named by the Wilkes Expedition with no apparent record of the name source. A name in local use in the past was *Goose Point*.

Spalding Lock and Dam (Garfield/Whitman counties) *see* Lower Granite Dam

Spanaway (*S.28;T.19N;R.3E*)

One of the earliest settlements in Pierce County, east of Spanaway Lake, 10 miles south of Tacoma. The name is from the original Indian name of Spanaway Lake, which was *Spannuch*, which means "On the shore of lake." Evidently it was named by officials of Hudson's Bay Company.

Spanaway Lake (*T.19N:R.3E*)

A 262.4-acre lake directly east of Fort Lewis Army Post, 1 mile southeast of McChord Field, west central Pierce County. The lake includes Daron Island at its north end. Another name which was in use in 1854, was *Bush Elier Lake*. (*see* Spanaway)

Spanaway Park (*T.19N;R.3E*)

A 339-acre park and picnic ground, directly east of Spanaway Park and Fort Lewis Army Post, northwest Pierce County. (*see* Spanaway)

Spangle (*S.4;T.22N;R.43E*)

One of the oldest settlements in the Inland Empire, 19 miles south of Spokane, in Spangle Township, south central Spokane County. This was a stop-off on the Mullan Road. In 1862, the first structure was built on a pre-emption claim. The first permanent resident was William Spangle, a Civil War veteran, who came in 1872. On June 18, 1879, the town was platted by L. W. Rima of Spokane Falls and named for William Spangle by officials of Northern Pacific Railway Company. Prior to platting, settlers called the place *Pine Grove*. The original Indian name was *N-soy-akin*, meaning "crawfish."

Spangle Creek (*Ts.22,23N;R.43E*)

The stream of the creek rises in the southern part of Spangle Township, south central Spokane County; flows northward 16 miles through Spangle to Latah Creek at Duncan. (*see* Spangle)

Spanish Camp Creek (*T.25N;R.15E*)

The stream of the creek heads at Ladies Pass, north of Cape Horn, Wenatchee National Forest, west central Chelan County; flows 3 miles southwest to Icicle Creek. Forest Supervisor A. H. Sylvester used an old name -- *Spanish Camp* -- which applied to an open range near the head of the creek.

Spar Point (*S.4;T.17N;R.10W*)

North shore point of Grays Harbor, directly west of Hoquiam, southwest Grays Harbor County. In 1841, the name was given by the Wilkes Expedition as a descriptive term. The shoreline has been altered since that time so that the point cannot be identified.

Spectacle Lake
(*Ss.24,25;T.23N;R.12E*)

High mountain lake, 3 miles east of Cascade Mountain summit, at head of West Fork, Coopers Creek, northwest Kittitas County. The lake is in a rugged, glaciated area, and shaped so that it has a distinct resemblance to a pair of spectacles.

Spedis (*T.2N;R.14E*)

Site of an old Indian fishing village, 9 miles west of Wishram, north bank of Columbia River, south central Klickitat County. The S.P.&S. Railway siding at this place is named for an Indian patriarch, Bill Spedis, a descendant of Wishram chiefs.

Speelyai Creek (*Ts.6,7N;Rs.3,4E*)

The stream of the creek rises south of Merrill Lake, southeast Cowlitz County; flows 10 miles south to Lake Merwin. This is the Indian word for "coyote." In this case, the creek was named for an Indian chief who had adopted the coyote's name.

Speiden Island (San Juan County) *see* Spieden Island

Spencer Canyon (*T.25N;Rs.20,21E*)

A Wenatchee National Forest canyon which heads near the east boundary of the forest, southeast Chelan County; it extends 2-1/2 miles to Spencer Lake and on to the Columbia River. It was named for G. E. Spencer, Chelan County Assessor, who owned a ranch and orchard at the canyon's mouth.

Spencer Lake (*S.31;T.25N;R.21E*)

Small lake in Spencer Canyon, 2 miles southwest of Entiat, 1/2 mile east of Columbia River, southeast Chelan County. (*see* Spencer Canyon)

Spencer Lake (*S.4;T.35N;R.1W*)

A 64-acre lake, maximum depth 72 ft., 1/2 mile east of Thatcher, on central Blakely island, east San Juan County. The lake is privately owned. It was locally named for a homesteader who claimed 160 acres here in 1886. Alternate names are *Wildwood Lake* and *Thatcher Lake.*

Spencer Spit (*S.12;T.35N;R.1W*)

Sand spit which almost reaches Frost Island, on the northeast shore of Lopez Island, north end of Lopez Sound, southeast San Juan County. (*see* Spencer Lake, San Juan County)

Sperry Peak (*S.10;T.29N;R.10E*)

A Mt. Baker National Forest peak, elevation 6,200 ft., 5-1/2 miles northwest of Monte Cristo, east central Snohomish County. It was named in the days of mining excitement for A. D. (Dick) Sperry, an early prospector in the area.

Sphinx (Jefferson County) *see* East Peak, Mt. Olympus

Spickard Peak
(*Ss.9,10;T.40N;R.12E.uns*)

Glacial peak, elevation 8,994 ft., at the head of Silver Creek, 2-1/2 miles south of the Canadian boundary, northeast Whatcom County. The original name was *Glacier Peak*, which often was confused with a larger peak by the same name in Snohomish County. In 1961, the name was changed at the suggestion of the Seattle Physicians' Committee for a North Cascades National Park, to honor Dr. Warren Spickard, Seattle physician and conservationist, who was killed in climbing Mox Peak in this general area. (USBGN)

Spider Glacier (*T.31N;R.16E*)

A Wenatchee National Forest glacier at the head of West Fork, Phelps Creek, directly southeast of Lyman Glacier at Cascade Mountain summit, northwest Chelan County. This somewhat imaginative name was applied by Jimmy Naughten, a mining engineer in this area for Royal Development Company.

Spieden Bluff (*S.2;T.36N;R.4W*)

Spieden Island bluff (on the west cape), Spieden Channel, northwest San Juan County. In 1859 -- as in the case of Spieden Channel -- Capt. Richards of the British admiralty survey extended Wilkes' name for Spieden Island to this feature. Wilkes' name was for William Spieden, purser in U.S. Sloop-of-war *Peacock*. The name was chosen by Lieut. Cmdr. Ringgold of the Wilkes Expedition. As in many such cases, the possessive form has been dropped in subsequent mapping and charting. The Lummi Indian name was *Wha-tith*, meaning "upright rock which tumbled on side."

Spieden Channel (*T.36N;Rs.3,4W*)

Channel between Spieden and San Juan Islands, directly north of Roche Harbor, northwest San Juan County. (*see* Spieden Bluff)

Spieden Island (*T.36N;Rs.3,4W*)

Narrow, 3-mile-long island on Spieden Channel, 1 mile north of the north end of San Juan Island, northwest San Juan County.

Spiketown (*S.15;T.19N;R.6E*)

Former coal mining town on South Prairie Creek, 1-1/2 miles south of Buckley, north central Pierce County. It was developed by William D. C. Spike of American Coal Company. The present name is for him. Another name, carried on some maps, was *Morristown.*

Spillei (Cowlitz County) *see* Yale

Spillnin (Okanogan County) *see* Nespelem

Spion Kop (*S.34;T.38N;R.37E*)

A 3,000-ft. peak between Kettle and Columbia rivers, about 2-1/2 miles west of Bossburg, northwest Stevens County. In 1902, it was thought to be an entire mountain of marble, valuable for building. The rock later was identified as dolomite, the basis for magnesite production. It was named by mining interests for a hill in South Africa which became famous during the South African War of 1899-1902, commonly called the Boer War.

Spipen (Yakima County) *see* Naches River

Spire Lake
(*Ss.26,27N;T.33N;R.13E.uns*)

A Mt. Baker National Forest lake, 1-1/2 miles west of Cascade Mountain summit, at the head of Bachelor Creek, directly west of Spire Peak, southeast Skagit County. It was named for Spire Peak, a towering mountain to the east, elevation 8,200 ft.

Spire Mountain (*S.35;T.28N;R.11E*)

A 6,065-ft. peak between Howard and Bear creeks, 3 miles southeast of Galena, southeast Snohomish County. The name was given by miners because of the mountain's sharp peak.

Spirit Lake (*T.9N;R.5E*)

A Gifford Pinchot National Forest lake, 1,300-ft. deep, elevation, 3,199 ft., 6 miles northeast of Mt. St. Helens summit, northwest Skamania County. The lake and adjoining area were once attractive to sportsmen and tourists; but since the eruption of Mt. St. Helen's in May, 1980, Spirit Lake has been devastated. The bottom of the lake is mostly white pumice. Aside from the main lake, over 6 miles-long, there are 30 smaller lakes in the area. The name relates to Indian superstitions. Local natives firmly believed that the lake was haunted, as well as the slopes of Mt. St. Helens; and the superstition spread to some of the early white settlers. Indian outcasts, called *Siatcoes*, may have been the basis for the legends.

Spirit Lake *(S.14;T.9N;R.5E)*

Community on south shore of Spirit Lake (lake), directly north of Mt. St. Helens, northwest Skamania County. On October 27, 1910, the post office name was changed from Spirit Lake to *Lange* to honor the postmaster, R. C. Lange. The original name, however, remains on standard maps and highway travel maps, except those issued by Washington state.

Split Rock *(S.8;T.22N;R.13W.uns)*

Pacific Ocean rock, 1-1/2 miles offshore from Quinault Indian Reservation, northwest Grays Harbor County. In 1889, it was named by Davidson of the U.S. Coast Survey. It is descriptive, as a distinct split appears when viewed from the west or northwest.

Spokane *(Ts.25,26N;Rs.42,43E)*

City of about 41 sq. miles, elevation, 1,890 ft., at the falls of Spokane River, 90 miles south of Canadian boundary, central Spokane County. Several trading posts, owned by Pacific Fur Company, The North West Company, and Hudson's Bay Company, operated in the vicinity from 1810 until 1826. Permanent settlement started in 1871 when J. J. Downing, S. R. Scranton, and R. M. Benjamin built a sawmill near Spokane Falls. On February 13, 1878, the town was platted as *Spokane Falls*, and in 1881, was incorporated under the same name, by act of the Territorial Legislature, which was dated November 29. In 1890, when the town was reincorporated, the city council altered the name to its present form. This name appears to be from the Indian tribal designation, *Spehkunne*, meaning "Children of the Sun" or "Sun People." It evidently derives from Indians who formerly lived in a village at the foot of Spokane Falls. When they fished at the falls, they stood in a rainbow or halo of light formed by sunlight striking a cloud of mist. An alternate source of the name is from Illum Spokane, an elderly chief of Middle Spokans, who lived near the falls a long time.

Spokane Air Force Base (Spokane County) *see* Fairchild Air Force Base

Spokane Army Air Depot (Spokane County) *see* Fairchild Air Force Base

Spokane Bridge *(S.1;T.25N;R.45E)*

Railroad town 14 miles east of Spokane, close to the boundary of Idaho, east central Spokane County. In the 1860s, it had a boom period because of mining excitement, at which time A. C. Kendall established a trading post. The name is descriptive, as an extensive bridge crosses the Spokane River here. In 1864, the first bridge was built.

Spokane County

A northeast Washington county. It is bounded on the west by Lincoln and Stevens counties; on the north by Stevens and Pend Oreille counties; on the east by Idaho; and on the south by Whitman County. On January 29, 1864, it was created from part of Stevens County by act of the Territorial Legislature. Fifty townships, each with township government, distinguish this county from others in the state. (*see* Spokane)

Spokane Falls *(S.17;T.25N;R.43E)*

Important and scenic falls in the center of Spokane, in the Spokane River, directly below Havermale Island, Spokane County. In this series of falls, the total drop is approximately 150 ft. Since 1871, they have been used for power purposes and were the feature around which Spokane was built. The Indian name was *Stluputqu*, meaning "swift waters." In 1805, Lewis & Clark referred to the falls as *Skeetsomish*. In 1811, David Thompson used the name *Skeetshoo*. (*see* Spokane)

Spokane Falls (city) (Spokane County) *see* Spokane

Spokane House (Spokane County) *see* Fort Spokane

Spokane Indian Reservation *(Ts.27-29N;Rs.35-40E)*

A 141,380-acre reservation, bounded on the west by Columbia River; on the south by Spokane River; on the east by Chamokane Creek; and, on the north by the 48th parallel of latitude, southwest Stevens County. On January 18, 1881, President Hayes established the reservation by executive order. (*see* Spokane)

Spokane Plains Battlefield *(T.25N;R.40E)*

Historic site near Deep Creek, 12 miles west of Spokane, west central Spokane County. Troops under Col. George M. Wright fought an allied force of Spokane, Coeur d'Alene, Palouse,

and Pend Oreille Indians on September 5, 1858. A monument marks the approximate location of this battle. (*see* Spokane)

Spokane River

The stream of this important river rises in Idaho's Lake Coeur d'Alene; flows 15 miles west to east central Spokane County near Spokane Bridge; it continues west and northwest through the center of the county and is bordered in its lower course by Stevens County on the north, Lincoln County on the south. Then it enters the Columbia River near that river's Elbow Bend. From source to mouth the total drop is 1,083 ft. The river's lower course was flooded for 35 miles in the reservoir created by Grand Coulee Dam. (*see* Spokane)

Spoon Lake (King County) *see* Shadow Lake

Sportsman Lake *(S.33;T.36N;R.3W)*

A 66-acre lake, maximum depth 10 ft., northeast San Juan Island, 3 miles northwest of Friday Harbor, west San Juan County. An early name was *Lake Tucker*, for Judge J. E. Tucker, a San Juan settler and a representative in the first state legislature. The present name is descriptive, as there is excellent bass fishing for local sportsmen. An alternate name is *Jesus Reservoir*. (USBGN)

Sprague *(Ss.23,24;T.21N;R.38E)*

Town 2 miles east of Colville Lake, 45 miles southwest of Spokane, extreme southeast Lincoln County. The town has declined somewhat from the boom period which it experienced during the days of railroad construction in the 1880s. It was named by North Pacific officials for Gen. John W. Sprague, director of the railway, and at one time general manager of the western division. An earlier name was *Hoodooville*, for a local character nicknamed "Hoodoo Billy" Burrow.

Sprague County (Lincoln County) *see* Lincoln County

Sprague Lake *(Ts.20,21N;Rs.37,38E)*

Lake between Sprague, southeast Lincoln County and Keystone, northeast Adams County. It is an enlargement of Cow Creek, extending 6 miles from southwest-to-northeast, and serving as a recreation spot for local people. It was formerly called *Colville Lake* and *Lake Colville*. The Indian name was *Silkatkwu*. In a 1954, the present name was approved by USBGN. (*see* Sprague)

Spray Creek *(Mt. Rainier National Park)*

The stream of this short creek rises at the foot of Flett Glacier, in Spray Park, northwest zone of the park; flows west to North Mowich River. The name is for Spray Falls which is in the creek. In 1883, trail builders named both creek and falls when the Bailey Willis Trail was built nearby. The name is descriptive because the falls breaks into a mass of spray when it plunges into the creek. (USBGN)

Spray Falls *(Mt. Rainier National Park)*

This waterfall, the highest and most beautiful on the north side of Mt. Rainier, is in Spray Creek, 3/4 mile from its junction with North Mowich River, in Spray Park. *(see* Spray Creek*)*

Spray Park *(Mt. Rainier National Park)*

Park at the headwaters of Spray Creek, above Spray Falls, northwest of the foot of Flett Glacier, northwest sector of the park. The park is dotted with small lakes and covered with flowers in season. *(see* Spray Creek*)*

Spring Beach *(S.34;T.22N;R.2E)*

Vashon Island beach on the island's southwest tip, West Passage, extreme southwest King County. In 1903, this feature was named by H. B. Ritz of Tacoma when he started a summer resort here on a 200-acre tract. The name was inspired by beautiful springs that emerge on the beach.

Spring Creek *(T.7N;Rs.37,38E)*

The stream of the creek rises on Blacksnake Ridge, in Blue Mountains, southeast Walla Walla County; flows 8 miles northeast to join Dry Creek near Buroker. It was named for the many springs in which it heads on the northwest slope of Blue Mountains.

Spring Creek (Stevens County) *see* Sheep Creek

Spring Creek *(S.5;T.7N;R.37E)*

Rail point on Spring Creek, 6 miles northeast of Walla Walla, southeast Walla Walla County. The railroad station here was named by Northern Pacific officials for the creek which crosses their railroad here.

Spring Passage *(T.36N;R.3W)*

Passage between Jones Island and the southwest end of Orcas Island, central San Juan County. In 1858, this name was charted by Capt. Richards, RN, and

is one of few names given by him on which no origin appears. This name, however, has been adopted by the U.S. Coast Survey.

Spring Valley (Stevens County) *see* Fruitland

Springdale *(S.34;T.30N;R.40E)*

Town in the Colville River Valley, 5 miles west of Loon Lake, on Sheep Creek, south central Stevens County. The land on which Springdale is located was homesteaded by Charles O. Squires in 1888, and the Spokane Falls & Northern Railway called their station *Squires City* when it was built through here. Settlers had the name changed by petition to its present form -- a name contrived for reasons which are not of record. There are, however, many subterranean streams in this part of the valley, some of which emerge as springs.

Spruce *(S.26;T..27N;R.11W)*

Community on Hoh River at the mouth of Spruce Creek, northwest Jefferson County. The name was chosen by John Huelsdonk, first postmaster, and by other local settlers as a post office name on June 18, 1904, because of the predominance of spruce timber in the area.

Spud Lake (Lewis County) *see* Newaukum Lakes

Spukwush, Spuckwush Creek (Mt. Rainier National Park) *see* Spunkwash Creek

Spunkwush Creek *(Mt. Rainier National Park)*

The stream of this short creek runs through a deep canyon and heads in an area of small lakes at the south base of Chenius Mountain, and in Crescent Lake to the south; flows northwest to Carbon River, near Alice Falls, northwest quarter of the park. The original Klickitat Indian name, which has been retained, means "A large number of small streams." The reference is to several short tributaries that feed the stream. Alternate spellings that have been used are *Spukwush* and *Spuchwush.* (USBGN)

Spurgeon Creek *(S.15;T.17N;R.1W)*

The stream of the creek rises east of Offuts Lake, central Thurston County; flows 7-1/2 miles northwest to Deschutes River. The stream was named for a pioneer who claimed land along the creek.

Squaib Bay (Kitsap County) *see* Miller Bay

Squak (King County) *see* Issaquah, Lake Sammamish

Squak Mountain *(S.4;T.23N;R.6E)*

A 1,980-ft. peak, 2 miles south of Issaquah, west central King County. *(see* Issaquah*)*

Squak Slough (King County) *see* Sammamish River

Squalus Point (Jefferson County) *see* Hazel Point

Squamish Harbor *(T.27N;R.1E)*

West shore harbor in a rather large, triangular bay, 4 miles south of Port Ludlow, east central Jefferson County. In 1841, it was named *Suquamish Harbor* for the Indian tribe of that name, by the Wilkes Expedition. The name has since been altered, probably by cartographers.

Square Bay (Skagit County) *see* Boat Harbor

Square Lake *(S.16;T.23N;R.1E)*

A 7.9-acre, swampy lake, 4-1/2 miles southwest of Port Orchard, south central Kitsap County. The only apparent reason for this geometrical name is that the lake is in the shape of a rather perfect circle.

Squaw Bay; Squaw's Bay (Skagit County) *see* Fidalgo Bay

Squaw Bay *(Ss.33,34;T.36N;R.2W)*

Narrow, tongue-shaped inlet on the southeast shore of Shaw Island, on Upright Channel, central San Juan County. An early name was *O'Hare Cove*, for a family of early settlers. The present name relates to Indian occupancy, and the fact that Indian women dug and dried clams here for many generations.

Squaw Butte Lake (Skamania County) *see* Meadow Lake

Squaw Lake *(Mt. Rainier National Park)*

Group of small lakes at the head of Devil's Dream Creek, east side of Indian Henrys Hunting Ground, southwest slope of Mt. Rainier, southwest quarter of the park. The lake is 3 acres, elevation 5,200 ft. The name was well-chosen because the wife of Sotolick, nicknamed "Indian Henry," often camped here while her husband hunted on upper slopes. (USBGN)

Squaw Tit *(S.15;T.14N;R.19E)*

Hill 7-1/2 miles northeast of Yakima, north central Yakima County. This somewhat descriptive name was applied by early cattlemen who displayed a scientific interest in the anatomy of Indian women.

Squalicum Creek *(T.38N;Rs.2,3E)*

The stream of the creek rises in Squalicum Lake, southwest Whatcom County; flows west and southwest 10 miles to Bellingham Bay, northern outskirts of Bellingham. The name is a compound of 2 Indian words -- *Squalla*, the dog salmon, and *cum*, meaning "place." Hence, "Place of the dog salmon." An alternate name, no longer used, was *Qualla Creek*.

Squalicum Lake *(S.4;T.38N;R.4E)*

A 33-acre, swampy lake, drained by Squalicum Creek, 6-1/2 miles northeast of Bellingham, near Squalicum Mountain, southwest Whatcom County. (*see* Squalicum Creek)

Squalicum Mountain
(S.13;T.38N;R.3E)

Peak 3 miles northeast of Bellingham, directly north of Lake Whatcom, southwest Whatcom County. (*see* Squalicum Creek)

Squillchuck State Park *(T.22N;R.20E)*

A 290-acre tract with campgrounds, on Squillchuck Creek, 7 miles southwest of Wenatchee, extreme south end of Chelan County. State officials adopted the Indian name of the creek on which the park is located.

Squire Creek *(Ts.31,32N;R.9E)*

The stream of the creek rises near Three Fingers, north central Snohomish County; flows 12 miles north to North Fork, Stillaguamish River, 4 miles west of Darrington. In 1890, it was named for an early resident, Squire Stewart.

Squires City (Stevens County) *see* Springdale

Squowh (King County) *see* Issaquah

Stafford Creek *(T.17N;R.10W)*

The stream of the creek rises 2-1/2 miles south of South Channel, Grays Harbor; flows north to the bay, southwest Grays Harbor County. It was named for one of the first residents in

this area by local use. In 1841, the Wilkes Expedition named it *Typha Creek*, with no record of the person for whom it was named.

Stafford Falls *(Mt. Rainier National Park)*

These falls are located directly south of the confluence of Chinook Creek and Ohanapecosh River, 4-1/2 miles north of Ohanapecosh Hot Springs, southeast area of the park. The unofficial name is for William Stafford, an early park ranger.

Staley *(S.28;T.14N;R.45E)*

Town 5 miles south of Pullman, southeast Whitman County. It was named by officials of Northern Pacific Railway Company for Mr. and Mrs. D. L. Staley, pioneer owners of the townsite.

Stam Island (Skagit County) *see* Pass Island

Stampede *(S.35;T.21N;R.11E)*

Construction town when the tunnel was bored through the mountains, at the west portal of Northern Pacific Railway's Stampede Tunnel, 1-1/2 miles west of Cascade Mountain summit, southeast King County. The name is presumed to have originated from an incident which occurred during the clearing between southeast Kie over the summit, when a hard-driving foreman told a trail crew, "No work, no eat!" The workmen are said to have dropped their tools and stampeded down the mountain.

Stampede Pass *(S.24;T.21N;R.11E)*

A 3,925-ft. at the head of Green River drainage to the west, Yakima River drainage on the east, at Cascade Mountain summit, 2-1/2 miles south of south end of Keechelus Lake, Kittitas and King counties. On March 19, 1881, the pass was discovered by Virgil Bogue, a location engineer for Northern Pacific Railway Company. He sought a location for building a temporary line over the Cascades to reach Tacoma quickly, thus saving land grants that the railway was to receive from the public domain if they reached a western terminus by a certain date in 1887. (*see* Stampede)

Stampede Tunnel
(Ss.24,26;T.21N;R.11E)

Tunnel at Stampede Pass area, Cascade Mountain summit, between southeast King County on the west, and west central Kittitas County on the east. In 1888, the tunnel was built by Northern Pacific Railway Company to replace the temporary switchbacks over the mountain that were built in 1887. (*see* Stampede)

Standard *(S.32;T.38N;R.5E)*

Lumber camp between Clipper and Acme, 1/2 mile east of South Fork, Nooksack River, southwest Whatcom County. The original name was *Green's Spur*. In 1908, the post office name was changed to the present form, through the influence of O. M. Rosseau, who was postmaster and also general manager of Standard Lumber & Shingle Company here, which is no longer in existence.

Stanwood *(T.32N;R.3E)*

Town near the mouth of Stillaguamish River, extreme northwest Snohomish County. The town has a large Scandinavian population. In 1877, when a post office was established, the name was *Centerville*. In the early 1900s, the post office name was changed because the first name was so common that postal deliveries were confused. The present name is the family name of the first postmaster's wife, Clara Stanwood Pearson.

Star (Okanogan County) *see* Starr

Starbo Camp *(Mt. Rainier National Park)*

Small, attractive park, elevation 6,000 ft., in Glacier Basin, north slope of Mt. Rainier, northeast of Inter Glacier, north central zone of the park. Before the park was established, a water-powered sawmill and a prospective mine were operated here. The name is for a miner who camped and mined here for years.

Starbuck *(S.13;T.12N;R.37E)*

Town on Tucannon Creek, 2 miles south of Snake River, extreme northwest Columbia County. This was once an important railroad town. In 1905, the O.W.R.&N. shops had a monthly payroll of over $20,000. When introduction of Mallet locomotives eliminated the need for adding "helper engines" to trains at this point, Starbuck declined and many of the buildings were moved to Walla Walla. The town was named for Gen. W. H. Starbuck, a "Nantucket Yankee" and early railroad financier. He donated a bell to the first church built here, in acknowledgment of the honor paid him.

Starr *(S.25;T.29N:R.23E)*

Railway station on the Columbia River, 12 miles southwest of Brewster, extreme southwest Okanogan County. The railroad station at this place was named by the Great Northern for R. W. Starr, a prominent orchardist from whom the railroad acquired a right-of-way. Some maps use the incorrect name of *Star.*

Starr Hot Springs (Snohomish County) *see* Garland Mineral Springs

Starr Rock *(T.37N;R.2E)*

Bellingham Bay rock, on Bellingham waterfront, southwest Whatcom County. The rock was named for the steamer *George E. Starr*, which struck here on August 25, 1888.

Startup *(S.35;T.28N;R.8E)*

Village 11 miles east of Monroe, at the junction of Wallace and Skykomish Rivers, south central Snohomish County. Its first name was *Wallace*, for Wallace Lumber & Manufacturing Company, which operated here. In 1901, the present name was substituted because of confusion with Wallace, Idaho. The name is for George G. Startup, who owned and operated the sawmill.

Starve-out Valley (Snohomish County) *see* North Fork, Stillaguamish River

State Soldiers Home Pond (Pierce County) *see* Soldiers Pond

Stayman *(S.4;T.26N;R.22E)*

Community on Columbia River, 32 miles northeast of Wenatchee, east central Chelan County. It was named for a species of apple that is produced heavily in this area, the Stayman Winesap.

Steamboat Island *(S.28;T.20N;R.2W)*

Island at the mouth of Totten Inlet, 1/2 mile west of Hope Island, extreme north central Thurston County. The name, applied by local settlers, is for a fancied resemblance between the island and a steamboat.

Steamboat Lake (Cowlitz County) *see* Blue Lake

Steamboat Prow *(Mt. Rainier National Park)*

Cliff northeast of Mt. Rainier's summit, southwest end of The Wedge, which splits Winthrop and Emmons glaciers into separate ice rivers. It is in the central zone of the park, 2 miles northeast of the summit, elevation 9,702 ft. In 1896, this descriptive name was chosen by Prof. I. C. Russell because the pointed cliff appeared to be buffeting a sea of ice. (USBGN)

Steamboat Rock *(S.3;T.28N;R.29E)*

Village north of Grand Coulee, 9 miles west-by-south of Grand Coulee Dam, northeast Douglas County. It was named for Steamboat Rock (rock formation) 2-1/2 miles southeast in Grant County. The site is on the north edge of Banks Lake, the equalizing reservoir impounded above South Dam.

Steamboat Rock *(Ts.27,28N;R.29E)*

Large, mesa rock in the equalizing reservoir 9 miles southwest of Grand Coulee Dam, northeast Grant County. Once this was an island in the course of the glacier-diverted Columbia River. It was named for an imagined resemblance to a huge ship.

Steamboat Slough *(T.33N;Rs.3,4W)*

One of several branches of the Skagit River which discharge into the shallow waters of Skagit Bay, on the Skagit Delta, southwest Skagit County. The name is for its extensive use by sternwheel steamboats that navigated the Skagit River in early days. In the early 1880s, this was the only Skagit River channel that was not blocked by driftwood and snags.

Stearnsville *(S.26;T.20N;R.12W)*

Almost deserted town 3 miles east of the seacoast, 1 mile east of Aloha, west central Grays Harbor County. At one time this was a center of shingle manufacturing. It was named by Northern Pacific Railway officials for J. O. Stearns, president of Stearns Lumber & Shingle Company.

Steel Mountain (Jefferson County) *see* Mt. Steel

Steele Harbor (Pierce County) *see* Still Harbor

Steep Creek *(T.24N;R.17E)*

The stream of the creek heads on the northeast slope of Icicle Ridge, Wenatchee National Forest, central Chelan County; flows northeast to Wenatchee River at south end of Tumwater Canyon. The name was applied by Forest Supervisor A. H. Sylvester to describe the steep descent of the creek from mountain to river.

Steep Point *(S.13;T.36N;R.3W)*

South end point of Orcas Island's western peninsula, on North Pass, north central San Juan County. In 1858, this name was charted by British admiralty surveyor, Capt. Henry Richards. It is a descriptive name applied to this point with very high bluffs.

Stehekin *(S.36;T.32N;R.17E.uns)*

Resort area on east shore of Lake Chelan, near its north end, Chelan National Forest, north Chelan County. The Indian name means "the pass" or "the way through." An earlier name was *Pierce's River.*

Stehekin River *(Ts.33,34N;Rs.15-17.uns)*

The stream of the river heads in several small lakes near Cascade Pass, Cascade Mountain summit, northwest Chelan County; flows southeast into the north end of Lake Chelan. (*see* Stehekin)

Steigerwald Lake *(T.1N;R.4E)*

Narrow, 3.7-mile-long lake, parallel to Columbia River, east of Washougal, extreme southeast Clark County. It was named for an early settler, but carried several other names in early years, including *Herzog's Lake, Shepherds Lake,* and *Steigerwald Slough.*

Steigerwald Slough (Clark County) *see* Steigerwald Lake

Steilacoom *(S.6;T.19N;R.2E)*

Oldest incorporated town in the state, on Nisqually Reach, 3 miles south of Fox Island, northwest Pierce County. The Indian name of a local tribe that lived on Steilacoom Creek has been retained. Hudson's Bay Company officials recorded the name as *Chil-a-coom*. Other white settlers and explorers spelled the name variously as *Chel-a-cum, Tail-a-coom, Skil-a-coom, Stiil-le-quem, Ch-til-acum,* and *Chil-a-coom.* The name appears to have been applied first to the creek, later to the town. Its meaning was "Flowers here."

Steilacoom Creek *(Ts.19,20E;R.2E)*

The stream of the creek heads in Steilacoom Lake, directly north of Gravelly Lake, northwest Pierce County; flows 1-1/2 miles north to Chambers Creek. (*see* Steilacoom)

Steilacoom Lake *(S.3;T.19N;R.2E;S.34;T.20N;R.2E)*

A 1-1/2 mile-long lake 3 miles west of Steilacoom, west central Pierce County. The lake is bordered with country homes. (*see* Steilacoom)

Steilacoom Waterway *(S.29;T.20N;R.2E)*

Inlet at the mouth of Chambers Creek, on Nisqually Reach, 1 mile northeast of Steilacoom. The first name of this inlet was *Heath Bay,* for an Englishman who leased a farm here from Hudson's Bay Company for sheep raising. In 1846, it first appeared on a chart of the area drawn by Capt. R. N. Inskip. (*see* Steilacoom)

Steliko Canyon *(T.26N;R.20E)*

A Wenatchee National Forest canyon, extending 3 miles east from Entiat River, east central Chelan County. This feature was named by Forest Supervisor A. H. Sylvester for an Entiat Indian chief.

Stella *(S.12;T.8N;R.4W)*

Hamlet at the mouth of Germany Creek, north bank of Columbia River, 9 miles west of Longview, southwest Cowlitz County. It was named for a daughter of Richard Packard who established a store here in 1880.

Stensgar Creek (Stevens County) *see* Stranger Creek

Stephens (Spokane County) *see* Tyler

Steptoe *(S.2;T.17N;R.43E)*

Small trading center, 10 miles north of Colfax, on Cottonwood Creek, central Whitman County. It was named for Lieut. Col. Edward J. Steptoe, U.S. Army, who suffered defeat by Indian forces on May 17, 1858, near Rosalia,

14 miles to the north. This disastrous retreat is often mentioned as "The Battle of Steptoe Butte." An early name for the place was *Steptoe Station.*

Steptoe Butte *(Ss.19,20,29,30;T.18N;R.44E)*

Granite and basalt mountain, elevation 3,673 ft., in upper Palouse River basin, 11 miles north-by-east of Colfax, northeast Whitman County. This is the most prominent landmark in the county. A tract of 136 acres on the butte has been developed as Steptoe Butte State Park. The summit was a lookout point for both Indians and white combatants during the Indian Wars. In 1888, James H. ("Cashup") Davis built a two-story hotel with solar observatory at the summit. After the place had been destroyed by fire, the sheriff of Whitman County sold almost the entire butte for $2,000 in the early part of 1902. An earlier name for the peak was *Pyramid Butte.* (*see* Steptoe)

Steptoe Butte State Park (Whitman County) *see* Steptoe Butte

Steptoe Canyon *(Ts.11,12N;R.45E)*

The canyon heads 1-1/2 miles south of Colton, extreme southeast Whitman County; extends south-by-west 8-1/2 miles to Snake River, 2 miles north of Alpowa. The canyon carries an intermittent creek. (*see* Steptoe)

Steptoe City (Walla Walla County) *see* Walla Walla

Steptoe Rapids *(S.1;T.11N;R.44E)*

Rapids in Snake River, 11-1/2 miles below Clarkston, extreme southeast Whitman County. (*see* Steptoe)

Steptoe Station (Whitman County) *see* Steptoe, Cashup

Steptoeville (Walla Walla County) *see* Walla Walla

Sterling *(S.27;T.35N;R.4E)*

Settlement 2 miles northeast of Burlington, on Skagit River, west central Skagit County. In the days of river navigation on the Skagit, this place was called *Ball's Landing* for Jesse B. Ball, a pioneer logger and rancher. The present name appears to have no particular meaning.

Stetattle Creek *(Ts.37,38N;Rs.12,13E.uns.)*

The stream of the creek rises in Azure lake, 1 mile east of Mt. Terror, southeast Whatcom County; flows southeast to Skagit River, just west of Diablo Dam. The name was applied to this creek by British Columbia Indians who fought with local Indians in this area. The creek was a boundary line between coastal Indians and those of the interior. The name means "wild people" or "bad people."

Stevens (Spokane County) *see* Tyler

Stevens *(S.12;T.36N;R.37E)*

Short-lived place on the Columbia River, between the old town of Kettle Falls and the falls in the Columbia River by the same name, northwest Stevens County. In the 1890s, it was platted for the sole purpose of taking the county seat away from Colville. The place had only one building, and folded up when the plan failed. The name was borrowed from that of the county.

Stevens Canyon *(Mt. Rainier National Park)*

Deep, 4-mile-long canyon, extending from the foot of Stevens Glacier southeasterly to within 1 mile of Muddy Fork, Cowlitz River, southeast zone of the park. The canyon has a "U-shaped" profile and forms the bed of Stevens Creek. It was named for Gen. Hazard Stevens, who made the first recorded sucessful ascent of Mt. Rainier on August 17, 1870, in company with P. B. Van Trump. (USBGN)

Stevens County

County in the northeast corner of Washington state. It is bounded on the north by British Columbia; on the west by Ferry County; on the south by Lincoln and Spokane counties; and on the east by Spokane and Pend Oreille counties. (*see* Stevens Canyon)

Stevens Creek *(T.26N;R.13E)*

The stream of the creek rises at Stevens Pass, south side of the Cascade Mountain summit at that point; flows 1-1/2 miles north to Nason Creek, Wenatchee National Forest, southwest Chelan County. It was named by Forest Service Supervisor A. H. Sylvester for its origin in Stevens Pass.

Stevens Creek *(Ts.21-22N;R.10W)*

The stream of the creek rises 7 miles south of Quinault Lake, north central Grays Harbor County; flows south to Humptulips River near Humptulips. In the summer of 1880, the name was given by surveyors for Harry Stevens who settled here some years earlier.

Stevens Creek *(Mt. Rainier National Park)*

The stream of the creek rises at the foot of Stevens Glacier, southeast zone of the park; flows south and southeast through Stevens Canyon to Muddy Fork, Cowlitz River, near the south Park boundary. (USBGN) (*see* Stevens Canyon)

Stevens Glacier *(Mt. Rainier National Park)*

Ice field which constitutes the east lobe of Paradise Glacier at the head of Stevens Canyon, southeast slope of Mt. Rainier, south central zone of the park. (*see* Stevens Canyon)

Stevens Lake (Snohomish County) *see* Lake Stevens

Stevens Pass *(Ss.13,14;T.26N;R.13E)*

Relatively low pass, elevation 4,061 ft., at the Cascade Mountain summit, between the headwaters of Nason Creek on the east and South Fork, Skykomish River on the west. It was named for John F. Stevens, Great Northern Railway engineer, who built the railway through this pass in the early 1890s.

Stevens Peak *(Mt. Rainier National Park)*

A 6,511-ft. peak in the south area of the park, 3 miles south of Stevens Canyon, 1-1/2 miles north of the park's south boundary. (*see* Stevens Canyon)

Stevens Ridge *(Mt. Rainier National Park)*

A 5,653-ft. ridge extending southeast from a point near the foot of Paradise Glacier, for a distance of about 5 miles parallel to Stevens Canyon which it borders on the northeast. (*see* Stevens Canyon)

Stevenson *(S.36;T.3N;R.7E)*

Town on a low bluff above Columbia River near Cascade Locks, south central Skamania County. The first settler was L. F. Iman, who built a water-powered sawmill in 1852. In 1880, the railroad station was named by Northern Pacific Railway officials for George H. Stevenson who settled in that same year in the Cascades, but moved here when flooded out at the lower location. An early name was *Stevenson's Spur*.

Stevenson Lake *(S.1;T.2N;R.7E)*

An 84-acre lake near the town of Stevenson, close to the north bank of Columbia River, south central Skamania County. The lake is an enlargement of Rock Creek, near its mouth. It was named for Stevenson, which it adjoins on the west. (*see* Stevenson)

Stewart Slough *(S.13;T.14N;R.10W)*

Slough directly south of Range Point, at the south entrance to Willapa River, northwest Pacific County. It was locally named for a pioneer who lived near the slough and was drowned in its waters in 1867.

Stewart's Island (San Juan Island) *see* Stuart Island

Stiak Run (Cowlitz County) *see* Martin Island

Still Harbor *(T.20N;R.1E)*

Northeast shore harbor on McNeil Island, Carr Inlet, northwest Pierce County. Names that appear on early maps of the area, applying to this feature, are *Julin's Bay* and *Johnson Bay*. A later name, *Steele Harbor*, was for an early settler, and evidently was altered to the present name through error or intention.

Still Park *(T.31N;R.1E)*

Area on central Whidbey Island near Prairie Center, Island County. This old place, not shown on recent maps, was named for Judge Lester Still, a local landowner who brought the first automobile to Whidbey Island.

Stillaguamish (Snohomish County) *see* Silvana

Stillaguamish Lake *(S.7;T.28N;R.6E)*

Lake directly north of Snohomish, southwest Snohomish County. The first name used by white settlers was *Blackman's Lake*, for Blackman Brothers, who built the first logging railroad in the state from Snohomish to the lake in the 1870s. The present name is of Indian origin. It is a modification of the name *Sta-luk-qua-mish*, meaning ''River people,'' a tribal designation.

Stillaguamish Peak *(Ss.10-12,15;T.30N;R.10E)*

A 1-1/2 mile-long ridge, elevation 5,682 ft., 4 miles northeast of Silverton, west central Snohomish County. (*see* Stillaguamish Lake)

Stillaguamish River *(Ts.30-34N;Rs.4-10E)*

The North Fork of the river rises in the mountains of south central Skagit County, Mt. Baker National Forest; flows south into Snohomish County, then west to join South Fork, near Arlington. The South Fork rises near Big Four Mountain, east central Snohomish County; flows west and northwest to North Fork. The combined river heads west to Port Susan and Skagit Bay at Stanwood. (*see* Stillaguamish River)

Stillwater *(S.4;T.25N;R.7E)*

Community 2 miles north of Tolt, in Snoqualmie River valley, north central King County. In 1910, the name was chosen by the first postmaster, H. Butikofer, when a post office was installed. The community started as a large logging camp, and most of the loggers came here from Stillwater, Minnesota.

Stimson Crossing *(S.33;T.31N;R.5E)*

Railroad point 4 miles north of Marysville, at the previous crossing of the Great Northern Railway and Stimson Timber Company's logging railroad, northwest Snohomish County. It was named for Stimson Timber Company, which logged extensively here in the early days of local sawmilling.

Stink Lakes *(S.32;T.20N;R.8E)*

Group of 3 shallow lakes, total 3 acres in size, 3-3/4 miles east of Enumclaw, south central King County. The name leaves little to the imagination. These lakes recede in the late summer, exposing a layer of decaying vegetable matter along the shores.

Stockade Bay (San Juan County) *see* Buck Bay

Stony Hill (San Juan County) *see* Rosario Hill

Stony Point *(S.28;T.14N;R.10W)*

Willapa Harbor point, 1 mile southwest of Bruceport, northwest Pacific County. It was locally named for a heavy outcropping of basaltic rock.

Storm King Mountain *(S.8;T.37N;R.32E)*

A Colville National Forest peak, elevation 5,326 ft., 4-1/2 miles northwest of Republic, northeast Ferry County. Originally it bore the rather ordinary name of *Granite Mountain* which was changed to the present form because of the frequency of thunderstorms around its summit.

Stormy Creek *(Ts.27,2N;Rs.19,20E)*

The stream of the creek heads on Stormy Mountain, in Chelan Mountains, Wenatchee National Forest, central Chelan County; flows 5-1/2 miles southwest to Entiat River. It was named for Stormy Mountain by Forest Service personnel.

Stormy Mountain *(S.29;T.28N;R.20E)*

A 7,219-ft. peak on the boundary between Chelan and Wenatchee national forests, at the south end of Devil's Backbone, Chelan Mountains, central Chelan County. The appropriate name was evidently applied by U.S.G.S. surveyors when they used the peak for a primary triangulation station.

Story Creek *(T.21N;R.16E)*

The stream of the creek flows from Teanaway Ridge, 5 miles west to Teanaway River, near Casland, northwest Kittitas County. It was named for a pioneer named Story who homesteaded in Section 32, at the mouth of this creek.

Straight Creek *(T.32N;R.11E)*

The stream of the creek heads in 2 forks on Whitechuck Mountain, Mt. Baker National Forest, northeast Snohomish County; flows 5-1/2 miles north to Suiattle River. It was named by Forest Service personnel because its channel is relatively straight, especially compared with that of Circle Creek, directly to the east.

Strait of Georgia (Whatcom,San Juan counties) *see* Georgia Strait

Strait of Juan de Fuca

A 90-mile-long waterway between Canada and the U.S., average width 13 miles; it extends from the Pacific Ocean at Cape Flattery to the vicinity of Port Townsend in the U.S. and Victoria in British Columbia, Clallam, Jefferson, and San Juan counties. The waterway was named for a Greek sailing master, Apostolos Valerianos, who called himself Juan de Fuca, and who claimed that he discovered this strait in 1592 while employed by the Spanish government to find the fabled and non-existent *Straits of Anian*. His claim is accepted by some authorities and is strongly rejected by others. In 1788, the strait was charted as *John de Fuca Strait*, by John Meares. Spanish explorers named this feature *Seno de Santa Rosa* and *Estrada de Juan de Fuca*. In 1787, Capt. Charles William Barkley was the first to name the strait as it is now designated. (USBGN)

Strandell *(S.36;T.40N;R.4E)*

Settlement 1-1/2 miles southwest of Nooksack, near Nooksack River, northwest Whatcom County. It was named for Andrew Strandell, a Swedish pioneer, who built a sawmill here in the late 1890s, and who platted a townsite on May 3, 1904.

Stranger Creek *(T.32N;Rs.35-37E)*

The stream of the creek rises on Colville Indian Reservation, in North Twin Lake, east central Ferry County; flows east 13 miles to the Columbia River south of Inchelium. It was named for a pioneer Scottish-Indian family who spelled their name *Stensger* -- the present name being a corruption of the former one.

Stranger Creek *(T.33N;Rs.37,38E)*

The stream of the creek rises 2 miles northeast of Maud, west central Stevens County; flows 7 miles southwest to the Columbia River at Gifford. In 1880, it was named for John Stensgar, an extraordinary Indian on the Colville Indian Reservation.

Stranger Mountain *(Ss.22-23;T.32N;R.36E)*

A Colville Indian Reservation peak, with two distinct elevations of 3,046 ft. and 2,770 ft. The mountain is located south of Stranger Creek, 5 miles east of Twin Lakes, east central Ferry County. (*see* Stranger Creek/Ferry County)

Strawberry Bay *(S.31;T.36N;R.1E)*

Rosario Strait bay on the southwest coast of Cypress Island, west central Skagit County. On June 6, 1792, the bay was named by Lieut. W. R. Broughton of the Vancouver Expedition, for the abundance of strawberries around it. The Indian name was *Tutl-ke-teh-nas*.

Strawberry Island *(S.25;T.34N;R.1E)*

Very small island in the central reach of Deception Pass, directly north of Ben Ure Island, northern limit of Island County. It was locally named for an abundance of wild strawberries here. On some recent maps, the island is not shown.

Strawberry Island *(S.31;T.36N;R.1E)*

A Rosario Strait island, on the west coast of Cypress Island, at the entrance to Strawberry Bay, northwest Skagit County. In 1841, it was charted by the Wilkes Expedition as *Hautboy Island*, using a common name for a species of strawberry that grows here -- *Fragaria elatio*. The U.S. Coast Survey translated it to the present name. An early local name was *Loon Island*.

Stray Dog Canyon *(Ts.31-32N;R.36E)*

Colville Indian Reservation canyon with an intermittent stream which heads between Meteor and Covada, then sinks above Covada, rises again beyond that place to flow into the Columbia River below the site of former Turtle Rapids, east central Ferry County. From 1898 to 1920, this canyon was the scene of much mining activity. Local tradition specifies that it was named for a stray dog that was shot here by a miner.

String Town (Kitsap County) *see* East Bremerton, Manette

Stringtown *(T.17N;R.5E)*

Former settlement in the Ohop Valley, south central Pierce County. The name now applies only to a north-south road along the west side of the valley. Pioneer settlers used this name because their homes were built along one road in a string.

Stringtown *(Ss.12,13;T.21N;R.45E)*

Settlement, much diminished, at the south end of Rock Creek Valley, 5 miles northeast of Latah, southeast Spokane County. Local settlers applied this name because the settlement was strung out along Painter Road, almost to the Idaho line.

Striped Peak *(S.22;T.31N;R.8W)*

Mountain 1 mile east of Tongue Point on Crescent Bay, north central Clallam County. On July 4, 1790, this peak was named *Punta de Salvi* by Manuel Quimper. In 1846, the present name was placed on British Admiralty charts by Capt. Henry Kellett, for a stripe or well-marked line visible on the hill from the Strait of Juan de Fuca.

Strongs River (Wahkiakum County) *see* Elokomin River

Stuart *(S.32;T.26N;R.7E)*

Small farming community 3/4 mile northeast of Snoqualmie River, north central King County. It was named for Elbridge Amos Stuart, founder of Carnation Company and Carnation Farms.

Stuart Island *(T.37N;R.4W)*

Haro Strait island, 3 miles northwest of San Juan Island, extreme northwest San Juan County. In 1791, this island was included with Waldron and several others in the area as *Islas de Moraleja* when named by Lieut. Juan Francisco de Eliza. In 1841, it was named *Stuart's Island* by Cmdr. Wilkes for Frederick D. Stuart, captain's clerk on the *Peacock*. An alternate version of the naming is that Capt. Richards, RN, placed it on British Admiralty charts in 1858 to honor Capt. Charles Edward Stuart of Hudson's Bay Company, who traded and navigated here between 1853 and 1863. The Lummi Indian name was *Qunnis*, meaning "whale."

Stubey Creek (Clallam County) *see* Stukey Creek

Stuck *(S.24;T.21N;R.4E)*

Site of a notable Indian village in very early pioneer days, 1 mile south of Auburn, between Stuck and White rivers, southwest King County. The name is that of an old Indian village site on the river *St-ax*. The meaning is "plowed through," and relates to an Indian legend of 2 whales in a landlocked prehistoric lake north of Sumner. They made a dash for freedom and bored their way through to Puget Sound.

Stuck River *(Ts.20,21N;Rs.4,5E)*

River between the White River, south of Auburn, and Puyallup River near Sumner, King and Pierce counties. Since 1906, it has been a part of White

River when that river broke its banks to flow into Stuck River, 1 mile east of Auburn. Originally Stuck River was 10 miles long, and suffered bad floods until it was recently controlled by Mud Mountain Dam. (*see* Stuck)

Stujack Creek *(T.31N;R.11E)*

The stream of the creek rises on Mt. Baker National Forest, northeast Snohomish County; flows 2 miles north to Whitechuck River at Leanto. This very short creek was given the combined names of 2 members of an early survey party, whose names were Sturat and Jackson.

Stukey Creek *(S.18;T.29N;R.7W.uns)*

The stream of the creek heads on the southeast slope of Happy Lake Ridge, Olympic National Park, central Clallam County; flows 1-1/2 miles east to Lake Mills (Elwha Reservoir). It was locally named for a pioneer settler. An unofficial alternate name is *Stubey Creek*.

Sturgeon Creek
(ss.20,29;T.30N;R.5E)

The stream of the creek rises on Tulalip Indian Reservation, 2 miles northwest of Marysville; flows south to Quilceda Creek, Snohomish County. Local Indians called the creek *Duh-kwuh-ti-ad-sib-dub*, meaning that sturgeon could be caught here. Early settlers settled for the English translation.

Sturgeon Island (Wahkiakum County) *see* Puget Island

Sturtevant lake *(S.28;T.25N;R.5E)*

A 10-acre lake 1-1/2 miles east of Bellevue at the head of Mercer Slough, west central King County. The lake discharges into Lake Washington through Mercer Slough. The name is for a very early settler on the lake. Other names once in use were *Bellvue Lake* and *Mid Lake*.

Stutzi Island (Wahkiakum County) *see* Jackson's Island

Success Cleaver *(Mt. Rainier National Park)*

Long, narrow wedge of rock between South Tahoma Glacier on the northwest and Pyramid and Success Glaciers on the southeast, southwestern slope of Mt. Rainier. It was named for Point Success at its upper extremity, 3/4 mile from Mt. Rainier's summit. (USBGN)

Success Glacier *(Mt. Rainier National Park)*

Small glacier, 1-mile-long, elevation 10,600 ft., which heads in a glacial cirque on south cliff of Success Cleaver; extends to Kautz Glacier, of which it is a lobe, on the south slope of Mt. Rainier, central zone of the park. (*see* Point Success)

Sucia Island *(T.38N;R.2W)*

Glacially-formed, northwest-southeast strips of land in the Strait of Georgia, 2-1/2 miles north of Orcas Island, extreme north San Juan County. This was once a famous smugglers' hideout, but is now a haven for pleasure boats. In 1791, the name was applied by Juan Francisco de Eliza as *isla Sucia*, which has a Spanish meaning of "foul." It was applied in the nautical sense of "reefy or muddy," as pertaining to navigational hazards. In 1841, Cmdr. Wilkes changed that name to *Percival Group*, to honor Capt. John Percival, a naval hero of the War of 1812. Capt. Kellett changed the name back to *Sucia* on British Admiralty charts in 1847. The Lummi Indian name for the islands was *Klow-co-me-ing*, meaning "Mussels on the rocks."

Sudbury *(S.18;T.7N;R.35E)*

Railroad point at confluence of Mud and Dry creeks, 5 miles northwest of Walla Walla, south central Walla Walla County. Superintendent J. G. Cutler of Washington & Columbia River Railway named the station for his former home in Massachusetts.

Suez River (Clallam County) *see* Sooes River

Sugarloaf Peak *(S.11;T.26N;R.18E)*

A Wenatchee National Forest peak at the south end of Entiat Mountain range, 6 miles east of Wenatchee River, central Chelan County. The name, slightly descriptive of the mountain's shape, was applied by early settlers and has become generally accepted.

Suiattle Glacier *(T.30N;R.13E)*

Glacier at the head of Suiattle River, southeast slope of Glacier Peak, extreme northeast Snohomish County. It was named by The Mountaineers after a local Indian band.

Suiattle Pass *(T.31N;R.14E)*

A 5,983-ft. pass at Cascade Mountain summit, between Chelan County and northeast Snohomish County. From the pass, Suiattle Creek leads to the west and Railroad Creek to the east. (*see* Suiattle Glacier)

Suiattle River
(Ts.30-33N;Rs.10-13E.partly uns)
The stream of the river heads on the southeast slope of Glacier Peak, northeast Snohomish County, between Suiattle and Chocolate glaciers; flows around the east and north slopes of Glacier Peak, then northwest into Skagit County to Sauk River. A local name in early days was *Miner's Creek.* (*see* Suiattle Glacier)

Suicide Point *(S.6;T.16N;R.13E.uns)*
A Bumping River point, 2 miles northeast of Bumping Lake, northwest Yakima County. It is named for the suicide of a laborer on Bumping Dam project -- the man having leapt from this point into the river in 1909.

Suise Creek *(T.21N;R.6E)*
The stream of this small creek enters Green River from the north at the site of a state salmon hatchery, southeast King County. This is the Indian name for the site, which was occupied in the winter by Skopamish or Green River Indians. They had two "longhouses" here, and a salmon weir in the creek. It is shown on some older maps as *Sus Creek* or *Soos Creek.*

Sullivan Lake *(Ts.38-39N;R.44E)*
Large, 3-mile-long lake, average width 1/2 mile, 4 miles southeast of Metaline Falls, just inside Kaniksu National Forest boundary, north central Pend Oreiille County. At the north end of the lake is a Forest Service ranger station. The lake is named for an early prospector, Michael R. O. Sullivan, who came here in the early 1860s and who located many mining claims in the area.

Sullivan Slough *(Ts.33,34N;Rs.2,3E)*
Saltwater slough which enters Skagit Bay, directly east of La Conner, extends northeast about 6-1/2 miles, southwest Skagit County. It is quite marshy in the lower reaches. Navigable in early days, this slough was named for a pioneer settler.

Sulphur Creek *(T.32N;Rs.12-14E.partly uns)*
The stream of the creek rises on the west slope of Bannock Mountain, at the Cascade Mountain summit, Mt. Baker National Forest, extreme northeast Sno-

homish County; flows 10-1/2 miles west and southwest to Suiattle River. It was named for hot sulphur springs on the creek's bank, 2 miles upstream from its confluence with Suiattle River.

Sulphur Creek *(T.37N;R.8E)*
The stream of the creek heads in Easton Glacier, south slope of Mt. Baker, south central Whatcom County; flows southeast to Baker Riiver at the head of Lake Shannon. The name was given by local residents because the moraine drift is impregnated with native sulphur.

Sulphur Mountain
(Ss.27,28;T.32N;R.13E.uns)
A Mt. Baker National Forest peak, elevation 6,697 ft., 6 miles west of Cascade Mountain summit, 9 miles north of Glacier Peak summit, northeast Snohomish County. The peak was named by surveyors for Sulphur Creek to the north. (*see* Sulphur Creek)

Sulphur Mountain Lake
(S.20;T.32N;R.14E.uns)
A Mt. Baker National Forest lake, elevation 5,200 ft., 1 mile north of Sulphur Mountain summit, northeast Snohomish County. It was named for Sulphur Creek which drains the lake. (*see* Sulphur Creek)

Sulphur Springs (Lewis County) *see* Packwood

Sultan *(Ss.31,32;T.28N;R.8E)*
Town at the confluence of Sultan and Skykomish rivers,,7 miles east of Monroe, south central Snohomish County. In the 1870s, the place was named by miners and prospectors for the chief of a Snohomish sub-tribe who lived on the Skykomish River. His name was *Tsultad* or *Tseul-tud,* which the miners twisted into the present name.

Sultan River *(Ts.28,29N;Rs.8,9,10E)*
The stream of the river rises near Hard Pass, east of Monte Cristo, Snoqualmie National Forest, south central Snohomish County; flows 16 miles west and southwest to Skykomish River at Sultan. (*see* Sultan)

Sumas *(T.41N;R.4E)*
Town at the Canadian boundary, 23 miles northeast of Bellingham, north central Whatcom County. Once a boom town in the Fraser River gold rush, it is now the location of U.S. Customs and Immigration Service. The name comes

from that of a Cowichan indian tribe who lived on Sumas Lake, River, and Prairie. Their word, *Sm-mess* means "land without trees" and referred to Sumas Prairie. Like many other pioneer towns, it once attached "City" to its name.

Sumas City (Whatcom County) *see* Sumas

Sumas Mountain *(Ts.39,40N;Rs.4,5E)*
A 2,000-ft. peak, 5 miles south of Sumas, northwest Whatcom County. Once this was the scene of mining industry. (*see* Sumas)

Sumas River *(Ts.39-41N;R.4E)*
The stream of the river rises 4 miles southeast of Nooksack, northwest Whatcom County; flows north to cross the Canadian boundary at Sumas, then to Fraser River. (*see* Sumas)

Summer Falls *(S.15;T.23N;R.28E)*
Waterfall at the north end of Long Lake Reservoir, northeast Grant County. The location is the site of a prehistoric natural waterfall, with a vertical drop of 165 ft. It is now fed from an equalizing reservoir at the rate of 3,150,000 gallons per minute during summer months. The name was chosen by irrigation officials because the falls are active only during the summer.

Summer Land (*Mt. Rainier National Park*)
Rugged, rocky mountain park on the northeast slope of Mt. Rainier, at the head of Fryingpan Creek, between Fryingpan Glacier and Goat Island, central zone of the park. It is a natural park, elevation 5,900 ft., with many alpine trees and flowers. In 1888, this poetic name was chosen by Maj. E. S. Ingraham because of the park's delightful location and surroundings, and for its beautiful display of flowers during summer months. (USBGN)

Summit *(S.11;T.18N;R.5W)*
Settlement at the summit of Black Hills, 8 miles west of Olympia, southeast Grays Harbor County. It was named because it is on the highest elevation between Olympia and Grays Harbor.

Summit Lake (Chelan County) *see* Top Lake

Summit Lake *(S.15;T.26N;R.13E)*
One of 5 Grace Lakes, directly west of Cascaade Mountain summit, 1-1/4 miles west of Stevens Pass, extreme

northeast King County. This lake covers 6 acres. The name describes the lake's location near the Cascade summit. An alternate name, also probably descriptive, is *Mosquito Lake*.

Summit Lake *(S.20;T.37N;R.1W)*

Long, narrow 10-acre lake, elevation 2,200 ft., on the east lobe of Orcas Island, northeast San Juan County. The name is for the lake's location near the summit of Mt. Constitution.

Summit Lakes *(T.14N;Rs.11,12E.uns)*

Group of approximately 100 small glacial lakes, elevation 4,500 ft. or higher, in mountain meadows on both sides of Cascade Mountain summit, north of White Pass, Snoqualmie National Forest, northwest Yakima and northeast Lewis counties. Some of the lakes are unnamed, others bear fanciful and interesting titles, such as Jug, Deerhead, Dumbell, Frying Pan, and Dancing Lady.

Sumner *(Ss.24,25;T.20N;R.4E)*

Town in the Puyallup Valley, 7-1/2 miles east of Tacoma, north central Pierce County. In 1876, the town was named by the Hon. L. F. Thompson, for Sen. Charles Sumner, when the first post office was established. The original Indian name was *Sta-hu.*

Sun Lakes State Park *(S.12;T.25N;R.27E)*

A 2,400-acre state park, 6 miles southwest of Coulee City, below Dry Falls, northwest Grant County. The park includes 7 lakes: Blue, Park, Falls, Deep, Perch, Rainbow, and Reflection. This park is on the site of an ancient waterfall which was far greater than Niagara. The vertical fall is estimated to have been 427 ft., and the width almost 3 miles.

Sundale *(S.28;T.3N;R.20E)*

Railroad station 25 miles east-by-south of Goldendale, on Columbia River, southeast Klickitat County. The name was chosen by L. W. Hill and C. M. Levy, officials of S.P.&S. Railway. It is quite descriptive, especially in summer months.

Sunday Creek *(Ts.20,21N;R.11E)*

The stream of the creek rises on the west slope of Cascade Mountain summit, directly south of Stampede Tunnel; flows 7 miles southwest to Green River, Snoqualmie National Forest, southeast King County. In 1881, it was named for

Virgil G. Bogue, locating engineer for Northern Pacific Railway. He "discovered" the creek on a Sunday.

Sundown Lake *(S.25;T.24N;R.7W)*

A 3-acre lake near Sundown Pass, Olympic National Park, 15-1/2 miles east of Lake Quinault, southeast Jefferson County. The lake is at the head of Graves Creek, named for nearby Sundown Pass.

Sunne (Pierce County) *see* Gertrude

Sunnyside *(T.2N;R.4E)*

Settlement about 14 miles east of Vancouver, north of Little Washougal River, southeast Clark County. It was named by Mrs. Hampton C. Blackwood, wife of a very early homesteader, for the clear atmosphere of this hilly country, and its illusion of being above the clouds when fog filled the valley.

Sunnyside *(S.32;T.38N;R.4E)*

Community on the east shore of Lake Whatcom, directly north of Towanda, southwest Whatcom County. On January 14, 1889, it was named by T. J. Smith when he submitted a plat. His townsite was on the sunny side of the lake.

Sunnyside *(S.25;T.10N;R.22E)*

Town 36 miles southeast of Yakima, east Yakima County. In 1893, the settlement was founded by Walter N. Granger of Sunnyside Canal Company. In 1904, it was platted as a townsite. In 1898, The Dunkards, or Church of the Brethren, came here in numbers, establishing their own telephone line and bank. In 1904, Zionists came from Illinois to establish a strong colony. In 1893, the present name was applied by Granger because land irrigated by the canal slopes toward the mid-day sun. A nickname is "Holy City," which seems fitting for a town that supported 22 churches at one time.

Sunrise Creek *(Mt. Rainier National Park)*

The stream of the creek rises in several branches on the east slopes of Sourdough Mountain, and on the north slope of Sunrise Ridge; flows 5-1/2 miles northeast to White River, northeast corner of the park. The stream was named for Sunrise Ridge, which the rays of early sunrise touch long before they reach the surrounding country. (USBGN)

Sunrise Lake *(Mt. Rainier National Park)*

Small lake, elevation 5,500 ft., on Sunrise Ridge, east side of White River Park, northeast quarter of the park. It was named for Sunrise Ridge.

Sunrise Park *(Mt. Rainier National Park)*

A 3-mile-long park, average width 3/4 mile, on a plateau at the foot of the south slope of Sourdough Mountain, northwest quarter of the park. This is a high, grassy mountain meadow from which an excellent view may be seen to the east and north. The feature was once called *Yakima Park*, because Yakima Indians used the meadow long ago for berry-picking and horse racing. The name was changed to the present form because some officials considered that it was being confused with the city of Yakima. Yakima citizens are not happy about the change. The Indian name was *Me-yah-ah-pah*, meaning "place of the chief." This referred to Chief Owhi of the Yakimas, who was very partial to this meadow.

Sunrise Point *(Mt. Rainier National Park)*

A 6,120-ft. vista on Sunrise Ridge, 2 miles below Sunrise Park, northeast quarter of the park. This is rated as the most spectacular viewpoint in the park and may be reached by highway. Among the points visible from here are Mt. Adams, Mt. Baker, Mt. Stuart, Glacier Peak, and 3 glaciers. It was named for Sunrise Ridge.

Sunrise Ridge *(Mt. Rainier National Park)*

A 6,100-ft. ridge extending east and northeast from Sourdough Mountain, between Sunrise Creek and White River, northeast area of the park. It is actually a spur of Sourdough Mountain. The name is descriptive. (USBGN)

Sunset (King County) *see* Naco

Sunset *(S.26;T.19N;R.42E)*

Town on Cottonwood Creek, 5 miles west of Thornton, north central Whitman County. The name was chosen as poetic by Joseph Conatzer, pioneer stockman, when he platted the townsite on November 16, 1888.

Sunset Amphitheater *(Mt. Rainier National Park)*

Glacial mass, elevation 12,522 ft., on the west slope of Mt. Rainier below

Liberty Cap, at the head of Puyallup Glacier, central zone of the park. The name was chosen because at this high altitude, the last rays of the setting sun touch the landscape.

Sunset Hill *(Ts.25,26N;R.3E)*

One of Seattle's 12 "official" hills, with bluffs rising to 305 ft., facing Shilshole Bay, near Golden Gardens, northwest Seattle. The name was chosen by residents because sunsets over the Olympic Mountains reflect on thousands of windows in a spectacular manner. An attempt was made to apply this name to all of Ballard, but it did not "take."

Sunset Park *(Mt. Rainier National Park)*

Region of many small lakes and abundant flowers, elevation 4,556 ft., between South Mowich and North Puyallup rivers, close to the park's west boundary, west central area of the park. The name is descriptive because from this vantage point on the west slope of Mt. Rainier, the full effect of sunsets is enjoyed. (USBGN)

Sunshine *(S.5;T.11N;R.10W)*

Abandoned settlement on Stanley Channel, at the mouth of Naselle River, southwest Pacific County. The name was chosen by Robert Miller when he established a sawmill here in 1884. After 10 years of operation, the sawmill failed and the settlement faded away.

Sunshine *(S.11;T.14N;R.45E)*

Community 3-1/2 miles east of Pullman, 2-1/2 miles west of Idaho boundary, southeast Whitman County. It was named for nearby Sunshine Creek, according to local residents.

Sunup Lake *(S.6;T.30N;R.12E)*

A 1/2-acre lake, elevation 5,300 ft., Mt. Baker National Forest, 4-1/2 miles east of Sauk River, east central Snohomish County. This very small lake was named by a Forest Service crew who camped here in the early 1930s, and who were awakened by bright, early morning sunshine.

Suquamish *(T.26N;R.2E)*

Village with a high percentage of Indian population at the west end of Port Madison Bay, on Port Madison Indian Reservation, northeast Kitsap County mainland. Chief Sealth (Seattle) is buried in a Catholic cemetery here, under the baptismal name of "Noah Sealth." The name is an alteration of the original Indian name, *Suk-wa-bish*, which included "Old Man House" to the south, near Agate Pass. When the Indian Reservation was established, this town was called *Bartow*, for A. A. Bartow, an early Indian agent for the reservation. In 1910, the name was changed to the present form, when Ole Hanson, later mayor of Seattle, developed beach property in this vicinity for a summer home area. The choice of this name was his. (USBGN)

Suquamish Indian Reservation (Kitsap County) *see* Port Madison Indian Reservation

Surnomish Settlement (Skagit County) *see* La Conner

Surprise Lake *(S.16;T.25N;R.13E)*

A 28.4-acre Snoqualmie National Forest lake, 1 mile west of Cascade Mountain summit, 2-3/4 miles south of Scenic, extreme northeast King County. This is one of 2 Scenic Lakes, with Glacier Lake. The lake is in a deep depression and the surprise happens when it pops into view as climbers approach. An alternate name is *Lower Scenic Lake*

Surprise Lakes
(Ss.13,14,23,24;T.7N;R.8E.uns)

Group of 15 lakes and ponds, total 17 acres, maximum depth 12 ft., on Gifford Pinchot National Forest, 10 miles north of Big Lava Bed, central Skamania County. The name evidently is due to the fact that the lakes are concealed by surrounding forests, and are not visible until one almost reaches the shores.

Surveyors Lake *(S.17;T.22N;R.11E)*

A 5.1-acre lake, 2 miles south of Snoqualmie Pass, at the head of Rockdale Creek, directly north of the west portal of Milwaukee Railroad's Cascade tunnel, east central King County. This name was suggested to the USBGN for approval by The Mountaineers when railroad surveyors slashed a survey line to the south end of the lake. (USBGN)

Sus Creek (King County) *see* Suise Creek

Sutherland Canyon
(Ts.22,23N;Rs.22,23E)

Canyon branching north from Moses Coulee for a distance of about 1/4 mile to the vicinity of Wallace Stool, southwest Douglas County. This feature carries the name of pioneer brothers John H. and George D. Sutherland, who settled here in the 1880s.

Sutico *(S.10;T.13N;R.7W)*

Former logging camp on Mill Creek, 8-1/2 miles southeast of Raymond, east central Pacific County. The name is a combination of the first 2 letters in each of the 3 words in Sunset Timber Company. That logging firm had a camp here for many years.

Sutter Lake, Sutter Mill Pond (King County) *see* Laughing Jacobs Lake

Sutter Mountain *(Ss.3,4;T.34N;R.9E)*

Peak 3 miles southwest of Rockport, near Skagit River, central Skagit County. It was locally named for John Sutter, an early settler here.

Swadhums Creek *(T.20N;R.3E)*

The stream of this very short creek, now obliterated, flowed into Commencement Bay from the vicinity of Puyallup Avenue in Tacoma. The Indian name, which was retained by early residents, means "Lowland people."

Swakane Creek
(Ts.24,25N;Rs.19,20E)

The stream of the creek rises on the south slope of Chumstick Mountain, southeast Chelan County; flows 10 miles southeast to Columbia River near Lincoln Rock. This original Indian name for the stream has been retained by cartographers and other naming agencies.

Swamp Creek *(Ts.26,27N;R.4E)*

The stream of the swampy, meandering creek rises near Martha Lake, southwest Snohomish County; flows south through King County to Sammamish River, near its mouth. The descriptive name was applied by early settlers along the creek. The original Indian name was *Tulq-ab*, meaning "The other side of something."

Swamp Creek *(S.31;T.17N;R.14E)*

The stream of the creek rises northeast of Little Bald Mountain on Snoqualmie National Forest, northwest Yakima County; flows 5 miles northeast to Naches River. This descriptive name was substituted for the original name of *Cow Creek* by Forest Service personnel.

Swan Bay *(Ss.10,11;T.30N;R.15E)*

An east shore bay of Lake Ozette, at the mouth of Big River, west central Clallam County. The bay was named for James G. Swan, a noted pioneer writer and explorer, who explored and mapped

Lake Ozette in 1861.

Swan Lake (Clallam County) *see* Ozette Lake

Swan Lake (King County) *see* Lake Youngs (Youngs Lake)

Swansea (Okonogan County) *see* Monse; Brewster

Swantown *(T.18N;R.2W)*

Abandoned settlement directly east of the first inhabited area of Olympia (now part of that city), north central Thurston County. On early maps it is shown as *Swan Town*, and was named for John M. Swan, who settled here in 1850.

Swauk Creek *(Ts.19-21N;R.17E)*

The stream of the creek rises at Blewett Pass, on boundary of Chelan and Kittitas counties; flows 18 miles south to Yakima River, 11 miles southeast of Ellensburg. This creek was the scene of much early gold mining -- both for placer and quartz gold. Some sporadic mining still takes place. The Indian name appears to have the meaning of "deep," which seems not too appropriate for this stream. In 1854, Capt. George McClellan mapped this creek as *Schwock River*.

Swauk Pass (Chelan County) *see* Blewett Pass

Swauk Prairie *(T.20N;R.17E)*

Settlement between Teanaway River and Swauk Creek, 9 miles east of Cle Elum, central Kittitas County. This was once a mining community of some importance. (*see* Swauk Creek)

Swede Heaven (Snohomish County) *see* Segalson Creek

Swift Creek *(T.30N;R.11E)*

The stream of the creek rises in the mountains, 7 miles northwest of Monte Cristo, Mt. Baker National Forest, central Snohomish County; flows 3 miles northeast *of* Sauk River near Bedal Camp. It was named by local homesteaders because of the rapid flow during almost the entire year.

Swift Creek *(Ts.37-39N;R.9E)*

The stream of the creek heads in Austin Pass, south of Mt. Baker Lodge, Mt. Baker National Forest, central Whatcom County; flows south between Mt. Baker and Mt. Shuksan to Baker River, 1 mile west of Baker Lake. This name evidently was chosen by Forest Service personnel, and is quite descriptive.

Swift Reservoir *(S.28;T.7N;R.5E.uns)*

An artificial reservoir, 4,588.8 acres, maximum depth 380 ft., on North Fork, Lewis River, 28-1/2 miles northeast of Woodland, west central Skamania County. It was named for Swift Creek which enters the river here, by Puget Sound Power & Light Company when that corporation created the reservoir.

Swifts Bay *(T.35N;Rs.1,2W)*

Semi-circular bay, with Port Stanley on the south side, at the northeast end of Lopez Island, directly south of Humphrey Head, central San Juan County. The name was given locally for a family who settled here in 1862.

Swinomish Channel *(Ts.33,34N;R.2E)*

Shallow, saltwater arm of Puget Sound, which extends north from Skagit Bay to the south end of Padilla Bay, a distance of 6 miles, southwest Skagit County. Until 1954, when the present name was substituted, the accepted name for this feature was *Swinomish Slough*. The name is for the Swinomish Indian tribe, who live on the reservation to the west of the channel and are a branch of the Skagit nation. (USBGN)

Swinomish Indian Reservation *(Ts.33,34N;R.2E)*

A 4,973-acre reservation between Swinomish Slough and Skagit Bay, west central Skagit County. It is bounded on the west by Similk Bay at the north end of the reservation. Most of the acreage is divided into individual allotments. On January 22, 1855, the reservation was created by the Point Elliott Treaty. On September 9, 1873, it was enlarged by an executive order. (*see* Swinomish Channel)

Swinomish (town) Skagit County *see* La Conner

Swinomish Slough (Skagit County) *see* Swinomish Channel

Swofford *(S.23;T.12N;R.3E)*

Settlement 10 miles southwest of Morton, central Lewis County. It was named for T. K. Swofford, who owned a large farm here in 1887, and who was the first postmaster when a post office was established in 1890.

Sylopash Point *(S.2;T.25N;R.2W)*

West shore point of Hood Canal, at the mouth of Dosewallips River, 1 mile northeast of Brinnon, southeast Jefferson County. In 1841, Wilkes used the original Indian name when he charted this area. In 1847, Capt. Henry Kellett extended this name to *Dosewallips River*, but his nomenclature did not persist.

Sylvan *(S.25;T.21N;R.1E)*

Small settlement on the northeast shore of Fox Island, 4 miles west of Tacoma, on Hales Passage, northwest Pierce County. In 1888, it was named *Sylvan Glen* by Mrs. C. J. Miller, who chose a really poetic name. In 1891, when a post office was established, the name was cut to its present form.

Sylvan Glen (Pierce County) *see* Sylvan

Sylvan Grove (Kitsap County) *see* Pleasant Beach

Sylvester Creek *(T.20N;R.9E)*

The stream of the creek rises west of Cougar Mountain, 2-1/2 miles northwest of Maywood, southeast King County; flows 2-1/2 miles south to Green River, Snoqualmie National Forest. The creek originally bore the name of an early squatter, Forsythe. It was changed by Prof. A. H. Landes of The Mountaineers to honor A. H. Sylvester, an outstanding Forest Supervisor on Wenatchee National Forest.

Sylvia Falls *(Mt. Rainier National Park)*

Waterfall in Stevens Creek, near the park's south boundary, southern part of Stevens Canyon, south central zone of the park. The falls were named by William Stafford, who admired them so completely that he attached his sweetheart's name to them. (USBGN)

Syue (Snohomish County) *see* Skiou Point

T

Table Mountain
(Ss.24,25;T.39N;R.8E.uns)

A Mt. Baker National Forest peak, elevation 5,300 ft., between Mt. Baker and Mt. Baker Lodge, central Whatcom County. In 1914, the name was chosen by Finley Roberts and Lou Darrow, evidently with the idea that the name was descriptive.

Tabook Point *(S.16;T.26N;R.1W)*

West side point of Toandos Peninsula, on Dabob Bay, 6 miles southeast of Quilcene, east central Jefferson County. In 1841, the point was named by the Wilkes Expedition, using an Indian name which may have been the same as applied to Tarboo Creek and Tarboo Bay.

Tac-a-lac-Lake (Skamania County) *see* Taklahk Lake

Tacoma *(Ts.20,21N;Rs.2,3E)*

One of the major cities of the Pacific Northwest, on Commencement Bay at the mouth of Puyallup River, north central Pierce County. The pioneer settlement began in 1852 with an isolated sawmill on Commencement Bay. The number of Indian names applied to the site by various tribes and bands are almost infinite. They include *Che-bau-lip*, *Ta-co-be*, *Ta-co-pe*, *T'kope*, *Ta-qo-bid*, *Ta-co-bud*, and *Tsa-la-te-litch*. Prior to 1868, the growing town had been called *Puyallup* and later *Commencement City*. In that year the present name, taken from Theodore Winthrop's *The Canoe and the Saddle*, was suggested by Philip Ritz, a Northern Pacific Railway official. The name was adopted through the influence of Gen. Morton Matthew McCarver, who was a leader in developing the city. It resembles many of the Indian names that were applied to the site before the first settlers arrived.

Tacoma Harbor (Pierce County) *see* Commencement Bay

Tacoma Pass *(S.23;T.20N;R.12E)*

Cascade Mountain summit pass, elevation 3,500 ft., between headwaters of Green River on west and Yakima River on east. (*see* Tacoma)

Taftsonville *(T.23N;R.1E)*

A very old settlement (not shown on modern maps) near San de Fuca, west central Whidbey Island, Island County. Founded in 1851, it was named for Martin and Christian Taftson, who settled here that same year, by the Surveyor General of Washington Territory when he mapped the island in 1859.

Tahk Prairie (Klickitat County) *see* Camas Prairie

Tahlequah *(S.2;T.21N;R.2E)*

Extreme south end point of Vashon Island, across Dalco Passage from Tacoma, southwest King County. The present name is a modification of the original Indian name for this place southwest of Quartermaster Harbor. A local name for the place is *Clam Cove*.

Taholah *(S.25;T.22N;R.13W)*

Community on the Pacific Ocean, at the mouth of Quinault River, 9 miles north of Moclips, northwest Grays Harbor County. It was named for a Quinault Indian chief, *Ta-ho-o-la*. The old Indian village on this site was called *Kwinailth*. For a brief period the place was known as *Granville* or *Grenville*.

Tahoma *(T.22N;R.6E)*

Small community directly east of Maple Valley, central King County. The name was concocted by residents who used the first 2 letters of 3 nearby towns -- Taylor, Hobart, and Maple Valley.

Tahoma Creek *(Mt. Rainier National Park)*

The stream of this ice-cold, swift torrent rises at the foot of Tahoma and South Tahoma Glaciers, southwest slop of Mt. Rainier; flows southwest to Nisqually River, and is almost as large as that river at the junction. The name used is the Indian word for "snow-covered mountain." An unofficial early name was *Rainier Creek*. (USBGN)

Tahoma Glacier *(Mt. Rainier National Park)*

One of 6 very large glaciers out of 28 on the mountain and within the park. This glacier originates in Sunset Amphitheater, a large cirque with precipitous walls on the southwest slope of Mt. Rainier; it extends 5-1/2 miles southwest from the mountain's summit to the headwaters of South Puyallup River. It was named for Tahoma Creek. On September 12, 1947, the U.S. Marine Corps League asked the secretary of the interior to have the name changed to *U.S. Marines Memorial Glacier*, in memory of 32 marines who were killed on the glacier in a plane crash on December 10, 1946. This name did not become official. (USBGN) (*see* Tahoma Creek)

Tahoma Peak (Mt. Rainier National Park) *see* Liberty Cap

Tahoma Vista *(Mt. Rainier National Park)*

A 3,458-ft. viewpoint northeast of Lake George, 6-1/2 miles by trail from Nisqually Entrance, southwest zone of the park. The place offers an excellent scenic view. (*see* Tahoma Creek)

Tahuya *(T.24N;R.3W))*

Community in Mason County. The name is derived from the Twana Indian words *ta* and *ho-i*, meaning "that done," in reference to something that took place at this site in the early days.

Tahuya Lake *(S.17;T.24N;R.1W)*

Shallow, marshy lake, 17.9 acres, 9 miles west of Charleston, 1-1/2 miles west of Green Mountain, southwest Kitsap County. It should not be confused with Tahuya Lake, Mason County. (*see* Tahuya)

Tahuya River *(Ts.22-24N;Rs.1-3W)*

The stream of the river rises directly west of Tahuya Lake, southwest Kitsap County; flows southwest to Hood Canal at the Great Bend, Mason County. In the early 1890s, this stream was locally known as *Jahnvan Creek*. (USBGN) (*see* Tahuya)

Taklahk Lake *(T.9N;R.10E.uns)*

A 35.5-acre lake, elevation 4,341 ft., 7-1/2 miles northwest of Mt. Adams summit, at head of East Canyon Creek, northeast Skamania County. The lake is in a high mountain meadow. Its Indian name refers to the superstition that the lake is haunted by spirits of wild dogs. Traditionally the older Yakima tribesmen would never turn their backs to the lake, because the dogs would emerge from the water to attack. Alternate names are *Taklahk Pond* and *Tac-a-lac Lake*.

Taklahk Pond (Skamania County) *see* Taklahk Lake

Takup Point (*S.36;T.30N;R.3W*)

East shore point of Sequim Bay, 2-1/2 miles north of Blyn, northeast Clallam County. In 1841, the point was named by the Wilkes Expedition and is a distortion of the Indian name, *T'kope,* meaning "white." The point is covered by a 2-ft. layer of very white clam shells. Local names that have been applied from time to time are *Travis Spit* for a settler named Bob Travis, and *Hardwick Point* for another early resident.

Tala Point (*S.10;T.28N;R.1E*)

East entrance point to Port Ludlow (bay) on Hood Canal, northeast Jefferson County. In 1841, it was named by the Wilkes Expedition, using the original Indian name *Tahla*.

Talapus Lake (*S.3;T.22N;R.10E*)

A 17.8-acre lake, 4-1/2 miles west of Snoqualmie Pass, east central King County. The name means "coyote" in Chinook Indian jargon. An alternate name is *Blue Lake*.

Tallant Creek (*T.33N;R.25E*)

The stream of the creek rises in Leader Reservoir, south central Okanogan County, 5-1/2 miles west of Okanogan; flows southeast 6 miles to Okanogan River near Chiliwist. The creek was named for Nathan ("Kentucky") Tallant, an early settler on land along the creek.

Tam Tam Ridge (*Ts.9,10N;Rs.43,44E*)

Ridge which extends from east Garfield County into Asotin County, a distance of 4-1/2 miles, between Dry Gulch and Charlie Creek Fork. This Indian name has been used since pioneer days although the oldest inhabitants do not know its meaning.

Tamanos Mountain (*Mt. Rainier National Park*)

A 6,800-ft. peak, 1/2 mile northwest of Owyhigh Lakes, between Wright and Shaw creeks, east central area of the park. The name chosen is from early Indian nomenclature. It has the meaning of "evil spirits, taboo," in Chinook Indian jargon. (USBGN)

Tamarack Creek (*T.25N;R.19E*)

The stream of the creek heads on the southeast slope of Chumstick Mountain, Wenatchee National Forest, southeast Chelan County; flows 5 miles in a wide curve to Roaring Creek. It was named by Forest Ranger John Brender for the numerous stands of western larch, which often is called tamarack in error.

Tampico (*S.18;T.12N;R.16E*)

Settlement on Ahtanum Creek, 11 miles west-by-south of Yakima, central Yakima County. The name is reported to have been placed on this settlement by A. D. Elgin, a pioneer cattleman, for a town of that name where he once lived. That would apply to towns in 6 states, with Texas the best bet.

Taneum Creek (*Ts.18,19N;Rs.14-17E*)

The stream of the creek rises in 2 main forks, Wenatchee National Forest, west central Kittitas County; flows 26 miles east to Yakima River near Thorp. The Indian word, *Teh-N-Am* or *Pteh-Num* apparently has the meaning of "Stream coming from high mountains," which is appropriate in this case.

Tanglewood Island (*S.35;T.21N;R.1E*)

An 18-acre canoe-shaped island, northeast of Fox Island, in Hale Passage, northwest Pierce County. This tiny island has borne 5 names, other than the original Indian designation: *Ellen's Isle, Grant Island, Grave Island, Hoska Island* and the present poetic name. Until 1933, it was owned by the Hoska family of Tacoma and their name was used during the period of ownership. In 1933, it was purchased by Dr. Schultz and called *Grave Island* by him, because it was a burial ground of the Nisqually Indians for many years. On June 26, 1947, it was again re-named when it acquired the present designation.

Tanwax Lake (*Ss.14,23;T.17N;R.4E*)

A 172.8-acre lake, maximum depth 30 ft., 3 miles southwest of Kapowsin, south central Pierce County. In 1857, the lake was mapped by the Surveyor-General of the territory as *Tanwux Lake,* using this Indian name which means *neck.* In 1859, the name was changed to the present form by the same Surveyor-General.

Tanwux Lake (Pierce County) see Tanwax Lake

Tapteal (Tap-Teil) River (Yakima County) *see* Yakima River

Tarboo (Jefferson County) *see* Dabob

Tarboo Bay (*T.27N;R.1W*)

Narrow extension of Dabob Bay to the north, 1 mile long, east central Jefferson County. The bay retains the original Indian name, pronounced *Tar-a-boo.*

Tarboo Creek (*T.28N;R.1W*)

The stream of the creek heads 5 miles south of south end of Port Discovery Bay; flows 6 miles south to Tarboo Bay, northeast Jefferson County. (*see* Tarboo Bay)

Tarboo Lake (*Ss.7,18;T.28N;R.1W*)

A 21.6-acre lake, 8 miles west of Port Ludlow, 3 miles south of south end of Port Discovery Bay, northeast Jefferson County. An alternate name is *Cord Lake.* (*see* Tarboo Creek)

Target Lake (*S.7;T.32N;R.11E*)

A Mt. Baker National Forest lake, 7-1/2 miles northeast of Darrington, at the head of All Creek, north central Snohomish County. The lake was named by Forest Service personnel because it was the target for the first air-drop of fire-fighting supplies on Mt. Baker National Forest, on July 22, 1938.

Tato Falls (*Mt. Rainier National Park*)

Waterfall on the west side of Nisqually Glacier, a small tributary of Nisqually River, just above Glacier Trail, southwest zone of the park. Ethan Allen, an early superintendent of the park, chose this name for his daughter, Rachel, whose nickname was *Tato.* (USBGN)

Tatoosh Island (*T.33N;R.16W*)

Rocky island, including a lighthouse, weather, and naval station in Pacific Ocean, 1 mile north of Cape Flattery, extreme northwest Clallam County. In 1857, the lighthouse was installed to guide ships entering the Strait of Juan de Fuca. In 1788, Capt. John Meares named the island *Tatootche* when he was entertained there by Chief Tatootche. The Chinook name means *Thunder Bird,* or *nourishing beast,* as the island was the legendary home of that huge creature. In Makah language the name is *Tu-tutsh.* In 1790, Alferez Manuel Quimper, who came here on a Spanish expedition named it *Isla de Tutusi.* Other names that have been used briefly are *Chardi Island, Green Island,* and *Opa Jecta.*

Tatoosh Lakes (*S.9;T.14N;R.9E*)

Two connected lakes, elevation 5,000 ft., on the northeast side of Tatoosh

Ridge, 7-1/2 miles north of Packwood, northeast Lewis County. One lake covers 10 acres and the other 2-1/2 acres. (*see* Tatoosh Island)

Tatoosh Range *(Ts.14,15N;R.9E)*

Long mountain range adjoining Rainier Park, between Cowlitz, Paradise, and Nisqually rivers, It extends from Eagle Peak, east of Longmire, east and southeast across the park, and about 5 miles into northeast Lewis County. Elevations of higher peaks in this range are over 6,900 ft. (USBGN) (*see* Tatoosh Island)

Tatsolo Point *(S.14;T.19N;R.1E)*

East shore point of Nisqually Reach, 4 miles southwest of Steilacoom, northwest Pierce County. In 1841, the point was named by the Wilkes expedition. The name source is not clear, but there is some evidence that there was Hudson's Bay Company influence in the naming.

Tatugh *(S.25;T.24N;R.2E)*

Low, pebbly point on the west side of Blake Island, west central Kitsap County. In 1858, it was named by Capt. George Davidson of U.S. Coast Survey, who used the original Indian name, meaning *milk*, although the reason for applying it to this point is unknown. The name does not show on recent maps.

Taunton *(S.8;T.15N;R.28E)*

Railroad station 1-1/2 miles north of Saddle Mountains, extreme southwest Adams County. It was named by H.R. Williams, vice-president of Chicago, Milwaukee & St. Paul Railway Company for Taunton, Massachusetts.

Taylor *(S.3;T.22N;R.7E)*

Community 6 miles east of Maple Valley, 3-1/2 miles west of Hober, in Cedar River Valley, central King County. There was much coal mining and the manufacture of brick and sewer tile here. In 1893, the Oregon Improvement Company founded and named the town for William T.W. Taylor, an official of Denny-Renton Clay & Coal Company. Taylor also founded the town of North Bend.

Taylor Bay (Pierce County) *see* Taylors Bay

Taylor Ridge *(Ts.38-39N;R.35E)*

A 6-mile-long ridge, elevation 6,211 ft., Colville National Forest, 20 miles northeast of Republic, northeast Ferry County. It was named by Forest Service personnel for Worth E. Taylor, a forest ranger who died on February 9, 1924, as a result of gassing in WWI. A former name was *Big Boulder Ridge* (USBGN)

Taylors Bay *(Ss.26,35;T.20N;R.1W)*

North shore bay of Nisqually Reach, 1-1/2 miles south of Longbranch, northwest Pierce County. It was named by local settlers for a British sailor who settled here in pioneer days. On certain state records, this feature is called *Taylor Bay.*

Tchannon (Columbia County) *see* Tucannon

Tchinom Point (Kitsap County) *see* Chinom Point

Teahwhit Head *(S.32;T.27N;R.15W)*

Pacific Ocean head, 4 miles south of Quillayute River mouth, extreme northwest Jefferson County. The original Indian name has been retained, but in a modified form. As pronounced by local Indians, the name should be spelled *T-seal-tla-ok.* It means *creek falling over a high bluff.*

Teanaway *(S.33;T.20N;R.16E)*

Settlement 4 miles east of Cle Elum, near junction of Teanaway and Yakima Rivers, central Kittitas County. This roadside settlement was a fairly important town at the time of gold excitement in Blewett Pass to the northeast. The Indian name translates to *place of fish and berries.* The present name is evidently adapted to English spelling and pronunciation, from *Yannoinse* or *Tannoinse.*

Teanaway River *(Ts.20-22N;Rs.14-16E)*

The stream of the river rises in 3 main branches on Wenatchee National Forest, north central Kittitas County; flows in a general southerly direction 31 miles to Yakima River at Teanaway. Its upper tributaries drain an expansive mountain area with peaks towering to over 6,000 ft. (*see* Teanaway)

Teekalet (Kitsap County) *see* Port Gamble

Teekalet *(S.6;T.27N;R.2E)*

Old Indian village was on the present site of Port Gamble at the west entrance to Port Gamble Bay, north Kitsap County. In 1853, when a large east coast lumber company decided to build a sawmill here, they moved the Indian village across the bay to Point Julia. Later the village was called *New Boston,* and the area was purchased for a reservation in 1936. The Indian name of the original town means *brightness of the noonday sun.*

Teekalet Bluff *(S.6;T.27N;R.2E)*

North shore bluff of mainland, on Hood Canal, west of Port Gamble, Kitsap County. (*see* Teekalet)

Tekoa *(SSs.17,20;T.20N;R.45E)*

Town on Latah Creek (Hangman Creek), 27 miles northeast of Colfax, extreme northeast Whitman County. A pioneer woman suggested the name from a Biblcal source, Tekoah, or Tekoa having been a town in Judah, 12 miles south of Jerusalem, 6 miles south of Bethlehem. Translation of the Hebrew word, often mistaken for an Indian name, is *sound of trumpet.*

Telegraph Road

Telegraph line built from Portland, Oregon and Seattle through northwest Washington, British Columbia, and Alaska to a point on the Bering Sea. The line was never completed, but was put into operation in its northern reaches. Its purpose was to connect the United States with England via the Bering Sea, Russia, and intermediate points to the English Channel, then by cable to London. In the 1860s, it was partly in operation, but was abandoned when a cable was successfully laid across the Atlantic Ocean in 1866. Parts of road or trail along which the line was built may be found in Whatcom County. Also, the name *Telegraph* was applied to several geographical features in the state which were on or along this line. The name is descriptive, because a road had to be built along the line in order to bring construction materials. Alernate names were *Old Telegraph Road, Telegraph Trail,* and *Collins Overland Telegraph.*

Telegraph Slough *(T.34N;Rs.2,3E)*

One of several tidewater sloughs that drain into the south end of Padilla Bay, on Skagit Flats, west central Skagit County. It was named for its location on the Collins Overland Telegraph Line. (*see* Telegraph Road)

Telegraph Trail (Wash. state reference/west. Wash./Canada/Alaska) *see* Telegraph Road

Telford *(S.4;T.25N;R.35E)*

Small settlement 12 miles north of Davenport, central Lincoln County. It was named for M.A. Telford, a prosperous rancher, where a post office was established here on July 4, 1909. The railroad station at this point had been known both as *Telford* and *Fellows*.

Ten Mile *(S.16;T.39N:R.3E)*

Small community in Ten Mile Township, 10 miles north of Bellingham over the route of Old Telegraph Road. (*see* Ten Mile Creek)

Ten Mile Creek *(T.39N:Rs.2,3E)*

The stream of the creek heads between Wahl and Goshen, northwest Whatcom County; flows 12 miles west through Barrett Lake to Nooksack River. In 1858, the creek was named by soldiers from Fort Bellingham who were stationed here to protect works on Caribou Trail against Indian attack. Their station was miles from Fort Bellingham over the Old Telegraph Road.

Ten Mile Creek *(T.35N;R.32E)*

The stream of the creek rises 10 miles south of Republic, Colville National Forest, west central Ferry County. Many of the tributaries of San Poil River, south of Republic, are named for their river distance from that town. In addition to this creek others so named are 13, 17, 19, 21 and 23 mile creeks.

Ten Mile Creek *(Ts.8-10N;Rs.45,46E)*

The stream of the creek rises 2 miles southeast of Anatone, east central Asotin County; flows north-by-east 18-1/2 miles to Snake River, directly north of Weissenfels Ridge. It was named by miners because it is 10 miles by river from Lewiston, Idaho. An alternate name, still used by local Indians, is *Antone Creek*.

Ten O'Clock Creek *(Ts.22,23N;R.11W)*

The stream of the creek rises in the northeast quarter of Quinault Indian Revervation; flows south 8 miles to Quinault River, northwest Grays Harbor County. When mail was carried by a horseback rider from Quinault to Queets, the mail carrier planned to reach this creek by ten o'clock in the morning to maintain his schedule. He named the creek accordingly.

Tenalquot Prairie *(Ts.16,17N;Rs.1W,1E)*

Series of park-like prairies with interspersed groves of coniferous trees, on Willamette Meridian, 12 miles southeast of Olympia, south central Thurston County. This Indian name means *the best yet.* It refers to a legend in which the coyote searched for a good home for poor Indian tribes who lived in California.

When he told them that he had found *the best yet,* they migrated here together. Game, water, and timber were abundant in earlier days.

Tenas Creek *(Mt. Rainier National Park)*

The stream of the creek rises on the southwest slope of Mt. Wow, extreme southwest corner of the park; flows southwest into Nisqually River, just west of the park boundary. The name is from Chinook Indian jargon, and means *small* As applied to this stream, it is quite descriptive. (USBGN)

Tenas Creek *(T.33N;R.11E)*

The stream of the creek rises in Boulder Lake, southeast Skagit County; flows 8 miles west to Suiattle River, 2 miles north of Snohomish County boundary. The name was evidently chosen to contrast with Big Creek, directly north. (*see* Tenas Creek)

Tenas George Canyon *(T.24N;R.20E)*

A Wenatchee National Forest canyon, which heads near Government Corral, at the east boundary of the forest, southeast Chelan County; extends 4-1/2 miles southeast to Columbia River. It was named for an Indian who lived in the canyon during pioneer days.

Tenas Mary Creek *(T.40N;Rs.32-33E)*

The stream of the creek heads in the extreme northwest corner of Ferry County; flows 3-1/2 miles west to Kettle River, north of Toroda. Little Mary was an Indian resident in the Toroda area in early days. (*see* Tenas Creek)

Tenasket (Okanogan County (*see* Tonasket

Tenino *(T.16N;1R.1W)*

Town 12 miles south of Olympia, south central Thurston County. In pioneer days this place was a junction of military roads between Fort Vancouver and Fort Steilacoom. It had been a meeting place of Indian trails before settlers arrived. The Indian name means *fork* or *junction,* and probably referred to the Indian trail crossings. Typical pioneer legends ascribe the name source to: (1) the figures *10-9-0* on a railroad survey stake here; (2) the same numbers on a railway locomotive that operated on this lne. Pioneers had powerful imaginations and usually a rough-and-ready sense of humor.

Tenino Junction *(S.30;T.16N;R.1W)*

Northern Pacific Railway junction,

directly south of Tenino, south central Thurston County. It was established in 1873. (*see* Tenino)

Tennant Lake *(Ss.29,32;T.39N;R.2E)*

A 43-acre lake in Ferndale Township, 3/4 mile southeast of Ferndale northwest Whatcom County. It was locally named for John A. Tennant, a pioneer surveyor and homesteader, who made the first plat of Ferndale. It is in a shallow, marshy basin, and has a tendency to vary in size.

Terminal City (Stevens County) *see* Northport

Termination Point *(S.35;T.28N;R.1E)*

An entrance point to Hood Canal, west shore, 3 miles east of Shine, east central Jefferson County. In 1841, the name was chosen by Cmdr. Charles Wilkes, for the point's location at the north termination of Hood Canal.

Terra Vaugh (Kitsap County) *see* Harper

Terrell Creek *(T.39N;Rs.1E,1W)*

The stream of the creek rises 4 miles northwest of Ferndale, northwest Whatcom County; flows northwest and west 6-1/2 miles to Birch Bay. (*see* Lake Terrell)

Texas City (Texas Ferry) (Whitman County) *see* Riparia

Texas Ponds *(Ss.1,12;T.33N;R.9E)*

Two ponds which cover 6 acres, 8 miles south of Rockport, Mt. Baker National Forest, southeast Skagit County. These upper and lower ponds were named by U.S. Forest Service personnel for a Texan who attempted to homestead here near the turn of the century. Alternate names on some maps are *McMillan Lake* or *McMillen Lake.*

Texas Rapids *(S.32;T.13N;R.38E)*

Snake River rapids near Riparia, above Texas Ferry, northwest Columbia County. The name has been in use since before 1893, and is reported to have been chosen by a Texan who came here after the Civil War.

Thatcher *(S.4;T.35N;R.1W)*

Small settlement on the west shore of Blakely Island, 2 miles north of Thatcher Pass, southeast San Juan County. It was named for Thatcher Pass, which was named to honor Capt. Decatur for his capture of the British frigate *Macedonian* in the War of 1812.

Thatcher Lake (San Juan County) *see* Spencer Lake

Thatcher Pass *(T.35N;R.1W)*

Pass between Blakely and Decatur islands, east central San Juan County. This pass, used by ferries through the San Juan Islands, was named in 1854 by the U.S. Coast Survey, cancelling the name given by Cmdr. Wilkes in 1841 -- *Macedonian Crescent* -- (for the water surrounding Decatur Island.) (*see* Thatcher)

That Mountain (Mt. Rainier National Park) *see* Denman Peak

The Badlands *(T.25N;R.16E)*

Series of talus slopes that cover over a section of land, Wenatchee National Forest between Painter Creek and Battle Canyon, southwest Chelan County. The name was applied by sheepmen who found no grazing in this area.

The Bench *(Mt. Rainier National Park)*

Rock bench between Tatoosh Range and Stevens Canyon, 1-1/2 miles southeast of Reflection Lakes, south central area of the park. This descriptive name was chosen by park officials.

The Breakers (Pacific County) *see* Breakers

The Brothers *(Ss.13,14;T.25N;R.4W)*

High peak, with 4 small glaciers and a double summit, Olympic Primitive area, 4 miles north of Mason County boundary, southeast Jefferson County. In 1856, the name was chosen by Capt. George Davidson of U.S. Coast Survey. He named the twin peaks for Arthur and Edward Fauntleroy, brothers of his fiancee, Ellinor.

The Burn (Grays Harbor County) *see* Neilton

The Burn (Snohomish County) *see* Darrington

The Castle *(Mt. Rainier National Park)*

A 6,500-ft. peak in Tatoosh Range, south of Stevens Canyon, south central zone of the park. The name originated in the earlier period of park development and was given because of the peak's fancied resemblance to an ancient, stone castle (USBGN)

The Dalles *(T.2N;R.13E)*

Now largely eliminated by The Dalles Dam, this series of waterfalls was in Columbia River, between south central Klickitat County and Oregon. The falls constituted the greatest obstacle to Columbia River navigation in early days. They were 12 miles long, with an 81-ft. drop at low water stage. Celilo Falls, at the head of the series, had a 20-ft. drop. The name applied by early French-Canadian voyageurs in the employ of fur trading companies, was *Les Dalles*, or *Flagstones*. Huge sheets of basaltic rock, polished by the river current, reminded them of stone paving used in eastern Canadian cities for roads and streets. Other early names used by explorers and fur traders were: *Les Grand Dalles de la Columbia, Long Narrows, Big Chutes, The Narrows, Columbia Falls, Great Falls of the Columbia*, and *Five-Mile Rapids*.

The Dome (Mt. Rainier National Park) *see* Columbia Crest

The Egypt Country (Lincoln County) *see* Egypt

The Fan *(Mt. Rainier National Park)*

Small lake, elevation 5,406 ft., on the southeast slope of Mt. Rainier, southwest of Cowlitz Glacier's terminus, between Williwakas Creek and Muddy Fork, Cowlitz River, south central zone of the park. The name was chosen by park rangers and is quite suggestive of the lake's contour. An unofficial, alternate name is *Fan Lake*. (USBGN)

The Lagoon *(S.32;T.31N;R.6W)*

A 19-acre pond at the west end of Ediz Hook, in Port Angeles Harbor, north central Clallam County. The pond is used for log storage and is truly a saltwater lagoon.

The Landing (King County) *see* Fall City

The Narrows (Klickitat County) *see* The Dalles

The Narrows *(Ts.20,21N;R.2E)*

Channel, 4 miles long, not less than 1 mile wide, bordering Tacoma on the northwest, between West and Hales passages, northwest Pierce County. The channel is subject to strong tide rips. In 1841, the name *Narrows* was applied by the Wilkes Expedition. In 1847, the name was expanded to the present form by Capt. Henry Kellett. It is quite descriptive.

The Palisades *(Ss.28,33;T.39N;R.7E)*

Cliffs on the northwest slope of Mt. Baker, directly east of Glacier Creek, central Whatcom County. This quite descriptive name was chosen by Charles E. Lindberry, county engineer, while surveying a trail from Glacier to Mt. Baker.

The Pointers *(T.35N;R.1W)*

A group consisting of Black Rock, Pointer Island, and Lawson Rock at the east entrance of Thatcher Pass, southeast San Juan County. In 1841, the name was charted by Cmdr. Wilkes because the group of rocks pointed to the entrance of Thatcher Pass.

The Pyramid (Whatcom County) *see* Mt. Degenhardt

The Ramparts *(Mt. Rainier National Park)*

Steep cliff on the southeast face of Rampart Ridge, directly northwest of Longmire Springs, southwest zone of the park. It includes glacial cirques and moraines, waterfalls, and rugged canyons. (*see* Rampart Ridge) (USBGN)

The Rustler Creek (Jefferson County) *see* Rustler River

The Sisters *(T.37N;R.1W)*

Very small island group in an elongated cluster, on the Strait of Georgia, 2 miles northeast of Orcas Island, northeast San Juan County. Six of the group are bare rocks, rather than islands. The largest and most northerly is called *Lone Tree Island*. In 1790, they were named *Islas de Aguayo* by Lieut Juan Francisco de Eliza, for one of the many names of the Spanish Viceroy. In 1841, Cmdr. Wilkes charted them as *Sisters*. His descriptive name has been altered to the present form by later coast surveyors.

The Sphinx (Mt. Rainier National Park) *see* McClure Rock

The Tooth *(S.30;T.33N;R.11E)*

Sharp, fin-like projection on the ridge between Chair Peak and Denny Mountain, 2 miles northwest of Snoqualmie Pass, east central King County. It was named by The Mountaineers. The place resembles a tooth or fang. This name was sent to USBGN for approval. Alternate names that have been used are *Denny Horn* and *Denny Tooth*.

The Wedge (*Mt. Rainier National Park*)

Sharp, rocky mountainous projection which divides Winthrop and Emmons Glaciers on the northeast slope of Mt. Rainier. Its point, Steamboat Prox, has an elevation of 9,702 ft. and is a very sharp divider of the glaciers. In 1896, the very descriptive name was chosen by Prof. I. C. Russell and explorers Willis, Ainsworth, Williams, and Smith who were with him. (USBGN)

The Willows (*S.34;T.26N;R.5E*)

Community 3 miles northeast of Kirkland, on Sammamish River, northwest King County. It was named by officials of Northern Pacific Railway for a heavy growth of willow trees along the river.

Theon (*S.19;T.8N;R.46E*)

Crossroads settlement 3 miles northeast of Anatone, central Asotin County. In 1880, it was founded by Daniel Theon Welch, who platted the town on May 15, l884. It was the given middle name of the founder.

Theosophy Ridge (*Mt. Rainier National Park*) *see* Reese's Camp

Theseus Lake (*S.7;T.27N;R.15E*)

A Wenatchee National Forest lake, southeast side of Labyrinth Mountain, between Lake and Rainy Creeks, directly east of Minotaur Lake, northwest Chelan County. (*see* Minotaur Lake)

Thiel (*S.25;T.8N;R.34E*)

Railway station 8 miles northwest of Walla Walla, south central Walla Walla County. Northern Pacific Railway Company acquired a right-of-way here from Fred W. Thiel, and named the station for him.

Think O' Me Hill (*T.17N;R.9W*)

Hill adjoining Aberdeen and overlooking the city, southwest Grays Harbor County. The hill was named for a brand of cigars. An Aberdeen cigarmaker used this name for his cigars and placed a large sign on the hilltop to advertise them.

Third Creek (*T.39N;R.34E*)

The stream of this short creek rises on the Colville National Forest, 8 miles east of Curlew, north central Ferry County. It is the third tributary to enter West Deer Creek above Curlew and another of the numerically named creeks in Ferry County, along with First and Sec-

ond creeks. The total length of the creek is 2 miles.

Third Lake (*S.16;T.20N;R.7E*)

A 2-acre lake, 3-1/2 miles east of Enumclaw, southwest King County. The name indicates the fact that it is one of 3 numbered lakes in fairly close proximity.

Thirteen Mile Mountain
(*S.26;T.35N;R.33E*)

A Colville National Forest peak, elevation 4,851 ft., at the head of Thirteen Mile Creek, 10 miles southeast of Republic, west central Ferry County. Its name is borrowed from that of the creek which enters the San Poil River 13 miles by river below Republic.

Thomas (*S.36;T.22N;R.4E*)

Settlement between Kent and Auburn, 18 miles south of Seattle, southwest King County. It was named for John W. Thomas, brother-in-law of Seattle pioneer Charles C. Terry. Thomas took a Donation Land Claim of 310 acres here and was the first settler in the White River Valley. Before the settlement was named for him, Thomas called the place *Pialsche* for a local Indian whose name was "Curly Nelson."

Thompson (*S.31;T.31N;R.25E*)

Village (which does not appear on recent maps), which was 3-1/2 miles northeast of Brewster, south central Okanogan County. It was named for John Thompson who owned a cattle ranch and a cable ferry on the Okanogan River near Monse in pioneer days. He also was the first postmaster of the place named for him.

Thompson Cove (*S.17;T.19N;R.1E*)

Small bay on the south tip of Anderson Island, on Nisqually Reach, west central Pierce County. In 1846, it was first mapped by Capt. R. N. Inskip and placed on British Admiralty charts. Inskip chose the name of Rev. Robert Thompson, chaplain of *HMS Fisgard*.

Thompson Creek (*T.34N;R.21E*)

The stream of the creek rises on Thompson Ridge, Chelan National Forest, southwest Okanogan County; flows 6 miles east to Methow River, 3 miles south of Winthrop. It was named for George L. Thompson, who once held a championship belt for teller of the tallest tales. From his fantastic stories, and those of other gifted old-timers, came the local name of *Liars Creek*.

Thompson Creek (*T.39N;R.7E*)

The stream of the creek rises on the north slope of Mt. Baker, Mt. Baker National Forest, north central Whatcom County; flows 5-1/2 miles north and west to Glacier Creek. It was locally named for one of the first homesteaders in the vicinity.

Thompson Lake (*T.28N;R.30E*)

Once a lake, now innundated in the equalizing reservoir of Grand Coulee Dam, below Electric City, northeast Grant County. It was named for a pioneer who had his home on the outskirts of what is now Electric City.

Thompson Rapids (*Stevens County*) *see* Rickey Rapids

Thompson Ridge (*Ts.37-38N;R.36E*)

A Colville National Forest ridge, 6 miles long, which runs parallel to Kettle River, at a distance of 3-5 miles from that stream, northeast Ferry County. Several features in this forest were named for Forest Service officers or employees. This one was named for Perry A. Thompson, formerly on the Colville, who became an assistant to the Chief of the Forest Service in Washington, D.C.

Thomson Canyon (*Chelan County*) *see* Thomson Creek

Thomson Creek (*T.26N;R.17E*)

The stream of the creek heads in a gulch at the east end of McCue Ridge, Wenatchee National Forest, central Chelan County; runs 2-1/2 miles southeast to Skinney (Skeeny) Creek. It was named by Forest Supervisor A. H. Sylvester for James Thomson whose farm was located at the creek's mouth.

Thornton Creek (*T.26N;R.4E*)

The stream of the creek rises in Ronald Bog, northwest King County; flows southeast into Lake Washington at Matthews Beach, north of Sand Point. It is reported to have been named for an early homesteader on the creek. The local Indian name was *Tu-xu-bid*.

Thornwood (*S.24;T.36N;R.4E*)

Small settlement 5 miles north of Sedro-Woolley, northwest Skagit County. The name was chosen for a station of the Northern Pacific Railway Company. Officials of that railway named it for W. J. Thorne, an early settler.

Thorp (*S.10;T.18N;R.17E*)

Community near Yakima River, 8 miles northwest of Ellensburg, central Kittitas County. In 1885, the town was founded by F. Mortimer Thorp, and was platted as a townsite in 1892. The name was chosen by Northern Pacific Railway officials to honor Milford A. Thorpe, a member of this famous pioneer family.

Thrall (*S.30;T.17N;R.19E*)

District 4-1/2 miles south of Ellensburg, near Yakima River, southeast Kittitas County. The name was chosen by railway officials to honor Nelson C. Thrall, chief clerk to the general manager of Northern Pacific Railway Company in 1883.

Three Brothers (*S.7;T.22N;R.17E*)

A 7,370-ft. peak between Ingalls and Nigger Creeks, south central Chelan County. The mountain was so named because it has a triple summit.

Three Corner Lake
(*S.31;T.36N;R.3W*)

A 2.8-acre, privately owned lake, in the central area of San Juan Island, 5 miles northwest of Friday Harbor, southwest San Juan County. Closed to the public, the lake's name is descriptive. An alternate name is *Triangle Lake*.

Three Fingers (*S.18;T.31N;R.9E.uns*)

Three-spired peak, 7 miles northeast of Gold Basin, Mt. Baker National Forest, north central Snohomish County. It was named for its configuration; a local name is *Three Finger Mountain*.

Three Fools Creek
(*T.39N;Rs.14-16E.uns*)

The stream of the creek heads on the slope of Three Fools Peak, Cascade Mountain summit, northeast Whatcom County; flows west to Lightning Creek, 3 miles east of Ross Lake. It was named by Bellingham Bay citizens for 3 inexperienced prospectors who found *fool's gold* in the creek in the 1890s, and who brought it to New Whatcom as genuine gold.

Three Fools Peak
(*S.8;T.39N;R.17E.uns*)

A 7,645-ft. mountain, North Cascade Primitive Area, at the Cascade Mountain summit, at the head of Three Fools Creek, between Whatcom and Okanogan counties. (*see* Three Fools Creek)

Three Forks (*Whitman County*) *see* Pullman

Three Lakes (*S.5;T.24N;R.8W*)

Three small lakes, total area 2 acres, in Paradise Valley at the head of Big Creek,

Olympic National Park, south central Jefferson County. The name is obviously descriptive.

Three Lakes (*S.4;T.36N;R.7E*)

Three lakes close together and connected, elevation 4,000 ft., 9 miles north of Hamilton, extreme north central Skagit County. One lake covers 4 acres, and each of the others are 1 acre. The name is descriptive.

Three Lakes (*S.3;T.28N;R.6E*)

Former mill town 3-1/2 miles northeast of Snohomish, near Panther Lake, southwest Snohomish County. It was once a busy lumber and shingle manufacturing town. In 1903, it was named by John Lauderyon for 3 small lakes near the town — Panther, Storm, and Flowing lakes.

Three Mile Creek (*T.28N;R.35E*)

The stream of the creek rises on the west bank of Columbia River, southeast Ferry County; enters that river 3 miles above the mouth of Spokane River. In the early days of the county's mining boom, this numbered creek provided some excitement because of the placer gold it yielded. This Colville Indian Reservation creek was named for its distance upstream from the mouth of the Spokane River.

Three Prune Creek (*T.25N;R.8W*)

The stream of the creek rises in several small lakes, 11 miles south of Mt. Olympus, Olympic National Park, south central Jefferson County; flows east 3-1/2 miles to North Fork, Quinault River. The name is borrowed from that of Three Prunes Camp near the stream's headwaters. A party of The Mountaineers camped here before WWI and ran out of food; they had 3 prunes each for breakfast.

Three Prune Lakes
(*S.28;T.25N;R.8W.uns*)

Three small lakes, total 2-1/2 acres, 12 miles northeast of Lake Quinault, at the head of Three Prune Creek, southeast Jefferson County. (*see* Three Prune Creek)

Three Spits (*Kitsap County*) *see* Bangor

Three Tree Points (*King County*) *see* Point Pully

Thunder Creek (*Ts.29,30N;R.15E*)

The stream of the creek heads at Tenpeak Mountain, Cascade Mountain summit, northwest Chelan County; runs 4 miles southeast to White River. This

name was applied by Forest Supervisor A. H. Sylvester because of many electrical storms in this area.

Thunder Lake (*S.35;T.30N;R.14W*)

Round, 12-acre lake, 8 miles north of Forks, southwest Clallam County; it is named for Thunder Creek, which feeds and drains it. (*see* Thunder Creek)

Thunder Lakes (*S.22;T.36N;R.8E*)

Two, connected lakes, 2 acres each, about 1,000 yds. apart, 6 miles east of Concrete, north central Skagit County. One lake has an elevation of about 4,000 ft., the other is 4,300 ft. (*see* Thunder Creek)

Thurston County

A 719-sq. mile, west central Washington county. It is bounded on the north by Mason County; on the east by Pierce County; on the south and west by Lewis and Grays Harbor counties. On January 12, 1852, it was founded while Washington was part of Oregon Territory. The county was named for Samuel R. Thurston, Oregon's first territorial delegate to Congress.

Tibbetts Creek (*T.24N;R.6E*)

The stream of the creek rises on Cougar Mountain, 2-1/2 miles south of Lake Sammamish; flows 3-1/2 miles south into the south end of the lake. The creek was named for *General* George W. Tibbetts, who bought 160 acres near the creek's mouth, and operated a boathouse in early days. (USBGN)

Tidewater (*S.34;T.21N;R.3E*)

Railroad station on Commencement Bay in Tacoma, near Ruston. In 1890, the place was named *Prescott* by Northern Pacific Railway officials. In 1910, they changed to the present name and closed the station in 1915. It is not on recent maps.

Tieton (*S.18;T.14N;R.17E*)

Town 12 miles northwest of Yakima, north central Yakima County. The name is borrowed from that of Tieton River (*see* Tieton River)

Tieton Reservoir
(*T.13N;Rs.13,14E.partly uns*)

A 7-mile-long reservoir, 200 ft. high, west of Rimrock Dam, on Tieton River, Snoqualmie National Forest, northwest Yakima County. The reservoir is impounded back of Rimrock Dam, whose purpose is to supply water for irrigating the lower valley. An alternate name is *Rimrock Lake*. (*see* Tieton River)

Tieton River
(Ts. 12-14N;Rs. 10-16E.partly uns)

The stream of the river rises in Goat Rocks Primitive Area near Cascade Summit, at Tieton Pass and Tieton Peak, Yakima County; flows northeast in 2 forks through Snoqualmie National Forest into Tieton Reservoir; then east-by-north to join Naches River, 5 miles west of Naches. Two Indian names applied to this stream, as in the multiple naming of streams by Indians throughout the Pacific Northwest. East of the Cascades, the common name in use was *Shanwappum*, meaning *milky water*, and was appropriate for this glacial river. The present name is a corruption of *Taitinapam*, which relates to a tribe in Cowlitz River Valley on the west slope of Cascades, who spoke the Yakima language and were affiliated with Naches Indians. The river itself appears to have been named *Tai-Tin* by this tribe.

Tiffany Lake *(S.22;T.37N;R.23E)*

Small mountain lake, Chelan National Forest, 1-1/2 miles north of Tiffany Mountain, 13 miles northwest of Conconully, north central Okanogan County. It is named for William Tiffany of a wealthy New York family, who camped at the base of the mountain with 2 brothers and other well-to-do young men, for 2 years. He was killed in the Spanish-American War.

Tiffany Mountain *(S.27;T.37N;R.23E)*

A Chelan National Forest peak, elevation 8,275 ft., 12 miles northwest of Conconully, central Okanogan County. (*see* Tiffany Lake)

Tiflis *(S.8;T.18N;R.30E)*

Community 7 miles north of Warden near Lind Coulee, southeast Grant County. It was named by H. R. Williams, vice president of Chicago, Milwaukee & St. Paul Railway, because of the many settlers from the Trans-Caucasian city of Tiflis on the Kura (capital of Georgia when Russia took over that kingdom in 1799).

Tiger *(S.29;T.37N;R.43E)*

Crossroads settlement on the west bank of Pend Oreille River, 48 miles north of Newport, 3-1/2 miles south of Ione, west central Pend Oreille County. In 1905, the place was established as a trading post by a pioneer named Yoder, who also was the first postmaster. The stern-wheeler steamers on the river stopped at Tiger during that period. No tigers terrorized Tiger. The place was named for a hardy pioneer named George Tiger, the first settler here, who homesteaded on the bank of the river about 1900.

Tiger Lake *(S.32;T.24N;S.5;T.23N;R.1W)*

A 109-acre lake, 9-1/2 miles southwest of Bremerton, northeast Mason and west central Kitsap counties. About 103 acres of the lake's area are in Mason County; with only 6 acres in Kitsap County. The name was of local selection, evidently to match Panther Lake, directly to the west.

Tillicum *(S.21;T.29N;R.2E)*

Village on Fort Lewis Army Post, adjoining American Lake on the south, central Pierce County. This locally chosen name is the Chinook jargon word for "friends, relatives." This euphonious word has been applied to many places and several organizations in the Pacific Northwest.

Tillicum Creek *(T.26N;RT.19E)*

The stream of the creek heads south of Sugarloaf Mountain, Wenatchee National Forest, central Chelan County; flows 5 miles northeast to Indian Creek, with several long branches. Forest supervisors used this name, in connection with the naming of nearby Indian and Kloochman Creeks -- "An Indian must have a friend and a wife" (Kloochman). (*see* Tillicum)

Tillicum Point *(Mt. Rainier National Park)*

Northwest end point of Ptarmigan Ridge, elevation 6,654 ft., 5-1/2 miles northwest of Mt. Rainier's summit, northwest zone of the park. (USBGN) (*see* Tillicum)

Tilton (Lewis County) *see* Alpha; Bremer

Tilton River *(Ts.12,13N;Rs.2-5W)*

The stream of the river rises northwest of Glenoma, central Lewis County; flows through Morton to Cowlitz River, 3-1/2 miles north of Mayfield. In 1857, the name was chosen by Gov. I. I. Stevens for Maj. James Tilton, first surveyor-general of Washington Territory. He later was an engineer for Northern Pacific Railway Company, locating many of that railway's branch lines.

Timothy Meadows
(Ss.4,5;T.18N;R.13E)

Mountain meadow on Snoqualmie National Forest, north side of Naches River, 5 miles east of Cascade Mountain summit, extreme southwest Kittitas County. The meadow was named by settlers because of the abundance of wild timothy here.

Tin Cup Joe Creek *(Ts.23,24N;R.10E)*

The stream of this short creek rises in Derrick Lake, Snoqualmie National Forest, east central King County; flows 2 miles northeast to Middle Fork, Snoqualmie River. In the 1890s, this stream was named by local miners for a roving prospector whose nickname was "Tin Cup Joe." Many names of this type are found in Washington state wherever there was early mining and prospecting.

Tinkham Peak *(S.31;T.22N;R.11E)*

A 5,356 ft.-mountain, 6-1/2 miles south of Snoqualmie Pass, 3/4 miles southeast of Abiel Peak, at Cascade Mountain summit, east central King and extreme northwest Kittitas County. On June 15, 1916, this peak was named by The Mountaineers. It was in honor of Abiel W. Tinkham, who made an important reconnaisance through Yakima Pass, directly to the south, in January 1854, on orders from Gov. Isaac I. Stevens. Abiel made the trip on snowshoes, accompanied only by 2 Indians, after Capt. George B. McClellan had failed to get through. (USBGN) (*see* Abiel Peak)

Tinpan Mountain *(T.31N;R.17E.uns)*

A 8,100-ft. peak on Chelan Ridge, between Railroad Creek and headwaters of Entiat River, 5 miles southeast of Holden, northwest Chelan County. The peak is on the boundary between Chelan and Wenatchee national forests. Forest Supervisor A. H. Sylvester, in applying this name, said that it was "Just a name for a feature needing naming."

Tiny Lake *(S.2;T.39N;R.11E.uns)*

Small Mt. Baker National Forest lake, elevation 6,100 ft., at the headwaters of Little Beaver Creek, northeast Whatcom County. This is an appropriate name for a lake that covers only 2/10ths of an acre.

Tipsoo Lake *(Mt. Rainier National Park)*

An 8-acre lake in Tipsoo Basin, elevation 5,314 ft., 3 miles east of Cayuse Pass, 1/2 mile west of Chinook Pass, extreme east central zone of the park. The lake is fed by springs and snow melt, and is ice-free for only a few weeks during the summer. This Indian name means "grassy lake." It has been spelled *Tupso* and *Tipso*, but the present spelling is official. (USBGN)

Tiptop Hill *(S.28;T.37N;R.4W)*

West side hill of Stuart Island, between Reid Harbor and Haro Strait, extreme northwest San Juan County. The name was given by U.S. Coast Survey for the name of their triangulation station on this 640-ft. hill.

Titakoclos Creek
(Ss.6,7;T.33N;R.15W)

The stream of the creek rises on north side of Archawat Peak, Cape Flattery, Makah Indian Reservation, extreme northwest Clallam County; flows 1-1/2 miles northwest ot Strait of Juan de Fuca near Classet. It discharges in a waterfall by the same name. On modern maps the stream may appear as *Beach Creek*, a white man's substitute for the original Indian name.

Titakoclos Waterfall
(S.6;T.33N;R.15W)

Small waterfall on Makah Indian Reservation, Cape Flattery, at the mouth of Titakoclos Creek, Strait of Juan de Fuca, extreme northwest Clallam County. The fall takes its name from the creek. (*see* Titakoclos Creek)

Titusi bay (Pierce County) *see* Filucy Bay

Titusville (King County) *see* Kent

Tivoli Island *(T.30N;R.15W)*

Small, timbered island owned by National Park Service, near the south end of Lake Ozette, west central Clallam County. It was named for an amusement center in Copenhagen by a Danish settler named Nielsen.

Tiye Point *(S.25;T.20N;R.1W)*

South entrance point to Filucy Bay, on Pitt Passage, northwest Pierce County. In 1841, the point was named by Cmdr. Wilkes and is evidently his version of the original Indian name *Titusi*.

Toad Lake *(Ss.11,14;T.38N;R.3E)*

Small, wooded lake, 29.7 acres, 2,700 ft. long, on a hilltop 1-1/2 miles north of the north end of Lake Whatcom, 5 miles northeast of Bellingham, southwest Whatcom County. In 1884, it was named by George Nolte, an early resident, for the abundance of toads around the lake. *Emerald Lake*, the present name, may be less descriptive, but is certainly more poetic.

Toads Coula Creek (Okanogan County) *see* Toats Coulee Creek

Toandos Peninsula *(Ts.25-27N;R.1W)*

A 10-mile-long peninsula, 2 miles wide north-south, between Dabob Bay and Hood Canal, east central Jefferson County. IN 1841, this feature was first mapped by the Wilkes Expedition. The record indicates that it was named for an Indian tribe who was found here and could have been *Twana*. A creditable source is also found in the name of a Pope & Talbot ship that came to Port Gamble in 1859, and was named *Toando*. There is no verification, however, that the peninsula was named after this vessel. It reached Port Townsend on March 29, 1859.

Toat (Toad) Coulee Creek (Okanogan County) *see* Toats Coulee Creek

Toats Coulee Creek
(Ts.38-40N;Rs.24,25E)

The north fork of this creek rises near the Canadian boundary southwest of Chopaka; the middle and south forks originate on the former Sinlahekin Game Refuge, north central Okanogan County. The combined stream flows east to Sinlahekin Creek, 2 miles north of Loomis. The name is from the Indian word *Toats-coula*, meaning "sucker." Variations that have been applied to this creek are *Toat Coulee Creek, Toads Coula,* and *Toad Coulee.*

Tocosos River (Clallam County) *see* Sail River

Todd Bay (Pacific County) *see* Knappton

Toe Point *(T.38N;R.2W)*

East end point of Patos Island, Georgia Strait, extreme north central San Juan County. In 1859, the descriptive name was placed on British admiralty charts by Capt. Richards, RN. It has become official.

Toke Point *(S.18;T.14N;R.10W)*

Settlement on the south side of a 3-mile spit, at the north entrance to inner Willapa Harbor, northwest Pacific County. The point is famous for oysters and the name is used commercially. It was named by early settlers for an old Indian chief who was an expert canoe navigator and a competent guide.

Tokeland *(T.14N;R.11W)*

Settlement on a narrow, 3-mile spit at the north entrance to Willapa Harbor,

northwest Pacific County. It is the center for commercial crab fishing and also a summer resort. (*see* Toke Point)

Toketie Lake *(S.19;T.33N;R.12E)*

A 17-acre lake, elevation 5,200 ft., maximum depth 40 ft., 14-1/2 miles northeast of Darrington, southeast Skagit County. This is a descriptive Kalepuya Indian name meaning "pretty."

Tokio *(S.22;T.20N;R.36E)*

Community 8 miles northeast of Ritzville, northeast Adams County. In 1888, it was named *Iona* by officials of Northern Pacific Railway Company, who changed the name to *Tracy*, in 1905, then again to the present form in 1906. The reasons for this multiple choice have not been determined. Adding to the name complex is the fact that the post office here was once called *Wheatland*.

Tokul Creek *(Ts.24,25N;R.8E)*

The stream of the creek rises 6 miles north of the community of Snoqualmie Falls, north central King County; flows 7-1/2 miles south and southwest to Snoqualmie River, 1 mile below Snoqualmie Falls (falls). It runs in a deep canyon and the water is quite dark in color. The name is from the Indian word *Tu-kwa-l*, which has the meaning "very dark water."

To-Kwak-Sose (*Clallam County*) *see* Snow Creek

Toleak Point *(S.20;T.27N;R.14W)*

Pacific Ocean point 2 miles south of Giants Graveyard, 9 miles south of Quillayute River's mouth, northwest Jefferson County. The name is a distortion of the Clallam word for "mussel," which is *To-luks*. It evidently was the original Indian name for this point.

Toledo *(Ss.18,19;T.11N;R.1W)*

Very old town on Cowlitz River, 15 miles south of Chehalis, southwest corner of Lewis County. It had 3 previous names -- *Plomondoe's Landing, Cowlitz Landing*, and *Warbassport*. The present town occupies the site of a Donation Land Claim owned in the 1850s and later by August Rochon and his wife, Celeste. The present name was given by Celeste Rochon for a pioneer sidewheel steamer operated by Capt. Oren Kellogg of Kellogg Transportation Company. (*see* Warbassport)

Toliva Shoal *(S.30;T.20N;R.2E)*

Nisqually Reach shoal, south of Fox

Island, 1 mile south of Gibson Point, northwest Pierce County. In 1841, this name was charted by the Wilkes Expedition. In 1846, Capt. R. N. Inskip used the name *Scarboro Shoals* on a British Admiralty chart of the area. Wilkes' name was favored by the U.S. Coast & Geodetic Survey, and has become accepted.

Tolmie Creek *(Mt. Rainier National Park)*

The stream of the creek rises at the head of Ranger Creek, north of Eunice Lake, 3 miles south of the park's north boundary, northwest corner of the park. It has the same name source as Tolmie Peak. Prof. Bailey Willis chose this name in 1883, for Dr. William Fraser Tolmie, Hudson's Bay Company factor and surgeon at Fort Nisqually from 1833 until the late 1850s. Dr. Tolmie was the first white man of record to explore Mt. Rainier and the surrounding area. In August, 1833, accompanied by 5 Indians, he climbed the peak that now bears his name. (USBGN)

Tolmie Lake *(Mt. Rainier National Park) see* Eunice Lake

Tolmie Peak *(Mt. Rainier National Park)*

A 5,939-ft. peak directly north of Eunice Lake, 1-1/4 miles northwest of Mowich Lake, northwest corner of the park. (*see* Tolmie Creek)

Tolo *(S.18;T.25N;R.2E)*

Settlement on west Bainbridge Island, east shore of Port Orchard Bay, central Kitsap County. In 1890, it was named by Martin Anderson, a homesteader, for a sailing ship that was built in that period at Hornbeck's Spit in Kitsap County.

Tolt *(King County) see* Carnation

Tolt *(S.16;T.25N;R.7E)*

Small town 18 miles south of Monroe, 6 miles east of Lake Sammamish, north central King County. In 1902, the town was platted by W. H. Lord, and named for the original word *Tolthue*, an Indian band who lived here. In 1917, it was re-named *Carnation* by the state legislature on an agreement with E. A. Stuart of Carnation Company to install a milk-condensing plant here if the name were so changed. In the early 1950s, after the Carnation plant had ceased operations, citizens requested a change back to the original name. Others

wanted to retain the name, Carnation. Both are carried on some recent maps.

Tolt River *(Ts.25,26N;Rs.7-10E)*

The stream of the river rises 8 miles west of Skykomish, in 2 forks, north central King County. The forks join 2 miles east of Lake Joy; flow 7 miles southwest to Snoqualmie River. The river is now a part of Seattle's water supply. The name is the white man's interpretation of the Indian word *H-lalty*, as used by the Snoqualmie tribe for the river. The surveyor general of Washington Territory mapped it as *Tolthue River* in 1857.

Tolthue River *(King County) see* Tolt River

Tomar *(S.27;T.6N;R.30E)*

Area on north bank of Columbia River opposite Van Skinner Island, 16 miles south of Kennewick, extreme southeast Benton County. The name is for one of the leaders of the Walla Walla Indians in pioneer days, stated to have been the second ranking chief.

Tomlinson Falls *(Mt. Rainier National Park)*

Waterfall in a tributary of Pyramid Creek which drains Pyramid Glacier, southwest slope of Mt. Rainier, southwest quarter of the park. The feature was named by The Mountaineers at the suggestion of one of the members, Charles A. Bieson. It was to honor Maj. O. A. Tomlinson, superintendent of the park between 1923 and 1941.

Tommy Creek *(T.28N;R.18E)*

The stream of the creek rises in 2 branches in Devil and Two Little Lakes on Wenatchee National Forest, north central Chelan County; drains eastward into Entiat River. Prior to 1908, the stream was named by Forest Ranger James McKenzie who did not state for which man he named the feature.

Tomyhoi Lake *(Whatcom County) see* Tommyhoy Lake

Tomyhoy Creek *(T.40N;Rs.8,9E.uns)*

The stream of the creek heads north of Welcome Pass, Mt. Baker National Forest, extreme north central Whatcom County; flows northwest through Tomyhoy Lake to Chilliwack River, British Columbia. It was named for Tomyhoy Mountain. The name is from the Indian word for "high mountain," and has been variously spelled as *Tomahoi*,

Tomohoy, Tomyhoi, and even *Tamania*. The British Boundary survey named it *Big Skookum*. British Columbia Indians used the name *Put-hish-go-hop*.

Tomyhoy Lake *(Ss.7,8;T.40N;R.9E.uns)*

Lake between Tomyhoy Mountain and Red Mountain, 1-1/2 miles south of the Canadian boundary, north central Whatcom County. On one issue of county maps, it is erroneously shown as *Tomhoy Lake.* (*see* Tomyhoy Creek)

Tomyhoy Mountain *(S.12;T.40N;R.8E.uns)*

A Mt. Baker National Forest peak, elevatiion 7,869 ft., 1-1/2 miles south of Canadian boundary, north central Whatcom County. The peak is glaciated on the north and east. (*see* Tomyhoy Creek)

Tomyhoy Peak *(Whatcom County) see* Tomyhoy Mountain

Tonasket *(S.16;T.37N;R.27E)*

Town on the east bank of Okanogan River, 17 miles south of Oroville, 21 miles south of the Canadian boundary, northeast Okanogan. The place was named for To-nas-ket, an intelligent and dignified chief of the Okanogan Indians. For the first school to be established in this area, he donated land that had been used as his camp in former days. Other names that have been used are *Tenasket* and *Dry Gulch*. (USBGN)

Tonasket Creek *(T.40N;Rs.27,28E)*

The stream of the creek rises in 2 branches which start near Kipling and on Haley Mountain, northeast Okanogan County; flow west 10 miles to Okanogan River, south of Osoyoos Lake, Colville National Forest. (*see* Tonasket)

Tongue Point *(Whatcom County) see* Semiahmoo

Tongue Point *(S.21;T.31N;R.8W)*

East entrance point to Crescent Bay, Strait of Juan de Fuca, north central Clallam County. In 1847, this name was placed on British Admiralty charts by Capt. Henry Kellett. It is descriptive as the point has a definite tongue-like shape. The name has been confirmed by U.S.C.&G. Survey.

Tono *(S.16;T.15N;R.1W)*

Very small settlement 2-1/2 miles southeast of Bucoda, extreme south central Thurston County. Officials of O.W.R.&N. Railway preferred brief names for stations. They stated, when they chose this name, that it was an abbreviation for "ton of coal."

Tookanan *(Columbia County) see* Tucannon

Tooth *(King County) see* The Tooth

Top Lake *(S.28;T.28N;R.14E)*

A 20-acre lake, located a few ft. east of Cascade Mountain summit, 1 mile west of Fall Mountain, Wenatchee National Forest, northwest Chelan County. The original name was the much-used *Summit Lake*. Assistant Forest Supervisor C. J. Conover chose this name to avoid repetition.

Topinish *(Yakima County) see* Toppenish

Toppenish *(Ss.3,4,10;T.10N;R.20E)*

Town 15 miles southeast of Yakima, southeast Yakima County. For many years this was the headquarters of Yakima Indian Reservation and the town caters strongly to Indian trade. The surrounding area is extremely fertile. In 1885, the original Indian name for this place was applied to the railroad station by Northern Pacific Railway Company. As spelled, it is a corruption of *Thappahn-ish*, which means "people of the trail which comes from the foot of the hills." In 1853, Capt. George McClellan mapped the place as *Sahpenis*. On some old maps the name is spelled *Topinish*.

Toppenish Creek
(Ts.9,10N;Rs.14-21E)

The stream of the creek rises on Yakima Indian Reservation near Signal Peak, southwest Yakima County; flows east to join Yakima River, 1 mile southeast of Granger. An early name used by the surveyor general of Washington Territory in 1859 was *Pisko*. This name, or an alternate version -- *Pisco* -- is a Yakima tribal word meaning "river bend." (*see* Toppenish)

Toroda *(S.27;T.40N;R.32E)*

Former mining town, Colville National Forest, 4-1/2 miles south of the Canadian boundary, 10 miles west of Curlew, on the Kettle River at the confluence of Toroda Creek, extreme northwest corner of Ferry County. The town has a colorful history. Among other claims to fame, it is the burial place of the world-wide adventurer Ranald McDonald, whose life has been made the subject of a well-written book.

A local legend regarding the name origin is that the word is an Indian pronunciation of "Dorothy", for Dorothy McDonald, a descendant of famous Angus McDonald of Hudson's Bay Company. A more logical choice is the Indian name for the place, *To-Ro-Tee*. On various maps and records the name has been misspelled *Taroda, Tarota, Tarroda,* and *Teroda*. A formerly used name is reported to have been *Lynch*. (USBGN)

Toroda Creek *(Ts.38-40N;Rs.31-32E)*

The stream of the creek rises near Wauconda, northeast Okanogan County; flows north-by-east for 35 miles into northwest Ferry County, to enter Kettle River at Toroda. The last 5 miles are in Ferry County. The creek was named for the town by the same name in Ferry County. An earlier name was *Meadow Creek*, which hardly is appropriate. (*see* Toroda)

Toroda Mountain *(S.29;T.38N;R.31E)*

A Colville National Forest peak, 1-1/2 miles southwest of Old Toroda, northeast Okanogan County. (*see* Toroda)

Torrent Creek *(S.15;T.38N;R.12E.uns)*

The stream of the creek rises at Elephant Butte, Mt. Baker National Forest, 6 miles north of Diablo Lake, east central Whatcom County; flows 1-1/2 miles southeast to Stetattle Creek. It was named for the swift and irregular water flow, due to a rough, steep channel.

Totem Pass
(Ss.20,29;T.32N;R.14E.uns)

A Mt. Baker National Forest pass, 2 miles west of Cascade Mountain summit, 3 miles northwest of Suiattle Pass, between Sulphur and Canyon Creeks, extreme northeast Snohomish County. The pass was named by Forest Service personnel because of the totem-like appearance of a nearby rock.

Totten Inlet *(Ts.19,20N;Rs.2,3W)*

Inlet 6 miles northwest of Olympia, 9 miles long, average width 1/2 mile. It serves as a part of the boundary between Thurston and Mason counties and the south end of the inlet has a separate name, *Oyster Bay*. In 1841, it was named by the Wilkes Expedition for Midshipman George M. Totten, who performed exploratory work here. (USBGN) (*see* Oyster Bay)

Touchet *(Columbia County) see* Dayton

Touchet *(S.34;T.7N;R.33E)*

Community at confluence of Touchet and Walla Walla rivers, 17 miles west of Walla Walla, southwest Walla Walla County. This place was settled in a very early period by French-Canadians who had come to the region with fur trading companies. The name is believed to have been from the French *toucheur* or cattle drover, or from the French verb *toucher*, one meaning of which is "to drive, to strike with a whip." Cattle and horse raising were important activities in pioneer days along Touchet River.

Touchet River *(Ts.7-9N;Rs.33-40E)*

The stream of the river heads in south central Columbia County; flows north to join South Fork, near Dayton, then west through Waitsburg and south to Walla Walla River near Touchet. In May 1906, Lewis & Clark named this stream *White Stallion River* for a fine horse given them by Walla Walla Indians. (*see* Touchet)

Toulou Creek *(T.38N;R.37E)*

The stream of the creek rises in Pierre Lake, Colville National Forest, northwest Stevens County; flows 9 miles south to the Kettle River at Barstow. It was named for a prominent local Indian family.

Toulou Mountain
(Ss.19,30,31;T.39N;R.37E)

Double-summit mountain, Colville National Forest, 2 miles east of Kettle River, 2-1/2 miles southeast of Orient, northwest Stevens County. The two peaks in a heavily mineralized area have elevations of 3,441 and 3,537 ft. (*see* Toulou Creek)

Toutle Lake (Cowlitz County) (*see* Silver Lake

Toutle River *(Ts.9,10N;Rs.2W-4E)*

The stream of the river rises in 2 branches, west Skamania County; flows west over 40 miles through north Cowlitz County to Cowlitz River north of Castle Rock. The name is from a local Indian tribal designation, *Hullooetell*. In 1841, Wilkes simplified that name to *Toutle*, and his title has remained.

Towal *(S.8;T.3N;R.18E)*

Former town and present railway station 12 miles southeast of Goldendale, near north bank of Columbia River, south central Klickitat County. The railway station at this point was named for *To-whal* or *Too-wal*, a Klickitat Indian, who, of course, is listed as having been a chief.

Towanda *(S.4;T.37N;R.4E)*

Small suburban area on the east shore of Lake Whatcom, southwest Whatcom County. It was named by settlers for the Indian term *Ta-wun-de-unk*, meaning "at burial place." As in the case of most Indian names, the spelling was changed to suit the white man's pronunciation.

Tower Rock Beaver Ponds
(S.18;T.11N;R.8E)

A series of shallow beaver ponds in a tributary of Cispus River, east of Tower Rock, southeast Lewis County. The total area is about 3 acres The por s were named for nearby Tower Rock.

Towhead Gap *(S.26;T.14N;R.7E)*

Gap 5 miles south of Nisqually Entrance to Mt. Rainier National Park, north central Lewis County. The name is for a "towhead" deer which a U.S. Forest Service ranger shot in this gap.

Towhead Island *(S.17;T.36N;R.1E)*

Rosario Strait island, directly north of the north tip of Cypress Island, northwest Skagit County. An early name for this very small, rocky island was *Cypress Rock*, although the trees that covered it were actually junipers. In 1854, it was also named *Rock Island* by the U.S. Coast Survey, a fairly descriptive name. The source of the present locally chosen name is not recorded. (USBGN)

Township 21-9 *(T.21N;R.9W)*

Township of forest land on the east and west forks of Humptulips River, central Grays Harbor County. On this area stood the greatest commercial stand of natural timber in the entire world, mostly Douglas fir. This timber was harvested and the land is growing a second crop. The township is known to loggers and foresters throughout the Pacific Northwest.

Tracy (Adams County) *see* Tokio

Tracy Point *(Ts.29,30N;R.41E)*

Loon Lake point, southwest Stevens County. It was named for the notorious outlaw Harry S. Tracy, who cleared land and cut cordwood here at the turn of the century, before embarking on a criminal career.

Tracyton *(S.34;T.25N;R.1E)*

Residential community on the east shore of Dyes Inlet, 1-1/4 miles north of Bremerton, central Kitsap County. The town was locally named for Benjamin Franklin Tracy, who was secretary of the navy, 1889-1893.

Tradedollar Lake *(S.18;T.10N;R.5E)*

A 12.1-acre, Gifford Pinchot National Forest lake, elevation 3,552 ft., at the head of Tradedollar Creek, northwest of Spirit Lake, northwest Skamania County. It was locally named for Tradedollar Creek, which drains the lake.

Tradition Lake *(S.35;T.24N;R.6E)*

A 19.2-acre, swampy lake high on a ridge, 1-1/4 miles east of Issaquah, King County. The lake is now used as part of Issaquah's water system, with limited access. The interesting tradition that concerns this small lake is that of early government land surveyors who were forced to leave portions of their lines unsurveyed because the place was too heavily infested with snakes to allow them to proceed. There probably are factual grounds for this story, as snakes are found around the lake in enormous numbers during the spring and early summer, feeding on frogs that are hatched in the lake shallows.

Trafton *(S.29;T.32N;R.6E)*

Small settlement 5 miles northeast of Arlington on North Fork, Stillaguamish River, northwest Snohomish County. Prior to 1890, the town's first name was *Glendale*. In 1890, the post office changed to the present name because of confusion with Glendale, Oregon and with Glendive, Montana. Trafton was the choice of George Estabrook, who owned the townsite. He attached the abbreviation for "town" to the first syllable of Trafalgar, a famous square in London.

Trail Lake (King County) *see* Rainbow Lake.

Trail of Shadows *(Mt. Rainier National Park)*

Foot trail around the edge of Longmire Meadows, which passes by the original Longmire cabin, southwest quarter of the park. The name is descriptive because the trail passes through thick forest cover. It is reported to have been named by an early party of hikers, who were impressed by the deep shadows caused by overhanging trees. The name is unofficial.

Traitors Inlet *(S2;T.16N;R.11W)*

South channel inlet of Grays Harbor, at the mouth of Johns River, southwest Grays Harbor County. It was named by the Wilkes Expedition when Indians who were hired to help survey parties refused to work and threatened violence in July and August, 1841.

Tramp Harbor *(T.22N;R.3E)*

East shore harbor of Vashon and Maury islands, on East Passage, directly northeast of Quartermaster Harbor across a narrow sand spit. The name was applied by local travelers who carried small boats across the spit from Quartermaster Harbor to Tramp Harbor. It was quite a tramp, unless there were several persons to assist. It is shown on maps published in 1894 as *Trump Harbor*.

Trap Creek *(T.12N;R.8W)*

The stream of the creek heads 5 miles southwest of Nalpee, central Pacific County; flows northeast and north to Willapa River at Nalpee. The name is of local origin and relates to the large amount of trap-rock along the stream.

Trap Lake *(S.10;T.25N;R.13E)*

A Wenatchee National Forest lake at the head of Trapper Creek, 1 mile east of Cascade Mountain summit, southwest Chelan County. The name was selected by Forest Supervisor A. H. Sylvester to harmonize with Trapper Creek.

Trapper Creek *(T.25N;R.13E)*

The stream of the creek heads 1 mile east of Cascade Mountain summit; flows 5 miles east to Icicle Creek through Grass Lake, Wenatchee National Forest, southwest Chelan County. (*see* Trap Lake)

Travis Spit (Clallam County) *see* Long Spit

Treble Point (Pierce County) *see* Point Treble

Trede Lake (Whatcom County) *see* Fountain Lake

Tree Bluff *(T.31N;R.10W)*

Headland on Strait of Juan de Fuca, 5 miles east of mouth of Pysht River, north central Clallam County. Originally this headland was covered with heavy, old-growth forest, but the timber has been harvested now. In 1847, this descriptive name was placed on British Admiralty charts by Capt. Henry Kellett.

Treen Lake *(S.36;T.27N;R.6E)*

A 1-acre lake in Snoqualmie River, 4-1/2 miles south of Monroe, southwest

Snohomish County. It was named for Lewis A. Treen, formerly assistant forest supervisor of Snoqualmie National Forest. On February 2, 1937, Treen died after 26 years on national forests. (USBGN)

Treen Peak *(S.18;T.24N;R.11E)*

A Snoqualmie National Forest peak, elevation 5,800 ft., due east of Snoqualmie, 1-1/2 miles northwest of Nordrum Lake, between Taylor River and Middle Fork, Snoqualmie River, northeast King County. *(see* Treen Lake)

Triad Creek *(T.30N;R.14E.uns)*

The stream of the creek rises in 3 branches at Cascade Mountain summit, near Buck Creek Pass, Mt. Baker National Forest, northeast Snohomish County; flows 3 miles northwest to Suiattle River at the foot of Glacier Peak. In 1920, the name was chosen by A. H. Sylvester, supervisor of Wenatchee National Forest, because of the 3 distinct forks near the creek's source.

Triangle Cove *(S.6;T.31N;R.3E)*

Northeast shore cove of Camano Island, east central Island County. In 1841, the cove was named by the Wilkes Expedition; the name is descriptive because of the inlet's distinctly triangular outline.

Triangle Lake (San Juan County) *see* Three Corner Lake

Trico Mountain Lake (King County) *see* Basin Lake

Trinidad *(S.7;T.20N;R.23E)*

Village near the Columbia River, 6 miles west of Quincy, southwest Grant County. It was named for a Colorado town of the same name, because of supposedly similar topography.

Trinity *(S.27;T.30N;R.16E)*

Mining camp at the confluence of Phelps Creek and Chiwawa River, 20 miles north of Leavenworth, Wenatchee National Forest, northwest Chelan County. The Royal Development Company established a mine and a campsite here many years ago and chose this name for the place in 1937.

Trixie Falls *(Mt. Rainier National Park)*

Waterfall on the southeast slope of Mt. Rainier, near the head of Basalt Creek in Cowlitz Park, southeast quarter of the park. The name was chosen by Park Superintendent Ethan Allen for the daughter of former Park Superintendent

E. S. Hall. (USBGN)

Trosper Lake *(S.4;T.17N;R.2W)*

Lake 1 mile southwest of Tumwater, on the west side of Bush Prairie, central Thurston County. The lake was named in pioneer days for an early settler on Bush Prairie who raised cattle and sheep.

Troublesome Creek *(T.28N;R.11E)*

The stream of this mountain creek rises in Blanco Lake, Snoqualmie National Forest, southeast Snohomish County; flows 5 miles southwest to North Fork, Skykomish River. Early prospectors and miners used this name because of their difficulty in fording this swift creek. The name has also been applied to a nearby mountain in the same mineralized area.

Troublesome Mountain *(Ss.14,15;T.28N;R.11E)*

A Snoqualmie National Forest peak, elevation 5,430 ft., 1-1/2 miles northwest of Garland Mineral Springs, southeast Snohomish County. The mountain is in a heavily mineralized area. *(see* Troublesome Creek)

Trout Creek (Ferry/Okanogan counties) *see* Turner Creek

Trout Lake (Cowlitz County) *see* Merrill Lake

Trout Lake *(S.34;T.21N;R.4E)*

An 18.1-acre lake, 4 miles southwest of Auburn, southwest King County. This name is so commonly used for Pacific Northwest lakes that it loses any significance. It can mean: 1) There were trout in the lake in the past; 2) There are trout in it now; 3)Trout may be planted in the lake at some later day; or, 4)People fish the lake for trout but don't catch any. An alternate name is *Jovita Lake.*

Trout Lake *(Ss.15,16;T.6N;R.10E)*

A 3/4 mile-long lake, 1/4 mile average width, in an area of ice caves, on Trout Lake Creek, 18 miles north of White Salmon, extreme northwest Klickitat County. *(see* Trout Lake, King County)

Trout Lake *(S.22;T.6N;R.10E)*

Community directly southeast of Trout Lake (lake), near confluence of White Salmon River and Trout Lake Creek, extreme northwest Klickitat County. the name was taken from that of the adjoining lake.

Troutdale *(S.1;T.20N;R.8E)*

Railway station on Green River, 18 miles west of Cascade Mountain summit, south central King County. This ornamental name was selected by officials of Northern Pacific Railway Company when a station was established here.

Truax *(Spokane County) see* Fairfield

Truax *(S.30;T.13N;R.44E)*

Railway station on north bank of Snake River, 20 miles south of Colfax, southeast Whitman County. It was named by officials of O.W.R.&N. Railway for Maj. Truax, who owned a river bar on the opposite shore of Snake River in Garfield County.

Trump Harbor (King County) *see* Tramp Harbor

Tsa-Tsa-Dakh (Clallam County) *see* Fuca Pillar

Tshletshy Creek *(Ts.24,25N;Rs.8,9,10W)*

The stream of the creek rises in Paradise Valley, Olympic National Park, south central Jefferson County; flows 14 miles northwest to Queets River. This Indian name is a modification of the Chehalis term *Tsa-lot-chi* or *Tus-lot-shee,* meaning "to pull up, roots and all." It refers to a Salish legend of the powerful Chinook wind.

Tskutsko Point *(S.5;T.25N;R.1W)*

Southwest point of Toandos Peninsula, on Dabob Bay, southeast Jefferson County. In 1841, the point was named by Cmdr. Charles Wilkes as *Tskulsko Point,* evidently in an effort to record a local Indian name. Over the years, the "l" has become a "t." *(see* Hazel Point)

Tsuga Lakes *(S.22;T.21N;R.9E)*

Two adjacent lakes on Snoqualmie National Forest, 5-1/2 miles south of Cedar Lake, southeast King County. One lake covers 5.6 acres, and the smaller covers 1.4 acres. The name obviously is for the hemlock timber surrounding the lakes, as Tsuga is the generic name for all species of hemlock. An alternate name is *Scotty's Lake.*

Tsugawa Brothers Reservoir *(S.32;T.5N;R.2E)*

A 15-acre lake, 4-1/2 miles east of La Center, northwest Clark County. It is named for the owners of the land on which it is located.

Tucannon *(S.3;T.12N;R.37E)*

Settlement on south bank of Snake River, 1 mile southeast of Pataha, extreme northwest Columbia County. The name is a distortion of the Indian appellation *tukanin*, which in Nez Perce means "bread root." The Indian bread root, "kouse" or "couse," was an important food source. Lewis and Clark called this stream *Ki-moo-e-nimm* and also *Kimooenem*, and described it in detail in their entries for May 3, 1806. This name evidently had the meaning of "abundance of bread root." Legends that are interesting but unverified, include a story of 2 cannons which were presumed to have been buried along the Tucannon River. Another legend states that the name is for 2 canyons that meet in the stream's lower course. Thus, aside from the official name which was accepted by the USBGN for Tucannon River and the town, the following have also been used on maps and in print: *Two Canyon, Tucanon, Tchannon, Twocannon, Tukanon, Tookanan, Tukanin, Kinnooenim, Kimooenim,* and *Ki-moo-e-nimm.* (USBGN)

Tucannon River *(Ts.8-12N;Rs.37-42E)*

Long river with numerous names which rises in the Blue Mountain area of Umatilla National Forest, southwest Garfield County; flows through Columbia County from southeast to northwest, for over 50 miles to Snake River at Tucannon. (*see* Tucannon)

Tucanon (Columbia County) *see* Tucannon

Tucker *(S.26;T.9N;R.2W)*

Railway station on Cowlitz River, 3-1/2 miles south of Castle Rock, northwest Cowlitz County. In 1888, this place was named *Tucker's* by Northern Pacific Railway, when a station was established here. The name is for a settler from whom the railway acquired a right-of-way. It was later shortened to the present form.

Tucker Lake (San Juan County) *see* Egg Lake

Tucquala Lake (Kittitas County) *see* Fish Lake

Tukanin (Columbia County) *see* Tucannon

Tukannon Post Office (Garfield County) *see* Chard

Tukey *(S.32;T.30N;R.1W)*

Resort community on the east shore of Port Discovery Bay, on Quimper Peninsula, northeast Jefferson County. Originally it was a camp for the production of hewed ships-knees, later a water landing and inn on the road to Port Townsend. Now it is a fashionable resort -- Chevy Chase. It was named for John F. Tukey, who established the camp and landing in 1852. It also was known as *Tukey's Landing* and later as *Saints' Rest.* It is shown on a recent county map, in egregious error, as *Turkey.*

Tukey's Landing (Jefferson County) *see* Tukey, Chevy Chase, Saints' Rest

Tukwila *(S.23;T.23N;R.4E)*

Town 2-1/2 miles west of Renton, west central King County. It was formed by merging several townsite plats in 1902 and 1903. In 1905, when a post office was established, Joel Shomaker, later mayor of the town, suggested the Indian name, *Tuck-wil-a,* which means "land of hazelnuts." Postal authorities accepted the name in its present, shortened form. The town seal is a cluster of 3 hazelnuts in the husk.

Tulalip *(S.22;T.30N;R.4E)*

Community on the north shore of Tulalip Bay, 5 miles west of Marysville on Tulalip Indian Reservation, west central Snohomish County. This is the reservation headquarters. The name is an Indian word with English spelling. *Duh-hlay-lup* means "a wide bay with a small mouth," which is quite descriptive of the bay on which this town is located.

Tulalip Bay *(S.27;T.30N;R.4E)*

North end bay of Port Gardner Bay, on Tulalip Indian Reservation, 6 miles northwest of Everett, west central Snohomish County. The small bay is almost land-locked. (*see* Tulalip)

Tulalip Indian Reservation *(Ts.25,30N;Rs.4,5E)*

A 22,490-acre reservation directly west of Marysville, on Port Susan and Port Gardner Bay, west central Snohomish County. On January 22, 1855, this reservation was established by an executive order of December 23, 1873. (*see* Tulalip)

Tum Tum *(S.30;T.28N;R.41E)*

Community on Long Lake Reservoir in the Spokane River, southeast Stevens County. The name, from Chinook jar-gon, stems from "thump thump," and refers to the heart or spirit.

Tumacs Mountain *(S.8;T.29N;R.14E)*

Peak directly east of Cascade Mountain summit, at the headwaters of Cascade Creek, west central Chelan County. The mountain was named by Forest Service Supervisor A. H. Sylvester for 2 Scottish sheepherders who raced their bands each year to early range on the mountain. The 2 Macs were McDuff and McAdam.

Tumtum Mountain (Mt. Rainier National Park) *see* Tumtum Peak

Tumtum Peak *(Mt. Rainier National Park)*

An isolated, 4,678-ft. peak, between Tahoma and Kautz creeks, 2-1/2 miles east of Nisqually Entrance, southwest corner of the park. Mountain goats may often be seen on its slopes. The Indian name, from Chinook jargon, means "heart." It is suggestive of the mountain's contour. (USBGN)

Tumwata Creek (Jefferson County) *see* Tumwater Creek

Tumwater *(S.27;T.18N;R.2W)*

First American settlement on Puget Sound, on Deschutes River, adjoining Olympia on the south, central Thurston County. Indian names for the place, relating to the falls in Deschutes River and in several dialects, were *Tum-chuck, Tum-wa-ta,* and *Spa-kwatl.* Each had the meaning of "strong water" or "water fall." In 1845, when Col. Michael T. Simmons and 31 Kentuckians settled here, they called the place *New Market.* Other names that have been used are *Falls River* and *Des Chutes.* The present name is well established and is a modification of the Indian *Tum-wa-ta.*

Tumwater Canyon *(Ts.24,25N;R.17E)*

A Wenatchee National Forest canyon, 9 miles long, 1 mile deep, which carries a rapid, boiling torrent, in the Wenatchee River from Chiwawa Creek to Leavenworth, south central Chelan County. Forest Supervisor A. H. Sylvester chose an Indian name which means "rough water."

Tumwater Creek *(T.30N;R.6W)*

The stream of the creek rises south of Port Angeles in the foothills, Clallam County; flows north-by-east to Port Angeles Harbor. The Indian name means "waterfall" or "cascade" in Chinook jargon. In pioneer days, the stream was named *Fraser Creek* for an early settler, Joe Fraser. Later it was re-named *Nelly's Run*, for a daughter of pioneer Norman R. Smith.

Tumwater Creek *(T.27N;R.11W)*
The stream of the creek rises north of Peak 6, Olympic National Park, northwest Jefferson County; flows 4-1/2 miles west to Bogachiel River. (*see* Tumwater)

Tumwater Falls *(S.27;T.18N;R.2W)*
Waterfall in Deschutes River at Tumwater, 2-1/2 miles from entry into Budd Inlet, north central Thurston County. The Indian name was *Spakwatl*, meaning "strong water." In 1829, Hudson's Bay Company employees called this feature *Puget Sound Falls*. In 1841, the Wilkes Expedition used the name *Shutes River Falls*. (*see* Tumwater)

Tunnel (Chelan County) *see* Tunnel City

Tunnel City *(S.8;T.26N;R.15E)*
Once a town near Berne at the east portal of Cascade Tunnel, southwest Chelan County. In 1897, the town was built for workers on Great Northern tunnel construction and called "the wickedest place in the world." In 1900, it was abandoned and destroyed by fire shortly afterward. The name chosen by Great Northern Railway officials is descriptive.

Tunnel Creek *(S.26;T.26N;R.13E)*
The stream of the creek rises on the west side of Cascade Mountain summit, 2 miles south of Great Northern Railway's Cascade Tunnel near Stevens Pass; flows 4 miles to Tyre River, Snoqualmie National Forest, northeast King County. It was named for the tunnel near which it originates. This creek should not be confused with one by the same name in Kittitas County.

Tunnel Creek *(S.9;T.22N;R.11E)*
The stream of the creek rises at Cascade Mountain summit, 2 miles south of Snoqualmie Pass; flows 1-1/2 miles east to Coal Creek. This very short stream was so named by The Mountaineers on June 15, 1916, because it is close to the Snoqualmie tunnel of Chicago, Milwaukee & St. Paul Railway. (USBGN)

Tunnel Island *(S.28;T.23N;R.13W)*
Pacific Ocean island at the mouth of

Raft River, 5 miles south of Queets, northwest Grays Harbor County. In 1855, this rock island was named *Raft Rock* by U.S. Coast Survey for nearby Raft River. In 1887, it was charted as *Arch Island* by U.S. Coast & Geodetic Survey for an arched opening in one of 2 small projections on the south end. The present, official name is for the same opening and was named by later surveyors. (USBGN)

Tupso Lake *(S.36;T.34N;R.10E)*
A 4-acre lake, elevation 4,500 ft., at the head of Grade Creek, 9-1/2 miles south of Marblemount, southeast Skagit County. The name means "grass" in Chinook Indian jargon. It obviously refers to swamp grass and reeds that grow along the lake margin.

Tupso Lakes *(S.5;T.31N;R.8E.uns)*
Group of 3 lakes, on Mt. Baker National Forest, 11 miles northeast of Granite Falls, northwest Snohomish County. The largest lake covers 2 acres. Chinook Indian jargon for this lake means "grass." It probably refers to swamp grass and reeds that grow along the lake shores.

Turk *(Ss.35-36;T.30N;R.37E)*
Settlement on Adler Creek, 6 miles east of the Columbia River, southwest Stevens County. It was founded by a company which owned and operated the Turk Mine here during the 1890s. The name is for the Turk Mine, for which it was founded as a supply point and to house the mine crew.

Turn Island *(S.18;T.35N;R.2W)*
San Juan Channel island, east of the east extremity of San Juan Island, central San Juan County. In 1841, Cmdr. Wilkes named this feature *Salsbury Point*, not realizing that it actually was an island. His name was for Francis Salsbury, captain-of-the-top in one of the expedition's ships. In 1858, Capt. Richards, RN, charted it under the present name because the island was a turning point in San Juan Channel. His name was adopted by U.S. geographers.

Turn Point *(S.20;T.37N;R.4W)*
Northwest end point of Stuart island, on Haro Strait, northwest San Juan County. In 1859, this name was placed on British Admiralty charts by Capt. Richards, RN, because it is located at a turning point in Haro Strait.

Turner *(S.30;T.11N;R.40E)*
Railway station 8 miles northeast of Dayton, north central Columbia County. The name is for Benjamin M. Turner who owned the land at this place, and who filed a townsite plat on January 17, 1902, when the O.W.R.&N. Railway extended a spur line from Dayton.

Turner Creek *(T.38N;Rs.31-32E)*
The stream of this small creek rises on west slope of Hardscrabble Mountain, northwest Ferry County; flows west to join Toroda Creek, 1 mile south of Bodie, northeast Okanogan County. Some early maps carry the unimaginative name of *Trout Creek*. The accepted name is for A. C. Turner, who homesteaded near the creek's mouth. (USBGN)

Turner Mountain *(T.28N;R.16E)*
A Wenatchee National Forest peak, between Chiwawa River and Raging Creek, southeast of Schaefer Lake, northwest Chelan County. It was named by Forest Supervisor A. H. Sylvester for Lieut. Turner, U.S. Army, who was a member of a calvary command that attacked Indians here in August, 1858.

Turnours Bay (Pierce County) *see* Filucy Bay

Turtle Back Range *(T.37N;R.2W)*
Orcas Island range on the western peninsula of the island, elevation 1,497 ft., extending about 5 miles southwest and northeast, north central San Juan County. In 1859, this name was placed on British admiralty charts by Capt. Henry Richards, RN. The profile of the range as viewed from the east, has a remarkable resemblance to a turtle.

Turtle Rapids *(T.33N;R.37E)*
Columbia River rapids, between Daisy on the east bank and Inchelium on the west bank. According to settlers who lived in this vicinity before the rapids were flooded, there were many turtles here, hence the name. An alternate possibility is that the rapids may have been named for a number of black-looking bedrock islands, both large and small, which Lieut. Thomas W. Symons described in his 1882 "Report of an Examination of the Upper Columbia River."

Tuscohatchie Creek
(Ss.35,36;T.23N;R.10E)
The stream of the creek heads in Tuscohatchie Lake, north slope of Granite Mountain, 3 miles west of Sno-

qualmie Pass; flows a short distance to the northwest, forming the headwaters of Pratt River. It was named by The Mountaineers for the lake in which it heads.

Tuscohatchie Lake
(S.36;T.23N;R.10E)

Two, connected lakes, north slope of Granite Mountain, 3 miles west of Snoqualmie Pass, east central King County. The upper lake is 58.3 acres, the lower 31.8 acres. The lake was named by The Mountaineers.

Tuton (Benton County) *see* Longview

Tuxpam River (Snohomish County) *see* Snohomish River

Twality District

One of 4 districts established by the provisional government of Oregon on July 5, 1843, when Oregon Territory was formed. It included all of western Washington, and the part of Oregon which was west of Willamette River. This was an administrative district. The name comes from the Indian word *Twha-la-ti*, meaning "land without trees," which is applied to several Oregon features as *Tualatin*.

Twelve Mile Bar *(T.38N;R.38E)*

These shoals were in the Columbia River, 11 miles by river below Little Dalles, on the east bank, Stevens County. The bar was flooded by the reservoir created by the Grand Coulee Dam. The name, like many on the upper Columbia River, denotes the number of miles above the Kettle Falls at which the feature was located.

Twelve Mile Creek *(T.28N;Rs.14,15E)*

The stream of the creek rises on the southeast slope of Poe Mountain, Wenatchee National Forest, west central Chelan County; flows south-by-east 2 miles to Little Wenatchee River. It was named by Forest Ranger S. Rice, because the creek's mouth is 12 miles from Wenatchee Lake.

Twenty Two Lake *(S.27;T.30N;R.8E)*

A 44.1-acre lake, elevation 2,460 ft., 9-1/2 miles east of Granite Falls, near Gold Basin, central Snohomish County. The lake was named for Twenty Two Creek, which drains it. An alternate name is *Canyon Lake*.

Twin *(T.31N;R.10W)*

Small settlement on Strait of Juan de Fuca, 20 miles west of Port Angeles, at the mouth of Twin River, north central Clallam County. It was named for its position at the mouths of West Twin and East Twin rivers.

Twin Harbors State Park
(T.16N;R.12W)

An 87-acre park on Pacific Ocean, 2 miles south of Westport, southwest Grays Harbor County.

Twin Lakes (King County) *see* Deception Lakes

Twin Lakes (Pierce County) *see* Meeker Lakes

Twin Lakes *(T.28N;R.16E)*

Two adjoining lakes on Wenatchee National Forest, in a deep cleft between Chiwawa Ridge and Dirtyface Mountain, northwest Chelan County. The lakes drain northwest into Napeequa River.

Twin Lakes *(S.8;T.26N;R.3W)*

Two lakes, 7 acres each, about 800 ft. apart, 9-1/2 miles southwest of Quilcene, east central Jefferson County. The 2 lakes are named Harrison and Karnes.

Twin Lakes *(Ss.6,7;T.27N;R.1E)*

Two lakes, 4-1/2 acres each, 1,700 ft. apart, 1 mile west of Hood Canal, 5 miles southwest of Port Ludlow, extreme east central Jefferson County. The names, Deep Lake and Pheasant Lake, have been applied locally to one or the other of these twins.

Twin Lakes *(S.21;T.37N;R.1W)*

Two connected lakes on the east lobe of Orcas Island, 1 mile northeast of Mt. Constitution summit, northeast San Juan County. One of the lakes is 8 acres, the other 3 acres.

Twin Lakes
(S.3;T.28N;S.34;T.29N;R.11E)

Two connected lakes, elevation 4,700 and 4,800 ft., respectively, maximum depth 50 ft., 2 miles south of Monte Cristo, 12 miles northeast of Index, southeast Snohomish County. Lower, or Little Twin Lake covers 24-1/2 acres. Upper, or Big Twin Lake is 68.8 acres.

Twin Lakes *(S.1;T.31N;R.12E)*

Two small lakes in close proximity, joined by a stream, on the lower northwest slope of Glacier Peak, Mt. Baker National Forest, northeast Snohomish County.

Twin Lakes *(S.16;T.40N;R.9E.uns)*

Two deep, connected lakes, elevation 5,180 and 5,200 ft., respectively, on Mt. Baker National Forest, at the head of Swamp Creek, 3-3/4 miles northeast of Shuksan, north central Whatcom County. Upper Twin covers 17 acres; Lower Twin 20 acres.

Twin Peaks *(S.19;T.30N;R.11E)*

Two Mt. Baker National Forest peaks, elevation 5,995 and 5,725 ft., respectively, 1-1/4 miles northwest of Monte Cristo Lake, east central Snohomish County. The descriptive name is quite accurate.

Twin River *(Ts.30,31N;R.10W)*

The streams of these 2 creeks rises northwest of Lake Crescent, central Clallam County; flow north to the Strait of Juan de Fuca at Twin. East Twin and West Twin have separate mouths, about 1/2 mile apart. The name is very descriptive and is locally chosen. In 1790, Manuel Quimper named one or both streams *Rio de Canel*, for Sebastian Canel, an outstanding Spanish naval officer.

Twin Sister Mountain (Whatcom County) *see* Twin Sisters Range

Twin Sisters Range *(T.37N;R.6E)*

A 6-mile-long mountain range, extending from 10 miles southwest of Mt. Baker summit, to Whatcom-Skagit county boundary, south central Whatcom County. There are glaciers on the north part of this range. North Twin Mountain has an elevation of 6,570 ft.; South Twin is somewhat higher, elevation 6,932 ft. The peaks are sufficiently similar to warrant the name.

Twin Tits (Columbia County) *see* Milk Shakes

Twin Wells (Adams County) *see* Hatton

Twisp *(S.17;T.33N;R.22E)*

Town at the confluence of Methow and Twisp rivers, 35 miles northwest of Pateros, west central Okanogan County. The town is dependent on logging and sawmilling. On July 30, 1897, it was platted as *Gloversville* by H. C. Glover on whose homestead it was located. On June 29, 1899, the town was re-platted by Amanda B. Burger as *Twisp*. The name is a modification of the Indian word *T-wapsp*, the meaning of which is obscure.

Twisp Lake *(T.34N;R.18E.uns)*

Very small mountain lake, directly east of Sawtooth Range summit, southwest Okanogan County. It is the source of South Fork, Twisp River, on the Okanogan National Forest. (*see* Twisp)

Twisp Mountain *(T.34N;R.18E.uns)*

A Chelan National Forest peak, on the Sawtooth Range summit, between the heads of North Fork and South Fork, Twisp River, west central Okanogan County. (*see* Twisp)

Twisp Pass *(T.34N;R.18E.uns)*

A Chelan National Forest pass, on the Sawtooth Range summit, north of Twisp Mountain, between North Fork and South Fork, Twisp River, west central Okanogan County. (*see* Twisp)

Twisp River *(Ts.33,34N;Rs.18-22E)*

The stream of the river rises in Twisp Lake, at Sawtooth Range summit, near Twisp Mountain and Twisp Pass, southwest Okanogan County; flows southeast and east 30 miles to Methow River at Twisp. (*see* Twisp)

Two Lakes *(S.21;T.20N;R.8E)*

Two small lakes, total only 1-1/2 acres, 9 miles east of Enumclaw, just below a lookout station on Grass Mountain, south central King County. The name is mathematically descriptive.

Two Lakes *(T.10N;R.11E.uns)*

Two shallow lakes, elevation 4,285 ft., on Yakima Indian Reservation, 2 miles east of Cascade summit, southwest Yakima County. The lakes are joined by a creek and drain into the West Fork, Fish Lake Stream. The latter is shown as *Lake Stream*, in error, on some maps. The name aptly applies to the joint lakes, as they are separated only by a few hundred feet.

Two Little Lakes *(T.28N;R.18E)*

Two small mountain lakes in close proximity, at the head of Tommy Creek, 2 miles southwest of Kelly Mountain, Wenatchee National Forest, north central Chelan County. The name developed by long use among sheepmen, and finally became the accepted designation.

Two Rivers *(S.34;T.8N;R.31E)*

Community 12 miles southeast of Pasco, southeast Walla Walla County. This railroad point had a boom period in the 1920s, based on irrigation with water pumped from Snake River. The irriga-tion company became bankrupt when farmers were unable to pay for water. In 1905, the name was chosen by railway company officials because the town was between the Walla Walla and Snake rivers. "Three Rivers" would have been equally appropriate, as it is close to the Columbia.

Twocannon (Columbia County) *see* Tucannon

Twocanyon (Columbia County) *see* Tucannon

Tye (Snohomish County) *see* Monroe

Tye City (Snohomish County) *see* Monroe

Tye Lake *(S.10;T.26N;R.13E)*

Glacier-fed, 3-acre lake at the headwaters of Tye River, 1-3/4 miles northwest of Stevens Pass, near Cascade Mountain summit, northeast King County. It was locally named for a locating engineer employed by Great Northern Railway.

Tye River *(T.26N;Rs.11-13E)*

The stream of the river heads at the west slope of Cascade Mountain summit, directly west of Stevens Pass, northeast King County; flows southwest and west to join Foss and Beckler rivers, forming the South Fork, Skykomish River. (*see* Tye Lake)

Tyee *(S.34;T.30N;R.13E)*

Community 12 miles east of Lake Ozette, in Soleduck Valley near Lake Pleasant, west central Clallam County. This name from the Chinook jargon means "chief, headman," or anything which is quite superior.

Tyee Creek *(T.27N;R.19E)*

The stream of the creek heads at the south base of Tyee Mountain, Wenatchee National Forest, central Chelan County; flows 3 miles southeast to Entiat River. The stream borrowed its name from Tyee Mountain by local usage.

Tyee Lake (Clallam County) *see* Lake Pleasant

Tyee Mountain *(S.5;T.27N;R.19E)*

A Wenatchee National Forest peak, elevation 6,688 ft., 2 miles west of Entiat River, on the divide between Entiat and Mad rivers, central Chelan County. An early hunter and trapper is said to have first used the name which later came into common use locally. (*see* Tyee)

Tyee Peak *(Mt. Rainier National Park)*

A 6,030-ft. peak at the southeast end of Chenius Mountain, north of Yellowstone Cliffs, north central zone of the park. (USBGN) (*see* Tyee)

TyKel Cove *(S.28;T.19N;R.2W)*

West shore cove of Budd Inlet, 2-1/2 miles north of Olympia, north central Thurston County. It was named for George TyKel, a pioneer who took a Donation Land Claim on upland adjoining Budd Inlet. On early maps and records this feature is called *TyKel's Cove*. The present name is a simplification.

Tyler *(S.5;T.22N;R.40E)*

Village 10 miles southwest of Medical Lake, southwest Spokane County. The place was founded by the Northern Pacific Railway Company while building the Pend Oreille Division and was platted on June 7, 1882 under the name of *Stevens*. The earlier name has appeared on some maps as *Stephens*. The name was changed to the present designation by Northern Pacific Railway Company officials. Information from that source states that the present name is "for a damage claimant in Montana." If this is correct, Tyler has the distinction of being the only place in the state that was named for a suer.

Tyler Glacier (Mt. Rainier National Park) *see* North Mowich Glacier

Typha Creek (Grays Harbor County) *see* Stafford Creek

Tyree *(S.19;T.30N;R.9E)*

Former logging camp on Mt. Baker National Forest, between Gold Basin and Weigle on South Fork, Stillaguamish River, central Snohomish County. The place was named for Jacy Tyrer, a timberman who logged here and ran a sawmill at Robe. The misspelling has never been corrected.

Tyrell's Prairie (Thurston County) *see* Hawks Prairie

Tzee-sa-ted Cove (Jefferson County) *see* Pleasant Harbor

U

U.S. Atomic Energy Commission Reservation

Federal reservation which extends for an average of 30 miles north-south, 25 miles east-west; it also extends on both sides of the Columbia River from Vernita, near Priest Rapids, south to the vicinity of Pasco, Benton, Grant, Franklin counties. The reservation is for testing and experimenting with atomic energy, the chief activity centering around Hanford. The name is often abbreviated to U.S.A.E.C. Reservation.

U.S. Creek *(Ts.37-38N;R.35E)*

The stream of this patriotic creek heads north of Scar Mountain, Colville National Forest, north central Ferry County; flows 8 miles northeast to Boulder Creek. After the Colville National Forest was established, but before the creek had been named, a local packer, Ed Smith was asked for its name. He replied that it was *Uncle Sam's creek,* and the name stuck.

U.S. Marines Memorial Glacier (Mt. Rainier National Park) *see* Tahoma Glacier

U.S. Military Reservation
(Ts.12-16N;Rs.19-23E)

Large range extending from Yakima River on west to Columbia River on east, northeast Yakima and southeast Kittitas counties. Almost 12 townships have been reserved for military purposes, particularly the testing of artillery weapons.

U.S. Mountain *(S.6;T.37N;R.35E)*

A Colville National Forest peak, elevation 6,230 ft., 16 miles northeast of Republic, directly northwest of U.S. Creek, north central Ferry County. It was named for its proximity to U.S. Creek. (*see* U.S. Creek)

Ucunas

Washington state shore of the Strait of Juan de Fuca, Clallam and Jefferson counties. In 1792, the name was applied by members of the Galliano Expedition. The meaning and the reason for naming an entire coastline are obscure.

Umatilla National Forest

A 321,932-acre forest in the southeast corner of the state, in the Blue Mountains area, within Columbia, Garfield and Asotin counties. The major part of the forest is in Oregon. Headquarters are in Pendleton, Oregon. It is one of 18 national forests included in Region 6 of the U.S. Forest Service, with Portland, Oregon headquarters. In 1908, it was established from Heppner National Forest and a part of Blue Mountains National Forest. In 1925, all of Wenaha National Forest was added. It was named for Umatilla River in Oregon, by U.S. Forest Service officials. The name is for the Umatilla Indians, a group of tribes who lived along Umatilla River in Oregon, and on the adjacent banks of Columbia River. Among many spellings of this name by explorers are You-matella, You-malo-lam, Umatallow, Umatilah, Umatella, Ewmitilly, and *Eu-o-tal-la.* The spelling now used is that charted by Cmdr. Charles Wilkes in 1841.

Umatilla Rapids *(Ss.9-11;T.5N;R.28E)*

Columbia River rapids now modified by the basin created back of McNary Dam. Their location before flooding was between Oregon and southeast Benton County, for a distance of 1-1/2 to 3-1/2 miles east of Plymouth. In 1805, the Lewis & Clark Expedition named these rapids *Musselshell Rapids,* a name intended to describe the numerous mussels at this point in the river. (*see* Umatilla National Forest)

Umatilla Reef *(T.34N;R.16W.uns)*

Very dangerous navigational hazard at the mouth of the Strait of Juan de Fuca, about 1 mile northwest of Duncan Rock. It was named for *S.S. Umatilla* which ran aground on the reef on February 9, 1884.

Umptanum *(S.20;T.16N;R.19E)*

Railway siding on west bank of Yakima River, 17 miles north of Yakima, south central Kittitas County. The original name of this place was used by Northern Pacific Railway when a station was established in 1885. The variation in spelling between the name of this town and of Umtanum Creek, indicates the difficulty of translating Indian language into English words. Each of these has the same meaning of *contentment.* It refers to the fact that because snow melted quite early in the year, deer came down to Umtanum Creek in plentiful numbers. There was plenty of food for the tribesmen.

Umtanum (Kittitas County) *see* Umptanum

Umtanum Creek *(T.16N;Rs.17-19E)*

The stream of the creek rises in Manashtash mountain, south central Kittitas County; flows 20 miles southeast to Yakima River, 17 miles north of Yakima. (*see* Umptanum)

Uncas *(S.25;T.25N;R.2W)*

Community 1/2 mile south of the south end of Port Discovery Bay, northeast Jefferson County. The original name of the place was *Junction.* When the Port Angeles & Western Railway objected to this name, it was changed to the name of a friendly Indian Chief. (USBGN)

Underwood *(S.23;T.3N;R.10E)*

Townsite on west bank of White Salmon River at its confluence with Columbia River, extreme southeast Skamania County. It is named for Andoniram Judson Underwood, a veteran of the Yakima Indian wars, who settled here in 1875 and who platted the townsite in the fall of 1881.

Unfried *(S.25;T.11N;R.43E)*

Hamlet on Alpowa Creek, 3 miles southwest of Alpowa, east central Garfield County. In 1911, the town had a post office, but the place is not shown on most current maps. It was named for the first postmaster, Fred W. Unfried.

Unfried Ridge
(Ss.22,23,27;T.9N;R.42E)

An Umatilla National Forest ridge, in Blue Mountains, 4 miles north of Tucannon River, south central Garfield County (USBGN) (*see* Unfried)

Unicorn Peak *(Mt. Rainier National Park)*

A 6,939-ft. mountain in Tatoosh Range, 1 mile north of the park's south boundary, south central area of the park. This massive peak, with a rock chimney, is the tallest in the Tatoosh Range. It was named by park officials for a *horn* of rock at the summit. (USBGN)

Union Flat *(Ts.15,16N;Rs.38-43E)*

A 70-mile-long flat, from the southeast extremity of Whitman County, northwest and west through the county to Palouse River, 5-1/2 miles west of Lacrosse, following the course of Union Flat Creek. This area was settled soon after the termination of the Civil War and this name echoes the influence of northern sympathizers. Rebel Flat, and Rebel Flat Creek, a few miles to the north, were named in the same period by adherents of *The Lost Cause.*

Union Flat Creek
(Ts.15,16N;Rs.38-43E)

The stream of the creek heads in the extreme southeast corner of Whitman County; flows northwest and west 72 miles to Palouse River, 12 miles northeast of Palouse Falls. the stream completely bisects the county through its central area. (*see* Union Flat)

Union Gap *(Ss.5,8;T.12N;R.19E)*

Town 4 miles south of Yakima, directly north of Union Gap (gap), in Ahtanum Ridge, central Yakima County. The town extends along a highway south of Yakima and is on the site of old Yakima City. When that town refused concessions demanded by the Northern Pacific Railway in 1884, the railroad established a station 4 miles to the north and started a new town, North Yakima. Most of Yakima City eventually moved to North Yakima. That name was later changed to *Yakima.*

Union Gap *(S.5;T.12N;R.19E)*

Prehistoric water gap, through which the Yakima River flows, 3 miles south of Yakima, through the east end of Ahtanum Ridge, central Yakima County. This is the route of a state highway and is a spectacular scenic feature from a distance. The Indian name was *Pah-h-ta-cute.* Settlement started here in the 1860s, and mostly after the termination of the Civil War. (*see* Union Gap)

Union Mills *(S.22;T.18N;R.1W)*

Once a sawmill town, now a scattered settlement at the north end of Long Lake, 4 miles east of Olympia, northeast Thurston County. In 1910, it was named by F. J. Shields and F. A. Leach for Union Lumber Company and the sawmill which they operated here.

Union Peak *(S.25;T.27N;R.13E)*

A Cascade Mountain summit peak, between the heads of Rainy Creek and Rapid River, on the Chelan-Snohomish county boundary. It was named by Forest Supervisor A. H. Sylvester, who did not record the reason for his choice.

Union Ridge (Clark County) *see* Ridgefield

Unity (Pacific County) *see* Ilwaco

Upper Baker River Reservoir (Whatcom County) see Baker Reservoir (Upper)

Upper Burnt Boot Lake (King County) *see* Iceberg Lake

Upper Crystal Lake (Mt. Rainier National Park) *see* Crystal Lake

Upper Curtis Glacier
(T.39N;R.9E.uns)

Northwest slope glacier of Mt. Shuksan, north of Sapphire Glacier, central Whatcom County. The glacier was named by the Mountaineers for Asahel Curtis, mountaineer and photographer. Lower Curtis Glacier was named by the same group and for the same person.

Upper Granite Lake (Skagit County) *see* Granite Lake No. 4

Upper Lake Creek
(Ts.12,13N;Rs.10,11E)

The stream of the creek rises on the northwest slope of Old Snowy Mountain at the Cascade summit, extreme east central Lewis County; flows 7 miles northwest into Packwood Lake, in the Goat Rocks Primitive Area. It was named locally because it flows into the upper, or south end of the lake.

Upper O'Neil Creek *(T.25N;R.6W)*

The stream of the creek heads in O'Neil Pass, 2 miles north of Mason County boundary, southeast Jefferson County; flows 2 miles northwest to Quinault River. (*see* O'Neil Creek)

Upper River *(T.23N;R.9E)*

Settlement on South Fork, Snoqualmie River, 11 miles southeast of Snoqualmie, central King County. This place was named for Herbert S. Upper who owned timberland here, by Philo Rutherford, who cruised Upper's timber.

Upper Scenic Lake
(Ss.16,21;T.25N;R.13E)

High mountain lake 1 mile west of Thunder Mountain, on Cascade Mountain summit, northeast King County. This lake drains into Lower Scenic Lake to the north. It was named for the town of Scenic, 3-1/2 miles north of the lake. (USBGN)

Upper Scenic Lake (King County) *see* Glacier Lake

Upper Surprise Lake (King County) *see* Glacier Lake

Upright Channel *(Ts.35,36N;R.2W)*

Passage between the north end of Lopez Island and the southeast shore of Shaw Island, central San Juan County. Canoe Island, mid-channel, reduces this passage almost to river width. In 1841, the passage was named *Frolic Strait* by Cmdr. Wilkes for the British brig *Frolic* which was captured on October 18, 1812, by the U.S. Sloop-of-war *Wasp.* Wilkes's name was replaced by the present name which was first placed on a chart by Capt. Richards, RN, in 1858.

Upright Head *(S.36;T.36N;R.2W)*

North end head of Lopez Island, in Upright Channel, central San Juan County. In 1841, Cmdr. Wilkes named this feature *Point Lloyd* for Wiliam Lloyd, captain-of-the-top in one of the expedition's ships. It was changed to the present name by U.S. Coast Survey, for the channel in which it is located.

Upthascap River (Mt. Rainier National Park) *see* Carbon River

Urban *(S.10;T.36N;R.1E)*

Cluster of houses on the east shore of Sinclair Island, extreme northwest Skagit County. It was named by a settler, L. U. Stenger, for his son, Urban.

Urban Island (Skagit County) *see* Sinclair Island

Ure's Island (Island County) see Ben Ure Island

Useless Bay *(Ts.28,29N;Rs.2,3E)*

Southwest shore bay of Whidbey Island, southwest Island County. In 1841, the name was applied by the Wilkes Expedition. It is quite appropriate, as the bay is so shallow that it is almost dry at low tide, and offers no protection from prevailing winds.

Usk *(S.32;T.33N;R.44E)*

Crossroads community on the Pend Oreille River's west bank, 14 miles northwest of Newport, south central Pend Oreille County. On June 9, 1903, it was platted as a townsite by George H. Jones. In 1890, Usk was a lively logging center when the post office was established. Destructive logging methods have almost destroyed the forest economy of the area. One of the assets here is a bridge across the river. In 1890, the place was named by George H. Jon, first postmaster, for the Usk River in Wales.

Utah Rock *(T.35N;R.3W)*

Southwest shore rock of San Juan Island, near False Bay, southwest San Juan County. This name was given many years ago by personnel of Puget Sound Marine Station at Friday Harbor, honoring the state of Utah. This name and many from the same source must be considered unofficials, as marine station names did nothing to have their designations recognized by any official agency.

Utsalady *(T.32N;R.2E)*

Scattered settlement on Utsalady Bay, at the north end of Camano Island, 6 miles west of Stanwood, northeast Island County. In the 1850s and 1860s, this was a very important sawmill town. The name is a distortion of the original Indian term, which means *place of the berries*. The Chinook jargon word *Ollalie* first referred to salmon berries only, but later was applied to all species of edible berries. The dialect word *Uts* means *place*. A typical pioneer legend regarding this name refers to a Scotsman who expected a *blessed event* in his family, and who ardently hoped for a son. When the child was born, the father shouted from the bedroom window. *It's a laddy!* This myth is still regarded as truth by a few local oldtimers.

V

Vader *(S.9;T.10N;R.2W)*

Town on Olequa Creek, 20 miles south of Chehalis, southwest Lewis County. The original name, *Little Falls* , was changed to *Sopenah* by Northern Pacific Railway officials, as they had a town by the same name on their line. Citizens who disliked the name, petitioned the legislature to change the name to Toronto. A dispute resulted, with a compromise agreement to name the town for a German resident named Vader. When that name was adopted, Herr Vader was insulted and moved to Florida.

Vail *(S.26;T.16N;R.1E)*

Community 16 miles southeast of Olympia, southeast Thurston County. There is a tree farm and the logging headquarters of Weyerhaeuser Company here. It was named for William Vail who owned farmland and timber holdings in the vicinity, by an early logger named Cosby.

Valentine *(S.25;T.12N;R.43E)*

Settlement 4 miles northwest of Alpowa, 5 miles west of Snake River, east central Garfield County. It was named for Alphonso S. Vallen, who was the first postmaster here.

Valley *(S.23;T.31N;R.40E)*

Community on the Colville River, 8 miles north of Springdale, central Stevens County. On July 29, 1891, it was platted by Daniel C. Corbin, railroad builder, when the Spokane Falls & Northern Railway was built through here. The town was named by Corbin because it is in the Colville Valley at the entrance of the main valley to the north.

Valley City (King County) *see* Algona

Valley Creek *(T.30N;R.6W)*

The stream of the creek rises in ''The Foot Hills,'' 5 miles south of Port Angeles Harbor; flows north through a mountain valley to the harbor. It was named for its course through the valley back of Port Angeles. An older name is *Warriner's Creek*, for Warriner Smith of a noted pioneer family.

Valley Grove *(S.19;T.8N;R.36E)*

Hamlet on Dry Creek, 6 miles north of Walla Walla, south central Walla Walla County. In 1879, the settlement was established by Mr. and Mrs. Charles McInroe who chose this pleasant name when a railroad station was built through here in 1881.

Van Asselt *(S.28;T.24N;R.4E)*

Community in the Duwamish River Valley, south of Seattle, on the east bank of Duwamish River, west central King County. The community centered around a large brick and sewer-pipe plant at the turn of the century. It was for Henry Van Asselt, a pioneer of 1851, on whose Donation Land Claim the place was located. It is not shown on recent maps.

Van Buren *(S.17;T.40N;R.4E)*

Township 2-1/2 miles south of the Canadian boundary, 3 miles southwest of Sumas, northwest Whatcom County. It was named for the first settler, who became a postmaster when a post office was established in 1900.

Van Horn *(S.13;T.35N;R.8E)*

Settlement 1-1/2 miles southeast of Concrete on the Skagit River, at the mouth of Jackman Creek, north central Skagit County. It was locally named for James V. Van Horn, who operated a shingle mill on Jackman Creek. He also owned a hotel and a store in Van Horn.

Van Horn Creek *(Mt. Rainier National Park)*

The stream of this short creek rises in the north central zone of the park; flows northeast into West Fork, White River, near the park's north boundary. The name was chosen by Park Ranger Thomas E. O'Farrell for Rev. F. J. Van Horn, a member of The Mountaineers who was on a Mountaineer's expedition in this area during the summer of 1909. (USBGN)

Van Trump Canyon *(Mt. Rainier National Park)*

Canyon on the south slope of Mt. Rainier, which carries the waters of Van Trump Creek; the canyon heads at the terminus of Van Trump Glacier, extends 5 miles southwest to Longmire, south central zone of the park. It was named for P. B. Van Trump, who accompanied Gen. Hazard Stevens in the first record- ed ascent of Mt. Rainier, on August 17, 1870. (USBGN)

Van Trump Creek *(Mt. Rainier National Park)*

The stream of the creek heads at the terminus of Van Trump Glacier, south slope of Mt. Rainier, south central zone of the park; flows about 5 miles southwest to Nisqually River, north of Ricksecker Point. (*see* Van Trump Canyon)

Van Trump Glacier *(Mt. Rainier National Park)*

Relatively short glacier on the south slope of Mt. Rainier, between Kautz and Wilson Glaciers at the head of Van Trump Creek; it constitutes the source of that stream. (*see* Van Trump Canyon)

Van Trump Park *(Mt.Rainier National Park)*

Natural mountain park, elevation 5,500 ft., at the foot of Van Trump Glacier, between Van Trump Creek and Kautz Glacier and Creek, southwest quarter of the park. (*see* Van Trump Canyon)

Van Wyck *(S.10;T.38N;R.3E)*

Railroad point 3 miles northeast of Bellingham, on Squalicum Creek, southwest Whatcom County. In 1891, when a post office was established here, the name was chosen by Postmaster Felmeley. It was to honor Alexander VanWyck, one of the oldest settlers.

Van Zandt *(S.8;T.38N;R.5E)*

Former lumber camp on South Fork, Nooksack River, 5 miles south of Deming, west central Whatcom County. In 1892, the place was named when a post office was established. It was for J. M. Van Zandt, the first postmaster, who homesteaded here in 1883.

Vance *(S.22;T.12N;R.7E)*

Community 20 miles southeast of Morton, on Siler Creek in the ''Big Bottom'' country, east central Lewis County. It was named for U.S. Senator Zebulon Baird Vance by J. S. Siler, when he applied for the post office and suggested its name. In the same year, 1885, Sen. Vance secured a 30-mile extension of the mail route, from Mossyrock into the ''Big Bottom'' Country.

Vancouver *(T.2N;R.1E)*

City on north bank of Columbia River, southwest Clark County. It is on a site occupied by Hudson's Bay Company's Fort Vancouver from 1824 until 1849. On March 15, 1854, a Territorial Legislature act passed, naming this place *Columbia City* and made it the county seat of Clark County. In 1855, the second session of the legislature changed the name back to the present designation. It is to honor Capt. George Vancouver who explored the Columbia River in 1792. The town inherited the name from Fort Vancouver, which had been named by Sir George Simpson on March 19, 1825. Serious suggestions have recently been made that the name be changed to *Fort Vancouver*, in order to avoid confusion with the name of Vancouver, B.C. Opponents of this idea declare that the Canadian city should change its name, as it was founded more recently than the American city.

Vancouver Lake *(Ts.2,3N;R.1E)*

Triangular lake, 3 miles long, 2 miles average width, elevation 2,580 ft., 3 miles northwest of Vancouver, Washington, on the flood plain of Columbia River, southwest Clark County. It was named for Capt. George Vancouver when mapped in 1856 by William Preston and other government surveyors.

Vancouver Point (Jefferson County) *see* Carr Point

Vancouver Trout Hatchery Pond *(S.3;T.1N;R.2E)*

One-acre, spring-fed pond 6-1/2 miles east of Vancouver, south central Clark County. This small pond adjoins Biddle Lake and drains into it. Washington State Game Department uses the pond for rearing trout. It was named for the city of Vancouver, Washington. (*see* Vancouver)

Vancouver's Straits (Wash. state reference/Northwest Washington) *see* Rosario Strait

Vanderfords Harbor (Pierce County) *see* Wollochet Bay

Vanson Lake *(S.27;T.11N;R.5E)*

A 10-acre lake, maximum depth 40 ft., elevation 4,150 ft., 1/2 mile southwest of Vanson Peak, south central Lewis County. The lake was named for Vanson Peak. Alternate names are *Star Lake* and *Hanson Lake*.

Vantage *(S.20;T.17N;R.23E)*

Community on west bank of Columbia River, 25 miles east of Ellensburg, southeast Kittitas County. A ferry across the Columbia River was established here by W. D. Van Slyke in pioneer days. A bridge replaced the ferry. Flooding by the Wanapum Dam at Priest Rapids caused a change in the location of this town. The name given to this point is presumed to be in recognition of the fact that this has always been a vantage point for crossing the river.

Vashon *(S.30;T.23N;R.3E)*

Community on north central Vashon Island, southwest King County. This is the island's main trading center. It was named for Capt. James Vashon, RN, who later became an admiral in the British Navy. Vancouver had served under Vashon in the West Indies.

Vashon Island *(Ts.21-23N;Rs.2,3W)*

Well-populated island, 14 miles long, in southern Puget Sound, between West Passage and East Passage, southwest King County. On May 29, this island was named by Capt. George Vancouver. (*see* Vashon)

Vashon Point *(S.6;T.23N;Rs.2,3E)*

North end point of Vashon Island on West Passage, southwest King County. In 1841, the point was named *Vashon's Point* for Vashon Island. The possessive form was dropped on latter mapping. On some older maps it appears as *Point Vashon*

Vassar *(S.15;T.17N;R.34E)*

Wheat elevator 4 miles east of Lind, central Adams County. It was named for Vassar College at Poughkeepsie, New York, by H. R. Williams, vice-president of Chicago, Milwaukee & St. Paul Railway Company.

Vaughn *(S.34;T.21N;R.1W)*

Scattered settlement of summer homes and farms on the north shore of Vaughn Bay, northwest Pierce County. It was named for William D. Vaughn, the first recorded settler, who settled and logged here in 1871.

Vaughn Bay *(T.21N;R.1W)*

East shore bay of Case Inlet, 1-1/2 miles east of Grapeview, northwest Pierce County. This tidal bay is bordered by summer homes and small farms. (*see* Vaughn)

Veazey (King County) *see* Veazie

Veazey Station (King County) *see* Veazie

Veazie *(S.8;T.20N;R.7E)*

Railroad point 3 miles northeast of Enumclaw, south central King County. In 1890, it was named by Northern Pacific officials for Thomas Veazie of Veazie & Russell Logging Company, who had a log-loading spur here at the time. The place appears on some maps as *Veazie Station* or *Veazey*.

Vega. *(S.17;T.19N;R.1E)*

Hamlet on Oro Bay, at southeast point of Anderson Island, west central Pierce County. It was named for Vegatorp, Sweden, by Bengt Johnson, the first postmaster, to honor his birthplace.

Velox *(S.6;T.25N;R.45E)*

Rail point 8 miles east of Spokane and 6 miles west of the Idaho boundary, east central Spokane County. It was named by a Northern Pacific Railway employee, Arthur S. Glendinning, for Harry Velox, a race horse which was owned by his father on western circuits in the 1890s.

Velvet (Station) (Stevens County) *see* Frontier

Venatchee Creek (Asotin County) *see* Menatchee Creek

Vendovi Island *(S.18;T.36N;R.2E)*

Small, rounded island, 220 acres, 2 miles south of Lummi Island, at the west limit of Samish Bay, northwest corner of Skagit County. In 1790, this island, with Sinclair Island directly to the west, received the name of *Islas de Aguayo* from Dionisio Galiano. In 1841, the present name was given by Cmdr. Charles Wilkes for a Fiji Islander who was a prisoner on one of his ships, having been arrested for the murder of an American seaman in the Fiji Islands. The name of this Fiji chief was Vendovi. A local name, used in the past, was *Hog Island*.

Venersborg *(S.34;T.4N;R.3E)*

Settlement 15 miles northeast of Vancouver, 1-1/2 miles southwest of Bells Mountain, central Clark County. In 1910, this name was chosen by members of Swedish Land & Colonization Company when that organization purchased 1-1/4 acres of land from Weyerhaeuser Timber Company for development. A local name for this settlement in 1910 was *The Colony*. Names that were in use before the colony was established were *Alpine* and *Bells Mountain*.

Venice *(S.8;T.25N;R.2E)*

Community on east shore of Port Orchard Bay, west central Bainbridge Island, north central Kitsap County. In 1908, it was named by local residents, for Venice, California. At that time, Venice boasted a 780-ft. dock, longest in Puget Sound.

Venice *(T.14N;R.10W)*

Settlement on Toke Point, at the southeast extremity of a 3-mile sand spit near the north entrance to Willapa Harbor, northwest Pacific County. The name was given by early residents because of the normally quiet and rather shallow water offshore.

Ventura *(S.5;T.36N;R.19E.uns)*

Mining camp on Okanogan National Forest, 2 miles south of Robinson, on the Methow River at the mouth of Lost Creek, west central Okanogan County. During the mining boom of 1895, the place was named by miners. Many, including some Mexicans, were from California. It seems probable that the Spanish name for *fortune* or *venture* may have been applied by them.

Vera *(S.25;T.25N;R.44E)*

Small trade center and gardening area, 1 mile northwest of Sprague, east central Spokane County. The place was named for Vera McDonald, by her father who assisted in platting the townsite. On April 10, 1911, this name was used for the first post office when it was established. On July 31, 1912, the post office was discontinued. On June 1, 1923, when reestablished, the post office was named *Veradale*. This town appears on recent maps, including those published by the State Highway Department as *Vera*.

Veradale (Spokane County) *see* Vera

Verlot *(S.15;T.30N;R.8E)*

Small settlement in the Gold Basin area, on South Fork, Stillaguamish River, Mt. Baker National Forest, central Snohomish County. It was named for the man who built the first mill here, and who founded the settlement.

Vermontville *(S.20N;T.23N;R.3E)*

Vanished settlement on the present site of Clan Acres, northeast end of Vashon Island, southwest King County. It is reported to have been named by settlers from Vermont, who established residence here in pioneer days.

Vern (Lewis County) *see* Glenoma

Verndale (Lewis County) *See* Glenoma

Vernon (Garfield County) *see* Columbia Center

Vesper Peak *(Ss.9,10;T.29N;R.10E)*

A Snoqualmie National Forest peak, 6 miles northwest of Monte Cristo, at the head of Vesper Creek, east central Snohomish County. The record shows that this mountain was named by early prospectors, although these hardy explorers usually gave less gentle and poetic names to landscape features.

Vesta *(S.32;T.16N;R.7W)*

Scattered, small settlement on North River, 9 miles south of Montesano, south central Grays Harbor County. In 1882, this place was named when a post office was established. It was named by pioneer Milton Dwinelle for his wife, Vesta.

Vesta Creek *(T.16N;Rs.6,7W)*

The stream of the creek rises 5 miles north of Blue Mountain, southeast Grays Harbor County; flows southwest to North River near Vesta. *(see* Vesta)

Victim Island *(S.17;T.36N;R.2W)*

Island 1 mile southeast of Deer Harbor in West Sound, near the west shore, north central San Juan County. In 1858, it was charted under this name by Capt. Richards, RN, because it showed evidence of massacre of local Indians by invading Haidahs.

View *(S.28;T.5N;R.2E)*

Settlement 9 miles east of Woodland, north central Clark County. In the early 1890s, the settlement was established and called *Mountain View*. The name was shortened to the present form when a post office was installed in 1894.

Village Creek *(T.33N;R.15W)*

The stream of the creek rises in high country 3 miles west of Neah Bay, on Makah Indian Reservation, extreme northwest Clallam County; flows east to Neah Bay at Neah Bay village. In 1792, first building erected in Washington State by white men. It was named by early Indian traders because of its mouth on the shore of Neah Bay at the site of a Makah village. An earlier name was *Neah Creek*.

Village Point (Kitsap County) *see* Restoration Point

Village Point (Pacific County) *see* Chinook Point

Village Point *(S.5;T.37N;R.1E)*

Northwest shore point of Lummi Island, southwest Whatcom County. Indians had extensive salmon fisheries here in early days and commercial fishing interests once operated a large number of destructive fish traps. In 1841, the point was named by Wilkes although it does not appear on his charts. He named it for the large Indian village of split-board huts here. In the 1890s, a post office was established and named *Carlisle*.

Villard *(S.13;T.8N;R.30E)*

Railroad point 5 miles southeast of Pasco, adjacent to Lake Wallula, southwest Walla Walla County. It was named for Henry Villard, outstanding railroad promoter of the 1890s.

Vimy Ridge
(Ss.31,32;T.29N;R.13E.uns)

A 6,352-ft. ridge directly southwest of Cascade Mountain summit, near Wards Pass, extreme east central Snohomish County. The ridge was named for famous battle site in WWI.

Vineland (Asotin County) *see* Clarkston

Vine Maple Valley (King County) *see* Maple Valley

Vineland *(T.11N;R.46E)*

Platted tract of land directly south of Clarkston, Asotin County. It was promoted as farmland by Lewiston Water & Power Company. The name chosen by the company suggests a fertile and prosperous agricultural area.

Viola Creek *(T.18N;Rs.8,9E)*

The stream of the creek heads on Independence Ridge, directly north of Mt. Rainier National Park's north boundary; flows 4-1/2 miles northeast of West Fork White River, northeast Pierce County. The name is for Viola Belyea, a popular early resident.

Violet Point *(S.3;T.30N;R.2W)*

East point of Protection Island, in the Strait of Juan de Fuca, extreme northeast Jefferson County. In 1841, the point was named by Wilkes. It is probable that it was named for the presence of violets, as Wilkes named a bluff on the same island *Daisy Bluff*. His exploration of this island would have been at a time when native flowers were in bloom.

Virden *(S.27;T.20N;R.17E)*

Hamlet on Swauk Creek, 10 miles east of Cle Elum, north central Kittitas County. It was named for a pioneer resident, G. D. Virden.

Virginia City (Okanogan County) *See* Brewster

Virginia City *(S.23;T.30N;R.24E)*

This almost forgotten town was on the Columbia River, 1/2 mile south of the present town of Brewster, south central Okanogan County. On July 10, 1893, it was platted by Francis Green and *Virginia Bill* Covington, and served as a river port until Brewster (Bruster) eclipsed it. It was named by Covington for his native state.

Vista (Lincoln County) *see* Fishtrap

Vista *(S.5;T.8N;R.29E)*

Railroad station 5 miles west of Kennewick, east central Benton County. In 1889, this station was named *Relief* by Northern Pacific Railway because *helper* or relief engines were added to heavy trains here. In 1908, after more powerful locomotives eliminated the need for 2 engines, the Northern Pacific changed the name to the present form. This name is presumed to describe the view of the surrounding landscape.

Vista Creek *(T.31N;Rs.13,14E.uns)*

The stream of the creek rises on the glaciated northeast slope of Glacier Peak, Mt. Baker National Forest, northeast Snohomish County; flows 4-1/2 miles northeast to Suiattle Creek. The stream was named by Forest Ranger Stoner, because of a natural straight opening in the trees along the creek, giving an unobstructed view of Glacier Peak from points along the Suiattle trail.

Viti Rocks *(T.36N;R.1E)*

Rocks between Vendovi Island and the south end of Lummi Island, in Georgia Strait, southwest Whatcom County. In 1841, these rocks were named by Cmdr. Charles Wilkes for the Viti Islands, now called the Fiji Islands. Aboard his ship he had a prisoner from those islands, a native chief who had killed an American seaman. The prisoner's name -- Vendovi -- was applied to nearby Vendovi Island. This appears to be a case where crime paid.

Volcano Point *(Island County) see* Double Bluff

Von Geldern Cove *(Ss.25,36;T.21N;R.1W)*

Small bay on the west shore of Carr Inlet, northwest Pierce County. The community of Home adjoined the cove to the west. On some recent maps the cove is called *Joe's Bay*, a local name for a resident who drowned here. On other maps the spelling is *Von Geldren* or *Von Gelden*, in error. Von Geldern was a pioneer land claimant on the cove.

Vulcan *(S.4;T.11N;R.22E)*

Settlement on the east bank of Columbia River, directly below Cabinet Rapids, extreme southwest corner of Douglas County. The place is in a very hot, sandy area. It was named for the Roman god of fire because of intense heat in summer months.

Vulcan *(S.4;T.40N;R.33E)*

A 5,300-ft. peak, 1 mile south of the Canadian boundary, 8 miles north of Curlew, northwest Ferry County. The name derives from indications of iron ore discovered on the mountain by early prospectors.

W

Waada Island *(Ss.1,2;T.33N;R.15W)*

Island on the east side of Neah Bay, Makah Indian Reservation, extreme northwest Clallam County. It is connected with the west shore of the bay by an artificial breakwater. In 1841, it was named *Neah Island* by Cmdr. Charles Wilkes of the Wilkes Expedition, using the name of the bay in which it is located. In 1846, Capt. Henry Kellett placed it on British Admiralty charts as *Wyadda Island*, using the Makah Indian name. Other spellings of the name, found on various maps and records, include *Waadah*, *Waaddah*, *Wa-dah*, and *Wa-a-dah*. The present name received U.S. Coast Survey approval in past years, and is now approved by USBGN.

Waadah Island (Clallam County) *see* Waada Island

Waatch *(S.12;T.33N;R.15W)*

Formerly an active Makah village, now in disuse, at Waatch River mouth, Makah Indian Reservation, extreme northwest Clallam County. The name is that of a tribal branch of the Makah nation, and is properly pronounced "Wa-a-tch." The name was used by Gov. Stevens in a treaty concluded on January 31, 1855.

Waatch Point *(S.19;T.33N;R.15W)*

Point on Pacific Ocean, 3-1/2 miles southeast of Cape Flattery at Waatch River mouth, Makah Indian Reservation, extreme northwest Clallam County. A very old Indian name for the place was *Ar-kut-tle-kower*. (*see* Waatch)

Waatch River *(T.33N;R.15W)*

More a tidal slough than river, this low, swampy, winding stream rises north of Makah Peaks, Makah Indian Reservation, extreme northwest Clallam County; flows westerly to the north end of Mukkaw Bay on Pacific Ocean. On some maps it is marked as *Waach River* or *Waatch Slough* (*see* Waatch)

Wabash *(S.33;T.15N;R.2W)*

Area 1 mile north of Centralia, northwest Lewis County. In 1908, the place was named by Northern Pacific Railway officials for the Wabash River.

Wagnersburg *(S.6;T.24N;R.21E)*

Railroad station on Columbia River, 14 miles north of Wenatchee, southeast Chelan County. The place was named for E. Wagner, a pioneer orchardist, who developed a remarkable irrigation system on his holdings here.

Wahatis Peak *(S.10;T.15N;R.26E)*

Highest point in Saddle Mountains, elevation 2,696 ft., 6 miles north of Wahluke, southeast Grant County. The name, spelled *Wahattus* on some maps, is the Indian word for the peak, meaning "lookout place."

Wahkiakum County

This very small county on Columbia River near its mouth, in extreme southwest Washington, is bounded on the north by Lewis and Pacific counties; on the east by Cowlitz County; on the west by Pacific County; and, on the south by Columbia River. Most of its area is in second-growth forest. On April 25, 1854, it was founded by Washington Territorial Legislature as *Wakiacum* County, taken from part of Lewis County. The name was that of both an Indian tribe and their chief, of Chinookian blood; it means "tall timber" or "big trees." Although unexplained, the spelling alteration evidently was made to more closely reproduce the Indian pronunciation.

Wahkiakus *(S.19;T.4N;R.14E)*

Settlement on Klickitat River, 2-1/2 miles east of Klickitat, west central Klickitat County. It was named for Sally Wahkiakus, a local Indian woman, who was considered "quite a character."

Wahl *(S.36;T.39N;R.3E)*

Very small settlement 7 miles northeast of Bellingham, west central Whatcom County. It was named for John Wahl, an 1882 pioneer.

Wahluke *(S.10;T.14N;R.26E)*

Settlement on Columbia River's north bank, at the upstream end of White Bluffs area, southwest Grant County. It is within the U.S. Atomic Energy Commission Reservation. The original Indian name means "watering hole" or "watering place."

Waiilatpu *(S.31;T.7N;R.35E)*

National historical monument on Walla Walla River, near the mouth of Mill Creek, 4 miles west of Walla Walla, Walla Walla County. In 1836, Dr. Marcus Whitman and his party built mission structures here; in 1847, they were partially destroyed and abandoned as a mission site, when Cayuse Indians killed Whitman and others. It is now administered by National Park Service. Translation of the Indian name is "place of the rye grass." An alternate name is *Whitman Mission*.

Waits Lake *(Ss.17-20;T.31N;R.40E)*

Lake with an area of about 1 mile, elevation 1,959 ft., 6-1/2 miles southwest of Chewelah and 2-1/2 miles west of Valley, south central Stevens County. It was named for George *Waitt*, who, in 1873, claimed land on the lake's east shore where the small settlement of Waits is located.

Wait's Mill (Walla Walla County) *see* Waitsburg

Waitsburg *(T.9N;R.37E)*

Town on delta of Touchet River and Coppei Creek, 16 miles northeast of Walla Walla, extreme east central Walla Walla County. In 1859, Robert Kennedy became the first settler. In 1869, the town was platted, and, in 1881, municipal government was organized. It was named for Sylvester M. Wait, who built the first flour mill here in 1865. Prior to that time, the place had been called *Delta*, *Wait's Mill*, and *Wait's Crossing*.

Waketickeh Creek *(T.24N;R.3W)*

The stream of the creek rises 2-1/2 miles west of Hood Canal, near the south boundary of Jefferson County; flows south and east to Hood Canal, 1 mile north of Hama Hama River mouth, through northeast Mason County. The Indian name means "we don't like it," and relates to the drowning of several Indians in a freshet at the creek's mouth. (USBGN)

Wakiacum County (Wahkiakum County) *see* Wahkiakum County

Walan Point *(S.24;T.30N;R.1W)*

Northwestern extremity of Indian Island in Port Townsend Bay, northeast Jefferson County. In 1841, Cmdr. Charles Wilkes named the feature *Flag Point*. At the same time, Wilkes named the entrance to Kilisut Harbor *Walan Passage*. The name Walan was transferred to this point at a later time.

Waldron *(T.37N;Rs.2,3W)*

Irregularly-shaped island, covering about 5 square miles, 2 miles northwest of Orcas Island's northwest shore, across President Channel, north central San Juan County. In 1841, it was named by Lieut. Cmdr. Ringgold of the Wilkes Expedition, for Thomas W. Waldron, captain's clerk on *U.S.S. Porpoise*, one of the expedition's ships. Previous names were *Shi-ish-uney*, used by Lummi Indians, and *Isla Lemos*, charted by Spanish explorers.

Wales (Snohomish County) *see* Monroe

Walker *(S.13;T.11N;R.33E)*

Railway station on the east bank of Snake River, at the mouth of Walker Canyon, 25 miles northeast of Pasco, extreme northwest Walla Walla County. When Northern Pacific Railway Company installed a station here in 1908, they named it for William H. Walker, from whom they acquired a right-of-way.

Walker Lake *(S.34;T.21N;R.7E)*

A very small body of water, covering 11.6 acres, 1-1/2 miles southeast of Cumberland, south central King County. It was locally named for Davis Walker, who settled on the lake in 1890. An alternate name, carried on county maps, is *Crow Lake*.

Walkers *(T.28N;R.40E)*

Stretch of prairie without definite boundaries, extending along Chamokane Creek and adjoining the east boundary of Spokane Indian Reservation, south central Stevens County. It is south of Springdale and includes the town of Ford. The name is for Elkanah Walker, who, with Cushing Eells, established an Indian mission on the prairie in 1838.

Walla Walla *(T.7N;Rs.35,36E)*

City in the center of Walla Walla Valley, on Mill Creek, southeast Walla Walla County. In 1856, a fort for protection against Indian attacks was built on the creek; during the following year, a village built up around the fort. On January 11, 1859, an act of the Territorial Legislature approved the name *Walla Walla City* When it boomed in 1862 during the Idaho gold rush, the village was incorporated and platted from land in A. J. Cain's claim. The town is now the trade and banking center for a rich, agricultural area. The Indian name translates as "place of many waters," referring to the many tributaries of Walla Walla River, and the abundant small streams and springs in the vicinity. Previous names were *Steptoeville* and Steptoe City, for Lieut. Col. Edward J. Steptoe, who fought in the 1850s Indian wars. (USBGN)

Walla Walla County

This county in southeast Washington is bounded on the north by Franklin County; on the east by Columbia County; on the south by Oregon; and, on the west by Benton and Franklin counties. On April 25, 1854, it was created from a portion of Skamania County, by an act of the Territorial Legislature. The county covers 1,288 square miles, and produces fruit, grain, vegetables, and livestock, as well as production from a large paper mill. (*see* Walla Walla)

Walla Walla River
(T.6N;Rs.31-34E)

The stream of the river heads in Mill Creek and a multitude of other streams which converge near Walla Walla, southeast Walla Walla County; flows west through Touchet to Lake Wallula, near Wallula. Although only a little over 30 miles long, the river is important commercially and historically. (*see* Walla Walla)

Wallace (Snohomish County) *see* Startup

Wallace Island (Pierce County) *see* Anderson Island

Wallace Lake *(S.20;T.28N;R.9E)*

Lake 3 miles north of Gold Bar, on North Fork, Wallace River, south central Snohomish County. (*see* Wallace River)

Wallace River *(Ts.27,28N;Rs.9,10E)*

The stream of the river rises on the west side of Ragged Ridge, south central Snohomish County; flows 10 miles west to Skykomish River, near Gold Bar. It was locally named for Wallace Joe, an Indian who was the first permanent settler on the river.

Wallace's (Cowlitz County) *see* Kelso

Wallacut River *(T.10N;R.11W)*

The stream of this very short river heads 3 miles north of Baker Bay, southwest Pacific County; flows southwest to Columbia River at Ilwaco. The name is a distortion of the Indian designation *Walihut*, meaning "place of stones." The north side of the river, near its mouth, is heavily banked with small, smoothly-worn boulders. Hudson's Bay Company employees used the course of the stream as a portage route, and called it *Knights River*.

Wallula *(T.7N;R.31E)*

Pioneer town originally located north of the junction of Walla Walla and Columbia rivers, Walla Walla County. With the completion of McNary Dam in 1954, the area was flooded in Lake Wallula. From 1818 until 1857, the site was occupied by fur trading posts and forts owned successively by North West Company and Hudson's Bay Company. A river town called *Wallula Landing* was established in 1859; then in March 1862, the town of Wallula was named and platted by J.M. Vansycle and S. W. Tatem. When Northern Pacific Railway built through the area in 1882, a town called *Wallula Junction* was built one mile to the east. This Walla Walla Indian word has the same meaning as Walla Walla in Nez Perce language, namely "plenty of water" or "place of many waters," an appropriate description of the original location which was thoroughly supplied with water from many sources.

Wallula Junction (Landing) (Walla Walla County) *see* Wallula

Walmouth Head (Hill) (San Juan County) *see* Watmough Head

Walton Lake (Snohomish County) *see* Wallace Lake

Walupt Lake *(T.11N;R.11E)*

A one-square-mile lake, elevation 3,921 ft., at the head of Cispus River into which it drains, south end of Goat Rocks Primitive Area, extreme southeast Lewis County. The Yakima Indian name relates to a tradition among the Yakimas that wild dogs live on the lake bottom, and attack any person who turns his back to the lake. The older Indian generation say that they back away from the lake.

Walville *(S.6;T.12N;R.5W)*

Lumber "ghost" town 28 miles

southwest of Chehalis, southwest Lewis County. Timber in the area was depleted some years ago. In 1903, it was locally named for the lumber firm Walworth & Neville Company, taking the first syllable of Walworth and the last of Neville. An older name for the place is *Rock Creek*, taken from the creek on which it is located.

Wana (Snohomish County) *see* Cicero

Wanapum Dam (*Ts.13-15N;R.23E*)

A 7,800-foot-long hydroelectric and irrigation dam at Beverly Gap on Columbia River, extreme southwest Grant County and extreme northeast Yakima County. It is built by Grant County Public Utility District. In 1949, American soldiers, who were held prisoners of war by the Japanese in World War II, requested the dam be named for Gen. Jonathan M. Wainwright. Instead, it carries the name of an Indian tribe which lived along Columbia River at this point; the word means "the river people." The Wanapums once numbered over 3,000, but now are reduced to 8 full-blooded tribesmen. They have no reservation, as they never entered into a treaty with the United States. No war, no treaty; no treaty, no reservation.

Waneta (*S.17;T.9N;R.23E*)

Small settlement 3-1/2 miles north of Mabton, southeast Yakima County. In 1901, it was named for Waneta Harader, daughter of J. Ward Harader, a local settler. On some maps, it is spelled *Wanita*, *Wanetta*, or *Juanita*. An earlier name was *Sage Valley*.

Wanicut Lake (Okanogan County) *see* Wannacut Lake, Wehesville

Wanlich Creek (*T.37N;Rs.7,8E*)

The stream of the creek heads on the southwest slope of Mt. Baker, west of Sulphur Butte, south central Whatcom County; flows 4-1/2 miles southwest to South Fork, Nooksack River. It was named for Martin C. Wanlich, a pioneer prospector, who explored the creek from 1887 until 1890.

Wannacut Lake (*T.39N;R.26E*)

An irregular, 2-mile-long lake 6 miles southwest of Oroville, north central Okanogan County. A post office of the same name existed in early mining days near the south end of the lake. Both are said to have been named for Edward *Wanicutt*, a well-known prospector and mine owner in Okanogan County. It has

been called *Wanacott, Wanicot, Wannacott, Wannicut, Wennacutt, Wanicut* and *Wonacot*. (USBGN)

Wannacut Lake (*T.39N;R.26E*)

Post office for early-day miners once located at the south end of Wannacut Lake, north central Okanogan County. It later was supplanted by Wehesville. (*see* Wannacut Lake (lake))

Wapaloosie Mountain (*Ss.26,35;T.37N;R.34E*)

Colville National Forest peak, elevation 7,026 ft., 12 miles east of Republic, north central Ferry County. In 1907, the name for this towering mountain was given by Hayse Houghland, first ranger on the Republic District of Colville National Forest. Houghland used the term for any very extraordinary feature; in this case, the name became permanent.

Wapato (*S.10;T.11N;R.19E*)

Town on Yakima Indian Reservation, 10 miles southeast of Yakima, central Yakima County. When Northern Pacific Railway established a station in 1885, the town, which was an early trading center for Indians and white settlers, was called *Simcoe*. On October 24, 1902, a townsite was platted; the name used was that of the Indian potato, *wapato*, or arrowroot (*Sagittaria latifolia*). This native root was a very important food for local Indians, and is still harvested by some of the older natives in Yakima Valley.

Wapato Creek (*T.20N;Rs.3,4E*)

The stream of this small, winding creek heads at Sumner, central Pierce County; flows 10 miles northwest to Commencement Bay at Tacoma. (*see* Wapato)

Wapato Lake (*S.29;T.20N;R.3E*)

A small, narrow lake covering 28.2 acres, surrounded by Wapato Municipal Park in Tacoma, directly south of South Tacoma business district, Pierce County. (*see* Wapato)

Wapowety Cleaver (*Mt. Rainier National Park*)

Triangular, pointed rock island between Kautz and Wilson Glaciers, on Mt. Rainier's south slope, 1-1/2 miles below the summit, central zone of the park. It is a glacial divider, which borders the upper reach of Kautz Glacier on the east. Lieut. A. V. Kautz named the area for an Indian, who guided him in an

attempt to reach Mt. Rainier's summit between July 8 and 15, 1857. (USBGN)

Warbassport (*Ss.18,19;T.11N;R.1W*)

An early name for the settlement at the present site of Toledo on Cowlitz River, 15 miles south of Chehalis, southwest Lewis County. In the 1850s, it was an important landing on the river, and was used extensively by pioneers who traveled from here by trail to Puget Sound. The first name was *Plomondoe's Landing*, for a French-Canadian employee of Hudson's Bay Company. Somewhat later, the name was changed to *Cowlitz Landing*, a descriptive designation. When E. D. Warbass installed a trading post and started the nucleus of a town, the name was again changed in his honor. The present name is *Toledo*.

Ward (*S.21;T.36N;R.38E*)

Small settlement at the location of St. Francis Regis Mission, 2 miles east of the present town of Kettle Falls, northwest Stevens County. In 1903, the name was given when the second post office was established, and was named for Thomas Ward, an early settler here. The railroad station is called Goodwin.

Warden (*Ss.10,15,16;T.17N;R.30E*)

Town 14 miles southeast of Moses Lake (town), southeast Grant County. It has gained appreciably as a result of recent irrigation developments in the area. Chicago, Milwaukee & St. Paul Railway officials named the town for one of their important stockholders.

Warm Beach (*S.13;T.13N;R.3E*)

A resort and summer colony on Port Susan, 6 miles south of Stanwood, west central Snohomish County. A one-mile tidal runout creates warm water on incoming tides, which gives reason for the name. An alternate name is *Birmingham*.

Warm Beach Lake (Snohomish County) *see* Martha Lake

Warm Creek (*T.38N;Rs.6,7E*)

The stream of the creek rises in Thunder Glacier, on the west slope of Mt. Baker, central Whatcom County; flows 6 miles west to Middle Fork, Nooksack River. It was named by pioneer settlers, who certainly chose an inappropraite name for a glacial stream.

Warner (*S.16;T.19N;R.45E*)

Settlement on Willow Creek, 6 miles southwest of Tekoa, northeast Whitman

County. It was named for William Warner, who settled here in 1898, secured a railroad siding, and built a grain warehouse within a one-year period.

Warnick *(S.2;T.39N;R.6E)*

Small sawmill town on North Fork, Nooksack River, between Maple Falls and Glacier, north central Whatcom County. In 1903, it was named for an engineer, who surveyed the Sumas extension of Bellingham Bay, and British Columbia.

Warriner's Creek (Clallam County) *see* Valley Creek

Warrior Peak *(T.26N;R.4W)*

An Olympic National Park peak, elevation 7,300 ft., 1 mile north-northwest of Mt. Constance, east central Jefferson County. In 1890, it was named by Lieut. Joseph P. O'Neil, although the records do not give his name source. (USBGN)

Warwick *(S.25;T.3N;R.14E)*

Spokane, Portland, & Seattle Railway station on Swale Canyon, 11 miles southwest of Goldendale, southwest Klickitat County. It was named for W. S. Warwick, an early sheriff and landowner.

Washington (state)

On November 11, 1889, this state was admitted to statehood as the 42nd State of the Union by United States Congress, with much the same boundaries as at present. It extends from Pacific Ocean on the west, to Idaho on the east; and, from Oregon on the south, to the Province of British Columbia on the north. Prior to statehood, it had been a part of Oregon Territory, and later became Washington Territory, including Idaho and part of western Montana. In 1863 and 1864, Idaho and Montana were separated.

When admitted as a territory on March 2, 1853, the name *Columbia* was suggested in Congress. Rep. Richard H. Stanton of Kentucky amended the bill by striking out Columbia and inserting Washington, to honor the first President of the United States. In 1852, *Washingtonia* had been suggested by Sen. Stephen A. Douglas. In 1955, Dr. Bror L. Grondal of the University of Washington also suggested that name, in order to dispel the confusion of the state with the nation's capital, but received little support.

At one time, an unsuccessful attempt was made to combine eastern Washington and eastern Oregon under the name *Lincoln*. The confusion which exists under the present name may be minimized when citizens of eastern states become slightly familiar with the geography of the United States of America.

Washington Cascade *(Mt. Rainier National Park)*

Series of rapids in Paradise River, above Narada Falls, 15 miles east of Nisqually Entrance, south central zone of the park. On August 24, 1893, the rapids were named for the State of Washingon by Henry Schwargel of Tacoma. (USBGN)

Washington Channel (San Juan County) *see* San Juan Channel

Washington Colony
(S.30;T.38N;R.3E)

A short-lived colony at the mouth of Whatcom Creek in Bellingham, Whatcom County. Established in 1883, it took its name from Washington state. The word "colony" survived in the name of a wharf on the Bellingham waterfront.

Washington Harbor (Clallam County) *see* Sequim Bay

Washington River (Skamania County) *see* Lewis River

Washington Sound (San Juan County) *see* San Juan Archipelago

Washingtonia *see* Washington (state)

Washougal *(S.8;T.1N;R.4E)*

Town on Columbia River's north bank, on the lower stretch of Washougal River, 17 miles east of Vancouver, southeast Clark County. Early names were *Parker's Landing*, *Point Vancouver*, and *Washoughally Camp*. Attempts to combine this town with Camas as *Twin City* have met with little success. The Indian name was first placed on Washougal River, and means "rushing water," which is quite appropriate.

Washougal Lake *(S.17;T.2N;R.4E)*

A 1/2-acre lake 5 miles north of Washougal, draining into Little Washougal River, southeast Clark County. Named for the town of Washougal, the lake appears on few maps. (*see* Washougal)

Washougal Ponds *(S.15;T.2N;R.5E)*

Three numbered, artificial lakes in

Washougal River, 10-1/2 miles northeast of Washougal, Skamania County. Ranging from 1-1/2 acres to 4 acres, the lakes are used for salmon-rearing by State Department of Fisheries. (*see* Washougal)

Washougal River *(Ts.1,4N;Rs.4-6E)*

The stream of the river rises in high country south of Lookout Mountain, southwest Skamania County; flows southwest through Clark County to Columbia River at Camas. In 1805, Lewis and Clark called the stream *Seal River* when they saw a large number of seals at the river's mouth. (*see* Washougal)

Washtucna *(S.33;T.15N;R.36E)*

Town 5 miles west of Palouse Falls on Palouse River, southeast Adams County. In the early 1890s, it was founded by the L. L. Bassett family. The name is taken from an Indian word said to mean "many waters," and was applied by Palouse Indians to a large spring on the townsite. Local tradition states that the town and valley were named for "Chief Washtucna," who is not otherwise identified.

Washtucna Lake (Franklin County) *see* Lake Kahlotus

Wasp Island (San Juan County) *see* McConnell Island

Wasp Islands *(T.36N;R.3W)*

Group of islands in San Juan Channel between the western extremities of Orcas and Shaw islands, central San Juan County. They include McConnell, Reef, Cliff, Yellow, Coon, Low, Nob Islands and Cormorant Rock (Bird Rock). In 1841, the group was named by Cmdr. Charles Wilkes, for the U.S. Sloop-of-war *WASP*, in which Cmdr. Jacob Jones captured the British brig *Frolic* in the War of 1812. In 1859, Capt. Richards charted the islands, retaining the name Wasp for the largest of the group, and naming the others as listed above.

Wasp Passage *(S.19;T.36N;R.2W)*

A narrow pass between Crane Island and the northwest end of Shaw Island, central San Juan County. It is used by ferries and by other shipping. (*see* Wasp Islands)

Watch Mountain *(T.13N;R.7E)*

A 4,833-ft. mountain extending 2-1/2 miles from east to west, 2-1/2 miles north of Randle, east central Lewis

County. It was named by pioneer J. T. Chilcoat, for a large watch which he lost on the peak. It is reported to have been the only timepiece in Randle in early days.

Watering River (Pierce County) *see* Sequalitchew Creek

Waterloo *(S.11;T.33N;R.37E)*

Small settlement on McGees Creek, 2 miles east of Columbia River and 17 miles south by west of Kettle Falls, west central Stevens County. In 1894, it was founded as a farm community. The first postmistress was a well-beloved character called "Grandma" Tipton; she was known as the greatest talker in the region. The name was applied to the post office because any person who tried to talk her down met his Waterloo.

Waterman *(S.17;T.24N;R.2E)*

Town on the east shore of Port Orchard bay, directly across from East Bremerton, east central Kitsap County. It was named for Delos Waterman, who homesteaded land here in 1904.

Waterstown, Watertown (Garfield County) *see* Pataha

Waterville *(Ss.21,22;T.25N;R.22E)*

Town at the foot of Badger Mountain, 6 miles east of Columbia River, west central Douglas County. In 1883, the place was founded by A. T. Greene, who entered a land claim to acreage which later included the Waterville townsite. In 1886, the townsite was established on 40 acres donated by Greene for the purpose. An early name was *Jumper's Flat*. The present name was applied when the townsite was platted, because of the excellent water secured from a 30-foot well on Greene's ranch.

Watmough Head *(S.2;T.34N;R.1W)*

Hamlet on the southeast end of Lopez Island, directly south of Watmough Bay, southeast San Juan County. In 1841, it was named by Cmdr. Charles Wilkes, for Lieut. John Goddard Watmough, U.S. Army, who was wounded at Ft. Erie during the War of 1812. The name has been misspelled on some subsequent maps as *Walmouth Head, Walmouth Hill*, and *Walmough Head*. The original Indian name for the place was *Noo-chaad-kwun*.

Watsak Point (Island County) *see* Snatelum Point

Watsok Island (Skagit County) *see* Rosario Head

Watson Lakes *(T.37N;R.9E)*

Two high-altitude lakes north of Mt. Watson, at the head of Noisy Creek, Mt. Baker National Forest, south central Whatcom County. The group is nestled at the foot of Mt. Watson, for which they were named. Big Watson Lake, also called East Watson, covers 45.8 acres; Little Watson Lake covers 18 acres.

Wauconda *(S.1;T.37N;R.30E)*

Community 18 miles northwest of Republic, east central Okanogan County. Originally established at the Wauconda Mine, it was later moved to a location near the head of Toroda Creek. Named for the mine, the Indian term means "master of life." Some informants state that the natives believed that this being dwelt in nearby mountains, which they greatly revered. The town should not be confused with old Wauconda, which is 2-1/2 miles southeast.

Waughop Lake (Pierce County) *see* Mud Lake

Wauhaukaupauken Falls *(Mt. Rainier National Park)*

Falls in Ohanapecosh River, at the foot of Ohanapecosh Glacier below Indian Bar, southeast quarter of the park. The original Indian name for the feature, which has been retained in its magnificent length, means "spouting water." (USBGN)

Waukee (Adams County) *see* Macall

Waukon *(S.26;T.24N;R.39E)*

Railroad station 9 miles south of Reardon, east central Lincoln County. It was named by railroad officials when the Spokane, Portland & Seattle Railway was built through here; the name origin is obscure.

Wauna *(S.22;T.22N;R.1E)*

Small settlement on the north shore of Henderson Bay, at the head of Carr Inlet, 3-1/2 miles north of Gig Harbor, northwest Pierce County. In 1906, it was named by Mary F. White when she was appointed postmistress. She chose the Indian name, which means "mighty" or "strong."

Waverly *(S.3;T.21N;R.44E)*

Once a busy town in Waverly Township, 21 miles southeast of Spokane, southeast Spokane County. From

1898 until 1911, the town was very active because of a sugar factory financed by the Corbin interests. Now, however, it is almost a ghost town. In 1879, the name was chosen by Saville Farnsworth and Fred Buckmaster, for their former home town in Iowa.

Wawa Point *(S.24;T.26N;R.2W)*

A west shore point of Dabob Bay, west entrance to Jackson Cove, southeast Jefferson County. The original Indian name means "talk" or "speak" in Chinook jargon.

Wawawai *(S.3;T.13N;R.43E)*

Village on the north bank of Snake River, at the mouth of Wawawai Canyon, 16-1/2 miles south of Colfax, south central Whitman County. The name is a Walla Walla Indian word meaning "council ground."

Way Luwa (Asotin County) *see* Grand Ronde River

Wayhut Lake *(S.14;T.27N;R.11E)*

A 5.8-acre lake, elevation 4,000 ft., 9 miles north of Skykomish, Snoqualmie National Forest, south central Snohomish County. The Chinook Indian jargon name means "road," "path," or "trail." Evidently, the lake was originally a stopping point on an important Indian trail through this area. An alternate name is *Oyhut Lake*.

Wayside *(S.12;T.27N;R.42E)*

Pioneer hamlet on Half Moon Prairie, 18 miles north of Spokane, central Spokane County. Reports from 1887 indicate that it was named by Joseph S. Fea, a homesteader, who also operated a general store and served as the first postmaster. The reason for the name choice probably was that the place was a stop-off point on a stage line from Spokane to Colville.

Weatherwax *(S.36;T.22N;R.8W)*

Settlement in the upper Wynooche River drainage basin, 1-1/2 miles west of Camp Grisdale, Olympic National Forest, northeast Grays Harbor County. It was named for George Weatherwax, a Grays Harbor pioneer.

Weatherwax Basin *(T.22N;Rs.7,8W)*

An extensive, high-altitude valley in the upper Wynooche River drainage area, directly southeast of Fitzgerald Peak, Olympic National Forest, northeast Grays Harbor County. (see Weatherwax)

Webb Hill *(T.21N;R.4W)*

A hill north of Shelton, on the road to Hood Canal, central Mason County. It was named for Thomas Webb, whose 1852 Donation Land Claim included the hill.

Weber *(S.31;T.19N;R.31E)*

Settlement in Weber Coulee, 28 miles west of Ritzville, northwest Adams County. It was named for Jacob Weber, the first settler and first postmaster.

Weber Coulee *(Ts.18,19N;R.31E)*

The coulee rises near Schrag, northwest Adams County; extends westerly into Grant County. (*see* Weber)

Webster Point *(T.25N;R.4E)*

A west side point of Lake Washington, at the entrance to Union Bay, in Seattle, King County. It was named for the operator of an early shingle mill at a nearby railway point. Alternate names used earlier were *Laurel Point* and *Whiskey Point*. The Indian name was *Cebu-lt*, meaning "dry."

Wehesville *(Ss.23,24;T.39N;R.26E)*

An old mining camp on Palmer Mountain, 1 mile south of the south end of Wannacut Lake, northeast Okanogan County. Established in 1892, it was settled by 4 brothers of Prussian origin: Prof. Ferdinand P. Wehe, Col. August M. W. Wehe, Capt. Albert C. Wehe, and Postmaster George Wehe. They ran the entire town, including the post office; the place was named for them.

Weikel *(S.11;T.13N;R.17E)*

Northern Pacific Railway station on Cowiche Creek, 5 miles northwest of Yakima, north central Yakima County. It was named by railway officials, for George Weikel, from whom they acquired a local right-of-way. On certain maps the name appears as *Wiekel*.

Weikswood *(S.9;T.16N;R.6W)*

Logging community 10 miles south of Elma, at the head of Vesta Creek, southeast Grays Harbor County. Established by Weyerhaeuser Timber Company, it was named by F. W. Byles, manager of Weyerhaeuser's Clemons Branch, for Carl Weiks, logging superintendent at the camp. Byles added the "wood" for good measure.

Weissenfels Ridge *(T.8N;R.46E)*

A 6-mile-long, north-south ridge 2 to 5 miles west of Snake River, east

central Asotin County. It carries the name of William P. Weissenfels, who settled in the vicinity in 1878.

Welch Ridge *(S.23;T.9N;R.42E)*

Umatilla National Forest ridge in Blue Mountains, 5 miles south of Peola, south central Garfield County. The name origin is reported to be for an early U.S. Forest Service employee. (USBGN)

Welcome *(S.27;T.39N;R.5E)*

Small settlement on North Fork, Nooksack River, 1/2 mile northwest of Kulshan, southeast Whatcom County. In 1888, it acquired the middle name of the first postmaster, John Welcome Riddle, as suggested by Robert L. Kline of Bellingham.

Welland *(S.30;T.9N;R.33E)*

Northern Pacific Railway station 16 miles east of Pasco, west central Walla Walla County. Railway officials named the station for Welland, in the Canadian Province of Ontario, but no reason was given for their choice.

Wellington *(S.5;T.26N;R.13E)*

A railway point at the west portal of an abandoned railway tunnel through Cascade Mountains, King County. In 1910, it was the site of a disastrous snowslide, which killed 118 persons who were aboard a stalled passenger train. The name was chosen at random by officials of Great Northern Railway Company. Later known as *Tye*.

Wellman Basin *(T.32N;R.9E)*

Basin at the head of Ashton Creek, Mt. Baker National Forest, 4 miles southwest of Darrington, north central Snohomish County. It was named for A. Wellman, who prospected here in early days.

Wellpinit *(S.35;T.38N;R.38E)*

Community 3-1/2 miles north of Spokane River, southeast Stevens County. It is the only town of its size on Spokane Indian Reservation, and includes tribal headquarters and an Indian school. During World War I, the name was changed from *Germania* to the present name, which is a Nez Perce Indian word meaning "water gushing." It was so called because an underground stream burst out here, and was a source of good water in early days.

Wells (Chelan County) *see* Azwell

Wells Creek *(T.39N;R.8E)*

The stream of the creek heads near the foot of Mazama Glacier and Coleman Peak, northeast slope of Mt. Baker, Whatcom County; flows northwest to North Fork, Nooksack River, Mt. Baker National Forest. It was locally named for Hamilton C. Wells, a civil engineer and prospector, who, in the 1880s and '90s, explored the creek.

Wells Creek Falls (Whatcom County) *see* Mazama Falls

Wenas *(S.13;T.16N;R.16E)*

Town on Wenas Creek, 20 miles northwest of Yakima, north central Yakima County. In early days, the area surrounding the town was a favorite hunting place for Indians. The Indian name means "last camping." It is spelled *Wenass* on some early maps.

Wenas Creek *(Ts.14,15N;Rs.17-19E)*

The stream of the creek heads in southwest Kittitas County; flows southeast 27 miles to join Yakima River, 6 miles north of Yakima. (USBGN) (*see* Wenas)

Wenass (Yakima County) *see* Wenas

Wenatchee *(Ss.3,10;T.22N;R.20E)*

City on Columbia River, at the confluence of Wenatchee River, southeast Chelan County. It is a fruit center, and presumed to be the geographic center of the state. The name is from the original Indian designation, which was *We-na-tcha* or *We-na-tchi*, meaning "river issuing from a canyon." In 1805, Lewis and Clark used the word *Wahnahchee* in referring to this location.

Wenatchee Creek (Asotin County) *see* Menatchee Creek

Wenatchee Lake *(9T.27N;Rs.16,17E)*

A 5-mile-long lake, average width 1 mile, on Wenatchee River, 15 miles north of Leavenworth, central Chelan County. (*see* Wenatchee)

Wenatchee National Forest

A 1,523,346-acre forest in east central Cascade Mountains area, bordering the summit to the east, Chelan and Kittitas counties; adjoining Skagit, Snohomish and King counties at the summit. Forest headquarters are at Wenatchee, and administration is under Region 6 of U.S. Forest Service, with Portland, Oregon, headquarters. In 1908, the forest was created from a part of Washington National Forest, which was established in 1897. The name was taken from Wenatchee River by U.S. Forest Service officials in Washington, D.C. (*see* Wenatchee)

Wenatchee Pass (*S.32;T.28N;R.14E*)

Cascade Mountain summit pass at the head of Lake Creek, 1/2 mile south of Top Lake, between Chelan and Snohomish counties. The 4,075-ft. elevation compares with 4,061 ft. at Stevens Pass. In 1912, it was named by U.S. Forest Supervisor A. H. Sylvester, for Wenatchee River and Lake. (*see* Wenatchee)

Wenatchee Ridge
(*Ts.27,28N;Rs.15,16E*)

Ridge extending 8 miles from Irving Peak to the junction of White and Little Wenatchee rivers, Wenatchee National Forest, northwest Chelan County. The name was applied by U.S. Forest Supervisor A. H. Sylvester, because the ridge is in the watershed of Little Wenatchee River. (*see* Wenatchee)

Wenatchee River
(*Ts.23-28N;Rs.14-20E*)

The stream of the river rises at Wards Pass, on the east slope of Cascade Mountain summit; flows southeast to Columbia River at Wenatchee, Chelan County. The stream passes through Wenatchee Lake in its course. (*see* Wenatchee)

Wenberg State Park (*T.31N;R.4E*)

A 55-acre park on Puget Sound, 18 miles northwest of Everett, between Warm Beach and Lakewood, northwest Snohomish County. It offers camping, swimming, fishing, and clam digging. The name is for Oscar Wenberg of East Stanwood, state legislator who helped create the park.

Wesley (*T.40N;R.3E*)

Once a town adjoining the town of Lynden, northwest Whatcom County. In 1884, the town was platted, then abandoned four years later. It took the first name of Wesley L. Lawrence, who settled here in 1872.

Wesley Junction (*S.32;T.11N;R.20E*)

Northern Pacific Railway junction 2-1/2 miles northwest of Toppenish, southeast Yakima County. In 1912, it was named by railway officials for a prominent cattle-raising Indian family.

West Bank (*S.27;T.38N;R.2W*)

Bank in 3-1/2 fathoms in Strait of Georgia, 1-1/2 miles west of Sucia Island, north central San Juan County. In 1858, it was charted under the present name by U.S. Coast Survey. In the same year, it was charted as *Plumper's Reef* by Capt. Henry Richards, R.N., for the name of the steam sloop which he commanded in survey work.

West Bremerton (*T.24N;R.1E*)

Town across Sinclair Inlet from Bremerton, central Kitsap County. In 1890, the place was platted by S. H. Barbee as *Port Orchard, for Port Orchard bay. The following year, Port Orchard Investment Company platted an adjoining tract as Charleston, for U.S.S. Charleston,* an armored cruiser. The first post office was named Charleston. In 1893, the 2 towns merged as Port Orchard. In 1903, the State Legislature changed the name of the combined town to *Charleston* It is now known by its present name.

West Cady Creek (*T.28N;Rs.12,13E*)

The stream of the creek rises in 2 main branches at Cascade Mountain summit, Snoqualmie National Forest, southeast Snohomish County; flows 8 miles west to Skykomish River, near Garland Mineral Springs. It was named for Capt. Cady, who built a military trail over nearby Cady Pass at Cascade Mountain summit. The town of Snohomish was originally called Cadyville in his honor. This stream should not be confused with Cady Creek, Wenatchee National Forest, Chelan County. (USBGN)

West Creek (Jefferson County) *see* West Fork, Dosewallips River

West Deer Creek (*T.39N;Rs.33-35E*)

The stream of the creek heads on the north slope of Sentinel Butte, Colville National Forest, Ferry County; flows 8-1/2 miles west to Kettle River, 1-1/2 miles below Curlew. The name distinguishes this stream from East Deer Creek, just across the mountain summit, north central Ferry County. When a western mountain stream is named for any wild animal, one may be quite sure that there were plenty of them around at the time. More than 20 names in the state include "deer." (USBGN)

West Fork (*S.11;T.34N;R.32E*)

Small settlement on Colville Indian Reservation, elevation 1,968 ft., at the junction of San Poil River and the river's West Fork, 13 miles south of Republic, west central Ferry County. In the 1890s, it had a short mining boom. The name is descriptive of its location. An earlier name in local use was *LeRoi's.* Another early name was *Alkire,* for a pioneer who operated a livery stable and stage station here.

West Fork, Dosewallips River
(*Ts.25,26N;Rs.4,5W*)

The stream of this tributary heads in Anderson Pass, Olympic National Park, east central Jefferson County; flows 8 miles northeast to Dosewallips River. An unofficial name, carried on some maps, is *West Creek.* (USBGN) (*see* Dosewallips River)

West Fork, Dungeness River (Clallam County) *see* Gray Wolf River

West Fork, Straight Creek (Snohomish County) *see* Black Creek

West Fork, White River (*Mt. Rainier National Park*)

The glacial stream of this tributary rises near the foot of Winthrop Glacier, north slope of Mt. Rainier, north central zone of the park; flows 9 miles north of the park to White River, Pierce County. (USBGN) (*see* White River)

West Kelso (Cowlitz County) *see* Catlin

West Passage (*Ts.22,23N;R.2E*)

A 14-mile-long passage, average width 1 mile, between Vashon Island, King County, and Kitsap County mainland to the west. In 1841, the original name *Colvos Passage* was applied by Cmdr. Charles Wilkes, for Midshipman George W. Colvocoressis, a member of the Wilkes Expedition. The present name was charted later by U.S. Coast Survey, and is in more general use than the name chosen by Wilkes.

West Peak, Mt. Olympus
(*T.27N;R.8W.uns*)

One of 2 major peaks on Mt. Olympus, elevation 7,915 ft., Olympic National Monument, north central Jefferson County. (*see* Mt. Olympus)

West Point (*T.25N;R.3E*)

A lighthouse reservation under U.S. Coast Guard control, on a low, sandy spit at the extreme west tip of Lawton Peninsula, northwest Seattle, King County; extends from Ft. Lawton to Puget Sound, between Elliott and Shilshole bays. In 1841, it was named by

Cmdr. Charles Wilkes, because it points due west. The Duwamish Indian name was *Oka-dz-elt-cu*, meaning "thrust far out." (USBGN)

West Richland *(T.9N;R.28E)*

Town 3 miles west of Richland, in Hanford A.E.C. Project area, east central Benton County. In 1953, the towns of Enterprise and Heminger City were combined under this name, which is in Greater Richland Community.

West Rock *(S.28;T.25N;R.3W.uns)*

One of 3 rocky peaks, with North Rock and East Rock, on the east wall of Cabin Creek Cirque, Olympic National Forest, 5 miles west of Bellview, southeast Jefferson County. It was named for its position on the wall of the cirque. (USBGN)

West Seattle *(T.24N;R.3E)*

A southwestern part of Seattle, extending south along Puget Sound from Elliot Bay, King County. Portions of this extensive district have had earlier names, including *Lamb's Point*, *Freeport*, and *Milton* or *Milltown*. The Indian name for the area along Elliott Bay was *Squ-ducks*, meaning "high point of land continuing into water."

West Sound *(T.36N;R.2W)*

A 3-mile inlet on the southwest side of Orcas Island, north central San Juan County. In 1841, it was named *Guerriere Bay* by Cmdr. Charles Wilkes, for a British ship captured by *U.S.S. Constitution* during the War of 1812. In 1858, that name was replaced when the present name was charted by Capt. Henry Richards, British Admiralty surveyor. The name is in relation to East Sound, Orcas Island, several miles east. The Lummi Indian name for the inlet was *Al-lay-ling*.

West Sound *(S.9;T.36N;R.2W)*

Small settlement on the east shore of West Sound, north side of White Beach Bay, San Juan County. It was named for the body of water on which it is located. (*see* West Sound (inlet))

West Tenino *(S.23;T.16N;R.1W)*

Northern Pacific Railway station 12 miles south of Olympia, southwest Thurston County. In 1914, the name was applied by railway officials, because the station is a short distance west of Tenino. It does not appear on recent maps.

Westcott Bay (San Juan County) *see* Westcott Creek

Westcott Creek *(T.36N;R.4W)*

Tidal stream at the northwest end of San Juan Island, directly south of Roche Harbor, northwest San Juan County. In 1858, it was charted under the present name by Capt. Henry Richards, R.N., for George Blagdon Westcott, R.N., paymaster on *HMS Bacchante*. In 1912, it was charted as *Westcott Creek* by U.S. Coast Guard Survey; in 1921, the same agency charted it under the present name.

Weston *(S.21;T.20N;R.11E)*

Small community at the headwaters of Green River, west end of Northern Pacific Railway's Cascade Mountain tunnel, 3-1/2 miles west of the summit, east King County. In 1915, it was abandoned as a railroad construction center by the railway. The name, given by railway officials, was to contrast with Easton on the east side of the mountains, which was the eastern terminus of the tunnel.

Westport *(S.7;T.16N;R.11W)*

Town on a large spit at the south entrance to Grays Harbor, southwest Grays Harbor County. It is headquarters for the fishing and crabbing fleet, and a mecca for sports fishermen. The present name is descriptive of the town's location. Other names used over the years include *Peterson's Point*, *Chehalis City* and *Ft. Chehalis*. The latter name is for a fort which was established here in 1860, before the town was platted. The fort was built to protect settlers against Indian attack, but never went into action.

Westport Lake (Grays Harbor County) *see* Chohassett Lake

Wetmore Slough *(T.24N;R.4E)*

Small, shallow bay on the west shore of Lake Washington, directly south of Mt. Baker district, in Seattle, King County. It was named for Frank Wetmore, a Seattle pioneer of the 1860s. The Indian name was *Ska-bo*, meaning "milk" or "nipple."

Whale Rocks *(S.16;T.34N;R.2W)*

A scattered group of bare rocks 1 mile southwest of Davis Bay, southwest end of Lopez Island, south central San Juan County. The rocks are included in Geese Islets, together with Long Island, Buck Island and Mummy Rocks. In 1858, they were named by Capt. Henry

Richards, R.N., on British Admiralty charts.

Whatcom *(Ts.35,36N;Rs.1,2E)*

Town on the site of present-day Bellingham. On October 27, 1903, it was one of 4 towns on Bellingham Bay which merged to form Bellingham. (*see* Whatcom Falls)

Whatcom County

This county in northwest Washington is bounded on the north by British Columbia; on the east by Okanogan County; on the south by Skagit County; and on the west by Puget Sound. It contains 2,151 square miles. On March 9, 1854, the county was created by the Territorial Legislature from a portion of Island County. Township government exists in 25 townships. The name derives from the Lummi Indian word *What-coom*, meaning "noisy, rumbling water," as applied to Whatcom Falls. From older Lummi dialect pronunciation, the name should be spelled *N-wh-ah-tk-hm*

Whatcom Creek *(T.38N;Rs.1,2E)*

The stream of the creek rises in the city of Bellingham, southwest Whatcom County; flows 4 miles west to Bellingham Bay, from the north end of Lake Whatcom. Whatcom Falls is at the outlet. (*see* Whatcom County)

Whatcom Falls *(S.30;T.38N;R.3E)*

Falls at the mouth of Whatcom Creek on Bellingham Bay, in the city of Bellingham, southwest Whatcom County. In 1853, a water-powered sawmill was established at this site. (*see* Whatcom County)

Whatcom Lake (Whatcom County) *see* Lake Whatcom

Wheatland (Adams County) *see* Tokio

Wheeler *(S.15;T.19N;R.29E)*

Small settlement 4 miles east of Moses Lake (town), southeast Grant County. It inherited its name from an older town, 4 miles southeast, which was named by a settler, for the street on which he had lived in St. Paul, Minnesota.

Wheeler Creek *(T.39N;R.36E)*

The stream of this very short creek heads on the north slope of North Boulder Ridge, Colville National Forest, northeast Ferry County; flows 2 miles east by north to East Deer Creek. It was named by U.S. Forest Service personnel, for Eugene Wheeler, whose employment on Colville National Forest started in 1908.

Wheeler Hill *(T.21N;R.20E)*

Hill on a divide between Squillchuck and Stemilt creeks, 5 miles south of Wenatchee, southeast Chelan County. It was named for the Peter Wheeler family, which, in 1885, homesteaded here.

Wheeler Mountain *(T.32N;R.7E)*

A sprawling mountain covering a wide area 4 miles southeast of Oso, north central Snohomish County. It was named for Robert Wheeler, a Civil War veteran; in September 1887, he had claimed 160 acres in this vicinity.

Whelan *(S.14;T.15N;R.45E)*

Hamlet 4 miles east of Pullman, 3-1/2 miles west of the Idaho border, extreme east central Whitman County. The original name of this small place was *Branam,* but was changed to the present name because of confusion with Branham, Whatcom County. Northern Pacific Railway officials applied the name to the station, for an engineer named Whelan in their employ.

Whetstone *(S.35;T.11N;R.39E)*

Settlement 7 miles northeast of Dayton, northeast Columbia County. It takes its name, as do the nearby creek and hollow, from Thomas W. Whetstone, who, in 1861, moved to the hollow with his family.

Whetstone Creek *(T.11N;R.39E)*

The stream of this intermittent creek follows Whetstone Hollow, south Columbia County and Walla Walla County. (*see* Whetstone, Whetstone Hollow)

Whetstone Hollow
(Ts.10-11;Rs.37-39E)

The draw heads near Whetstone, central Columbia County; trends 12 iles west and southwest, to Touchet River near Prescott, Walla Walla County. (*see* Whetstone)

Whidbey Island
(Ts.28-34N;Rs.1W-4E)

A 235-square-mile island, with Deception Pass to the north; Skagit Bay, Saratoga Passage and Possession Sound to the east; Possession Sound and Admiralty Inlet to the south; Admiralty Inlet and Strait of Juan de Fuca to the west, Island County. It rates as the second largest island in the lower 48 states. On June 24, 1792, it was named by Capt. George Vancouver, for Joseph Whidbey, master of the ship *Discovery,*

who proved it to be an island by exploring through Deception Pass. In older records and on maps, the island has borne many names, including *Whidby, Whidby's, Whitbey, Whitbey's,* and the Indian name *Tscha-kole-chy.*

Whidby Island, Whidby's Island (Island County) *see* Whidbey Island

Whiskey (Whisky) Creek
(Ts.8-9N;Rs.37,38E)

The stream of this intermittent creek rises near Walla Walla County line, southwest Columbia County; flows 15 miles northwest to Touchet River, near Huntsville, through Walla Walla County and an angle of Columbia County. The name origin traces back to pioneer days, when 3 lawless characters lived at a trail crossing of the creek, and traded whiskey for Indian cayuses. Their names were William Bunten, George Ives and George ("Clubfoot George") Lane. In 1860, they sold out and moved to Montana, where, in 1864, they were hanged by vigilantes.

Whiskey Point (King County) *see* Webster Point

Whiskey Rock *(S.14;T.21N;R.38E)*

Old trading post just beyond the one-mile limit of Sprague, southeast Lincoln County. In 1880, it was founded by E. M. Kinnear and Patrick Wallace, supplying railroad construction camps at Sprague, when Northern Pacific Railway was building through here. The precise location was due to the railroad's rule that no liquor could be sold within one mile of Northern Pacific camps. The name, not shown on recent maps, was for the chief commodity handled by Kinnear and Wallace. The post was of relatively short duration.

Whisky Dick Creek *(T.18N;Rs.21,22E)*

The stream of the creek rises north of Whisky Dick Mountain, east central Kittitas County; flows 14 miles east to Columbia River, north of Vantage. The creek drains part of an area reserved for rocket motor tests; in May 1961, 2,500 acres were acquired by a Seattle firm for this purpose. The typical pioneer name might have some reference to the fact that the stream is intermittent, making water a scarce commodity in the dry season.

Whisky Dick Mountain
(S.29;T.18N;R.21E)

Isolated peak, elevation 3,873 ft., 15

miles east of Ellensburg and 10 miles west of Columbia River, east central Kittitas County. (*see* Whisky Dick Creek)

Whistling Pig Creek *(T.28N;R.18E)*

The stream of the creek rises on the north side of Cougar Mountain, Wenatchee National Forest, central Chelan County; flows 4 miles west to Mad River. The name was applied by sheepmen, for the mountain marmot which is often called "whistling pig."

Whitbey Island, Whitbey's Island (Island County) *see* Whidbey Island

Whitcomb *(S.35;T.5N;R.24E)*

Settlement 1-1/4 miles north of Columbia River, on the south side of Canoe Ridge, extreme southwest Benton County. The original name, *Luzon,* was changed to the present name at the suggestion of 2 landowners, James A. Moore and G. Henry Whitcomb, in honor of the latter.

White Beach Bay *(S.9;T.36N;R.2W)*

Small bay on the west shore of West Sound, Orcas Island, north central San Juan County. In 1858, it was first mapped on British Admiralty charts by Capt. Richards. The name is descriptive of the bay's very white beach of sand or shell.

White Bluffs *(S.31;T.14N;R.27E)*

Former town 7 miles northwest of Hanford, near the north end of U.S. Atomic Energy Commission Reservation, north central Benton County. It was named for white bluffs of diatomaceous earth along Columbia River, which reach up to 500 ft. in height.

White Brant Island (Clark County) *see* Lady Island

White Cliffs *(T.34N;R.2W)*

Bluffs on the west shore of Lopez Island, 2 miles northwest of Richardson, south central San Juan County. In 1858, the quite descriptive name was first mapped on British Admiralty charts by Capt. Richards. The place does not appear on recent maps.

White Creek *(T.30N;R.6W)*

The stream of the creek rises 3-1/2 miles south of Port Angeles Harbor, east Clallam County; flows north to that harbor, directly east of Port Angeles. In 1859, it was named for Capt. John White, who settled on land through which the creek flows. He placer-mined the creek for gold -- with little success. On certain older maps, it is named *Yennis Creek* or *Ennis Creek*. The latter name is properly applied to a creek directly to the east.

White Creek *(T.34N;R.10E.uns)*

The stream of the creek heads at Illabot Peaks, Mt. Baker National Forest, southeast Skagit County; flows 6 miles, in a wide circle, to Sauk River. The name was locally applied for George White, who homesteaded in 1884 near the creek's mouth.

White Glacier (Mt. Rainier National Park) *see* Winthrop Glacier

White Horse Mountain *(S.32;T.32N;S.5;T.31N;R.9E)*

A 6,820-ft. peak 4-1/2 miles southwest of Darrington, north central Snohomish County. In 1894, it was named by W. C. Hiles, Darrington's first postmaster. He noticed that the snow melting on the mountain slope each spring created a snow image of a horse.

White Mountain (No. 1) *(Ts.28,29N;Rs.15,16E)*

Long ridge, without pronounced peaks, extending about 7 miles from White River to Napeequa River, Wenatchee National Forest, northwest Chelan County. It was named by Forest Supervisor A. H. Sylvester, for the rather light-colored granodiorite rock, of which the mountain is largely composed. It should not be confused with White Mountain at Cascade Mountain summit, Chelan County.

White Mountain (No.2) *(S.5;T.29N;R.14E)*

A 6,986-ft. peak at Cascade Mountain summit, directly north of White Pass, on the boundary of Chelan and Snohomish counties. It was named by Forest Supervisor A. H. Sylvester for its prevalent snow cover. It should not be confused with White Mountain near White River, Chelan County.

White Mountain *(Ss.19,20,29,30;T.35N;R.35E)*

A Colville National Forest peak, elevation 6,927 ft., 16 miles southeast of Republic, central Ferry County. Most mountains with this name were so designated because of snowcaps; this one, however, was named for large, white granite outcroppings on the upper half of the slope.

White Pass *(Ss.7,8;T.29N;R.14E)*

A 5,901-ft. pass at Cascade Mountain summit, at the head of White River, directly south of White Mountain, on the boundary of Snohomish and Chelan counties. It was named by Forest Supervisor A. H. Sylvester for its proximity to White River and White Mountain.

White Pass *(S.2;T.13N;R.11E.uns)*

A 4,500-ft. pass, traversed by a state highway, at Cascade Mountain summit, between the headwaters of Clear Fork, Cowlitz River on the west, and Tieton Basin on the east, Lewis and Yakima counties. It was named for Charles W. White, a civil engineer, who discovered the saddle while working for Northern Pacific Railway Company. He later laid out the streets of New Tacoma, Washington Territory.

White Pine Creek *(T.26N;R.15E)*

The stream of the creek heads near the junction of Icicle Ridge and Cascade Mountain summit, southwest Chelan County; flows 8 miles northeast to Nason Creek, near Gaynor. Prior to 1902, it was named by local settlers. Pine timber is plentiful in the area, although it is doubtful there could be stands of white pine in this vicinity.

White River *(Ts.27-30N;Rs.14-16E)*

The stream of the river heads on the east slope of Cascade Mountain summit, Wenatchee National Forest, northwest Chelan County; flows southeast 25 miles to Wenatchee Lake. Because it is glacier-fed, the water is milky in color during spring and summer. The name derives from the original Indian name *Na-pe-qua*, meaning "white water." The Indian term is now used to designate the river's north fork.

White River *(Ts.17-21N;Rs.5-10E)*

The stream of the river rises in a glacial run-off area, in 2 forks on north and northeast slopes of Mt. Rainier; flows 15 miles north to join Greenwater River, west through Mud Mountain Reservoir and Dam. It continues northwest into south King County, then south to Puyallup River at Sumner. It joined Green River south of Auburn until 1906, when it broke out of its channel and followed Stuck River channel in its present course. The name describes the milky color of the river's water, caused by a burden of glacial flour. The Indian name was *S'kamish*, meaning "mixed water."

White River (post office) (King County) *see* O'Brien

White River (town) (Pierce County) *see* Buckley

White River Glacier *(T.30N;R.14E)*

A southeast slope glacier of Cascade Mountain summit, at the head of White River, Wenatchee National Forest, northwest Chelan County. The live glacier, with extensive ice and snow fields, was named by Forest Supervisor A. H. Sylvester, for its location at the head of White River.

White River Glacier (Mt. Rainier National Park) *see* Emmons Glacier

White River Junction *(Mt. Rainier National Park)*

Point at the junction of Mather Memorial Hwy. and Sunrise Park (Yakima Park) Hwy., northeast zone of the park. The name was given because this highway fork is directly east of White River.

White River Mill Pond (King County) *see* Boise Lake

White River Park *(Mt. Rainier National Park)*

Natural alpine park extending about 3 miles, from Sunrise Ridge, north to Brown Park, at the head of Sunrise Creek, northwest zone of the park. It contains several small lakes which are drained by Sunrise Creek, a tributary of White River. The name was chosen because the park is in the White River drainage basin. (USBGN)

White River Siding (Pierce County) *see* Buckley

White Rock (San Juan County) *see* Pointer Island

White Salmon *(S.19;T.3N;R.11E)*

Town on hillside above Columbia River's north bank, directly across from Hood River, Oregon; southwest Klickitat County. When a post office was established in 1872, it was named for White Salmon River, directly west. Rivalry with Bingen, a town directly adjoining White Salmon on the southeast and on Spokane, Portland, and Seattle Railway line, caused the station to be marked with both town names. Efforts to combine the towns have been made for many years, but so far have proven fruitless. In 1931, Bingen took the matter of naming the railway station to court, without satisfaction to either town.

White Salmon Creek (Okanogan County) *see* Salmon Creek

White Salmon Glacier
(T.8N;R.10E.uns)

A west slope glacier of Mt. Adams, from about 7,500 ft. to the summit, with the head in extreme western Yakima County, and lower reaches in Mt. Adams Wild Area, east Skamania County. Two lobes of the glacier are joined in the lower reaches. (*see* White Salmon River)

White Salmon River
(Ts.3-10N;Rs.9,10E)

The stream of the creek rises on the west slope of Mt. Adams, northeast Skamania County; flows south to Columbia River at Underwood, a total distance of about 40 miles, northwest Klickitat County. The name was given for the salmon entering the stream to spawn, whose flesh changed color from red to pinkish white. The original Indian name was *Nikepun.* In 1805, Lewis and Clark called the river *Canoe Creek,* for the numerous Indians fishing the stream from canoes.

White Stallion River (Walla Walla County) *see* Touchet River

White Swan *(S.5;T.10N;R.17E)*

Townsite on Simcoe Creek, 20 miles southwest of Yakima, Yakima Indian Reservation, central Yakima County. This place had been inhabited by Indians for generations before white men invaded their domain. When Ft. Simcoe & Western Railway built through here, several stores were established, and, in 1910, the townsite was platted. It now boasts a substantial sawmill which subsists on timber from the reservation. The name is for the Indian leader White Swan, whom white men called Joe Stwire.

Whitechuck Lake *(S.33;T.32N;R.11E)*

Two small lakes, elevation about 5,000 ft., on the northeast side of Whitechuck Mountain, north central Snohomish County. It was named for Whitechuck Mountain, which was named for Whitechuck River. (*see* Whitechuck River)

Whitechuck Mountain
(S.5;T.31N;R.11E)

A 6,935-ft. peak at the head of Straight Creek, 14 miles northwest of Glacier Peak summit, northeast Snohomish County. It was named for White-

chuck River, 2 miles south. (*see* Whitechuck River)

Whitechuck River
(Ts.30,31N;Rs.10-12E)

The stream of the river rises in several small branches on the west slope of Glacier Peak, northeast Snohomish County; flows 15 miles west to Sauk River, 9 miles southeast of Darrington. It was named for the water's milky color, caused by a heavy burden of glacial flour, in combination with the Chinook jargon word "chuck" for water.

Whitehorn Point (Whatcom County) *see* Point Whitehorn

Whitelow *(S.4;T.14N;R.45E)*

Community on Paradise Creek, 1 mile southeast of Pullman, southeast Whitman County. In pioneer days, it was named for M. W. Whitlow, who built a warehouse here, and who owned a nearby farm.

Whiteman Cove *(S.15;T.20N;R.1W)*

East shore cove of Case Inlet, 12 miles north of Olympia, northwest Pierce County. The name *Whiteman's Cove* was chosen by pioneer settlers, for the first white man, named Reed. He claimed land on the cove, and became a permanent resident with his Indian wife. The name appears on certain recent maps, in error, as *Whitman Cove.*

Whiteman's Cove (Pierce County) *see* Whiteman Cove

Whites *(S.20;T.18N;R.5W)*

Railway station in Chehalis River valley, on Wildcat Creek, 4 miles northeast of Elma, southeast Grays Harbor County. It was named by Northern Pacific Railway officials, for Allen White, who built a sawmill here in 1890, and operated it for many years.

Whitestone Lake
(Ss.7,17,18,20;T.38N;R.27E)

Narrow, 2-mile-long lake 1 mile north of Whitestone Mountain, 5-1/2 miles north of Tonasket, northeast Okanogan County., It is a winter sports area, with public access. The name derives from nearby Whitestone Mountain's pale, ghostly cliffs.

Whitestone Mountain
(Ss.19,20;T.38N;R.27E)

A 2,867-ft. peak 1 mile south of Whitestone Lake, 5 miles north of Tonasket, northeast Okanogan County.

With Whitestone Lake, it constitutes a winter sports area. A poetic name applied to the peak is *Whitestone Phantom.* (*see* Whitestone Lake)

Whitman *(S.31;T.7N;R.35E)*

Settlement 7 miles west of Walla Walla, north of Walla Walla River, south central Walla Walla County. It was established between 1847 and 1855, near Waiilatpu (Whitman) Mission, by French-Canadians, or "Free French," who had served out their terms with Hudson's Bay Company. At that time it was known as *Frenchtown.* The present name is for Dr. Marcus Whitman, who established a mission at Waiilatpu in the winter of 1836, and was killed there on November 29, 1847, by Cayuse Indians.

Whitman Cove (Pierce County) *see* Whiteman Cove

Whitman County

This county in southeast Washington is bounded on the north by Lincoln and Spokane counties; on the east by Idaho; on the south by Asotin, Garfield and Columbia counties; and on the west by Adams County. On November 29, 1871, it was created from a portion of Stevens County by the Territorial Legislature. It is essentially a farming county, raising an abundance of wheat, dry peas and livestock on its 2,167 square miles. (*see* Whitman)

Whitman Crest *(Mt. Rainier National Park)*

Sharp, narrow ridge between Whitman and Ohanapecosh glaciers, 3-1/2 miles east of Mt. Rainier summit, southeast of Little Tahoma Peak, central area of the park. (USBGN) (*see* Whitman)

Whitman Dam (Walla Walla County) *see* Ice Harbor Dam

Whitman Glacier *(Mt. Rainier National Park)*

The wide, short ice field heads in a rocky triangle east of the park; extends about 3/4 mile southeast on the east slope of Mt. Rainier, between Ingraham and Ohanapecosh glaciers. (USBGN) (*see* Whitman)

Whitman Mission (Walla Walla County) *see* Waiilatpu

Whitney *(S.7;T.34N;R.3E)*

Hamlet on Telegraph Slough, near the south end of Padilla Bay, 7 miles northwest of Mt. Vernon, west central

Skagit County. In 1882, it was founded as *Padilla* by Rienzie E. Whitney. When Great Northern Railway came through the area in 1890, the town was moved to the railway, and the name was changed to that of the town's founder.

Whitney Island *(T.34N;R.3E)*

Small island in Padilla Bay, on tidelands north of Swinomish Slough, north central Skagit County. (*see* Whitney)

Whitney Point *(S.7;T.26N;R.1W)*

A west shore point of Dabob Bay, directly south of the mouth of Quilcene Bay, east Jefferson County. It was locally named for Robert S. Whitney, a Nova Scotian, who was the first logger in the area. Other names for the feature have been *Whitney Spit* and *Point Whitney*.

Whitney Spit (Jefferson County) *see* Whitney Point

Whitstran *(S.29;T.9N;R.25E)*

Railroad stop 3 miles northeast of Prosser, west central Benton County. The name was reportedly applied by Northern Pacific Railway officials, for a landowner from whom right-of-way was acquired.

Whittier *(S.26;T.21N;R.12E)*

Railroad station 3 miles southeast of Keechelus Lake's south end, northwest Kittitas County. It was named for John Greenleaf Whittier by some poetic soul in the employ of Chicago, Milwaukee & St. Paul Railway.

Whittier Peak *(S.7;T.28N;R.15E)*

Wenatchee National Forest peak at the headwaters of Ibex Creek, 6 miles east of Cascade Mountain summit, northwest Chelan County. It is one of 5 peaks in the area which Forest Supervisor A. H. Sylvester named for early American authors. He named this one for John Greenleaf Whittier.

Whollochett Bay (Pierce County) *see* Wollochet Bay

Whoopemup Hollow *(S.36;T.10N;R.37E)*

Hollow near Huntsville, 2 to 5 miles north of Waitsburg, west central Columbia County. In 1880, it was named by local residents because of a rowdy element living in the place.

Wickersham *(S.31;T.37N;R.5E)*

Small settlement on Samish River, 3 miles southeast of the south end of Lake Whatcom, southwest Whatcom County.

Formerly an important lumber and shingle production community, it was named for Noah and William Wickersham, who filed homesteads here about 1885.

Wickswood (Grays Harbor County) *see* Weikswood

Widgeon Lake *(S.23;T.4N;R.1W)*

Lake on Bachelor Island, adjoining Canvasback Lake on the south, 1-1/2 miles west of Ridgefield, west central Clark County. It was named, as was Canvasback Lake, for a native species of wild duck.

Wiekel (Yakima County) *see* Weikel

Wieletpu (Walla Walla County) *see* Waiilatpu

Wigwam Camp *(Mt. Rainier National Park)*

A 5,300-ft. camp area on the lower, southeast slope of Mt. Rainier, in Indian Henrys Hunting Ground, southwest quarter of the park. In the early period of park use, the camp consisted of tents and log cabins, and was operated for tourists by George B. Hall. The place was named for the camp.

Wilbur *(Ss.7,18;T.26N;R.33E)*

Town 70 miles west of Spokane, in San Poil Mining District, on Goose Creek, northwest Lincoln County. In 1887, it was founded by Samuel Wilbur Condit, homesteader. The original name *Goosetown* was for Sam Condit's nickname, "Wild Goose Bill," and was applied to his trading post here. He is presumed to have shot into a flock of "wild" geese, killing a neighbor's gander. In 1889, the name was changed to its present form, for Condit's middle name.

Wilbur Creek *(Ts.14,15N;R.44E)*

The stream of the creek heads 3 miles southwest of Pullman, southeast Whitman County; flows northwest 7-1/2 miles to Union Flat Creek. The creek, intermittent in its upper course, was named for C. D. Wilbur, an early settler.

Wilburton *(S.33;T.25N;R.5E)*

Community 1-1/2 miles east of Bellevue, between Lake Washington and Lake Sammamish, northwest King County. It was named for Manley Wilbur, president of Wilbur Logging Company and part-owner of the townsite.

Wilburville (Wilberville) (Whitman County) *see* Elberton

Wilcox *(S.2;T.15N;R.42E)*

Town 8 miles southwest of Colfax, 7-1/2 miles north of Snake River, south central Whitman County. When a post office was established in 1886, it was named for Robert Wilcox, first postmaster.

Wild Goose Pass *(Ss.25,26;T.39N;R.8E.uns)*

Mt. Baker National Forest pass between Table Mountain and Colman Peak, central Whatcom County. In very early days, it was named for a flock of wild geese trapped here by an early snow.

Wild Goose Rapids *(S.33;T.7N;R.47E)*

Rapids in Snake River, about 4 miles above the mouth of Grande Ronde River, between southeast Asotin County and west Idaho. They were named by early river navigators, for a futile attempt to take a stern-wheel steamer upstream through these fast and rock-stewn waters -- a "wild goose chase."

Wild Horse Creek (Walla Walla County) *see* Mud Creek

Wild Rose *(S.3;T.27N;R.43E)*

Prairie in Denison Township, on Wethey Creek, 12 miles north of Spokane, northwest Spokane County. A pioneer, named Hazard, selected this flowery designation for the abundance of wild roses around the countryside.

Wildcat Lake Pothole (King County) *see* Wildcat Lakes

Wildcat Lakes *(Ss.11,12;T.23N;R.10E)*

A 53.7-acre upper lake and an 18.9-acre lower lake, 1,500 ft. apart, 5 miles and 5-1/4 miles northwest of Snoqualmie Pass, Snoqualmie National Forest, east central King County. Wildcat Lake Pothole, 150 ft. from the lower lake, covers less than 1/2 acre. The name is taken from Wildcat Creek, which drains them.

Wilder Creek *(T.36N;R.23E.uns)*

The stream of the creek rises on the east slope of Old Baldy Mountain, Okanogan National Forest, central Okanogan County; flows 4 miles southeast to Salmon Creek. In the early 1890s, it was named for Hiram A. Wilder, who came to Okanogan County in 1891, and had mineral prospects here until 1892. In 1894, he worked the Northland mines, north of Conconully.

Wildhorse Creek *(Ts.25,26N;R.15E)*

The stream of the creek heads on the north slope of Icicle Ridge, near Frosty Pass, Wenatchee National Forest, southwest Chelan County; flows 5-1/2 miles north to Whitepine Creek. The very old name was evidently applied by early stockmen, when bands of wild horses were in the area.

Wildwood *(S.5;T.11N;R.3W)*

Settlement on South Fork, Chehalis River, 7 miles southwest of Winlock, southwest Lewis County. On August 24, 1889, a post office was established, and Thomas C. Naylor, first postmaster, devised the descriptive name. Before that date, it was known as *South Boistfort.*

Wildwood Lake (San Juan County) *see* Spencer Lake

Wildwood Pond *(S.13;T.22N;R.2E)*

An artificial, 1.7-acre reservoir in Fisher Creek, west of Burton, central Vashon Island, King County. Those who created the pond chose a rather fancy name for this artificial feature. An alternate name is *Ernst Reservoir.*

Wiley *(S.6;T.12N;R.18E)*

Community in Ahtanum Valley, 10 miles southwest of Yakima, central Yakima County. In 1871, Hugh Wiley homesteaded here; in 1910, his son Wallace named the town *Wiley City,* when he platted a townsite on the Wiley homestead. The name was later shortened to its present form, when the chances of its becoming a city were remote.

Wilkeson *(S.27;T.19N;R.6E)*

Farming town on Wilkeson Creek, 3 miles southwest of Buckley, north central Pierce County. It was once an important producer of coal and sandstone quarry rock. On May 8, 1877, it was named for Samuel Wilkeson, secretary of the board of Northern Pacific Railway Company, by a resolution of the board.

Willaby Creek *(Ts.22,23N;R.9W.uns)*

The stream of the creek rises 4 miles south of Lake Quinault, north central Grays Harbor County; flows north and west to Lake Quinault, at the settlement of Willaby Creek. It was named by local settlers, for one of the original homesteaders in the area.

Willame Creek *(T.13N;Rs.8,9E)*

The stream of the creek rises on Skate Mountain, northeast Lewis County; flows 8 miles to Cowlitz River, at Packwood. The name is adapted from the Indian word *Wa-ll-a-met,* meaning "running water." It appears as *Willamette Creek* on some older maps.

Willamette Creek (Lewis County) *see* Willame Creek

Willapa *(S.28;T.14N;R.8W)*

One of the oldest communities in the state, on Willapa River, 3 miles southeast of Raymond, north central Pacific County. In early days, it was the head of navigation on Willapa River, and a supply point for Willapa Valley, until railroads were built. The first name was *Woodard's Landing,* for Samuel Lowell Woodard, the first settler, who came here in 1852. When postal service was established, the present name became official. It is for the *Whilapah* Indian tribe, now extinct. (USBGN)

Willapa Bay *(Ts.10-13N;Rs.10,11W)*

Large, shallow bay extending south from Goose Point to Tarlett Slough, west Pacific County. In pioneer days, it was an abundant source of native oysters. The original Indian name was *Atsmitl,* a Chehalis tribal designation. In the period of Spanish exploration, it was charted as *Ensenada de Mal Arrimo* by Jose Martinez de Zayas. Early settlers and oyster harvesters used the name *South Bay,* as suggested by James Swan. On July 5, 1788, Capt. John Meares, a British fur trader, named it, very appropriately, *Shoalwater Bay.* Dislike of that name resulted in a switch to the present name, which is for the Whilapa Indian tribe, which lived around the bay when the first white explorers arrived. (USBGN) (*see* Willapa)

Willapa Harbor *(T.14N;Rs.10,11W)*

Bay extending from the mouth of Willapa River to Pacific Ocean, northwest Pacific County. In 1841, it was mapped by Cmdr. Charles Wilkes as *Useless Bay,* because of its shoals and shallow stretches. Early settlers gave it the descriptive name *North Bay.* The present name was applied when this area became an important lumber-producing center. (*see* Willapa)

Willapa River *(Ts.12-14N;Rs.6-9W)*

The stream of the river heads in Willapa Hills, near Pluvius, east Pacific County; flows 30 miles west and north-

west to Willapa Harbor at South Bend. (*see* Willapa)

Willapacific *(S.6;T.14N;R.9W)*

Unsuccessful town on the north shore of Willapa Harbor, at the mouth of Willapa River, northwest Pacific County. It was boomed in 1900, and many lots were sold to remote investors. Promoters called it *Venice of the Northwest,* but it faded and died within a few years. The combination name was devised by town promoters.

William Point *(S.28;T.36N;R.2E)*

Extreme north point of Samish Island, facing Samish Bay, northwest Skagit County. It extends into Samish Bay, marking the south entrance of Bellingham Bay, Whatcom County. In 1792, the point was named *Punta de Solano* by Dionisio Galiano. Later that year, it was charted as *Point William* by Capt. George Vancouver, for Sir William Bellingham. (USBGN) (*see* Bellingham Bay)

Williams Canyon (Chelan County) *see* Ollala Canyon

Williams Creek *(T.20N;R.17E)*

The stream of the creek rises on Snowshoe Ridge, north central Kittitas County; flows southwest 7 miles to Swauk Creek. In early days, a great deal of placer gold was recovered in this area. The name is for one of the first miners to operate on the creek.

Williams Creek (Chelan County) *see* Raging Creek

Williams Point (King County) *see* Point William

Williamson Rocks *(T.34N;R.1E)*

Rocks off the west shore of Fidalgo Island, 1 mile south of Allan Island, west central Skagit County. In 1841, they were named by the Wilkes Expedition, for John G. Williamson, a gunner in one of the expedition's ships.

Williamson's Landing (Skagit County) *see* Lyman

Willis *(S.9;T.19N;R.34E)*

Formerly a post office 9 miles west by north of Ritzville, north central Adams County. It took its name from John A. Willis, a prominent farmer, who, in 1892, was appointed postmaster.

Willis Glacier (Mt. Rainier National Park) *see* North Mowich Glacier

Willis Wall *(Mt. Rainier National Park)*

Mass of steep, rock cliffs on the north slope of Mt. Rainier, 1 mile north of the summit, at the head of Carbon Glacier, central area of the park. It is surrounded by glaciers, and subject to very heavy snow avalanches in summer. It was named for Prof. Bailey Willis, who, in 1881 and 1883, explored the north side of Mt. Rainier. (USBGN)

Williwakas Creek *(Mt. Rainier National Park)*

The stream of the creek heads in Williwakas Glacier, southeast of Paradise Glacier, southeast slope of Mt. Rainier, southeast area of the park; flows southeast and east to Muddy Fork, Cowlitz River, north of Stevens Ridge. (USBGN) (*see* Williwakas Glacier)

Williwakas Glacier *(Mt. Rainier National Park)*

Small glacier adjoining Paradise Glacier at its southeast end, on the southeast slope of Mt. Rainier, southeast area of the park. It was named by George Weikel of Yakima, who evidently shortened the Indian name for the glacier, which was *Williwilliwakus.* (USBGN)

Willoughby Rock *(S.8;T.22N;R.13W.uns)*

A large rock and several smaller ones in Pacific Ocean, 1 mile offshore from Quinault Indian Reservation, northwest Grays Harbor County. In 1887, the name was mapped by U.S. Coast & Geodetic Survey; their records fail to show the origin.

Willow Creek *(T.30N;R.16E)*

The stream of this small creek heads on the west slope of Entiat Mountains, Wenatchee National Forest, northwest Chelan County; flows 3 miles southwest to Chiwawa River. Prior to 1908, the local name was appropriately applied, as most of the streams in the area have heavy stands of willow on their banks.

Willow Creek (Spokane County) *see* Dartford Creek

Willow Lake (lake) (Spokane County) *see* Four Lakes

Willows *(S.16;T.30N;R.1W)*

Site of Crown Zellerbach's paper mill on Glen Cove, Port Townsend Bay, northeast Jefferson County. It was on the Albert Briggs donation land claim, and later became a country club. Members of Port Townsend Country Club named it for 2 willows, which were planted here as cuttings by a sea captain, who brought them from the site of Napoleon's imprisonment on St. Helena.

Wilma Creek *(T.27N;R.18E)*

The stream of this short creek heads at Miners Ridge; flows 2 miles to Mad River, Wenatchee National Forest, central Chelan County. It was named by Forest Ranger John Brender, for one of his 2 daughters; he named Alma Creek for the other.

Wilmon Peaks (Snohomish County) *see* Monte Cristo Peak

Wilmot Creek *(Ts.30-32N;Rs.34-36E)*

The stream of the creek rises about 4 miles west of Twin Lakes, and drains part of a remote cattle country on Colville Indian Reservation, southeast Ferry County; flows southeast for 24 miles to . Columbia River, 11 miles north of Spokane River's mouth. During the 1890s, the creek valley was heavily prospected by early miners. It was named for Lew P. Wilmot, an adventurous, early settler and miner, who was one of the first county commissioners. On some early maps, the creek is called *Wilmont Creek.*

Wilson Creek *(Ts.18-20N;Rs.18,19E)*

The stream of the creek rises 16 miles north of Ellensburg, north central Kittitas County; flows southerly 19 miles to Yakima River, near Ellensburg. It was named for a pioneer, who settled here in 1886, and lived with Indian "Chief" Shushuskin near the creek's mouth. The original name was *Nanum Creek.*

Wilson Creek (Chelan County) *see* Sevenmile Creek

Wilson Glacier *(Mt. Rainier National Park)*

Ice field between Van Trump and Nisqually Glaciers, on the south slope of Mt. Rainier, south central area of the park. Its melt is discharged into the upper waters of Nisqually River. The name is for A. D. Wilson, who, in 1870, made the second recorded ascent of Mt. Rainier with Samuel F. Emmons. (USBGN)

Wilson Point *(S.20;T.20N;R.1W)*

Southeast point of Hartstene Island, on Cases Inlet, southeast Mason County. In 1841, it was named by Cmdr. Charles Wilkes, for Thomas Wilson, sailmaker's mate.

Wilson Point (Jefferson County) *see* Point Wilson

Wind River *(Ts.3-6N;Rs.7,8E.uns)*

The stream of the river heads in McClellan Meadows, Gifford Pinchot National Forest, central Skamania County; flows south and southeast 28 miles to enter Columbia River at Home Valley. About 1853, the name was applied by pioneers because prevailing winds sweep up and down Columbia River, constantly blowing through the rocky canyon where the river runs much of its course. An earlier name, applied in 1806 by Lewis and Clark Expedition, was *Cruzatte River,* for Peter Cruzatte, one of the party.

Windandtide Lake (Snohomish County) *see* Picnic Point Lake

Windust *(S.8;T.12N;R.33E)*

Railroad point on Snake River, 7 miles south of Kahlotus, east central Franklin County. It was named by Northern Pacific Railway Company officials, for James O. Windust, owner of a ferry which operated across the river.

Windy Arm *(S.20;T.29N;R.7W.uns)*

Small peninsula on the east shore of Lake Mills (Elwha Reservoir), Olympic National Park, central Clallam County. The locally-applied name is quite descriptive. An unofficial name is *Elk Point.* (USBGN)

Windy Creek *(T.27N;R.19E)*

The stream of the creek rises at the south base of Tyee Mountain, Wenatchee National Forest, central Chelan County; flows 4 miles south to Mad Creek. The descriptive name was mapped by Forest Service personnel.

Windy Lake *(S.23;T.23N;R.10E)*

A 5.7-acre lake 1/2 mile southwest of Kaleetan Lake, Snoqualmie National Forest, east central King County. According to those who live in the area, the name is quite descriptive.

Winesap *(S.16;T.26N;R.21E)*

Community on the west bank of Columbia River, 6 miles north of Entiat, east central Chelan County. In 1909, a post office was established, and the name suggested was *Coles View,* to honor Postmistress Elizabeth Cole. Postal authorities objected to two words, and, from a submitted list, picked the present name. It is for the species of apple which is most popular in this orchard area.

Wing Point *(S.25;T.25N;R.2E)*

An east shore point of Bainbridge Island, at the north entrance to Eagle Harbor, east central Kitsap County. In 1841, it was named by Cmdr. Charles Wilkes, on the same day he named Eagle Harbor and Bill Point, which is across the bay from this point. Evidently, Wilkes related the two points to the "eagle" in Eagle Harbor

Winlock *(T.12N;R.2W)*

Formerly a logging and sawmill center, now a famous egg-producing area in Olequa Valley, on Olequa Creek, southwest Lewis County. In 1873, it was named by Northern Pacific Railway officials, for Gen. Winlock W. Miller, a U.S. Army officer sent to Washington Territory during the 1850s Indian wars. He was a close friend of Gov. I. I. Stevens.

Winslow *(Ss.26,27;T.25N;R.2E)*

Ferry dock, business district and ship-repair yard on the north shore of Eagle Harbor, Bainbridge Island, east central Kitsap County. On August 11, 1890, a post office was established here, and named *Madrone* at the suggestion of Postmistress Cynthia C. Williams. The area is well stocked with native Madrona trees *(Arbutus menziesii)*. On January 27, 1903, the name was changed to the present designation, for Winslow Hall, who, in 1902, established a ship-building yard here with his brother Henry.

Winsor *(T.26N;R.5E)*

Platted area near Bothell, extreme northwest King County. In 1888, it was laid out by the sons of Judge Richard Winsor; it was named for the judge, who had purchased the land. The area does not appear on recent maps.

Winston *(S.29;T.12N;R.2E)*

Settlement 1/2 mile southwest of Mayfield, on Winston Creek, central Lewis County. It was locally named for T. R. Winston, who, in 1875, settled here.

Winston Creek *(Ts.11,12N;Rs.2-4E)*

The stream of the creek rises between Green and Winters mountains, south central Lewis County; flows west by north 16 miles to Cowlitz River, 1 mile west of Mayfield. (*see* Winston)

Winters Lake *(S.21;T.28N;R.8E)*

A 11.2-acre lake 3 miles northeast of Sultan, Snoqualmie National Forest, south central Snohomish County. It is reported to have been named for a pioneer homesteader in this area.

Winthrop *(S.2;T.34N;R.21E)*

Town at the junction of Methow and Chewack rivers, west central Okanogan County. It is an entry point to the upper Methow Valley for hunters and fishermen. In 1890, it was named by Congressman John L. Wilson, for Theodore Winthrop, author of *The Canoe and the Saddle*.

Winthrop Glacier *(Mt. Rainier National Park)*

Very large, active ice field between Carbon and Emmons Glaciers, extending north from Mt. Rainier summit to West Fork, White River, and to Winthrop Creek, a distance of about 5 miles, central zone of the park. The surface is very uneven, with domes of resistant rock, which are coated and recoated with ice. Steamboat Prow divides it from Emmons Glacier and the much smaller Inter Glacier. It was named for writer Theodore Winthrop, who viewed the glacier in 1853, and described it in *The Canoe and the Saddle.*(USBGN)

Winton *(S.21;T.26N;R.17E)*

Railway spur in Dardanelles Pass, 5 miles south of Wenatchee Lake, Wenatchee National Forest, central Chelan County. Prior to 1908, this Great Northern Railway spur was used for loading wood products, and was called *Wood Spur*. It later was changed to the present name by railway officials.

Winton Station *(Chelan County) see* Winton

Wirkkala Ponds *(S.4;T.10N;R.9W)*

Two ponds, covering a total of about 3 acres, 1 mile north of Naselle, southwest Pacific County. The name is for Oscar Wirkkala, an outstanding pioneer logger and inventor, who came to Pacific County from Finland in his youth.

Wiser Lake
(S.1;T.39N;R.2E;&S.6;T.39N;R.3E)

A low-altitude lake in 2 segments, totaling 123 acres, 9 miles north of Bellingham, 1 mile south of Nooksack River, northwest Whatcom County. It drains southwest to Nooksack River. The lake was locally named for the first

settler on the lake, Jacob Wiser, a colorful frontiersman.

Wishkah *(S.2;T.18N;R.9W)*

Village on Wishkah River, 5-1/2 miles north of Aberdeen, adjoining the north end of Aberdeen Gardens, south central Grays Harbor County. (*see* Wishkah River)

Wishkah River *(Ts.17-21N;Rs.8,9W)*

The stream of the river rises on Wishkah Watershed, between Wynooche and Humptulips rivers, northeast Grays Harbor County; flows south 26 miles to Grays Harbor, at Aberdeen. The name is a distortion of the Indian word *Woosh-kla*, meaning "stinking water" or "stink river." Indian legend relates that a whale swam some distance up this river and died.

Wishram *(S.17;T.2N;R.15E)*

Railroad division point on the north bank of Columbia River, 15 miles southwest of Goldendale, directly upstream from the location of Celilo Falls, before inundation, Klickitat County. It was formerly a trading place, where Wishram Indians dealt with Indians from the Inland Empire, and also with tribesmen from lower Columbia River. The name is a Chinook dialect word, meaning "louse" or "flea."It applied to the location and to the Indians who were permanent residents at this river point. Names in other Indian dialects were *Niculuita* and *Tlaqluit*.

Withrow *(S.34;T.26N;R.24E)*

Town 13 miles northeast of Waterville, central Douglas County. It was named for J. J. Withrow, a prominent rancher, who settled here before the small settlement was established as a town.

Wolf Creek *(T.29N;R.7W)*

The stream of the creek rises south of Hurricane Hill, Olympic National Park, central Clallam County; flows west to Lake Mills (Elwha Reservoir). On July 16, 1890, it was named by Seattle Press Expedition, for a wolf they killed on the creek, near Elwha River.

Wolfnite Mountain *(Okanogan County) see* Wolframite Mountain

Wolframite Mountain
(T.40N;R.22E.uns)

Mineralized peak in North Cascade Primitive Area, at the head of Ashnola River's east fork, north central Okanogan County. It was named for tungsten ore, which was found here. An incorrect name on some maps is *Wolfnite Mountain*. (USBGN)

Wolfred *(S.32;T.32N;R.45E)*

Small settlement and railroad loading point close to Pend Oreille River, 5 miles northwest of Newport, southeast Pend Oreille County. It was named for Fred Wolf, a militant editor of *Newport Miner*; the name is a reversal of his surname and given name.

Wollochet *(S.31;T.21N;R.2E)*

Small settlement on the east shore of Wollochet Bay, Hales Passage, northwest Pierce County. The Indian name, which has been retained, means "squirting clams."

Wollochet Bay *(T.21N;R.2E)*

North branch of Hales Passage, terminating at Artondale, northwest Pierce County. In 1841, the bay was named *Vanderford's Harbor* by Cmdr. Charles Wilkes, for Pilot Benjamin Vanderford of the flagship *Vincennes*, who died during the cruise. The present Indian name appears on older maps with the spelling variation *Whollochet*. (*see* Wollochet)

Wolverine Creek
(Ss.31,32;T.32N;R.18E)

The stream of the creek heads 2-1/2 miles west of Lake Chelan, north central Chelan County; flows east to Lake Chelan, 3 miles north of Lucerne. It was named by Andy Crumbine, a prospector and trapper, who caught a black wolverine at the mouth of the creek.

Wonder Creek (Jefferson County) *see* Lost Creek

Wonderland Trail *(Mt. Rainier National Park)*

Horse-and-foot trail around Mt. Rainier, slightly over 100 miles long. It reaches many outstanding, scenic spots in the park, and requires a guided 7- to 10-day trip. Shelter cabins are spaced at 8- to 12-mile distances along the trail. The poetic name was devised by park officials, and is quite descriptive.

Wood Lake *(S.34;T.7N;R.8E.uns)*

A 12.5-acre lake, elevation about 5,000 ft. and maximum depth 15 ft., Gifford Pinchot National Forest, 7-1/2 miles north of Big Lava Bed, central Skamania County. A dense growth of timber around the lake makes the name

quite descriptive. An alternate name is *Woods Lake*.

Wood Spur (Chelan County) *see* Winton

Woodard Creek (Thurston County) *see* Woodward Creek

Woodard's (Spokane County) *see* Millwood

Woodards Landing (Pacific County) *see* Willapa

Woodburn Hill *(S.1;T.1N;R.3E)*

Hill 1 mile northeast of Camas, southeast Clark County. The Scottish term was applied by a Scottish pioneer, Mrs. George Mitchell, for the abundance of low-growing shrubs in the vicinity, especially along small streams.

Wooded Island
(Ss.14,23;T.11N;R.28E)

Island in Columbia River, 9 miles north of Richland, between east central Benton and Franklin counties. It is stated that the name, given by pioneer settlers, was for a fairly heavy growth of cottonwood timber in which many species of birds nested.

Wooded Island (San Juan County) *see* Skipjack Island

Woodinville *(S.9;T.26N;R.5E)*

Community near the north end of Lake Washington, in Sammamish Valley, northwest King County. It was named for the M. D. Woodin family, 1872 pioneers.

Woodland *(S.24;T.5N;R.1W)*

Town on North Fork, Lewis River, 8 miles south of Kalama, south Cowlitz County. In 1850, the site was occupied as a Donation Land Claim by Squire Bozarth, who called it *Woodland Farm*. It was shortened to the present name when the town was established.

Woodland (Thurston County) *see* Lacey

Woodlawn (Whatcom County) *see* Agate Bay

Woodman *(S.8;T.29N;R.1W)*

Settlement on the east shore of Port Discovery Bay, 5 miles southwest of Port Townsend, northeast Jefferson County. It was locally named for James O. Woodman, who came here from Portsmouth, England, and remained for over 60 years.

Woodruff *(S.34;T.28N;R.6E)*

Small settlement 4 miles southeast of

Snohomish, southwest Snohomish County. It was named for George L. Woodruff, general manager of Three Lakes Lumber Company and superintendent of the company's logging railroad, Washington & Western Railway.

Woods Lake (Skamania County) *see* Wood Lake

Woods Prairie *(T.18N;R.1W)*

Prairie north of Chambers Prairie, including the present site of Lacey, north central Thurston County. In pioneer days, it was named for Isaac Wood, who came here in 1852, the area's first settler.

Woodward Bay *(S.18;T.19N;R.1W)*

West shore bay of Henderson Inlet, at the mouth of Woodward Creek, 4 miles northeast of Olympia. north central Thurston County. It was named for Harvey Rice Woodward; on March 1, 1853, he had filed a Donation Land Claim here.

Woodward Creek *(S.18;T.19N;R.1W)*

The stream of the creek rises east of Olympia in north central Thurston County; flows almost due north to Henderson Inlet at Woodward Bay. Earlier names for the stream, now in disuse, are "Pattison Creek" and "Patterson Creek." (USBGN) (*see* Woodward Bay)

Woody Island *(T.33N;R.26E)*

Island in Okanogan River, directly south of Okanogan, central Okanogan County. It is a community park area for county-wide rodeos, horse races and fairs. The name is for O. H. Woody, founder of the *Okanogan Independent*, and publisher of that paper for 40 years.

Woolloomooloo Creek *(T.34N;R.25E)*

The stream of the creek rises in Neville Range, central Okanogan County; flows northeast 3 miles to Salmon Creek, 9 miles northwest of Okanogan. Carrying the burden of 8 "O"'s, the creek was named during the Okanogan gold rush by Australian miners, for a bay in Sydney Harbor.

Workman Creek *(T.17N;Rs.6,7W)*

The stream of the creek rises south of Montesano, southeast Grays Harbor County; flows northeast to Chehalis River, 1-1/2 miles south of Elma. On the 1857 maps of the surveyor general of Washington Territory, the stream is mapped as *Mason's Creek*. The present name is for an early settler on land adjoining the creek.

Wormald State Park *(S.23;T.4N;R.4E)*

Wilderness area on East Fork, Lewis River, southwest of Jack Mountain, east central Clark County. On June 18, 1927, it was deeded to the state for park purposes by State Sen. Joseph Wormald. The park is named for him.

Wormel Gulch *(T.8N;R.45E)*

The gulch heads 2-1/2 miles northwest of Anatone, central Asotin County; trends northwest 2 miles to George Creek. It was named for Leonard J. *Wormell*, a "well-to-do and venerable gentleman," who settled here in 1880.

Wright Mountain (King County) *see* Mt. Wright

Wrights *(S.8;T.3N;R.13E)*

Railway station on Klickitat River, 19 miles west by south of Goldendale, southwest Klickitat County. When the station was established here by Spokane, Portland, & Seattle Railway, it was named for L. C. Wright, a local landowner.

Wrights Butte *(S.27;T.24N;R.41E)*

Butte in Four Lakes Township, directly southeast of Granite Lake, central Spokane County. It was named for Col. George Wright, USA, who defeated a strong band of allied Indian tribesmen on September 1, 1858, in the "Battle of Four Lakes." The battleground was at the base of this butte. An alternate name for this feature is *Wrights Hill*.

Wrights Hill (Spokane County) *see* Wrights Butte

Wyadda Island (Clallam County) *see* Waada Island

Wyam (Klickitat County) *see* Celilo Falls

Wye Lake *(S.2;T.22N;R.1W)*

A 37.9-acre lake 3-1/2 miles southeast of Belfair, southwest Kitsap County. The name is for a distinct "Y" branch at one end of the lake. An alternate name is *Y Lake*.

Wymer *(S.4;T.15N;R.19E)*

Railway station on Yakima River, 15 miles north of Yakima, southeast Kittitas County. In 1902, the station at this place was named *Canyon* by Northern Pacific Railway personnel. In 1912, it was changed to the present name to honor Seymour Wymer, a former pump operator here.

Wynooche, South Montesano (Grays Harbor County) *see* Montesano

Wynooche River *(Ts.17-23N;Rs.7,8W)*

The stream of the river heads in Olympic Primitive Area, extreme northeast Grays Harbor County; flows 51 miles south to Chehalis River, south of Montesano. The name is the original Indian designation, meaning "shifting sands." On March 1, 1854, the name was recorded by George Gibbs in Pacific Railroad Reports. (USBGN)

Wynooche Valley *(Ts.18-20N;R.8W)*

Valley extending north of Montesano, up Wynooche River approximately 16 miles, north central Grays Harbor County. Its boundaries are not well defined. (*see* Wynooche River)

Y

Y Creek *(T.29N;R.16E)*

The stream of the creek heads in upper Chiwawa River drainage area, Wenatchee National Forest, northwest Chelan County; flows 3-1/2 miles northeast through D Lake, to Chiwawa River. It was named by Forest Ranger Delmer S. Rice because it makes a distinct ''Y'' for 2/3 of its length.

Y Lake *(S.19;T.28N;R.8W.uns)*

A 5-acre lake, located in a perpetual snowfield in Seven Lakes Basin, Olympic National Park, south central Clallam County. It is named for its shape -- using a little imagination.

Yacolt *(S.2;T.4N;R.3E)*

Town 20 miles northeast of Vancouver, central Clark County. At one time, 2 post offices were in competition at this place, Yacolt and Garner. Eventually, they were combined under the present name. The Indian word means ''place abounding in evil spirits'' or''haunted place.'' It derives from an incident, many years ago, in which 5 Indian children were lost while picking wild berries.

Yacolt Reservoir *(S.6;T.4N;R.4E)*

A 1-1/2-acre, artificial lake 2 miles southeast of Yacolt, in Big Tree Creek, northeast Clark County. It is used for public water supply. The name is for nearby Yacolt Prairie. (*see* Yacolt)

Yakima *(T.13N;Rs.18,19E)*

City in Yakima River Valley, north central Yakima County. It is a very progressive trading center for a wide area of fertile country. In 1861, the settlement started at the north entrance to Union Gap. On December 1, 1883, it was incorporated as *Yakima City*. When Northern Pacific Railway Company failed to secure certain concessions from the town in 1884, they established a station 4 miles west, and moved over 100 buildings from Yakima City to the new townsite, free of charge. The new town was called *North Yakima*. On January 1, 1918, the State Legislature changed the name of North Yakima to Yakima, and the name of Yakima City to Union Gap. With subsequent growth, the two places have joined boundaries. Several author-ities have claimed divergent meanings of the Indian term *E-Yak-Kah-Ma* or *Yah-Ah-Ka-Ma*. A plausible translation is ''black bear,'' from *yah-kah*, meaning black bear, and the plural ending *ma*. The Bureau of American Ethnology has interpreted the term as meaning ''runaway,'' which tends to support an Indian legend of an Indian chief's erring daughter, who lived at Moxee. When the girl became pregnant out of wedlock, she moved to the Yakima River near Union Gap, either as a runaway or as a *deporte*.

Yakima City (Yakima County)*see* Yakima, Union Gap

Yakima County

This second-largest county in the state, in south central Washingon, is bounded on the north by Kittitas County; on the east by Grant and Benton counties; on the south by Klickitat County; and on the west by Skamania, Lewis and Pierce counties. For a brief period, its area was included in Ferguson County, which had been established in 1863 by the Territorial Legislature. On January 1, 1865, the legislature created this county by repealing its action on Ferguson County, giving it a smaller area than the latter. The county's 4,273 square miles includes irrigated valleys that produce excellent fruits and field crops. Other products are lumber, hops and livestock. (*see* Yakima)

Yakima Creek *(Mt. Rainier National Park)*

The stream of the creek rises near Sunrise Park, on the northeast slope of Mt. Rainier, northeast zone of the park; flows east, then plunges down the mountainside to White River, near the park's White River Entrance. It was named for the previous title of Sunrise Park, which was Yakima Park. (*see* Yakima)

Yakima Falls (Benton County) *see* Prosser

Yakima Indian Reservation *(Ts.6-12N;Rs.11-23E.partly uns)*

The state's largest reservation, covering 1,134,830-acre, with 500,000 acres in timberland, extending about 72 miles west to east from Cascade Mountain summit, east of Mt. Adams, to Mabton; and about 38 miles north to south from Ahtanum River, to Satus Pass, Yakima and Klickitat counties. In 1855, it was allotted to 14 tribes by a treaty with the United States, and was named for the largest tribe placed here at that time. (*see* Yakima)

Yakima Park (Mt. Rainier National Park) *see* Sunrise Park

Yakima Peak *(Mt. Rainier National Park)*

A 6,231-ft. peak on Cascade Mountain summit, overlooking Tipsoo Lake, Chinook and Cayuse passes, extreme east central zone of the park. In 1919, it was named by Asahel Curtis, for the Yakima Indian nation. (USBGN) (*see* Yakima)

Yakima River *(Ts.8-21N;Rs.11-28E)*

The stream of the river heads in Keechelus Lake, near Cascade Mountain summit, northwest Kittitas County; flows southeast through Ellensburg and south through Yakima, Yakima County; continues east through Benton County, with a northern loop before entering Columbia River, between Richland and Kennewick. Since 1811, some of the names applied to the river by Indians and white men include *Tapteal, Tap-teil, Nocktosh, Yahinse, Eyakama, Eyakemka, Yakama, Skaemena* and the present name. (*see* Yakima)

Yakima State Park *(T.12N;R.19E)*

A 213-acre park 3 miles southeast of Yakima, on Yakima River, central Yakima County. Camping and picnic facilities are available to the public. (*see* Yakima)

Yale *(S.24;T.6N;R.3E)*

Small community 1-1/2 miles north of Lake Merwin's east end, southeast Cowlitz County. The short name was selected by postal officials. An earlier name was *Spillel*, for nearby Spillel Creek.

Yale Lake (Cowlitz County) *see* Lake Merwin

Yale Reservoir *(T.6N;R.4E)*

An 8-mile-long, hydroelectric reservoir in Lewis River, 8 miles northeast of Yacolt, covering 2,022 acres in Clark County, and 1,779 acres in Cowlitz County. It was created by Pacific Power & Light Company as a unit in their Lewis River power development., and was named for the town of Yale. (*see* Yale)

Yardley *(S.14;T.25N;R.43E)*

Industrial district, built around railroad freight yards, adjoining Spokane on the east, Spokane County. in 1902, it was started by Northern Pacific Railway Company, and named by railroad officials for the company's yards.

Yarrow Point *(T.25N;R.5E)*

An east shore point of Lake Washington, 2 miles south of Kirkland, between Yarrow Bay and Cosy Cove, King County. It was named by Leigh S. J. Hunt, publisher of *Seattle Post-Intelligencer,* who owned the point and lived there from 1886 to 1895; he named it for a poem about this Scottish flower.

Yellepit *(S.8;T.6N;R.31E)*

Former town on the west bank of Columbia River, 15 miles south by east of Kennewick, southeast Benton County. The name is reported to be that of a "great chief" of the Walla Wallas, to whom Lewis and Clark presented "a medal, a string of wampum & handkerchief." Capt. Clark described him as "a bold handsome Indian, with a dignified countenance about 35 years of age, about 5 feet 8 inches high and well perpotiond." Capt. Lewis wrote that he was "a man of much influence not only in his own nation but also among the neighboring tribes and nations." On their return trip, Lewis and Clark received material assistance from him.

Yellow Island *(T.36N;R.3W)*

Arid island in Wasp Island group, directly south of McConnell Island, off the northwest point of Shaw Island, central San Juan County. The local name is for the typical color of the island's vegetation.

Yellow Lake *(S.14;T.24N;R.6E)*

Lake, varying from 5 to 25 acres, with an average area of 10-1/2 acres, 3 miles north of Issaquah, west central King County. The locally-applied name was chosen because the lake is silty and yellowish in color at high-water stages.

Yellowhawk Creek *(Ts.6,7N;Rs.35,36E)*

The stream of the creek rises directly south of Walla Walla (city); flows southwest 5 miles to Walla Walla River, south central Walla Walla County. The name is that of an early Walla Walla or Cayuse Indian, *Pe-Tum-Ro-Mus-Mus* or "Yellow Hawk," who was the leader of a local band.

Yelm *(T.17N;Rs.1,2E)*

Town on Yelm Prairie, 1-1/2 miles south of Ft. Lewis Army Post, 14 miles northeast of Tenino, east Thurston County. The name is from the Salish Indian word *chelm,* meaning "heat waves from the sun." Local Indians revered the sun as the cause of fertility. In 1873, Northern Pacific Railway officials named the place *Yelm Prairie,* which was later shortened to its present form.

Yelm Prairie *(T.17N;Rs.1,2E)*

Several square miles of farmland and irrigated orchards directly south of Ft. Lewis Army Post, in Yelm-McKenna area, east Thurston County. (*see* Yelm)

Yemoalt (Kitsap County) *see* Yeomalt

Yennis Creek (Clallam County) *see* White Creek

Yeomalt *(S.25;T.25N;R.2E)*

A settlement with many summer homes on the east shore of Bainbridge Island, north side of Yeomalt Point, east central Kitsap County. The name is a modification of the Indian designation *Yem-o-alt,* the meaning of which apparently relates to story-telling.

Yeomalt Point *(S.25;T.25N;R.2E)*

An east central shore point of Bainbridge Island, between Wing Point and Ferncliff, Kitsap County. Since first occupied in 1890, 2 names have been applied to the point: *Dead Man's Bar,* for a dead sailor whose body was found on the point; and *Finch's Sand Spit,* for the Finch family, who homesteaded 160 acres near the point in 1890. (*see* Yeomalt)

Yesler *(T.25N;R.4E)*

Once a town on Lake Washington and Union Bay, in the area now occupied by Laurelhurst, King County. In 1888, it was founded by, and named for, Henry Yesler as a sawmill town, with a school, post office, store and 2 churches. Yesler was a Seattle pioneer, who built the first steam sawmill on

Puget Sound in 1853, and served 2 terms as mayor of Seattle. (*see* Kent)

Yesler Hill *(T.24N;R.4E)*

One of Seattle's 12 "official" hills north of Jackson Street, east and south of the main business district, central Seattle, King County. It has 2 summits: one 234 ft. at 7th Ave. and Spruce St.; the other 256 ft. near Broadway and Tenth Ave. (*see* Yesler, Profanity Hill)

Yew (Snohomish County) *see* Maltby

Yocum Lake *(Ss.14, 23;T.36N;R.43E)*

Very small lake 32 miles northwest of Newport, 1 mile east of Pend Oreille River, central Pend Oreille County. It was named by members of a hunting party, when one of the hunters, "Shorty" Yocum, discovered the lake by pushing through the brush and falling into it.

Yoman Point *(S.34;T.20N;R.1E)*

A northeast shore point of Anderson Island, on Balch Passage, northwest Pierce County. In 1841, it was mapped and named by Cmdr. Charles Wilkes. His records do not give the name source, but practically all the names he applied, which were not descriptive or for regular Navy personnel, were for members of his expedition.

Young America (Stevens County) *see* Bossburg

Young Creek *(T.27N;R.19E)*

The stream of the creek heads on Tyee Mountain, Wenatchee National Forest, central Chelan County; flows 3-1/2 miles south to Mad River. The name, applied by Forest Supervisor A. H. Sylvester, is for Billy Young, who ranged sheep along the creek for many years.

Young Island *(S.33;T.35N;R.1E)*

Very small islet in Burrows Bay, in Fidalgo Island, between Burrows and Allan Islands, west central Skagit County. In 1841, it was named *Young's Island* by Cmdr. Charles Wilkes, for Ewing Young, an Oregon pioneer with whom he had recently visited. It has since been shortened to the present form.

Young's Island (Skagit County) *see* Young Island

Youngs Lake *(T.22N;R.5E)*

A 700-acre, artificial reservoir, maximum depth 72 ft., fed by Cedar

River, 4 miles west of Maple Valley, west central King County. It is part of Seattle's domestic water supply. Seattle city officials named it for L. B. Youngs, who planned the reservoir while employed by Seattle's water department.

Youngstown *(T.24N;R.3E)*

An industrial area south of Harbor Island, west of Duwamish River, West Seattle, King County. It includes a steel mill and other heavy industries. The original name of this Seattle suburb was *Humphries*. It later became known as *Young's Cove*, using the name of a landowner at the mouth of Longfellow Creek, which discharged into the cove. The present name was adopted when the area became industrialized.

Yukon Harbor *(S.34;T.24N;R.2E)*

Puget Sound harbor between Harper and Colby, 2-1/2 miles west of Blake Island, southeast Kitsap County. In 1841, Cmdr. Charles Wilkes named it *Barron's Bay*, for Commodore Samuel Barron, who served in Tripolitan War in 1805; some maps carried the name, in error, as *Barrow's Bay*. During the 1890s Alaska gold rush, the present name was adopted, for Yukon River.

Z

Z Canyon *(T.40N;R.43E)*

A remarkable canyon in Pend Oreille River, 2 miles south of the Canadian boundary, north central Pend Oreille County. Through this narrow chasm, only 18 ft. wide but 400 ft. deep, the river plunges at a terrific speed. The name is for the zig-zag contour of the canyon.

Zelatched Point *(S.29;T.26N;R.1W)*

An east shore point of Dabob Bay, near the south end of Toandos Peninsula, southwest Jefferson County. In 1841, the name was applied by Cmdr. Charles Wilkes, evidently using the original Indian name.

Ziegler Creek *(T.23N;R.9W)*

The stream of the creek heads 3-1/2 miles east of Quinault Lake; flows west to Quinault Lake, 1 mile south of Quinault, Grays Harbor County. It was named for one of the original homesteaders on the creek.

Zillah *(S.35;T.11N;R.20E)*

Town on the north bank of Yakima River, 16 miles southeast of Yakima, east central Yakima County. In 1892, it was founded; and, in the early 1900s, the townsite was platted by C. E. Mayne, a land promoter of Salt Lake City, Utah, and San Diego, California. It was named by Walter N. Granger, for the daughter of Thomas F. Oakes. In 1888, Oakes was vice president of Northern Pacific Railway Company, and later became president of that line.

Zindel *(T.7N;R.46E)*

Former town and post office near Snake River, about 2 miles from Rogersburg, southeast Asotin County. It was named for Martin W. Zindel, a former postmaster.

REFERENCES.

● Surveyor General's Office
◗ Land Office
⊞ Townships Subdivided
⊙ County Seats
▪ Cities, Towns
- - - Rail Road Limits
■ Military Reservations